geographic perspectives on urban systems

WITH INTEGRATED READINGS

CONTRIBUTING AUTHORS

Josephine Olu. Abiodun
Qazi S. Ahmad
Gwen Bell
Hans Blumenfeld
Larry S. Bourne
Colin Clark
Stanislaw Czamanski
Michael F. Dacey
Otis Dudley Duncan
Kazimierz Dziewonski
John Friedmann
William L. Garrison
Peter G. Goheen
Harold Goldstein
Gerald Hodge
Sven Illeris
Leslie J. King
Ira S. Lowry
Fred Lukermann
Duane F. Marble
Om P. Mathur
John Miller
Richard L. Morrill
R. M. Morse
Leon Moses
Elaine Neils
G. H. Peters
D. Michael Ray
Philip H. Rees
Joseph L. Schofer
James W. Simmons
M. C. K. Swamy
Robert H. T. Smith
Robert J. Tennant
Pierre de Visé
Harold W. Williamson

geographic perspectives on urban systems

WITH INTEGRATED READINGS

BRIAN J. L. BERRY

University of Chicago

FRANK E. HORTON

University of Iowa

prentice-hall, inc., englewood cliffs, new jersey

13–351312–2

Library of Congress Catalog Card Number: 72–86517

Current printing (last digit):

10 9 8 7 6 5 4 3 2 1

PRENTICE-HALL INTERNATIONAL, INC., *London*
PRENTICE-HALL OF AUSTRALIA PTY. LTD., *Sydney*
PRENTICE-HALL OF CANADA LTD., *Toronto*
PRENTICE-HALL OF INDIA PRIVATE LTD., *New Delhi*
PRENTICE-HALL OF JAPAN, INC., *Tokyo*

Printed in the United States of America

preface

At any time, any part of any discipline is a creation of the accidents of its evolution, of the interests and orientations of its adherents, and their relationships with scholars in surrounding fields. Urban geography is no exception. Subjects and ideas considered of central importance to the field have changed substantially over the years, and continue to do so.

As in other fields, change has not been smooth and continuous. Rather, a series of novel and unprecedented shifts in the concepts used by urban geographers has been separated by periods of relative intellectual quiescence. Each transformation was based upon a work or works sufficiently novel and exciting to attract young scholars from alternative lines of work, while leaving many unresolved problems for them to work on. Each resulted in a framework of ideas and premises accepted by the adherents, and created a particular *paradigm** of the field. In urban geography the paradigms have been those of environmentalism, regionalism, and currently, locational analysis.

*See Thomas S. Kuhn, *The Structure of Scientific Revolutions* (Chicago: The University of Chicago Press, 1962).

Within the framework of any paradigm, research workers generally devote themselves to "normal" scientific activity, such as:

1. Increasing the accuracy and scope of the facts shown to be of central importance to the paradigm's theory.
2. Comparing the theory with facts.
3. Articulating theory, resolving some of its ambiguities, and permitting the solution of problems to which it had previously only drawn attention.

The chapters of this book report the results of these three kinds of "normal" work by urban geographers who base their work on the premises of location theory. The principal purpose of this book is to introduce the student to these premises, and to the related concepts, facts, and analyses of this latter, most recent postwar paradigm.

No pretense is made that the volume is "complete." Obviously, no book can ever be so, particularly this volume, which began as a fairly conventional "reader" and developed on the editors' desks into a study with somewhat more continuity and consistency than normally is found in readers. Because the book deals with complex urban phenomena studied by research workers in a variety of fields, no claim is made, either, that the volume is "comprehensive." Rather, what is provided is an introduction to the *geographic* perspectives of urban *geographers* as they study urban phenomena within the framework of ideas provided by urban location theorists. There are obvious overlaps with other fields, notably economics and sociology; insights from these other disciplines are incorporated where relevant, however.

The book begins by reviewing the changing framework of ideas in the field, to emphasize that the "facts" considered significant at one time seldom remain so: concepts shift as one paradigm is transformed into another.

Because urban areas have themselves changed alongside the disciplines studying them, a second chapter explores the evolution of the American urban system. Just as the first chapter emphasizes the ingredients involved in the growth of the field, so the second considers the emergence of the phenomena studied by American urban geographers, with substantial emphasis upon the evolutionary processes, major system transformations, and the characteristics of the urban system and its environmental relationships at each stage of its development. Since the next decades seem destined to become periods of consciously planned urban development, the chapter concludes by considering possible future forms of urbanization.

In Chapters 3 to 7 the city is treated as an entity, part of a system of such entities interacting with and influencing each other. Among the topics considered are the sizes, types, dimensions of variation, hierarchical relationships, and spatial arrangements of cities. Emphasis switches from theory to empirical relationships, from methods of analysis to unsolved problems, from the United States to cross-cultural variations, and from present patterns to processes generating these patterns, within each chapter.

Similar varieties of subject matter and ranges of emphasis are also to be found in Chapters 8 to 13. In these chapters the focus is individuals, groups, and areas within cities. Problems of the definition, characterization, and dynamics of the city as a unit are combined with detailed explorations of its social geography, land use, and traffic patterns. Increasing attention is given to the decisions and events that sum to urban processes, and to the fact that urban patterns, viewed at any point in time, are but "snapshots" that freeze these processes at an instant. The reader's attention is also directed to contemporary social and physical planning problems, and to the geographic analyses that may contribute to their solution. To enable the student to draw comparisons and explore relationships between many types of geographic insights into contemporary urban patterns, processes and problems, most of the examples in Chapters 9 to 13 are of a single city, Chicago—perhaps the most studied city in the world.

We do not expect the student who reads this book to become an expert urban geographer overnight. The book will have served its purpose if it illustrates the geographic perspective in the study of cities, exemplifies the rich array of ideas now present in the discipline, and stimulates the reader to delve more deeply—to explore more thoroughly the processes that are so imperfectly understood today but which must be grasped if we are to adequately predict and control change to produce the higher-quality urban environments that we all desire.

BRIAN J. L. BERRY
FRANK E. HORTON

Hyde Park, Chicago
September, 1969

contents

CHAPTER 7

urban hierarchies and spheres of influence 169

CHAPTER 8

problems of defining the metropolis 250

CHAPTER 9

the urban envelope: patterns and dynamics of population density 276

CHAPTER 10

concepts of social space: toward an urban social geography 306

CHAPTER 1

emergence of urban geography: methodological foundations of the discipline

THE EARLY LITERATURE ON URBAN LOCATIONS

The formative years of the social sciences in the late nineteenth and early twentieth centuries were also the years in which urban studies first developed, thus providing the context for the geographer's emerging interest in cities. Many of the classic statements were preoccupied with the prevailing environmentalist orientation of geographic thought. Differences in philosophic stance among the social sciences, and systems of cities that changed with increasing rapidity during the developmental period of urban studies, were responsible for substantial conceptual variation, however, as well as dramatic conceptual change over the years, and these varying and changing perspectives were carried over into geography.

As appropriate a way as any to introduce the reader to the evolution and current status of urban geography, therefore, is to review the classical literary themes dealing with the location, size, and shape of cities—in effect, the intellectual heritage from and within which urban geography has grown and developed. Such a methodological introduction should serve to disabuse the student of the notion that there are "facts" about urban geography to be learned, apart from a tentative and changing set of concepts about what is meaningful in the many facets of cities that can be observed and recorded—indeed, it should impress on him that the *geographic* perspective is simply one among many.

Speculation in New City Locations

A dramatic beginning is offered by the literature that accompanied the actual establishment of American cities in the late eighteenth and early nineteenth centuries, as settlers moved across the Alleghenies and the urban system expanded westward. Speculators and town builders operated from practical notions about likely locations for successful commercial cities, and they, as well as later city boosters, were eager to publicize for particular cities descriptions of their physical advantages that would ensure success.

"Men in the East with surplus capital," writes Wade, "scanned maps looking for likely spots to establish a town, usually at the junction of two rivers, or sometimes at the center of fertile farm districts."[1] As the steps in picking city sites were simplified and more universally applied, the city advertisements also became more highly formalized in description and praise of sites and opportunities. By 1803 the promoter advertising in the *Augusta Chronicle* was able to apply the magic formula to his chosen City of Skunksburgh:

> Situated in Wilks county, not far from the junction of Pickett's main spring branch, and a Western fork, called the Slough, which runs in the rainy season. . . . This noble stream, by the use of proper and sufficient means, may be made navigable to the sea. It abounds in delicate minnows, a variety of terrapins, and its frogs, which, in size, voice, and movement, are inferior to none. . . . A noble bluff of 18 feet commands the harbor, and affords a most advantageous situation for defensive military works. This bluff slopes off into nearly a level, diversified only by the gentle undulations of surface, as will give a sufficient elevation for the principal public edifices. . . . The future advantages of this situation are now impossible to calculate. . . . To mercantile men, however, a mere statement of its geographical position is deemed sufficient, without comment. It stands on about the middle ground between Baltimore and Orleans, Charleston and Nickajak, Savannah and Coweta, Knoxville and St. Mary's, Salisbury and Cusseta, and between Little Heil on the Altamaha, and Telfico block house. A line of Velocipede stages will be immediately established from Skunksburg straight through the O-ke-fin-o-cau Swamp, to the southern-most point of the Florida peninsula; and, as soon as a canal shall be cut through the rocky mountains, there will be direct communication with the Columbia river, and thence to the Pacific Ocean. Then opens a theatre of trade bounded only by the Universe![2]

Daniel Drake, author of *Natural and Statistical View: A Picture of Cincinnati and the Miami Country* (1815), catalogued the natural advantages of the site of that city, which would become, he was sure, the "future metropolis of the Ohio . . . the permanent mart and trading capital,"[3] by virtue of its river and lake connections, and of the productivity of the Miami country and neighboring parts of Kentucky.

The question, Did cities grow because of natural advantages or local enterprise?, a "question central to all nineteenth century debate about the future course of American cities,"[4] was considered by Charles Francis Adams, Jr., in a comparison of Chicago and Boston in 1866. The rivalry between St. Louis ("a central mart, seated on the great southern water line of transport and traffic, by the river, the gulf, and the ocean . . . [the hub of] a great railroad wheel,"[5]) and Chicago ("If our National Wheel of commerce have its Hub immovably pivoted by Nature and by Art, should not Every Business Man know it?"[6]) was furthered in *Saint Louis: The Future Great City of the World* (1875) and *Chicago: Past, Present, Future* (1868).[7]

Early Theories concerning City Locations

Many popular writings enumerated the particular locational requisites and physical advantages best suited to the development of cities. It remained for the early theorists of urban location to begin to draw together and systematize such ideas in the latter part of the nineteenth century. In his Introduction to *The Theory of Transportation* (1894), Charles H. Cooley recognized the task explicitly:

> The present essay, then, is an attempt to put these two things together, to write a theory of transportation from a sociological standpoint.
>
> While many of the matters here treated have been and are the subject of unceasing discussion, others have received but small attention. This is particularly true of the theory of the location of cities, to which I have devoted a chapter. Indeed, I think that the analysis of the territorial relations of society offered . . . brings to view an important field of social research that has been much neglected. Since the work of Kohl, published in 1841, I know of no comprehensive and connected investigation of that branch of demography, or demographic sociology that treats of the forces and laws that determine the territorial distribution of persons and wealth. (*Note:* A good deal is now being done in this field by men who approach it from the side of geography. The most important work seems to be that of Professor Ratzel, *Anthropogeographie* [Part I, 1882; Part II, 1891]). Little is understood concerning the theory of settlement, the theory of the

location of towns and cities, or the laws that determine their size, the density of their population and their internal structure.

Certainly these inquiries have been neglected in the United States. Yet we have here the amplest possible material for working out this branch of science; ampler than has ever existed elsewhere. Within the memory of living men, for the most part, our country has been settled and our towns and cities have grown up,—not without the action of laws, which remain as yet unformulated.[8]

Adna F. Weber's 1899 book, *The Growth of Cities in the Nineteenth Century: A Study in Statistics*, described in 1963 as "a near classic and still not superseded statistical examination of urbanization in the western world in the nineteenth century,"[9] contains more complete references to the early writings of European scholars who had attempted to formulate theories of urban location as the industrial and transportation revolutions changed that continent:

The origin and location of towns is treated in a philosophic manner by Roscher in the introductory chapter of his work on commerce and industry: *System der Volkswirthschaft, dritter Band, Die Nationalokonomik des Handels und Gewerbefleisses, "Einleitung: Aus der Naturlehre des Stadtwesens im Allgemeinen."* Roscher further develops the theory of the location of cities in an essay "*Ueber die geographische Lage der Grossen Stadte*," published in his *Ansichten der Volkswirthschaft*, Vol. I. Cf. the work by J. G. Kohl, *Die geographische Lage der Haupstadten* and the latter's standard work, *Der Verkehr und die Ansiedelungen der Menschen in ihrer Abhängigkeit von der Gestaltung der Erdoberfläche*, 1843. This was written before the era of railways, however, and is in some respects superseded by the later works: E. Sax, *Die Verkehrsmittel in Volks: und Staatswirthschaft*, Vienna, 1878; A. de Foville, *De la Transformation des Moyens de Transport et ses Consequences economiques et sociales*, Paris, 1880. The most recent treatment is by a young American, Dr. C. H. Cooley, whose book (*The Theory of Transportation*, in Publications of the American Economic Association) will interest the general reader as well as the trained economist; it is by far the best study of the subject in English, but, like the others, is written from the standpoint of transportation. Sir James Stewart devotes a chapter of his *Inquiry into the Principles of Political Economy* to this subject ("What are the Principles which regulate the Distribution of Inhabitants into Farms, Villages, Hamlets, Towns and Cities?") Chap. ix in Vol. I of the *Works of Stewart*, edited by Gen. Sir J. Stewart, London, 1805. More recently the subject has been approached from the side of geography, e.g., Ratzel's *Anthropogeographie*, Vol. II, §§12–14, in which connection may also be mentioned a paper by Prof. W. Z. Ripley on "Geography and Sociology" (with bibliography) in the *Pol. Sc. Quar.*, X, 636–55.[10]

In his presentation of a theory of urban location, Cooley noted the effects of "military considerations . . . in early and warlike times," of "religious prestige," of "political forces," and of "the chance and possibly unwise selection of the first colonists."[11] He then continued:

Aside from these causes cities owe their origin entirely to economic forces. . . .

Of economic causes of cities the most general is pressure toward greater division of labor: the efficient use of natural forces is inseparable from the concentration of population and wealth. This cause acts independently of particular places and has of itself alone no action in fixing location.

Two influences chiefly determine the location of cities: local facilities for production and location relative to transportation. The former of these acts mostly through the coarser and primary manufacturing industries. The finer manufactures seek the most convenient centers of distribution, that is, of transportation.

Transportation, itself guided in its course chiefly by the earth's surface, is the main cause of the location of cities in an industrial society. The mode of its action is that *population and wealth tend to collect at a break in transportation;* the reason being in the first place the necessity for the material and symbolic machinery of transfer at breaks, and in the second the tendency of other economic activities to collect where that machinery exists.[12]

Cooley defined a "break" as "an interruption of the movement at least sufficient to cause a transfer of goods and their temporary storage." A "mechanical break" involves only a physical interruption of movement, and a "commercial break" includes a change in the ownership of the goods and so is of much greater importance. Breaks arise at necessary physical interruptions: at the junction of land transportation with water transportation, "the location of the greater number of commercial towns the world over"; along navigable rivers where they are most accessible from the land, perhaps at a pass or confluence with a smaller river, at fords or bridges, at the two sides of an isthmus, and at coastal and lake harbors; at the junction of two kinds of water transportation, "wherever the technical apparatus of vehicles and forces has to be changed," that is, "at that point in the course of rivers where seagoing vessels must be exchanged for lighter and shallower craft . . . the chief factor in determining the location of most commercial towns of the first class"; and also at the junction of two kinds of land transportation, railway and road intersections[13]:

> Thus in these days railways have much the same part in determining social development as formerly belonged to rivers. In their original location they are in great part influenced by the situation of existing cities; but once built they become themselves a cause of new cities, especially in those young countries where railroad building precedes population. The active towns are invariably placed on the line of the railway, and the precise location, if the surface is at all irregular or mountainous, is likely to be fixed by the point of intersection with an important earth road. The point where the railroad crosses a navigable river is of course favorable as being a place where the exchange between land and water movement takes place. The intersection of two railways has of itself no tendency to form a town, because there is no change in the kind of transportation, no necessary break [as at the borders of mountainous districts, and between desert or arid plains and fertile agricultural regions].[14]

Cooley, explicating his concept of the break, continues:

> It appears that the interruption is not necessarily due to a change in the natural features of the earth's surface, but may be simply the change from the vehicles of a small and scattered movement to those of a large and unified movement. Breaks of this sort are exceedingly important in land transportation, and exist wherever a number of small local movements come together and form by their junction a single large movement, or go to swell a large movement formed elsewhere. They correspond to the fact that the raw material of all commerce comes originally from the soil and must be collected at central points by the vehicles and at the convenient seasons of local transportation. So also whatever of local produce is consumed by the scattered population must be distributed by similar means. This sort of movement naturally takes on a radial form, the small local movements drawing together to a common point and contributing to the larger movement that takes place between that point and the others at a distance. At the point of junction of the larger and better equipped and organized long-distance transportation with the crude vehicles of local conveyance, there is necessarily an interruption of the movement. If the conditions are in every respect uniform, considerations of convenience tend to place these points of collection and distribution at the center of the tributary plain. The location of many towns and cities seems to be fixed by this requirement alone.[15]

A second major type of break is that due to political forces. "The obstacles to trade arising out of the non-industrial organization of many societies and particularly of international relations, often render it impracticable for merchants to extend their operations far into other countries than their own." In addition to determining locations of cities, the requirements of transportation also promote "the continual aggrandizement of the large towns at the expense of the smaller, by the removal to them of the mechanism of transfer and commercial exchange. From one point of view the number of breaks represents the expense of transportation, and the tendency to dispense with the smaller ones by means of interchange of vehicles, consolidation of lines, etc. is a part of the progress of the division of labor." Also, "the nucleus . . . of a commercial city tends strongly, though the tendency may be counteracted by adverse conditions, to become the seat of manufactures, of political power, and of the central institutions of all varieties of social organization."[16]

Weber also accepted the emphasis on transportation in his brief summary of "the fundamental theory . . . of the principles of city-location"[17]:

> The greatness of an inland city will depend on the size of the plain for which it is the natural centre of distribution, and in a second degree on the fertility of soil, which determines the number of inhabitants in the plain. The factor of chief importance in the location of cities is a *break in transportation*. . . . Every *great* city owes its eminence to commerce, and even in the United States, where the railways are popularly supposed to be the real city-makers, all but two of the cities of 100,000 or more inhabitants are situated upon navigable waters. . . . New York's primacy depends upon her location at the junction of land and water transportation; in New York occurs the change of ownership and transfer of goods in the commerce between Europe and the United States. If the water route could be extended inland to Chicago by means of a ship canal, Chicago would become the terminus of European commerce, and in the course of time would with scarcely any doubt take from New York the rank of commercial and financial centre of the New World, and prospectively, of the globe.[18]

Thus, early location theorists considered transportation to be the primary factor in city location: cities were found at breaks in transportation.

Environmentalism within Geography: Categories of City Sites

Weber's book belongs to the Studies in History, Economics, and Public Law of Columbia University, and Cooley's monograph appeared in the Publications of the American Economic Association. These first students of cities in America approached the location of cities as an economic problem, in the spirit of most of the founders of American towns, who had built for economic or commercial success. Both Cooley and Weber noted a new approach being taken by geographers, however, especially in the work of Ratzel, in which greater priority was assigned to the environment. William Z. Ripley, in his article "Geography as a Sociological Study," an early methodological presentation of the field, discussed the "widespread revival of interest in geographical studies . . . now under way among English-speaking peoples."[19]

> The geography that is attracting the historian today is that which is defined by Gonner as "the study of the environments of man." It is the geography of Guyot and of Ritter, enlightened by the newly developed sciences of anthropology, archaeology, sociology and even statistics. Call it "physiography"—defined by Professor Huxley as the science of man in relation to the earth, as distinct from geography, the science of the earth in its relations to man; "anthropo-geography," with Professor Ratzel; or "histo-geography," with other writers: all these names point to the same end. . . . In fact geography, in any of the familiar senses, is after all only one element in this new science, which is simply an attempt to explain the growing conviction so well expressed by Professor Giddings, "that civilization is at bottom an economic fact." As such the new discipline is subordinate to history and yet superior to it. It stands to history as anatomy does to art. . . . In this sense, then, geography becomes a branch of economic as well as of historical inquiry, deriving from that fact twofold importance.[20]

"Human history," he wrote, "may be resolved into three factors—environment, race and epoch," adding, "At the present day there is a pronounced movement toward a favorable reception . . . of the science which deals with environment in history"[21]:

> It is a branch of economics, with a direct bearing upon history and sociology. . . . "It is the point of contact between the sciences of nature taken all together and the branches of inquiry which deal with man and his institutions." . . . the science may, perhaps, be termed merely a mode of sociological investigation—the geographical as distinguished from the graphical method; and in this case there is no limit to its application. . . . With all its possibilities, however, this science must clearly recognize its own limitations, arising from the power of purely historical elements, of personality, of religious enthusiasm, and of patriotism. . . . Yet, even if it does not reach the grade of a predictive science, the study of the *milieu* cannot be neglected. One of its aims will always be to discover whether the historical development of a people is in harmony with its environment, and if not, whether it is a plus or minus factor in progress.[22]

In addition to his presentation of this "new geography," Ripley also considered the conflicts of opinion on the matters of heredity vs. environment, direct vs. indirect influences of the milieu, and escape from natural influences through cultural advances vs. progress in civilization with ever more specialized adaptation to natural resources. The last question was of increasing importance to later writers who considered the location of different types of cities and of particular cities. But it was this new geography described by Ripley, in contrast to that which had produced "topographical descriptions . . . miniature gazetteers . . . [and studies in] dynamic geology,"[23] that emerged as a major part of the social sciences in the late nineteenth and early twentieth centuries and whose proponents undertook the geographical discussion of the location of cities—a discussion of those critical features of the environment which have operated historically in the process of locating cities.

Ratzel's fundamental contribution to this work was acknowledged by leading urbanists in other fields. A summary of Ratzel's writing by Louis Wirth appears in *The City*, the classic series of position papers published in 1925 by the emerging Chicago School of urban sociologists:

> *Ratzel, Friedrich.* "*Die geographische Lage der grossen Stadte*," in *Die Grosstadt*, edited by Th. Petermann, Dresden, 1903: A thoroughgoing consideration of the location of types of cities by one of the earliest and most competent students of the subject. Offers the theory,

also held by Cooley, that cities arise at the end of a route of transportation, or at a juncture of several such routes, or at the point where one route of transportation joins another, where, for instance a land transportation route ends and a waterway begins. Ratzel also gives one of the earliest and soundest geographical definitions of the city: "A permanent condensation (or dense settlement) of human beings and human habitations covering a considerable area and situated in the midst (or at the juncture) of several routes of transportation."[24]

Ratzel's approach at this juncture appears indistinguishable from that of Cooley, with whom he shared a common antecedent, J. G. Kohl. The concern with "geographic" factors with which Ratzel is more closely associated appears in another work, *The History of Mankind*, Vol. I (1896) translated by A. J. Butler:

The effects of the craving for protection reach neither far nor deep, when the essence of it is only isolation; but when it tends to pack men together it gives rise to developments which have a wide and mighty bearing. The great cities which belong to the most marvellous results of civilization stand at the further end of the effects produced by this tendency to unite men and their dwellings about a single point. Nothing will enable us so well to recognize the power of the motive of defence as a glance at the situation of cities. We find fortified villages crowded together on the tops of mountains or on islands, in the bights of rivers or on tongues of land. Since most centres of habitation have been laid out at a time when a thin population was beginning to spread, and the danger of hostile invasions was vividly before their eyes, considerations of defence are often strongly stamped on their situation. . . .

[Another] cause to be considered is common interests in labour. These of course increase with the progress of economic division of labour, until they form the principal cause which decides the situation of an inhabited place. Even at primitive stages of culture large populations assemble temporarily in spots where useful things occur in quantity. . . if, when life has become settled, the population increases and division of labour comes in, larger habitations will spring up until such spots of the earth as are furnished by Nature with any special wealth will, as the highest stages of civilization are reached, show those unwontedly dense populations—400 and upwards to the square mile—which we meet in the fertile lowlands of the Nile and Ganges, in the coal and iron districts of Central and Western Europe, or in the goldfields of Australia and California.

The larger isolated aggregations, on the contrary, come into existence at definite points, which have become points where the streams of traffic meet or intersect. The wish for exchange of goods first causes the need for drawing as near as possible; traffic creates towns. Everywhere that Nature simplifies or intensifies traffic great assemblages of men spring up, whether as cities of the world like London, or market-towns like Nyangwe.

We assume by a kind of instinct a certain connection between cities and higher culture, and not without reason, since it is in the cities that the highest flower of our culture declares itself. . . . [A] certain material culture is independent of the highest intellectual culture and . . . cities help to serve that life of trade which is less dependent on culture. . . . If cities are an organic product of national life, they are now always the result of that race's own force to which they belong. There are towns of international trade. . . . So mighty is traffic that it bears with it the organization necessary to it into the midst of an alien nationality; so that again whole races which have become organs of traffic bear the stamp of town life on their brow. . . . The first conquerors of an inhabited country, again, are often compelled to live in towns, independently of traffic; feeling themselves secure only in close settlements. Then in later times these compulsory towns follow the natural requirements of trade, and change their situation. Premature foundation of towns is a symptom of young colonizations; in North and Central America we may find ruined cities of quite modern date.[25]

"Such spots of the earth as are furnished by Nature," "everywhere that Nature simplifies or intensifies traffic," are expressions of the "new geography" concerned with environmental influences on man's activities, of which Ripley wrote in 1895.

It was Ellen Churchill Semple who interpreted Ratzel's writing to Americans; she concentrated almost exclusively on environmental factors and principles, and created much of our contemporary image of environmentalism—that "Man is a product of the earth's surface,"[26] for example. This idea was taken up by American geographers as peculiarly their own at the turn of the century. Semple's 1897 article, "Some Geographic Causes Determining the Location of Cities," in the *Journal of School Geography*, emphasized the historical sequences of defensive and commercial locations, changing transportation technologies, the environmental determinants of trade accessibility, and mining and manufacturing resources. In her book *American History and Its Geographic Conditions* (1903), she included statements on the location of cities within this historical framework, and in *Influences of Geographic Environment* (1911), she presented a typology of commercial cities: coast, pass, piedmont, river, and seaport. Semple's idea of the city was very similar to that of Cooley's:

As society in general passed out of the militant stage into the industrial stage, this consideration—the needs of trade—came to outweigh all others. The modern city is essentially a center of industry and commerce, a point for collecting, producing, and distributing commodities of all kinds. Its location must be as accessible as possible, at the crossroads of the great world highways, in sharp contrast to the isolated, inaccessible sites of the militant past. It must be easily reached by land and sea, ocean steamer, river packet, canal boat, railroad and turnpike if it is to develop into a metropolis.[27]

But where Cooley emphasized breaks in transportation, Semple emphasized the types of physical obstacles causing these breaks, distinctive types of cities naturally appearing at these breaks to handle the needs of circulation, and also the support available to cities from the surrounding countryside:

Piedmont belts tend strongly towards urban development, even where rural settlement is sparse. Sparsity of population and paucity of towns within the mountains cause main lines of traffic to keep outside the highlands, but close enough to their base to tap their trade at every valley outlet. On the alluvial fans or plains of these valley outlets, where mountain and piedmont road intersect, towns grow up. Some of them develop into cities, when they command transverse routes of communication quite across the highlands . . . .

Piedmont cities draw their support from plain, mountain, and transmontane regions, relying chiefly on the fertile soil of the level country to feed their large populations.[28]

Wherever there is a decided bend in the direction of a river course, a necessity for some division of traffic arises.[29]

Natural advantages, always important and always desirable, have been made to take a secondary place since the introduction of the railroad. New towns are springing up where none of these advantages exist and where the site has little to recommend it as such except that there occurs the junction of several railroad lines and so excellent facilities for transportation.[30]

All seaport towns are on the world's greatest and cheapest highway, the ocean. Theirs is the first and greatest advantage. Their further development depends upon the area, fertility, and population of the back country which they command, and their means of communication with the same . . . . Coast cities develop because they are middlemen in the commerce of all the bordering continents . . . . New York and San Francisco are on opposite sides of the same country, command therefore the same area, and have equally good harbors; but while New York is connected by cheap waterways and almost level railroads with the interior, for San Francisco the high freight rates over the Rocky Mountains are prohibitive except for merchandise of small bulk and large volume, and the arid plains and highlands of the west can never support the same density of population as the fertile region which lies within the range of attraction of the Hudson River port. Moreover San Francisco's trans-oceanic connections are longer than those of New York, and the outbound cargo finds a far more restricted market than the highly progressive countries of Europe offer to the commerce of our Atlantic cities.[31]

Semple's work on commercial cities was paralleled by Vaughan Cornish's presentation of environmental considerations of political importance in his book *The Great Capitals: An Historical Geography* (1923):

A Great, or Imperial, Capital, is the headquarters of a Great Power, whether the Power be monarchical or republican. It has a double aspect, that of an Urban community with exceptionally wide interests, and a Geographical site with exceptional advantages. It is with the latter only that we are here concerned. For the purpose of this study the Natural Regions or districts of the World must be considered in relation to the Productive Areas from which supplies of men and material are obtained, the Lines of Communication along which these are moved, and the Natural Obstructions which hinder movement. Classified according to the predominance of one or other of these characters they fall into the three categories of natural Storehouses, Crossways, and Strongholds. The first is the original and fundamental character, the second and third dependent upon it, for easy movement and natural barriers are only important if there be inducement to develop or obstruct traffic. It is therefore the world's Storehouses of natural wealth which sooner or later determine the importance of Crossways and Strongholds.

An historical examination of imperial capitals shows that their district is usually either a Storehouse, or a far-reaching Crossways near a Storehouse, seldom a Stronghold. Their political geography has one outstanding character, a forward, as distinguished from a central, site. The Great Power both of ancient and modern times has always been an incorporation of several States, and the characteristic site of the imperial capital is in or adjacent to that Storehouse of the dominant community of the empire which is nearest to the principal foreign neighbour. When by the growth of the Empire the capital ceases to be in this position the government transferred its seat to another city or founded a new city. When, on the contrary, the advance of the frontiers left the capital in the same relative position the government did not change its seat. The sites of these enduring headquarters became great capitals in the fullest sense, the seat of great political power, cities with great population, and great centres of culture.

The initial capital of a federation of sovereign States is at a connection between the States themselves, not of the whole territory with foreign countries, but when the States consolidate the capital is in a forward position.

The requirements which place a sovereign capital in the forward area are suggested when we contrast its administration with that of a provincial capital. The domestic affairs of a province would be most conveniently conducted at the natural crossways of communication nearest to the centre of the district. The government of a sovereign State is, however, charged with the conduct of foreign as well as home affairs. Hence, its most convenient seat in times of peace is the natural crossways which provides the best junction of the home communications with those which lead across the most important frontier.

As every civilized country is engaged in foreign as well as home trade, the same conditions determine the site of the best commercial centre. In time of war the government has to be in a forward position in order to keep in touch with operations, but the presence of a large Urban population is an embarrassment. This drawback has attracted more popular attention than the advantage of a great junction of roads not far from the principal frontier (ensured by the forward position of the capital) which assists strategic concentration. The doctrine of the Forward Position of the capital, which is hoped this book will establish, is, however, not theoretical, but historical. The proof does not depend upon the explanations given above but upon the evidence in the following chapters, in which most of the chief examples of ancient and modern times have been examined.[32]

Urban Geography, by Griffith Taylor (1946), perhaps the most extreme of the environmentalist studies of cities, brought to an end such leanings in urban studies. Geography had embroiled itself, by the time he wrote his book, in a methodological debate over the precise definition of the field. Environmental determinism had been *disapproved* (but not *disproved*) by the majority of professionals in America by the 1930's, but Taylor declared himself for the environmentalists:

> The peculiar province of the geographer is to interpret the relation between man and his environment. For a generation there has been debate as to the closeness of this relationship, geographers being divided into two schools on the question. The Possibilists stress the human aspect of the relation, the Determinists the environmental factor. The present writer belongs to the latter school.[33]

His stand on the question led Taylor, in his "evaluation of the relation in regard to the three main types of human agglomeration . . . . Race, Nation and City,"[34] to produce an entire volume on city location and growth as affected by features of the natural environment, well illustrated by topographical maps and containing numerous examples:

> It will be of interest to many geographers to see what determined the writer to adopt the classification and order which is described in his book. . . . In the case of the present writer it is the site and the evolution which are of most interest. . . . I have endeavoured to describe processes and stages in some detail in the case of a few outstanding examples. . . . The later chapters take the *dominant feature of the environment as the key to the city*. . . . It seems more logical to use the unaltering character of the site as our chief determiner rather than the varied functions of the city.[35]

In the first part of the book, Taylor studies seven cities chosen for their latitudes—"in the broadest sense *latitude* is the variable which most controls human affairs"[36]—and asks the questions:

1. What induced man to settle in this region?
2. Why did he choose this particular site of all those available?
3. What kind of a settlement developed on the chosen site?
4. How far has the settlement progressed towards the climax stage, having in view the period since it was founded?
5. Can we decide where the environmental factors and where the human factors have played the greater part in the present pattern?[37]

In the second part, he discusses "the various classes of towns as controlled by their sites."[38] "It seems logical to the writer to discuss sites of towns in an order based essentially on varying importance of the topography."[39] His classes are cities at: hills; cuestas; mountain corridors; passes; plateaux; eroded domes; ports, including fiords, rias, river estuaries, and roadsteads; rivers, falls, meanders, terraces, deltas, fans, valleys, islands; lakes. All of these are "controlled primarily by the topography of their sites."[40] Those where the topography is less obvious are cities on plains, cleared out of forests, and in deserts. Cities developed to serve special human needs include mining, tourist, and railway cities, the first two being located in reference to special qualities in the environment. Miscellaneous types are: planned, ghost, boom, and suburban towns. Taylor's classification thus covers the types of commercial settings considered by Semple, other social and economic types of cities defined in the work of the land economists of the 1920's (see below), and the internal structure and development of the city also raised as a major question in the 1920's. His book is mainly built of descriptions of typical city features and patterns of growth at typical city sites, as, for example:

> In the early days all the region to the south of the Red River confluence was known as the Delta. New Orleans was the sole town for many decades in this large area. The delta was crossed by a maze of bayous, all of which could be reached fairly readily from the young settlement. A canal was cut (via the bayou) to the large lake Pontchartrain from the old French City, and this opened up much country to the north-east. "Down river" it was about 100 miles from the sea, and there was a large trade with Mexico and the West Indies in those early days. Tides had little effect in the crescent-shaped harbour; and the chief wharves, then as now, were on the northern concave side of the great bend of the Mississippi near the French city.
>
> There were three or four small settlements in the delta, such as Madisonville on Lake Pontchartrain, placed on a higher portion of the levee. At the time of the Purchase (1803) there was one cotton mill in the city. About this time there were ten sugar refineries in the valley, and one at New Orleans produced annually about 200,000 lbs. of load sugar. Lumber was important, and the planters cut mill races through the natural "levees" (i.e., high natural ridges bordering the senile river), and erected saw mills which worked continuously during flood periods. In 1803 the port exported flour, tobacco, salt beef, and cotton to the amount of 40,000 tons. Until 1820 the downriver trade originated chiefly in the Ohio River, whence flour was sent to New Orleans. About 1817, 287 barges came regularly to the city. In 1825 the commerce of New Orleans was worth seventeen million dollars, and by 1840 New Orleans was the fourth city in population in the United States.
>
> The plan of the city about 1803 . . . has a number of points of interest. There were a number of disadvantages, the chief being the low site, so that in floodtime there was always danger of the natural levees breaking and allowing the river to flood the lower parts of the city. . . . Sewage and drainage were very real difficulties in the early days, and accounted for the rather unhealthy reputation of New Orleans. Bienville founded the settlement in 1718, and the early French city was in the form of a rectangle, surrounded by the ramparts and bastions in the approved military style of the late 17th century. The central portion alongside the river was the Place d'Armes, and the streets within the ramparts were arranged in the conventional grid . . . .
>
> . . .
>
> . . . To-day the city extends for four miles up the river from the oldest quarter, and about two miles down stream. It has spread north along the Carondelet Canal as far as Lake Pontchartrain; and important suburbs such as Algiers and Gretna lie on the south bank of the river.
>
> One peculiarity of the western portion of the city is the radiating character of the streets . . . and the "fan" seems to be due to the streets being laid out at right angles to the curving meander of the river.[41]

The "Possibilists"

French geographers avowing the "possibilism" disavowed by Taylor, particularly Jean Brunhes and Max. Sorre, also considered the environmental settings of cities but stressed the human rather than the physical aspects of settlement patterns. While the general line of reasoning of the Kohl–Ratzel "transportation hypothesis" was accepted, the French inclined more to biological analogies and reasoning than to the geometric formulations of the Germans, in keeping with a Gallic orientation begun by Emile Levasseur. Brunhes' *Human Geography: An Attempt at a Positive Classification, Principles and Examples* (1920) was adjudged by Wirth to be:

> . . . the most comprehensive and basic work in human geography at the present time available. Discusses the city as a form of occupation of the soil. Describes the principles and gives many illustrations of the effect of location on the growth and the character of cities.[42]

Brunhes considered the city to be an unproductive occupation of the soil, whose geographical localization is influenced by "the same natural facts which influence the location of the house."[43] Natural facts described and illustrated with reference to the city were the sun, water as a source of food, as drinking water, and as a route, topographical conditions, forests, climatic conditions, the snow line, and limits of vegetation. These facts are in the nature of conditions tending to make life more or less supportable in a particular place:

> An intense historical life maintains a city in an environment which is geographically abnormal. . . . Still further, a definite political interest may create an entirely artificial establishment. . . . Finally there are cases where men, with deliberate purpose, create a settlement in a new country precisely in order that there may be no bonds with any earlier political interest. . . . When conditions are unfavorable to an urban establishment it seems that a more ingenious necessity and a more considerable human force are alone capable of overcoming the difficulty.[44]

More elements than just the topographical were included as environmental factors affecting city location; however, the general location involves a place within the framework of the circulation system:

> The concentration of habitations keeps pace with the concentration of paths of communication. The larger a city, the finer the network of roads which surround it. Inversely, the more physical conditions favor the concentration of roads at one point, the more possibilities of growth a city has. The essential needs of the inhabitants demand for their satisfaction a fine network of paths of communication. . . .
>
> In attaching roads to itself the city commands and maintains them. While a simple trail . . . may be very easily displaced, every great city, by becoming an almost necessary point of arrival and departure, fixes roads at least for a long time and gives a certain permanence to the main directions successively adopted by more and more modern types of paths of circulation.
>
> The road leads toward the urban center and depends upon it; but this constructed center also depends upon the road. The city creates the road; the road in its turn creates the city or re-creates it—that is, displaces it or changes its form.[45]

The Influence of Ecology on Physical Planning

The continuing emphasis of the French scholars was on the interdependence of the city and its social and physical environment. This ecological view was carried over into emerging urban planning in England, France, and the United States by Patrick Geddes in the years 1890 to 1925. Geddes was a teacher rather than a writer. For twelve successive summers he held seminars in Edinburgh for urbanists and city planners from all disciplines and all countries in Western Europe, plus the United States, in which he emphasized the organic approach to city planning—the harmonious relationships between city and region, between city and environment, and of land uses within cities, as well as the role of planning in achieving harmony where it did not exist. In particular, his idea laid the foundations of modern physical planning as the presumed means by which harmony can be achieved in the social life of cities. Among later scholars who acknowledged their debt to Geddes were Aurousseau, Unwin, Mark Jefferson, Patrick Abercrombie, who prepared the Greater London Plan, and Geddes' greatest American student and disciple, Lewis Mumford. Further, he was a major influence in the New York Regional Plan group of 1925, which involved Mumford, Clarence Stein, and Robert M. Haig. This group did much to stimulate modern city planning and to draw together some of the major concepts of urban land economics.

Urban Land Economics and the Emergence of Interest in City Structure

In spite of the influence of Geddes upon urban studies, the extremes of the environmentalist perspective and later reactions to it were creating considerable intellectual stress within geography during the 1920's and 1930's, for geography during this period became increasingly inward-looking. Ironically, Richard M. Hurd had, in 1903, already provided the beginnings of a more balanced view that generated a new discipline—urban land economics—and that was later to provide urban geographers with a way out of the methodological dilemmas involved in the environmentalist debate.

He wrote, on city locations and their determinants:

> The same factors create all modern cities; commerce and manufactures, with political and social forces, being everywhere operative, the chief difference in influence coming from variations in their relative power. . . .
>
> . . .
>
> Defense against enemies, the chief factor in primitive times creating cities, survived as an influence affecting

the first settlements in this country, the early forts on the Atlantic Coast and in the West drawing population around them in the same way that the Roman camps on the borders of the Danube and Rhine, and the Cossack camps in southern Russia started cities. With the establishment of civilized government the necessity for defence has vanished and population is concentrated either by commerce or manufactures, or by the less important political and social factors.

Commerce, or the distribution of commodities, involves their storage and transfer, and requires warehouses, docks and freight depots, while the population engaged in this business requires residences, shops and public buildings. Where the products handled are of low value, and the handling is a simple trans-shipment, the result of even a large flow of commodities in locating population at a point of trans-shipment may be small. It is when the transfer of goods is accompanied by a breaking of bulk or by a change of ownership, there being then added the complex mechanism of commercial exchange performed by importers, exporters, wholesalers, retailers, insurers, brokers and bankers, that wealth is accumulated and localized, with consequent power to control business for local benefit.

Manufactures are of constantly increasing importance in city growth, owing to the development of the factory system and the advantages of labor supply, transportation, and markets in the larger cities. Diversified manufactures are a creation of the last fifty years, the law of development being an evolution from a rough working of coarser forms of necessary articles in the newer sections of a country, through various grades of refining and specialization, to a great variety of necessaries and luxuries in the older and more populous sections. A city created soley by manufactures is a modern development.

Political forces operate to build up a city when it is the seat of national, state or county government, either legislative, executive or judicial, or all combined. The administration of government as a single factor has created but few cities, Alexandria furnishing an ancient example, St. Petersburg, Moscow and Washington later examples, and in this country a few state capitals being arbitrarily started, such as Columbus, O., Indianapolis, Ind., and Lincoln, Neb. Nevertheless the rapid growth of Berlin, London and Vienna has been largely due to the centralizing of national government in those cities. In many American state capitals, city growth is injured by public attention being diverted from business to politics.

All other factors creating cities may be broadly classed as social, cities being centres of culture and furnishing education, art, fashion, intellectual stimulus and amusements to their tributary country. The social factor operates in direct ratio to the size of the city, social ambition and opportunities constituting a steady attracting force through the various grades of cities, migration being from the farm to the village, from the village to the town and from the town to the city. Thus the fact that New York counts among its inhabitants the great majority of American millionaires is of vital importance in maintaining its luxurious standard of hotels, shops, theatres, clubs and restaurants, which in turn attracts the pleasure-seeking travelers of this country. Insofar as a city is a market or consuming centre, business is created and population attracted, cities in some cases being consuming points only, such as Atlantic City, St. Augustine, Newport, etc., where wealth is not created, but a city is required to minister to those distributing wealth.

All cities which have attained any considerable size include in varying proportions all the above factors of commerce, manufactures, political and social forces. In each city the sections built up by the different factors may be clearly distinguished, these flourishing or decaying according to the prosperity or decline of their special factors. Thus the railroads, docks and warehouses evidence the city's commerce; the factories its industrial energies; the retail shops the consuming power of the population; the residence sections the wealth, social grades and numbers of the citizens; and the buildings of public and semi-public utility the standard of civilization and civic pride of the city.

The underlying factors which start all the processes creating and distributing wealth are the energy and enterprise of the people, these being in the last analysis the sole sources of wealth.[46]

Hurd attached great importance to the notion that "Raw materials, waterways, favorable climate and other natural advantages are only indirectly decisive and always presuppose men to exploit them."[47]

Spelling out his ideas further, and extending the statement to internal structure and form, he said:

Cities originate at their most convenient point of contact with the outer world and grow in the lines of least resistance or greatest attraction, or their resultants. The point of contact differs according to the methods of transportation, whether by water, by turnpike or by railroad. The forces of attraction and resistance include topography, the underlying material on which city builders work; external influences, projected into the city by trade routes; internal influences derived from located utilities; and finally the reactions and readjustments due to the continual harmonizing of conflicting elements. The influence of topography, all-powerful when cities start, is constantly modified by human labor, hills being cut down, waterfronts extended, and swamps filled in, this, however, not taking place until the new building sites are worth more than the cost of filling and cutting. The measure of resistance to the city's growth is here changed from terms of land elevation or depression, and hence income cost, to terms of investment or capital cost. The most direct results of topography come from its control of transportation, the water fronts locating exchange points for water commerce, and the water grade normally determining the location of the railroads entering the city. As cities grow, external influences become constantly of less relative importance, while the original simple utilities develop into a multitude of differentiated and specialized utilities, tending constantly to segregate into definite districts.

Growth in cities consists of movement away from the point of origin in all directions, except as topographically hindered, this movement being due both to aggregation at the edges and pressure from the centre. Central growth takes place both from the heart of the city and from each subcentre of attraction, and axial growth pushes into the outlying territory by means of railroads, turnpikes and street railroads. All cities are built up from these two influences, which vary in quantity, intensity and quality, the resulting districts overlapping, interpenetrating, neutralizing and harmonizing as the pressure of the city's growth brings them in contact with each other. The fact of vital interest is that, despite confusion from the intermingling of utilities, the order of dependence of each definite district on the other is always the same. Residences are early driven to the circumference, while business remains at the centre, and as residences divide into various social grades, retail shops of corresponding grades follow them, and wholesale shops in turn follow the retailers, while institutions and various mixed utilities irregularly fill in the intermediate zone, and the banking and office section remains at the main business centre. Complicating this broad outward movement of zones, axes of traffic project shops through residence areas, create business subcentres where they intersect, and change circular cities into star-shaped cities. Central growth, due to proximity and axial growth, due to accessibility, are summed up in the power of established sections and the dynamic power of their chief lines of intercommunication.[48]

Further:

The continual readjustments in the life of a city, reflecting the total social relations of its inhabitants, lead to the concept of a city as a living organism. That such a concept is popularly held is shown by the common phrases, the "heart" of the city to represent the business centre, the "arteries" of traffic to represent the streets, the "lungs" of the city to represent the parks, and, to carry the similes further, the railroad depots and wharves may be called the mouths through which the city is fed, the telephone and telegraph lines its nervous system, while man in his residence has been likened by Spencer to a particle of protoplasm surrounding itself with a cell.[49]

And finally:

Underneath all economic laws, the final basis of human action is psychological, so that the last stage of analysis of the problems of the structure of cities, the distribution of utilities, the earnings of the buildings which house them, and the land values resulting therefrom, turn on individual and collective taste and preference, as shown in social habits and custom.[50]

Hurd's statement remains one of the clearest and best. Together with the foundations laid by Ratzel and Semple, who dealt with the modern city as an economic creation on the physical landscape, Cooley, who treated it as one element in a transportation system, and Cornish, who considered politically strategic locations, it led to the classical typology of city locations that emerged in the 1920's. As Weber had accepted the transportation theory and presented "facts" about cities accordingly, so the students of the city in the 1920's largely accepted and presented the "facts" of previous location theory in a textbook manner, as a necessary introduction to their main concern with the city itself. Then the internal structure of the city became the consuming interest of "urban" sociologists, land economists, and geographers:

Cities are a distinguishing mark of advanced civilizations. There have been careful studies of the political, social and legal aspects of this phenomenon of advanced civilizations since the beginning of scientific inquiry; it is passing strange that the study of the economic aspects of the physical structure itself, and of the uses to which its different parts are put, should not have received earlier attention.

A promising beginning of this study was made in 1903 with the publication of *Principles of City Land Values*, but for many years the study languished. It received a new impulse from the organization of the Institute for Research in Land Economics and Public Utilities in 1920; and in 1923 with the publication of the first edition of the present work, the study came again into the forefront.

Doubtless additional necessity for the study was indicated by the conditions prevailing throughout the country at the end of the Great War, when, due to the accumulated congestion and the tendency toward lateral expansion caused by the universal use of individual transportation, American cities began to develop with a rapidity that was astonishing. Changes in their internal structure were effected with no less rapidity and with as great an influence upon the value of the land.

Another impulse has come from the study of sociologists of what has come to be known as human ecology.

The objective of these studies appears to be that of discovering the relationships which exist between social organizations, customs, and the institutions and the positions which they occupy relative to each other. . . .

Attention on the problem has also been focused by geographers, by whom an attempt is being made to ascertain the relationship between urban communities and the natural features of the environment in which cities are found. More and more the attention of geographers appears to be turned toward the problems of urban geography.

For many years the great city planning movement in the United States concerned itself chiefly with elements of the aesthetic in the planning of cities. Latterly, however, there appears to be a tendency, also, for this great group of American thinkers to turn their attention more and more to the problem of uses and the functioning of land in urban areas . . . .

The premise upon which the current studies are being made is that the city is, after all, a natural phenomenon. As such, it is obedient to natural laws. Its growth is a natural growth, and the changes wrought by growth by careful observation can be classified and the natural laws governing them discovered.[51]

With this introduction, Stanley McMichael and Robert F. Bingham began their book *City Growth Essentials*. This book and *Urban Land Economics* by Herbert P. Dorau and Albert G. Hinman, published in the same year (1928), dealt primarily with factors affecting city land utilization and values. Both contain an introductory chapter on the location of cities, presenting a typology which also appeared in Henry C. Wright's *The American City: An Outline of Its Development and Functions* (1916), which was mainly a study of government, finance, and administrative problems.[52] As set forth in *Urban Land Economics*, the typology presents typical physical locations which offer advantages for major city functions:

A city is located where it is because the location offers some definite advantages for the satisfaction of whatever need or needs have given occasion for the city. Thus we see that the same social, political and economic factors that affect urbanization operate to determine the relative desirability or undesirability of various available sites for cities.[53]

Environment is only of significance within the context of some kind of need. Social factors that are satisfied by particular topographical features are the desire for defense, and for recreation, which "has occasioned that evaluation of climate and scenery which has established the resort cities."[54] Political factors affecting physical location are the centralization of authority and administration, and considerations of international strategy. Economic factors, the "most important in stimulating urbanization" and so "most important in locating cities" are natural resources for agriculture, fishing, lumbering, water power, and mining, and the opportunities for trade, the "most important economic factor influencing the choice of sites."[55] (McMichael also included religious shrines and manufacturing enterprises as factors.) The typology is by now most familiar, but an additional idea was introduced into the concept of city location by Dorau and Hinman, the idea of a distinction between *particular site* and *general situation:* "Thus the conclusion is reached that the general location of a city would be determined by the general economic, social, and political factors, chiefly the economic, while the specific site would be determined by the local physiographic character of the area."[56] This idea is illustrated by the examples of Chicago and Philadelphia:

It might seem somewhat out-of-the-ordinary that a city should find its origin in a swamp when more pleasant sites were available. However, the Chicago and Illinois rivers flowing into Lake Michigan were important canoe routes in the pioneer days, in fact the best from the Great Lakes to the Southern Mississippi. This fact determined the specific site of Chicago.[57]

Philadelphia owes its origin primarily to religious motives. However, Penn was careful to locate the city between two rivers, the Delaware and the Schuylkill, and close to the point where these rivers emptied into the ocean, forming a good harbor. This location insured the city importance as a trading center because the products of the hinterland follow the water route to the coast.[58]

When the problem of the internal structure of the city was approached, the question of actual site became important, especially to land economists and urban geographers; the smaller topographical details affecting utilization, land values, and city growth and expansion became important considerations along with the grosser features which initially determined the suitability of sites and eventually affected city success or failure. Dorau presents a brief summary of the physiographic factors influencing the direction of city growth:

With respect to their influence upon the direction of city growth, physiographic features may be classified as entirely advantageous, partly advantageous, or entirely disadvantageous. Thus the process of urban structural development involves: (1) proper conformation to the entirely advantageous features, (2) alteration, to better adapt, of the partly advantageous features, and (3) avoidance or destruction of the entirely disadvantageous features.

Cities quite normally follow the line of least resistance in their development. At the beginning, when the demand for land is not great, the town conforms itself to the advantageous features; in fact, the city has been located exactly where it is partly because of certain desirable features. As the town grows into a city and the demand for land increases, the process is begun of altering them to the city's needs. In both of these first two stages of growth the entirely disadvantageous features are avoided, let alone. Finally when the great city stage is reached and it becomes necessary to utilize every foot of land possible in the urban area, entirely disadvantageous features, physical obstacles, are removed where possible. Thus it is at the beginning that a city is limited by its physiography, and hence that these factors have the most influence in determining the direction of growth. As the city increases in size this limitation is more and more overcome and this factor becomes less influential.

The physiographic features which interfere with the free central and axial growth of cities from their points of origin may be classified again according to their physical nature as, (1) land features, such as hills, ravines, and rough, irregular surfaces, and (2) water features, such as harbors, lakes, rivers, creeks, and swamps.

As has already been noted, business sections grow up on level land and residential sections on land of moderate elevation, transport utilizes low land, industries occupy poor lands, often filled in, and recreational uses are developed around points of natural beauty. Thus to a considerable extent existing physiographic features can be conformed to. It is the sharp variations from the general topography which form the barriers to growth. Gradual hills may be utilized for fine residential sections without much change, but steep hills must be leveled or otherwise removed. The boring of a 12,000-foot tunnel under Twin Peaks in the city of San Francisco provided access to the center of the city from a large area, causing an urban growth toward the west.

Ravines may be utilized by transport lines and thus promote axial growth parallel to them, but unless they are narrow enough to be bridged easily or shallow enough to fill, growth across them is stopped. Likewise rough and irregular surfaces will be avoided until the demand for sites has become so great as to make it practicable to grade them.

Deep harbors and lakes are irremovable obstacles to city growth and, hence, form part of the outline of cities located on them. As has been pointed out, the waterfront serves as the base for rectangular platting in lake and ocean harbors. In the case of rivers, the usual growth is first along the river for a way, then back from the river, and finally across the river if it is not too wide and if there are good sites on the other side. If the city originates on an island, as in the case of Paris and of New York City, the sites on the island are developed very intensively before growth is carried across the water surfaces. Creeks have the same effect as rivers except that they are crossed or filled in more quickly. The ravine worn by the erosion of a creek often bars city growth except when its use by a transportation line promotes axial growth. Marshes limit the direction of growth in the case of smaller cities, but as cities become large and spread over the original level and moderate elevations, the demand for land may cause the marshes to be filled in. The Back Bay district of Boston is a striking example of filled-in marshy surface.

It is difficult to isolate and discuss the influence of physiography in determining the direction of city growth because it is so conditioned by economic forces. It was brought out in the discussion above that cities become freer from the limitation of physiography as they become larger because the increasing demand for land makes it practicable to remove natural obtacles. This is an economic consideration. It means that there are enough people able and willing to pay for sites a price sufficient to more than compensate the cost of removing the obstacles to the site.[59]

McMichael offers another typology, one based on internal topography alone:

1. The flat city, built upon a level plain or plateau.
2. The rolling type, with slight undulations in grade.
3. Hill cities, where steep grades are encountered.
4. Valley cities, flat in part, but with mountains or hills above them. Some cities may have topographical conditions which partake of almost all of the characteristics noted. Topographical features, which are actually handicaps in some respects, may be offset by greater advantages offered in other phases of a city's physical layout. For instance, a settlement may build upon several hillsides, yet this fault may be offset by the presence of a splendid harbor.[60]

Various effects of topography and general physical and climatic setting are noted: the cooling ocean breezes at Los Angeles which contrast with the heated valley at Pasadena; the scenic advantages of Minneapolis's chain of lakes; the necessity of dealing with waterfalls; soil conditions, as affecting building foundations, the growth of trees and shrubbery, and salubrity; and natural disasters.

> Cities lying along seashores, subject to visitations of tidal waves and hurricanes frequently invoke engineering genius to protect themselves from devastating elements. ... Residents of Miami, in 1926, after the disastrous hurricane, realized that a low, flat seaside city has little hope of successfully contending with such disasters when they occur ....
>
> Topography has a decided influence in the layout of the streets and highways of a city. ... In a city of the level type, square or rectangular street systems usually prevail, because there is nothing to prevent such a layout. Where hills and ravines intervene, winding streets and boulevards are often used.[61]

In addition to such effects on the physical appearance of a city,

> Topography may exert a definite influence upon the ultimate size of a city. Suburbanization is steadily going on in every large city, yet there is a constant growth in the central business district, filled up as it is with a miscellaneous class of buildings and businesses. Pittsburgh has for years been facing the problem of expanding its downtown business area but has found it extremely difficult to do so because it is hemmed in by two rivers. The city some years ago cut away a great hill to provide comparatively level land to be utilized for business purposes. ... The city which may grow uninterruptedly in all or several directions finds itself in a more fortunate position than the one which must, at large expense, surmount natural barriers before it can expand. Inability to grow naturally results in a pyramiding of land values in business districts which in turn affect living costs to some extent.[62]

URBAN GEOGRAPHY AT MID-CENTURY

Site and Situation

The dual notions of site and situation that crystallized in American urban land economics before the Second World War had become the central elements in American urban geography by 1950, distinguishing the perspectives of urban geography from, say, urban sociology, which also developed as a distinguishable field during the 1920's and 1930's with a central set of ecological ideas originally stimulated by work in plant ecology. (This approach is discussed more fully in Chapter 10.) Robert E. Dickinson, a leading British-American urban geographer, expressed the prevailing viewpoint of the profession when he wrote:

> The first task of the geographer in an urban study is to determine exactly the characteristics of the site and situation of the settlement. The site embraces the precise features of the terrain on which the settlement began and over which it has spread. This study demands thorough examination of the initial site that so often has been profoundly modified by human action, especially in the large city. ... The situation is usually taken to mean the physical conditions (as for the site) over a much wider area around the settlement. But of equal importance are the human characteristics of the surrounding country, since these affect the character and fortunes of the urban settlement. ... Having determined precisely the physical conditions of situation and site which affected the beginnings of the urban settlement, the geographer examines how, with the passage of time, the settlement utilizes, adapts itself to, and transforms these conditions in the process of its formation and expansion.[63]

Max. Sorre reiterated the view from the vantage point of French geography. The French roots were different, however, for in 1922 Raoul Blanchard had distinguished between general elements of situation, "phenomena in ensemble ... acting in order to promote or shackle the development of a human organism" and characteristics of local site, "purely local traits of the landscape."[64] Like Geddes, Blanchard related urban geography to planning, and he spoke of towns as living organisms in an environmental and historical context. His thinking substantially moulded subsequent French urban geography. Thirty years after Blanchard, Sorre ranged widely in the discussion of situation, considering latitude, which "does not appear to have a proper action on the development of cities," altitude, which "does not have a direct action on urbanization. It affects their birth and their progress in the measure in which it affects the general activity of men," and high densities of population, of which he wrote, "In total, the relation between the density of population and the development of cities is a gross enough approximation. The exceptions appear more interesting to the geographer than the rule."[65]

The position in relation to the different parts of a country, and especially in relation to the regions of consumption and production, and to the routes which unite them, is the capital element of the situation. Since Kohl (1841) geographers have insisted on this remarkable couple, the route and the city. . . . One might even think that this insistence has been occasionally a little extreme. A central position within a state, the command of a threatened front, are favorable situations for the birth of capitals. . . . But no less important is the facility of commercial linkages. Urbanization closely depends on mercantile activity, and the most important cities are localized within the bed of the great currents of circulation.

The study of the elements of the situation leads to a conception of veritable *urban lines*, of which the great valleys, the piedmonts, the desert borders, the coasts offer remarkable examples. . . . In the United States the states with the highest coefficients of urbanization are those on the Atlantic front, where four-fifths of the population reside in cities, followed by California, and then Washington and Oregon. They include an important proportion of the transportation and commercial workers of the United States. The analysis of the last historical generation of cities suggests the existence of urban regions which are above all else creations of industry. The geographer, when he studies these cities, is not solely concerned with isolated individual places. He describes ensembles, groups, lines or regions, and this view appears particularly fruitful. These ensembles do not embrace all cities; there are regional centers whose isolated development demands all our attention. Cities like Paris, like New York, present characters too singular to be treated only like a city of the Seine or a city of the American Atlantic series. But nonetheless that is what they are, and to understand them it is necessary to replace them within the urban ensemble. This would be necessary if only to understand the facts of competition. For there has always been the phenomenon of competition within these groups.

Let us return to the geographic couple route-city. The interdependence of these two facts explains itself on the map by the fanning out of routes of all types around the cities and also by the meeting of routes. This link is again marked by the influence of the route on the plan of the city and on its growth. We touch here on one of the essential aspects of urban morphology. . . .

Using the advantages of situation, cities do not obey a mathematical law in their distribution. . . . It remains to be said that the small regional centers are in general at comparable distances from each other: these distances being determined by the possibilities of transportation for a given state of circulation. This is a very general formula, which is worthwhile only for a time and for a given equilibrium of population and economy.[66]

Important elements of site were to Sorre: "those which carry an effective protection. . . . The idea of the force proper to a site is one of the most rooted in military art"; the command of a passage by land or river; the presence of water; salubrity; and the disposition of open flat spaces—"In reality this factor does not play in the fixation of the urban seed, which is related to other advantages. It is found in the development of the agglomeration and the evolution of the plan." Minor advantages were the presence of construction materials and the fertility of the land, though "the fertility of the soil which surrounds the cities is often in part their own creation."[67]

One cannot hold to a restrictive conception of the site. Most little cities and even a certain number of medium cities are constructed on one site—the site where they were born. But, when it gains in importance, the city passes beyond the limits of the topographical accident where it was fixed. . . . And even it does not grow except by annexing neighboring sites to the initial site. Not only for need of space, but because the elements which fixed the urban seed do not well assure its growth, because other functions are born for which the city searches sites with different properties. It is no longer only *one* site that it is necessary to consider, but a *complex of sites* juxtaposed or at least neighbors. . . .

For a general rule . . . in the topographical evolution, the importance of the detail . . . attenuates itself. The more the city grows, the more considerations of space pass to the foreground and supplant all the rest. This remark . . . suggests the idea of a certain relativity of geographical conditions.[68]

Inventory and Prospect: 1950

The importance of site and situation was reiterated by Harold M. Mayer in his review paper "Urban Geography" that appeared in *American Geography: Inventory and Prospect* (1954):

In urban studies the areal relations of a city are commonly examined from two different points of view, each representing a different degree of generalization. On maps of large scale the relation between the internal pattern of the city . . . and the features of the terrain are analyzed: on maps of smaller scale covering a much larger area the external relations of the city as a whole are analyzed. The close-up view reveals the characteristics of the site; the broader view reveals the characteristics of the situation. The significance of both site and situation must be examined historically for they may change radically, even in a short time, as a result of changes in the technology of transportation, changes in the general economic development of the country, or changes in the functions performed in the city.[69]

Mayer's paper represented an impressive stocktaking of American urban geography in 1950. He wrote:

Urban geographers approach the study of cities in different ways. They may be chiefly concerned with the city as part of the fabric of settlement. . . . They may examine the forms and patterns of settlement as of today, trace the evolution of the phenomena . . . [or] forecast the changes to come. Or they may approach the city as an economic phenomenon with associated social and political attributes, by seeking to identify the function or functions underlying city growth or decline, or the role of the city in the larger area it serves. Actually, most urban geographers combine these approaches.[70]

In his review, he recognized some of the European roots of American urban geography,[71] cited the early interest in the physical sites of cities,[72] the seminal contributions of Mark Jefferson on city sizes and distribution, and the concept of primacy,[73] as well as Robert Dickinson's work on city-region relations,[74] and alluded to attempts at generalization among urban geographers:

Several geographers have attempted to formulate empirically derived principles relative to the general distribution of cities, particularly in relation to their hinterlands or service areas. Walter Christaller's work on central places in Germany stimulated a further examination of this problem in the United States by Edward L. Ullman and others. G. K. Zipf and J. Q. Stewart have worked out mathematical rules pertaining to the distribution and support of population which have attracted wide attention. . . . Their conclusions, however, have aroused considerable controversy.[75]

In fact, however, Christaller considered his contribution to be a "general purely deductive theory to explain the size, number and distribution of towns in the belief that there is some ordering principle governing the distribution."[76] It was Zipf who was the empiricist, a philologist who became interested in rank-size relationships and the reasons for them. Stewart, an astronomer, attempted to develop "social physics" by transferring Newtonian concepts to geography. Geographer Ullman's paper, "A Theory of Location for Cities," was published in a sociological journal.[77]

What followed in Mayer's review was a listing of "major concepts" in the field of urban geography (many of these are discussed in the chapters that follow): urban functions (classifications of types of cities were discussed); supporting and tributary areas (nodal regions); site and situation; distribution of cities (central-place theory, rank-size regularities, and gravity models); economic base; internal form (Burgess's zonal ideas, Hoyt's sectors, and Harris and Ullmans' multiple nuclei); urban expansion and the rural-urban fringe; land uses; and size of cities. His essay concludes with "The Prospect." Possible trends in the years ahead are seen to be: more comparative studies of cities and greater attention to historical evolution of city forms and functions, to suburbs, urban ribbons, new towns, movement within cities, and the "third dimension." In contrast, Soviet geographers, who assessed their subject just a few years later, saw as their main task "the formulation and elaboration of laws concerning economic-geographic functions of cities."[78] This contrast is doubly ironic, for there is little evidence that Soviet urban geography has gained much in generality since 1950, whereas in the nearly two decades since *American Geography: Inventory and Prospect* was published a substantial formalization and generalization of American urban geography has taken place.

Recent Trends

Some of the elements of these changes in American urban geography were reviewed in three papers prepared for the interdisciplinary Committee on Research on Urbanization of the Social Science Research Council (1962 to 1964) by geographers Harold M. Mayer, Norton S. Ginsburg, and Brian J. L. Berry.[79] Mayer revised his earlier report, covering the same topics as he had in 1954, updating references, extending his treatment of central-place theory, and noting the entry of new techniques of analysis made possible by electronic computers. Ginsburg asked:

. . . whether the urbanization process is unidimensional or multidimensional and whether it is culturally and areally, as well as temporally, differentiated . . . the controversial issue . . . turns . . . on the relationships between value systems and social organization on the one hand, and the development of city systems and various types of urban morphological patterns, on the other.[80]

He then reviewed research in urban geography conducted in Sub-Saharan Africa and the Asiatic Triangle.

Berry chose to highlight the trends since 1955:

> Urban geography also has its "young men on new frontiers." The research of a growing group of these men appears, at first glance to be markedly different from that of other urban geographers in the recent past. Differences, however, occur in the ways in which research is undertaken rather than in basic objectives and concepts. Substantive foci of urban geography remain unchanged. Research on the "frontier" simply has greater theoretical orientation and shows increased reliance on quantitative analysis and modern digital computers. The "new frontier" is a decade old at most. . . . In this short time no dramatic contributions have been made. Most new studies have been preoccupied with testing existing concepts and theories.
>
> . . . Incisive mathematical and statistical methods have been introduced to the discipline . . . but use . . . has been limited by the availability of simple, concise, precisely stated concepts. Hence, the main concern . . . has been to begin putting the conceptual house in order.[81]

By the end of the decade a very different story could be told. Not only have there been major syntheses of existing concepts, but bold new theoretical departures have been made and valuable comparative empirical research has been completed. It is the purpose of this book to introduce the beginning student to these new developments in urban geography. Part of what follows is original text by the present authors, and part is readings from the work of others. Some sections are reviews of classical concepts; others may be new to both teacher and student. The attempt is to strike some mid-point between a textbook and a collection of readings.

We begin with an historical overview of the process of urbanization in America, to provide context, and then consider systems of cities and their regional relations, as well as the social and physical structure of cities and planning applications.

FOOTNOTES TO CHAPTER 1

1. Richard C. Wade, *The Urban Frontier: Pioneer Life in Early Pittsburgh, Cincinnati, Lexington, Louisville, and St. Louis* (Cambridge, Mass.: Harvard University Press, 1959), p. 30. Maurice Beresford records parallel considerations in the planting of new towns in England, Wales, and Gascony, in *New Towns of the Middle Ages* (London: Lutterworth Press, 1967), and also provides a substantial bibliography on the formation of new towns elsewhere. See, also Michael Benyah Essam, *The Fiat City and Regional Development* (Ithaca, N. Y.: Cornell University Press, 1968). Essam defines a "fiat" city as "a new town . . . deliberately created . . . in accordance with a carefully designed plan . . . to stimulate and control the development of commerce."

2. Quoted in *ibid.*(Wade), pp. 32–33.

3. Daniel Drake, *Natural and Statistical View: A Picture of Cincinnati and the Miami Country* (Cincinnati: Looker and Wallace, 1815). Quoted in Charles N. Glaab, *The American City: A Documentary History* (Homewood, Ill.: Richard D. Irwin, 1963), p. 47.

4. Quoted in *ibid.*, p. 188.

5. Quoted in *ibid.*, pp. 213–14.

6. Quoted in *ibid.*, p. 222.

7. L. U. Reavis, *Saint Louis: The Future Great City of the World* (St. Louis: C. R. Barns, 1876); and John S. Wright, *Chicago: Past, Present, Future* (Chicago: Horton & Leonard, 1868).

8. Charles H. Cooley, *The Theory of Transportation*, Publications of the American Economic Association, (Baltimore: American Economic Association), IX, No. 3 (1894), 5–7.

9. Glaab, *The American City*, p. 180.

10. Adna F. Weber, *The Growth of Cities in the Nineteenth Century: A Study in Statistics* (New York: The Macmillan Company, 1899), p. 172.

11. Cooley, *The Theory of Transportation*, pp. 90–91.

12. *Ibid.*, pp. 91, 99–100.

13. *Ibid.*, pp. 91–95.

14. *Ibid.*, pp. 95–96.

15. *Ibid.*, pp. 97–98.

16. *Ibid.*, pp. 93, 98–99.

17. *The Growth of Cities*, p. 172.

18. *Ibid.*, pp. 172–74.

19. In *Political Science Quarterly*, X, No. 4 (December, 1895), 636–37.

20. *Ibid.*, pp. 638–39.

21. *Ibid.*, p. 636.

22. *Ibid.*, pp. 651–54.

23. *Ibid.*, p. 638.

24. Louis Wirth, "A Bibliography of the Urban Community," in *The City*, eds. Robert E. Park and Ernest W. Burgess (Chicago: University of Chicago Press, © 1925), p. 177.

25. (New York: The Macmillan Company, 1896), pp. 112–13.

26. Ellen Churchill Semple, *Influences of Geographic Environment on the Basis of Ratzel's System of Anthropo-Geography* (New York: H. Holt and Company, 1911), p. 1.

27. Ellen Churchill Semple, "Some Geographic Causes

Determining the Location of Cities," *Journal of School Geography* I, No. 10 (October, 1897), p. 228.

28. Semple, *Influences of Geographic Environment*, pp. 527–28.

29. Semple, "Some Geographic Causes," p. 229.

30. *Ibid.*, p. 231.

31. Ellen Churchill Semple, *American History and Its Geographic Conditions* (Boston: Houghton Mifflin Company, 1903), pp. 341–42.

32. (London: Methuen & Co. Ltd., 1923), pp. vii-ix.

33. Thomas Griffith Taylor, *Urban Geography: A Study of Site, Evolution, Pattern and Classification in Villages, Towns and Cities* (London and New York: Methuen & Co. Ltd. and E. P. Dutton & Co., 1949), p. 3.

34. *Ibid.*

35. *Ibid.*, p. 8.

36. *Ibid.*, p. 15.

37. *Ibid.*, p. 10.

38. *Ibid.*, p. 11.

39. *Ibid.*, p. 12.

40. *Ibid.*

41. *Ibid.*, pp. 225–27.

42. Wirth, "A Bibliography of the Urban Community," p. 178. Among Emile Levasseur's earlier studies were *La Population française*, 3 vols. (Paris: A. Rousseau, 1889–1892).

43. Jean Brunhes, *Human Geography: An Attempt at a Positive Classification, Principles and Examples*, trans. I. C. LeCompte (Skokie, Ill.: Rand McNally & Co. 1920), p. 131. See also P. Vidal de la Blache, *Principles of Human Geography*, ed. Emmanuel de Martonne, trans. Millicent Todd Bingham (New York: H. Holt and Company, 1926).

44. *Ibid.*, pp. 165–66.

45. *Ibid.*, pp. 169–71.

46. Richard M. Hurd, *Principles of City Land Values* (New York: The Record and Guide, 1903), pp. 13, 19–21.

47. *Ibid.*, p. 21.

48. *Ibid.*, pp. 13–15.

49. *Ibid.*, p. 16.

50. *Ibid.*, pp. 17–18.

51. Stanley McMichael and Robert F. Bingham, *City Growth Essentials* (Cleveland: Stanley McMichael Publishing Organization, 1928), pp. 5–6.

52. (Chicago: 1916).

53. Herbert P. Dorau and Albert G. Hinman, *Urban Land Economics* (New York: The Macmillan Company, 1928), p. 44.

54. *Ibid.*, p. 45.

55. *Ibid.*, pp. 46–48.

56. *Ibid.*, p. 59.

57. *Ibid.*, p. 56.

58. *Ibid.*, pp. 57–58.

59. *Ibid.*, pp. 76–78.

60. In McMichael and Bingham, *City Growth Essentials*, p. 101.

61. *Ibid.*, pp. 102–8.

62. *Ibid.*, p. 109.

63. "The Scope and Purpose of Urban Geography: An Assessment," in Harold M. Mayer and Clyde F. Kohn, eds., *Readings in Urban Geography* (Chicago: University of Chicago Press, 1959), pp. 12–13.

64. Raoul Blanchard, "Une Méthode de Géographie Urbaine," *La Vie Urbaine*, IV (1922), 301–19.

65. Max. Sorre, *Les Fondements de la Geographie Humaine*, III, *L'Habitat: Conclusion Générale* (Paris: 4. Colin, 1952), pp. 202–4, by permission of Librairie Armand Colin.

66. *Ibid.*, pp. 204–7.

67. *Ibid.*, pp. 207–11.

68. *Ibid.*

69. Eds. Preston E. James and Clarence F. Jones (Syracuse, N. Y.: Syracuse University Press, 1954), pp. 148–49.

70. *Ibid.*, p. 143.

71. Mayer also referred to the earliest American urban geography, H. P. Tappan, *The Growth of Cities: A Discourse* (New York: American Geographical and Statistical Society, 1855).

72. E.g., R. D. Salisbury and W. C. Alden, *The Geography of Chicago and Its Environs* (Chicago: Geographic Society of Chicago, 1920).

73. In particular, Jefferson's "The Law of the Primate City," *Geographical Review*, XXIX, No. 2 (April, 1939), 226–32.

74. Dickinson wrote *City, Region and Regionalism* (London: Routledge & Kegan Paul, Ltd., 1947).

75. Mayer, "Urban Geography," p. 145.

76. Quoted in Brian J. L. Berry and Allan Pred, *Central Place Studies* (Philadelphia: Regional Science Research Institute, 1961).

77. J. Q. Stewart, "Empirical Mathematical Rules Concerning the Distribution and Equilibrium of Population," *Geographical Review*, XXXVII, No. 3 (July, 1947), 461–85; E. L. Ullman, "A Theory of Location for Cities," *American Journal of Sociology*, XLVI, No. 6 (May, 1941), 853–64; and G. K. Zipf, "The Hypothesis of the Minimum Equation as Unifying Social Principle," *American Sociological Review*, XXII, No. 6 (December, 1947), 627–50.

78. V. V. Pokshishevskiy, "Geography of Population and Populated Points," *Soviet Geography: Accomplishments and Tasks*, pp. 141–50. Translation published as Occasional Publications No. 1 of the American Geographical Society, New York, 1962.

79. The papers are, respectively, "A Survey of Urban Geography" (pp. 81–114), "Urban Geography and 'Non-Western' Areas" (pp. 311–46), and "Research Frontiers in Urban Geography" (pp. 403–30) in P. M. Hauser and L. F. Schnore, eds., *The Study of Urbanization* (New York: John Wiley & Sons, Inc., 1965).

80. *Ibid.*, p. 311.

81. *Ibid.*, p. 403.

CHAPTER 2

urbanization and environment: changes in the nature of the urban system

The concepts of urban geographers changed during the late nineteenth and early twentieth centuries for several reasons. Not only were ideas modified because more was learned about cities, but even as they were being studied the cities themselves were changing. The classical contributions to urban geography emphasized interrelationships of city location, size, and shape with transportation and environmental factors. Theories of urban phenomena used very simple environmental causes for explanations. But later students thought these explanations lacking in power and elegance, and perhaps part of the reason was the growing complexity of the urban scene. The geographers responded by disapproving environmentalism although, unfortunately for the development of the field in the years preceding the Second World War, without providing any alternative body of theory. In the 1930's, in particular, geography lapsed into empirical studies concerned simply with description and classification of the characteristics of urban centers, at a time when other fields were developing new theoretical frameworks for the study of cities. Much of the difference was accounted for by the fact that geographers were continually concerned with the complexities of regional differences, whereas scholars in other fields were more willing to sacrifice detail by making simplistic assumptions which enabled them to begin to build up theoretical frameworks, albeit primitive ones.

In the postwar years the balance was somewhat redressed, as a wide range of urban location theories was introduced into geography. Yet these theories swung to the opposite extreme of the descriptive geography of the 1930's. Each was based on an extreme simplification—the *ceteris paribus* assumption of a uniform plain containing no environmental differences whatsoever.

With few exceptions even today, urban location theorists continue to find solace in models of urban systems and city structure constructed on unbounded uniform plains, and delight in the beautiful tessellations of the "central-place hierarchy" and graceful negative exponential "distance-decay patterns" (as we shall see in later chapters that review these concepts). For such theoreticians conveniently sidestep environmental issues, as well as questions about the changing nature of the urban system and the processes by which cities have grown and developed.

Yet no number of assumptions can avoid the fact that there is an environmental context within which behavior occurs.[1] As Perloff notes, "the *urban environment* is a contained (but not closed) highly interrelated *system* (or subsystem) of natural and man-made elements in various mixes." At the interface of these natural and man-made elements one finds the "urban resource endowment."[2]

The composition of this resource endowment is rooted in the determinants of final demand—in consumer preferences and income distribution—and in the contemporaneous organization and technology of production. As they change, so does the resource endowment. And as the endowment changes, so does the urban system, which generates further changes in final demand in a circular and cumulative sequence in which causes merge into consequences and consequences become causes, and in which it is no longer possible to distinguish that which is natural and that which is man-made. The complexity is awesome, yet there is need to contend with it, to introduce order and gain new insight. A fresh look at the classical environmentalist ideas may therefore be warranted, using a newer systems framework which is consistent with contemporary modes of scientific thought, one that emphasizes both the social definition of resources and the complexity of the interdependencies. We shall focus first on the evolution of the American urban system and on the relation between patterns of regional growth and changing definitions of natural resources. The student will want to explore the similarities and differences between the American experience and that of other parts of the world.

EVOLUTION OF THE AMERICAN URBAN SYSTEM

Several stages of "natural resources that count" can be cited in the history of the American economy.[3] In the agricultural period, the natural endowment most valued was arable land, and the environmental components most valued were water and favorable climate. During industrialization, mineral resources became paramount. In the twentieth century, service activities and amenity resources have become increasingly important.

Natural resources, in a socio-economic sense, are those elements of the natural environment that have use to man and the supply of which is less than the demand for them. In our contemporary urbanized society we can also identify "new" resources, including as a minimum pure air and water, breathing space, adequate open spaces, and other amenities. These are the resources that count in crowded urban areas. Since the last third of the twentieth century seems destined to become a period of conscious urban development, in part as a response to the shortage of these new resources, it seems appropriate that we should begin to understand the nature of the system in which such new resources have been defined, their interrelationships and the extent to which they are direct products of growth and change within the urban system, so that we can then go on to understand the purposes of planning.

Is there a way to introduce order without retreating to the uniform plain in the manner of the urban location theorists? One can order a complex universe in several ways, namely:

1. By creating typologies and by classifying and arranging examples, as was done by urban geographers in the 1930's and 1940's.
2. By tracing common developmental processes, despite many differences between types.

In this chapter we do both, but the typologies of cities are shown to be logical outcomes of the growth processes that have shaped urban systems. Therefore, we emphasize the developmental processes rather than the types of cities that are the outcomes of these processes.

Summarizing extensive research on the development of the American urban system, John R. Borchert concluded:

> Throughout the evolution of the present pattern of American metropolitan areas two factors, great migrations and major changes in technology, have particularly influenced the location of relative growth and decline. Both factors have repeatedly been given specific geographical expression through their relationship to resource patterns. Major changes in technology have resulted in critically important changes in the evaluation or definition of particular resources on which the growth of certain urban regions had previously been based. Great migrations have sought to exploit resources—ranging from climate or coal to water to zinc—that were newly appreciated or newly accessible within the national market. Usually . . . the new appreciation or accessibility has come about, in turn, through some major technological innovation.[4]

Several stages of urban evolution are readily distinguishable, and in considering them we can capture the essentials of the growth process.

Mercantile Beginnings

America's oldest cities were the mercantile outposts of an area rich in resources whose exploitation was organized by the developing metropolitan system of Western Europe. The initial impulses toward independent urban growth came at the end of the eighteenth century, when towns were becoming the outlets for capital accumulated through commercial agriculture as well as the centers from which colonial development of the continental interior proceeded. Arable land was the resource that counted in regional growth. Regional economies developed a certain archetype: a good deepwater port was the nucleus of an agricultural hinterland well adapted to the production of a staple commodity in demand on the world market. The potential growth of a region depended on the extent and richness of the hinterlands accessible to it's port (see Fig. 2–1). The distribution of economic activity before 1840 was a function of the expansion of nucleated agricultural regions into the vacuum of the unsettled continent (see Figs. 2–2, 2–3, and 2–4).

It was during this expansion that New York established itself as the national metropolis (see Figs. 2–3 and 2–4), a position it was never to lose, by setting the terms under which exportable surpluses were marketed, imports obtained, and by which industries in the interior of the continent could secure credit. New York was the one colonial center which had good interior connections for both exports and imports. Boston and Charleston were prevented from exploiting the interior by physical barriers; Baltimore and Philadelphia were able to import with ease, but movement of exports to them from the interior was too costly because of the difficulty of crossing the Appalachian Mountains; New Orleans was well-suited to control the riverine internal trade but far distant from the areas which supplied domestic manufactures and from the heart of the domestic consumer market.[5] The prototype of the American metropolis was thus a port strategically located on long-distance oceanic or riverine trade routes, providing a range of mercantile services, and determining the terms of trade.

FIGURE 2–1. Status of American urban centers in 1790 correlated with population potentials (contoured in thousands of persons per mile) and with the location of the "urban frontier" in 1790. *Sources:* Data indicating the relative status of urban centers in Figs. 2–1 through 2–9 were adapted from John R. Borchert, "American Metropolitan Evolution," *Geographical Review*, LVII, No. 3 (July, 1967), 324. The information on population potentials in Figs. 2–1 through 2–9 is drawn from William Warntz, "Macroscopic Analysis and Some Patterns of the Geographical Distribution of Population in the United States, 1790–1950," in W. L. Garrison and D. F. Marble, eds., *Quantitative Geography*. (Evanston, Ill.: Northwestern Studies in Geography, 1967), pp. 191–218. High population potentials, of course, index high degrees of accessibility to the nation's population, so that in 1790 the highest status centers were located in the areas that were most central. The information on the location of the urban frontier in Figs. 2–1 through 2–6 is adapted from Fred Lukermann, "Empirical Expressions of Nodality and Hierarchy in a Circulation Manifold," *East Lakes Geographer*, II (August, 1966), 17–44. Lukermann defined the urban frontier as that area which, in the previous decade, displayed the greatest growth in the relative status of its urban centers. In 1790 the Eastern Seaboard was experiencing such growth. (The U.S. base map used for the illustrations in this book is courtesy of Goode's Map Series, University of Chicago.)

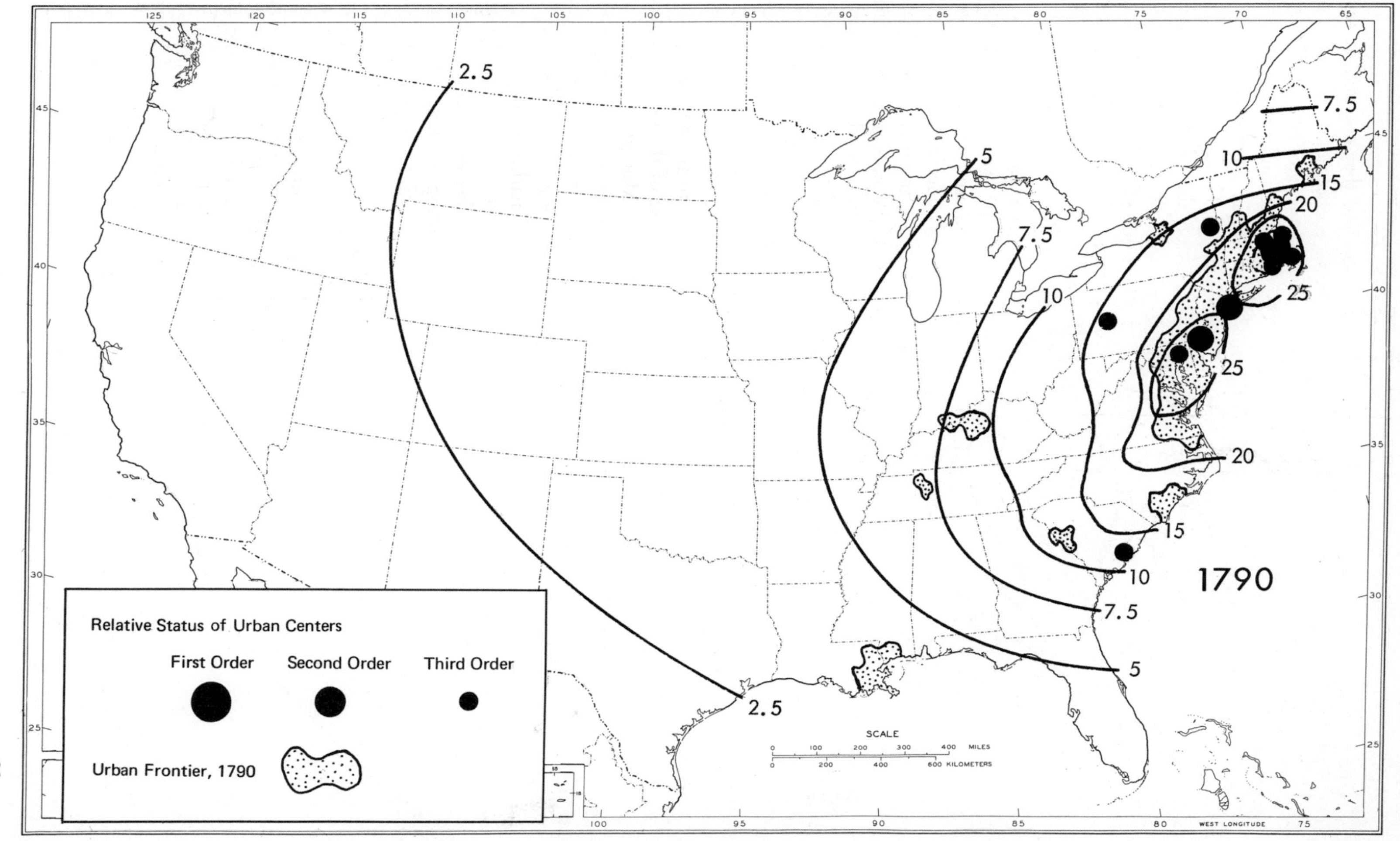
1790
Relative Status of Urban Centers
First Order
Second Order
Third Order
Urban Frontier, 1790
2.5
5
7.5
10
15
20
25
SCALE
MILES
KILOMETERS
WEST LONGITUDE

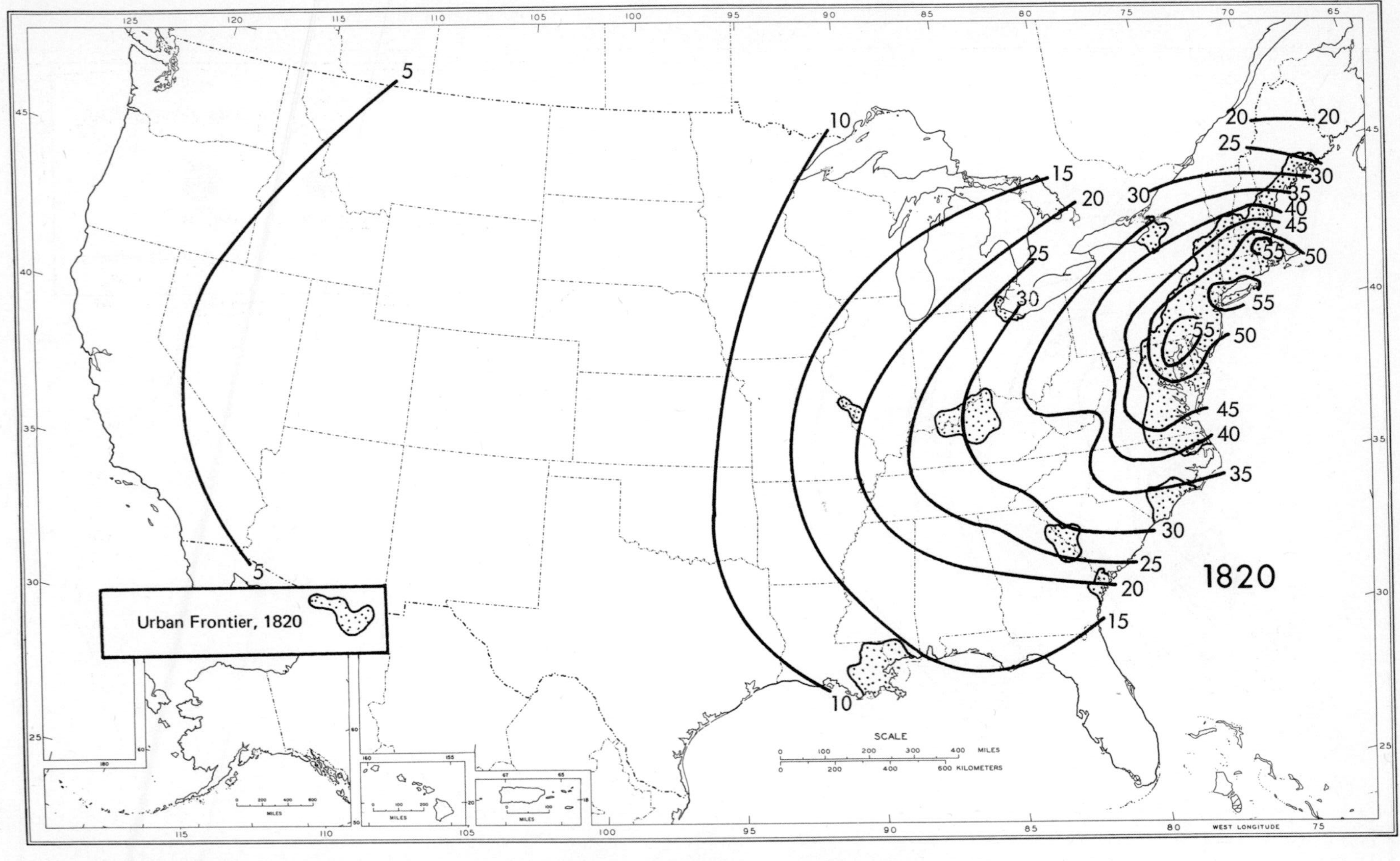

FIGURE 2–2. Population potentials in 1820 *(in thousands of persons per mile)*. Note the increasing densities along the east coast as well as the westward spread of the urban frontiers. Whereas Boston had the greatest potential in 1790, three east coast metropoli had equal status by 1840. *Source:* See caption for Fig. 2–1.

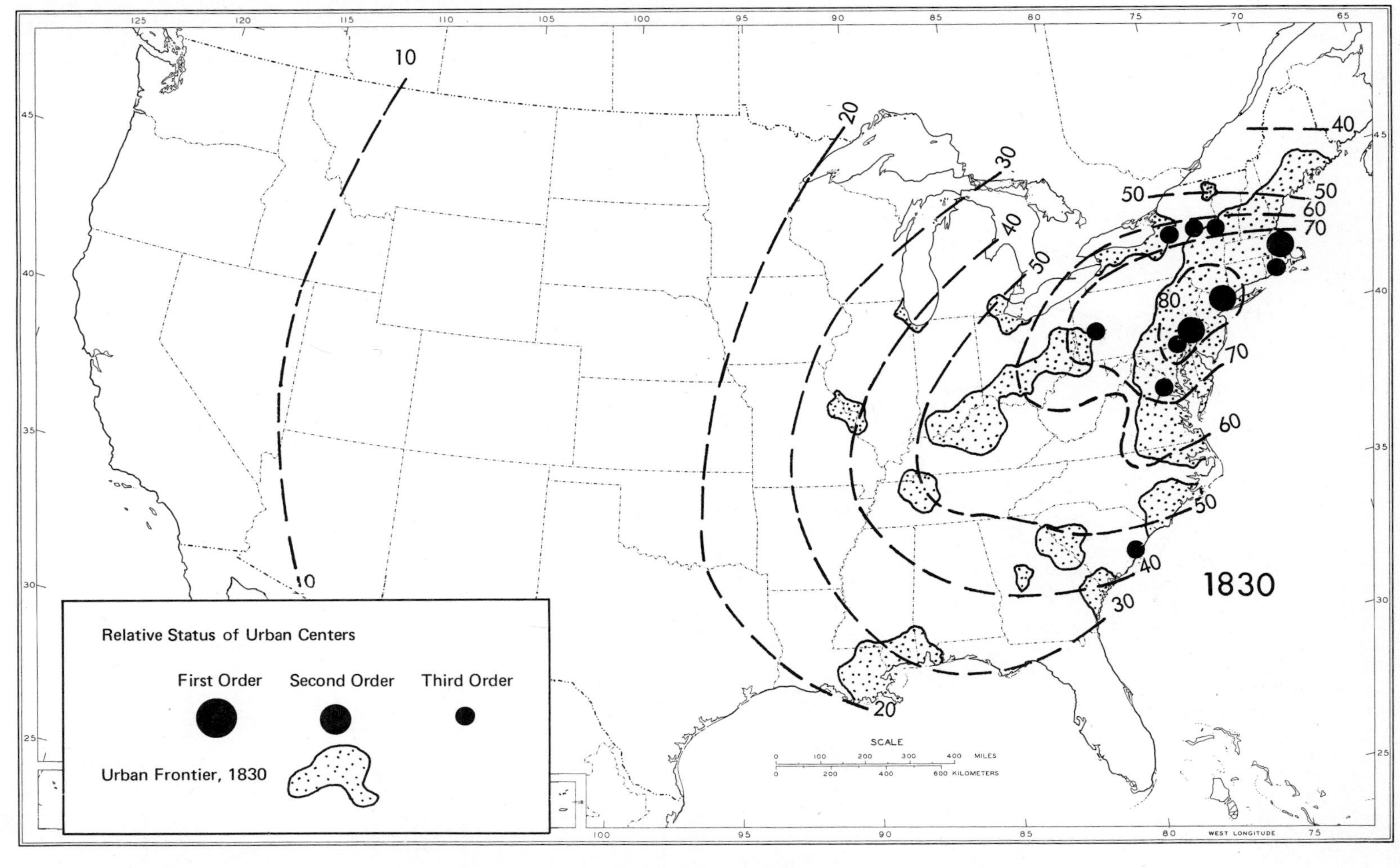

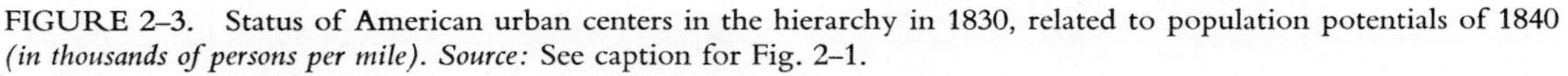
FIGURE 2–3. Status of American urban centers in the hierarchy in 1830, related to population potentials of 1840 *(in thousands of persons per mile). Source:* See caption for Fig. 2–1.

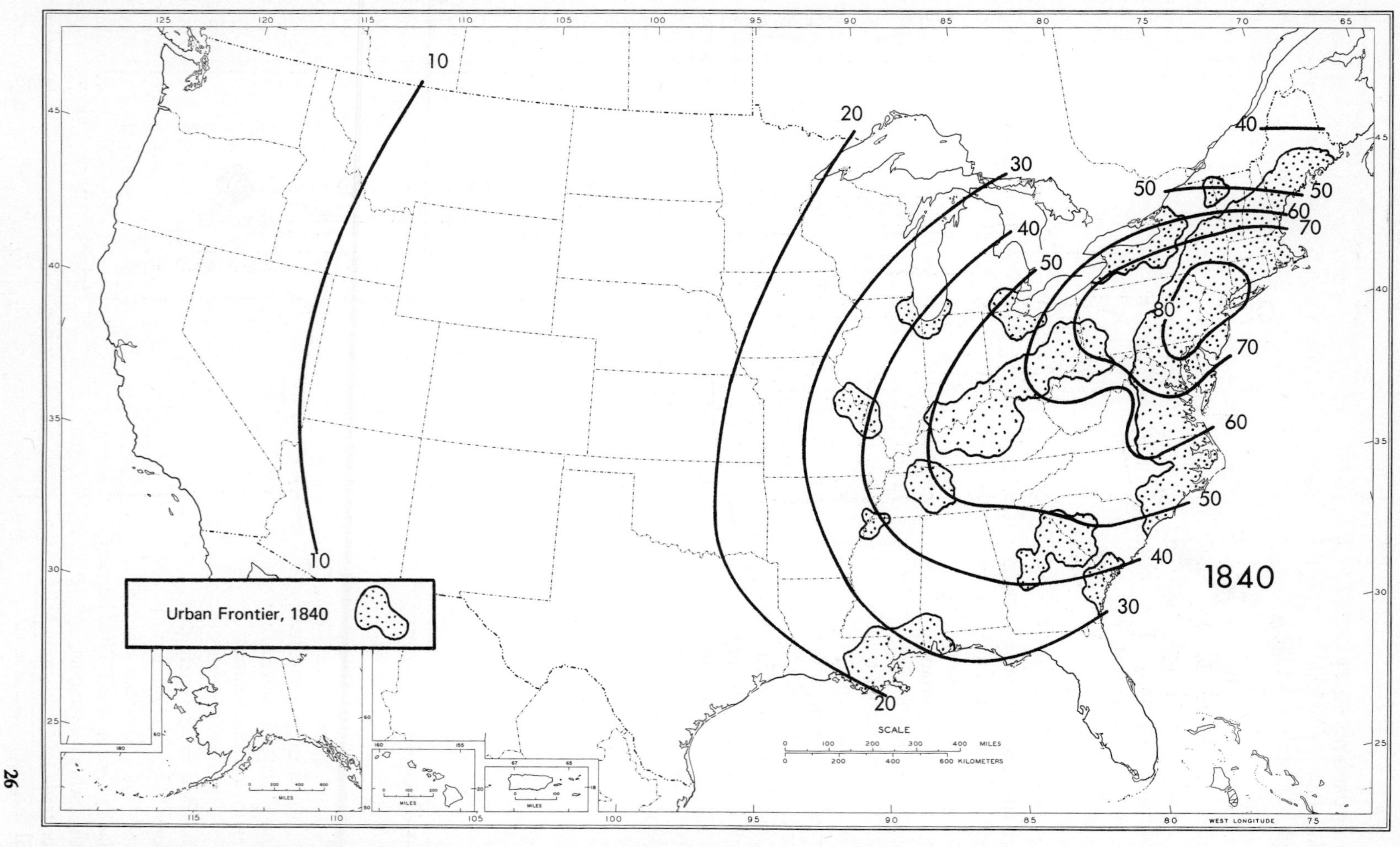

FIGURE 2–4. Population potentials in 1840 *(in thousands of persons per mile)*. The greatest potential is now centered in New York, and the trans-Appalachian spread of population has continued. *Source:* See caption for Fig. 2–1.

Much of the early theory on the importance of transportation to urban location (from Kohl through Cooley) was written about exactly such cities.

This expansion of the economy—dominated by agricultural resources but centered in the cities—set the stage for subsequent developments by establishing a geography of markets, transport routes, and labor force that conditioned succeeding growth. The system that developed thus persisted as the environmental context of the changes that followed,[6] although of course the increase and spread of population continued and the rapid construction of railroads and the expansion of processing industries gave rise to new centers of rail transportation and manufacturing such as Cincinnati, Chicago, and St. Louis—gateways to the agricultural regions of the midwest. As in the east, shipments of goods demanded by farmers and the assembly of their produce for the regional, national, and international markets proceeded in and out of the national and regional metropoli through the organizational medium of a central-place hierarchy comprising regional capitals, smaller cities, towns, villages, and hamlets.[7] (Chapter 7 is devoted to a consideration of central-place concepts.)

Industrial Transformation

But new resources became important between 1840 to 1850 and onwards, and new locational forces came into play, although it was not until 1899 that Adna Weber began to theorize about them. Foremost was a growing demand for iron, and later steel, and along with it a rapid elaboration of productive technologies. The juxtaposition of coal, iron ore, and markets afforded the impetus for the growth of manufacturing in the northeastern United States, localized there both by factors in the physical environment (minerals) and by environmental components created by the prior growth of the urban system (linkages to succeeding stages of production, in turn located closer to markets). Manufacturing cities such as Buffalo, Cleveland, Detroit, and Pittsburgh grew apart from the earlier centers that had dominated long-distance trade, although some of the older commercial metropli were able to capture a share of the new manufacturing base. The heartland of the American manufacturing belt developed westwards from New York, in the area bounded by the iron ores of Lake Superior, and the Pennsylvania coalfields, on the one hand, and by the capital, entrepreneurial experience, and engineering trades of the northeast, on the other. At the same time New York solidified its dominance in financial, entrepreneurial, and specialized manufacturing functions. The heartland became not only the heavy industrial center of the country, but has remained the center of national demand, continuing to determine patterns of market accessibility (see Figs. 2–5 through 2–9).[8]

Relationships between the Heartland and the Hinterlands

The heartland had initial advantages of both excellent agricultural resources and a strategic location in respect to minerals. Later it grew into the urbanized center of the national market (see Figs. 2–10 and 2–11). Subsequent metropolitan growth has been in a pattern organized around this national core region. Since 1869, there has been a stable pattern of growth of manufacturing employment among the states.[9] Continued spread of population and agriculture over the continent has pulled processing and servicing activities and new urban growth with them (see Fig. 2–7). However, the dominant effects in urban development proceeded from the sustained growth of the minerals economy until well into the twentieth century. Thus, a process of "circular and cumulative causation"[10] strengthened and maintained the relationship of the national heartland to the hinterlands—of the core to the periphery—and the new metropolitan centers that emerged did so in consequence of the over-all growth, outward spread, and spatial integration of the economy.

Before 1900, New Orleans, San Francisco, and Minneapolis grew, respectively, as commercial gateways to the Gulf and the Mississippi basin, the central valley of California, and the mid-continental plains. Between 1900 and 1940, Los Angeles grew as the trade and service center for southern California, while Kansas City emerged in the central plains. Since 1940, Seattle has grown in the Pacific Northwest, and Dallas, Houston, and

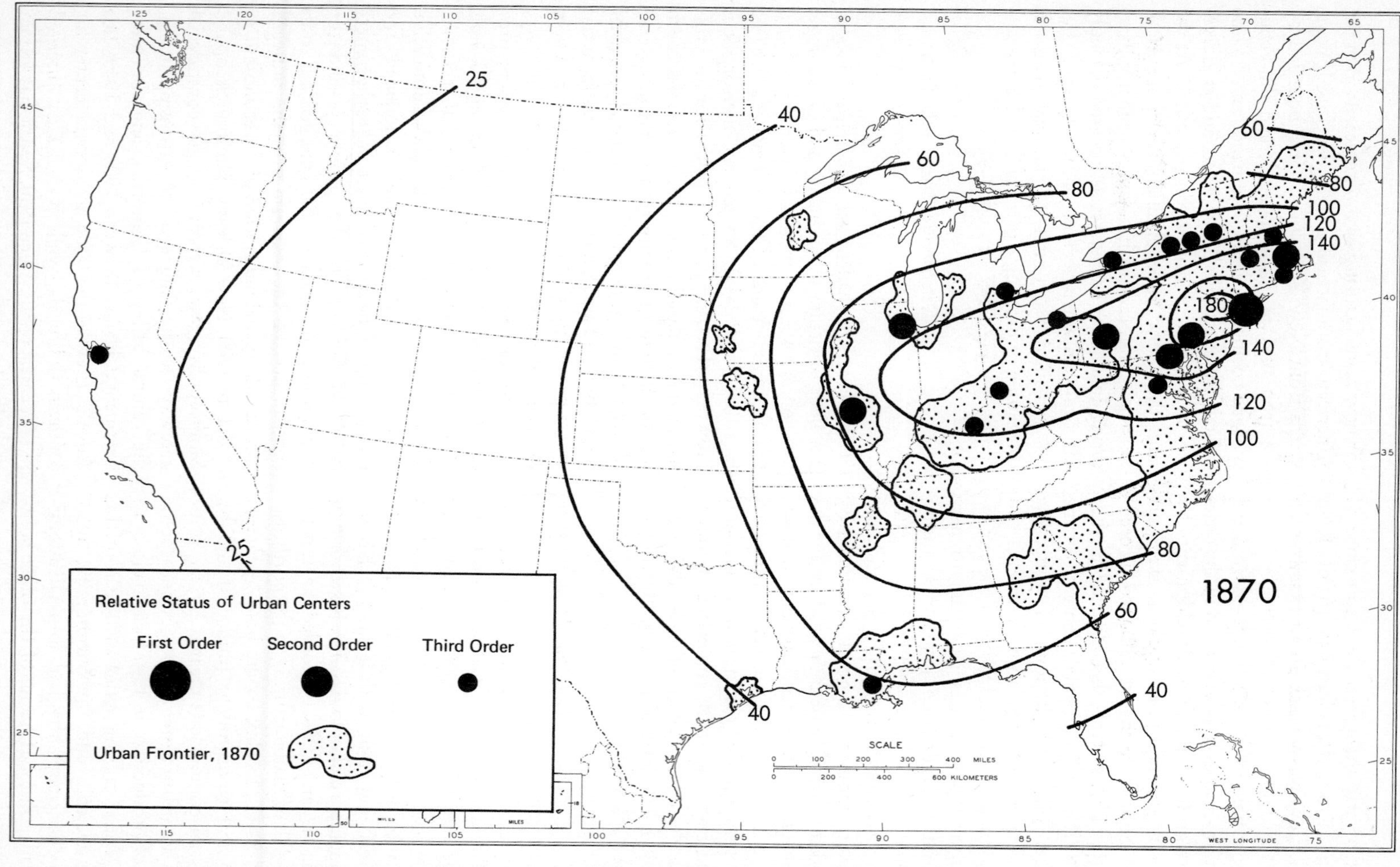

FIGURE 2–5. Population potentials in 1870 *(in thousands of persons per mile)*. Many urban centers achieved new status between 1830 and 1870. The growth of the manufacturing belt and the agricultural midwest stand out clearly. New York has moved ahead to first-order status, and population potential outlines the northeastern heartland. *Source:* See caption for Fig. 2–1.

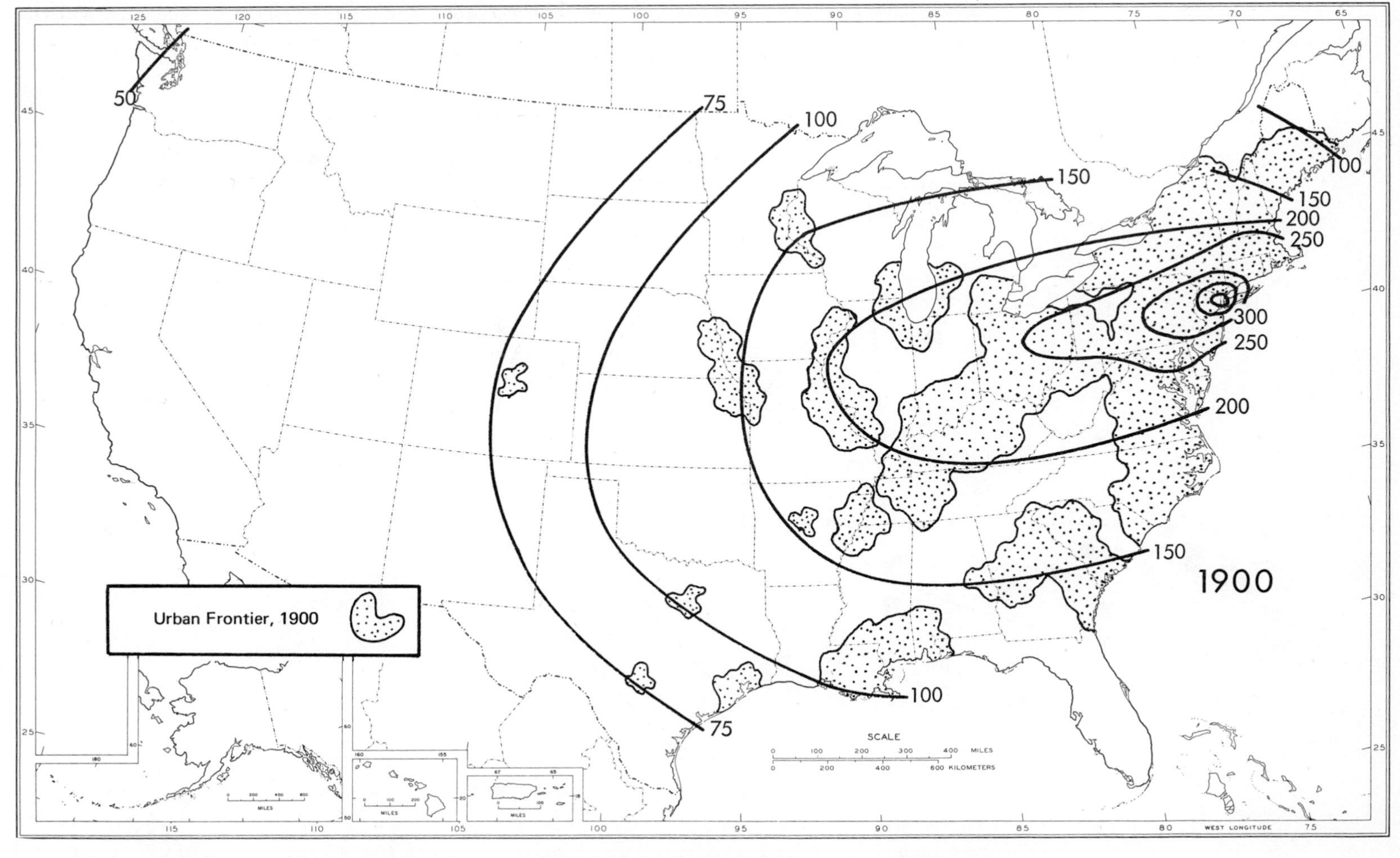

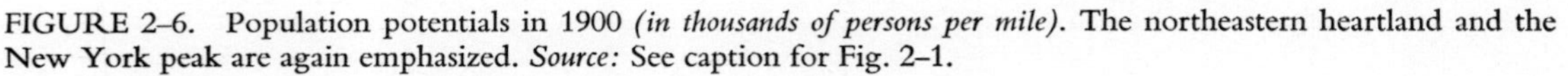

FIGURE 2–6. Population potentials in 1900 *(in thousands of persons per mile)*. The northeastern heartland and the New York peak are again emphasized. *Source:* See caption for Fig. 2–1.

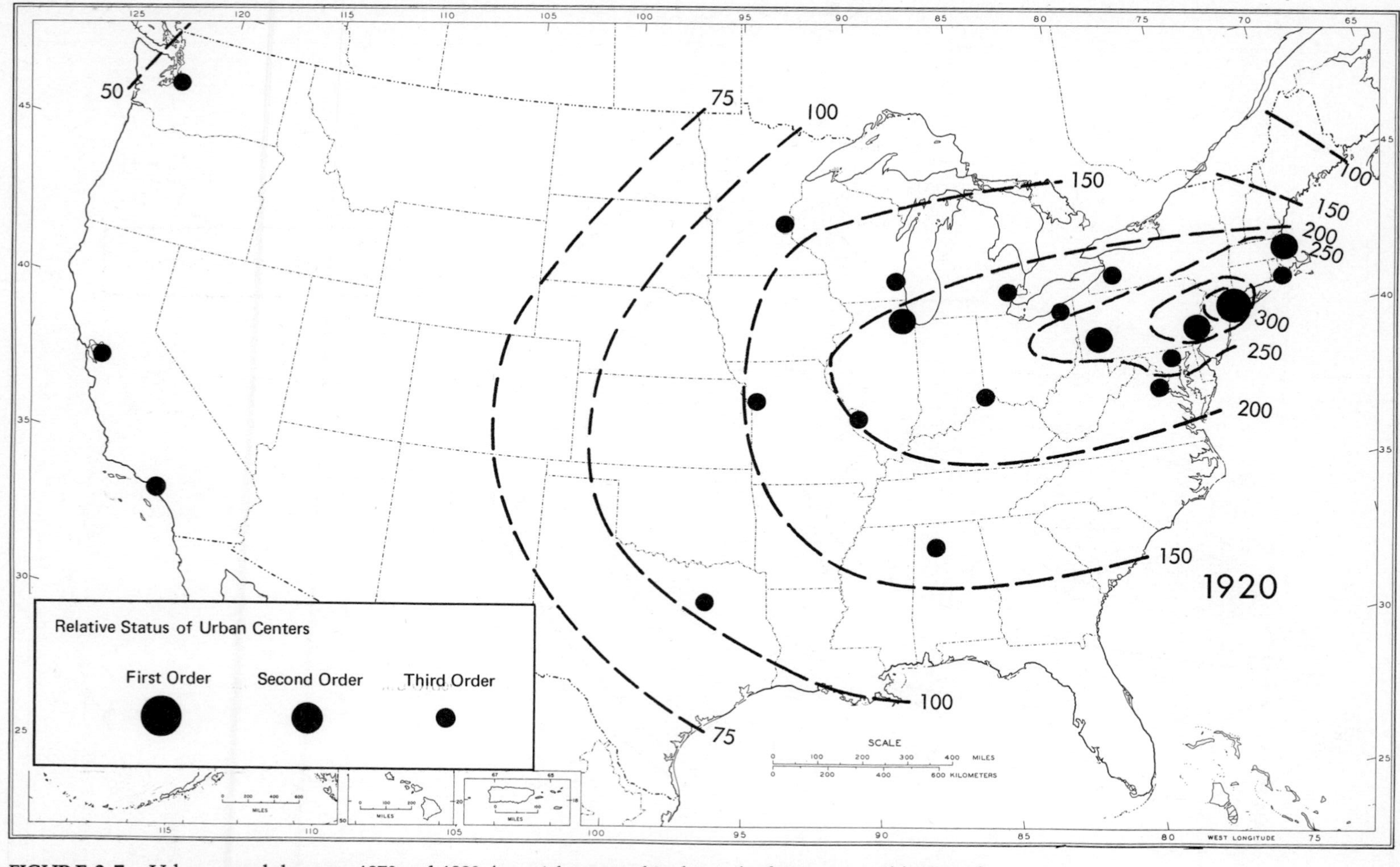

FIGURE 2–7. Urban growth between 1870 and 1920 *(potentials contoured in thousands of persons per mile)*. Note the emergence of the commercial metropoli of the plains and the west coast. *Source:* See caption for Fig. 2–1.

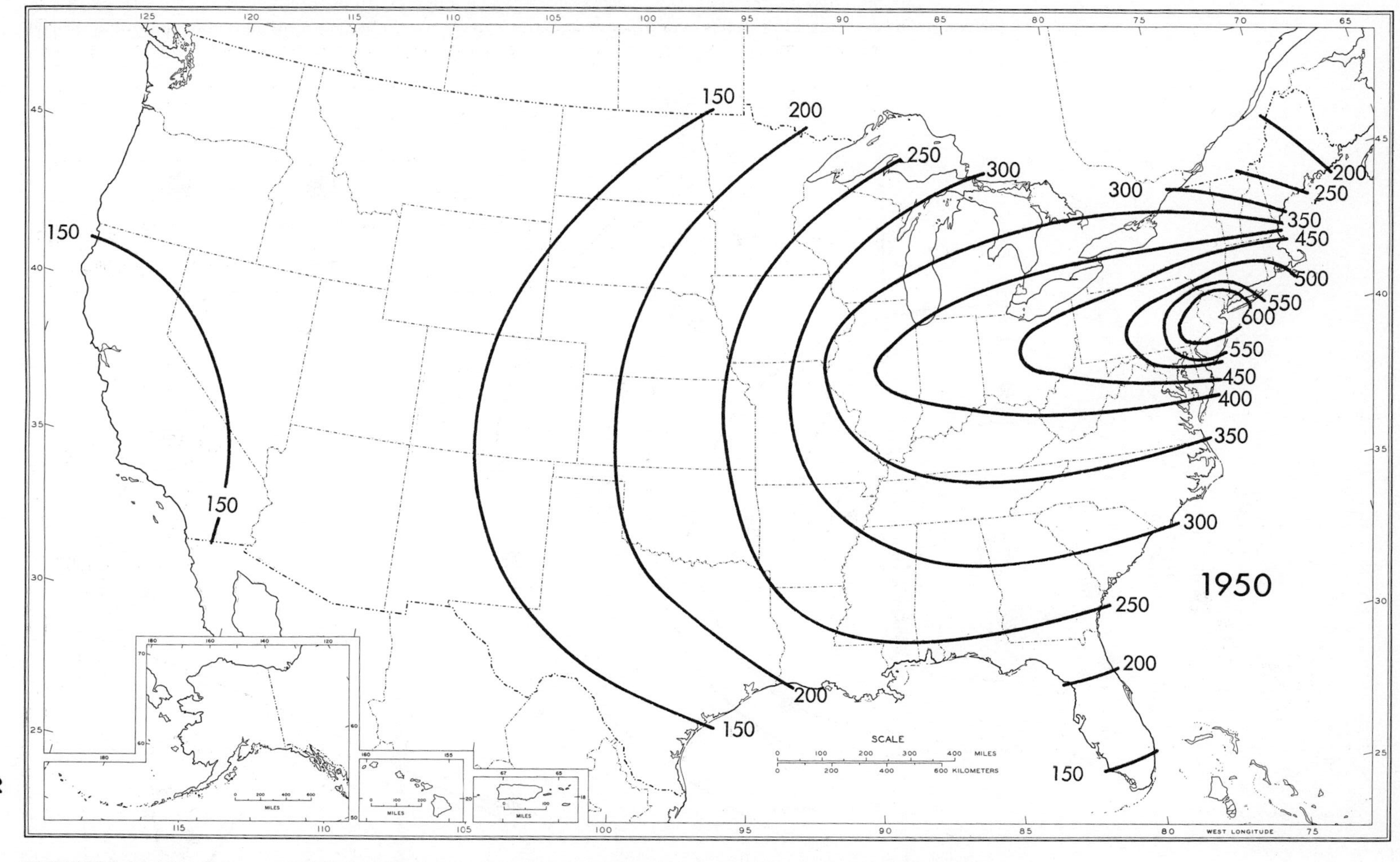

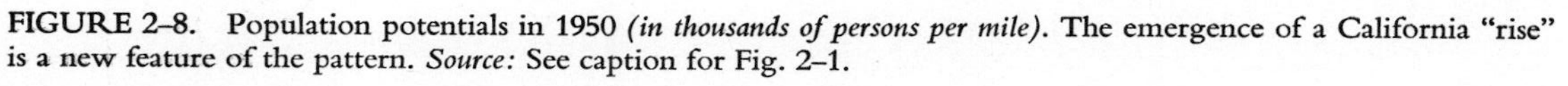

FIGURE 2–8. Population potentials in 1950 *(in thousands of persons per mile)*. The emergence of a California "rise" is a new feature of the pattern. *Source:* See caption for Fig. 2–1.

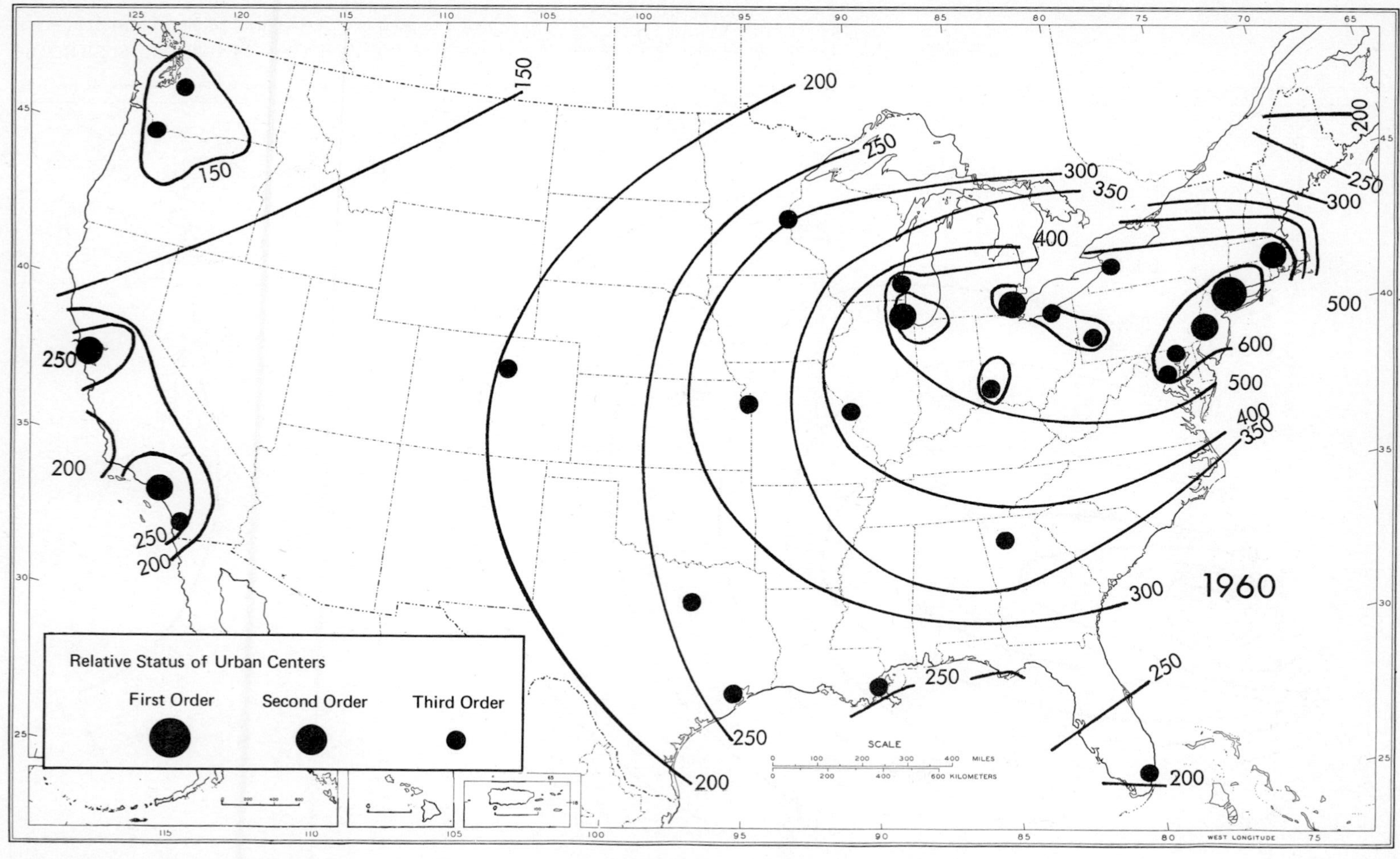

FIGURE 2–9. Population potential in 1960 *(in thousands of persons per mile)*. Between 1920 and 1960, the manufacturing belt metropoli and cities in the far west, Gulf coast, and Florida rose to new status. Population potentials reveal several western peaks and a greater differentiation within the northeastern manufacturing belt heartland. *Source:* See caption for Fig. 2–1.

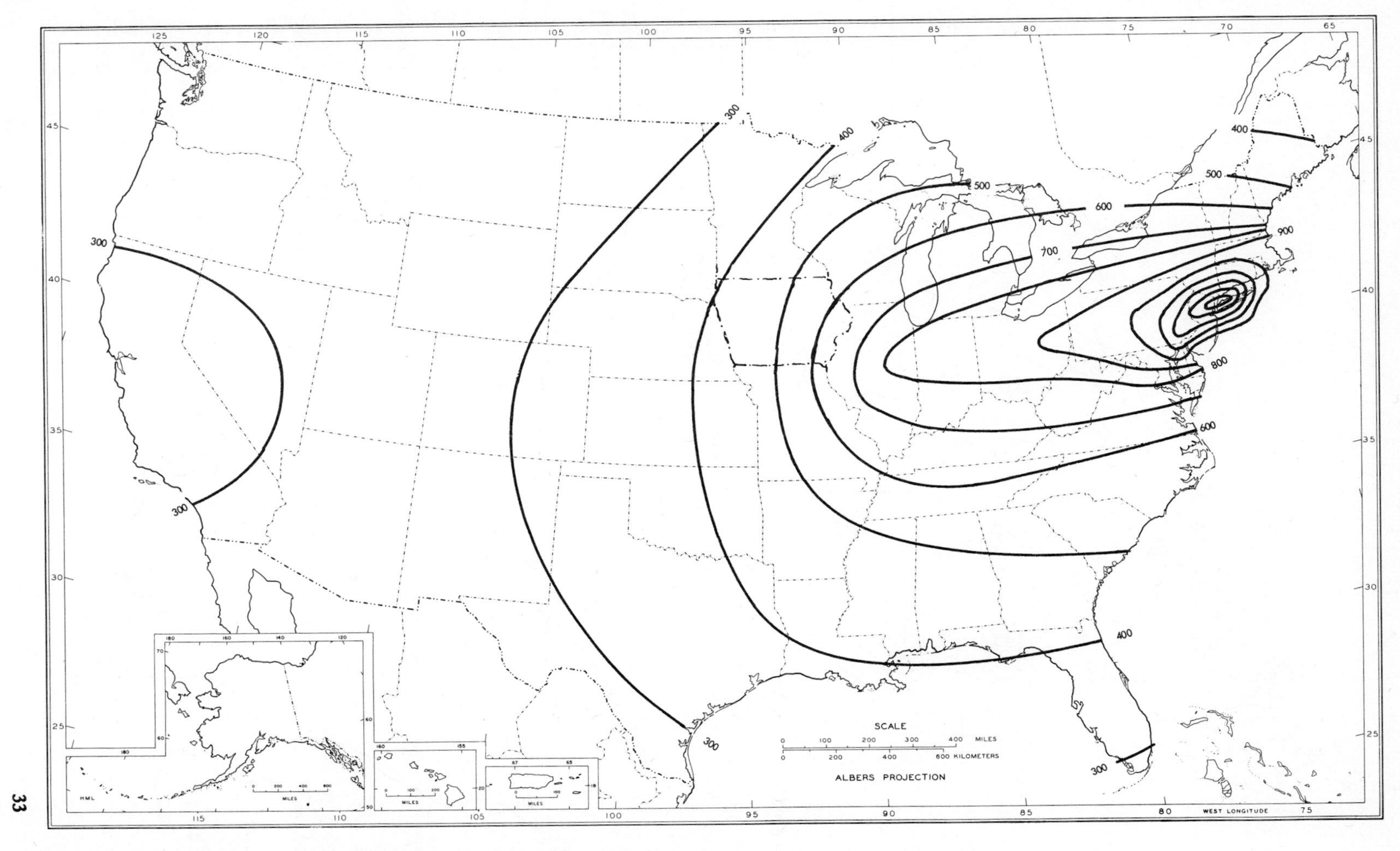

FIGURE 2–10. Income potentials in 1956 *(in millions of dollars per mile)*. Note that this measure of access to the national market is patterned in the same way as population potentials. *Source:* Adapted from William Warntz, *Macrogeography and Income Fronts* (Philadelphia: Regional Science Research Institute, 1965) p. 14.

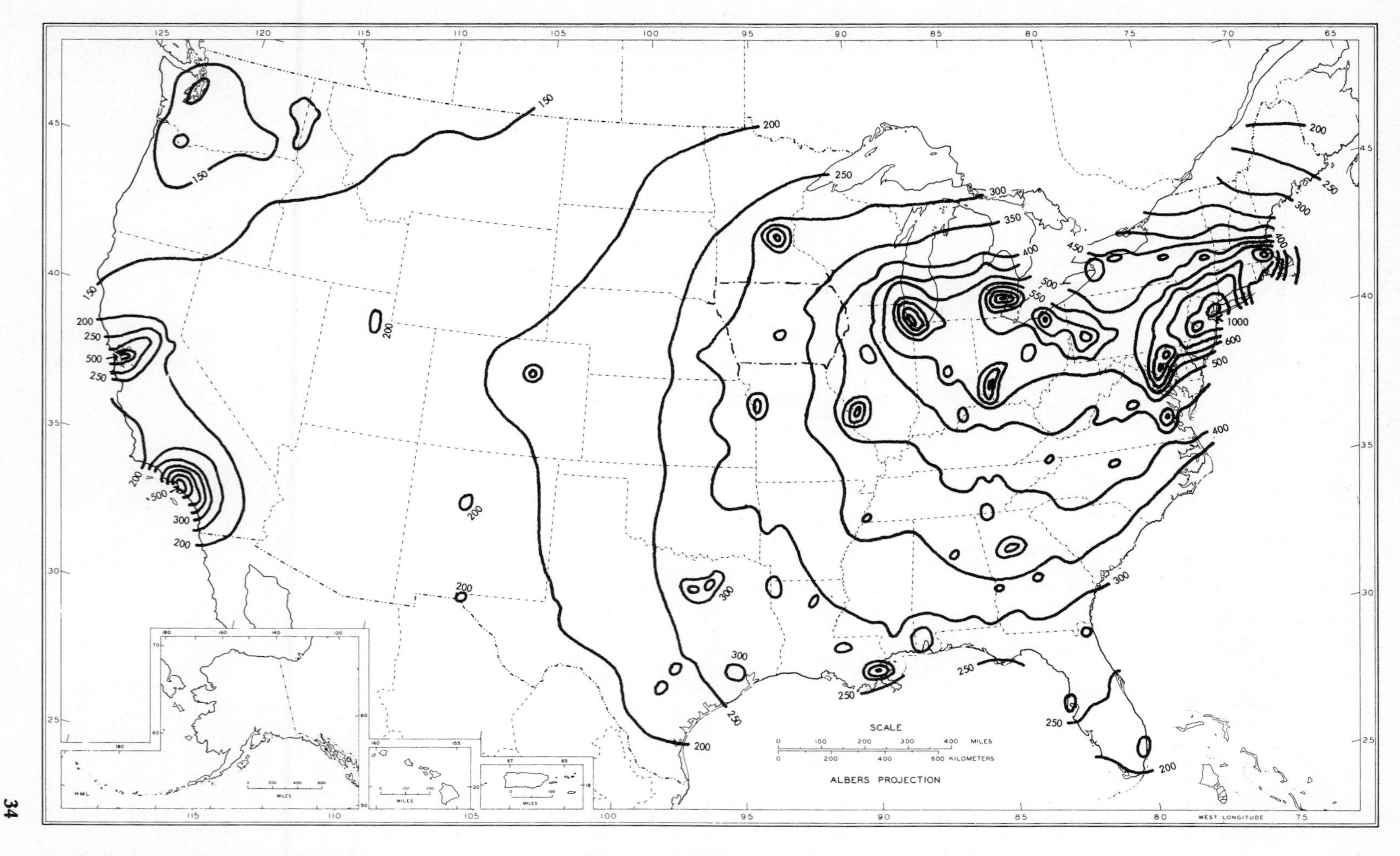

FIGURE 2–11. Details of population potentials in 1960 *(in millions of persons per mile)*. County population data were taken from the U.S. Census and used by William Warntz to generate this surface, to show local metropolitan peaks against the overall configuration of accessibility to the nation's population. *Source:* See caption for Fig. 2–10.

Phoenix have grown in Texas and the southwest. These represent an elaboration and deepening of subnational economies, built upon the geographic pattern of activity brought about by the shifts of interregional resources after 1850, although they also reflect the relative decline of mineral resource activities in the national economy and the increasing significance of the service sector (see Figs. 2–7 and 2–8).

In each case, the basic conditions of regional growth were set by the heartland. It served as the lever for successive development of newer peripheral regions by reaching out to them as its input requirements (needs) expanded, thus fostering economic specialization of regional roles in the national economy. The heartland experienced cumulative urban-industrial specialization, while each of the hinterlands found its comparative advantage in narrow and intensive specialization in a few resource subsectors, only diversifying when the extent of specialization enabled them to secure markets large enough to support profitable local enterprise. Flows of raw materials inward, and of finished products outward, articulated the whole.[11]

The spatial dimensions of the national economy thus became:

> . . . a great heartland nucleation of industry and the national market, the focus of large-scale national-serving industry, the seedbed of new industry responding to the dynamic structure of national final demand, and the center of high levels of per capita income. . . . Radiating out across the national landscape are the resource-dominant regional hinterlands specializing in the production of resource and intermediate outputs for which the heartland reaches out to satisfy the input requirements of its great manufacturing plants. Here in the hinterlands, resource-endowment is a critical determinant of the particular cumulative advantage of the region and hence its growth potential.[12]

Amenities and Services

Since 1950, the growth of the service sector, the increase in the number of "footloose" industries (including the final processing of consumer goods using manufactured parts, and the aircraft, aerospace, and defense industries), the rapid emergence of a "quaternary" sector of the economy (e.g., the research and development industry), the expansion and interregional migration of the non-job oriented population (e.g., retirees who more to Florida, Arizona, and California), and the over-all rise in real incomes, have all served to produce yet another transformation of the economy and the urban system—one based upon new amenity resources. Advantages for economic growth have been found around the "outer rim" of the country, in regions and places relatively well endowed with such amenities[13] as advances in technology have reduced the time and costs involved in previous heartland-hinterland relationships. The advantages have been cumulative, for regional growth within the context of the national pattern of heartland and hinterland relationships had brought these regions to threshold sizes for internal production of a wide variety of goods and services at the very time that changes in the definition of urban resources made possible the rapid advance of the peripheries, based upon their superior factor endowments. Hence the explosive metropolitan growth of the south, southwest, and west (see Fig. 2–9).

Studies of employment shifts in the national economy from 1950 to 1960 provide graphic evidence of this growth and place it within the context of continuing and cumulative national trends. The differences in the relative growth of cities and of regions in that decade can be attributed to two principal causes:

1. An "industry mix" effect, whereby areas fortunate enough in 1950 to have a large share of their workers employed in the nation's rapid-growth industries would be the ones to show the most rapid growth.
2. A "competitive shift" effect, according to which the rapid-growth industries grow most rapidly in the areas best endowed with the resources they need, and slow-growth industries become gradually concentrated in areas with superior endowments of more traditional resources.

It is possible to take any industry and calculate, for any area and time period, the way that industry changed because of these two factors (the method is described at length in Chapter 4). This was done for thirty-two sectors of the American economy in two ways: first, for all 3,102 counties; and second for each of the 212 Standard Metropolitan Statistical Areas (SMSA's) of 1960.[14] A careful analysis of these data showed certain consistent patterns of change, both in cities and in the groups of counties comprising their dependent regions:

First, there was *cumulative growth based on the industry mix*. The rapid-growth sectors of the economy in 1950 to 1960 were market-oriented manufacturing, wholesaling, retailing, and services. Because of the legacy of past development, much of the expansion of these sectors had to take place in the metropoli of the heartland. But the relatively rapid growth of population in the south and west, as the continued development of the heartland stimulated further expansion of the hinterlands, also led to the growing participation of the nation's periphery in these newer sectors of the economy (cf. Figs. 2–12 and 2–9). Clearly, the principal patterns of growth in the decade from 1950 to 1960 were due to an industry mix effect.[15] And because the same relative rates of growth imply widely different absolute amounts of development when the baseline numbers differ, the changes due to industry mix had the effect of promoting further concentration of development in the heartland, together with further centralization in the nation's metropolitan areas.

Second, there was a *redistribution based on competitive shifts*. There were, on the one hand, substantial competitive shifts in the light manufacturing and service sectors. At the level of metropolitan areas, these shifts led to deconcentration of growth, toward the peripheral ring of Florida, Texas, the southwest, and the west. The county data showed that wherever in the nation such shifts took place, they favored lower-density suburban-type locations, thus fostering *decentralization* within the metropolitan areas (see Fig. 2–13). On the other hand competitive shifts in agriculture led to increasing concentration of production in certain areas along with withdrawal of land from farming in others (see Fig. 2–14).[16]

The important conclusion is that by far the majority of American cities changed much like the nation in the decade from 1950 to 1960—simply on the basis of the relative growth of the industries already there.[17] However, a few groups of SMSA's showed substantially different trends. The largest group was of cities in Florida, Arizona, Texas, and California, plus Denver, Las Vegas, and Reno. These have been the main beneficiaries of the competitive shifts. Most of the other changes are industry-specific (e.g., the textile towns of Fall River-New Bedford, Paterson-Clifton-Passaic, Pawtucket-Providence, the mining towns of Wilkes-Barre, Johnstown, and Scranton), or they are related to spectacular military shifts (e.g., in San Diego, Seattle, Norfolk, and Washington, D.C.). Finally, the nation's principal metropoli—New York, Chicago, Los Angeles, Detroit, Philadelphia, Boston, and San Francisco—experienced continued growth due to industry mix, but underwent some loss of competitive strength in the central city while their suburban peripheries grew. Every indication is that the types of shifts now taking place in the economy will impel further changes of similar kinds. The final section of this chapter presents one prediction of what the resulting urban pattern of the country is likely to be.

PATTERNS OF URBANIZATION AND URBAN INFLUENCE IN 1960

By the 1960's the United States had been completely metropolitanized as a result of these

FIGURE 2–12. Growth due to the industry mix: 1950 to 1960. Intensities are based upon a factor analysis of data on industrial change due to differing industrial growth rates and competitive shifts in the economy. The areas shaded black showed the greatest growth and those shaded with dots the next highest growth rates. *Source:* Figs. 2–12 through 2–14 are drawn from Brian J. L. Berry, *Strategies, Models, and Economic Theories of Development in Rural Regions* (Washington, D.C.: U.S. Government Printing Office, 1967).

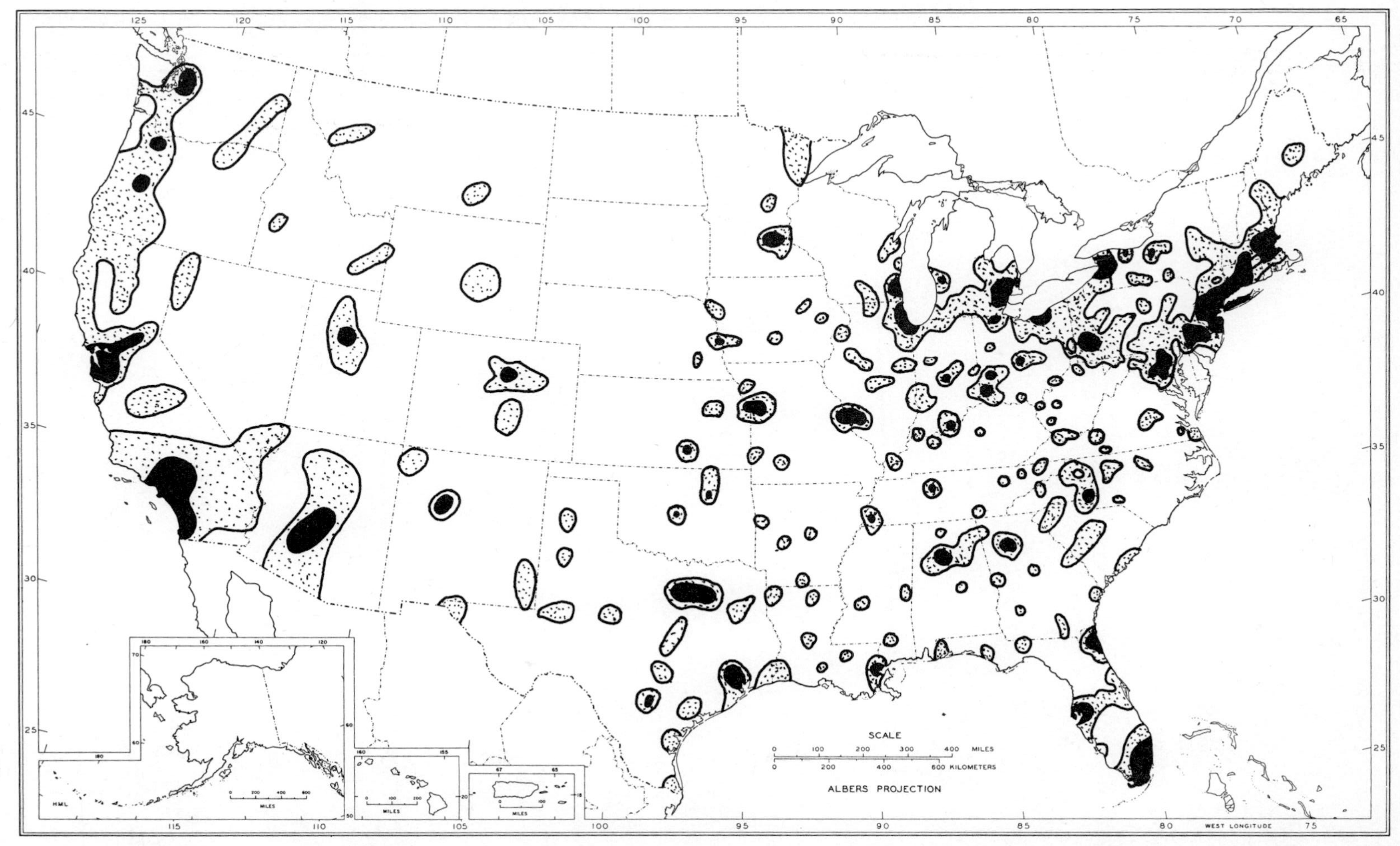
SCALE
0 100 200 300 400 MILES
0 200 400 600 KILOMETERS
ALBERS PROJECTION
WEST LONGITUDE

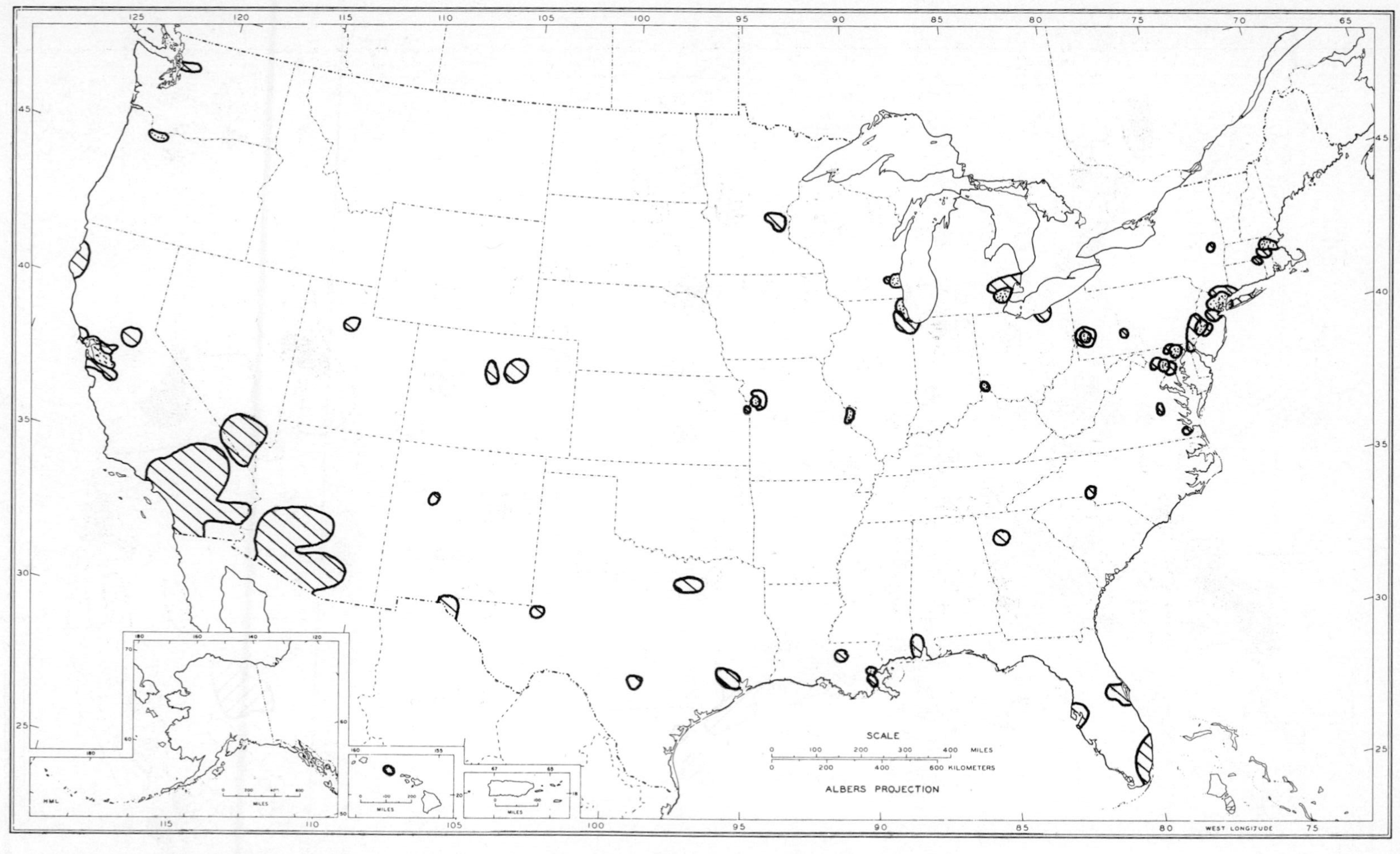

FIGURE 2–13. Change due to "Competitive Shifts": 1950 to 1960. The dotted areas experienced relative losses; the cross-hatched areas in the metropolitan suburbs, the southwest, and the south gained. For a concise definition of competitive shifts, see the section on "Shift Analysis" in Chapter 4. *Source:* See caption for Fig. 2–12.

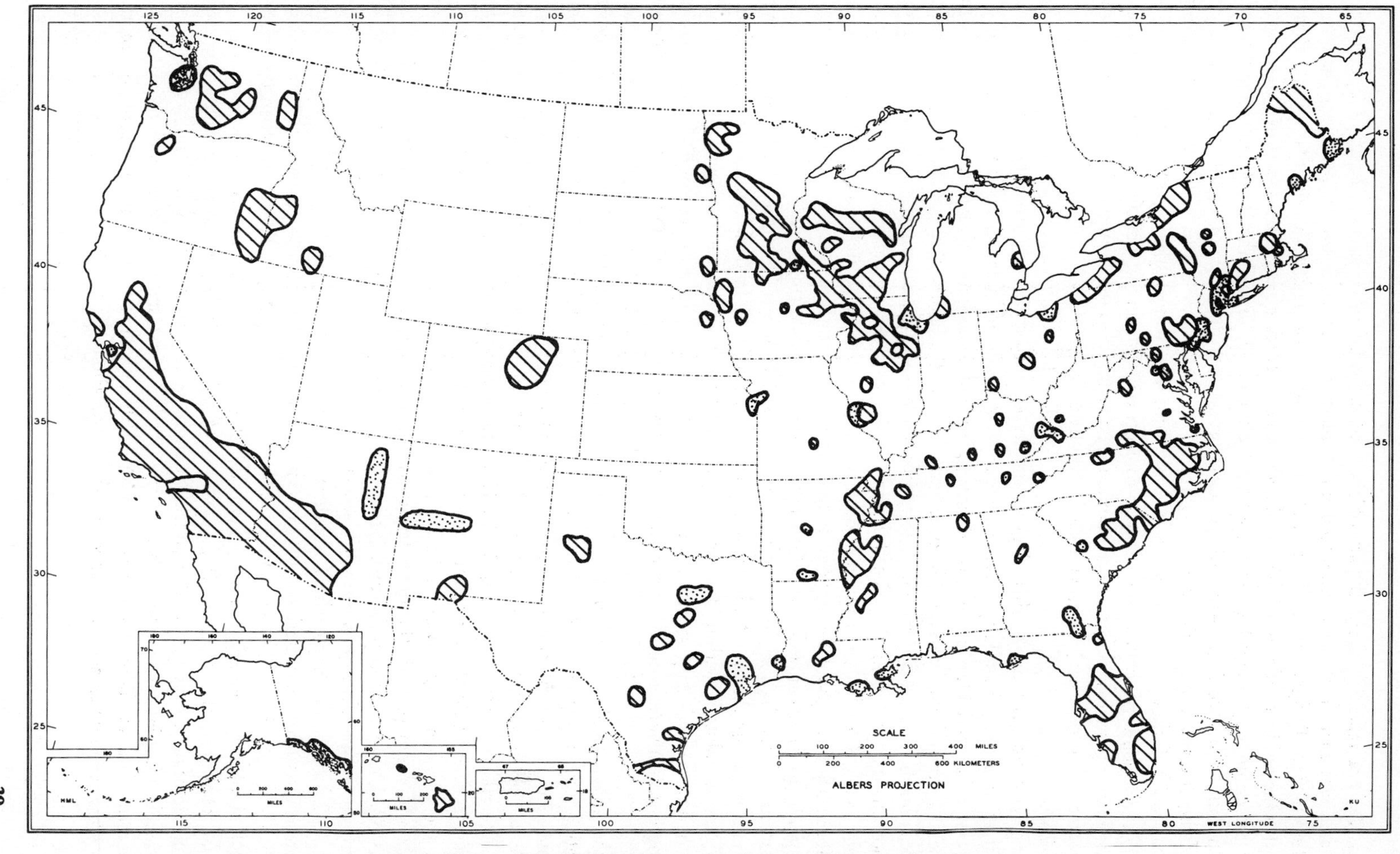

FIGURE 2–14. Relative change in agriculture: 1950 to 1960. Lines indicate areas of competitive gain; dotted areas suffered competitive losses. *Source:* See caption for Fig. 2–12.

processes. Only a relatively limited part of the nation's area was characterized as "metropolitan" by the Bureau of the Budget (see Fig. 2–15), but the fact was that the residents of most of the populated parts of the country journeyed to metropolitan jobs on a daily basis (see Fig. 2–16). Many segments of the country lay simultaneously within more than one of these commuting areas (see Fig. 2–17), although of course the degree to which local labor participated in the metropolitan labor market declined in each case, with distance (see Fig. 2–18).

Varying rhythmically with this degree of participation in metropolitan labor markets were a variety of other variables: population density, the value of farmland and buildings, income and educational levels, rates of migration, patterns of population change, and unemployment (see Figs. 2–19 and 2–20). Clearly, metropolitan centers mould social life throughout the nation, in well-marked gradients of urban influence. Generally, urban centers of less than 25,000 have no local impact on these gradients. Additionally, the patterns are involuted within the inner-city ghettos of the nation's largest cities, dropping with progression inwards from the inner suburban ring.[18]

On the other hand, the economic base of urbanization varies along the lines of heartland and hinterland. An analysis of county employment structure in 1960 produced relevant maps.[19] The industrial heartland stands out (see Fig. 2–21). The predominant orientation to agriculture remains only in the plains and the western basins (see Fig. 2–22 and compare with the unshaded areas in Fig. 2–16). Urban areas in the plains, west and south, are most dependent on the tertiary sector (see Fig. 2–23); and the Appalachian, southern, and western interurban peripheries have the least such dependence (see Fig. 2–24 and compare with Fig. 2–26). Similar relations are seen in the familiar functional classification of cities (Fig. 2–25). The manufacturing heartland is surrounded by mixed retail-industrial metropoli, whereas the southwestern and southern rims have urban centers whose economies are dominated by the retail and service sectors. Each group reflects a phase of growth and a particular pattern of resource-orientation during that phase. Because manufacturing agglomerations led to regional clusters of cities, the heartland evidences the greatest complexity of commuting patterns (see Figs. 2–17 and 2–18), whereas the hinterlands, with the widest spacing of metropoli and the greatest interurban peripheries have the greatest concentration of counties in economic distress (see Fig. 2–26).

The heartland-hinterland patterns are perhaps most clearly shown by measures of potential population or income, indices of accessibility to national markets. Tideman has proved that potential maximization, under certain elasticity conditions, produces profit maximization (generally, where marginal production cost is insignificant compared to unit transport cost),[20] which is reason enough to account for the maintenance of the manufacturing belt.[21]

The Duncans go further.[22] They show that the proportion of land in farms, the proportion of farmland in crops, and the density of farm population are functions of accessibility to the national system as measured by potentials, and a measure of land quality. On the other hand, per acre value of crops and farmland values (which indicate intensity of production) vary with proximity to a metropolitan center. Yet the correlation between density of population and land quality is negative: farm densities are higher in the northeast where general access is greater than in the naturally superior farmlands of the Midwest and south. Lower natural endowments are offset by opportunities for employment away from the farms.

Similarly, nonmetropolitan manufacturing drops off with general accessibility to the heartland more so for the fabricating than the processing industries. The association between the level of activity and general accessibility to an urban center is weaker, but still significant, for other resource-extracting activities such as coal mining, although their location is obviously governed by availability of the resource.

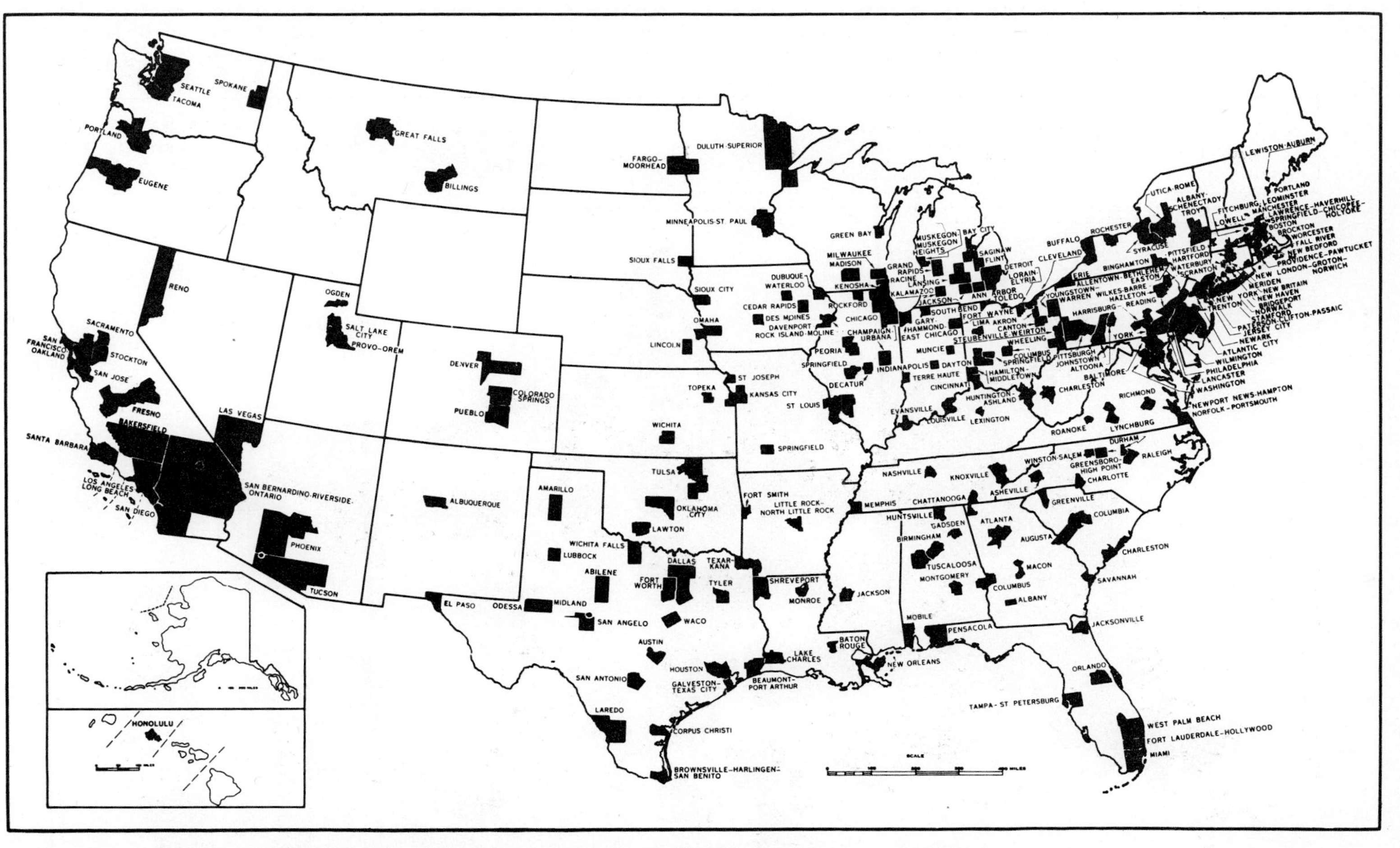

FIGURE 2–15. Standard Metropolitan Statistical Areas: 1960. The zones shaded black cover the counties designated "metropolitan" in 1960 by the U.S. Bureau of the Budget. *Source:* U.S. Bureau of the Budget, *Standard Metropolitan Statistical Areas* (Washington, D.C.: U.S. Government Printing Office, 1967).

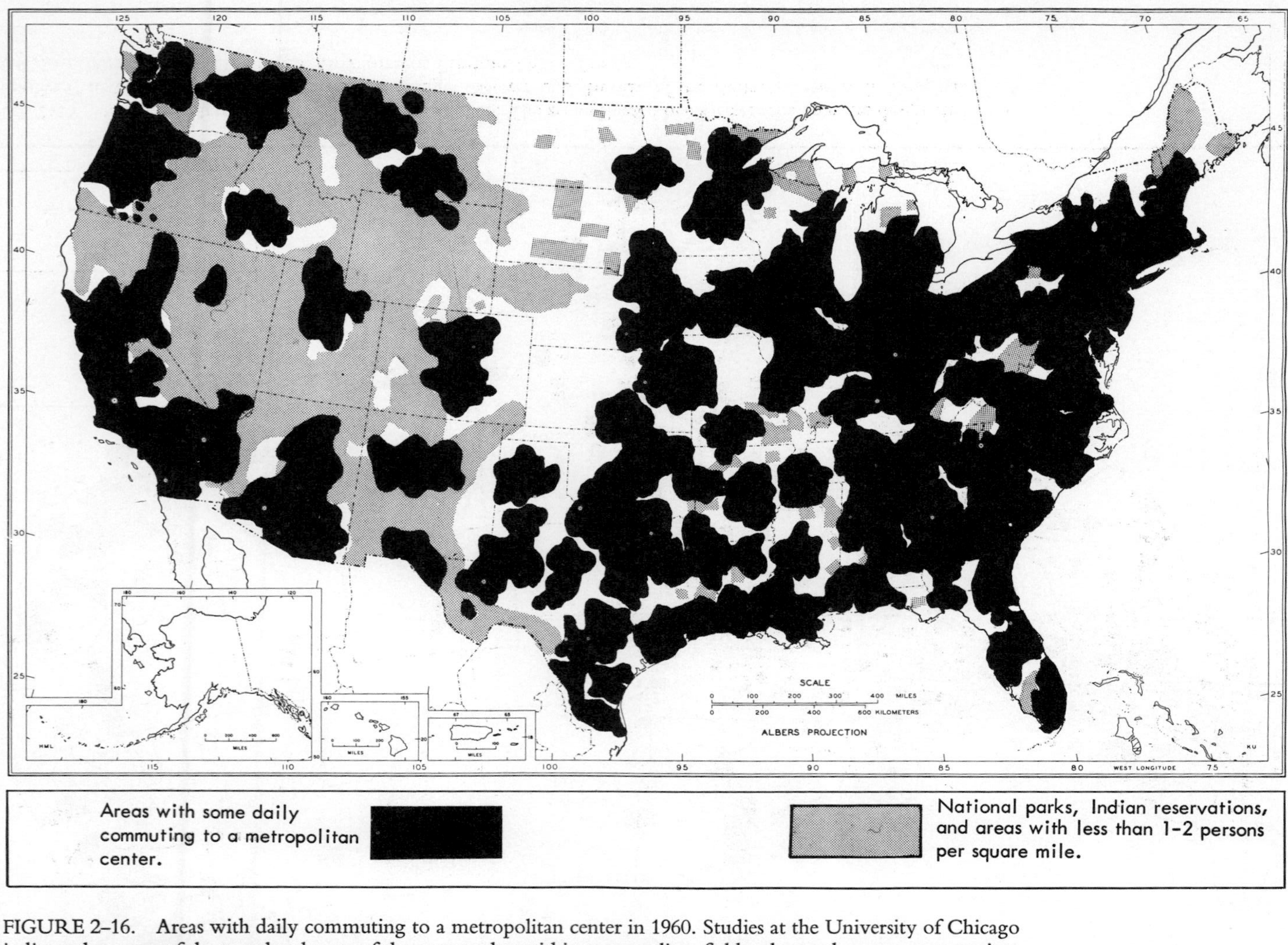

FIGURE 2–16. Areas with daily commuting to a metropolitan center in 1960. Studies at the University of Chicago indicate that most of the populated parts of the country lay within metropolitan fields whence there was commuting. *Source:* Figures 2–16 through 2–20 first appeared in Brian J. L. Berry, *Metropolitan Area Definition: A Re-evaluation of Concept and Statistical Practice* (Washington, D.C.: Bureau of the Census Working Paper No. 28, 1968).

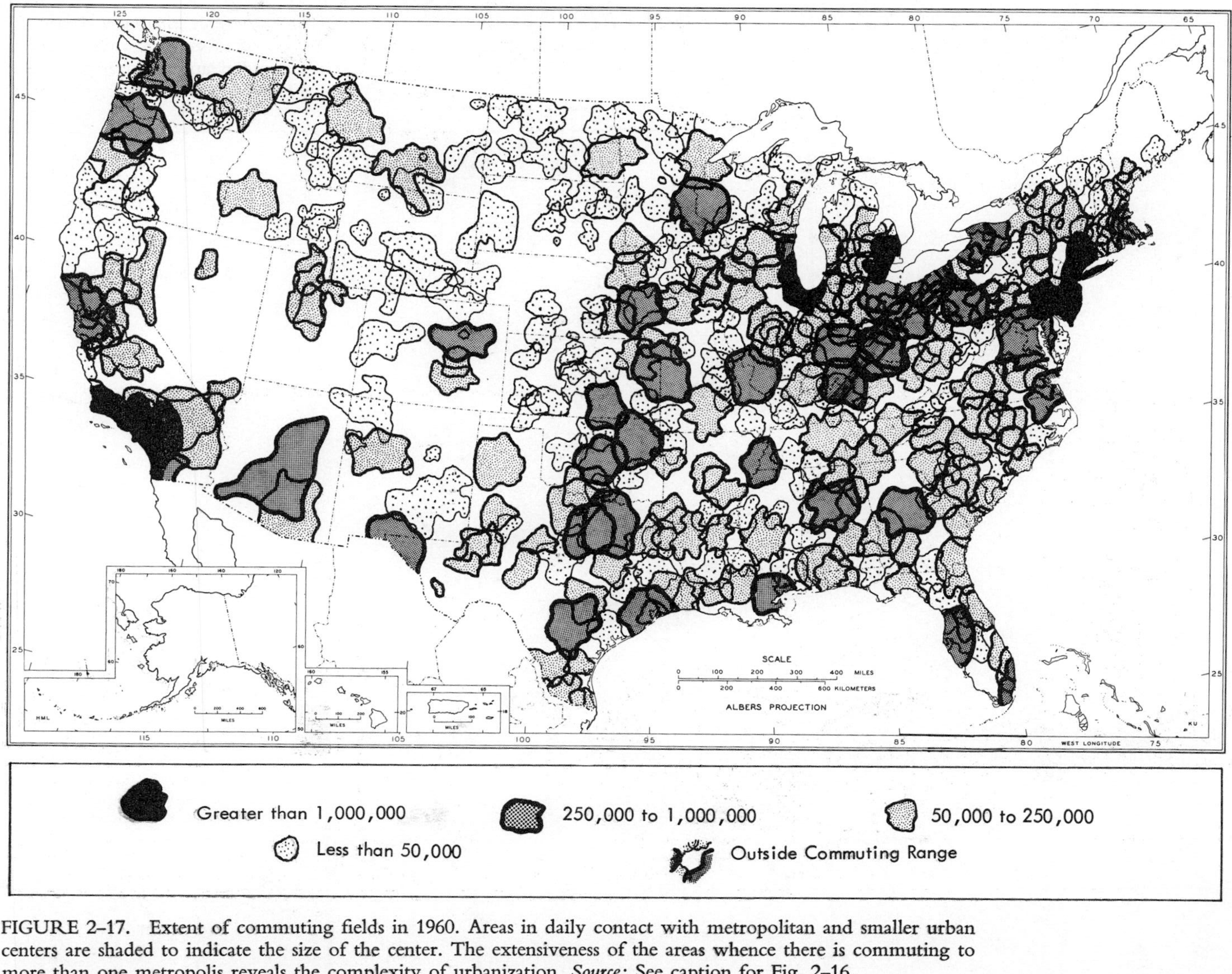

FIGURE 2–17. Extent of commuting fields in 1960. Areas in daily contact with metropolitan and smaller urban centers are shaded to indicate the size of the center. The extensiveness of the areas whence there is commuting to more than one metropolis reveals the complexity of urbanization. *Source:* See caption for Fig. 2–16.

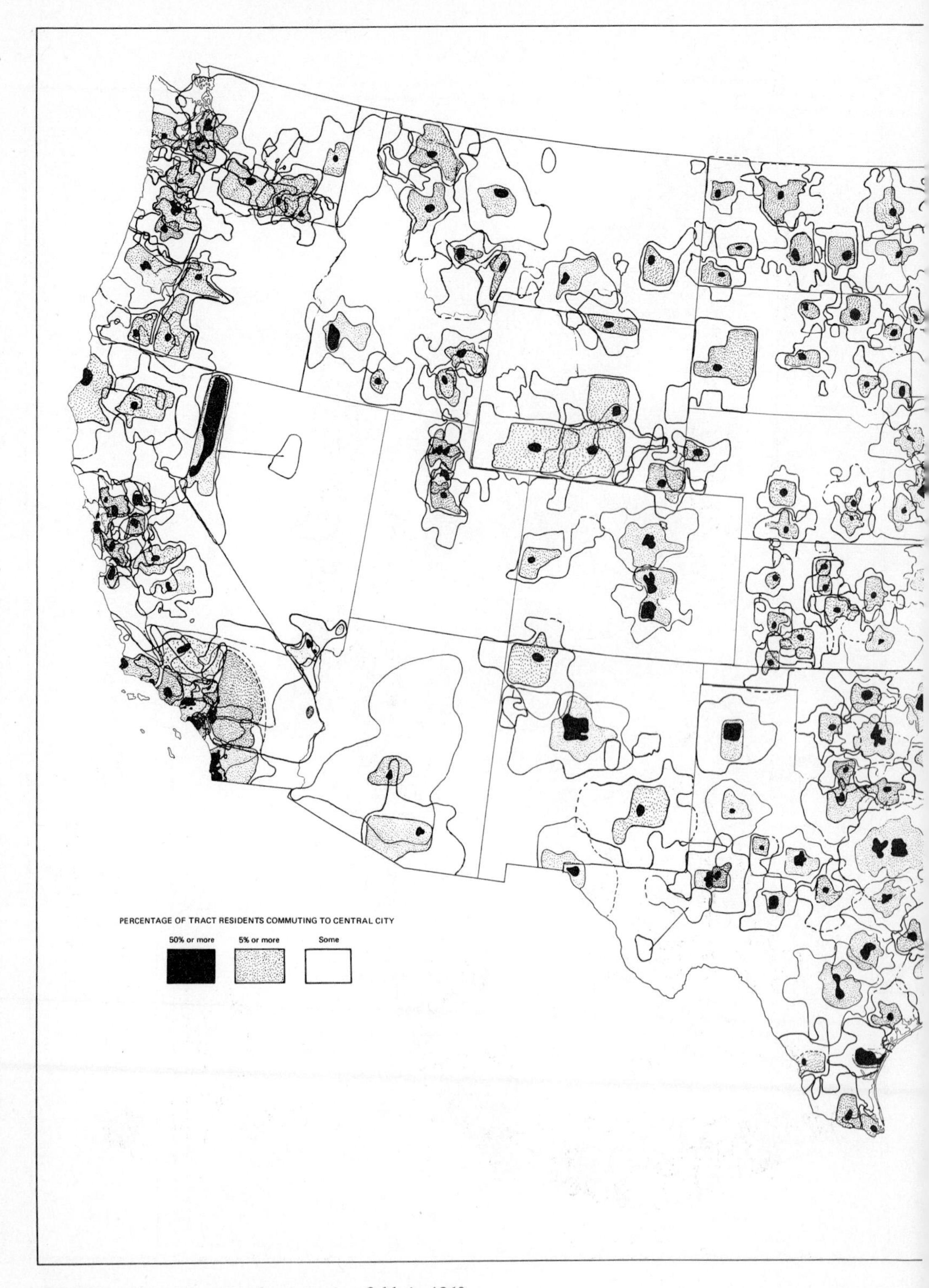

FIGURE 2–18. Intensity of commuting fields in 1960.
Source: See caption for Fig. 2–16.

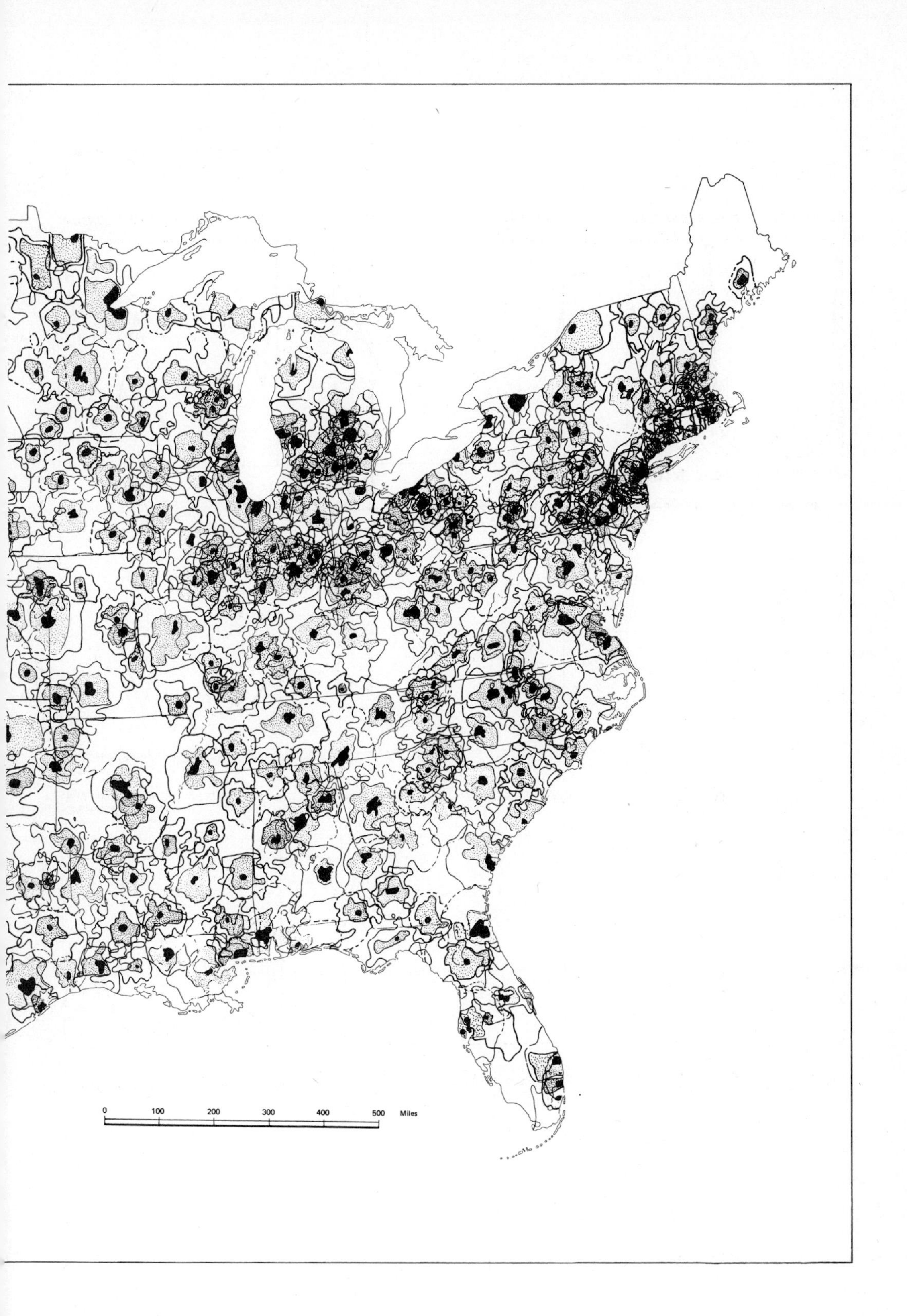
0
100
200
300
400
500
Miles

FIGURE 2–19. Gradients of urban influence on a traverse from Des Moines to St. Louis. *Source:* See caption for Fig. 2–16.

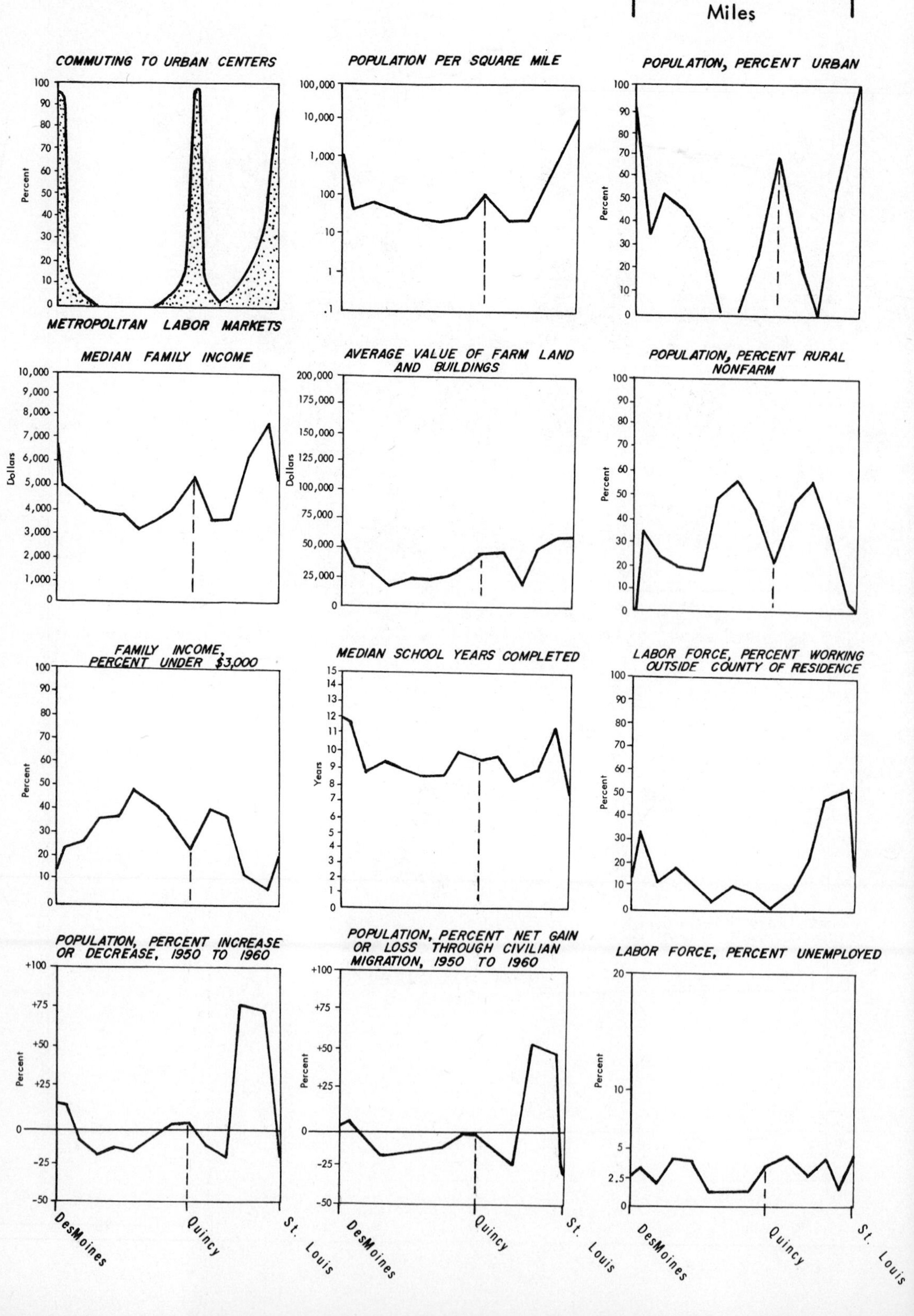

FIGURE 2–20. Gradients of urban influence on a traverse between Des Moines and Jefferson City. *Source:* See caption for Fig. 2–16.

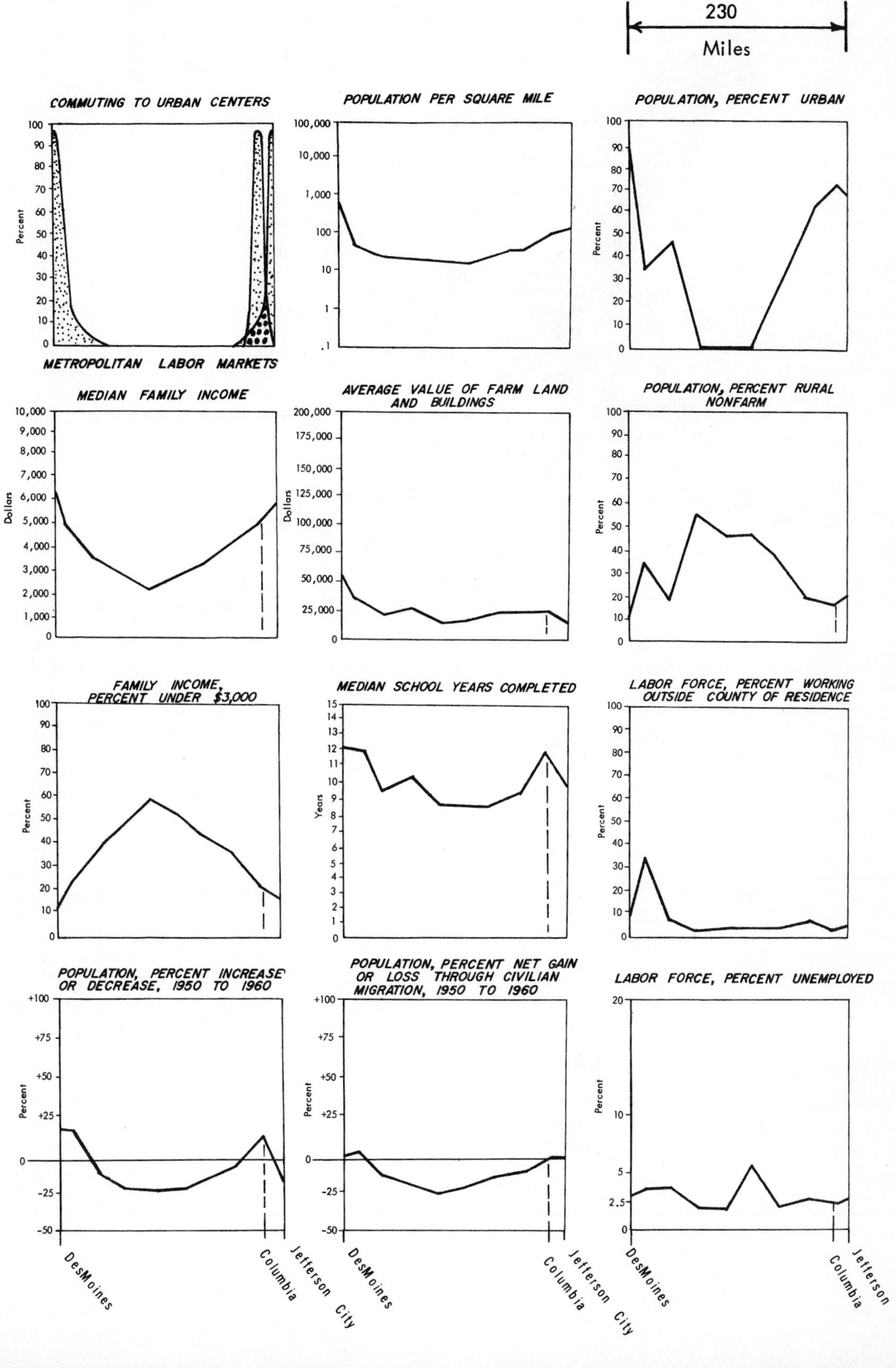

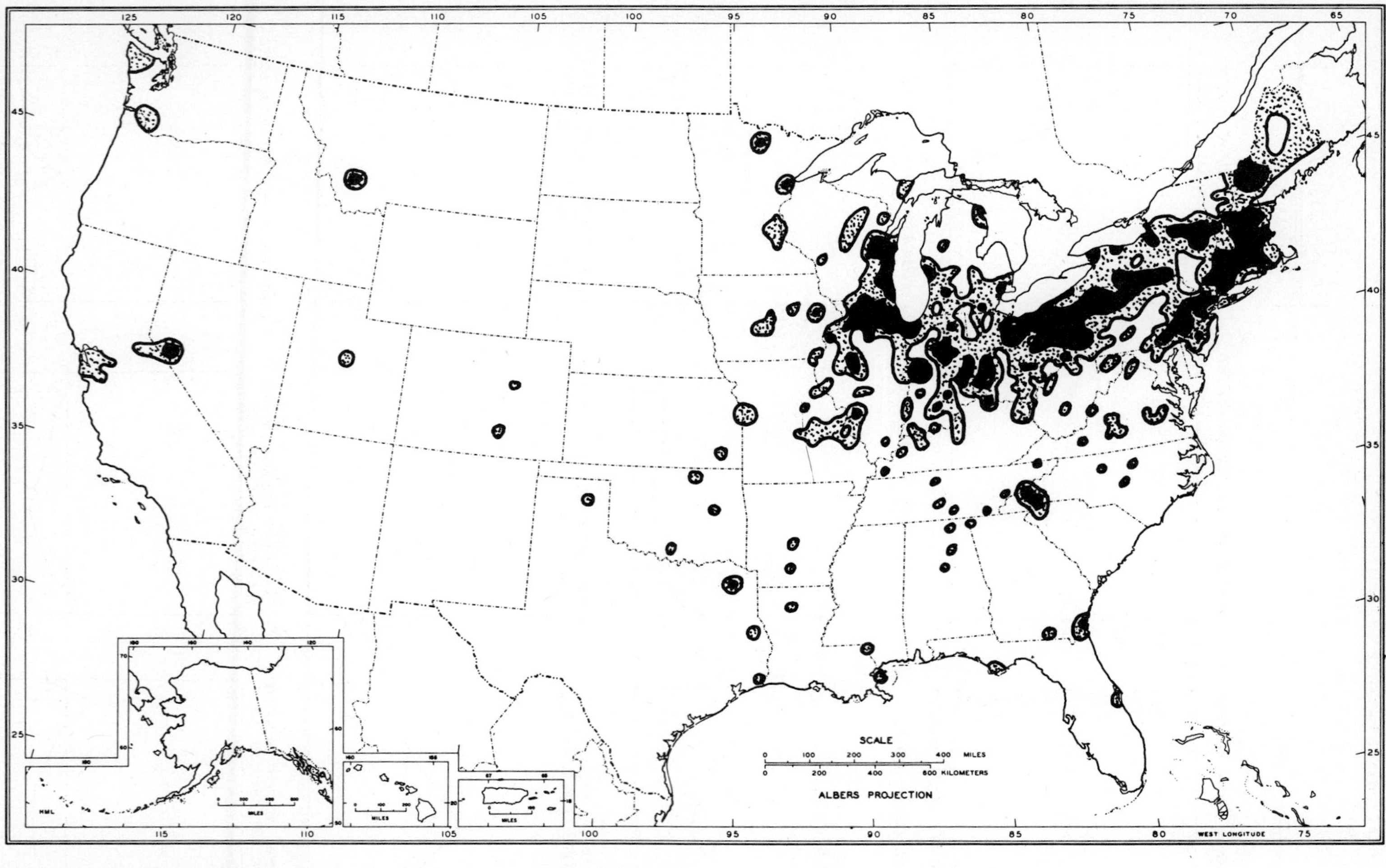

FIGURE 2–21. Areas least dependent upon agriculture in 1960. The intensities are based upon factor scores created in a principal axis factor analysis of county employment data. The darkest shades indicate the least dependence on agricultural employment. *Source:* Figs. 2–21 through 2–24 are from Brian J. L. Berry, *Strategies, Models, and Economic Theories of Development in Rural Regions*, Agriculture Economic Report No. 128, Department of Agriculture (Washington, D.C.: U.S. Government Printing Office, 1967).

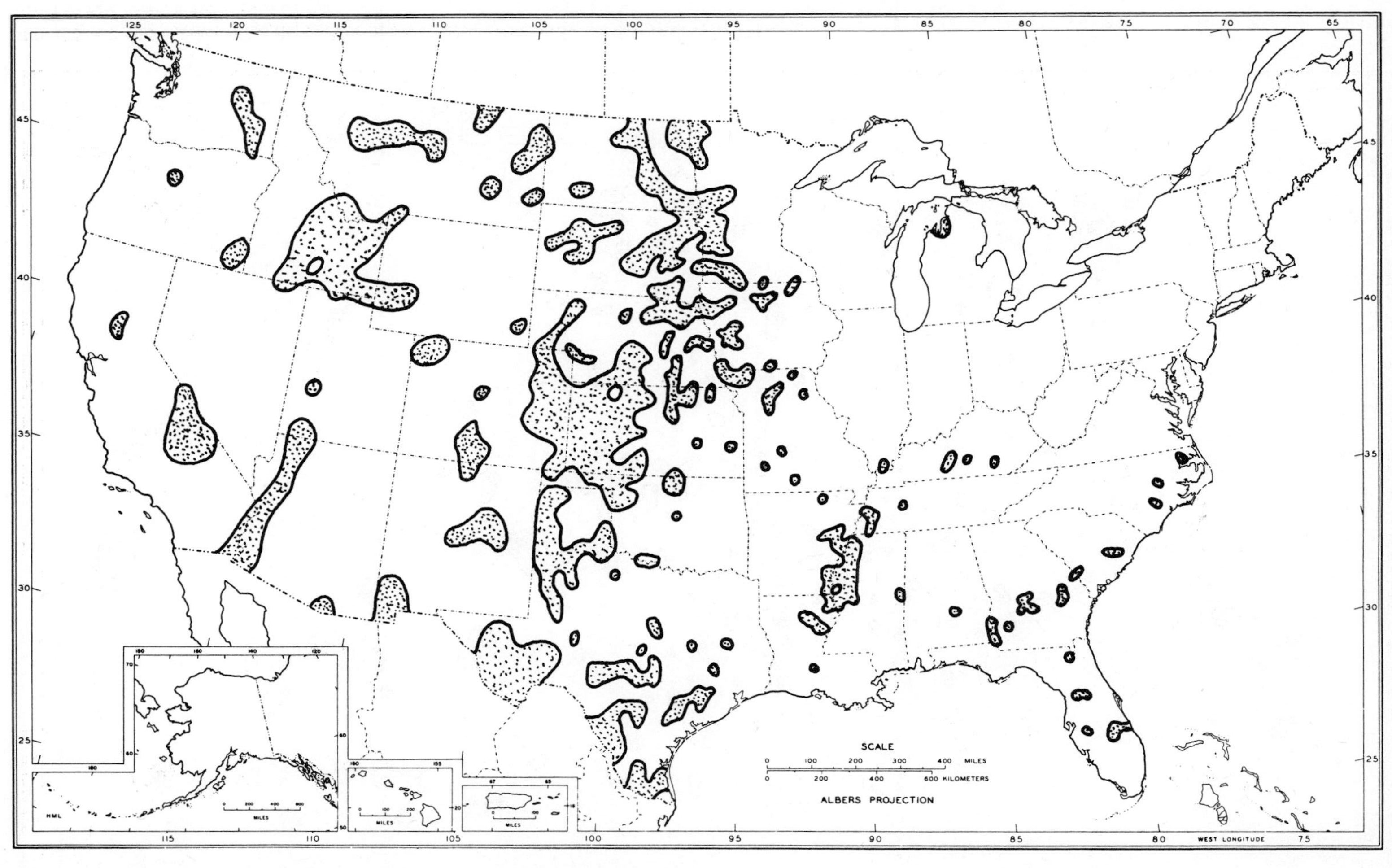

FIGURE 2–22. Areas most dependent upon agricultural employment in 1960.
Source: See caption for Fig. 2–21.

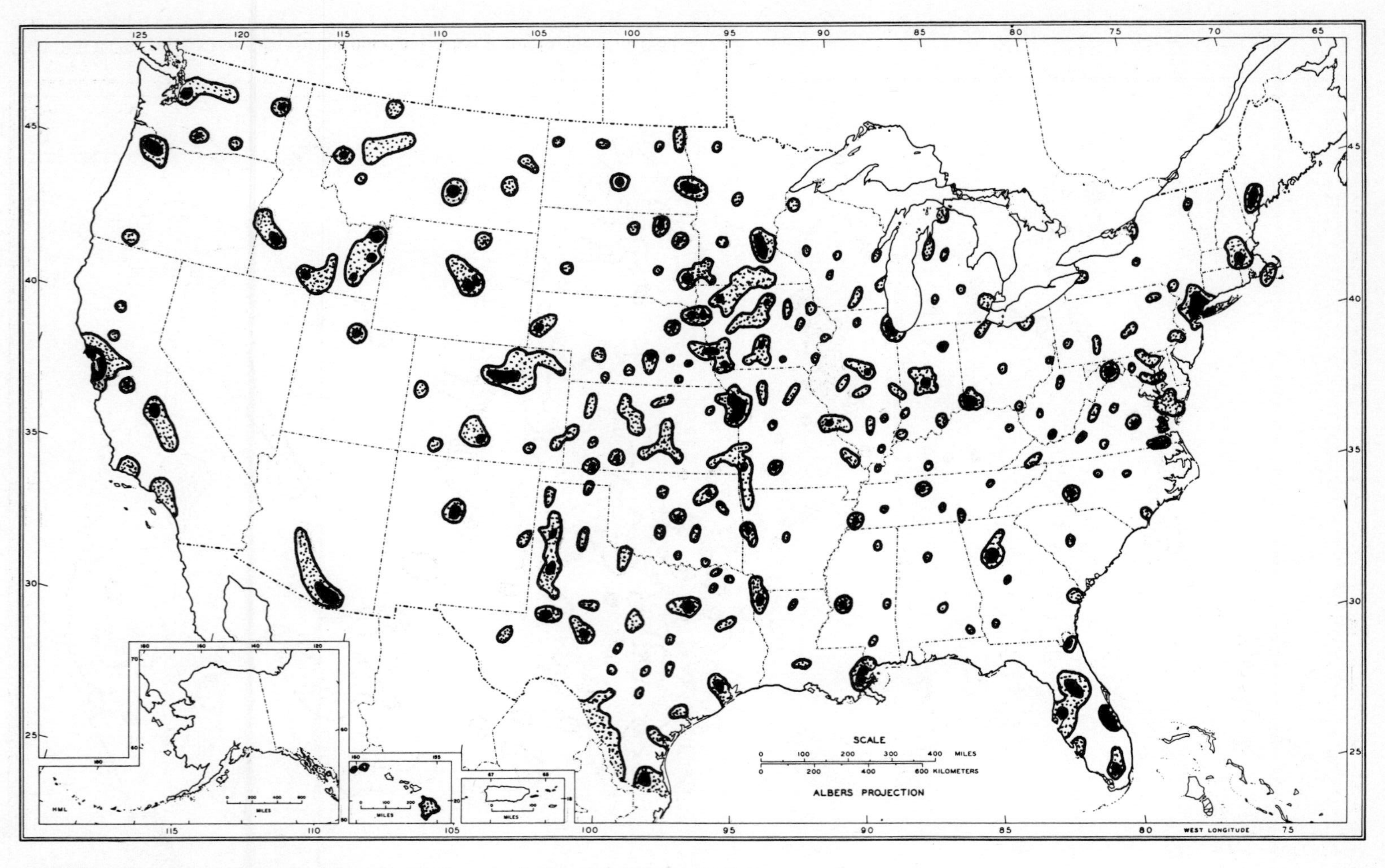

FIGURE 2–23. Areas most dependent upon employment in the tertiary sector in 1960.
Source: See caption for Fig. 2–21.

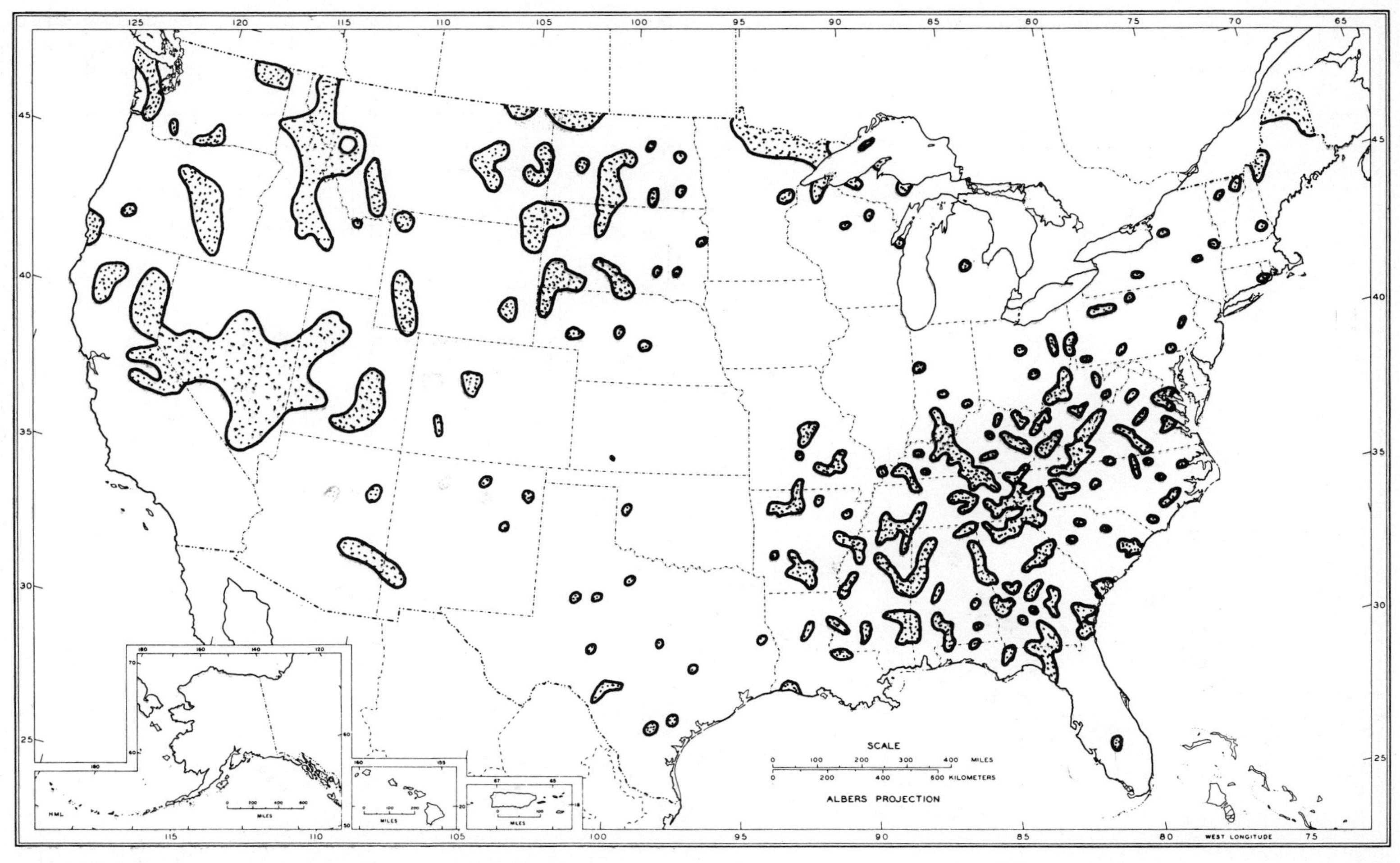

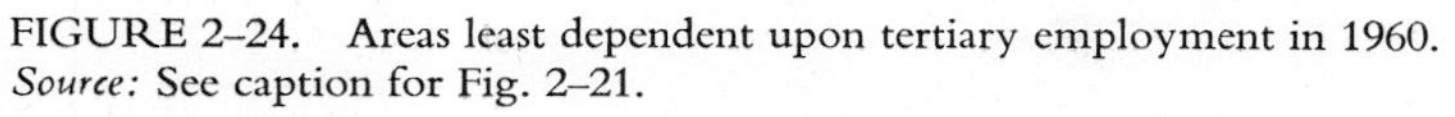

FIGURE 2–24. Areas least dependent upon tertiary employment in 1960.
Source: See caption for Fig. 2–21.

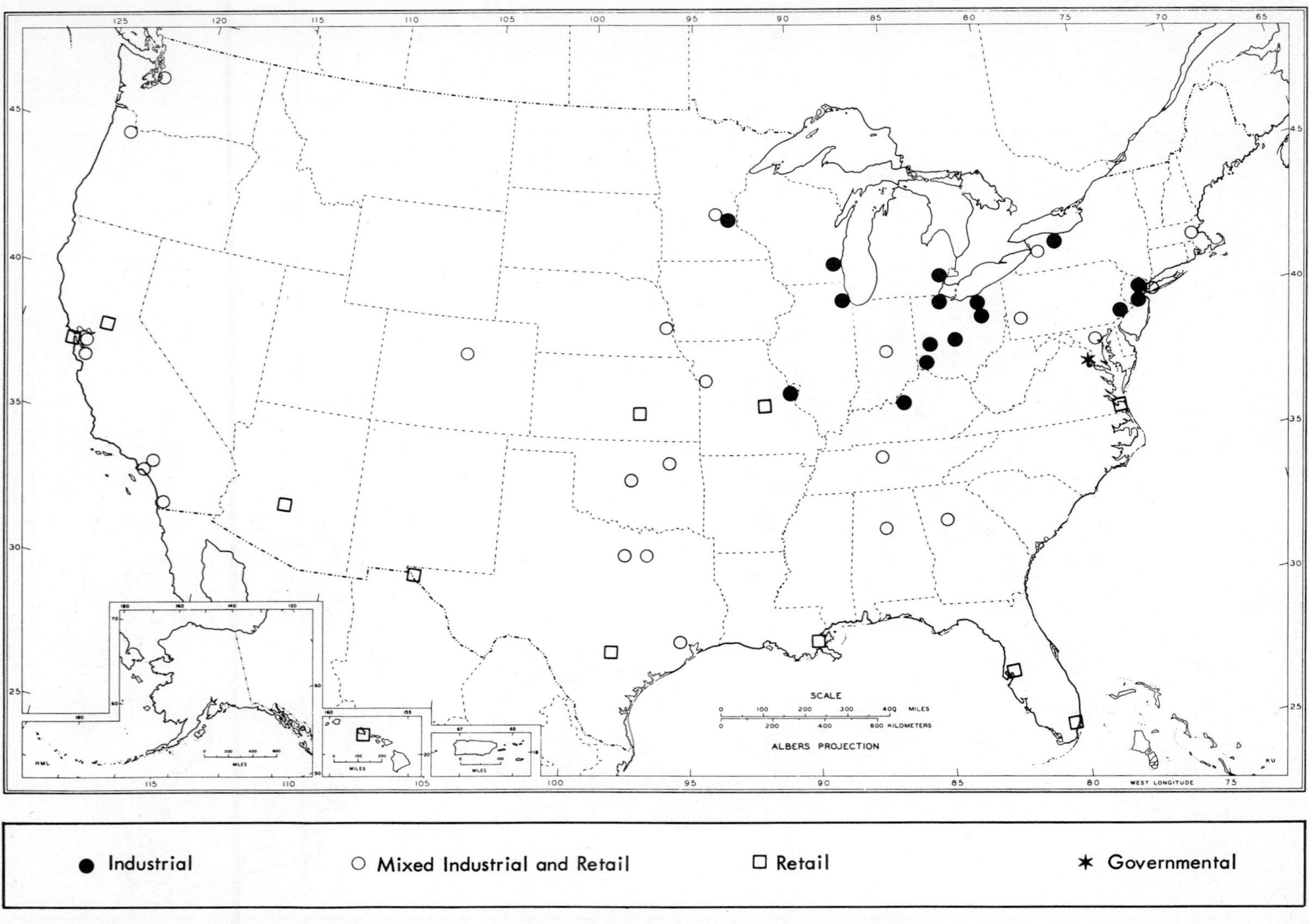

FIGURE 2–25. Principal functional classification of cities of over 250,000: 1960. *Source:* From data tabulated in the International City Managers' Association *Municipal Yearbook: 1967* (Washington, D.C.: ICMA, 1967).

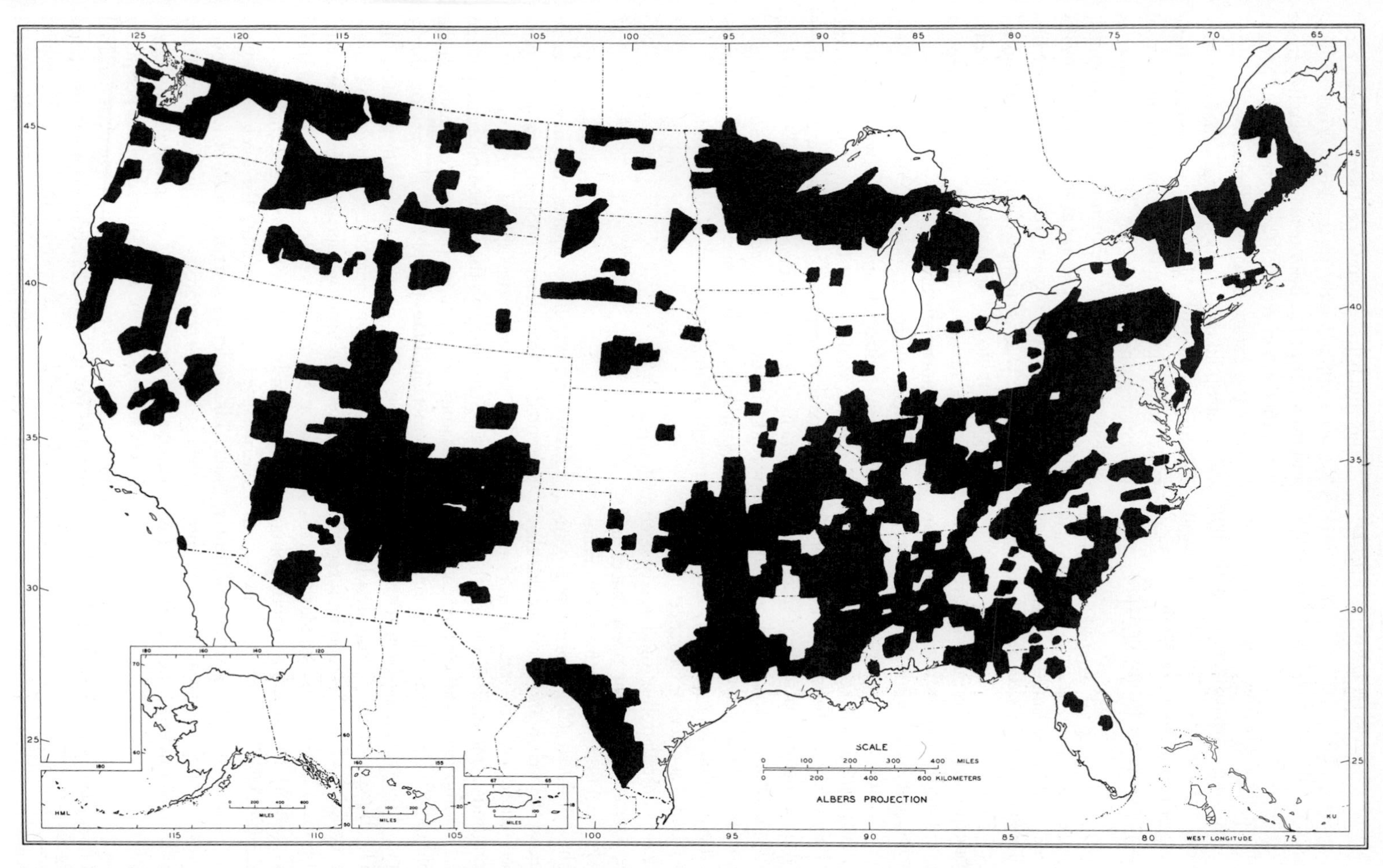

FIGURE 2–26. Counties in economic distress in 1964. Note the inverse relationship between income and participation in metropolitan labor markets. These 1,225 counties—containing 49,000,000 people—qualify for federal public works grants and regional development aid by reason of high unemployment and low average income. *Source:* Brian J. L. Berry and Peter Goheen, *Metropolitan Area Definition: A Re-evaluation of Concept and Statistical Practice* (Washington, D.C.: Bureau of the Census Working Paper No. 28, 1968).

*THE URBAN FIELD**

In Search of a New Image

Observation of these processes of urbanization has led to growing dissatisfaction with the historical concept of the city. Don Martindale, in his brilliant introduction to Max Weber's essay, *The City*, has composed a fitting epitaph:

> The modern city is losing its external and formal structure. Internally it is in a state of decay while the new community represented by the nation everywhere grows at its expense. The age of the city seems to be at an end.[23]

Various concepts have been put forward in the endeavor to capture the expanding scale of urban life. "Metropolitan region," "spread city," "megalopolis," "ecumenopolis"—each attempt to redefine the new reality has led to a broader spatial conception. Behind these efforts lies an awareness of the constantly widening patterns of interaction in an urbanizing world. And modern utopian constructs have been equally intent on fitting city concepts to the possibilities created by our communications-based society. Clarence Stein's *Regional City* is a constellation of moderately sized communities separated by great open spaces and bound closely together by highways.[24] Frank Lloyd Wright's *Broadacre City* represents a complete melding of the urban and rural worlds that, without pronounced centers, would uniformly dissolve throughout a region.[25] Both see the city as an essentially unlimited form of human settlement, capable of infinite expansion. None of the new concepts, however, has been completely successful. The Bureau of the Census has had to redefine the concept of a metropolitan region, from "metropolitan district" to "standard metropolitan area" (SMA) to "standard metropolitan statistical area" (SMSA) in order to keep pace with our improved understanding of what constitutes the fundamental ecological area of urban life, and it is still reexamining the question (see Chapter 8).[26]

*Reprinted from John Friedmann and John Miller, "The Urban Field," *Journal of the American Institute of Planners*, XXXI, No. 4 (November, 1965), 312–19, with the permission of the authors and editor.

The much looser conception of "spread city" has been applied only to the New York region, and no attempt has been made to generalize from it to other urban areas.[27] Jean Gottmann's "Megalopolis" is a geographic place name for the chain of metropolitan giants along the Boston-Washington axis.[28] Although later writers have taken it as a generic term for contiguous metropolitan regions, the concept, lacking precision as well as generality, has frequently been misapplied. One writer has gone so far as to extend its meaning to the entire region from Phoenix to Minneapolis.[29] His "midwest Central Megalopolis" is a geographic and conceptual absurdity. Finally, C.A. Doxiadis's "ecumenopolis" is no concept at all, but a poetic vision.[30]

Scholars, therefore, are left in a quandary. "Modern metropolitan trends," wrote the late Catherine Bauer Wurster, "have destroyed the traditional concept of urban structure, and there is no new image to take its place."[31] Yet none would question the need for such an image, if only to serve as the conceptual basis for organizing our strategies for urban development.

The Enlarged Scale of Urban Life

However, as the evidence we have already presented shows clearly enough, it is now possible to interpret the spatial structure of the United States in ways that will emphasize a pattern consisting of: (1) metropolitan areas; and, (2) the inter-metropolitan periphery. Except for thinly populated parts of the American interior, the inter-metropolitan periphery includes all areas that intervene among metropolitan regions that are, as it were, the reverse image of the trend towards large scale concentrated settlement that has persisted in this country for over half a century. Like a devil's mirror, much of it has developed a socio-economic profile that perversely reflects the very opposite of metropolitan virility.

Economically, the inter-metropolitan periphery includes most of the areas that have been declared eligible for federal area redevelopment assistance (ARA).[32] This is illustrated in Fig. 2–26, which shows the geographic extent of substandard income and high unemployment areas relative to the urbanized regions of the United States.[33] Situated almost entirely outside the normal reach of the larger cities, these areas are shown to be clearly peripheral. They have a disproportionately large share of low-growth and declining industries and a correspondingly antiquated economic structure. Nevertheless, one-fifth of the American people are living in these regions of economic distress.

Demographically, the inter-metropolitan periphery has been subject to a long-term, continuous decline (see Fig. 2–27). This trend reflects the movement of people to cities, especially to the large metropolitan concentrations. Although the smaller cities on the periphery have to some extent benefited from migration, their gains have been less, on the average, than for all urban areas.[33] In addition, migration from economically depressed regions has been highly selective, so that the age distribution of the remaining population has become polarized around the very young and very old. In Appalachia, for example, the two million people who left the region during the 1950's were, for the most part, drawn from the productive age groups from 18 to 64. At the same time, the population over 65 years old increased by nearly one-third.[34] In some areas, recorded death rates now actually exceed birth rates.[35]

Socially, the standard indices of education and health are substantially lower along the periphery than in metropolitan areas. The quality of public services has deteriorated (though their per capita cost has increased), the housing stock is older, and the level of educational attainment is significantly below the average for metropolitan America. Rapid and selective outmigration, a declining economic base, the burden of an aging population, and low incomes have rendered many peripheral communities helpless in their desire to adapt to changing circumstances in the outside world. The remaining population is frequently short both on civic leadership and hope. They can neither grasp the scope of the events that have overtaken them nor are they capable of responding creatively to the new situations.[36]

FIGURE 2–27. Population change between 1950 and 1960 (by county). *Source:* Adapted from John Friedmann and John Miller, "The Urban Field," *Journal of the American Institute of Planners*, XXXI, No, 4 (November, 1965), 312–90.

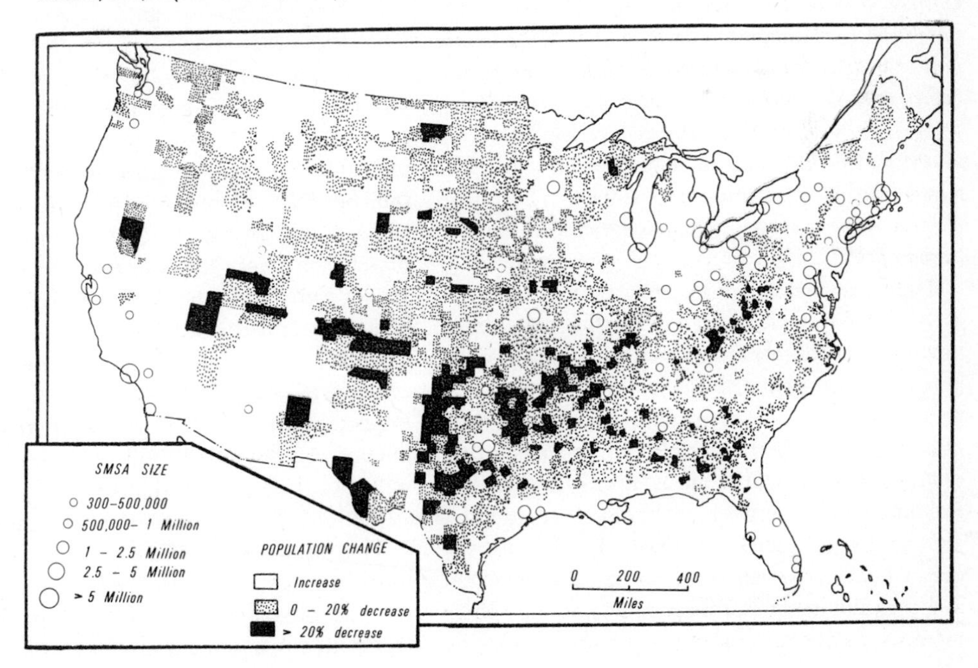

Politically, many peripheral areas have lost their ability to act. They are fragmented, disorganized, and without effective economic leverage. The Area Redevelopment Administration [and now the Economic Development Administration] has for a number of years been at work in these regions on a county by county basis (itself a fragmented strategy) and now the Appalachia program has been launched amidst much fanfare. Yet neither of these programs has adequately recognized the relationship between metropolitan cores and their peripheries, so their scale, though ambitious, has been dwarfed by the extent of the social and economic problems of the periphery.

The emergence in large sections of the country of the inter-metropolitan periphery as a major problem area has been the direct result of the concentration of people and activities around closely contiguous metropolitan cores. Growth in and around these cores has drawn off the productive population, economic activities, and investment capital of the periphery, but the forces of urbanization are now in the process of reversing this trend.[37]

Looking ahead to the next generation, we foresee a new scale of urban living that will extend far beyond existing metropolitan cores and penetrate deeply into the periphery. Relations of dominance and dependency will be transcended. The older established centers, together with the intermetropolitan peripheries that envelop them, will constitute the new ecological unit of America's post-industrial society that will replace traditional concepts of the city and metropolis. This basic element of the emerging spatial order we shall call the "urban field."

The urban field may be viewed as an enlargement of the space for urban living that extends far beyond the boundaries of existing metropolitan areas—defined primarily in terms of commuting to a central city of "metropolitan" size—into the open landscape of the periphery. This change to a larger scale of urban life is already underway, encouraged by changes in technology, economics, and preferred social behavior. Eventually the urban field may even come to be acknowledged as a community of *shared* interests, although these interests may be more strongly oriented to specific functions than to area. They will be shared because to a large extent they will overlap and complement each other within a specific locational matrix. Because urban fields will be large, with populations of upwards of one million, their social and cultural life will form a rich and varied pattern capable of satisfying most human aspirations within a local setting.

It is no longer possible to regard the city as purely an artifact, or a political entity, or a configuration of population densities. All of these are outmoded constructs that recall a time when one could trace a sharp dividing line between town and countryside, rural and urban man. From a sociological and, indeed, an economic standpoint, what is properly urban and properly rural can no longer be distinguished. The United States is becoming a thoroughly urbanized society, perhaps the first such society in history. The corresponding view of the city is no longer of a physical entity, but of a pattern of point locations and connecting flows of people, information, money, and commodities.

The idea of an urban field is similarly based on the criterion of interdependency. It represents a fusion of metropolitan spaces and nonmetropolitan peripheral spaces centered upon core areas of at least 300,000 people and extending outwards from these core areas for a distance equivalent to two hours' driving over modern throughway systems (approximately 100 miles with present technology). This represents not only an approximate geographic limit for commuting to a job, but also the limit of intensive weekend and seasonal use (by ground transportation) of the present periphery for recreation. Between 85 and 90 per cent of the total United States population falls within the boundaries of this system while less than 35 per cent of the total land area of the country is included. These are facts of signal importance, for as the area of metropolitan influence is substantially enlarged nearly all of us will soon be living within one or another of the 70-odd urban fields of the United States.[38]

The choice of core areas of at least 300,000 inhabitants as a basis for delineating urban fields requires some justification. Karl Fox, for instance, recommends a reduction of central city size to

25,000 or less for his proposed set of Functional Economic Areas which, in a sense, is alternative to our concept of a system of urban fields.[39]

The threshold size of 300,000 was suggested to us by the work of Otis Dudley Duncan and his associates. According to Duncan, a Standard Metropolitan Area of 300,000 people in the United States in 1950:

> . . . marked a transition point where distinctively "metropolitan" characteristics first begin to appear. Adequately to describe the base of the "urban hierarchy" —consisting of almost all urban centers smaller than this size—one would have to shift the emphasis from "metropolitanism" to other principles of functional differentiation.[40]

Although the SMA's of 1950 are not equivalent to the SMSA's of 1960, the two concepts are similar enough to suggest the possibility of a transfer of Duncan's threshold size to the SMSA. An additional consideration was the expectation that core regions of this size and larger will continue to expand over the next several decades and will consequently generate a vast demand for various uses of intermetropolitan space.

The urban field of the future, however, will be a far less focussed region than today's metropolitan area. The present dominance of the metropolitan core will become attenuated as economic activities are decentralized to smaller cities within the field or into the open country, but because proximity will continue to account for a good deal of local interaction, the urban field will be a coherent region.

To define this region on a map, the main criterion should be that exchange relations *within* each field are more intensive than among them, during the course of an entire year. The calculation of this measure on an annual basis instead of at a single point in time is important because some of the functional relationships among subareas may be subject to seasonal variations. The enjoyment of summer and winter recreation areas is the outstanding example of this phenomenon. These areas should be allocated to that realm whose population makes the most intensive use of them.

It is important to recollect what this projected geographic expansion of urban living space will accomplish. First, it will turn the resources of the inter-metropolitan periphery to important uses by existing metropolitan populations; second, as the periphery becomes absorbed into the urban field, it will be eliminated as a distinctive problem area. The remaining parts of the United States will either remain in low density agrarian uses or revert to wilderness for the enjoyment of distant populations.

Forces Underlying the Emergence of Urban Realms

Our case for the urban field rests on two propositions. The first is that the future growth of population in the United States will take place almost exclusively within the areas we have defined as urban fields. The second is that within each urban field substantial centrifugal forces will propel the settlement of population and the location of activities from existing metropolitan centers into the present periphery.

One of the clearest national trends of the past few decades has been that of increasing demographic concentration. Most of the discussion, however, has emphasized the pulling together of people in metropolitan and coastal regions. It has been less well publicized that the great majority of counties that lost population during the 1950's are predominantly rural and lie outside the boundaries of any urban realm. The gains have occurred almost entirely within these boundaries, though not exclusively in metropolitan counties. We have no reason to expect this trend to be reversed during the coming generation.

In 1960, an estimated 150,000,000 Americans lived in potential urban fields. We have projected their number to more than double the present number by the year 2000. This increase of 150,000,000 to 180,000,000 will have to be accommodated within roughly the same area. The question arises as to where, within a given field, this population will be living. In approaching this question, we are mindful of the New York Metropolitan Region Study which for 1985 foresees as many people living in the "outer ring" as in the central core. This outer ring extends as far as 100 miles from New York City and is not today part of the daily life of the metropolis.[41] Elaborating on this startling projection, Raymond Vernon writes that employment and population trends

> . . . cast doubt on any image of the Region as a gaint cluster of human activity held together by a great nub of jobs at the center. Instead . . . [they afford] a picture of a Region in which the centripetal pull is weakening. This, in turn, means a further modification of the over-simplified picture of the Region as a ring of bedroom communities in the suburbs emptying out their inhabitants every morning to the central city. Incomplete and misleading as this picture is today, it promises to be even more misleading in the decades ahead. . . . And the chronic complaint of the outlying areas that they lack an "economic base" may continue to lose some of its realism and force.[42]

Vernon has foreshadowed the appearance of an urban field that would have New York City as its core. What are the forces, then, which suggest this occupancy of the periphery by people and activities, not only for New York, but for all other core regions in the United States? And what specific forms will it assume?

The main pull, we submit, is the increasing attractiveness of the periphery to metropolitan populations. It has space, it has scenery, and it contains communities that remain from earlier periods of settlement and preserve a measure of historical integrity and interest.

Demand for these resources will be generated by three main trends: increasing real income, increasing leisure, and increasing mobility. Although these trends are familiar, brief discussion of them will help to suggest their cumulative impact.

The President's Council of Economic Advisors estimates that output per man-hour may undergo a three-fold expansion by the year 2000.[43] Holding constant both working hours and labor force participation rates, this would raise average family income (in today's prices) to approximately $18,000. Although there is every reason to expect that part of the potential gains in income will be taken in the form of greater leisure through a combination of shorter working hours, longer vacations, later entry into the labor force, and earlier retirement, the prospective rise in wealth is still very substantial. If present patterns of consumption are any guide, we can expect a good share of this new wealth to be devoted to the purchase of space, privacy, travel, education, culture, and various forms of recreative leisure.

The present allocation of leisure time is distributed among numerous activities. The Stanford Research Institute reports that already 50,000,000 Americans are actively participating in amateur art activity; that 32,000,000 are musicians, and 15,000,000 are painters, sculptors, and sketchers. There are more piano players than fishermen, as many painters as hunters, and more theater goers than boaters, skiers, golfers, and skin-divers combined.[44]

The U.S. Department of Health, Education, and Welfare has published statistics showing that new museums, including aquariums and zoos, are being established at the rate of one every three days, and that one-third of all existing musuems in the country have been opened since 1950.[45] Other cultural activities have shown equally phenomenal gains. For instance, there are now 1,400 symphony orchestras in the United States, compared to only 100 in 1920.

These new cultural facilities are more mobile, more intimate, and more dispersed than their predecessors. They are different from the grand centers of high culture left in our central cores by nineteenth century cultural ideology.

Participation in outdoor sports is likewise on an impressive scale. In 1964, there were an estimated 38,000,000 boaters, 20,000,000 campers, 7,000,000 skiers, and an equal number of golfers. Skiing enthusiasts alone have jumped by 600 per cent during the past ten years. And attendance in official park and forest areas has been rising at a cumulative annual rate of about 10 per cent.

With increasing leisure time available, the prospects for the future show no abatement in these activities. For the mass of the people, nearly two-thirds of their waking hours will be essentially in free, unstructured time. It is therefore not surprising that the Outdoor Recreation Resources Review Commission has predicted in their news releases a tripling in the overall demand for recreation by the year 2000. For the hedonistic leisure society we are becoming, this estimate may indeed be a conservative one.

The combined trends in income and leisure are bound to arouse great popular interest in the periphery, but their full effect will be transmitted through the increased mobility which our technology affords.

The gradual lifting of constraints which during the industrial era packed jobs and people into tightly confined urban spaces will encourage what Jean Gottman has called the "quasi-colloidal dispersion" of activities throughout the urban field.[46] Impending communications technologies suggest the possibility of relaxing the need for physical proximity in distribution, marketing, information services, and decision-making.

A few examples may be cited. Computers which keep business inventories and send information on replenishment items over TV or telephone are now technically feasible. They may also be used to alert suppliers to periodically recurring needs for product service. In retailing, a major revolution is in the making, as videophones have been developed that can transmit images of products and convert these images on signal into photographic reproductions. The use of coded cards to send information, order items, and transfer funds by telephone has already passed the laboratory stage and no doubt will soon be introduced on the market.

Transport technology continues to advance toward greater speed and versatility. Supersonic and short-distance jets, automated highways, and rail transport which moves at several hundred miles an hour through densely built-up regions, are expected to pass from drawing board to commercial application within ten to twenty years. The result will be a further shrinkage of the transportation surface and vastly increased accessibility on a national scale no less than within each urban field.

One effect of increased accessibility especially worthy of note is the estimated 3,500,000 to 7,500,000 acres which will be opened up for urban development when the federal interstate highway program is completed. This land newly available for urbanization will represent a major resource to the national economy.

The combined effects of greater income, leisure, and mobility will be felt, by virtue of these arguments, primarily on the present periphery of metropolitan regions, as demand for the use of its resources are vastly intensified. Some of these uses are shown below. They are distinctly urban in character.

Uses of the Intermetropolitan Periphery

RECREATION
- camps
- parks
- forests
- wilderness areas
- nature sanctuaries
- resorts
- outdoor sport areas
- quietist retreats

INSTITUTIONS
- boarding schools
- junior colleges
- universities
- museums
- cultural centers
- scientific research stations
- conference centers
- hospitals
- sanatoria
- government administrative offices

COMMUNITIES
- holiday communities
- retirement communities
- vacation villages
- art colonies
- diversified "new towns"
- historical communities
- second home areas

ECONOMIC ACTIVITIES
- agro-business
- space-extensive manufacturing plants
- research and communications-based industries
- mail order houses
- warehouses
- insurance companies
- jet airports

Emerging Life Styles of the Urban Field

The projected incorporation of the periphery into the urban realm will be accompanied by significant changes in American patterns of living. On the whole, we expect that these changes will be evaluated favorably. Derogatory slogans, such as "sprawl" and "scatteration," bandied about in ideological campaigns, will have to be discarded in any serious search for what it means to live on the new scale. Although not all the consequences can be foreseen now, a few merit closer attention. We shall restrict our comment to only three of them: a wider life space on the average; a wider choice of living environments; and a wider community of interests.

A wider life space. The effective life space of an individual includes all the geographic areas within which his life unfolds. It includes his home and its immediate vicinity; his place of work or schooling; the places in which he does his shopping and engages in leisure activities; the more distant places to which he travels for business, recreation, or learning; the residence areas of the friends and relatives he visits; and the connecting paths over which he travels to reach his destination.

It is possible to map these spaces for individuals—distinguished by age, sex, and socio-economic status—as well as for entire communities. These maps would show which areas of the total available space are actually being used by different parts of the population as well as the intensity of their use. An important feature of these maps would be data relating to the percentage of the individual's total annual time spent at different localities and travelling over various routes. A further distinction with regard to the seasonality of use could be made.

Such maps for an urban field would reveal greatly expanded and more complexly structured systems of life spaces for the total population compared to existing patterns. The higher speeds, greater versatility, and lower costs expected in transportation and communication during the next few decades will encourage a dispersion of people and activities throughout the urban field and a further thinning out of metropolitan core areas on an unsurpassed scale. Technological innovations will make it possible to substitute mobility for location. The strong likelihood that this will occur is suggested by foreseeable changes in patterns which underlie the location decisions of families and firms.

For individual families, locational decisions will be increasingly influenced by larger incomes that will permit the purchase of more space, more privacy, and more transportation; by a growing concern with the qualitative aspects of life, especially with the quality of the physical environment; by the gradual relaxation of the puritanical distinction between work and play, especially among professional and business elite groups; and by the desire for an environment that will permit a richer family life. All of these forces will tend to render the intermetropolitan periphery more attractive as a place to live, and help to tie it more closely into the urban field.

The location of business firms will encounter fewer economic constraints within the urban field than at present. This is especially true for the new kinds of service activities—professional, managerial, research- and communications-based—which are the leading edge of a post-industrial society. Urban infrastructure and services will be nearly ubiquitous throughout the urban field; the pressing need for physical propinquity among firms is declining; and the expansion and improvement of transport and communication services will tend to make regional as well as national markets equally accessible. If only those economic factors that operate generally throughout a given field are taken into account, thereby excluding local subsidies or differences in local tax structure, which provide only small and temporary advantages, it is possible to assert that firms may locate nearly at random throughout the field, subject only to the constraint of labor force distribution. Location of the labor force will then become a primary determinant in business location decisions, with the result that firms will be attracted in increasing numbers into what is now the inter-metropolitan periphery. Firms as well as families will substitute mobility and machine-interposed communications for location.

A wider choice of living environments both for resident and nonresident use and more interchange among environments. The urban field offers a heterogeneous landscape, consisting of metropolitan cores, small towns, and varied open spaces. Within it, a wide variety of living environments may be sought and created. There is nothing rigid or predetermined about the physical form of the field: rather, it may be viewed as a mosaic of different forms and micro-environments which coexist within a common communications framework without intruding spatially on each other.

For the family, the urban field offers a far greater choice of living environments than do the old metropolitan areas. Alternatives include country and in-town living, perhaps combined, through a steep increase in the frequency of second homes for year-round use; single family dwellings and apartment towers; dense metropolitan clusters and open countryside; new towns and towns with an historical tradition; and functionally specialized communities.

No part within the urban field is isolated from another. There is rather an easy-going interchange among all the parts, encouraged not only by the wider distribution of population but also by the larger amounts of time available for the pursuit of leisure. All areas are located no further than two hours' driving distance from old metropolitan cores. And although these cores will lose much of their present importance to the people of the field as functions are decentralized, they will continue for at least a few more decades to attract many people to the activities that are traditionally carried out within them, such as major educational and governmental institutions, famous museums, outstanding music, artistic, and sport events. Many cultural facilities, however, will be dispersed throughout the realm and many metropolitan services will become available at any point within it through extended distribution systems. At the same time, easy access to other urban fields can be provided through a regional system of airports capable of handling short-distance jets and vertical take-off craft. High-speed rail transport may be a significant means for inter-realm travel in some parts of the country, such as the "Northeast Corridor."

A wider community of interests. The already noted increase in the effective life space of the population suggests that each person will have interests in happenings over a larger segment of the field than at present. In the course of a year, he may actively participate in the life of a number of spatially defined local communities. As a result, he is likely to be less concerned with the fate of the community where he resides and more with activities that may be scattered throughout the field but are closest to his interests, leading to a stronger identification on his part with the realm as a whole at the cost of a declining interest in purely local affairs. (In some places, this loss may be offset by the smaller size of his resident community which would encourage more active participation in problem-solving.) We foresee continuation of the present trend toward a cosmopolitanization of values, attitudes, and behavior, with politically relevant behavior organized principally along functional lines, and with the governing of local communities passing increasingly into the hand of professionals.

FOOTNOTES TO CHAPTER 2

1. Norbert Wiener implies in several of his works on cybernetics that the environment might best be conceived as a myriad of "To Whom It May Concern" messages from which it is necessary to make a selection. See, for example, *The Human Use of Human Beings* (Boston: Houghton Mifflin Company, 1964). See also Emrys Jones, "Cause and Effect in Human Geography," *Annals of the Association of American Geographers*, XLIV, No. 4 (December, 1956), 369–77.

2. Personal correspondance with the author.

3. The framework of the present discussion is that of Perloff. See Harvey S. Perloff, "Modernizing Urban Development," *Daedalus*, XCVI, No. 3 (1967), 789–800. See also H. Perloff and L. Wingo, "Natural Resource Endowment and Regional Economic Growth," in J. J. Spengler, eds., *Natural Resources and Economic Growth* (Washington, D. C.: Resources for the Future, Inc., 1961), pp. 191–212. A similar picture of the stages of urban evolution is found in Lewis Mumford, *The Urban Prospect* (New York: Harcourt, Brace & World, Inc., 1968).

4. John R. Borchert, "American Metropolitan Evolution," *Geographical Review*, LVII, No. 3 (July, 1967), 324.

5. Beverly Duncan and Stanley Lieberson, *Metropolis and Region in Transition* (Washington: Resources for the Future, Inc., 1967); John R. Borchert, "American Metropolitan Evolution," *The Geographical Review*, LVII, No. 3 (July, 1967), 301–23.

6. See, by William Warntz, *Macrogeography and Income Fronts* (Philadelphia: Regional Science Research Institute, 1965); and "Macroscopic Analysis and Some Patterns of the Geographical Distribution of Population in the United States: 1790–1950," in W. L. Garrison and D. F. Marble, eds., *Quantitative Geography* (Evanston, Ill.: Northwestern Studies in Geography, 1967), pp. 191–218.

7. For a full introduction to the central-place concept, see

Brian J. L. Berry, *Geography of Market Centers and Retail Distribution* (Englewood Cliffs, N. J.: Prentice-Hall, Inc., 1967).

8. See Chauncy D. Harris, "The Market as a Factor in the Localization of Industry in the United States," *Annals of the Association of American Geographers*, XLIV, No. 4 (December, 1954), 315–48; and Edward L. Ullman, "Regional Development and the Geography of Concentration," *Papers of the Regional Science Association*, IV (1958), 179–98.

9. George H. Borts, *Patterns of Regional Economic Development in the United States, and their Relation to Rural Poverty*, Report to the National Advisory Commission on Rural Poverty, Department of Agriculture (Washington, D. C.: U. S. Government Printing Office, 1967).

10. Allan Pred, *The Spatial Dynamics of U.S. Urban-Industrial Growth: 1800–1914* (Cambridge, Mass.: The M.I.T. Press, 1966), p. 25.

11. See Edward Ullman, *American Commodity Flows* (Seattle: University of Washington Press, 1957).

12. Perloff and Wingo, "Natural Resource Endowment," p. 211.

13. See Edward L. Ullman, "Amenities as a Factor in Regional Growth," *The Geographical Review*, XLIV, No. 1 (January, 1954), 119–32.

14. The analyses were performed for Edgar S. Dunn, Jr. A preliminary report on the county analysis is in Brian J. L. Berry, *Strategies, Models and Economic Theories of Development in Rural Regions*, Agriculture Economic Report No. 128, Department of Agriculture (Washington, D. C.: U. S. Government Printing Office, 1967).

15. It is thus no accident that Wilbur Thompson gets excellent results using industry mix as his principal independent variable in predicting levels, distribution, and stability of urban incomes, and the consequent growth of a city. See "Internal and External Factors in the Development of Urban Economies," mimeographed paper presented at 1967 Washington Conference of the Committee on Urban Economics, Resources for the Future, Inc.

16. Maps are to be found in Berry, *Strategies, Models*.

17. This is consistent with the notion of growth of systems in accordance with a "law of proportionate effect," which can be inferred from the parallel rank-size regularities in 1950 and 1960. See Brian J. L. Berry, "Cities as Systems within Systems of Cities," *Papers of the Regional Science Association*, X (1964), 147–63, and also Chapter 3 of the present work.

18. Brian J. L. Berry, "Degree of Metropolitan Labor Market Participation as a Variable in Economic Development" (to be published by the Economic Development Administration).

19. The Analysis was made for Edgar S. Dunn, Jr. See Berry, *Strategies, Models*.

20. Nicolaus Tideman, "Transport Cost vs. Market Potential" (Unpublished paper, Center for Urban Studies, University of Chicago, 1967).

21. See Chauncy D. Harris, "The Market as a Factor.

22. O. D. Duncan *et al.*, *Metropolis and Region* (Baltimore: John Hopkins University Press, 1956).

23. Max Weber, *The City* (New York: The Free Press, 1958), p. 62.

24. Clarence S. Stein, "A Regional Pattern for Dispersal," *Architectural Record*, CXXXIV, No. 3 (September, 1964), 205–6.

25. Frank Lloyd Wright, *The Living City* (New York: Horizon Press, Inc., 1958).

26. The review of methods of defining the metropolitan region was conducted by Brian J. L. Berry for the Social Science Research Council Committee on Areas for Social and Economic Statistics. The results are presented in Chapter 8 of this book.

27. See the *Christian Science Monitor* (Boston), November 14, 1964, p. 3.

28. Jean Gottmann, *Megalopolis* (New York: Twentieth Century Fund, 1961).

29. Herman G. Berkman, *Our Urban Plant: Essays in Urban Affairs* (Madison: The University of Wisconsin Extension, 1964), pp. 4–5.

30. It is the final stage in the hierarchy of living spaces. See, e.g., "The Ekistic Grid," *Ekistics*, XIX, No. 112 (March, 1965), 210.

31. "The Form and Structure of the Future Urban Complex," in *Cities and Space*, ed., Lowdon Wingo, Jr., Published for Resources for the Future, Inc. (Baltimore: The Johns Hopkins Press, 1963), p. 73.

32. Eligibility criteria were rather complicated. ARA has been replaced by EDA, the Economic Development Administration. They are fully stated in Area Redevelopment Administration, Department of Commerce, *Summary List of Redevelopment Areas and Eligible Areas: Public Works Acceleration Act* (Washington, D. C.: U. S. Government Printing Office, 1964).

33. See Ray M. Northam, "Declining Urban Centers in the United States: 1950–1960," *Annals of the Association of American Geographers*, LIII, No. 1 (March, 1963), 50–59.

34. Appalachian Regional Commission, *Appalachia* (Washington, D. C.: U. S. Government Printing Office, 1964).

35. Economic Research Service, Department of Agriculture, *Recent Population Trends in the United States with Emphasis on Rural Areas*, Agricultural Economic Report No. 23 (Washington, D. C.: U. S. Government Printing Office, 1963), pp. 24–25.

36. Harry M. Caudill has documented this physical and social deterioration of declining inter-metropolitan peripheral areas in his able study of eastern Kentucky, *Night Comes to the Cumberlands* (Boston: Little, Brown and Company, 1962). See especially Chap. XX, "The Scene Today," pp. 325–51.

There is evidence that this is not an isolated phenomenon. The *New York Times*, March 21, 1965, reports that "hundreds of Texas towns and smaller cities that once drew incomes from agriculture are finding few farmers left today to trade in their stores and banks. Massive depopulation has been the rule." Only in a few communities where agressive local leadership has grasped opportunities in regional and national markets has the decline been decelerated. According to the University of Texas's Bureau of Business Research, regional and national corporations do not find these communities attractive areas for investment.

Disintegration of morale and of physical facilities, a depressed economic climate, was also characteristic of large parts of the inter-metropolitan periphery of western Massachusetts within the dynamic "megalopolis" described by Gottmann. A regional study of this area by M.I.T. students elicited a general expression of the disintegration of communities in the comments of local citizens: "People feel," one citizen volunteered, "it is a second rate town. Young people get it from their parents." "The people move out, leave their houses vacant, and after a while they look dingy." "We are in a rut. We have an inferiority complex." "Young people don't plan to stay." "Look at those vacancies on Main Street."

37. The Economic Research Service of the Department of Agriculture, in a study of the effects of metropolitan growth trends on rural counties, asserts:

...the existence of a large, dense, and growing urban population in a region tends to create conditions of population growth in rural counties of the same region. This is true not only because an ever-larger number of the rural counties are within commuting range of urban centers, but also because more distant counties are affected by the accession of businesses or residents who do not need frequent commutation to the city but whose work or choice of residence is related to the city—especially the large metropolitan city. These are counties beyond "exurbia" which the geographer Wilbur Zelinsky has referred to as the "urban penumbra." *Recent Population Trends*, p. 14.

38. It is significant to note that if all present SMSA's of between 200,000 and 300,000 people were to reach the critical threshold size of 300,000 during the next generation, only a small expansion of the area now included in urban realms would occur. Most of these centers are located within or close to the edge of an existing urban realm and are thus encompassed by the boundaries we have provisionally defined.

39. For a recent statement by Fox, see "Programs for Economic Growth in Non-Metropolitan Areas," mimeographed paper prepared for the Third Conference on Regional Accounts, Miami Beach, Fla., November 19–21, 1964.

40. Otis D. Duncan *et al.*, *Metropolis and Region*, Published for Resources for the Future, Inc. (Baltimore: The Johns Hopkins Press, 1960), p. 275.

41. The total population of the "core" (New York City's four major boroughs and Hudson County) in 1985 is estimated by Vernon to be 7,810,000, a decline of almost a half-million from the 1955 population. The population of the outer ring (90 minutes from Manhattan to up to 30 miles beyond that) is estimated to be some 7,809,000, an increase of over 300 per cent. See Raymond Vernon, *Metropolis:* 1985 (Cambridge, Mass.: Harvard University Press, 1960), p. 221.

42. *Ibid.*, p. 224.

43. See the Council's 1964 *Annual Report*, as reported in the *Christian Science Monitor* (Boston), January 28, 1965.

44. Ralph Lazarus, "An 'Age of Fulfillment,'" in *ibid.*, February 6, 1964.

45. Josephine Ripley, "U. S. Cultural Crescendo," in *ibid.*, January 1, 1965.

46. Gottman, *Megalopolis*, p. 217.

CHAPTER 3

the distribution of city sizes

Another index of the extent to which the urban fields form a national system in the United States is provided in Fig. 3–1. This diagram shows a *rank-size distribution*—that is, the populations of the urban fields have been ranked in decreasing order of size (the largest urban field is given rank 1) and plotted in a graph which has the logarithm of population on the ordinate and logarithm of rank on the abscissa. A variety of authors, notably J. Q. Stewart and G. K. Zipf, have argued that if the plot of observations in such a graph forms an approximately straight line with a slope of −1, an integrated national system of cities is indicated.[1] In Fig. 3–1 an approximately straight-line relationship does exist down to a population of 250,000, the size of urban region argued (in the latter part of Chapter 2) to constitute the minimum threshold scale for economic and social viability in contemporary, metropolitanized America. Other correlates of city size are shown in Figs. 3–2 and 3–3.[2]

RANK SIZE VS. PRIMACY

There are, however, other ideas about city sizes. Zipf stated the rank-size relationship mathematically as follows:

$$P_r = \frac{P_1}{r^q}$$

Verbally, this says that the population of the rth ranking city P_r equals the population of the largest city P_1 divided by rank r raised to an exponent q (the slope of the line in the diagram) which generally has a value very close to unity. He derived the relationship empirically, but then argued that when it held throughout a country, it indicated that national unity is maintained through an integrated urban system.

At roughly the same time as Zipf advanced the concept of rank-size regularity to describe the distribution of city sizes, Mark Jefferson introduced the concept of the "primate city." Primacy

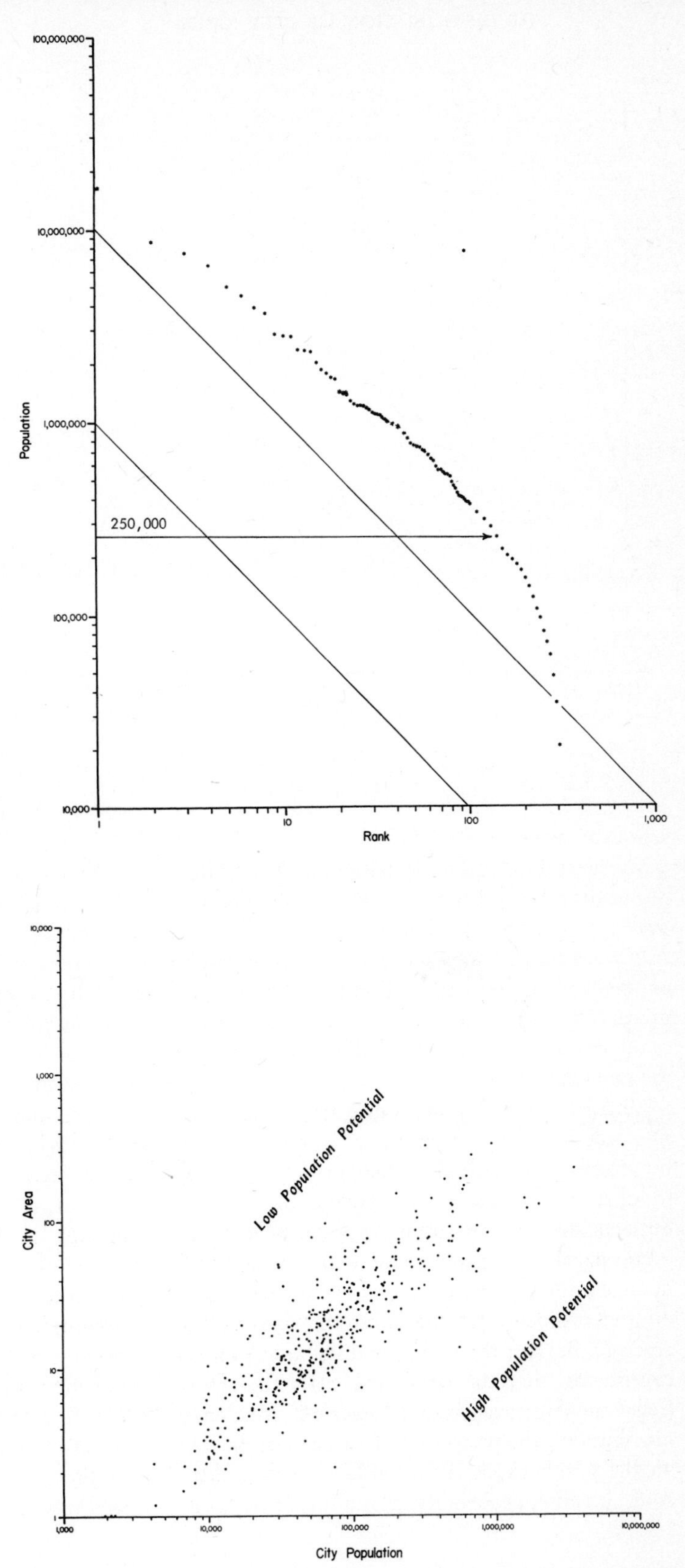

FIGURE 3–1. Rank-size distribution of American labor markets in 1960. The labor markets were defined using commuting data as the smallest subdivisions of the county in which, on a daily basis, all of the residents have both their home and workplace, so that the daily commuting trip does not cross the boundaries of the area. *Source:* Brian J. L. Berry, *Metropolitan Area Definition: A Re-evaluation of Concept and Statistical Practice,* (Washington, D.C.: Bureau of the Census Working Paper No. 28, 1968).

FIGURE 3–2. Relation between city area and population: 1960. *Source:* Graph prepared at the Center for Urban Studies, University of Chicago, using U.S. Census data.

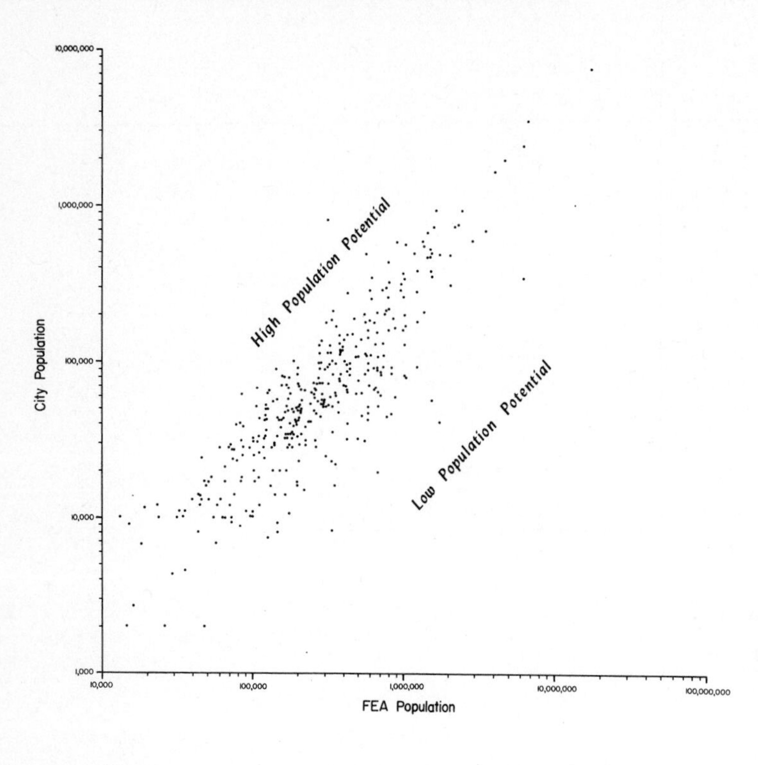

FIGURE 3–3. Relation between population of city and population of Functional Economic Areas: 1960. *Source:* Graph prepared at Center for Urban Studies, University of Chicago, using U.S. Census data.

is present, according to Jefferson, when the largest city is several times the population of the one that is second in rank. Later authors have applied the term to the whole distribution of cities of different sizes. Primacy, they say, exists when a stratum of small towns and cities is dominated by one or more very large cities and there are fewer cities of intermediate sizes than would be expected from the rank-size rule.[3]

Whether a distribution conforms to the rank-size rule or displays primacy is determinable by observation and measurement. One way is to plot the cumulative percentage of cities of different sizes on logarithmic–normal probability graph paper (i.e., graph paper with a scale based upon cumulative areas under the normal curve on the ordinate and logarithm of size on the abscissa). Because the rank-size distribution shows consistently that the larger the cities the fewer (what the statisticians call a "reverse-J" frequency distribution), the plot should form a straight line on the graph paper if the rank-size rule holds.[4] And, because probability graph paper is used, the degree of deviation from rank-size regularity can be measured with relative ease.

This might be argued to be measurement for measurement's sake if it were not for the fact that rank-size regularities have been associated with the existence of integrated systems of cities in economically advanced countries,[5] whereas primate cities have been associated with "over-urbanization," with the superimposition of colonial economies on underdeveloped countries, and with political and administrative controls of indigenous subsistence and peasant societies.[6] However, the question of the empirical reality of rank-size distributions has also been raised.[7] To complicate the matter, Jefferson did not develop the idea of a primate city with the dual economies of Asia in mind.[8]

Some synthesis is evidently required, both to resolve the conceptual issues and to introduce the reader to patterns of urbanization and city-region relationships that may be substantially different than those in the United States (which were discussed in Chapter 2). It is also possible that there are systematic cultural variations in city-size relationships. In this chapter, therefore, we shall first consider the city-size distributions of thirty-eight different countries. The processes linking urbanization, economic development, and city size will then be explored in detail in a case study of Poland that is made all the more interesting because of post-war attempts to control and direct urban changes through planning. Finally in this chapter, we shall return to the United States and try to show that the diffusion of innovations down the system of city-sizes is the means by which growth and change are transmitted throughout the economy and integrated national development is achieved and maintained.

City-Size Distributions in Thirty-eight Countries

Figures 3–4 through 3–9 contain curves best fitting the city-size distributions in thirty-eight different countries. These thirty-eight were selected simply on the basis of convenience of access to data. Each plot is of cumulative frequencies on lognormal probability paper, so that if the city-size distribution is lognormal (rank-size), the curve assumes the form of a straight line. The cumulative frequencies obtained were for cities with populations exceeding 20,000, and for six size classes: 20,000–50,000; 50,000–100,000; 100,000–250,000; 250,000–500,000; 500,000–1,000,000; and over 1,000,000. All the regions of the world except Africa are well represented, and that because very few African countries have many cities of over 20,000. Since we have comparable urbanized area statistics only for cities of over 100,000, the statistics used refer to populations of the legal "city proper," excluding suburbs.

Thirteen of the thirty-eight countries have lognormally-distributed city sizes (see Figs. 3–4 and 3–5). The higher any of these thirteen curves on the graph, the greater the percentage of small cities in that country; the steeper the slope, the smaller both the country and its largest city. Among the thirteen are very large countries (e.g., China), very small countries (e.g., Switzerland), highly developed countries (e.g., the United States), and underdeveloped countries (e.g., Korea). It is noticeable that countries with long urban traditions (e.g., India and China) and highly developed countries (e.g., the United States and West Germany) have very similar city-size distributions.

There are fifteen countries with primate city-size distributions (see Figs. 3–6 and 3–7). Note the shape of the curves: lognormally distributed lesser city sizes are followed by a gap because cities of intermediate size are absent, and then there is a rapid cumulation to one or several primate cities. Mexico, for example, has lognormally distributed city sizes up to an urban population of 250,000, and then there is a considerable gap followed by a primate capital city of over 1,000,000 people. In Ceylon, the gap comes earlier and the capital is smaller. In Japan, the gap comes later and indicates the absence of cities in the size bracket 500,000 to 1,000,000; in this case there are several larger cities. The gap need not be a void: in Spain and Sweden, there is merely a considerable deficiency of cities of intermediate size. Thailand and Guatemala are limiting cases in which the lower lognormal distribution is absent; instead, there are a few cities of 20,000 to 50,000 people, followed by a considerable gap and a single large primate city. All fifteen countries are small, but they cover a wide range, from underdeveloped Thailand through countries with dual and peasant economies to countries with highly specialized agricultural economies such as Denmark and the Netherlands.

Nine countries have city-size distributions intermediate between lognormal and primate (see Figs. 3–8 and 3–9). All display some primacy, but none are without cities of intermediate size. Some (e.g., Norway and Canada) approach lognormal. Others are almost primate (e.g., Malaya and Pakistan). In Australia and New Zealand the deficiency is not in cities of middling size, but in smaller cities. Figure 3–9 also includes the special case of England and Wales, where primate cities are grafted on top of a complete lower lognormal distribution. This intermediate group also includes countries of a variety of sizes and at a variety of levels of development.

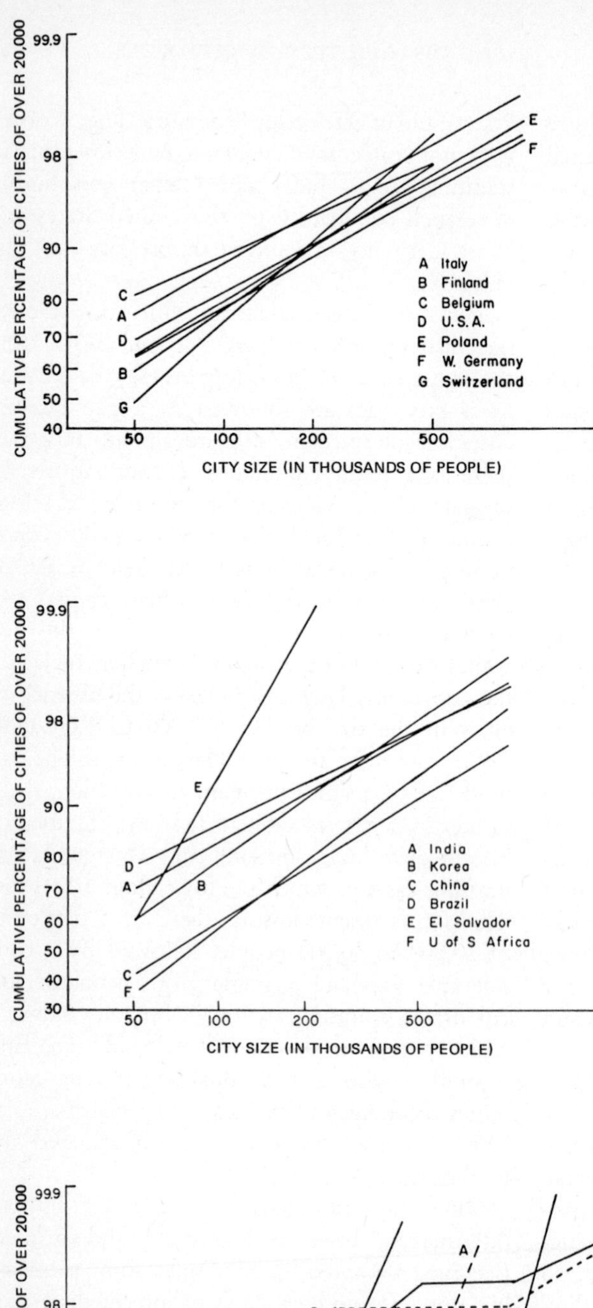

FIGURE 3–4. Seven lognormal (rank-size) distributions. *Source:* Figs. 3–4 through 3–12 are drawn from Brian J. L. Berry, "City Size Distributions and Economic Development," *Economic Development and Cultural Change*, IX, No. 4 (July, 1961), 573–88.

Figure 3–5. Lesser developed countries may also have lognormal city-size distributions. *Source:* See caption for Fig. 3–4.

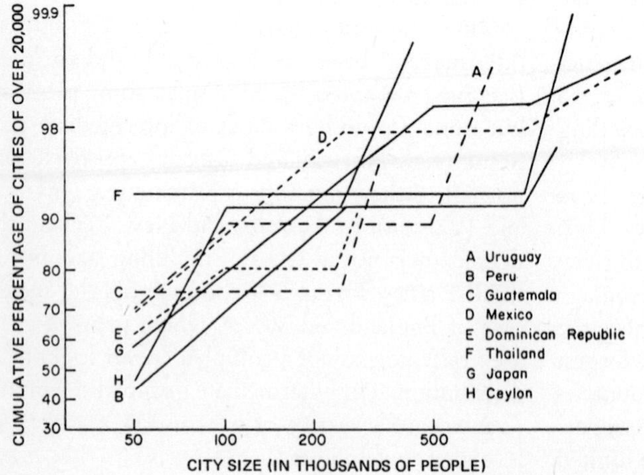

FIGURE 3–6. Eight primate distributions. *Source:* See caption for Fig. 3–4.

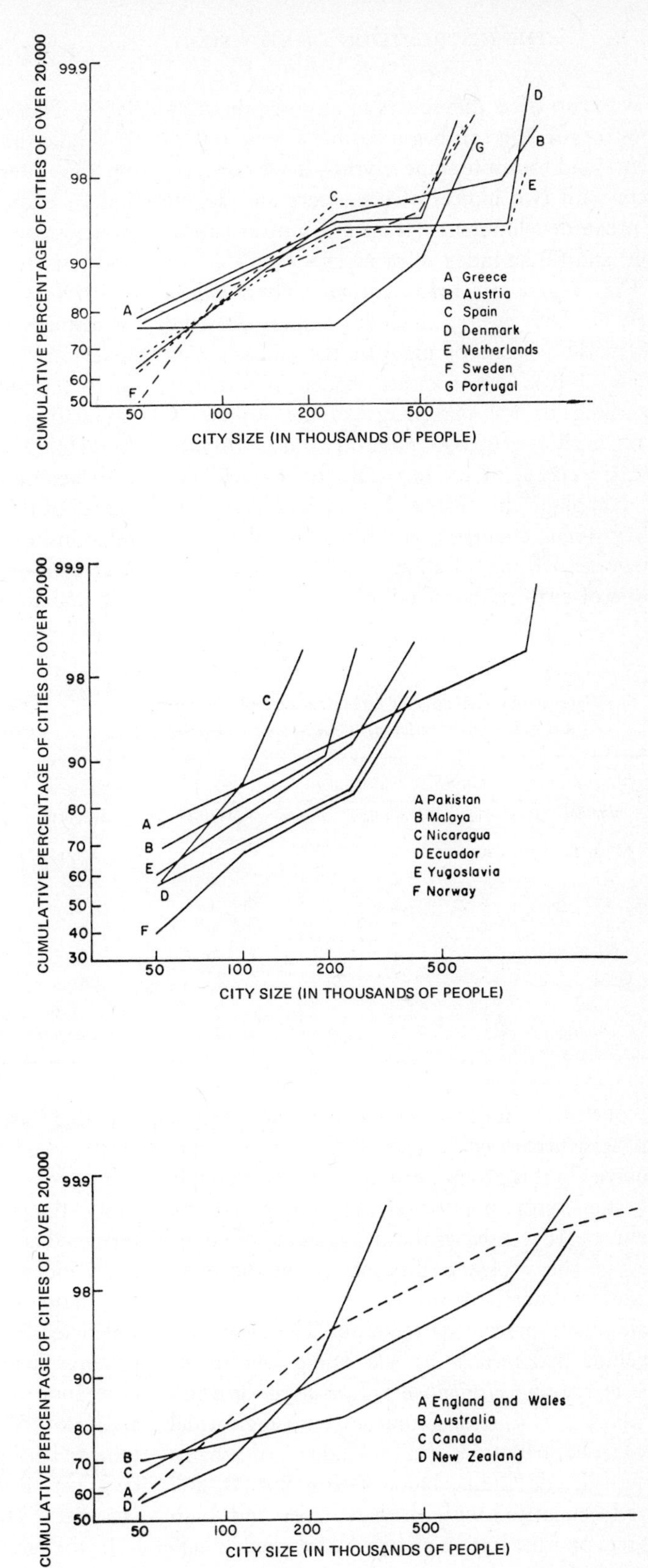

FIGURE 3–7. More developed countries may also have primate distributions. *Source:* See caption for Fig. 3–4.

FIGURE 3–8. Six distributions intermediate between lognormal and primate. *Source:* See caption for Fig. 3–4.

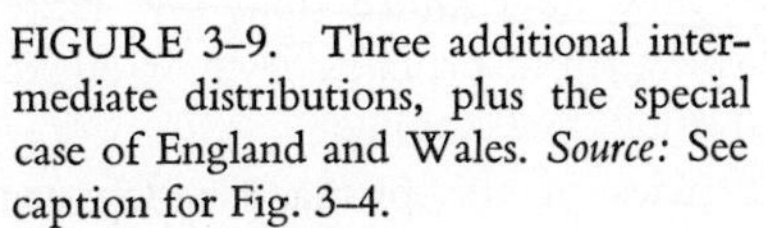

FIGURE 3–9. Three additional intermediate distributions, plus the special case of England and Wales. *Source:* See caption for Fig. 3–4.

What do these differences in city-size distributions mean? We can begin to make sense out of them—and to refute some myths—if we compare them with two indices of the nature and degree of urban development: (1) an index of urbanization; and (2) an index of primacy.

The degree of urbanization. The *Atlas of Economic Development*[9] includes a map showing the world pattern of urbanization (shown here as Fig. 3–10). Countries are shaded in this map according to the percentage of the population living in cities of 20,000 and more, and are divided into six classes of urbanization for convenience of mapping. In Table 3–1 we cross-classify thirty-seven countries according to these six categories of urbanization and the three categories of city-size distribution.

TABLE 3–1

Comparison of Degree of Urbanization and Type of City-size Distribution of Thirty-seven Countries

Degree of Urbanization	*City-Size Distribution*			*Total Countries*
	Rank-Size	*Intermediate*	*Primate*	
Most	4	2	5	11
2	2	2	1	5
3	1	2	3	6
4	4	2	3	9
5	2	1	3	6
Least	—	—	—	—
Total countries	13	9	15	37

None of the thirty-seven countries falls within the "least urbanized" category because very few countries in this group possess more than a couple of cities with populations exceeding 20,000. A chi-square test shows the arrangement of countries in the cross-classification to be not significantly different from an arrangement which could have arisen at random. Therefore we conclude that *there is no relationship between the type of city-size distribution and the degree to which a country is urbanized.* Countries with lognormal city-sizes distributions and low indexes of urbanization include China, India, Korea, Poland, and Brazil; countries with primate cities and high degrees of urbanization include Spain, the Netherlands, Denmark, Sweden, Japan, and Uruguay. Australia and New Zealand are the most urbanized of the intermediate cases. All these countries fail to exhibit the commonly hypothesized but nonexistent relationship between urbanization and rank-size regularities.

Primacy. The *Atlas*[10] also includes an index of primacy which is very similar to that used by Jefferson,[11] namely, the ratio of the population of the largest city in a country to the combined population of the first four cities (see Fig. 3–11). In Table 3–2 we cross-classify thirty-seven countries according to city-size distribution and six classes of this primacy index. There is an obvious relationship: *countries with the lowest primacy indices have rank-size city-size distributions and countries with the highest have primate city-size distributions.*

TABLE 3–2

Comparison of Degree of Primacy and Type of City-size Distribution of Thirty-seven Countries

Degree of Primacy	*City-Size Distribution*			*Total Countries*
	Rank-Size	*Intermediate*	*Primate*	
Most	—	—	8	8
2	1	1	2	4
3	1	2	1	4
4	1	—	2	3
5	6	2	—	8
Least	4	4	2	10
Total countries	13	9	15	37

But there are also anomalies: Spain, the Netherlands, Sweden, and Japan have primate distributions yet low primacy indices, because they have more than one large city above the gaps in intermediate city size; countries with a high primacy index and a primate distribution have only one large primate city. This anomaly reflects a deficiency of the *Atlas* index: it only indicates primacy when a country has a single primate city. Intermediate Australia, New Zealand, Canada, and Yugoslavia also have low primacy indices because they have more than one large city, yet all display some primacy if their entire city size distributions are studied.

If the deficiencies of the primacy index are

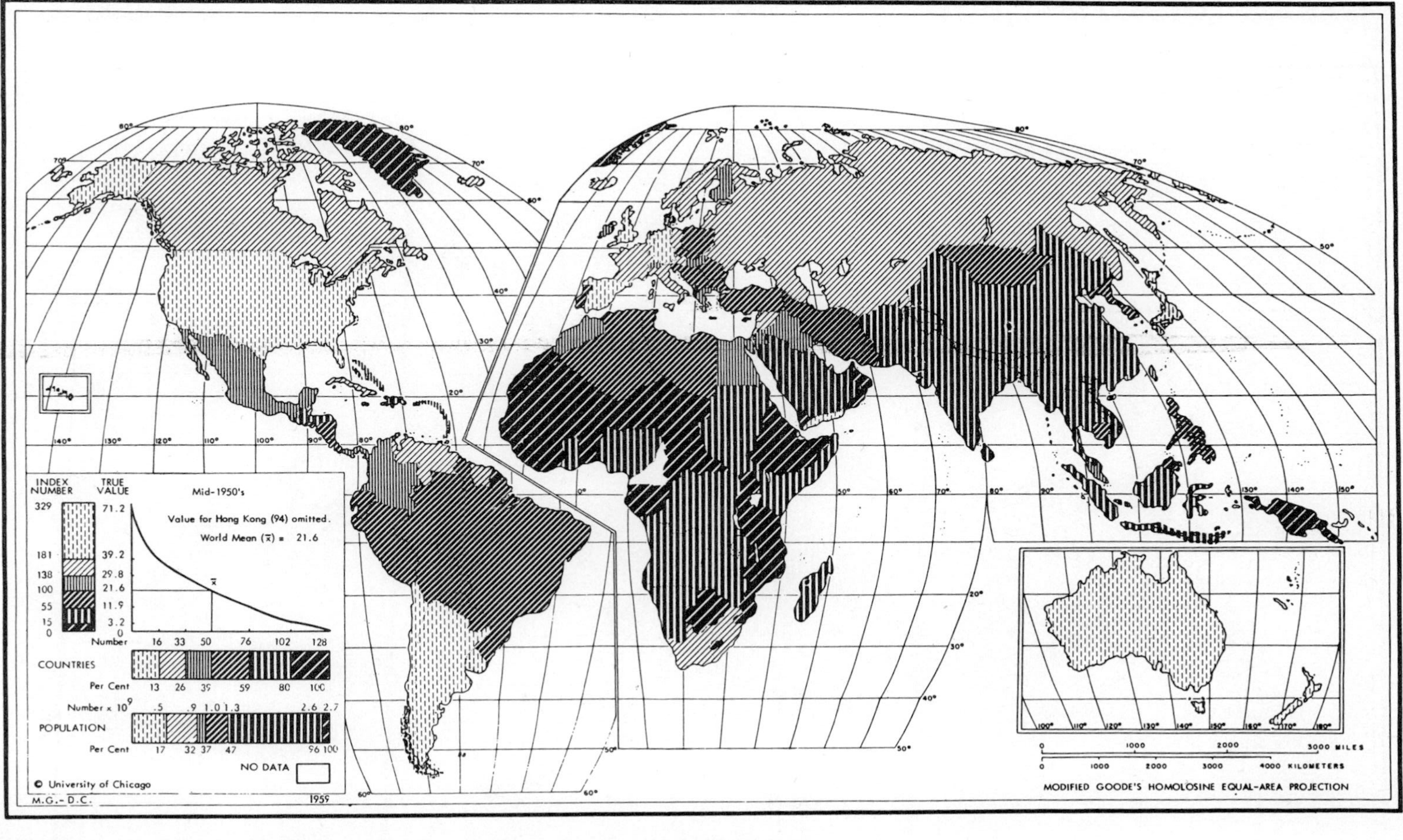

FIGURE 3–10. Urbanization: Percentage of the world's population in cities of 20,000 and more.
Source: See caption for Fig. 3–4.

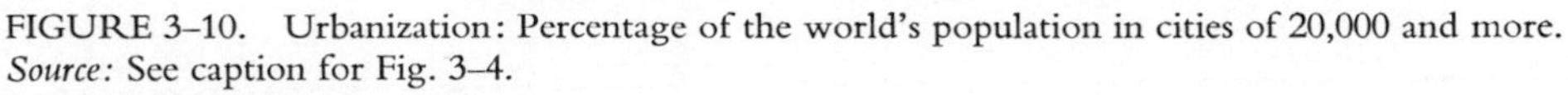

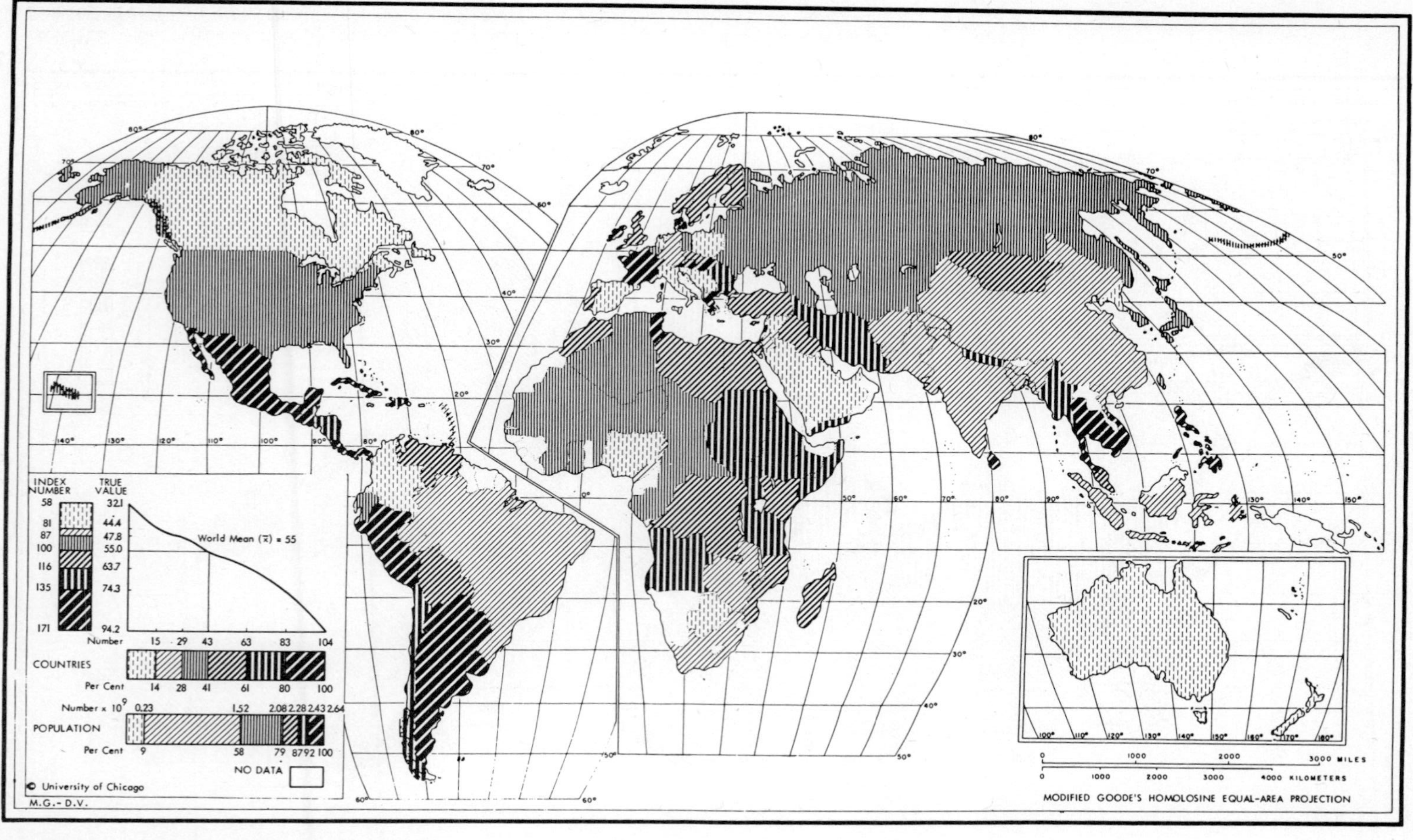

FIGURE 3–11. Urbanization: A measure of primacy.
Source: See caption for Fig. 3–4.

taken into account in an interpretation of Fig. 3–11, however, the map throws light on the differences in city-size distributions which we have exposed. Countries which have until recently been politically or economically dependent on some outside country tend to have primate cities which are the national capitals, the cultural and economic centers, often the chief port, and the focus of national consciousness and feeling. Small countries which once had extensive empires also have primate cities which are on the one hand the former capitals of the empires (e.g., Vienna, Madrid, and Lisbon) and, on the other hand, centers in which such economies of scale may be achieved that cities of intermediate size are not called for. Countries with more than one large city are either (e.g., Canada, Australia, and New Zealand) effectively partitioned into several city-regions dominated by very similar primate cities or else (e.g., Sweden, Spain, the Netherlands, and Japan) they have several large specialized cities which are complementary rather than duplicative. Countries with the lowest degrees of primacy, and therefore with lognormally distributed city sizes, include many which are considerably industrialized as well as those with long traditions and histories of urbanization.

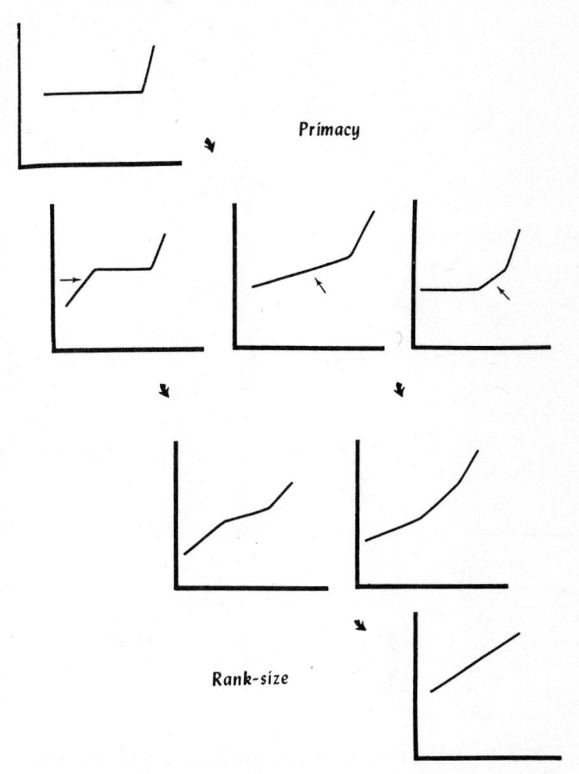

FIGURE 3–12. A developmental model city-size distributions. *Source:* See caption for Fig. 3–4.

A model of city-size distributions. Given the above evidence, a simple graphic model may be proposed which places the several types of city-size distributions on a scale between the limiting cases of primacy (e.g., Thailand) and lognormality (e.g., the United States). The model is presented in Fig. 3–12.

A rationale for the model comes from the work of Simon, who showed that lognormal distributions are produced as limiting cases by stochastic growth processes.[12] Berry and Garrison argued that, as a limiting case, a lognormal distribution is a "condition of entropy," defined as a circumstance in which the forces affecting the distribution are many and act randomly within the context of growth proportionate to size of city. This contrasts with other distributions which are simpler in that they are produced by fewer forces.[13]

We assume that primacy is the simplest city-size distribution, affected by but few simple strong forces. Thus, primate cities are either "orthogenetic" political and administrative capitals, "heterogenetic" capitals of the emerging nations, or empire capitals.[14] At the other extreme, rank-size distributions are found when, because of complexity of economic and political life or the age of the system of cities, many forces affect the urban pattern in many ways and the only systematic influence upon size is the expectation that all cities will grow at the same rate.

In Fig. 3–12, the intermediate distributions are arranged on the scale from primacy to lognormality. Three intermediate subcategories are evident: those with more small cities than the primate, those with more medium-sized cities, and those with more large cities. In addition, two stages in the intermediate progression from primate to rank-size distribution are pictured.

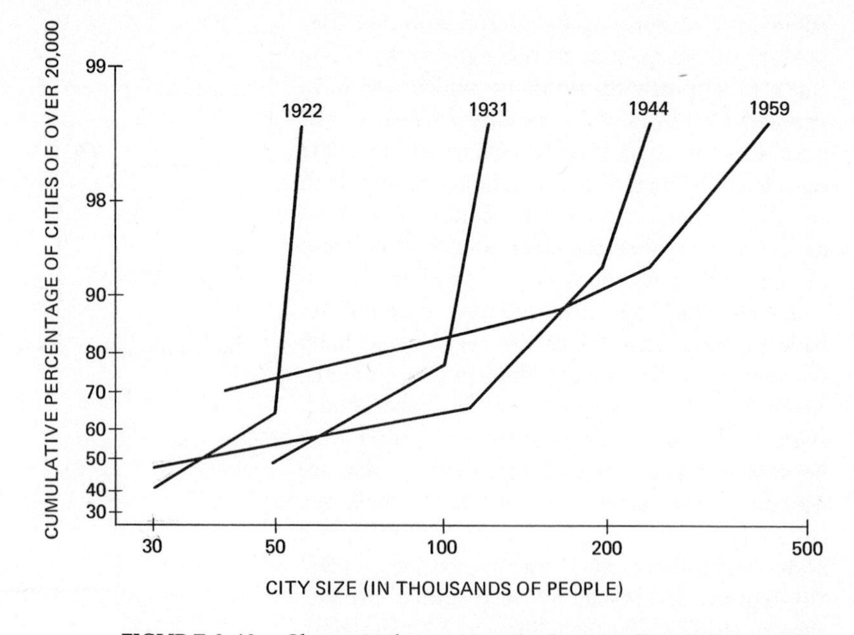

FIGURE 3–13. Change in the city-size distribution of Israel. *Source:* Gwen Bell, "Change in City Size Distribution in Israel," *Ekistics*, XIII (1962), 103.

The model in effect proposes a major hypothesis: increasing entropy is accompanied by a closer approximation of a city size distribution to lognormality. Common sense suggests several sub-hypotheses: fewer forces will affect the urban structure of a country: (1) the smaller the country is; (2) the shorter is the history of urbanization in the country; and (3) the simpler is the economic and political life of the country and the lower its degree of economic development. The converse of each sub-hypothesis also follows.

In the simple orderly cases most cities perform essentially the same set of functions, whether political or concerned with rudimentary economic activities. As complexity increases so do urban functions—cities may have political functions, be centers on transport routes, be specialized centers of primary or secondary economic activities, or be central places performing tertiary economic functions. At the highest levels of development a country will contain many specialized cities performing one or several of these functions; when the cities are viewed in the aggregate, a condition of entropy will be seen to obtain within the limits of the urban growth process.

The limited data available from our previous discussion seem to bear out several of the sub-hypotheses. Countries with rank-size distributions include urban industrial economies (e.g., Belgium, United States), larger countries (Brazil), and countries with long histories of urbanization (India and China). Intermediate distributions, but nearly rank-size, characterize countries which are larger (e.g., Canada) and which have both primary and secondary commercial specialities Australia and New Zealand) or at least are considerably commercialized. The more primate of the two intermediate stages is found in small countries engaged in the primary production of a relatively few commodities (e.g., Austria, Sweden, Netherlands, Denmark) or with some commercialization superimposed on a subsistence or peasant agricultural system (dual economies such as Ceylon, Mexico, and the Dominican Republic). Primacy characterizes small countries with simple subsistence economies (e.g., Thailand), or is associated with the presence of an empire capital (Portugal).

Further, historical changes in city-size distributions appear to follow the trends suggested in the model. As we can see in Fig. 3–13, which shows changes in Israel, the city-size distribution has become increasingly linear as the country has developed economically.[15]

*A CASE STUDY: URBANIZATION IN CONTEMPORARY POLAND**

The complexity of the processes linking urbanization, economic development, and the distribution of city sizes may be clarified somewhat by means of a case study of Poland, which possesses long traditions of urban life, a comparatively rapid growth rate (see Table 3–3), and is characterized by definite planning efforts to control and direct these changes.

The growth of urban population in Poland throughout the nineteenth and in the twentieth centuries, although interrupted by wars and social and economic upheavals, was steady (see Table 3–4). In the last ten years it has been especially rapid, the direct result of planned industrialization of the national economy. In fact, greater growth was observed only in Soviet Russia in the years 1926 to 1939, and there its cause, in addition to industrialization, was the collectivization of the agricultural economy. In the years 1950 to 1960, the increase of urban population in Poland amounted to 450,000 annually, while in the years 1870 to 1900 it was only 75,000. The recent increase is practically equal to the total natural increase of population, while in the inter-war period it was below 60 per cent, and at the end of the nineteenth century below 36 per cent. Before 1914, 100,000 persons emigrated from Poland annually, so that the degree of urbanization tends to be somewhat overstated for that period, in addition. Today, there are few who leave, and today's rate of urbanization exceeds both past urbanization and emigration combined.

The French geographer, Pierre George, in his book *La ville, le fait urbain à travers le monde*,[16] classified countries on the basis of the percentage of their population living in cities. Countries with urban populations under 20 per cent of the total population are defined by him as territories of old, agricultural civilizations, where urbanization is just beginning. In the 20 to 40 per cent class are the European agricultural countries as well as other countries where industrialization of the economy has already started. In the over-40 per

*Reprinted from Kazimierz Dziewonski, "Urbanization in Contemporary Poland," *Geographia Polonica*, III, No. 1 (January, 1964), 37–56, with the permission of the author and editor.

TABLE 3–3

Percentage of Urban Population in Various Countries

Year	*U.S.A.*	*England and Wales*	*France*	*Sweden*	*Denmark*	*U.S.S.R.*	*Poland within the Frontiers of 1960*	*Poland within the Frontiers of 1937*
1850	15.3	50.2	25.5	10.1	20.9	(1851) 7.8	—	13.6
1860	19.8	54.6	28.9	11.3	23.4	(1863) 10.6	—	—
1870	25.7	61.8	31.1	13.0	24.9	—	23.2	16.9
1880	28.2	67.9	34.8	15.1	28.1	—	—	—
1890	35.4	72.0	37.4	18.8	33.2	—	—	—
1900	39.7	77.0	40.9	21.5	38.2	(1897) 11.5	(1897–1900) 26.6	(1897–1900) 25.1
1910	45.7	78.1	44.2	24.8	40.3	—	—	29.7
1920	51.2	79.3	46.3	29.5	44.2	(1917) 15.6	(1921–1925) 32.8	(1921–1925) 27.2
1930	56.2	80.0	(1926) 49.1	32.5	43.9	(1926) 17.9	(1931–1933) 35.5	(1931–1933) 32.1
1940	56.5	—	(1946) 53.2	(1945) 42.3	47.4	(1939) 32.8	(1946) 31.8	(1937) 34.5
1950	59.0	(1951) 81.0	(1954) 56.0	48.0	—	—	39.0	—
1960	—	—	—	(1959) 51.0	—	(1959) 47.9	48.1	—

Sources: N. P. Gist and L. A. Halbert, *Urban Society* (New York: Thomas Y. Crowell Company, 1938); W. S. Woytinsky and E. S. Woytinsky, *World Population and Production* (New York: The Twentieth Century Fund, 1953), p. 124; and others.

TABLE 3-4

Population and Urban Population of Poland in the Years 1800–1960

	1800 (estimated)	*1850 (estimated)*	*1870 (estimated)*	*1897–1900 General Censuses*	*1910 (estimated)*	*1921–1925 National General Censuses*	*1931–1933 National General Censuses*	*1937 (estimated)*	*1946 Provincial Census*	*1950 National General Census*	*1960 National General Census*
Poland within the frontiers of 1937.											
Total population (*in hundred of thousands*)	90	136	169	251	297	272	321	345	—	—	—
Urban population (*in hundreds of thousands*)	—	—	—	50	—	67	87	—	—	—	—
Percentage of population, urban	—	—	—	19.9	—	24.6	27.4	—	—	—	—
Poland within the frontiers of 1960.											
Total population (*in hundreds of thousands*)	—	—	175	237	—	266	297	321	239	250	297
Urban population (*in hundreds of thousands*)	—	—	41	63	—	87	105	—	74	96	141
Percentage of population, urban	—	—	23.2	26.6	—	32.8	35.5	—	31.8	39.0	48.1

Sources: Data for Poland within the frontiers of 1937, from *Encyklopedia Nauk Społecznych* (*Encyclopedia of Social Sciences*), Vol. III, Population Table 13, p. 633, Central Statistical Office, *Concise Statistical Yearbook for 1935.* Data for the year 1870, and within the frontiers of 1960, compiled by F. Osowski. Data for the years 1897–1900, 1921–1925, and 1931–1933, within the frontiers of 1960, compiled by K. Pudło-Palonka. Data for the years 1946, 1960, from Central Statistical Office, *Statistical Yearbook: 1961,* Table 1 (21).

cent class George found three separate groups of countries: traditional industrialized states of Western Europe ([with urbanization] indices of 40 to 60 per cent); new countries whose development takes place through the growth of new big towns; and, finally, the U.S.S.R., where urbanization is closely connected with new industrialization. On this comparative basis, in the last ten years Poland has passed from the class of European agricultural states to the class of the U.S.S.R.

Structure of Urban Growth

At present, urban growth is heterogenous in its origin and structure. Generally speaking, it is composed of three elements: natural increase, influx from the countryside together with repatriation from abroad, and change of administrative status (i.e., change of urban boundaries and creation of new towns). Data collected and published for the years 1950 to 1959 indicate that natural increase was responsible for 41 per cent of the total urban growth; rural immigration for 19 per cent, external immigration for about 1 per cent, and changes in administrative status for the remaining 40 per cent.

The most characteristic of these indices is that of natural increase. Usually it is assumed that the index of natural increase for urban areas is well under the same index for rural areas and therefore also less than the average for the whole country. This was certainly true for pre-war Poland when the urban index was no more than half the rural (8.4 and 16.7 per cent in 1931 and 1932). But in the post-war years indices for both urban and rural areas have been practically the same. It is only in the last few years that the rural index has again gained over the urban one although the difference so far is not as great as before the war (in 1960: 13 per cent and 16 per cent). This high natural growth is due to several causes, among which the fall in death-rate—the result of the improvement in sanitary conditions—and the post-war increase in number of births should be mentioned. However, economic factors should not be omitted. In fact, they are probably the most important. The general rise in living conditions, due in the beginning to the changes brought about by the social revolution and later additionally increased through the great progress in the industrialization of the country, played the decisive role. A specific influence was exerted by the educational policies of the present government. When practically all the costs of education on all levels are covered from social funds, the parents are released from otherwise very heavy financial burdens and worries.

The growth of towns as a result of the influx of rural population was, according to the statistical data, comparatively small. Part of it is hidden by inclusion under the heading of change in administrative status. It was still great enough to take from the rural areas all natural increase of manpower. In the future it is expected that this will continue, perhaps even at an increased rate. However, there exist obvious limits to such migrations. At present, in spite of war losses in Polish agriculture, especially in the central part of the country, there is a very definite underemployment (or hidden unemployment). With further emigration of rural population the stage will be reached when this underemployment will turn into a labour shortage, however. The advent of difficulties due to deficits in manpower will probably be the starting point for stronger mechanization of agriculture. However, it also means that the importance of this factor of urban growth will diminish in the more distant future.

The most doubtful, although obvious and potent sources of increase in indices of urbanization, are the changes in the administrative status, especially in municipal boundaries. Nevertheless they should not be omitted. At the worst these legal changes were nothing else than a recognition of already established realities. In the remaining cases the change of administrative status marks new developments in town construction or at least in urban housing. In future, such changes will easily dominate over all others.

Structure of the Urban Network

As in all other countries, the urban population in Poland is not evenly spread. There is a great diversity of towns and cities of various functions, character, status, and size. Many geographers have tried to bring some order in to what seemed to be at the first glance only an accidental grouping, loosely connected with the road and railroad networks. For that purpose they used one or another of the various theories of settlement—of W. Christaller or of A. Lösch, of Homer Hoyt, E. Ullman and C. D. Harris, or of B. J. Berry and W. L. Garrison, of W. J. Davidovich, and many others. Although in the interpretation of realities observed in smaller areas these theories and related concepts proved to be serviceable and fairly satisfactory tools of analysis, for the whole of Poland they failed to provide a reasonable basis of comparison. In fact divergences between regional settlement networks, palimpsests of various historical periods and processes seem to raise serious questions as to the validity of their theoretical assumptions.

A more satisfactory tool for analysis of urbanization on both national and regional levels is the "rank-size rule." It is an empirically established rule and there exist several divergent interpretations of its meaning, ranging from the opinion

FIGURE 3–14. Classification of Polish towns by rank and size: 1950 and 1960. The curves on the left represent data ordered by administrative units; those on the right, data summed together for each metropolitan area or conurbation disregarding their administrative division. *Source:* Figs. 3–14 through 3–18 are from Kazimierz Dziewonski, "Urbanization in Contemporary Poland," *Geographia Polonica*, III, No. 1 (January, 1964), 37–56.

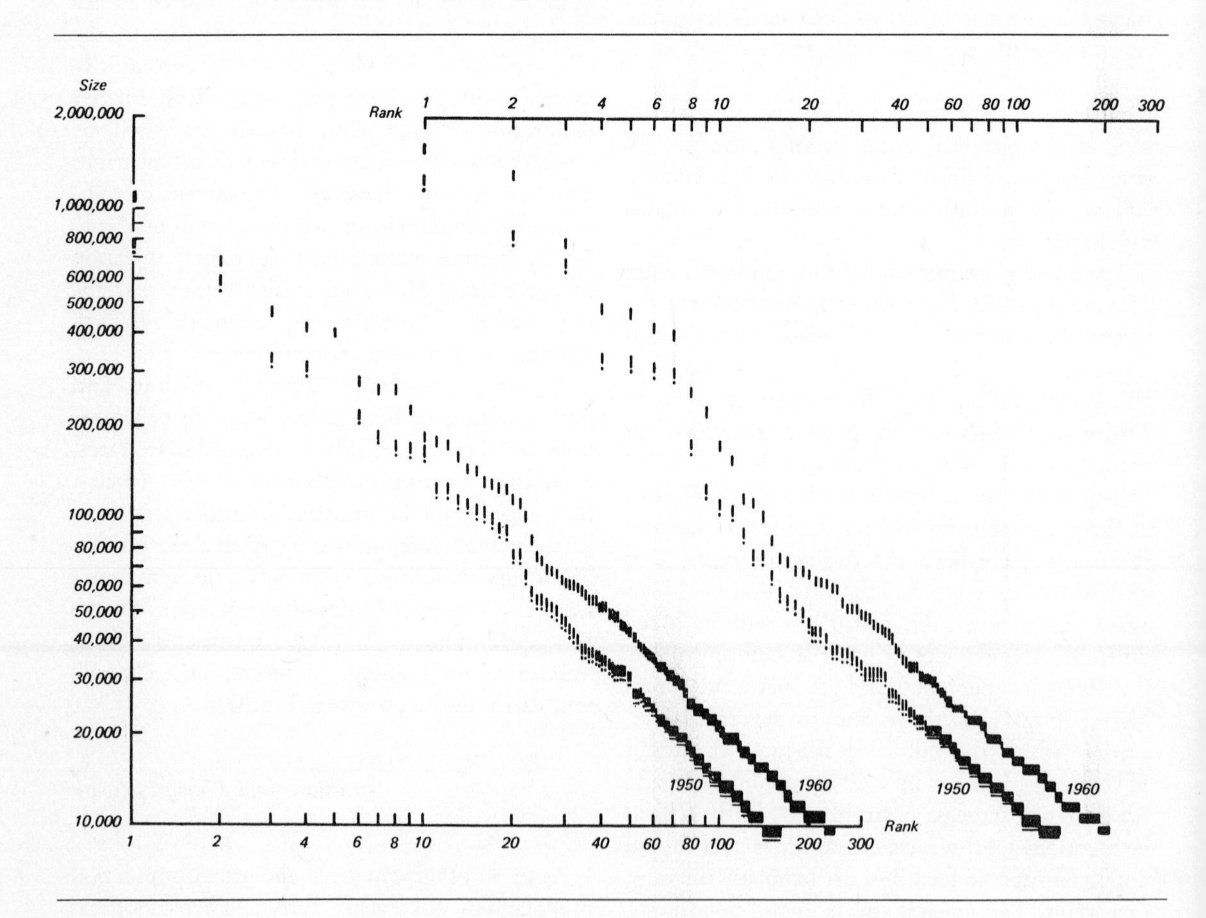

of G. K. Zipf, who sees in it the reflection of "unifying (i.e., centralizing) power," to the opinion of H. A. Simon, supported by B. J. Berry and W. L. Garrison, that it is a result of the law of entropy. Graphs for Polish towns, collated nationally and regionally on a double logarithmic scale according to this rule, demonstrate rather remarkable regularities and characteristics. As we can see in Fig. 3–14, the graph for all Polish towns in 1960 has an exceptionally regular shape, forming almost a straight line. According to the probability interpretation of Simon, this marks an ideally balanced structure of the urban network, without almost any influence of strongly deforming forces. In fact, the same graph for 1950 shows some evidences of underdevelopment at the left end of the curve. It is a reflection of the destruction of Warsaw and of its uncompleted reconstruction.

. . .

Graphs for each of the regions of Poland (Fig. 3–15) may be grouped into three classes: (1) the regular ones characteristic of areas with evenly developed urban networks and with slight preponderance of the main urban center (the voivodships of Katowice, Cracow, Poznań, Wroclaw, and Szczecin); (2) the skewed ones characteristic of areas where the main urban center is growing at the expense of others, especially the middle-sized towns (the voivodships of Warsaw, Łódź, Gdańsk, Bydgoszcz, Lublin, Białystok and, in smaller degree, of Rzeszów, Olsztyn and Opole); and finally (3) the irregular ones characteristic of areas without a clearly crystallized main urban center (the voivodships of Kielce, Koszalin and Zielona Góra). In fact, in these last areas the largest city is not the seat of the voivodship administration. As a result, within the generally balanced urban network certain areas of lesser and greater irregularities may be distinguished.

Geographically, the central, eastern, and northeastern parts of the country show marked growth of the largest cities at the expense of smaller towns. Areas without clearly crystallized main urban centers are located between or on the peripheries of the regions with well-balanced urban networks.

Parallel problems to that of the primacy of the largest city are those of density of towns of various types and classes of importance. This density is, however, extremely variable—in fact so much so that it is impossible to explain it within the framework of Christaller's theory [see Chapter 7]. For instance, the general density of towns varies by voivodships from 11.6 to 36.8 per thousand people per square kilometer (average density being 22.7), and the density of towns over 5,000 inhabitants varies from 6 to 27.4 (average, 12.5). The largest densities are characteristic of the western and southern regions; the smallest, of the eastern, northern, and central ones. Greater densities of the urban network are clearly connected with areas of stronger regional economy and also with wealth of natural resources, both mineral and agricultural.

An additional aspect of the urban network is found in the journey to work. Partial analysis of statistical data indicates that this phenomenon is extremely complicated. Along with the cases where longer journeys to work mark areas displaying special types of interrelations between urban settlements, there are others where the journey to work represents only the first, passing stage of urbanization. Usually, where the present large industrial plants, concentrated in few and larger centers, have grown out of formerly dispersed manufactures or even older industrial trades and handicraft (i.e., in the southern parts of the country), they form a permanent feature of the urban settlement. On the other hand, in the southeastern, central, and northern parts, the second type prevails. There the journey to work is perhaps a temporary phenomenon, which will vanish in future when the housing difficulties in the towns are completely overcome and the industrial population moves from the countryside to newly developed residential districts. The western parts of the country, especially Lower Silesia, are characterized by the almost complete lack of long-distance commuting.

. . .

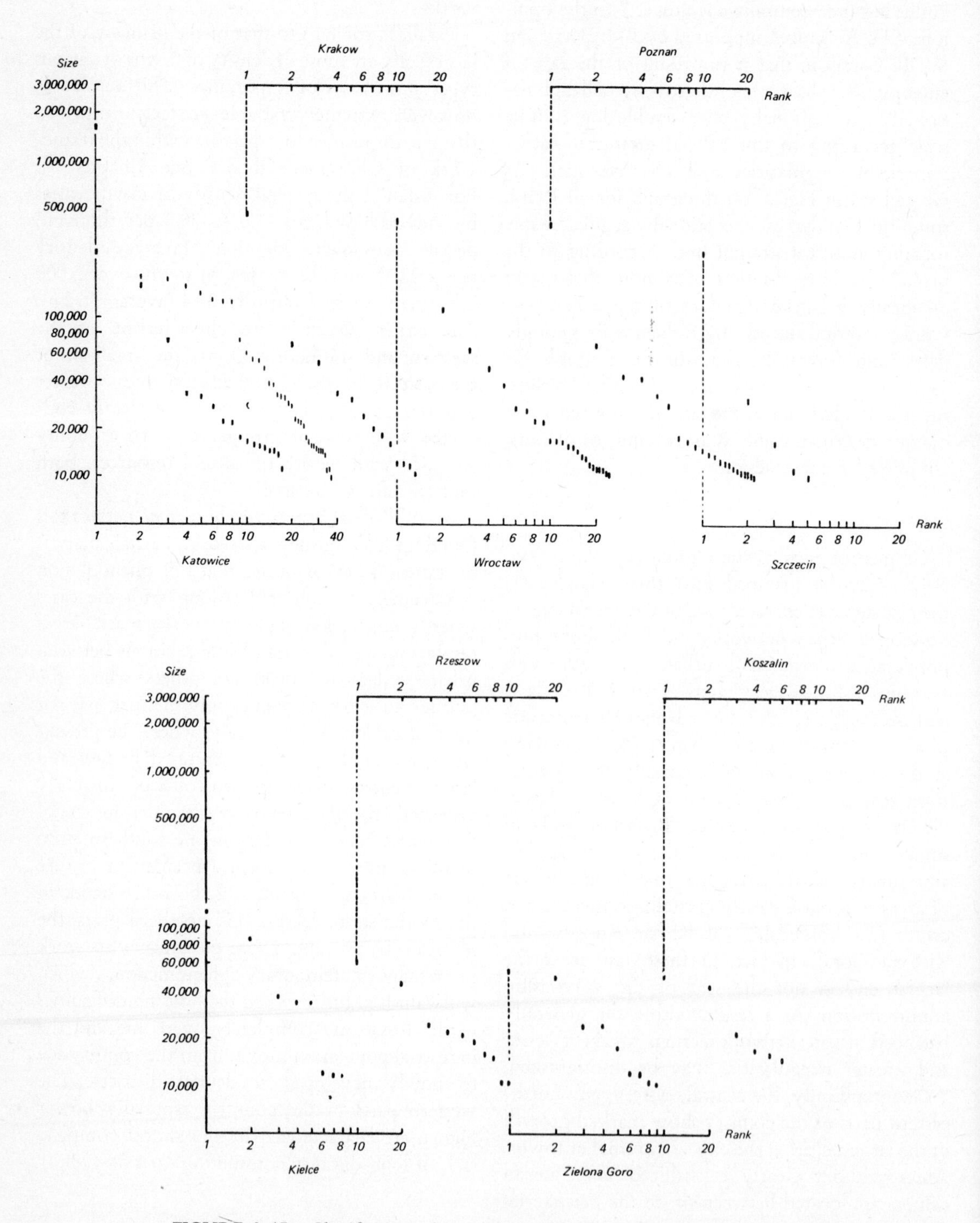

FIGURE 3–15. Classification of towns by rank and size in each voivodship of Poland in 1960. (See explanation of data in Fig. 3–14.) *Source:* See caption for Fig. 3–14.

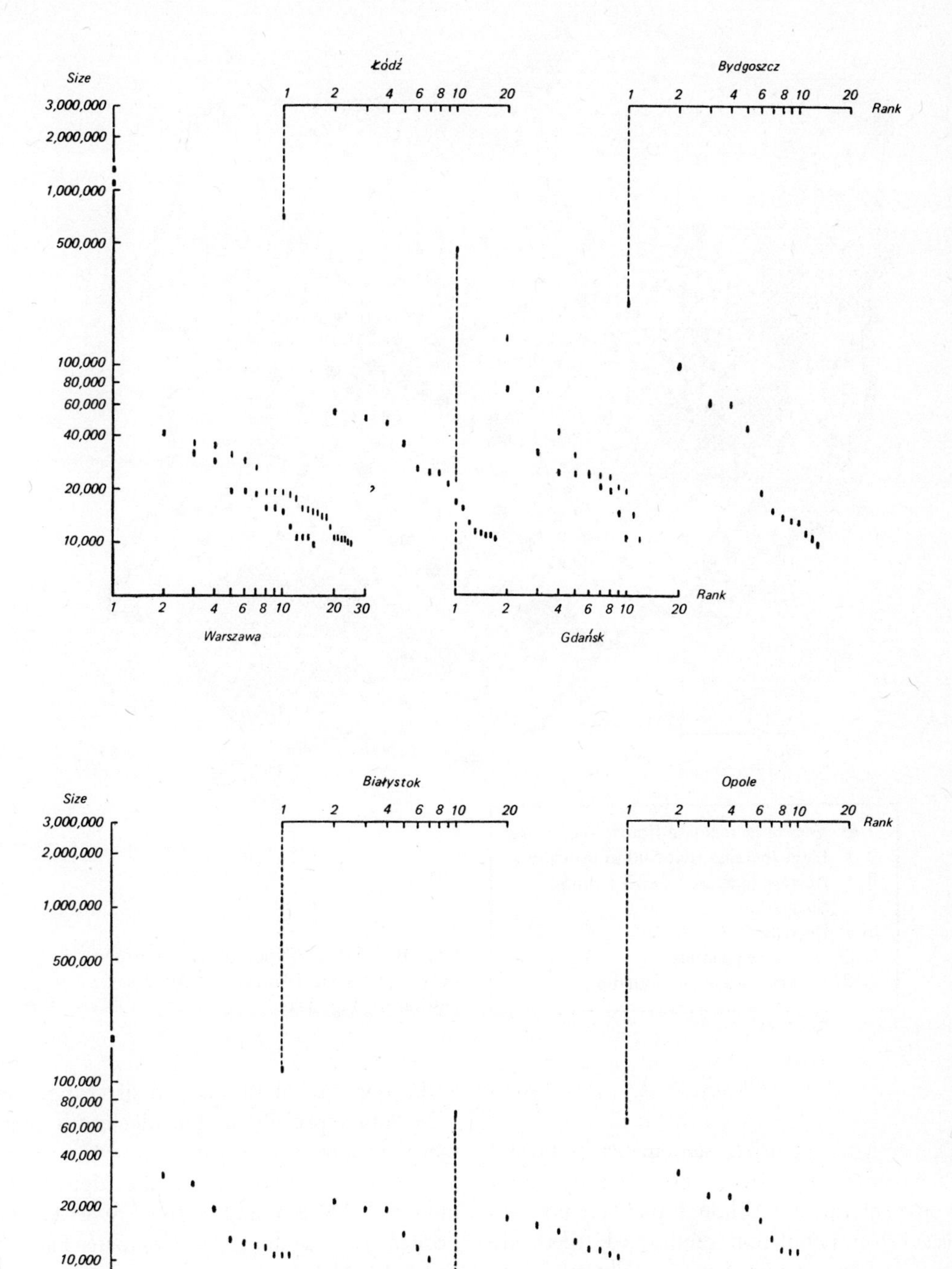
Size
3,000,000
2,000,000
1,000,000
500,000
100,000
80,000
60,000
40,000
20,000
10,000
Łódź
Bydgoszcz
Rank
Warszawa
Gdańsk
Białystok
Opole
Lublin
Olsztyn
1 2 4 6 8 10 20 30

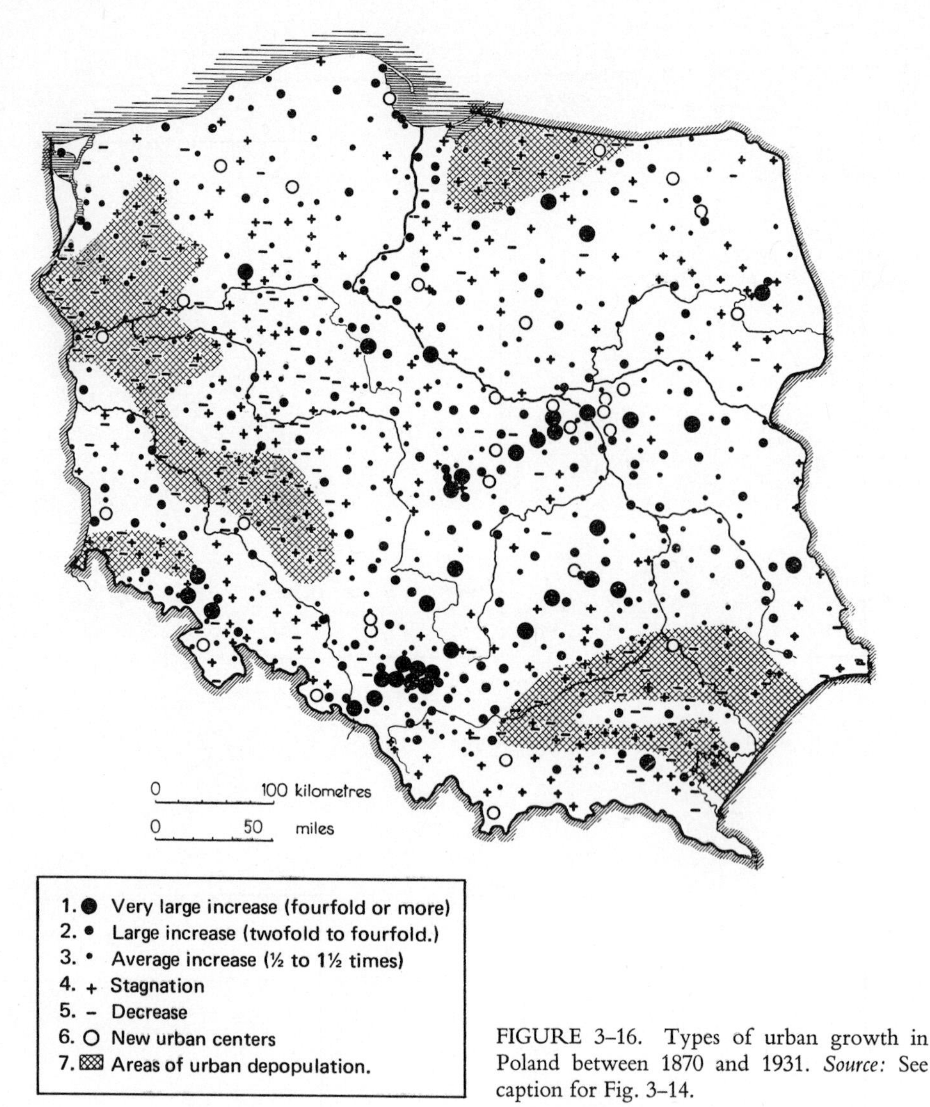

FIGURE 3–16. Types of urban growth in Poland between 1870 and 1931. *Source:* See caption for Fig. 3–14.

Changes in the Urban System

The network of urban settlements in Poland is changing and the changes are not proportionally or evenly spread. Although there are no areas where urban population diminished (there are however a few sporadic cases of small towns with decreasing population), the whole central part of Poland (the voivodships of Łódź, Katowice, Poznań, Bydgoszcz, Opole, and Warsaw) is, in comparison with the remaining areas, characterized by below-average growth rates. This is the opposite of the pattern of change before 1939, and especially in the nineteenth century, when progress in urbanization was strongest in the central areas (i.e., in the Upper Silesian Industrial District and around Warsaw, Łódź, Poznań and Bydgoszcz). Compare Figs. 3–16 and 3–17. Moreover, the changes between towns belonging to different population categories vary in different regions. As a result, the final distribution of growth is more diversified than at first glance would seem to be possible.

The proportional growth of towns of all classes

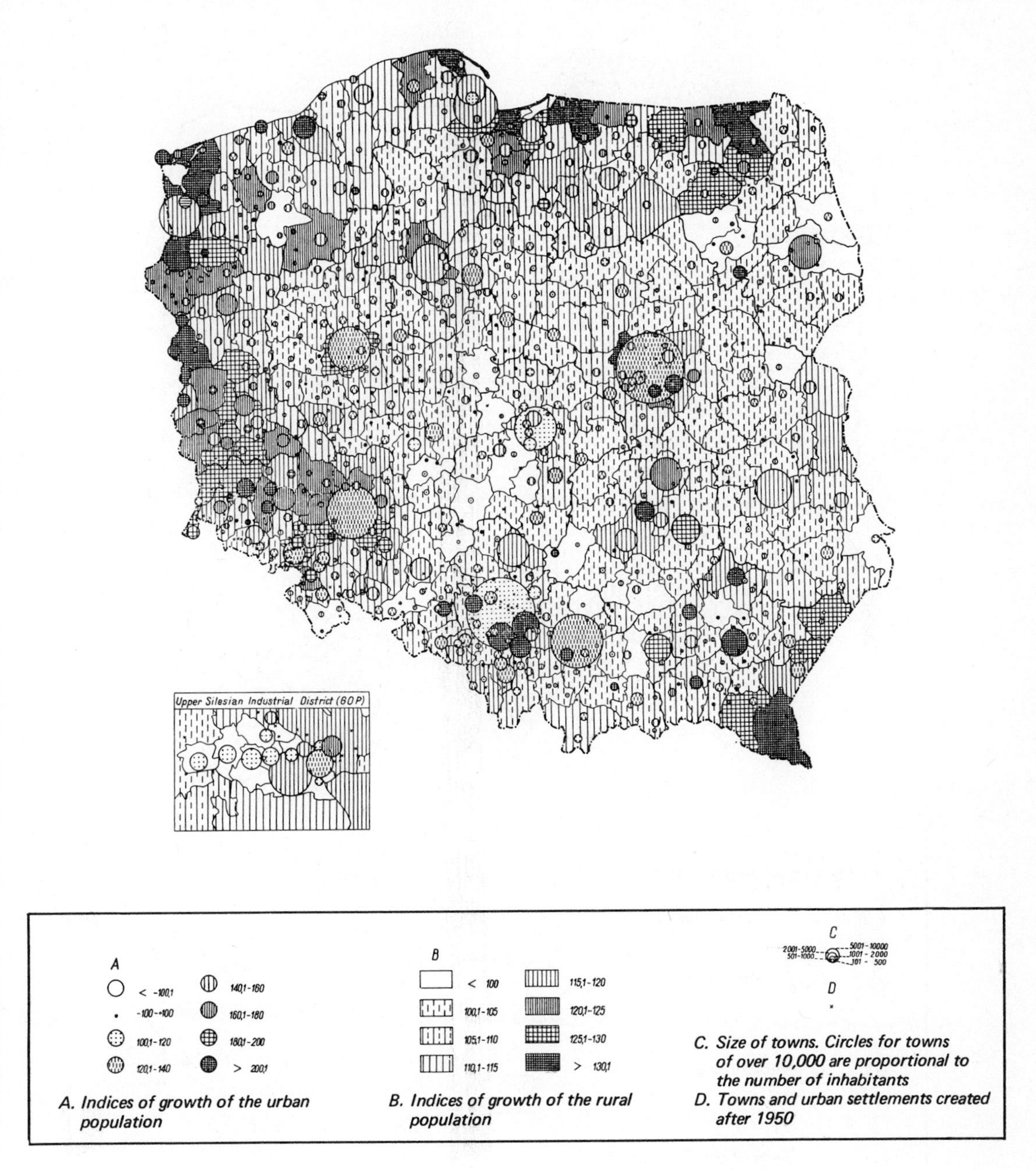

FIGURE 3–17. Changes in the urban and rural population of Poland between 1950 and 1960. *Source:* See caption for Fig. 3–14.

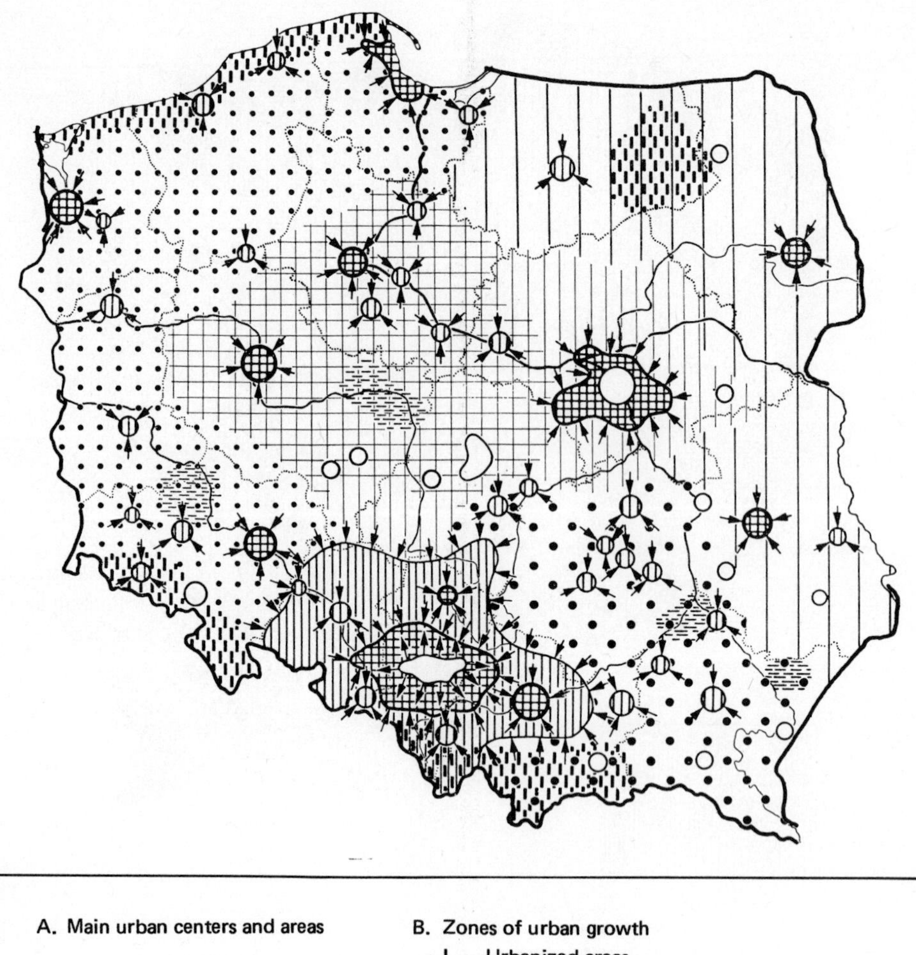

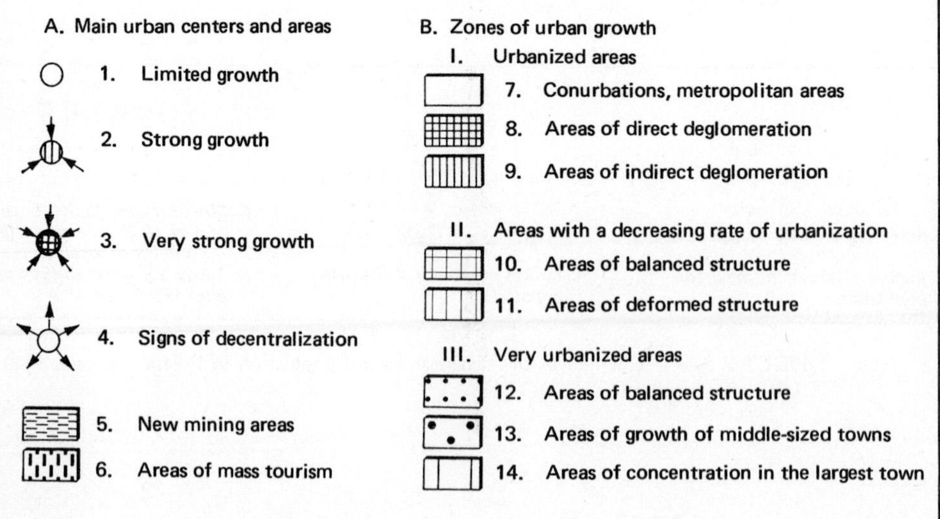

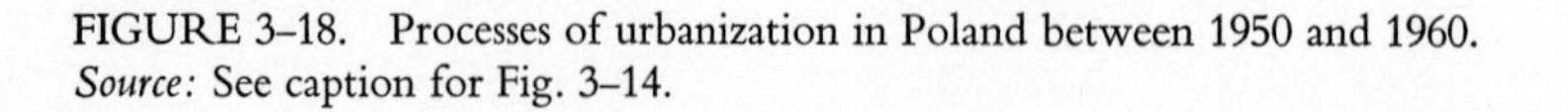

FIGURE 3–18. Processes of urbanization in Poland between 1950 and 1960.
Source: See caption for Fig. 3–14.

was evident in the territories recovered after the war (in some areas the growth of small towns was even greater than that of larger ones); in the eastern voivodships, urban growth was concentrated to a very high degree in the main city, and the middle-sized towns developed the most in the southeastern regions. There were several reasons for these differences: (1) planned industrialization created development in specific areas and centers; (2) rates of natural growth varied with regions, being highest in the west and north; and (3) differences in housing and in living conditions made some places more attractive than others. See Fig. 3–18.

One additional fact should also be noted. The southern voivodships of Katowice, Opole, and at least partly of Cracow form an integrated economic region and their urban network developed in a characteristically interrelated manner. Three concentric zones can be distinguished. The central core, composed of nineteen cities of about 1,500,000 inhabitants, forms a classical mining and industrial conurbation (the Upper Silesian Industrial District) which is slowing down in growth. The first ring includes the area of the greatest present mining, industrial and urban growth. This development is taking place in middle-sized towns and industrial settlements. Within this area, new satellite towns for the overspilling population from the central area are under construction. The third zone is composed of large districts developing around their own large urban center. Here planned industrial development is greatest and urban growth well over the average, although less than within the inner ring.

Similar development is taking place in the metropolitan area of Warsaw, but there the full stage of decentralized development has not yet been reached. So far only two concentric zones can be distinguished—the central core (the city of Warsaw itself) and the suburban zone. But already there are signs of new developments in the outer area: some subregional urban centers such as Płock and Siedlce are showing signs of an increased rate of growth.

. . .

The present trends of urbanization in Poland are thus probably typical of countries with developed traditions of urban life but passing through a period of very intensive modern industrialization. However, growth is more rational and structurally more balanced than in many other countries. This is seen in the limited growth of the capital, and in the existence and development of numerous large and middle-sized towns, as well as in the vitality of small towns. However, there are regional variations both in the existing network and in its present changes. These are caused by: (1) variability of the geographical environment, especially in the distribution of natural resources; (2) variation in the time of development of the settlements, especially from the point of view of the density of the network of the settlements (a network based on the distribution of *gród* [burgh] organizations dating from the early Dark Ages, and which was fully developed in Silesia in the twelfth, thirteenth, and fourteenth centuries, in Wielkopolska and in Malopolska as well as in Pomerania between the thirteenth and fourteenth centuries, in Mazowsze in the fourteenth, fifteenth, and sixteenth centuries, and in Podlasie and Mazury in the sixteenth or in some areas even in the eighteenth century); (3) the great differences in the functions and sizes of towns in various regions, due to the development of industrial towns and settlements dating from the second half of the eighteenth century right up to the present time; (4) the division of the whole territory of Poland, divided for about a hundred and fifty years, into parts of three states completely different in their political, social, and economic structure and life; and finally (5), the differences in the population structure of various parts of the country, resulting from the postwar resettlement and recent migrations.

All of these elements find their final expression in the regional structure of the urban network, both existing and developing. Definite settlement regions and, in other cases, separate zones of settlements may be distinguished. They are: (1) The Upper Silesian and Cracow Region; (2) the heterogeneous zone of below-average urbanization, including the voivodships of Łódź,

Poznań, Bydgoszcz, and Warsaw (including the whole metropolitan area of Warsaw); (3) the zone of greatest urbanization, including three different types of areas—first, areas of balanced development of urban networks (the western and northern voivodships); second, areas of the largest growth of middle-sized towns where there is limited growth or even stagnation of small towns (the voivodships of Rzeszów and Kielce, as well as the eastern part of the voivodship of Cracow), and third, areas of increasing concentration of urban population in the main urban center (the voivodships of Białystok and Lublin).

Effectiveness of Planning Policies

The picture of contemporary urbanization in Poland involves certain additional questions: To what degree is it a result of planning? And how far is it due to spontaneous growth, perhaps even impeded by the planned intervention? To answer these questions it is necessary to describe, at least shortly, the proclaimed aims of planning as well as the means used for their fulfillment, and then to compare them with the results obtained.

The programs of balanced economic and social decentralization, as well as some kind of unification between urban and rural ways of life, were among the principal elements of the ideology of early Utopian socialists, such as Owen and Fourier. This preference for decentralized development passed through Friedrich Engels to Marxist socialism. Although in the U.S.S.R. the construction of the socialist society and economy involved the necessity of an originally opposed use of a strongly centralized state organization, the ideological postulate of decentralization was never abandoned and may easily be found in all the statements and plans concerned with the development of national economies in the U.S.S.R., and, after the Second World War, in other socialist countries. However, the need for the existence and preservation of big cities, especially national capitals, was tacitly admitted later, and in some cases their further development was ardently supported.

Starting from such ideological bases, the Six-Year Plan for the Development of Polish National Economy, prepared and approved in the years 1947 to 1949, contained on the one hand a very ambitious program for decentralized industrial development, involving complete transformation of many backward areas and smaller urban centers and, on the other (easily understandable under Polish conditions), complete reconstruction of Warsaw which, as a result of war destruction, had been reduced to one-third of its former population and had had its central areas and all its industrial plants completely destroyed. Thus, in the plan itself two opposite tendencies were included: to develop the backward or retarded areas, and to concentrate new investments in the capital. The chief means for realizing the plan was the erection of new industrial plants. All other investments, especially in housing, were to be secondary, following in the wake of new industries.

However, following the period from 1950 to 1955, some very serious modifications and corrections had to be made. First, it was found that the proposed program of production could be achieved in many cases by modernizing existing plants. Difficulties were experienced in organizing big constructional enterprises and in finding qualified labor for new factories far from existing centers. Moreover, the rule that new services, especially new housing, were to follow the new industrial development led to strong pressures for changes in industrial locations on behalf of the existing large towns and other concentrations of industrial population. (A good example such a shift is the final location in Warsaw of big steel works formerly planned for one of the smaller towns within a radius of about 100 kilometers of the capital.) As a result, the whole program for the decentralization of industry and more balanced urban development was deferred. On the other hand, when it was found that the rapid influx of population into the largest industrial and urban agglomerations tended to worsen living conditions, means for controlling the growth of those cities were introduced, including strict limitations on the admission of new inhabitants, the correlation of the number of new jobs and new residents, and a reduction in the number of government offices and officials. Further modifications of policies were connected with the political changes of 1956. A general readjustment of the economic plan led to increases in funds for new services as well as to a certain weakening of the rule: "New industries first, then the services." This consequently diminished the pressure from existing agglomerations for new industrial developments. Moreover, to correct the obvious faults and mistakes in centralized planning, many powers and corresponding funds were transferred to regional and local authorities.

This evolution, which began around 1956, is still continuing, although at a somewhat slower rate than was originally provided. At the same time, an increase in the number of experienced planners led to better prepared, more realistic plans and proposals. However, the awareness that the economic reality did not conform to the original program left a certain malaise both among planners and in the whole community. This, in turn, led to a critical revaluation of the aims and means of regional planning which is still under discussion.

CITY SIZE AND THE DIFFUSION OF INNOVATIONS IN THE UNITED STATES

The general regularity of rank-size distributions clearly results from the growth processes that have operated. It is useful to think (to return to the American case) of a national system which extended and developed in a heartland-hinterland fashion, of a system of cities that increased numerically as well as in size as the nation grew, and of individual urban fields that expanded and took shape as the growth process ran its course.

There are three scales at which change takes place—national, regional, and local. That is: (1) the growth of the nation at large, leading both to polarized development (heartland and hinterlands) and to a national system of metropolitan centers; (2) an urban hierarchy within each metropolitan region; and (3) urban fields, or gradients of influence of each urban center on its surrounding hinterland. The different regional types and networks of cities arise from their age and stage of development within this matrix, from the manner in which innovation and diffusion processes have operated in this systems framework.

Innovation and Development

One can view development as being made up of a series of elementary innovations that occur in cities. Groups of these innovations merge into innovative clusters and, finally, into linked systems of evolutionary innovations that successively replace one cultural paradigm by another until they culminate in an "epochal innovation" that produces a "revolutionary" change.[17] Thus, one can talk of the technological innovations that ultimately accumulated to create the industrial transformation of the earlier mercantile paradigm of American urbanization, and the more recent replacement of the industrial paradigm by one related to services and communications.

The frequency of innovation is a function of the probability of interaction or information exchange in open systems—particularly large cities or urbanized regions—so that what develops in one phase of growth becomes the environment of subsequent phases, and powerful pressures for system maintenance are generated. The developmental process, therefore, has its origin in a relatively small number of "poles of change," or core regions, and spreads outwards from these to the peripheral areas. Core region or heartland development is, as a result, self-reinforcing in a pattern of "circular and cumulative causation,"[18] due to such "feedback" elements in the developmental process as the net flow of natural, human, and capital resources from the hinterlands to the heartland; information flows due to size and change at the core; linkages involving innovations that breed others by creating new demands; the creation of necessary conditions for innovation; the transformation of values into those accepting greater change through innovation; and scale, urbanization, and localization economies.

The Polarization of Growth

Spatially, then, polarized development can be seen to have taken place in the United States in a system with New York at its center, with a core industrial and consumption region in the northeastern manufacturing belt, spanning a variety of urban places supported mainly by their manufacturing function. Connections between this heartland and the specialized hinterlands surrounding it have been maintained by a network of commercial metropoli that have articulated commodity flows between core and periphery and have set the terms of trade.[19] Beneath them, successively lower orders of central places have organized the supply and assembly functions for the surrounding peripheral areas.[20]

The rate of innovation is greatest in the heartland, and is systematically transmitted outwards from it into the hinterlands.[21] Thus, in the United States, one should expect change to take place: (1) nationally, outwards from the manufacturing belt; (2) down the urban hierarchy; and (3) outwards from any urban center into its surrounding urban field. However, the propensity of newer centers to adopt innovations and assume new forms more rapidly than older centers of comparable size, located in regions which grew at an earlier time, should be recognized, for following Perloff's analysis[22]:

1. Relative change in the urban system in any time period is based upon activities and resources new in the national economy, rather than upon redistribution of existing activities. This is the basis of the emergence of new centers and regions and the shift in relative size of the old.
2. New centers, growing rapidly during a particular phase of urban growth, always have a concentration of the newer lines of economic activity—the growth sectors of the current phase of technology—and are found in regions well endowed with resources valued by those growth sectors.
3. City character and structure are a record of the epoch of initial growth, and subsequent success in capturing lines of activity new upon the national scene.[23]
4. Since the phase of growth associated with iron and steel, the dominant national pattern in the American urban system has been that of a manufacturing-belt heartland and surrounding resource-oriented hinterlands, complemented, at the regional level, for each metropolitan center, by an analogous center-periphery (or distance-decay) phenomenon, which is then repeated at the successively more local scales of each level of the urban hierarchy downward from the metropolis.[24]

The operative processes can be seen in the sequences and transitions of technology used to move people and goods within cities, and the way they relate to the national growth process and diffusion mechanisms.

Borchert identifies four principal epochs in American metropolitan growth, separated by changes in technology crucial in the location of urban development and the internal features of urban morphology: (1) "sail–wagon" (1790 to 1830); (2) "steamboat and iron horse" (1830 to 1870); (3) "steel rails and electric power" (1870 to 1920); and (4) "auto–air–amenity," which could also be called "internal combustion engine and the shift to services" (1920 to the present).[25] (Chapter 2 was devoted to the growth and change of the national urban system as the country developed through these phases.) Paralleling the system transformation, a series of shifts in the internal structure of cities took place—from the preindustrial walking-and-wagon form, to the industrial city in which jobs remained centralized but residential areas had spread out and become differentiated, to the post-industrial decentralization of both residences and workplaces.

In the preindustrial phase there had been water-related expansion of the national urban system along the Mississippi-Ohio system and the Great Lakes, as well as the beginning of the blanketing of the country by a network of railroads and rail-related commercial centers. The internal growth of the cities, however, still was constrained by the internal means of transportation—essentially walking, or horse and wagon. Urban activities, despite good reasons for decentralization—the prices of land, labor, and capital—were forced by primitive means of moving goods short distances overland to remain as close as possible to port facilities and later to railroad terminals.[26] Workers of all grades were forced to live close to work in crowded, mixed, residential-commercial-industrial areas.[27]

But during the time that the economy was being transformed industrially, and the dynamics of industrial growth were being added to the commerce–related expansion of the urban system, the street railway was invented in New York (1851). Although workplaces were still confined, by the limitations of horses and wagons, to port and railroad-related locations at (and radiating from) the city center, this revolutionary innovation permitted residences to be decentralized.[28] The industrial city came into being—not simply because of the new economic base, but because the industrial transformation coincided with a new means of moving people, and this in turn led to the segregation is different parts of the city of land uses that had previously been intermixed, together with the socio-economic differentiation of residential areas according to principles of both centrality and axiality. According to Hurd, this meant cities in which:

The land which is most convenient is first utilized, and that which is less convenient is made of service in accordance with its diminishing facilities. Since convenience means economy in time and cost, the value in any piece of land will represent the cost saved and the pleasure obtained by its use, as compared with the use of land worth nothing multiplied by the number and economic quality of the people for whom the saving is made. Thus the value of all urban land ranges from that which least serves the smallest number of people of the lowest economic quality, up to the highest economic quality.

Since value depends on economic rent, and rent on location, and location on convenience, and convenience on nearness, we may eliminate the intermediate steps and say that value depends on nearness. The next question is, nearness to what?—which brings us to the land requirements of different utilities, their distribution over the city's area and the consequent creation and distribution of values.[29]

New York, as we have just noted, installed its street railway in 1851. By 1865, the largest of the older cities and the new industrial and commercial-manufacturing centers of the emergent

FIGURE 3–19. Urban centers installing street railways: 1851 to 1865. *Source:* Figs. 3–19 through 3–22 are from Arthur J. Krim, "The Innovation and Diffusion of the Street Railway in North America" (master's thesis, University of Chicago, 1967).

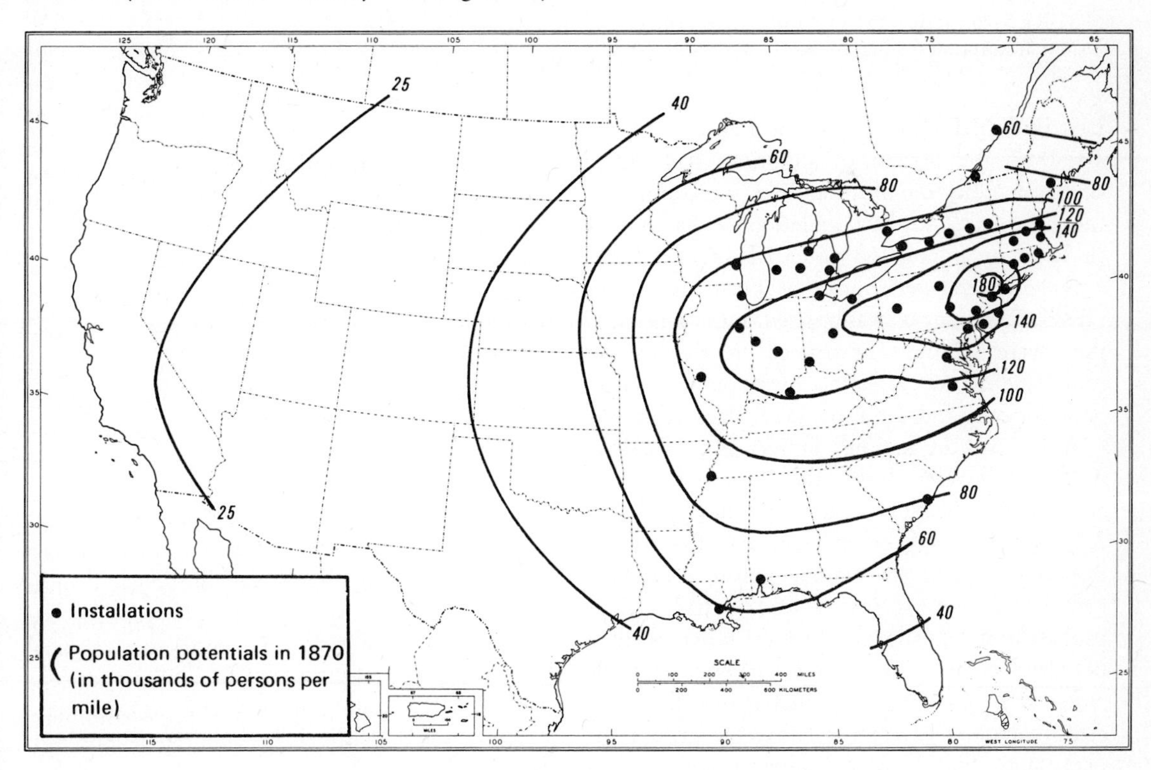

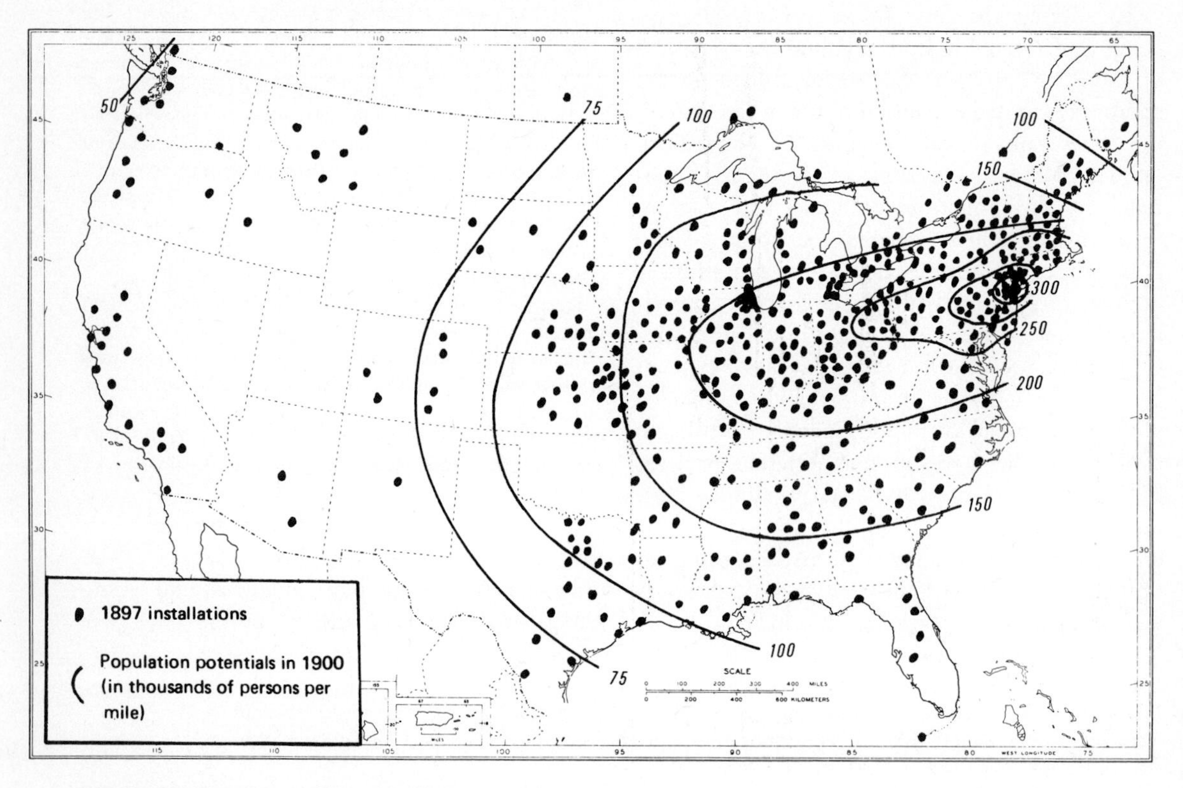

FIGURE 3–20. Street railway installations in 1897.
Source: See caption for Fig. 3–19.

heartland had also adopted it (see Fig. 3–19). By 1897, the pattern of adoptions had spread outward from the heartland in a pattern that mirrored access to the population of the country (indexed by population potentials in Fig. 3–20). Early adopters used horses or mules as motive power. Later, steam was applied, but steam facilities were seldom constructed in the smaller hinterland centers after the invention of electricity. Not only did diffusion take place from the heartland to the nation's hinterlands, however; it also followed down the urban hierarchy according to the city-size distribution (Fig. 3–21). Additionally, two other elements affected the diffusion sequences: smaller, newer hinterland centers that were growing rapidly had greater probabilities of adopting street railways than heartland cities of a comparable size; and the closer a small city to a metropolis that had already adopted a street railway, the greater the probability that it would adopt it sooner than more distant places within the urban field.[30]

A similar heartland-large city pattern characterized electric interurban railway installations (see Fig. 3–22). These permitted further residential decentralization until the 1930's, when their function, and that of the street railways, was gradually replaced by buses and the private automobile in the areas shown in Fig. 3–22. In cities of more recent growth, the automobile dominated from the start.

Each of these subsequent developments in personal transportation took place within the context of the industrial city. They were *evolutionary* innovations permitting increased residential differentiation based on life cycle, social status, and ethnicity (see, in Chapter 10, the discussion of social space). Given the central-axial layout of places of employment, and the concentration of development in central areas made possible by the inventions in building technology of the 1870's and 1880's (e.g., the steel-frame

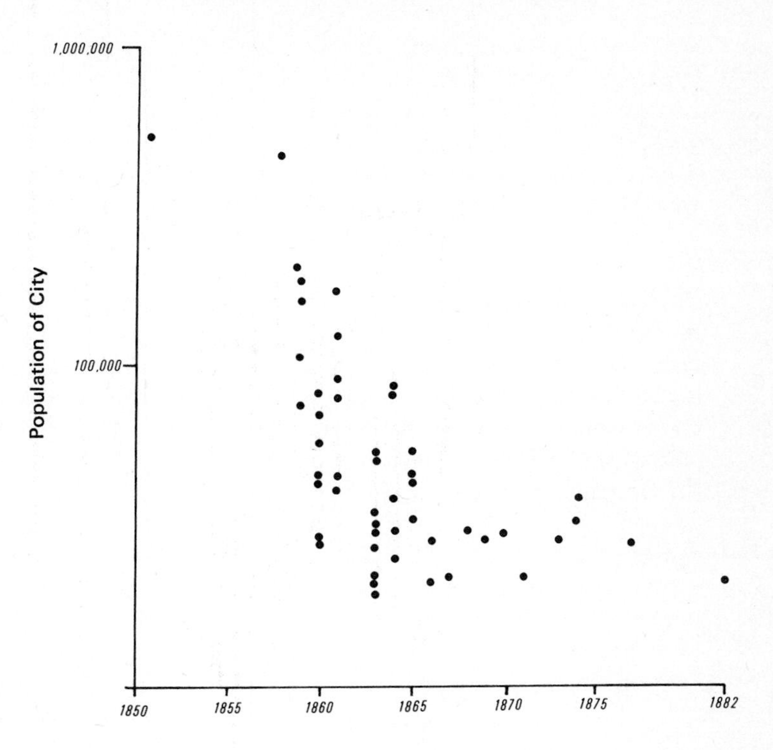

FIGURE 3–21. Diffusion of street railway adoptions down the urban hierarchy: 1851 to 1880. *Source:* See caption for Fig. 3–19.

FIGURE 3–22. All known electric interurban railway routes. *Source:* See caption for Fig. 3–19.

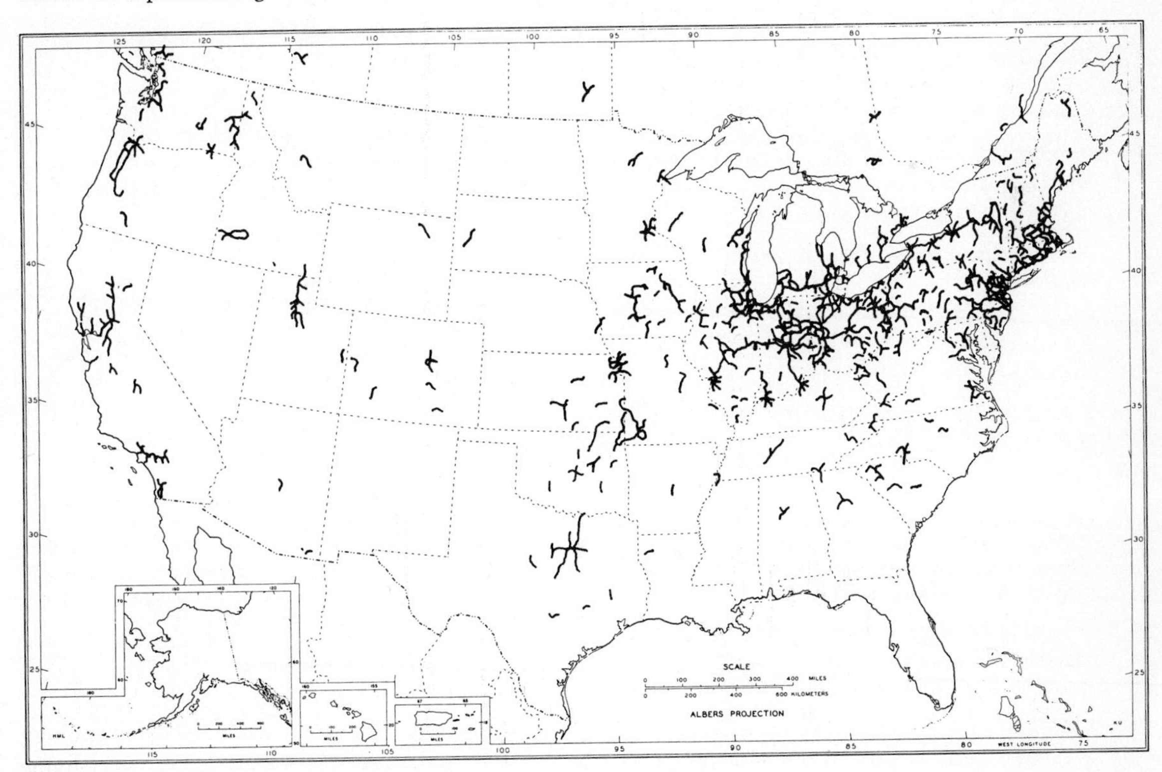

skyscraper and the elevator), they supported the familiar ecology of the industrial city.

It was not until the combination of truck transportation and new interstate highways was felt in the years after the Second World War, at a time when new economic growth was based on footloose industries (e.g., in the final stages of processing and in the service sectors) that places of employment began to decentralize substantially.[31] It was this combination of elements that led to the next urban revolution: the growth of the postindustrial city in which industries, workers, and the nonjob oriented population have all been seeking out new amenity resources, and in which the overlapping commuting fields depicted in Chapter 2 grew. The process involves both push and pull, for the essence of the large industrial city is concentration and density—an absence of open space, intense crowding, increasing problems of environmental pollution, and so forth.[32] Large industrial cities have also been the principal sources of blue-collar employment, with attendant accumulations of people on the lowest rungs of the status system in deteriorating, crowded, and riot-prone slums. New industries and the white-collar middle class characteristically avoid such areas.[33] Thus, the revolutionary innovations of the post-1950 period imply substantial changes in system form, rather than the system-maintenance of evolutionary sequences. There is growth of certain parts at the expense of others. In any case, however, it is the system that provides the environmental context for the changes.[34]

The new challenges are substantial and many. At the very time that the pull of new urban resources is toward decentralization within urban regions and continued deconcentration by hinterland growth along the southern and western rims of the continent, an observer such as Jean Gottmann concludes that, for the nation's great urban concentrations, "increased crowding has become the indispensable alternative to decay.[35]

FOOTNOTES TO CHAPTER 3

1. See John Q. Stewart, "Empirical Mathematical Rules concerning the Distribution and Equilibrium of Population," *The Geographical Review*, XXXVII, No. 3 (July, 1947), 461–85; and George Kingsley Zipf, *National Unity and Disunity* (Bloomington, Ind.: Principia Press, 1941), and *Human Behavior and the Principle of Least Effort* (Reading, Mass.: Addison-Wesley, 1949).

2. The relationships are that city areas (A) vary directly with their populations (S_c), and inversely with potential population (i.e., with whether the area is in the core or the periphery); and that populations of urban fields (S_M) vary directly with both the size of the central cities and with potential populations (P).

Relevant equations are:

$$\begin{aligned} \log A &= 0.78 + 0.82 \log S_c - 0.396 \log P \\ r^2 &= 0.80 \\ S_e &= 0.196 \\ \log S_M &= -0.2 + 0.71 \log S_c + 0.53 \log P \\ r^2 &= 0.81 \\ S_e &= 0.21 \end{aligned}$$

3. See Mark Jefferson, "The Law of the Primate City," *The Geographical Review*, XXIX, No. 2 (April, 1939), 226–32. The second usage is found, e.g., in the discussion in UNESCO, *Report by the Director-General on the Joint UN/UNESCO Seminar on Urbanization in the ECAFE Region* (Paris: UNESCO, 1956).

4. This statement is valid when a variable exponent is allowed. See Martin J. Beckmann, "City Hierarchies and the Distribution of City Size," *Economic Development and Cultural Change*, VI (April, 1958), 243–48; Brian J. L. Berry and William L. Garrison, "Alternate Explanations of Urban Rank-Size Relationships," *Annals of the Association of American Geographers*, XLVIII, No. 1 (March, 1958), 83–91; Herbert A. Simon, "On a Class of Skew Distribution Functions," *Biometrika*, XLII (1955), 425–40; and J. Aitchison and J. A. C. Brown, *The Lognormal Distribution* (Cambridge: Cambridge University Press, 1957). The truncated lognormal is used here rather than the Yule distribution because both are similar in form and because subsequent analysis is facilitated by use of lognormal probability paper. See also the discussion of E. N. Thomas, "Additional Comments on Population–Size Relationships for Sets of Cities," in W. L. Garrison and D. F. Marble, eds., *Quantitative Geography* (Evanston, Ill.: Northwestern Studies in Geography, 1968).

5. See Zipf, *National Unity* and *Human Behavior*; Brian J. L. Berry, "An Inductive Approach to the Regionalization of Economic Development," in *Essays on Geography and Economic Development*, ed., Norton Ginsburg (Department of Geography, University of Chicago, Research Paper Number 62, Chicago, 1960), pp. 78–107; and UNESCO, *Report by the Director-General*. See also Beckmann's "City Hierarchies"; and Berry and Garrison's "Alternate Explanations," which argue for the compatibility of Christaller-Lösch type hierarchies and ranked sizes distributions.

6. UNESCO, *Report of the Director-General*, ascribes the over-urbanization of Asian economies to: (1) excessive immigration; and (2) the superimposition of a limited economic development of a colonial or semi-colonial type, creating dual economies and primate cities which contrast with systems of cities in the west. It was reported that primate cities have paralytic effects upon the development of smaller urban places and tend to be parasitic in relation to the remainder of the national economy.

7. C. Stewart, in "The Size and Spacing of Cities," *The*

Geographical Review, XLVIII, No. 2 (April, 1958), 222–45, argues that there are marked divergences from Zipf's rank-size rule that in any country the *n*th ranking city has a population of 1/*n*th that of the largest city because, for 72 countries in the world and for major political divisions within the six largest countries, the theoretical 1.0: 0.5: 0.33: 0.25: 0.20 ratios of the sizes of the five largest cities are not found. Using Sweden and Denmark as his examples, and citing four time periods for each, he argues that there is, instead, an *S*-shaped distribution of towns by size (pp. 230–31). The comments of F. T. Moore on Zipf's limiting case, "A Note on City Size Distributions," *Economic Development and Cultural Change*, VII (October, 1959), 465–66, are also germane.

8. See Jefferson, "The Law of the Primate City."

9. See Brian J. L. Berry, "A Statistical Analysis," in *Atlas of Economic Development*, ed. Norton Ginsburg (Chicago: Univerity of Chicago Press, 1961), Part 8.

10. *Ibid.*, p. 36.

11. Jefferson, "The Law of the Primate City."

12. See Simon, "Skew Distribution Functions." The thesis is that a lognormal or closely-related distribution holds when, over a period of time, cities have grown at a given rate (the "law of proportionate effect") with only random deviations in the case of particular cities.

13. Berry and Garrison, "Alternate Explanations."

14. We use the terms "orthogenetic" and "heterogenetic" in the original sense of Redfield and Singer, realizing that they are subject to debate. See Robert Redfield and Milton Singer, "The Cultural Role of Cities," *Economic Development and Cultural Change*, III (October, 1954), 53–73.

15. The graph is from Gwen Bell, "Change in City Size Distribution in Israel," *Ekistics*, XIII (1962), 103, with the permission of the author and editor. She writes,

> In lognormally graphing the distribution changes in 1922, 1931, 1944, and 1959, the hypothetical model seems to be borne out in reality. Until 1931, the distribution was that of a predominant primate city, although it changed from Jerusalem in 1922 to Tel Aviv-Jaffa in 1931. The 1944 and 1959 curves would then seem to follow the changes suggested in Berry's developmental model towards a rank-size order. During this same time, Israel, although a very small nation, has been developing into a highly complex industrial one.

16. Pierre George, *La ville, le fait urbain à travers le monde* (Paris: Presses Universitaires, 1952).

17. See John R. P. Friedmann, *Regional Development Policy* (Cambridge, Mass.: The M. I. T. Press, 1966), and his "A General Theory of Polarized Development," draft manuscript (Santiago: Ford Foundation Urban and Regional Development Advisory Program in Chile, June, 1967).

18. Allan Pred, *The Spatial Dynamics of U. S. Urban-Industrial Growth: 1800–1914* (Cambridge, Mass.: The M. I. T. Press, 1966), p. 25.

19. See Edward Ullman, *American Commodity Flows* (Seattle: The University of Washington Press, 1957).

20. See Brian J. L. Berry, *Geography of Market Centers and Retail Distribution* (Englewood Cliffs, N. J.: Prentice-Hall, Inc., 1967).

21. See Edward L. Ullman, "Regional Development and the Geography of Concentration," *Papers of the Regional Science Association*, IV (1958), 179–98.

22. Harvey S. Perloff *et al.*, *Regions, Resources and Economic Growth* (Baltimore: Johns Hopkins Press, 1960).

23. Beverly Duncan, *Metropolis and Region in Transition* (Washington: Resources for the Future, Inc., 1968).

24. See Berry, "A Statistical Analysis"; Peter Haggett, *Locational Analysis in Human Geography* (London: Edward Arnold (Publishers) Ltd., 1965); and Melvin W. Reder, "The Theory of Occupational Wage Differentials," *American Economic Review*, VL (1955), 832–52. Eugene Smolensky, extending Reder, describes the economic mechanism which promotes diffusion by filtering or "trickling down" the urban size-ratchet as follows:

> The higher the capital-labor ratio in a region the higher the employment level at any wage rate of the unskilled and at any given social minimum; therefore, the smaller the number of involuntarily unemployed. The implication of this is that in any general expansion the high income region will reach a rising floor to the wage-rate first. As a consequence, some industries will be priced out of the high income labor market and there will be a shift of that industry to low-income regions. The significance of this shift of industry lies not so much in its direct, but in its indirect effects. If the boom originated in the high income regions, as is highly likely, then the multiplier effects will be larger in the initiating region although the relative rise in income may be greater in the under-developed region. But, more interestingly, the induced effects on real income and employment may be considerably greater in the low-income region and/or if the rise in output per worker would be greater. Both are likely from the same source—decreasing cost due to external economies. If the boom stemming from urbanization of the labor force can be maintained, industries of higher labor productivity will shift into the low income region and some industries will be driven out of the county.—["Poverty Policy and Pennsylvania," paper presented to the Pennsylvania Economic Association (June, 1965)].

25. John R. Borchert, "American Metropolitan Evolution," *The Geographical Review*, LVII, No. 3 (July, 1967), 324.

26. See Leon Moses and Harold F. Williamson, "The Location of Economic Activity in Cities," *American Economic Review*, LVII, No. 2 (May, 1967), 211–22. Parts of this paper are reproduced in Chapter 12 of the present volume.

27. See Gideon Sjoberg, *The Preindustrial City* (New York: The Free Press, 1960).

28. Arthur J. Krim, "The Innovation and Diffusion of the Street Railway in North America" (Master's thesis, University of Chicago, 1967).

29. Richard M. Hurd, *Principles of City Land Values.* (New York: The Record and Guide, 1924), pp. 12–13.

30. Krim, "The Street Railway."

31. See Moses and Williamson, "The Location of Economic Activity in Cities."

32. See William P. Lowry, "The Climate of Cities," *Scientific American*, CCXVII (1967), 15–23.

33. See Moses and Williamson, "The Location of Economic Activity in Cities."

34. Borchert, in his essay "American Metropolitan Evolution," notes the increasing problem of residual structures dating from earlier times. Andrew Wilson notes that the immigration to Tucson in response to the climatic advantages has ironically contributed to that city's high unemployment rates. See "The Impact of Climate on Industrial Growth: Tucson, Arizona, A Case Study," in W. R. D. Sewell, ed., *Human Dimensions of Weather Modification* (Department of Geography Research Paper No. 105, University of Chicago, 1966), pp. 249–60.

35. Jean Gottmann, *Megalopolis* (New York: Twentieth Century Fund, 1961), p. 632.

CHAPTER 4

*theories and techniques for studying urban and regional growth**

At this juncture an aside is appropriate, to apprise the student of the theoretical and technical skills he will have to master if he is to progress beyond the materials in this book and become a productive research worker on the frontiers of urban geography, contributing important new findings about the growth of urban systems. We have talked a good deal in the previous chapters about urban and regional growth. Exactly what are the various theories of growth? How does one go about studying the growth phenomenon? Are there public policy implications? These are the questions addressed in this chapter.

Since whole books have been written about each theory and technique, we can at best provide only a quick overview here, in the expectation that the reader has been (or will be) exposed to these relevant ideas and methods in much greater detail elsewhere. The beginning student may wish to read only the sections "Theories of Urban and Regional Growth," "Shift Analysis," and "Economic Base Analysis," because many of the other sections may, in providing a compact summary, be too formal and concise.

*The bulk of this chapter is from Brian J. L. Berry, *Strategies, Models and Economic Theories of Development in Rural Regions*, Agriculture Economic Report No. 127, Department of Agriculture (Washington, D.C.: U.S. Government Printing Office, 1967).

THEORIES OF URBAN AND REGIONAL GROWTH

For consistent explanations of patterns of urban and regional growth within the context of national growth, one must turn to the insights provided by economic theory. In a recent review of theories of regional development, Anthony Scott[1] concluded that trade and location theories are suggestive but not really helpful in understanding the dynamics of growth because the conclusions drawn from these theories have traditionally depended on the assumption that available inputs of the factors of production are not mobile among regions, i.e., that the supply of land, labor, and capital in each region (its factor endowment) is fixed and may not be augmented or depleted by interregional shipments.[2] Scott sees a version of the staple theory as the most useful one among the alternates. Whether this conclusion is valid in the context of the growth of one or a sample of rural regions or urban places as distinct from national growth is debatable, however. Location theory is certainly relevant to the examination of the strengths and weaknesses of particular cities and regions as attempts are made to develop these cities and regions by both private and public groups interested in taking action that will increase growth rates.

Trade Theory

Trade theory was initially developed to deal with movements of goods among nations, but most of it also applies to movements of goods among regions or cities of a nation. In its classical or Ricardian form, this theory focuses on the "comparative advantage" of nations for specialization in one or another line of production. Comparative advantage is based on relative productivity. Modifications of the theory lead to the prediction that higher incomes will accrue to the nation with the greatest absolute advantage.

This classical theory does seem to account for trade flows and for spatial differences in wealth at any point in time, yet it fails to explain why nations have particular types of relative productivity advantage and why all nations produce a certain amount of most products.

Attempts to apply trade theory to regions were made by both Heckscher and Ohlin. Heckscher based his argument upon regional differences in production functions.[3] Ohlin, on the other hand, assumed that from region to region production functions and the quality of resources were identical, attributing relative productivity advantages to differences in "factor endowment," i.e., in the supplies of land, labor, and capital available. Refinements of his theory led to the explanation of differences in average incomes of regions in terms of differences in factor endowments,[4] yet, left unexplained by the theory are the observable facts that wage differentials tend to disappear and that factor inputs are mobile among regions. Neither fact is admitted in even a refined version of Ohlin's theory. Ohlin provides a satisfactory basis for explaining differences among regions at any point in time, but fails to account for the effects of change. Other theories must be sought to provide the more general framework that is needed.

Location Theory

Location theory was developed out of the need to explain and predict the location of economic activities (for an elaboration in the urban context see Chapters 5, 7, and 12). It provides either the medium for ex-post-facto rationalization of the "survival of the fittest" within an "adoptive" economic system (in the sense of Alchian)[5] or the basis for "adaptive" planning whereby businessmen can analyze and comprehend the economic system and make rational choices concerning location of their firms.[6] This theory embraces three levels of observation: (1) location of a firm; (2) the location of groups of firms so they will be in a stable competitive situation in relation to each other; and (3) the location of sets of activities, such as different kinds of agricultural land use, in relation to each other so that all activities bear a stable competitive relationship.

First, let us consider location of a single firm. Here, location theory stems from Weber's theory of industrial location. In this theory, the locational problem is formulated as one of cost minimization. Cost schedules are examined to determine the proportion of total costs accounted for by different elements: transportation of raw materials; labor; processing as affected by internal economies of scale of production and external economies of the size of the agglomeration within which the plant is located; and transportation of finished products to market. The spatial variability of each of these elements for each industry is studied, and the least-cost mix for industries of different kinds is determined. Different cost mixes lead to different locational orientations of industries of different kinds: raw material orientation, market orientation, labor orientation, and so forth. In the tradition of Weberian theory, analysis of the various cost levels in a region in relation to those of other regions can provide valuable information on what industries are likely to be successful. However, the basic shape of economic space is taken as given; firms simply adjust to it. A dynamic theory of the location of the firm has yet to be constructed.

At the second level of observation, the theories of Christaller and Lösch apply.[7] Examining the interactions of conditions of entry of business firms (thresholds) and drawing power (range in terms of maximum market areas), Christaller and Lösch provide a solution to the problem of a competitive locational equilibrium for a set of firms of the same type and scale. They then show how firms of different types agglomerate into urban centers. A number of discrete types of agglomerations exist; these are organized into an urban hierarchy connected by patterns of dominance of the smaller centers by the larger in a regular, nested arrangement. These assumptions lead to deductions about the increased polarization of activities in the larger urban centers. Structural changes in the economic environment, such as a technological advance in agriculture, may cause marginal firms at different levels in the hierarchy to fail. In this event, the market is likely to be captured by the output of more efficient firms at higher levels in the hierarchy, the competitive process thus leading to further centralization.

At the third level of observation are Von Thünen's theories of location and land use, which were recently expanded and refined by Edgar S. Dunn and William Alonso.[8] These theories deal with allocation of uses to the land in terms of rents, in a competitive bidding process.

Export or Staple Theory[9]

To come closer to a theory of urban and regional development that accounts for changes in the shape of the space economy, someone must explain why entrepreneurs and capital move from region to region. Some assert that owners of wealth shift quickly and readily to those investments which, taking into account risks and taxes, yield the greatest net returns. Migration is explained by both the "pull" of greater expectations elsewhere and the "push" of displacement from zones of inferior incomes and opportunity. Both are discounted by some function of distance, so that migration rates vary directly with the size of the push and pull and inversely with distance. Furthermore, the value of land and other resource endowments of regions change through time because of changes in the population, the standard of living, tastes, technology, and because exploitation of nonrenewable resources leads to progressive depletion. It is in the context of these changes that Scott writes:

> Some general theory of regional fortunes must take into account not only . . . factors, techniques, and demand, but also their growth over time, as in population growth, innovation and opulence and . . . their change through space, as in labor and capital migration, the diffusion of new techniques, and the opening of new regional markets.[10]

The export, or staple model, originally developed for application to the problem of the settlement of undeveloped regions, approaches this goal. The assumption is that growth in an unsettled region can be explained in terms of the region's main export commodity or staple.

Staple theory emphasizes migration of the factors of production, arguing that factor endowment can better be explained by factor migration than by local generation. Factors come to a region in response to the high returns offered by a staple export; growth comes when advancing technology reduces unit costs, or when expanding demand increases rates of return.

The size of a region affected by a given industry, according to the traditional staple theory, depends upon the land-using characteristics of the industry. We must add, however, that this statement should be extended to cover the land-using characteristics of those activities affected by production and consumption of the staple. There is also a superstructure of "residentiary" activities such as retail shops and service centers which are secondary in that they do not export their sales, but which, rather, depend on the staple because they come into existence to serve workers employed in staple industries. The location of residentiary activities is fundamental to a definition of the "impact region" of the staple, because the area affected by growth of the staple comprises the region within which its workers live, together with the region from which these workers obtain their everyday needs.[11]

If the staple industry continues to grow and, if along with it, the residentiary activities of the dependent region expand sufficiently, these secondary activities may, through the internal and external economies of increasing scale of firms and size of agglomerations of industry, become export staples. It is at this point that the region "takes off" into self-sustained growth. But whether a region has reached the point of self-sustained growth may not be apparent unless the original staple industry falters or dies. If this eventuality leads only to temporary disturbances and reallocations of factors, then regional growth has become self-sustaining.

The regional development of staple industries is primarily a function of national economic growth, although the converse is often asserted by proponents of the export staple theory. Staple theory describes the mechanism by which the national endowment is allocated among industries in response to changing demands. A reallocation requires the abandonment of some resources and locations and the development of others, so that the developmental process embodies, as integral parts, both regional growth and decline. In either case, the region is that area affected by both the basic and residentiary components of staple activities.

Thompson's concept of the "urban size-ratchet" is relevant in this context.[12] Thompson argues that the growth rates of small regions are highly variable, but that the larger the region (1) the more likely it is to have continuous, self-sustained growth; and (2) the more likely the growth rate is to approximate that of the nation. Specifically, when the population of urban centers exceeds 250,000 (refer back to Chapters 2 and 3), these centers display all of the characteristics of self-sustained growth and carry forward their entire labor market—that region within effective commuting distance of the city's main employment centers.

Thompson continues his argument by stating that the export staples of these continually growing regions do not remain constant. There are always some current changes in the industry mix; for, the essence of growth is continuous innovation. Urban nodes have satisfied the agglomerative conditions necessary for continuing development and exploitation of new kinds of staples, which subsequently "filter down" the urban hierarchy to smaller centers, and spread outwards from the centers of change to the periphery.

Thus, according to staple theory, it is the continual introduction of new staple industries, possible in the large urban agglomerations, and the conjoint filtering down and diffusion outwards of older staple industries, that have led to the urban orientation of the nation. The lagging segments of the rural periphery are those regions least able to benefit from such filtering and diffusion.

GROWTH FORECASTING

The techniques currently available for forecasting urban or regional growth make direct use of one or more facets of the trade, location, or staple theories. Each available method assumes that the regions for which forecasts are required have already been defined, that good historical data are available, and that historical relationships will continue to hold in the future. Most forecasting methods link regional fortunes to those of the nation and are predicated upon the hypothesis that a solution to the basic economic problem of optimal area development requires public and private investment at levels high enough to at least maintain the competitive position of the area's export industries and to provide for the growth of both export and local markets at a rate equal to or greater than the rate of increase in regional labor productivity.

Shift Analysis (the Spatial Allocation or Components-of-Growth Approach[13]*)*

One of the simplest analytical approaches is based on a study of three main components of growth: (1) that part attributable to national growth; (2) that part attributable to the difference between rates of growth of the mix of industries in the region and the national rate of growth of all industries; and (3) that part due to differences between the rates of growth of the industries within any particular region and the rates of growth of the same industries in other regions. Symbolically, this may be expressed as:

$$d_{ij} = g_{ij} + k_{ij} + c_{ij} \tag{1}$$

where: g_{ij} = the national growth element for industry i in region j

k_{ij} = the industry-mix effect for industry i in region j

c_{ij} = the regional competitive effect for industry i in region j

d_{ij} = the absolute change in employment between two points in time for industry i in region j (that is, $E_{1960} - E_{1950}$).

For example, consider industry i in region j between 1950 and 1960:

Year	*Employment on April 1 (in Thousands)*
1950	42.8
1960	59.0
Change	16.2

Now, the national rate of growth between 1950 and 1960 was 0.1548; for industry i, it was 0.3112; and for industry i in region j it was 0.3787.

Let: r = the national rate of growth (0.1548)

r_i = the national rate of growth in industry i (0.3112)

r_{ij} = the rate of growth of industry i in region j (0.3787)

E_{1950} = employment in 1950

E_{1960} = employment in 1960

Then:
$$g_{ij} = E_{1950} \times r = 42.8 \times 0.1548 = 6.6 \text{ thousands}$$

$$k_{ij} = E_{1950} \times (r_i - r) = 42.8 \times (0.3112 - 0.1548) = 6.7 \text{ thousands}$$

$$c_{ij} = E_{1950} \times (r_{ij} - r_i) = 42.8 \times (0.3787 - 0.3112) = 2.9 \text{ thousands}$$

$$d_{ij} = E_{1960} - E_{1950} = 59.0 - 42.8 = 16.2 \text{ thousands}$$

Finally:
$$d_{ij} = g_{ij} + k_{ij} + c_{ij}$$
$$16.2 = 6.6 + 6.7 + 2.9$$

This example was worked out in terms of employment. However, the same method could have been used to analyze many other kinds of shifts—for example, a change in the sources of regional income. And clearly if the calculation is made for each industry in a region, one can obtain by addition the total industry-mix effect and the total competitive shift effect for the region.

If it is assumed that the shift coefficients will be the same in the future, they can be used to make direct employment forecasts. Alternatively, the industry-mix and competitive shift coefficients can be used as independent variables in econometric models such as Matilla's regional interaction unemployment-migration model.[14] The inclusion of additional information will permit more refined regional forecasting. For example, the effect of national growth may be obtained from forecasts of growth in national employment. Similarly, the effect of industry mix can be obtained from industry-specific forecasts. Careful comparative cost analysis based on Weber's location theory will indicate the probable competitive position of a region. By combining these three, one can make forecasts of aggregate growth.

Economic Base Analysis

Theoretical and empirical findings to date all stress the importance of export activity as a determining factor in urban economic growth. Any city within a specialized economy must import to survive, and, to pay for its imports, it must in turn export to other regions. Thus, a basic sector of urban activity will be the production of goods and services for export. Another sector consists of output activity that, because of convenience and comparative cost, will always be local (e.g., retailing and repair services). If the city is in equilibrium, with imports equaling exports and with local (residentiary) output just equaling demand, the question is, on which sector will the equilibrium most depend? Export activity will be the most important, especially in the short run, according to staple or export theory. Urban export activities essentially limit residentiary activities, unless these too become a part of the city's exporting base. Fluctuation in the level of urban exports is a prime cause of changes in urban economic activity. Consequently, forecasts of urban economic activity may be based on multipliers which relate residentiary activities to exports.

In economic base analysis, certain activities are classified as exogenous. These comprise the export industries whose fortunes are determined by forces outside the city or region. All other industries are classified as endogenous or residentiary. The fortunes of these industries are determined by internal forces which can be represented by a multiplier linking the export sector to total regional activity. This multiplier is estimated by observing historical relationships between export activity and total regional activity. Then, given estimates of the future magnitude of export activity, application of the multiplier will yield a forecast of the total regional activity.

In a simple economic model, we have:

$$Y_r = f(Y_t) \qquad (2)$$

and

$$Y_t = Y_r + E$$

where: Y_t = total urban or regional employment or income

Y_r = employment or income in the residentiary (local, endogenous, "nonbasic") sector

E = employment or income in the export (exogenous, "basic") sector

In its most elementary form, economic base analysis hypothesizes simple homogeneous relationships expressing the level of residentiary activity as a constant proportion, k, of the total, i.e.:

$$Y_r = kY_t$$

so that:
$$Y_t = \left(\frac{1}{1-k}\right)E = mE$$

and so that m, the multiplier, $\dfrac{1}{1-k} = \dfrac{1}{1-\left(\dfrac{Y_r}{Y_t}\right)}$

$$= \frac{Y_t}{E} = \frac{Y_r + E}{E} = 1 + \frac{Y_r}{E}$$

The weaknesses of this type of analysis are many and well known. There are difficulties in allocating activities to the export and residentiary sectors. External money flows into a region are generally unaccounted for. The handling of indirect effects is unclear. The basic/nonbasic multiplier mixes economic concepts and thereby cuts across the conventional Keynesian multipliers. The sensitivity to fluctuation of an export base will be greater, the smaller the area. In relatively large areas, the multiplier will approximate that of the nation. (This suggests the importance of finding the appropriate size of region for base analysis.) There is some contradiction in the logic of base analysis and shift analysis. Base analysis projects the base and then applies the resulting rate to the residentiary sectors. Shift analysis develops separate rates of change for both basic and residentiary functions. Thompson's "ratchet effect" shows that once a city has reached a given size, its continued growth may be assured apart from the original base, through innovation of new bases.

Intersectoral Input-Output Analysis (Area Accounts and Multipliers)

A logical extension of economic base analysis is input-output analysis, which provides a complete structural description of the transactions taking place within a region during some period and which links each intermediate flow among sectors of the regional economy to exogenous demand.

Consider the economic system to be made up of n sectors. The sectors may be arrayed in a double-entry table, each sector appearing on the column side as a purchaser of goods and services from the other sectors and on the row side as a supplier of products to other sectors. The conventional ordering is to put the n sectors in the first rows and columns of the matrix and to reserve the last columns for the so-called "final sectors": household expenditures, government purchases, private capital formation, and exports. These final sectors are often treated as exogenous parts of the model.

The array appears as follows:

Supplying Sectors	*Purchasing Sectors* 1	2	3	. . . n	*Final Demand Sectors* Y_i ($i = 1, 2, \ldots, m$)	*Total Output*
1	x_{11}	x_{12}	x_{13}	x_{1n}	Y_1	$X_{1.}$
2	x_{21}	x_{22}	x_{23}	x_{2n}	Y_2	$X_{2.}$
3	x_{31}	x_{32}	x_{33}	x_{3n}	Y_3	$X_{3.}$
.	.	.	.	.	.	.
.	.	.	.	.	.	.
.	.	.	.	.	.	.
n	x_{n1}	x_{n2}	x_{n3}	x_{nn}	Y_n	$X_{n.}$
V_j	V_1	V_2	V_3	V_n	—	—
Total	$X_{.1}$	$X_{.2}$	$X_{.3}$	$X_{.n}$	—	—

In the array x_{ij} is the sales of sector i to sector j, V_i is the value added by sector i, and $X_{i.}$ is the total sales of sector i.

This accounting system displays consistency because of the following balance conditions:

1. *Row balances:* When total output is measured, operationally, in value terms $X_i p_i$ (where p_i is price per unit), the following relationship exists:

$$X_{i.}p_i = \sum_{j=1}^{n} x_{ij}p_i + y_i p_i$$

2. *Column balances* (similar to row balances):

$$X_{.i}p_i = \sum_{i=1}^{n} x_{ij}p_i + v_i$$

3. *Over-all balance:*

$$X_{.i} = X_{i.}$$

As in economic base analysis, it is then assumed that the amount of goods and services delivered by any sector i to the other sectors is a linear and homogeneous function of the output levels of the purchasing sectors j. That is,

$$x_{ij}p_i = a_{ij}X_{.j}p_j$$

where the coefficients a_{ij}, calculated in some time period t as

$$a_{ij} = \frac{x_{ij}p_i}{X_{.j}p_j}$$

represent the *direct* requirement of the products of any sector i per unit of output of any other purchasing sector j.

Assuming that the entire $n \times n$ system A of technical coefficients a_{ij} remains constant through time, then one can write, for the $n \times n$ intersectoral portion of the input-output array X plus the vectors representing the final sectors Y:

$$X = AX + Y$$

which becomes:

$$Y = (I - A)X$$

where I is an $n \times n$ identity matrix.

Furthermore: $X = (I - A)^{-1}Y$

The coefficients in the matrix $(I - A)^{-1}Y$ represent the *direct plus indirect* requirements of the products of any sector i per unit of final demand for the products of any other sector j. Thus, the output level of each productive sector is related to the final demand for finished products supplied by all other sectors, and the elements of $(I - A)^{-1}$ are multipliers in the intersectoral case analogous to the multiplier $m = 1/(1 - k)$ used in the two-sector economic base analysis described earlier.

Input-output analysis is usually applied by forecasting exogenously the levels of final demand. The application of the multiplier matrix $(I - A)^{-1}$ to these levels yields estimates of the gross output of each producing sector required to meet the direct (export) and derived (endogenous, including residentiary) demand originating with the initial increase in each final demand specified.

The problems of this kind of analysis are many. Some are similar to those of economic base analysis. Data on interindustry flows are scarce. Linear homogeneous relationships do not necessarily obtain, and technical coefficients may well be unstable through time. Production functions may be irregular, stepped, or "lumpy," rather than continuous over time. On the other hand, the input-output method of analysis is more general than the economic base method. It provides specific multipliers for each industry. Hence, when used in the correct context, it may provide findings of considerable value.

Interregional, Intersectoral Input-Output Analysis

Intersectoral input-output analysis may be extended to interregional models. Where there are R regions for which regional detail is needed for the forecasts, the matrix of technical coefficients is $Rn \times Rn$, with cells $x_{si,tj}$, representing the direct requirements of the products of sector i in region s per unit of output of purchasing sector j in region t. Final demand vectors are thus disaggregated by sector and region (they might represent an area divided into subregions, or a nation into regions). However, one may still write:

$$X = (I - a_{si,tj})^{-1}Y$$

so that exogenous forecasts of final demands produce estimates of the required production levels of every industry i in all regions s.

In general, because of the unavailability of data on interregional, intersectoral flows, this method of analysis is seldom likely to be operational. It has all of the problems associated with the simpler single-region intersectoral models, which, of course, involve nothing more, for the large area or nation than the "collapse" over-all regions of the $Rn \times Rn$ matrix (i.e., $x_{si,tj}$) to the $n \times n$ matrix (x_{ij}), plus additional problems resulting from regional detail. At the national level, arguments for short-run stability of technical coefficients can be made because they are tied to the current technology and prices. But at the regional level, stability also implies that the ratio of regionally produced intermediate flows to imported flows remains stable at different levels of demand. The technical coefficients and multipliers in an interregional model are blends of conventional technical coefficients and interregional trade coefficients. The stability of trade coefficients in particular is open to question. On the other hand, compared with simple economic base analysis and the intersectoral model, interregional input-output analysis has the advantage of making it possible to estimate not only the total impact of a given change (as in economic base analysis) and the industrial composition of that impact (achieved, for a single region, by intersectoral input-output analysis), but also the regional location of the impact. A capability is thus provided for estimating regional impacts within the context of national growth forecasts or goals.

Regional, intersectoral, input-output models have been prepared for single cities such as St. Louis and Philadelphia, and for states such as California and Iowa. Little attention has been paid to developing a consistent set of models to blanket all regions of the United States simultaneously. Additional information needed to reflect regional variations includes:

1. Differences in production techniques
2. Differences in regional consumption functions
3. Differences in estimates of regional sales to final demand sectors
4. Variations in sources of supply, by sector, for each region

But the formulation of the model involves a questionable assumption: inputs for a given sector in one region require fixed proportions of output from other sectors in other regions. Changes in the shape of the space economy and changes in regional flows might constrain the use of the model to short-run applications. Leontief and Isard have attempted to solve this problem.[15] In their "balanced models," the solution involves three steps:

1. Solving a national input-output table for all sectors exogenous to the regions into which the nation is to be divided.
2. Allocating the national output among regions (Leontief assumed this to be in the same proportions as in the past).
3. Given estimates of regional final demand, solving for each region to obtain total regional production, including residentiary output.

Isard has proposed gravity models as a means of allocating output among regions.

A variant is provided by Chenery's model for the Italian economy.[16] Input-output matrices are provided for the nation and for each region. A region's supply coefficients for each commodity are the fraction of total input furnished by each of the other regions, so that there is a single trade coefficient for each region by particular type of commodity imported. The assumption is that if imports of a commodity are needed as inputs by regional industries, the proportion of imports of the commodity will be the same for all industries in the region.

Each of these may be subjected to the same general order of criticism. However, it is worth noting John Meyer's general conclusions about the utility of this form of analysis:

> The fact still remains that with all its problems and difficulties input-output does have the advantage of being an empirically workable model that provides an organizational framework and set of consistency checks that are difficult to achieve with less formal techniques. The danger does exist . . . that preoccupation with the empirical detail involved in establishing these models may lead to an oversight of importance . . . that . . . leads to grossly inaccurate results . . . . Still this is not an intrinsic shortcoming of the model as such . . . [but] a question of what constitutes a proper allocation of research resources in regional analysis. . . . Finally, it must be recognized that input-output and economic base analyses, with all their short-comings and deficiencies, are the tools most invariably relied upon at the present time when actual empirical work in regional economics must be performed.[17]

Econometric Models

The central ideas of input-output social accounting tables can be incorporated into models comprising sets of equations that can be used to study the evolution of the regional economy.

One example was developed for the Iowa economy by Wilbur Maki.[18] It comprises fifty major equations showing the chain of events from capital consumption and labor utilization to the disposition of business income among households, government, and business. Of the fifty main equations, twenty disaggregated into as many as seven subequations (one for each of seven sectors in an abbreviated interindustry transactions table), so that the complete model consists of some 170 equations. These equations are connected sequentially. Some constituent variables are affected by current conditions, whereas others are predetermined for any given year either on the basis of the previous year's activity or by forecasting from national or regional phenomena that lie entirely outside the influence of State policies and programs. Running this model on a computer, Maki produced a yearly series of estimates for variables of interest, constructed a 1974 social accounts table, estimated year-to-year effects of changes in labor productivity and market demand, and explored the regional implications of changes in government expenditures and receipts in relation to changes in the distribution of business incomes, resource productivity, and market shares of export industries.

Econometric models of the kind developed by Maki to study the economy of Iowa will play an increasing role in regional analysis for several reasons. They draw on and use the essential ideas and methods of the simpler forecasting procedures. Yet they order these methods sequentially so that the regional growth process may be seen as it takes place through time, and as growth itself modifies the parameters of subequations and accounting schemes.

Simulation Models

The models discussed so far are deterministic. No allowance was made for a range of possible outcomes and for random disturbances of the growth process. Sometimes complicated models which contain probability distributions are called "simulation models." The geologist who uses a sandpile to show how fluvial erosion works is in a sense using a simulation model. An econometric model, since it replicates a growth process, is also a simulation model. We frequently reserve the term "simulation" for models which admit to the high "noise" level of social and economic life. Simulation models, then, may incorporate time-dependent probability processes in which the distributions of probable outcomes are specified. Solutions may be achieved in a Monte Carlo fashion: a random number is selected which prescribes an outcome from among the possible outcomes as arrayed in a probability distribution. A sequence of such choices, with later decisions in part a function of earlier choices, simulates the process being considered.

Urban economists are turning to the development of simulation models more rapidly than are economists concerned with regional problems. However, several significant applications of simulation models analysis to regional studies could be cited.[19]

DEVELOPMENTAL PROGRAMMING

Forecasting procedures can be used to predict probable regional growth, and, in a larger spatial framework, to indicate viable and lagging areas and to reveal meaningful growth matrices. With these procedures, the research worker can replicate growth processes. Forecasts made on the basis of different sets of assumptions about investment patterns, for example, can facilitate the study of the costs and benefits of the alternatives. Yet, they cannot tell the research worker what investment patterns meet given sets of goals and lead to optimal use of funds, or whether welfare aims are realized in the achievement of some economic optimum.

For optimizing the level of relevant decision variables, we turn to programming procedures. According to Meyer, "mathematical programming is without question the best of the tools employed in modern regional analysis from a strictly conceptual point of view if one believes in a reasonably pervasive economic rationality."[20] Two illustrative examples, discussed below, are the Heady-Skold spatial programming of agricultural locations, showing how optimal interregional allocations may be achieved, and the Spiegelman-Baum-Talbot activity analysis of a small rural region, which exemplifies the evaluation of multiple policy objectives.[21]

Spatial Programming

Heady and Skold studied five agricultural systems that compete for use of the land of the United States—wheat, feedgrain rotations, feedgrain-soybean rotations, soybeans, and cotton. They calculated the production costs of each system in each of 144 producing areas, the yields of each, and the land available for each kind of production. They then made a forecast for 1975. Using a projected population of the United States of 230,000,000 and assuming real incomes would be 50 per cent higher than they are now, they computed consumption requirements at that time in thirty-one consuming areas of the United States (each of which is a group of four or five producing areas). Transport costs for each crop to each consuming area from each producing area were also calculated.

They then sought to determine the production and interregional trade pattern of each of the five activities that would meet 1975 demands, while simultaneously minimizing joint costs of agricultural production, processing, and transportation. Relatively straightforward application of linear programming to the spatial allocation and trading problem which had been posed provided the answers. Maps of production patterns and trade flows were created. Required withdrawals of land from production were specified.

The over-all model comprises 401 equations and 1,925 variables, excluding "slack" vectors. The equations include 144 total land area restraints, 105 soybean area land restraints, 58 cotton area land restraints, and 94 area demand restraints. The 1,925 column vectors in the coefficient matrix include 134 for wheat production, 144 for feedgrain production, 105 for feedgrain-soybean production, 105 for soybean production, 58 for cotton production, 31 for transforming wheat to feed grain, 549 each for wheat and feedgrain transportation, and 430 for oilmeal production.

Major problems encountered by the authors included data accumulation, computer capacity, and, conceptually, the fact that regional demands are given rather than determined endogenously in terms of prescribed consumption functions. The analysis resulted in the specification of optimum production patterns and trade flows of the various crops and total and regional land requirements and surpluses.

Activity Analysis

In the study by Spiegelman, Baum, and Talbot, a highly disaggregated form of linear programming was used to determine, for a five-county area incorporating a small trade center and its tributary region, the following:

1. The amount of outside financing needed to achieve the planned increase in income and consumption.
2. The mix of new manufacturing and agricultural activities that would achieve these increases with the least cost in outside financing.
3. The best techniques of production to employ where alternative techniques are available.
4. The amount of technological change required in existing economic sectors, especially agriculture.
5. The amount of labor, of different levels of skill, required for the plan, and any shortage or surplus in the local labor force.
6. The amount of local capital formation required.
7. The variations in the costs and content of the plan that would result from varying the assumptions concerning outmigration.

A ten-year time span was selected for the development analysis, and the model was stated in terms of planning increases in production above existing levels to meet targets of increased income and consumption, with the assumption of equilibrium at full use of capital.

The core of the model is an input-output matrix for alternative economic activities. The authors use alternative technologies, alternative scales, and joint products to enrich the model.

To run the model, targets for population, income, and local consumption in the tenth year were given, together with size and composition of the local labor force, constraints on natural resource use, and export demand. The model estimates income generated by the development program, activities to be included, net foreign balance on capital and current accounts, fixed investment required by industry and government, and the labor surplus and deficit by type.

The model has 586 columns (activities) and 239 rows (balance equations). Of the 586 columns, 339 represent real activities (manufacturing, 62; agricultural production, 32; agricultural conversion, 13; other production, 15; export activities, 129; and import activities, 88. The remaining 247 columns represent "slack" variables. Of the 239 rows, 115 are equations showing flows of commodities, and 124 are "dummy" equations for exports. The solution obtained minimized total foreign funds required for the program, while achieving targets subject to the constraining goals and targets for population and income. This emphasized what the authors believed to be the scarcest resource in a depressed area: capital. To the extent that this is not the relevant criterion for a region seeking to grow, this may be the major limitation in applying the resulting estimates. The solution was forced into the competitive range by assigning appropriate prices to import and export activities.

In evaluating their results, the authors found many important implications for public policy formulation in the five-county study area. The results provided the basis for determining the magnitude of capital requirements for the proposed plan, suggested the need for shifting developmental goals, and indicated a scarcity of skilled labor and managerial personnel. The authors considered the "activity-analysis" planning model to be extremely useful, and pointed out the need for obtaining solutions under varying economic conditions and resource structures to learn more about the sensitivity of the planning requirements. They saw that, in the long run, the very high costs of preparing matrices of technical coefficients could be spread over many studies, because technological requirements are liable to be constant over many areas for industries of similar scale. Further, they pointed out the flexibility provided by the method in evaluating requirements of alternative goals.

With such programing techniques, it is clear that one can come closer to satisfying the requirements of regional policymakers for information than is possible with other techniques. Furthermore, these techniques can be used either in an interregional context, as was done by Heady and Skold, or to provide detailed estimates of capital requirements and the like of small urban regions, properly defined, as was done by Spiegelman, Baum, and Talbot.

Moreover, above and beyond immediate value to the policymaker, it should be clear that an impressive arsenal of technique is available to the urban geographer who wants to understand the complexities of urban and regional development processes and their relationships to national growth. (The student who wishes to progress rapidly to the research frontiers of the field will find it necessary to master at the very minimum the theory and methods touched upon briefly in this aside.)

FOOTNOTES TO CHAPTER 4

1. Anthony Scott, "Policy for Declining Regions: A Theoretical Approach," *Areas of Economic Stress in Canada*, eds. W. D. Wood and R. S. Thoman (Kingston: Queens University Centre for Industrial Relations, 1965), pp. 73–93.

2. See John S. Chipman, "A Survey of the Theory of International Trade," *Econometrica*, XXXIII, No. 4 (December, 1965), 477–519.

3. Eli Heckscher, "The Effect of Foreign Trade on the Distribution of Income," *Readings in the Theory of International Trade*, eds. H. S. Ellis and L. A. Metzler (Philadelphia: Blakiston Co., 1949), pp. 272–300.

4. Bertil Ohlin, *Interregional and International Trade* (Cambridge, Mass.: Harvard University Press, 1933).

5. A. A. Alchian, "Uncertainty, Evolution and Economic Theory," *Journal of Political Economy*, LXIII, No. 2 (June, 1950), 211–21.

6. For a more detailed discussion, see W. Isard, *Location and Space Economy* (New York: John Wiley & Sons, Inc., 1956); and R. M. Lichtenberg, *One Tenth of a Nation* (Cambridge, Mass.: Harvard University Press, 1959).

7. Walter Christaller, *The Central Places of Southern Germany* (Englewood Cliffs, N. J.: Prentice-Hall, Inc., 1966); and August Lösch *The Economics of Location* (New Haven: Yale University Press, 1954).

8. Peter Hall, ed., *Von Thünen's Isolated State* (London: Pergamon Press, 1966); Edgar S. Dunn, Jr., *The Location of Agricultural Production* (Gainesville, Fla.: University of Florida Press, 1954); and William Alonso, *Location and Land Use* (Cambridge, Mass.: The M. I. T. Press, 1964).

9. For a more detailed discussion, see W. A. Mackintosh, "Innis on Canadian Economic Development," *Journal of Political Economy*, LXI, No. 2 (June, 1953), 185–94.

10. Scott, "Policy for Declining Regions," p. 78.

11. Karl A. Fox and T. Krishna Kumar, "Delineating Functional Economic Areas," eds. Wilbur R. Maki and Brian J. L. Berry, *Research and Education for Regional and Area Development* (Ames, Ia.: Iowa State University Press, 1966), pp. 13–55.

12. See Wilbur Thompson, *A Preface to Urban Economics* (New York: John Wiley & Sons, Inc., 1965).

13. See Lowell D. Ashby, *Regional Change in a National Setting* (U. S. Department of Commerce, Staff Working Paper No. 7, 1964); and John M. Matilla, *A Methodology of Comparative Analysis of Regional Growth: Some Technical Notes* (U. S. Department of Commerce, Staff Working Paper No. 8, 1964).

14. John Matilla, "A Regional Interaction Unemployment-Migration Model" (Unpublished manuscipt, Office of Business Economics, U. S. Department of Commerce, 1965).

15. Walter Isard et al., *Methods of Regional Analysis* (Cambridge, Mass.: The Technology Press, 1960).

16. Hollis B. Chenery, *The Structure and Growth of the Italian Economy* (Rome: U. S. Mutual Security Agency, 1953).

17. John R. Meyer, "Regional Economics: A Survey," *American Economic Review*, LIII, No. 1 (January, 1963), 19–54.

18. Wilbur R. Maki and Brian J. L. Berry, eds., *Education and Research for Regional and Area Development* (Ames, Ia.: Iowa State University Press, 1965).

19. See the May, 1965, issue (XXXI, No. 2) of the *Journal of the American Institute of Planners* for examples of the use of both econometric and simulation models in forecasting the growth of urban regions.

20. Meyer, "Regional Economics," p. 53.

21. Earl O. Heady and Melvin D. Skold, "Analyses to Specify the Regional Distribution of Farm Production," in Maki and Berry, *Regional and Urban Development;* Robert G. Spiegelman, E. L. Baum, and L. E. Talbot, *Application of Activity Analysis to Regional Development Planning*, Department of Agriculture, Technical Bulletin No. 1339 (Washington, D. C.: U. S. Government Printing Office, 1965).

CHAPTER 5

types of cities and the study of urban functions

National development processes lead to differences in regional growth patterns as a result of the historical sequence of growth, differences in local resources, and consequent differences in the industry mixes of regions. In turn, cities within each region are made up of a series of "layers" reflecting the initial epoch of regional growth and the subsequent competitive position of the region. Because, in turn, differing economic bases support different mixtures of social groups and classes, distinctive types of cities with markedly different outlooks develop in different regions, creatures of their varying growth histories and resource orientations.[1]

It is thus important to review what has been learned in one of the more important traditional fields of urban geography—*functional town classification*—which deals with the structure and distribution of urban functions, to provide a basis for exploring other facets of the distinctiveness of different types of cities later in the book.

*FUNCTIONAL TOWN CLASSIFICATION**

The functions of towns have been investigated within a number of conceptual frameworks, including central place theory[2] and the urban economic base.[3] It might be asserted that the geographical study of urban functions is well accommodated within these two frameworks, but if this claim is accepted, it becomes necessary to explain the need for functional classifications of towns. Such studies abound in the geographical literature,[4] and apparently are accepted as a legitimate part of the field of urban geography.[5] No problem is posed, of course, if the functional classifications are concerned with identifying

*Reprinted from Robert H. T. Smith, "Method and Purpose in Functional Town Classification," *Annals of the Association of American Geographers*, LV, No. 3 (September, 1965), 539–48, with the permission of the author and editor.

spatial regularities in the distribution and structure of urban functions. But after a thorough review of a large number of these studies, one is drawn to the conclusion that specific geographic objectives—or, for that matter, objectives in general—usually are difficult to discern in the statements of purpose appearing in functional classifications of towns.[6] The following is a typical example: "The purpose of this paper is to contribute to a better understanding of the functions of Japanese urban settlements."[7]

Wilson justly complains that:

> With a limited number of exceptions [and I suspect Wilson errs on the side of generosity by allowing *any* exceptions] the service or functional classifications of urban areas so popular among geographers over the last fifteen years have proved to be ends in themselves rather than points of departure for further research into the character of urban settlements.[8]

This lament has been summarized succinctly by Duncan and his co-authors of *Metropolis and Region*, who write that "the purposes for which functional classifications are designed are seldom made explicit, and often-times little is done with them after they are finished."[9]

Since these studies ostensibly are concerned with a feature of towns, the explanation of whose distribution and structure is sought through at least two other conceptual approaches, surely it is not too much to expect more of them than the pedagogic objective apparent in such criticisms as Wilson's and embodied in such statements of purpose as Watanabe's.

A second feature that becomes apparent on review is the bewildering array of methodologies that has been employed to group towns into functional classes. Too often it appears that a major purpose of these studies (if not *the* major purpose) has been the development and presentation of a different classificatory methodology as an end in itself. Indeed, Duncan and his co-authors were prompted to remark that:

> In examining representative studies in functional classification one is impressed by the apparent complexity of the detailed criteria by which cities are grouped into types or categories, the variation of these criteria from one study to another, and the consequent variation in results.[10]

The wide selection of functional classifications of towns clearly needs to be reviewed,[11] paying close attention to methodology and objectives. . . .

The Methodology of Functional Town Classification

At the outset a distinction should be made between *qualitative* and *quantitative* methods,[12] to separate those approaches using precise numerical data from those which do not. Of the qualitative classification schemes, Aurousseau's is doubtless the best known.[13] Through what must have been a combination of general observation and logical deduction, Aurousseau postulated six urban functions: administration; defense; culture; production; communication; and recreation. He noted that while a combination of these functions was performed by any given city, one function usually tended to overshadow the rest. Thus he enunciated the concept of functional differentiation and specialization.[14] A similar approach, with a marked emphasis on the evolution of towns and the importance of physical site factors, has been adopted by several subsequent workers,[15] although Trewartha's discussion of the functions of Chinese cities used fewer categories,[16] and Hance's recent study of tropical African cities related function explicitly to location.[17] The basic weakness of this approach is encountered when one tries to decide, *from general observation*, whether a particular town belongs in one category or another; but in all fairness it should be noted that when precise data are unavailable, there is simply no alternative to this approach.

Studies employing quantitative standards of classification are far more numerous. On the assumption that the occupational or industrial structure of a town's labor force reflects those economic, political, and social activities in which the residents of the town engage, industry employment or occupational data[18] have been manipulated in various ways to establish groups of towns with similar functional specializations. "Specialization" implies an amount or proportion of the labor force in a given industry category which exceeds by a certain margin some predetermined minimum level.[19] In answer to Nelson's question, "How large a percentage of the labor force must be employed in a particular service [function] to make the performance of the service far enough above normal to warrant separate classification?"[20] one finds that there is agreement on neither the magnitude of these threshold values nor on the methods of their selection. For example, classification as a manufacturing city was effected in three different studies as follows:

1. In the now classic analysis of American cities by Harris, 30 per cent or more of the employed labor force (occupational figures) in manufacturing was required.[21]
2. In contrast, Nelson's service classification of American cities set 43.11 per cent (the urban-complex average, 27.07 per cent, plus one standard deviation, 16.04 per cent) as the minimum proportion of the labor force indicating manufacturing specialization.[22]
3. In Aagesen's analysis of Danish towns, 50 per cent of the active labor force in manufacturing was accepted as the critical threshold.[23]

These studies illustrate admirably three different methods of selecting threshold values for a classification, on the basis: of (1) the occupational structure of (intuitively) well-defined types of cities; (2) arithmetic means or some other statistically defined quantity; or (3) arbitrary majority quantities, often, though not always, 50 per cent.

In the first method, functional specialization is identified by a concentration of the labor force in a particular employment or occupational category; threshold values are determined "on the basis of an analysis of cities of well recognized types."[24]

In an attempt to exclude local service employment, Harris assigned higher threshold percentages to some functions than to others,[25] a feature which is said to make the consistent application of his method difficult.[26] While concern has been expressed that Harris failed to identify the "well recognized types,"[27] his threshold values have been used with slight modification by numerous writers.[28]

The use of arithmetic means or other statistically defined quantities is appealing because one tends to feel that as such quantities supposedly are representative of the "average" or "normal" city, their use is valid beyond dispute. Indeed, in an examination of some essentially structural characteristics of the labor force of Netherlands towns, Steigenga claimed that "only the average or total of the whole urban society . . . can be used as a measure of comparison."[29] And although Watanabe was equally insistent that "an essentially 'common' or 'average' functional structure of urban settlements should not be assumed,"[30] many writers have interpreted an above-average concentration of the labor force in one industry category as indicative of functional specialization.[31] In some studies, dispersion measures have been employed to identify nonsignificant variations above and below the average.[32] This is, of course, a desirable refinement, but deviation measures frequently involve assumptions about the nature of the distribution of the values to which they are applied which, if not met, can render the results meaningless.[33] Still other classifications identify specialization by the use of medians, quartiles, or deciles, thus relying more on the rank order of the array of values regardless of their size.[34] The intuitive appeal of this method of identifying specialization has already been noted, but one should realize that although the arithmetic mean is a precisely defined quantity, if it is not representative of the values from which it is calculated (that is, if these are many small but a few large values, or vice versa), then it is no less an arbitrary yardstick than a value drawn at random.[35]

The simplest way of identifying so-called single-function towns is to select that industry category in which 50 per cent or some smaller but quite substantial proportion of the labor force is concentrated. This approach is characteristic of many European studies,[36] and when data are available for only three employment categories such as service, manufacturing, and primary (agricultural, etc.) activities (as apparently is often the case in Europe), the classifications frequently are presented on triangular graphs.[37] In a number of these studies an attempt was made to apply the classification only to that proportion of a town's labor force engaged in basic activities, so that identification of the town's *basic* functions was ensured.[38] However, methods of separating basic from nonbasic employment when one is working with census data are still far from satisfactory, and Kosinski (one of the main protagonists of *basic* classifications of towns) refers to the "dangers of subjective classification of the town's labor force into basic and non-basic group [sic]."[39] In addition, the validity of using a standard 50 per cent or similar figure is questionable, especially when it is applied to data representing the number of people rather than the value of their output. This latter objection, however, can be raised against all methods of identifying functional specialization that have been discussed so far.

If the *immediate* purpose of a classification is to divide an array of towns into a series of classes so that functional similarity is maximized within but minimized between the groups, it will not necessarily be achieved through any of the three procedures discussed above. For example, consider a situation where a series of towns is to be classified on the basis of employment in manu-

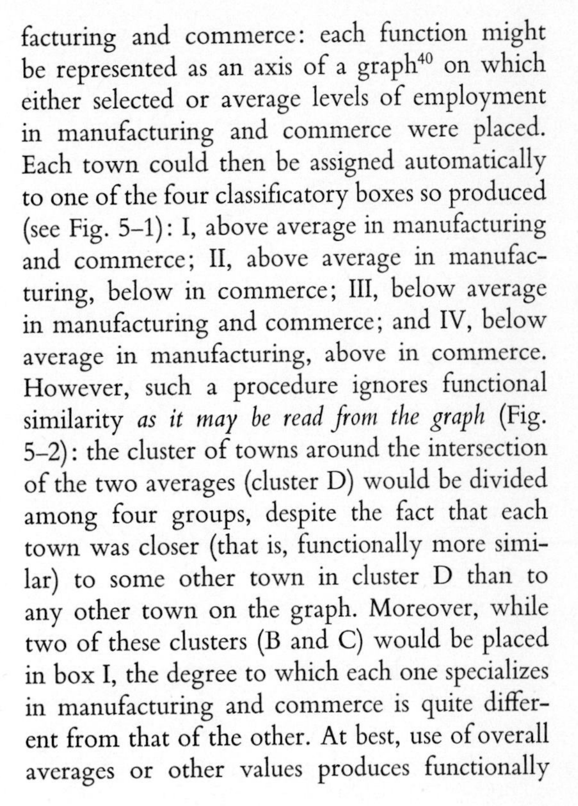

facturing and commerce: each function might be represented as an axis of a graph[40] on which either selected or average levels of employment in manufacturing and commerce were placed. Each town could then be assigned automatically to one of the four classificatory boxes so produced (see Fig. 5–1): I, above average in manufacturing and commerce; II, above average in manufacturing, below in commerce; III, below average in manufacturing and commerce; and IV, below average in manufacturing, above in commerce. However, such a procedure ignores functional similarity *as it may be read from the graph* (Fig. 5–2): the cluster of towns around the intersection of the two averages (cluster D) would be divided among four groups, despite the fact that each town was closer (that is, functionally more similar) to some other town in cluster D than to any other town on the graph. Moreover, while two of these clusters (B and C) would be placed in box I, the degree to which each one specializes in manufacturing and commerce is quite different from that of the other. At best, use of overall averages or other values produces functionally

FIGURE 5–1. Four classificatory boxes created to assign towns to types automatically, using averages. *Source:* Figs. 5–1 and 5–2 are from Robert H. T. Smith, "Method and Purpose in Functional Town Classification," *Annals of the Association of American Geographers*, LV, No. 3 (September, 1965), 539–48.

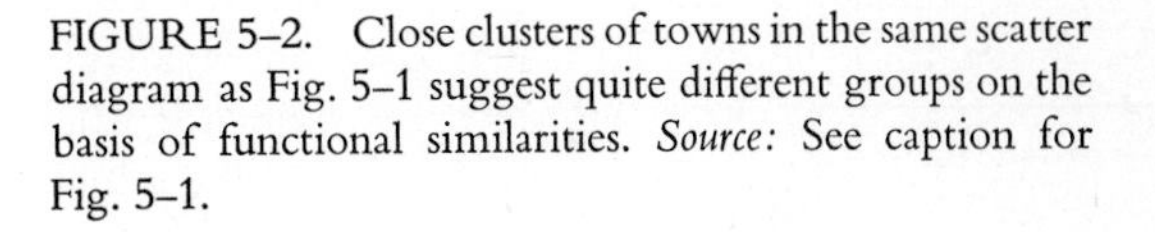

FIGURE 5–2. Close clusters of towns in the same scatter diagram as Fig. 5–1 suggest quite different groups on the basis of functional similarities. *Source:* See caption for Fig. 5–1.

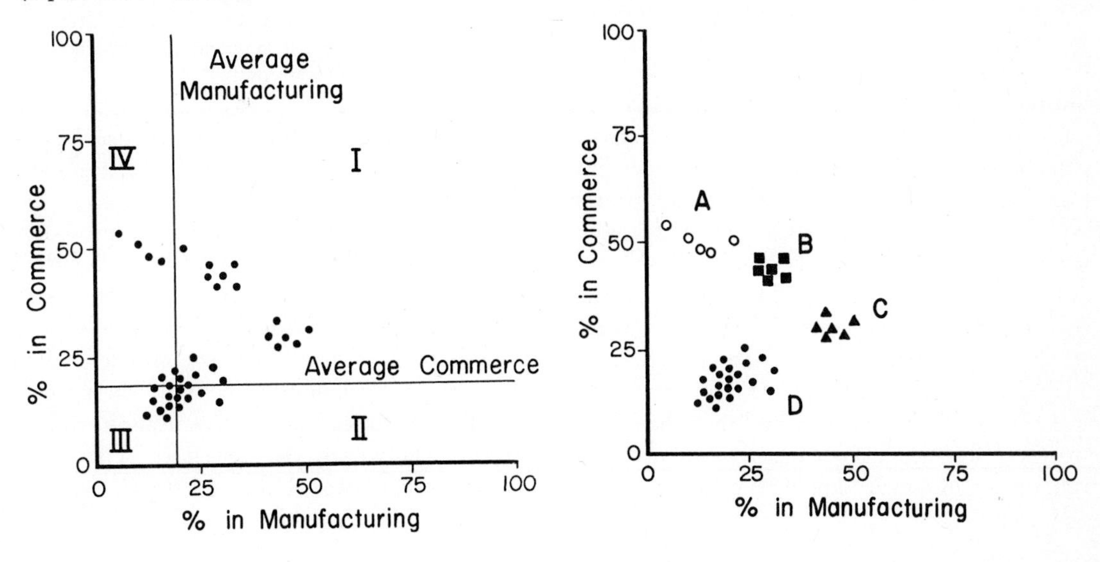

heterogeneous groups; at worst, significant functional combinations may be concealed. It is surprising, to say the least, that le Guen, Enequist, and Tuominen did not attach any real significance to the clusters of points which may be discerned on their triangular graphs, especially as one objective of the analysis of proportions by means of a triangular graph is "to establish the existence or otherwise of groups of similar places [towns] so that some sort of classification can be produced."[41] This was an even greater oversight when one realizes that by plotting the towns with reference to the three sides of the triangle, both the simple graphic representation and the mechanics of clustering on distance proximity are made so much easier because of the absence of the third dimension.

Although this straightforward grouping or classification procedure has been used frequently,[42] the examples given in Figs. 5–1 and 5–2, and even in the triangular graphs, might appear to grossly oversimplify the situation for the simple reason that occupations usually are reported in many more than two or three categories. Certainly the problem of selecting classificatory standards "becomes still more difficult when we undertake different functions together,"[43] but the same clustering principle underlying the examples given above may be applied when data are available for more than three industry categories for each town. In a situation involving m towns for which we have occupational statistics for n industry categories, the $m \times m$ between-town correlation matrix would first be obtained. Cluster or linkage analysis of the $m \times m$ matrix would yield as many groups as there were reciprocal pairs of towns.[44] If a sufficient level of generalization had not then been reached, the process would be repeated, using a measure of between-group similarity such as Mahalanobis' D-square.[45] An alternative approach would involve reducing the n industry categories to their p (where $p < n$) basic sources of variation, by factor analysis. For each of the m towns, a score on the p factors would be obtained, and then the $m \times m$ matrix of distances between each town and every other town in p space would be calculated, using the analogy from Pythagoras' theorem. Groups could then be formed by cluster analysis.[46] The functional characteristics of each group may be identified by noting marked clustering of group members above or below the urban-complex average (or some other acceptable yardstick) for each industry category. In this way, those functions in which a town is specialized or underspecialized, or in which there is no significant concentration (some towns high and some low) may be identified; single and multiple specializations will be obvious, as will those functions which have not played a significant part in allocating towns to the group under consideration.[47] In fact, urban-complex averages seem to be more useful for describing groups of towns derived inductively than as a basis for initial classification.

Other multivariate approaches are available, and while there is nothing sacred about the two presented here, a compelling reason for their use often is the availability of suitable computer programs. It is, however, of cardinal importance that a technique of grouping which allows simultaneous consideration of variation in *all* industry categories (i.e., a multivariate technique) be employed, that averages, "typical" structures, or majority percentages be avoided in the process of classification itself, and that:

> . . . the choice among alternative procedures of functional classification . . . be based primarily on the demonstrated greater relevance or predictive power of one classification in comparison to its alternatives. . . . Considerations of aesthetics, simplicity, convenience, and intuitive appeal should be secondary.[48]

The Objectives of Functional Town Classification

Perhaps more important than mere procedure is the question of purpose, especially if it is agreed that the objectives (other than pedagogic, that is) of the classification should be known *before* it is performed. If the objectives are defined in advance, some relationship between the purpose and the categories of the classification will be ensured.[49] However, the objectives of an overwhelming majority of the functional classifications of towns rarely extend beyond the pedagogic.[50] Geographers usually are content to simply *report* their results verbally and almost always cartographically; Lal noted in his concluding remarks that:

. . . with the exception of four uni-functional cities, all the Indian cities are multifunctional in nature. . . . Accordingly, 12 cities are specialized in two functions, 23 in three, and 28 in four or more functions.[51]

The maps and statements often are accompanied by general observations on the areal location of different functional groups; thus Enequist observed "a certain correlation between the economic character of the Swedish countryside and the type of agglomeration. The industrial areas usually contain industrial centers of all sizes,"[52] and Hart, writing about the functions of cities in the American South, concluded that "*Manufacturing Cities* (M) are concentrated primarily in the Piedmont textile belt."[53]

Indeed, there would be considerable cause for concern if either Enequist or Hart had found manufacturing cities anywhere else but in manufacturing areas, and in the light of observations such as these,[54] the critical comments of Duncan and his co-authors are well deserved:

. . . most of the contributors to the literature on functional specialization have noted broad regional groupings of their functional classes and have offered general interpretations of this form of regional differentiation. . . . Whether the ad hoc rationalization of such vague findings greatly advances the understanding of the location-function nexus may be questioned.[55]

The formidable collection of functional studies that has accumulated over the years attests to the popularity of such studies among geographers. Yet apart from map presentation of their results, there is very little to distinguish them from contributions to this field by workers in other disciplines such as sociology and economics.[56] Conceivably, some students have taken their rationale for functional classifications from statements such as these:

Cities serve manifold functions in the economy and culture of a people. All cities have some functions in common; all cities have some functions that are peculiar to their site and situation, to the people whom they serve; and all cities have some functions peculiar to their development and their history; hence cities may be classified more effectively on the basis of their functions as criteria than perhaps according to any other attribute.[57]

But it is difficult to see why *any* functional classification rather than a classification on some other basis should be more "effective," especially when the purpose for classifying is undefined. As Duncan wrote, "there is little need for yet another functional classification of cities, however ingenious its methodology."[58]

The classification procedure that is adopted should produce groups of towns about which the greatest number, most precise, and most important statements can be made for the *differentiating* and *accessory* characteristics.[59] And more generally, to be justified on other than pedagogic grounds, *any* classification should be relevant to a well-defined problem or class of problems. Thus when towns are classified according to function (the *differentiating* characteristic), we not only want to be able to say something about the function or combination of functions typical of that group; knowledge of membership in any one group should automatically carry with it knowledge of additional characteristics of the towns in that group.[60] It is not difficult to deduce that there are at least two spatial characteristics associated with town functions. First, if we agree that there is some spatial order to the distribution of economic activities in general,[61] then surely we can expect to find distributional characteristics of towns in similar functional classes that are peculiar to those classes. Second, given the notion that function implies at the simplest level a complementary relationship between a town and its hinterland,[62] different functional classes ought to be associated with different types of hinterland areas. Classification of towns by function (the *differentiating* characteristic) might lead to the formulation of generalizations about the location pattern of towns (one *accessory* characteristic) and the relationship between towns with particular functions and their hinterlands (another *accessory* characteristic). Thus functional classifications of towns become relevant to the problems of town distribution and hinterland relationships.

Procedures for the precise description of point distribution patterns are available in statistics based on the average distance to nearest neighbor of the same type.[63] By comparing actual average distance to nearest neighbor with the expected average distance (where the expected distance is calculated from the Poisson function), town distribution patterns may be described precisely as agglomerated, random, or uniform (hexagonal or evenly spaced), thus providing a first approximation to statements on locational and distributional characteristics.[64] Similarly, using the Chi-square distribution, one can test whether the location of group members in different hinterland zones reflects either chance occurrence or a significant concentration.[65] Such an analysis is clearly unnecessary and even inappropriate for groups of towns whose locations coincide with the occurrence of immobile resources and which support extractive industries exploiting these resources (e.g., mining towns).[66] That analyses such as these may require intensive fieldwork to establish the nature and extent of a town's hinterland and detailed statistical analysis to test the relationships observed are essentially procedural matters; a functional classification of towns devoid of these or similar objectives has only a tenuous claim to a legitimate place in the geographic literature.

Admittedly, functional town classifications per se, regardless of the disciplinary affiliations of the author, may be of considerable pedagogic value. Thus it is useful to know that all except four Indian cities are multifunctional in nature,[67] although this piece of information on its own has little, if any, geographical relevance.[68] If geographers are going to employ classification as a tool in the study of urban functions, then the basic principles of classification procedures and objectives should be adhered to; it is no less than absurd to argue that "Geography is not a subject in which the ordinary classifications of science are either possible or desirable."[69]

*EXAMPLE: THE FUNCTIONS OF AUSTRALIAN TOWNS**

While there appear to be grounds for hoping that in the future classifications might provide ordered descriptions *and* a basis for statements about specific geographic problems,[79] there seems merit, therefore, in presenting an example of the modern approach to functional town classification described earlier, if only for pedagogic purposes. Thus, we now turn to a systematic description, by way of example, of the way Australian towns vary in their function. Wherever appropriate, references to spacing and hinterland relationships are made.

Now clearly, many kinds of classifications of Australian towns *could* be constructed, and the example presented here is limited because it focuses upon data that are relevant in the context of contemporary socio-economic theory. In dealing with the growth and location of Australian towns, this choice of data may be apt, but for other purposes another data set might be more appropriate.

The Method Chosen

The assumption was made that the number of people employed in various industry groups gives an accurate indication of the significance of that function in a town. From the 1954 Census of Population[71] data on twelve industry groups in 422 Australian towns (ranging in size from Sydney with 1,863,161 inhabitants to Edithburg in South Australia with a population of 477) were selected (see Table 5–1). These data were recorded initially as percentages of each town's labor force; transformed to standard scores using the appropriate parameters reported in Table 5–1, they provided the raw material for the classification. An expression of functional similarity between each town and every other town was obtained by regarding each town as one of 422

*Reprinted from Robert H. T. Smith, "The Functions of Australian Towns," *Tijdschrift voor Economische en Sociale Geografie*, LVI, No. 3 (May-June, 1965), 81–92.

TABLE 5–1

Selected Parameters of the Proportion of the Labor Force in 12 Classes of Industry in 422 Australian Towns: 1954

Occupational Class	*Mean*	*Standard Deviation*	*Coefficient of Variation*
Primary production	10.01	7.92	.79
Mining and quarrying	3.81	12.60	3.31
Manufacturing	19.02	11.91	.63
Electricity, gas, water and sanitary services	2.15	4.26	1.98
Building and construction	12.12	6.36	.52
Transport and storage	7.41	5.83	.79
Communication	3.05	1.28	.42
Finance and property; Business services	2.46	1.05	.43
Commerce	18.44	5.35	.29
Public authority and professional activities	11.78	5.64	.48
Amusements, hotels, cafes, personal services, etc.	8.16	2.89	.35
Other; Inadequately described; and not stated	1.52	1.10	.72

Source: Census of the Commonwealth of Australia: 30th June, 1954, Vols. I-VI, Part 5; "Population and Occupied Dwellings in Localities" (Canberra: Government Printer, 1955).

variables and each of the twelve industry group standard scores for each town as one of twelve observations. Then, the 422 by 422 matrix of ("variable" or town) simple correlation coefficients contained the desired measures. Linkage analysis on this matrix produced 91 groups of towns, ranging in size from 2 to 17 members.[72] These 91 groups were generalized to 17 groups by clustering the 91 by 91 matrix of Mahalanobis' D^2 measures.[73]

This classification procedure derived an array of mutually exclusive groups of towns such that, in a given group, each member was functionally more similar to another town in that group than to any other town in the urban complex. However, a problem was encountered in identifying the characteristic functional features of each group, and in the absence of an alternative threshold value, the average employment level in each industry category for all 422 towns was adopted as a meaningful quantity (see Table 5–1).[74] The problem was then reduced to observing significant differences between this set of averages and the composite industry structure of the 17 groups of towns. Measures such as the standard deviation were irrelevant because of the nature of the distribution of the industry proportions, and significance tests were similarly invalid because each group could not correctly be regarded as a random sample from the larger population of Australian towns. Eventually, a simple observational procedure was followed: if all or most of the members of a group had proportions of employment in, for example, manufacturing well above the average for all towns, a specialization in the manufacturing function was noted for that group. Conversely, marked clustering below the average value was interpreted as underspecialization. Relatively even distribution of group members both above and below the urban complex averages indicated that the particular industry category in question was relatively unimportant in allocating towns to this particular group. Even though this procedure represented a marked departure from the rigorous research design followed previously, it was considered the most suitable for this particular situation; the underlying reasoning is similar to that employed in identifying the basic dimensions of variation extracted by factor analysis.

Australian Towns Classified

There is a notable tendency in the literature to refer to single-function towns. This feature was evident in Aurousseau's pioneering work, and has persisted in many subsequent studies,[75] so that it has become commonplace to speak of "manufacturing towns," "resort towns," and "trade towns."[76] For Australian towns, this characteristic proved to be more the exception than the rule and, for example, of three groups of towns specialized in manufacturing employment, only one was notably underspecialized in all other industry categories. In the presentation of the results of the classification, subheads such as manufacturing, transportation, and mining will

TABLE 5–2

Average Within-Group Proportions of Employment in 12 Classes of Industry in 422 Australian Towns: 1954

Group Number	Descriptive Title	Number of Towns	Total Inhabitants per Group	Percentage of Total Inhabitants of 422 towns	Primary Production	Mining and Quarrying	Manufacturing	Electricity, Gas, Water, Sanitary Services	Building and Construction	Transport and Storage	Communication	Finance, Property, Business	Commerce	Public Authority and Professional	Amusements, Hotels, Cafes, Personal Services	Unidentified
422	Australian Towns				10.01	3.81	19.02	2.15	12.12	7.41	3.05	2.46	18.44	11.78	8.16	1.52
1	Manufacturing	50	634,229	8.99	5.98	1.90	43.03	1.60	9.33	5.64	1.94	1.73	13.48	8.77	5.36	1.40
2	Manufacturing	17	5,045,595	71.50	3.93	0.41	30.16	1.98	10.42	6.92	2.35	3.31	19.46	13.19	6.88	1.06
3	Manufacturing	11	33,278	0.47	9.21	3.86	26.40	1.58	10.00	5.22	3.12	2.55	16.33	11.16	7.56	3.01
4	Service	31	72,612	1.03	16.61	0.38	8.34	1.31	14.29	7.68	3.86	2.57	20.69	11.62	10.99	1.67
5	Service	24	51,940	0.74	16.10	0.29	10.36	1.25	11.43	6.43	3.58	2.76	21.57	11.81	10.50	4.25
6	Service	22	82,041	1.15	7.50	0.33	16.60	1.79	13.14	6.93	4.58	4.06	21.10	13.83	8.82	1.32
7	Service	11	64,610	0.92	8.84	0.14	20.69	1.34	10.96	5.37	2.47	2.63	22.95	12.94	9.62	2.16
8	Service	9	14,205	0.20	8.68	0.23	16.46	1.73	12.17	4.77	5.57	3.29	25.12	12.17	8.92	1.05
9	Service	82	315,219	4.47	8.68	0.49	14.97	1.79	16.48	5.77	3.20	2.99	22.97	12.16	8.86	1.34
10	Resort	19	55,041	0.78	15.57	0.49	13.73	1.73	15.64	5.86	2.40	2.11	18.15	9.25	13.45	1.64
11	Resort	6	35,468	0.50	5.66	0.64	15.30	1.71	13.94	5.35	3.47	3.00	18.85	16.42	14.23	1.13
12	Transport	23	70,213	0.99	6.65	0.51	15.34	1.58	10.55	25.84	2.95	1.68	15.65	10.40	7.25	1.57
13	Communication	15	25,383	0.34	12.97	1.04	18.64	1.66	12.23	8.73	5.60	2.27	16.88	11.22	7.38	1.42
14	Mining	25	148,629	2.11	1.34	50.49	11.64	1.19	4.36	4.59	1.35	0.97	11.16	7.40	4.69	0.84
15	Utilities	15	53,981	0.76	6.60	3.36	16.09	17.41	13.65	6.08	3.45	2.10	16.42	8.40	5.42	1.03
16	Administration	34	299,717	4.24	6.00	0.66	16.53	1.76	10.94	9.43	2.97	2.46	17.65	21.88	8.07	1.32
17	Primary production	28	57,019	0.81	27.91	0.79	18.11	0.96	10.42	5.47	2.42	2.03	14.59	9.23	6.74	1.41

Source: *Census of the Commonwealth of Australia: 30th June, 1954*, Vols. I-VI, Part 5: "Population and Occupied Dwellings in Localities" (Canberra: Government Printer, 1955).

be used, but only in certain instances will these refer to clear-cut cases of single-function towns.

Manufacturing Towns

The three groups of towns recording specialization in manufacturing employment are shown in Fig. 5–3, and the average within-group employment levels are given in Table 5–2. Towns in Group 1 (Fig. 5–3) might be termed "manufacturing" towns proper, as the average employment level in all other occupational categories is well below the average for Australian towns. These within-group averages accurately represent the situation, and for most towns whose levels of employment in given industry categories fall above the over-all averages, there is a valid explanation. For example, Mossman lies well above the primary production average, yet this is a reflection of the importance of sugar cane production and processing in the area.[77] Similarly, the above average proportions in mining and manufacturing at Portland and Kandos are explained by the location of cement producing plants in both towns, which would call for a large labor force in both mining and manufacturing. The group includes such centers of heavy industry as Newcastle, Wollongong, and Whyalla. However, many of the towns are noted for food processing of various kinds: meat-packing establishments are present

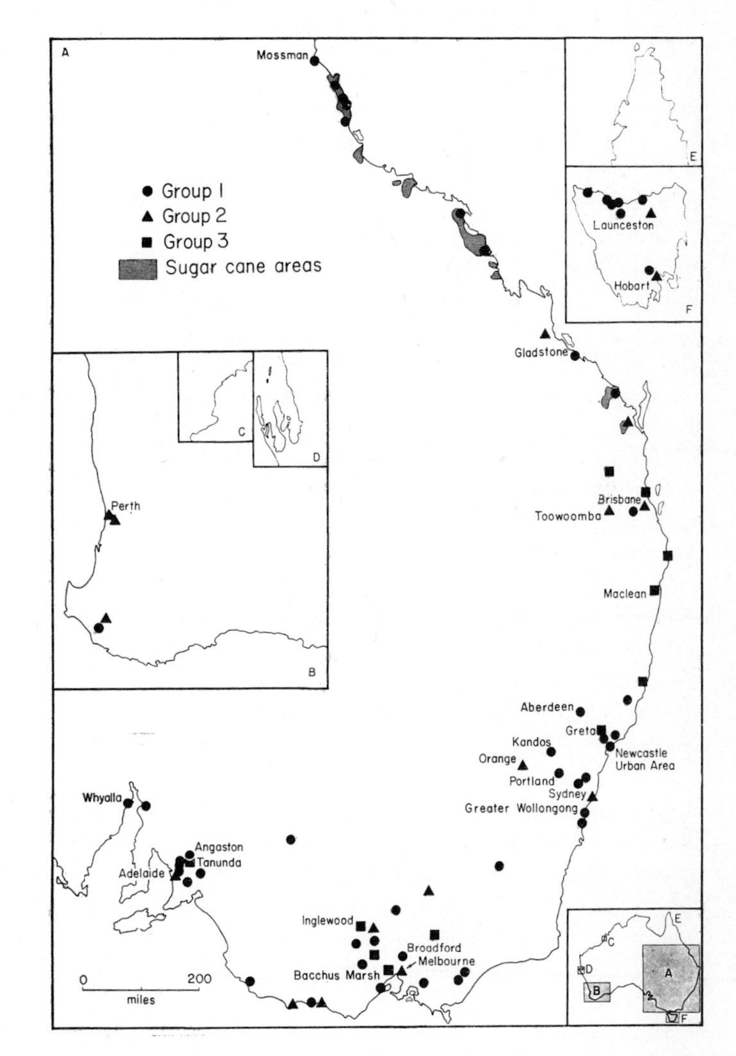

FIGURE 5–3. The manufacturing towns of Australia. *Source:* Figs. 5–3 through 5–8 are from analysis reported in Robert H. T. Smith, "The Functions of Australian Towns," *Tijdschrift voor Economische en Sociale Geografie*, LVI, No. 3 (May-June, 1965), 81–92.

in Aberdeen and Gladstone; Angaston is located in a wine producing area,[78] while a variety of food processing industries is represented in some of the Group 1 towns on Tasmania's northern coast.[79] In addition, textile factories are located in certain country centers (for example, in Broadford).

The 17 towns in Group 2 are markedly different: they have industry specializations in addition to manufacturing and with an average population of almost 300,000, they are consistently larger than Group 1 towns. The fifty members of Group 1 in contrast record a mean population of only 12,700. Included are the state capital cities and some larger country centers such as Launceston, Orange, and Toowoomba. Commercial and administrative functions are here combined with manufacturing, and employment levels in finance and property, commerce, and public authority and professional are well above average (see Table 5–2). As might be expected, there is a marked lack of specialization in primary production and mining.

Group 3 comprises eleven towns which share a manufacturing specialization with Groups 1 and 2, but which are not consistently underspecialized in all other employment classes (like Group 1), and which do not have markedly strong commercial and administrative functions (like Group 2). Some of the towns combine mining activities with manufacturing, as in Greta (coal) and Bacchus Marsh (brown coal); others, such as Tanunda, record a primary production specialization related to the local production of wine.[80] Maclean and Inglewood are anomalous in that the proportion of their labor force engaged in manufacturing is well below both the national average and the general level for the group. It could be that the relatively high proportion of their labor force engaged in primary production was sufficient to allocate them to this group. Most towns cluster below the average for transportation and building and construction employment, but this characteristic is shared with Groups 1 and 2. Although it helps little in interpretation, it is well to note that Group 3 towns record a consistently high proportion in the unidentified category.

There appear to be three groups of manufacturing towns: one group of single function manufacturing towns comprising centers of heavy industry, primary processing and textile manufacturing; a second group of much larger towns where commercial, financial, professional and administrative functions are combined with the manufacturing specialization (most of the members are large port cities which offer obvious advantages to manufacturing industry);[81] a third group of manufacturing towns which display neither an additional specialization in commerce and administration, nor consistent underspecialization in other categories.

Service Towns

Within the limits of the census terminology, it frequently was difficult to select an appropriate name for a number of groups sharing a common employment specialization. This very problem was encountered with Groups 4, 5, and 6 (Fig. 5–4*a*) and Groups 7, 8, and 9 (Fig. 5–4*b*). All six record above average employment levels in commerce (see Table 5–2) but vary considerably in additional specializations and underspecializations, and in population (see Table 5–3). The term "service centers" appeared the most accurate, especially as the manufacturing function was well below average for 5 of the 6 groups (see Table 5–2).

TABLE 5–3

Average Population of Groups of Service Centers

Group	*Mean*	*Standard Deviation*	*Coefficient of Variation*
4	2,131	1,144	0.54
5	2,164	1,628	0.75
6	3,729	3,759	1.01
7	5,874	4,414	0.75
8	1,578	748	0.47
9	3,861	3,257	0.84

Groups 4 and 5 contrasted sharply with the remaining four by possessing—in addition to the commercial function—an above average proportion of their labor force in primary production. A relatively large proportion of the local labor force employed as farm workers could account for this,[82] although there are alternative explanations.[83] There are few cases where employ-

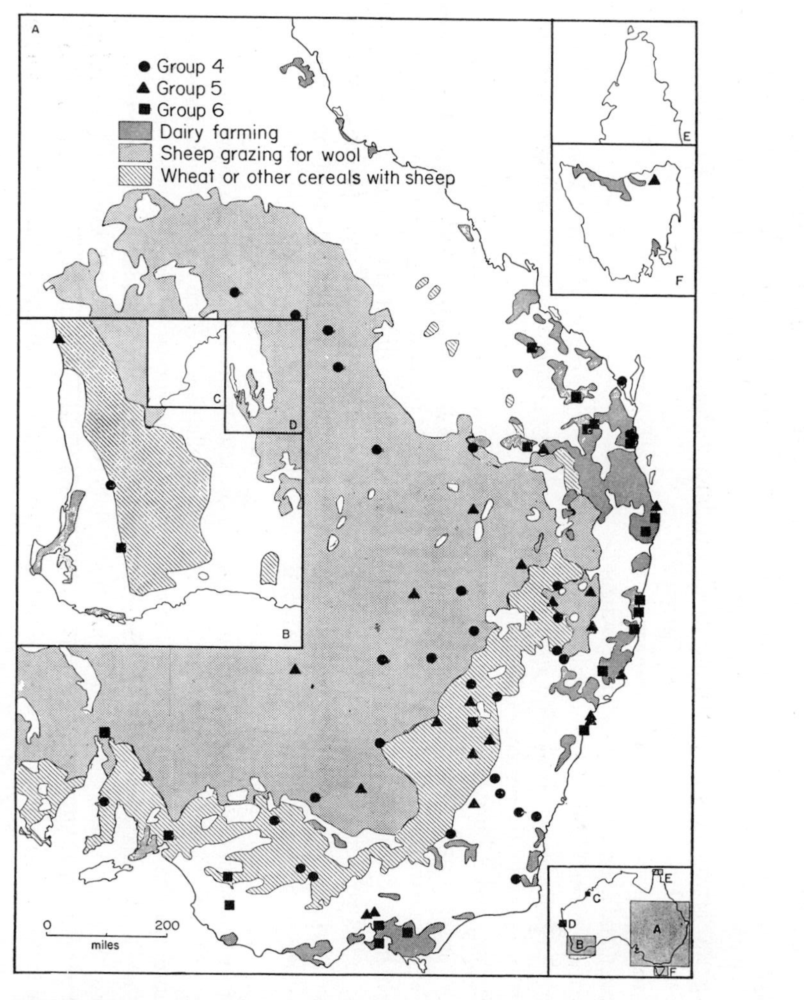

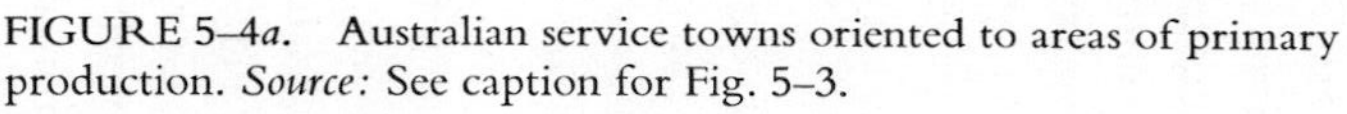

FIGURE 5–4*a*. Australian service towns oriented to areas of primary production. *Source:* See caption for Fig. 5–3.

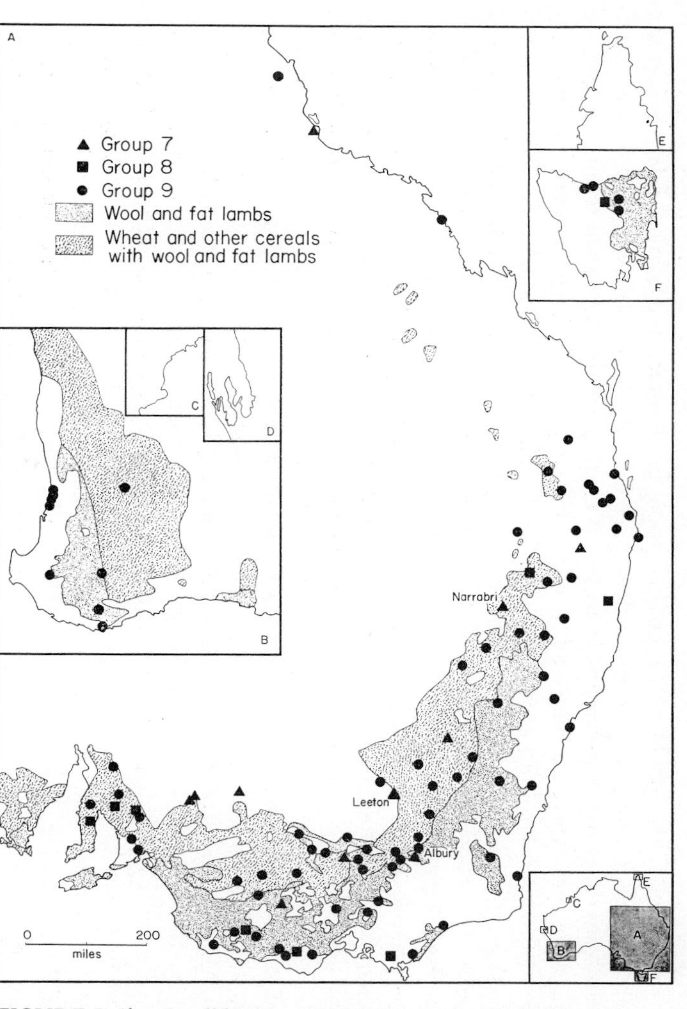

FIGURE 5–4*b*. Small highly specialized service towns (Group 8) and large, more highly diversified service towns (Groups 7 and 9). *Source:* See caption for Fig. 5–3.

ment in forestry or fishing could be responsible for this above average concentration, and in fact most of the towns in Group 4 are located in areas of mixed sheep and wheat farming and wool production (see Fig. 5–4*a*). Both groups are well above average in employment in amusements, hotels, cafes, and personal service, but have few further distinguishing characteristics.

The twenty-two towns in Group 6—on the average larger than those just discussed—also seem best described as service centers, but the primary production specialization noted for Groups 4 and 5 is here replaced by an emphasis on financial, public authority, and professional functions. Most of these towns are located in the intensive dairy farming areas in eastern Australia, and have a peculiar combination of commercial and service functions characteristic of large towns with a productive hinterland.

Groups 7 and 9 in Fig. 5–4*b* are considerably larger than the 77 service towns already discussed (see Table 5–3) and may be expected to provide a greater range and variety of goods and services. In both groups, employment in primary production is below average, a generalization which is supported with relatively few exceptions after examining the actual values in relation to the national means. However, these two groups contrast markedly in terms of manufacturing employment, and in fact, the average employment in manufacturing in Group 7 (comprising predominantly large towns: cf. Tables 5–3 and 5–2) is reflecting, for example, the presence of flour milling at Narrabri and Albury, and fruit and vegetable canning at Leeton. While employment in building and construction in towns in Group 9 is much higher than for Group 7, professional and administrative functions are much more pronounced in Group 7 than in Group 9, perhaps because of the greater availability of educational and medical services in larger centers. The tendency for the towns in Group 9 to cluster in areas of wheat with wool and fat lamb production is much more marked then for Group 7 towns (see Fig. 5–4*b*). The small service towns comprising Group 8 differ notably by combining an emphasis in communication employment with a pronounced underspecialization in transportation, but in other employment categories do not contrast too sharply with the other service towns.

There is on the Australian scene a number of different classes of service centers, varying with population size, additional functional specialization, and type of hinterland. One class (Groups 4 and 5) carries an emphasis on primary production as well as its commercial specialization. Members of a group of larger service centers (Group 6) cluster in the coastal dairying areas of eastern Australia, and specialize in commercial, financial, and professional functions. In the extremely small service centers (Group 8), both primary production and manufacturing are under-represented, as is transportation, but the level of employment in commerce is high and varies less than for the other five groups (see Table 5–2). There is a final class of quite large service towns (Groups 7 and 9) which have consistently low employment levels in primary production, but which differ strikingly in the degree of manufacturing specialization. Finally, the towns in all six groups display significant concentrations in particular land use zones,[84] and it may be concluded that for Australian service towns, there is an observable relationship between town function and type of tributary area.

Resort Towns

While two groups of towns have well above average proportions of their labor force in amusements, hotels, cafes, and personal services (see Fig. 5–5), Group 10 apparently comprises two different kinds of towns with this common specialization: those with an above average proportion of employment in primary production, some in inland pastoral areas (Bourke, Warren, Mitchell, and Cunnamulla) and some with a coastal location (Port Macquarie, Ulladulla, and Narooma), and a second class comprising truly resort settlement, such as South Coast,[85] Sorrento, Healesville, and Warburton, which have only small proportions of employment in primary production. Thus, a distinction appears in Group 10 between coastal resort towns where fishing is and is not important. Also, the similarity between the inland and coastal towns lies only in

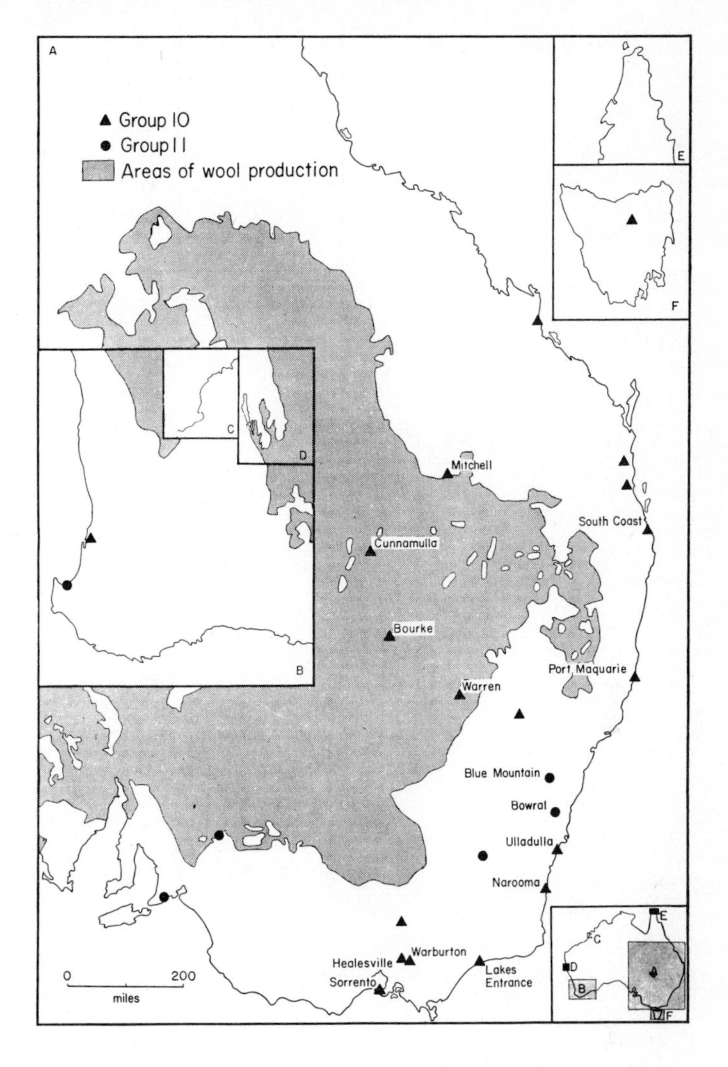

FIGURE 5–5. The resort towns of Australia. *Source:* See caption for Fig. 5–3.

the level of employment in amusements, hotels, cafes, and personal service, *not* in resort functions. Only such inland towns as the Blue Mountains complex and Bowral (Group 11) are known to have a specific resort function. The high level of employment in this category in inland pastoral centers is difficult to explain, and these towns should be excepted from the "resort" class.

Both Groups 10 and 11 record above average proportions in building and construction, and only four of the 19 towns in Group 10 and one of the six in Group 11 fall below the appropriate national average. However, they contrast sharply in the public authority and professional function (see Table 5–2), and the much higher level in Group 11 perhaps reflects the larger average size of towns (6,000 as against 3,000).

A single, close-knit group of resort towns does not emerge, and within the larger group of towns specializing in recreation and service employment, there is considerable variation in additional functions, so much so that the accuracy of the term "resort" in describing all the towns in Group 10 must be qualified considerably.

Transport and Communication Towns

Groups of towns with a marked specialization in either transport (Group 12) or communication (Group 13) employment are shown in Fig.

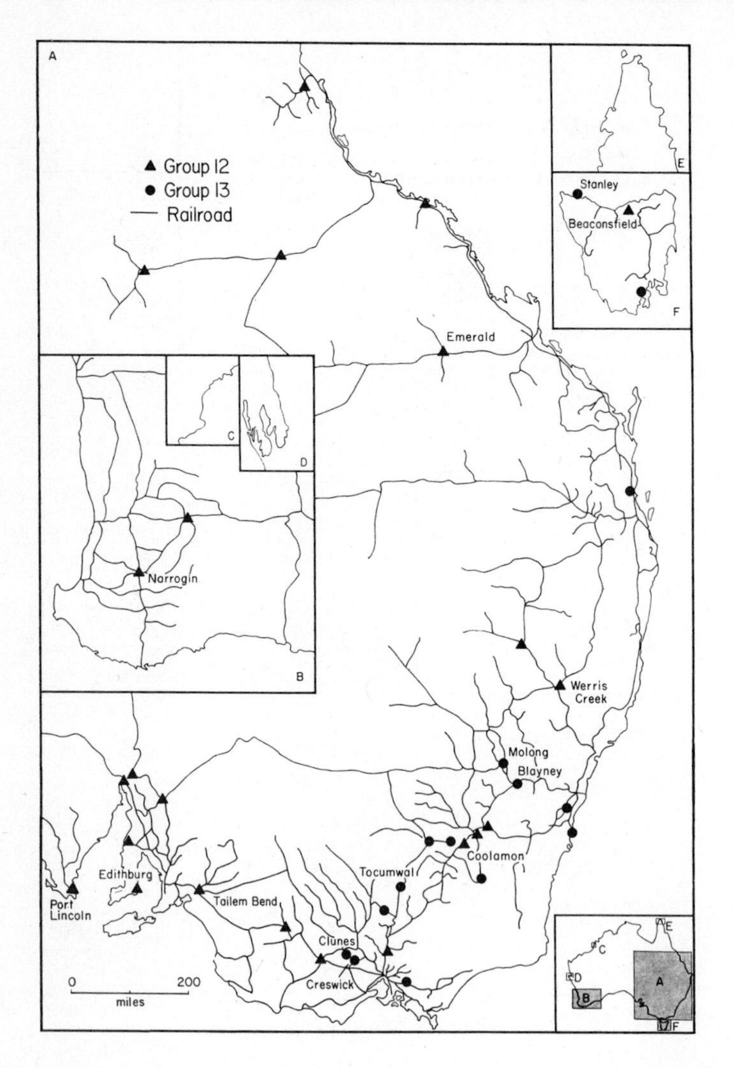

FIGURE 5–6. The transport towns (Group 12) and communication towns (Group 13) of Australia. *Source:* See caption for Fig. 5–3.

5–6. The 23 members of Group 12 record proportions of their labor force in transportation ranging from 13.3 per cent to 48.7 per cent, well above the urban complex average of 7.41 per cent. Many of these centers are railroad junctions, such as Emerald, Werris Creek, Tailem Bend, and Narrogin, although there are certain exceptions to this generalization. For example, Edithburg is a small port, and although Port Lincoln marks the terminus of a railroad line, port functions are also important here.[86] Beaconsfield in northern Tasmania, neither a railroad junction nor the site of a port, is a clear exception. As the change to diesel locomotives becomes more complete, some of the towns in 1954 sites of maintenance and repair shops for steam locomotives may record a substantial decline in the importance of the transport function. Members of Group 12 have relatively small proportions of their labor force in financial and commercial services, in primary production, and in manufacturing; they may be considered correctly as a group of single function centers, performing few other functions for their hinterlands.

Towns in Group 13 have employment levels in communication which are consistently above average (see Table 5–2), but there is no other industry group in which all members record a marked specialization. Some centers such as Tocumwal and Stanley perform additional transportation functions, the former being a railroad junction between the N.S.W. standard and the Victorian broad gauge system, the latter a minor port serving a confined hinterland in northwestern Tasmania. Creswick and Clunes have 30 per cent of their labor force in manufacturing, while Molong and Coolamon record an additional specialization in primary production. This irregular pattern is typical of all other industry groups with some towns above and some below the national average.

The term "transportation town" appears to describe appropriately the large group of predominantly inland railroad centers, and the implication of single function is not incorrect. Some towns in the communication group also record transportation functions and it is well to note that subsidiary transportation services are provided by certain towns not included in Group 12.

Mining and Utility Towns

Australian mining towns already have been the subject of intensive study,[87] although as a different classification method was employed in the present study, there is some variation in the results. As is shown in Fig. 5-7, many of the mining towns (Group 14) are associated with the extraction of coal; such is the case for the cluster of towns north of Sydney and for Lithgow, Collins-

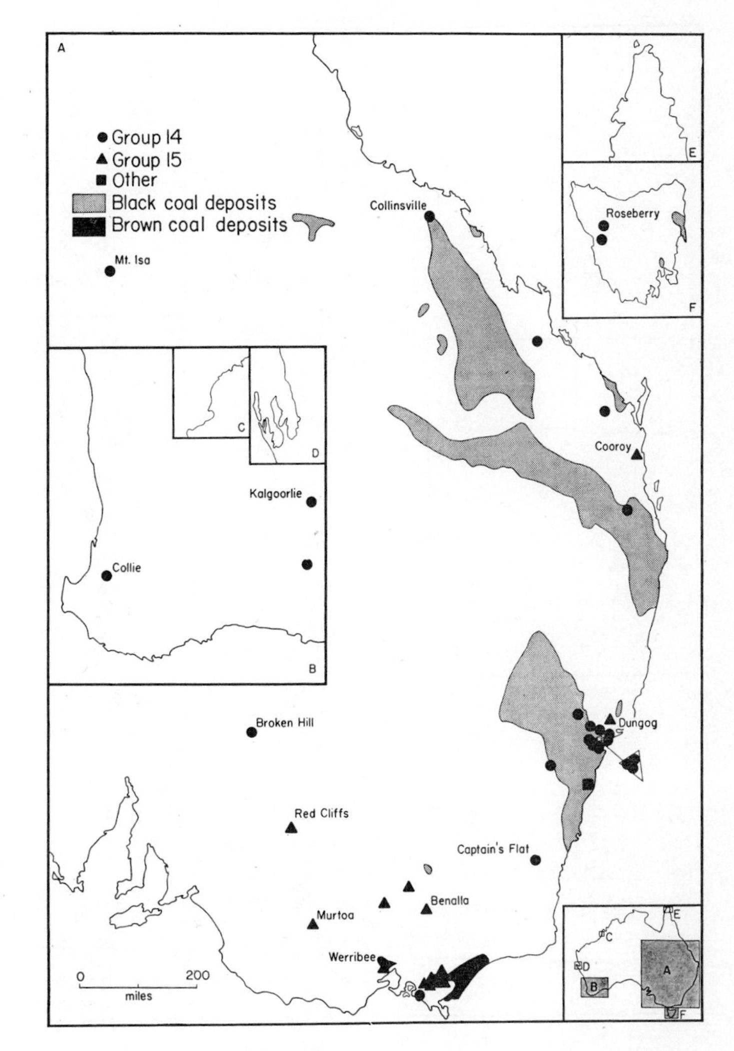

FIGURE 5-7. The mining towns (Group 14) and utility towns (Group 15) of Australia. *Source:* See caption for Fig. 5-3.

ville, Rosewood, and Collie. Well known exceptions to this generalization are Kalgoorlie in Western Australia (gold), Broken Hill, Captain's Flat, and Mt. Isa (lead and zinc), and Roseberry in Tasmania (copper and lead). With very few exceptions, these towns are underspecialized in every other industry category, although certain centers such as Lithgow and the coal mining towns north of Sydney do record above average proportions in manufacturing.

The utility towns (Group 15) with a marked specialization in employment in electricity, gas, water, and sanitary services, display the most concentrated distribution of any group discussed so far. The near neighbor statistic for this group is 0.2390, and the observed distance to nearest neighbor in the same group, 94 miles, differs significantly from the expected mean distance separating a random distribution of this density.[88] Almost half the group members are located on the brown coal deposits of the Latrobe Valley in southeastern Victoria. In some towns here, almost half the labor force is employed in activities associated with electricity generation; also, the proportion in manufacturing and mining is frequently quite high, reflecting the local extraction of brown coal and the manufacture of briquettes.[89] The remaining towns in this group are either associated with water treatment and irrigation projects (Werribee and Redcliffs), or are

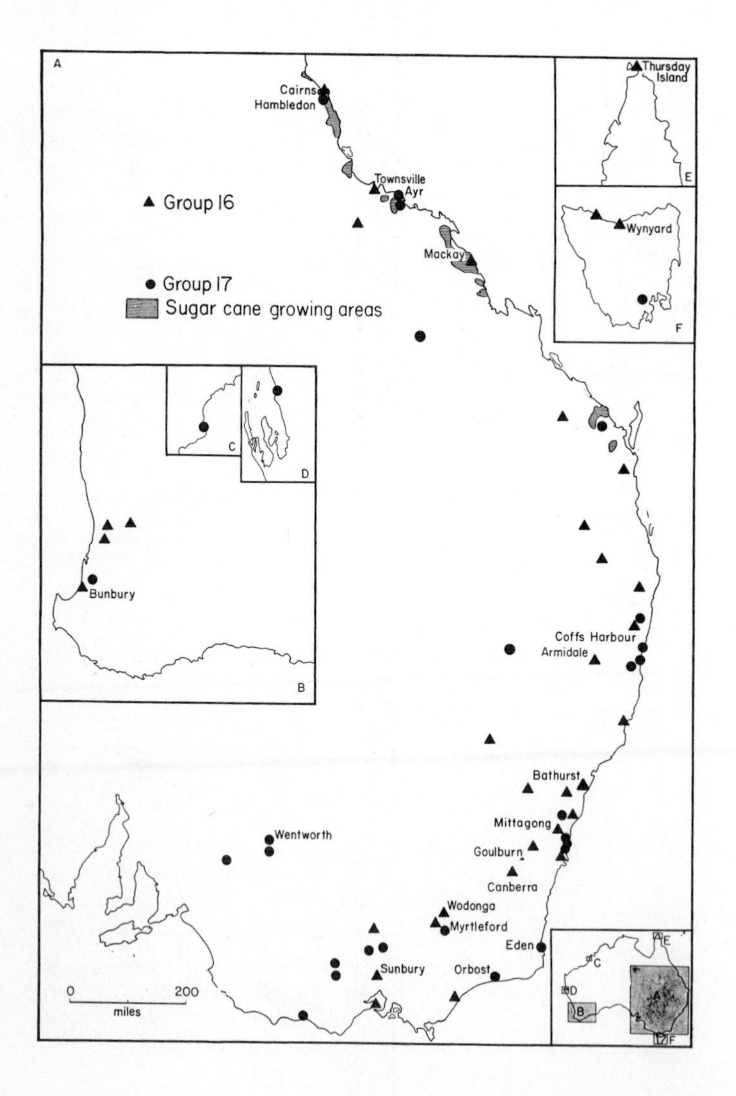

FIGURE 5–8. The professional and administrative towns (Group 16) and primary production towns (Group 17) of Australia. *Source:* See caption for Fig. 5–3.

centers where gas works are located (Benalla), and power is either generated or transmitted (Cooroy and Dungog). These towns are not markedly specialized in any additional function, although employment in building and construction tends to be well above average.

Professional and Administrative Towns

For Group 16 (Fig. 5–8), comprising 34 towns with an average population of almost 5,000, there is a marked concentration of employment in the public administration, professional and educational industry group. In fact, the only town where this proportion was below the national average was Bunbury in Western Australia. In Canberra and Thursday Island, a relatively large number of people employed in government services was responsible for this concentration, while in towns such as Sunbury and Goulburn the presence of large hospitals, mental homes, and correctional institutions nearby required a higher than average proportion of employment in this industry group. Some towns were allocated to this group because of large numbers in education; Mittagong (boarding schools), Bathurst (schools and a teacher training college), and Armidale (both schools and a teacher training college, in addition to a university). A number of towns provided transportation functions; thus, Cairns, Townsville, Mackay, and Bunbury are ports, and Goulburn, Wodonga, and Wynyard are rail centers of some significance. While employment in primary production and mining was predominantly below average, there appeared to be no marked clustering either above or below the urban complex average in the remaining categories, and towns in this group can not be described accurately as specialized single function centers.

Primary Production Centers

The dominant function of towns in Group 17 (see Fig. 5–8) seems to be the extraction and, in some cases, initial processing of primary products other than minerals, and the proportion of the labor force in primary production is well above average (see Table 5–2). This group differs from Groups 4 and 5 in that the additional specialization in commercial services is absent, indicating clearly that the emphasis is on production, not service. Some towns are located in areas of sugar cane production and milling, such as Ayr and Hambledon. Fishing and fish canning are important activities at Eden, while the local production of fruit and vegetables with the aid of irrigation along the Murray River near Wentworth probably accounts for its presence in this group. Such towns as Orbost and Myrtleford in Victoria are located in predominantly forest areas. Most of the members of this group are under represented in other industry categories, and are characterized by a single specialization, even though some initial processing may be performed.

*MANUFACTURING AS AN URBAN FUNCTION: THE NEED FOR A NATIONAL VIEWPOINT**

Clearly, many interpretive difficulties were faced in the foregoing example, for functional classifications per se are full of paradoxes. One that is worthy of elaboration is that a strictly regional viewpoint is inadequate for understanding manufacturing as an urban function within a region. A regional interpretation can be valid only as it supplements and ties into the notion of a national system of cities. Our argument and evidence, therefore, are consistent with the contention of Pappenfort[90] that urban and metropolitan functions are interregionally organized in a total "ecological field." General support for the position taken here as well as valuable clues for further research are found in a paper published by Chauncy D. Harris some years ago—a rare instance of a contribution which represents a genuine break-through in understanding a complex problem.[91] Harris showed that the principal factor in the remarkably persistent concentration of manufacturing activity in the northeastern

*Reprinted from Otis Dudley Duncan, "Manufacturing as an Urban Function: The Regional Viewpoint," *Sociological Quarterly* (1959), 75–86, with the permission of the author and editor.

manufacturing belt is the superior accessibility of manufacturing-belt locations to the national market. He also calls attention to the fact that the belt itself represents a large share of that market. A second type of result provides independent corroboration of our general thesis. Winsborough[92] presents data which are most easily interpreted on the supposition that as far as manufacturing functions are concerned, the urban hierarchy in the United States is a truly national one, and not a mere summation of similar regional hierarchies. The pattern of variation in manufacturing industry structure by city size is a hierarchic one when the nation is taken as the universe of study, but not when individual regions are examined (see the final section of this chapter).

The paper by Harris not only emphasizes the dominant national pattern of manufacturing localization; it also points to sources of regional deviation from that pattern. Manufacturing industries which are strongly oriented to sources of raw-material input, those serving specialized regional markets, and those whose costs of transporting both input and output are negligible may exhibit sporadic localization somewhat independently of generalized accessibility to the national market. Moreover, the sector of processing industries does not locate with respect to market potential in the way that the remainder of manufacturing does.

Case Study: The West North Central Region

To illustrate how these hypotheses and assumptions may be applied in interpreting the situation of a particular region, the occurrence of manufacturing activity in the larger urban and metropolitan centers of the West North Central geographic division, as defined by the Bureau of the Census, may be examined.[93]

As an indicator of generalized accessibility to the national market, we employ population potential, computed according to the proposal of J. Q. Stewart.[94] The potential values we use actually are those observed in the general vicinity of the respective cities, not the values that one would find at their cores. Stewart and Warntz[95] have used the term "base potential" for this kind of measurement. While some investigators have chosen to work with "market potential" or "income potential," wherein population is weighted by some index of purchasing power,[96] we have relied on population potential unweighted by any economic quantity.

Let us consider first the nonmetropolitan centers of 25,000 to 50,000 inhabitants in 1950 (i.e., those outside Standard Metropolitan Areas or metropolitan State Economic Areas). Taking manufacturing activity as the dependent variable and the indicator of accessibility as the independent variable, we find that the regression of the percentage of the employed labor force engaged in manufacturing (Y) on population potential in 10,000 persons per mile (X) is $\hat{Y} = 0.796X - 0.98$, for the 149 nonmetropolitan cities of the indicated size in the United States as a whole. The corresponding correlation coefficient is 0.62, indicating a moderate goodness-of-fit for the regression equation. According to that equation, an increase of population potential of 10,000 persons per mile is accompanied, on the average, by an increase in the percentage engaged in manufacturing of 0.8 points.

With this relationship established for the country as a whole, we may take a closer look at the eighteen nonmetropolitan centers of 25,000 to 50,000 inhabitants in the West North Central division. Table 5–4 lists them, giving for each its proportion engaged in manufacturing and the deviation of that proportion from the one expected on the basis of the foregoing regression equation. It will be observed that the deviations are quite small for at least half of these cities. The fact that the majority of the West North Central cities are below the average in percentage in manufacturing for the entire universe (23.6 per cent) seems to be accounted for satisfactorily by the fact that most of them are at locations which are below average in population potential.

The deviations from the expected relationship—particularly the positive ones—are likewise of interest from a regional standpoint. Table 5–4 indicates for each sizable deviation what its most important source appears to be. Most significant is the finding that each city with an unexpectedly high proportion in manufactur-

TABLE 5–4

Percentage of Employed Persons Engaged in Manufacturing, Nonmetropolitan Cities of 25,000–50,000 Inhabitants, West North Central Division of the United States: 1950

City	Percentage in Manufacturing: Actual	Percentage in Manufacturing: Deviation from Regression Estimate*	Source of Deviation
Clinton, Ia.	37.2	11.9	Food and kindred products; chemicals and allied products
Ottumwa, Ia.	34.8	11.9	Meat products; nonelectrical machinery
Dubuque, Ia.	36.4	11.1	Food (meat and kindred products); lumber and wood products; agricultural machinery and tractors
Winona, Minn.	28.3	8.6	Food and kindred products
Fort Dodge, Ia.	23.9	3.4	—
Hutchinson, Kans.	16.5	– 0.8	—
Burlington, Ia.	24.2	– 1.1	—
Mason City, Ia.	23.3	– 1.2	—
St. Cloud, Minn.	17.0	– 2.7	—
Rapid City, S.D.	9.9	– 2.7	—
Grand Forks, N.D.	9.8	– 3.5	—
Fargo, N.D.	9.2	– 4.1	—
Joplin, Mo.	16.0	– 4.5	—
Salina, Kans.	11.7	– 5.6	—
Jefferson City, Mo.	13.3	–12.8	State capital
Rochester, Minn.	6.1	–13.6	Medical center
Columbia, Mo.	6.1	–19.2	University center
Iowa City, Ia.	4.4	–20.9	University center

Source: Bureau of the Census, Department of Commerce, *1950 Census of Population* (Washington, D.C.: U.S. Government Printing Office).
*See text for regression equation.

ing has a major fraction of its manufacturing employment assigned to the food and kindred products industry. Now, food products is an example par excellence of what we call a "processing" (as opposed to a "fabricating") industry—i.e., one a major part of whose input is raw materials. While processing industries are not necessarily oriented to raw materials in a locational sense, they frequently are so oriented, owing to the high weight per unit value of input, which leads them to locate so as to minimize transfer charges on input. That a West North Central location should be a strategic location for at least some food processing industries requires little argument. We find yet another processing industry, lumber and wood products, playing an important role in one city with an unexpectedly high level of manufacturing activity, and one industry, chemicals and allied products, whose classification is at least marginal to the processing category, playing a similar role. Almost equally significant is the finding that where manufacture of machinery attains sufficient importance to come to our attention in this analysis, it is likely to be a kind of machinery that may be oriented to a regionally specialized market: according to the *1954 Census of Agriculture* there are more tractors on farms in Iowa than in any other state.

In summary, manufacturing specialization in nonmetropolitan cities of 25,000 to 50,000 inhabitants in the West North Central division is relatively infrequent owing to the region's comparatively low accessibility to the national market. Where such specialization does occur, it reflects an orientation of the leading manufacturing indus-

TABLE 5–5

Percentage of Employed Persons Engaged in Manufacturing in Standard Metropolitan Areas of 100,000 to 300,000 Inhabitants, West North Central Division of the United States: 1950

SMA	Percentage in Manufacturing: Actual	Percentage in Manufacturing: Deviation from Regression Estimate*	Source of Deviation
Waterloo, Ia.	38.7	17.6	Meat products; agricultural machinery and tractors; miscellaneous machinery
Davenport, Ia.—Rock Island–Moline, Ill.	40.1	11.1	Agricultural machinery and tractors
Cedar Rapids, Ia.	29.6	6.5	—
Wichita, Kansas	27.0	6.2	—
Sioux City, Ia.	20.5	4.3	—
Duluth, Minn.—Superior, Wis.	16.1	−2.0	—
Lincoln, Nebr.	13.1	−3.1	—
Des Moines, Ia.	20.4	−4.1	—
Topeka, Kans.	13.7	−4.5	—
Springfield, Mo.	14.0	−7.1	—

Source: Bureau of the Census, Department of Commerce, *1950 Census of Population* (Washington, D. C.,: U.S. Government Printing Office).
*See text for regression equations.

TABLE 5–6

Location Quotients for Broad Manufacturing Industry Categories in Individual Standard Metropolitan Areas (SMA's) of 100,000 to 300,000 Inhabitants, West North Central Division, and in Combined SMA's of 100,000 to 250,000 Inhabitants, United States: 1950

	*Industry Category (Type of Resource Use and Type of Market)**					
	First Stage		*Second Stage*		*Indirect*	
SMA's	*Nonfinal* (2)	*Final* (3)	*Nonfinal* (4)	*Final* (5)	*Nonfinal* (6)	*Final* (7)
36 SMA's of 150,000 to 250,000 inhabitants	1.2	1.0	1.1	1.0	1.3	1.3
Duluth, Minn.—Superior, Wis.†	0.3	0.7	1.0	0.7	0.4	0.3
Davenport, Ia.—Rock Island–Moline, Ill.	0.5	0.9	0.4	0.5	3.0‡	0.3
Des Moines, Ia.	0.4	1.1	0.4	0.6	1.1	0.7
Wichita, Kans.	1.0	1.2	0.2	0.3	0.6	7.0‡
38 SMA's of 100,000 to 150,000 inhabitants	0.6	1.6	1.5	1.0	1.0	0.9
Lincoln, Nebr.	0.4	0.8	0.1	0.2	0.6	1.6‡
Topeka, Kans.	0.4	2.2‡	0.1	0.2	0.7	0.1
Springfield, Mo.	0.6	1.3	0.2	1.1	0.4	0.2
Cedar Rapids, Ia.	1.7‡	3.8‡	0.2	0.3	1.5‡	0.1
Sioux City, Ia.	0.4	5.1‡	0.1	0.5	0.6	0.2
Waterloo, Ia.	0.2	6.8‡	0.3	0.5	1.9‡	0.3

Source: Otis Dudley Duncan et al., *Metropolis and Region* (Baltimore: The Johns Hopkins Press, 1960), pp. 213–19. Nonmanufacturing categories are omitted.
*See text for discussion of industry categories and location quotients.
†1950 population was 253,000.
‡Specialization is discussed in the text.

tries to regionally specialized raw material input or to regionally localized markets, at least in part.

An analysis parallel to the one just summarized is reported in Table 5–5, which considers the smaller standard metropolitan areas (SMA's) in the region (omitting two, St. Joseph, Missouri, and Sioux Falls, South Dakota, which were below 100,000 in population in 1950 and for which detailed industry statistics were not reported). At the national level we find that the regression of percentage in manufacturing (Y) on population potential (X), for the 36 SMA's of 150,000 to 250,000 inhabitants is given by $\hat{Y} = 0.904X + 0.06$, and for the 38 SMA's of 100,000 to 150,000 inhabitants by $\hat{Y} = 0.981X - 6.37$. The respective correlation coefficients are 0.78 and 0.59. Table 5–5 indicates that most of the SMA's in the West North Central division lie close to the regressions for their respective size groups (the Duluth-Superior SMA had a population of 253,000 in 1950, slightly beyond the size range used in computing the regression, but this probably has little importance in the present context). The analysis of deviations leads to a conclusion much like the one above. Only two SMA's in the region have strikingly high deviations from expectation. In both, manufacture of agricultural machinery is prominent, and in one the meat processing industry is of leading importance. Again, we conclude that the moderately low levels of manufacturing activity characteristic of the region are due primarily to average or lower accessibility to the national market. Exceptions reflect orientation to regionally specialized sources of input and markets.

Thus far we have examined manufacturing specialization only from the standpoint of aggregate employment in all manufacturing industries. However, a city may specialize in a particular industry without showing up with an unusually high proportion employed in all manufacturing. For a more detailed appraisal of manufacturing specialization, therefore, we turn to the information in Table 5–6. Here (as in Table 5–7) manufacturing industries are grouped into six broad categories. One basis of classification is type of input. Industries making much use of raw materials are classified as "first stage resource users"; those depending heavily on first stage resource users for input are called "second stage resource users"; and those whose input has already gone through extensive processing or preliminary fabrication are termed "industries for which resources are only indirectly significant." The other basis of classification is type of market—whether products on the whole are destined for other manufacturers, or whether they are ready for distribution to the final consumer. This second classification is rather arbitrary in some instances and cannot always be interpreted literally.[94] . . . The data are in the form of "location quotients." This statistic is defined as the percentage of the employed labor force in a given category in a given areal unit divided by the corresponding percentage in the United States as a whole. Location quotients appreciably in excess of unity are interpreted as indications of industry specialization.

The first salient finding is that specialization in "first stage resource using" (processing) industries, particularly those producing for final markets,

TABLE 5–7

Rank Correlations of Location Quotients for Manufacturing Industry Categories with Population Potential, SMA's 100,000 to 250,000 Inhabitants, United States: 1950

*Industry Category**	*38 SMA's of 100,000 to 150,000*	*36 SMA's of 150,000 to 250,000*
2. First stage resource users; production for nonfinal market	−.44	−.53
3. First stage resource users; production for final market	−.37	−.13
4. Second stage resource users; production for nonfinal market	.32	.21
5. Second stage resource users; production for final market	.36	.64
6. Resources of indirect significance; production for nonfinal market	.48	.69
7. Resources of indirect significance; production for final market	.55	.59

Source: Based upon data developed in the preparation of Otis Dudley Duncan et al., *Metropolis and Region* (Baltimore: The Johns Hopkins Press, 1960).
*See text for definitions of categories.

is not uncommon in the region. Moreover, even where such specialization is lacking, location quotients tend to run higher than for "second stage resource users." Regional orientation to both input and markets is suggested by these comparisons. This suggestion is supported when we identify the particular industries largely accounting for the specializations: meat products in Topeka, Cedar Rapids, Sioux City, and Waterloo, and grain-mill products in Cedar Rapids. In Category 6—industries using resources "only indirectly" to produce for "nonfinal markets"—two instances of specialization reflect manufacture of agricultural machinery and tractors. This industry, which is sizable in Davenport-Rock Island-Moline and Waterloo, is perhaps not correctly classified as having "nonfinal markets." In any case, we have already pointed to the probable regional factor in this specialization. In Cedar Rapids, the Category 6 specialization comprises miscellaneous machinery and electrical machinery, equipment, and supplies; and in Waterloo, miscellaneous machinery accompanies agricultural machinery and tractors.

In Category 7—industries producing for final markets and using resources only indirectly—we find but two instances of specialization. These reflect the large-scale employment in aircraft and parts manufacture in Wichita, and the manufacture of watches, clocks, and clockwork operated devices in Lincoln. The former is a notoriously footloose industry in which transfer costs, though presumably not negligible, apparently have not been of primary locational importance. The latter is an instance of an industry in which transfer costs for both input and output are low in relation to value of product.

It appears that this study of detailed manufacturing industries affords no cause for revising the earlier conclusions concerning the nature and circumstances of manufacturing specialization in the West North Central states. The discovery of rather frequent specialization in processing industries—Categories 2 and 3—in this region comes as no surprise. Table 5–7 shows that on a national basis the processing categories are negatively correlated with population potential. This is quite contrary to the case for industries at more advanced stages of production which, like all manufacturing industries combined, show appreciable positive correlations with potential.

The last collection of data we wish to consider concerns the larger SMA's of the West North Central division, those having more than 300,000 inhabitants in 1950—St. Louis, Minneapolis-St. Paul, Kansas City, and Omaha. The nation's SMA's in this size group have been subjected to detailed study, and a typological classification of metropoli has been set forth at some length.[98] The discussion here will be oriented to the categories of this classification. Taking the SMA's of the entire United States as the universe of discourse, it turns out that there is virtually no correlation between level of manufacturing activity and indicators of what are identified as distinctively metropolitan functions: financial activities, business services, and wholesale distribution. Note that the correlation is not negative but is rather essentially zero. Thus if we identify "metropoli" as large cities strongly specialized in "metropolitan" functions, these cities may or may not be specialized in manufacturing. The two possibilities are about equally likely.

Taking this finding into account, the classification makes a basic distinction between centers in which the level of manufacturing activity is high and manufacturing industries are prominent in the industry profile, and those in which manufacturing is subordinate in importance to the trade, service, and transportation functions. Among the former, three groups are distinguished: "diversified manufacturing centers with metropolitan functions" (*D*), "diversified manufacturing centers with few metropolitan functions" (*D-*), and "specialized manufacturing centers" (*M*). The second major grouping includes the "regional metropoli" (*R*), and the "regional capitals" (*C*). These five types account for the bulk of all SMA's between 300,000 and 3,000,000 inhabitants, but it is necessary to recognize such "special cases" (*S*) as the nation's capital, the resort center Miami, and some centers specializing in national defense activities. Finally, the five largest SMA's are regarded as "national metropoli" (*N*).

The West North Central division does not include a metropolis of national rank (*N*), and it lacks an example of the miscellaneous *S* category. In conformity with our earlier findings, it also turns out to be lacking in *M* and *D* centers, those with heavy specialization in manufacturing to the exclusion or virtual exclusion of metropolitan functions involving strong regional orientations. The four largest SMA's in the region, then, appear in the remaining three categories. Minneapolis-St. Paul and Kansas City are classified as *R* centers (regional metropoli) on the basis of highly developed trade, service, and financial functions clearly oriented to surrounding areas roughly identifiable as their hinterlands. Similar characteristics, on a smaller scale, justify the classification of Omaha as a regional capital. St. Louis is the only large metropolis in the region classified as a manufacturing center, but it is clearly one with strongly developed metropolitan functions; thus it is placed in the *D* category.

For two of the four West North Central SMA's, the story on manufacturing is short: in both Kansas City and Omaha, the only manufacturing industry large enough to stand out in the industry profile is meat products.[99] This activity, of course, is oriented to hinterland agricultural pursuits and ties these cities to the region in which they are located. The same industry likewise appears in the profiles of Minneapolis-St. Paul and St. Louis. However, in the latter cities it is of lesser relative importance, being found in conjunction with a variety of manufacturing industries, not all of which exhibit so clear a regional orientation. Minneapolis-St. Paul has one other prominent processing industry—beverage production. The remainder of its profile manufacturing industries fall in Category 6, resources of indirect significance, production for nonfinal market. St. Louis likewise specializes in beverage production, but it is a truly diversified manufacturing center, with profile industries in five of the six manufacturing categories. Situation in a region of only moderate accessibility to the national market, therefore, appears to be somewhat less of a handicap to the development of manufacturing in these two SMA's than in the smaller SMA's of the region. Is it only a coincidence that both are located at the extreme eastern edge of the West North Central division and that the St. Louis SMA actually extends into the East North Central division? We may note as a special advantage of St. Louis its exceptionally favorable combination of rail and water transport facilities—an advantage not typical of cities in the West North Central Region.

*MANUFACTURING ACTIVITIES RELATED TO CITY SIZE**

Not only are urban and metroplitan functions interregionally linked in a total "ecological field," as shown in the previous section, however. There remains (and, indeed, current changes in economic activity are increasing) the structuring of these activities according to city size; most industries appear, today, to be concentrated in particular population-size classes of cities.

Here the evidence is quite problematic, though. Except for two major contributions by Duncan[100] and Morrissett,[101] locational analyses to date have produced little evidence to distinguish ubiquitous types of industries from what may be singularly representative of particular sizes of urban center. Most discussions have been devoted to expositing a two-tier classification of industries, that is, those which have least freedom in their locations, and those which are footloose in character. Their locational attributes have been explained in relation to the classical factors of production, in terms of the relative costs of transporting inputs to industry and outputs of consumers, and in terms of agglomeration and external economies. Even this classification is being eroded with greater application of science and technology so that industries which formerly were locationally sensitive are no longer so. In fact, the whole spectrum of industrial locations under the impact of continuing technological change is becoming unresponsive to the classical and neo-classical locational models, which might suggest that the locational behavior of industries is being influ-

*Reprinted from R. M. Morse, O. P. Mathur, and M. C. K. Swamy, *Costs of Urban Infrastructure as Related to City Size in Developing Countries* (Palo Alto, Calif.: Stanford Research Institute, 1968), pp. 175–90, 377–85, with the permission of the authors.

enced to an increasing degree by noneconomic phenomena. Lösch's[102] prologue that the actual location may not necessarily coincide with the rational location is one of the many expressions to indicate the qualified validity of locational theories.

Duncan analyzed U.S. Census data for 1950 to show that industry composition differs with size-of-place groups, using an "index of dissimilarity," and extended his exposition to what he calls a complete urban hierarchy. The hierarchic pattern, he concludes:

> ... is largely accounted for by the tendency of extractive, processing, and local service industries to relate inversely to city size and the complementary tendency of fabricating and non-local service industries to relate directly to city size. The conclusion must be phrased in terms of the particular industry classification used, however.[103]

Morrissett keyed his contribution to establishing quantitative relationships between "sporadic" and "ubiquitous" industries and city size,[104] and for this purpose utilized Alexandersson's[105] k values (ratios which show, for different industries, the proportion of industry activity required as a minimum to supply a city's own population with goods and services).

Evidence for the United States

New evidence is presented in Table 5–9, which is organized according to the classification of industries presented in Table 5–8. In developing these tables a four-digit classification of American industries in city-size groups in 1954 was used and location quotients were computed for each industry, using the formula:

$$LQ = \frac{\text{Percentage of industry } i \text{ employment in size of place } j}{\text{Percentage of total U. S. population in size of place } j}$$

TABLE 5–8

Classification of United States Industries by City Size

Category	*Description*	*City Population Class (1950)*	*Employment Criterion (1954)**	*Equivalent Location Quotient*
1	Very high incidence in large cities	500,000 or more	50% or more	2.82 or more
2	High incidence in large cities	500,000 or more	35–50%	2.00 to 2.81
3	High incidence in medium cities and substantial in smaller cities	100,000–499,999 10,000–99,999	50% or more, of which at least ⅖ were in cities of 100,000 to 499,999	1.69 or more
4	High incidence in smaller cities and substantial in medium cities	10,000–99,999 100,000–499,999	50% or more, of which at least ⅗ were in cities of 10,000 to 99,999	1.53 or more
5	Wide incidence in all size cities	(a) Over 2,500 (b) Over 10,000	Category determined by location quotient	.75 or more† .75 or more†
6	High incidence in small cities outside metropolitan areas	10,000–49,999	50% or more outside SMAs, 15% or more in cities of 10,000 to 49,999	‡
7	High incidence in smallest cities	2,500–9,999	Category determined by location quotient	2.00 or more†
8	Wide incidence in nonurban as well as urban places	Less than 2,500	Category determined by location quotient	.75 or more†
9	High incidence in nonurban places, within and outside metropolitan areas	Less than 2,500	50% or more	1.21 or more

*Percentage in the specified city size class or classes.
†Not meeting the criteria for other categories.
‡Not available.

TABLE 5–9

Locational Categories of Manufacturing Industry as Related to Size of Place, United States: 1954

SIC 1954	Industry Title	Total Industry Employment 1954 (in Thousands)	Percentage within SMA's	Location Quotient for Places with 1950 Population of: 500,000 or More	100,000–499,999	50,000–99,999	10,000–49,999	2,500–9,999	All Other	Dominant Locational Characteristic
Percentage of U.S. Population, 1950:			56.1	17.7	11.8	5.9	13.7	9.7	41.2	
1. Very high incidence in large cities										
2013	Prepared meats	45.0	90.6	2.92	1.79	0.69	0.53	0.35	0.30	NM
2045	Flour mixes	5.6	96.4	3.33	1.14	1.68	.89	.12*	.05*	U
2071	Confectionery products	66.8	90.3	2.88	1.67	1.47	.81	.37	.15	NM
2082	Beer and ale	81.3	74.7	3.27	2.07	.83	.58	.29	.05	LM
2095	Flavorings	10.6	92.1	2.99	1.81	1.05	.73	.30	.16	NM
2253	Knit outerwear mills†	46.4	78.7	2.85	1.00	1.47	.72	1.10	.20	E
2311	Men's and boys' suits and coats	119.0	85.1	3.36	1.36	.39	.60	.97	.11	E
2323	Men's and boys' neckwear	9.5	95.9	4.21	.92	1.02	.40	.18	.03	E
2325	Men's and boys' cloth hats	8.1	82.4	3.39	1.36	.37	.42	*n.a.*	*n.a.*	E
2333	Dresses, unit price	143.3	91.9	3.63	.91	.81	.72	.63	.11	E
2337	Women's suits, coats, and skirts	96.0	91.2	3.55	1.22	.83	.47	.64	.13	E
2338	Women's neckwear and scarves	1.7	(90–95)	4.56	.34	1.22	*n.a.*	*n.a.*	*n.a.*	E
2339	Women's outerwear, *n.e.c.*	25.4	85.4	3.06	1.09	.66	.76	.95	.23	E
2351	Millinery	20.2	94.9	4.31	.52	.93	.16*	*n.a.*	.08*	E
2363	Children's coats†	14.4	91.1	2.99	.94	1.02	1.24	.80	.13	E
2371	Fur goods	10.0	97.8	5.39	.11	.05	.16	*n.a.*	*n.a.*	E
2384	Robes and dressing gowns†	11.0	77.4	2.98	.95	.66	.87	1.37	.16	E
2385	Waterproof outer garments	12.9	79.0	2.95	1.11	1.34	.64	.61	.30	E
2387	Belts	12.6	90.4	3.89	.87	.80	.41	.52	.13	E
2391	Curtains and draperies	14.0	92.2	3.02	2.15	.66	.72	.41	.08	E
2395	Tucking, pleating, and stitching	6.5	98.0	4.90	.20	.34	.28*	.12*	.06	E
2396	Trimmings and art goods	17.8	86.8	3.57	.30	*n.a.*	1.55	.30*	.16	E
2397	Embroideries, except Schiffli	5.7	98.1	4.70	.28	.64	.42*	.23*	.03	E
2493	Mirror and picture frames	5.2	90.4	3.95	1.04	.20	.61	.04*	.09*	E
2519	Household furniture, *n.e.c.*	1.3	84.3	4.01	.53	*n.a.*	.77*	*n.a.*	.08*	E
2721	Periodicals	62.4	95.9	3.65	1.15	1.12	.87	.12	.05	I
2741	Miscellaneous publishing	18.4	94.1	3.34	1.42	1.17	.65	.54	.08	E
2761	Lithographing	77.7	92.4	3.01	1.77	1.12	.69	.41	.13	E
2771	Greeting cards	21.3	89.5	3.27	1.28	1.53	.64	.08	.21	E
2781	Bookbinding	17.2	96.3	4.20	1.25	.88	.27	*n.a.*	*n.a.*	E
2789	Miscellaneous bookbinding work	3.3	99.2	4.97	.71	*n.a.*	.12	*n.a.*	.03	E
2791	Typesetting	14.6	98.4	4.19	1.51	.63	.18	.03	.04	E
2792	Engraving and book plating	7.5	95.7	3.09	2.53	.69	.33	.19	.12	E
2793	Photo-engraving	17.7	95.4	3.70	1.76	1.03	.42	.09	.02	E
2794	Electrotyping and stereotyping	8.0	96.0	4.21	1.37	.39	*n.a.*	*n.a.*	.07*	E
2891	Printing ink	7.6	97.9	3.19	1.53	.44	.71	.76*	.12*	E
3171	Handbags and purses	22.9	88.1	3.46	.52	.64	1.25	.31	.21	E
3199	Leather goods, *n.e.c.*	4.6	92.4	3.76	.67	.69	.78	.26	.20	U
3298	Statuary and art goods	1.7	89.0	4.07	.93	.14	.45*	.22*	.14	E
3465	Enameling and lacquering	5.5	92.6	3.12	1.58	.46	.53*	.14*	.33	E
3467	Engraving on metal	3.5	90.5	3.18	.88	.78	.74*	.61	.08*	E
3555	Printing trades machinery	12.0	91.4	2.93	1.08	1.88	.71	.44	.25	LS
3616	Electrical control apparatus	79.3	91.2	2.97	.61	1.73	.85	.90	.24	I
3942	Dolls	15.1	95.5	4.21	.79	.83	.44	.15	.09	E
3953	Hand stamps and stencils	5.7	92.1	3.16	2.08	.61	.50	.49*	.04	U
3962	Artificial flowers	7.3	85.7	3.81	.88	.42	.55	.38	.21	E
3987	Lampshades	5.0	94.3	3.99	.71	1.20	.40*	.01*	*n.a.*	E
3994	Hairwork	1.7	99.5	4.62	.37	.20	.81*	*n.a.*	.02*	E
3995	Umbrellas, parasols, and canes	3.2	(95–100)	3.60	1.73	1.73	*n.a.*	.27	*n.a.*	E

SIC 1954	Industry Title	Total Industry Employment 1954 (in Thousands)	Percentage within SMA's	Location Quotient for Places with 1950 Population of: 500,000 or More	100,000–499,999	50,000–99,999	10,000–49,999	2,500–9,999	All Other	Dominant Locational Characteristic
2. High incidence in large cities										
2052	Biscuits and crackers	44.8	89.9	2.16	2.39	1.71	.74	.69	.16	LM
2098	Macaroni and spaghetti	7.1	92.4	2.52	1.96	1.03	.77	1.74*	.21*	U
2099	Miscellaneous food preparations	72.0	80.8	2.03	2.14	1.61	.90	.46	.22	LM
2331	Blouses	43.0	83.4	2.81	.75	.76	.84	1.34	.30	E
2342	Corsets and allied garments†	38.8	77.4	2.13	1.39	1.56	1.21	1.14	.22	E
2361	Children's dresses†	32.5	82.6	2.31	1.08	1.70	.87	1.01	.36	E
2369	Children's outerwear, *n.e.c.*†	30.6	78.6	2.66	.99	1.27	.97	1.17	.22	E
2386	Leather and sheeplined clothing	5.4	86.1	2.71	1.44	1.19	1.34	*n.a.*	*n.a.*	E
2393	Textile bags	12.1	92.7	2.60	2.90	1.22	.48	.10*	.07*	LM
2399	Textile products, *n.e.c.*	18.0	82.8	2.61	1.25	2.00	.91	.52	.24	E
2514	Metal house furniture†	29.6	74.6	2.11	1.11	.71	2.02	.97	.20	LM
2541	Partitions and fixtures	38.1	85.0	2.42	2.00	.83	.63	.57	.35	LM
2563	Venetian blinds	9.4	87.1	2.41	2.15	1.49	.71	.75	.14	LM
2691	Die cut paper and board	12.3	83.0	2.39	.70	.44	2.35	.94	.14	U
2751	Commercial printing†	200.2	86.2	2.50	1.87	1.31	.96	.67	.15	E
2782	Blank books and paper ruling	8.6	74.3	2.64	1.03	1.14	.38*	1.90*	*n.a.*	U
2842	Cleaning and polishing preparations†	18.0	93.3	2.07	1.55	1.92	.69	1.28	.29	I
2851	Paints and varnishes	56.6	96.0	2.58	1.97	.80	.95	.64	.17	I
2893	Toilet preparations†	24.8	92.4	2.49	1.16	1.86	.69	1.07	.27	I
2894	Glue and gelatin	6.8	88.4	2.05	.85	.31	2.12	.42*	.28*	NM
3161	Luggage	15.9	88.8	2.57	2.46	.59	.64	.38	.24	E
3293	Gaskets and asbestos insulation	12.8	86.3	2.52	.46	.20	1.30	1.06	.50	U
3341	Secondary nonferrous metals†	15.8	95.7	2.21	1.17	.95	1.02	.51	.55	LM
3411	Tin cans and other tinware	55.2	94.0	2.79	1.56	.68	.76	.47	.32	LM
3463	Metal stampings†	128.2	83.7	2.24	1.28	.88	1.41	.82	.31	NM
3468	Plating and polishing	36.1	84.7	2.50	1.59	1.17	1.15	.49	.25	E
3471	Lighting fixtures	45.1	76.0	2.68	.69	.81	1.44	.59	.35	LM
3495	Screw machine products†	35.0	87.1	2.02	1.14	1.31	1.22	.90	.43	NM
3499	Fabricated metal products, *n.e.c.*†	18.1	78.5	2.03	.86	.83	1.18	.80	.61	U
3565	Industrial trucks and tractors	15.8	75.8	2.32	1.02	.76	.88	.67	.58	NM
3567	Industrial furnaces and ovens	8.4	86.9	2.25	1.79	1.49	.85*	*n.a.*	.26*	NM
3591	Valves and fittings, except plumbing†	75.0	81.4	2.11	1.42	1.51	1.41	.91	.20	NM
3592	Fabricated pipe and fittings†	12.7	89.4	2.19	.92	1.90	.71	1.32	.41	NM
3699	Electrical products, *n.e.c.*	8.5	80.3	2.14	.70	2.05	.74*	.16*	.50	U
3811	Scientific instruments	45.3	96.0	2.26	1.14	.63	.34	.92	.71	LS
3821	Mechanical measuring instruments	69.4	84.6	2.31	1.68	.73	.99	.64	.37	LS
3911	Jewelry	23.5	95.0	2.24	2.58	.54	1.13	.12	.24	E
3963	Buttons	8.5	65.5	2.62	.90	*n.a.*	.93*	.76	.51	E
3981	Brooms and brushes	16.8	80.9	2.23	1.58	.73	1.29	.54	.35	I
3993	Signs and advertising displays	33.6	88.7	2.71	1.75	1.32	.85	.44	.17	E
3999	Miscellaneous products, *n.e.c.*	20.8	81.3	2.20	1.87	.32	1.50	.67	.24	U
3. High incidence in medium cities, substantial in small										
2011	Meat packing plants	220.2	78.8	1.18	2.21	2.22	1.23	.26	.50	NM
2027	Fluid milk and other products	177.3	70.2	1.17	2.00	1.78	1.46	.92	.40	LM
2041	Flour and meal	29.0	58.3	.88	1.92	1.58	1.65	1.56	.36	NM
2051	Bread and related products	246.3	82.9	1.99	2.47	1.66	1.20	.46	.12	LM
2121	Cigars	38.5	88.2	1.23	3.19	2.31	.94	.64	.06	I
2515	Mattresses and bedsprings	32.1	93.1	2.19	2.63	2.88	.50	.08	.04	LM
2522	Metal office furniture	16.1	70.5	.53	2.58	1.98	2.31	.60	.27	U
2561	Window and door screens	4.4	79.3	1.39	2.95	.44	1.01	1.12	.33	U

SIC 1954	Industry Title	Total Industry Employment 1954 (in Thousands)	Percentage within SMA's	Location Quotient for Places with 1950 Population of: 555,000 or More	100,000–499,999	50,000–99,999	10,000–49,999	2,500–9,999	All Other	Dominant Locational Characteristic
2641	Paper coating and glazing	27.7	72.3	.73	2.15	2.22	1.15	.80	.61	U
2711	Newspapers	281.8	73.3	1.86	1.97	1.59	1.39	.98	.15	LM
2896	Compressed and liquefied gases	10.4	90.1	1.58	2.89	1.34	.60*	.25*	.33	I
3011	Tires and inner tubes	92.7	86.0	*n.a.*	3.77	*n.a.*	1.55	*n.a.*	.38	I
3099	Rubber industries, *n.e.c.*	132.5	75.7	.68	2.53	1.24	1.50	1.18	.46	U
3192	Saddlery, harness, and whips	1.3	56.1	.65	3.25	.46	.84	2.38*	.26	U
3291	Abrasive products	22.3	88.6	1.09	1.78	2.63	.99	.27	.68	U
3351	Copper rolling and drawing	41.9	83.6	1.00	2.82	.90	1.93	.59	.16	LM
3431	Plumbing fixtures and fittings	30.6	68.2	1.18	2.73	.71	1.31	.94	.39	NM
3441	Structural and ornamental work	116.3	89.5	1.22	2.46	1.56	1.39	.64	.36	LM
3443	Boiler shop products	74.4	83.8	.92	1.97	1.39	1.72	1.02	.45	LM
3541	Machine tools	81.0	81.0	1.61	2.48	1.53	1.14	.87	.22	NM
3571	Computing and related machines	56.7	85.0	.79	2.87	*n.a.*	2.75	*n.a.*	*negl.*	LS
3585	Refrigeration machinery	128.3	77.5	.74	2.97	1.42	.91	.80	.55	NM
3613	Electrical measuring instruments	33.0	88.8	1.06	2.26	4.59	.42	.20	.29	LS
3614	Motors and generators	112.0	84.6	1.11	2.06	2.95	1.15	1.34	.24	U
3831	Optical instruments and lenses	12.7	97.4	1.05	3.97	.64	.64*	.06*	.48	U
3861	Photographic equipment	58.1	95.1	1.29	4.28	1.46	.72	.04	.12	I
3912	Jewelers' findings	5.4	98.5	.52	3.97	*n.a.*	1.78*	*n.a.*	.23*	E
3961	Costume jewelry	27.7	98.4	2.23	3.40	.63	.96	.02	.07	E
	4. High incidence in small cities, substantial in medium									
2034	Dehydrated fruits and vegetables	7.0	68.3	.28	1.53	2.70	1.28	2.23	.53	NM
2081	Bottled soft drinks	91.6	64.0	1.15	1.99	1.86	1.87	1.14	.20	LM
2131	Chewing and smoking tobacco	7.5	90.5	1.06	2.44	6.34	.42*	*n.a.*	*n.a.*	NM
2397	Schiffli machine embroideries	5.7	98.1	1.14	.29	3.53	2.10*	1.60*	.23*	E
2431	Millwork plants	68.7	61.3	.84	1.63	1.37	2.06	1.23	.43	NM
2532	Professional furniture	5.5	51.2	1.23	.40	1.12	3.76	.21*	.08*	I
2699	Paper and board products, *n.e.c.*	73.2	75.0	1.34	1.03	2.56	1.66	1.18	.35	U
2822	Intermediates and organic colors	32.7	70.0	.81	.32	.49	3.15	.24*	.69*	I
2932	By-product coke ovens	31.9	95.3	.80	1.31	2.19	2.24	.34	.54	NM
3111	Leather tanning and finishing	43.5	65.2	1.11	1.06	.90	2.61	.85	.45	LM
3131	Footwear cut stock	20.1	61.8	1.28	.38	3.02	2.34	.46	.45	U
3221	Glass containers	48.4	50.6	*n.a.*	.80	2.02	1.76	1.98	.50	NM
3312	Steel works and rolling mills	518.7	93.5	.58	1.09	2.88	1.83	.60	.70	NM
3321	Gray-iron foundries	133.9	68.4	.66	1.25	2.98	1.69	1.51	.45	NM
3322	Malleable-iron foundries	23.4	52.1	.77	1.30	3.71	2.45	*n.a.*	*n.a.*	NM
3323	Steel foundries	55.1	88.0	1.07	.86	3.31	1.50	1.41	.42	LM
3391	Iron and steel forgings	39.8	92.3	1.38	1.16	2.59	2.16	.40	.32	NM
3392	Wire drawing	54.9	80.4	.53	1.57	1.90	3.07	.47	.35	NM
3442	Metal doors, sash, and trim	43.3	81.9	1.74	1.69	1.17	1.87	.70	.24	NM
3519	Internal combustion engines	51.8	59.5	1.30	.82	.59	3.76	.59	.03	U
3522	Farm machinery, except tractors	74.4	55.9	.54	1.03	1.41	2.53	2.00	.39	NM
3531	Construction and mining machinery	75.7	77.9	1.02	1.87	2.63	1.75	.91	.28	NM
3559	Special-industry machinery, *n.e.c.*	47.0	78.7	1.12	1.90	1.03	2.42	.73	.28	U
3561	Pumps and compressors	60.3	72.4	.93	1.66	.97	2.45	.68	.44	U
3569	General industrial machinery, *n.e.c.*	27.9	85.6	1.13	1.41	1.85	1.96	.85	.42	U
3593	Ball and roller bearings	48.7	76.8	.99	1.92	1.98	2.31	.12	.18	U
3615	Transformers	41.0	89.7	.97	.58	4.10	3.12	.54	.09	U
3621	Electrical appliances	48.6	70.7	1.64	1.00	2.22	1.96	.64	.31	NM
3662	Electronic tubes	71.0	67.2	.41	.76	2.98	2.34	1.88	.38	LS
3717	Motor vehicles and parts	649.3	91.2	1.40	1.79	3.19	1.04	.69	.35	NM
3729	Aircraft equipment, *n.e.c.*	180.9	90.8	1.10	1.67	1.44	1.61	.66	.58	I
3731	Ship building and repairing	109.5	80.0	1.37	1.58	2.14	1.88	.73	.06	NM

SIC 1954	Industry Title	Total Industry Employment 1954 (in Thousands)	Percent-age within SMA's	Location Quotient for Places with 1950 Population of: 500,000 or More	100,000–499,999	50,000–99,999	10,000–49,999	2,500–9,999	All Other	Dominant Locational Charac-teristic
5. Wide incidence in all size cities: (A) over 2,500; and (B) over 10,000 population										
	A. All size cities over 2,500 population									
2024	Ice cream and ices	36.5	75.7	1.98	1.75	1.68	1.19	1.03	.19	LM
2031	Canned seafood	15.1	55.4	1.41	1.20	.80	1.08*	1.00*	.69	NM
2035	Pickles and sauces	21.9	64.9	1.69	1.22	1.07	.99	1.30	.57	U
2293	Paddings and upholstery filling	9.1	85.9	1.88	1.28	1.42	1.48	1.11	.30	U
2329	Men's and boys' clothing, *n.e.c.*	90.8	52.1	1.18	1.68	1.14	1.40	1.95	.35	LU
2334	Dresses, dozen price	54.5	65.9	1.63	1.47	1.86	1.34	1.35	.28	E
2341	Women's and children's underwear	73.4	65.8	1.95	.94	.85	1.20	1.72	.40	E
2512	Household furniture, upholstered	56.0	64.4	1.31	1.58	1.14	1.56	1.80	.31	LM
2531	Public building and related furniture	14.0	55.6	.84	1.91	1.03	1.47*	1.47*	.37	I
2671	Paperboard boxes	133.0	81.7	1.86	1.69	1.27	1.31	.76	.35	LM
2899	Chemical products, *n.e.c.*	21.4	88.4	1.74	1.75	1.47	.87	.97	.45	U
3142	House slippers	10.9	62.1	1.42	.76	1.17	1.26	1.61*	.33*	U
3361	Nonferrous foundries	73.5	78.4	1.66	1.20	1.44	1.31	1.53	.37	NM
3399	Primary metal industries, *n.e.c.*	25.1	94.1	1.48	.91	1.51	1.36	1.57	.50	NM
3423	Hand tools, *n.e.c.*	23.4	63.4	1.04	1.39	1.80	1.66	1.03	.53	NM
3439	Heating and cooking equipment, *n.e.c.*	75.3	75.6	1.57	1.47	1.46	1.69	.79	.38	U
3444	Sheet metal works	50.2	85.2	1.75	2.05	1.27	1.22	.90	.29	LM
3489	Wirework, *n.e.c.*	59.9	82.8	1.94	1.06	1.45	1.45	.88	.40	NM
3542	Metalworking machinery	59.5	80.6	1.31	1.40	2.20	.91	1.69	.44	NM
3544	Special dies and tools	77.4	90.0	1.95	1.47	2.02	.96	.77	.40	E
3551	Food products machinery	33.2	75.5	1.92	.95	2.20	1.38	.89	.34	U
3563	Conveyors	32.4	78.9	1.49	.82	1.00	1.66	1.94	.40	U
3566	Power transmission equipment	49.6	83.2	1.92	1.87	1.19	.93	1.22	.30	U
3589	Service and household machines, *n.e.c.*	10.4	87.9	.97	1.16	2.68	1.47	.98*	.49	U
3594	Industrial patterns and molds	19.9	85.1	1.85	1.81	1.22	1.39	.77	.30	E
3599	Machine shops	103.7	77.1	1.69	1.19	1.20	1.42	.89	.50	LM
3619	Electrical industrial apparatus, *n.e.c.*	15.0	76.3	.92	1.27	2.59	1.26	2.14	.37	LS
3949	Sporting and athletic goods	28.9	64.8	1.55	1.11	.80	1.89	1.24	.41	LM
3952	Lead pencils and crayons	5.0	69.5	1.62	1.25	1.27	*n.a.*	1.19*	.34	U
3971	Plastic products, *n.e.c.*	92.0	78.9	1.52	1.19	1.22	1.45	1.07	.53	U
3988	Morticians' goods	16.7	70.1	1.62	2.04	1.22	1.12	1.73	.19	U
	B. All size cities over 10,000 population									
2097	Manufactured ice	20.9	55.4	.80	1.98	1.63	1.79	.30	.28	LM
2295	Coated fabric, except rubberized	8.5	79.4	.91	1.64	1.25	1.83	.52*	.49*	E
2392	House furnishings, *n.e.c.*	36.2	56.9	1.99	1.01	.76	.95	.59	.72	E
2394	Canvas products	13.5	79.7	1.93	2.42	1.59	1.04	.56	.21	U
2732	Book printing	22.7	74.4	1.93	1.31	1.36	1.75	.19	.40	E
3429	Hardware, *n.e.c.*	88.3	85.8	1.50	1.48	2.25	1.01	.42	.60	NM
3494	Bolts, nuts, washers, rivets	53.7	91.8	1.84	1.69	1.34	1.04	.70	.45	NM
3553	Woodworking machinery	12.0	70.6	1.26	1.66	1.03	1.75	.65	.51	U
3564	Blowers and fans	18.1	87.8	1.59	1.66	1.80	2.01	.37	.25	U
3579	Office and store machines, *n.e.c.*	20.8	94.4	1.99	1.60	1.20	1.72	*n.a.*	*n.a.*	NM
3611	Wiring devices and supplies	43.2	90.7	1.86	2.35	.78	1.18	.64	.30	U
3631	Insulated wire and cable	14.4	75.4	.85	1.96	2.08	1.05*	.38*	.48	I
3661	Radios and related products	294.0	82.0	1.90	1.38	1.37	1.32	.65	.42	U
3691	Storage batteries	15.7	88.6	1.67	1.57	2.25	1.63	.48*	.15*	I
3941	Games and toys, *n.e.c.*	38.2	85.4	1.69	1.50	1.68	1.13	.72	.49	E
3964	Needles, pins, and fasteners	23.2	74.9	1.52	2.51	.75	1.79	.25	.30	E

SIC 1954	Industry Title	Total Industry Employment 1954 (in Thousands)	Percentage within SMA's	Location Quotient for Places with 1950 Population of: 500,000 or More	100,000–499,999	50,000–99,999	10,000–49,999	2,500–9,999	All Other	Dominant Locational Characteristic
6. High incidence in small cities outside metropolitan areas										
2015	Poultry dressing plants	46.2	29.9	.36	.78	.88	1.43	2.09	.96	NM
2021	Creamery butter	21.0	23.2	.31	.78	.88	1.28	2.30	.98	NM
2023	Concentrated milk	13.3	13.4	.06	.39	.37	1.41	3.39	.97	NM
2033	Canned fruits and vegetables	119.8	46.7	.56	1.27	.66	1.34	1.91	.83	NM
2036	Packaged seafood	12.2	38.6	.71	1.37	.46	1.66*	.77	.89	NM
2037	Frozen fruits and vegetables	21.4	29.0	.11	.44	.19	1.88	2.27	1.07	NM
2141	Tobacco stemming and redrying	18.8	46.1	*n.a.*	1.25	4.71	2.53*	1.46*	.17	NM
2223	Thread mills	13.9	30.6	.41	.69	.64	2.07*	2.63	.38*	LU
2224	Yarn mills, cotton system	85.3	15.8	*n.a.*	.22	1.07	1.47	2.64	1.06	LU
2233	Cotton broad-woven fabrics	296.2	24.4	.08	.52	1.59	1.41	1.79	1.12	LU
2234	Synthetic broad-woven fabrics	90.0	40.5	.18	.73	1.58	1.16	1.61	1.15	I
2252	Seamless hosiery mills	63.4	35.1	.15	.78	1.00	2.25	2.86	.58	LU
2273	Carpets and rugs, except wool	11.5	32.3	.58	.54	.46	3.29	1.57	.49	I
2298	Cordage and twine	12.3	44.4	1.20	.72	*n.a.*	1.71	1.15*	.83	NM
2321	Men's dress shirts and nightwear	108.3	45.0	.83	.95	1.27	1.66	2.55	.46	E
2382	Fabric work gloves	10.1	22.3	.27	1.09	*n.a.*	1.51	3.94*	.55	LU
2432	Plywood plants	39.2	17.6	*n.a.*	.92	*n.a.*	2.07	1.68*	1.05	NM
2444	Wooden boxes	39.5	39.0	.53	.86	1.10	1.34	2.11	.85	LM
2511	Wood furniture, not upholstered	124.9	42.0	.64	1.08	1.32	1.72	2.31	.54	I
2611	Pulp mills	57.7	21.6	*n.a.*	.36	.44	1.49	2.40	1.14	NM
2612	Paper and paperboard mills	142.2	43.3	.14	.55	1.36	1.69	1.95	1.00	NM
2613	Building paper and board mills	16.4	50.0	.18	.88	.78	1.79	2.00	.92	NM
2872	Fertilizers, mixing only	12.0	47.5	.35	1.11	.95	1.53	1.70	.92	LM
2881	Cottonseed oil mills	13.7	37.6	*n.a.*	1.29	1.81	1.85	2.41	.59	NM
3141	Footwear, except rubber	219.4	43.7	.80	.41	1.92	2.18	2.09	.47	I
3229	Pressed and blown glassware, *n.e.c.*	41.9	32.7	.18	.32	.34	3.61	1.96	.55	NM
3255	Clay refractories	14.5	38.6	.49	*n.a.*	.39	1.75	1.36	1.15	LM
3275	Mineral wool	10.2	42.4	.16	1.27	.53	3.57	.26	.29	U
3281	Cut-stone and stone products	21.6	36.9	.58	.86	.49	2.07	1.25	.88	NM
3581	Domestic laundry equipment	22.1	40.5	*n.a.*	1.13	*n.a.*	2.65	2.36	.06	NM
3641	Engine electrical equipment	46.3	39.2	.43	1.80	.08	3.28	1.80	.20	U
7. High incidence in smallest cities										
2222	Yarn throwing mills	11.8	58.8	.73	.84	1.54	1.90	2.15	.51	LU
2251	Full-fashioned hosiery mills	60.2	51.6	.46	.92	1.15	1.52	3.12	.57	LU
2254	Knit underwear mills	31.3	57.9	.46	1.36	2.44	1.06	3.09	.41	LU
2256	Knit fabric mills	16.8	58.3	.86	.98	1.03	1.34	2.39	.62	E
2322	Men's and boys' underwear	9.4	25.2	.31	.47	*n.a.*	1.99*	2.69*	.61	LU
2327	Separate trousers	51.7	53.0	1.26	1.10	.68	1.23	2.41	.50	E
2328	Work shirts‡	7.0	16.7	.07	*n.a.*	*n.a.*	.58*	5.50*	.53*	LU
2441	Fruit and vegetable baskets	6.7	20.9	.07	.24	*n.a.*	1.29	2.23*	1.17	LM
2521	Wood office furniture	5.5	61.4	.99	1.09	.22	1.48	3.42	.36	I
2674	Fiber cans, tubes, and drums	12.1	71.7	1.20	1.44	1.68	1.34	2.07	.33	LM
2889	Animal oils, *n.e.c.*	2.3	29.0	.43	.31	.42	.69	3.18	1.11	NM
2952	Roofing felts and coatings	15.7	92.7	1.06	1.31	1.17	.96	2.70	.47	NM
3152	Leather work gloves	2.5	35.7	1.06	.98	*n.a.*	1.09*	3.10	.49	I
3269	Pottery products, *n.e.c.*	9.6	60.9	.62	.84	.61	1.45	2.69	.72	U
3292	Asbestos products	22.0	86.8	1.07	.31	.80	.77	2.33	.96	U
3521	Tractors	64.7	92.6	1.05	.43	2.93	1.37	3.25	.21	NM
3713	Truck and bus bodies	18.7	56.8	1.02	1.06	1.47	1.73	2.60	.29	NM
3722	Aircraft engines	167.4	96.5	.94	.51	.66	.86	2.26	.96	I

SIC 1954	Industry Title	Total Industry Employment 1954 (in Thousands)	Percentage within SMA's	Location Quotient for Places with 1950 Population of: 500,000 or More	100,000–499,999	50,000–99,999	10,000–49,999	2,500–9,999	All Other	Dominant Locational Characteristic
8. Wide incidence in nonurban as well as urban places										
2026	Fluid milk	14.1	59.2	.71	.89	1.07	1.27	1.22	1.00	LM
2241	Narrow fabric mills	25.7	66.7	.83	1.11	2.64	1.09	1.04	.77	E
2261	Finishing textiles, except wool	79.3	59.6	.45	1.27	1.66	1.23	.91	1.01	E
2499	Wood products, *n.e.c.*	38.6	39.3	.59	.80	.71	1.20	1.80	1.02	U
2661	Paper bags	33.3	69.7	1.35	1.22	.92	.95	.82	.86	NM
2871	Fertilizers	19.7	73.3	.59	1.52	1.12	1.26	.64	1.01	LM
2886	Grease and tallow	11.5	73.8	1.61	1.31	1.17	.76	.54	.81	LM
2951	Paving mixtures and blocks	4.4	72.1	.76	1.04	.76	1.63	.98	.92	LM
3295	Minerals, ground or treated	7.7	76.9	.76	1.25	1.59	1.06	.54	1.04	U
3297	Nonclay refractories	8.6	67.3	1.05	*n.a.*	1.32	.74	1.21*	1.06	U
3491	Metal barrels, drums, and pails	10.6	96.1	1.41	.92	1.49	1.38	.40*	.75*	LM
3545	Metal working machinery attachments	44.9	79.4	1.60	.92	1.49	1.04	.62	.77	E
9. High incidence in nonurban places										
A. Within metropolitan areas										
2084	Wines and brandy	5.7	62.9	.85	.24	.39	.64	.68	1.57	NM
2819	Inorganic chemicals, *n.e.c.*‡	97.0	61.1	.30	.25	.95	.74	.29	1.78	NM
2824	Synthetic rubber§	8.5	88.5	*n.a.*	.84	*negl.*	*n.a.*	*n.a.*	1.39*	NM
2829	Organic chemicals, *n.e.c.*	67.5	74.5	.36	.28	1.19	1.36	.51	1.45	I
3241	Cement, hydraulic§	39.8	56.1	.37	.86	*n.a.*	*n.a.*	.87	1.50	LM
3352	Aluminum rolling and drawing§	36.8	66.3	.37	.25	*n.a.*	.79*	.15*	1.28	NM
B. Outside metropolitan areas										
2022	Natural cheese	13.9	13.8	.25	.25	.19	.82	2.08	1.46	NM
2061	Raw cane sugar	3.1	0	0	0	0	*n.a.*	*n.a.*	2.18	NM
2063	Beet sugar	11.0	12.9	0	0	0	*n.a.*	*n.a.*	2.28	NM
2411	Logging camps and contractors	75.5	6.3	.01	.05	.03	.34	.71	2.13	NM
2421	Sawmills and planing mills	321.2	10.8	.02	.33	.12	.61	1.13	1.83	NM
2422	Veneer mills	12.8	20.8	*n.a.*	.76	.68	1.09	1.88*	1.25	NM
2423	Shingle mills	2.5	24.7	*n.a.*	1.22	*negl.*	1.20*	1.15	1.39	NM
2424	Cooperage stock mills	3.4	10.2	*n.a.*	.36	*negl.*	1.52*	1.34*	1.47	NM
2433	Prefabricated wood products	11.5	48.7	.34	1.09	1.12	.79	1.24	1.25	NM
2491	Wood preserving	12.1	43.3	.25	.86	.46	1.10	1.55	1.28	NM
2825	Synthetic fibers§	61.1	33.7	*n.a.*	*n.a.*	*n.a.*	*n.a.*	*n.a.*	1.83	NM
2826	Explosives§	32.5	49.7	*n.a.*	*n.a.*	*n.a.*	*n.a.*	*n.a.*	1.68	I
3251	Brick and hollow tile	32.4	46.8	.14	.58	.75	.79	.90	1.62	LM
3254	Clay sewer pipe	9.6	29.2	.19	.49	.47	.66*	2.11*	1.32	U
3259	Structural clay products, *n.e.c.*	5.0	27.7	.24	.33	.02	.47*	.75*	1.79	U
3272	Gypsum products	11.0	47.7	.85	.43	*n.a.*	.69*	*n.a.*	1.52	NM
3274	Lime	8.0	16.9	*n.a.*	.16	*n.a.*	.23	.53	2.11	U
10. Industries which do not meet criteria for the above categories										
2025	Special dairy products	7.3	53.7	1.39	.14	.88	.93	2.76	.71	NM
2042	Prepared animal feeds	59.9	56.1	.66	1.70	1.85	1.24	1.53	.62	NM
2085	Distilled liquor	21.5	61.4	1.01	1.69	*n.a.*	.36*	*n.a.*	1.18	I
2093	Margarine	2.6	77.5	1.85	3.41	0	*n.a.*	*n.a.*	.55*	U
2211	Scouring and combing plants	7.0	71.3	.65	*n.a.*	3.46	*n.a.*	*n.a.*	1.42	LU
2212	Yarn mills, wool, except carpet	17.8	55.0	.25	.66	4.27	.36*	1.58	.98	LU
2213	Woolen and worsted fabrics	62.5	45.8	.40	.43	1.53	.54*	1.08*	1.25	E
2281	Fur-felt hats and hat bodies	8.2	59.9	1.55	.57	*n.a.*	4.11	*n.a.*	.12	I
2294	Processed textile waste	5.8	76.5	1.35	.92	*n.a.*	2.11	.38*	.60	U
2381	Fabric dress gloves	4.5	41.7	1.62	.54	*n.a.*	2.78	1.64*	.21	E

SIC 1954	Industry Title	Total Industry Employment 1954 (in Thousands)	Percent-age within SMA's	Location Quotient for Places with 1950 Population of: 500,000 or More	100,000–499,999	50,000–99,999	10,000–49,999	2,500–9,999	All Other	Dominant Locational Charac-teristic
2445	Cooperage	3.7	75.3	1.48	3.04	.51	.42	.82	.51	LM
2823	Plastics materials	41.1	71.7	.39	1.10	.46	1.79	.42	1.18	I
2834	Pharmaceutical preparations	76.6	90.2	1.88	.88	.63	1.25	1.09	.60	I
2841	Soap and glycerin	25.8	99.2	1.72	3.41	1.14	.20	1.46	.14	I
2897	Insecticides and fungicides	6.5	78.6	.46	1.42	1.47	.60	1.23	1.12	U
2911	Petroleum refining	153.1	78.8	.58	.30	1.76	1.09	1.24	1.19	NM
2992	Lubricants, *n.e.c.*	8.2	94.0	1.77	2.89	.76	.56	.30	.48	NM
3231	Products of purchased glass	21.6	65.9	1.84	1.36	.46	.89	.97	.65	LS
3261	Vitreous plumbing fixtures	9.2	54.5	*n.a.*	1.76	*n.a.*	1.58	1.98*	.70	NM
3271	Concrete products	60.4	65.0	.49	1.31	1.64	1.45	1.30	.82	NM
3421	Cutlery	15.1	71.7	1.58	2.26	.31	1.27	.81	.45	LM
3422	Edge tools	7.1	76.0	1.71	1.70	2.81	.45	1.06	.40	NM
3493	Steel springs	7.1	92.0	1.72	1.49	.17	2.20*	.94*	.09*	NM
3532	Oil-field machinery and tools	33.7	78.8	1.95	1.86	.51	1.01*	.09*	.43	NM
3552	Textile machinery	36.6	59.8	.56	1.36	1.58	1.58	1.43	.71	NM
3554	Paper industries machinery	15.0	59.5	.79	1.26	1.93	2.66	.95	.34	U
3715	Truck trailers	16.4	87.5	1.23	2.27	*n.a.*	.25*	2.52	.37	NM
3716	Automobile trailers	11.1	50.4	.50	.48	.73	1.44	1.66	1.10	NM
3732	Boat building and repairing	16.9	51.2	.43	1.19	.58	1.42	1.90	.90	NM
3799	Transportation equipment, *n.e.c.*	1.6	61.3	.36	.91	4.53	1.49*	.47*	.53	U

Sources: The first 10 columns are based on Business and Defense Services Administration Office of Area Development, Department of Commerce, *Metropolitan Area and City Size Patterns of Manufacturing Industries, 1954*, Area Trend Series No. 4 (Washington, D. C.: U.S. Government Printing Office, 1959), pp. 12–21. Dominant Locational Characteristics in the last column are adapted from Robert M. Lichtenberg, *One Tenth of a Nation* (Cambridge, Mass.: Harvard University Press, 1960).
*Represents part but not all of the industry's employment in this size group because data for some cities is not available.
†Also well distributed in other size cities.
‡Distribution of over 10 per cent of this industry's employment is not available.
§This industry meets the criterion of having 50 per cent or more of total industry employment in nonurban places, though the city size distribution for more than 10 per cent of employment is not available.
n.a. = not available.
n.e.c. = not elsewhere classified.
negl. = negligible, less than .005.
Classes of Dominant Locational Characteristics are as follows:
E: External economics
I: Inertia
LM: Transport costs, sectional or local market
LS: Labor costs and supply, skilled labor
LU: Labor costs and supply, unskilled labor
NM: Transport costs, national market
U: Unclassified

These quotients were inspected, together with the percentage distribution of American employment in the various industries by city-size group, and a classification of industries by city size into nine groups was produced (Table 5–8). Next, Lichtenberg's classification of industries according to "dominant locational characteristic" was added.[106]

The principal features of the results are as follows:

1. Very high incidence in large cities (500,000 or more). Industries with very high incidence in large cities are of three types: food and beverages, apparel and other nonstandardized consumer products, and printing. Industries of the first type—prepared meats, flour mixes, confectionery products, beer and ale, and flavorings—decline in incidence with remarkable regularity from large to medium-size and smaller places, and their dominant locational characteristic is national market orientation. Very high location quotients for many clothing industries reflect in particular the dominance of New York, and the externalities present in that city. Printing and publishing industries reflect forward linkages to commercial users and engender noteworthy backward linkages. For example, the only chemical or machinery industries very often found in large cities are printing ink and printing trades machinery!

2. High incidence in large cities (500,000 or more). Nearly half the industries in this category are similar to types in Category 1, food, apparel, and printing. Two important types are added: chemical end-products, and fabricated or assembled light metal products. Chemical end-products produced by this group are paints and varnishes, toilet preparations, cleaning and polishing preparations, and glue and gelatine. Metal products include metal house-furniture, lighting fixtures, fabricated pipe and fittings, valves and fittings (except plumbing), mechanical measuring instruments, and scientific instruments. Metal stampings, tin cans and other tinware, and plating and polishing are also prominent industries, implying direct linkages with many of the consumer end-products manufactured in this city size group.

Virtually all products of very high or high incidence in large cities are compact and light in weight, with transport costs being very low in relation to the value added by manufacture. This product characteristic permits shipment to regional or national markets, contributing to the strong position of major cities as distribution centers for such industries.

The relatively high labor intensity required in the manufacture of Category 1 and 2 products is also evident. These industries are among those employing the highest number of employees per unit of value added.

3. High incidence in medium cities (100,000–499,999); substantial in smaller cities (10,000–99,999). Machinery industries, conspicuously absent from Categories 1 and 2, abound in the medium and smaller cities. Category 3 includes machine tools, computing and related machines, refrigeration machinery, and motors and generators. Important food product industries in this category are meat-packing plants, fluid milk and other products, flour and meal, bread and related products. Other heavy industries of high incidence in medium-sized cities include tires and inner tubes, copper rolling and drawing, plumbing fixtures and fittings, and structural and ornamental work.

4. High incidence in smaller cities (10,000–99,999); substantial in medium (100,000–499,999). Basic producer goods, including metals, machinery, and transport equipment, are especially prominent in cities of 10,000 to 99,999. Basic metal industries include steel works and rolling mills, foundries, forgings, and wire drawing. Machinery and electrical equipment industries include farm machinery (except tractors), construction and mining machinery, special purpose and general industry machines, internal combustion engines, pumps and compressors, transformers and electrical appliances. The city subclass 50,000 to 99,999 has location quotients of 3.19 for motor vehicles and parts, and 2.14 for ship building and repairing.

5. Wide incidence in all sizes of cities. Industries with location quotients of 0.75 or more in all city-size classes, but without any quotient meeting the criterion for high incidence in any single class, meet the test of wide incidence in cities of all sizes. The floors used were (a) 2,500; and (b) 10,000 population. Not surprisingly, this category displays the widest industrial heterogeneity among the nine locational categories. Thirteen major industry groups are represented.

Important metal, machinery, and electrical industries in this category include nonferrous foundries, heating and cooking equipment, sheet metal and wire work, bolts, nuts, washers and rivets, metalworking, food products machinery, special dies and tools, conveyors, power transmission equipment, wiring devices and supplies, and radios and related products. Machine shops, a prominent service industry, are also central to this category. In ten of the industries just cited, 75 to 85 per cent of industry employment in 1954 was within metropolitan areas. About 90 per cent of employment in the other three industries was in SMA's.

By contrast, the metropolitan share of most widely distributed consumer nondurable manufactures was from 52 to 66 per cent. Among these are the largest consumer-product industries in this locational category: men's and boys' clothing not elsewhere classified, dresses sold by the dozen, women's and children's underwear, upholstered household furniture, house furnishings, and sporting and athletic goods. The metropolitan employment share in these industries corresponds directly with the metropolitan share of total population, 56 per cent, contrasting significantly with the 85 to 95 per cent metropolitan share of employment in those apparel industries whose incidence is high in large cities.

In interpreting these locational contrasts, it is to be noted that apparel industries which are widely found in all sizes of cities use more labor per unit of value added, and pay lower hourly wages, than the apparel industries which are concentrated in large cities. Wage differentials are an important factor in these locational differences. Apparel and household product industries which are well distributed in all sizes of cities are also characterized by a lower value added, in relation to transport costs, than are the specialty clothes or brand-name apparel and consumer chemical products which are made largely in big cities. This suggests closer market orientation of consumer goods with high transport costs in relation to value added.

Neither the consumer products nor the varied metal-working and machinery industries in Category 5 can be said to require a "minimum" or "critical" size city. Consumer industries in this category appear able to operate without the benefit of external economies provided by metropolitan status. That the multi-component metal and machinery manufactures in this category are found more in metropolitan areas, on the other hand, can be associated with the advantages of external economies and of proximity to purchasing and distribution agencies.

6. High incidence in small cities (10,000–49,999) outside metropolitan areas. Industries prominent in small, nonmetropolitan cities are of two main kinds: transport-sensitive resource processing, located so as to reduce the weight, bulk, and/or perishability of major raw materials; and low-paying, labor-intensive manufacturing. Agriculturally based industries include canned and frozen fruits and vegetables, poultry dressing, creamery butter, concentrated milk, and cottonseed-oil mills. Forest-based industries are pulp, paper, paperboard and building-paper mills, plywood, wooden boxes, and wood furniture (not upholstered). Pressed and blown glassware, clay refractories, and cut stone and stone products complete the resource-based industries in this category.

Textile mills make their first prominent appearance in this city size group: cotton yarn, cotton and synthetic broad-woven fabric, and seamless hosiery mills. Footwear and men's dress shirt and nightwear industries are also substantial employers in small, nonmetropolitan cities.

7. High incidence in smallest cities (2,500–9,999). Hosiery, knitwear, and selected men's apparel including separate trousers and work shirts evidence the importance of textile and apparel manufactures in the smallest as well as the small cities. The differences between the two locational categories are not pronounced. Many industries which meet the nonmetropolitan small city criteria of Category 6 have even higher location quotients in the smallest cities, those of 2,500 to 9,999. Of note are aircraft engines, tractors, and truck and bus bodies: the first two are found almost entirely in metropolitan areas, but body building is distributed exactly in proportion to the distribution of population between metropolitan and nonmetropolitan areas.

8. Wide incidence in nonurban as well as urban places; and 9. High incidence in nonurban places (less than 2,500). Category 8 industries are perhaps the most ubiquitous, with respect to size of place, tending to nonurban location but not in sufficient numbers to establish clear locational characteristics. Fluid milk, textile finishing (except wool), fertilizers, and metal working machinery attachments suggest the diversity of this small array of manufactures.

Much clearer in significance are those industries with predominantly nonurban locations, divided in Table 5–9 between metropolitan and nonmetropolitan locations. Six of these have over 50 per cent employment inside, and 17 outside, standard metropolitan areas.

The high incidence of heavy chemicals and of chemical intermediates in nonurban places is the most striking feature of this locational category. Inorganic chemicals, organic chemicals, synthetic fibers, explosives, and synthetic rubber are major industries having 57 to 75 per cent of their employees in places of less than 2,500, or locational quotients of 1.39 to 1.83 for such locations. No basic chemical industries meet the criteria for urban locational categories. The heavy chemicals just cited include substantial nonmetropolitan as well as metropolitan employment. Their employment percentages within SMA's in 1954 were, in decreasing order: synthetic rubber, 89 per cent; organic chemicals, 75 per cent; inorganic chemicals, 61 per cent; explosives, 50 per cent; and synthetic fibers, 34 per cent.

To basic chemicals must be added hydraulic cement, and aluminum rolling and drawing, as heavy industries of a high nonurban incidence. Cement exactly matches the 56 per cent metropolitan share of population in employment distribution, while aluminum rolling is somewhat above, at 66 per cent employment inside SMA's. These locational patterns document the tendency of heavy processing industries to choose plant sites some distance removed from urban population centers, to meet special requirements of space, materials and process control, transport, waste disposal, and safety. Resource-based food, wood, and clay product industries complete the nonurban location category.

Industries not classified by location. Size-of-place distributions of thirty-three industries in 1954 did not fall within the criteria established to define locational categories. Several of these industries display other regularities of location in respect to size of place, but the rest show little locational consistency. Location quotients for these unclassified industries may be examined in Category 10 of Table 5–9.[107]

Summary findings. This locational taxonomy reveals great diversity in the relationship of industries to size of place. Only a few summary findings can be drawn, therefore, without aggravating the risk of unwarranted aggregative statements.

1. Over the spectrum of urban and nonurban place sizes, food and beverage products as a whole are of the widest incidence. But individual food industries display sharply divergent locational pulls, some, as we have seen, concentrating in the largest cities, some in medium-sized or small cities, others in rural places. Transport, marketing, and processing characteristics of individual industries would require examination to explain these locational contrasts.
2. Apparel, fabricated metal products, and wood products including furniture are widely distributed over all sizes of urban places. Certain apparel industries are of very high or high incidence in the largest cities; others are bound in the smallest cities outside metropolitan areas. Most metal fabricating industries display wide distribution in urban places, though a few are primarily found in large cities. Wood product industries are more evenly spread in places of all size, including rural places.
3. Consumer product industries, largely encompassed in the two previous paragraphs, are far more eclectically located than producer or intermediate goods industries, with respect to size of place. Each of the more basic industries is associated with a narrower range of city size groups, as follows.
4. Basic metals, machinery, and transport equipment are of high incidence especially in cities of 10,000 to 99,999. Certain machinery industries are generally found in medium-sized cities; others are more widely distributed than primary metals or transport equipment in cities of all size. Three important transport industries are located in the smallest cities. Aluminum rolling is predominantly nonurban.
5. Heavy chemicals are predominantly nonurban. They are slightly more drawn to nonurban localities in metropolitan than in nonmetropolitan areas, but are also found in nonmetropolitan areas.
6. Textile mills are oriented strongly to the small cities and to nonurban locales, in many instances outside metropolitan areas.
7. Industries strongly oriented to raw materials, such as pulp, paper, and paperboard, or stone, clay, and glass products, are of high incidence in the small and smallest cities as well as in nonurban places outside metropolitan areas.
8. Frequent exceptions to these size of place patterns are observable in the detailed industry lists in Table 5–9. The unclassified industries listed in Category 10 are also instructive. Useful insights on urban advantages and disadvantages for specific manufactures can be

gained by the scrutiny of industry-wide city-size distributions, in conjunction with traditional industrial location analyses.

Data for Two States in India

Similar location quotients are shown for two states in India (Uttar Pradesh and the Punjab) in Table 5–10 to provide additional evidence to compare with the American case. Inspection of these added materials leads to the following conclusions:

First, there is a high incidence of dairy, bakery, sugar, beverages, cordage-rope-twine, cotton ginning, footwear, wood, paper, glass, and pottery industries in the smaller-sized urban centers of Punjab, and of beverage, sugar, wood, structural clay products, glass, and pottery industries in Uttar Pradesh. The quotients for these industries (excepting structural clay products) in other size groups are below 1, further signifying a strong orientation to small urban centers. Examining the characteristics of these industries, it may be observed that cotton ginning, wood, paper, pottery, and sugar industries are heavily drawn to specific nodes of resource availability, all these resources being either weight-losing or perishable. Economically and rationally, their locations are principally determined by resource distribution. The role of small towns as collection centers for raw materials of the region is a factor in the location of these industries. The consideration that explains the location of the cordage–rope–twine industry is either nearness of the resource or nearness to the consuming centers: in the former case, the raw material used may be grass, while hessian may be the raw material if the product is manufactured close to the markets. In Punjab, this industry is characteristic of small centers, while in Uttar Pradesh, small and large centers share the total employment in this industry. The high incidence of bakery, beverages, and footwear industry in the small centers of Punjab is more attributable to historic reasons than to size advantage or any other locational consideration. No technologically advanced industrial activity is associated with the smallest urban centers.

The medium-sized group of urban centers has but few industries in India. In Punjab, there is a concentration of professional, scientific, and control instruments in this size category,[108] the same industries being characteristic of large-sized urban centers of Uttar Pradesh. No other clear relationships are seen for this size group. It is when we move to the next higher category of urban centers (over 250,000) that the industrial composition becomes heterogeneous and typically includes more manufacturing than processing operations. Obvious illustrations are metal and machinery, motorcycles and bicycles, aircraft parts, and specialized production of photographic materials, watches and clocks, and musical instruments. Other industries oriented to this size of urban center are cotton textiles, knitting, basic industrial chemicals, soft drinks, tanneries, and rubber products. This structure bespeaks specialization, extended market areas for products which require a minimum level of technology for manufacturing, and other economies associated with size. It is these which differentiate a large from a small city.

Second, in the smaller-sized urban centers, industries which are found seldom or only moderately are nonmetallic mineral products, pottery, cordage-rope-twine, canning and preservation of fruits, and sugar refineries—incidentally, all relatively inflexible in location. Perishability or weight reduction play an overwhelmingly important part in the location of these industries. The manufacture of railroad equipment and miscellaneous chemicals has location quotients ranging between 2 and 3 for medium-sized urban centers in Uttar Pradesh.

There is far greater industrial diversification in the large-sized urban centers: the significant concentrations of leather products, motor vehicle parts, big sized castings and forgings, cocoa and chocolate, and chemicals are examples.

Third, conforming to the twin test of ubiquity, a number of industries are widely dispersed in different city-size groups (see Table 5–10). These are flour and rice milling, ice making and cold storage, structural clay products, repair of motor vehicles, castings and forgings of different sizes,

TABLE 5–10

Location Quotients for Selected Indian Industries by City Size: 1965

Industry Code	Industry Description	Location Quotients in Sizes								
		Punjab				Uttar Pradesh				
		250,000–500,000	100,000–250,000	50,000–100,000	20,000–50,000	500,000–1,000,000	250,000–500,000	100,000–250,000	50,000–100,000	20,000–50,000
20	Food Manufacturing Industries, Except Beverages									
202	Dairy products	—	—	1.35	1.88	1.21	0.22	1.96	0.31	0.99
203	Canning and preserving of fruits and vegetables	0.70	—	2.93	—	0.39	1.72	1.34	1.62	0.37
205–1 205–2	Flour mills Rice mills }	1.05	1.84	0.66	0.68	1.14	0.16	0.50	1.54	1.69
206	Bakery products	0.09	—	—	3.04	2.85	0.54	0.63	—	—
207	Sugar factories and refineries	—	—	2.66	0.69	0.003	0.06	0.50	0.92	3.77
208	Cocoa, chocolate and confectionary	—	—	—	—	2.11	—	1.45	0.99	—
209–2 &3 209–8	Edible and hydrogenated oils Cold storage and ice-making }	1.59	0.45	1.01	0.92	1.17	0.57	0.68	0.57	1.79
21	Beverage Industries*	—	—	3.42	—	0.81	0.12	1.23	1.01	1.86
214	Soft drinks and carbonated water	—	—	—	—	3.68	—	—	—	—
22–220	Tobacco Manufacturers	—	—	—	—	0.58	—	3.98	—	0.28
23	Manufacture of Textiles									
231–1	Cotton textiles	2.67†	0.06	1.20	0.29	2.92	0.09	0.21	0.41	0.45
231–3	Woolen textiles	—	—	—	—	2.64	—	1.15	—	0.27
232	Knitting mills	4.86	—	0.03	—	3.59	0.08	—	—	0.04
233	Cordage, rope and twine	—	—	3.42	—	2.39	—	—	2.46	—
239	Textiles not elsewhere classified	—	5.52	—	—	2.22	0.18	0.76	0.49	0.72
239–1	Cotton ginning and pressing	0.05	0.11	1.18	1.93	1.98	—	1.90	0.18	0.30
24	Manufacture of Footwear, Other Wearing Apparel and Made-up Textiles	0.13	—	3.33	—	3.66	—	0.02	—	—
25	Manufacture of Wood Except Furniture	0.34	0.18	3.01	0.03	0.48	0.18	0.35	4.46	0.67
26–260	Manufacture of Furniture and Fixtures	1.10	2.87	0.70	0.16	0.30	2.69	0.39	0.16	1.54
27–271	Manufacture of Paper and Paper Products	0.11	0.24	3.20	—	2.17	1.13	0.25	0.44	0.42
28–280	Printing, Publishing and Allied Industries	2.87	1.20	0.63	0.04	1.43	0.98	2.11	0.04	0.03
29	Manufacture of Leather and Fur Products Except Footwear									
291	Tanneries and leather finishing	3.00	—	—	1.20	3.41	0.04	—	0.16	0.19
293	Leather products except footwear	2.59	—	—	1.46	2.73	1.09	—	0.36	—
30–300	Manufacture of Rubber Products	2.19	0.01	1.36	0.48	0.30	4.27	0.44	0.17	0.03

Code	Industry									
31	Manufacture of Chemicals and Chemical Products									
311	Basic industrial chemicals	3.55	0.22	0.41	0.36	1.52	1.51	0.49	0.04	0.99
313	Paints, varnishes and lacquers	1.05	0.04	1.88	0.70	‡	—	—	—	—
319	Miscellaneous chemicals	—	—	—	—	0.81	1.23	2.21	0.15	0.45
33	Manufacture of Non-Metallic Mineral Products									
331	Structural clay products	1.24	1.04	1.17	0.67	1.61	—	—	3.95	—
332	Glass, and glass products	0.10	0.06	3.32	—	0.25	0.21	0.16	4.67	0.98
333	Pottery, china and earthenware	—	0.23	1.68	1.45	1.49	—	0.43	2.42	0.83
339	Non-metallic mineral products not elsewhere classified	0.56	—	0.62	2.18	0.85	1.17	2.78	—	—
34	Basic Metal Industries									
341–3	Castings and forgings	2.10	0.30	0.80	0.88	2.31	0.30	0.68	0.92	0.27
342	Non-ferrous basic metal industries	0.99	2.51	0.87	0.28	2.64	0.13	0.98	0.22	0.17
35–350	Manufacture of Metal Products Except Machinery and Transport Equipment	3.41	0.20	0.54	0.34	1.37	0.82	1.63	0.65	0.28
36–360	Manufacture of Machinery Except Electrical	3.76	0.42	0.68	0.28	1.97	0.79	1.07	0.42	0.23
37–370	Manufacture of Electric Machinery, Apparatus, Appliances and Supplies	0.51	0.62	1.80	0.77	1.50	1.22	0.53	1.28	0.37
38	Manufacture of Transport Equipment									
382	Railroad equipment, including wagons and coaches	2.42	0.23	1.22	0.34	1.85	0.06	2.41	0.07	—
383	Motor vehicles and parts	—	—	—	—	2.29	1.28	0.70	—	—
384	Repair of motor vehicles	1.67	1.35	0.51	0.82	1.54	0.68	0.80	0.65	1.02
385	Motorcycles and cycles	4.71	—	—	0.46	§	—	—	—	—
386	Aircraft	—	—	—	—	3.45	—	—	0.44	—
389	Transport equipment not elsewhere classified	—	—	—	—	0.87	4.06	—	—	—
39	Miscellaneous Manufacturing Industries									
391	Professional, scientific and controlling instruments	0.44	4.50	0.33	—	3.18	0.15	0.53	—	—
392	Photographical and optical goods	—	—	—	—	3.68	—	—	—	—
393	Watches and clocks	—	—	—	—	—	5.32	—	—	—
395	Musical instruments	—	—	—	—	3.68	—	—	—	—
399	Industries not elsewhere classified	2.07	0.39	1.29	0.39	1.49	0.65	1.21	0.47	0.83

Sources: List of Registered Factories, Uttar Pradesh and Punjab, 1965; industry codes used here have been adapted from the Classification of India Industries, as published in the *Annual Survey of Industries*, Vol. 1, Appendix II (Calcutta, India: Central Statistical Organisation, 1961).

*Beverage industries do not include soft drinks, which is a subcategory.

†Cotton textiles category includes woolen textile manufacturing for Punjab.

‡Included in miscellaneous chemicals.

§Included in transport equipment "not elsewhere classified."

nonferrous metal products, electric appliances, and beverage industries. An analysis of the characteristics of these industries shows that ice making (cold storage) and repair of motor vehicles are highly localized types of activities, in the sense that the final consumption of their products and services is linked primarily with the area of production. In these cases, the means of transferability is extremely low. Structural clay products, which involve heavy transportation costs, also tend to be manufactured for limited areal demands. Customarily, in order to meet at least the demands of a nonbasic nature, nearly all sizes of urban centers have casting and forging operations, as well as facilities for manufacturing electric household appliances and similar equipment. This is true also of various kinds of nonferrous metal products. The significant point to note is that manufacturing operations for the same product differ in scale, in technology, and in management with variation in the size of urban centers.

Judging from the characteristics of the above industries, it is quite apparent that they essentially are related to the community's own needs. Their occurrence in cities of all sizes indicates that there are no inhibitions imposed by the size of urban centers on their location. In fact, they may constitute the minimum industrial structure of any size of town.

Comparative Observations

Four broad comparisons stand out from this information concerning Indian and American industrial patterns:

1. In the smallest cities, very similar types of industries are found, attracted particularly to resources by transport considerations. In small American towns, wage differentials in the South have contributed to attraction of textile manufactures on a major scale, a feature not evident in India except perhaps in incipient form.
2. Industries classed as ubiquitous in the United States are more numerous than in India, and more diversified in manufacturing characteristics.
3. The high incidence of machinery and metal manufactures in American cities of 10,000 to 100,000 and 100,000 to 500,000 is a particular contrast to the present locational distribution of these industries in India. It can be inferred that U. S. cities of this size have achieved an adequate base of labor skills, specialized supplier industries, and communication links to attract such producer goods industries, whereas Indian cities have not.
4. Prominent heavy industries—both chemical and basic metal—are often nonurban in character in the United States. The incentive to be outside municipal areas probably arises from considerations of space, zoning, and tax obligations. Evidently the physical infrastructure of these industries demands present volume or quality requirements that enable individual plants or complexes to achieve their own economies of scale.

FOOTNOTES TO CHAPTER 5

1. See Richard E. Engler, Jr., *The Challenge of Diversity* (New York: Harper & Row, Publishers, 1964).

2. See B. J. L. Berry and A. Pred, *Central Place Studies: A Bibliography of Theory and Applications*, Bibliography Series, No. 1 (Philadelphia: Regional Science Research Institute, 1961), pp. 15–18.

3. See Harold M. Mayer *et al.*, "The Economic Base of Cities," in *Readings in Urban Geography*, eds. H. M. Mayer and C. F. Kohn (Chicago: University of Chicago Press, 1959), Section 4, pp. 85–126.

4. For an extensive list of these studies, see Berry and Pred, *A Bibliography;* and R. H. T. Smith, "The Functions of Australian Towns," in *Tijdschrift voor Economische en Sociale Geografie*, LVI, No. 3 (May-June, 1965), 81–92. Selected American and European functional studies are mentioned in I. Sandru, V. Cucu, and P. Poghirc, "*Contribution géographique à la classification des villes de la République populaire roumaine*," *Annales de Géographie* LXXII, No. 390 (March-April, 1963), 162–63, 185. Recent Studies of Soviet cities are reviewed in R. J. Fuchs, "Soviet Urban Geography: An Appraisal of Postwar Research," *Annals of the Association of American Geographers*, LIV, No. 2 (June, 1964), 282–83.

5. Section 5 of Mayer and Kohn, *Readings*, is entitled "Classification of Cities," but both classifications included are functional in nature.

6. There are, of course, exceptions. For example, a study of fifty United States metropolitan districts with more than 250,000 people was carried out to see whether the "economic character" of a community had any relevance in "planning aeronautical demand"—Civil Aeronautics Administration, "Economic Character of Communities" (mimeographed, U. S. Department of Commerce, 1948). Similarly, the functions of twenty-seven towns in southern New South Wales were found to be associated partly with the level of goods receipts at those towns—see R. H. T. Smith, *Commodity Movements in Southern New South Wales* (Canberra: Department of Geography, Australian National University, 1962), pp. 112–14.

7. Y. Watanabe, "An Analysis of the Function of Urban Settlements Based on Statistical Data: A Functional Differentiation Vertical and Lateral," *Science Reports of the Tôhoku University*, Seventh Series (Geography), No. 10 (September, 1961), 63. See also G. le Guen, "*La structure de la population active des agglomérations françaises de plus de 20,000 habitants:*

Méthode d'Étude: Résultats," *Annales de Géographie*, LXIX, No. 374 (July-August, 1960), 355.

8. M. G. A. Wilson, "Some Population Characteristics of Australian Mining Settlements," *Tijdschrift voor Economische en Sociale Geografie*, LIII, No. 5 (May, 1962), 125.

9. O. D. Duncan *et al.*, *Metropolis and Region* (Baltimore: The Johns Hopkins University Press for Resources for the Future, Inc., 1960), p. 35.

10. *Ibid.*, p. 34.

11. The present Chapter is not concerned with classifications of towns on the basis of characteristics other than functions as, for example, in G. Taylor's "Environment, Village and City: A Genetic Approach to Urban Geography; with Some Reference to Possibilism," *Annals of the Association of American Geographers*, XXXII, No. 1 (March, 1942), 58–65. The comprehensive study of British towns by C. A. Moser and W. Scott, *British Towns: A Statistical Study of Their Social and Economic Differences*, University of London Centre for Urban Studies, Report No. 2 (London and Edinburgh: Oliver and Boyd, 1961), is much broader in scope than a specifically functional classification, although its methodology resembles very much what is recommended later in this paper. See also Fuchs, "Soviet Urban Geography."

12. See A. Lal, "Some Aspects of Functional Classification of Cities and a Proposed Scheme for Classifying Indian Cities," *National Geographical Journal of India*, V, No. 1 (March, 1959), 12; and K. N. Singh, "Functions and Functional Classification of Towns in Uttar Pradesh," *ibid.* (September, 1959), 130.

13. M. Aurousseau, "The Distribution of Population: A Constructive Problem," *Geographical Review*, XI, No. 4 (October, 1921), 563–92.

14. Cf. J. W. Webb, "Basic Concepts in the Analysis of Small Urban Centers of Minnesota," *Annals of the Association of American Geographers*, XLIX, No. 1 (March, 1959), 55.

15. See, for example, H. Rees, "A Functional Classification of Towns," *Journal of the Manchester Geographical Society*, LII (1942–1944), 26–32; V. A. Janaki, "Functional Classifications of Urban Settlements in Kerala," *Journal of the Maharaja Savajirao University of Baroda*, III (1954), 81–114; and A. A. Mints and B. S. Khorev, "*Opyt ekonomiko-geografitcheskoi tipologii sovetskikh gorodov*" ("An attempt at Economic-Geographic Typology of Soviet Cities"), *Voprosy Geografii*, VL (1959), 72–88.

16. G. T. Trewartha, "Chinese Cities: Origins and Functions," *Annals of the Association of American Geographers*, XLII, No. 1 (March, 1952), 69–93. See also M. Santos, "Functional Classification of the Agglomerations in the Cacao Zone of Bahia," *Eighteenth International Geographical Congress (1956), Abstracts of Papers* (Rio de Janeiro: Brazilian National Committee, 1959), p. 124; and K. H. Stone, "Populating Alaska: The United States Phase," *Geographical Review*, XLII, No. 3 (July, 1952), 402–4.

17. W. A. Hance, "The Economic Location and Function of Tropical African Cities," *Human Organization*, XIX (1960), 135–36.

18. "Employment" statistics are collected at the place of work; "occupational" statistics are collected from the place of residence. Obviously, occupational data can be distorted by intracity and intercity commuting patterns. However, most population censuses record occupational rather than employment statistics for a variable number of industrial categories.

19. "Specialization" is elsewhere defined in terms of basic and nonbasic economic activities. See O. D. Duncan and A. J. Reiss, Jr., *Social Characteristics of Urban and Rural Communities, 1950* (New York: John Wiley & Sons, Inc., 1956), p. 12.

20. H. J. Nelson, "A Service Classification of American Cities," *Economic Geography*, XXXI, No. 3 (July, 1955), 189–210, quote from p. 194.

21. C. D. Harris, "A Functional Classification of Cities in the United States," *Geographical Review*, XXXIII, No. 1 (January, 1943), 86–99.

22. See Nelson, "A Service Classification," p. 195.

23. A. Aagesen, *The Population*, in *Atlas of Denmark*, ed. N. Nielsen (Copenhagen: C. A. Reitzels Forlag, 1961), II, 89–92.

24. Harris, "A Functional Classification," p. 87. The classification used by Duncan and Reiss in "Social Characteristics" should perhaps be included in this category, although for certain industry groups they used decile and quintile values to establish thresholds.

25. Harris, "A Functional Classification." In a number of studies of urban functions, the basic-nonbasic division of urban economic activities is incorporated to a greater or lesser extent. Perhaps the best-known example is G. Alexandersson, *The Industrial Structure of American Cities* (Lincoln: University of Nebraska Press, 1956).

26. H. M. Mayer, "A Commentary on the Study of Urban Functions," *Revista Geográfica*, XVIII, No. 44 (1956), 85.

27. See Nelson, "A Service Classification," p. 194.

28. See, for example, G. M. Kneedler, "Functional Types of Cities," *Public Management*, XXVII (1945), 197–205; *The Municipal Yearbook* (Chicago: International City Managers Association, years 1945 to 1950); J. F. Hart, "Functions and Occupational Structures of Cities of the American South," *Annals of the Association of American Geographers*, XLV, No. 3 (September, 1955), 269–86; M. G. A. Wilson, "Australian Mining Settlements," pp. 125–32; and H. J. Keuning, "*Een Typologie van Nederlandse Steden,*" *Tijdschrift voor Economische en Sociale Geografie*, XLI (1950), 187–206.

29. W. Steigenga, "A Comparative Analysis and a Classification of Netherlands Towns," *Tijdschrift voor Economische en Sociale Geografie*, XLVI (1955), 108.

30. Watanabe, "An Analysis."

31. L. L. Pownall, "The Functions of New Zealand Towns," *Annals of the Association of American Geographers*, XLIII, No. 4 (December, 1953), 332–50; F. Conway, "The Industrial Structure of Towns," *Manchester School of Economic and Social Studies*, XXI (1953), 154–64; O. Tuominen, "*Zur Geographie der Erwerbe in Finnland,*" *Fennia*, LXXVIII, No. 3 (1955); and Webb, "Small Urban Centers of Minnesota," pp. 55–72.

32. The standard deviation was used in this context by Nelson, in "A Service Classification," and Singh, in "Functions and Functional Classification," (he duplicated Nelson's study design for the towns of Uttar Pradesh). It was used in a slightly different way by the Civil Aeronautics Administration, in "Economic Character of Communities."

33. See W. L. Garrison, "Some Confusing Aspects of Common Measurements," *Professional Geographer*, VIII, No. 1 (January, 1956), 4–5.

34. Lal, "Classifying India Cities," pp. 12–24; Duncan and Reiss, "Social Chracteristics"; and Alexandersson, *American Cities*.

35. For example, of the nine arrays of industry percentages manipulated by Nelson, the arithmetic mean is truly representative of only one, Retail Trade. See Nelson, "A Service Classification," Fig. 1, p. 192.

36. See J. Kostrowicki, "*O funkcjach miastotwórczych i*

typach funkcjonalnych miast" ("Basic Function of Towns"), *Przeglad Geograficzny*, XXIV, No. 1 (1952), 7–64; L. Kosinski, "*Zagadnienia struktury funkcjonalnej miast polskich*" ("On the Functional Structure of Polish Towns"), *ibid.*, XXX, No. 1 (1958), 58–96, and "*Klasyfikacja funkcjonalna wiekszych miast polskich według stanu z roku* 1950" ("Functional Classification of the Larger Towns in Poland"), 573–85; le Guen, "*Agglomérations françaises*"; Sandru, Cucu, and Poghirc, "*Des villes de la République*," pp. 162–85; G. Enequist, "*Tätorternas Yrkessammansättning*" ("Types of Urban Settlements"), *Svensk Geografisk Arsbok*, XXXI (1955), 139–56, "The Habitation of Sweden," in International Geographical Union, *Eighth General Assembly and Seventeenth International Congress, Washington, D. C., August 8–15, 1952* (Washington: U. S. National Committee for the I. G. U., 1957 [?]), and "*Tätorternas Øch Landsbygdens Näringstyper*" ("Types of Agglomerations and Rural Districts," *Atlas Øver Sverige* (*Atlas of Sweden*) (Stockholm: Svenska Sällskapet för Antropologi Øch Geografi, 1957), pp. 59–60: 1 to 59–60: 8; and A. Aagesen, *The Population.*

37. For example, in le Guen's, "*Des agglomérations françaises*"; Tuominen's, "*Erwerbe in Finnland*"; Enequist's work (see ftn. 36, *supra*); and Sandru, Cucu, and Poghirc, "*Des villes de la République.*"

38. See, for example, Kostrowicki, "Basic Function of Towns"; Kosinski, "Polish Towns"; and le Guen, "*Des agglomérations françaises.*"

39. Kosinski, "Polish Towns," p. 96.

40. The procedure of plotting points (towns) on a two-dimensional graph with orthogonal axes is strictly correct only if the correlation coefficient between the two variables is not significantly different from zero. See B. J. L. Berry, "The Impact of Expanding Metropolitan Communities upon the Central Place Hierarchy," *Annals of the Association of American Geographers*, L, No. 2 (June, 1960), 112–16.

41. G. C. Dickinson, *Statistical Mapping and the Presentation of Statistics* (London: Edward Arnold, 1963), p. 34. One other European worker has used the clusters, however—see M. Rochefort, "*Détermination des types de villes d'un réseau urbain*," *Eighteenth International Geographical Congress* (1956), *Abstracts of Papers* (Rio de Janeiro: Brazilian National Committee, 1959), pp. 121–22.

42. See, for example, L. J. King, "The Functional Role of Small Towns in Canterbury," *Proceedings of the Third New Zealand Geography Conference* (Palmerston North), 1961, pp. 139–49, Figs. 2 and 3; Berry, "On the Central Place Hierarchy," Fig. 2; and J. W. Webb, "The Natural and Migrational Components of Population Changes in England and Wales: 1921–1931," *Economic Geography*, XXXIX, No. 2 (April, 1963), 130–48, Figs. 8, 9, and 11.

43. Singh, "Functions and Functional Classifications."

44. Other methods of group formation which do not carry this restriction are discussed in B. J. L. Berry, "Grouping and Regionalizing: An Approach to the Problem Using Multivariate Analysis," in *Quantitative Geography*, ed. W. L. Garrison (Evanston, Ill.: Northwestern Studies in Geography, 1968), pp. 219–51.

45. This procedure was used by Smith in "The Functions of Australian Towns," and a similar approach may be found in B. J. L. Berry, "Ribbon Developments in the Urban Business Pattern," *Annals of the Association of American Geographers*, XLIX, No. 2 (June, 1959), 145–55. Berry discusses this general type of classification procedure in "A Note Concerning Methods of Classification," *ibid.*, XLVIII, No. 3 (September, 1958), 300–303.

46. This general approach is outlined in B. J. L. Berry, "A Method for Deriving Multi-Factor Uniform Regions," *Przeglad Geograficzny*, XXXIII, No. 2 (1961), 263–79. A recent example of its application is given in D. M. Ray and B. J. L. Berry, "Multivariate Socio-Economic Regionalization: A Pilot Study in Central Canada," a paper read to the Canadian Political Science Association Conference on Statistics, Charlottetown, Prince Edward Island, June, 1964 (Mimeographed). Examples of both types of approaches to classification are contained in L. E. Newman, "An Employment Classification of Urban Centers in Southern Illinois" (M. A. thesis, Southern Illinois University, Carbondale, 1962).

47. Smith, "The Functions of Australian Towns."

48. Duncan *et al.*, *Metropolis and Region*, p. 35.

49. Thus, although one must give credit to H. J. Nelson, "Some Characteristics of the Population of Cities in Similar Service Classifications," *Economic Geography*, XXXIII, No. 2 (April, 1957), 95–108, for using his classification as a "point of departure for further research into the character of urban settlements" (Wilson, "Australian Mining Settlements"), one cannot help but ask whether more might not have been learned about the spatial variation in features of population had the classification been designed originally with this in mind. In fact, one might even argue that the various aspects of population studied by Nelson might better be regarded as *accidental* characteristics of the classification (the terminology is that of M. G. Cline, "Basic Principles of Soil Classification," *Soil Science*, LXVII [1949], 83).

50. Wilson, in "Australian Mining Settlements," comments generally on this situation, and a specific example is available in Watanabe, "The Function of Urban Settlements."

51. Lal, "Classifying Indian Cities," p. 24; see also le Guen, "*Des agglomérations françaises*," p. 366, on industrial towns.

52. Enequist, "Types of Agglomerations, pp. 59–60: 6. In his discussion of "urban regional groups," le Guen draws attention to "*la prépondérance de la fonction industrielle*" in the North around Lille, and to the social and commercial functions of towns on the Mediterranean littoral (le Guen, "*Des agglomérations françises*," pp. 368–69). See also Harris' discussion of manufacturing towns, "Cities in the United States," p. 90.

53. Hart, "Cities of the American South," p. 280.

54. Although Pownall pays some attention to the distribution of New Zealand towns in different functional classes, his discussion is largely superficial and involves either the identification of specific towns ("meat freezing works at Waitara and Patea"), reference to regional groupings ("The greatest concentration of major transport centers is located near the center of the North Island along the Main Trunk Railway"), or noting the interisland distribution of towns ("Of the seventeen towns in this class [primary industrial] the South Island has no less than 59 per cent.")—"New Zealand Towns," pp. 340, 341, and 342, respectively. Enequist's discussion of Swedish towns is much less satisfactory because it is in the framework of *län*, or Parish boundaries; see "Types of Agglomerations," pp. 59–60: 7.

55. Duncan, *et al.*, *Metropolis and Region*, p. 35.

56. See, for example, Conway, "The Industrial Structure of Towns," quoted in R. E. Wakeley, *Types of Rural and Urban Community Centers in Southern Illinois*, Area Services Bulletin No. 3 in the series *Human and Community Resources of Southern Illinois* (Southern Illinois University, 1963 [?]); P. B. Gillen, *The Distribution of Occupations as a City Yardstick* (New York:

King's Crown Press, 1954); and Duncan and Reiss, *Urban and Rural Communities*. Both sociologists and economists have attempted to incorporate city size into functional studies; see C. Schettler, "Relation of City Size to Economic Services," *American Sociological Review*, VIII, No. 1 (January, 1943), 60–62; and C. Clark, "The Economic Functions of a City in Relation to Its Size," *Econometrica*, XIII, No. 1 (January, 1945), 97–113.

57. "Urban Functions," *Economic Geography*, XXI, No. 2 (April, 1945), Editorial facing p. 79. One can well raise the question of "more effective" for what? The same doubt arises when one considers the following statement by K. Dziewónski: "The development of a logically consistent and realistic typology is one of the more important tasks essential for the progress of urban geography"—"Typological Problems in Urban Geography," in *Twentieth International Geographical Congress Abstracts*, ed. F. E. I. Hamilton (London: Nelson, 1964), pp. 321–22. For a more complete discussion of this typology, see Dziewónski, "Typological Problems in Urban Geography," *Geographia Polonica*, No. 2 (1964), 139–44.

58. Duncan *et al.*, *Metropolis and Region*, p. 36.

59. Again the terminology is that of Cline, "Soil Classification," p. 82.

60. "Through accessory [additional] characteristics one multiplies the number of statements about each class and increases the significance of the classes formed." *Ibid.*, p. 82.

61. Few would dispute this in the light of the large and growing literature on the theory of the location of agricultural, manufacturing, and tertiary activities.

62. "Cities exist primarily to provide goods and services for the people who live outside the urban boundaries. No city can exist purely as a self-sufficient unit; it is a focus or area of concentration for a variety of activities serving areas beyond the city itself"—H. M. Mayer, "Geography and Urbanism," *Scientific Monthly*, LXIII (1951), 1–12, quoted in *Readings in Urban Geography*, eds. Mayer and Kohn, pp. 7–8. Also, "The support of a city depends on the services it performs not for itself but for a tributary area. . . . The service by which the city earns its livelihood depends on the nature of the economy of the hinterland," C. D. Harris and E. L. Ullman, "The Nature of Cities," *Annals of the American Academy of Political and Social Science*, CCXLII (November, 1945), 7–17, quoted in Mayer and Kohn, *op. cit.*, footnote 3, p. 277. Webb recognized the important relationship between a town's hinterland and its function, but he incorporated this more into the mechanics of the classification procedure than into the interpretation and evaluation of the classification, Webb, "Small Urban Centers of Minnesota," pp. 55–58.

63. See P. J. Clark and F. C. Evans, "Distance to Nearest Neighbor as a Measure of Spatial Relationships in Populations," *Ecology*, XXXV (1954), 445–53.

64. This sort of analysis is applied to some groups of towns in Smith, "The Functions of Australian Towns."

65. *Ibid.*

66. *Ibid.*

67. Lal, "Classifying Indian Cities."

68. In his entertaining critical discussion of "commercial geography," Stephen Leacock in *The Boy I Left Behind Me* (London: The Bodley Head, 1947) made a distinction between "information" and "study." I would equate the latter with "knowledge" and suggest that however commendable such classifications as Lal's are in providing a convenient and ordered description of towns in an area, their contribution to geographical knowledge is limited and even ephemeral. Lal himself recognized that a functional classification had implications for city distribution: "Such a classification can be of value in analyzing the spatial distribution of cities of various functional types" ("Classifying Indian Cities," p. 24), yet he neglected to perform such an analysis himself.

69. Aurousseau, "The Distribution of Population," p. 571.

70. In his introduction, Smith notes a variety of earlier studies of particular Australian towns, among them: H. W. H. King, "Armidale, N.S.W. A Standard 'Australian' Service Town: Its Evolution, Morphology and Changing Functional Character," in *New England Essays*, ed. R. F. Warner (Armidale: University of New England, 1963), pp. 96–117. Smith also notes that Solomon has discussed Hobart as a port (R. J. Solomon, "External Relations of the Port of Hobart: 1804–1961," *The Australian Geographer*, IX, No. 1 [March, 1963], 43–53); and that Britton presented a similar analysis for Port Kembla, N.S.W (John N. H. Britton, University of Sydney and the Geographical Society of New South Wales, 1962). He also cities H. W. White, ed., *Canberra: A Nation's Capital* (Sydney: Angus and Robertson, 1961), pp. 467–86; John H. Shaw, *The Urban Evolution of Wagga Wagga* (Armidale: Department of Adult Education, University of New England, 1960); R. J. Solomon, "Broken Hill: The Growth of Settlement, 1883–1956," *The Australian Geographer*, VII, No. 5 (August, 1959), 181–92; and R. G. Golledge, "Observations on the Urban Pattern and Functional Role of Newcastle, N.S.W.," *Tijdschrift voor Economische en Sociale Geografie*, LIII, No. 3 (March, 1962), 72–78.

Predominantly large towns, Smith observed, are discussed in the following papers: Raymond Bunker, "The Metropolis in Australia," in *Readings in Urban Growth*, pp. 18–37; G. J. R. Linge, *The Future Work-Force of Canberra* (Canberra: National Capital Development Commission, 1960); J. Achterstraat, "*De Steden in Australie*," *Tijdschrift voor Economische en Sociale Geografie*, LI, No. 3 (March, 1960), 65–70, and "*De Steden in Australie:* II," *ibid.*, LII, No. 4 (April, 1961), 94–106; Clifford M. Zierer, "Brisbane River Metropolis of Queensland," *Economic Geography*, XVII, No. 4 (October, 1941), 327–45, "Industrial Area of Newcastle, Australia," *ibid.*, XVII, No. 1 (January, 1941), 31–49, "Melbourne as a Functional Center," *Annals of the Association of American Geographers*, XXXI, No. 4 (December, 1941), 251–88, and "Land Use Differentiation in Sydney, Australia," *ibid.*, XXXII, No. 4 (December, 1942), 255–308.

Mining centers have been the subject of two papers: Clifford M. Zierer, "Broken Hill: Australia's Greatest Mining Camp," *ibid.*, XXX, No. 1 (March, 1940), 83–108; and Murray G. A. Wilson, "Some Population Characteristics of Australian Mining Settlements," *Tidschrift voor Economische en Sociale Geografie*, LIII, No. 5 (May, 1962), 125–32.

Other studies include: A. J. McIntyre and J. J. McIntyre, *Country Towns of Victoria: A Social Survey* (Melbourne: Melbourne University Press, 1944); E. C. Chapman, "The Ports of Central and North Queensland," Unpublished paper read to Section P of the Australian and New Zealand Association for the Advancement of Science (Brisbane, 1961); R. S. Dick, "Five Towns of the Brigalow Country of South-Eastern Queensland," *University of Queensland Papers*, I (1960), "Variations in the Occupational Structure of Central Places of the Darling Downs, Queensland," *ibid.*, No. 2 (1961); Herbert W. H. King, *The Urban Hierarchy of the Southern Tablelands, New South Wales* (Ph. D. dissertation, Australian National University, 1955), "The Canberra-Queanbeyan Symbiosis:

A Study of Urban Mutualism," *Geographical Review*, XLIV, No. 1 (January, 1954), 101–18; and Robert H. Smith, *Commodity Movements in Southern New South Wales* (Canberra: Department of Geography, Australian National University, 1962), pp. 112–14.

71. *Census of the Commonwealth of Australia, 30th June, 1954*, Vols. I-VI, Part 5: "Population and Occupied Dwellings in Localities" (Canberra: Government Printer, 1955). At the time of final analysis and writing—the latter half of 1963 and early 1964—the 1961 Census figures were unavailable.

72. The method is identical to that used by Brian J. L. Berry in "Ribbon Developments in the Urban Business Pattern," *Annals of the Association of American Geographers*, XLIX, No. 2 (June, 1959), 145–55. Berry discusses linkage or cluster analysis in "A Note Concerning Methods of Classification," *ibid.*, XLVIII, No. 3 (September, 1958), 300–303.

First, the well-known product-moment correlation coefficient was employed. It was obtained for all possible pairs of towns on the basis of the proportion of employment in each industry category:

Towns	*Industry*			*Categories*	
	1	2	3	. . .	12
1					
2					
3					
.					
.					
.					
422					

Thus, the correlation coefficient was available for town 1 with town 2, 1 with 3, 1 with 4, . . . , 1 with 422; and for 2 with 3, . . . , 2 with 422; . . . , and for 421 with 422. That pair of towns recording the highest mutual correlation coefficient with each other (i.e., "reflexives") was selected; in the following matrix of the five largest towns (1, Sydney; 2, Melbourne; 3, Brisbane; 4, Adelaide; 5, Perth), this is 1 and 2.

	1	2	3	4	5
1	1.00	*.98*	.86	*.97*	.76
2	*.98*	1.00	.91	.96	.81
3	.86	.91	1.00	.89	*.93*
4	.97	.96	.89	1.00	.85
5	.76	.81	*.93*	.85	1.00

Then, towns which recorded their highest correlation coefficient with either town 1 or 2 would be added to the cluster. This process would continue until no new towns remained to be added, and the entire procedure would be repeated with a new pair of reflexives; and so on until all towns had been allocated to a group. Here, there are two groups:

$4 \rightarrow 1 \longleftrightarrow 2$ Group 1

$3 \longleftrightarrow 5$ Group 2

For this particular study, much of the operation described above was performed on a CDC 1604 computer, using a program written especially for this purpose. Other methods of clustering are discussed in Brian J. L. Berry, "Grouping and Regionalizing: An Approach to the Problem Using Multivariate Analysis," in *Quantitative Geography*, ed. William L. Garrison (Northwestern Studies in Geography, 1967).

73. Berry, "A Note Concerning Methods of Classification." Mahalanobis' D^2 statistic was used in precisely the same manner as the correlation coefficients. Whereas before, the problem had been to allocate the 422 towns to a set of (91) groups, the problem here was to generalize the 91 groups to a smaller set (17, as it happened) of clusters. In this case, linkage analysis was performed on a smaller matrix of D^2 statistics. D^2 is the sum of the differences between the transformed mean values of each variable for each group. The transformation takes into account over-all and group estimates of dispersion.

Thus, D^2 between groups 1 and 2 =

$$(X_1^* - X_2^*) + (Y_1^* - Y_2^*) + (Z_1^* - Z_2^*) + \ldots$$

where X^*, Y^*, and Z^* are the transformed mean values of variables X, Y, and Z in groups 1 and 2. Computational procedure is discussed in most intermediate and advanced statistics textbooks (e.g., Palmer O. Johnson and Robert W. B. Jackson, *Modern Statistical Methods: Descriptive and Inductive* [Skokie, Ill.: Rand McNally & Co., 1959], pp. 448–54), and an historical note on the development of this type of measure is available in M. G. Kendall, *A Course in Multivariate Analysis* (New York: Hafner Publishing Co., Inc., 1961), pp. 111–16.

74. Steigenga claims that "only the average or total of the whole urban society . . . can be used as a measure of comparison," W. Steigenga "A Comparative Analysis and a Classification of Netherlands Towns," *Tijdschrift voor Economische en Sociale Geographe*, XLIV (1955), 108.

75. Marcel Aurousseau, "The Distribution of Population: A Constructive Problem," *Geographical Review*, IX, No. 4 (October, 1921), 563–92. See also comments in John W. Webb, "Basic Concepts in the Analysis of Small Urban Centers of Minnesota," *Annals of the Association of American Geographers*, XLIII, No. 1 (March, 1953), 55–72.

76. See, for example, Edward J. Taaffe, "Air Transportation and United States Urban Distribution," *Geographical Review*, XLVI, No. 2 (April, 1956), Fig. 7, p. 232.

77. Norman J. King, "The Sugar Industry," in *Introducing Queensland*, ed. W. H. Bryan *et al.* (Brisbane: Australian and New Zealand Association for the Advancement of Science, 1961), pp. 48–49.

78. Keith W. Thompson, "The Settlement Pattern of the Barossa Valley, South Australia," *The Australian Geographer*, VII, No. 1 (May, 1957), 54–55.

79. See G. J. R. Linge, "The Location of Manufacturing in Australia," in *The Economics of Australian Industry, Studies in Environment and Structure*, ed. Alex Hunter (Melbourne: Melbourne University Press, 1963), pp. 18–64.

80. Thompson, "The Settlement Pattern."

81. Linge, "The Location of Manufacturing."

82. McIntyre and McIntyre, *Country Towns of Victoria*, pp. 49–63, 69.

83. Dr. G. M. Neutze of the School of General Studies, Department of Economics, Australian National University, has suggested that this might be due to the fact that the census enumeration area for many country towns is much larger than the actual town itself, and would therefore include many

people whose occupation was farming. Dick has commented on this problem in some detail. See "Variations in the Darling Downs," p. 39.

84. The frequency table below records the number of towns from each group of service centers located in particular zones of land use, as read from Department of National Resources, *Atlas of Australian Resources*, "Dominant Land Use" (Canberra, 1957). The scale used is 1: 6 million. A test of whether these distributions are random can be made with the chi-squared statistic: First, one calculates the expected distribution of towns, which may be based on two different assumptions: (1) that there are equal numbers of towns in each zone; or (2) that the number of towns in each zone is proportional to its area. The second hypothesis seemed more appropriate in this instance, and the value of chi-squared, for all six groups, was significant at the 1 per cent level of confidence for 7 degrees of freedom.

	Group					
Land Use	*4*	*5*	*6*	*7*	*8*	*9*
Wool	11	6	1	2		3
Wheat with wool and fat lambs	10	7	3	3	4	24
Wool and fat lambs	5	3	2	2	1	13
Dairy cattle	1	1	13		3	20
Sugar cane	2	1		1		2
Fruit, etc.		2		3	1	14
Timber	1	4	3			6
Intensive breeding and fattening of beef cattle	1					
Total	31	24	22	11	9	82

85. The term "South Coast" refers to a group of resort towns on the Queensland coast south of Brisbane. There is a similar implication when "Blue Mountains" is used.

86. Department of National Resources, *Atlas of Australian Resources*, "Ports and Shipping" (Canberra, 1957). Scale 1: 6 million.

87. Wilson, "Some Population Characteristics of Australian Mining Centers."

88. For a description and explanation of the use of the near neighbor statistic, see P. J. Clark and F. C. Evans, "Distance to Nearest Neighbor as a Measure of Spatial Relationships in Populations," *Ecology*, XXXV (1954), 445–53. In calculating the density of the distribution, the populated area of Australia (about 921,000 sq. m.) was used. For a discussion of the problems in selecting meaningful study area for near neighbor analysis, see: A. Getis, "Temporal Land Use Pattern Analysis with the Use of Nearest Neighbor and Quadrat Methods," *Michigan Inter-University Community of Mathematical Geographers Discussion Papers*, No. 1 (1963), 4–5 (Mimeographed).

89. M. G. A. Wise, "The Changing Latrobe Valley: The Impact of Brown Coal Mining," *Australian Geographical Studies*, I, No. 1 (April, 1963), 31–38.

90. Donnell M. Pappenfort, "The Ecological Field and the Metropolitan Community: Manufacturing and Management," *American Journal of Sociology*, LXIV (1959), 380–85.

91. Chauncy D. Harris, "The Market as a Factor in the Localization of Industry in the United States," *Annals of the Association of American Geographers*, XLIV, No. 3 (September, 1954), 315–48.

92. Hal H. Winsborough, "Variations in Industrial Composition with City Size," *Papers and Proceedings of the Regional Science Association*, V (1959), 121–31.

93. See also Otis Duncan *et al.*, *Metropolis and Region* (Baltimore: The Johns Hopkins Press, 1960).

94. See, e.g., his paper, "Empirical Mathematical Rules Concerning the Distribution and Equilibrium of Population," *Geographical Review*, XXXVII, No. 3 (July, 1947), 461–85; reprinted in *Demographic Analysis*, eds. J. J. Spengler and O. D. Duncan (New York: The Free Press, 1956). The map of isopotential lines used here appears in O. D. Duncan's, "The Measurement of Population Distribution," *Population Studies*, XI, No. 1 (July, 1957), 27–45, and in his "Population Distribution and Community Structure," *Cold Spring Harbor Symposia on Quantitative Biology*, XXII (1957), 357–71.

95. John Q. Stewart and William Warntz, "Physics of Population Distribution," *Journal of Regional Science*, I, No. 1 (Summer, 1958), 99–123.

96. See, e.g., Harris, "The Market as a Factor"; and William Warntz, "Measuring Spatial Association with Special Consideration of the Case of Market Orientation of Production," *Journal of the American Statistical Association*, LI (December, 1956), 597–604.

97. Duncan *et al.*, *Metropolis and Region.*

98. *Ibid.*

99. See Philip Neff and Robert M. Williams, "The Industrial Development of Kansas City" (Kansas City: Federal Reserve Bank of Kansas City, 1954), mimeographed.

100. O. D. Duncan, *Metropolis and Region* (Baltimore: The Johns Hopkins Press, 1960).

101. Irving Morrissett, "The Economic Structure of American Cities," *Papers and Proceedings, Regional Science Association*, IV, 1958.

102. August Lösch, *The Economics of Location* (New Haven: Yale University Press, 1954), p. 4. He further elaborates this point to say that "it would be dangerous to conclude that what is must also be rational since otherwise it could not exist, and that any theoretical determination of the correct location would therefore be superfluous."

103. Duncan, *Metropolis and Region*, p. 66.

104. Morrissett, "The Economic Structure of American Cities," pp. 239–56.

105. Gunnar Alexandersson, *The Industrial Structure of American Cities: A Geographic Study of Urban Economy in the United States* (Lincoln: University of Nebraska Press, 1956).

106. Robert M. Lichtenberg, *One-Tenth of a Nation* (Cambridge, Mass.: Harvard University Press, 1960), pp. 31–70, 252–71. Classificatory factors used are: external economies; transport costs, creating locational pulls toward either sectional or national markets; supply and costs of skilled and unskilled labor; and inertia. Of 446 industries examined, 91 were unclassified.

107. Size of place distributions for 10 per cent or more of industry employment are not available for 135 additional industries covered in the 1954 manufacturing census. No attempt was made to assign these industries to location categories.

108. Several cities of the region are characterized by a high degree of specialization in a relatively narrow group of industries. Examples are: hosiery in Ludhiana; rubber footwear in Jullundur; brass utensils and goods in Jagadhri and Moradabad; mathematical, surveying, and drawing instruments in Roorke; scientific instruments in Ambala; and glass bangles in Firozabad.

CHAPTER 6

basic dimensions of urban systems

The study of urban functions captures only a limited number of the ways in which towns and cities vary and change. Recently, urban geographers (aided by developments in multivariate analysis and by the manipulative abilities of modern computers) have extended their studies of urban characteristics to include simultaneous consideration of much wider ranges of variables, including the social characteristics of the residents and the physical properties of the structures in which they live. The results of their studies indicate that there are in fact but a few basic ways in which cities vary. The large numbers of characteristics which may be collected for each town show high degrees of intercorrelation, indicating that whole groups of variables are giving exactly the same information about town-to-town variations. Each group of characteristics, in effect, behaves like the multiple symptoms of more a fundamental "syndrome" or "dimension" of variation. Using multivariate analysis to study the patterns of interrelationship among the characteristics, we can isolate the basic dimensions. The type of multivariate analysis used most commonly is called factor analysis, and factor analysts call the "syndromes" or "dimensions" the common *factors* or *principal components* of city-to-city variation.

Two of the earliest of such studies dealt with British towns and Indian cities, respectively.[1]

BRITISH TOWNS

Moser and Scott sought to classify British towns into a few relatively homogeneous categories, or to see whether such a classification makes sense. Their analysis dealt with the 157 legal towns (local authority areas) of England and Wales with populations greater than 50,000 in 1951, containing half the population of England and Wales. Sixty variables, falling into eight major categories, were used in the analysis: population size and structure (7 variables); population change (8); households and housing (15); economic characteristics (10); social class (4); voting behavior (7); health (7); and education (2).

There were four stages to the analysis. In the first, the diversity of British towns in terms of each of the 60 variables was studied. The second stage involved the study of simple relationships between 57 of the variables, through the medium of a 57 × 57 correlation matrix.

In the third stage, the principal components were analysed to find the basic patterns according to which the towns vary, "because the many series that describe towns are not independent—they overlap in the story they tell. . . . [T]owns with a high proportion of heavy industry tend . . . to have low 'social class' . . . , a substantial Labour vote, high infant mortality, and so on."[2] "The essence [of the analysis was] to investigate how much of the total variability exhibited in the [57] primary variables [could] be accounted for and expressed in a smaller number of new independent variates, the principal components."[3] The results were striking—only four basic dimensions accounted for more than 60 per cent of the covariance of the 57 variables to be seen in the correlation matrix.

The four components were identified as: *social class; growth patterns from 1931 to 1951; growth patterns from 1951 to 1958;* and *overcrowding*. Each town was given an index value (factor score) based on these basic dimensions. The 157 × 4 table was then used in stage four of the study, the classification of towns, instead of the original 157 × 57 table, because the essential variability of the towns with respect to the original 57 characteristics had been captured, synthesized, and summarized in the 4.[4]

To classify the towns, scatter diagrams were prepared, using the four dimensions as axes and plotting the towns as points. Clearly, the closer were any two points in the diagram, the more similar the towns. Then, by inspection, 14 groups of towns (clusters of points) were identified. These fall into three main categories:

1. *Resorts, administrative and commercial centers.*
   a. Seaside resorts
   b. Spas, professional and administrative centers
   c. Commercial centers
2. *Industrial towns*
   a. Railway centers
   b. Ports
   c. Textile centers of Yorkshire and Lancashire
   d. Industrial towns of the Northeast and Welsh mining towns
   e. Metal manufacturing centers
3. *Suburbs and suburban-type towns*
   a. Exclusive residential suburbs
   b. Older mixed residential suburbs
   c. Newer mixed residential suburbs
   d. Light industrial suburbs, national defense centers, and towns within the influence of large metropolitan conurbations
   e. Older working-class industrial suburbs
   b. Newer industrial suburbs[5]

Two unique cases were not classified: London A. C. and Huyton-with-Roby (the Liverpool suburb with the most rapid rate of growth in England and Wales).

INDIAN CITIES

Ahmad followed a similar procedure for 102 Indian cities with populations exceeding 100,000, and 62 variables, with the exception that he classified the towns by mathematical means, using the computer, rather than by visual inspection.

He found that 10 dimensions were required to account for over 70 per cent of the correlations among his variables. The 8 most important he described as follows:

> What are these dimensions of variation of Indian cities? Indian cities differ from each other in terms of (1) a north-south regionalism based on female labor force and sex ratio; (2) generalized accessibility; (3) compactness; (4) occupational structure (commercial versus industrial); (5) rural orientation; (6) city size; (7) population change; and (8) east-west regionalism based on occupational and migration characteristics, sex ratio and degree of clustering. Together the dimensions summarize the story of Indian urbanization as told by the 62 variables, at least 70 per cent of it.[6]

Ahmad compared his results with those of other studies, such as Moser and Scott's, and made some interesting generalizations.

*Which Are the Basic Factors?**

Granting that each study utilizes a set of variables which often are very much different from those of the other, [which] renders any comparison of the results extremely difficult, one generalization can still be made. It seems that five factors—size, the specific set of economic specialities, population change, density, and some social characteristics such as income and literacy—are sure to emerge as independent differentiating elements of urban systems in any situation, Western or non-Western, unless the variables related to these factors are omitted [from the initial data matrix to be analyzed] . . . .

It is not surprising that the factor of population size appears in almost all the cases under review. The sociological significance of "size" has been stressed quite often in the literature.[7] City-size or "the size of community," according to Duncan, "is closely connected with whatever it is that produces a hierarchy."[8] City-size seems to play a significant role in India's urban system. . . . The large urban centers of India are characterized among other things by relatively large areas, greater "generalized accessibility"[9] [higher potentials], greater accessibility to the railroad network, high ratio of telephone connections, and a high proportion of in-migrants, more particularly those in the age-groups 15 to 34 and 35 to 59 years. The characterization of large cities with greater accessibility is quite significant in the context of systems of cities, which, according to Berry, are "entities of interacting, interdependent parts,"[10] for it means that the larger cities play more central roles in these systems, in accordance with their size. This relationship may be seen in yet another way, for such cities serve as mediating agencies between populations involved in exchange relationships. Obviously, the mediating function of the city cannot be fulfilled without facilities for movement. "Transport routes and carriers must bring spatially separate populations within easy access of one another if exchange is to take place."[11] Once again, attention is drawn to the structure of the size factor, in other words, to the interrelationship of city size and various measures of accessibility and communication media. Thus, our empirical finding has a definite theoretical base.

Here, it would be interesting to recall some of the observations of Duncan about relationships of characteristics to size:

1. The larger the SMA [Standard Metropolitan Area], the more likely it is to have a diversified, i.e., less specialized, industrial structure.
2. [R]esource-extraction and first stage resource-using industries are more highly developed in the less accessible SMA's, while second stage resource using industries and manufacturing industries making little direct use of resources are more conspicuous in the more accessible SMA's.
3. The proportion of the labor force employed in manufacturing in hinterland SEA's [State Economic Areas] is found to increase with rising values of population potential (generalized accessibility) and also with increasing proximity to a metropolitan center.[12]

These observations seem to have validity in the context of Indian urbanization as well. The first generalization is true to all the major metropolitan centers of India with the possible exception of Ahmedabad.

The second generalization is only partly true of India or Indian cities. The major metropolitan centers in India, which also have greater accessiblity, do not have the same high concentration of manufacturing activity in terms of the proportion of total labor force of the city, as witnessed in the more industrialized countries of the world. The present stage of industrial development in India reflects a dominant role of centralized planning and control so far as location of industries is concerned. Despite planned development, it seems that the present is just a transitional phase and in the long run the market will be the dominant factor in the location of industry in India. Even now, such metropolitan centers as Ahme-

*Reprinted from Q. Ahmad, *Indian Cities: Characteristics and Correlates*, Research Paper No. 102, Department of Geography, University of Chicago, 1965, pp. 114 ff., with the permission of the author and editor.

dabad, Bombay, Delhi, Calcutta, Bangalore, Madras, Kanpur, and Poona have considerable manufacturing activity. This leads us to Duncan's third generalization which, as he himself states, is in conformity with the observation of Harris that manufacturing is concentrated toward areas of high "market potential," and with the finding of Bogue that beyond a certain critical point intensity of manufacturing activity falls off as distance from the center of the metropolitan region increases. [The reader may wish to refer back to the discussion in Chapter 5—eds.] The validity of this generalization is reflected in the location of manufacturing centers in proximity to a major metropolitan center. In particular, note the location of cities in proximity to the metropolitan centers of Calcutta, Bombay, and Ahmedabad, most of which have considerable industrial activity.

Conversely, cities which have considerable proportions of workers in all categories of services (tertiary activity) are found either outside or on the margins of the zone of maximum generalized accessibility.

Last though not the least in importance is the first component, north-south regional differentiation by sex, the most fundamental characteristic of Indian urbanization. As noted before, this component accounts for the largest proportion of total variance of 102 Indian cities. According to the 1961 census, all cities except Eluru (Andhra Pradesh) had fewer women than men. The general paucity of women is again a characteristic of Indian or South Asian cities. However, cities in South India—Kerala, Madras, Mysore, and Andhra—have relatively larger number of females than cities in the north, particularly those of the Punjab, Uttar Pradesh, Madhya Pradesh, Bihar, West Bengal, and Assam. Cities in the states of Rajasthan, Gujarat, and Maharashtra occupy an intermediate position between the north and south extremes. Attempts have been made recently to give tentative reasons for the disparity in the female-to-male ratio in different regions of India. However, the fact that cities with relatively more balanced sex ratios are located in the four southern states which are also linguistic states, with Malayalam, Tamil, Kanarese, and Telegu (all Dravidian languages) as the prevalent languages, it is argued, does *not* imply that the disparity in sex ratio is a reflection of the difference in the cultures of the two areas, namely north (the Aryan culture areas) and south (the Dravidian culture area). Instead the emphasis is placed on such factors as male-selective migration to the manufacturing and administrative centers of northern and western India, as well as to destinations outside India, in-migration of relatively larger proportions of females from rural areas in the south, and the extremely small proportion of Muslims in the south.[13] The large participation of women in the labor force of southern cities is ascribed to two other factors—high literacy and greater proportion of Christian population in the south.[14]

Another major research finding is related to the grouping characteristics of Indian cities. For the first time, as a result of this study it has been possible to discern systematic spatial variations of the characteristics of Indian cities based on certain well-defined dimensions. Of particular interest is the north-south regional differentiation of cities by sex (female employment and sex ratio), literacy rate, and certain types of urban services. Equally interesting is the east-west regional differentiation of cities in terms of a number of characteristics, particularly migration. Cities in the western part of India have a relatively higher proportion of inmigrants from other urban centers, lower proportions of migrants from rural areas, lower proportions of workers, higher ratios of females to males, and higher proportions of female migrants than cities in the east. The western and eastern cities are also differentiated in terms of their distribution pattern. The Western cities are scattered while the eastern cities, as in the extremely clustered nature of the Calcutta conurbation, are concentrated.

Yet another regional pattern embraces cities located in the Andhra-Madras littorals. These are characterized by large female employment, high sex ratios, very high proportions of female inmigrants and in-migrants from rural areas, large proportions of workers engaged in primary activity, low employment in manufacturing, relatively small population size, small area, and high density of dwellings per unit area.

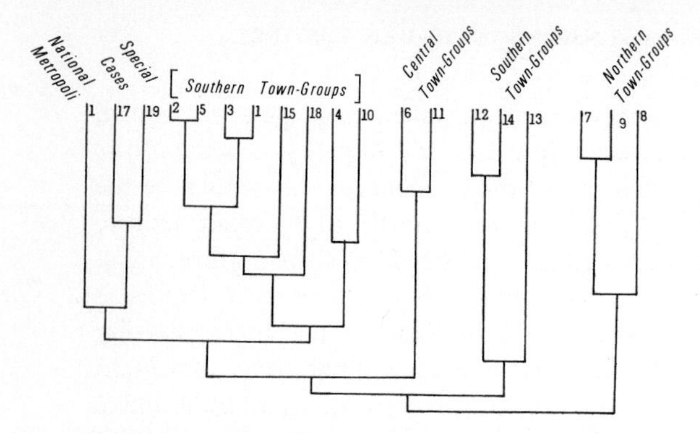

FIGURE 6–1. Indian town-groups: The linkage tree. *Source:* Figs. 6–1 and 6–2 are from Q. Ahmad, *Indian Cities: Characteristics and Correlates*, Research Paper No. 102, Department of Geography, University of Chicago, 1965.

[Finally, the analysis showed that] Indian cities fall into five *major* groups: (1) the national metropoli of Bombay, Delhi, and Calcutta; (2) Calcutta suburbs, a cluster of eight cities of more than 100,000 population; (3) northern cities; (4) southern cities; and (5) cities with generally central location, including most of the cities of Rajasthan, Madhya Pradesh, and a few cities of Maharashtra and other states of India. [These, in turn, are composed of 19 regional sub-groups

FIGURE 6–2. Regional sub-groups of Indian towns. *Source:* See caption for Fig. 6–1.

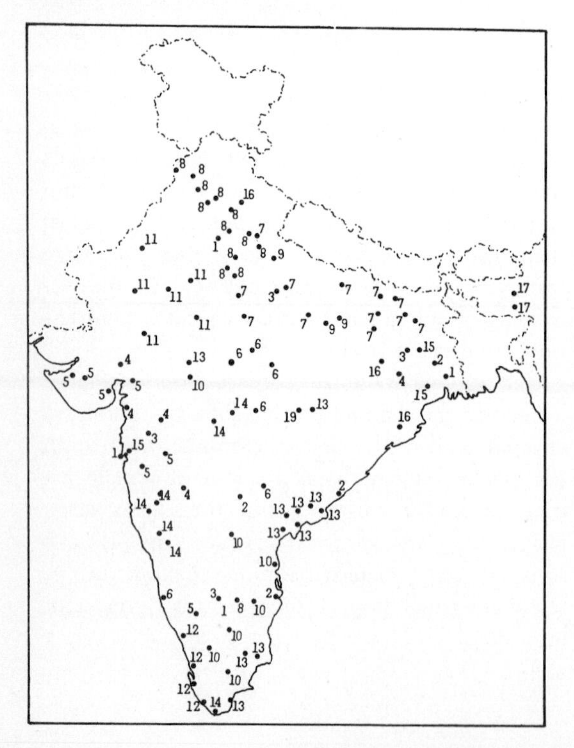

(see Figs. 6–1 and 6–2), since the] statistical groups which were established showed a marked regionalization. The statistical analysis, therefore, has high geographic quality. However, with the availability of more elaborate and refined set of data on Indian cities, it would be useful to repeat this analysis. Two principal points of emphasis remain: (1) the consistency of the components or dimensions of variation; (2) the regional structure of Indian cities. The significance of the regional structure in terms of cultural attributes and historical trends should be properly assessed.

*A CANADIAN CASE STUDY**

The studies of British towns and Indian cities were exploratory in the sense that they were not structured around any hypotheses or the testing of any theory. In fact, these studies appear conspicuously devoid of any reference to theory. What they have achieved is an extension of the type of empirical analysis suggested, for example, by Price in the 1940's.[15] Given the advantages of modern computer facilities in the analyzing of data matrices too large and formidable for hand manipulation, these recent studies have been able to focus on a wider spectrum of the complexities of modern urban society and, as a consequence, the dimensions which they identified appear more basic and general than those emphasized in earlier studies.

The empirical findings are both significant and provocative. On the one hand, they provide valuable information as to the underlying structures of different urban systems and there should emerge from such comparative studies a wealth of generalizations concerning urban systems as they exist at different times and places. On the other hand, as a set of empirical statements unattached to any theoretical structure, they prompt a concern for further investigations which might provide a linkup between such urban theory as exists and these empirical findings on urban structure.

*Reprinted from Leslie J. King, "Cross-Sectional Analysis of Canadian Urban Dimensions: 1951 and 1961," *Canadian Geographer*, X, No. 4 (December, 1966), 205–24, with the permission of the author and editor.

This case study has both of the above goals in view. A number of empirical findings concerning the urban dimensions in Canada are discussed for two points in time, 1951 and 1961. At the same time, an attempt is made to review the findings in the light of some generalizations concerning the growth and development of urban systems.

The Model of Urban Dimensions

In the previous studies, the basic model involved the projection of a set of observations relating to cities from an original m-variable space ($x_1, x_2, x_3 \ldots x_m$), into another r-variable space of basis ($y_1, y_2 \ldots y_r$). This latter space will be referred to henceforth as the "urban-dimensions space." In the case of the principal-components solution, r is equal to m, while in the factor-analysis approach, where estimates of the communalities have been inserted along the principal diagonal of the correlation matrix, r is usually less than m.[14] The question of what to use as estimates of the communalities is a vexing one within the context of factor analysis. The Hadden and Borgatta study employed the coefficients of multiple determination obtained by regressing each variable in turn on all of the other (m-1) variables. This same approach has been adopted in geographic research with the argument that the "random noise" within the system is reduced as a consequence.[15] There are at least two points of dissent which might be raised with regard to this argument. First, it is by no means certain that all of the so-called noise is eliminated simply by using the coefficient of multiple determination. All that this approach ensures is that the covariance will be emphasized, but much of this still may be quite spurious as far as meaningful urban relationships are concerned. Second, the "unique" variance which is dismissed in using the communality estimates, in this case (1-r^2), may not be noise in the total urban system. Indeed, it may be related quite closely to variables which are not included in the set under study. A great deal more understanding of urban relationships would seem to be required before such communality estimates can be employed confidently.

Both the principal components and factor analysis solutions yield correlations or "loadings" between the original variables and the new components or factors, and also scores for the cities on the components or factors. An examination of the loadings particularly, and also of the scores, allows for empirical interpretations to be given to the new variables or dimensions. It is generally the case that such interpretations are possible only for the first few factors or components, for example, the first 5 to 10 in studies based upon an original set of 50 to 60 variables.[18] In principal-components analyses and principal-axes factor solutions these first few dimensions account for most of the variance, or covariance as the case may be, and hence they are of sufficient importance in this regard to warrant subsequent consideration at the expense of the others. This is not to overlook the fact that the remaining components or factors do help account for a portion of the original variance or covariance, but in terms of the associated loadings for these dimensions they tend to appear simply as mathematical artifacts and often are difficult to interpret within the context of the urban system. Furthermore it is on these latter dimensions that the effects of noise in the data set become pronounced and interpretation is made all the more difficult as a result.

There appear to be at least four major features of this urban-dimensions model which warrant further study, especially from the point of view of their sensitivity to changes in the urban system over time. These aspects of the model are discussed below.

First, there is the question of how the urban dimensions themselves behave over time. They may remain stable: Hadden and Borgatta, and Ahmad were able to demonstrate such stability in the dimensions of their systems when different city-size classes were considered.[19] Another study has confirmed the temporal stability of the dimensions noted by Price in his 1942 work.[20] Also, it might be noted that Berry has suggested that the dimensions of broader regional systems are stable over time, and it might be argued that the same should hold true for urban systems.[21] At the same time, however, this postulate of stability would seem to contradict much of what is already known concerning the dynamics of urban systems. While the theory in this area of research is still only weakly structured, there exist some low-level generalizations which are suggestive of a nonstationary character for most urban systems. For example, it is recognized that most societies, and in particular those of North America, are becoming increasingly oriented toward the metropolis. Indeed, the notion of "megalopolis" has far wider implications than its spatial expression alone might suggest. Concomitant with this emergence of metropolitan growth poles, there have evolved within the metropolitan centers very complex organizational forms, detailed patterns of interdependence, sophisticated communication media, high levels of tertiary employment, and considerable socioeconomic stratification. Variables which serve to index these characteristics should serve also to identify certain dimensions of metropolitanization in the model outlined above. Over time, these dimensions should show up more clearly in the variable loadings, and there should be a sharp differentiation on these dimensions between the cities located within or near the metropolitan complexes and the other urban centers.

On this first point also, one of Schnore's conclusions concerning the comparative socio-economic status of central cities and suburbs might be noted. Schnore comments:

> Sheer age of settlement has emerged as the best predictor of the direction of city-suburban differences in socio-economic status. Older urbanized areas tend strongly to possess peripheral populations of higher socio-economic standing than found in the central cities themselves. In contrast, newer cities tend to contain populations ranking higher on education, occupation, and income than their respective suburbs.[22]

This being the case, it might be anticipated that the suburban dimensions would emerge more clearly over time, and that the positions of individual communities on these dimensions would change as the cities became older.

Finally, with respect to the dynamics of an urban system, the fact must be noted that urban trends are seldom independent of developments in the surrounding regions. Comparative levels of regional economic development, for example, do find expression in the urban system and changes in the urban dimensions over time may reflect, in part, new or changed economic orientations within some regions. This will almost certainly be the case where the regional economy is geared to the exploitation of some particular factor of production and where the region's comparative advantage is disappearing. Cities dependent upon mining activities or labor-intensive manufacturing activities may show marked changes in their positions on certain urban dimensions as a result of these economic trends.

The preceding sentence points up the second feature of the urban dimensions model which should be discussed. It is that even allowing for the fact that the interpretations of the dimensions may not change over time, suggesting some stability in their form, the scores of individual cities on these dimensions might vary considerably. These changes would reflect new socio-economic or locational orientations for the cities concerned, and the possibility of such changes has already been mentioned with regard to suburban and resources-oriented communities.

A third feature of the model is a corollary of the second. In the urban-dimensions space each city is represented as a point and since the solutions discussed earlier yield orthogonal dimensions which define this space, the distances between points can be used as indices of their similarities. Presumably there will be some tendencies towards clusterings of the points and these clusterings will define groupings of the cities in the urban-dimensions space. If the bases of this space change over time, or if the positions of different cities on any of the dimensions change, then these groupings may vary accordingly.

The fourth and final feature of the model to be noted is that the basic form of a dimension may remain comparatively stable over time but the loadings of different variables on this dimension may vary from one time to another. Such a possibility would seem all the more likely when the dimensions are given only broad interpretations. For example, in the Hadden and Borgatta study the first factor is identified as indexing "socio-economic status," and it is conceivable that this same interpretation might show up in different analyses notwithstanding the fact that the loadings of particular variables on the dimension had changed.

In the following discussion of the Canadian urban system as it existed in 1951 and 1961, all of the above four features of the urban-dimensions model are examined. The study focusses upon the 106 cities which in 1951 had populations in excess of 10,000. For these cities there are available fairly comparable data for the two years, relating to more than 50 economic, demographic, social, and locational characteristics.[23] These two sets of data are analyzed by principal-components analysis and a grouping algorithm,[24] and the results for the two years are compared below.

Dimensions of the Canadian Urban System: 1951

As much as 83 per cent of the original total variance in the set of 52 variables for 1951 is accounted for by twelve components. The higher loadings for these components are presented in the columns of Table 6–1. An examination of these loadings and the corresponding component scores allows for fairly detailed interpretations to be given to the first six of these components. By contrast, the interpretations of components seven through twelve pose many conflicting questions, some of which may stem from the presence of random noise in the system.

The first component indexes the youthfulness of the female population in the cities. The highest positive loadings are for the percentage of women aged 15 to 39, percentage of population aged five years and over with more than eight years of schooling, and percentage of total population in the active labor force. The highest negative loadings are for: males per 100 females, taxes levied per capita, and percentage of manufacturing labor force in petroleum and coal products. Aside from these, there are also high negative loadings for many of the other employment and demographic variables. These loadings suggest that the component is indexing particularly the youthfulness of the female population in the nonmanufacturing and less densely populated cities. This interpretation is confirmed by the plotting of the component scores on the vertical axis in Fig. 6–3*a*. The cities of British Columbia and of the prairie and maritime provinces generally rank high on the scale. At the lower end of the scale are most of the cities of Quebec along with a few "exceptional" cases from among the Ontario cities.

The socio-economic character of the second component is reflected in the high positive loadings for percentage of population aged 65 and over, percentage of population of English ethnic origin, percentage of population aged five years and over with more than eight years of schooling, percentage of occupied dwellings single detached, retail sales per capita, and percentage of dwellings with autos. This component appears to index the service role of many comparatively isolated communities located outside Quebec. The negative loadings add weight to this interpretation as do the component scores. The cities of British Columbia and the prairie provinces again show up at the upper end of the scale (see Fig. 6–3*a*). In this case, the grouping of the cities of Quebec at the lower end of the scale is even more pronounced than on the first dimension.

Frontier location and a closer economic orientation to primary activities is indexed by the third component. The associated characteristics of youthful population, employment dominated by primary activities and the manufacturing of wood and paper products, and locations remote from the metropolitan areas, are found to varying degrees in the cities of Edmundston, Glace Bay, Jonquiere, New Waterford, Prince Albert, Rimouski, Rouyn, and Timmins. These are the cities which rank high on this scale (see Fig. 6–3*b*), while at the lower end of the same scale are the metropolitan communities of Hamilton, Toronto, Montreal, Outremont, Forest Hill, and Mount Royal.

The fourth component is identified with urban manufacturing in the smaller cities located outside of the major metropolitan complexes. These cities also are ones in which the proportions of occupied dwellings classed as owner-occupied or single-detached are high. The cities with high scores on this dimension are Kitchener, Oshawa, Stratford, Waterloo, Welland, and Woodstock. It is noteworthy that, in addition to these very high values among the Ontario cities, there is a general concentration of the cities of that province at the upper end of the scale (Fig. 6–3*b*).

TABLE 6–1

Loadings for First Twelve Components: Canada, 1951

Variable	Component I	II	III	IV	V	VI	VII	VIII	IX	X	XI	XII
% women aged 15–39	.91											
% total population aged 65 and over		.58					−.43					
% total population aged 14 and under		−.48	.50			−.35						
% total population French ethnic origin		−.88										
% total population English ethnic origin		.78										
Number males per 100 females	−.97											
% population aged 5 and over with more than 8 years schooling	.59	.63										
Population immigrating from overseas in previous decade	−.74											
Age of city					−.41					−.30	.39	
Size of city	−.80						.38					
City population density	−.82						.35			.20		
% occupied dwellings single detached		.62		.44	.35							
% occupied dwellings owner occupied		.49		.46	.36		−.39		.31			
% occupied dwellings occupied over 10 years	−.60				−.33							
% occupied dwellings needing major repairs	−.52					.55			−.32			
% occupied dwellings with mechanical refrigeration			−.69									
% occupied dwellings with automobile		.65	−.40	.39		−.33						
Average number persons per room	−.61							−.36	.45	−.25		
Total retail sales per capita		.60			−.51							
New wholesale sales per capita		.51		−.45						−.26		
Number branches of banks	−.86											
% wage-earners earning over $4,000 annually	−.79				.34							
Assessed value for taxation per capita			−.39					.27		−.61		
Taxes levied per capita	−.90							.24				
Gross debenture per capita	−.61			.31			−.49					
% total population in active labor force	.55						.52					
% total labor force in primary industry	−.60		.49					.29				
% total labor force in manufacturing		−.51	−.49	.46						−.25		
% total labor force in transportation, storage, etc.	−.79						−.43					
% total labor force in construction											−.41	−.30
% total labor force in retail, wholesale	−.71											
% total labor force in finance, insurance, etc.	−.83							.28				
% total labor forces in public and private services				−.40		−.54					.33	
% manufacturing labor force in textiles, clothing, etc.		−.48			−.34	−.32						
% manufacturing labor force in wood, paper, etc.			.38					−.42				−.35
% manufacturing labor force in all metal products						.35		.31		−.40		.32
% manufacturing labor force in transportation equipment					.40			−.30				
% manufacturing labor force in electrical apparatus	−.84											
% manufacturing labor force in non-metallic minerals	−.81											
% manufacturing labor force in petroleum and coal products	−.90											
% manufacturing labor force in chemicals											−.30	−.53
% female labor force in manufacturing	−.50	−.46	−.44									
% labor force in proprietary, managerial, and professional occupations					.37	−.52	.44					
Distance to nearest central city of a Metropolitan Area			.66					.30				
Member of Metropolitan Area			−.41	−.67								
Located on Canadian National Railway network			−.38					−.33				
Served by commercial airline				−.65								
Having port facilities				−.31	.41						.30	
Number cities in 50 mile radius		−.42	−.70									
Number cities in 100 mile radius		−.46	−.75									
Distance to closest of Montreal, Toronto, Vancouver		.44	.45									
Number of through highways			−.49	−.56								

Source: Tables 6–1 through 6–4 are from Leslie J. King, "Cross-Sectional Analysis of Canadian Urban Dimensions: 1951 and 1961," *Canadian Geography*, X, No. 4 (December, 1966), 205–24.

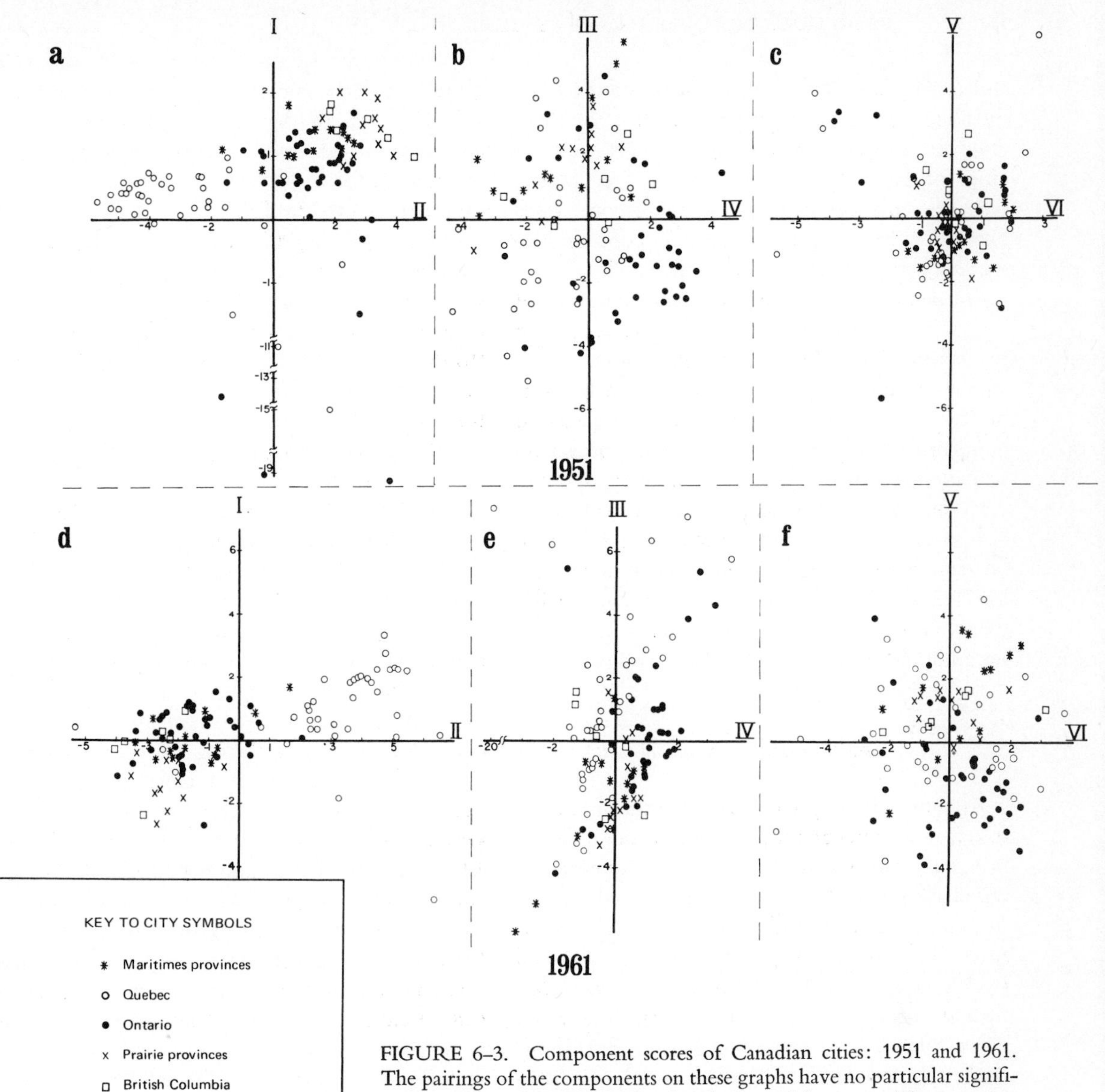

FIGURE 6–3. Component scores of Canadian cities: 1951 and 1961. The pairings of the components on these graphs have no particular significance and are adopted only for the plotting of the scores. The scores are standardized for each of the first six components. *Source:* Leslie J. King, "Cross-Sectional Analysis of Canadian Urban Dimensions: 1951 and 1961," *Canadian Geographer*, X, No. 4 (December, 1966).

Two aspects of urban structure show up on the fifth dimension. The first is the occupational and housing correlates of the suburban communities. Noteworthy in this respect are the positive loadings for the variables: percentage of occupied labor force in proprietary, managerial, and professional occupations, percentage of total wage-earners earning over $4,000 annually, percentage of occupied dwellings single-detached, and percentage of occupied dwellings owner-occupied. There are correspondingly high scores for such communities as Forest Hill, Leaside, Mount Royal, and North Vancouver (Fig. 6–3*c*). The second facet of this dimension is that of manufacturing employment geared to the production of transportation equipment, and the role of the city as a port.

The sixth component is an employment-housing dimension, reflecting an emphasis upon manufacturing employment in metals production, and comparatively high proportions of occupied dwellings in need of repair. The first of these emphases shows up in the higher scores for the cities of Hamilton, Sydney, Sault Ste. Marie, Oshawa, and Windsor, while the second finds expression in the high scores for communities such as Jacques-Cartier, Levis, and Sorel.

On neither the fifth nor the sixth component is there any clear grouping of the cities according to their provincial location (see Fig. 6–3*c*).

For the remaining components no clear interpretations are possible. The seventh appears to be identified strongly with the labor-force participation ratio; the eighth with nonmetropolitan location, metals manufacturing, and urban financial structure; the ninth with aspects of urban housing; the tenth with urban population density; the eleventh with the age of the city; and finally, the twelfth with metals manufacturing. However, on all of these dimensions other loadings tend to weaken these interpretations.

Structural Affinities among Cities: 1951

Attention already has been focussed upon the relative positions of certain cities on the different urban dimensional scales. Now the question is raised as to how the 106 cities are located relative to one another in the total urban dimensions space. For the purposes of this discussion, all twelve components mentioned above are considered to form the basis of the urban-dimensions space. Since these twelve components are orthogonal or uncorrelated, the distances between city-points in the dimensions space can be regarded as measures of their similarities. A matrix of these distances, computed as Mahalanobis' D^2 statistics, is derived and used in a stepped grouping of the cities.[25] At the first step, the two observations closest together are grouped and their individual rows and columns in the distance matrix are replaced by a single row and column containing the distances from the centroid of the two-member group to the other cities. Then at successive stages of the grouping, individual cities or existing groups are linked on the basis of minimizing the increment to within-group distance. This grouping procedure has no single analytic solution and if pursued to the end results in only one group of all 106 cities. In this study, the grouping was terminated when only one single member group remained. The result was the set of eleven city groups presented in Table 6–2.

On the whole, the grouping of the cities is consistent with the accepted broad regional divisions of the country. The first group includes many of the cities located on the eastern "industrial frontier." These cities without exception, rank very low on the second, but generally high on the third, urban dimension. Very similar dimensional profiles although with even higher scores on the third dimension and often positive scores on the second, are characteristic of the industrial cities which form the second group.

The regional concentration in southern Ontario of the members of the third group is conspicuous. Most of these cities have high scores on the fourth, and to a lesser extent on the first components.

The fact that they typically have positive scores on all of the first three components seems to account for the next grouping of cities, which are located in the prairie and maritime provinces. However, the larger metropolitan centers in these regions, specifically, Calgary, Edmonton, Halifax, and Saint John, fall in another group along with Montreal, Quebec, Ottawa, and Toronto. Significantly, the smaller incorporated communities located within the Montreal and Toronto metropolitan complexes do not group with their parent central cities. The Montreal suburban cities comprise a fairly separate group notwithstanding the inclusion of Sillery and Eastview, while Forest Hill and Leaside from the Toronto area group with the Montreal suburb of Mount Royal. However, the high-income Montreal community of Westmount does not group with any of the suburban communities. This appears to be a function of the very low scores which it has on the first and sixth components. Galt has a very similar profile to Westmount on the urban dimensions.

The smaller urban communities, located in the province of Quebec, which generally have very low scores on the second component, group together and, in a sense, provide a mirror image of the grouping of the Ontario cities.

TABLE 6–2

City Groupings: Canada, 1951

1
Arvida
Shawinigan
Chicoutimi
Rouyn
Jonquiere
Thetford
Edmundston
Hull
Trois Rivières

2
Glace Bay
New Waterford
Sault Ste. Marie
Trail
Sydney
Sudbury
Timmins

3
Barrie
Orillia
Trenton
Belleville
Chatham
St. Thomas
Owen Sound
Stratford
Niagara Falls
Sarnia
Brantford
Guelph
Brockville
Peterborough
Woodstock
Cornwall
Waterloo
Welland
Oshawa
St. Catharines
Hamilton
London
Windsor
Mimico
New Toronto

4
Brandon
Regina
Saskatoon
Lethbridge
Medicine Hat
Moose Jaw
Prince Albert
Fort William
Port Arthur
Penticton
Charlottetown
Fredericton
Truro
Pembroke
Dartmouth
North Vancouver
New Westminster
Victoria

5
Calgary
Edmonton
Moncton
St. Boniface
Vancouver
Winnipeg
Halifax
Ottawa
Kingston
St. Johns
Saint John
Montreal
Quebec
Toronto

6
Eastview
Sillery
Outremont
Lachine
Longueuil
Lasalle
St. Laurent
Verdun
Jacques-Cartier
Montreal North
St. Michel

7
Forest Hill
Leaside
Mount Royal

8
Westmount
Galt

9
Cap-de-la-Madeleine
Grand'mere
Magog
Victoriaville
Sorel
Drummondville
Granby
St. Jerome
Valleyfield
Joliette
Sherbrooke
St. Hyacinthe
St. Jean

10
Kitchener
North Bay

11
Levis

Source: See note to Table 6–1.

Finally, there are two anomalies among the groups. In the case of Kitchener and North Bay, extremely low scores on the first component account for their similarity. Levis on the other hand, has a unique profile with a low score on the first component and high scores on both the fifth and sixth dimensions.

Stability in the Form of the Dimensions: The 1961 Analysis

Unfortunately, it was not possible to obtain, for 1961, measurements on all of the variables considered in the 1951 analysis. However, the 54 variables which were available related to the same general demographic, social, economic, and locational facets of the urban system, and the problems of comparability which exist do not appear serious within the context of this study.

The principal-components solution reveals that the first eleven components account for 83 per cent of the original total variance, precisely the same level as was achieved on the first twelve components in the 1951 solution.

An examination of the loadings of these components (see Table 6–3) provides only weak support for the contention that the urban dimensions are stable over time.

The first component in this case is identified strongly with urban manufacturing, especially textile manufacturing. In addition, many of the inverse loadings suggest that it is identified with weakly developed urban structure as regards urban finance and services. The communities ranking high on this dimension are all located within Quebec and include Magog, Grand'mere, Granby, Victoriaville, Cap-de-la-Madeleine, and Drummondville. It is interesting to note that while this textile-manufacturing dimension did not show up in the same positive way in the earlier analysis, it was present as a type of dual to the second dimension. It will be recalled that the dimension in question was identified with the service role of many communities located outside Quebec, and that as a consequence, the Quebec cities ranked low on that dimension. Now in the 1961 analysis this dimension is flipped over, the Quebec communities rank high, and western cities such

TABLE 6-3

Loadings for First Eleven Components: Canada, 1961

Variable	Component I	II	III	IV	V	VI	VII	VIII	IX	X	XI
% women aged 15–39		.66									
% total population aged 65 and over		−.67		−.49		.24					
% total population aged 14 and under		.57	−.65								
% total population French ethnic origin		.89									
% total population English ethnic origin		−.79		.32							
Number males per 100 females				−.79	−.34	−.29		−.29			
% population aged 5 and over with more than 8 years schooling		−.51		.54							
Population immigrating from overseas in previous decade			.44	−.77							
Age of city						.40	−.48				
Size of city			.37	−.85							
City population density			.61		.42		−.33				
% occupied dwellings single detached			−.46		−.41						
% occupied dwellings owner occupied		−.66	−.38		−.46						
% occupied dwellings occupied over 10 years			−.35			.34		.63			
% occupied dwellings needing major repairs			−.60			.44					
% occupied dwellings with mechanical refrigeration				.92							
% occupied dwellings with automobile				.78							
Average number of persons per room		.76	−.47								
Median value of dwelling			.64	.47							
Total retail sales per capita	−.84						.25				
% wage-earners earning over $4,000 annually											
Number branches of banks	−.44				−.33	−.76	−.42		−.24	−.38	
General expenditure per capita	−.92										
Property taxes levied per capita	−.65	−.41		.32							
Market rating index		−.56				.26	.29	−.41		.27	
Disposable income per capita	−.94										
Building permits, 1961 value	−.87									−.22	
% total population in active labor force		−.49	.58	.33							
% total labor force in primary industry	−.47		−.44					.26	−.28		
% total labor force in manufacturing	.36	.40			−.68						
% total labor force in transportation, storage, etc.	−.92										
% total labor force in construction	−.88										
% total labor force in retail, wholesale		−.43			.44						
% total labor force in finance, insurance, etc.	−.95										
% total labor force in public and private services		−.51			.58						
% manufacturing labor force in textiles, clothing, etc.	.26	.45				.46	.35				
% manufacturing labor force in wood, paper, etc.								.26	.24	−.66	
% manufacturing labor force in all metal products					−.33	−.36	−.39		−.43		.32
% manufacturing labor force in transportation equipment							−.35		.75		
% manufacturing labor force in electrical apparatus*											
% manufacturing labor force in non-metallic minerals	−.86										

Variable	Component I	II	III	IV	V	VI	VII	VIII	IX	X	XI
% manufacturing labor force in petroleum and coal products	−.86										
% manufacturing labor force in chemicals							.21		−.29		−.75
% female labor force in manufacturing		.49	.35		−.50	.38					
% labor force in proprietary, managerial and professional occupations		−.42	.44			−.42	.43				
Distance to nearest central city of a Metropolitan Area	−.54		−.55								
Member of a Metropolitan Area	−.66		.48								
Located on Canadian National Railways network	−.66								.22		
Served by commercial airline	.90										
Having port facilities			.36				−.46	.28			
Number of cities in 50 mile radius		.54	.56								
Number of cities in 100 mile radius		.56	.58		−.40						
Distance to closest of Montreal, Toronto, Vancouver	−.84										
Number of through highways			.65								

Source: See note to Table 6–1.
*No significant loading.

as Brandon, Calgary, Regina, Saskatoon, Vancouver, and Winnipeg rank low on the dimension (see Fig. 6–3*d*).

The second dimension for the 1961 analysis is clearly identified with the Quebec population structure. Apart from the fact that the variable—percentage of women aged 15–39—loads positively on both dimensions, this component appears as a mirror image of the first component in the 1951 analysis. The variables which load positively on this 1961 dimension, such as percentage of the population aged 14 and under, and average number of persons per room, were inversely related to the 1951 dimension and, conversely, variables which now show strong negative loadings, for example, percentage of the population aged five years and over with more than eight years of schooling, and percentage of the total population in the active labor force, were related positively to the 1951 dimension. The scores on this second component show the differentiation between the cities in Quebec at the upper end of the scale and the remaining cities of Canada (see Fig. 6–3*d*).

The third dimension is identified with metropolitan socio-economic structure. There are positive loadings for the variables: population density, population immigrating from overseas in the previous decade, median value of dwellings, percentage of the total population in the active labor force, number of through highways, and the number of towns within a 50- and a 100-mile radius. The high scores on this dimension are confined to Montreal and its satellite communities of Mount Royal, Outremont, and Westmount; to Toronto and its satellites Forest Hill and Leaside; and finally, to Sillery which is located within the Quebec City metropolitan area (Fig. 6–3*e*). This dimension had no real counterpart in the 1951 analysis, and while its appearance among the 1961 dimensions provides no strong support for any general statement concerning trends in the Canadian urban system, its emergence is at least consistent with some of the comments made earlier concerning the changing orientation of urban society.

Aspects of the residential role of many communities appear to be indexed on the fourth component. The positive loadings are also suggestive of comparatively high socio-economic status, and it is noteworthy that the highest scores on the dimension are for the communities of Mount Royal, Leaside, Forest Hill, Mimico, Westmount, and Brockville. The Ontario cities in general rank high on this component (Fig. 6–3*e*). This dimension is very similar in form to the fifth one identified in the 1951 analysis, although now the metropolitan association again appears more pronounced.

The fifth component is identified principally with the service function of many older and comparatively isolated communities. Employment in the service activities shows up clearly, while the positive loading of "population density" suggests that the cities ranking high on this dimension will be long-established urban centers. The high scores for Quebec, Halifax, St. Johns, and Charlottetown are consistent with this interpretation. The high scores for Outremont and Eastview can be attributed to a very high population density in the former case, and a very high level of service employment in the second. This dimension shows some similarity in form to the second dimension identified in the 1951 analysis, although now the employment component in the service role of the isolated communities is emphasized more clearly. Most of the Ontario cities are located at the lower end of this urban scale (see Fig. 6–3*f*).

The sixth component appears to index certain aspects of urban depression, in the sense that there are high positive loadings for the variables: age of city, percentage of dwellings occupied more than ten years, and percentage of dwellings in need of major repair, and a strong inverse relationship with the percentage of total wage-earners earning more than $4,000 annually. The association with textile manufacturing appears to be a fairly strong one. The component scores confirm this latter relationship with respect to such cities as Drummondville, Granby, Magog, and St. Hyacinthe. The older central cities of Montreal and Toronto also rank high on this dimension, as do some other scattered communities including Charlottetown, Galt, Saint John, Stratford, and Truro (see Fig. 6–3*g*). This dimension was not so apparent in the 1951 analysis. The variable "per cent of dwellings in need of major repair" did show up on the sixth component in that analysis but there was not the same strong association with the ages of the city and housing, and low income levels, as is the case for 1961.

Once again, the pattern of loadings on the remaining components makes interpretation difficult. In the case of the seventh component, for example, there is strong identification with employment in the managerial, professional, and technical occupations, while at the same time, there is a positive association with employment in textile manufacturing. The eighth component shows a similar dualism, with percentage of dwellings occupied for more than ten years, and, again, employment in the managerial, professional and technical occupations, both loading positively. The ninth component however, is clearly identified with the manufacturing of transportation equipment, while the tenth is identified with metals manufacturing, the market rating index, and the number of through highways. Finally, employment in metals manufacturing and textiles are the only variables to show positive loadings greater than 0.2 on the eleventh component. Apart from the fact that metals manufacturing employment tends to show up in both sets, these last few components in the 1961 analysis show little resemblance in form to their 1951 counterparts.

City Groupings: 1961

The fact that the important urban dimensions have changed somewhat in form over the decade, does not preclude the possibility that the basic groupings of the cities may have remained fairly stable. This possibility seems all the more likely given the strong regional associations which showed up in the 1951 groupings. These regional clusters in the urban-dimensions space may well persist even though the bases of the space have changed and the relative locations of the clusters in the space may have altered. This possibility is examined with respect to a grouping of the cities derived in the same way as before and with the same number of groups being recognized. The eleven groups for 1961 are presented in Table 6–4.

TABLE 6–4

City Groupings: Canada, 1961

Group	Cities
1	Chicoutimi, Rouyn, Jonquiere, Thetford, Edmundston, Rimouski, Hull, Timmins
2	Arvida, Glace Bay, New Waterford, Sault Ste. Marie, Trail, Sydney, Sudbury
3	Barrie, Orillia, Trenton, Belleville, Chatham, St. Thomas, Owen Sound, Stratford, Niagara Falls, Brantford, Guelph, Brockville, Peterborough, Woodstock, Waterloo, Galt, Kitchener
4	Brandon, Regina, Saskatoon, Lethbridge, Medicine Hat, Moose Jaw, Prince Albert, Penticton, Charlottetown, Fredericton, Truro, Pembroke, Calgary, Edmonton, St. Boniface, Winnipeg, Vancouver, North Bay, Ottawa, London, Kingston, Moncton
5	Cap-de-la-Madeleine, Grand'mere, Magog, Victoriaville, Sorel, Drummondville, Granby, St. Jerome, Valleyfield, Joliette, St. Hyacinthe, St. Jean, Trois Rivières, Jacques-Cartier, Montreal North, St. Michel, Cornwall
6	Forest Hill, Leaside, Mount Royal, Outremont, Westmount
7	Montreal, Toronto
8	Dartmouth, Levis, Halifax, St. Johns, Saint John, Eastview, Quebec, Verdun, Hamilton, New Toronto, Mimico, Lachine, Longueuil, Lasalle, St. Laurent, Sarnia, Shawinigan
9	Fort William, Port Arthur, New Westminster, North Vancouver, Victoria, Oshawa, St. Catharines, Windsor
10	Sherbrooke
11	Sillery

Source: See note to Table 6–1.

The two groups of frontier industrial cities are virtually unchanged from the earlier listing [cf. Table 6–2]. Group 1 now has Timmins as a member in place of Arvida, and Shawinigan and Trois Rivières no longer appear in this group. The cities in this group generally have high scores on the second and to a lesser extent on the first component, while ranking low on the third dimension. The second group differs from its 1951 counterpart only in the fact that Arvida has replaced Timmins as a member. These seven cities are important for metals production. They rank low on the third dimension as do the cities in Group 1, but since they are located, with the exception of Arvida, outside of Quebec, they do not show the same high rankings on the second dimension as did the members of Group 1. The fact that these two groups have remained distinct over the decade may be a reflection of the relative immaturity of the urban system and of the fact that as a network the system is not a highly connected one. In other words, these cities still depend very strongly on the development of local natural resources or on a particular basic industrial function. This attachment is reflected in the demographic, social, and economic character of these cities and it serves to differentiate them from the more diverse and mature urban centers found elsewhere in Canada. The second point is that the urban pattern in Canada is essentially a linear one with two major concentrations in the Eastern Townships of Quebec and in southern Ontario. As a consequence the marginal or frontier location of certain cities on the urban network is conspicuous and, in the case of the cities in the first groups, this location factor strengthens the separation of these centers from the other cities in the dimensions space.

A grouping of the cities of Ontario which showed up in the 1951 analysis is duplicated only partially in the 1961 analysis. The group is now a much smaller one but there is a more noticeable concentration of the member cities in the southern Ontario region. The cities involved typically have high scores on the fourth dimension, that of residential socio-economic status. Significantly, many of the cities located on the margins of this urban region in southern Ontario, for example,

Sarnia, North Bay, Kingston, and Ottawa, which in 1951 had been grouped with the southern Ontario cities, now belonged to some other group. Again, the effect of the distance variable is important in this regard, for these more remotely located cities have fairly high rankings on the fifth dimension, the service function of older and comparatively isolated communities. The strengthening of the southern Ontario cluster in the urban-dimensions space is significant and it points up the need for further studies aimed at investigating the links and transactions which exist between the cities of such a group. Apparently there is a well defined urban sub-system here which is relatively homogeneous in terms of the attributes considered in this study.

Some of the Ontario cities mentioned above, namely North Bay, Kingston, and Ottawa, group with the cities of the prairie and maritime provinces in 1961. A very similar grouping of the latter cities was apparent in 1951 but now with the addition of such cities as Calgary, Edmonton, St. Boniface, and Winnipeg, it appears as an even stronger group in terms of its locational association. As was noted above with respect to the Ontario cities that fall into this group, the member cities have relatively high rankings on the fifth dimension, the service function of older and comparatively isolated communities.

The general tendency for there to be stronger regional contiguity effects associated with the 1961 groups, compared to their 1951 counterparts, is supported in the case of the fifth group which includes many of the smaller cities of Quebec. This group now includes, in addition to most of the cities in the Eastern Townships, some of the Montreal suburban communities, Cornwall which grouped formerly with the Ontario cities, and Trois Rivières which was grouped with the industrial communities in 1951. Without exception, the cities in this group ranked relatively high on the first two urban dimensions.

A grouping of the higher socio-economic suburban communities located within the Montreal and Toronto metropolitan areas is even more pronounced in 1961 than it was a decade earlier. The group now includes Forest Hill and Leaside from the Toronto area, and Mount Royal, Outremont, and Westmount from the Montreal area. These cities all have comparatively high scores on the third and fourth dimensions, namely, metropolitan socio-economic structure, and high socio-economic residential status. The two central cities of Toronto and Montreal, however, remain as a separate group. Together these cities have negative scores on the first, fourth, and sixth components, and comparatively high positive values on the third and fifth dimensions.

The eighth and ninth groups are not as clearly identified in terms of any strong locational associations. The seemingly heterogeneous character of these groups stems in part from the arbitrary decision to consider a set of eleven groups. If the grouping procedure had been terminated at an earlier level, then the eighth group would have appeared in two parts, the one involving the cities of Dartmouth through Verdun inclusive in the list, and the other, the cities of Hamilton through Shawinigan inclusive. The cities in the first of these two subgroups ranked high on the fifth dimension, the service function of older and comparatively isolated communities, and it is noteworthy that four of the communities in this subgroup are metropolitan areas located in the Maritimes. The cities belonging to the second group generally had positive ratings on the second, third, and fourth components, this pattern being most pronounced in the case of the four suburban communities belonging to the Montreal metropolitan area. Group 9 includes two metropolitan areas, Windsor and Victoria, which have at least similar relative locations compared to the main urban network; four other major urban areas, namely, Fort William and Port Arthur, the two lake-port cities, Oshawa which has a similar manufacturing structure to that of Windsor, and St. Catharines; and finally, two of Vancouver's suburban communities, North Vancouver and New Westminster. These nine cities generally have low scores on all six important urban dimensions.

There remain, for 1961, two single-member groups. In the case of Sherbrooke, a low score on the first component and a high score on the second account for its separation. Sillery on the other hand, has very low scores on the second and fourth dimensions.

These findings not only throw new light on the Canadian urban system, but they also complement those of previous studies of urban systems in contributing towards a better understanding of urban structure and the sensitivity of related models to changes in the urban system over time.

The comparison of cross-sectional results from principal-components analysis cannot be taken too seriously, particularly when, as in this case, no attempt has been made to examine closely the degree and direction of changes in the correlation matrix.[26] Many of these correlations are also undoubtedly spurious while others are probably inflated by nonlinearity in the observed relationships. But, these limitations notwithstanding, the comparison of the two sets of results in this study has pointed up some interesting conclusions.

First, it seems essential that more analysis be undertaken with a view to examining the stability of urban dimensions over time. The results obtained here would suggest that these dimensions are not stable in form, and that over time they may reflect the changing orientations of urban society. The fact that a metropolitan scale showed up more clearly in 1961 than in 1951 is suggestive of the types of changes in the form of the dimensions that might be sought for more carefully. There are available more sophisticated designs, including three-way factor analyses and factor-matching procedures, which would be applicable in this context.[27] A second question that arises is that of interpreting the "flipping-over" of the urban dimensions that was noted in this study. This may well be only a mathematical consequence of the procedures and order by which the principal components are extracted. However, it may also be suggestive of stronger relationships among certain of the variables and this possibility warrants further study.

Finally, the stability of the relative locations of cities in the urban-dimensions space is significant. This was apparent in the persistence of certain city-groupings from one analysis to another, even though the bases of the urban-dimensions space had altered somewhat. Of particular importance is the fact that within many of these groupings there were strong regional contiguities among the member cities. In some other fields of urban research, particularly in the study of central place systems, the tendency towards order has been well established.[28] In the language of systems analysis this has been identified as a condition of "macroscopic negentropy" which constrains the system from reaching its most probable state.[29] It may well be that on the broader level of a national urban system in all its complexities, a similar tendency towards order exists and that the developing contrasts between the regional groupings of cities may be regarded as further examples of "deviation amplifying processes" within the system.[30] Again, the evidence provided here on this question is meager and more research is needed on the precise nature of these regional contrasts and the trends affecting them. This case study, hopefully, has raised more questions along such lines than it has answered.

FOOTNOTES TO CHAPTER 6

1. C. A. Moser and W. Scott, *British Towns: A Statistical Study of their Social and Economic Differences* (Edinburgh and London: Oliver and Boyd, 1961); Q. Ahmad, *Indian Cities: Characteristics and Correlates*, Research Paper No. 102, Department of Geography, University of Chicago, 1965. A similar study of the United States was made earlier by D. O. Price, "Factor Analysis in the Study of Metropolitan Centers," *Social Forces*, XX, No. 4 (December, 1942), 449–55. A more recent exercise in the American case is J. K. Hadden and E. F. Borgatta, *American Cities: Their Social Characteristics* (Skokie, Ill.: Rand McNally & Co., 1965).

2. Moser and Scott, *British Towns*, p. 3.

3. *Ibid.*, p. 66.

4. *Ibid.*, p. 80.

5. *Ibid.*, pp. 84–88.

6. Ahmad, *Indian Cities*, pp. 112–13.

7. See Amos Hawley, *Human Ecology* (New York: The Ronald Press, 1950), pp. 122–23; Duncan, *Metropolis and Region*, pp. 23–81; and Leo F. Schnore and David Varley, "Some Concomitants of Metropolitan Size," *American Sociological Review*, XX, No. 3 (August, 1955), 408–14.

8. O. D. Duncan *et al.*, *Metropolis and Region* (Baltimore:

The Johns Hopkins University Press, 1960), p. 81.

9. The term is borrowed from *ibid.*, p. 10. See also Chapter 5 of this book.

10. Brian J. L. Berry, "Cities as Systems within Systems of Cities," *Papers of the Regional Science Association*, XIII (1964), 147–65.

11. Schnore and Varley, "Some Concomitants of Metropolitan Size," p. 409.

12. *Metropolis and Region*, pp. 12, 15.

13. Note that the Muslim population, in general, suffers from a highly unbalanced sex ratio (more males to females). There is a far greater proportion of Muslims in the north as compared with the south.

14. More than 70 per cent of the total Christian population of India (10,726,350) is located in the four southern states of Andhra, Madras, Mysore, and Kerala. The last mentioned state has the largest proportion of Christian population of any states in India (21.22 per cent).

15. Price, "Factor Analysis."

16. For a discussion of principal components and factor analyses, see D. N. Lawley and A. E. Maxwell, *Factor Analysis as a Statistical Method* (London: Methuen, 1963).

17. B. J. L. Berry, "A Synthesis of Formal and Functional Regions using a General Field Theory of Spatial Behavior," in *Spatial Analysis*, eds. B. J. L. Berry and D. F. Marble (Englewood Cliffs, N. J.: Prentice-Hall, Inc., 1968).

18. This is an empirical observation, not a mathematically justified position.

19. Hadden and Borgatta, *American Cities*, pp. 38–66; Ahmad, *Indian Cities*.

20. S. M. Perle, "Factor Analysis of American Cities: A Comparative Study" (unpublished M. A. thesis, University of Chicago, 1964).

21. Berry, "A Synthesis of Formal and Functional Regions," p. 5.

22. L. F. Schnore, *The Urban Scene* (New York: The Free Press, 1965), pp. 212–13.

23. These data were taken from the *Census of Canada for 1951 and 1961; The Business Year Book* (Toronto: Government of Canada, 1952, 1961); *Canadian Municipal Financial Statistics* (Toronto: Bureau of Municipal Research, 1951, 1961); and the *Atlas of Canada* (Ottawa: Government of Canada, 1957).

24. The basic grouping algorithm is discussed in J. H. Ward, "Hierarchical Grouping to Optimize an Objective Function," *Journal of the American Statistical Association*, LVIII (June, 1963), 236–44. See also B. J. L. Berry, "A Method for Deriving Multi-Factor Uniform Regions," *Przeglad Geograficzny*, XLIII, No. 2 (1961), 263–79.

25. The D^2 statistic is discussed in C. R. Rao, *Advanced Statistical Methods in Biometric Research* (New York: John Wiley & Sons, Inc., 1952), pp. 354–55.

26. For a discussion of the problems associated with comparison of factor structures see Lawley and Maxwell, *Factor Analysis*, pp. 6, 92–93.

27. L. R. Tucker, "Implications of Factor Analysis of Three-Way Matrices for Measurement of Change," in *Problems in Measuring Change*, ed. C. W. Harris (Madison: University of Wisconsin Press, 1963), 122–37.

28. B. J. L. Berry, "Cities as Systems within Systems of Cities."

29. *Ibid.*, p. 159.

30. *Ibid.*, p. 160.

CHAPTER 7

urban hierarchies and spheres of influence

Already, the notion of an urban hierarchy has emerged in the discussions of city size and urban functions. Two ideas about the urban system are intertwined here, nodality and hierarchy.

THE URBAN HIERARCHY*

[Discussions of cities frequently refer to] the *nodal* character of locational pattern and the *hierarchical* structure of distribution as measured by size of function. Unfortunately, very few articles define either word but take the terms as given. The concept of hierarchy is the least defined of the two and the most troublesome, especially in a locational context.

*Reprinted from Fred Lukermann, "Empirical Expressions of Nodality and Hierarchy in a Circulation Manifold," *East Lakes Geographer*, II (August, 1966), 17–44, with the permission of the author and editor.

Articles concerned with the rank-size problem [see Chapter 3] assume hierarchy to mean simply order of size-rank. Articles concerned with the functional level of cities assume hierarchy to mean that restricted functions are higher in level (i.e., the-higher-the-fewer). "Restriction" is here measured in three ways: (1) by the number of cities having the function; (2) by the size of the population served by the function; and (3) by the area of the population served by the function. The concept of hierarchical control (higher over lower, few over many, *in seriatim*) is generally implicit, but seldom explicitly stated. That is, it is generally understood that something within a hierarchical structure is controlled (outside of the structure it cannot function), but seldom is the *line* of command specified as it should and must be. The old mechanistic problem of "action at a distance" is an ever-present, but unvoiced, problem in practically all . . . urban function studies. Eventually, however, the physical link between the population and the service must be specified. Merely counting functions, establishments, or population is not sufficient; the flow line must eventually be plotted.

As part of a system, a hierarchical unit has two attributes that should be distinguished: its relationships to a higher order unit is one of part to whole, to a lower unit of whole to part. That is, going up the hierarchy, lower parts are incorporated in the wholes above. Going down the hierarchy, wholes are divided into parts and separated out. Thus, despite the over-all characteristics of control, each hierarchical level has autonomy over orders below itself, while being a dependent of those above. In yet another context, a hierarchy could be conceived in a similar manner as levels of generalization from the higher abstract to the lower specific.

The concept of nodality is more clearly defined in the geographic literature, but not necessarily always in the same terms. Nodality is best defined as the place of greatest convenience. The qualities of nearest, closest, most central do not specify nodality exclusively and, in most contexts, leave room for ambiguity. Curry's definition is probably the most exact in contemporary literature and has the added capability of being specifically formulated. The value of nodality is determined by the number of possible services rendered, goods procured, contacts made, etc., at a place without additional movement or circulation after the initial trip.[1]

Nodality can, thus, be defined as a behavioral act of man, not simply a geometric point or circulation intersect. In behavioral terms, a nodal location is that place where the individual has the greatest freedom to interact. Such a definition involves both population density and areal accessibility, as well as functional availability. Expressed in locational terms, nodality and hierarchy are conceptually analogous. A spatial hierarchy is the specification of a nodal system or pattern.

Physical access usually defines the point of most convenience and, with functional availability, is a necessary concomitant of interaction. As in the definition of hierarchy, the definition of nodality must involve physical circulation and movement. The mere enumeration of route intersects, population, and functions, in themselves, does not define nodality. The flow of people, goods, and messages, as well as their exchange and interaction must eventually be stipulated.

Hierarchical structure and nodal pattern are, in a very exact sense then, the consequences and indices of the division of labor and territorial specialization. Adam Smith made very clear that the relation between the degree of division of labor and specialization was limited by the size of the market. It follows that the market, both as to population size and areal spread, is dependent on the presence of institutions of exchange and a transportation-communication medium. Hierarchy and nodality, in turn, are dependent on and limited by the nature of the route grid and the extent of the circulation manifold.

In urban systems analysis it would seem, obviously, to follow that some specification of all three elements (hierarchy, nodality, and circulation) is mandatory.

*CENTRAL-PLACE THEORY**

What Lukermann feels is mandatory has been accomplished by central-place theory. In central-place theory the term "central place" has meant "urban center." In the past the theory sought to account for these urban centers. It consisted of a series of assertions and definitions, logical consequences of which were a hierarchical ranking of urban centers according to function (e.g., hamlets, villages, towns, and cities) and associated market areas and transportation networks.

Concern with the full array of urban centers and associated market areas and transportation routes remains basic to central-place theory. Important recent work has shown the usefulness of the theory in understanding the spatial structure of retail and service business, however (whether this business be located in alternate urban

*Reprinted from Brian J. L. Berry and William L. Garrison, "Recent Developments of Central Place Theory," *Papers and Proceedings of the Regional Science Association*, IV (1958), 107–20.

centers or in shopping districts within cities), and the content of the theory thereby has been increased. These changes have resulted in an increased generality of the application of the theory (i.e., the theory may be more widely used; it serves as a theory of tertiary activity) and a more powerful theory (i.e., its assertions are more plausible; its logical consequences are more explicit). The elaboration of these results is the purpose of the ensuing discussion.

Initial Formulation of the Theory

Schemes explaining urban growth and arrangement are many in number. Most of these likely stem from common origins. It seems, thus, that generic roots of central-place theory extend in many directions and are joint with those of competing schemes. That these things may be true is taken for granted in the present discussion, which simply begins with the pragmatically taken position that central-place theory began with Walter Christaller in 1933. To begin with Christaller and outline the chief contributions of subsequent workers is a sufficient statement of the theory for present purposes. The complete statement of the growth of the theory awaits [a] definitive work on the development of ideas about urbanism.

Central-place theory as formulated by Walter Christaller[2] and presented by Edward Ullman[3] is relatively well-known.[4] The content of the theory may therefore be stated in a summary way with an outline of its definitions, relationships, and consequences:

1. Terms defined included:
   a. A central place.
   b. A central good.
   c. A complementary region.
2. Relationships specified included:
   a. Variations in prices of central goods as distance from point of supply changes.
   b. Explicit extremization behavior in the distribution and consumption of goods (e.g., goods are purchased from the closest place).
   c. Inner and outer limits for the range of distances over which central goods may be sold.
   d. Relationships between the number of goods sold from a central place and the population of that place.
3. A statement which used the terms defined and relationships specified (within the simplifying assumption of homogeneous distribution of purchasing power in all areas) and described the arrangement of central places and complementary regions was made.

Essential features of this statement were:

1. Hexagonal market areas for any set of central goods.
2. Overlapping sets of hexagons. The hexagons overlap in such a way that larger hexagonal market areas (resulting from a set of central goods) are divided into smaller hexagons when supplied by other central goods. The smaller hexagons nest into the larger according to a rule of threes (this is the K-3 network described by Lösch).
3. Transportation routes serving the system of cities.

These elements were included by Christaller so that he could construct a "general purely deductive theory" to explain the "size, number, and distribution of towns" in the belief that "there is some ordering principle governing the distribution." Christaller considered that his theories "could also be designated as the theory of location of urban trades and institutions," to be placed beside Thünen's[5] theory regarding the location of agricultural production and theory regarding location of industries developed by Weber.[6] An abstract of relevent parts of his treatise that previously appeared in Berry and Pred's bibliography of central-place studies follows:

The crystallization of mass about a nucleus is part of the elementary order of things. Centralistic principles are similarly basic to human community life. In this sense the town is a center of a regional community and the mediator of that community's commerce; it functions, then, as the central place of the community.

Central places vary in importance. Those of higher order dominate larger regions than those of lesser order, exercise more central functions, and therefore have greater centrality. For all, however, "the sum of the distances which rural residents travel to the central place is the smallest conceivable sum."

The goods and services provided by the central place because it is central are known as central goods and services. Higher order goods are offered at central places of higher order, and lower order goods at places of both higher and lower order.

The region for which a central place is the center should be called the complementary region; it includes relationships in both directions—town to country and country to town. Complementary regions are likewise of higher and lower order. They are hard to determine because they differ for different types of goods, undergo periodic and seasonal variation, and consistently overlap neighboring complementary regions at the periphery. Distance plays a vital role in any determination of complementary regions, especially "economic distance," measured in time and cost. The range of a good is the farthest distance a dispersed population is willing to go in order to buy a good offered at a place. This range will take on a lower limit if there is competition from another center.

A decisive fact in the development of central places is the net income which inhabitants earn. There is a functional relationship between the size of a central place on the one hand and the sizes of the complementary region, its population and income on the other.

Central goods offered at a larger place have a larger range than those offered at smaller, and the fact that a central place is larger or smaller has an immediate influence on the range of a central good because more types of central goods are offered at a center of higher order. The possibility that on a single trip several types of goods may be offered simultaneously has the same effect as a general price decline in goods offered by larger towns.

Every type of good has its special range, which differs at different central places and is not the same in all directions from the same center, but varies according to objective and subjective economic distance. More basically, range is determined by: (1) the size and importance of the center and the spatial distribution of population; (2) the price-willingness of purchasers; (3) subjective economic distance; and (4) quantity and price of the good at the central place. The range is actually a ring with an upper limit beyond which a good can no longer be obtained from a center, and a lower limit which is determined by the minimum amount of consumption which is necessary before production or offering the central good will pay.

There is a system of central places comprising several size-types, determined in general by the spatial effects of the upper and lower limits to the range of central goods. According to this *marketing or supply principle*, if the assumption of a homogeneous plain with equal access in all directions is made, complementary regions become hexagonal, and lower order centers and their complementary regions "nest" within those of larger centers according to a rule of threes. In this system the relations between size, spacing, functions and hierarchical interdependence in the system of central places are determined precisely. Seven levels to the hierarchy are postulated from the level of hamlet to world-city, based upon south German evidence. This strict mathematical scheme is, of course, as imperfect as the simplifying assumption, and reality may be approached by recognizing price differences, differences in population distribution, etc. Note the strong parallel between size and frequency of central places and intensity of traffic, but it is the former which determine the latter, and not viceversa.

The system of central places developed on the basis of range of central goods used the assumption that all areas were able to be served from a minimum of central places; therefore the principle on which the system was developed can be called the *marketing or supply principle*. But there are other factors. *The principles of traffic* say that the distribution of central places is at an optimum where as many important places as possible lie on one traffic route between larger towns, the route being established as cheaply as possible. Complementary regions then "nest" according to a rule of fours. Principles of traffic are fundamentally linear, those of marketing spatial. *The political-social (administrative) principles* are based upon ideas of separation of complementary regions for purposes of protection, or of distinction which implies clear-cut administrative control. In this case "nesting" follows a rule of sevens. Figure 7–1 depicts the patterns that result from the operation of each of the three principles.

The three principles determine, each according to its own laws, the system of central places. Two of them are economic and one is political. Under certain circumstances one or the other principle may dominate, but mostly they have to fight for predominance, a predomi-

FIGURE 7–1. The system of central places after the marketing, administrative, and transportation principles. *Source:* B. J. L. Berry and A. Pred, *Central Place Studies*, after Walter Christaller, *Das Grundgerust der Räumlichen Ordnung in Europa* (Frankfurt: Waldemar Kramer Verlag, 1950).

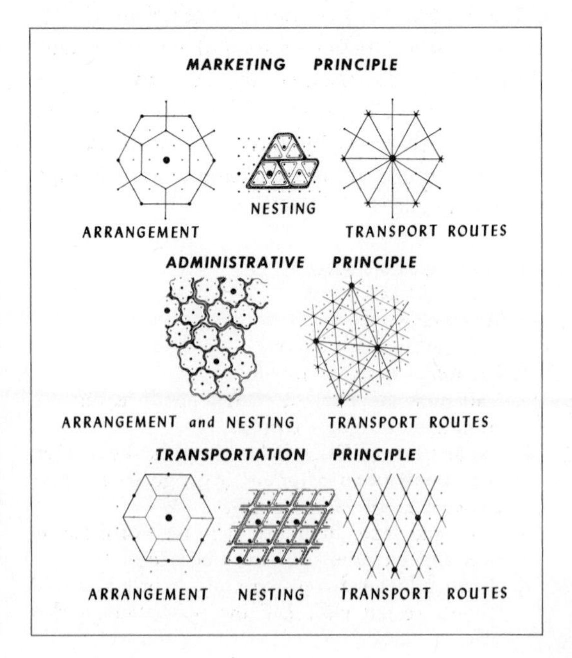

nance which depends upon the operation of dynamic processes—of short-run, periodic, and seasonal fluctuations, and longer-run secular changes.[7]

Christaller then discusses the central-place systems of southern Germany. On the basis of this discussion he evaluates his theory; we return to this evaluation:

We may call (the three principles) laws of distribution of central places, or laws of settlement, which fundamentally determine the location of a central place with astonishing exactness.

The chief and uncontested range of the principle of marketing lies in the prevalent agricultural provinces. Dominance of the principles of traffic per se, depends upon orientation to real traffic flows not related to the marketing of goods; in many cases pseudo-traffic orientation may also be found, as along valleys or on the margins of mountains. Dominance of the sociopolitical or administrative-separation principle is hard to prove; it can only be established by historical study. But wherever two low order places lie close together in a place where we might predict a higher order center to be, the probability exists that the separation principle is operative. Generally, both the latter principles must operate together with that of marketing; the marketing principle is the chief law, and the transport and administrative principles are secondary laws of deviation.

Many deviations not explainable by any of the principles are nevertheless explainable by economics: (1) a whole system may be raised to a higher or lower level with general wealth and a dense population or general poverty and a sparse population; (2) spacing may be enlarged or compressed by the relative strength of any one system and adjacent systems; (3) depending upon the economic base of the area in question, there may be more or less of centers of any order.

Deviations from population: centrality ratios may be of a local nature, viz: spas, mining towns, dormitory suburbs, etc. Similarly, local price differences, international borders, etc., may result in differences in the subjective evaluation of the importance of distance.

Other deviations are not explainable by economics. One class must be explained historically, for example in the foundations of sovereign nobility or of religious sites or of industrial towns. Another class depends upon circumstances of physical geography. Yet another class is of a military character. And so on.[8]

Generalization by August Lösch

A good portion of August Lösch's now classic *Die räumliche Ordnung der Wirtschaft*[9] was given to an evaluation and extension of notions of the arrangement of central places. Lösch's additions to the ideas of Christaller fall into three major divisions.

1. The explicit statement of two aspects of the system:
   a. The derivation of spatial demand cones.
   b. Verification of the hexagonal-shaped complementary region as the "best" shape where purchasing power was uniformly distributed.
2. Clear linking of the arrangement of transportation routes among cities to central place notions.
3. The extension of the special case of a K-3 network to a more general description of a system containing all possible relationships of evenly spaced central places and nests of hexagonal shapes of complementary regions. In the system he develops, he maintains:
   a. That consumer movement must be minimized.
   b. That no excess profits can be earned by any firm.

Lösch further asserts, but does not demonstrate, that one outcome of his system is a specialized type of hierarchical class system of central places, both as sources of central goods and as nodes in the transport network.

Recent Developments

As initially developed, central-place theory related only to alternate urban centers and the transport network linking urban centers. The statement was in terms of homogeneously distributed purchasing power (hence, the hexagonal trade areas) and, thus, restricted in applicability in more realistic situations. Such assumptions as the absence of excess profits in the system were troublesome. Recent work shows however:

1. That central-place theory is definitely more viable when reformulated in terms of a series of simple concepts.
2. That reformulation in terms of these concepts enables a hierarchical structure to be developed without the assumptions of uniformity concerning purchasing power which are basic to the arrangement of hexagonal trade areas. One consequence of this is that the theory become applicable to areas within cities as well as areas without.
3. That the notion of elimination of excess profits can be relaxed.

Empirical work associated with these developments has shown how they simplify the problem of the empirical verification of the theory.

The concept of the range of a good. A concept with an important role in present central-place theory is that of "the range of a central good." This range delineates the market area of a central place for the good. It has a lower limit which incorporates threshold purchasing power for the supply of the good (see below) and an upper limit beyond which the central place is no longer able to sell the good. Each good will have different limits to its range because of competition between central places supplying the good (in the case of the upper limit) and differing internal economic characteristics of the supplying firms which determine threshold (in the case of the lower limit).

The concept of threshold. There is some minimum size of market below which a place will be unable to supply a central good. This is the point where sales are large enough only for the firm to earn normal profits. This minimum scale, the lower limit of the range of a central place, is the minimum amount of purchasing power necessary to support the supply of a central good from a central place, and is here termed the "threshold sales level" for the provision of that good from the center.

The spatial structure of the hierarchy of central places. It can be argued that *whatever* the distribution of purchasing power (and whether in open countryside or within a large metropolis) a hierarchical spatial structure of central places supplying central goods will emerge. This argument requires only the concept of range and threshold just given.

For the sake of exposition assume an area to be supplied with n types of central goods. Let these be ranked from 1 to n in ascending order of threshold sales requirements. The central place supplying good n will require the largest market area (in terms of purchasing power) to support it. Let a central place supplying good n be called an A center.

As many A centers will exist in the area as there are threshold market areas to support firms supplying good n. These firms compete spatially, hence are distributed so as to supply their own threshold most efficiently. If total sales levels are an exact multiple of thresholds for good n, firms will earn only normal profits, and these *only if* they minimize costs by: (1) locating so to minimize distribution costs if the product is delivered; or (2) locating so to minimize consumer movement if the consumer comes to purchase the products.

If sales in the whole area are slightly greater than an exact multiple of threshold, but not great enough to justify another A center, then excess profits may be earned.

The question arises as to how good $n - 1$ will be provided. Presumably, it will be supplied from the A centers, which have sought out the most efficient points of supply. Too, there will be advantages from association with other establishments providing central goods. The threshold of good $n - 1$ is less than that of good n and hence, spatial competition determines market areas (these are delimited by upper limit ranges) and excess profits may be earned. This argument will hold for good $n - 2$, down to good 1.

But there may be one or more goods, say good $n - i$, in which case the interstitial purchasing power located between threshold market areas of A centers supplying good $n - i$ will themselves reach threshold size. In this case greater efficiency is reached if a second set of centers, which may be termed B centers, supply the good. These B centers again locate most efficiently in relation to their threshold market area. If the market area is just at the threshold only normal profits are earned by firms supplying good $n - i$; if part-multiples of the threshold are present, some excess profits are earned. Good $n - i$ may be termed a *hierarchical marginal good.* B centers will also provide lower threshold goods, $n - (i + 1)$ through good 1.

Let us assume that good $n - j$ $(j > i)$ is also a hierarchical marginal good, supporting a third set of central places designated as C places. These are a lower order of central places and provide only goods $n - j$ through good 1.

The pattern of provision of goods by centers in this hierarchical system may be displayed in an array (see Table 7-1). The table displays how sets of goods build up hierarchies of types of central places. For example, the set of C places and places

TABLE 7–1

How* n *Goods Are Supplied by* M *Centers

	Goods				
Centers	$n^*, n-1, \ldots$	$n-i^*, n-(i+1), \ldots$	$n-j^*, n-(j+1), \ldots$	$\ldots$	$k^*, (k-1), \ldots 1$
A	X	X	X	...	X
B		X	X	...	X
C			X	...	X
.				.	.
.				.	.
.				.	.
M					X

Source: Brian J. L. Berry and William L. Garrison, "Recent Developments of Central Place Theory," *Papers of the Regional Science Association*, IV (1958), 107–20.
*Indicates hierarchical marginal good. *X* indicates the set of goods supplied by the center.

in the tributary areas of *C* places rely upon either *B* or *A* places for goods $n - i$ to $n - (j - 1)$ and upon *A* places for goods *n* to $n - (i - 1)$. *B* places rely upon *A* places for goods *n* to $n - (i - 1)$. All places will be located at the point from which they most efficiently serve tributary areas with central goods.

Yet at the same time excess profits may be earned in the system. Where *n* goods are provided, it is likely that the hierarchical marginal firm will tend to earn only normal profits. This is the firm which satisfies Lösch's condition that excess profits shall be at a minimum. However, all supramarginal firms in the hierarchy will have the opportunity to earn excess profits to the extent that they are able to compete spatially with other firms for the sub-threshold purchasing power which exists *between* threshold market areas in the spatial system.

The question may quite properly be raised, Why argue for a step hierarchy of functions and one with excess profits (profits over and above normal profits) when a system without excess profits can be posited (by Lösch), using the notion of nested hexagonal trade areas? The argument used was presented because recent empirical work indicates it is more like reality than the alternate argument. Examples of relevant empirical findings follow.

*THE URBAN HIERARCHY OF A DEVELOPING COUNTRY: NIGERIA**

The need for an objective approach to the empirical problem of determining the hierarchy of central places has long been felt by many urban geographers. Such an approach was suggested in 1958 by Berry and Garrison,[10] and in 1962 by Berry and Barnum.[11] Recently, Grove and Huszar put forward a method designed for studying the problem in a developing country.[12] However, a careful investigation of their book reveals major deficiencies. In the following paragraphs an alternative method is proposed which removes these defects, and the method is applied to a developing country [Nigeria].[13]

We make no assumption as to which settlement should be treated as an urban center. Only after the grouping and analysis do we identify settlements that qualify as urban centers. Such new concepts as functional distances between settlements, functional interaction between settlements, and the functional magnitude of settlements are discussed.

The hierarchical system of centers emerges from

*Reprinted from Josephine Olu. Abiodun, "Urban Hierarchy in a Developing Country," *Economic Geography*, XLIII, No. 4 (October, 1967), 347–67, with the permission of the author and editor.

Christaller-Lösch[14] deductions based on a theoretical model of the spatial distribution of centers in an economic landscape. In recent years several studies have been undertaken in both developed and developing areas to test the idea. For a summary of previous work in this field, the reader is referred to the review by Berry and Pred.[15] Those who doubt the reality of a class system of centers drew attention to the a priori methods of many of these studies. Vining's[16] criticism of Brush's[17] study is a case in point. Having pointed out the arbitrariness of Brush's classification, he drew the implication that instead of centers being arranged in a hierarchical class system, they are differentiated along a continuum.

Berry, Barnum, and Tennant[18] in an objective approach to the problem noted that both a continuous system and a hierarchical system of centers may be found, depending on the scale of the inquiry. However, their approach assumes the availability of accurate population data, which in turn restricts its applicability to only those areas where such conditions can be satisfied.

In a recent study on Ghana, Grove and Huszar[19] put forward a method for studying the problem in a developing country. The essence of their method is that the existence or otherwise of any hierarchical class system of centers can be tested merely by "adding up the points awarded to the services in each center" and fitting on to the graph of such a summary, the so-called "crucial curve" merely by inspection. This approach incorporates some serious defects. By adding up the points awarded to a center in respect to each of the functions, the assumption is being made that all the functions considered are commensurable (or have been made commensurable). A close examination of the functions the authors considered shows that this condition is far from being satisfied. A second defect is that the fitting of the curve by inspection introduces quite arbitrary decisions and since this curve is "crucial" to their interpretation of central-place theory, their deductions are likewise liable to subjectiveness.

A classification process which considers the variables individually meets the first defect. The other is avoided by a systematic grouping procedure which aims at maximum uniformity within groups and minimum uniformity between groups. The use of variables that have not been ascertained to be mutually independent seems unsatisfactory. One consequence of the use of such variables is the danger of overestimation. It is only through the technique of multivariate analysis that we can ensure that the variables used in the classification of centers are mutually independent and, thus, that no overestimation occurs.

A Brief Outline of the Method

If the hierarchical concept implied in central-place theory holds good for any region of study, i.e., that we would expect a classification of the relative importance of the settlements of the region in terms of the central functions each performs to result in a well-defined hierarchy of centers, then such information must be contained in any complete assemblage of the available data of the centeral functions for the settlements of the region. Let us denote this assemblage by the array $A(p, q)$ such that:

$$A(p,q) = \begin{bmatrix} a_{11} & a_{12} & \cdot & \cdot & \cdot & a_{1q} \\ \cdot & \cdot & \cdot & \cdot & \cdot & \cdot \\ \cdot & \cdot & \cdot & \cdot & \cdot & \cdot \\ \cdot & \cdot & \cdot & \cdot & \cdot & \cdot \\ \cdot & \cdot & \cdot & \cdot & \cdot & \cdot \\ a_{p1} & \cdot & \cdot & \cdot & \cdot & a_{pq} \end{bmatrix}$$

where p is the number of settlements, q denotes the number of the central functions, and a is the observed value of each central function for each settlement.

The associated correlation matrix[20] of central functions will then be of the form:

$$C(q,q) = \begin{bmatrix} 1 & & & & & \\ c_{21} & 1 & & & & \\ c_{31} & \cdot & 1 & & & \\ \cdot & \cdot & \cdot & 1 & & \\ \cdot & \cdot & \cdot & \cdot & 1 & \\ c_{q1} & \cdot & \cdot & \cdot & \cdot & 1 \end{bmatrix}$$

In this form, the correlation matrix C also contains complete information regarding the variability of the central functions among themselves. The off diagonals (usually less than unity) give the correlation between one central function and the other, while the diagonal elements (which must be approximately unity) give self-correlation. The key point of the method of component analysis lies in obtaining, without any loss of details, a new set of variables (principal components) in terms of which the correlation matrix C becomes the following:

$$C(q,q) = \begin{bmatrix} k_1 & & & & \\ & k_2 & & & \\ & & \cdot & & \\ & & & \cdot & \\ & & & & \cdot \quad k_q \end{bmatrix}$$

Such new variables with zero intercorrelation must be mutually independent. The diagonal terms of C', usually the eigenvalues, are known to be a measure of the importance of the corresponding principal components.[21] Since it is known in linear transformation theory that the sum of the diagonal terms, i.e., the spur of a real symmetric matrix is invariant under a linear transformation, the sum of the eigenvalues will, therefore, in all cases of component analysis, be equal to the number of the original primary variables. This provides a useful check on the accuracy of the computation.

It is evident from the correlation matrix C that the primary variables are not generally independent of one another. Thus, the use of the independent variables ensures that each principal component considered introduces new details hitherto unaccounted for. The main problem of component analysis is, therefore, one of determining the diagonal terms of the matrix $C'(q,q)$ and the corresponding principal components.

The functional score according to each principal component of importance is then easily calculated for each settlement.

One of the simplifications afforded by this method, therefore, occurs when any of the diagonal elements is zero for the corresponding principal component will then be redundant. Further simplification also occurs when just one, two, three, or even more of the diagonal elements constitute a very large proportion, say 70 to 80 per cent of the total variability. When such is the case, the corresponding principal components alone will suffice for the determination of the hierarchy.

Centrality

Ideas vary as to how the centrality of a place can be measured. What constitutes centrality must be defined relative to the conditions prevailing in the area under study. The idea of assessing centrality by the number of a particular single service, e.g., the number of telephones installed (Christaller), or bus service frequency,[22] if applied to a developing country, could lead only to unrealistic conclusions. Such functions as banking or insurance, telephone service, self-service laundry, or even a hotel, regarded in the developed countries as ordinary basic services, must in the developing countries of Africa be associated with higher order centrality. Moreover, no single central function that might be taken as a significant median of the importance of other central functions has at present a sufficiently wide distribution as to be a reliable guide of the relative importance of settlements. In such a case, the use of a single central function would be misleading; the author holds that centrality in the area under study must depend on the quality (variety and type) of the central functions available. It is also worth mentioning that such classifications as are based on a single central function are of limited use.

Selection of Data

The study area for this analysis is in southwestern Nigeria, a region of rather numerous population centers (see Figs. 7–2 and 7–3). However, any functional classification of urban centers based exclusively on population can only be a purely arbitrary and crude measure of their relative importance. It is, therefore, essential that we consider the central functions offered by each settlement. It is worthwhile to note that the type of central functions that determine an urban center would depend a good deal on the level of economic development in the area under study. The social, administrative, and cultural level, as well as the entertainment habits of the area, would also influence the type of data selected. In a developed

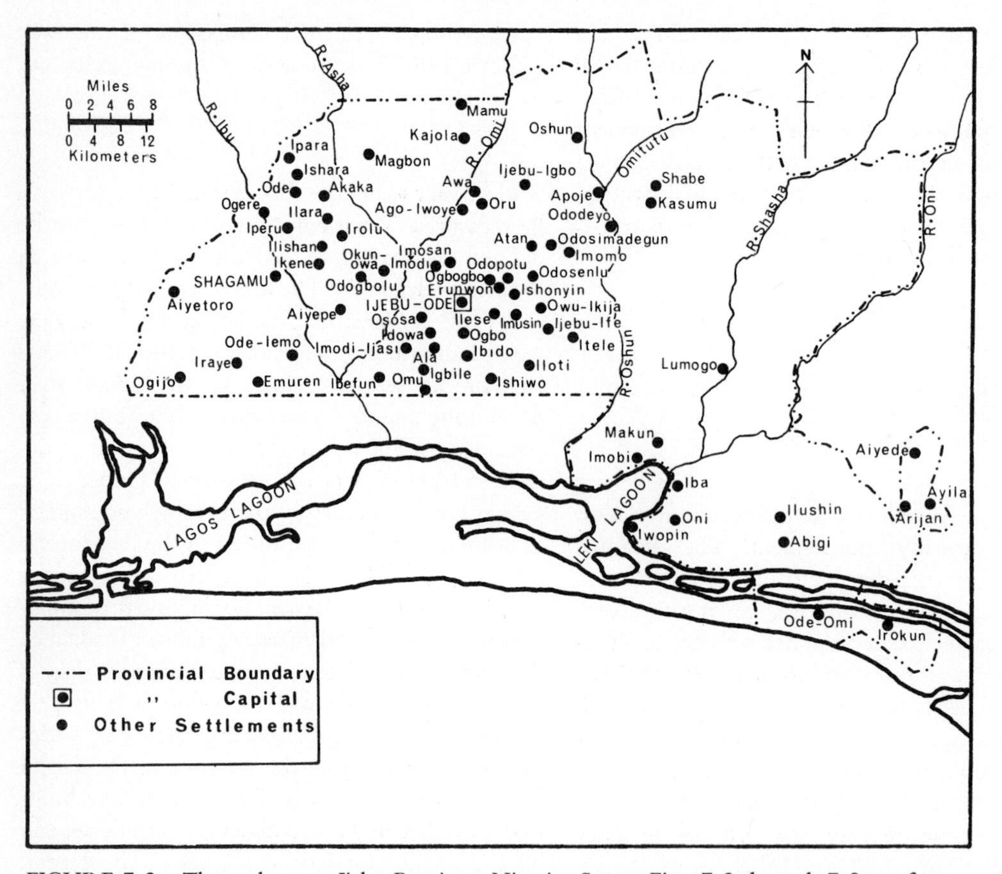

FIGURE 7–2. The study area: Ijebu Province, Nigeria. *Source:* Figs. 7–2 through 7–9 are from Josephine Olu. Abiodun, "Urban Hierarchy in a Developing Country," *Economic Geography*, XLIII, No. 4 (October, 1967), 145–54.

area, for instance, the existence of three or more banks[23] may be needed to indicate an urban center; but in a developing country, the existence of even one bank indicates a center of a high order of importance.

Another problem which confronts an investigator of the present topic in such an area is the general lack of data or the difficulty of collecting it. Functions such as daily newspaper circulation are of limited application and moreover data on this is difficult to obtain. Similarly, the data on urban retail shops is not available and is very difficult to collect by a single investigator over such a wide region. The distribution of representative retail company stores has been used. We may note, however, that markets rather than urban retail shops form the characteristic retail channel in the area under study for the distribution of products (especially food products) from the surrounding countryside and also for the distribution of certain imported products such as textiles and hardware, though the tendency toward local retail stores in imported products is increasing, particularly in the large urban centers.

A distinction needs to be made, however, between periodic markets and daily markets. From a local knowledge of the area, we know that while the periodic markets are characteristic of rural settlements, it is the daily markets that characterize the urban settlements. To be useful in a study such as ours, therefore, data on markets must be those relating to daily markets. At the moment the relevant data is not completely available, but effort is being made to fill the gaps, and this function will be included in the wider study of which the present is a part. The assumption is made that the

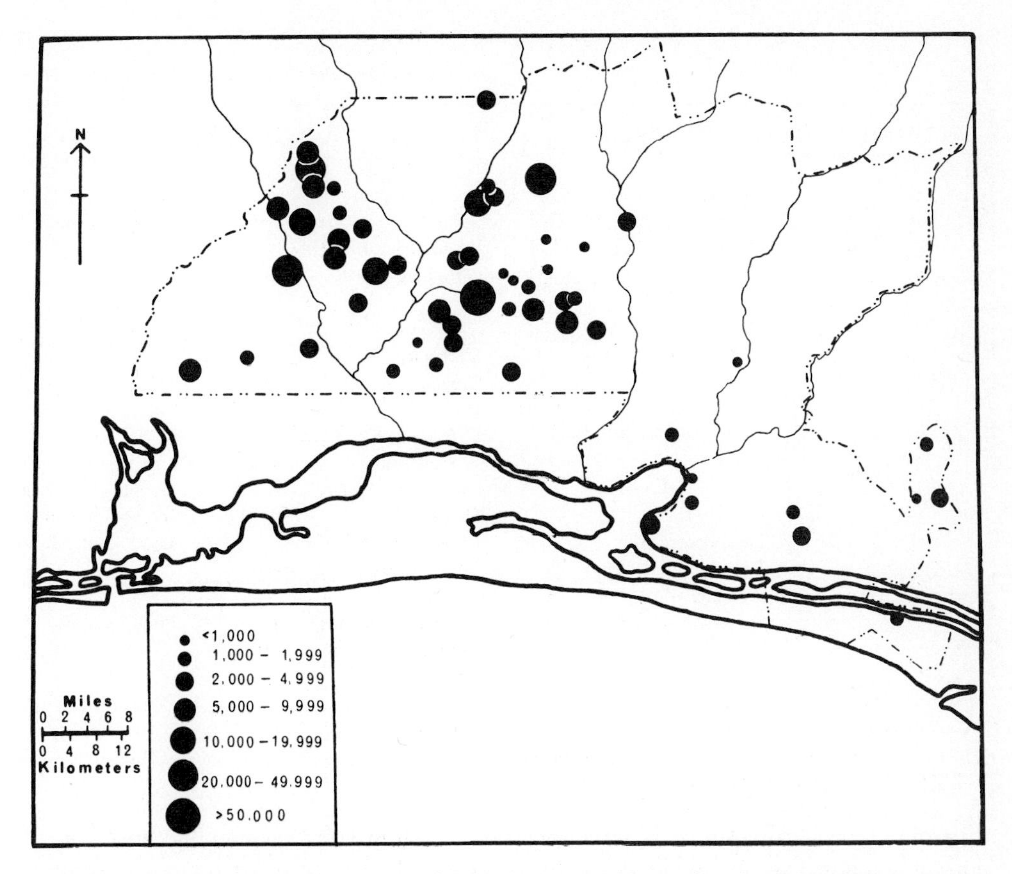

FIGURE 7–3. Population distribution of Ijebu Province, Nigeria (based on the 1963 Census). *Source:* See caption for Fig. 7–2.

pattern they express conforms with those resulting from the combination of the 28 central functions considered in the present study.

The Weighting of Variables

The problem of determining the hierarchy of central places and that of determining the threshold population for each central function need not be synonymous, as is sometimes implied, but may be treated as aspects of the same theory, the latter being always complementary to the former. When the main interest lies exclusively on testing the existence or otherwise of a hierarchy of centers, it would suffice without loss of any vital detail to ignore the volume and consider only the quality and the presence or absence of central functions.

Three classes of central functions are considered in the present study (see Table 7–2). In a study of this type, the need for maintaining a balance between the different groups of central functions—economic, social, administrative, entertainment, etc.—deserves recognition. As more information becomes available it would be possible to make improvements along this line. At the moment we are handicapped by the lack of relevant data.

To assume that all central functions are of equal level of significance, does not appear realistic. The practice of awarding one or zero depending on the presence or absence of a function in a settlement irrespective of the type of function, therefore, seems inadequate. It is, therefore, essential to give consideration to differences in the level of functions where such exist. In this locality, for instance, it is common knowledge

TABLE 7–2

Weighting and Classification of Services in Nigerian Centers

	Class I	*Class II*	*Class III*
Weighting score	*10*	*5*	*1*
	Hospital	Special hospital	Dispensary
	University and Technical college	Secondary grammar school and Grade II teacher training college	Secondary modern school
	—	—	Rediffusion
	—	—	Piped water
	—	Electricity	—
	—	Cinema	—
	—	Banking	—
	U.A.C. wholesale store	U.A.C. (commercial) branch store	—
	—	Cooperative society	Cooperative society
		Shops	Licensed buying agents
	Local court "A"	Local court "B"	Local courts "D" and "C"
	Divisional and city council	Local, district and urban council	—
	—	Police headquarters	Police station
	—	Government treasury	—
	—	Public library	—
	"A" post office (G.P.O.)	"B" post office	Postal agency

Source: Tables 7–2 through 7–5 are from Josephine Olu. Abiodun, "Urban Hierarchy in a Developing Country," *Economic Geography*, XLIII, No. 4 (October, 1967), 347–67.

that some centers can adequately serve their area with only a postal agency, while others by virtue of their importance would be expected to possess a General Post Office. To award the same score to both functions is to reduce them to the same level of significance. We, therefore, weighted central functions (in Table 7–2), bearing in mind the prevailing conditions in the study area. A General Post Office with all facilities including telephone exchange, public holiday and Sunday openings, has been allocated 10 points, while a postal agency is allocated 1 point. The intermediate type, with no telephone exchange and no Sunday and public holiday openings but having all the other facilities, has been allocated 5 points. Where no distinction can be made within the type of service, the local conditions have been the factor considered in classifying the function. Electricity in an advanced country for instance, is regard as a basic service, but in the developing countries of Africa, it indicates a center of some importance[24] and it has therefore been placed in the intermediate class of central functions.

It is worth mentioning, however, that a service such as piped water is not necessarily indicative of the importance of a place. Settlements located near the source of distribution of the service may possess it while settlements known to be relatively more important may lack such a service. This occurs in the case of Odopotu, Ilaporu, and Alemafo, which have the service, while Odogbolu, which is much farther from the source of distribution to Ijebu-Ode (the provincial capital), lacks the service, though Odogbolu is locally recognized as the most important both in terms of central functions performed and of population. It is among the objectives of this study to highlight such anomalies and suggest remedies.

Two notes of clarification need to be made at this point. The first concerns the distinction between the weighting of the primary variables and their statistical standardization. A function that exists to the same degree in every settlement ceases to be useful in defining the relative importance of settlements. The statistical standardization of each central function emphasizes its ubiquity and hence its importance due to its scarcity in the area. On the other hand, it is the weighting of the central function that takes account of its quality. For instance, a United Africa Company wholesale store and a Co-operative Society shop, which have identical distribution within the Province, attained the same degree of importance under statistical standardization. However, the classification (Table 7–2) shows the U.A.C. wholesale store as a function of greater economic importance. It is only through such a weighting device that distinctions due to quality have been achieved. The second point concerns the allocation of weighting scores. Shall we arrive at the same results under different weighting scores? A tentative answer to this question is that there is no reason why the same order of hierarchy should not reproduce, as the question of the allocation of weighting scores is merely one of the choice of a measure. The choice of a measure will however affect the ease with which groups of the hierarchy are identified. This point is the subject of a thorough investigation now in progress and it is hoped that a satisfactory answer to this question would be possible in a subsequent paper.

Application of the Method

In assembling the data, no assumption is made as to which settlement should be treated as an urban center. All settlements came on the list by virtue of possessing any of the functions being considered. Only after analyzing the grouping do we identify urban centers. In Table 7–3 we have obtained the correlation matrix of the central functions. A thorough investigation of Table 7–3 and Fig. 7–4 reveals several points of interest. Outstanding among these is the fact that of the 406 coefficients of correlation, 376 are positive. This indicates that, if we take any pair of functions, there is a general tendency for the probability of the existence of one in a settlement to increase as that of the other increases.

First, let us consider the pattern described by the banking profile (see Fig. 7–4). This shows a high degree of positive correlation (.882) between banking and hospital in terms of their distribution within the province. In other words, there is a distinct tendency for the two to occur in association; where there is one there is likely to be the other. The same pattern is exhibited by the following pairs of central functions:

1. Banking and Secondary Grammar School	.840
2. Banking and Secondary Modern School	.748
3. Banking and Local Court "B"	.916
4. Banking and "A" Post Office	.860
5. Banking and Divisional Council	.882
6. Banking and Library	.740
7. Banking and Cinema	882

However, great caution should be exercised in interpreting these coefficients. As usual, we need to remember that such deductions are subject to the limitations of statistical generalization. For instance, though from a common knowledge of conditions in this province one would expect, as the pattern shows, that a settlement with a General Post Office would be such a focus of the economic life of the area as to need banking facilities, the same deductions could not be asserted in relation to banking and secondary grammar school. This is particularly so since, with the general upsurge in the demand for educational facilities, it is a common feature for communities to build their own secondary grammar school either for local prestige or to meet a limited local demand which otherwise cannot attract interest from the regional authorities (e.g., Imushin Grammar School was established as a result of local pressure). Though such a move eventually enhances the importance of that settlement, it cannot by itself make it an economic proposition for a banking establishment. The exact relationship between banking and secondary grammar school in this province is difficult to establish without reference to the threshold population for each of them. Since our emphasis here is on testing the validity of the hierarchical concept of centers, we defer further consideration of this point to a later work. All that could be said in such a case is that while there is a high probability that a secondary grammar school exists where there is a bank, the converse need not hold in this province.

An exception to the general positive trend in the relationship between central functions is the pattern described by the dispensary profile (see

TABLE 7–3

Correlation Matrix of Central Functions of Settlements in a Nigerian Province

	X_1	X_2	X_3	X_4	X_5	X_6	X_7	X_8	X_9	X_{10}	X_{11}	X_{12}	X_{13}	X_{14}	X_{15}	X_{16}	X_{17}	X_{18}	X_{19}	X_{20}	X_{21}	X_{22}	X_{23}	X_{24}	X_{25}	X_{26}	X_{27}
X_1	1.000	....	....	....	....	....	....	....	....	....	....	....	....	....	....	....	....	....	....	....	....	....	....	....	....	....	....
X_2	0.49	1.000	....	....	....	....	....	....	....	....	....	....	....	....	....	....	....	....	....	....	....	....	....	....	....	....	....
X_3	0.556	0.964	1.000	....	....	....	....	....	....	....	....	....	....	....	....	....	....	....	....	....	....	....	....	....	....	....	....
X_4	0.49	1.000	0.964	1.000	....	....	....	....	....	....	....	....	....	....	....	....	....	....	....	....	....	....	....	....	....	....	....
X_5	0.697	0.02	0.128	–0.02	1.000	....	....	....	....	....	....	....	....	....	....	....	....	....	....	....	....	....	....	....	....	....	....
X_6	0.49	1.000	0.964	1.000	–0.02	1.000	....	....	....	....	....	....	....	....	....	....	....	....	....	....	....	....	....	....	....	....	....
X_7	0.916	0.396	0.465	0.396	0.862	0.396	1.000	....	....	....	....	....	....	....	....	....	....	....	....	....	....	....	....	....	....	....	....
X_8	0.639	0.426	0.48	0.426	0.478	0.426	0.629	1.000	....	....	....	....	....	....	....	....	....	....	....	....	....	....	....	....	....	....	....
X_9	0.000	0.000	0.000	0.000	0.000	0.000	0.000	0.000	0.000	....	....	....	....	....	....	....	....	....	....	....	....	....	....	....	....	....	....
X_{10}	0.495	0.155	0.217	0.155	0.387	0.155	0.449	0.618	0.000	1.000	....	....	....	....	....	....	....	....	....	....	....	....	....	....	....	....	....
X_{11}	0.882	0.702	0.673	0.702	0.486	0.702	0.862	0.607	0.000	0.387	1.000	....	....	....	....	....	....	....	....	....	....	....	....	....	....	....	....
X_{12}	0.49	1.000	0.964	1.000	–0.02	1.000	0.396	0.426	0.000	0.155	0.702	1.000	....	....	....	....	....	....	....	....	....	....	....	....	....	....	....
X_{13}	0.422	0.206	0.289	0.206	0.294	0.206	0.341	0.504	0.000	0.435	0.294	0.206	1.000	....	....	....	....	....	....	....	....	....	....	....	....	....	....
X_{14}	0.49	1.000	0.964	1.000	–0.02	1.000	0.396	0.426	0.000	0.155	0.702	1.000	0.206	1.000	....	....	....	....	....	....	....	....	....	....	....	....	....
X_{15}	0.882	0.702	0.673	0.702	0.486	0.702	0.862	0.607	0.000	0.387	1.000	0.702	0.294	0.702	1.000	....	....	....	....	....	....	....	....	....	....	....	....
X_{16}	0.231	–0.014	0.199	–0.014	0.702	–0.014	0.396	0.245	0.000	0.155	–0.02	–0.014	0.206	–0.014	–0.02	1.000	....	....	....	....	....	....	....	....	....	....	....
X_{17}	0.06	–0.117	–0.063	–0.177	0.000	–0.117	–0.097	0.335	0.000	0.351	–0.167	–0.117	0.252	–0.117	–0.167	0.117	1.000	....	....	....	....	....	....	....	....	....	....
X_{18}	0.474	0.232	0.325	0.232	0.331	0.232	0.384	0.535	0.000	0.6	0.331	0.232	0.654	0.232	0.331	0.232	0.235	1.000	....	....	....	....	....	....	....	....	....
X_{19}	0.214	0.134	0.188	0.134	0.191	0.134	0.222	–0.032	0.000	0.174	0.191	0.134	0.014	0.134	0.191	0.134	–0.164	0.171	1.000	....	....	....	....	....	....	....	....
X_{20}	0.84	0.798	0.836	0.798	0.458	0.798	0.778	0.633	0.000	0.455	0.882	0.798	0.405	0.798	0.882	0.203	–0.083	0.497	0.236	1.000	....	....	....	....	....	....	....
X_{21}	0.748	0.861	0.908	0.861	0.395	0.861	0.699	0.638	0.000	0.341	0.811	0.861	0.434	0.861	0.811	0.277	–0.015	0.43	0.146	0.907	1.000	....	....	....	....	....	....
X_{22}	0.000	0.000	0.000	0.000	0.000	0.000	0.000	0.000	0.000	0.000	0.000	0.000	0.000	0.000	0.000	0.000	0.000	0.000	0.000	0.000	0.000	0.000	....	....	....	....	....
X_{23}	0.74	0.362	0.479	0.362	0.516	0.362	0.598	0.462	0.000	0.335	0.516	0.362	0.355	0.362	0.516	0.362	0.046	0.411	0.091	0.607	0.586	0.000	1.000	....	....	....	....
X_{24}	0.86	0.569	0.67	0.569	0.811	0.569	0.941	0.642	0.000	0.409	0.811	0.569	0.363	0.569	0.811	0.569	–0.069	0.408	0.236	0.844	0.829	0.000	0.636	1.000	....	....	....
X_{25}	0.000	0.000	0.000	0.000	0.000	0.000	0.000	0.000	0.000	0.000	0.000	0.000	0.000	0.000	0.000	0.000	0.000	0.000	0.000	0.000	0.000	0.000	0.000	0.000	0.000	....	....
X_{26}	0.369	0.511	0.497	0.511	0.004	0.511	0.257	0.533	0.000	0.368	0.439	0.511	0.451	0.511	0.439	–0.099	0.188	0.392	0.068	0.509	0.57	0.000	0.208	0.303	0.000	1.000	....
X_{27}	0.543	0.266	0.373	0.266	0.379	0.266	0.44	0.466	0.000	0.435	0.379	0.266	0.434	0.266	0.379	0.266	0.22	0.508	0.208	0.538	0.493	0.000	0.484	0.467	0.000	0.457	1.000
X_{28}	0.882	0.702	0.673	0.702	0.486	0.702	0.862	0.607	0.000	0.387	1.000	0.702	0.294	0.702	1.000	–0.02	–0.167	0.331	0.191	0.882	0.811	0.000	0.516	0.811	0.000	0.439	0.379

Source: See note to Table 7–2.
Note: The three central functions with zero coefficients of self-correlation are nonexistent in this province. They have been retained here for uniformity and possible comparison with other provinces being studied where these functions exist. The effective number of variables for this province is therefore 25.

Key:

X_1 Banking
X_2 Cooperative society shop
X_3 Cooperative society licensed buying agent for primary products
X_4 United Africa Company wholesale store
X_5 United Africa Company branch store
X_6 Local court "A"
X_7 Local court "B"
X_8 Local court "C"
X_9 Local court "D"
X_{10} Local and district council
X_{11} Divisional council
X_{12} Police headquarters
X_{13} Police station
X_{14} Government treasury
X_{15} Hospital
X_{16} Special hospital
X_{17} Dispensary
X_{18} Electricity
X_{19} Piped water
X_{20} Secondary grammar school
X_{21} Secondary modern school
X_{22} University
X_{23} Public library
X_{24} General post office
X_{25} "B" post office
X_{26} Postal agency
X_{27} Rediffusion
X_{28} Cinema

Fig. 7–4). This shows a high frequency of inverse correlation with other central functions. Fifty per cent of the negative correlation coefficients occur with this service, which indicates that this service does not in general depend on the occurrence of other central functions. It has been regarded as a basic service and its distribution is determined more by the need to serve the whole population in the area than by economic factors.

As one would expect, the strength of the correlation varies between different central functions. The low correlation revealed in Table 7–3 and Fig. 7–4 between piped water and other variables (none greater than ±.236) indicates that this function is not necessarily a good measure of the relative importance of settlements. As already noted, settlements of very little importance such as Odopotu, Ogbogbo, and Ilaporu have the service, while relatively more important settlements such as Odogbolu and Okun-Owa lack it. It seems there is a case for providing such settlements with the service. The variables with which the pattern of electricity profile exhibits high correlations are all administrative functions, which indicates, as one would expect, that the distribution of this service is more related to administrative and political factors, since in this province the distribution of electricity is more in the nature of a social service than a function of economic demand. There is as yet no widely distributed industry of importance making a demand for this service. Areas to the west of the province are well served with the service, whereas in the east and southeast the service is limited in distribution to the important settlements.

Similarly, the distribution of postal facilities in this province is far from being adequate, as could be seen from the lack of any "B" Post Office and the concentration of the General Post Offices in the three major settlements—Ijebu-Ode, Shagamu, and Ijebu-Igbo. Also significant is the need for more retail distribution stores. This demand

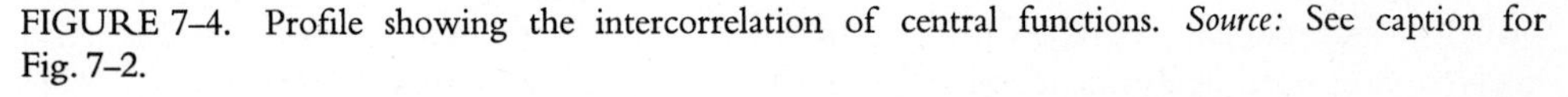

FIGURE 7–4. Profile showing the intercorrelation of central functions. *Source:* See caption for Fig. 7–2.

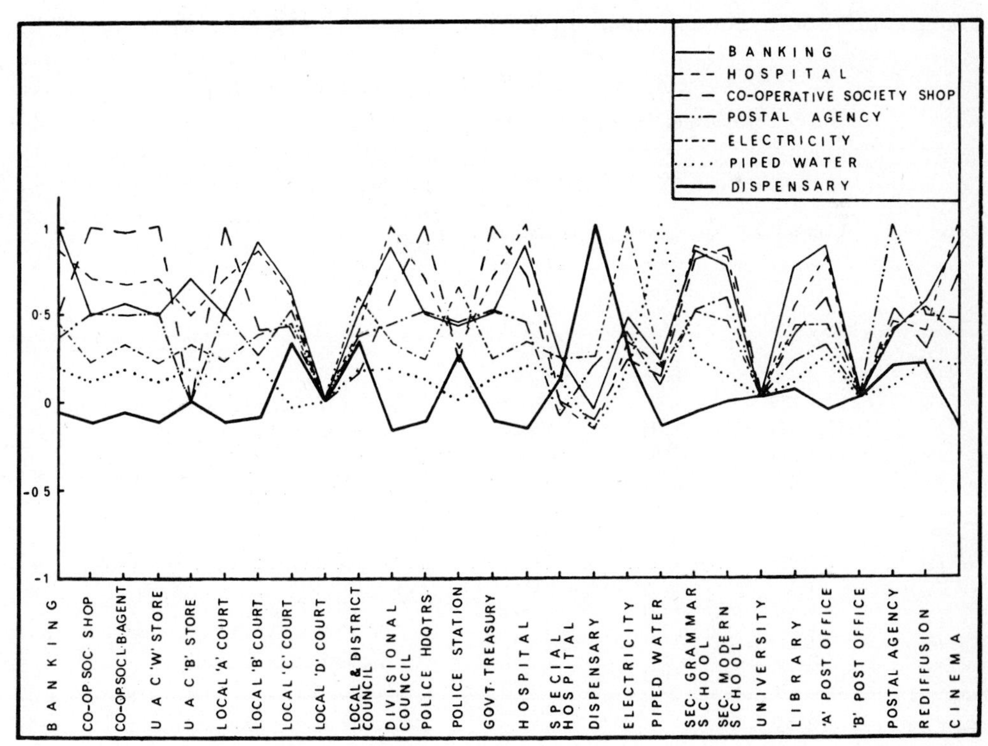

could be met by a wider distribution of cooperative retail stores and the encouragement of local participation in the cooperative movement.

A closer study of Table 7–3 shows that the pattern described by cooperative society shop and local court "A," and again by hospital and divisional council are identical. This raises the question of whether, in each pair, one variable could be a sufficient substitute for the other and whether we can eliminate one without loss of detail in describing the variation between the settlements. It is only through further analysis by the multivariate technique, i.e., component analysis, that such questions can be satisfactorily answered.

Table 7–4 shows the principal components and the extent to which each accounts for the total variation of the original primary variables and hence the variability between the settlements in terms of the central functions they perform. Sixteen new variables or principal components have been obtained instead of the original 28 primary variables. Thus, a reduction in the dimension of the problem has been attained. Since the principal components obtained by component analysis are statistically uncorrelated, each introduces information not accounted for by any other. The first principal component has the maximum variance, accounting for 52.735 per cent of the total variation. The second component has the next largest variance, 15.279 per cent, and so on in descending order. The first two principal components account for 68.014 per cent of the total variation, while the first four account for 82.179 per cent. This means that the first four principal components will adequately describe the hierarchy of settlements in this Province. In fact, we can, to a good degree of accuracy, describe the hierarchy of settlements in this Province in terms of the first two[25] principal components (see Fig. 7–5).

TABLE 7–4

Contributions of Principal Components

Principal Components	Eigenvalue	*Percentage Variability* Component	Cumulative
P1	13.184	52.735	52.735
P2	3.82	15.279	68.014
P3	2.182	8.727	76.741
P4	1.359	5.438	82.179
P5	1.086	4.344	86.523
P6	0.753	3.01	89.533
P7	0.644	2.574	92.107
P8	0.575	2.301	94.408
P9	0.41	1.641	96.049
P10	0.35	1.401	97.45
P11	0.261	1.046	98.496
P12	0.218	0.871	99.367
P13	0.06	0.238	99.605
P14	0.046	0.183	99.788
P15	0.043	0.171	99.959
P16	0.01	0.041	100.000

Source: See note to Table 7–2.

The identification of each new principal component depends on the strength of the correlation coefficients between it and the original primary variables. Figure 7–6 illustrates the relationships between the first four principal components and the primary variables. The lack of any strong loading for any of the primary variables on the first principal component makes it difficult to label it in terms of a single central function or of any particular type of functions. Another feature of interest is that apart from the very low (−0.009) negative loading for dispensary, all the other correlations on this first pattern are positive. This first component may therefore be thought of as giving weight to the over-all general importance of settlements. The second principal component gives the greatest weight to economic and administrative functions, while the third and fourth principal components give the greatest weight to social services.

Functional Distances of Centers

In Fig. 7–5, the junction of points is an accurate measure of the functional distances[26] between the settlements. That is, a measure of the extent to which the settlements are alike or unlike, in terms of the central functions they perform. This result is in excellent accord with observations. Ijebu-Ode, which is the provincial capital, stands high in the graph relative to other settlements, while the settlements known to be of little importance show a clustering below, near the point of origin. Between these two extremes lie the other settle-

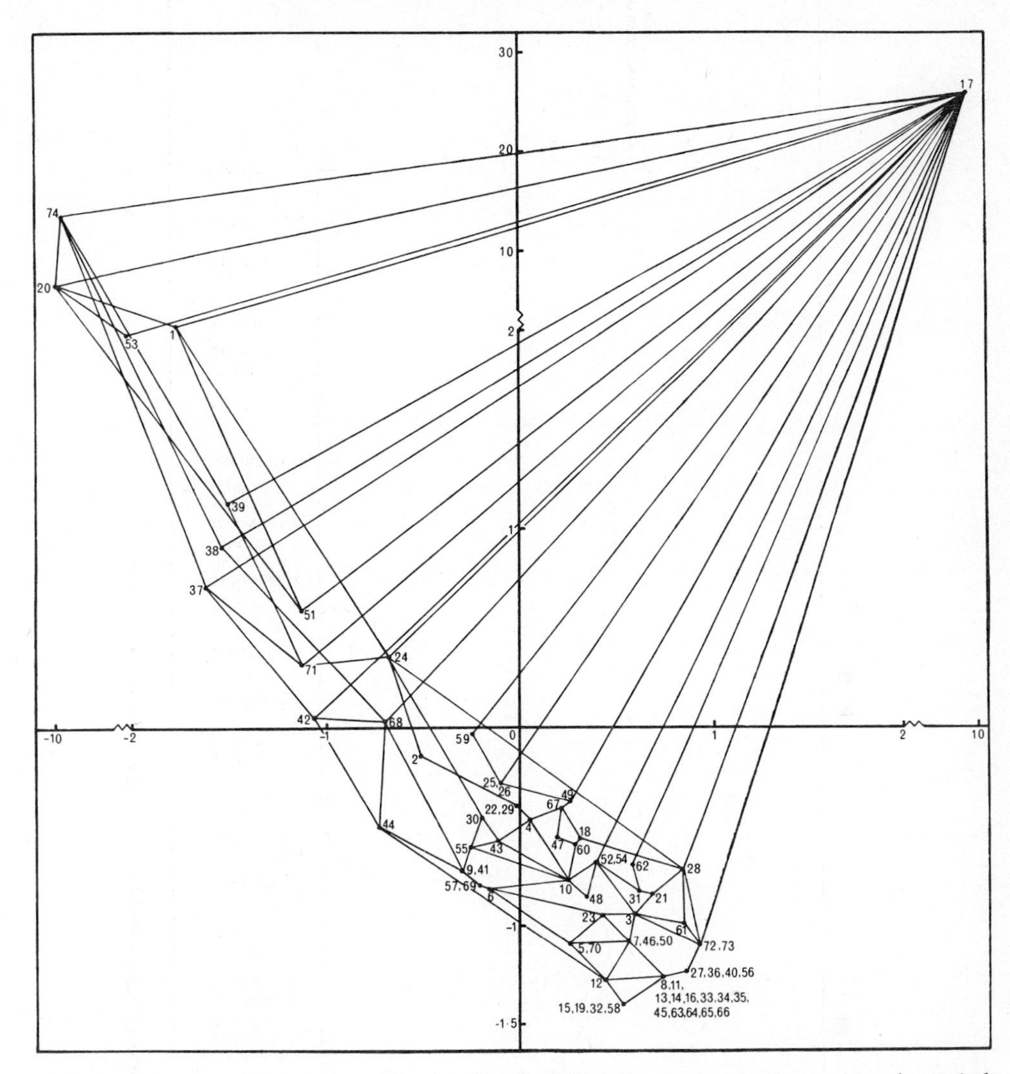

FIGURE 7–5. Functional distance of centers. The first principal component is shown along the vertical axis, while the second principal component is shown along the horizontal axis. Breaks in scale in the above diagram on the horizontal axis are denoted by standard symbols. The cluster of settlements about the point of origin has been magnified twenty times. *Source:* See caption for Fig. 7–2.

ments, at varying distances from one another. Their separations determine the degree of their functional similarity.

Another feature of this graph is its interpretation in terms of the interaction between the settlements. The more unlike the settlements are in terms of the central functions they perform, the stronger is the potential interaction between them. The converse also holds. However, to bring the element of reality into this interpretation, the actual spatial relationship between the settlements must be dominant.

Functional Magnitude of Centers

The concept of functional magnitude of settlements is a hitherto unexplored aspect of service centers. It is a measure of the importance of a

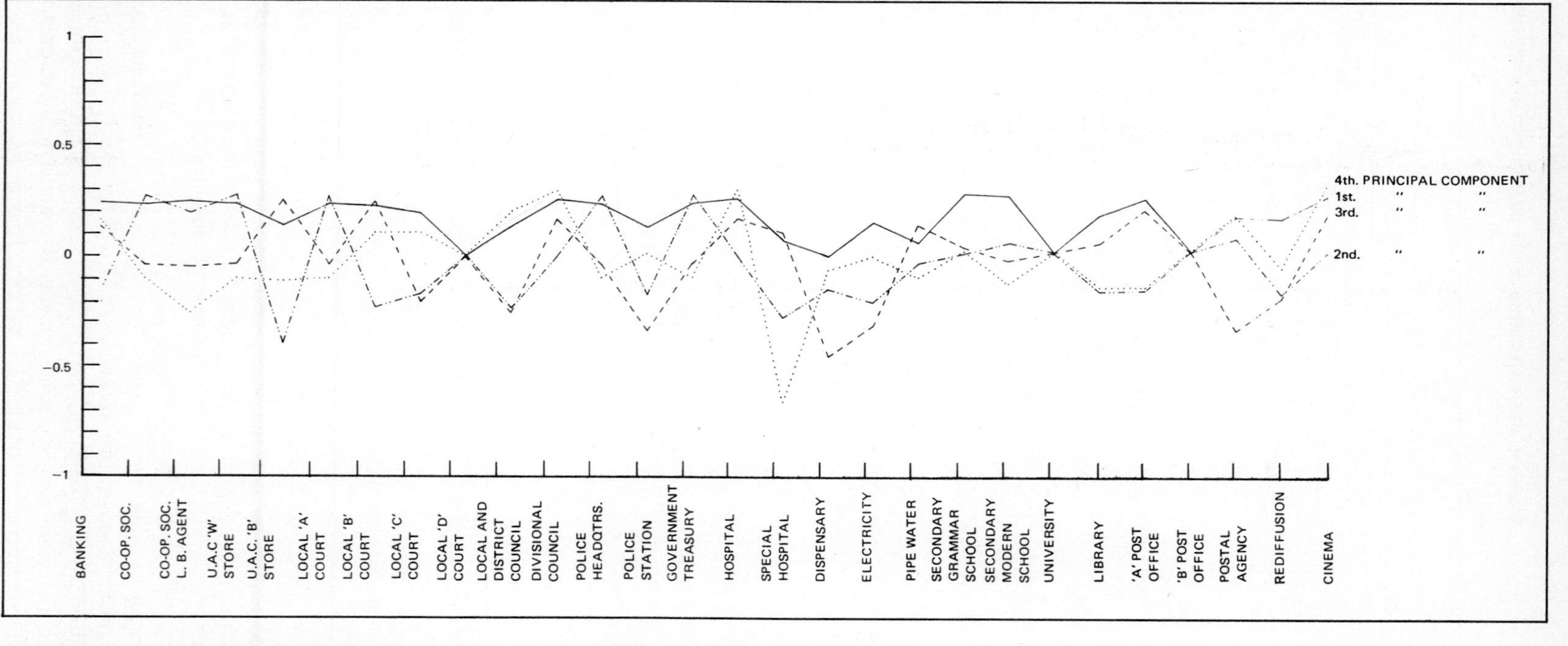

FIGURE 7–6. Profile showing the "loadings" of the primary variables on the first principal components.
Source: See caption for Fig. 7–2.

settlement in terms of all the central functions under consideration. To the urban geographer interested in the rational distribution and redistribution of services within an area, it provides a valuable and interesting guide. It could also be of great assistance to a potential industrialist. Its greatest advantage lies in the fact that it provides a common base from which the settlements concerned can be assessed at a glance (see Fig. 7–7).

Figure 7–7 shows the overwhelming importance of Ijebu-Ode, the provincial capital, as a major service center. It is followed by Shagamu, Ijebu-Igbo, and Ago Iwoye in order of importance. At the other end is a sort of skyline of centers not so well endowed with central functions. Between these two groups are those centers with a medium range of central functions. Where we are interested in a rational distribution of services, a further examination of the services available and the spatial distribution of these centers would suggest which centers need to be provided with more or less services, and the types needed. Again to the potential investor, the graph indicates where certain industries might best be located in this province. Ijebu-Ode and Shagamu, for instance, provide immediate attraction.

Grouping

The problems arising from the grouping of settlements are too well known to be further discussed here, except to note that almost all the previous treatments have so far fallen short of being completely satisfactory. The basic aim of any efficient grouping device is to classify logically and methodologically, in one group, settle-

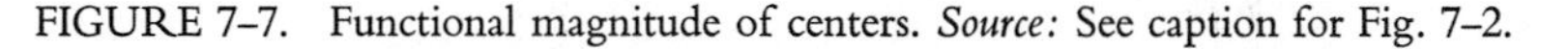

FIGURE 7–7. Functional magnitude of centers. *Source:* See caption for Fig. 7–2.

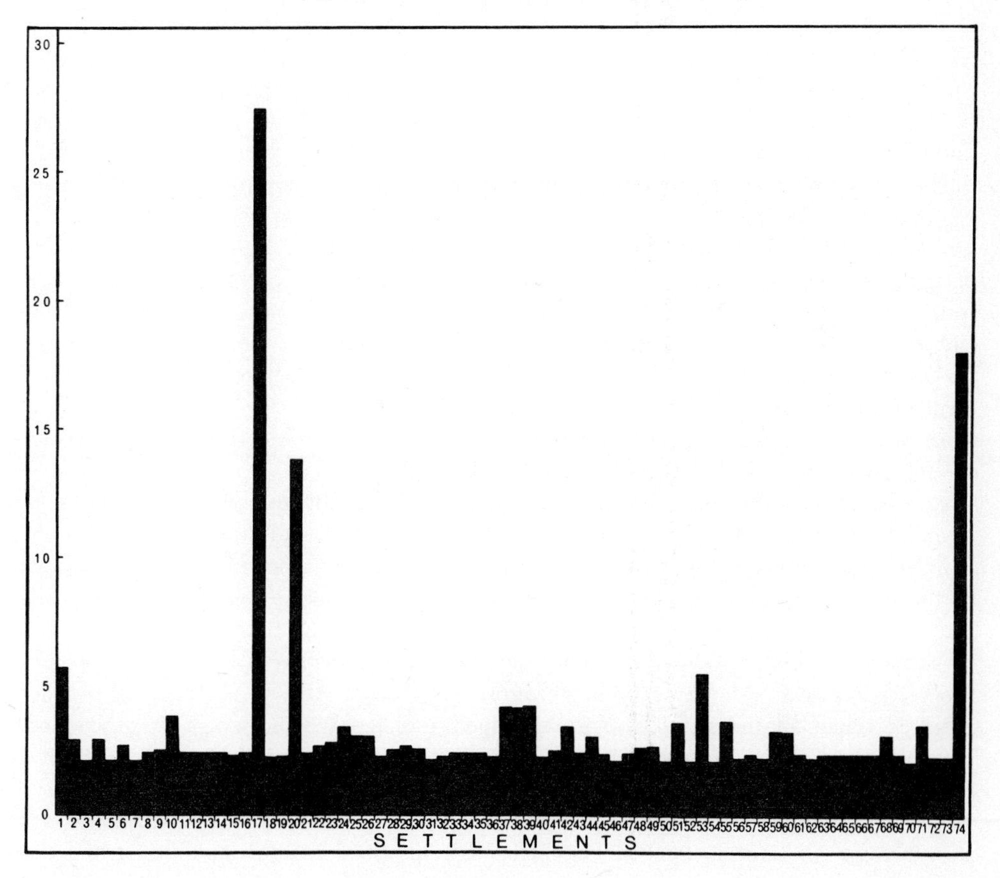

ments that are most similar. When two or three independent variables are involved, a graphic representation of the settlements greatly facilitates the identification of the groups that may be present. However, when several independent variables, say p ($p > 3$), are to be considered, a graphic representation in a p dimensional space becomes impossible and it is then necessary to apply a more analytical process. In this study, we begin the grouping by thinking in terms of the relative functional distances between the settlements, when we define as a measure of the similarity between any pair of settlements in terms of the central functions they perform.

These functional distances were calculated and assembled in a 74 by 74 matrix D, whose element d_{ij} is the functional distance between settlements i and j. D is therefore symmetrical:

$$D = \begin{bmatrix} d_{11} & d_{12} & \cdot & \cdot & \cdot & d_{1\,74} \\ d_{21} & \cdot & \cdot & \cdot & \cdot & \cdot \\ \cdot & \cdot & \cdot & \cdot & \cdot & \cdot \\ \cdot & \cdot & \cdot & \cdot & \cdot & \cdot \\ \cdot & \cdot & \cdot & \cdot & \cdot & \cdot \\ d_{74\,1} & \cdot & \cdot & \cdot & \cdot & d_{74\,74} \end{bmatrix}$$

since d_{ij} is the same as d_{ji}.

The settlements are then grouped systematically, beginning with the least distant and thus, the most similar pair. This pair is placed at the mean point of their original separation. This operation, of course, alters the relative distances between the new group and the remaining settlements, while the distances between the latter settlements remain unaltered. To obtain the distance of this new group from each of the remaining settlements or group of settlements, we take the mean distance to the two settlements comprising the new group. In terms of the distance matrix, this involves combining the two rows and the two columns relating to the two settlements involved, into one row and one column respectively. Thus the dimension of the array is reduced by one each time the process is repeated. Maximum generalization is achieved when all the settlements are grouped into one, i.e., a 1×1 matrix is attained.[27] In the present study this was achieved at the 73rd step. However, a close examination of the grouping steps before this stage is reached (see Fig. 7–8) enables distinct groups to be identified. A good knowledge of the area under study greatly facilitates such an identification.

It is worth noting that in Fig. 7–8, settlement 17 (i.e., Ijebu-Ode, the provincial capital) stood alone throughout the analysis until the last step in the grouping process (i.e., the stage of maximum generalization), while, on the other hand, less important settlements were being grouped and re-grouped together (e.g., the settlements in Group 5). The latter group is distinctive at step 65. This is to be expected from Fig. 7–5 (based on the first two principal components accounting for 68.014 per cent of the total variability), which shows the large functional distance between Ijebu-Ode and the other settlements. The settlements in Group 2 stood in a similar relationship to those in Group 4 or any other group (see Fig. 7–8).

This grouping process exhibits any hierarchy that may be present. Among the great advantages of this linkage analysis is that groups are objectively derived by an inductive process, while also insuring maximum homogeneity within groups and maximizing between group differences. This technique, when coupled with the facility of a high speed electronic computer, makes it possible to consider as many dimensions of variability as may be thought desirable and for any number of settlements. In this work we have taken into account 100 per cent variability. It is interesting to note that the grouping process in Fig. 7–8 took only .8 minute on the IBM 7090 computer.

General Discussion

The distribution of settlements in the groups identified is illustrated in Fig. 7–9. A comparison of this figure with Fig. 7–3 lends weight to the finding that a hierarchy of centers does exist in this area. An outstanding feature of Fig. 7–9 is the pre-eminence of Ijebu-Ode, the only First-order Center. Around it cluster Fifth-order Centers or villages beyond which the other grades of centers become distinctive.

Of great significance to regional planning are the functional characteristics of the different grades in the hierarchy and the spatial distribution of

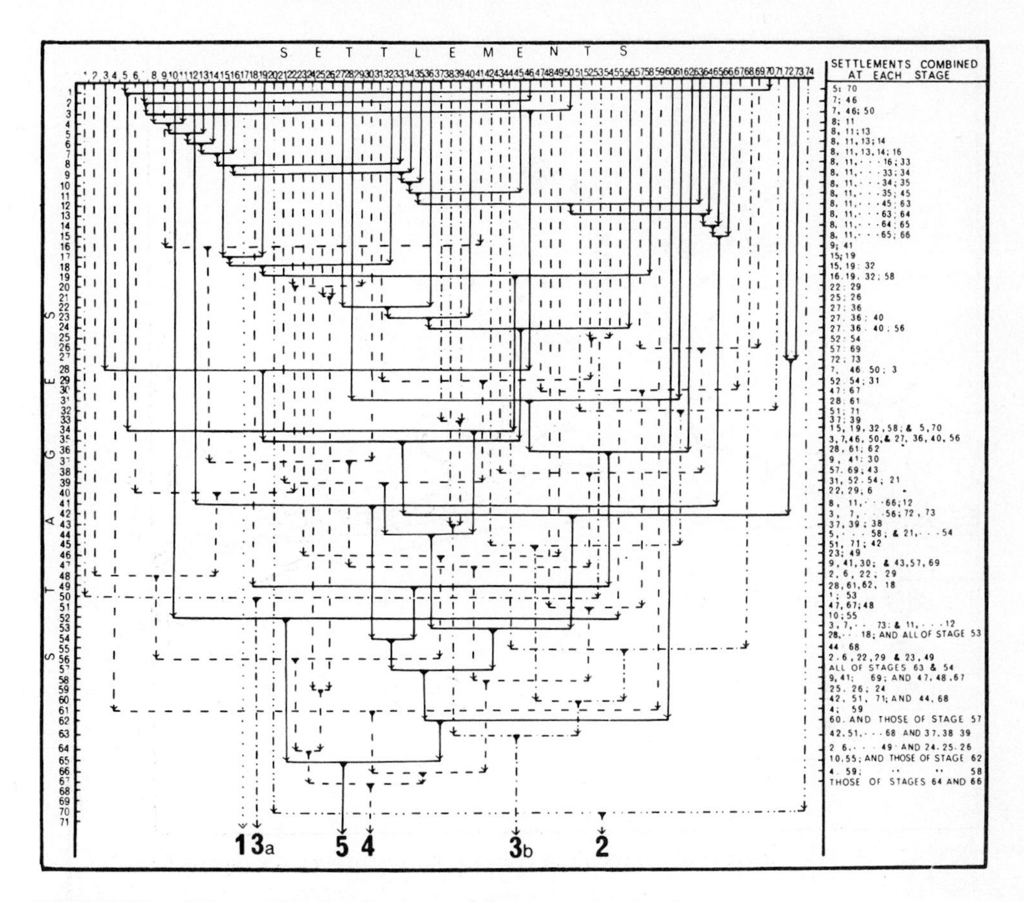

FIGURE 7–8. Diagram showing the stages of the systematic grouping.
Source: See caption for Fig. 7–2.

these centers. Table 7–5 shows the variety of central functions characteristic of each group and further emphasizes the existence of a hierarchy of centers in this province.

TABLE 7–5

Variety of Central Functions Characteristic of Each Grade of the Hierarchy

Order of Centers	Number of Characteristic Functions			
	Class I	*Class II*	*Class III*	*Total*
1	5	10	7	22
2	1–3	8	6–7	16–17
3	—	2–3	5–7	7–10
4	—	0–1	2–5	3–5
5	—	—	1–2	1–2

Source: See note to Table 7–2.

Again, Ijebu-Ode, the only First-order Center, has all the central functions considered except special hospital (maternity hospital), dispensary, "B" post office, United Africa Company branch store, a local court "D," and a university. The latter does not exist anywhere in the province, being a high order of service whose location is decided upon at national and regional levels. The only three universities in southwestern Nigeria are located in centers of greater importance, better accessibility to other parts of the region, and better facilities than this provincial capital. The absence of the first five functions may be explained by the fact that they are services that are already available in the higher-order establishments of these type of functions. The settlement possesses these higher order establishments.

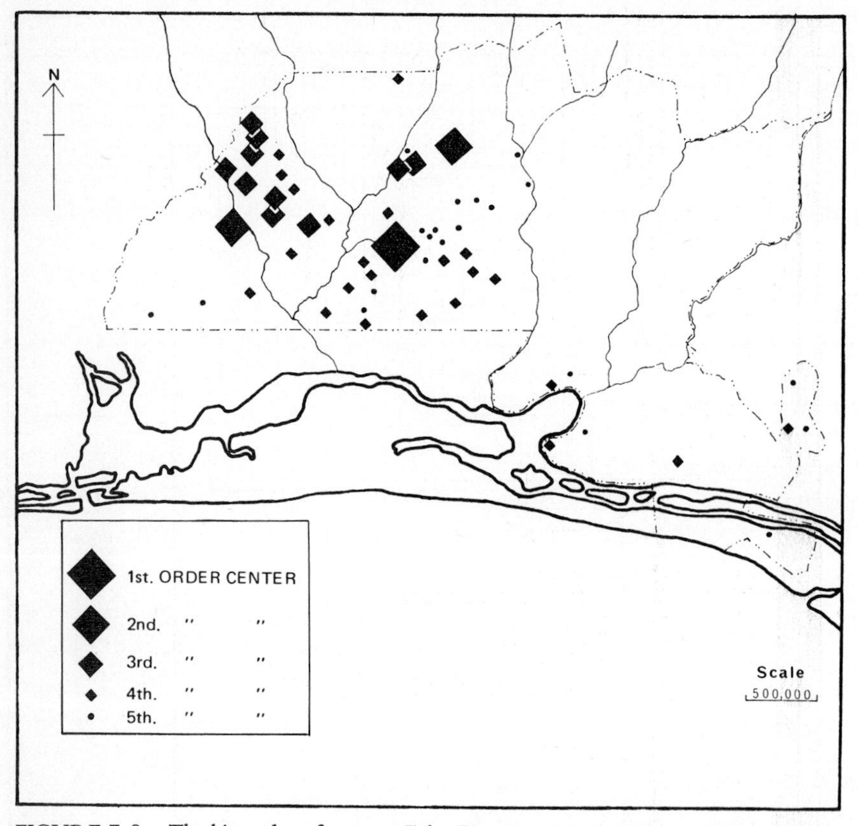

FIGURE 7–9. The hierarchy of centers: Ijebu Province, Nigeria. *Source:* See caption for Fig. 7–2.

The next higher group, the Second-order Centers, are characterized by a predominance of Class II central functions (see Table 7–2) and fewer Class I functions than in the group of First-order Centers. A complete absence of any Class I central functions and not less than two Class II functions characterize those Centers of the Third order. All are centers having a local or a district council and all have electricity and at least a grammar school.

In the Fourth-order Centers, we find a low level of local administration, in particular a local court "C." A dispensary and a postal agency are also characteristic. These are the small urban centers and the large rural centers. The last group in the hierarchy—the Fifth-order Centers, or the villages, are characterized by at least one and not more than two Class III functions. Thirteen of the 36 settlements in this group have no other function besides piped water. Apoje, for instance, which has both piped water and a dispensary is an experimental farm settlement established by the Western Nigeria Development Corporation.

Perfect uniformity in terms of population and the number of central functions is of course difficult to obtain in any group of several centers. The Fourth-order Centers provide an example: Here, we have large rural centers such as Ikija, Isiwo, and Iloti grouped together with small urban centers such as Imusin and Ososa. This occurs because the former type of settlements are more similar to the latter type than to the next lower group of centers.

Although 52 per cent of the total population of Ijebu Province may be classified as urban dwellers (23 per cent of which are domiciled in Ijebu-Ode), a striking feature of the spatial distribution of the centers presented by Figs. 7–2 and 7–9 is the absence of any urban center of importance east of Oshun River. This is reflective of the fact that the Oshun River had long remained a barrier to the eastward advancement of settlements in this province. The area had therefore remained an extensive forest reserve, sparsely populated, and providing rich sources of commercial timber. It is worth noting that in this vast area extending over more than one-third of the total area of this province, only ten settlements qualified for inclusion in the present study. Of these, four are in the lowest grade of urban centers, while the remaining are villages. However, with the recent opening of the Lagos–Ijebu-Ode–Benin–eastern Nigeria road across River Oshun, through this forest region, we may expect the development of more urban centers in response to the advantages provided by this new major line of communication.

Theoretical Discussion

Table 7–6 shows that the structure of settlements in Ijebu Province follows the rule that holds for regions with the same structure when *K* has the value 3.

TABLE 7–6

Number of Settlements in Regional System with* K = *3

Size-Class of Place	*Theoretical Number of Places*	*Actual Number of Places in Nuremberg (Christaller)*	*Actual Number of Places in Ijebu Province (Present Study)*
0	486	462	—
1	162	105	—
2	54	60	36
3	18	23	25
4	6	10	10
5	2	2	2
6	1	1	1

Source: J. O. Abiodun and W. Christaller, *The Central Places of Southern Germany*, trans. Carlisle Baskin (Englewood Cliffs, N. J.: Prentice-Hall, Inc., 1967).

The good agreement between the number of centers in the first three high grades [Classes 4, 5, and 6] in Christaller's Nuremberg and the present study is remarkable. However, in Size-class 2 the deviation is obvious. Also, the absence of any settlement in Size-classes 1 and 0 should be noted. This may be due to the fact that many of the hamlets that could have been considered did not appear for consideration since they do not possess any of the functions under consideration. This reflects the fact that the provision of services to this class of settlements is less widely distributed than in the developed countries. However, the table confirms that a hierarchy of settlements does exist in the province. The structure of settlements conforms to that which occurs in an agrarian based economy.

*CONSUMER TRAVEL, THRESHOLDS, AND THE RANGES OF GOODS: CULTURAL VARIABILITY**

To date, little attention has been given to the effects of cultural differences on consumer travel and the relevance and relativity of the range and threshold concepts. One important exception is Murdie's study of cultural differences in consumer travel in the Ontario Counties of Waterloo and Wellington.[28] Murdie's main finding is that size of center, which is generally the most important factor influencing travel, has little effect on the distance travelled by Mennonities, who generally patronize the closest centers.

It is not surprising that significant differences in consumer travel behavior should exist between modern Canadians and Old Order Mennonites who use modern techniques and machinery only for farming. Equally intriguing are the question of cultural differences in consumer travel between two groups of "modern" Canadians, the French-Canadian and the English-Canadians in Eastern Ontario, and the opportunity to compare the

*Reprinted from D. Michael Ray, "Cultural Differences in Consumer Travel Behavior in Eastern Ontario," *Canadian Geographer*, XI, No. 3 (September, 1967), 143–56, with the permission of the author and editor.

Gary Nadon, Brendon M. Hamill, Carl Smith, Graham Murchie, Willard Smith, and Kenneth Ramraji of the Department of Geography, University of Ottawa, conducted desire-line maps. Robert Carstens, Geographer, Spartan Air Services Limited, prepared additional maps. John S. Lewis, Statistician, Spartan Air Services Limited, developed and programmed the mathematical analyses.

central-place system of bicultural Eastern Ontario with the results of other studies of the central-place hierarchy of South Dakota, Southwest Iowa, and Chicago, to see what emerges of general interest concerning notions of range and threshold.

The Study Area

The Eastern Ontario bicultural area studied lies between Ottawa and Cornwall, and covers the interfluve of the upper St. Lawrence and Ottawa Rivers. The first extensive European occupancy occurred at the turn of the eighteenth century when United Empire Loyalists settled the Upper St. Lawrence Valley. After the mid-eighteenth century, heavy French-Canadian migration followed across the provincial boundary and along the Ottawa Valley. The two ethnic groups are geographically separated, partly because the French-Canadians formed many of their own settlements and partly because English-Canadians left communities with heavy French-Canadian in-migration (see Fig. 7–10).

Central-Place Functions and Consumer Travel

A sample of 500 farmers in the study area was interviewed in 1964 to determine what market center they preferred for a list of consumer services, and the manner and frequency of their shopping. The pattern of their travel as consumers is displayed by drawing desire lines from the farm residence directly to the central place providing each service. These consumer-travel maps suggest five levels of central place which are termed, for convenience: hamlets, offering only the lowest services, such as food and auto repair; villages, distinguished by banking services; towns, which also offer medical and legal services; cities, with dental services; and regional capitals, distinguished by optical services.

The study area is divided into four zones, English and French core zones, and English and French marchland zones (see Fig. 7–11). Cultural differences in consumer travel are evaluated first by examining maps of consumer travel, and then by analyzing the means and variances of consumer travel from each of the four zones for the seven distinguishing central functions.

Food services. Food services are considered a hamlet-level function and are offered in the smallest central places. The consumer-desire lines form a symmetric pattern of consistent travel to the closest center (see Fig. 7–12). The few exceptions, where consumers ignore an intervening opportunity, are explained by multi-purpose travel, particularly among English marchland families, and by cultural preferences—a few French-Canadian farmers preferring French-Canadian centers to closer English stores. Measurement of the desire lines does not indicate any significant cultural difference in consumer travel for these low-order services, though the mean and variance of the distance traveled by the English marchland families is higher than in any other zone because of their multi-purpose travel to Ottawa (see Table 7–7).

TABLE 7–7

The Mean and Standard Deviation of the Distance Traveled by Consumers in Four Cultural Zones of Canada

	French-Canadian				*English-Canadian*			
	Core		*Marchland*		*Core*		*Marchland*	
Services	$\bar{x}$	δ	$\bar{x}$	δ	$\bar{x}$	δ	$\bar{x}$	δ
Food	3.37	1.75	3.25	2.00	3.66	2.17	4.85	4.23
Auto	4.03	2.61	5.07	5.05	4.31	3.16	5.13	4.32
Bank	3.39	1.66	4.24	2.83	4.32	2.43	6.14	5.44
Medical	5.63	4.79	5.24	2.96	5.23	3.01	7.62	5.50
Legal	6.27	7.43	11.34	9.23	7.44	4.40	14.12	6.39
Dental	11.27	9.03	12.14	6.11	6.71	3.71	11.20	7.11
Optical	29.56	4.42	22.82	3.31	20.40	9.20	21.31	3.43

Source: Tables 7–7 and 7–8 are from D. Michael Ray, "Cultural Differences in Consumer Travel Behavior in Eastern Ontario," *Canadian Geographer*, XI, No. 3 (September, 1967), 143–56. See Fig. 7–11 for map of cultural zones.
$\bar{x}$ = mean average of distance traveled.
δ = standard deviation of distance traveled.
Distances are the desire-line distances in miles.

The hamlet-level functional regions, indicated by the perimeters of the desire lines, are related in size to the population of the centers. The functional regions of the smallest centers are nested within the trade areas of the larger centers to form

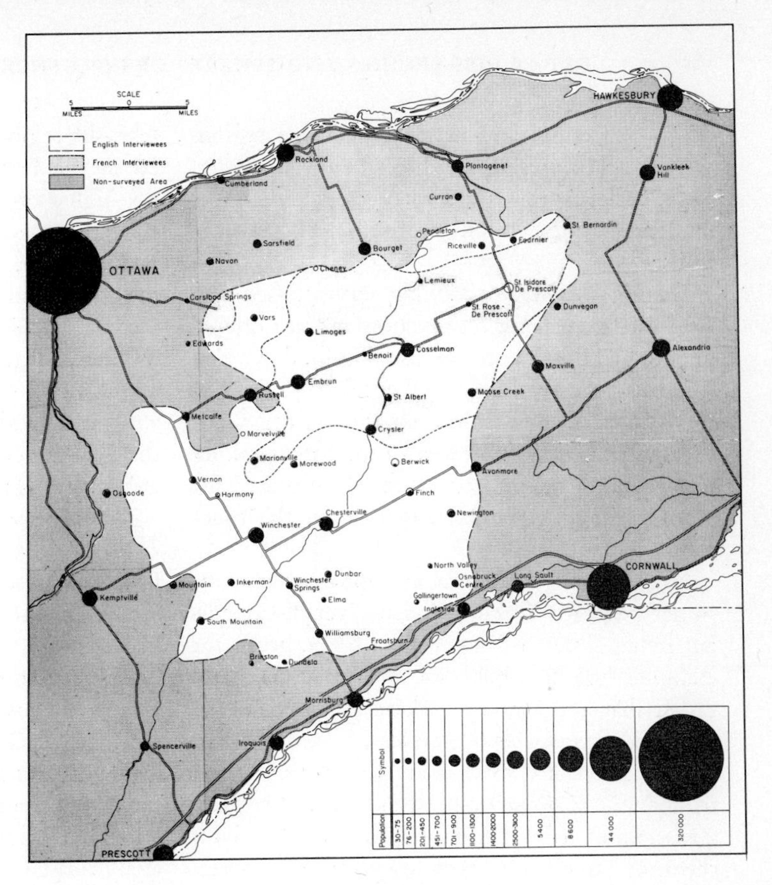

FIGURE 7–10. Ethnic origin of people interviewed in the Eastern Ontario study. *Source:* Figs. 7–10 through 7–19 are from D. Michael Ray, "Cultural Differences in Consumer Travel Behavior in Eastern Ontario," *Canadian Geographer*, XI, No. 3 (1967), 143–56.

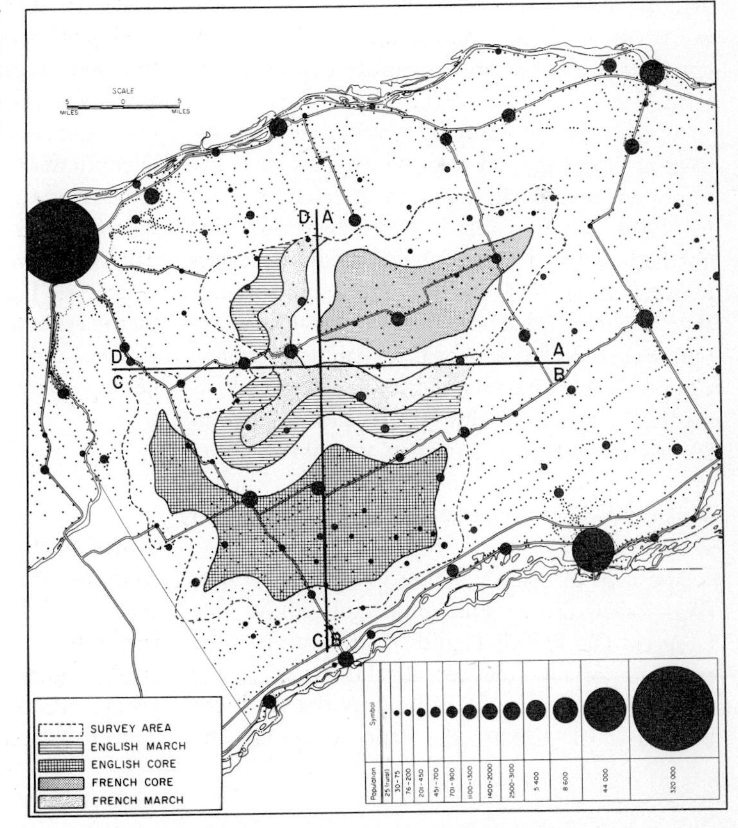

FIGURE 7–11. The distribution of population and cultural zones in Eastern Ontario. *Source:* Data from unpublished Dominion Bureau of Statistics material and Eastern Ontario Development Center. See also caption for Fig. 7–10.

enclaves. Examples of nested or enclave regions are Limoges-Embrun, and Inkerman-Winchester. Such enclave centers are early casualties in the inter-urban competition to provide central functions.

Banking services. Banking services (see Fig. 7–13) are a village-level function and are offered in only half of the centers providing food services. The villages have captured the nested regions of the hamlets lying within their trade areas. Consequently, the travel patterns for food and banking services are very similar, and the drop-out of the hamlets simplifies rather than realigns the functional regions.

No cultural preferences are apparent in consumer travel for banking services. French-Canadians living closer to Russell than to Embrun, for example, use the Bank of Nova Scotia there rather than the Caisse populaire at Embrun.

Medical and legal services. Medical and legal services are town-level functions. Travel to them is a consciously weighted rather than a random or habitual decision, as is the case with the more frequently used lower-order services. Convenience is no longer the primary determinant of consumer travel; quality of the service can outweigh proximity, and consumer-desire lines cross each other to produce more complex patterns.

As convenience shopping gives place to comparison shopping, and as proximity becomes less important than quality, cultural differences begin to play an obvious role in travel behavior. The northern limit of Chesterville's medical services region (see Fig. 7–14) extends to the ethnic boundary; it thereby includes the English-Canadians who travel to Chrysler for their banking services. Chrysler's banking region is bisected and its medical clientele exclusively French-Canadian. Similarly, the French physician at Embrun serves French patients beyond Vars, while English patients at Vars travel to the English physician at Russell.

The map of consumer travel for legal services (Fig. 7–15) also reveals important ethnic differences. The French-English boundary plays the same important role for legal services as for medical services, again delimiting the northern boundary of Chesterville, and bisecting the Chrysler region. Moreover, legal services, provided in the French-Canadian area by *notaires*, are not higher order than medical services. Only St. Albert in the French-Canadian area has a doctor but no *notaire*. In the English-Canadian area, on the other hand, legal services are higher order than medical services; Russell, Metcalfe, Osgoode, Williamsburg, and Finch all have physicians but no laywers. Average distance traveled is higher and variance of distance traveled is lower in both the English core and marchland zones than in either of the French zones.

Dental services. Dental services (see Fig. 7–16) are a city-level function. In the French-Canadian area, Casselman alone has dental services which are provided by the English dentist from Hawkesbury. The nearest French-Canadian dentists are in Ottawa and Cornwall and there is extensive consumer travel to those centers from the French-Canadian area. Consequently, the average distance traveled is substantially higher for dental than for legal services.

In the English-Canadian area, by contrast, there are dentists at Winchester, Chesterville, and Avonmore, and average distance traveled is lower for dental services than for legal services.

Optical services. The Ottawa and Cornwall functional regions meet for optical services, which are a regional capital function. Both Ottawa and Cornwall are bicultural, so that cultural differences in consumer travel are not evident. The functional regions of Casselman, Winchester, and Chesterville fall entirely within the Ottawa region. The pattern of areal functional organization is fully nested (see Fig. 7–17) such that the region served by the regional capital subdivides into city, town, village, and hamlet subregions in turn.[29] This nesting agrees with other empirical work.

Structural Differences in Consumer Travel

Structural differences in the over-all pattern of consumer travel can be determined by statistical analysis of the distances traveled by each farm family for each of the seven services. The farm-family observations are allocated to different groups according to the cultural zone in which they are located.

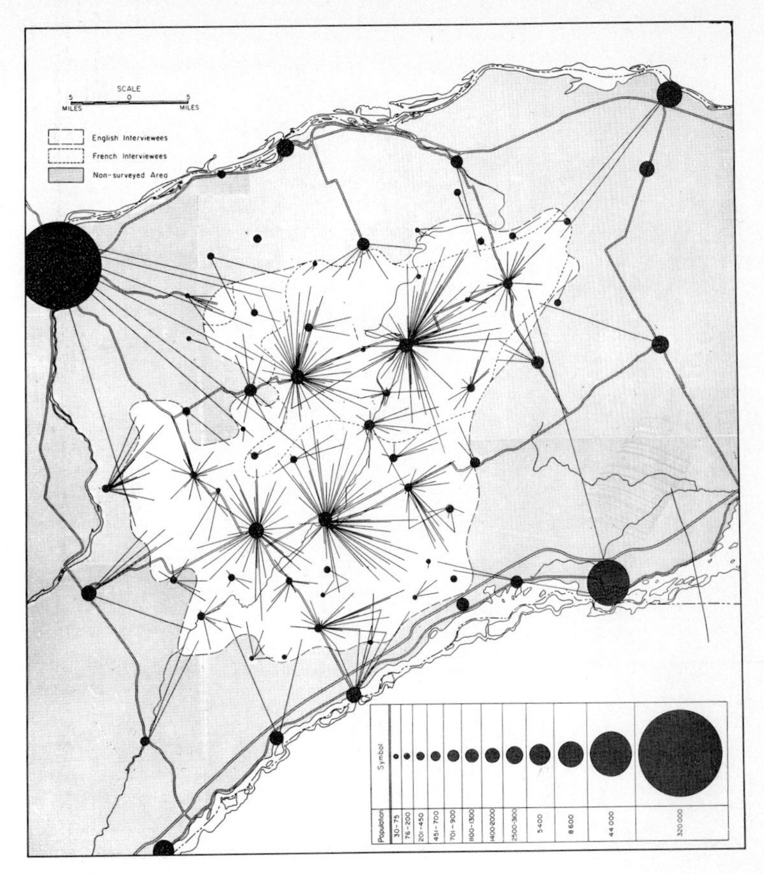

FIGURE 7–12. Patterns of food shopping in Eastern Ontario. *Source:* See caption for Fig. 7–10.

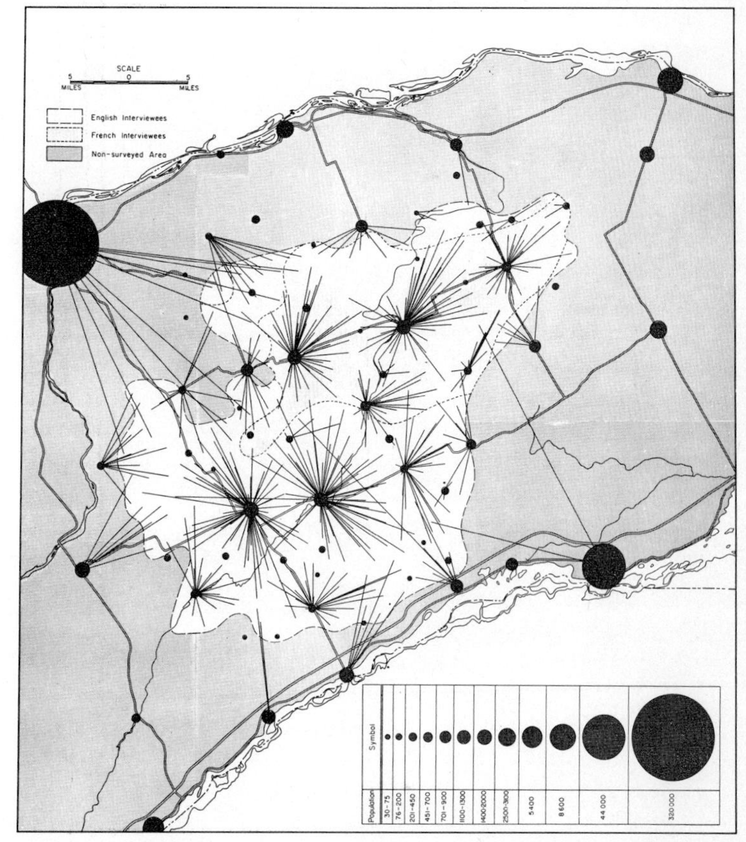

FIGURE 7–13. Travel to the bank in Eastern Ontario. *Source:* See caption for Fig. 7–10.

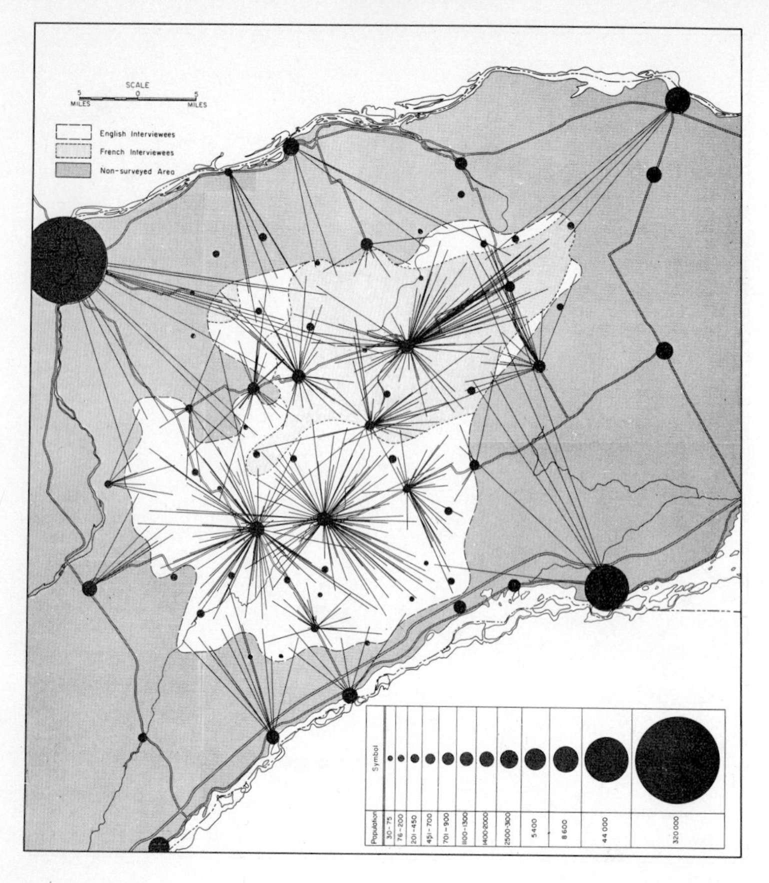

FIGURE 7–14. Travel for medical services in Eastern Ontario. *Source:* See caption for Fig. 7–10.

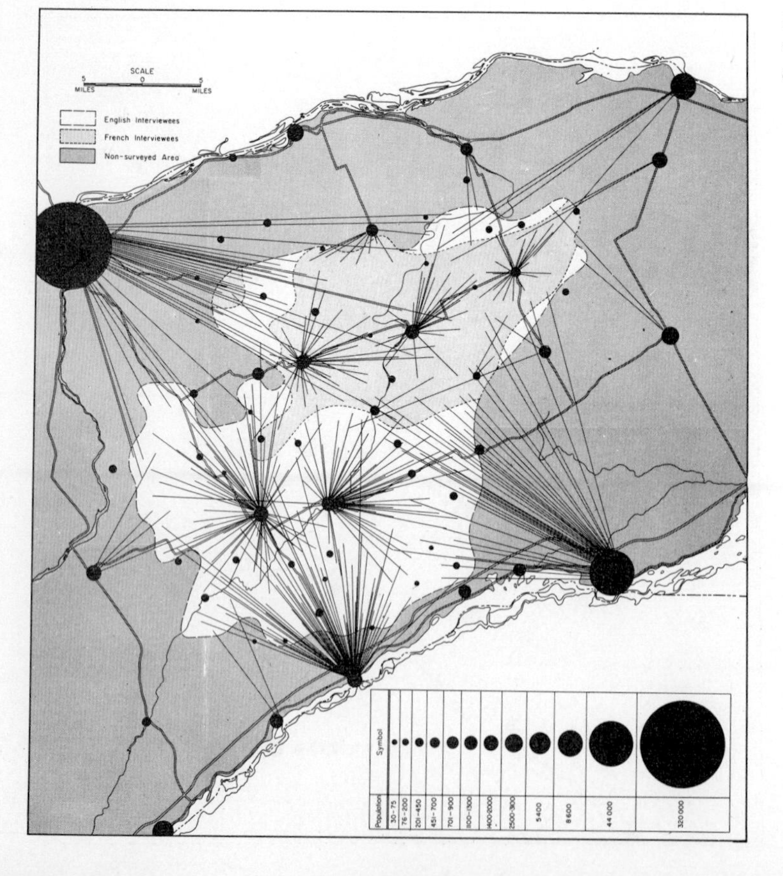

FIGURE 7–15. Travel for legal services in Eastern Ontario. *Source:* See caption for Fig. 7–10.

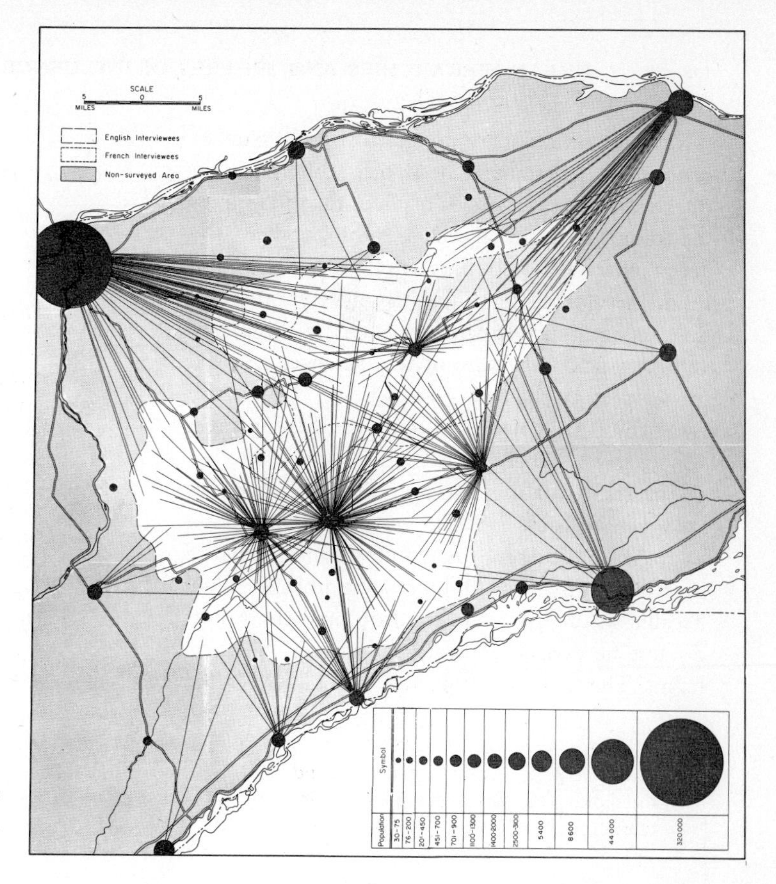

FIGURE 7–16. Travel to the dentist in Eastern Ontario. *Source:* See caption for Fig. 7–10.

FIGURE 7–17. Travel to the optician in Eastern Ontario. *Source:* See caption for Fig. 7–10.

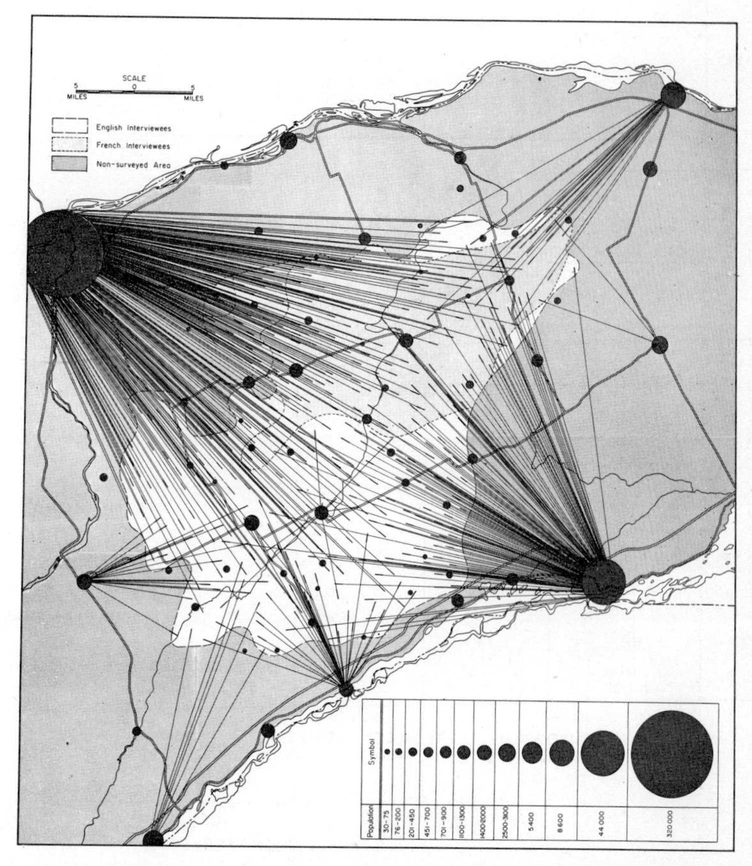

Two hypotheses are tested for each pair of groups. The first hypothesis tests differences in the covariance structure of trip length, and ignores the mean distances traveled, which reflect the geographic location of the farm families in relation to the service centers. The second hypothesis is that no significant differences occur in the means and covariance structure of the distances traveled for services by the two groups being tested. Any two groups are considered to have different travel behavior only where both tests are significant.

The results of the tests for the first hypothesis are given in Table 7–8. The results for the second hypothesis, testing means and covariance structure of trip length, are all highly significant solely because of differences in location, and the results do not necessarily indicate differences in travel habits. The first pair of groups, a test between the

TABLE 7–8

Cultural Differences in Consumer Travel in Canada

*Groups Tested**	*Significance of Difference in Variation in Trip Length*
1. English core (Quadrangle B)† and English core (Quadrangle C)*	
2. English marchland and French marchland	‡
3. English core and French core	†
4. All English and All French	†
5. English core and English marchland	†
6. French core and French marchland	‡
7. Both marchlands and Both cores	†

Source: See note to Table 7–7.
*See Fig. 7–11.
†Significant at the 99% level.
‡Significant at the 95% level.

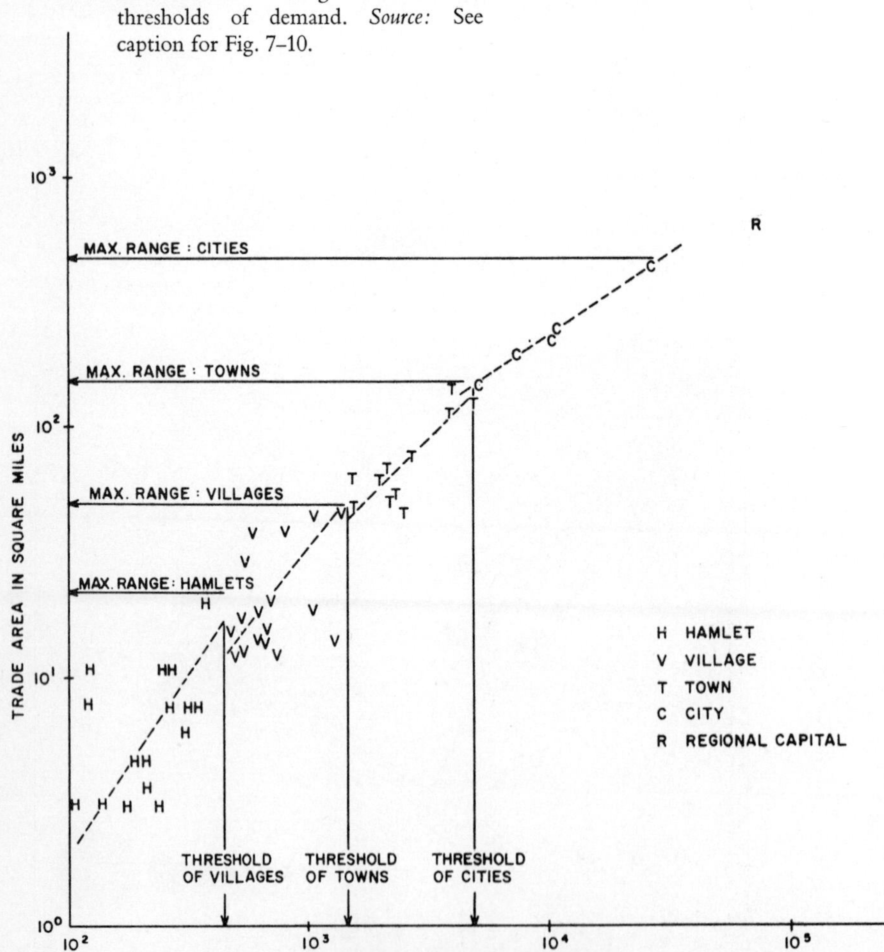

FIGURE 7–18. Range of services and thresholds of demand. *Source:* See caption for Fig. 7–10.

two halves of the English core, is a methodological test. It gives highly significant results for the second hypothesis (geographic location related to destinations), but nonsignificant results for the first hypothesis (trip length covariance structure). This test indicates the homogeneity of the pattern of travel in the English core zone.

Further tests indicate highly significant differences in the structure of consumer travel between the French and the English zones, and between the combined marchlands and the combined core zones.

The Central-Place System

The central-place system in the Eastern Ontario study area is illustrated by plotting, for the largest trade area of each central place, the population served against the area served (see Fig. 7–18). The graph indicates the range of the good and the threshold for the five levels of central place on the hierarchy. The "range of the good" is the maximum distance which consumers travel for a particular good or service. The "threshold" is the condition of entry for a good or service, and equals the minimum sales volume required to support that good or service. The graph suggests a single central-place system in which the maximum range for any level of the hierarchy is set by the threshold at which the additional functions of the next higher level of the hierarchy can be supported. French and English centers appear randomly intermingled within the system. No English-French dichotomy is evident.

In Fig. 7–19, this graph is superimposed on the central-place systems distinguished for the South-

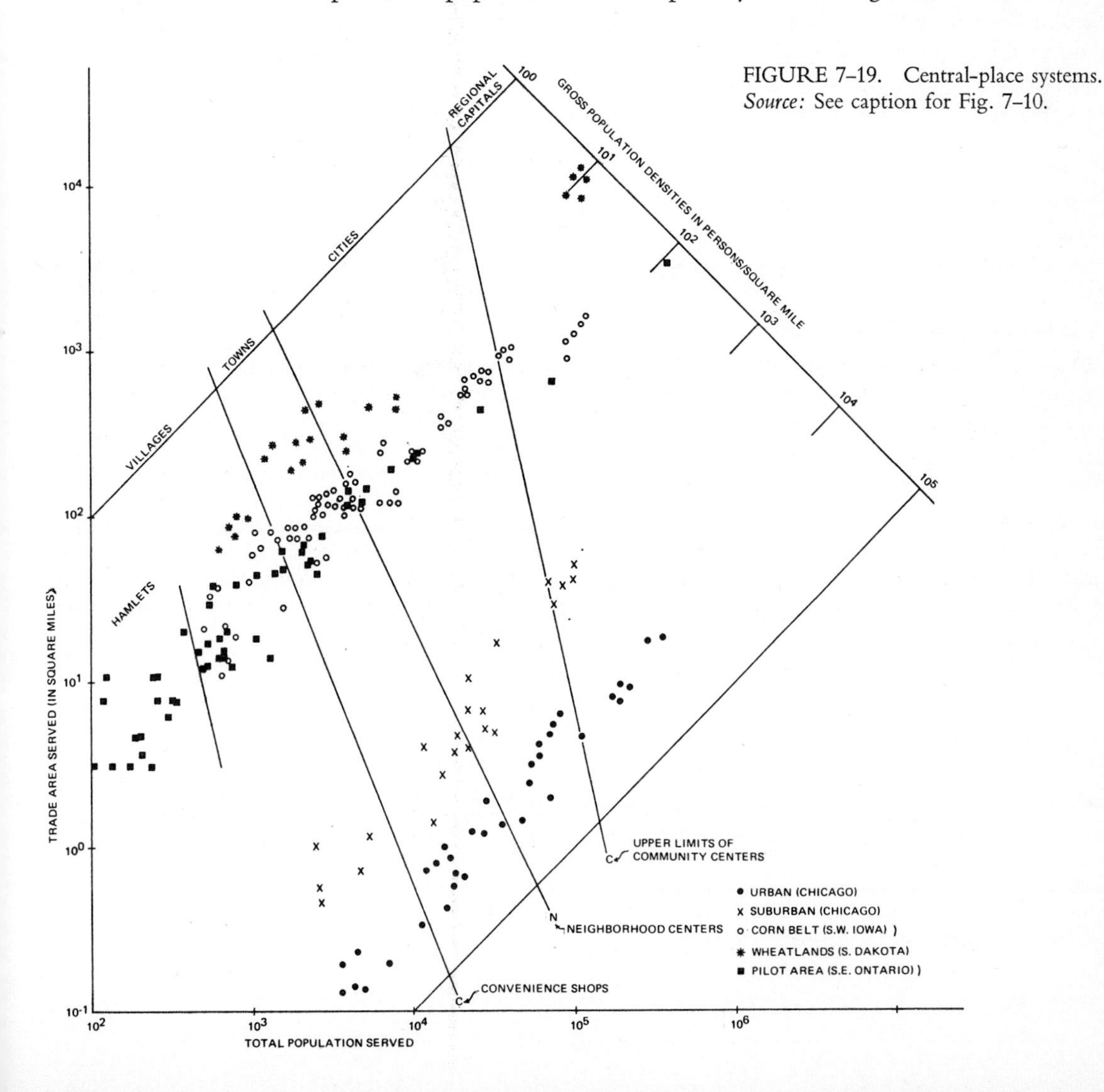

FIGURE 7–19. Central-place systems. *Source:* See caption for Fig. 7–10.

west Iowa portion of the corn belt, the South Dakota portion of the spring wheat belt, and for a group of urban and suburban communities in the Chicago Metropolitan area. The graph reveals a distinct central-place system for each of these agricultural regions, as well as for the urban and suburban communities. Differences in these systems are controlled by the regional population densities. In particular, diminishing population densities produce increases in the area served by centers of any rank, matched by corresponding decreases in the total population served. The structure of these systems shows a remarkably consistent pattern. The hierarchies for the wheat and corn belts, and for the urban and suburban communities have been identified by use of direct factor analysis. The levels of the hierarchy are linked by straight lines which intersect the Eastern Ontario system at the points suggested by changes in central functions performed. Cultural differences do not appear to affect the central-place hierarchy of Eastern Ontario.

*HIERARCHIES OF FUNCTIONAL REGIONS: THEORETICAL MODELS AND EMPIRICAL EVIDENCE FOR DENMARK**

Trade areas based on consumer travel were shown in the previous section. In this section we extend the idea, and add theoretical models of functional regions—similar areas delimited on the basis of all kinds of spatial interactions—so that trade areas are but a special case. In its widest sense, the notion of interaction may include transfer of persons, goods, capital, and information. However, in what follows we only deal with retail trade and other services, as well as transportation and telecommunications, which to a large extent are based on trade and services and whose geographical patterns closely coincide with the geographical patterns of retail trade and other services. Further, this analysis of hierarchies of functional regions is restricted to only the main features of interaction systems, namely the *biggest* interaction flow originating from each place. These "biggest interaction flows" join centers, and the system they form may be described through a mapping of centers and watersheds, to delimit nodal regions or hinterlands.

*Reprinted from Sven Illeris, "Funktionelle Regioner i Danmark Omkring 1960," *Geografisk Tidsskrift*, LXVI (1967), 225–51, with the permission of the author and editor.

Models

To describe the frictional effects of distance of various kinds of interaction, the gravity model may be used:

$$I_{ij} = \frac{m_i m_j}{d_{ij}^{\,a}} \tag{1}$$

in which I_{ij} = the interaction between the places i and j,

m_i and m_j = the masses of places i and j, measured in some meaningful way,

d_{ij} = the distance between i and j, measured in some meaningful way,

a = an exponent.

From this formula, the location of the hinterland boundary between centers A and B can be

FIGURE 7–20. Construction of theoretical hinterland boundary. The field strength of a center at a point is defined as the centrality of the center, divided by the distance between the center and the point, raised to a given power. Around each center, concentric circles are drawn at the distances where the field strengths are, say, 25, 15, 10, 5, etc. The theoretical hinterland boundary between two centers, A and B, each surrounded by its set of concentric circles, may then by constructed as a circular line through the intersection points of concentric circles with equal field strengths. The center of the circular line will be on the prolongation of the line connecting the two hinterland centers. *Source:* Figs. 7–20 through 7–30 are from Sven Illeris, "Funktionelle Regioner i Danmark Omkring 1960," *Geografisk Tidsskrift*, LXVI (1967), 225–51.

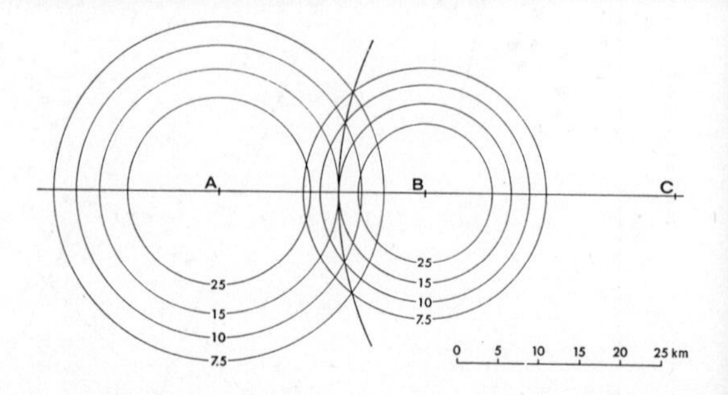

derived, understood as the locus of points with equal amounts of interaction with A and B (see Fig. 7–20). The boundary has the form of a circle, whose center C is placed on the prolongation of the line AB, in the distance from A:

$$AC = \frac{\sqrt[\frac{a}{2}]{m_A}\,1}{\sqrt[\frac{a}{2}]{m_A} \div \sqrt[\frac{a}{2}]{m_B}} \qquad (2)$$

The radius of the circle is:

$$r = \frac{1}{\sqrt[\frac{a}{2}]{m_A} \div \sqrt[\frac{a}{2}]{m_B}} \sqrt[a]{m_A m_B} \qquad (3)$$

in which m_A and m_B = the "masses" of the centers A and B
1 = the distance between A and B
a = the exponent.

Application to the Case of Denmark

Previous empirical research on Denmark's urban hierarchy reveals a 103-center-level and a 4-center-level.[31] For the former, the measurement of mass used to characterize each center was an estimate of "basic" or "nonlocal" tertiary employment.[32] Measuring distances as the crow flies, excepting that measurements do not cross the sea but follow the shortest landwards route, three alternative models were fitted, using exponents of 3, 2, and 1.5. The results are shown in Figs. 7–21, 7–22, and 7–23.

The models on the higher hierarchical level, assigning high-order hinterlands to the 4 major centers, need not be so detailed as the low-order models. It was found sufficient to calculate the theoretical interaction flows—according to Eq. (1)—between 100 districts and the 4 centers. The "masses" of the centers are measured by their population in 1960. The distances were measured as time distances by road, assuming an average speed of 60 kilometers per hour—on motor-ways 80 kilometers per hour, with the addition of timetable crossing times for ferry connections. The value of the distance exponent was alternatively fixed as 2, 1.5, and 1.

The resulting models show that if the distance friction in high (see Fig. 7–24), the biggest interactive flows of most of the Jutland districts will be directed towards the main Jutland centers of Århus and Ålborg, while the Funen districts will be assigned to the high-order hinterland of Odense. In the southwestern corner of Jutland, however, the field strength of Copenhagen will outweight those of the west Danish centers. In this model as well as in the alternative ones. Copenhagen will dominate all east Danish districts.

In the model with a distance exponent of 1.5 (see Fig. 7-25), a higher number of districts will show more theoretical interaction with Copenhagen than with the west Danish centers. The high-order hinterland of Copenhagen thus expands to include the southwestern half of Jutland. If the distance friction is small (Fig. 7-26), most districts will be assigned to Copenhagen. Århus, Odense, and Ålborg will only carve out small influence zones with radii of 25 to 40 kilometers.

Empirically Determined Hinterlands

A large amount of empirical material on hinterlands on various levels has been assembled by the National Planning Secretariat and the Communal Reform Commission. It includes the following studies:

1. A delimitation of the hinterlands of shopping goods' centers, based on interviews with shopkeepers in 1959.
2. Various studies of retail hinterlands, based on interviews with consumer households or key persons representing the consumers.
3. Statistics on telephone calls from various sample periods between 1951 and 1961.
4. Statistics on mail sendings from a sample period in 1967.
5. Statistics on railway passenger tickets for the years 1961 to 1962 and 1963 to 1964.
6. Origin-destination studies of road traffic, carried out in eastern and northern Jutland in 1956 and 1957.
7. A mapping of local newspapers' coverage in 1962.

Both low-order and high-order empirically determined hinterlands, delimited in these seven ways, coincide to a very high degree. Since each

FIGURE 7–21. Model of 103 hinterlands about 1960 (distance exponent: 3). Each hinterland boundary forms the locus of points with equal amounts of interaction with the neighboring centers. *Source:* See caption for Fig. 7–20.

FIGURE 7–22. Model of 103 hinterlands about 1960 (distance exponent: 2). Each hinterland boundary forms the locus of points with equal amounts of interaction with the neighboring centers. *Source:* See caption for Fig. 7–20.

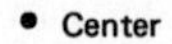

● Center

⌣ Theoretical hinterland boundary

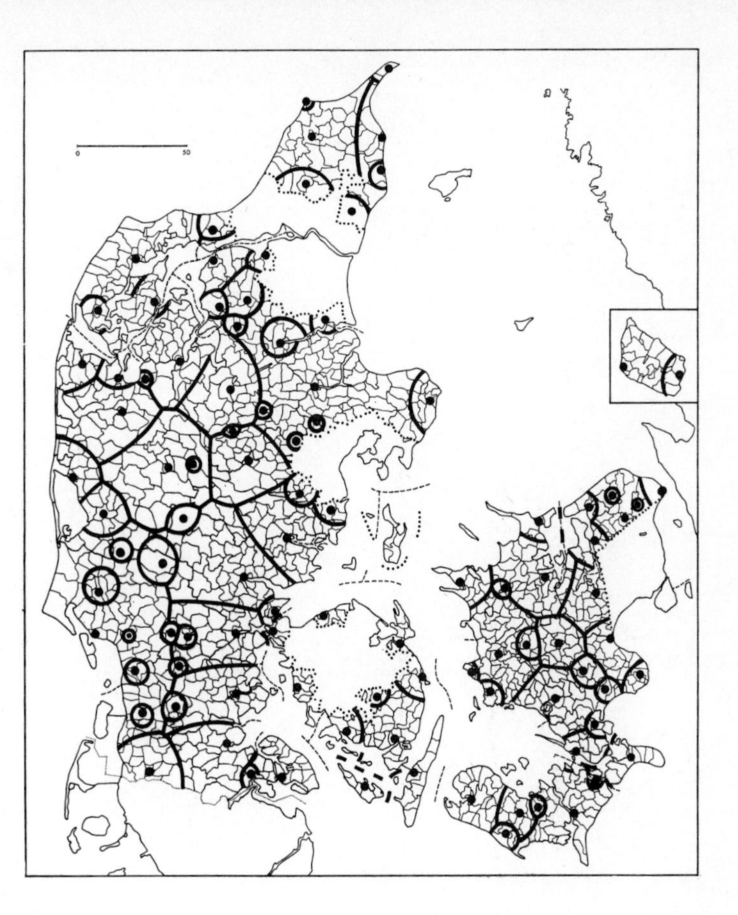

FIGURE 7–23. Model of 103 hinterlands about 1960 (distance exponent: 1.5). Each hinterland boundary forms the locus of points with equal amounts of interaction with the neighboring centers. *Source:* See caption for Fig. 7–20.

FIGURE 7–24. Model of high-level hinterlands: 1960 (distance exponent: 2). Each district is assigned to the hinterland of the high-level center with which it has the greatest amount of interaction. *Source:* See caption for Fig. 7–20.

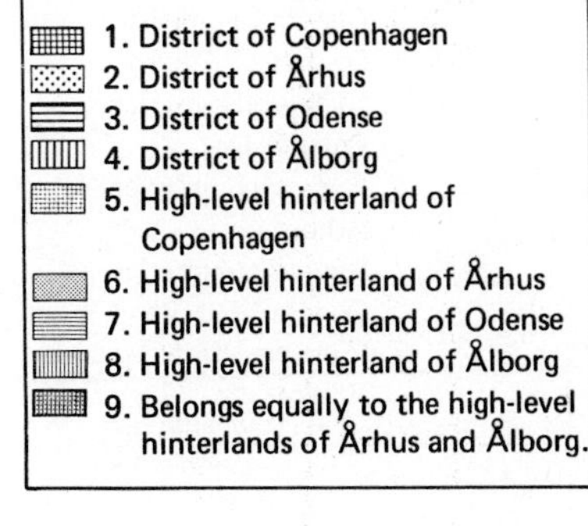

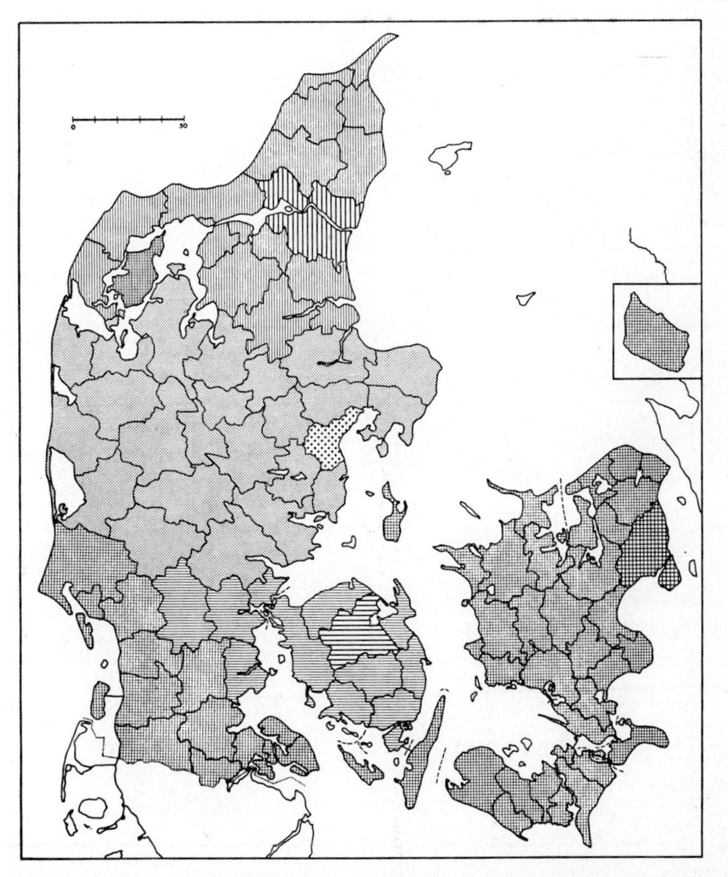

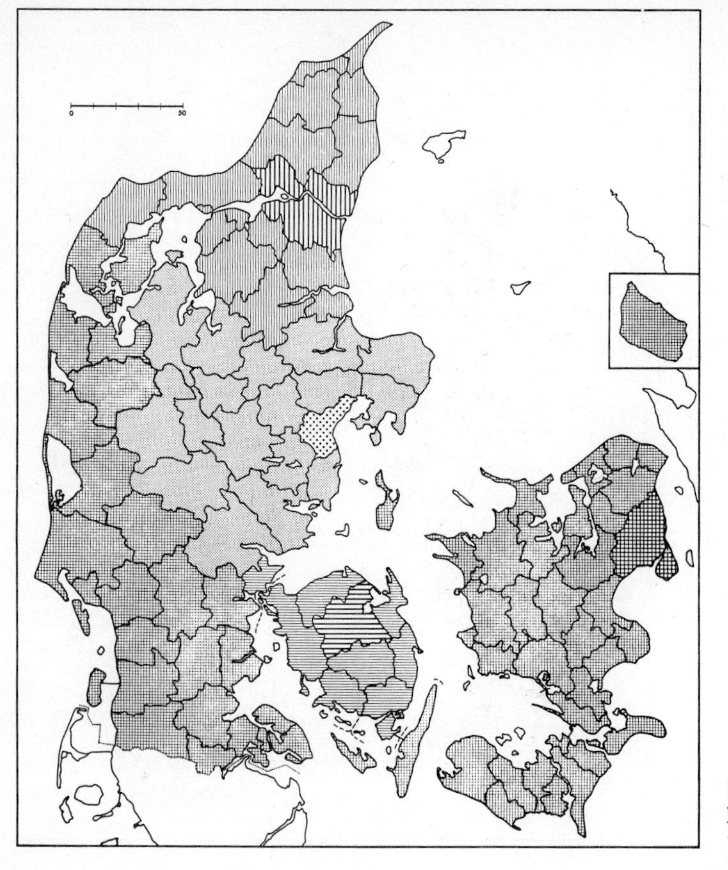

1. District of Copenhagen
2. District of Århus
3. District of Odense
4. District of Ålborg
5. High-level hinterland of Copenhagen
6. High-level hinterland of Århus
7. High-level hinterland of Odense
8. High-level hinterland of Ålborg

FIGURE 7–25. Model of high-level hinterlands: 1960 (distance exponent: 1.5). *Source:* See caption for Fig. 7–20.

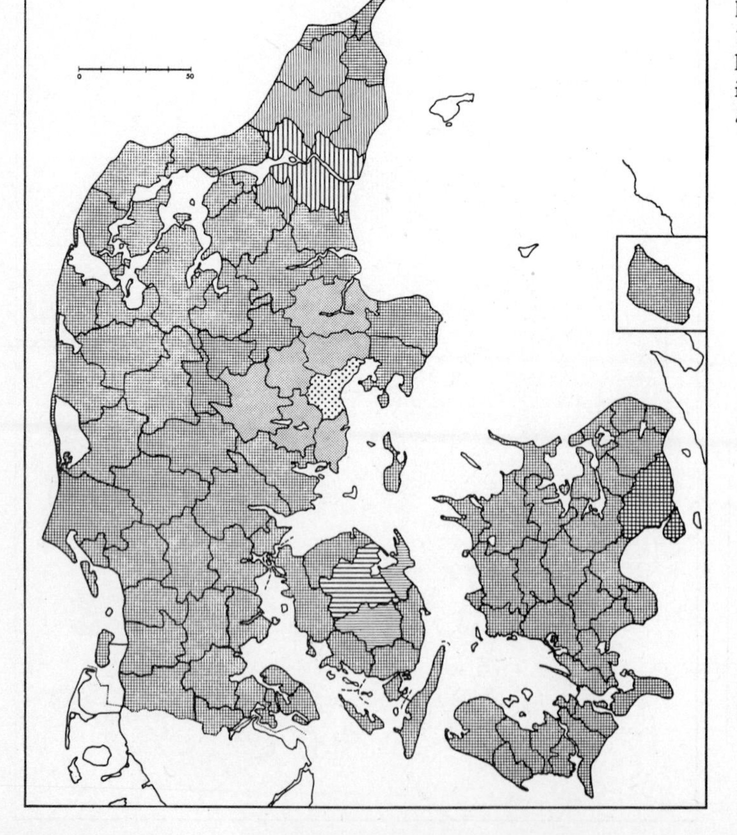

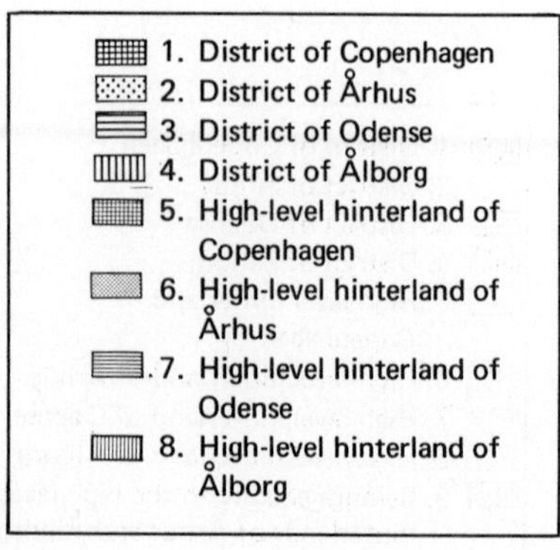

FIGURE 7–26. Model of high-level hinterlands: 1960 (distance exponent: 1). Each district is assigned to the hinterland of the high-level center, with which it has the greatest amount of interaction. *Source:* See caption for Fig. 7–20.

of the studies has its individual drawbacks, the information was merged to synthesize hinterland delimitations. The empirical data enable us to distinguish categories of 103 low-level, 43 medium-level, and 4 high-level hinterlands.

On a low-medium level, 103 centers can be chosen, and synthesizing hinterlands assigned to them (Fig. 7–27). The smallest unit assigned to a hinterland is normally the commune, since most of the seven individual studies are based on communes. However, in some cases, when one commune contains two telephone exchanges or post offices, it has been possible to use smaller units. The set of 103 hinterlands may be said to form a maximum set of hinterlands in Denmark on this level.

A minimum set of medium-level hinterlands has been assigned to 43 centers (Fig. 7-28). The units are the same as the ones in the map of 103 hinterlands.

To the 4 high-order centers, high-order empirically determined hinterlands have been assigned in Fig. 7–29. Data on telephone calls, mail, and railway trips from low-order centers are part of the information on which the delimitation can be based; but statistics on interactive flows from larger telephone, railway, and road traffic districts can also be applied. As the smallest units assigned to high-order hinterlands, it has therefore been necessary to apply a set of 67 very schematic districts. Figure 7–29 shows that the west Danish centers of Århus, Odense, and Ålborg have high-order influence zones consisting of Central-Eastern Jutland, Funen, and Northern Jutland respectively. Southern and Western Jutland, as well as East Denmark, belong to the high-order influence zone of Copenhagen.

Comparisons between Theoretical and Empirically Determined Hinterlands

The delimitations of 103 theoretical hinterlands in Figs. 7–21 to 7–23 may be compared to the delimitation of 103 empirical hinterlands in Fig. 7–27. However, the theoretically determined hinterlands have been delimited on a continuous plane, and in order to make a comparison possible, transformations of the models are necessary. Each commune—or part of commune—in the models has to be assigned undivided to the theoretical hinterland in which its population center of gravity is placed. It may then be calculated for each model, what share of its smallest units (communes or parts of communes) belongs to the same hinterland as in the empirical delimitation.

The comparisons show that in the model with a distance exponent of 3, 5 per cent of the smallest units have been assigned to a different hinterland than in the empirical delimitation. In the model with a distance exponent of 2, 10 per cent of the smallest units diverge from the empirical map, and in the model with distance exponent 1.5, 15 per cent of the smallest units diverge.

The 4 theoretical high-order hinterlands in Figs. 7–24 to 7–26 may be compared to the empirically determined high-order hinterlands in Fig. 7–28. In order to make comparisons possible, the 100 districts of the theoretical models have been combined to form 67 districts, corresponding to the ones of the empirical delimitation. The comparisons show that in the model with a distance exponent of 2, 30 per cent of the districts have been assigned to a different high-order center than in the empirical delimitation. The model with a distance exponent of 1.5 proves to be the best one, 12 per cent of the districts diverging from the empirical picture; while in the model with a distance exponent of 1, 20 per cent of the districts diverge.

Discussion

The functional delimitation of regions may have several practical applications, e.g., as a base for administrative divisions. Such divisions need to be unchanged over a considerable period of time. If the theoretical models are accepted as describing the hinterland pattern with sufficient accuracy, and if knowledge about change in the parameters of the model can be obtained from other sources—which is quite often the case—the models may form a basis for predicting the stability of the hinterland pattern. Thus expensive repetitions of empirical studies may be saved because the centralities of central places more often than not develop in parallel ways, thus causing little

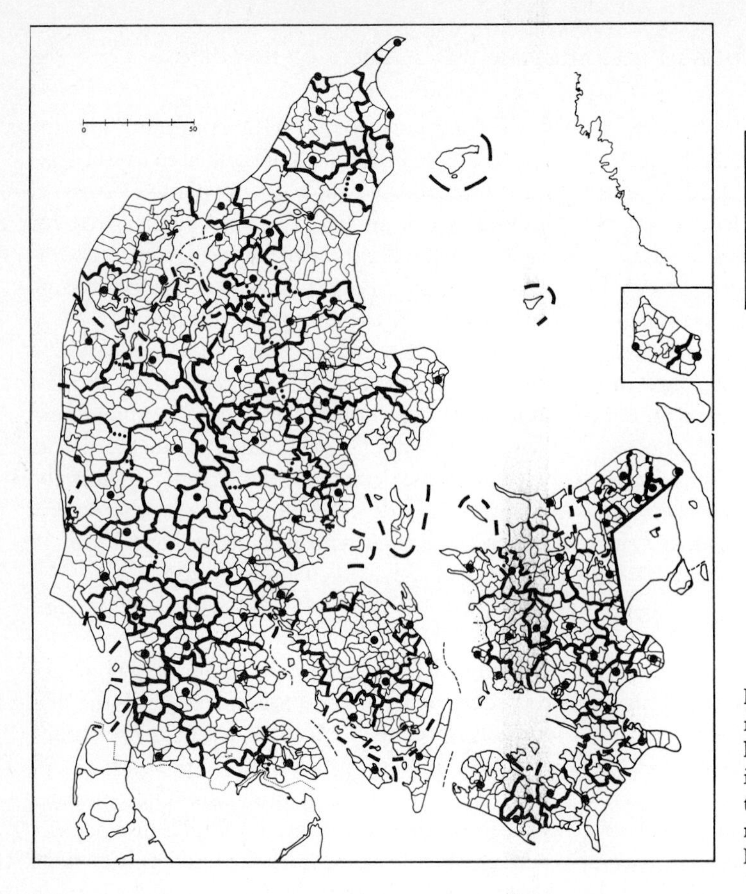

FIGURE 7–27. Empirically determined hinterlands about 1960. The hinterland delimitation is based on investigations of retail trade, services, telephone calls, mail shipments, and railway tickets. *Source:* See caption for Fig. 7–20.

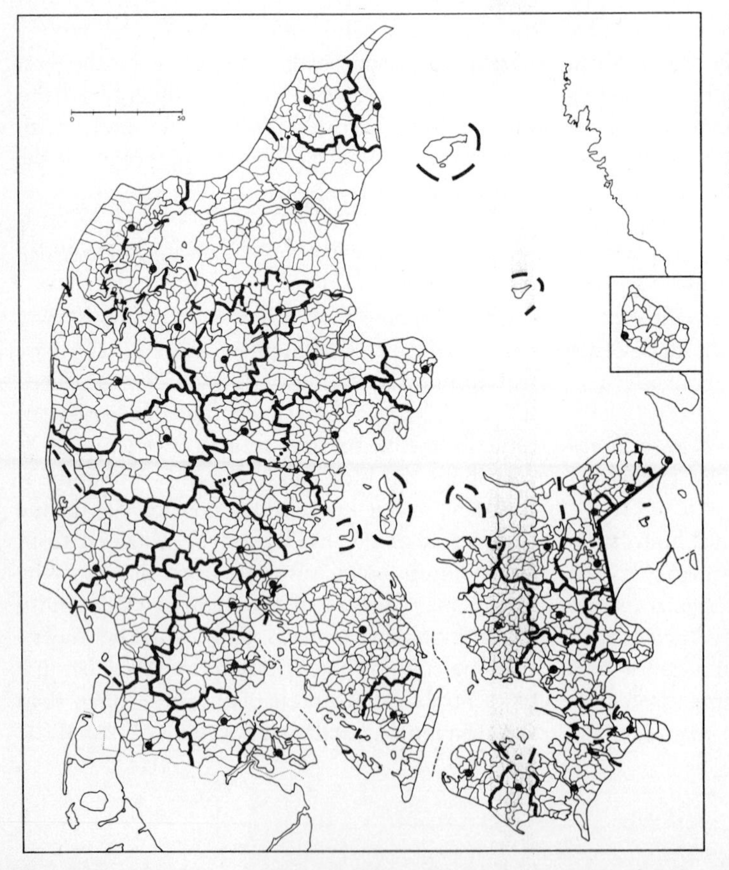

FIGURE 7–28. Forty-three empirically determined hinterlands about 1960. The hinterland delimitation is based on investigations of retail trade, services, telephone calls, mail shipments and railway tickets. *Source:* See caption for Fig. 7–20.

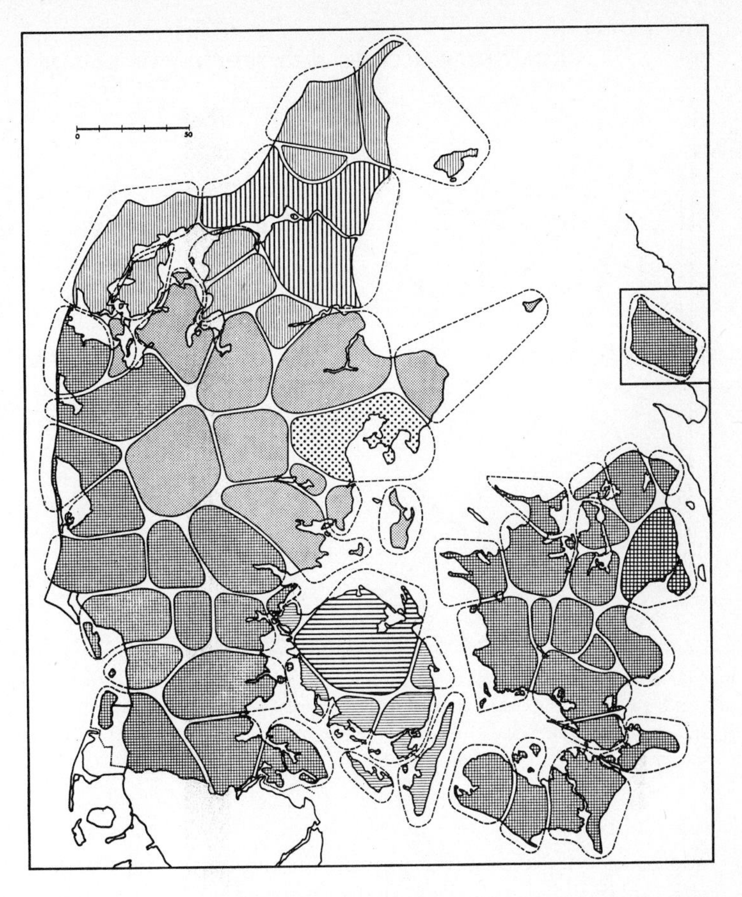

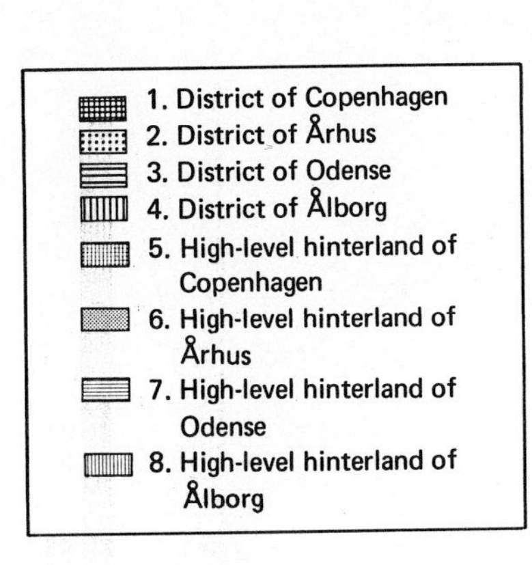

FIGURE 7–29. Four empirically determined high-level hinterlands about 1960. Each of the schematic districts is assigned to the hinterlands of the high-level center with which the district and its central town have most connections, according to investigations of telephone calls, mail shipments, railway trips, and road traffic. *Source:* See caption for Fig. 7–20.

shifting in the location of the theoretical hinterland limits. It is clear that improved transportation —such as private car ownership—tend to lower the distance exponent. However, even a change in the distance exponent from 3 to 1.5 does not displace the hinterland limit between roughly equal centers by more than a few kilometers (see Fig. 7–30). Thus the hinterland limits between centers of more or less equal influence may be foreseen to be rather stable, even with greatly increased mobility. Experiences from the abolition of the 1864 to 1920 Danish-German frontier and from the construction of long bridges in the 1930s tend to confirm the stability of hinterland limits. When the distance exponent is lowered, the hinterland limit between centers with very different centralities is displaced considerably in the direction of the weaker center, however. Thus with an increase in mobility, the hinterlands of the weakest of the present centers may dwindle to almost nothing, emphasizing the strong pressures toward centralization implicit in current technological change.

*THE PREDICTION OF TRADE CENTER VIABILITY: THE CASE OF THE NORTHERN GREAT PLAINS**

Nowhere have the changes in the urban hierarchy predicted by the gravity models been as pronounced in actual fact as in the Great Plains of North America. The form of the space economy in rural parts of the Great Plains has changed dramatically in the past twenty years. There are fewer farmers and fewer, but much larger, farms, and the farms have been highly mechanized and commercialized with a consequent altering of the kinds and volume of goods and services needed on the farm. Improvements in means of movement have tended to make rural people less dependent upon their local trade centers for these goods and services, even when they can be supplied. Expanding farm incomes in the region

*Reprinted from Gerald Hodge, "The Prediction of Trade Center Viability in the Great Plains," *Papers and Proceedings of the Regional Science Association*, XV (1965), 87–115, with the permission of the author and editor.

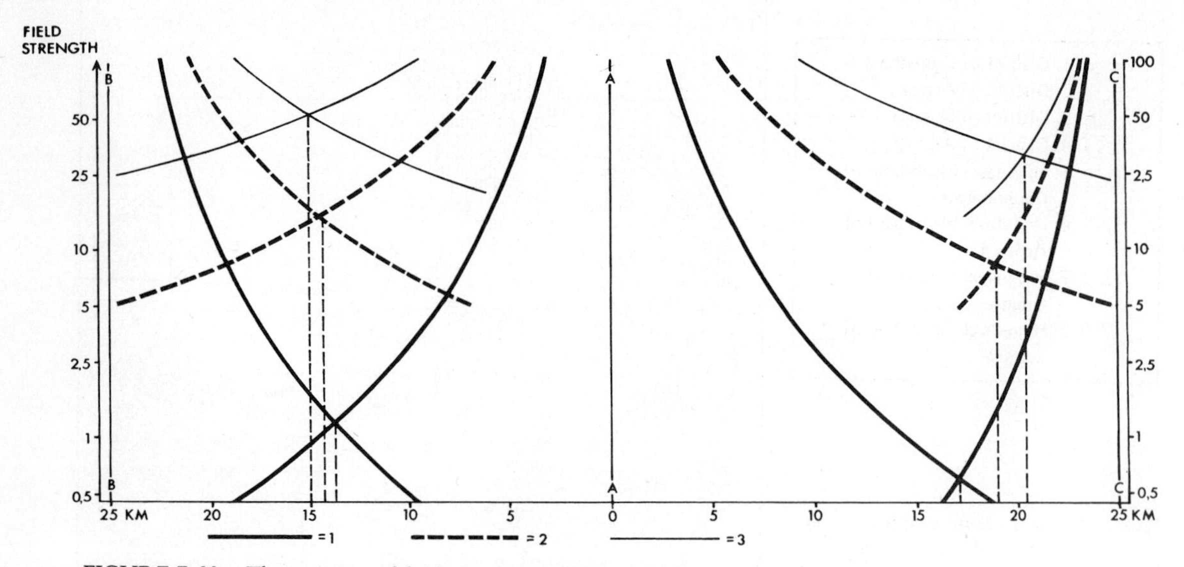

FIGURE 7–30. The variation of field strength with distance from the centers. The diagram shows centers A, B, and C to be evenly spaced 25 kilometers apart on the abscissa. Center A has a centrality index of 3000, and B and C, respectively, 1650 and 300. Variations in field strengths with distance exponents 1, 2, and 3 are plotted. *Source:* See caption for Fig. 7–20.

combined with increases in physical and attitudinal mobility have allowed an exposure to and created a demand for more specialized goods and services in both the public and private sectors. These changes have engendered many efforts aimed at reassessing the efficacy of the spatial arrangements in the public sphere, such as for local government, education, health care, transportation, and grain marketing and storage.[33]

This concern turns upon the problem of creating and maintaining a satisfactory living environment for the farm and small town residents of this region in the context of so dispersed a settlement pattern. No one part of this problem is more important than that concerning the future of the many small trade centers one finds so liberally distributed in the countryside. These trade centers are important focal points for social and economic activity in the region; besides being places of residence for many, they are places for marketing farm produce and distributing farm supplies and they are places for social interaction and cultural fulfillment for the people of town and country. But unlike urban centers in metropolitan complexes, these trade centers cannot count on growing. Indeed, many have disappeared and many more face the same fate or at the very least will have their ability to perform even their normal functions sharply curtailed. From almost all points of view, continuing decline of trade centers and dispersion of the settlement patterns in the Great Plains means higher costs for rural residents to maintain their present standard of living, which is, even now, inferior in most respects to their urban counterparts.

"The handwriting is on the wall for a good many of these (small) towns," a contemporary observer of the region has commented.[34] If this prophecy is valid, and for the Canadian province of Saskatchewan where 15 per cent of all centers disappeared in the past two decades it appears to be, then the public policy implications are many. Within individual communities thus affected, the closure of business establishments results in a loss of investment, of tax revenue, and of employment. Commercial decline often presages the diminution of the community as a location for public facilities, and it certainly affects the population holding power of the center with the consequent loss in housing investment. In terms of the state or provincial government, trade center decline poses the possibility of facilities at some locations having to close, as with schools and hospitals; it almost always means changes in travel patterns and thus affects highway needs.

If there is to be an adequate response to the problems of trade center decline by public authorities, there must be, at a minimum, some way of distinguishing the prospects for growth or decline —*the viability*—of trade centers. The present study addresses itself to the analytical problem of how such a prognostication might be made. The ultimate aim of this study is to help provide greater understanding of the changes in the trade center system of the Great Plains, as well as to provide a base of information and methodology that could be useful in planning for the space-economy of the region. To this end, the following sections in this paper describe, respectively, the development of the analytical framework, the pace and incidence of change in the trade center system, the derivation of a predictive model using a combined factor and multiple regression analysis, and the implications for both policy and theory.

While acknowledging differences between the trade center systems of various parts of the Great Plains, in, for example, Missouri, Kansas, North Dakota, Saskatchewan, or Alberta, there is enough similarity to warrant limiting the investigation to one portion of the large region.[35] Thus, in this study, the focus is the Province of Saskatchewan in the Northern Great Plains. Its problems of trade center change are typical of those affecting states to the south and provinces to the east and west. Observations, for the period 1941 to 1961, of the modifications in the pattern of trade centers are central to this study. For this is the period that has seen agriculture in the Great Plains transformed almost completely into large-scale, mechanized operations.

Analyzing Trade Center Viability

The literature on the subject of trade center change is very inconclusive. A large group of literature, mainly from rural sociology, shows a lack of general agreement about whether trade centers actually are declining and, if so, to what extent.[36] A second group of relevant writings is concerned with central-place theory; this provides descriptive models of trade center systems but not of the change in the systems.[37] A third group of writings is largely problem-oriented regarding changes in the region's agriculture and rural life but lacks a systematic analytical base.[38] In all the literature, only a few deal more or less directly with the particular problem of diagnosing trade center viability. The main usefulness of the literature is in its raising of a number of issues for which the present study attempts to provide some analytical clarity.

The first issue concerns whether trade centers really are declining. The lack of clarity on this issue stems from the lack of appropriate or, at least, comparable measures of trade center change. Much of the literature uses population change to measure viability among trade centers. This is not a satisfactory measure of viability viewed either in terms of analytical method (dozens of trade centers are too small to be recorded in official censuses) or in terms of the true nature of trade center functioning. Trade centers in this region exist to serve primarily the commercial needs of a limited, surrounding, agriculturally-based population. Their possibilities for population growth are restricted largely to the inflow of farmers choosing to reside in town rather than in the surrounding countryside. Only a few centers experience population growth as a result of an expansion in their nonfarm economic base. Moreover, the inflow of farm families means no more than the transfer of an originally dispersed hinterland population to a point of central residence.

For the present study, change in retail service level of a trade center is used to measure growth or decline of that center. This measure has the advantage not only of data being available for all centers (through Dun and Bradstreet directories) but also of being a direct reflection of the meaning of *trade* center. It measures changes in the quality which is basic to a trade center's existence—its power to attract patrons for its business establishments. A seven-point ordinal scale, developed for this study but similar to others used in this region, was used to classify centers according to configurations of increasingly more specialized goods and services offered by centers. A trade center was said to "decline" if it shifted downward one or more classes; a trade center was said to experience "demise" or to "disappear" if it shifted downward below the threshold of the lowest functional class. Similarly, a center "grew" if it shifted upward one or more classes. Allowance was made in the scale for changes in configurations of trade center functions, as between the beginning and the end of the period 1941 to 1961.

Two other issues raised by the literature have engendered the analytical framework used herein. The first of these concerns the validity of a number of tentative hypotheses about the nature of trade center change in the writings consulted, i.e., it is most prevalent in proximity to large centers; it is directly related to the population size or retail service level; it is occurring most in certain classes of centers. These and similar hypotheses have been made operational and have been tested for all the trade centers in Saskatchewan at both the beginning and end of the period. This constitutes the deductive analysis portion of this study; its results are described in the succeeding section of this paper. The other issue raised in the literature stems from the conclusions in a number of studies that the key relationships governing trade center change are more complex than those of population size, retail service level, or location just alluded to. By evidence and inference, such variables as a history of sustained population growth, good access to rail and highway transportation, a high level of community services, presence of a high school and hospital, a high ratio of nonagricultural employment, and a high level of education among the population have been suggested as improving the chances for survival of centers. To explore the notion that trade center decline is related to differences in community environment requires an inductive analysis. A factor analysis was employed to determine which variables went with which. The resultant clusters of variables (factors) were treated as independent variables describing trade center environment in a multiple regression model in which the dependent variable was the change in number of retail firms between 1941 and 1961.

The deductive and inductive analyses were conducted separately but are complementary approaches to the question of diagnosing trade center viability. The deductive analysis consisted of viewing changes in retail service level of centers in terms of several hypotheses regarding anticipated changes in functional distribution and in location and spacing of centers. It viewed all 906 trade centers extant in Saskatchewan in 1941. Thus it was possible to gain the aggregate picture of trade center change for all classes of centers and for each class for the past twenty years. The deductive analysis was limited, for reasons of data, to the relations of retail service changes to functional distribution and location. Nevertheless, it provides an illumination of key trends regarding the amount, location, and kind of trade center decline from which extrapolations can be made for future periods.

The inductive analysis provides the possibility that trade center decline in specified centers could be predicted rather than just decline by class of center or general location. For this analysis, only the incorporated trade centers were included, 473 in all. Thirty-five variables for each of these centers were subjected to a principal-axis type of factor analysis. The thirty-five variables were condensed by this method to three dimensions (factors) that were statistically independent (orthogonal) of one another and along which each trade center in the sample could be arrayed and positions of all centers could be compared. The inductive analysis was further extended to include a regression model to determine to what extent, if any, community differences as indicated by the factor analysis were related to trade center decline. The position of a center on each of the three factors was treated as an independent variable, while the dependent variable was change in retail service level from 1941 to 1966.[39] Thus, for any designated center, for which a factor score has been obtained, the inductive analysis provides the potential of predicting future trade center performance. Further substance can be added to the prediction by taking into account the variables which dominate the factor analysis scales.

Finally, the analysis undertaken for this study is premised on the need for planning of the changes in the space-economy of Great Plains' areas. The present analysis is explicitly directed at solving the planning problem of regulating the pace and incidence of change in trade center systems which, if left to chance the evidence indicates, are tending to unsatisfactory spatial distributions of activities. The methodology, therefore, aims not only at deriving an understanding of the basic characteristics of changes in trade center systems in general, but also aims at deriving analytical results which planners in the region may find immediately useful.

Changes in the Trade Center System: 1941 to 1961

Observations of changes in the Saskatchewan trade center system are organized with respect to the following five hypotheses which have been tested:

1. Trade centers ranking low in the retail service hierarchy at the beginning of the period lost rank more rapidly than higher ranking centers between 1941 and 1961.
2. Between 1941 and 1961, the number of centers at both extremes of the retail service hierarchy increased relatively to centers in the middle range of the hierarchy.
3. The density of small trade centers in both 1941 and 1961 decreases with increasing proximity to larger centers, and/or the rate of decline of small trade centers between 1941 and 1961 increases with increasing proximity to larger centers.
4. The characteristic spacing of trade centers in any one class for the period 1951 to 1961 is increasing for centers at the lower end of the retail service hierarchy and decreasing for centers at the upper end of the hierarchy.
5. Where trade centers at the same class situated adjacent to one another were separated by less than the average spacing for the class in 1941, one or more of the centers experienced either relative or absolute decline by 1961.

The retail service hierarchy to which most changes are linked consists of a system of seven types of trade centers. From the highest to the lowest functional level they are primary wholesale and retail centers, secondary wholesale and retail centers, complete shopping centers, partial shopping centers, full convenience centers, minimum convenience centers, and hamlets.[40] The distribution of these centers and some of their characteristics as of 1961 are given in Table 7–9 and Fig. 7–31.

TABLE 7–9

Major Characteristics of Trade Centers in Saskatchewan: 1961

Type of Center	*Number of Centers*	*Median Population† (in Thousands)*	*Range of Population (in Thousands)*	*Average Number of Establishments*	*Index of Sales Volume†*
Primary wholesale and retail	2	103.80	95.5–112.1	1,414.0	2,000‡
Secondary wholesale and retail	9	10.00	5.2– 33.2	232.0	500
Complete shopping	29	1.80	0.9– 4.0	58.5	100
Partial shopping	85	0.61	0.3– 1.4	26.1	35
Full convenience	100	0.36	0.2– 1.6	16.5	13
Minimum convenience	150	0.21	0.08– 0.7	9.9	7
Hamlet	404	0.05	0.03– 0.3	3.3	2
All trade centers	779	0.15	2.03–112.1	17.1	—

Sources: Dun and Bradstreet, *Reference Book*, January, 1961, and Census of Canada, and (for Tables 7–9 through 7–20), Gerald Hodge, "The Prediction of Trade Center Viability in the Great Plains," *Papers and Proceedings of the Regional Science Association*, XV (1965), 87–115.

*Population of unincorporated centers has been estimated.

†Derived from data for a limited number of centers; index computed as ratios of sales volume in complete shopping centers.

‡Or more.

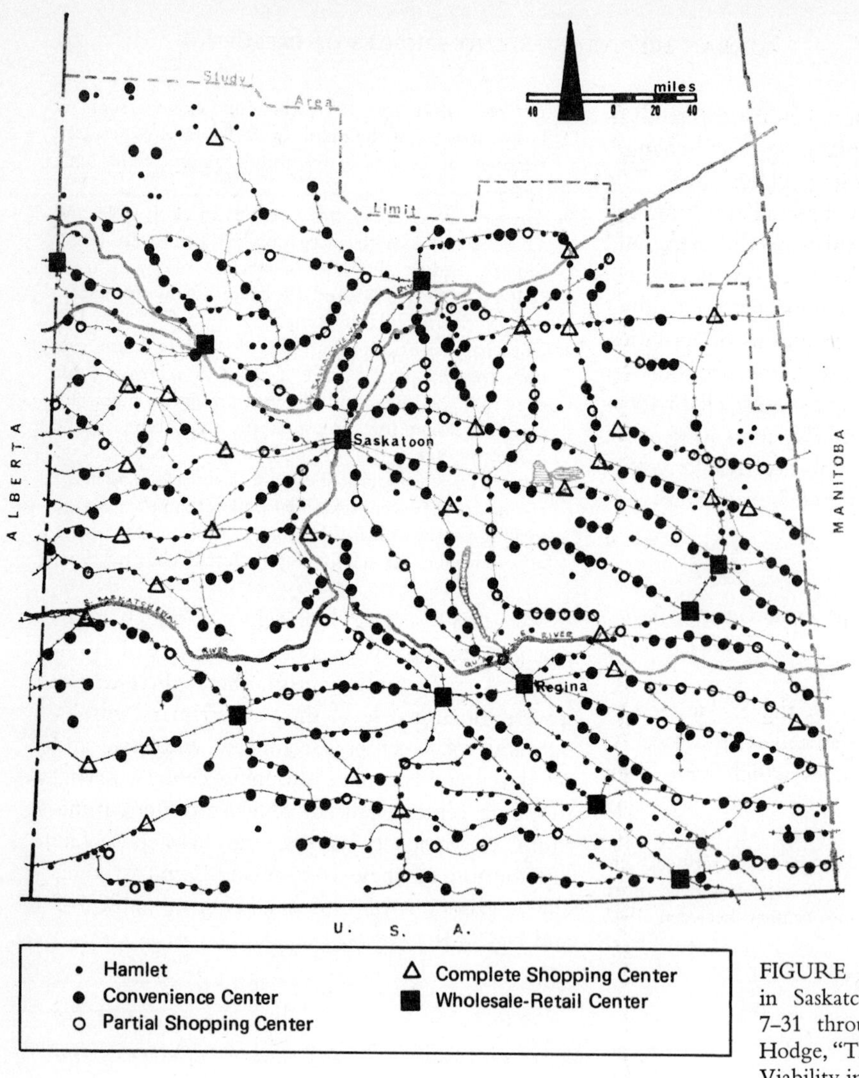

FIGURE 7–31. Trade center system in Saskatchewan: 1961. *Source:* Figs. 7–31 through 7–35 are from Gerald Hodge, "The Prediction of Trade Center Viability in the Great Plains," *Papers and Proceedings of the Regional Science Association*, XV (1965), 87–115.

From the table, it is evident that there is a close correlation between retail service level of a center and its population size. But there is also a wide range of population within any trade center class, which indicates that the strength of a center may depend upon other characteristics of the center and its surrounding area as well as on the center's size. It is also clear that the frequency distribution does not conform to the theoretical expectations of a hexagonal trade center system, such as propounded by Christaller, either in total number of centers or the number expected in each class. (In a complete hexagonal system the number of centers of any given rank is equal to twice the number of all higher ranking centers.) Figure 7–31 further confirms the lack of regular hexagonal pattern of centers in Saskatchewan. Indeed, the characteristic pattern is a linear one that was fostered by the extensive railway building the province experienced in its settlement period of 1900 to 1930. The fairly regular spacing of centers along the rail lines arose with the establishment of trade centers at the grain collection points located by the railroads every six to ten miles. Similar forces helped shape the pattern of trade centers in all of the grain growing areas of the Great Plains.

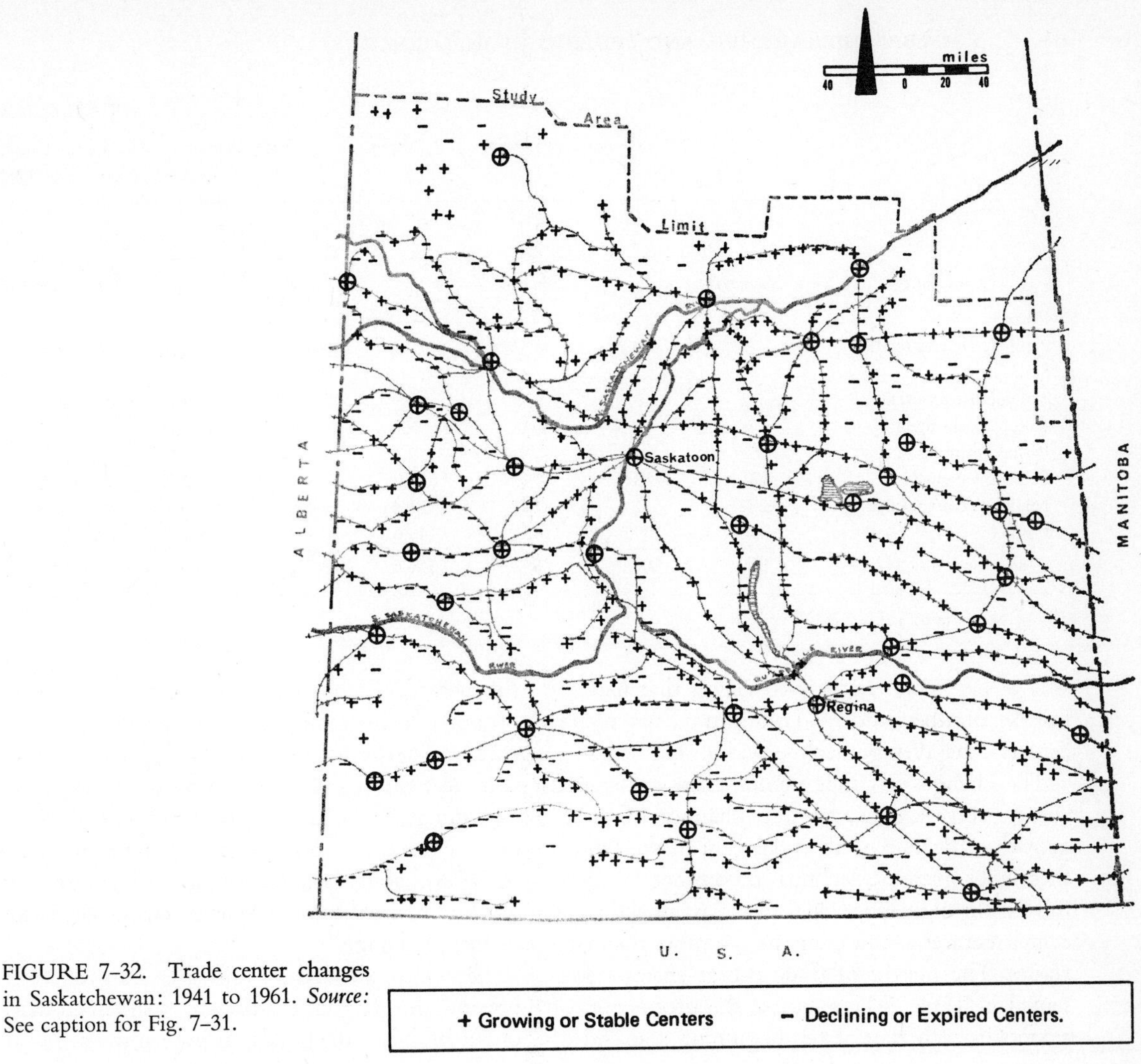

FIGURE 7–32. Trade center changes in Saskatchewan: 1941 to 1961. *Source:* See caption for Fig. 7–31.

Changes in the number and distribution of trade centers. Since 1941, when Saskatchewan recorded its largest number of extant trade centers, 909, there has been a decrease of 127, or 14 per cent. The decade 1941 to 1951 was the first time the province experienced a net loss in trade center numbers; although 69 new centers emerged in that decade, 83 expired. In the succeeding decade, the net loss was still greater: 16 new centers and 129 centers disappearing. Besides outright disappearance of many centers, the system suffered considerable decline among its centers in the same two decades—142 declined in commercial status in the 1941 to 1951 period, and 148 more declined in the following decade. Thus, the past twenty years have seen an increase in the rate of both decline and disappearance among trade centers in the province. Furthermore, these changes have been general across Saskatchewan, as can be seen in Fig. 7–32.

Viewing the changes in terms of trade center classes, four classes experienced net increases in numbers in the past twenty years, two classes had net decreases in numbers, and one class (the primary wholesale and retail centers of Regina and Saskatoon) remained constant (see Table 7–10). Of the four classes that had net gains in numbers—secondary wholesale and retail, complete shopping centers, partial shopping centers, and hamlets—the unweighted average increase

TABLE 7–10

Changes in Number and Proportion of Trade Centers by Functional Class: Saskatchewan, 1941-1961

Type of Center	*1941*		*1951*		*1961*		*% Change 1941–1961*
	Number	*%*	*Number*	*%*	*Number*	*%*	
Primary wholesale and retail	2	0.2	2	0.2	2	0.3	0.0
Secondary wholesale and retail	5	0.6	8	0.9	9	1.2	80.0
Complete shopping	26	2.9	23	2.6	29	3.7	11.6
Partial shopping	57	6.3	66	7.4	85	10.9	49.2
Full convenience	171	18.9	169	18.9	100	12.7	−41.5
Mininum convenience	287	31.8	191	21.4	150	19.4	−47.8
Hamlet	358	39.3	433	48.6	404	51.8	12.8
All trade centers	906	100.0	892	100.0	779	100.0	−14.0

Source: See note to Table 7–9.

was 18 per cent. Of the two classes that had net losses in numbers—full and minimum convenience centers—the average decline was 45 per cent.

The changes in trade center classes tabulated above were largely one-step changes of either growth or decline. Only 3 per cent of the centers that either grew or declined in commercial status moved through more than one class in the trade center hierarchy, and none moved more than two classes. The matrix of trade center changes presented in Table 7–11 indicates the proportion of centers in each class at the beginning and end of the period. Each row of the matrix gives the proportion in each class (as specified by the columns) at the end of 1961 period, given that they were in one class (as specified by the rows) at the beginning of the period. It is not unrealistic to think of these proportions as a matrix of transitional probabilities and, although this has not been done here, use these in a Markov chain calculation of future change.[41]

There are, altogether, only five non-zero cells beyond the diagonals adjacent to the main diagonal; the latter diagonals indicate movements of

TABLE 7–11

Changes in the Proportion of Classes of Trade Centers in Saskatchewan from 1941-1961

Class of Center 1941	*Class of Center in 1961*							
	Expired by 1961	*Hamlet*	*Minimum Conven-ience*	*Full Conven-ience*	*Partial Shopping*	*Complete Shopping*	*Secondary Wholesale and Retail*	*Primary Wholesale and Retail*
New center (1942–1951)	**48**	52						
Hamlet	46	**52**	02					
Minimum convenience	02	63	**27**	07	01			
Full convenience		−6	28	**39**	26	01		
Partial shopping			02	19	**63**	16		
Complete shopping					12	**73**	15	
Secondary wholesale and retail							**100**	
Primary wholesale and retail								**100**

Source: See note to Table 7–9.

only one class. The three classes in which two step changes occurred include the full and minimum convenience centers which experienced both growth and decline of this degree in some of their centers and the partial shopping centers which showed a few centers declining by this degreee. The proportions of centers in each class which remained stable in the twenty-year period are revealed through the percentages in the main diagonal. It can be seen that each of the three lowest ranking types of centers had the least stability. In each of these classes, there are also large entries in the diagonal immediately to the left of the main diagonal thereby indicating that the lack of stability is due to substantial decline or demise occurring in these classes.

The data generally substantiate the thesis that small trade centers (low in the retail service hierarchy) are declining faster than large trade centers, our first hypothesis. However, what might have been expected, an increasing rate of decline for each successively lower rank of center, is not borne out by these findings. Hamlets are declining at a higher rate, but it is only two-thirds the rate of decline of minimum convenience centers and is less than for the full convenience centers as well. Apparently the most unstable groups of centers are the two types of convenience centers.

Some of the literature reviewed for this study drew the inference that trade center systems in rural areas were changing so that commercial needs of rural people were being served increasingly by only two types of centers, those serving local day-to-day needs and those serving specialized needs of large areas. This prompted the formulation of our second hypothesis, and tests were made for this phenomenon in Saskatchewan. Again referring to Table 7–11, there may be evidence of an emerging pattern like that hypothesized. Local, day-to-day needs may be met adequately in centers much like the present hamlets. The latter class has shown a high degree of stability compared to the two classes above it. Today there are one-third less convenience centers than hamlets, whereas twenty years ago there were almost 30 per cent more. Changes at the upper end of the trade center hierarchy are not as clear as for the lower end, however. Excluding the two provincial centers, Regina and Saskatoon, there has been an increase in the number and proportion of partial shopping, complete shopping, and secondary wholesale-retail centers since 1941. But there does not appear to be any strong tendency towards the convergence of all higher ranking centers into one type of shopping center providing specialized goods and services over large areas. Another possibility is suggested by the large increase in number and proportion (almost 50 per cent in both cases) of partial shopping centers. The latter centers may develop a special role as an intermediate level shopping center for rural residents much as do "community shopping areas" or "shopping plazas" for residents in a large city. Moreover, partial shopping centers have been developing at remarkably regular intervals, and their characteristic spacing is just over twenty-two miles. This puts them easily within twenty minutes drive of rural residents at the extremes of their trading areas. A third, or upper, level of center specialization might then be postulated on the basis of this data. But, in short, the second hypothesis is not borne out.

Before leaving the matter of changes in the trade center hierarchy, there are two other facets of change revealed in Table 7–11 that deserve mention. First, there is the somewhat ambivalent behavior among centers at the middle of the hierarchy. Full convenience centers shifted almost equally up and down; to some extent, but less pronounced, this behavior is repeated by the partial and complete shopping centers. This seems to be a clear indication of the state of flux in the current organization of the Saskatchewan trade center system, particularly in its middle range. Second, there is a high mortality among the centers that emerged subsequent to 1941. Of the latter, which were shown to be present in 1951, fully 48 per cent had disappeared by 1961. The tenuous existence of small centers generally in the region, and the fact that these new centers were mostly very small, probably accounts for their high rate of demise.

Changes in the spatial distribution of trade centers. The third hypothesis was that decline of small trade centers is greater with increasing proximity to large centers. Large centers were assumed to be complete shopping centers and other higher-ranking centers. The effect of proximity to large centers on small centers has been examined in two ways: the change in density of small centers in the period and the change in commercial status. In each case, concentric zones of zero to ten miles, ten to fifteen miles, and fifteen to twenty miles are the organizing principle for the data. The results of these tests are found in Tables 7–12 and 7–13.

TABLE 7–12

Change in Density of Small Trade Centers in Relation to Distance from Large Centers in Saskatchewan: 1941–1961

Distance	*1941 (Number per 1,000 sq. mi.)*	*1961 (Number per 1,000 sq. mi.)*	*Percentage of Change*
Within 10 miles	5.2	4.0	−23.1
10 to 15 miles	7.6	6.3	−17.1
15 to 20 miles	8.2	7.3	−11.0
Provincial average: all small centers	7.2	6.2	−16.7

Source: See note to Table 7–9.

TABLE 7–13

Rate of Decline among Small Trade Centers in Relation to Distance from Large Centers in Saskatchewan: 1941–1961

Distance	*Hamlet*	*Minimum Convenience**	*Full Convenience*	*Partial Shopping*	*All Small Centers*
Within 10 miles	55	81	43	100	61
10 to 15 miles	51	65	50	29	55
15 to 20 miles	36	38	24	29	38
Provincial average: all locations	46	58	34	23	51

Source: See note to Table 7–9.
*In percentages.

The data show that, in 1941 as well as in 1961, the density of small trade centers decreased with increasing proximity to large centers, thus corroborating the first point of the third hypothesis. Not until the distance was between ten and fifteen miles was the average provincial density for small centers reached in either 1941 or 1961. That this is the reflection of the debilitating effect of large centers on small nearby centers (not just the phenomenon of large centers having larger trade areas in the same goods and services dispensed by small centers) is shown by the fact that the densities of the small centers declined faster than the provincial average in both the zero to ten and ten to fifteen mile zones. There is clearly a zone of attrition of small centers up to ten miles around large centers, and the indications are that attrition may soon extend much farther out.

The data show, conversely, that small centers beyond the fifteen mile zone are much less likely to decline in density than those that are closer to a large center. This condition holds despite the fact that the small centers in the fifteen to twenty mile zone are much closer together than in the province as a whole. It would seem that, at least up to this time, the spatial or trade area integrity of small centers beyond fifteen miles is more secure.

Another way to view the effect of large centers on small centers is to examine the rate of decline in retail service levels among the various classes of small centers in the same three concentric zones, the second point of our third hypothesis. In Table 7–13 the evidence is that, for all small centers within ten miles of a large center, the rate of decline was more than 20 per cent higher than for small centers regardless of location. In the next zone out, decline of small centers was still higher than the provincial average. Small centers continued to decline in the outer zone, fifteen to twenty miles, but the rate was considerably below the provincial rate. Again, centers above the hamlet level fared worst in the period, i.e., centers more nearly in competition with their neighboring large center.

Observations made of recent changes in agriculture and rural life—depopulation, increased physical mobility, and expanded farm incomes—suggest the possibility of complementary changes in the spacing of trade centers. Depopulation reduces the number of consumers in any given trade center hinterland, thereby causing disadvantage to those centers most dependent upon a certain volume of customers to support their businesses—that is, those centers supplying day-to-day needs, such as hamlets and convenience centers. Increased mobility and income favor shopping in more distant centers offering specialized goods and services, such as partial shopping centers and above. Our fourth hypothesis is predicated on the notion that centers at the lower end of the retail service hierarchy are less in demand and so are becoming fewer and more widely spaced, and that the rising demand for goods and services of higher-ranking centers is bringing more of them into existence and at lesser intervals than heretofore. Table 7–14 presents the results of testing this hypothesis.

TABLE 7–14

Characteristic Spacing of Trade Centers of the Same Class in Saskatchewan: 1941 and 1961

Type of Center	*1941**	*1961**	*Percentage of Change*
Primary wholesale and retail	144	144	—
Secondary wholesale and retail	119.8	67.5	−43.7
Complete shopping	40.4	39.5	− 2.2
Partial shopping	25.9	22.5	−13.5
Full convenience	15.4	19.8	+22.2
Minimum convenience	10.3	13.5	+31.1
Hamlet	9.1	9.6	+ 5.5

Source: See note to Table 7–9.
*Miles apart.

In general, the fourth hypothesis is borne out: small trade centers are farther apart today than in 1941 and large centers are closer together. But other than for the general division into small and large centers, there is not a fully consistent pattern of change in the characteristic spacing of trade centers such as by increasing retail service level, by changes in density of centers, or by changes in numbers in each class. In some cases, changes in spacing appear to have been affected by areally selective tendencies. For example, complete shopping centers, although growing in numbers by more than 25 per cent since 1941, tended to emerge in areas of the province where the spacing of centers of this kind was already small. Hence, the characteristic spacing of this class of center decreased only slightly. And, as already noted, small trade centers in proximity of large centers have declined much faster than similar centers located elsewhere, and this adds further to the increase in spacing of small centers since those located close to large centers were already more widely spaced. In other cases, changes in spacing appear to be affected by local spatial tendencies, such as closeness of like-centers, or by nonspatial factors such as the population composition in the locale.

Figure 7–31 clearly shows the existence of considerable variety in the sequence of different types of trade centers in the linear arrangements that characterize the spatial distribution of centers in Saskatchewan. The variety was no less evident in 1941. Then, as now, there were many instances of two or more similar centers situated adjacent to one another along the rail lines. Given the regular spacing of centers due to the grain collection points, any pair of centers not separated by one of either higher or lower rank is almost by definition spaced less than the average distance apart for their class. The fifth, and final, hypothesis suggested that adjacent similar centers must then share their patrons and that this might prove weakening to one or both centers of the pair. Table 7–15 gives the results of applying such a test to all pairs of adjacent similar centers in the four types of centers at the lower end of the retail service hierarchy where such spacing was found in 1941.

Of the 190 pairs of similar trade centers spaced less than the mean apart for their class, 79 per cent experienced relative decline. In some cases, both centers declined, and, in other cases, one center grew and the other declined. Of the four types of lower-ranking centers, the hamlet was less affected by below-average spacing than centers in the three classes immediately above which were in comparable situations. It was also found that the rate of decline was considerably greater among centers with such spacing than for all centers of the same class. Of hamlets thus situated, 66 per cent declined from 1941 to 1961, compared to 46 per cent for all hamlets in the same period. Similar differentials of decline were found for the other types of centers studied.

The data presented in the preceding sections established the fact of fundamental changes in the

TABLE 7–15

Effect of Spacing on Adjacent Pairs of Similar Small Trade Centers in Saskatchewan: 1941–1961

Type of Trade Center	Number of Pairs of Adjacent Centers	Pairs Spaced below Mean*					
			No Change		Decline†		
		Number of Pairs	Number	%	Number	%	
Hamlet	91	87	25	29	62	71	
Minimum convenience	78	73	10	14	63	86	
Full convenience	26	26	5	20	20	80	
Partial shopping	5	5	—	—	5	100	
Total	200	190	40	21	140	79	

Source: See note to Table 7–9.
*See Table 7–14 for characteristic spacing.
†One center of pair declined or grew, or both declined.

Saskatchewan trade center system. Changes are occurring in the number of centers, the distribution of various types of centers, the density and spacing of centers, and in the performance of trade centers in certain spatial situations. These are key trends which, if they continue into the future, will significantly affect the Saskatchewan space-economy. An extrapolation of these trends will be left to the concluding section of this paper, but it is important to note here the limitations of the foregoing analysis. Projections of aggregates of all centers or classes of centers with regard to amount, kind, and location of trade center change can be made through this type of analysis. It cannot, however, help predict with precision, for example, which center of a pair spaced less than the mean distance will decline; it cannot tell us which full convenience centers will grow into partial shopping centers and which will survive. Nor can such a deductive analysis tell us which *traits* of trade centers, other than size and location, make them more conducive to growth or decline. To achieve the latter answers would have meant framing and testing innumerable hypotheses, many of which would have covered only unique situations. In order to broaden the perspective on declining trade centers, an inductive was also used; it employed a factor analysis and is reported in the next section.

Community Environment and Trade Center Viability

Many arguments from the literature on trade centers and other experience make it seem reasonable to pursue the issue that there are strong and explicable associations between the environments of trade centers and their pattern of growth and decline. The essence of these arguments is that trade centers differ from one another with respect to their environments in strategic ways that affect their ability to survive. This immediately opens up a wide realm of conjecture about the relevant influences in the environment affecting trade center decline. Indeed, in discussions in Saskatchewan preliminary to choosing a method to analyze viability, over fifty environmental variables were suggested as important to the question. The analytic problem is to determine in what "strategic and relevant" ways trade centers differ from one another, given the many possible variables against which community differences can be measured.[42] We need to do more than just recognize that such relationships exist; we need to specify the nature and strength of them and how they are related to trade center change. A factor analysis is used here to help clarify the structural relations among observable environmental characteristics. A multiple regression model is used to determine the extent to which trade center decline is related to community differences.

Dimensions of trade center communities. Thirty-five measures of community environment in the Saskatchewan portion of the Great Plains were selected for analysis. Using the technique of principal-axis factor analysis, they were condensed mathematically to three dimensions along which the individual trade centers could be arrayed, given their special configurations of characteristics. The factor analysis did not simply sort the thirty-five measures into three groups containing a certain number of characteristics in each; rather each factor gathered together statistically independent clusters of characteristics on the basis of their intercorrelations. The analytical procedure used to arrive at these dimensions is described below in terms of the variables, the universe of trade centers, the computational method, and the interpretation of the factors.

THE VARIABLES. Many variables appear to play a part in a trade center's growth or decline. Of over fifty initially investigated, many had to be rejected for lack of data despite their apparent relevance (i.e., community leadership, farm income, nonfarm employment). Others were discarded to avoid duplicate measures of the environment. Those finally selected are given in Table 7–16. Unless otherwise mentioned, the measure refers to the area within the municpal boundaries of incorporated trade centers.

Each variable was transformed into quantitative terms so that it maintained linear properties. In some cases, the variables lent themselves to numerical transformation easily as with population size or value of grain shipments. In others, the numerical measures were derived from two facets of the variables as with the many percentage and per capita measures. Still others required new scales to be conceived for the occasion, as in the railroad accessibility and level of utilities measures. Ordinal scales were sufficient in such cases.

THE UNIVERSE OF TRADE CENTERS. A total of 473 trade centers comprised the sample studied in the factor analysis. They were all of the incorporated cities, towns, and villages in Saskatchewan as of 1962, except the four largest cities. The most populous of the centers studied had just over

TABLE 7–16

Variables Used in the Factor Analysis

Demographic
1. Population size, 1961.
2. Population density, persons per gross acre, 1961.
3. Population growth rate, 1951–1961.
4. Percentage of population under 15, 1961.
5. Percentage of population over 65, 1961.
6. Sex ratio, 1961.
13. Rural population growth in the locale, 1951–1961.*
18. Rural population density in locale, 1961.

Physical development
7. Value of private investment per capita, 1961.
8. Value of investment in public utilities per capita, 1960.
9. Level of utilities index, 1960.
10. Value of private buildings per gross acre, 1961.
25. Quality of high school, 1962.
26. Hospital beds per capita, 1962.

Central-place role
11. Number of commercial establishments, 1961.
12. Distance to nearest similar center, 1961.
22. Distance to nearest neighboring center, 1961.
23. Distance to nearest regional center, 1961.
24. Distance to nearest provincial center, 1961.
29. Value of grain shipped through center, 1958.
30. Quality of rail service, 1962.
31. Highway usage at the center, 1962.

Local government quality
14. Value of local government payroll per capita, 1960.
15. Value of physical assets of the community per capita, 1960.
16. Value of local government services per capita, 1960.
17. Percentage of expenditure on administration, 1960.

Economic base
19. Agricultural land potential index, 1961.
20. Average size of farm in locale, 1961.
21. Average annual wheat yield (1941–1961) in locale.
28. Manufacturing employment, 1961.

Social
27. Membership in community cooperatives, 1961.
32. Number of professional people in the population, 1962.
33. Percentage of adults with grade eight or better education in center, 1961.
34. Percentage of adults with grade eight or better education in locale, 1961.
35. Percentage of population on social aid, 1961.

Source: See note to Table 7–9.
*Locale refers to surrounding rural municipality.

12,000 residents and the least populous had just over thirty residents. This sample represents nearly 61 per cent of the total number of trade centers extant in the province in 1961. The remainder are unincoporated, which means they are excluded from most formal data sources relied on by this study. The primary difference between these two groups is that among the incorporated places are found six types of trade centers, from hamlets to secondary wholesale-retail centers. Among the unincorporated centers are found only hamlets and minimum convenience centers; in the sample studied only 52 per cent were in the latter two categories, compared to 71 per cent in the province as a whole. The basic limitation of using any sample less than the total universe is that those not studied would have to be similarly factor analyzed in order to derive factors for them and to be able to array them on the dimensions of community environment. It was presumed that the inclusion of the generally smaller unincorporated centers, had this been possible, would not have significantly altered the results of the factor analysis.

In order to determine the effects of the local agricultural base and rural population base on the trade center, several measures of the surrounding rural municipality were included. Rural municipalities in Saskatchewan are about eighteen miles square, on the average, or a little more than one and one-half times as large as a trade area for hamlet-level goods and services. This makes them highly suitable for reporting locality characteristics of the agriculture and population.

THE COMPUTATIONAL METHOD. A rank-order matrix was constructed from the original data matrix; that is, each of the 473 communities received a rank equivalent to its numerical score on each of the thirty-five variables. Rankings were used for a number of reasons: (1) several different measurement scales were used; (2) many of the data had log-normal distributions, since most of the centers were small and generally of the same size; and (3) ranked data are not as highly demanding statistics, thus more consistent with the level of precision known to exist for the data. Rank-order correlations were calculated for each pair of variables according to Spearman's technique.[43] This constituted the input for the factor analysis.

Principal axis factor analysis, using Hotelling's iterative procedure, was employed in the calculation of the factors.[44] The correlation matrix, 35×35 was reduced to nine principal axes.[45] The nine factors were, according to this method, orthogonal. Together they accounted for 71.1 per cent of the variance present in the original correlation matrix.[46] Among the individual variables the explained variance was high: thirty-four of the thirty-five items had more than 50 per cent of their variance explained by the nine factors; twelve variables had over 80 per cent of their variance explained.

A further refinement of the factor matrix was achieved by rotating the factor matrix to orthogonal simple structure, according to the varimax criterion.[47] This process results in a maximization of the variance of the factor loadings of the variables on a factor. The procedure renders a new factor matrix in which each factor is described in terms of only those variables with which it is most highly correlated. The result, then, is a further economy in the number of truly relevant variables and affords greater ease of interpretation. For example, the principal axis solution extracted six factors that appeared relevant, and the varimax rotation reduced this to three factors. The varimax factor matrix is presented in Table 7–17.

INTERPRETING THE FACTORS. The factors extracted in the analysis resulted from the "collapse" of highly correlated items into distinctive clusters of variables. Each factor is made up of a linear combination of all variables in which the factor loadings are analogous to regression coefficients in a multiple regression equation. The factor loading is thus the measure of the degree of closeness between the variable and the factor. The largest loadings, either positive or negative, suggest the meaning of the dimension; positive loadings indicate the variable increases as the dimension increases; negative loadings indicate a decrease in the variable as the dimension increases.

The highlights of the three new dimensions of trade center environment are discussed below. An attempt is made to name them, but this should not be considered binding. It is in the nature of factor analysis that the real meaning comes out of the

TABLE 7–17

Rotated Orthogonal Factor Loadings for Trade Center Variables

	Varimax Factors									
	Urban Size	*Farm Size*				*Urban Density*				*Communa-lities*
Trade Center Variables	V_1	V_2	V_3	V_4	V_5	V_6	V_7	V_8	V_9	h^2
1. Population	67	−16	11	−23	−03	48	28	−16	−08	89
2. Population density	31	−07	13	−16	04	82	01	01	04	83
3. Population growth	19	15	38	−35	14	42	38	13	02	68
4. Population 15 and under	−02	09	88	07	13	−04	−01	04	22	85
5. Population 65 and over	08	−09	−86	−06	07	−08	08	15	13	81
6. Sex ratio	−24	18	−01	−05	60	−16	04	−08	−14	50
7. Physical investment	17	28	−45	53	04	06	−27	−04	19	71
8. Utilities investment	72	23	−01	13	−21	08	13	09	01	67
9. Utilities quality	88	14	03	10	23	21	24	00	20	99
10. Building quality	29	10	−11	14	−01	82	−14	−01	11	84
11. Retail level	67	−21	−03	−21	−01	52	19	−16	−06	87
12. Retail dominance	−02	05	00	00	−05	−03	11	07	79	66
13. Rural population growth	07	64	09	18	16	02	16	02	06	51
14. Local government payroll	79	06	−15	07	−01	04	−05	−10	−06	67
15. Community assets	75	23	−12	25	−20	07	08	06	−05	75
16. Local services	45	−06	−05	13	11	−01	−11	−66	−05	69
17. Local goverrnment adminis-tration	25	12	−07	−02	26	−33	−10	63	−05	67
18. Rural population density	13	−82	09	21	19	−03	16	00	−02	80
19. Agricultural land potential	17	−12	19	76	15	05	11	11	−25	77
20. Average farm size	04	89	00	−14	12	00	−09	03	19	87
21. Average wheat yield	16	−76	02	33	27	01	00	−06	01	80
22. Distance nearest center	−05	07	−14	−04	15	16	39	−27	38	44
23. Distance regional center	37	−01	−06	−55	25	12	−19	12	−01	58
24. Distance provincial center	11	−03	13	−18	24	08	−28	−17	55	54
25. High school quality	65	−11	10	−22	−01	43	18	−14	−09	75
26. Hospital quality	69	01	03	−04	39	35	14	−08	20	82
27. Cooperative participation	22	04	07	09	76	16	11	07	27	75
28. Manufacturing employment	79	−02	04	04	35	23	21	−07	15	87
29. Value grain shipped	32	13	−05	35	−01	58	06	−18	−04	61
30. Rail accessibility	29	−03	−04	09	13	02	66	05	05	53
31. Road accessibility	31	−06	03	05	08	−04	68	−03	−04	58
32. Professional people	66	−22	03	−16	−03	37	22	−14	−09	73
33. Educational attainment, town	22	65	17	19	18	−06	−07	11	−09	60
34. Educational attainment, farm	10	76	04	22	16	01	05	11	−07	69
35. Social aid load	36	−22	15	−14	13	−06	01	−57	10	57
*Absolute contribution of factor**	692	394	208	208	183	319	186	151	154	
Percentage contribution of factor	28	16	8	8	7	13	7	6	6	

Source: See note to Table 7–9.
Decimal points have been omitted.
*The sum of the squared factor loadings.

degree to which extant community relationships are described by the factors. The names, therefore, are descriptive labels, and, indeed, each factor is a mathematical statement of relationships of all the environmental variables used in the analysis.

DIMENSION 1: URBAN SIZE (V_1). This dimension has significant loadings on eleven of the thirty-five measures.[48] High positive loadings on items of population size, level and investment in utilities, level of retail services, quality of high school and hospital, manufacturing employment, number of professional people, assests of the community, and local government payroll clearly distinguish a syndrome of *urban* characteristics in this dimension. Lesser loadings on population density, community services, and social aid case load further support this interpretation. Moreover, it seems to point up distinctions between centers more or less on the basis of size. The absence of high loadings on any of the various measures of agricultural development suggests that a high degree of urban development in this region is not dependent upon the local agricultural base. It is also noteworthy that none of the four locational variables emerges with high loadings among these urban characteristics, thus indicating that urban development is not significantly associated with either relative isolation or proximity to other centers.

DIMENSION 2: FARM SIZE (V_2). The second dominant dimension distinguishes those communities in which there has been a high degree of the adaptation of the farming in the locale to the exigencies of a highly mechanized and commercialized agriculture, as exemplified by the large farm. High positive loadings on average farm size, rural population growth, and educational attainment of country and town indicate a willingness and ability to make adjustments. High negative loadings on farm population density and average wheat yields indicate, respectively, that density decreases with increasing farm size and that adjustment to larger farm size is more advanced in areas of low yield.

DIMENSION 3: URBAN DENSITY (V_6). This dimension is characterized by high loadings on population density and quality of buildings (the value of buildings per acre). Also closely associated with this factor, and significantly different from the Urban Size dimension, are the variables of population growth and value of grain shipments. The variables of population size, high school quality, and number of professional people also show up as closely associated with this factor. This dimension appears to describe another aspect of urban development. It is by definition orthogonal to the dimension of Urban Size, although some variables are collinear. Trade centers characterized by this trait would display compact development as well as possess a range of commercial buildings which represent relatively higher private investment than other centers. Such centers are growing in population and are focal points for grain shipments.

The three dimensions extracted in this analysis account for most of the variance in the twenty-four of the original thirty-five variables. They also account for nearly 60 per cent of the variance in the factor matrix. The remaining factors each contain no more than two variables with significant loadings, and, furthermore, they resist easy interpretation on other than the grounds that they reflect unique trade center situations. We can also say that as many as eleven variables of those studied play little or no important role in distinguishing among trade centers in the province. Hence, we are left with three factors in terms of which each trade center may be classified; these can be viewed as *environmental traits* which each center possesses to one degree or another.

The relative position of each center on the three dimensions was established in order to determine whether some fundamental structure of trade center communities had been derived or whether the factors were only mathematical conveniences. Factor scores in the form of canonical variates were obtained for each center by using the original rank of the center on each variable and the factor loadings of the variables. Thus, a center's score on Dimension 1 = (.67) (rank of center in the population size) + (.31) (rank of center in population density) + (.19) (rank of center in population growth), and so on through all thirty-five variables. Scores for centers on Dimensions 2 and 3 were obtained in the same manner.

An examination of center scores indicated that

these dimensions did represent basic structural features of trade center environment in Saskatchewan. Dimensions 1 and 3 each mirror the province's pattern of urbanization; the largest and most well-developed places fall high on these two scales and the converse is true for the typical small hamlet. Furthermore, there is a strong correlation between the position of centers on the two scales, ($r = .87$). Dimension 2 reveals centers arrayed by agricultural regions such as soil and climatic zones. Two of the dimensions thus provide a way of describing urban aspects of trade center development, and the other of describing trade-center relationships to the local agricultural base.

Community differences and trade center change. The three apparently valid dimensions of trade center communities may now be tested to determine whether, and to what degree, they are associated with trade center change. If, as claimed at the outset, trade center change is dependent upon certain features in the community environment, then the canonical variates may be treated as independent variables in a multiple regression model which tests this hypothesis. In a regression equation of the typical form, the Y_i are the dependent variables of trade center change, and the X_j are the canonical variates on each of the three dimensions.

Two regression analyses were completed,[49] one to determine the ability to predict change in retail service level, Y_1, and the other to predict change in population, Y_2. Changes in retail service level for the regression analysis were measured in terms of changes in the number of business firms from 1941 to 1961. The latter scale was used because it could be calibrated more finely than one using just change in trade center class. Population change was also measured for 1941 to 1961. For each of these dependent variables, an index was constructed on which 100 equaled no change in the period, less than 100 equaled decline, and greater than 100 equaled some degree of growth. The variables used in the analyses are listed in Table 7–18.

The results of the regressions show a rather inconclusive picture regarding the relationship of community environmental differences, as measured by the factor scores and trade center changes in the 1941 to 1961 period. Table 7–19 presents these results. On the one hand, they indicate several highly significant statistical relationships, i.e., at less than the .001 level. The position of centers on the Urban Density scale is highly significant in terms of both dependent variables. The position of centers on the Farm Size scale is also highly significant with respect to Y_1, but shows no strong relationship to Y_2 population change. Centers on the Urban Size scale show a significant relationship, at the .05 level, with both dependent variables. On the other hand, the coefficients of determination, R^2, obtained in both regressions are not overly large. The regression

TABLE 7–18

Variables Used in Two Regression Analyses

Y_1 = Index of change in number of retail and service establishments in the center, 1941 to 1961.
Y_2 = Index of population change, 1941 to 1961.
x_1 = Canonical variates for trade centers on factor one, V_1.
x_2 = Canonical variates for trade centers on factor two, V_2.
x_3 = Canonical variates for trade centers on factor three, V_6.
b_0 = The intercept of Y at $x = 0$.
B_j = Amount to be added to an estimate of Y_i if trade center has a value of unity on x_j variable.

Source: See note to Table 7–9.

TABLE 7–19

Results of Two Regression Analyses

Independent Variables	*Regression Y_1 Change in Number of Retail Firms*		*Regression Y_2 Change in Population*	
	B_j	*T Value*	B_j	*T Value*
X_1 Urban size	0.1397	1.7888*	−0.1728	−2.0927*
X_2, Farm size	−0.1458	−3.8306†	0.0385	0.3869
X_3, Urban density	0.4161	5.3084†	0.0789	8.8872†
Intercept b_0	42.74		84.79	
R_2 Coefficient of determination	0.3308		0.3175	

Source: See note to Table 7–9.
*B_j is significant at the 5 per cent level.
†B_j is significant at the 0.1 per cent level.

model, insofar as these coefficients are presumed to be measures of the power of the model to predict, is slightly more powerful in predicting change in the number of retail firms, .3308, than change in population, .3175. However, the exploratory nature of this investigation, the tentativeness of the hypotheses leading up to it, and the fact that several highly significant relationships were found seem to justify pursuing these results further.

An examination of the substance of the regression relationships reveals that the position of a trade center on the Urban Density scale is more closely related to trade center change (of either kind) than a center's position on the other two scales. The linear relationship that can be derived from the results — $Y_1 = 42.74 + .4161(x_3)$ — is presented in Fig. 7–33. That is, the analysis suggests that it is a particular aspect of urban development, as measured by this scale, that is important in determining the growth or decline, the viability, of trade centers. The scale, it will be remembered, is dominated by two items: gross population density of the built-up area of the center and the assessed valuation, or private physical investment, per acre over the same area. The scale is also structured on several other items of an urban or central place nature. Although several of the items are also found highly weighted on the Urban Size scale, the cluster of variables on the Urban Density scale is statistically and substantively different from the former scale. Indeed, the generally weaker relationship of the Urban Size scale to trade center change suggests that size of a trade center alone is not sufficient to guarantee its viability.

It is not surprising that there is considerable association manifested between the degree of urban development as measured by the Urban Density scale and performance of a trade center as a commercial place. We have become, even in agricultural regions, a highly industrialized and urbanized society. Economic development in North America acts to intensify the possibilities for growth at urban places. But it is also axiomatic that not all centers can expect to share in the possibilities for growth; many, whose urban accoutrements are meager and quality of physical development is not high, start with a handicap in attracting investment and population. The particular qualities of urban development that are associated with trade center viability must be determined and the status of communities measured. The dimension of Urban Density seems to provide important clues in this direction even if it does not provide a definitive answer.

The usefulness of the Urban Density scale in making predictions about trade center viability may be given further credence upon comparison with results obtained in the deductive analysis.

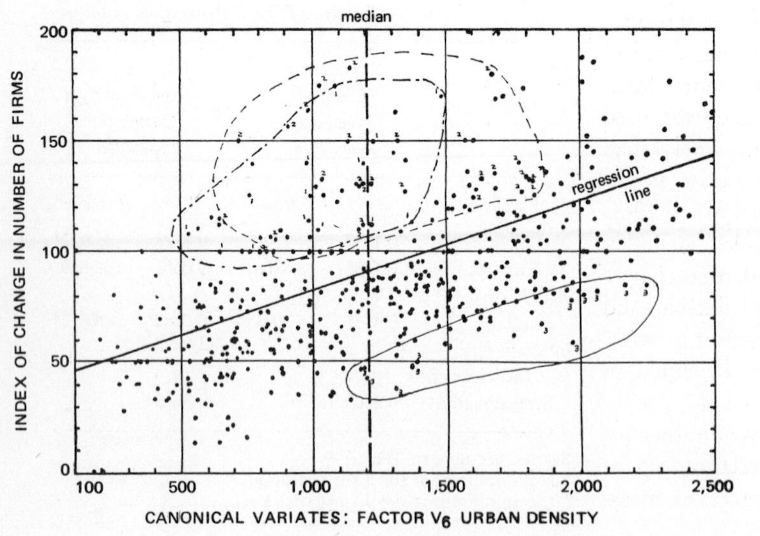

FIGURE 7–33. Urban density and trade center changes in Saskatchewan: 1941 to 1961. *Source:* See caption for Fig. 7–31.

First, it can be ascertained how well the scale distinguishes those classes of trade centers we know to be experiencing decline, and, second, it can be ascertained if the scale distinguishes centers known to be vulnerable to decline according to their location. The two classes known to be experiencing the greatest degree of decline in the 1941–1961 period, i.e., minimum convenience centers and hamlets, in most cases have factor scores below the median. Hamlets, in 85 per cent of the cases fall into the lowest two quintiles, and 87 per cent of the minimum convenience centers are in the lowest three quintiles. Full convenience centers, apparently reflecting their tendency to experience both growth and decline, have large proportions above and below the median. The remaining higher classes of centers have scores mostly in the top two quintiles; only 11 per cent of the partial shopping centers have scores below the top two quintiles.

Trade center performance derived from the deductive analysis also shows that small trade centers are more vulnerable to decline when in close proximity to large centers. Two-thirds of the centers in the sample located within ten miles of a large center have factor scores that put them in the lowest two quintiles, and 95 per cent of such centers are no higher than the third quintile. In the ten-to-fifteen mile zone, two-thirds of the centers in the sample have scores in the lowest two quintiles, but, because centers in this zone are less subject to decline, almost 20 per cent in this zone are in the top two quintiles. The fifteen-to-twenty mile zone shows no regular pattern of scores, much as it shows no regular pattern of trade center changes. The fairly high coincidence of results between the deductive analysis and the factor analysis seems to justify substantial confidence in the validity of the Urban Density scale to make measurements that have significance in determining trade center viability.

This leads naturally to the question of calibrating the scale of Urban Density in relation to trade center viability. To be most useful we would like to know which points on this scale set off different degrees of viability so that the individual centers could be related. It must be remembered that the factors are only ordinal in nature, and, in deference to the limits of ordinal scaling and to the tentative results of the inductive analysis, a division of scale values only into quintiles has been chosen. It is important to note that the quintile divisions coincide closely with values on the index of change in retail firms which are meaningful for describing growth and decline of centers (see Table 7–20).

Many of the apparent inconsistencies of high index of change values among centers in the low quintiles and low index values in high quintiles can generally be explained by differences in subre-

TABLE 7–20

Calibration of the Urban Density Scale in Terms of Changes in Retail Service Level

Trade Center Quintile		*Index of Change in Number of Retail Firms**		*Scale Value Urban Density*	
Number	*Number of Centers*	*Range*	*Mean*	*Range*	*Suggested Level of Viability*
1 (top)	94	58–226	115	1771–3501	Good
2	95	50–169	96	1381–1770	Moderately good
3	95	33–183	89	1031–1380	Transitional
4	95	16–300	78	690–1030	Moderately poor
5 (bottom)	94	1–116	55	107– 689	Poor
Complete scale	473	1–300	87.6	107–3501	

Source: See note to Table 7–9.
*Index of 100 equals no change, 1941–1961; more than 100 equals growth; less than 100 equals loss in number of retail firms.

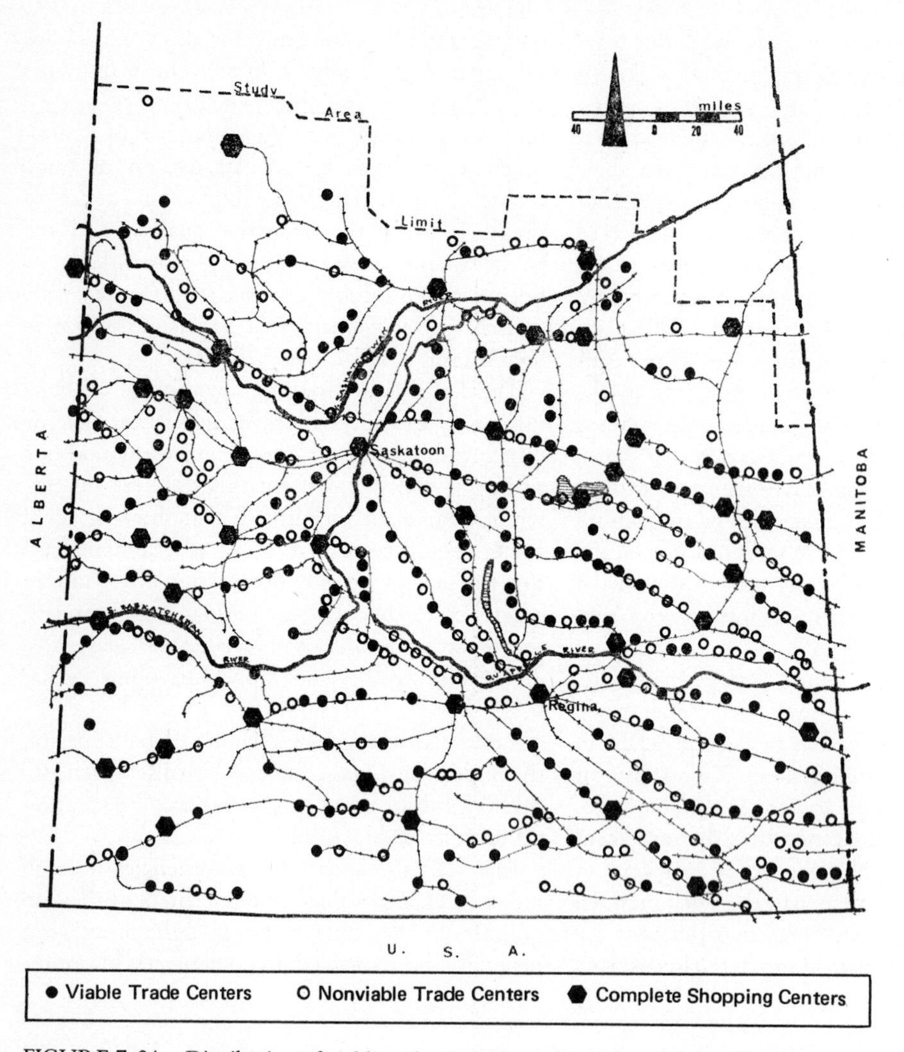

FIGURE 7–34. Distribution of viable and nonviable trade centers (in incorporated places only). *Source:* See caption for Fig. 7–31.

gional development and by unique local conditions. For example, most of the centers exhibiting a high rate of growth in the number of retail firms but also having low scores on the Urban Density scale are likely to be one of two types: they are either centers that are located in recently developed areas of the northern fringe of the province, or they are centers that have been subject to the effects of recent expansion in the exploitation of natural resources such as oil or potash. In both such situations, the demands on the community to expand its range of retail services has outstripped the ability to acquire urban accoutrements. A number of centers that have high scale values of urban density combined with a low index of change are known to be centers that reached a fairly high degree of urban development before 1941 but have since declined in retail level because of the competition of nearby cities. The effect of identifying these three types of centers on the regression graph dramatically reduces the scatter of the data, Fig. 7–33.

Finally, it is possible to map the incidence of trade center viability according to positions on the Urban Density scale. Figure 7–34 presents the graphic picture of trade center viability for the 473 incorporated centers used in the factor analysis. They have been classified in terms of Viable and Nonviable with respect to factor scores above and below the median, respectively. Although this does not provide a rating for all centers in the province, it is reasonable to assume that the remaining unincorporated centers, which are generally very small and poorly developed, would be rated as Nonviable by this scale. The map's most striking feature is the regularity in spacing of the Viable Centers. They are approximately fifteen miles apart on the average. And according to this map there are no regions of nonviability in the province; rather, there appears to be a "filtering out" of the Nonviable Centers in all areas resulting in this regular spacing.

Implications for Policy and Theory

On the basis of the deductive analysis, it is possible to suggest what the future holds for the Saskatchewan trade center system. Four conclusions seem warranted (see Fig. 7–35). First, the number of centers will decrease by 110 to 180; the first number assuming a continuation of the aggregate rate of change from 1941 to 1961 and the second assuming that the rate of decline among hamlets continues to rise as it has since 1941. Second, the two types of convenience centers will all but disappear in the next two decades, while partial and complete shopping centers will grow by 20 to 30 per cent in number. Third, except for a limited amount of "suburbanization" around the largest cities, small trade centers will likely disappear within a radius of ten miles of large

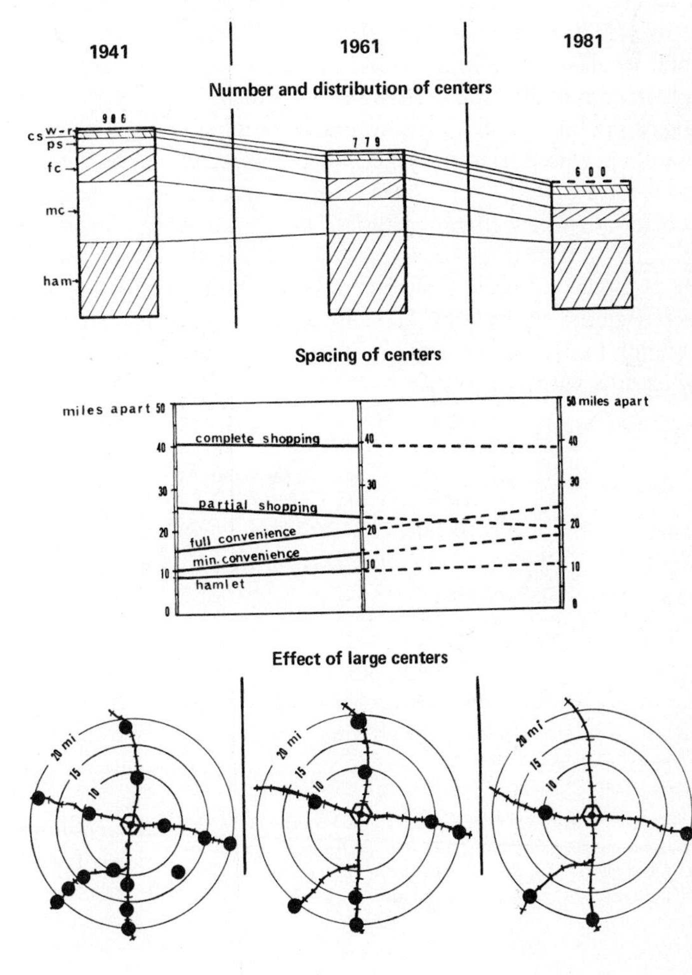

FIGURE 7–35. Projected changes in trade centers. *Source:* See caption for Fig. 7–31.

trade centers and will show substantial decline in areas up to fifteen miles away. Fourth, as the thinning out of small centers continues, rural residents will have to travel as much as one-third farther to reach a center offering day-to-day needs. Higher-order centers may not be much closer together but will be more regularly spaced.

The Urban Density scale which proved to be the most significant of those derived in the factor analysis helps to provide a substantive basis for understanding the lack of viability in trade centers. The scale is constituted of several variables that impinge on important public policy areas, and these might be amenable to policy decisions to alter the prospects for growth or decline among selected centers. For instance, the scale gives considerable weight to two measures of density both of which are areas of direct concern in community planning. The importance of the center as a grain shipment point is also strongly related to its viability, according to the scale. This last point would seem to come under consideration in light of current discussions on the abandonment of branch rail lines. Lastly, the importance of a high school and a hospital to a trade center as evidenced by the scale suggests the need for a location strategy regarding these facilities. In all these cases, it will have to be a strategy that allows both the possibility of decline of trade centers hosting such facilities as well as the allocation of the facilities to strengthen the position of centers which it is wished to sustain.

*ADVANCED CONCEPTS: A PROBABILITY MODEL FOR CENTRAL-PLACE LOCATIONS**

The applicability of central-place theory is limited by two major weaknesses. On one hand, the theory pertains only to urban systems composed of central places providing service and market activities; it does not incorporate such important urban activities as manufacturing, nor does it take into account such important economic aspects of urbanization as agglomeration and scale economies. On the other hand, the theory is algebraic and, hence, deterministic rather than probabilistic; because it does not allow for any deviations from precisely stated relations and locations, there is no chance of accumulating evidence verifying the theory. This section is directed to the latter limitation as it pertains to the location of central places.

An important property of the theory is the honeycomb network of central places. Some students reject the hexagonal pattern, but without providing an alternative system; most students, however, accept the hexagonal properties. Although it is unimaginable that any urban system conforms exactly to the hexagonal pattern, [the fact that] many empirical studies have reported patterns in approximation to theory is interpreted as an underlying or pervasive tendency towards the honeycomb network, and deviations from the idealized pattern [are thought to] occur because various physical, economic, and political conditions required by the theory are not satisfied in the real world. There is no statement on central places that makes explicit such deviations or that describes the resulting pattern of places.

What is needed is the formulation of a central-place model that allows for deviations from the precise lattice locations. This model is consistent with many classical aspects of central-place theory while possessing characteristics more likely to be found in the real world. Deviations from the hexagonal network are obtained by interpreting the lattice as an equilibrium state, whereas the realized locations of central place are stochastic (random) displacements from the lattice positions.

As in central-place theory, central places are treated as punctiform entities. This probabilistic central-place model is formulated as a type of two-dimensional stochastic point process obtained by combining a random element with the hexagonal point lattice. Lattice points identify equilibrium positions, and the realized position of each central-place point is defined by a random displacement from its equilibrium

*Reprinted from Michael F. Dacey, "A Probability Model for Central Place Locations," *Annals of the Association of American Geographers*, LVI, No. 4 (December, 1966), 550–68, with the permission of the author and editor.

position. The displacement is defined by a vector, and the angular and distance components of this vector are random variables. To obtain the realized position of a central-place point, the origin of the vector is placed at that place's equilibrium position and the location of the displaced point is given by the angular and distance components of the vector. The probability law describing vector displacement may be selected so that central-place points tend to be located in the neighborhood of their equilibrium positions, and the resulting point pattern retains, at the visual level, the underlying hexagonal structure. Alternatively, for a large mean displacement distance the hexagonal genesis of the resulting point pattern is vestigial.

A stochastic process generating this type of point pattern is identified, and the resulting pattern is described by the spacing between neighboring points. The general form of spacing measures is obtained and this expression may be used with a variety of probabilistic interpretations for central-place patterns. Because these results are too general for numerical analysis, one type of stochastic process, contained within the general model, is considered in detail. The displacement from equilibrium position is related to the normal probability law and this Gaussian formulation is probably the basic stochastic interpretation of central-place theory. Although some statements of spacing measures are obtained in closed form, other results are mathematically intractable (for this writer, at least) and a Monte Carlo experiment for estimating spacing measures is also described.

The Basic Model

An explicit statement of the postulates and theorems of central-place theory has been given by Dacey.[50] For this interpretation of central places, only the basic locational property is required: the points representing central places form the vertices of equilateral triangles.

Let H denote this hexagonal point lattice, and by choosing an arbitrary lattice point as origin of the lattice, labeled 0, all other points in H may be identified by vectors. Let $h(u, v)$ denote an element of H, and the vector identification of this point is:

$$\cdot u\vec{i} + v\vec{j} \cdot \tag{1}$$

where u and v are specified integers and $\vec{i}$ and $\vec{j}$ are vectors of unit length and separated by an angle of $2\pi/3$ radians.

Using brackets to denote a collection, the point set H may be identified as:

$$H = \{ \cdot u\vec{i} + v\vec{j} \cdot \} \tag{2}$$

where u and v run through the set of integers.

The prediction of a hexagonal network for central places is predestined to rejection upon empirical investigation, because it is inconceivable that any observed pattern of places conforms precisely to the lattice structure. Some degree of realism is obtained by considering an imperfect central-place system. An imperfect central-place system is obtained by using a shock or disturbance effect to displace each point from its exact lattice site to a nearby location. For this construction, the hexagonal lattice identifies equiblibrium positions of central-place points whereas the realized positions of central-place points are the outcomes of the displacements.

Let M denote the point set obtained as the outcome of the displacement of each point in H. There is a one-to-one correspondence between elements of M and H, and let $m(u, v)$ denote that element of M which corresponds to $h(u, v)$. The symbol $(\vec{rt})_{uv}$ is the vector notation for the displacement associated with the point $h(u, v)$.

The disturbed or displaced point $m(u, v)$ may be identified as:

$$\cdot u\vec{i} + v\vec{j} + (\vec{rt})_{uv} \cdot \tag{3}$$

and the collection of displaced points is:

$$M = \{ \cdot u\vec{i} + v\vec{j} + (\vec{rt})_{uv} \cdot \} \tag{4}$$

The point set M identifies an imperfect central place system.

The displacement vector $(rt)_{uv}$ may be defined in different ways. For development of a probabilistic central-place model, $(\vec{rt})_{uv}$ is interpreted as having a specified probability distribution. Although not an inherent limitation, it is assumed for this study that all displacements are outcomes from a single probability distribution. This means only stationary processes are studied, and this is reflected in the notation by replacing $(\vec{rt})_{uv}$ with the briefer symbol rt, so that M may be defined as:

$$M = \{ \cdot u\vec{i} + v\vec{j} + r\vec{t} \cdot \} \qquad (4a)$$

Spacing measures on M are obtained first for the displacement vector defined by an arbitrary population. There is a more detailed discussion of the special case of a normally distributed distance component and a uniformly distributed angular component.

Distance Relations in M: *General Case*

The major results obtained in this section are expressions for: (1) the distance from an arbitrarily selected point of M to the *ith* nearest point; and (2) the distance from an arbitrarily selected coordinate location to the *jth* nearest point. To obtain these results it is assumed that points are generally displaced only a short distance (relative to the translation period of the hexagonal lattice) from their equilibrium positions; hence, displaced points tend to be located in the neighborhood of their equilibrium positions. This is not viewed as a severe restriction; if this assumption is not tenable, an imperfect central-place model is probably not a useful formulation for central places.

The reasons for describing M by order distances may not be clear, though the reason for not using mean distance between points in M is obvious. The M contains an infinite number of points in a conceptually unbounded plane and the expected distance between any two arbitrarily selected points is infinite. To obtain a mean distance with finite value, it is necessary to define distance measures for points in a bounded region or by a locational property identifying specific types of points. The ordering of distances from an origin point or sample locus is particularly convenient for summarizing both observed and theoretical point patterns; theoretical patterns because order distance may be derived with not overly restrictive conditions and observed patterns because measured distances may be ordered even though the equilibrium positions of points may not be known.

Point to point distances. In the following discussion it is convenient to use rectangular coordinates, largely because the expression for distance between two points has a simpler form than in polar coordinates. The distribution function of distance between two arbitrary points is found, and this result is related to the hexagonal point lattice.

Let $Y = (y, y')$ and $Z = (z, z')$ denote two points with distribution functions $F(Y)$ and $G(Z)$, respectively. The probability that the distance between the two points is not greater than R is obtained by integrating the product of the two density functions over an offset circle with radius R:

$$F(R) = \int_{-\infty}^{\infty} \int_{D_1} dF(Y)\, dG(Z) \qquad (5)$$

where D_1 is the disk defined by:

$$(y - z)^2 + (y' - z')^2 \leq R^2$$

Integrals of the form of Eq. (5) have been extensively studied in terms of coverage and bombing problems. Guenther and Terragno recently reviewed this literature and provided an extensive bibliography.[51]

Points in M are distributed around specified lattice positions so that a more explicit expression for distance may be obtained. Let $X_0 = (a + x, b + y)$ and $X_0' = (a + a' + x', b + b' + y')$ denote two points in M with equilibrium positions (a, b) and $(a + a', b + b')$, respectively. The two points have the same distribution function for distance about their lattice positions and differ only by having equilibrium positions separated by a distance $(a'^2 + b'^2)^{1/2}$. Since the displacement vector is independent of location, X_0 and X_0' have the same relative positions as the points $X = (x, y)$ and $X' = (a' + x', b' + y')$. Accordingly, to evaluate the distance between any two points with equilibrium position distance k $(k^2 = a'^2$

$+ b'^2$) apart, the points X and X' may be considered. The equilibrium position of X is taken as the origin of the lattice, and the equilibrium position of the other point is offset a distance k. Let $F(X, 0)$ and $F(X', k)$ denote the distribution functions of the points X and X', respectively, about the origin of the lattice.

Then, the integral of Eq. (5) may be written in the more explicit form:

$$F(R; k) = \int_{-\infty}^{\infty} \int_{D_2} dF(X; 0)\, dF(X'; k) \quad (6)$$

where $k^2 = a'^2 + b'^2$, and D_2 is the disk defined by:

$$(x - a' - x')^2 + (y - b' - y')^2 \leq R^2$$

For the purposes of this analysis near neighbor distances are most interesting, and distance from X to its six neighboring points is obtained. Let X'_i, $i = 1(1)6$, denote the position in M of any one point with equilibrium position unit distance from the origin of the lattice. The distribution function for X is $F(X; 0)$ and the distribution function for any X'_i is $F(X'; 1)$. The probability that X and any X'_i, are within distance R is obtained from Eq. (6) by putting $k = 1$.

Suppose the displacement is defined so that with probability approaching 1 each displaced point is closer to its equilibrium position than to any other lattice site; that is, the distribution functions are such that:

$$F(.5; 0),\ F(.5; 1) \approx 1 \quad (7)$$

Then, with probability approaching 1, the six nearest points to a selected point X in M will be points displaced from lattice sites unit distance away and, hence, with the common distribution function $F(R, 1)$. Under these assumptions, distance from an arbitrary point X to each of the six nearest points in M has the distribution function $F(R, 1)$. Since the displacements are independent events, the six distances may be interpreted as a sample of size six from a single population. The six observations are ordered from shortest to longest, and let $F(R_{i6}; 1)$ denote the distribution of the *ith* smallest distance. From properties of order statistics it is known that the density function of R_{i6} is:

$$dF(R_{i6}; I) = \frac{6!}{(i-1)!\,(6-i)!} F^{i-1}(R; 1) \times [1 - F(R; 1)]^{6-i} dF(R; 1) \quad (8)$$

when $i = 1(1)6$.

Assuming that the displacement distance is small relative to the lattice dimension, Eq. (8) is, to a high approximation, the density function of distance from an arbitrary point in M to the *ith* nearest point. This expression may be evaluated analytically for displacement vectors defined by at least some probability distributions.

Locus to point distances. Point to point order distances are only one type of spacing measure used to describe a pattern. A second spacing measure is based upon distance from a sample point randomly located in the pattern to the *ith* nearest point belonging to the pattern. Spacing measures from sample points are obtained, and to avoid confusion between sample points and points legitimately belonging to M, a sample point is called a locus.

Suppose a locus is randomly placed within a hexagonal lattice. Because of the periodicity of a lattice, this locus is necessarily placed in an equilateral triangle with sides of unit length and vertices defined by points of the hexagonal lattice. Further, the three nearest lattice points to the locus are vertices of the equilateral triangle in which the locus is located. By assuming, as for point to point distance, that the displacement distance is small relative to the translation period of the lattice, distance from the locus to the three nearest points in M is derived.

First, consider a locus A' with fixed location (a', b') in M and a point $X' = (x, y)$ with equilibrium position distance ω from A'. Let $F(X'; 0)$ denote the distribution function of X' around its equilibrium position. Then, the probability, written $G(Z; \omega)$, that A' and X' are within distance Z is given by the integral of $F(X'; 0)$ over an offset circle with radius Z, or:

$$G(Z; \omega) = \int_{D_3} dF(X'; 0) \quad (9)$$

where D_3 is the disk defined by:

$$(x - a')^2 + (y - b')^2 \leq Z^2$$

The integral in Eq. (9) differs from that in Eqs. (5) and (6) because the position of one point, the locus A', is fixed.

Let A denote a sample locus, and it does not have a fixed position; instead, the distance from A to the equilibrium position of point X' is a random variable. Denote by $F(\omega)$ the probability that A is less than distance ω from a specified equilibrium position. The probability that A and X' are within distance R is obtained by integrating Eq. (9) with respect to ω; that is, since the order of integration is arbitrary:

$$\begin{aligned} G(R; \omega) &= \int_{D_3} \int_{-\infty}^{\infty} dF(X'; 0)\, dF(\omega) \\ &= \int_{-\infty}^{\infty} G(Z; \omega)\, dF(\omega) \end{aligned} \tag{10}$$

The distribution function of ω is found by a simple geometric derivation and is given in Dacey.[52] The result is:

$$\begin{aligned} F(\omega) &= \frac{2\pi\omega^2}{3\sqrt{3}}, \qquad \left[0 < \omega < \frac{\sqrt{3}}{2}\right] \\ &= \frac{2\pi\omega^2}{3\sqrt{3}} - \left(\frac{4\omega^2}{\sqrt{3}}\right) \times \cos^{-1}\left(\frac{\sqrt{3}}{2\omega}\right) \\ &\quad + 2\left(\omega^2 - \frac{3}{4}\right)^{1/2}, \left[\frac{\sqrt{3}}{2} < \omega < 1\right] = 0 \\ &\qquad [\text{elsewhere}] \end{aligned} \tag{11}$$

The distribution function $G(R; \omega)$ applies to the distance from A to each of the three points displaced from lattice points forming vertices of the triangle containing A. Since displacements are independent, distances from A to the three displaced points are independent observations from the same population. When these distances are ordered from shortest to largest, they are order statistics from $G(R; \omega)$. Let $G(R_{j3}; \omega)$ denote the distribution function for the *jth* order distance and from properties of order statistics:

$$\begin{aligned} dG(R_{j3}; \omega) &= \frac{3!}{(j-1)!(3-j)!} \times G^{j-1}(R; \omega) \\ &\quad \times [1 - G(R; \omega)]^{3-j} \times dG(R; \omega) \end{aligned} \tag{12}$$

when $j = 1(1)3$.

Assuming that the displacement distance is small relative to the lattice dimension so that Eq. (7) holds, $G(R_{j3}; \omega)$ is, to a high approximation, the distribution function of distance from a randomly located locus to the *jth* nearest point in M. In terms of formal mathematical structure, this integral is not appreciably more difficult to evaluate than the corresponding integral in Eq. (8) for point to point distances; however, in practice, numerical evaluation may be more difficult because Eq. (12) generally yields expressions not as well-known as those obtained from Eq. (8).

Spacing ratio. The index for *gth* order spacing measures is obtained by taking the ratio of the expectations of point to point and locus to point distances. In symbols, the *gth* order index is:

$$S_g = \frac{\int R\, dF(R_{g6}; 1)}{\int R\, dG(R_{g3}; 1)} \qquad [g = 1(1)3] \tag{13}$$

Although I cannot construct a proof, I believe it is correct to assert that for any M having a displacement vector with a uniformly distributed angular component the S_1, at least, is greater than unity.

The spacing ratio is a particularly useful measure for summarizing an observed point pattern. For comparison of observed and theoretical point patterns, observed point to point order distances must be in the same metric as values calculated for M. The usual procedure for standardizing observed distances is to multiply each measured distance by the square root of density of points. However, standardized distances are subject to sampling and other types of error because an accurate estimate of the density of points on an actual map pattern is frequently difficult to obtain. The spacing ratio does not require standarized distances because the quotient of two measurements in arbitrary (but the same) units is automatically expressed in standardized units directly comparable with theoretical measurements on M. For this reason spacing ratios are the recommended basis for evaluating the correspondence of calculated values to an observed map pattern, but this recommendation may not always be practical because the sampling distribution of S_g may be difficult to determine.

Distance Relations in M*: Normal Distribution*

The determination of spacing measures for a specified M requires, on one hand, the identification of the distribution function underlying the displacement vector $\vec{rt}$ and, on the other hand, evaluation of the distribution functions $F(R_{i6}; k)$ and $G(R_{j3}; \omega)$. The evaluation of these integrals is considered for the special case where $m(u, v)$ is normally distributed around $h(u, v)$. To say that a point is "normally distributed" around a fixed point in two-dimensional space is not an unambiguous statement and two interpretations are considered.

The probability distributions considered in this section may be summarized in the following way. Let r and t denote the distance and angular components of the disturbance vector $\vec{rt}$. The angle t, measured in radians, is uniformly distributed in the range 0 to 2π. The distance r, measured in the metric of the lattice H, depends upon a specified parameter σ, and the quantity r/σ has the Helmert distribution with either 1 or 2 degrees of freedom or, alternatively, the quantity r^2/σ^2 is distributed as chi-square with 1 or 2 degrees of freedom. These alternative expressions for displacement of central place points are obtained by interpreting the normal probability law in terms of polar and rectangular coordinates.

Displacement may be defined by the polar coordinates r' and t. The angular component t is uniformly distributed in the range 0 to π, and the distance component r' is normally distributed with mean 0 and standard deviation σ. Alternatively, t is uniformly distributed in the range 0 to 2π, and r' has the folded half-normal distribution with parameter σ. Density functions for the latter conditions are:

$$\begin{cases} dF(t) = (2\pi)^{-1} & [0 < t < 2\pi] \\ dF(r') = \left[\dfrac{\sqrt{2}}{\sigma\sqrt{\pi}}\right] \times e^{-r'^2/2\sigma^2} & [\sigma > 0] \\ & [0 < r' < \infty] \end{cases} \quad (14)$$

The circular normal or uncorrelated bivariate normal distribution may also be used to define displacement. An orthogonal $X - Y$ axis is superimposed over the hexagonal lattice H and the metric is defined by the translation period of the lattice. The probability that a point is within x units of its equilibrium position on the X axis is:

$$F(x) = \frac{1}{\sigma_x(2\pi)^{1/2}} \int_{-x}^{x} e^{-x^2/2\sigma_x^2} dx$$

and the probability that the point is displaced y units from its equilibrium position on the Y axis is:

$$F(y) = \frac{1}{\sigma_y(2\pi)^{1/2}} \int_{-y}^{y} e^{-y^2/2\sigma_y^2} dy$$

In order to satisfy the requirement that the angular component is uniformly distributed, it is necessary that $\sigma = \sigma_x = \sigma_y$. Put $p^2 = x^2 + y^2$. The density functions of t and p are:

$$\begin{cases} dF(t) = (2\pi)^{-1} & [0 < t < 2\pi] \\ dF(p) = \dfrac{pe^{-p/2\sigma^2}}{\sigma^2} & [\sigma > 0] \\ & [0 < p < \infty] \end{cases} \quad (15)$$

The Helmert distribution with parameters n and σ may be written:

$$dF(x; n, \sigma) = \frac{2x^{n-1}}{(2\sigma^2)^{n/2}\Gamma\left(\dfrac{n}{2}\right)} e^{-x^2/2\sigma^2}$$

So, r' has the Helmert distribution when $n = 1$ and p has the Helmert distribution when $n = 2$.

The distribution of x may also be written in terms of the chi-square distribution with parameter n:

$$dF(x; n, \sigma) = dH\left(\frac{x^2}{\sigma^2}; n\right) = \frac{x^{n-1/2}e^{-x^2/2}}{2^{n/2}\Gamma\left(\dfrac{n}{2}\right)}$$

So, r'^2/σ^2 and p^2/σ^2 have chi-square distributions with 1 and 2 degrees of freedom, respectively. In order to use the well-tabulated chi-square distribution, measures on M are frequently related to standardized distance squared.

The two interpretations of "normally distributed" may be considered in one formulation by specifying that the angular component t of the disturbance vector is uniformly distributed in the range 0 to 2π and the distance component r of the disturbance vector has the Helmert distribution with parameters n and σ; if $r = r'$ then $n = 1$, and if $r = p$ then $n = 2$. The following notation is used to identify the various formulations that have been mentioned: M refers to any stochastic interpretation of central-place locations. The two Gaussian formulations for central-place locations are denoted by $M(n, \sigma)$; the n has the value 1 or 2 and σ denotes the single parameter defining each of the two models.[53]

The specification of the displacement variable as an n dimensional normal distribution eases the analytic task because this imperfect central-place model may be stated as a special case of the extensively studied integral of the normal distribution over an offset circle. This integral occurs frequently in the class of problems referred to as coverage and bombing. Available results are used here without needless repetition of derivations; basic references are Germond and Weil, and a series of articles by Rubin provide a definitive description of the spherical normal distribution.[54]

A frequently studied problem, in the coverage and bombing literature, in the terminology of this report, concerns the distance from a displaced point to an offset point with fixed location or (what is the same problem) the distance from a point with fixed location to a point displaced from an offset position. This particular coverage problem is identical to the statement preceding Eq. (9) of finding the distance from a sample locus with fixed location to a displaced point. The spacing measures obtained in this report pertain, however, to distance between two displaced points or between a displaced point and a point with variable location. The formal mathematics of these problems and the coverage problem are, however, identical. First, the integral for distance between two displaced points differs from the integral for distance between a displaced point and a fixed point only by a scale factor. Second, the integral for distance between a sample locus and a displaced point differs from the integral for distance between two displaced points only by definition of one distribution function; that is, instead of two displaced points one point is treated as a randomly located locus. Using these relationships, closed forms for $F(R, k)$ and $G(R, \omega)$ are obtained directly from the coverage literature. These distributions and their related order statistics are stated first. Then, numerical evaluations are considered. Finally, there is an evaluation of the range of values of σ for which order statistics are accurate approximations to measures on $M(n, \sigma)$.

Point to point distances. Having specifically identified the displacement variables, notation is changed slightly to reflect known parameters. The probability that a displaced point $m(v, u)$ in $M(n, \sigma)$ is within distance r of its equilibrium position $h(u, v)$ is denoted by $F(r; n, \sigma)$. Because the distribution function is the same for every point in $M(n, \sigma)$, it is not necessary to distinguish various equilibrium positions. So, the probability that any $m(u, v)$ is within distance r of $h(u, v)$ is:

$$F(r; n, \sigma) = \int_0^r \frac{\left(\frac{x}{\sigma}\right)^{n-1} e^{-x^2/2\sigma^2}}{\sigma\Gamma\left(\frac{n}{2}\right)2^{(n-2)/2}}\, dx \qquad (16)$$

Let $H(r^2/\sigma^2; n)$ denote the chi-square distribution with n degrees of freedom.

Then:

$$F\left(\frac{r}{\sigma}; n, \sigma\right)H = \left(\frac{r^2}{\sigma^2}; n\right) \qquad (17)$$

The distribution function for standardized distance between two points in $M(n, \sigma)$ with equilibrium positions distance k apart is denoted by $F(R/\sqrt{2}\sigma; k, n)$. As the point lattice H has been defined $k = 1$, but for subsequent analysis it is convenient to give k other values. The $F(R/\sqrt{2}\sigma; k, n)$ is obtained from Eq. (6) by substituting Eq. (16) for $F(X; 0)$ and a corresponding function for $F(X'; k)$.

Using the relationship between the integral for point to point distances in $M(n, \sigma)$ and integrals of the normal distribution over an offset circle, the distribution function for point to point distances is known to be:

$$F\left(\frac{R}{\sqrt{2\sigma}}; k, n\right) = H\left(\frac{R^2}{2\sigma^2}; k^2, n\right) = \int_0^{R^2/2\sigma^2} \frac{e^{-(x^2+\lambda^2)/2}}{2^{n/2}} \times \sum_{a=0}^{\infty} \frac{x'^{2(n/2+a-1)}\lambda^{2a}}{\Gamma\left(\frac{n}{2}+a\right)2^{2a}a!} dx'^2 \tag{18}$$

where $\lambda^2 = k^2/2\sigma^2$.

Equation (18) is the noncentral chi-square distribution with n degrees of freedom and offset parameter λ^2.

The distribution function for the order distance R_{i6} for point to point measurements on $M(n, \sigma)$ is obtained from Eq. (8) by substituting $F(R/\sqrt{2\sigma}; k, n)$ for $F(r; 1)$, or, in symbols:

$$dF\left(\frac{R_{i6}}{\sqrt{2\sigma}}; k, n\right) = \frac{6!}{(i-1)!(6-i)!} \times F^{i-1}\left(\frac{R}{\sqrt{2\sigma}}; k, n\right) \times \left[1 - F\left(\frac{R}{\sqrt{2\sigma}}; k, n\right)\right]^{(6-i)} \times dF\left(\frac{R}{\sqrt{2\sigma}}; k, n\right) \tag{19}$$

It follows directly from Eq. (18) that Eq. (19) is the standardized *ith* order statistic in sample size six from a population distributed as noncentral chi with parameters n and λ^2.

Locus to point distances. Locus to point distances in $M(n, \sigma)$ are more difficult to derive, and I have had no success in obtaining locus to point order distances. Let $G(R/\sigma; \omega, n)$ denote the probability that the average standardized distance from a randomly located locus A to the points displaced from the three nearest lattice points to A is less than R/σ. Assuming that $k = 1$ and that the restriction of Eq. (7) holds, so that the mean displacement distance is small relative to the translation period of the lattice, then it is not difficult to show that:

$$G\left(\frac{R}{\sigma}; \omega, n\right) = \frac{1}{2}\int_0^1\int_0^{R/\sigma} v\left(\frac{\sigma v}{\omega}\right)^{\frac{1}{2}(n-2)} \times e^{-(v^2+\omega^2/\sigma^2)/2} I_{\frac{1}{2}(n-2)}\left(\frac{v\omega}{\sigma}\right) dF(\omega)dv \tag{20}$$

where $I_z(x)$ is the modified Bessel function of order z.

The integration with respect to ω is not formally difficult but the number of terms in the resulting expression yields, for this writer at least, a prohibitively complex expression for the distribution function for order distance. The probable strategy is to find a simpler expression to approximate the upper range of $F(\omega)$. Because I have not found a suitable approximation, the following paragraph is restricted to numerical evaluation of point to point order distances.

Numerical evaluation of point to point distances. The integrals in Eqs. (18) and (19) are not elementary, and brief comments on the evaluation of these equations are made.

The probability distribution $F(R/\sqrt{2\sigma}; k, 1)$ for point to point distances reduces to a well-known form. It has been shown that $R^2/2\sigma^2$ has a noncentral chi-square distribution with one degree of freedom and noncentrality parameter $k^2/2\sigma^2$. It is then known (for example, see Eisenhart and Zelen)[55] that the quantity $s = (R - k)^2$ has a gamma distribution with shape parameter 1/2 and scale parameter $4\sigma^2$, that is, the probability density function of s is

$$dF(s) = \frac{\left(\frac{s}{\beta}\right)^{-1/2} e^{-8/\beta}}{\beta\sqrt{\pi}} \tag{21}$$

where $\beta = 4\sigma^2$.

So, the cumulative distribution of the transformed distance s may be obtained from tables of the gamma function such as Pearson or Harter.[56]

In a similar manner, the order distance R_{i6} may be related to the *ith* order statistic from a population with the density function of Eq. (21). Denote these transformed order statistics by s_{i6}, and $s_{i6} = (R_{i6} - k)^2$. The cumulative distribution of the order statistics from the gamma distribution were tabulated by Gupta and the values of low order moments are found in Harter.[57]

The bivariate normal case, $n = 2$, does not reduce to a simple expression. However, a recent article by Grubbs contains a nontechnical discussion of the evaluation of $F(R/\sqrt{2\sigma}; k, 2)$.[59] He cited available tables and identified known approximations to Eq. (18). These approximations treat the noncentral chi-square variate as a scaled-up central chi-square variate. Accordingly, order distances may be approximated by order statistics from a chi-square distribution with appropriate parameters.

Evaluation of the approximation to order statistics. The integrals used in this paper are of two kinds. One class gives distance between two displaced points, and the other class gives order distances from a displaced origin point to other displaced points. The second class of integrals is particularly relevant to distance relations in the central-place model $M(n, \sigma)$. The derivation of these order distances from the first class of integrals involved a critical assumption, and the validity of this assumption needs evaluation.

The assumption is that *ith* order distance in $M(n, \sigma)$ is given by the *ith* smallest observation in a sample of six distances between points displaced from nearest neighbor equilibrium positions. This condition is satisfied if each displaced point is, with probability approaching 1, closer to its equilibrium position than to any other equilibrium position, and Eq. (7) insures that this condition holds with probability approaching 1. Equation (7) is probably too restrictive, but it is difficult to evaluate the required integrals to determine the range of values of σ for which this condition is approximated. In lieu of an analytic solution, a Monte Carlo experiment was used.

A Monte Carlo experiment was used to estimate the probability that one or more of the sixth neighbors of an arbitrary origin point in $M(n, \sigma)$ are not displaced from nearest neighbor equilibrium positions. For this experiment a set of nineteen points was used. The center point was the origin from which measurements were taken; the other eighteen points corresponded to the nearest, second nearest, and third nearest rings of six lattice points each. More distant rings of lattice points were not required for the values of σ that were examined. Results were expressed in standardized distance units by defining parameters of the hexagonal point lattice so that the mean density of points per unit area was unity. This put the three rings of equilibrium positions at, approximately, the following distances from the origin: 1.0746, 1.8612, and 2.1491. The displacement of points and measurement of distances was programed for an IBM 709 computer. To reduce computing time, but without affecting results, four lattice points were positioned on a line at distances 0, 1.0746, 1.8612 and 2.1491, and one point was displaced from each lattice point. Distances were measured from the point displaced from 0 to the three other displaced points. Each observation consisted of six sets of these three measurements, and the eighteen distances were ordered from smallest to largest. For each value of σ, 100 observations were taken and the proportion of times the *ith* order distance was not the *ith* order statistic from a nearest neighbor lattice position was obtained. These values are listed in Table 7–21, where $\sigma = .1(.1).4$ for $M(1, \sigma)$ and $M(2, \sigma)$, and they provide estimates of the proportion of cases that do not conform to the assumptions underlying the derivation of order distances.

TABLE 7–21

Estimated Percentage* of ith Order Distances in M(n, σ) That Are Not the ith Order Neighbor for Points Displaced from Nearest Neighbor Equilibrium Positions

σ	1	2	3	4	5	6
			$M(1, \sigma)$			
.1	0	0	0	0	0	0
.2	0	0	0	1	2	12
.3	0	1	4	11	24	41
.4	4	6	18	32	51	75
			$M(2, \sigma)$			
.1	0	0	0	0	0	0
.2	1	2	7	18	28	50
.3	3	6	18	41	65	87
.4	12	27	48	63	84	99

Source: Tables 7–21 through 7–27 are from Michael F. Dacey, "A Probability Model for Central Place Locations," *Annals of the Association of American Geographers*, LVI, No. 4 (December, 1966), 550–68.

*Percentages were obtained from a simulation described in the text.

The data in Table 7–21 indicate that nearest neighbor distances in $M(1, \sigma)$ may be approximated quite accurately for values of σ as large as 0.4 but that higher order distances are free from bias only when σ is relatively small, certainly less than .2. For $M(2, \sigma)$, the corresponding value of

σ is substantially smaller. The value of σ critical to interpretation of $M(n, \sigma)$ probably lies between .1 and .2. If an observed urban pattern is approximated by a model for which, say, $\sigma < 0.2$, there is an inferential basis for asserting that the observed pattern corresponds to this stochastic central-place model. Since each observed location is, with high probability, closer to its equilibrium position than any other equilibrium position, the observed pattern approximates the equilibrium state defined by central-place theory. If, however, an $M(n, \sigma)$ corresponds closely to an observed point pattern for large values of σ, the correlation between observed and calculated values may be an indication that the urban system is in a pronounced state of disequilibrium or the correlation may be specious. This latter condition could happen if a point pattern having properties similar to $M(n, \sigma)$, for large σ, were generated by more than one type of stochastic process.

Monte Carlo Estimation of Spacing Measures

A Monte Carlo procedure for estimation of order distances in $M(n, \sigma)$ is given for two reasons. First, the distribution function for locus to point order distance was not derived and this distance is useful for summarizing both theoretical and observed point patterns. Second, order distances obtained from the parent populations with the distribution functions of Eqs. (18) and (20) provide a summary description of the point set $M(n, \sigma)$ only for assumptions of an unbounded Euclidean plane and for displacement vectors with a mean distance component small relative to the translation period of the lattice. If either or both of these two conditions are not satisfied, spacing in $M(n, \sigma)$ is not given by Eqs. (18) and (20), and appropriate expressions are difficult to obtain. When analytic methods fail, numerical estimates frequently may be obtained by simulation of properties underlying the intractable equation. A Monte Carlo approach is described that yields estimates of point to point and locus to point order distances for more general conditions than required for derivation of Eqs. (18) and (20).

Specification of a synthetic point pattern. The Monte Carlo method generates a synthetic point set, called $M^*(n, \sigma)$, that has properties specified for $M(n, \sigma)$. The generation of this point set and the estimation of order distances utilized a program written for the CDC-3400 which is titled HEXLAT. A brief description of HEXLAT identifies the essential characteristics of the simulation procedure.

HEXLAT is initiated by specifying: (1) the number of rows, a, and columns, b, on the hexagonal point lattice; and (2) parameters of the probability law defining the displacement vector. This probability law is either a half-normal ($n = 1$) or a circular normal ($n = 2$) and has the single parameter σ. All parameters are reduced to a standarized unit obtained by spacing nearest neighbor lattice points so that there is an average of one lattice point per unit area. The distance between nearest neighbor lattice points in standard units is, accordingly, $\sqrt{2}/\sqrt[4]{3} = U$, say. HEXLAT constructs the hexagonal point lattice of ab points and uses pseudo-random numbers and normal deviates to generate the point set $M^*(n, \sigma)$.

A difficulty in generating a synthetic $M(n, \sigma)$ is that displaced points corresponding to lattice positions close to the edge of the lattice may be displaced away from the lattice so that these points are dispersed over a larger area than the lattice and, hence, the density of displaced points is, in effect, less than the density of lattice points. To keep the displaced points within a confined area, the hexagonal lattice is mapped onto a torus. One way to visualize this mapping is to center the hexagonal lattice on a rectangle with sides of length aU and bU^{-1}. Opposite edges of the rectangle are joined so that the resulting figure, called a torus, has no edges or boundaries. Because the torus has no edges, sources of areal or boundary biases are reduced.

This toroidal mapping produces a surface with area ab that contains exactly ab lattice points and ab displaced points. The specification of a and b is not entirely arbitrary. If these dimensions are small relative to σ, the realized position of a displaced point may be more than halfway around the torus so that the point approaches its equilibrium position from the "opposite" direction. In order to avoid this type of bias in the estimation of the first six order distances, each side of the rectangle should have a length not less than $6\sigma U$ units although a longer length is preferred.

***Distance measures on* M.** HEXLAT generates the point set $M^*(n, \sigma)$ on a torus. Spacing measures may be obtained from the toroidal construction or the torus may be "cut" to obtain the original rectangle with dimensions aU and bU^{-1}. Except when σ is small, certainly less than 0.1, these two procedures yield different spacing measures. If the toroidal construction is retained, conditions of the unbounded plane are approximated; if the rectangular area is used, the spacing measures describe the pattern of displaced points in a bounded rectangular region.

For the rectangular area, distance between the points (x_1, y_1) and (x_2, y_2) is, of course, $[(x_1 + x_2)^2 + (y_1 - y_2)^2]^{1/2}$. The toroidal distance between these two points may be obtained in the following manner:

1. Compute $(x_1 - x_2)^2$, $(x_1 - x_2 - aU)^2$ and $(x_1 - x_2 + aU)^2$, and denote the minimum value by x_m.
2. Compute $(y_1 - y_2)^2$, $(y_1 - y_2 - b/U)^2$ and $(y_1 - y_2 + b/U)^2$, and denote the minimum value by y_m.

the toroidal distance between the points (x_1, y_1) and (x_2, y_2) is $(x_m + y_m)^{1/2}$.

For estimation of point to point measures, the distances (either Euclidean or toroidal) from each displaced point in $M^*(n, \sigma)$ to all other displaced points are computed. The distances from each point are ordered from shortest to longest and the *ith* order distance is the *ith* member of each array. The collection of *ith* order distances may be summarized by a frequency distribution or by moments; these results from $M^*(n, \sigma)$ provide estimates of point to point distance in $M(n, \sigma)$.

Locus to point distances are obtained by locating a collection of sample points randomly and independently within the rectangle. Euclidean or toroidal distances are obtained from each locus to all points of the pattern. The distances from each locus are ordered from shortest to longest and the *jth* order distance is the *jth* member of each array. The collection of *jth* order distances may be summarized by a frequency distribution or by moments; these results from $M^*(n, \sigma)$ provide estimates of locus to point distance in $M(n, \sigma)$.

Examination of the Iowa Urban Pattern

Central-place theory formulates on a homogeneous, unbounded plane the locations of centers of service and marketing activities. Because mining, transportation, manufacturing, and similar activities are excluded, central-place systems are probably restricted to predominantly agricultural regions where the economic support of cities and towns is largely the provision of goods and services to the rural population. For these reasons central-place systems are commonly applied to rural areas having relatively uniform climatic and physical properties. Iowa satisfies the agricultural and homogeneity conditions as adequately as any medium size region and has been a favored study region. Evaluation of the empirical validity of this probabilistic formulation of central place locations uses a pattern of Iowa cities and towns.

For comparison of $M(n, \sigma)$ with the pattern of places in Iowa, a collection of places needs to be designated and summary distance measures on the Iowa pattern must be obtained that are comparable with theoretical measurements. An appropriate test is not easy to design, largely because the classical formulation of central-place theory contains many terms that are not explicitly defined. For example, there is no a priori method for determining the central places in a given study region. As such, any empirical examination of the theory is as much a test of working definitions as a test of the theory itself.

The Iowa pattern selected for empirical examination was defined arbitrarily, though the definitions conformed to the operational procedures current in urban geographic research. The pattern was formed by the larger cities and towns in Iowa as defined by the US Bureau of the Census in 1950. However, to emphasize the areal content of the central place model, the places used for test of the model satisfied the census definition of place and, in addition, were areally distinct. For larger places, urbanized areas were used. Smaller places recognized by the Bureau of the Census but contiguous (as seen from a map) to a larger place were combined to form a single place for the purposes of this analysis. Thus, the Iowa urban pattern was defined by areally distinct places.

The urban system for analysis was defined by the ninety-nine largest, areally distinct places. The use of the N largest places was a reasonable interpretation of central-place concepts, but putting $N = 99$ was completely arbitrary. This number was selected simply because Iowa had ninety-nine counties and it is not unreasonable to assume that each county had at least one central place.

Data from the 1950 census were used, instead of the more recent 1960 data, because the earlier census was, for other purposes, extracted from census publications in a form suitable for analysis. However, the ninety-nine largest, areally distinct places for 1950 and 1960 differ only by three places and it is not believed that there are significant differences between the two patterns.

The distance measures summarizing this Iowa urban pattern were obtained from a toroidal mapping. The state of Iowa cannot be mapped onto a torus without distorting distances. A torus is commonly obtained by folding together edges of a regular polygon with $2n$ edges. To obtain a regular polygon it is convenient to delimit a rectangular region that contains all or part of the Iowa urban pattern. For this analysis the largest rectangle, with an east-west orientation, contained entirely within the state of Iowa was used. This rectangle contained seventy-nine of the ninety-nine largest places, and this collection of areally distinct places was used to test the probabilistic model.

All measurements on the Iowa urban pattern were obtained from the toroidal mapping of the rectangular region and, henceforth, the urban system in this rectangle is equated with the Iowa urban system. The advisability of mapping a study region onto a torus is an immediate question. To the geographer who believes "east is east and west is west, and never the twain shall meet," the joining of opposite boundaries of the study region may constitute a first-order geographic sin. To sin or not to sin—if that is the question—depends upon properties of the phenomena under study, characteristics of the region containing this pattern, and the nature of the hypotheses under consideration. If the underlying locational process is known or assumed to be stationary, then any two subregions may be treated as identical with respect to this process and the joining of opposite edges is legitimate. If a locational process having a directional trend or areal bias is known or assumed, a toroidal mapping is inappropriate because the joining of opposite edges may combine border regions with quite different areal properties.

The toroidal mapping of the Iowa study region was used because, on one hand, the theoretical collection of points M is generated by a stationary process and, on the other hand, Iowa was selected for analysis because relatively homogeneous conditions prevailed throughout the state. If the homogeneity assumption is in fact satisfied, measurements on the Iowa urban pattern in the rectangular region probably reflect the statewide pattern and, possibly, spacing of larger, areally distinct places in the larger Midwestern agricultural region having physical and economic conditions similar to Iowa.

The model M identifies spacing relations in a point set, whereas cities and towns are obviously not punctiform entities. For measurement of distances between places or from sample loci to places, it is convenient to treat places as points. The point corresponding to a place was identified as the geographic center of that place, as visually determined from a map. This method may produce measurement error, and the level of error is evaluated below. All distance measurements on Iowa refer to the collection of geographic centers of the seventy-nine places contained within the rectangular region. The terms *place* and *point* are used synonymously.

Toroidal distances were obtained from each of the seventy-nine places to its six nearest neighbors. Also, 400 loci were randomly located in the rectangle and toroidal distances were obtained from each locus to the six nearest places. These measurements are in arbitrary units and, for comparison with theoretical measurements, a standardized unit distance is required.

Standardized distance may be obtained by multiplying observed distances by the square root of the density of places, where density is expressed in the same metric as the measured distances. The value for density was obtained simply by dividing the number of places, seventy-nine, by the area of the torus. This estimate of density is not completely satisfactory; this value and the estimate of density obtained for ninety-nine places in the state of Iowa are not exactly the same, and small changes in the location of the boundaries of the torus would change the estimate of density.

Errors arising from the estimation of density are eliminated by use of the spacing ratios, S_g, defined in Eq. (13). Because an estimate of density is not required, spacing ratios are probably the preferred basis for comparing observed and calculated values. The ratio values are, however, influenced to some degree by the specification of the torus. Moreover, the evaluation of differences between observed and calculated ratios requires a substantially more sophisticated analysis than used for this report.

The Iowa urban pattern of ninety-nine largest, areally distinct places is summarized in Table 7–22. Order distances were obtained from the toroidal mapping of the rectangular region containing seventy-nine places and all measurements were standarized by the observed density of seventy-nine places in the torus. Mean distances for the first six orders of neighbors are listed for point to point and locus to point relations. These distances are expressed in approximate miles to give an indication of the magnitudes involved in terrestrial space. The six lowest order spacing ratios are also listed.

An indication of the accuracy of these distances was obtained. The source of greatest error was the location of the geographic centers required to reduce places with areal extent to punctiform entities. The geographic center of places and a rectangular study region were located independently on two maps and the coordinates of places were determined. Measurements on both patterns were obtained by use of a program written for the CDC-3400 which yields order distances for points located on a torus. Corresponding *ith* order mean distances from the two patterns differed by substantially less than the unit of measurement. On this basis, it is concluded that there is negligible measurement error in the Iowa place to place measurements. The locus to point distances are of course subject to sampling error.

TABLE 7–22

Toroidal Distances for 79 of the 99 Largest, Areally Distinct Places Located in the Largest Rectangle Contained within Iowa: 1950

	Distance in Standardized Units			*Distance in Approximate Miles*		
	Point to Point	*Locus to Point*				
Order	*Mean*	*Mean*	*Standard Error*	*Point to Point*	*Locus to Point*	*Spacing Ratio*
1	.68	.43	.01	16	10	1.58
2	.87	.70	.01	21	17	1.24
3	1.01	.88	.01	24	21	1.15
4	1.17	1.06	.01	28	25	1.10
5	1.30	1.20	.01	31	29	1.08
6	1.42	1.33	.01	34	32	1.07

Sources: Distances were calculated from a base map titled *Iowa: Minor Civil Divisions–Townships*, Bureau of the Census. See also note to Table 7–21.

The value of density of places required to obtain standard units was calculated from the area of the torus. Measuring unit was 1/60th of an inch or approximately .008 standard units. Geographic centers of places were located independently on two maps; standardized point to point mean distances obtained from the two maps differed at each order by less than $0.5 \cdot 10^{-5}$. Locus to point distances were calculated from one of the two maps, and 400 randomly located loci were used.

The toroidal representation of the Iowa urban pattern is a basic data set for evaluation of central place and other models for urban systems. To aid in evaluation of this model, and other models that may be subsequently formulated, several properties of the toroidal measurements on the seventy-nine largest, areally distinct places in Iowa were tabulated in standardized units: Table 7–23 gives the second, third, and fourth moments about zero origin for the first six orders of point to point and locus to point distances, Table 7–24 gives the frequency distributions for the first six orders of point to point measurements, and Table 7–25 gives the six lowest orders of frequency distributions of distances from 200 sample loci.

TABLE 7–23

Comparison of Low Order Moments of Order Distance Measures on the Iowa Urban Pattern, M*(1, .35) and M*(2, .35)

Point to Point Measures				Locus to Point Measures			
Order	*Iowa*	*M*(1, .35)*	*M*(2, .25)*	*Order*	*Iowa*	*M*(1, .35)*	*M*(2, .25)*
			Second moment				
1	.50	.50	.41	1	.22	.20	.21
2	.78	.82	.82	2	.52	.52	.51
3	1.04	1.12	1.13	3	.81	.81	.82
4	1.39	1.42	1.42	4	1.15	1.15	1.15
5	1.73	1.72	1.73	5	1.48	1.47	1.45
6	2.04	2.04	2.08	6	1.79	1.78	1.79
			Third moment				
1	.39	.39	.38	1	.14	.11	.12
2	.72	.77	.78	2	.41	.40	.41
3	1.10	1.21	1.23	3	.77	.77	.78
4	1.69	1.72	1.73	4	1.28	1.26	1.28
5	2.34	2.29	2.30	5	1.85	1.82	1.78
6	2.99	2.96	3.04	6	2.47	2.40	2.43
			Fourth moment				
1	.31	.33	.31	1	.09	.06	.07
2	.67	.74	.76	2	.34	.32	.32
3	1.20	1.32	1.35	3	.76	.75	.75
4	2.11	2.11	2.05	4	1.46	1.41	1.44
5	3.23	3.07	2.94	5	2.36	2.27	2.21
6	4.45	4.33	4.19	6	.3.44	3.27	3.33

Sources: Iowa values were obtained from a base map titled *Iowa: Minor Civil Division-Townships*, Bureau of the Census. See also note to Table 7–21.
$M^*(n, \sigma)$ was calculated from 500 observations from a simulation described in the text.

Calculated Spacing Measures for Iowa

There is no a priori basis for deciding whether $M(1, \sigma)$ or $M(2, \sigma)$ has a higher level of correspondence to the Iowa urban pattern; so, both models were examined. Conditions under which Eqs. (18) and (20) may be used to obtain point to point and locus to point order distances in $M(n, \sigma)$ have been stated, and Table 7–21 identifies the approximate ranges of σ for which these conditions are satisfied. The values of σ which approximate first order point to point distances in Iowa (.68) fall outside of this range for both $M(1, \sigma)$ and $M(2, \sigma)$. The immediate conclusion was that the Iowa urban pattern does not closely approximate the equilibrium state defined by the hexagonal lattice of central-place theory, though an $M(n, \sigma)$ may have close correspondence to the observed pattern.

To examine the level of correspondence, estimates for $M(n, \sigma)$ were obtained by Monte Carlo simulation of the synthetic point set $M^*(n, \sigma)$. The previously described analytic methods yield at most six orders of point to point distances and three orders of locus to point distances. The simulation procedure HEXLAT is not restricted to these orders, and for a torus with sufficiently large dimensions, estimates of high order distances may be obtained. The present analysis used the six lowest orders of point to point and

TABLE 7–24

Frequency Distributions of Point to Point Order Distances for Iowa Urban Pattern, M*(1, .35) and M*(2, .25)

Interval	*Iowa*	*M*(1, .35)*	*M*(2, .25)*	*Interval*	*Iowa*	*M*(1, .35)*	*M*(2, .25)*
	Order 1				*Order 2*		
0–.1		.3	.3	0–.1			
–.2		.9	.6	–.2			
–.3		2.5	3.8	–.3			
–.4	6	5.8	5.4	–.4		.2	
–.5	11	6.6	7.7	–.5	1	.3	.2
–.6	7	12.3	10.4	–.6	3	2.7	2.8
–.7	20	13.0	13.9	–.7	9	7.1	7.9
–.8	14	14.1	15.6	–.8	15	11.9	13.9
–.9	9	10.1	10.6	–.9	10	16.3	16.9
1.0	11	9.5	7.3	1.0	26	22.6	15.6
1.1	1	3.5	2.2	1.1	11	12.0	12.6
1.2		.2	1.1	1.2	3	5.2	6.8
1.3		.2		1.3	1	.6	1.7
				1.4		.2	.5
	Order 3				*Order 4*		
0–.6		.2		0–.6			
–.7	1	.8	.6	–.7			
–.8	6	1.6	3.3	–.8	1		
–.9	7	7.1	8.2	–.9	1	.9	.9
1.0	22	18.2	17.1	1.0	10	6.0	6.6
1.1	26	20.4	21.0	1.1	20	12.5	14.5
1.2	10	22.0	16.0	1.2	18	23.5	20.0
1.3	4	7.1	8.4	1.3	13	20.4	21.3
1.4	2	1.6	3.3	1.4	11	12.2	11.4
1.5	0	.2	1.1	1.5	1	2.7	4.1
1.6	0			1.6	2	.8	.3
1.7	1			1.7	2		.2
	Order 5				*Order 6*		
0–.9	1			0–.9			
1.0	1	.6	.5	1.0			
1.1	8	4.3	4.0	1.1	2	.6	.6
1.2	18	12.8	9.6	1.2	9	3.0	2.1
1.3	15	19.4	23.1	1.3	10	11.2	7.4
1.4	9	24.0	23.7	1.4	14	19.4	21.8
1.5	16	12.0	13.1	1.5	20	21.8	23.2
1.6	8	4.9	4.1	1.6	13	15.0	15.3
1.7	2	.9	.8	1.7	3	6.5	6.3
1.8	0		.2	1.8	7	1.1	2.2
1.9	1			1.9	1	.3	

Sources: Iowa values were obtained from a map titled *Iowa: Minor Civil Division-Townships*, Bureau of the Census. See also note to Table 7–21.

$M^*(n, \sigma)$ was calculated from 500 observations from a simulation described in the text. Because of rounding errors, columns do not necessarily sum to 79.

***Frequency Distributions of Locus to Point Order Distances for Iowa Urban Pattern,* M*(1, .35) *and* M*(2, .25)**

Interval	*Iowa*	*M*(1, .35)*	*M*(2, .25)*	*Interval*	*Iowa*	*M*(1, .35)*	*M*(2, .25)*
		Order 1				*Order 2*	
0–.1	16	16.0	7.2	0–.1			
–.2	39	36.8	45.6	–.2		2.4	1.6
–.3	70	44.8	56.8	–.3	7	1.6	3.2
–.4	71	84.8	85.6	–.4	12	8.8	17.6
–.5	66	86.4	76.8	–.5	38	34.4	28.0
–.6	61	67.2	56.0	–.6	60	59.2	62.4
–.7	32	39.2	40.0	–.7	82	96.8	96.8
–.8	25	19.2	22.4	–.8	75	83.2	81.6
–.9	13	5.6	8.0	–.9	80	72.0	62.4
1.0	6		.8	1.0	27	27.2	29.6
1.1	1		.8	1.1	15	12.0	10.4
				1.2	2	2.4	5.6
				1.3	1		.8
				1.4	1		
D†		.068	.038	D		.031	.043
Pr‡		>.10	>.10	Pr		>.10	>.10
		Order 3				*Order 4*	
0–.5	2	2.4	4.8	0–.5			
–.6	21	12.8	12.0	–.6			
–.7	42	42.4	34.4	–.7	6	2.4	2.4
–.8	65	65.6	56.8	–.8	16	16.0	16.0
–.9	92	90.4	102.4	–.9	49	33.6	46.4
1.0	83	86.4	90.4	1.0	85	82.4	72.8
1.1	51	52.8	56.8	1.1	93	101.6	95.2
1.2	25	36.0	36.8	1.2	66	98.4	91.2
1.3	11	9.6	4.8	1.3	47	45.6	48.8
1.4	6	1.6	.8	1.4	27	17.6	24.0
1.5	2			1.5	10	1.6	3.2
				1.6	1	.8	
D		.021	.055	D		.054	.046
Pr		>.10	>.10	Pr		>.10	>.10
		Order 5				*Order 6*	
0–.8	2	1.6		0–.8			
–.9	5	0	5.6	–.9	2		
1.0	36	21.6	27.2	1.0	6	4.0	.8
1.1	73	60.0	64.8	1.1	29	10.4	13.6
1.2	97	101.6	110.4	1.2	56	46.4	50.4
1.3	76	116.0	105.6	1.3	91	104.8	100.0
1.4	54	72.8	54.4	1.4	86	119.2	118.4
1.5	37	24.0	28.0	1.5	59	85.6	74.4
1.6	14	1.6	3.2	1.6	49	21.6	33.6
1.7	3	.8	.8	1.7	13	8.0	8.8
1.8	2			1.8	4		
1.9	1			1.9	5		
D		.082	.062	D		.104	.072
Pr		.10	>.10	Pr		.025–.01	>.10

Sources: Iowa values were obtained from a base map titled *Iowa: Minor Civil Divisions-Tounships,* Bureau of the Census. See also note to Table 7–21.

†*D* denotes the Kolmogorov-Smirnov statistic for a two sample test computed from Iowa and $M^*(n, \sigma)$.

‡*Pr* denotes the approximate tabulated probability level of *D* for samples of sizes 400 and 500.

$M^*(n, \sigma)$ was calculated from 500 observations from a simulation described in the text.

locus to point distances. The arbitrary selection of six orders was made because of the obvious relation to the hexagonal lattice.

Because properties of the spacing measures are not known, it was necessary not only to estimate properties of $M(n, \sigma)$ by simulation but first, by an iterative or trial and error procedure, to estimate the values of σ that provide the best or, at least, good levels of correspondence to the Iowa data. Measurements on $M(n, \sigma)$ are sensitive to changes in σ, at least for or $<.5$. This means that goodness-of-fit between observed and calculated values depends, in part, on the accuracy in estimating σ. For values which approximate the Iowa pattern, a change in σ produces an inverse change of equivalent size in first order point to point distances. It was initially decided to examine $M^*(n, \sigma)$ by .05 augments of σ and to select for more detailed analysis the $M^*(1, \sigma)$ and $M^*(2, \sigma)$ which gave the best fits to the nearest neighbor point to point measurements in Iowa. The results obtained from the $M^*(n, \sigma)$ did not necessitate changes in this plan.

Values of σ which have relatively high correspondence to the Iowa pattern are .35 for $n = 1$ and .25 for $n = 2$. Mean distances and the spacing ratios for $M^*(1, .35)$ and $M^*(2, .25)$ are listed in Tables 7–26 and 7–27, respectively. Order distances for the two $M^*(n, \sigma)$ were obtained from five patterns, each containing 100 lattice points and 100 sample loci. Comparable Iowa data are listed and the differences between

TABLE 7–26

***Comparison of Iowa Urban Pattern and* M*(1, .35)**

	Iowa		*M*(1, .35)*		*Difference between Iowa and M*(1, .35) Means*		
Order	*Mean*	*Standard Error*	*Mean*	*Standard Error*	*Standard Units*	*Per Cent of Iowa*	*Approximate Miles*
			Point to Point Distances				
1	.68	—	.674	.009	.006	0.9	0.1
2	.87	—	.889	.007	.019	2.2	0.5
3	1.01	—	1.049	.006	.039	3.9	0.9
4	1.17	—	1.185	.006	.015	1.3	0.4
5	1.30	—	1.304	.006	.004	0.3	0.1
6	1.42	—	1.424	.006	.004	0.3	0.1
			Locus to Point Distances				
1	.43	.01	.417	.008	.013	3.0	0.3
2	.70	.01	.700	.007	.000	—	—
3	.88	.01	.885	.007	.005	0.6	0.1
4	1.06	.01	1.060	.007	.000	—	—
5	1.20	.01	1.207	.006	.007	0.6	0.2
6	1.33	.01	1.327	.006	.003	0.2	0.1

Spacing Ratios

Order	*Iowa*	*M*(1, .35)*
1	1.58	1.62
2	1.24	1.27
3	1.15	1.19
4	1.10	1.12
5	1.08	1.08
6	1.07	1.07

Sources: Iowa values are from Table 7–23. See also note to Table 7–21.
M(1, .35)* values were calculated from 500 observations from a simulation described in the text.

TABLE 7–27

Comparison of Iowa Urban Pattern and M*(2, .25)

	Iowa		*M*(2, .25)*		*Difference between Iowa and M*(2, .25) Means*		
Order	*Mean*	*Standard Error*	*Mean*	*Standard Error*	*Standard Units*	*Per Cent of Iowa*	*Approximate Miles*
			Point to Point Distances				
1	.68	—	.660	.010	.020	2.9	0.5
2	.87	—	.890	.007	.020	2.3	0.5
3	1.01	—	1.051	.007	.041	4.1	1.0
4	1.17	—	1.185	.006	.015	1.3	0.4
5	1.30	—	1.308	.006	.008	0.6	0.2
6	1.42	—	1.437	.006	.017	1.2	0.4
			Locus to Point Distances				
1	.43	.01	.419	.008	.011	2.6	0.3
2	.70	.01	.694	.008	.006	0.9	0.1
3	.88	.01	.890	.007	.010	1.1	0.2
4	1.06	.01	1.063	.007	.003	0.3	0.1
5	1.20	.01	1.196	.006	.004	0.3	0.1
6	1.33	.01	1.332	.006	.002	0.2	0.1

Spacing Ratios

Order	*Iowa*	*M*(2, .25)*
1	1.58	1.58
2	1.24	1.28
3	1.15	1.18
4	1.10	1.11
5	1.08	1.09
6	1.07	1.08

Sources: Iowa values are from Table 7–23. See also note to Table 7–21.
$M^*(2, .25)$ values were calculated from 500 observations from a simulation described in the text.

observed and calculated values are stated in standardized units, percentage of the Iowa values and approximate miles. Tables 7–23 to 7–25 list additional data obtained from the two simulations.

Interpretation of Results

Evaluation of the degree of correspondence between observed and calculated values should take into account that, on one hand, the Iowa values are accurate only up to scale (because the specification of the boundaries of the torus was arbitrary) and, on the other hand, the theoretical values provide (probably) good fits but not best fits to the observed Iowa data (because of the highly inefficient procedure for estimating σ). The first source of error may or may not be biased towards increasing the levels of correspondence between observed and calculated values; the latter source of error does not inflate the latter source of error does not inflate the degrees of correspondence and probably produces lower levels of correspondence than obtained by a more efficient estimating procedure. Considering these limitations, the levels of correspondence of both sets of calculated values to the observed Iowa values listed in Tables 7–23 through 7–27 must be judged sufficiently high to encourage further work on probabilistic formulations of central-place patterns. More formal evaluation of the levels of correspondence is difficult.

Because M is a probabilistic model, evaluation of the levels of correspondence between the Iowa pattern and the two $M^*(n, \sigma)$ by standard statistical goodness-of-fit tests may be suggested. There are, however, two major obstacles to the use of statistical methods; one concerns the nature of the Iowa data and the other concerns the formulation of hypotheses or, more accurately, the lack of hypotheses.

The Iowa urban pattern consists of seventy-nine points or places, and point to point measurements were obtained by ordering measurements from all points to all other points. Consequently, the point to point measurements are census rather than sample data. Statistics is largely concerned with the evaluation of hypotheses for data subject to sample variation, and statistical tests are generally inappropriate for census data. The locus to point measurements are subject to sample variation and the Kolmogorov-Smirnov statistic for a two sample test was calculated for each of the locus to point frequency distributions (Table 7–25). With the advantage of hindsight a smaller class interval for the locus to point frequency distributions would have provided more information. Tabulated probability levels corresponding to these statistics are also listed, but the meaning attached to these probabilities is not clear.

Statistical methodology is directed to sample data and, in addition, is primarily concerned with the evaluation of sets of exclusive and all inclusive hypotheses where values may be assigned to the commission of various types of errors. At this stage of the analysis few hypotheses and no meaningful evaluation of errors are available. The primary concern is simply whether to continue or terminate this research. Although this is a common and basic question, statistical methodology is not equipped to provide answers. In a provocative study, Anscombe recognized this stage of research and the need to evaluate objectively the advisability of continuation or termination of an investigation, but admitted that statistics does not provide adequate guidance to the researcher.[59] Evidently evaluation of the results in Tables 7–23 through 7–27 reduces to personal judgment.

In terms of simply comparing observed data with values calculated from either model, I [M. F. Dacey, ed.] believe the evidence strongly urges continuation of this research, and my study of probabilistic central-place models is continuing. The similarity of results from $M^*(1, .35)$ and $M^*(2, .25)$ is not surprising because displacement distances for both models are described by the same probability law, i.e., the Helmert distribution with n degrees of freedom.

The evaluation of a model is not necessarily limited to comparison of observed and calculated values. Geographers have classically demanded theoretical justification for a substantive interpretation of a process which appears to "work" or "fit." At this conceptual level the present stochastic interpretation of central place patterns is not satisfactory. Parameters have not been given substantive interpretations (so that σ was estimated from the observed measurements rather than from knowledge about the Iowa landscape), and no theoretical justification was provided for displacement from an equilibrium state. Whereas each urban geographer will undoubtedly supply his own criticisms of this model, here one basic deficiency is examined.

The hexagonal lattice of classical central-place theory is derived under very strong assumptions about geographic and economic conditions. Although it is not at all clear that such conditions are ever approximated in the real world, if the theory has empirical significance such conditions must be approximately satisfied. Where such conditions are approximated, it is reasonable to expect that the resulting arrangement of central places conforms approximately to the hexagonal lattice arrangement. The degree of similarity to the hexagonal point lattice evidently may be measured by the value of σ which best describes a point pattern, because as σ goes to 0 the pattern of displaced points approaches the regular hexagonal point lattice, and as σ goes to ∞ it may be shown that the displaced point pattern approaches a completely random point pattern. If an observed pattern and $M(n, \sigma)$ have a high correspondence for small values of σ, this suggests that the equilibrium positions defined by the hexagonal lattice are a close approximation to observed positions. Alternatively, if correspondence between the patterns requires a relatively large value of σ, then the equilibrium condition is a poor approximation to realized positions. Large values of σ may occur because the hexagonal lattice defines an equilibrium state though the observed system is in a pronounced state of disequilibrium. Alternatively, an $M(n, \sigma)$, with σ large, may correspond closely to an observed pattern for factors unrelated to central-place theory. This specious correlation would occur, for example, if more than one type of areal process were capable of generating a point pattern with properties similar to $M(1, \sigma)$ or $M(2, \sigma)$.

These alternatives presume a decision on the values of σ that are relatively small and relatively large. One way to evaluate the magnitude of σ is by the degree to which neighborhood relations on the hexogonal lattice are maintained by the displaced points. This consistency is indicated by the proportion of near neighbors in the displaced pattern which do not have nearest neighbor equilibrium positions (Table 7–21). A value of σ may be considered small if there is a high probability that the six nearest neighbors in the displaced point set have nearest neighbor equilibrium positions. The probability level ajudged high is undefined, but for the present analysis precise definitions are not necessary. Interpolation in Table 7–21 indicates that in $M(1, .35)$ over half and in $M(2, .25)$ nearly three-quarters of the origin points do not have six neighbors displaced from nearest neighbor equilibrium positions. These proportions clearly are not small. This leads to the conclusion that: (1) a displaced central-place model describes the Iowa urban pattern though the Iowa pattern is in a strong state of disequilibrium; or (2) the utility of this stochastic interpretation of central-place theory is limited to description of the urban pattern but has no explanatory implications to the locational process underlying the urban pattern. The present analysis does not permit objective evaluation of the relative merits of these two contradictory conclusions.

FOOTNOTES TO CHAPTER 7

1. L. Curry, "The Geography of Service Centers within Towns: The Elements of an Operational Approach," *Proceedings of the I.G.U. Symposium in Urban Geography*, ed. K. Norborg, *Lund Studies in Geography*, Series B. Human Geography, No. 24 (Lund, Sweden: Gleerup, 1960), pp. 31–53.

2. Walter Christaller, *Die zentralen Orte in Süddeutschland: Eine ökonomischgeographische Untersuchung uber die Gesetzmässigkeit der Verbreitung und Entwicklung der Siedlungen mit städtischen Funktionen* (Jena: Gustav Fischer Verlag, 1933).

3. E. L. Ullman, "A Theory of Location for Cities," *American Journal of Sociology*, XLVI, No. 2 (May, 1941), 853–64.

4. For a complete treatment of the theory, with examples, see Brian J. L. Berry, *Geography of Market Centers and Retail Distribution* (Englewood Cliffs, N.J.: Prentice-Hall, Inc., 1967). Brian J. L. Berry and Allan Pred, *Central Place Studies: A Bibliography of Theory and Applications* (Philadelphia: Regional Science Research Institute, 1961), contains an exhaustive list of related work.

5. Peter Hall, ed., *Von Thünen's Isolated State* (London: Pergamon Press, 1966).

6. Alfred Weber, *Theory of the Location of Industries* (Chicago: University of Chicago Press, 1929).

7. Berry and Pred, *Central Place Studies*, pp. 15–17.

8. *Ibid.*, p. 17.

9. Translated by W. H. Woglom and W. F. Stolper as *The Economics of Location* (New Haven: Yale University Press, 1954).

10. B. J. L. Berry and W. L. Garrison, "The Functional Bases of the Central Place Hierarchy," *Economic Geography*, XXXIV, No. 2 (April, 1958), 145–54.

11. B. J. L. Berry and H. G. Barnum, "Aggregate Relations and Elemental Components of Central Place Systems," *Journal of Regional Science*, IV (1962), 35–68.

12. D. J. Grove and L. I. Huszar, *The Towns of Ghana* (Accra: Ghana Universities Press, 1964).

13. The research work reported here is part of a much wider study of southwestern Nigeria, comprising the western and Midwestern regions of Nigeria and the Federal Territory of Lagos.

14. Christaller, *Die zentralen Orte in Süddeutschland;* Lösch, *The Economics of Location.*

15. Berry and Pred, *Central Place Studies.*

16. R. Vining, "A Description of Certain Spatial Aspects of An Economic System," *Economic Development and Cultural Change*, III, No. 2 (April, 1955), 147–95.

17. E. Brush, "The Hierarchy of Central Places in Southwestern Wisconsin," *Geographical Review*, XLIII, No. 3 (1953), 380–402.

18. B. J. L. Berry, H. G. Barnum, and R. J. Tennant, "Retail Location and Consumer Behavior," *Papers and Proceedings of the Regional Science Association*, IX (1962), 65–106.

19. Grove and Huszar, *The Towns of Ghana.*

20. It is assumed that each of the columns in the array $A(p, q)$ has been standarized to unit variance.

21. See M. G. Kendall, *A Course in Multivariate Analysis* (London: Charles Griffin & Company, Ltd., 1961).

22. See A. E. Smailes, "The Urban Hierarchy in England and Wales, *Geography*, XXIX, No. 1 (January, 1944), 42.

23. *Ibid.*

24. Where a settlement, by virtue of its accidental location along a line of distribution, possesses a function which it would otherwise have lacked, say electricity, the score of 5 or less

for that function would not significantly affect its importance as there are still 27 other functions to be considered.

25. This result seems rather encouraging if we note that in Moser and Scott's analysis it needed the first four principal components to attain 60 per cent of the total variance, which was all that they considered in their classification of towns. See C. A. Moser and W. Scott, *British Towns: A Statistical Study of their Social and Economic Differences* (Center for Urban Studies, Report No 2, London, 1961).

26. Details of the calculations will be found in the author's Ph. D. thesis (University of London), in preparation.

27. See B. J. L. Berry, "A Method for Deriving Multi-Factor Uniform Regions," *Przeglad Geograficzny*, XXXIII, No. 2 (1961), p. 273.

28. R. A. Murdie, "Cultural Differences in Consumer Travel," *Economic Geography*, XLI, No. 3 (July, 1965), 211–33.

29. A. K. Philbrick, "Principles of Areal, Functional Organization in Regional Human Geography," *Economic Geography*, XXXIII, No. 4 (October, 1957), 306–36.

30. See B. J. L. Berry, *Geography of Market Centers and Retail Distribution* (Englewood Cliffs, N.J.: Prentice-Hall, Inc., 1968).

31. Sven Illeris, "*Danmarks byer som service centre*," *Byplan*, No. 70 (1960).

32. Sven Illeris, "The Functions of Danish Towns," *Geografisk Tidsskrift*, LXIII (1964), 203–36.

33. See A. H. Anderson, "Space as a Social Cost," *Journal of Farm Economics*, XXXII (1950), 411–30; Carl H. Kraenzel, *Great Plains in Transition* (Norman: Oklahoma University Press, 1955); Saskatchewan, Royal Commission on Agriculture and Rural Life, *Movement of Farm People*, Report No, 7 (Regina: Queen's Printer, 1956); Dwight Nesmith, "Cities Crowding: Countryside Losing," *U.S. News and World Report*, May 7, 1962; and John R. Borchert, *The Urbanization of the Upper Midwest: 1930–1960*, Urban Report No. 2, (Minneapolis: Upper Midwest Economic Study, 1963).

34. Nesmith, "Cities Crowding: Countryside Losing."

35. Cf. descriptions of subregional trade center systems in such works as Saskatchewan's Royal Commission on Agriculture and Rural Life, *Service Centers*, Report No. 12 (Regina: Queen's Printer, 1957); Brian J. L. Berry, H. Gardiner Barnum, and Robert J. Tennant, "Retail Location and Consumer Behavior," *Papers and Proceedings of the Regional Science Association*, IX (1962), 65–106; Anderson, "Space as a Social Cost"; and Borchert, *Urbanization of the Upper Midwest*.

36. For example, C. E. Lively, *Growth and Decline of Farm Trade Centers in Minnesota: 1905–1930*, Agricultural Experiment Station Bulletin 287 (St. Paul, Minn., 1932); Edmund De S. Brunner, "Do Villages Grow?" *Rural Sociology*, I (1936), 506–9; Saskatchewan, Royal Commission, *Service Centers*, *ibid*, p. 127; and Edward H. Hassinger, "Factors Associated with Population Changes in Agricultural Trade Centers in Southern Minnesota, 1940 to 1950," (Ph. D. dissertation, University of Minnesota, 1956).

37. See, for example, Walter Christaller, *Die zentralen Orte in Süddeutschland* (Jena: Fischer, 1933); Rutledge Vining, "A Description of Certain Spatial Aspects of an Economic System," *Economic Development and Cultural Change*, III, No. 2 (April, 1955), 147–96; and Brian J. L. Berry and William L. Garrison, "Recent Developments in Central Place Theory," *Papers and Proceedings of the Regional Science Association*, IV (1958), 107–21.

38. Such as A. H. Anderson, *The Changing Role of the Small Town in Farm Areas*, Agricultural Experiment Station Bulletin 419 (Lincoln, Nebr.: 1953); Kraenzel, *Great Plains in Transition;* Saskatchewan, Royal Commission, *Service Centers.*; and John R. Borchert, *Trade Centers and Trade Areas in the Upper Midwest*, Urban Report No. 3 (Minneapolis: Upper Midwest Economic Study, 1963).

39. Shue Tuck Wong, in "A Multivariate Statistical Model for Predicting Mean Annual Flood in New England," *Annals of the Association of American Geographers*, LIII, No. 3 (September, 1963), 298–311, uses a similar statistical model.

40. These labels, used originally in the Upper Midwest Economic Study, *Trade Centers and Trade Areas*, are apt descriptions of the function of such centers.

41. See Glenn V. Fuguitt, "The Growth and Decline of Small Towns as a Probability Process," (Unpublished ms., Madison, Wisc., 1963).

42. Robert C. Wood, *1400 Governments* (Cambridge, Mass.: Harvard University Press, 1961), p. 218.

43. The computation was carried out on the IBM 704 EDPM, using a program written for the occasion.

44. The method is described in Benjamin Fruchter, *Introduction to Factor Analysis* (Princeton, N.J.: D. Van Nostrand Company, Inc., 1953), pp. 99 ff.

45. The computation was carried out on the IBM 1620 EDPM, using a program developed by Thomas C. Teeples, "Principal Axis Factor Analysis Using Hotelling's Iterative Procedure," IBM 1620 General Program Library, No. 6.0. 091, 1963.

46. The analysis was stopped at this point in accordance with a rule-of-thumb that holds factors explaining less than 5 per cent of the variance to be statistically unreliable.

47. The computation was carried out on the IBM 7094 EDPM, at the Computation Center of the Massachusetts Institute of Technology, Cambridge, Mass., using BIMD Program 19. The rationale for varimax factor matrix rotation is described in Henry F. Kaiser, "The Varimax Criterion for Analytic Rotation in Factor Analysis," *Psychometrika*, XXIII (1958), 187–200.

48. A factor loading of 0.40 is used here as a lower limit on significance. The literature is not explicit on such a limit, but obviously very little is added to the eigenvalues below 0.40.

49. The computation was carried out on the IBM 7094 EDPM, at the Computation Center, Massachusetts Institute of Technology, Cambridge, Mass. using BIMD Program 06, "Multiple Regression Analysis."

50. M. F. Dacey, "The Geometry of Central Place Theory," *Geografiska Annaler*, XLVII -B (1965), 111–24.

51. W. C. Guenther and P. J. Terragno, "A Review of the Literature on a Class of Coverage Problems," *Annals of Mathematical Statistics*, XXXV (1964), 232–60.

52. M. F. Dacey, "Measures of Distance from a Randomly Located Point to Neighboring Lattice Points for Rectangular and Hexagonal Point Lattices," Submitted to Defense Documentation Center as Technical Report No. 3, Geographic Information Systems, Department of Geography, Northwestern University (1965).

53. An unpublished but widely distributed mimeographed study describes another stochastic interpretation of central-place theory: see M. F. Dacey, "Imperfections in the Uniform Plane," Michigan Inter-University Community of Mathematical Geographers, No. 3 (1963).

54. F. Germond, *The Circular Coverage Function* (Santa Monica, Calif.: Rand Corporation, Report No. RM-330, 1950); H. Weil, "The Distribution of Radial Error," *Annals*

of *Mathematical Statistics*, XXV (1954), 168–70. A series of four articles by H. Rubin has the general title "Probability Content of Regions under Spherical Normal Distributions," *Annals of Mathematical Statistics*, XXXI (1960), 598–618 and 1113–21; XXXII (1961), 171–86; and XXXIII (1962), 542–70.

55. C. Eisenhart and M. Zelen, "Elements of Probability," in *Handbook of Physics*, eds. E. U. Condon and H. Odishaw (New York: McGraw-Hill Book Company, 1958), Chap. xii.

56. K. Pearson, *Tables of the Incomplete Function* (Cambridge: Cambridge University Press, 1922); H. L. Harter, *New Tables of the Incomplete Gamma Function Ratio and of Percentage Points of the Chi-Square and Beta Distributions* (Washington, D.C.: U.S. Government Printing Office, 1964).

57. S. S. Gupta, "Order Statistics from the Gamma Distribution," *Technometrics*, II (1960), 243–62. See also H. L. Harter, *Expected Values of Exponential, Weibull and Gamma Order Statistics*, Report AD 436763, Office of Technical Services, Department of Commerce (Washington, D.C.: U.S. Government Printing Office, 1964).

58. F. E. Grubbs, "Approximate Circular and Non-Circular Offset Probabilities of Hitting," *Operations Research*, XII, No. 1 (January, 1964), 51–62.

59. F. J. Anscombe, "Tests of Goodness of Fit," *Journal of the Royal Statistical Society*, B, XXV (1963), 81–94.

CHAPTER 8

problems of defining the metropolis*

In Chapter 2 it was concluded that a new concept was required to capture the nature of the metropolis in a post-industrial society, and in Chapter 7 the many technical difficulties of dealing with such terms as "village," "town," "city," and "metropolis" were outlined. We now turn to a more searching discussion of the changing attempts of the U. S. Bureau of the Census to define the nation's metropolitan areas, under conditions in which the scale and pattern of urban growth are being transformed continuously and with increasing rapidity. That the definitional problem is complex is illustrated by Fig. 10–9 (p. 325), which shows how, in the Chicago region, one is dealing with a variety of legal cities, each considerably less in size than the continuously built-up urbanized area, which sprawls across a built-up urbanized area, which sprawls across a series of metropolitan areas as defined by the Bureau of the Census, which in turn are smaller than the commuting area (labor market) of just the *central city* of Chicago. An additional case, that of Phoenix, is presented in Fig. 8–1. We hope, then, that from this discussion the student will begin to appreciate that, just as the "facts" of urban geography are determined by geographers' concepts, so the "data" are not absolute but dependent upon a whole series of prior decisions about definitions, some of which may be questionable.

*Reprinted from Brian J. L. Berry, Peter G. Goheen, and Harold Goldstein, *Metropolitan Area Definition: A Re-evaluation of Concept and Statistical Practice* (Washington, D. C.: U.S. Government Printing Office, U. S. Bureau of the Census Working Paper, 1968).

HISTORY OF THE DEFINITION OF METROPOLITAN AREAS IN THE UNITED STATES

Fundamental changes in the American way of life were recognized at the beginning of the century by the Bureau of the Census when, in 1910, it introduced the category *Metropolitan Districts* to its system of area classification. This marked the first use by the Bureau of the Census of a unit other than the corporate boundaries of a city for reporting data on urban population. The Metropolitan District of 1910, defined for every city of over 200,000 inhabitants and used by the Bureau with little alteration in 1920, 1930, and 1940, served basically to distinguish the urban population, whether located within the central city or adjacent to it, from the surrounding rural population. The idea behind the definition was in essence, that stated in 1932:

> [T]he population of the corporate city frequently gives a very inadequate idea of the population massed in and around that city, constituting the greater city, . . . and [the boundaries of] large cities in few cases . . . limit the urban population which that city represents or of which it is the center. . . . If we are to have a correct picture of the massing or concentration of population in extensive urban areas . . . it is necessary to establish metropolitan districts which will show the magnitude of each of the principal population centers.[1]

Almost as soon as the concept of "metropolitan" was introduced into statistical practice, as part of the attempt to capture "the greater city," there was dissatisfaction with the criteria, the definitions, used, or with the results of their application. It is inevitable that the delimitation, for statistical purposes, of any set of areas transcending conventional legal jurisdictions will become the subject of local protest and political pressure. Almost any set of statistics will attract a coterie of users, too, many of whom will find it inadequate for their particular purposes. The criteria used in formulating a concept as fundamental and important as "metropolitan" necessarily become the objects of academic evaluation and criticism. Moreover, society itself continues to change, so that even criteria and statistical areas that are valid representations of real conditions, just as surely cease to be so in the course of time. The result has been the successive modification of the definitional criteria.

Metropolitan Districts, which were defined, in 1940 for each incorporated city having 50,000 or more inhabitants, included adjacent and contiguous minor civil divisions or incorporated places having a population density of 150 persons or more per square mile.[2] In 1940, however, relatively few data were tabulated for minor civil divisions. At the same time, the various government agencies used no standard set of regions in reporting their statistics: for example, the *Industrial Areas* defined by the Census of Manufacturing and the *Labor Market Areas* used by the Bureau of Employment Security both differed from the Metropolitan Districts used by the Bureau of the Census.

In consequence, a further consideration was introduced in developing the *Standard Metropolitan Areas* (SMA's) of 1950: so that a wide variety of statistical data might be presented on a uniform basis.[3] The SMA consisted of one county, or of contiguous counties, containing at least one city of 50,000 inhabitants. The additional counties had to meet certain criteria of "metropolitan character" and of "social and economic integration" with the central city in order to be classified within an SMA. Various government agencies cooperated to collect and report data in terms of this statistical unit, for the SMA was by its very nature a compromise designed to facilitate uniform reporting of data. It differed from the old Metropolitan District in that it was not primarily based upon density of population. The introduction of the *Urbanized Area* in 1950 provided a unit that fit more closely to the idea of the Metropolitan District.

The *Standard Metropolitan Statistical Area* (SMSA) of 1960 embodies a slight revision of the SMA concept, the word "statistical" being added so that the character of the area being defined might be better understood. The primary objective of the SMSA, as stated, is to facilitate the utilization of a uniform area by all federal agencies which publish statistical data useful in analyzing metropolitan problems. The usefulness of the data has been related most especially to the fact that the SMSA takes into account places of industrial concentration (labor demand) and of population concentration (labor supply).[4]

Two important claims have been advanced for the SMSA. First, it provides a "standard" area composed of a large city and its closely integrated surrounding area which can be used by the Census Bureau and other government agencies when gathering, analysing, and presenting data.

Second, the classification distinguishes between metropolitan and nonmetropolitan areas, as places of residence, replacing the older distinctions between rural and urban, farm and nonfarm areas.[5]

The SMSA has indeed been used extensively as a reporting unit by government. The Censuses reporting data about SMSA's include Population, Housing, Manufactures, Business, and Governments; the government agencies using the SMSA as a reporting unit include the Bureau of Labor Statistics, the National Office of Vital Statistics, the Social Security Administration, the Federal Reserve Board, the Federal Communications Commission, the Department of Housing and Urban Development, the Department of Transportation, the Small Business Administration, the Defence Service Administration, and the Federal Bureau of Investigation. Other users include local planning agencies and sales and advertising concerns. Much nonstatistical use has also been made of the classification by local political organizations and boosters.

Many of the nongovernmental users of SMSA data assume that the areas defined as metropolitan represent, in some measure, trading areas for the metropolis.[6] Thus, the use of SMSA data to establish quantitative indices of potential sales market areas, to set comparative guidelines for contrasting markets and market penetration, and to allocate manpower for sales and promotion efforts in common. Local and regional planners find SMSA data useful especially because of the quantity of information provided that would otherwise be unavailable, and because the SMSA's are ready-made planning regions within which they can study broad trends relating to mobility, social and economic patterns, and land use.

Recently, as an outcome of the Demonstration Cities and Metropolitan Development Act of 1966, many kinds of requests for federal public works monies must first be submitted to regional metropolitan planning agencies designated by the federal government. The U.S. Bureau of the Budget has been given the responsibility for selecting the appropriate local planning agency for the relevant SMSA. New legal status has thus been given to a set of statistical areas which has been, like its predecessors, subject to intense criticism and to the pressures of continuing societal change.

THE 1960 STANDARD METROPOLITAN STATISTICAL AREA

The purpose of establishing the SMSA in 1960 was to set out objective criteria of a quantitative character, in order to define areas "in a manner which reflects the underlying social and economic realities."[7] In the words of the Bureau of the Budget:

> The general concept of a metropolitan area is one of an integrated economic and social unit with a recognized large population nucleus. To serve the statistical purposes for which metropolitan areas are defined, their parts must themselves be areas for which statistics are usually or often collected. Thus, each Standard Metropolitan Statistical Area must contain at least one city of at least 50,000 inhabitants. The Standard Metropolitan Statistical Area will then include the county of such a central city, and adjacent counties that are found to be metropolitan in character and economically and socially integrated with the county of the central city. In New England the requirement with regard to a central city as a nucleus still holds, but the units comprising the area are the towns rather than counties. The county (or town in New England) is the basic statistical unit. A Standard Metropolitan Statistical Area may contain more than one city of 50,000 population. The largest city is considered the nucleus and usually gives the name to the area. The name may include other cities in the area. Standard Metropolitan Statistical Areas may cross State lines.... One of the basic criteria for measuring economic integration to determine whether additional counties should be included in an area definition, is the relationship of place of residence to place of work, involving outlying counties and the county of the central city. The volume of worker commuting was determined on the basis of data from the 1960 Census of Population.
>
> The definitions presented here are designed to serve a wide variety of statistical and analytical purposes. Adoption of these areas for any specific purpose should be judged, however, in light of the appropriateness of the criteria by which they are defined.[8]

The Definitional Criteria

The definition of an individual Standard Metropolitan Statistical Area involves two considerations: (1) a city or cities of specified population to constitute the central city and to define the county in which it is located as the central county; and (2) economic and social relationships with contiguous counties which are metropolitan in character, so that the periphery of the specific metropolitan area may be determined. SMSA's may cross state lines, if necessary, in order to include qualified contiguous counties.

Population.

1. Each SMSA must include:
   a. One city with 50,000 or more inhabitants; or
   b. Two cities having contiguous boundaries and constituting, for general economic and social purposes, a single community with a combined population of at least 50,000, the smaller of which must have a population of at least 15,000.
2. If two or more adjacent counties each have a city of 50,000 inhabitants or more (or there are twin cities, as defined in 1*b*) and the cities are within twenty miles of each other (city limits to city limits), they will be included in the same area unless there is definite evidence that the two cities are not economically and socially integrated.

Metropolitan character. The criteria of metropolitan character relate primarily to the attributes of the county as a place of work or as a home for a concentration of nonagricultural workers:

3. At least 75 per cent of the labor force of the county must be in the nonagricultural labor force.
4. In addition, the county must meet at least one of the following conditions:
   a. It must have 50 per cent or more of its population living in contiguous minor civil divisions with a density of at least 150 persons per square mile, in an unbroken chain of minor civil divisions with such a density radiating from a central city in the area.
   b. The number of nonagricultural workers employed in the county must equal at least 10 per cent of the number of nonagricultural workers employed in the county containing the largest city in the area, or be the place of employment of 10,000 nonagricultural workers.
   c. The nonagricultural labor force living in the county must equal at least 10 per cent of the number of the nonagricultural labor force living in the county containing the largest city in the area, or be the place of residence of a nonagricultural labor force of 10,000.
5. In New England, the city and town are administratively more important than the county, and data are compiled locally for such minor civil divisions, towns and cities being the units used in defining SMSA's. Because smaller units are used and more restricted areas result, a population density of 100 persons per square mile is used as the criterion of metropolitan character.

Integration. The criteria of integration relate primarily to the extent of economic and social communication between the outlying and the central counties.

6. A county is regarded as integrated with the county or counties containing the central cities of the area if either of the following criteria is met:
   a. If 15 per cent of the workers living in the county work in the county or counties containing the central cities of the area; or
   b. If 25 per cent of those working in the county live in the county or counties containing central cities of the area.
7. Where data for Criteria 6*a* and *b* are not conclusive, related types of information are used, as necessary: newspaper circulation reports prepared by the Audit Bureau of Circulation; analysis of charge accounts in retail stores of central cities to determine the extent of their use by residents of the contiguous county; delivery service practices of retail stores in central cities; official traffic counts; the extent of public transportation between central cities and communities in the contiguous county; and the extent to which local planning groups and other civic organizations operate jointly.

Criticisms of Present Definitions

Each of the criteria used to define the SMSA has been subject to criticism from many points of view. It is clear from these comments that much of the dissatisfaction stems from the compromise nature of the concept as it has been defined. The criticisms then, are valuable challenges to and examinations of the bases of the criteria and their definitions.

Criticisms of the population criteria. Questions have been raised about the basis for the population criteria, the necessity of a minimum or a maximum limit to population, and the distances specified (in Criterion 2) for combining adjacent counties, each containing central cities, into a single SMSA. On a more basic level, there is disagreement concerning the relation between population thresholds and economic organization, brought out by Fox and Duncan.[9]

The application of Criterion 2, by which

adjacent counties each having a central city of 50,000 inhabitants or more within twenty miles of each other are included within the same SMSA, has resulted in conflicts with Criterion 6, the commuting criterion.[10] There are twelve cities with 50,000 or more inhabitants within twenty miles of each other which meet the commuting requirements and are classified together within one SMSA. There are nine cities of 50,000 or more inhabitants, within twenty miles of each other, which do not meet commuting requirements and are classified together as a single SMSA. There are seventeen cities of 50,000 or more, within 20 miles of each other, which are not classified within the same SMSA (one of these meets the commuting stipulation). Additionally, there are approximately forty counties that meet the criteria of metropolitan character, have populations exceeding 100,000, and are not included in any SMSA.

Some have argued that the urbanized area should be used as the population base instead of the central city.[11] A calculation based on urbanized area population would not be difficult since it is already done as a matter of course, but it would involve defining urbanized areas for many cities of less than 50,000 inhabitants.

The number 50,000 has itself been challenged on several scores. To Fox, that number seems too arbitrary and too large, since a great many smaller centers of local activity in rural areas will be missed, and the importance of size in the economic organization of space will thus be overemphasized.[12] Duncan, on the other hand, argues that a city of 50,000 is really too small to constitute a metropolitan center, and that larger areas, with central cities of about 300,000 people, are most meaningful in today's economic context.[13]

Criticisms of the criteria of metropolitan character. The criteria of metropolitan character have been subjected to much criticism and questioning. The criticisms arise, for the most part, from the vagueness of the concept. No full or adequate explanation has been enunciated by the Bureau of the Budget, although the social and economic connotations of the criteria have been subject to much debate. There is also a need for clarification of the spatial extent of the SMSA. Clearly, the compromises inherent in the present definition have contributed considerably to the confusion.

Even the most explicit sections of the criteria have been questioned. How does one justify a requirement that 50 per cent of the population live in contiguous minor civil divisions of a certain minimum population density? Further, how does one define the nonagricultural labor force? Where do part-time farmers fit in? Specific objections have been raised to the unique definition of the New England SMSA. Critics have suggested raising to 90 per cent the proportion of the labor force in a county which must be in the nonagricultural labor force, and then dropping Criterion 4 altogether.[14]

In reviewing the comments addressed to it, the Bureau of the Budget has found numerous inconsistencies of application and a bewildering variety of choices made possible because many counties do not meet a few of the criteria. For example, the Bureau of the Budget found thirty-eight counties otherwise qualifying as metropolitan which were excluded because of small total population, small labor force, or insufficient population density.

Besides the uncertainties about meaning, there are, first, specific questions about the apparent conflicts arising from defining metropolitan character in both economic and social terms, a disjunction pointed out by Fox, and by Friedmann and Miller.[15] Second, some aspects of the urban-rural distinction (a distinction long indistinct) still appear to be built into the language of the criteria for metropolitan character—density and size—introduced by Wirth.[16] Third, the definition ignores, except in the crudest sense, the question of the necessity for some landscape criteria by which to enunciate metropolitan character. The literature on metropolitan areas reveals a basic cleavage between the scholars who rely on some landscape element to form part of their definition and another group who find it unnecessary to include any specific reference to particular landscape features when discussing the concept. Included in the first group are Blumenfeld, Hawley, Friedmann and Miller, Pickard, and Schnore. [17]Among those in the second group are Isard and Kavesh, and Webber *et al.*[18]

The fact that the SMSA uses both social and economic criteria has created differing interpretations. It has been implied by some that the central county is both a place of work and a home for concentrations of nonagricultural workers, as well as being the primary trading area for the metropolis.[19] Are these conditions necessary for a county to be metropolitan in an economic sense? Some evidence, advanced by Borchert, indicates that the wholesale trading territories of large metropolitan areas are coterminous with areas of migration from farm to city (suggesting a correspondence of boundaries of several indicators of metropolitan economic influence), and that retail trade areas are coincident with the commuting areas of smaller places.[20] In agricultural areas and around the smaller central cities of the SMSA's, Borchert's findings notwithstanding, others have argued that the general trade area of the central city covers a more extensive terrain than any kind of extended migration or commuting zone.[21] Further information about commuting patterns will answer such questions, it is likely, however, that the patterns will vary in metropolitan areas of different sizes and in different parts of the country.[22] If one is speaking of a metropolitan economy, then it is clear that the larger SMSA's are underbounded. If one is speaking of activity patterns of individuals and groups living within metropolitan areas, the SMSA does not distinguish these: it is clear, from research, that there is little difference between groups included within metropolitan areas and some of those which are excluded.[23] The differences appear to be more distinct between workers engaged in urban pursuits and those engaged in rural, agricultural pursuits.[24] If by the metropolitan character of an area we mean the use made of its land by various groups, then it is clear that the sphere of influence of metropolitan dwellers extends far beyond the counties currently classified as metropolitan.[25] At this point the discussion reverts to the problem of interpreting what is meant by "metropolitan."

Criticisms of the criteria of integration. A review of the criticisms and comments concerning the criteria of integration reveals a lack of satisfaction with the current definition, based as it is only on commuting to or from the county containing the central city. General comment about the concept of metropolitan areas echoes this dissatisfaction, and there have been many suggestions that a more precise and detailed statement about economic and social integration within the metropolitan area must be made.

The percentages established by the Bureau of the Budget (Criteria 6*a* and *b*) have been questioned. The discrepancy (between 15 per cent and 25 per cent) seems particularly curious. The necessity for direct contact with the central county has been challenged by pointing out the lack of unified labor markets within large metropolitan areas.[26] The achievement of maximum accessibility throughout the metropolitan areas through reductions in the cost and time of travel has led to the suggestion that a commuting radius be established on the basis of the time taken to reach the central county or its central area.[27]

That integration can be defined without bringing in what is commonly thought to be metropolitan character is implicit in several of the classification schemes. The classifications suggested by Friedmann and Miller, and by Fox, revolve around a notion of integration which is not accompanied by the criterion of population density now closely associated with metropolitan character.[28] The two proposals will be discussed at greater length in the following section of this chapter, but it is well to note here that such schemes propose a radical alternative to our present concept of "metropolitan." Friedmann and Miller believe that the whole scale of urban life is changing as our technology and economy develop. Such an idea implies that the distinction between metropolitan and nonmetropolitan is no longer useful, and that a new and broad *urban realm* has come into being. The argument rests largely on the claim that the area in which a metropolitan population lives and conducts its social activities now encompasses a broad zone around the metropolitan centers. This zone, or realm, extends to, perhaps, a hundred miles from the central city and is defined as the limit for regular week-end or seasonal use. Within this area, the imprint of the urban dweller is of paramount significance. This realm is also largely coincident with areas of general economic health, they maintain.

Fox is concerned with small, functionally specialized regions which he considers to be the major facts of economic importance in the context of the regionalization of most of the country. Integration thus is often without metropolitan character since many of the smaller centers are too tiny or too sparsely populated to be classed as metropolitan. Fox posits the *Functional Economic Area* (FEA) as the economic building block of the regionalization of the United States.

Nevertheless, commentators always point out, in any discussion of the criteria of metropolitan character or integration, that the issues are bound together and that one's understanding of the one can hardly be divorced from the other.

Criticisms of area titles. Various local booster organizations have suggested modifications of titular designations, particularly with respect to the size limits imposed on the inclusion of place names in SMSA's.[29]

Building blocks. Suggestions for splitting large counties, for automatically classifying counties containing cities of 50,000 inhabitants as central counties, and for reconsidering the population density criteria for the inclusion of contiguous counties within the SMSA have also been made.[30]

General comments on the criteria. The whole idea of using distance as a major criterion of definition has been challenged by suggestions that time-distance measures ought to be used instead.[31] It has been suggested that self-sustaining economic growth of a region be made the basis of defining one level of metropolitan region and its central city.[32] Researchers who have sought to make trade areas out of the metropolitan regions defined by the Census Bureau have suggested that self-sufficiency with respect to local services be made the criteria for defining metropolitan areas.[33]

ALTERNATIVE CLASSIFICATION SYSTEMS

The various proposals for establishing new classification systems can be viewed as attempts to bring into focus the social or economic aspects of what the research workers consider to be a viable and useful concept of the metropolitan area. Definitions of "metropolitan" are often absent from the discussion, but all classifications can be considered as approaches to the regionalization of the country in terms which will highlight what are thought to be the important processes at work in the present scene. To begin with, three questions can be asked, the answers to which it will be useful to search for in the proposed new classifications schemes:

1. What areal bases are appropriate for defining metropolitan areas?

   On this point, there is generally unanimous opinion that the two aspects of the present classification of area—the economic and social—cannot now be defined meaningfully by outlining one set of regions which occupy a tiny fraction of the total land area and classifying it as metropolitan, and by outlining another region, occupying most of the land area, and classifying it as nonmetropolitan.
2. Can social and economic areas be mapped by using coincident boundaries, or must there be a separate classification of territory for each?

   About the second question there is less agreement. Some argue that the sphere of metropolitan economic influence is more widespread and general across the country than that of metropolitan social influence. Others, arguing from the facts of the greatly increasing mobility of metropolitan residents, state that the impact of metropolitan dwellers is everywhere evident if one examines the areas they visit and use regularly for recreation and other purposes.
3. Can all social communication be subsumed under a single category, an area outlining metropolitan residents' social activities? If the journey to work and the week-end holiday involve the use and habituation of greatly differing areas, should not two or more types of social region be defined, at least one based on day-to-day contact and the other on the more extensive territories infrequently occupied by city dwellers?

   The latter question makes it clear that one of the major problems involves the interpretation of the areal boundaries drawn on the map, especially since economic and social area boundaries apparently are so often not coincident. A much more explicit interpretation of these boundaries would seem warranted, no matter what decision is reached regarding the classification scheme.

Two schemes have been proposed which consider the over-all economic organization of the country. One is Bogue's, which emphasizes metropolitan dominance over an adjacent hinterland, and the other is suggested by Duncan *et al.*, who made a detailed empirical study of functional specialization in American cities.

Metropolitan Dominance

Bogue attempted to examine the hypothesis that the metropolis, by 1950, had come to dominate the social and economic organization of a technologically advanced society such as the United States.[34] The increased efficiency of transportation had presumably greatly extended the radius of convenient daily movement to and from the city, diffusing the urban mode of life over ever increasing areas. Distance, therefore, was considered to be the single most important determinant of the limits of areas of metropolitan dominance. Bogue proceeded to divide the entire area of the nation into "metropolitan communities," abstracting patterns of population distribution from various groupings of these communities. He began somewhat arbitrarily by selecting 67 metropolitan communities, each claiming as hinterland all the areas lying closest to itself.

Such an arbitrary division of the area among zones of dominance, however, ignores the differences of kind between the largest and the smallest metropolitan centers. What was meant by "metropolitan" was not defined, nor was the selection of 67 centers justified. And, because the distance relationships between the metropolitan centers in the northeast are different than in other areas, comparisons of the data based on distance zones are misleading: the comparisons are really of different sets of centers.[35] Bogue ignored the data on social interaction and so did not broach the second and third questions posed above. He included and labeled as "metropolitan" areas which are more extensive than those so labeled at present. Actually, without providing convincing supporting arguments, Bogue used the concepts of "metropolitan area" developed by Gras and McKenzie. Gras argued that in defining the metropolis, it was the hinterland that was the important element—and the sphere of commercial dominance that was particularly important. He stressed interdependence of function rather than size.[36] McKenzie sought to explore the dominance of the metropolitan city over the social organization of the surrounding areas.[37]

In a later work, Hawley utilized much the same conceptual framework of metropolitan dominance to test the adequacy of the SMA's as poles of population growth.[38] He arbitrarily selected a 35-mile radius from central cities and measured the population growth within this area to see the extent to which national growth was oriented to the metropoli. Over 90 per cent of the population's growth, he found, occurred within 25 miles of a central city, and the radius of that growth increased only slightly from 1900 to 1950.

Functional Specialization

Work on functional specialization and on areas of metropolitan economic influence was accomplished by Duncan and his associates.[39] Using as indicators of metropolitan influence wholesale trade, bank clearings, business service receipts, value added by manufacture, and retail trade, they found the larger metropoli to be much more diversified than the smaller. It was concluded that the critical population figure for the emergence of metropolitan character is 300,000. Above this level, metropolitan areas are generally diversified, while below it they are functionally specialized. A hierarchy of types of economic relations can be found, but at the highest level the whole nation is served by one set of metropolitan areas. A range of higher-order goods and services is provided by a metropolitan economy which is organized and directed by these great metropolitan centers.

Several other suggested schemes of classification have been based on the idea that the country can be divided up into a set of relatively small and somewhat independent local areas which accurately delineate, in economic or social terms, areas of distinct local identity. A few of these schemes are outlined below.

The Functional Economic Area (FEA)

The FEA is an attempt to set out, ecologically, the labor market areas of central cities, by defining around them a set of small towns and villages and farms which comprise the area of active commuting to the central city. According to Fox,[40] the chief proponent of this scheme, such an area forms a low density city characterized by the definite interaction of the various parts with the center. The FEA is conceived of as an independent unit, in terms of local services to the adjacent population. Fox maintains that the United States, outside of the largest metropolitan areas, can be divided into a series of such FEA's which approximate relatively bounded or closed labor market areas. By proceeding to recognize this fact, one can classify workers by place of residence *and* place of work and produce a set of FEA's with relatively little commuting from one to another.

Considerable data are required to achieve the classification, as well as some model of the economy based on an examination of the system of structural relations connecting the country and its parts. Flow data are especially necessary for the analysis. A central city of the order of 25,000 inhabitants or more is the crux of the FEA, which is seen as a product of local economies of size and specialized management. The argument amounts to a statement that areas of social significance in terms of intimate daily contact are co-extensive with areas meaningful in local economic terms.

The State Economic Area (SEA)

Bogue and Beale, in setting down a complete system of SEA's for the United States, state that they have subdivided the country into units which are homogeneous with respect to general livelihood and socio-economic characteristics.[41] They maintain a distinction between metropolitan and nonmetropolitan SEA's based on the Bureau of the Budget's definitions of metropolitan areas. Their data, evaluated by subjective procedures, consists of information on land use, industry, the social characteristics of the population, and the wide range of information available in the various censuses. Their building blocks are counties, and the SEA is the basic unit upon which a hierarchy of economic areas is built.

The particular areas defined by Bogue and Beale have been called into question by various scholars, as have their methods of delimitation, but the notion that the country can be subdivided into a set of relatively self-contained economic areas has not been questioned. As defined, however, the SEA provides little insight into any of the questions posed. Vining believes that the arbitrariness of the boundaries established for the SEA can be overcome only by examining commodity flows and functional hierarchies, rather than by assuming some arbitrary functional grouping of counties each of which is presumed to contain a distinctive economy.[42]

Urban Community of Interest Areas

The premise upon which this concept is based is that the great metropolitan areas are too large to constitute a single labor market area.[43] A new unit is called for, which is defined on the basis of generalized spheres with which communities and the immediate ties of families can be identified. The expectation is that, at least for the majority of urban dwellers, there is a definably regular pattern of daily activity which can be mapped and generalized. The important activities can be classed as the journey to work, ordinary shopping, and social trips.

This approach provides some answers to our first two questions. It defines social areas within the city which are small and clearly distinct from areas of economic influence. However, it assumes that for the family or community the area within which regular and frequent social activities are undertaken is coterminous with the area of economic activity.

The "non-place" urban realm. Here is another argument about social areas, one which comes to a different conclusion by examining the activities of a different class of urban dweller. For Webber,[44] the community of interest is no longer conditioned by propinquity, but is essentially "non-place." Travel is easy and interests diffuse, and simple mapping procedures can no longer plot out the urban spaces which a man inhabits, nor can they separate any urban realm from a rural one adjacent to it. His is a functionalist view, which regards the distinction of activity by place of activity as exaggerated. It is a plea for a new meaning of "community," based on the notion of interdependence. Such an argument seems most appropriate when one examines the activity patterns of upper-class, mobile persons whose activities are not as conditioned by factory, store, or office hours as those of most workers.

The urban field. The third of our questions is most directly answered in the propositions outlined by Friedmann and Miller in a discussion of the expanding scene in which urban residents live.[45] They argue that, because of increasing mobility, there can now be seen in this country, around what are customarily called urban places, vast areas which are influenced to a great degree by the activity of urban dwellers. These border areas contain a commuting population, but they also house, occasionally, the week-end traveler from the city. They have become, in short, economically and socially a part of the urban community. The outer metropolitan peripheries beyond this field, in contrast to the metropolitan peripheries, are the areas of economic stress and emigration, those places most characterized by substandard educational, medical, and service facilities. They are, in consequence, characterized also by a declining economic base, an aging population, and low incomes which serve to lock them in and make them helpless even though they may desire to adapt to changing circumstances.

The urban field is presented as an ecological unit which has been created by the increase in the real income, leisure time, and mobility of those people who occupy the country's great metropolitan centers. Similar conclusions were reached in the Upper Midwest Economic Study.[46]

EVIDENCE FROM DATA ON THE JOURNEY TO WORK IN 1960

We have seen that there is much dissatisfaction with present definitional practice and that, although many alternatives have been proposed, the extent of their agreement is slender. A period of thinking and reevaluation is in order, to establish what should be retained in present practice, and what ideas common to the alternative proposals should be put into practice.

Several qualities are apparently desirable in any alternative: (1) the criteria should reflect the underlying realities of the behavior of the population and the socio-economic structure of areas; (2) they should be simple expressions of the way these realities are conceptualized, leading to consistent, unambiguous classification of areas without compromising statistical standards; and (3) they should lend themselves readily to a range of practical applications, as meaningful regional units, within the framework of emerging national urban policy.

In view of the major thrust of criticisms of the 1960 criteria, these considerations lead us naturally to an analysis of the commuting patterns of the American population. We use the unpublished journey-to-work information collected in the 1960 Census of Population and Housing made available to us by the U.S. Bureau of the Census.

The Data about Commuting

In 1960, for the first time, the Census of Population and Housing included a question designed to determine the commuting behavior of the population of the United States. Item *P28* of the Household Questionnaire read:

P28. What city and county did he work in last week?
  a. City or town:____________
  b. If city or town, did he work inside the city limits? Yes_____No_____
  c. County:____________State:____________

Some questions in the census were asked of every family unit in the country. Others, the journey-to-work question among them, were asked in every fourth housing unit visited, and in group quarters (e.g., institutions), of every fourth person, to maintain the 25 per cent sampling rate. Most of the data were collected in two stages. An Advance Census Report (ACR) was sent to all occupied housing units throughout the country in the last week of March, 1960, to be completed and held for the census enumerator's visit. When the enumerator collected the ACR, he left at every fourth household the Household Questionnaire, to be completed and mailed to the District Office of the Bureau of the Census.

In the less densely settled areas of the country (over half the land area of the country, but containing only 20 per cent of the population), the enumeration was accomplished in a single stage, however, by enumerators who recorded the additional data for every fourth household on their initial visit.

Once the schedules had been assembled in the District Offices of the Bureau of the Census, the information on them was transcribed to special FOSDIC (Film Optical Sensing Device for Input to Computers) schedules by employees of the Bureau. These schedules were microfilmed, and the FOSDIC scanned the microfilms and converted the marks on the schedules directly into magnetic impressions on the tapes that were then used for the preparation of the census reports.

Household question *P28* was transcribed in the following manner:

P28a. If he worked last week (yes in *P22*) what city or town did he work in last week?
Not in a city ☐ skip to *P28c*
This city ☐
Different city (specify):____________
P28b. If city or town, did he work inside city limits?
Yes ☐ No ☐
P28c. What county and state did he work in?
This county ☐
Different county (specify):____________
state:____________

Four-digit codes were used to identify the cities and counties as places of work, according to the Bureau's Universal Area Code (UAC) for workplace locations. Approximately 4,300 UAC workplaces of the following classes are recognized:

1. Central cities of SMSA's
2. Other cities of 50,000 population or more
3. Counties including no towns classified under 1 or 2
4. Remainders of counties which have cities classified under 1 or 2
5. Minor civil divisions (MCD's) in the New England states

However, certain restrictions were applied in coding the data concerning workplaces in any segment of the country. Individual and household data were assembled into totals for each of the country's 43,000 Standard Location Areas (SLA's) —census tracts in tracted areas, and MCD's elsewhere. For the residents of each county in the country, it was then decided what initially appeared to be the thirteen most important UAC workplace locations. These thirteen UAC codes, plus "other" and "unknown" categories, were then used as the basis for aggregating the journey to work information for each SLA in the county. Thus, although theoretically the 1960 journey to work data were assembled into a 43,000 SLA × 4,300 UAC matrix of journey to work information, the SLA's were in fact grouped into some 4,300 county sub-matrices, each of which had only 13 columns and 2 balance categories.

Commuting Fields and Labor Markets

A reporting booklet could be prepared from these data for any UAC workplace (e.g., 3301, the City of Chicago), listing all SLA's sending commuters to it, and for each of the SLA's showing how many and what proportion of the resident workers traveled to each of its thirteen UAC most important alternative work places or fell into one of the balance categories. With such information in hand, it was possible to plot a map for each UAC and its surrounding territory, showing the percentage of the workers resident in each SLA who commuted to that UAC. Because of the regular decline of the commuting rate with distance, it was also possible to contour the percentages to depict the *commuting field* of that workplace. Figure 8–1 shows such a cone-like commuting field for UAC 3301, the City of Chicago. The outer limit of this field is described by a zero contour beyond which there is no reported inward commuting; this zero contour delineates the Chicago *labor market*: the area within which jobs and homes are brought into balance, the area which serves as a bounded "container" of the journey to work. The mapped boundary is, in a sense, a conservative limit because: (1) since the sample was only 25 per cent, there remains some probability that there are longer-distance commuters; and (2) in some areas the outer limit is depicted by the dotted lines of an "option limit," the point at which the data ran out. Beyond this point, their thirteen permitted SLA's did not include Chicago, even though there may

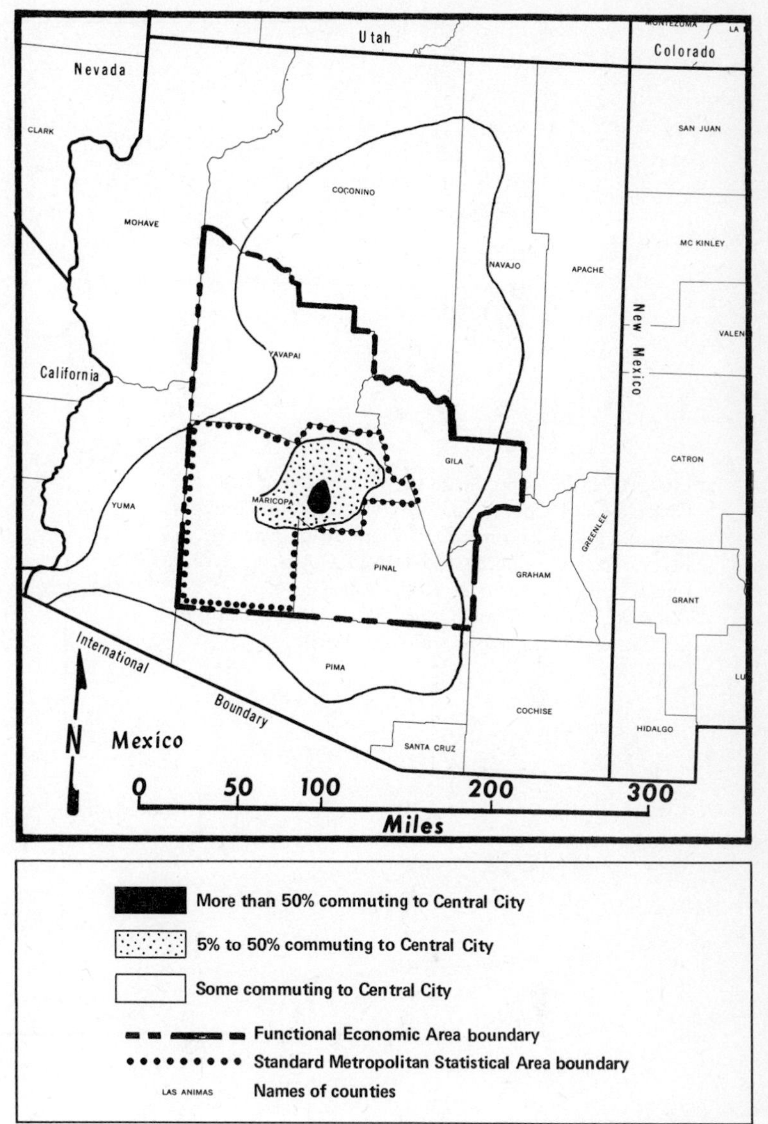

FIGURE 8–1. The commuting area, Standard Metropolitan Statistical Area, and Functional Economic Area of Phoenix, Arizona. *Source:* Primary data.

have been long-distance commuting to the city.

Commuting fields were mapped for every central city in an SMSA, for most urban centers in the 25,000–50,000 population range, and for many small places (see Chapter 2). Each field shows a gradual decay with distance; the greater the distance from the City of Chicago, for example, the smaller the proportion of the residents in an SLA who commuted to it. Figure 8–1 shows other features, too: "mountains" and "craters" in areas around the central city pick out the details of commuting suburbs and of outlying centers of employment.

In addition, there is a "bunching" of contours along the city limits, indicating a sharp discontinuity in the pattern of employment of residents on either side of the city limits. Figures 8–2*a* and *b* bring out the difference, amounting to at least 15, and sometimes as much as 40, percentage points. Chicago's workers are almost all part of Chicago's labor force, but just across the line into Cook County, there is apparently a sharp drop in the

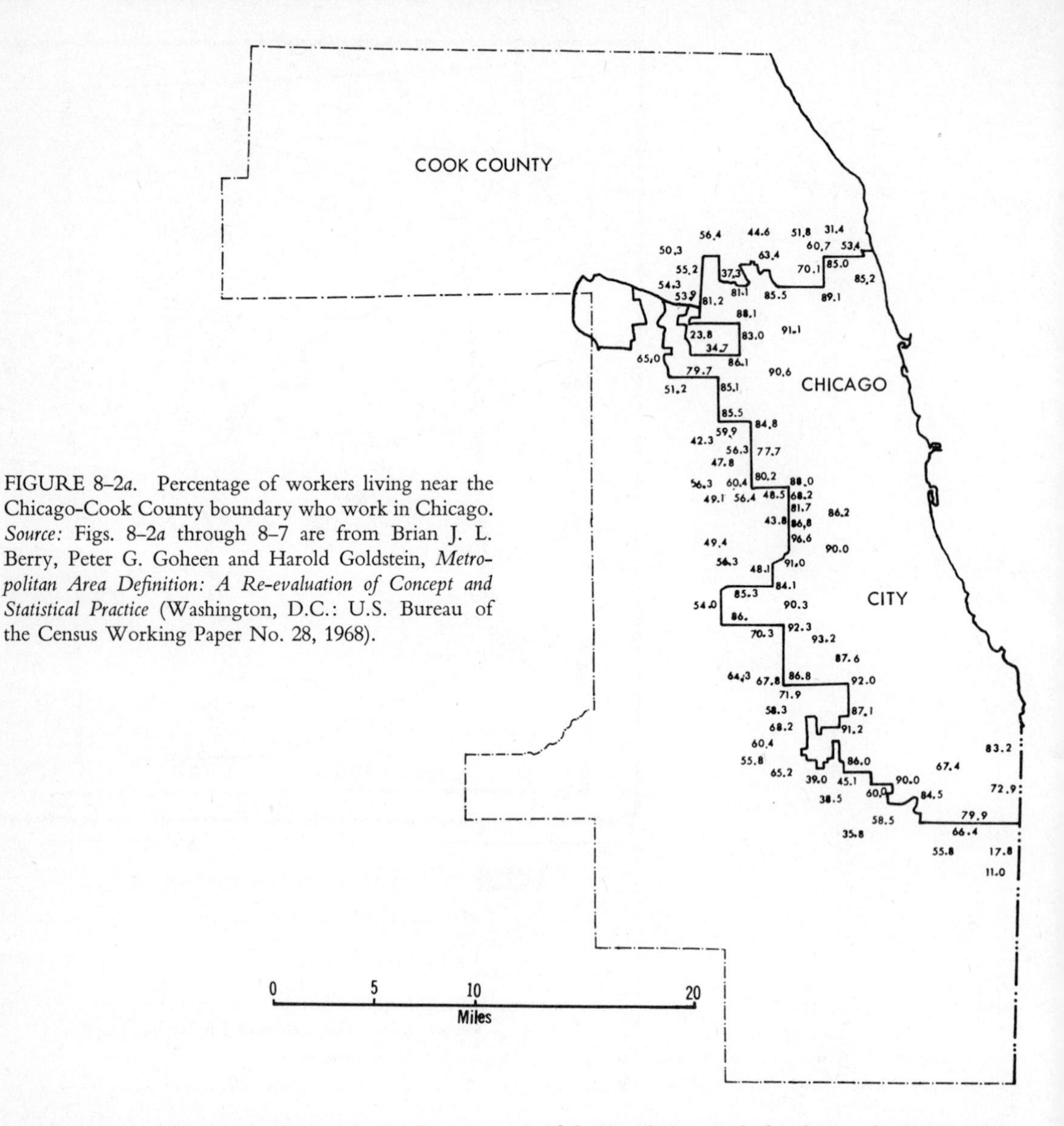

FIGURE 8–2*a*. Percentage of workers living near the Chicago-Cook County boundary who work in Chicago. *Source:* Figs. 8–2*a* through 8–7 are from Brian J. L. Berry, Peter G. Goheen and Harold Goldstein, *Metropolitan Area Definition: A Re-evaluation of Concept and Statistical Practice* (Washington, D.C.: U.S. Bureau of the Census Working Paper No. 28, 1968).

percentage of workers who have jobs in the city. The same holds true of Cook County (UAC workplace 3302): it seems to draw far more heavily, for its labor force, on Cook County residents near the boundary than on workers who live across it, in Chicago. Indeed, *in every case studied, the data reveal marked discontinuities along political boundaries.*

Why discontinuities? There are several reasons why such discontinuities might be expected to occur:

1. If the population worked at home, the UAC coding of workplaces would result in a 100–0 split along either side of a UAC boundary. In farming areas, then, a relatively sharp differential should be expected, in general, as the trip to work shortens, the probability that a commuter will cross a boundary will fall.
2. If adjacent counties have employment opportunities concentrated in central county seats, and commuters chose their residences with a sharp eye on distance from the job, the tradeoff between the two centers should coincide with the county boundary. This appears to be the case in many parts of the country, both for commuting and shopping.

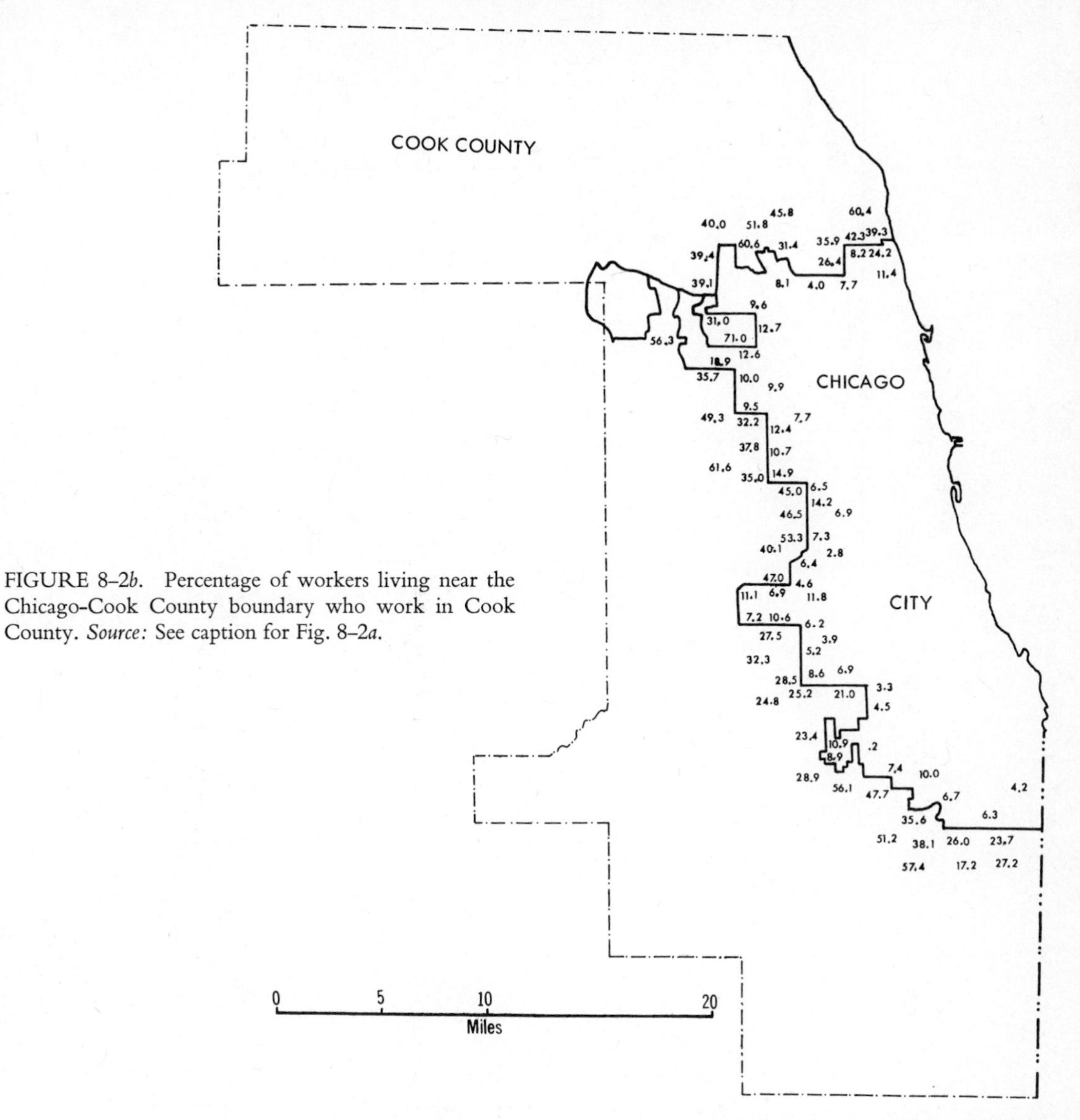

FIGURE 8–2*b*. Percentage of workers living near the Chicago-Cook County boundary who work in Cook County. *Source:* See caption for Fig. 8–2*a*.

Such reasons do not apply to situations like the Chicago–Cook County boundary, however. Here, we might argue that:

3. Suburban workers like to live as close to Chicago as possible without being within the city, and city workers prefer residences within the city, but choose not to reside one or two blocks over the city limits.

However, the boundaries create discontinuities even *within* cities. No amount of rationalization will wish away the same kind of differential along the Queens–Brooklyn boundary within New York City (Figs. 8–3*a* and *b*). Why, then, does such a boundary effect appear? What can explain the fact that, of those who live in Queens tracts bordering on Brooklyn, a median percentage of 47.6 work in Queens and only 17.6 in Brooklyn, whereas, of those living in Brooklyn tracts which border on Queens, a median percentage of 57.6 work in Brooklyn and only 12.1 in Queens? Some boundary effect of this kind has appeared in every commuting field studied in the U.S.—in

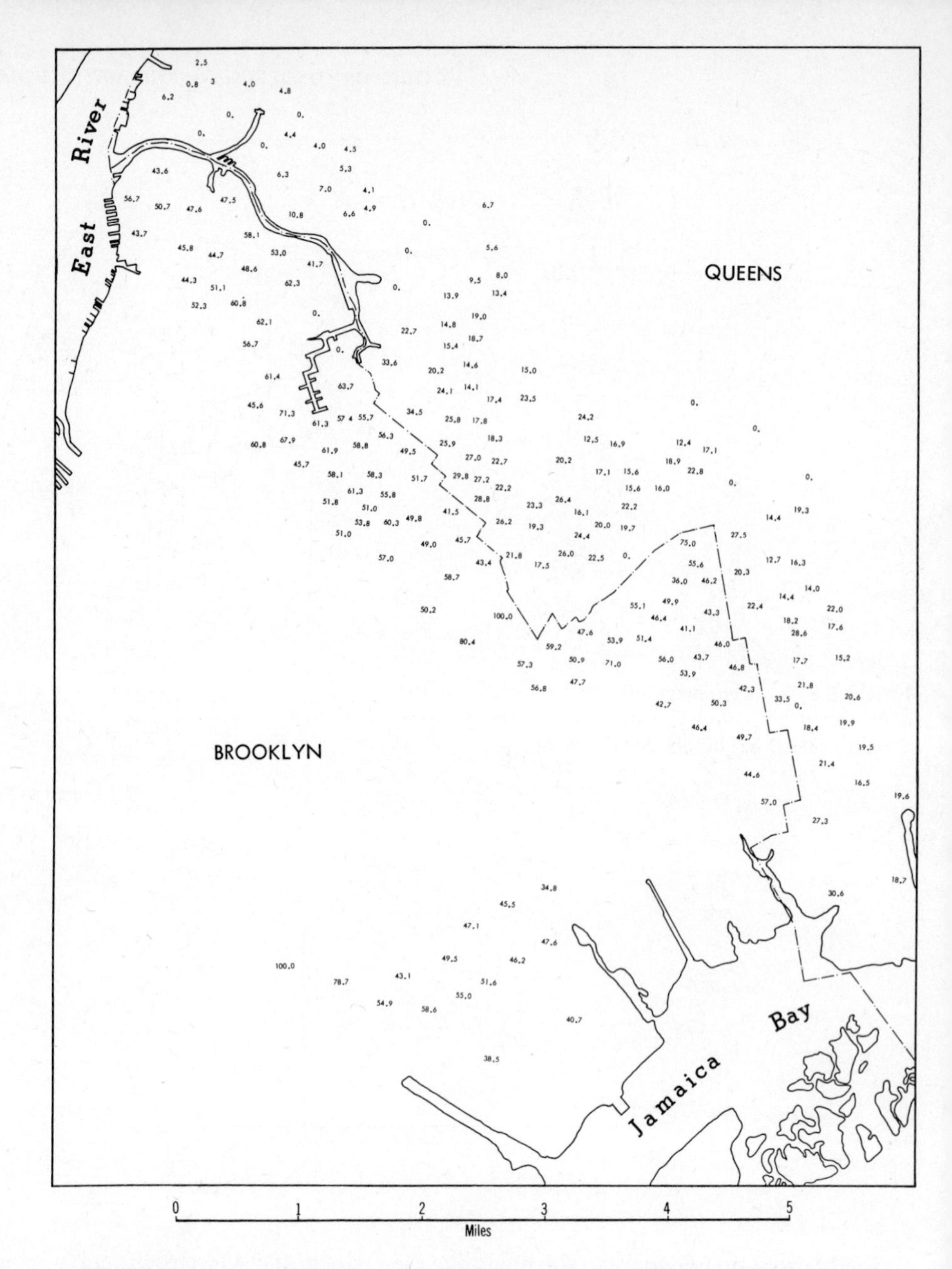

FIGURE 8–3*a*. Percentage of workers living near the Queens-Brooklyn boundary who work in Brooklyn. *Source:* See caption for Fig. 8–2*a*.

larger cities and smaller ones, in industrial areas and agricultural areas, in areas with natural boundaries and those with artificial boundaries. There have been no exceptions.

Systematic bias. Another possible explanation is that the boundary effects are due to systematic errors in the data. The Census Bureau's volume *Journey to Work* records one possible source of systematic bias introduced during the preparation of FOSDIC schedules from Household Questionnaires by census employees:

Some enumerators working in counties containing central cities of SMSA's, but outside the cities themselves, had failed to identify correctly these central cities as places of work. For the convenience of the enumerator and the coder, the FOSDIC document contained a

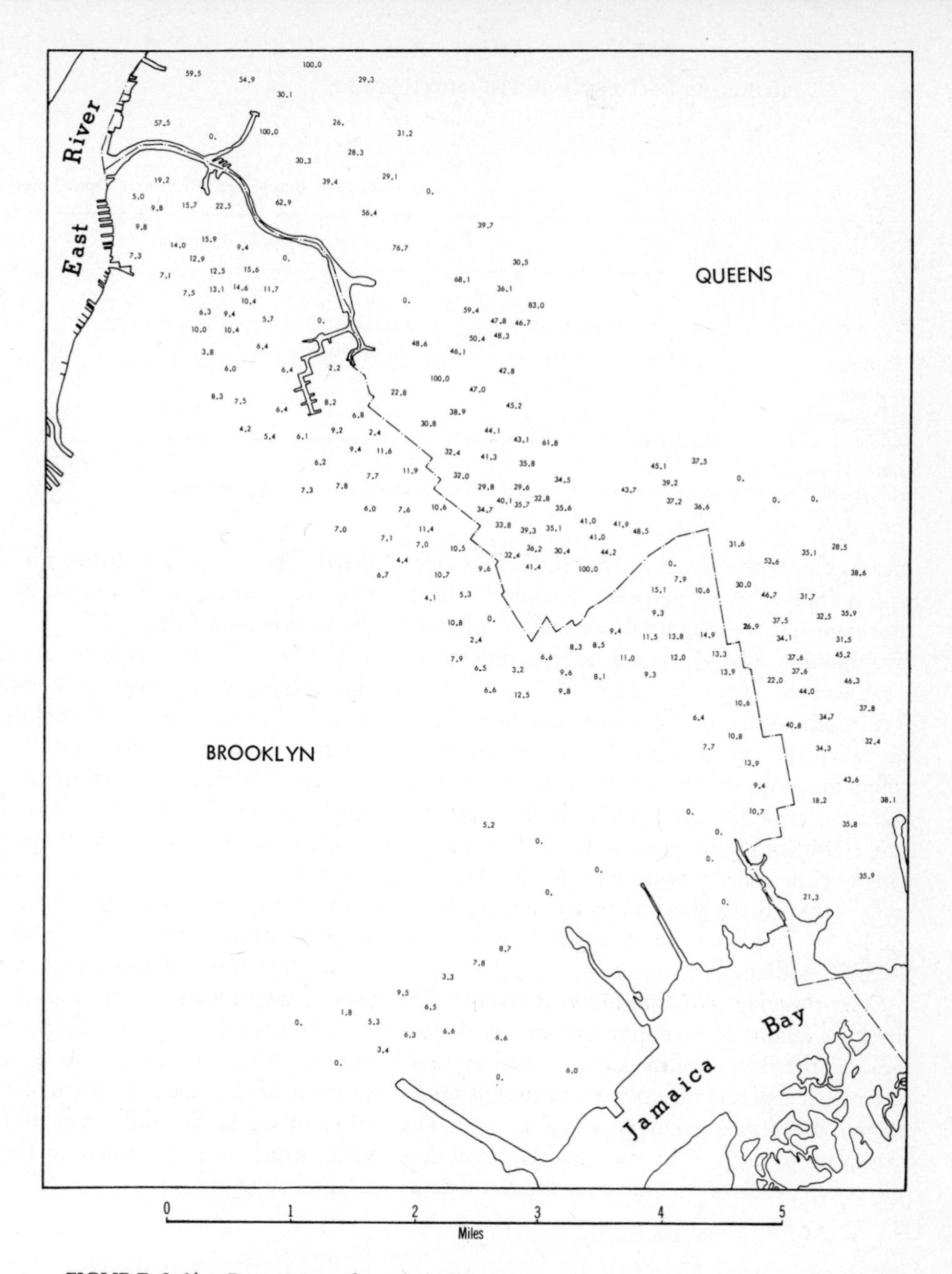

FIGURE 8–3*b*. Percentage of workers living near the Queens-Brooklyn boundary who work in Queens. *Source:* See caption for Fig. 8–2*a*.

circle labeled "this city" for indicating that the place of work was in the respondent's city or town of residence. Some enumerators understood this category to refer to a nearby large city and filled the circle when they should have written in the name of that city in *P28a*."[47]

An error of this type could obviously lead to the results obtained, for where "this city" or "this county" was checked, a respondent would be recorded as working in the UAC that he lived in. The Bureau of the Census reports the Shaker Heights data, which showed residents as employed in Shaker Heights rather than Cleveland; it was this well-known suburban dormitory instance that led to discovery of the error. A consistent 10 per cent bias toward coding the UAC of resid-

TABLE 8–1

Census Data from Employees' Responses about Location of Workplace

	Employee said he worked in:			
State	*"Same city"*	*"Same county"*	*Different county*	*Response is Type 9999**
Illinois	113 (71%)	23 (15%)	20 (12.5%)	3 (1.5%)
Indiana	24 (30%)	48 (60%)	6 (7.5%)	2 (2.5%)
Wisconsin	30 (67%)	4 (9%)	8 (18%)	3 (7%)

Source: Primary data.
*A Type 9999 response means that the employee has given two workplaces in different states.

ence as the workplace in the FOSDIC Schedules would lead to a 20 per cent boundary effect, approximately the magnitude seen of the Chicago discontinuity. The Queens-Brooklyn differential is substantially larger, however.

A similar source of error could have been introduced by the enumerators themselves, to compound the problem. Part *b* of item *P28* is the seemingly innocent question "inside the city limits?" Any consistent presumption in favor of one alternative or the other when the respondent did not really know would also lead to a boundary effect similar in character to a systematic bias in FOSDIC coding.

Cross-checking with employment records. To check the validity of the responses about workplace location, the Bureau of the Census asked a sample of employers across the country to submit information about their employees (Table 8–1). The workplace data given by the employer and employee were recorded on the same form and compared. The comparison forms for the same states (Illinois, Indiana, and Wisconsin) provided the results noted in Table 8–2.

The over-all disagreement between employee and employer responses is one-third (approximately the same rate as reported for the nation as a whole in the complete check). Most of these are Type 9999, i.e., either the employer or the employee put down two different workplaces in different states. Since instructions were for persons to mark the place where they spent the greatest number of hours, these disagreements may be misunderstandings. If they are not, it means that most of these Type 9999 differences were either initially reported by the interviewers or subsequently coded as "same city" or "same county," thus contributing to the systematic bias in favor of recording the place of residence as the place of work. The difference amounts to 25 per cent, which is very similar to the discontinuity at the boundaries.

TABLE 8–2

Cross-Checking the Data in Table 8–1 with Employers

		Disagreement			
State	*Agreement*	*Employee says he works in his home town: Employer disagrees*	*Employee says he works outside of his home town: Employer disagrees*	*Disagreement not having to do with home town*	*Response of either respondent is Type 9999**
Illinois	104 (66%)	3 (1.5%)	3 (1.5%)	8 (5%)	41 (26%)
Indiana	46 (57.5%)	0	4 (5%)	6 (7.5%)	24 (30%)
Wisconsin	36 (80%)	0	0	1 (2%)	8 (18%)

Source: Primary data.
*A Type 9999 response means that the respondent has given two workplaces in different states.

"Improvement" of the published statistics. The published commuting statistics reported in the volume *Journey to Work* were "improved" by the Bureau of the Census prior to printing because the coding error caused by the item, "this city" had been discovered:

> This alteration applied to entries for workers living in unincorporated parts of counties containing the central city of an SMSA (or other city with a population greater than 50,000). For these workers, a workplace code of "this city" was tabulated as the largest city in the county (this was not done for New England, New Jersey, and parts of Pennsylvania). Codes of "this city" for workers living in unincorporated areas outside counties containing central cities of SMSA's (or other city with a population greater than 50,000) were tabulated as "balance of county" since it was not clear what "this city" intended.[48]

Data for workers living in incorporated places were not edited, however, since it was believed that these data "were likely to be correct."

Following this editing, the Bureau of the Census concluded:

> It appears that the published statistics are substantially better than would be the case had the corrective edit been omitted. The number of workers residing outside central cities in the balances of central counties and working in the central cities appeared to be considerably understated before the correction and only a slightly overstated, in net effect, after the correction.[49]

It is unclear whether such a change actually corrects the systematic bias, however, especially if, in a proportion of the cases, the "this city" error worked in favor of the central city rather than against it. In such instances, the corrections could increase rather than eliminate the bias. For example, in the Hamilton-Middletown SMSA, Hamilton is the dominant city. As one moves from Hamilton towards Middletown, the percentage of people who work in Hamilton drops gradually, but close to Middletown there is a sharp rise. In fact, in a tract just out of Middletown, we find no one going to Middletown and an unusually high number of people going to Hamilton. These strange results may well be the result of well-intentioned attempts to correct the "this city" bias when "this city" was Middletown, not Hamilton.

Other Problems with the Commuting Data

There are three additional broad categories of error and inconsistency in the 1960 data on the journey to work: coding; inconsistent numerical results; and poor assignments and aggregations of workplaces. These should be recognized by anyone working with the commuting tapes.

There are numerous cases where the coding of the National Location Code records and the census tapes are in disagreement. Incorrect locational assignments can, in turn, lead to incorrect summaries of data about commuting characteristics and to improper mapping of commuting fields and labor markets.

Frequent cases of *numerical inconsistencies* are found. For example, the tape data for SLA 7213 (Petulama City) read:

Population	14,035
Commuters out	20,060
Employed population	18,560

And again, Los Angeles:

	AL11A	*AL11B*
Population	7,501	6,675
Commuters out	6,528	1,388
Employed population	29	576

The problems inherent in materials of this kind speak for themselves! There is much that must be done to correct the basic census tapes.

The only basis for the *allocation* of a UAC workplace to any SLA was proximity, but even then there were difficulties in census practice. For example, Putnam County, New York, is not an optional workplace for itself—thus we find some 60 per cent of the workers who live there work "elsewhere." Fairfield County, Connecticut (not part of an SMSA, UAC workplace locations 1668 to 1676), is not an optional workplace for itself. Some of its areas send over 90 per cent of their workers "elsewhere."

Putnam County, in addition to not being an optional workplace for itself, does not have adjacent counties to the north or west as options and goes three counties deep for optional workplaces in the other directions. Rockland County, New York, does not have adjacent New Jersey counties as optional workplaces. The Bronx, in New York City, has Stamford, Connecticut, but not nearer Greenwich, Connecticut as optional workplaces, although Stamford and Greenwich are very similar in size and other characteristics. Innumerable similar examples, taken from all parts of the country, could be cited.

This leads to the problems caused by nearby foreign nations. Cuba was a work location option for Dade County, Florida, (in the Miami SMSA). This is an interesting choice since there are zero workers listed as commuting to Cuba (as would be expected), yet there are people listed as working "elsewhere," meaning that at least one other work location that could have been used was eliminated from consideration. On the other hand, Canada is listed as an optional workplace in Macomb County (UAC work location 3409), in the Detroit SMSA, although nearer counties would seem more likely to send workers to Canada, as would Detroit itself. The results for Macomb County show zero workers commuting to Canada, which is probably not so. It thus seems that a deficiency in the data is that people working outside the country (certainly in Canada, and probably also Mexico) are not caught in the results.

Obviously, almost any county which contributes no workers to one of its thirteen possible workplaces but does send people "elsewhere" has not been assigned the best set of work locations.

In addition, in many SLA's, fewer than thirteen workplaces would account for all significant commuting trips, while some extra options would be desirable for others. New York City, for example, draws workers from a larger area than recognized by the data. Philadelphia has commuting trains to New York, yet the thirteen workplaces named for Philadelphians do not come near New York. On the other hand, in some of the agricultural areas of the country, as few as five options might account for all the significant commuting traffic.

The problem of *aggregation* is that, in some areas, distant work locations were lumped together and counted as one. Just how this was done can be illustrated by the New York City SMSA. In SLA's within the SMSA, all counties and boroughs were listed as separate work locations. However, in SLA's outside the SMSA, the five boroughs of New York City were aggregated into one work location. Nassau, Suffolk, Westchester, and Rockland counties were also aggregated into one work location—four counties that are not even contiguous and do not make up a unit that is meaningful in any way other than that they are the "other counties" in the New York SMSA. It is even questionable whether it is as meaningful to aggregate Richmond with the other boroughs of New York City as with its contiguous New Jersey county. And there are many other strange workplace assignments and aggregations that make it difficult to use the journey to work data.

Conclusions about Errors in the Journey to Work Data

In short, a substantial systematic bias overemphasizes the proportion of residents of any county or city who work in that county or city. The bias makes it difficult to analyze commuting within cities and leads to fictitious discontinuities along city and county limits. This bias, coupled with other sources of error and problems in the assignment of UAC workplaces, makes it necessary to exercise extreme caution in making fine analytic choices among alternatives based on these data. Any results of journey to work studies should be examined for the broad patterns they can indicate despite the bias, but fine discriminations should be examined with care and, indeed, suspicion.

GENERAL FEATURES OF THE COMMUTING FIELDS

If the commuting fields are studied in their broad outlines, however, interesting perspectives are gained on the realities of American society and economy. Each commuting field exhibits a fundamental property of the country's residential areas—*their degree of participation in metropolitan labor markets*. Each degree of participation is closely correlated with many other social and economic characteristics. The maps and related materials presented in Chapter 2 indicate the true nature and extent of the metropolitanization of the United States.

The contrast between the country's Standard Metropolitan Statistical Areas, as defined by the Bureau of the Budget, and the map showing the commuting fields of cities in 1960 (Fig. 2–17, p. 43) is immediately apparent. Whereas about 66 per cent of the nation resided in the SMSA's in 1960, 87 per cent lived within the commuting area of one of the central cities of the SMSA's, and many within more than one such area. Another 9 per cent lived in the commuting fields of the somewhat smaller urban centers that filled the populated gaps between the metropolitan labor markets. Only 4 per cent of the population lived outside these labor markets. In fact, then, in 1960 the populated parts of the nation were indeed completely metropolitanized—covered by a network of urban fields, and patterned socially and economically by them. It is clear, then, that:

1. The areas socially and economically integrated with the central cities are far more extensive than the SMSA's. This should be no surprise, in view of the criterion that 15 per cent of the workers in an SMSA must commute to the central county (criterion 6a), and the criteria of metropolitan character (criteria 3 to 5), which reduce and constrain the boundaries of the SMSA's. Moreover, in light of the commuting patterns and the related socio-economic gradients, these constraints appear to cut across continuous, correlated patterns rather than seek out real limits such as discontinuities or major transitional zones. The only such limit evident in the data about the journey to work occur where one commuting field leaves off and socio-economic behavior begins to respond to the pull of another central city.

2. Similarly, in the least densely populated parts of the nation's settled area, foci of the commuting fields are urban centers of less than 50,000 people (although in general, they must exceed 25,000 to have any effect on the socio-economic gradients flowing outwards from larger places).

3. At the other extreme, particularly in the manufacturing belt, labor markets overlap in elaborate ways. The urban regions of the "megalopolis" are highly complex, multi-centered entities.

At least three questions of definitional practice are raised in view of these considerations:

1. If the intent is to define economically and socially integrated units with a recognized large population nucleus, are the constraints of the criteria of metropolitan character and the 15 per cent commuting criterion desirable and reasonable?

In light of the evidence, we think not.

2. What is an appropriate minimum size for the central city of the statistical area? and indeed, is the size of the central city a valid population criterion?

Although one may want to start with the 50,000 size for historical reasons, the total population of the entire region is probably more interesting.

3. How is the complexity of the most densely populated parts of the country to be handled? Is a multi-centered urban region an appropriate substitute?

We think so, and suggest a comprehensive set of Consolidated Urban Regions. Clearly, no statistical unit based on single centers will be able to embrace the interdependent labor markets.

The steps taken in 1960 handled these issues by beginning with a previously defined set of centers, and building for each a metropolitan area composed of counties as building-blocks. The commuting criterion then identified the out counties potentially eligible for membership in each of the SMSA's, the criterion of metropolitan character leading finally to the elimination of some of the candidates. Lip-service was given to interdependencies by the creation of the New York and Chicago Consolidated Regions. The whole procedure was simple, straightforward, and easy to use.

FUNCTIONAL ECONOMIC AREAS AND CONSOLIDATED URBAN REGIONS

Are there equally simple alternatives that also start with the same population criterion, rely on counties as building blocks (one of the features of the journey to work data for small areas is that county units may be retained without undue loss of detail), but come closer to the real areas of daily journey to work interdependence?

We think that there are, and list below one set resulting from our research.

Proposed Definitions

Considerable experimentation with the journey to work data has led to the following set of definitions, which we feel goes a long way towards providing a viable series of alternatives:

1. *Commuting field:* An area encompassing all standard location areas sending commuters to a designated workplace area. The field varies in intensity according to the proportion of employees resident in each SLA who commute to the workplace, and may be depicted cartographically by contours that enclose all areas exceeding a stated degree of commuting. (There will be as many commuting fields as there are designated workplace areas.)
2. *Labor market:* All counties sending commuters to work in a given central county.
   a. *Central county:* The designated workplace area used to define a labor market.
   b. *Central city:* The principal city of a central county. (SMSA criteria 1 and 2 might be used to make 2*a* and *b* more specific.)
3. *Functional Economic Area:* All those counties within a labor market in which the proportion of resident workers who commute to a given central county exceeds the proportion who commute to alternative central counties. (There will be as many FEA's as there are central counties.)
4. *Consolidated Urban Region* (*CUR*)*:* Two or more FEA's in which at least 5 per cent of the resident workers of the central county of one commute to the central county of another. (No prior determination of the number of CUR's is possible, but application of the criterion to the 1960 data yield 31. See Fig. 8–4.)

FIGURE 8–4. Consolidated urban regions. Based upon 1960 population counts from the Census of Population. *Source:* See caption for Fig. 8–2*a*.

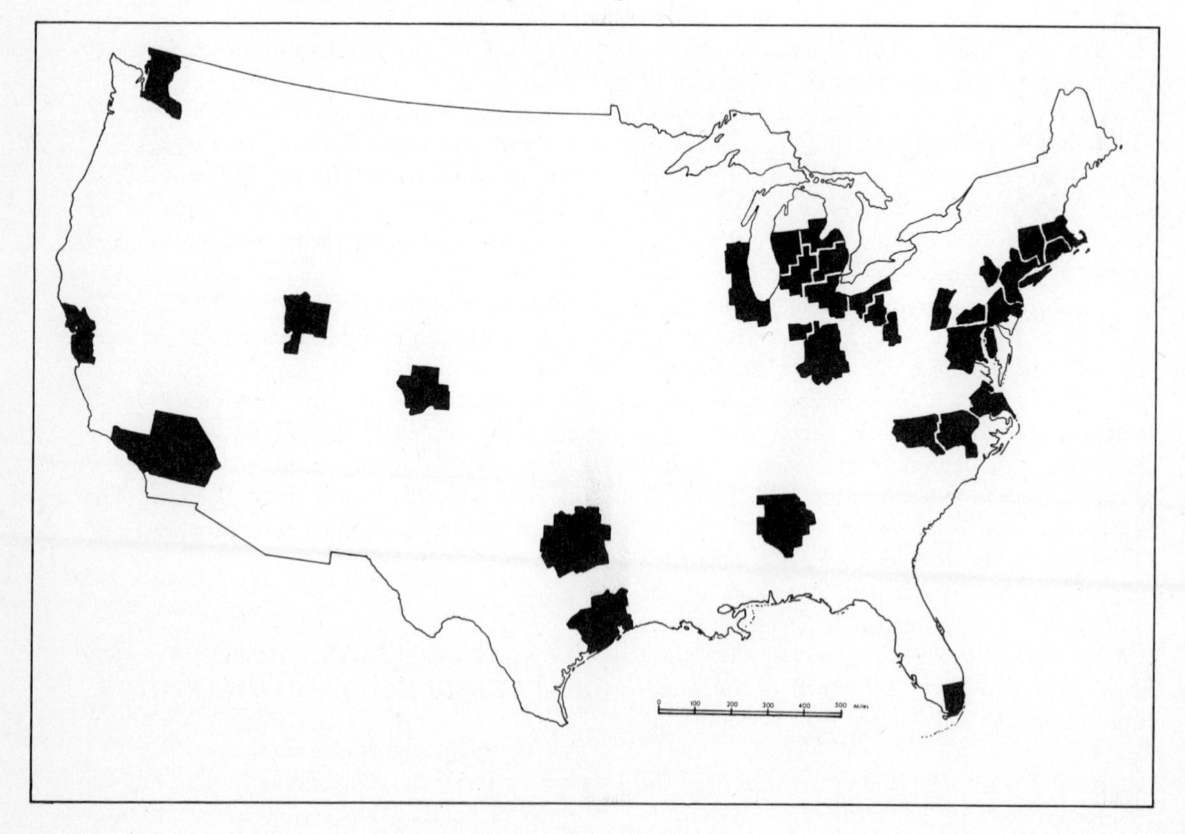

Variations

As experiments leading to this proposed system for defining a consistent set of CUR's and FEA's were carried on, many variations arose or were suggested.

Size of central city. The list of central cities can be limited to those exceeding 50,000, together with the other variants of SMSA criteria 1 and 2, or it might be extended to permit centers of, say, in the 25,000–50,000 range, thus including the FEA's. Or it might be extended even further downward, to try to exhaust the parts of the country with population densities exceeding 2 persons per square mile (as was done in Fig. 8–5). In that case, a final list of "integrated social and economic units" would include CUR's (constituent FEA's might be noted), FEA's of centers exceeding 50,000, and FEA's of smaller centers.

Minimum total population size and exhaustion of territory. The inclusion of other criteria in the definitional process can also be contemplated. One involves exhaustion of the national territory, once a list of CUR's and FEA's has been devised. Or, the list might be limited by requiring some minimum total population in each CUR or FEA. Yet a third, proposed by the Regional Economics Division of the Office of Business Economics of the Department of Commerce, is to combine these.

Hierarchical allocation. An alternative process may be illustrated by the case of Connecticut. Figure 8–6 shows the commuting fields of Connecticut's SMSA's. They overlap in complex ways, so that every part of the state lies simultaneously in *several* labor markets. To complicate matters further, New York's commuting field reaches into Stamford, Norwalk, and Bridgeport's labor markets and on into Waterbury and New Haven. Even plotting only those parts of the commuting fields within the 5 per cent contours on the same map reveals complicated overlaps.

On the other hand, the SMSA's vary considerably in size above the 50,000 population minimum used for admission to the list in 1960, and this fact may be used to resolve the state into an exhaustive system of Consolidated Urban Regions and Functional Economic Areas that are as self-contained as possible. The labor markets in Connecticut (Fig. 8–7) are laid down in order of size: New York, Hartford, New Haven, and so on. If a labor market (for example, Stamford) lies within an area already defined, it is ignored. Five per cent contours are used to indicate approximate locations of the equal centile contours of adjacent commuting fields. The labor markets of the smaller centers can be used to subdivide the larger consolidated areas so created, if desired.

"Cascading" of commuting fields. A variant of the classifiction first described involves making a more discriminating allocation of marginal counties to a given FEA, by "cascading." This process involves considering the proportion of resident workers who commute not only to the central county but to all counties already allocated to the FEA. Thus, for the first ring contiguous to the central county, the criterion used is commuting to the central county; for the second ring, it is commuting to the center plus the first ring; and so forth.

The Proposal and the Variants

The proposed definitions will lead to a list of economically and socially integrated units, since they make use of the daily journey to work data and identify relatively self-contained labor markets in the short run. One or another criterion of size will shorten or lengthen the list of areas. Slight modifications in the process of defining FEA's, for example by cascading, might sharpen the allocation of marginal counties. Hierarchical allocation might be a better way of creating consolidated regions than plotting cross-commuting between central counties. But each of these is a minor consideration compared with the prime issue that should now be apparent.

The regionalization used to create the 1960 SMSA's and the functional regionalization evidenced by commuting behavior are significantly different. A major choice must be made, for the 1960 classification does not produce fully integrated areas with a large population as its nucleus, even though this was the underlying concept.

FIGURE 8–5. Functional Economic Areas.
Source: See caption for Fig. 8–2*a*.

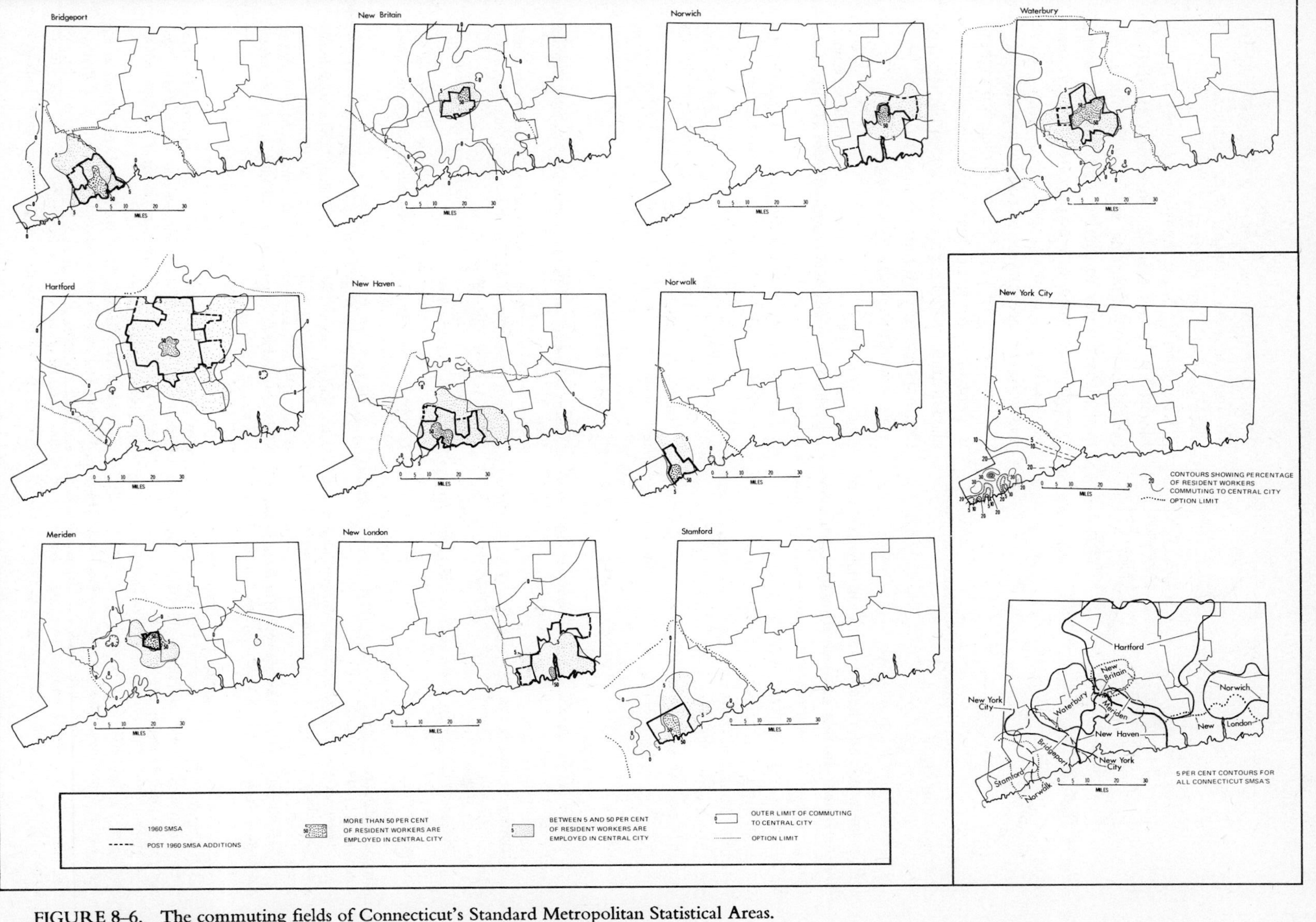

FIGURE 8–6. The commuting fields of Connecticut's Standard Metropolitan Statistical Areas.
Source: See caption for Fig. 8–2*a*.

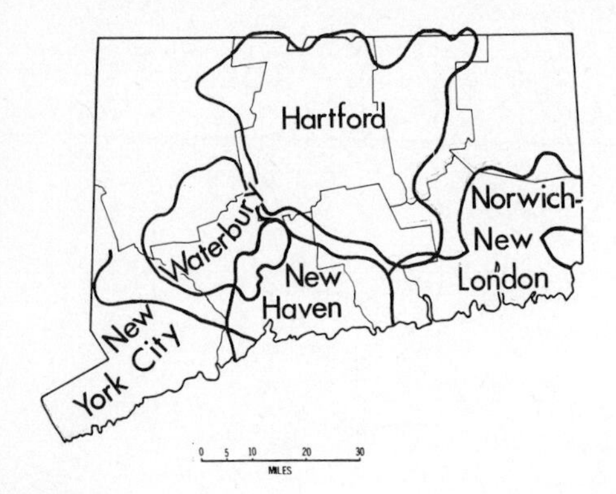

FIGURE 8–7. Labor markets of Connecticut. *Source:* See caption for Fig. 8–2*a*.

Is the intention to classify areas on the basis of *how they look*? In this case, continuation of present practice will suffice, and attention should be focused on the criteria of metropolitan character (although continuation of the practice of defining urbanized areas may be a more appropriate substitute). Alternatively, should the areas embrace people with *common patterns of behavior?* Then, commuting data dealing with daily behavior and the links between place of residence and place of work are relevant.

Comparability is not the issue, if county building blocks are used. Besides, there has been little consistency in definitional practice since the inception of attempts to define metropolitan areas. Nor should consistency be expected in a dynamic socio-economy in which patterns of organization and behavior are subject to continuing change.

There is a hard problem of choice, since there is general agreement that some form of area classification will be required for publication of summary statistics for some time to come.

We recommend the following:

1. County building blocks or equivalent units be retained as the basis of any area classification, in all parts of the country.
2. County-to-county commuting data be the basis of the classification of counties into functional economic areas.
3. FEA's be delineated around all central counties satisfying the existing SMSA criteria 1 and 2, and in addition be created for smaller regional centers in the less densely-populated parts of the country.

FOOTNOTES TO CHAPTER 8

1. Bureau of the Census, *Fifteenth Census of the United States: 1930, Metropolitan Districts* (Washington, D. C.: U. S. Government Printing Office, 1932).

2. Bureau of the Census, *Sixteenth Census of the United States: 1940*, Vol. I, *Population* (Washington D. C.: U. S. Government Printing Office, 1942).

3. Bureau of the Census, *Seventeenth Census of the United States: 1950*, Vol. I, *Population* (Washington D. C.: U. S. Government Printing Office, 1951).

4. See Otis D. Duncan, "Research on Metropolitan Population: Evaluation of Data," *Journal of the American Statistical Association*, LI (1956), 591–96.

5. Bureau of the Budget, *Standard Metropolitan Statistical Areas* (Washington, D. C.: U. S. Government Printing Office, 1964).

6. See Allen G. Feldt, "The Metropolitan Area Concept: An Evaluation of the 1950 S.M.A.'s," *Journal of the American Statistical Association*, LX (1965), 617–36.

7. Conrad Taeuber, "Regional and Other Area Statistics in the United States," Paper read at the Thirty-fifth Session of the International Statistical Institute (Belgrade, Yugoslavia: September, 1965, Mimeographed).

8. Bureau of the Budget, *Standard Metropolitan Statistical Areas*, p. 1.

9. Karl A. Fox, "Integrating National and Regional Models for Economic Stabilization and Growth," Paper read at a Conference on National Economic Planning, University of Pittsburgh, March 25-26, 1964 (Mimeographed); O. D. Duncan, *Metropolis and Region* (Baltimore: The John Hopkins Press, 1960).

10. See U. S. Bureau of the Budget, "Materials for Consideration in Review of SMSA Criteria" (Washington, D.C., February, 1966, Mimeographed).

11. For example, Nels Anderson, *Urbanism and Urbanization* (Leiden: E. J. Bull, 1964).

12. Karl A. Fox and Krishna T. Kumar "Programs for Economic Growth in Non-Metropolitan Areas" (Ames, Iowa, 1964, Mimeographed).

13. Duncan, *Metropolis and Region.*

14. Bureau of the Budget, "Review of SMSA."

15. Karl A. Fox and Krishna T. Kumar, "Delineating Functional Economic Areas for Development Programs" (Ames, Iowa, 1964, Mimeographed). Friedmann and Miller's article, "The Urban Field," reprinted in Chapter 2 of the present volume.

16. See Otis D. Duncan, "Community Size and the Rural-Urban Continuum," in *Cities and Society*, eds. Paul K. Hatt and Albert J. Reiss, Jr., 2nd ed. (New York: The Free Press, 1957), pp. 35–45. The reference is to Louis Wirth, "Urbanism as a Way of Life," *American Journal of Sociology*, XXXVIII (1938–1939), 1–24.

17. Hans Blumenfeld, "The Urban Pattern," *Annals of the American Academy of Political and Social Science*, CCCLII (March, 1964), 74–83; *idem*, "The Tidal Wave of Metropolitan Expansion," *Journal of the American Institute of Planners*, XX (1954), 3–14; *idem*, "The Dominance of the Metropolis," *Land Eco-*

nomics, XXVI (1950), 194–96; *idem*, "On the Concentric-Circle Theory of Urban Growth," *Land Economics*, XXV (1949), 208–12; *idem*, "On the Growth of Metropolitan Areas," *Social Forces*, XXVIII (1949), 59–64; Amos H. Hawley, *The Changing Shape of Metropolitan America* (New York: The Free Press, 1956); Friedmann and Miller, "The Urban Field"; Jerome Pickard, "Urban Regions of the United States," *Urban Land*, XXI, No. 4 (April, 1962), 3–9; Leo F. Schnore, *The Urban Scene* (New York: The Free Press, 1965); *idem*, "Municipal Annexations and the Growth of Metropolitan Suburbs: 1950–1960," *American Journal of Sociology*, LXVII (1961–1962), 406–17; *idem*, "Metropolitan Growth and Decentralization," *American Journal of Sociology*, LXIII (1957–1958), 171–80; *idem*, "The Growth of Metropolitan Suburbs," *American Sociological Review*, XXII (1957), 165–73; *idem*, "The Functions of Metropolitan Suburbs," *American Journal of Sociology*, LXI (1955–1956), 453–59.

18. See Walter Isard and Robert Kavesh, "Economic Structural Interrelations of Metropolitan Regions," *American Journal of Sociology*, LX (1954–1955), 152–62; and Melvin M. Webber *et al.*, *Explorations into Urban Structure* (Philadelphia: University of Pennsylvania Press, 1964).

19. Feldt, "The Metropolitan Area Concept."

20. John R. Borchert *et al.*, *Urban Reports*, Nos. 1, 2, 3 (1961–1963) (Minneapolis: Upper Midwest Economic Study).

21. Fox, "Integrating National and Regional Models."

22. Don J. Bogue, *The Structure of the Metropolitan Community* (Ann Arbor, Mich.: Horace H. Rackham School of Graduate Studies, 1949).

23. Conrad F. Taeuber and Irene B. Taeuber, *The Changing Population of the United States* (New York: John Wiley & Sons, Inc., 1958).

24. Otis D. Duncan and Albert J. Reiss, *Urban and Rural Communities of the United States* (New York: John Wiley & Sons, Inc., 1956).

25. Friedmann and Miller, "The Urban Field."

26. Bureau of the Budget, "Review of SMSA Criteria."

27. Friedmann and Miller, "The Urban Field."

28. *Ibid.*; Fox, "Integrating National and Regional Models."

29. Bureau of the Budget, "Review of SMSA Criteria."

30. *Ibid.*

31. Blumenfeld has propounded this idea in varions papers (see ftn. 17).

32. Duncan, *Metropolis and Region.*

33. Feldt, "The Metropolitan Area Concept"; Fox, "Integrating National and Regional Models."

34. Bogue, *Structure of the Metropolitan Community.*

35. See Blumenfeld, "The Dominance of the Metropolis."

36. N. S. B. Gras, *An Introduction to Economic History* (New York: Harper & Row, Publishers, 1922).

37. R. D. McKenzie, *The Metropolitan Community* (New York: McGraw-Hill Book Company, 1933).

38. "The Changing Shape of Metropolitan America."

39. *Metropolis and Region.*

40. Fox, "Integrating National and Regional Models."

41. Donald J. Bogue and Calvin L. Beale, *Economic Areas of the United States* (New York: The Free Press, 1961).

42. Rutledge Vining, "Delimitation of Economic Areas: Statistical Conceptions of the Spatial Structure of an Economic Sytem," *Journal of the American Statistical Association*, XLVIII (1953), 44–64.

43. B. J. L. Berry, W. Garrison, and K. Fox, "Urban Community of Interest Areas" (Unpublished paper, 1966).

44. Webber *et al.*, *Explorations into Urban Structure.*

45. Friedmann and Miller, "The Urban Field."

46. Borchert *et al.*, *Urban Reports.*

47. Bureau of the Census, *Journey to Work* (Washington, D.C.: U.S. Government Printing Office, 1965).

48. *Ibid.*

49. *Ibid.*

CHAPTER 9

the urban envelope: patterns and dynamics of population density

The commuting cone mentioned in Chapter 8 is repeated in an "envelope" of declining population densities with increasing distance from the core of the city. Some of the most significant theoretical contributions to urban geography have been made in recent years as an outcome of analysis of this urban envelope, and it is with more than passing interest that we now turn to the problem of describing the population density pattern of the metropolis. The relevance of the existing inductive generalizations is examined, and attempts are made to outline the theory embracing the processes that produce the empirical regularities. The implications are more general, however, for the densities at which people live may have profound effects on their lives, or so the classical urban ecologist or experimental psychologist would have us believe.[1] Chicago is taken as a case study, because in the chapters that follow, we describe that city's ecology and land use in some detail, thus providing the opportunity to explore these general implications.

*THE AXIOMS OF INTRA-URBAN STRUCTURE AND GROWTH**

Social scientists have arrived at fairly broad agreement that a single pattern of urban densities is repeated in a large number of very different cities.[2] This consensus of opinion has been summarized and extended into a system of equations by Berry[3] and Newling,[4] as follows.

The Decline of Population Densities with Distance from the City Center (Axiom 1)

In three dimensions the urban population density pattern approximates a cone, the vertical scale of which, density, is expressed in natural logarithms and the horizontal scale, distance from the center of the city, in arithmetic terms. If the cone is assumed to be regular and symmetric, then

*Adapted by Philip H. Rees especially for this book from his study *The Factorial Ecology of Metropolitan Chicago* (Master's thesis, University of Chicago, 1968), Appendix B.

the relationship between density and distance can be summarized as:

$$d_x = d_0 e^{-bx} \qquad (1)$$

where: d_x = population density
x = distance from the city center
d_0 = density at the city center
e = natural logarithmic base
b = density gradient

When the natural logarithm of density is used,[5] the equation becomes:

$$\ln d_x = \ln d_0 - bx. \qquad (2)$$

How well does this generalization fit the population pattern of Chicago? The map (Fig. 9–1) confirms that population densities do decline in a cone-like fashion from the center of the city (the intersection of State and Madison Streets) in general, though at different rates depending on the direction of traverse. Thus, the over-all density-distance decay graph (Fig. 9–1) can be decomposed into several sectoral components (Fig. 9–2).[6] The density gradient becomes steeper as one moves counter-clockwise around the metropolitan sectors from north to south (Table 9–1). This means that the city has spread out further towards the north and northwest than towards the southwest and south (though the picture may be somewhat distorted by the exclusion from consideration of the north west Indiana SMSA). The b value in Table 9–1, follows Winsborough,[7] and can therefore be considered an index of the *deconcentration* of the urban population. The northern part of the metropolis has proved to be a more attractive location for suburban development than the southern, probably as a result of its higher social prestige (see Chapter 10). Population is, however, more crowded at the center in the northern, western, and southern sectors than in the other two. The cardinal northern, western, and southern sectors laid down by the rectangular street grid were the sectors of earliest growth. In these sectors, too, the processes of physical redevelopment and population turnover have proceeded furthest, and they are now occupied by Negro residents in generally substandard, overcrowded housing, or by whites who live in blocks of new, high-rise apartments.

If the scatter of points on the density-distance graph is reduced by calculating the density of population within two-mile rings centered on State and Madison, a number of relationships become clear. Look at the summary diagram in Fig. 9–3. Between the center of the city, point X_0 and point X_1, densities increase to a peak; this peak has shifted outwards in the course of time (except between 1940 and 1950, when the processes of urban spread were temporarily slowed by wartime constraints on the housing industry). An exponential decline of density with distance from the center of the city, however, is characteristic of only that portion of the total gross population density curve lying between X_1 (the point at which densities peak) and the limit of the continuously built-up area (between

TABLE 9-1

The Decline of Population Density with Distance from the Center of Chicago, Whole SMSA and Five Sectors: 1960

		Sector				
*Parameters**	*Whole SMSA*	*North*	*Northwest*	*West*	*Southwest*	*South*
r	−0.908	−0.909	−0.930	−0.947	−0.900	−0.957
a	4.519	4.591	4.442	4.574	4.465	4.909
d_0	33.0	39.0	27.7	37.5	29.2	81.1
b	−0.056	−0.037	−0.050	−0.062	−0.063	−0.080

Source: Philip H. Rees, *The Factorial Ecology of Metropolitan Chicago* (Master's thesis, University of Chicago, 1968).
* r = Coefficient of correlation
a = Intercept of line of regression with density axis measured in $\log_{10}$ units
d_0 = Extrapolated central density (in thousand of persons per sq. m.)
b = Density gradient measured in units of $\log_{10}$ density/miles

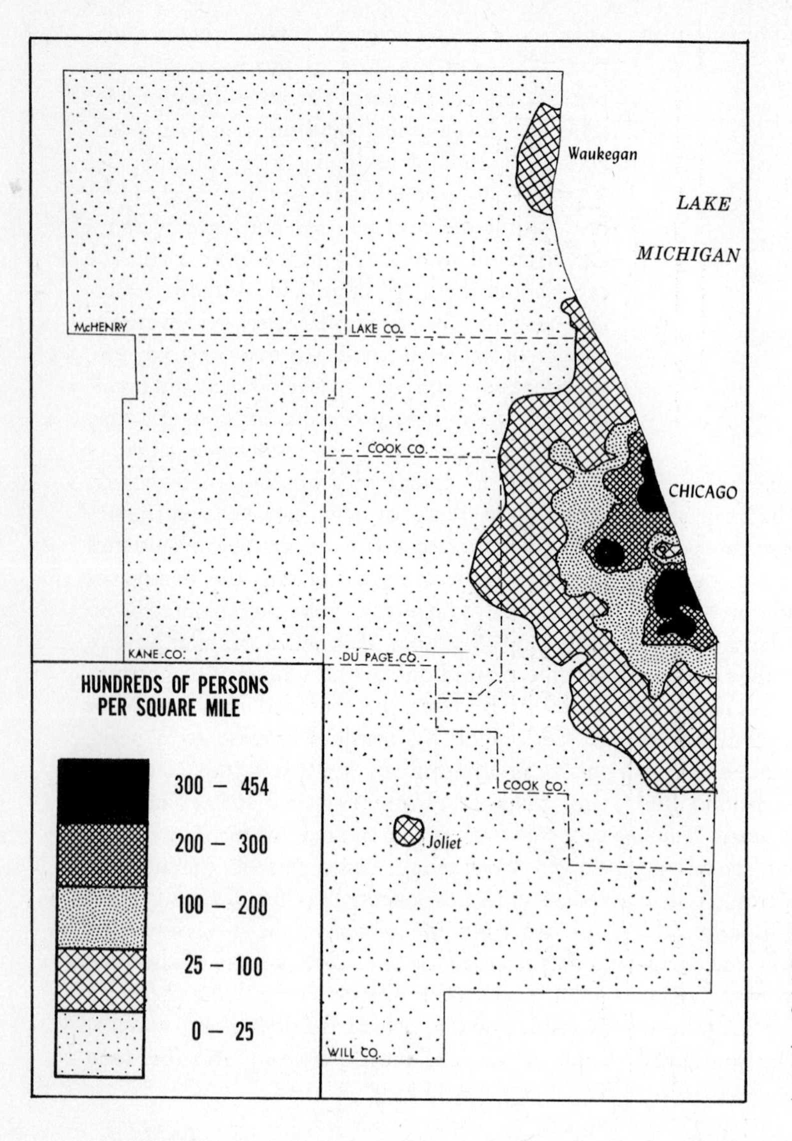

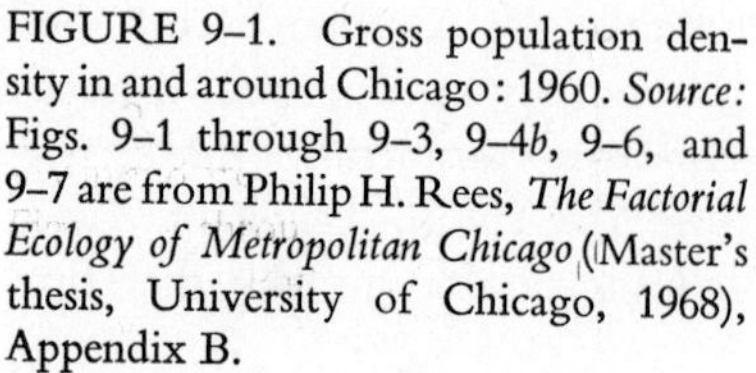
FIGURE 9–1. Gross population density in and around Chicago: 1960. *Source:* Figs. 9–1 through 9–3, 9–4*b*, 9–6, and 9–7 are from Philip H. Rees, *The Factorial Ecology of Metropolitan Chicago* (Master's thesis, University of Chicago, 1968), Appendix B.

points X_1 and X_2). Beyond that limit the density curve can be broken down into a number of components. The *total* population density curve (K) is seen to be an amalgam of suburban (J_1) and rural (M) density functions, and it declines in a curvilinear fashion rather than in the linear mode that characterizes the curve within the continuously urbanized area. However, one curve does continue to decline at the same rate as population within the limits of the continuously urban area: that is *urban* population density (L), at least until we reach the distance from the center of the city (point X_3 in Fig. 9–3), when it too changes slope. At this same point also "suburban" densities become "semi-independent town" densities which appear to be fairly constant with distance from Chicago.

Thus, although our single-equation model of the behavior of total population densities in the Chicago urban region proves to be an oversimplification, it is nevertheless true to say that in the area of the metropolis where most of the people live, a great crescent some 10 to 15 miles in width around the Loop, the axiom that density of popula-

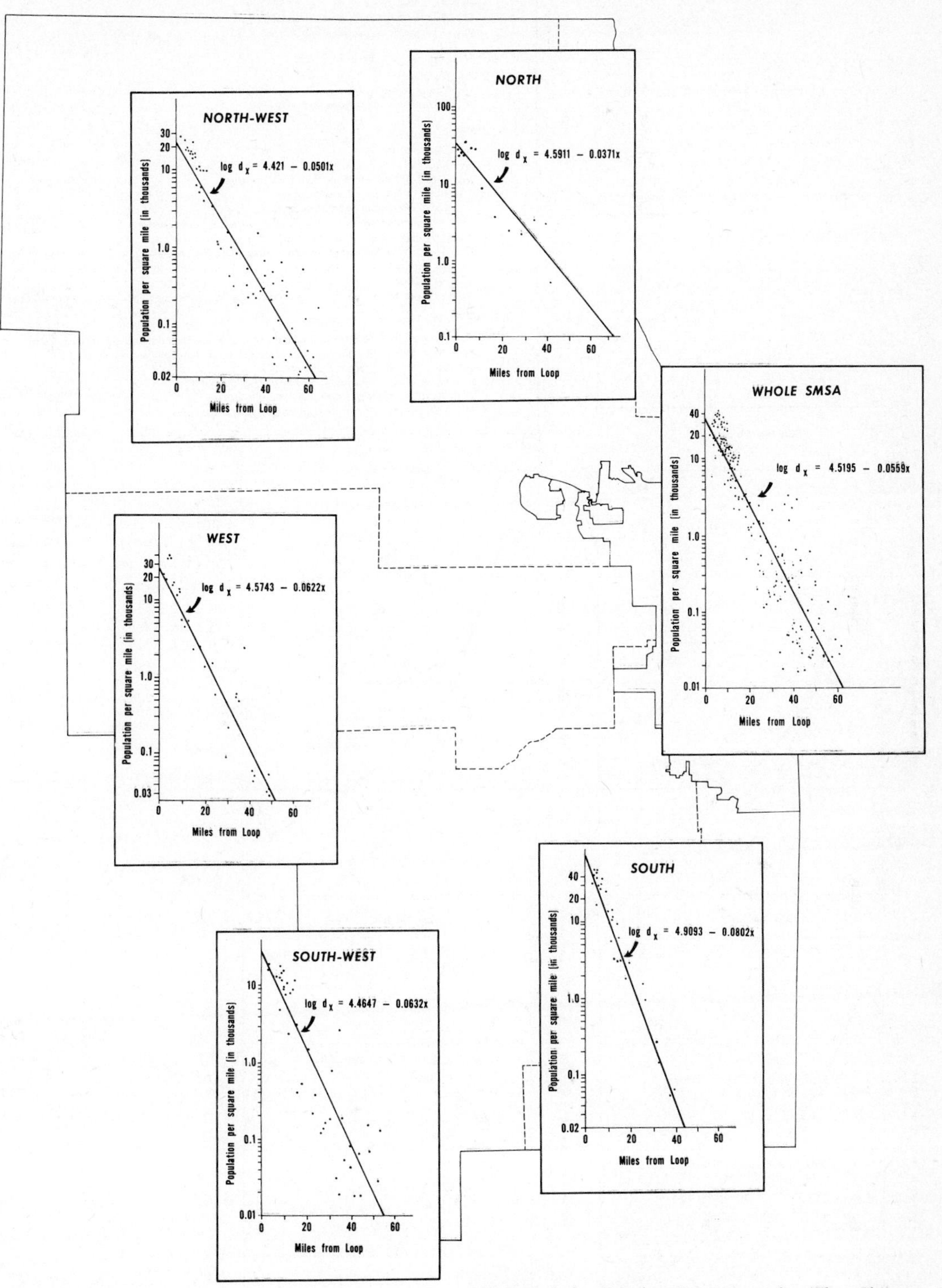

FIGURE 9–2. Density-distance graphs: The Chicago SMSA and five sectors, 1960. *Source:* See caption for Fig. 9–1.

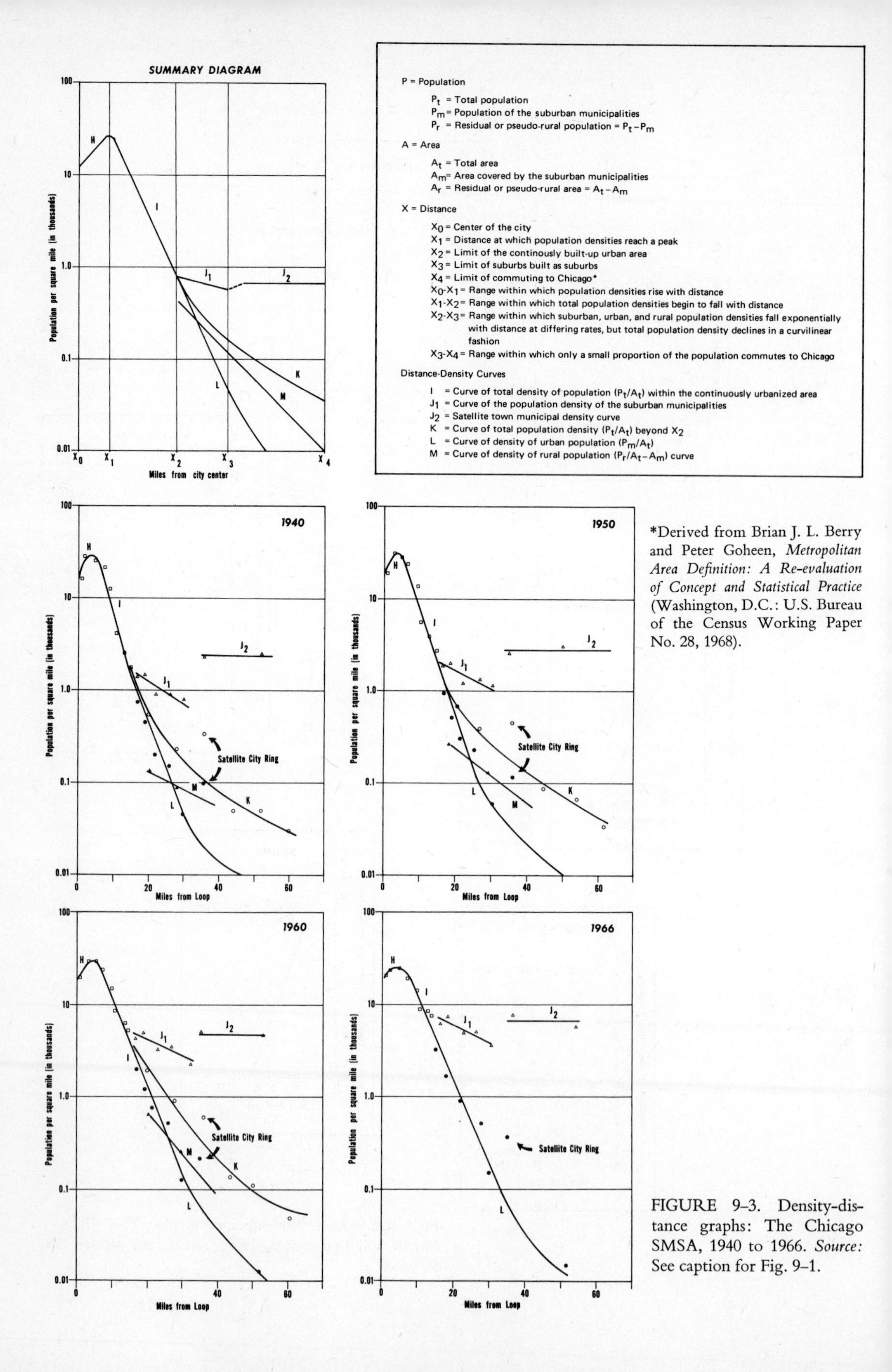

*Derived from Brian J. L. Berry and Peter Goheen, *Metropolitan Area Definition: A Re-evaluation of Concept and Statistical Practice* (Washington, D.C.: U.S. Bureau of the Census Working Paper No. 28, 1968).

FIGURE 9–3. Density-distance graphs: The Chicago SMSA, 1940 to 1966. *Source:* See caption for Fig. 9–1.

tion declines exponentially at a constant rate with distance from the city center is a fairly close approximation to the truth. Even beyond that point, the density at which people reside in continuously built-up suburbs continues to decline in the same fashion, but rural and small outlying town densities complicate the simplicity of the urban pattern. Making the assumption of constancy, then, we turn to the behavior of the density gradient over time.

The Density Gradient Declines with Time (Axiom 2)

The second axiom in the system says that the density gradient falls in the course of time (see Fig. 9–4) in the following manner:

$$b_t = b_0 e^{-ct} \qquad (3)$$

Expressed in natural logarithms, Eq. (3) becomes:

$$\ln b_t = \ln b_0 - ct \qquad (4)$$

where: b_t = distance–density gradient at time t
b_0 = distance–density gradient at time t_0
e = base of natural logarithms
c = exponent

Winsborough[8] presents two series of population density gradients for Chicago between 1860 and 1950. His calculations were checked for 1940 and 1950, and extended to 1960 and 1966 by the same method, i.e., the assignment of the population and community areas to two-mile rings of distance starting from the center of the

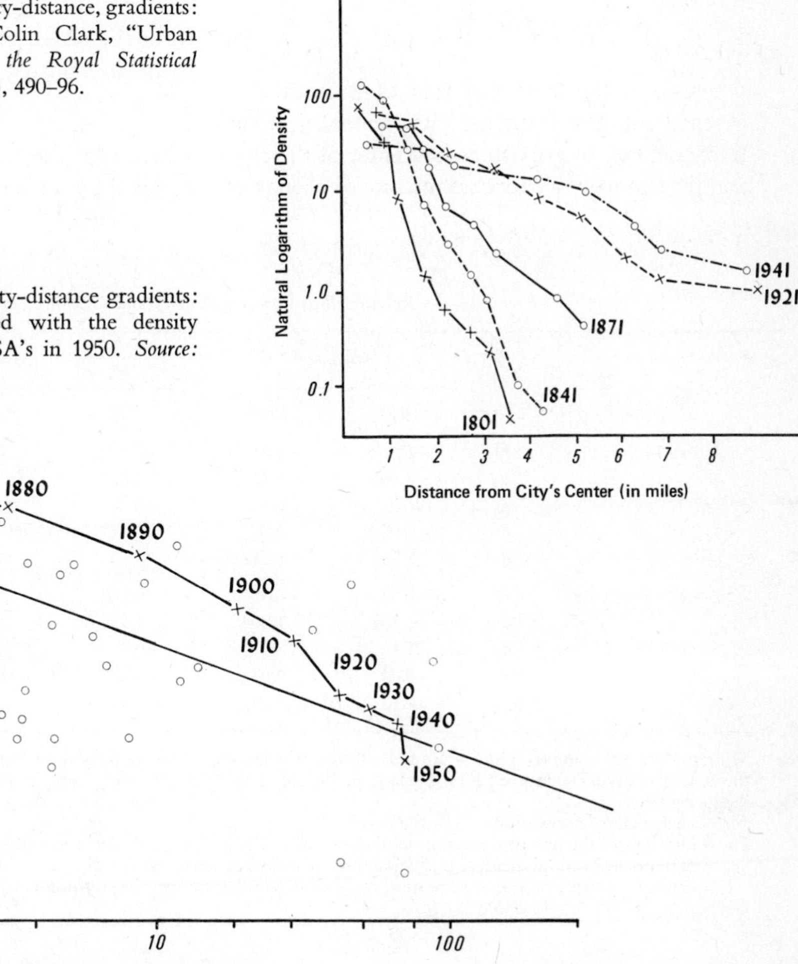

FIGURE 9–4*a*. Diminishing density-distance, gradients: London: 1801 to 1941. *Source:* Colin Clark, "Urban Population Densities," *Journal of the Royal Statistical Society*, Sec. A, CXIV, No. 4 (1951), 490–96.

FIGURE 9–4*b*. Diminishing density-distance gradients: Chicago: 1860 to 1950, compared with the density gradient of all United States SMSA's in 1950. *Source:* See caption for Fig. 9–1.

city. The results are presented in Tables 9–2 and 9–3, and Fig. 9–5. Although the data are not completely comparable (see notes to Fig. 9–5) it is clear that the total population density gradient does decline exponentially with time.

Thus, given the qualifications we have already noted, Newling's axioms of intra-urban growth and spatial structure can be said to hold for Chicago.

The Theorems of Intra-urban Growth and Spatial Structure

From the two axioms outlined above, Newling goes on to deduce a number of necessary consequences about the density of urban populations.[9]

The rule that intra-urban growth is allometric. The first theorem is that intra-urban growth is allometric. That is,

$$(1 + r_x) = (1 + r_o)e^{gx} \quad (5)$$

where r_x is the fractional rate of growth at a given distance x from the city center, r_o is the fractional rate of growth at the center of the city, and the exponent g expresses the rate of change of the rate of growth with distance from the center of the city.

Transformed into natural logarithms, the equation becomes:

$$ln\ (1 + r_x) = ln\ (1 + r_0) + gx \quad (6)$$

This relationship appears to hold for Chicago (see Fig. 9–6) out to a distance of about 13 to 15 miles from the Loop, but beyond that distance the rate of population growth declines with increasing distance from the center of the city. The maximum growth takes place at the margin of the continuously built-up area through the replacement of agricultural land by residential uses, and declines beyond that point with diminishing pressure for the conversion of rural into urban land uses.

The relation between density and the rate of growth. Since both density itself and its growth rate may be expressed as functions of distance from the city center, the growth rate of density is directly related to the level of density:

$$(1 + r_d) = ad^{-k} \quad (7)$$

where r_a is the fractional growth rate at density d; a is a parameter of the equation; and the expo-

TABLE 9–2

Relationships between Density and Distance from the Center of Chicago: 1940 to 1966

		*Winsborough**		*Present Study**			
Zones		*1940*	*1950*	*1940*	*1950*	*1960*	*1966*
0–2 to 14–16 miles	r†	−0.93	−0.95	−0.891	−0.911	−0.875	−0.917
	a	1.665	1.667	1.665	1.663	1.512	1.501
	d_0	46.2	46.5	46.2	46.0	32.5	31.7
	b	−0.07	−0.07	−0.087	−0.078	−0.052	−0.047
	g	5.85	6.51	5.00	5.60	8.36	9.10
2–4 to 14–16 miles	r†	−0.98	−0.98	−0.968	−0.978	−0.975	−0.974
	a	1.852	1.804	1.954	1.900	1.712	1.635
	d_0	71.1	63.7	89.9	79.4	51.5	43.1
	b	−0.09	−0.08	−0.113	−0.099	−0.070	−0.060
	g	4.76	5.48	3.84	4.38	6.20	7.29

Sources: Data for columns 3 and 4 from Halliman Winsborough, "A Comparative Study of Population Densities" (Doctoral thesis, University of Chicago, 1961), Table 2, p. 19. Columns 5 and 6 are compiled from primary data.

*$\log_{10}$ density

† r = coefficient of correlation

a = intercept of the line of regression with the density axis, measured in either $\log_{10}$ or $\log_e$ units

d_0 = extrapolated central density, in thousands of persons per square mile

b = density gradient, measured in units of $\log_{10}$ density/miles, or $\log_e$ density/miles

$g = -\log_{10}e/-b = -0.4343/b$

TABLE 9–3

Relationships between Density and Distance from the Center of Chicago: Further Results of the Present Study

Zones		*1940*	*1950*	*1960*		*Zones*		*1940*	*1950*	*1960*	
0–2 to	r*	−0.956	−0.967	−0.985		2–4 to	r*	−0.953	−0.964	−0.985	
56–64	a	1.329	1.389	1.442		56–64	a	1.342	1.400	1.400	
miles	d_0	21.3	24.5	27.7		miles	d_0	22.0	25.1	30.1	
	b	−0.054	−0.052	−0.048			b	−0.054	−0.052	−0.049	
	g	8.08	8.42	8.98			g	8.03	8.38	8.80	
		1940	*1950*	*1960*	*1966*			*1940*	*1950*	*1960*	*1966*
0–2 to	r*	−0.891	−0.911	−0.875	−0.917	2–4 to	r*	−0.968	−0.978	−0.975	−0.974
14–16	a	3.833	3.828	3.482	3.456	14–16	a	4.499	4.374	3.940	3.764
miles†	d_0	46.2	46.0	32.5	31.7	miles†	d_0	89.9	79.4	51.5	43.1
	b	−0.200	−0.179	−0.120	−0.109		b	−0.261	−0.228	−0.161	−0.137
		1940	*1950*	*1960*				*1940*	*1950*	*1960*	
0–2 to	r*	−0.956	−0.967	−0.985		2–4 to	r*	−0.953	−0.964	−0.985	
56–64	a	3.060	3.199	3.320		56–64	a	3.089	3.224	3.405	
miles†	d_0	21.3	24.5	27.7		miles†	d_0	22.0	25.1	30.1	
	b	−0.214	−0.119	−0.111			b	−0.125	−0.119	−0.114	

Source: Primary data.
* r = coefficient of correlation
a = intercept of the line of regression with the density axis, measured in either $\log_{10}$ or $\log_e$ units
d_0 = extrapolated central density, in thousands of persons per square miles
b = density gradient, measured in units of $\log_{10}$ density/miles, or $\log_e$ density/miles
$g = -\log_{10}e/-b = -0.4343/b$
† Expressed in log e units.

FIGURE 9–5. Density-distance gradient over time: Chicago: 1860–1966. *Sources:* 1860–1910: The values used are the b values in Table 1, Halliman H. Winsborough, "A Comparative Study of Urban Population Densities" (Ph.D. dissertation, University of Chicago, 1961); 1920–1950: The values used are the b values in Table 2, *ibid.*, p. 19; 1940–1966: The values used are the b values of the present study, reported in Table 9–2.

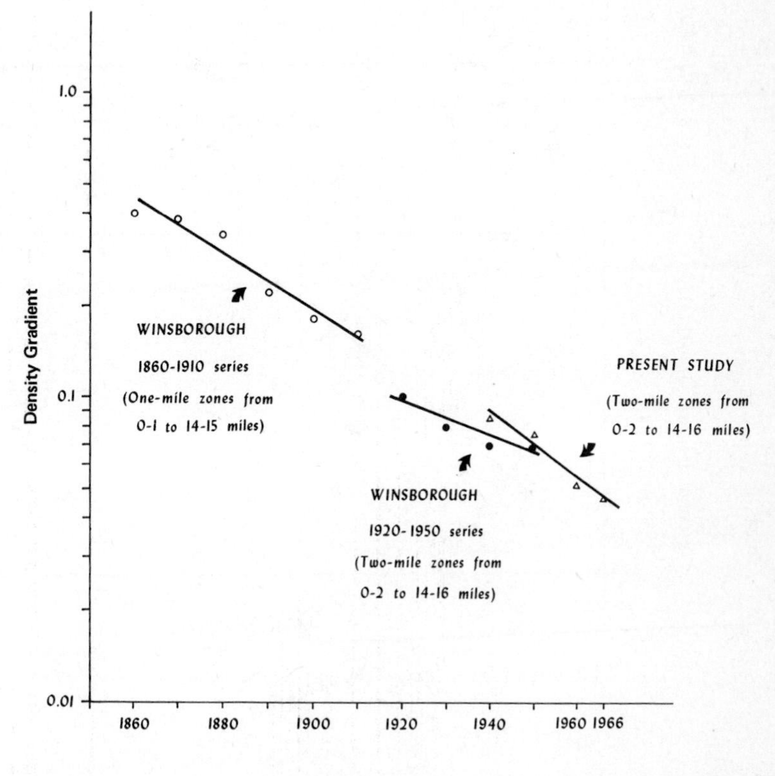

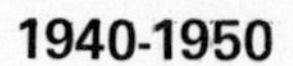

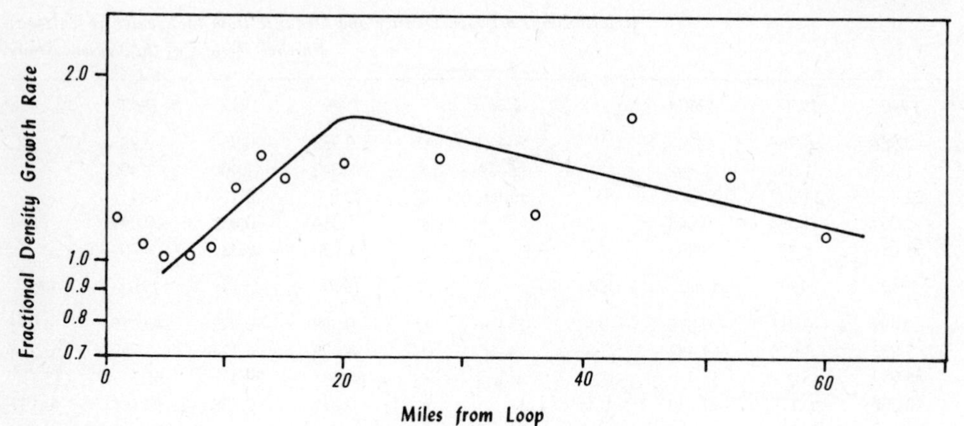

1950-1960

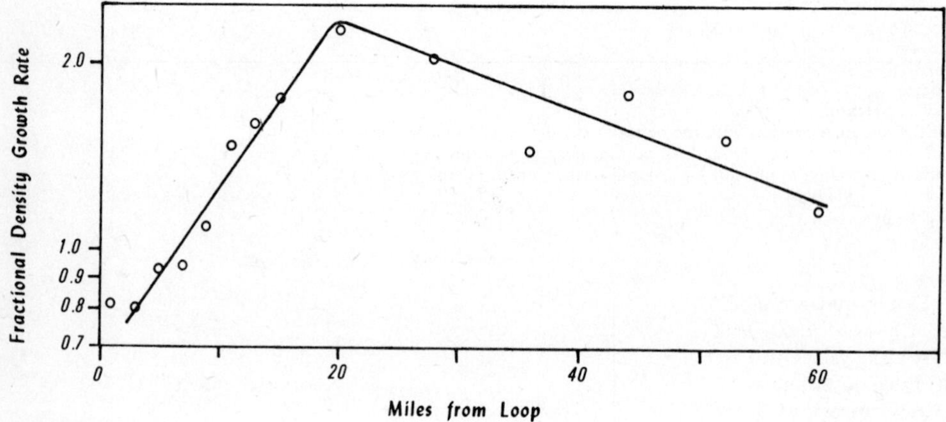

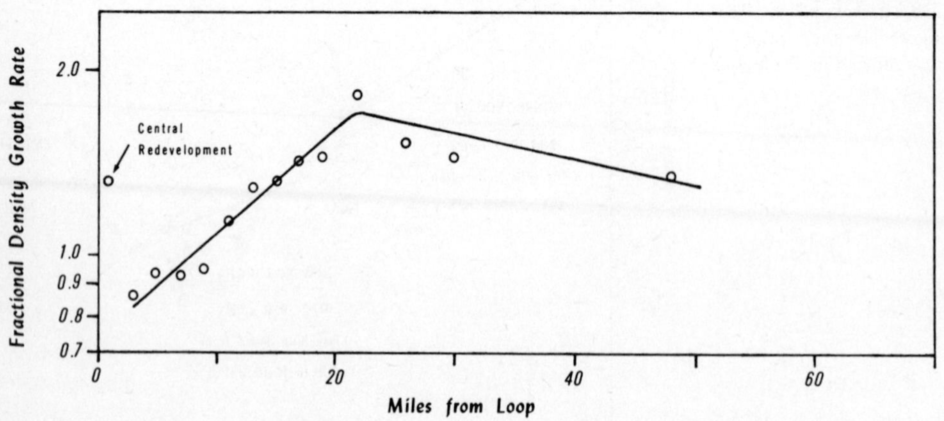

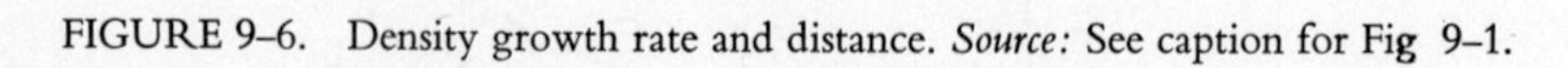
FIGURE 9–6. Density growth rate and distance. *Source:* See caption for Fig 9–1.

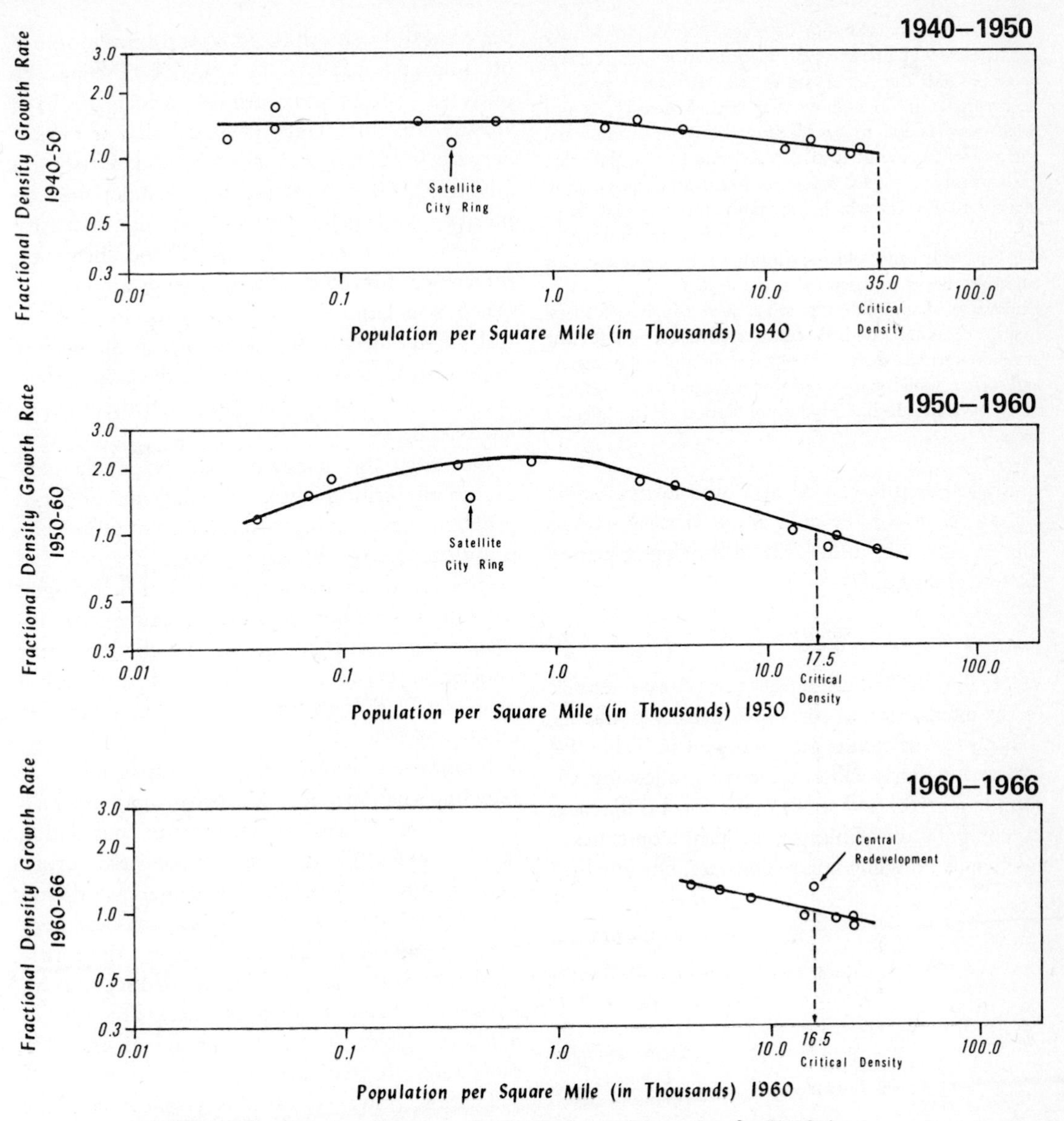

FIGURE 9–7. Density and its rate of growth. *Source:* See caption for Fig. 9–1.

nent k gives the rate of change in the rate of growth with respect to density.

Transformed into natural logarithms the equation reads:

$$ln\,(1 + r_d) = ln\,a - k\,ln\,d \qquad (8)$$

This relationship appears to hold for the Chicago metropolitan region down to a density of about 2,000 persons per square mile (see Fig. 9–7).[10] At lower densities in the rural peripheries of the urban region, there appears to be a positive association between growth rates and density levels.

Critical density. Newling goes on to argue that there exists a *critical* density which, if exceeded, will in time lead to a decrease in densities, and below which increases in density will continue. He argues strongly for a link between such a critical density and social conditions:

The inverse relationship between population density and the rate of growth, the identification of a critical density, and the observation that negative growth, occurring as it does above the critical density, is not solely attributable to competition between commercial and residential use of land, all lead one to speculate that perhaps there is indeed some optimum urban population density to exceed which inevitably incurs social costs. We may speculate that certain events in the history of the city will cause this optimum to be exceeded (for example, heavy immigration without a commensurate expansion of the housing stock and supply of social overhead capital), with deleterious consequences for the areas concerned (such as blight, crime and delinquency, and other social pathological conditions) and leading to an eventual decline in the population of the affected areas.[11]

Critical density can be measured in two ways: (1) by means of the rule about density and its rate of growth, using the following equation derived from Eq. (7):

$$d_c = a^{1/k} \tag{9}$$

where d_c is the critical density; or (2) by reference to the intersection of successive density gradients.

Both sets of results are presented in Table 9–4 and are in fairly close agreement, allowing for rounding errors and slight operational differences in computation. Chicago, in fact, comprises a case which Newling fails to consider, one in which the critical density shifts downward in the course of time and outward in space (paralleling the outward shift of peak densities which we have already noted).[12] Thus, the similarity of critical density in Kingston, Jamaica, and Pittsburgh (about 35,000 persons per square mile) may be merely a coincidence. Just as the decline in density gradients over time testifies to the increasing preference for low density living among the urban population (as well as to the increases in real income needed to achieve it), so the decline in the critical density is witness to the population's decreasing preference for living in densely populated areas.

TABLE 9–4

Critical Density Values (in Persons per Square Mile)

Density Used	*Growth Period*	*Critical Density Defined by Density-Growth Rule*
1940	1940–1950	35,000
1950	1950–1960	17,500
1960	1950–1960	16,500
Gradients Intersecting	*Critical Density Defined by Intersecting Density Gradients*	*Distance from City Center at Which Critical Density is Found (in Miles)*
1940, 1950	33,110	3.85
1950, 1960	18,200	6.49
1960, 1966	14,790	7.70

Source: Primary data.

Newling also suggests that when densities exceed the critical level, the incidence of social problems or pathologies increases far more than proportionately. Biological experiments, and even a casual comparison of maps of density and the rates of delinquency, crime, and mental illness, would seem to suggest that there is some association between crowding and these social problems, although the evidence is somewhat conflicting.[13]

Population estimates. The remainder of Newling's partial theory of urban growth in which he develops "rules of intra-urban population density growth" and an "exponential urban growth model" is predicated on the assumption that central density (d_0) remains constant over time, or, ignoring shifts in density in the innermost ring of the city, that critical density remains constant.[14] Since neither of these assumptions holds for Chicago over the period of attention these rules are inapplicable.

There is, however, a further implication of the theory of urban growth that is testable for Chicago. Densities in the urban region can be summed to give the volume of the cone, which, of course, equals the population of the urban region.

Integration of Eq. (1) to a marginal density d_{x^*} yields the total population within the margin of the urban region, at a distance x^* from the city center, defined by this marginal density:

$$P_{x^*} = \int_0^{x^*} d_0 e^{-bx}(2\pi x)dx \tag{14}$$

which is evaluated as:

$$P_{x^*} = 2\pi d_0 b^{-2}[1 - e^{-bx^*}(1 + bx^*)] \quad (15)$$

If we solve for x^* in Eq. (2) and substitute the solution into Eq. (15), we can rewrite Eq. (15) as:

$$P_{x^*} = 2\pi d_0 b^{-2}\left[1 - \left(\frac{d_{x^*}}{d_0}\right)\left(1 + ln\ d_0 - ln d_{x^*}\right)\right] \quad (16)$$

where P_{x^*} is the population of the urban region which resides between the center of the city and the distance x^* where the density is d_{x^*}.[15]

In Table 9–5 are presented Newling's calculations for Chicago based on Winsborough's density parameters, to which values for 1960 and 1966 have been added. The assumption of zero density at the perimeter undoubtedly exaggerates the population of the Standard Metropolitan Statistical Area (SMSA) and the urbanized area. The assumption of a marginal density of 2,000 inhabitants per square mile at the perimeter overestimates the urbanized area population (after 1920), an overestimation which reflects the growing depression at the center of the population density cone as nonresidential uses expand around the core. The Standard Metropolitan Area (SMA) or SMSA population is underestimated by the equation until about 1950, reflecting the fact that much of the SMSA area lay outside the metropolitan labor market before that date.

Total urban density. One final urban population density relationship deserves mention. Winsborough[16] proves that the over-all density of a city (total population divided by total area) is a function of d_0 (extrapolated central density) alone. The equation is:

$$D = \frac{P}{A} = \frac{2d_0}{ln^2\left[\frac{d_0}{L}\right]}\left[1 - \frac{\left(ln\left[\frac{d_0}{L}\right] + 1\right)}{\frac{d_0}{L}}\right] \quad (17)$$

where D is the over-all density of a city of P population and A area, and L is the density of population at the margin of the city.

The density gradient does not enter into the calculation at all, if the population of the city is known and if a constant marginal density is assumed for the city for which the population is known. In studies where attention is concentrated on only the degree of crowding at the center, over-all density therefore can be substituted for central density, thus avoiding much labor. If over-all density and population are known and the assumption of constant marginal density holds, then the equations might be used to calculate both central density and the density gradient. However, that would be equivalent to assuming that densities decline in a negative exponential fashion without bothering to test the proposition.

From a small number of basic assumptions concerning urban population densities, an elaborate system of descriptive equations can thus be derived. In the case of Chicago, the assumptions accord reasonably well with reality, and the

TABLE 9–5

Estimated Population of the Chicago Urban Region Compared with Actual Population of the SMA or SMSA, the Urbanized Area, and the Central City

	Population Estimates			*Actual Population*		
Year	*I**	*II†*	*III‡*	*SMA or SMSA*	*Urbanized Area*	*Central City*
1900	1.95	1.76	1.79	2.09	1.89	1.70
1910	2.47	2.23	2.18	2.75	2.53	2.19
1920	3.89	3.40	2.78	3.52	3.29	2.70
1930	5.31	4.64	3.36	4.68	4.43	3.38
1940	5.42	4.72	3.36	4.83	4.52	3.40
1950	6.43	5.53	3.50	5.50	5.05	3.62
1960§	6.68	5.58	3.19	6.22	5.46	3.55
1966§	7.72	6.26	3.05	—	—	—

Source: Bruce E. Newling, "Urban Growth and Spatial Structure: Mathematical Models and Empirical Evidence," *Geographical Review*, LVI, No. 2 (April, 1966), Table 3, p. 219; Table 4, p. 221.

*Estimated from Winsborough's density parameters (see Table 9–2), assuming that the density at the perimeter is zero and that the Chicago urban region occupies 53.5 per cent of a full circle.

†Estimated from Winsborough's density parameters, assuming that the density at the perimeter is 2,000 persons per sq. mi. and that the Chicago urban region occupies 53.5 per cent of a full circle.

‡Estimated from Winsborough's density parameters, assuming a radius of 10 miles and that the site of the city occupies 53.5 per cent of a full circle.

§Calculated from the density parameters of the present study (see Table 9–2) in the same manner as for earlier years.

derived equations have been verified. When the assumptions do not reflect real conditions as, e.g., Newling's assumptions of a constant critical density and a constant central density, the derivations have been rejected as irrelevant. A revision of the theory to include the more realistic assumptions of declining critical and central densities is therefore indicated.

*TEMPORAL AND CROSS-CULTURAL COMPARISONS**

The necessary revision of Newling's theory, suggested by Rees in the previous section, might be achieved by proceeding to broader contexts. Colin Clark argued that the negative exponential pattern of urban densities "appears to be true for all times and all places studied, from 1801 to the present day, and from Los Angeles to Budapest."[17] But central density d_0 and density gradients do vary from city to city, and even in the same city from time to time. Why should this be so?

First, certain relationships between these two parameters and city size are evident.

As x^* tends to a maximum as d_{x^*} tends to zero, Eq. (16) becomes:

$$P = 2\pi b^{-2} d_0 \tag{18}$$

or

$$d_0/P = b^2/2\pi \tag{19}$$

Expressed in logarithmic form, Eq. (19) reads:

$$\log (d_0/P) = \log (1/2\pi) + 2 \log b \tag{20}$$

If we plot $\log (d_0/P)$ against $\log b$, we obtain a straight line for Chicago for the period since 1900. However the relationship between d_0, b and P in the century since 1860 has undergone distinct changes. From Fig. 9–8*a*, we can see that the density of Chicago's population has passed through a series of behavior patterns. Also plotted on other parts of that diagram are similar d_0, b and P values for other cities. The possible variations in a city's population density pattern and in its total population over time are summarized so they can be compared to a number of theoretical behavior patterns in Fig. 9–8*b*.

But what is the basis of these different behavior patterns? Clearly, a more penetrating analysis of factors influencing central density and the density gradient is required. For purposes of analysis, Muth's data for United States cities may be used, since he has already provided the parameters d_0 and b for each in 1950.[18]

Cross-Sectional Analysis

The most obvious influence on population densities near the city center is the age and mode of development and building. Older cities built with small lots and subdivisions will have higher densities than cities built at other times with other modes of subdivision. Winsborough follows Boulding in arguing for the controlling influence of the timing of development on subsequent form: "At any moment the form of any object, organism, or organization is the result of its laws of growth up to that moment," and "Growth creates form, but form limits growth."[19]

But when holding size is constant, central density is related to the density gradient, which in its turn may be influenced by a variety of additional factors, including the size of the city (see Figs. 9–9 and 9–10). Thus central density is a function both of age and, as a composite surrogate for these other factors, of density gradient. A regression equation computed to quantify this functional relationship yielded the expression:

$$d_0 = 0.5302 + 0.6362 \text{ age} - 3.495\, b^{-1} \tag{21}$$

Both age, i.e., years since the city reached a population of 50,000, and density gradient were significant at the .01 level, and 61 per cent of the variance of d_0 was accounted for.[20] This is pleasing, since Muth's estimates of d_0 were subject to error, but it also indicates that additional factors should be investigated. A better measure of age should be found, probably one indicative of the nature of the growth process and accounting for differences in local transportation technology, in particular.[21]

*Reprinted from Brian J. L. Berry, James W. Simmons, and Robert J. Tennant, "Urban Populations: Structure and Change," *Geographical Review*, LIII (July, 1963), 389–405, with the permission of the authors and the editor.

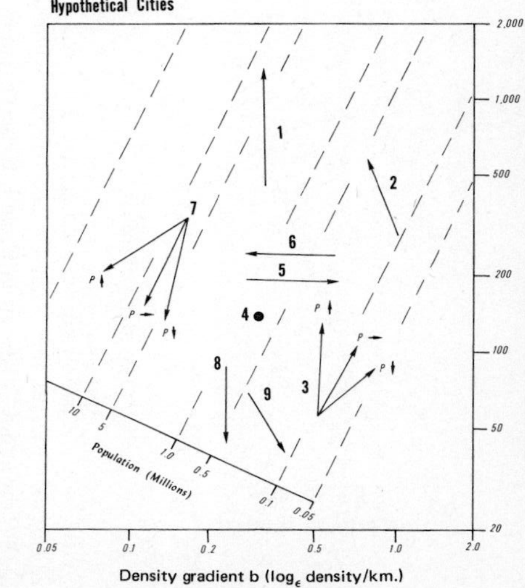
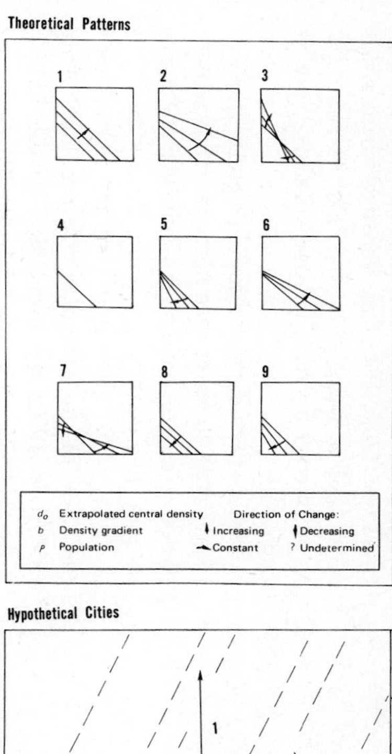

FIGURE 9-8. (*a*) The density-distance gradient and *d*/*P* for actual cities; and (*b*) theoretical density-distance gradients and *d*/*P*. *Source:* Original graphs prepared by Philip H. Rees.

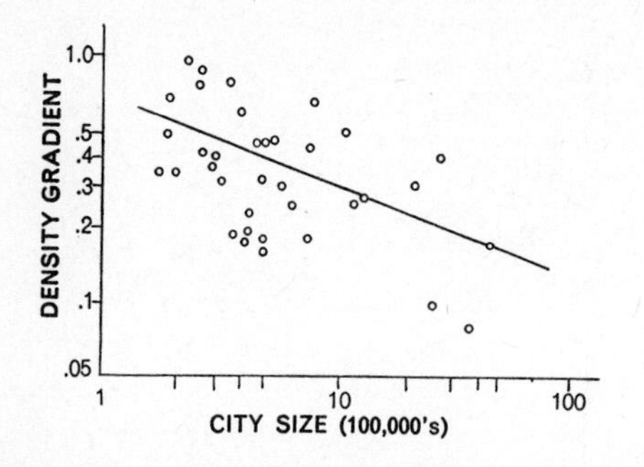

FIGURE 9–9. Relationship between the size and density gradients of cities in the United States: 1950. *Source:* Figs. 9–9 through 9–12 are from Brian J. L. Berry, James W. Simmons, and Robert J. Tennant, "Urban Populations: Structure and Change," *Geographical Review*, LIII (July, 1963), 389–405.

FIGURE 9–10. Relationship between the size and density gradients of selected Asian cities: Post-World War II. *Source:* See caption for Fig. 9–9.

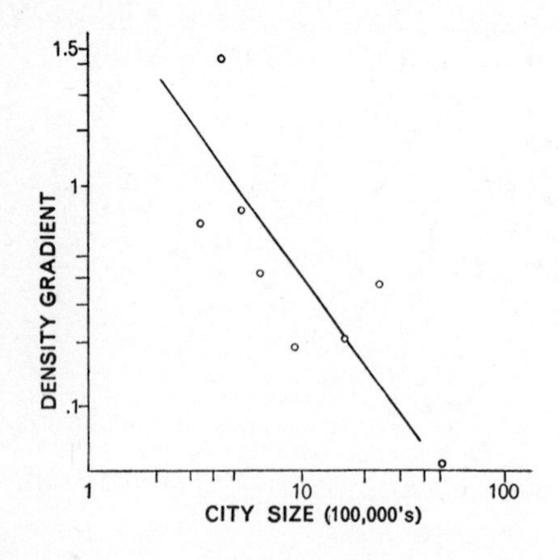

Rees' Eqs. (9–14) to (9–16) assume a circular city, the integration of Eq. (1) proceeding over the full 360° of the circle, and the city center being located at the center of the circle. Yet cities that conform to these assumptions are hard to find. Asymmetry and lopsidedness are common, elongations and crenulations many. Theoretically at least, one would expect the density gradient to diminish as such distortions of shape increase, because areas that would normally be occupied by certain densities are now no longer available, and uses that prefer these densities must move outward to the nearest available sites (though with some inevitable changes because of the effects of substitution). We must find out whether this is so, and if shape distortion, size of city, and so on interact to create the over-all density gradient.

Muth, after a detailed multiple regression analysis, rejected no fewer than nine different variables hypothesized to have some influence in determining the density gradient: density of local transit systems; quantity of local transit trackage; the area of the Standard Metropolitan Area (SMA) in 1950; the proportion of the SMA's growth from 1920 to 1950; median income; proportion of the SMA's sales in the central business district; proportion of substandard dwelling units in the central city; proportion of males employed in manufacturing in the urbanized area; and average density of the central city. Only the size of the SMA and the proportion of manufacturing outside the central city clearly appeared to bear significant relationships to b, though per capita car registrations showed a significant partial correlation, and the signs of the other variables included in his regression equation such as median income, indicated behavior in the right direction. Muth argued that size of city was significant only because other variables existed which were significant, and which could be approximated in sum by such a surrogate.[22]

This leads us to postulate that the density gradient is a function of the size of a city, distortion of its shape and the proportion of manufacturing outside the central city. A regression equation of the form:

$$\log b = 3.08 - 0.311 \log P - 1.0 \log A + 0.407 \log M \qquad (22)$$

resulted for the sample of forty-six United States cities. Only size of city (P) was significant at the .05 level, and scarcely 40 per cent of the variance of b was explained.[23] However, there is reason to believe that at such conventionally high levels of significance the risk of making errors of the other kind (rejecting true hypotheses) is somewhat too large for comfort, and there is thus reasonable doubt whether distortion of shape (A) and spatial pattern of employment in manufacturing (M) should be rejected, the more so since Muth did find M to be significant. A final decision cannot be made at this time, and further work is required. The only positive conclusion is to reiterate the relationship already found by Muth, and remarked briefly in passing by Clark,[24] that b diminishes as size of city increases, so that smaller cities are more compact than larger.

Cultural Differences

As Western cities grow, their density gradients, and therefore their compactness steadily decrease, whereas their central densities first increase and later decrease. But the same changes do *not* occur in non-Western cities. Figure 9–11 shows the density gradients and central densities of Calcutta from 1881 to 1951. Central density increased steadily and the urbanized area expanded, but the density gradient remained constant. This tendency towards increased overcrowding and the maintenance of a constant degree of compactness appears to be characteristic not only of a substantial part of the Indian urban scene[25] but also more generally in the non-Western world.

Figure 9–12 summarizes the cross-sectional variations (i.e., between regions or cultures at a point in time) and temporal patterns that may therefore be identified. At any point in time, the empirical regularities to be observed are the same for both Western and non-Western cities. But through time the patterns differ. In the West, central densities rise, then fall; in non-Western cities they register a continual increase. In the West, density gradients fall as cities grow; in non-Western cities they remain constant. Hence, whereas both the degree of compactness and crowding diminish in Western cities in time, non-Western cities experience increasing overcrowding, constant compactness, and less expansion at the periphery.[26]

Colin Clark[27] observed that there are "two possibilities for development, if the population is increasing. Either transport costs are reduced, enabling the city to spread out; or they cannot be reduced, in which case density has to increase at all points." In this, however, he was identifying the permissive factor accounting for the accelerated *sprawl* of Western vis-à-vis non-Western cities (on the supply side) rather than the real reason for the accompanying differentials in their density gradients (which is on the demand side).

Alonso[28] showed that the rich, in Western cities, live at the periphery on cheap land and consume

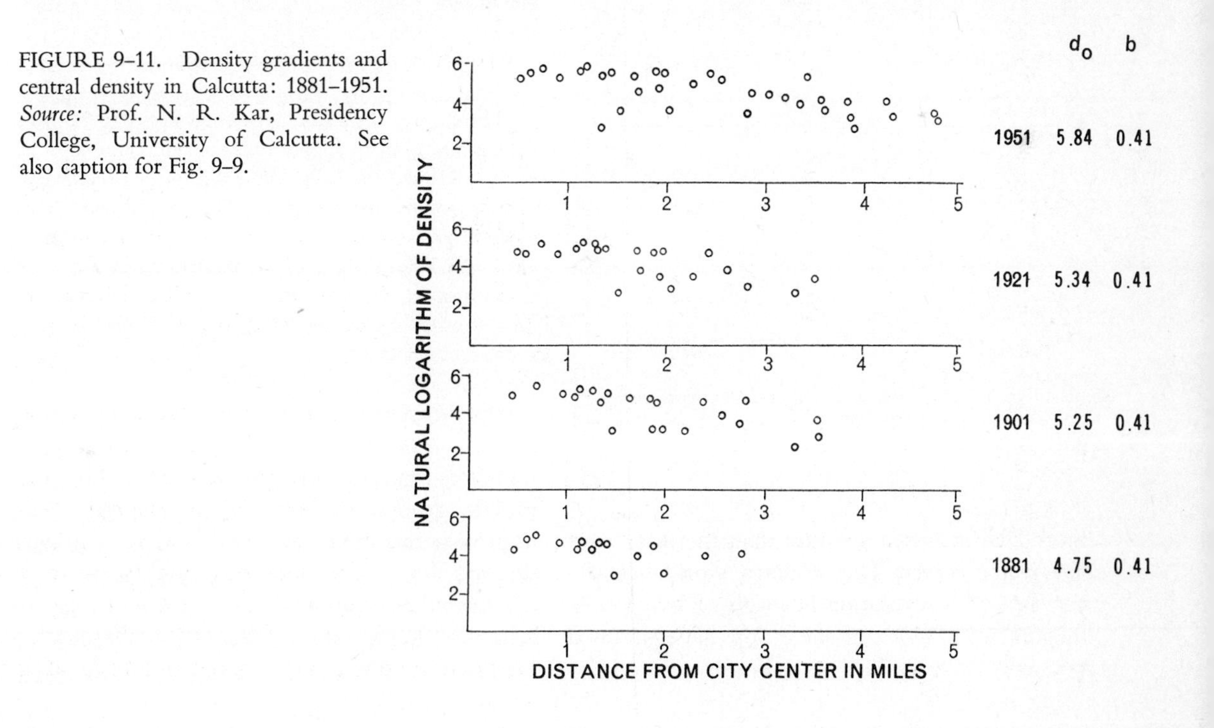

FIGURE 9–11. Density gradients and central density in Calcutta: 1881–1951. *Source:* Prof. N. R. Kar, Presidency College, University of Calcutta. See also caption for Fig. 9–9.

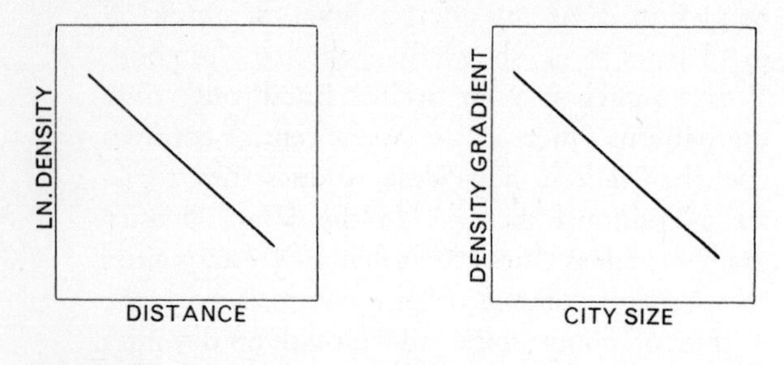

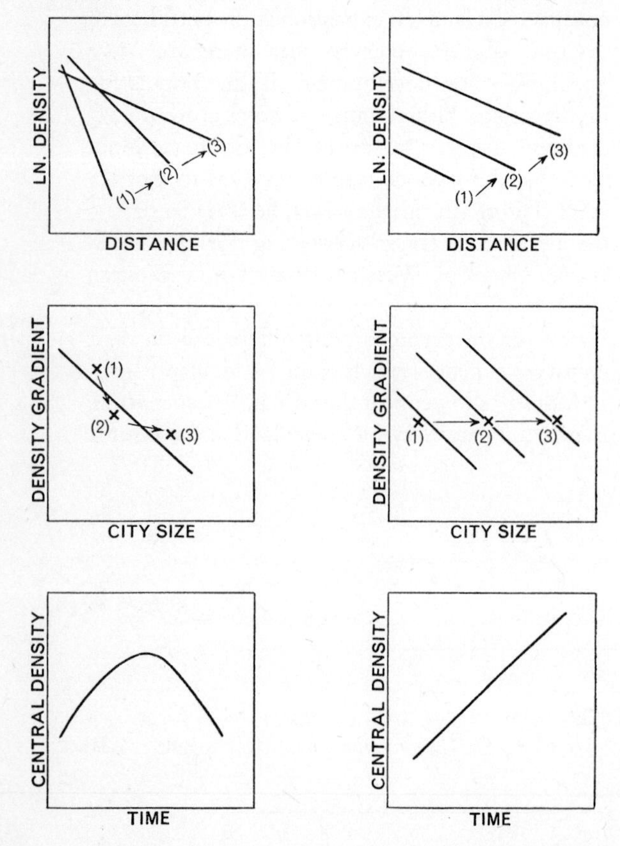

FIGURE 9–12. Cross-sectional and temporal comparisons, Western and non-Western cities. *Source:* See caption for Fig. 9–9.

more land at lower densities than the poor who live at the center. The Western world has also experienced a revolution in levels of living such that the richer, more mobile groups have increased not only numerically but also proportionally. Hence accelerated sprawl, facilitated by improved transportation systems, has been further stimulated by greater demand for peripheral, lower-density land, and there have been attendant reductions of the density gradient. The Western world has experienced significant changes in the nature of *demand* for residential land. Changed transport systems have merely ensured a supply adequate to meet the demand.

However, the socio-economic pattern of non-Western cities is markedly different. Sjoberg writes:

> . . . the feudal city's land use configuration is in many ways the reverse of that in the highly industrialized communities. The latter's advanced technology fosters, and is in turn furthered by, a high degree of social and spatial mobility that is inimical to any rigid social structure assigning persons, socially and ecologically, to special niches.[29]
>
> [There are] three patterns of land use wherein the non-industrial city contrasts sharply with the industrial type: (1) the pre-eminence of the "central" area over the periphery, especially as portrayed in the distribution of social classes; (2) certain finer spatial differences according to ethnic, occupational, and family ties; and (3) the low incidence of functional differentiation in other land use patterns.[30]

Chatterjee reiterates the regularity:

> The influence of the caste system is reflected in the usual concentration of the higher castes in the central areas of good residential localities, while the lower caste groups usually occupy the fringe. . . . The people still attach more importance to these centrally situated residential areas . . . . Thus, in spite of the modern development of road transport, the residential decentralization or movement towards the fringe outside the old residential areas is not very marked.[31]

If in Western cities the poor live at the center and the more mobile rich at the periphery, in non-Western cities the reverse is true. The least mobile groups occupy the periphery.[32] Any improvements in income will lead to a greater demand for central locations, and to increased overcrowding. Sprawl takes the form of the projection of the over-all surface outwards as densities increase throughout, into a periphery of degrading and depressing slums. The degree of compactness of the non-Western city remains, therefore, relatively unchanged, with the least mobile groups being located at the periphery. In spite of reductions in transport costs in non-Western cities, the groups located where the possibilities of saving are greatest are the groups least able to take advantage of the possibilities. Changes on the supply side occasioned by transport improvements are of little utility. The differences in the movement of central densities and density gradients through time are a function of the inverted locational patterns of the socio-economic groups in Western and non-Western cities and the attendant contrasts in their demand for residential land.

The two parameters, d_0 (central density, indicating concentration or crowding) and b (density gradient, indicating compactness), vary from city to city. In any temporal cross-section, central density appears to be determined by the growth history of the city up to that time, and the density gradient appears to be a function of city size.

Western and non-Western cities differ, however, in the ways in which d_0 and b change through time. In Western cities, d_0 increases, then decreases, and b steadily drops. Later stages are characterized by "deconcentration" (falling d_0) and suburbanization (falling b, or "decompaction"). Non-Western cities, however, experience continued increases in d_0 (overcrowding) and relative constancy of b (and hence, urban expansion without suburbanization in the Western sense). The contrast results from the differing patterns of location displayed by the higher and lower-level socio-economic groups in these cities.

Given the universal existence of the negative exponential density pattern, a large number of interesting applications become possible. Weiss,[33] for example, shows how the equations may be integrated with Zipf's rank-size rule for the United States to create a model that facilitates optimal location of market-oriented servicing units. The effectiveness of urban geography as an applied science is likely to increase as more such findings are produced, but only to the extent that the equations have an adequate theoretical base.

EXPLANATION OF THE INDUCTIVE GENERALIZATIONS

Apparently, the exponential decline of density with distance represents a condition of competitive locational equilibrium in a private housing market, and it may be derived from traditional theories of urban land economics under a set of very simple assumptions.

To develop the explanation, we examine first the particular components that go to make up population density, and then attempt to explain, with reference to land value theory, how these components vary with distance from the city center.

Winsborough's Accounting System

Winsborough[34] points out that gross population density (the measure we have been using in this chapter, of the density of people in a space) may be regarded as the product of a series of components, themselves made up of a more basic set of variables.[35] (Note: ftn. 35 contains an alternative to Winsborough's social accounting model.) With this insight, one can construct an accounting system which links population densities with the theory of urban land values. This theory, in turn, provides the basic theoretical foundation for the empirically derived exponential decay of urban population densities with distance from the city center, and for the set of derived relationships.

The accounting system is presented in Table 9–6. Each of the (logarithmic) components can be plotted against distance from the center of the city, and the contribution of their behavior to the over-all decline of gross densities with respect to distance assessed.

Gross and Net Densities Compared

The pattern of net densities (Fig. 9–13) looks very similar to that for gross densities (Fig. 9–1), though the values are much higher. Utilizing data gathered by the Chicago Area Transportation Survey (CATS), we can plot net population density against distance from the city center (Fig.

TABLE 9–6

An Accounting System for Population Density

Basic Variables

P = Population

FS = Floor space

R = Rooms

HU = Housing units

S = Structures

RA = Residential area

TA = Total area

Component Ratios

$\frac{P}{FS}$ = Population per unit of floor space

$\frac{FS}{R}$ = Floor space per room

$\frac{R}{HU}$ = Rooms per housing unit

$\frac{HU}{S}$ = Housing units per structure

$\frac{S}{RA}$ = Structures per unit of residential land

$\frac{RA}{TA}$ = Residential land per unit of all land

The Identities

1. Gross population density $\frac{P}{TA} = \frac{P}{FS} \cdot \frac{FS}{R} \cdot \frac{R}{HU} \cdot \frac{HU}{S} \cdot \frac{S}{RA} \cdot \frac{RA}{TA}$
2. Net population density $\frac{P}{RA} = \frac{P}{FS} \cdot \frac{FS}{R} \cdot \frac{R}{HU} \cdot \frac{HU}{S} \cdot \frac{S}{RA}$
3. Structure density $\frac{P}{S} = \frac{P}{FS} \cdot \frac{FS}{R} \cdot \frac{R}{HU} \cdot \frac{HU}{S}$
4. Housing unit density $\frac{P}{HU} = \frac{P}{FS} \cdot \frac{FS}{R} \cdot \frac{R}{HU}$
5. Room density $\frac{P}{R} = \frac{P}{FS} \cdot \frac{FS}{R}$
6. Floor space density $\frac{P}{FS} = \frac{P}{FS}$

Identities Expressed Logarithmically

1. $\log (P/TA) = \log (P/FS) + \log (FS/R) + \log (R/HU) + \log (HU/S) + \log (S/RA) + \log (RA/TA)$
2. $\log (P/RA) = \log (P/FS) + \log (FS/R) + \log (R/HU) + \log (HU/S) + \log (S/RA)$
3. $\log (P/S) = \log (P/FS) + \log (FS/R) + \log (R/HU) + \log (HU/S)$
4. $\log (P/HU) = \log (P/FS) + \log (FS/R) + \log (R/HU)$
5. $\log (P/R) = \log (P/FS) + \log (FS/R)$
6. $\log (P/FS) = \log (P/FS)$

9–14) in 1940 and 1956, and compare it with the equivalent curve of gross density, at least for 1940. The *net* density gradient steepened between 1940 and 1956 (or at least did not decrease), implying (1) that the level of *gross* densities increased through the process of conversion of vacant into residential land at lower densities than prevail on existing residential land and (2) that redevelopment of existing land used for residences was also at lower net densities than existed before redevelopment. In 1940 the gross density distance gradient was steeper than that of net densities, but in 1956 they were approximately equal (see Fig. 9–14) to a distance of about 11.5 miles from the intersection of State and Madison Streets. If the net *b* value were to exceed the gross *b* value,[36] then this might lead to the paradoxical deduction that, at some distance from the center of the city, gross densities exceed net. In fact, the slope of the net density curve changes at about 11.5 miles from the Loop, and thereafter the gradient is much gentler.

Gross and net densities are linked by the *RA*/*TA* ratio (residential land as a proportion of all land), which is plotted in various forms in Fig. 9–15. If we concentrate on the graphical material for 1940 for the moment[37] (Figs. 9–14 and 9–15), it becomes obvious that the departures of the actual

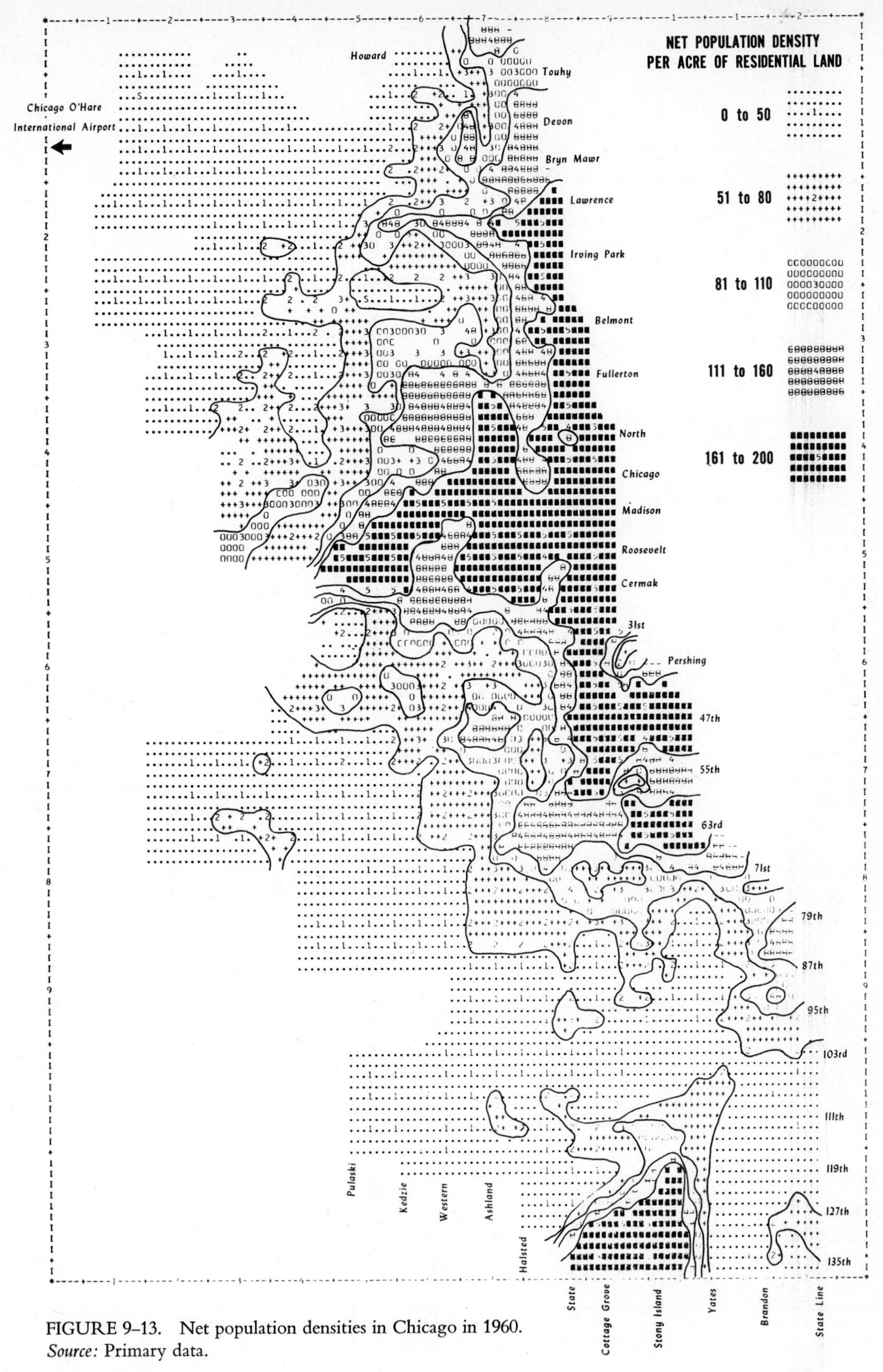

FIGURE 9–13. Net population densities in Chicago in 1960.
Source: Primary data.

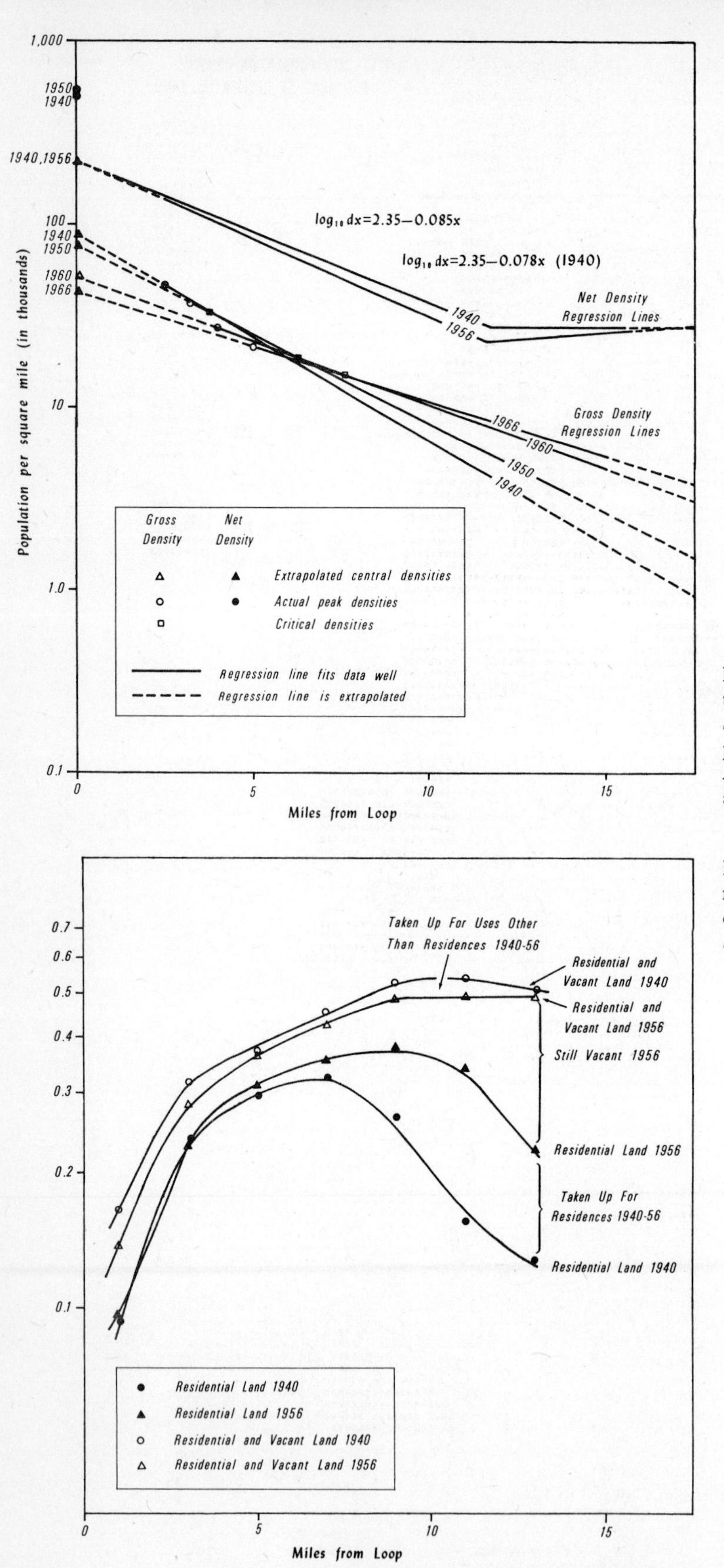

FIGURE 9–14. Gross and net population densities in Chicago: 1940 to 1966. *Source:* Data from Chicago Area Transportation Study, *Final Report*, I: *Survey Findings* (Chicago: Western Engraving and Embossing Company, 1959).

FIGURE 9–15. The use of land for residences at various distances from the center of Chicago: 1940 and 1956. *Source:* Primary data.

gross density-distance curve from the fitted regression line are a function of the variations in the proportion of residential land as we move away from the city center. This is shown in Fig. 9–16. In Zone I, actual gross density increases with distance because the proportion of land devoted to residences rises steeply with greater distance from the center. At the center of the city, commercial, industrial, and transportation users bid higher rents for land than residential users because they benefit more from centrality and resultant access to the rest of the metropolis than do residents.[38] The proportion of land in residential use remains roughly constant in Zone II, and the slope of the actual gross density curve approximates that of net density. In Zone II, also, the proportion of residential land begins to fall, and the actual gross density curve becomes somewhat steeper than the net. Net density becomes approximately constant (at some average density of single-family homes) in Zone IV, and the slope of the actual gross density curve slackens in response, despite the continued drop-off in the proportion of land devoted to residences.

The accounting system thus appears to work in its initial stages. We see that to explain the form of the gross density curve, it is necessary to explain why the proportion of land devoted to residences varies with distance from the city center and why the densities of people on residential land fall exponentially with distance from the center. Land value theory seems to provide the answer to both these questions.[39]

LAND VALUE AND LAND USE THEORY

A Model of Land Values and Population Density

There exists general agreement among students of land economics that land values are a function of the location of the lot within the city and the amenity value accorded the site, that is:

$$\text{land rent} = \text{location rent} + \text{amenity rent}.$$

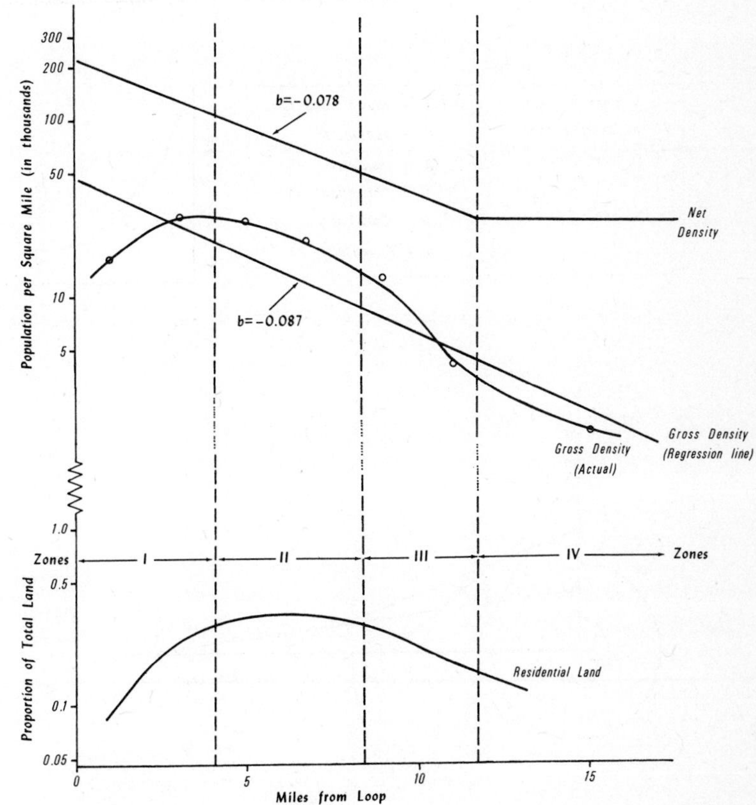

FIGURE 9–16. Gross density, net density, and the proportion of land devoted to residential use in Chicago. *Source:* Primary data.

Most attention has been devoted to a consideration of land values as location rents capitalized at the current interest rate. A causal chain may be built up in which the transport cost of the journey to centrally located work places (the dominant pattern in the industrial city) is linked to population densities via the distance-related land-value function and the capital/land ratio. The argument may be presented (with much simplification) in graphic form (see Fig. 9–17). Net savings in commuting costs accrue to the landowner (von Thünen type location rent),[40] and the profitability of the land to the landowner is reflected in the land value, which thus declines with distance from the center of the city. Since towards the center of the city land prices are high, little land and much capital will be used in order to equate their marginal productivities. Towards the periphery of the city, where land is much cheaper, the converse will be true. The occupation of the more remote structures (the physical expression of investment of capital) results in a decline of net residential densities with distance from the center of the city. The exponential form of the decay of density with distance is ultimately a function of the asymptotic increase in total transport costs with distance from the center of the city.

Land Value Theory

Mills presents a much more sophisticated version of this model for the derivation of land rent

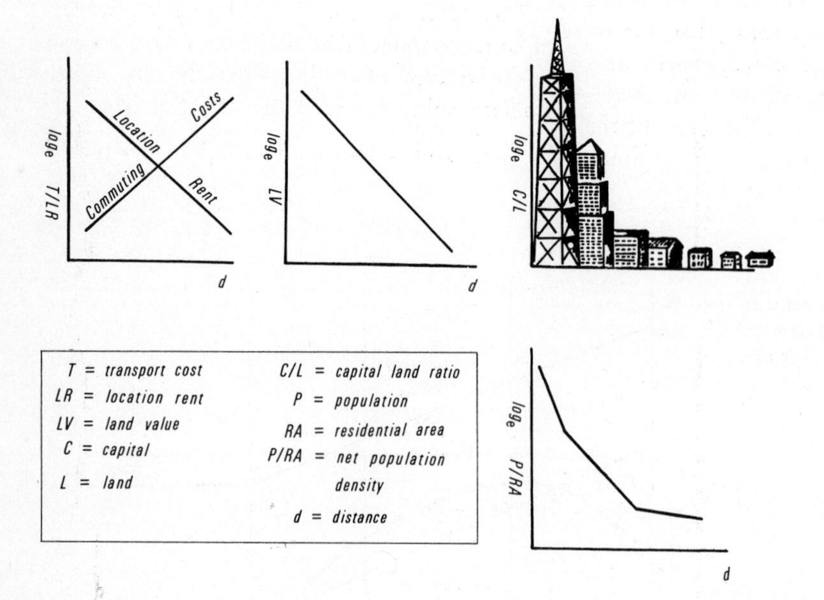

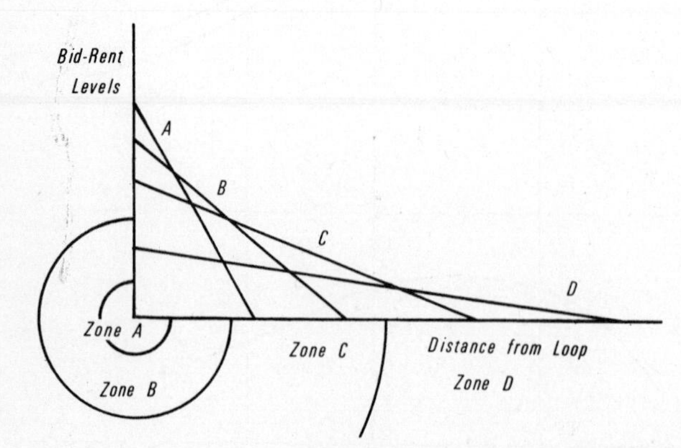

FIGURE 9–17. A model of land values and population densities. *Source:* Primary data.

from transport cost, given certain simplifying assumptions.[41] From a general equilibrium model encompassing production and transportation (with residential use being regarded as one form of output, to rest and refresh labor, e.g.) he deduces that:

$$R(u) = R_0 e^{-Au} \tag{23}$$

where: $R(u)$ = land rent at distance (u) from city center
R_0 = a constant of integration interpreted as land rent at the city center
e = natural base of logarithms
A = exponent
u = distance from city center

Mills also deduces that all land use densities are proportional to land rent,[42] so that, for example:

$$\frac{K_1(u)}{L_1(u)} = \left(\frac{c_1}{a_1}\right) \cdot \left(\frac{R(u)}{r}\right) \tag{24}$$

where: $K_1(u)$ = capital input on a site at distance u from city center
$L_1(U)$ = land input on a site at distance u from city center
c_1 and a_1 = coefficients in the marginal productivity equations
$R(u)$ = marginal productivity of land
r = marginal productivity of capital

One of those densities is population density.[43] (Note: ftn. 43 contains a long summary of Mills' model for the student who can follow the economic arguments and the mathematics.)

The explanation of the form of the residential land use curve involves the same concept of location rent, which can be explained as follows: different uses experience different savings in the cost of transportation through central location and therefore have different bid rent curves (see Fig. 9–17). Use A is able to outbid other uses for land within the first zone (Zone A), closest to the city center; use B outbids other uses in the second zone (B); C outbids others in the third zone; and D, in the fourth. The activities represented might be, respectively: central commercial (A); wholesaling and industrial (B); residential (C); and agricultural (D). The intersections in Fig. 9–17 do not represent points of abrupt change from one land use to another but rather thresholds in zones of transition at which one land use becomes more important than another. The curve showing the proportion of residential land (Fig. 9–16) takes the form that might be predicted by such a model.

Mills has, in fact, tested his land value model for Chicago, using Homer Hoyt's comprehensive estimates of land values in Chicago for five years—1836, 1857, 1873, 1910, and 1928—and his own sample of land values from Olcott's *Blue Book of Land Values* for 1966.[44] His results are reproduced in Table 9–7. The linear regression provides a poor fit; the two nonlinear equations fit much better and in part form the supporting evidence for his theoretical model.[45]

Initially (1836 to 1857), the city experienced an increase in the land value gradient and level of explanation afforded by distance, the result of rapid industrial growth around important interregional transport nodes in an era of inadequate means of intra-city transport of goods and people. Between 1857 and 1873, technical innovation in transportation (the street-car railway for commuters) led to a rapid decrease in the land value gradient, and a similar change again occurred between 1910 and 1928 (with the advent of the automobile for workers and the truck for goods).[46] These declines in the land value gradient over time parallel declines in the density gradient, lending support to our linkage of the two phenomena (see Fig. 9–18).[47]

The explanation of land value variability afforded by distance from the center of changes also weakens in time (after 1857), implying that distance from center of the city becomes less of a determining influence on land values as Chicago grows. Some of this decline (shown in Table 9–7) may be attributed to the increasing inaccuracy of the assumption that there is a single node or focus for the city. The effect of the geography of retailing within the city is to produce an "over-all ribbed or ridged cone (the business ribbons) bristled with minor cones of varying height (the shopping centers)."[48]

TABLE 9–7

Mills' Land Value Regressions for Chicago

Year	*Regression*	*Constant*	*Distance*	R^2
1836	linear	1016	−101.6	.0503
			(−3.2782)	
	log	5.799	−0.3986	.7836
			(−27.1104)	
	log-log	6.272	−1.936	.8284
			(−31.3073)	
1857	linear	6011	−575.1	.1911
			(−6.9412)	
	log	8.792	−.4874	.8597
			(−35.3627)	
	log-log	10.40	−2.873	.8509
			(−34.1262)	
1873	linear	24920	−2333	.2009
			(−7.2494)	
	log	10.05	−.3300	.7066
			(−22.4327)	
	log-log	10.34	−1.543	.6640
			(−20.3243)	
1910	linear	139800	−19220	.1386
			(−4.4658)	
	log	10.84	−.3275	.5867
			(−13.2685)	
	log-log	10.70	−1.300	.6828
			(−16.3365)	
1928	linear	182400	−15590	.1150
			(−4.2650)	
	log	11.85	−.2184	.4985
			(11.7969)	
	log-log	11.96	−.9886	.4551
			(−10.8135)	

Regression	*Constant*	*Distance*	*Zoned Commercial*	*Zoned Business*
Linear	3228	−217.8	−1531	1997
		(−3.4726)	(−1.6557)	(1.8720)
log	6.505	−.1147	−.3016	.8990
		(−4.8754)	(−.8693)	(2.2465)
log-log	6.692	−.6071	−.2217	.2707
		9.4496)	(−.7729)	(.7878)

Regression	*Zoned Services*	*Zoned Manufacturing*	*Zoned Residential*	R^2
Linear	−1262	−1335	−732.8	.2924
	(−1.2443)	(−1.2194)	(−0.6904)	
log	−.04778	−.2422	.2588	.3196
	(−.1256)	(−.5899)	(.6600)	
log-log	.0365	−.3060	.3316	.5276
	(.1153)	(−.9040)	(.9993)	

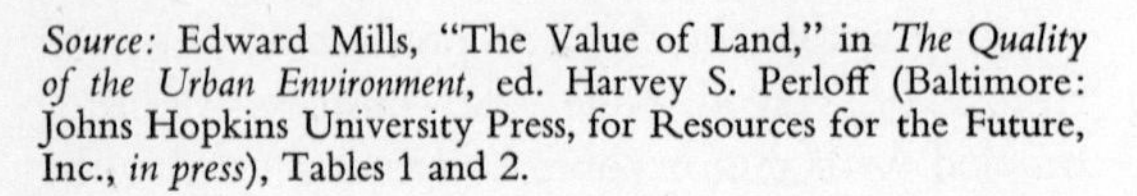
Source: Edward Mills, "The Value of Land," in *The Quality of the Urban Environment*, ed. Harvey S. Perloff (Baltimore: Johns Hopkins University Press, for Resources for the Future, Inc., *in press*), Tables 1 and 2.

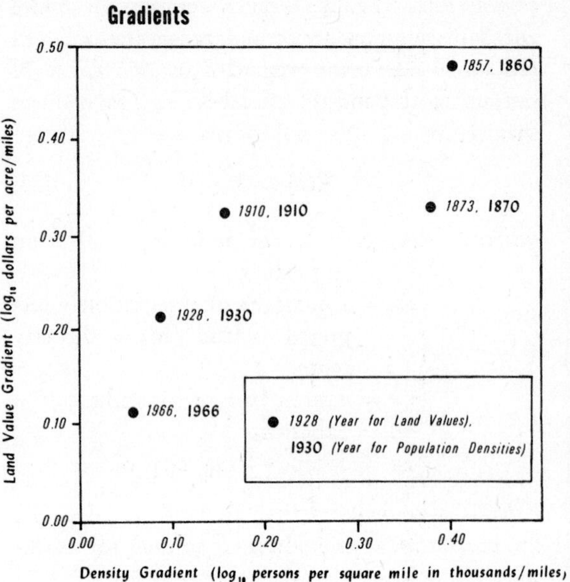

FIGURE 9–18. Land value and population density compared. *Source:* Primary data.

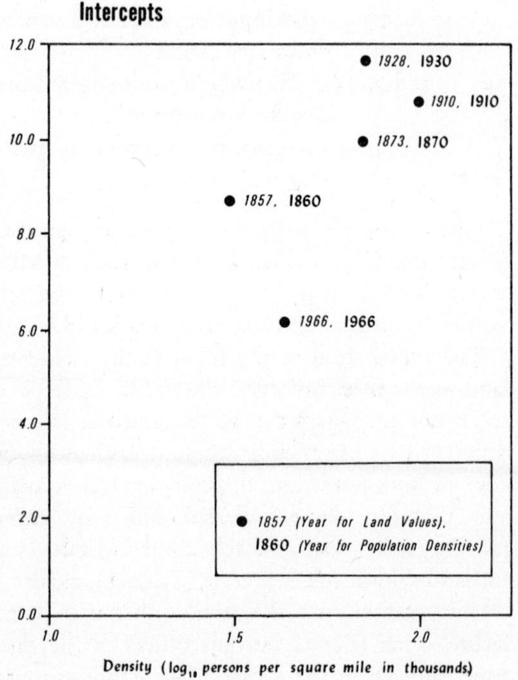

The retail centers and the dispersed industrial plants form workplace centers which will command their own residential location rents.[49] The precise influence of these dispersed workplace centers on the pattern of residential land values will depend on the location rents commanded by those centers.[50]

Amenity Rent

The other major influence leading to the distortion of the distance-decay relation of land values is the geographic variation in residential amenities. Harris, Tolley, and Harrell have investigated land values in Raleigh, North Carolina, in an effort to isolate the amenity component.[51] From land values at the center of the city they subtracted the value of land at the margin of the city and the value of travel savings.[52] The residual was regarded as a measure of the value of amenities and could be either negative or positive. To support their interpretation of this land value residual, they regressed it against a number of supply and demand variables that might reasonably be thought to be associated with amenity:

> Tenancy, zoning, and socio-economic class variables were supply-related variables found to be statistically significant. . . . Significant demand variables explaining amenity expenditures were income, family size, and structure type.[53]

An attempt to assess the various forces determining land values in Chicago has been made by Yeates, whose data (like Mills's) came from Olcott's *Blue Book of Land Values* measured in front-foot values.[54] These unfortunately fail to take into account lot or site size. Yeates adopts the following multiple correlation and regression model:

$$\log V_i = a + b_1 \log C_i + b_2 \log R_i + b_3 \log M_1 + b_4 \log E_i + b_5 \log P_i + b_6 N_i + e \quad (25)$$

where: V_i = front foot land value
C_i = distance to central business district
R_i = distance to nearest regional shopping center
M_i = distance to Lake Michigan
E_i = distance to nearest elevated train or subway station
P_i = population density
N_i = percentage of non-white population
e = error
i = "ith" sampling point

The results of this model are reproduced in Table 9–8. The explanatory power of the model declines over time, as does the regression coefficient of distance. This coefficient is one obtained from the regression of the logarithm of land value against the logarithm of distance, rather than against distance expressed arithmetically, the form

TABLE 9–8

Yeates' Regression Results

	1910	*1920*	*1930*	*1940*	*1950*	*1960*
Multiple r_2	77	65	37	34	24	18
b_1	−.837*	−.673*	−.268*	−.275*	−.268*	−.173*
b_2	−.038	−.122*	−.156*	−.134*	−.080	−.092*
b_3	−.450*	−.414*	−.367*	−.285*	−.227*	−.146*
b_4	−.248*	−.240*	−.214*	−.140*	−.152*	−.050
b_5	+.105*	−.008	+.039	+.044	−.016*	−.137*
b_6	+.005*	+.001	−.003*	−.002*	−.002*	−.002*
Correlation between log c_i and log p_i	−.63	−.56	−.23	−.18	−.20	+.04

Source: Maurice Yeates, "Some Factors Affecting the Spatial Distribution of Chicago Land Values," *Economic Geography*, XLI, No. 1 (January, 1965), 57–70.
*Significantly different from zero when $P = .05$.

suggested by the theory. In the latest year of the study, 1960, only within 1.5 miles of the intersection of State and Madison Streets were land values found to be strongly related to distance; towards the edge of the city, land values actually increase. Whether this situation persists into the inner suburbs is not known. It is doubtful whether $M_i + N_i$ measure amenity, as Yeates himself points out, so it is somewhat difficult to assess the relative influences of location and amenity on land values.

Conclusion

The empirical link between land values and population densities may be established by plotting the parameters of land value and population density against each other (see Fig. 9–18). The pattern of central values is not very clear, probably because at the center of the city we are comparing two very unlike things—largely commercial land values and extrapolated gross density—the latter of which tended to reach its peak earlier. But that the gradient declined in a consistent and parallel fashion in the century or so from 1857 to 1966 lends strong support to the theoretical conclusions outlined earlier in the chapter.

The makings of a wide-ranging descriptive and explanatory system for the pattern of population in a large metropolis have thus been shown to exist.

FOOTNOTES TO CHAPTER 9

1. See Halliman H. Winsborough, "The Social Consequences of High Population Density," *Law and Contemporary Problems*, XXX (Winter, 1965), 120–26; John B. Calhoun, "Population Density and Social Pathology," *Scientific American* (February, 1962), 139–48; and *idem*, "A Method for Self-Control of Population Growth among Animals Living in the Wild," *Science*, CIX (April, 1949), 333–35.

2. Colin Clark, "Urban Population Densities," *Journal of the Royal Statistical Society*, Series A, CXIV, No. 4 (1951), 490–96; *idem*, "Urban Population Densities," *Bulletin de l'Institute International de Statistique*, XXXVI, No. 4 (1958), 60–68; *idem*, *Population Growth and Land Use* (London: Macmillan & Co., Ltd., 1967); John Q. Stewart and William Warntz, "The Physics of Population Distribution," *Journal of Regional Science*, I (Summer, 1958), 99–123; Brian J. L. Berry, James W. Simmons, and Robert J. Tennant, "Urban Population Densities: Structure and Change," *Geographical Review*, LIII, No. 2 (July, 1963), 389–405; Halliman H. Winsborough, "A Comparative Study of Urban Population Densities" (Ph.D. dissertation, University of Chicago, 1961); Bruce E. Newling, "The Growth and Spatial Structure of Kingston, Jamaica" (Ph.D. dissertation, Northwestern University, 1962); Richard F. Muth, "The Spatial Structure of the Housing Market," *Papers and Proceedings of the Regional Science Association*, VII (1961), 207–20; *idem*, "The Variation of Population Density and Its Components in South Chicago," *Papers and Proceedings of the Regional Science Association*, XV (1965), 173–83; *idem*, "The Spatial Pattern of Residential Land Use in Cities" (Unpublished manuscript, September, 1964).

3. Brian J. L. Berry, "The Internal Structure of the City," *Law and Contemporary Problems*, XXX (Winter, 1965), 111–19, Bruce E. Newling, "Urban Growth and Spatial Structure: Mathematical Models and Empirical Evidence," *Geographical Review*, LVI, No. 2 (April, 1966), 213–25.

4. Bruce E. Newling, "A Partial Theory of Urban Growth: Mathematical Structure and Planning Implications" (Paper presented at the Latin American Regional Conference of the International Geographical Union, Mexico City, August, 1966).

5. It has been suggested more recently by Bruce E. Newling, in "Urban Populations: The Mathematics of Structure and Process" (Paper presented at the annual meeting of the American Association of Geographers, St. Louis, Mo., April 12, 1967), that a quadratic regression of the logarithm of density on distance is a better generalization, because it accounts for the density crater at the center of the city. Eq. (1) would thus become:

$$d_x = d_0 e^{bx-cx^2} \qquad (1a)$$

where b measures the instantaneous rate of change of density with distance at the center of the city and can be positive or negative. Equation (2) becomes:

$$ln\ d_x = ln\ d_0 + bx - cx^2 \qquad (2a)$$

For the present study, the linear version of the exponential equation seems more useful. The existence of systematic deviations from the line of regression is explained in terms of the interaction of the various components of gross population. Retention of the linear form also makes possible comparisons with similar studies of other cities.

6. These sectors represent merely a convenient spatial grouping of areas rather than slices of the metropolitan cake tied to the center by a commuting railroad or expressway. Pierre DeVise, in *The Social Geography of Metropolitan Chicago* (Chicago: Northeastern Illinois Metropolitan Area Planning Commission, 1964), pp. 54–55, distinguishes twelve sectors tied to railroads; in his *Suburban Factbook* (Chicago: Northeastern Illinois Metropolitan Area Planning Commission, 1964) some nine sectors are distinguished in the suburbanization of the metropolis in Illinois.

7. Winsborough,"A Comparative Study of Urban Population Densities."

8. *Ibid.*

9. Newling, "Urban Growth and Spatial Structure."

10. This is the marginal density which Newling found most useful in estimating SMSA populations from the density-distance Eqs. (1) and (2). The estimated population lying within a marginal density of zero was found to be larger than the census

population of the SMSA's; the estimates of population lying within a marginal density of 5,000 persons per square mile proved too large; a marginal density of 2,000 persons yielded approximately correct SMSA populations. See *ibid.*, and a later section of this chapter.

11. *Ibid.*, p. 225.

12. Poul O. Pedersen, *Modeller for Befolkningsstruktur og Befolkningsudvikling i Storbyomrader Specielt med Henblik pa Storkobenhavn* (Copenhagen: State Urban Planning Institute, 1967), p. 135, notes a similar downward shift in density, from approximately 52,000 persons per square mile in 1940 (an interpolated figure since all growth rates are positive) through 22,000 per square mile in 1950 to 14,000 in 1960.

13. Winsborough, "The Social Consequences of High Population Density," investigated the correlates of gross population density in 75 community areas of Chicago in 1950. The correlations with mortality, morbidity, and public assistance levels suggested that social problems were concentrated in the high density areas, but when the effects of the age structures and social status of community populations were held constant then the results were equivocal.

14. Newling, "A Partial Theory of Urban Growth," p. 14. From these assumptions, plus the assumptions that population density is a negative exponential function of distance from the center of the city and that the density gradient b is a negative exponential function of time, Newling deduces that density is a function of distance and time in the following way:

$$d_{x,t} = d_0 e^{-b_0 x e^{-ct}} \tag{10}$$

Further, that density is a function of the initial density and time:

$$d_{t-1} = (d_t/a)^{1/(1-k)} \tag{11}$$

Stated generally, the population density at any location at time $t + n$ is specified as:

$$d_{t+n} = a^{1/k} a^{-[(1-k)^n/k]} d_t(1 - k)^n \tag{12}$$

As n becomes very large, the expression $a^{-[(1-k)n/k]} d_t(1 - k)$ approaches unity, and

$$\lim_{n\to\infty} d_{t+n} = a^{1/k} \tag{13}$$

That is, the limiting density to which densities grow along a sigmoidal growth curve is the critical density.

15. The form of the equations is taken from Newling, "Urban Growth and Spatial Structure," pp. 215–16, and the the nomenclature from similar equations in Brian J. L. Berry, "Spatial Organization and Levels of Welfare: Degree of Metropolitan Market Participation as a Variable in Economic Development" (Paper prepared for the Economic Development Administration Research Conference, Washington, D.C., October 9–13, 1967), p. 11, in which he defines x^* as the distance at which densities become rural.

16. Winsborough, "A Comparative Study of Urban Population Densities."

17. Clark, "Urban Population Densities," p. 490.

18. Muth, "The Spatial Structure of the Housing Market."

19. Winsborough, "Comparative Studies of Urban Population Densities"; and K. E. Boulding," "Toward a General Theory of Growth," in *Population Theory and Policy*, eds. Joseph J. Spengler and Otis D. Duncan (New York: The Free Press, 1956), pp. 109–24. This is Boulding's "first principle of structural growth." Winsborough says that "the timing of growth affects the density patterns . . . different influences on the pattern of development at different times and the resultant structure of the city sets limits on its subsequent growth. . . . "

20. See James W. Simmons, "Relationships between the Population Density Pattern and Site of Cities" (Master's thesis, University of Chicago, 1962), for an elaboration of these results.

21. Winsborough, in "Comparative Studies of Urban Population Densities," shows that the implied central density of Chicago increased until 1900 or 1910 and decreased thereafter, apparently as a result of a change in local transport that superimposed its effects on the established growth processes. He also found the total population density of a city (D) to be positively correlated with the percentage of old dwellings, the size of the city, and the percentage of the population engaged in manufacturing, and negatively correlated with the percentage of one-family detached dwellings. For any city, he showed D to be a function of d_0, regardless of b; thus, by implication, d_0 is a function of age, population, and employment. In turn, we shall see that b is a function of the last two variables. For an analysis of declining urban densities in the U. S. in the decade 1950 to 1960, see Ronald R. Boyce, "Changing Patterns of Urban Land Consumption," *Professional Geographer*, XV, No. 1 (January, 1963), 19–24.

22. Muth, Spatial Structure of the Housing Market."

23. Simmons, "Population Density Pattern and Site of Cities." The index of shape distortion (A) was constructed as the ratio of the sum of distances of points arranged in a regular network, within the boundaries of the city's urbanized area, from the city center to the sum of distances of points, in the same regular network as from the center of a circle of the same area as the city. A is 1 for a perfectly circular city and increases with distortion of the shape. The index is highly sensitive to elongation or lopsidedness, but not to crenulations, and only slightly to a starfish pattern created by radiating transportation routes. It appears to be fairly highly correlated with physical distortions, especially the presence of water bodies; thus A is also an index of the influences of city sites on population density patterns. The correlation between A and a site index (S) was .584. S was defined as WT, where $W = 1 -$ (water area/total area) in a circle of the same area as the city, centered on the central business district, and $T = 1 -$ tan (average slope). $S = WT + 1$ in a circular city on a level plain. The greatest proportion of the covariance of A and S was accounted for by the W component, an indication that major distortions of shape are largely a function of location alongside bodies of water.

24. Clark, "Urban Population Densities."

25. See Roy Turner, ed., *India's Urban Future* (Berkeley: University of California Press, 1962). In a more recent study, John E. Brush has identified four types of density distribution in Indian cities, and some temporal differences in their density gradients. See "Spatial Patterns of Population in Indian Cities," *The Geographical Review*, LXVIII, No. 2 (July, 1968), 362–91.

26. Winsborough, in "Comparative Studies of Urban Population Densities," points out the problems of differentiating between "deconcentration" and "suburbanization" in Chicago. N. R. Kar, "Growth, Distribution and Dynamics of the Population Load in Calcutta" (Calcutta, 1962), describes the absence of suburbs around Calcutta.

27. Clark, "Urban Population Densities," p. 495.

28. W. Alonso, "A Theory of the Urban Land Market," *Papers and Proceedings of the Regional Science Association*, VI (1960), 149–58.

29. Gideon Sjoberg, *The Preindustrial City—Past and Present*

(New York: The Free Press, 1960), p. 103. See also pp. 95–103.

30. *Ibid.*, pp. 95–96.

31. A. B. Chatterjee, "Howrah: An Urban Study" (Ph.D. dissertation, University of London, 1960), p. 233.

See also John E. Brush, "The Morphology of Indian Cities," in *India's Urban Future*, pp. 57–70. Contrast this picture with that provided throughout the book by James M. Beshers, *Urban Social Structure* (New York, the Free Press, 1962). Paul Wheatley has pointed out (in conversation) that the larger Southeast Asian cities do not have what we have termed the "non-Western" socio-economic pattern, though the smaller and medium-sized towns do, and the result is that population redistribution follows the Western pattern in the larger cities.

32. The same social pattern is being repeated in new Indian towns. In Le Corbusier's plan for the new Punjab capital of Chandigarh in India, the best-quality residences are at the center and are graded outwards to the poorest at the periphery.

33. Herbert K. Weiss, "The Distribution of Urban Population and an Application to a Servicing Problem," *Operations Research*, IX (1961), 860–74.

Another interesting outcome of his model is that it made it possible to calculate how many people reside in the most densely settled parts of the U. S. For example, the 3,000 most densely occupied square miles today contain the homes of 45,000,000 people.

34. Winsborough, "Comparative Studies of Urban Population Densities," pp. 32–33.

35. Muth, in "The Spatial Pattern of Residential Land Use in Cities," discusses at length a somewhat similar concept of components of population density (see Chapter IX, "Components of Population Density in U.S. Cities," and Chapter X, "Population Density and Its Components in South Chicago"). Similarly, in "Metropolitan Population Decentralization" (Ph.D. dissertation, University of Michigan, 1967), Roy C. Treadway analyzes the social components of densities as follows:

$$\frac{P}{A} = \frac{U}{A} \cdot \frac{O}{U} \cdot \frac{H}{O} \cdot \frac{P}{H}$$

where: P = population
A = area
U = total housing units
O = the number of occupied housing units
H = household population

In one case study (Syracuse), he found that the density gradient (i.e., of P/A) was $-.4943$ in 1950 and $-.4367$ in 1960. In 1950 it was made up of the following components: $-.4832$ (U/A) $-.0118$ (O/U) $+.0084$ (H/O) $-.0077$ (P/H). In 1960, it was composed of $-.4432$ (U/A) $-.0086$ (O/O) $+.0213$ (H/O) $-.0026$ (P/H). Thus the components of the decadal gradient decrease of .0577 were .04 (U/A); .0032 (O/U); .0129 (H/O); and .0016 (P/H). Not only was population density related in a systematic fashion to distance, but so were its components, and the declining densities at the center were produced by the demolition or merger of housing units, increased vacancies, smaller households and a decreasing proportion of group quarters.

36. This was the case in 1956 if we use extrapolated b coefficients based on a regression using all zones.

37. Published data is most readily available for this year.

38. Some recent private redevelopment of land for residential use in or near the Loop (Marina Towers, Lake Shore East, John Hancock Center, Lake Point Tower, and 1160 South Michigan being the most conspicuous examples) seems to indicate that this may be changing. The suburbanization of formerly centrally located, metropolitan-wide activities has resulted in a somewhat less vigorous growth in the demand for office and retailing space in the central business district, and population growth at the center has resulted. The net densities that make possible the conversion to residential use of high-value land are, however, very high indeed (500,000 persons per square mile).

39. Among recent important materials on land value theory are the following: Richard Muth, "The Spatial Structure of the Housing Market," *Papers and Proceedings of the Regional Science Association*, VII (1961), 207–20; William Alonso, *Location and Land Use* (Cambridge, Mass.: Harvard University Press, 1964); Lowdon Wingo, *Transportation and Urban Land* (Washington, D.C.: Resources for the Future, Inc., 1961); Edwin S. Mills, "The Value of Land," in *The Quality of the Urban Environment*, ed. Harvey S. Perloff (Baltimore: Johns Hopkins University Press for Resources for the Future, Inc., *in press*); R. N. S. Harris, G. S. Tolley, and C. Harrell, "The Residence Site Choice" (mimeographed, North Carolina State University, 1968); Edwin S. Mills, "An Aggregative Model of Resource Allocation in a Metropolitan Area," *American Economic Review*, LVII, No. 2 (May, 1967), 197–210.

40. Peter Hall, ed., *Von Thünen's Isolated State* (London: Pergamon Press, 1968).

41. Mills, "The Value of Land," pp. 19–26. Other extensive discussions of the theory of land values are to be found in Muth, "The Spatial Pattern of Residential Land Use in Cities," Part I, Theoretical Analysis; and in D. E. Seidman, "An Operational Model of the Residential Land Market" (Unpublished paper, Penn-Jersey Transportation Study, 1964).

42. "The Value of Land."

43. To paraphrase Mills' arguments that lead to these conclusions:

1. There are constant returns to scale for production.
2. Homogeneous land stretches from the city center in all directions, except for a pie slice of $2\pi - \theta$ radians ($0 < \theta < 2\pi$) as far as urban users outbid rural users.
3. There are two kinds of activity and outputs in the city: production (including household activity); and transportation.
4. Production of transportation and all other goods is bought and sold in competitive markets.

The value of all other goods produced at u miles from the city center is given by:

$$X_1(u) = \bar{A}_1 L_1(u)^{a_1} . N_1(u)^{b_1} . K_1(u)^{c_1} \quad \text{where: } a_1 + b_1 + c_1 = 1 \tag{F1}$$

where X_1 = output; and L_1, N_1, and K_1 are inputs of land, labor, and capital, respectively. Equation (F1) is well known as the Cobb-Douglas production function.

The production function for transportation outputs is of the same form (but with different parameters):

$$X_2(u) = \bar{A}_2 L_2(u)^{a_2} . N_2(u)^{b_2} . K_2(u)^{c_2} \quad \text{where: } a_2 + b_2 + c_2 = 1 \tag{F2}$$

The competitive assumption applied to factor markets implies that the value of the marginal product of each factor is equal to its price. That is:

$$\left.\begin{aligned} a_2 p_2(u)\frac{X_2(u)}{L_2(u)} &= R(u) \qquad (a) \\ b_2 p_2(u)\frac{X_2(u)}{N_2(u)} &= w \qquad (b) \\ c_2 p_2(u)\frac{X_2(u)}{K_2(u)} &= r \qquad (c) \end{aligned}\right\} \quad (F3)$$

where $p_2(u)$ is the price per unit distance of transportation u miles from the center; $R(u)$ is the rental rate on land u miles from the center, to be determined by the model; and w and r are the wage rate of labor and the cost of capital respectively, assumed to be determined exogeneously and to be the same at all points in the urban area. From Eqs. (F2) and (F3) it can be shown that:

$$P_2(u) = A_2 R(u)^{a_1} \quad A_2 = [\bar{A}_2 a_2{}^{a_2} b_2{}^{b_2} c_2{}^{c_2}] - {}_1 w^{b_2} r^{c_2} \qquad (F4)$$

Now, the total cost $T(u)$ of shipping a unit of output at a distance u to the city center is:

$$T(u) = \int_0^u P_2(u')du' \qquad (F5)$$

The price received at the place of production for output is therefore $p_1 - T(u)$. Under the competitive assumption for production factor markets, we have the following marginal productivity equation for rent:

$$a_1[p_1 - (Tu)]\frac{X_1(u)}{L_1(u)} = R(u) \qquad (F6)$$

There are similar equations for w and r. That is:

$$p_1 - T(u) = A_1 R(u)^{a}{}_1 \qquad (F7)$$

where: $A_1 = [\bar{A}_1 a_1{}^{a_1} b_1{}^{b_1} c_1{}^{c_1}]^{-1} w^{b_1} r^{c_1}$

Now, total sales of industry are a decreasing function of p_1:

$$p_1 = a_1 X_1{}^{-c_1} \qquad (F8)$$

where X_1 is the area's total output:

$$X_1 = \int_0^k X_1(u)du \qquad (F9)$$

August Lösch, in his book *The Economics of Location* (New York: John Wiley & Sons, Inc., 1967), discusses this decline of sales as the price to the consumer increases with distance from the sales center, with respect to central place theory.

Given the condition that production and transportation exhaust all the land, then:

$$L_1(u) + L_2(u) = u \qquad 0 \leq u \leq k \qquad (F10)$$

where k is the margin of the urban area where nonurban users outbid urban users for land.

$$R(k) = Ra \qquad (F11)$$

If the right-hand side of Eq. (F4) is substituted into the right-hand side of Eq. (F5), and this is in turn substituted into Eq. (F7), the result is:

$$p_1 - A_2 \int_0^u R(u')^{a}1du' = A_1 R(u)^{a_1} \qquad (F12)$$

Differentiating once, the result is:

$$AR(u)^a + R'(u) = 0 \qquad (F13)$$

where: $A = A_2/a_1A_1$; $a = 1 + a_2 - a_1$.

When $a \neq 1$, this equation has the solution:

$$R(u) = [C - A(1 - a)u]^{1/1-a} \qquad (F14)$$

When $a = 1$, and $a_1 = a_2$, the solution of Eq. (F13) is:

$$R(u) = R_0 e^{-Au} \qquad (F15)$$

where the constant of integration has the interpretation of land rent at the city center, R_0. That $a_1 = a_2$ means that transportation and production each occupy about half of the land.

Data in Harland Bartholomew, *Land Uses in American Cities* (Cambridge, Mass.: Harvard University Press, 1955), indicate that transportation uses occupy about a third of all developed land in American cities, and about 40 per cent of all developed land not in parks or other public use. If the land occupied by sidewalks and pathways is added, the proportion of land occupied by transportation uses begins to approach the proportion assumed by Mills.

44. Mills, "The Value of Land," pp. 26–37; Homer Hoyt, *One Hundred Years of Land Values in Chicago* (Chicago: University of Chicago Press, 1933); G. H. Olcott, *Blue Book of Land Values* (Chicago: G. H. Olcott, Co., annual).

45. That is, if we accept the log rather than the log-log regression as being the correct form. Empirically there is little to choose between them; in the analysis of data from 1836 to 1928, and in one form of the analysis of 1966 data in which a sample of tracts from the Olcott *Blue Book* is used, the log-log form is significantly better than the log. Mills does not assess the implications of these results regarding his theoretical model.

46. The impact of the truck on intra-city and inter-city transportation of goods on the relative attractiveness to industry of various parts of the urban region is discussed by Leon F. Moses and Harold F. Williamson, Jr., in "The Location of Economic Activity in Cities," *American Economic Review*, LVII, No. 2 (May, 1967), 211–22.

47. A similar comparison of the behavior of central land values and central densities would be possible if Mills had converted his land values into real terms by dividing through by a price index.

48. Brian J. L. Berry *et al.*, *Commercial Structure and Commercial Blight* (Chicago: University of Chicago Department of Geography Research Paper No. 85, 1963), p. 14 and Fig. 3. It is the local differential rate of return to businesses associated with pedestrian traffic that accounts for these variations in land values on land devoted to retailing.

49. The dispersion of industrial plants to the suburbs in Chicago is described in Moses and Williamson, "The Location of Economic Activity in Cities."

50. The point is made by Harris, Tolley and Harrell, in "The Residence Site Choice," ftn. 3.

51. *Ibid.*

52. "Travel savings were computed at $1.55 per car hour, divided by the number of passengers and capitalized at a 7 per cent discount rate." *Ibid.*, p. 20.

53. *Ibid.*, p. 29.

54. Maurice Yeates, "Some Factors Affecting the Spatial Distribution of Chicago Land Values," *Economic Geography*, XLI, No. 1 (January, 1965), 57–70.

CHAPTER 10

*concepts of social space: toward an urban social geography**

What of the people who live at these differential densities? What are they like? Who lives where? Certain insights are forthcoming from everyday experience, but a more formal basis for understanding can be provided. The beginnings of this base came from studies in urban ecology and urban land economics, written very largely about Chicago, in Chicago, by faculty and students of the University of Chicago.

THE CLASSICAL MODELS

The Ecological View: Burgess's Concentric Zone Theory

It was work in plant ecology at the University of Chicago that provided the inspiration for fruitful urban research by sociologists and geographers at Chicago in the years between World Wars I and II. In Robert Park's essay on "Human Ecology"[1] the analogies are direct. He talks about "competition" between various population or interest groups in the metropolis, the "dominance" of one group in the "natural" or "functional areas"[2] of a metropolitan community, and the "invasion" of a natural area by a competing group, leading to "succession" and to the dominance of the area by a new group. Park points out, however, that though competition is relatively unrestricted in the biological world, in the human world it is restricted by conventions, laws, and institutions.

These urban ecological processes, Park said, derive their energy from the expansion of the city's population and the city's area in a concentric ringlike fashion over time. Observation (at first on an informal basis) of Chicago revealed

*Adapted by Philip H. Rees especially for this book from his study *The Factorial Ecology of Metropolitan Chicago* (Master's thesis, University of Chicago, 1968).

that the process of upward social mobility involved geographic migration: the population group which had resided in the city for the longest time would move from their original homes to newer homes in the city's periphery as their economic status improved; they would be replaced at the center of the city by new arrivals, to whom the older housing stock would "filter down." Thus, a distinctive spatial pattern of activity and residence zones, Burgess's concentric zones (see Fig. 10-1), emerged, the definitions of which are based on principal land use (Zone I, Commercial; Zone IIa, Industrial; Zones IIb to V, Residential), and within the residential category by the type of resident (Zone III, zone of workingmen's homes; Zone V, commuter's zone), both use and tenants changing in time as a result of the filtering down of property. The broadly defined zones are divided into smaller natural areas (see Fig. 10–1) on the basis of race (the Black Belt), or ethnicity (Little Sicily), or the type of residence (Residential Hotels).

The model is crude and unrefined, but it provided a set of ideas about urban spatial structure which could be empirically tested,[3] and a framework for the more detailed study of natural areas within the city.[4] The focus of interest of many of the Chicago monographs was the "disorganized" communities of the city (Skid Row, Hobohemia), the real and immediate problems of poverty and deviant behavior posed by such residential areas invoking a research response from the Chicago academic community.

A number of ideas were put forward to explain why it was that certain neighborhoods of the city persistently posed social problems even as a multitude of population groups moved through the neighborhoods in the processes of invasion and succession. Burgess considered that the relationship between mobility and individual behavior was central:

> [T]he mobility of city life, with its increase in the number and intensity of stimulations, tends inevitably to confuse and to demoralize the person. For, an essential element in the "mores" and in personal morality is consistency, consistency of the type that is natural in the social control of the primary group. Where mobility is greatest, and where in consequence primary controls break down, as in the zone of deterioration in the modern city, there develop areas of demoralization, of promiscuity, and of vice.[5]

But he missed the point of his own model of the city. The movement of people from one residence to another *as the city grows* is the very mechanism by which the zones and natural areas (disorganized or organized) are created.

Louis Wirth suggested, alternatively, that size, density, and heterogeneity are the key factors in explaining social disorganization.[6] He postulated that secondary and tertiary modes of interaction are substituted for primary modes in densely populated, large, heterogeneous cities,[7] but later scholars have shown that family life shows little propensity to wither away with urbanization.[8] The relation of the urban environment to the behavior of the urban population remains obscure in this classical stream of research.[9]

A Land Economist's View: Hoyt's Sector Model

An alternative model of the changing spatial structure of the city was put forward by Homer Hoyt.[10] On the basis of an intensive study of some 142 cities for which eight variables[11] were mapped by blocks, Hoyt was able to say that the high and low rent neighborhoods occupied distinct subareas of the city, and that these were not aligned concentrically about the city center but, rather, distributed in a sectoral fashion. The spatial pattern of the city's rental areas was determined, in Hoyt's view, by the choice of those who could afford the highest rents. They preempt the land along "the best existing transportation lines," "high ground—free from the risk of floods," and "land along lake, bay, river and ocean fronts where such water fronts are not used for industry."[12] Hoyt showed that high-grade residential areas of Chicago follow such a pattern (see Fig. 10–2), and that there is a concomitant tendency for the innermost parts of the high-rent sectors to become low-grade residential areas, except in the case of the Gold Coast. But Hoyt's view of the city is at best partial, constrained by his narrow focus of interest on housing

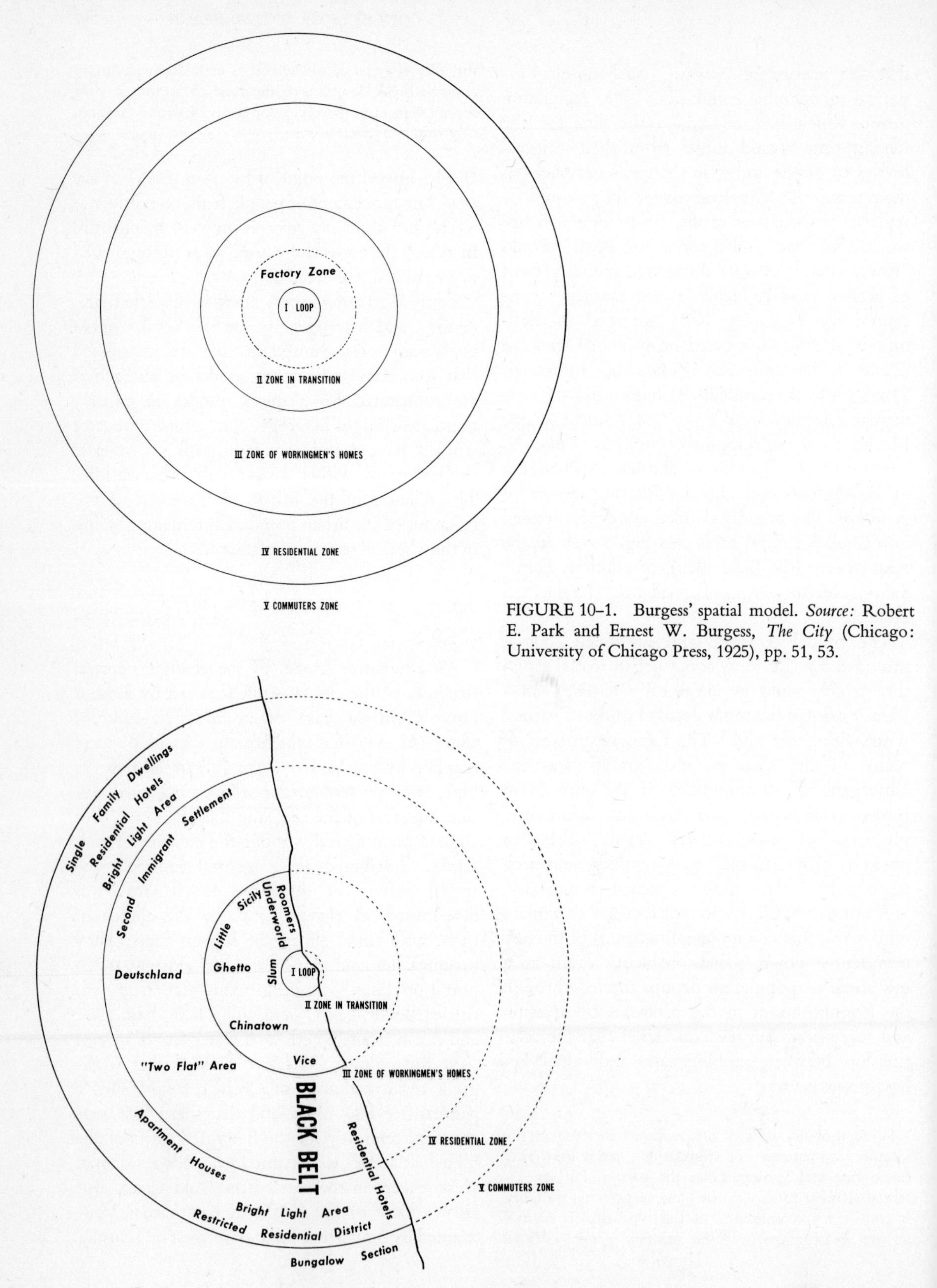

FIGURE 10–1. Burgess' spatial model. *Source:* Robert E. Park and Ernest W. Burgess, *The City* (Chicago: University of Chicago Press, 1925), pp. 51, 53.

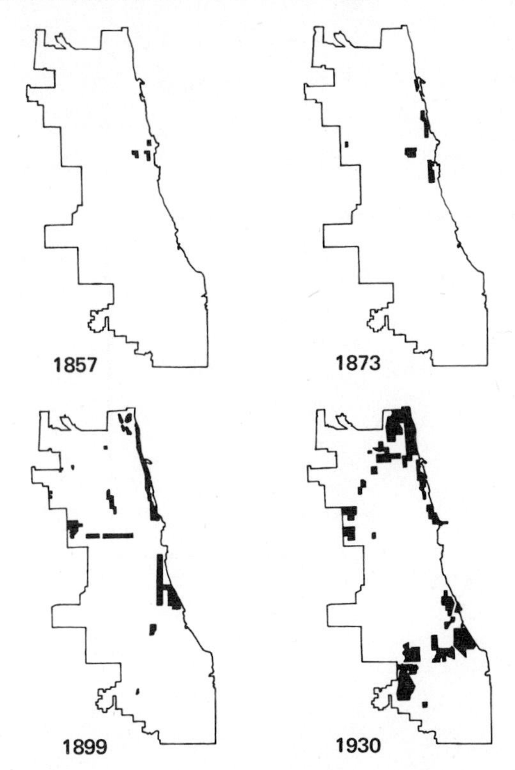

FIGURE 10–2. Growth of high-grade residential areas in Chicago. *Source:* Homer Hoyt, *The Structure and Growth of Residential Neighborhoods in American Cities* (Washington, D.C.: Federal Housing Administration, 1939), p. 830.

characteristics in general and on rent in particular. He gave little consideration to the characteristics of the inhabitants who occupied the structures.

Integration of the Spatial Models

There has been considerable discussion of the relative merits of these classical models of the spatial structure of the city's population.[13] There is an emerging consensus that, in Western metropoli born in the industrial age and populated by a variety of races or national groups, "the models are independent, additive contributors to the total socio-economic structuring of city neighborhoods."[14]

Those indices which measure the socio-economic status of individuals or groups vary principally by sector; those which measure the familial characteristics and age of the population vary principally by concentric zone; and those which isolate a minority group within the population show a tendency for that group to cluster in a particular part of the metropolis. Such is the conclusion of Anderson and Egeland in their analysis of the spatial variance of a number of socio-economic measures within four medium-sized American cities (Akron, Dayton, Indianapolis, and Syracuse).[15] The variables that were thought to measure social status were combined into a "social rank" index and those that were considered indicative of family status and degree of urban acculturation were combined into an index of "urbanization" in the manner originally developed by the social area analysts [whose work will be reviewed a little later]. An analysis of the variance of these two indices by sector and by concentric zone revealed that social rank varied principally by sector, and urbanization by concentric ring. The independent, additive nature of these two indices has been demonstrated through factor analysis of matrices of data about socio-economic variables in census tracts for many cities. ["Factorial ecology" of the city is discussed in subsequent paragraphs.] The dimensions that emerged from these analyses are exactly those posited by the social area analysts. A third dimension, corresponding to their "segregation index," is also present and describes the concentration of particular minority groups in limited neighborhoods of the city.

The sectoral patterning of the attributes of the neighborhood residents (e.g., education, occupation, and income) and of neighborhood structural characteristics (e.g., rent or value, and quality of housing)[16] is a product of the differing abilities of various income groups to bear the costs of the journey to work. The lower-income workers, because of their restricted budgets, must live close to their work, which is concentrated in the inner city around the central business district and along the rail and water routes radiating from the Loop.[17] The larger incomes of the higher-status workers give them the freedom to locate their homes in areas with more residential amenities—away from their places of work, away

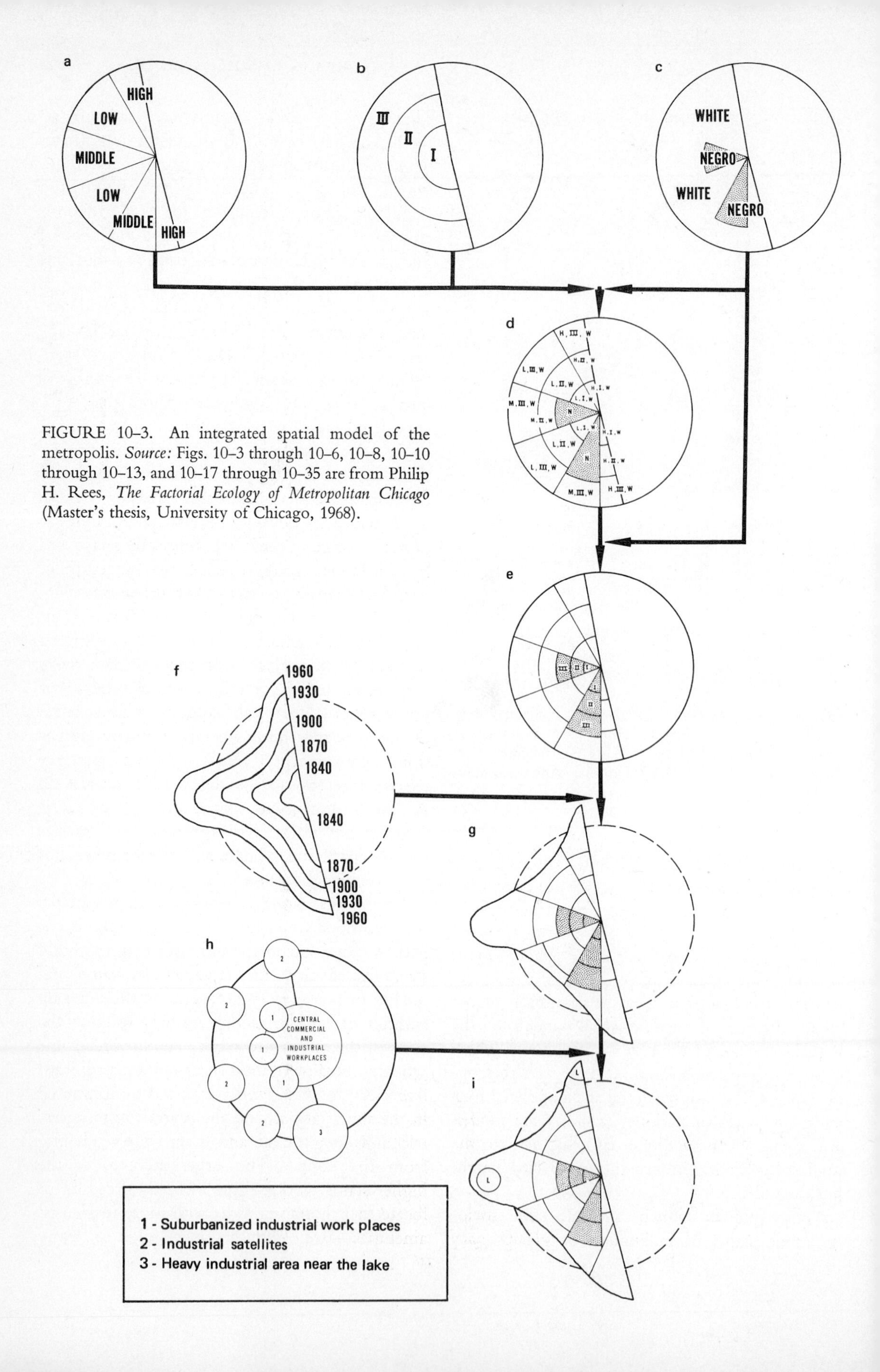

FIGURE 10–3. An integrated spatial model of the metropolis. *Source:* Figs. 10–3 through 10–6, 10–8, 10–10 through 10–13, and 10–17 through 10–35 are from Philip H. Rees, *The Factorial Ecology of Metropolitan Chicago* (Master's thesis, University of Chicago, 1968).

from the smoke and dirt of industry, and close to the amenities of lakeshore and open space.

The age structure of the population, average family size, and the participation of females in the labor force change as distance from the city center increases: young families locate further from the center than older families. This pattern is a response to the change in the ages and types of houses as distance from the center becomes greater—the houses are newer, and there are more predominantly single-family homes, as the city's center is left behind. It is the lower land values toward the urban periphery that make possible the construction of land-voracious single-family homes,[18] and the increasing real income of home buyers which makes possible their purchase. Finally, minority groups find themselves segregated from the rest of the population to a greater or lesser degree as a result of their recent arrival in the city, discrimination in the housing market, or through their own choice of homes in congenial communities.

This basic triad of spatially arranged social dimensions can be superimposed to form, at the intersections of sectors, zones, and segregated areas, *communities* of similar social, family, and ethnic status. Figure 10–3 is an idealized picture into which distortions can be successively introduced to approximate reality more closely.

However, there is a further complication. The zones within the segregated area occupied by the minority group do not have the same life cycle as other zones of the metropolis; the segregated area is a microcosm of the whole, compressed spatially, reproducing in minature the metropolitan-side pattern (Fig. 10–3*e*). This modified pattern is then further distorted by the way the city grew (Fig. 10–3*f*).[19] "Tear faults" develop as the earliest zones of the city are outwardly displaced and cross sectoral boundaries. Finally, the introduction of secondary nodes of workplaces—a heavy industrial area in the southern part of Chicago and industrial satellites in a crescent around the city—further changes the form of the model of the metropolitan region.[20] The influence of the suburbanization of industry, a trend characterizing the era of truck transport, electricity, and clean factories, is as yet unclear. The varying association between workplace and home location in different income classes may be changing. In Chicago, however, the legacy of the industrial past obscures the new and emerging spatial structure,[21] and the verification of the classic models and their spatial structure can still be the principal problem addressed in this study of Chicago in 1960.

*Behavioral Basis: The Residential Location Decision**

The attraction of the ecological view of the city is that it postulates a process of group competition and mobility that produces the spatial structuring of the city's population. In Hoyt's model, on the other hand, the operations of the real estate market[22] are not spelled out, though he does recognize the importance of the decisions of prestigious individuals in the location of the high-grade rental sector.

An alternative view of the processes producing the structuring may be proposed, however, involving the behavior of individuals and institutions. The inhabitants of the city are faced with a fundamental decision: where to live. The principal determinants of their choice of housing are three in number: the price of the dwelling unit (either rent or purchase price); the type of residence; and its location, both in terms of neighborhood environment and in relation to place of work. These determinants have parallels in the attributes of the individual making the choice of housing; the amount he is prepared to pay for housing, which depends on his income; the housing he needs, which depend on his marital status and family size (i.e., his stage in the life cycle); his life style preferences, which will affect the type of neighbor he wants; and finally, where he works and how close to the job he must live.[23] When the values of the two sets of characteristics match:

*Based in part on a lecture course (Urban Studies 371) given by Brian J. L. Berry at the University of Chicago, Winter, 1968—P. Rees.

Individual characteristics	*Housing characteristics*
Income	Price
Stage in life cycle	Type of home
Life style preferences	Neighbors; type of community institutions
Attitudes toward journey to work	Location with respect to the job

a decision to purchase housing will be made.

The most important determinant is undoubtedly income. A large family with many children may need a large single-family home, but unless their income is above the minimum required by the mortgage company, purchase of this type of home will not be possible. Similarly, low wages may make it essential for a worker to live near his place of employment in order to minimize the cost of the journey to work, and he may therefore be unable to satisfy his preferences about type of neighborhood.

It may be objected that other factors, such as the nature of the school system in the community or the location of the prospective home in relation to a golf course, play an important role in the decision, but these influences are significant only if the individual's income is large enough for him to be able to ignore the more basic determinants. Gans, in his participant-observer study of the inhabitants of a new suburban town in New Jersey,[24] asked a sample of Levittowners what their principal reason was for moving there: over 80 per cent gave house-related reasons for moving.

Gans's work contains many valuable illustrations of the way in which some of the determinants of residential choice operate. Prices in Levittown, New Jersey, ranged from $11,500 to $14,500.[25] In order to insure that he got paid for the houses he built, Levitt told his salesmen not to sell to would-be purchasers with incomes less than $5,500 a year. In fact, a small percentage of the house buyers did have lower incomes, but the majority earned more. His middle-range prices acted as a selection mechanism by attracting predominantly lower middle class families, along with small minorities of working class and upper middle class families.

The houses were free-standing, single-family residences, with three or four bedrooms. Not unnaturally, young couples with (or intending to have) children became their occupants. They were spacious and comfortable homes for a household of four or five members, and the surrounding yard provided a play area over which the mother could keep an eye from the kitchen window. Since Levittown was an entirely new settlement, there were no neighbors when the first inhabitants arrived, but the builder was careful to project a prestigious image in nearby Philadelphia (in order to counteract the unfavorable impression created by his other venture in the urban region, which had had trouble over racial integration and had suffered a subsequent decline in status), and for the first two years, until legal action forced Levitt to integrate the community, discrimination was practiced against prospective Negro buyers.

Thus, the residential location decision was (and is) clearly a product of the interaction of the home demander (the individual) and the house supplier (the construction company plus the institutional actor), a not unexpected conclusion! In turn, the individual choices of home builders and home buyers either create (in the case of a new community) or affect (in the case of an established community) the urban ecology, resulting in homogeneous areas containing similar sorts of people, areas which were called "natural" in the earlier ecological literature[26] and which are generally called "social" today. The character of these established social areas in turn influences the subsequent housing choices of subsequent occupants of the neighborhood, because people seek compatible neighbors who share the same views about life (particularly on such important questions as the way in which children should be brought up), and find compatibility by selecting their residence in the appropriate social area.

The choice of the type of house and community is only one part of the complete residential location decision, however. The housing consumer is also faced with the problem of locating his residence. This is decided in view of his job location, for the time and money spent in commuting have to be traded off against the relative benefits of living in alternative communities that meet, within budgetary constraints, his family's needs. The lower the income, the more constrained will be the choice. Thus, people of lower status live closer to their work than people of higher status.[27]

To summarize more generally (see Fig. 10–4), the individual or family occupies a position s_i in *social space*, determined by economic and family status. The household matches this position with that of a dwelling located in an analogous position h_i in housing space and in an equivalent community space c_i, whose axes comprise socio-economic status on the ordinate and familial characteristics on the abscissa.[28] From a range of possible communities in the same zone of community space, one dwelling in one community is selected on the basis of proximity to the job (if this is a constraint) or on the basis of other important neighborhood characteristics,[29] thus fixing the choices in real geographic or *physical space*. An orderly social geography results as like individuals make like choices, in response to regularities in the operation of the land and housing markets and the collaboration of similar individuals who act to exclude dissimilar people from their neighborhood or to restrict minority groups to particular areas. The autonomous suburb is the prime example of the process of exclusion,[30] and the ghetto the most glaring illustration of the process of exclusion.[31]

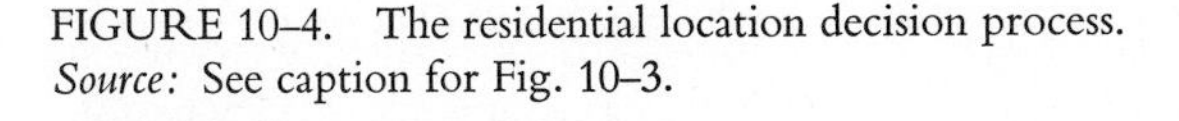

FIGURE 10–4. The residential location decision process.
Source: See caption for Fig. 10–3.

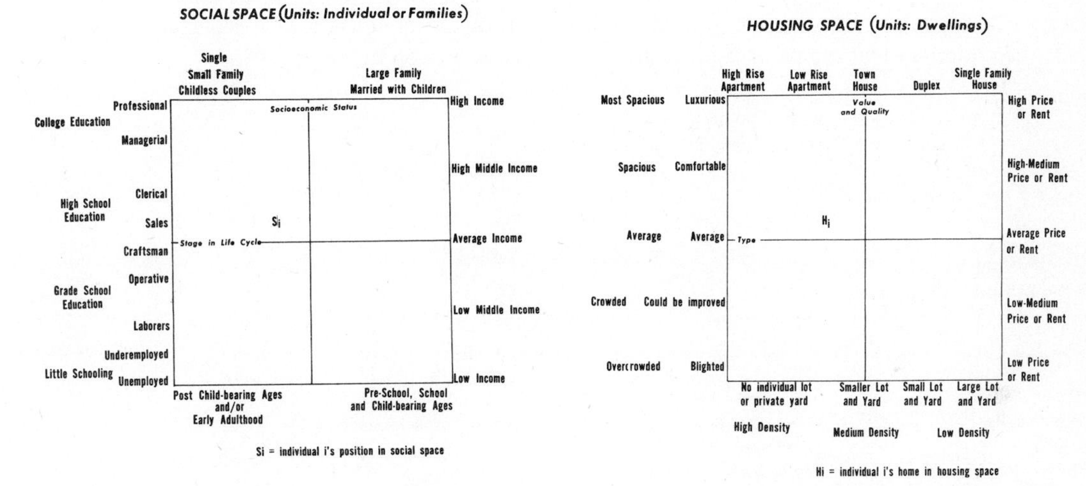

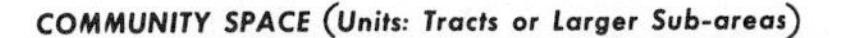

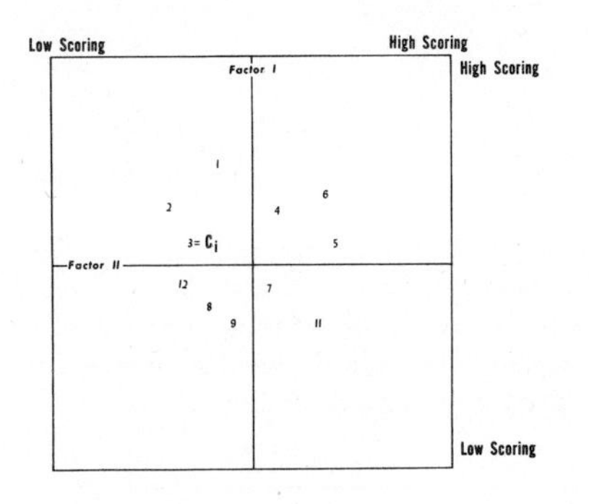

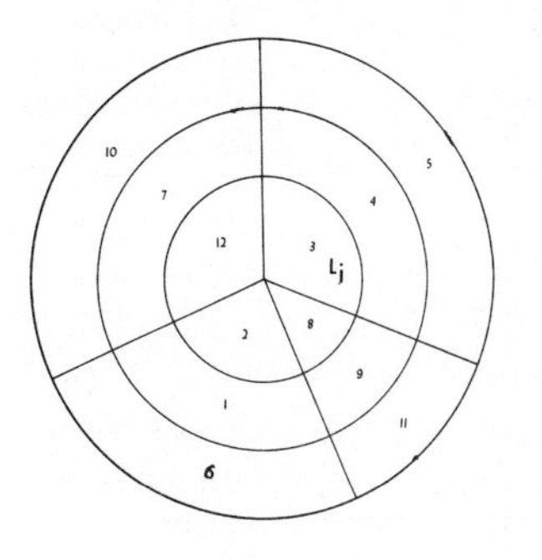

SOCIAL AREA ANALYSIS: A REVIEW OF SOME KEY PROBLEMS AND WORKS

The classic concern with a spatial basis for the differentiation of the city's population and the interest of those writing about the way people choose their homes have yet to be merged into a holistic framework that will make clear the linkages between the social, structural, and locational spaces of the city. Such a framework can be provided by a geographic interpretation of social area (factor) analysis.

There exists some semantic confusion about the term "social area analysis" which should be cleared up before some of the more important pieces of research are reviewed. An over-all view of the development of social area analysis is provided in Fig. 10-5. Figure 10–6 translates history into typology. These figures should aid the reader in understanding the paragraphs to follow.

Social Area Analysis

The term "social area analysis," strictly speaking applies only to that mode of analysis originally outlined by Eshref Shevky, Marianne Williams, and Wendell Bell in their studies of Los Angeles and San Francisco.[32] From a number of postulates concerning industrial society they derived three basic constructs which, they considered, described the way in which urban populations are differentiated (Table 10–1). The three constructs were called Social Rank by Shevky (and Economic Status by Bell), Urbanization (Family Status), and Segregation (Ethnic Status). They then proposed three indices, one per construct, made up of from one to three census variables—designed to measure the position of census tract populations on scales of economic, family, and ethnic status and to make possible the classification of census tracts into social areas based upon their scores on the indices.[33]

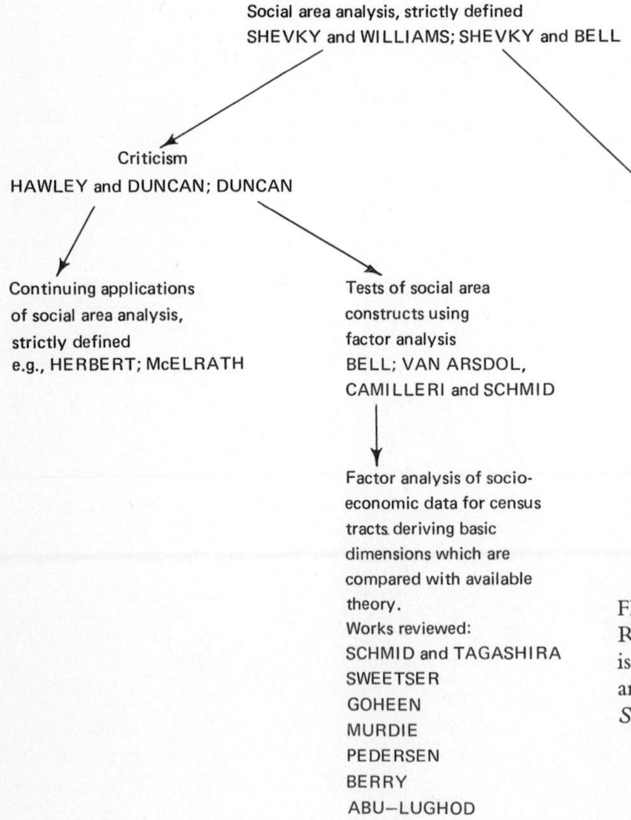

FIGURE 10–5. Development of social area analysis. Reference to each of the works mentioned in this figure is to be found in the footnotes to Chapter 10. Cluster analysis is Tryon's proposed alternative to factor analysis. *Source:* See caption for Fig. 10–3.

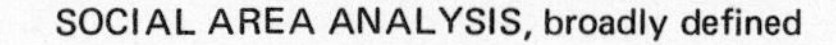

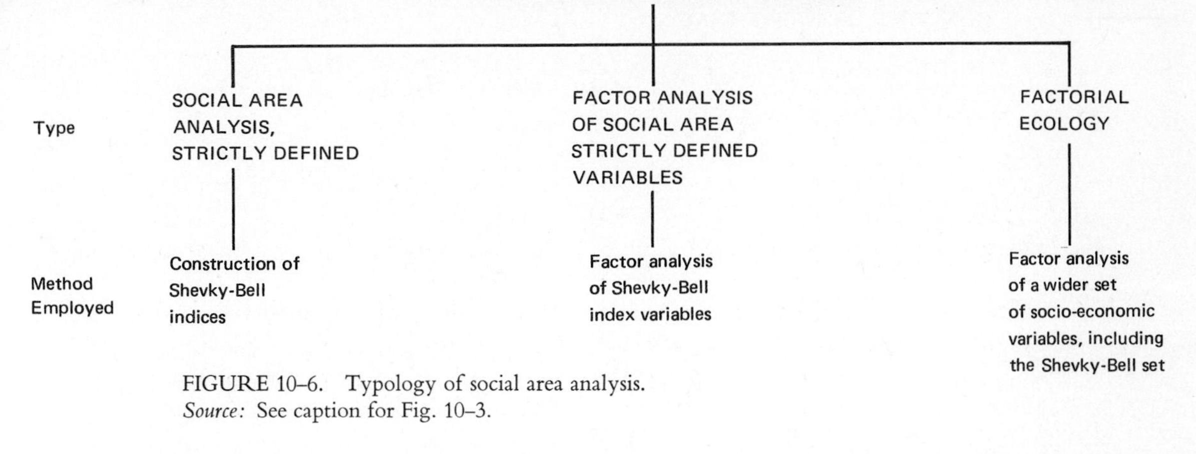

FIGURE 10–6. Typology of social area analysis.
Source: See caption for Fig. 10–3.

TABLE 10–1

Shevky and Bell's Steps in Construct Formation and Index Construction

Postulates Concerning Industrial Society (Aspects of Increasing Scale) (1)	*Statistics of Trends* (2)	*Changes in the Structure of a Given Social System* (3)	*Constructs* (4)	*Sample Statistics (Related to the Constructs)* (5)	*Derived Measures (from Col. 5)* (6)	
Change in the range and intensity of relations	→ Changing distribution of skills: Lessening importance of manual productive operations—growing importance of clerical, supervisory, management operations	→ Changes in the arrangement of occupations based on function	→ Social Rank (economic status)	→ Years of schooling Employment status Class of worker Major occupation group Value of home Rent by dwelling unit Plumbing and repair Persons per room Heating and refrigeration	→ Occupation Schooling Rent	Index I
Differentiation of function	→ Changing structure of productive activity: Lessening importance of primary production—growing importance of relations centered in cities—lessening importance of the household as economic unit	→ Changes in the ways of living—movement of women into urban occupations—spread of alternative family patterns	→ Urbanization (family status)	→ Age and sex Owner or tenant House structure Persons in household	→ Fertility Women at work Single-family dwelling units	Index II
Complexity of organization	→ Changing composition of population: Increasing movement—alterations in age and sex distribution—increasing diversity	→ Redistribution in space-changes in the proportion of supporting and dependent population—isolation and segregation of groups	→ Segregation (ethnic status)	→ Race and nativity Country of birth Citizenship	→ Racial and national groups in relative isolation	Index III

Source: Eshref Shevky and Wendell Bell, *Social Area Analysis: Theory, Illustrative Application, and Computational Procedures* (Stanford, Calif.: Stanford University Press, 1955), Table II–1, by permission of Stanford University Press.

Social area analysis, strictly defined, has been criticized both on theoretical grounds (the theory underlying the constructs) and for empirical reasons (the method of dimensioning the constructs).[34] In an effort to meet the empirical objections that the measures employed assumed the constructs to be correct and failed to provide a test of their validity, Bell used factor analysis to show that, in both Los Angeles and San Francisco, the census measures used in fact formed a structure consistent with Shevky's formulations.[35] Van Arsdol, Camilleri, and Schmid extended Bell's test of Shevky's model to some ten cities, six of which confirmed that Shevky's indices were valid measures of his constructs.[36] The fact that four cities did not confirm their validity, however, suggested that the existence of the constructs should be left to be empirically determined by the patterns of the variables rather than assumed. The logical extension of this argument is that many more variables detailing the socio-economic characteristics of census tract populations should be included in the study, and that factor analysis should be used to isolate the fundamental patterns of variation in the data, be they Shevky's and Bell's constructs and patterns or nay.[37]

Factorial Ecology[38]

The basic purpose of factor analysis as applied in urban ecology, is to reduce a matrix of n tracts by m variables to one of n tracts and r factors, where the number of *significant* (i.e., of practicable, interpretable importance)[39] factors, r, is less than m.[40] The r factors summarize the common patterns of variability in the data and make possible more concise statements about the population under consideration. The mathematical dimensions isolated are an objective outcome of the analysis, their interpretation depending upon the nature of the variables used in the analysis and the body of concepts or theory that is brought to bear. The theory provides the investigator with a set of expectations regarding the factor structure which can be compared to the actual set of factors produced. Such a comparison was made formally by Van Arsdol, Camilleri, and Schmid,[41] and somewhat less formally by later writers.

The variables employed. The variables that are most usually included in social area analyses (using the term broadly) are those that describe the characteristics of population groups living in small areas (i.e., census tracts). The characteristics which are regarded as important are those which social scientists have long studied and which the census has recorded for them, for example: 1 education, occupation, income, sex, age, membership in an ethnic or racial group—measures which apply to people themselves; and (2) the value of the home (or its rent), state of repair, plumbing facilities, and so forth—measures that apply to the dwelling unit. The physical and mental characteristics of individuals have not usually been included. Since the national census is the main source of information, the mix and range of variables included reflect census policy. The U.S. Bureau of the Census places rather more emphasis on individual attributes than on physical characteristics of structures; the British Registry Office, on the other hand, places more emphasis on housing conditions in order to meet the needs of planning authorities and local governments.

Case study: Seattle. A typical example is a study of Seattle by Schmid and Tagashira.[42] The primary orientation of the paper was methodological: The question posed was whether a smaller set of variables would, in fact, summarize the basic factors underlying a more elaborate set.

From an original matrix of 42 variables and 115 tracts, was produced a set of five interpretable factors: family status; socio-economic status; a "down-and-out" factor; residential stability; and racial status. In a second-stage factor analysis, 21 variables that showed "mixed" loadings or which "loaded" on factors which were not interpretable were eliminated. The same factors, with the exception of residential stability, were reproduced. In a final analysis, only 10 variables that loaded highly on family status, socio-economic status, and racial status were used, the authors arguing that the "down-and-out" or "skid row"[43] factor was essentially a special subcomponent of the family status concept. In this way, the principal social area dimensions proposed by Shevky and Bell were isolated: family status; socio-economic status; and racial status.

Schmid and Tagashira's finding that a smaller set of variables, carefully selected, will essentially reproduce the principal factors extracted from a much larger set is employed in our study of Metropolitan Chicago, as a labor-saving device in dealing with the 1,324 census tracts that cover the metropolis.

Study area. The proper area in which to conduct a social area analysis (the term is used broadly) is a matter which has received relatively little attention in the literature, and yet is of vital concern. Many studies have adopted the politically defined central city as a study area, without considering whether this is the most appropriate choice. Where the lines of the political city underbound a large portion of the metropolis, many suburbs are thereby omitted from the analysis. If the city overbounds its labor market, many rural areas without daily connection and involvement with the rest of the metropolis are included in the study. The proper area for study would seem to be a functional one, the unified housing and labor market of the metropolis. The urbanized area, together with the major commuting settlements beyond, suggests itself as appropriate.[44] Towards the conclusion of the study of Chicago which follows, we attempt to evaluate the effects of differing study areas on factor structures.[45]

Units used. There has been a continuing debate in the literature concerning the utility of ecological correlations, that is, correlations based on groups of people living in a set of areas.[46] Ecological correlation, if it is regarded as a way of measuring individual correlations, tends to exaggerate the magnitude of such associations. There are methods for estimating individual correlations from ecological correlations,[47] although usually in ecological studies such elaborate inference is not attempted—instead the author warns that his conclusions apply to population groups rather than individuals, because most studies are limited in their choice of unit to that made available by the Census authority. The results of a series of social area factor analyses of both individuals and various kinds of areal units in the city of Toronto in 1850 to 1900, however, seem to suggest that the factor structures produced are not made markedly different as the basic unit in the investigation is modified.[48] In the present study the link between individual and ecological correlation is made via the theory of residential choice.

Time-base of studies. Most factorial ecologies have been confined to one time period (the census date). Comparison of the evolution of the factor structure and of the temporal changes in the spatial patterning of the factors is of vital concern. Detailed studies of the changing City of Toronto in each decade from 1850 to 1900, in 1950 and 1960 and during the decade 1950 to 1960 are in preparation by Goheen,[49] Murdie,[50] and Berry and Murdie.[51] Murdie identifies a number of processes at work reordering the social geography of metropolitan Toronto in the decade from 1950 to 1960, the most important being suburbanization, ethnic change, and urbanization. An extension of the present study to show the changes which have taken place in Chicago over the years was not feasible.[52]

Cultural base of studies. Studies of American cities have, by and large, succeeded in isolating the three social factors related to areas of the city originally proposed by Shevky: socio-economic status, family status, and ethnic status. What of foreign cities? Do their census tract populations exhibit the same patterns of variation?

Pedersen's Study of Copenhagen is one of the most comprehensive urban ecological analyses to date.[53] From a matrix of 14 socio-economic variables of the population (related to age distribution, employment status, industry in which employed, household size, sex ratio, and female employment) and 76 zones of the city, three basic factors emerged in both 1950 and 1960, namely:

1. Urbanization or family status
2. Socio-economic status
3. Population growth and mobility

The first factor, when mapped and graphed, displayed the classic Burgess pattern of concentric rings; the second had a sectoral distribution, except that the population of the central zones of the city was of uniformly low status; the third was greatest in the zone of new suburban developments and the low-status areas of the inner city. Pedersen devotes a separate chapter to a detailed consideration of each of the three principal factors. Age structures in the communities of the city are considered as functions of the population growth and migration processes. Income differentials within the suburban portion of the metropolitan region are shown to have narrowed over time as the area has been converted from farmland into residences for city-dwellers, whereas the gap between inner city and suburban incomes has widened. Absent from Pedersen's findings is a differentiation of Copenhagen's population along linguistic or racial lines. Such differentiation does not exist in Denmark.

TABLE 10–2

Summary of Janet Abu-Lughod's "Necessary Conditions"

Factor Conditions	*Types of Variables Used*	*Necessary Conditions*
Socio-economic status factor	Education, Occupation, Income	1. "That the effective ranking system in a city be related to the operational definition of social status"; 2. "That the ranking system in a city be manifested in residential segregation of persons of different rank at a scale capable of being identified by the areal units of observation used in the analysis."
Family status factor	Family size, Portions of the age pyramid, Fertility	1. "That family types vary, either due to 'natural' causes such as those associated with sequential stages in the family cycle, or to 'social' causes such as those associated with other divisions in society, whether ethnic, socio-economic or other"; 2. "That subareas within the city are differentiated in their attractiveness to families of different types" at a scale capable of being identified by the areal units of observation used in the analysis.
Disassociation between socio-economic status and family status dimensions		Either: 1. That there exists little or no association between social class and family type; *or* 2. if there is some association between social class and family type, a. there is a clear distinction between stages in the family cycle, each stage being associated with a change of residence; b. "subareas within the city offer, at all economic levels, highly specialized housing accommodations especially suitable to families at particular points in their natural cycle of growth and decline" at a scale capable of being identified by the areal units of observation used in the analysis; *and* c. "Cultural values permitting and favoring mobility to maximize housing efficiency, unencumbered by the 'unnatural' frictions of sentiment, local attachments or restritive regulations."

Source: "A Critical Test for the Theory of Social Analysis: The Factorial Ecology of Cairo, Egypt" (Paper, Department of Sociology, Northwestern University, February, 1968), pp. 1–10.

Confirmation of the homogeneity of the population of the Scandinavian cities is found in Sweetser's comparison of Helsinki and Boston.[54] In addition to the basic social area dimensions, the Boston study yielded a number of ethnic dimensions (e.g., Irish Middle Class; Italian Blue Collar). The Swedish-speaking population of Helsinki, however, failed to load on a separate factor, but rather loaded on the socio-economic status factor, since it is of generally higher status than the Finnish-speaking population.

Studies of non-Western cities[55] highlight the cultural context of the American and Scandinavian factor structures, and have led recent investigators to try to isolate those basic conditions in the urban system, social and spatial, which are necessary in order to produce the observed factor structures. In a study of Cairo, Janet Abu-Lughod found that "no factorial separation between indicators of social rank and the indicators of family cycle stage could be obtained,"[56] in contrast with the normal separation of these two sets of indicators in factor analyses of American city data matrices. This led her to outline, in an extremely effective way, the conditions that were necessary and sufficient to produce the dimensions of socio-economic status and family status that are found to have independent existence in almost all American cities,[57] conditions that were not fulfilled in the case of Cairo. These conditions are outlined in Table 10–2. She writes:

> The disassociation between social rank and familism variables found in contemporary western cities in societies at the terminal stages of the demographic transition can be attributed to the reinforcing and cumulative effects of several conditions that "define" the nature of urban organization in such cities: (1) residential segregation according to modern ranking systems; (2) relatively low correlations between social rank and differences in fertility and family styles; and (3) high differentiation of residential sub-areas by housing types. To the extent that these conditions are not perfectly fulfilled, the vectors will not be totally disassociated.[58]

Thus, a study made from another cultural base (a "deviant" case) throws considerable light on the theoretical bases for the social area factor structures found in Western ("normal") cities.

The Factorial Ecology of Chicago: A Case Study

PREVIOUS LITERATURE

We now turn to a detailed, original case study of metropolitan Chicago. However, since there have been several prior social area analyses of Chicago, including social area analysis, sensu stricto, factor analysis of social area variables, and a factorial ecology of data relating to the legally defined urban places of the SMSA outside Chicago, it is appropriate first to review these contributions.

Social Area Analysis

McElrath and Barkey[59] performed a social area analysis (in the strict sense) of the Chicago metropolitan area in 1960. The spatial patterns displayed by the composite social area indices (with respect to the classic ecological models) were examined through an analysis of variance, with the following results: Urbanization varied by zone and by sector; social rank, by zone but not by sector; segregation, by sector but not by zone. However, since the method of social area analysis employed suffers, as we have already pointed out, from conceptual deficiencies, the conclusions of this study can only be regarded as tentative.

Factor Analysis of Shevky-Bell Variables

Kaufman[60] factor analyzed a set of seven variables (the Shevky-Bell set, with the exception that two variables in the "urbanization" index were substituted for one that was dropped) and confirmed the existence of the dimensions pro-

TABLE 10–3

Socio-Economic Factor Structure in Northeastern Illinois Metropolitan Area, 1960

Variables	Factors and Factor Loadings*								Community: h^2
	Size	*Social Status*	*Family Structure*	*New Suburbs*	*Distance Density*	*Housing Vacancy*	*Race*	*Density Residual*	
1. Population, 1960	.966	—	—	—	—	—	—	—	.993
2. Population, 1950	.416	—	.556	−.667	—	—	—	—	.939
3. Population, 1940	—	—	.607	−.432	—	—	—	—	.765
4. Area	.784	—	—	—	—	—	—	—	.950
5. Gross density (Variable 1/Variable 4)	.485	—	—	—	−.559	—	—	−.541	.901
6. Total number of residents employed	.946	—	—	—	—	—	—	—	.994
7. Housing units, 1960	.950	—	—	—	—	—	—	—	.988
8. Housing units, 1950	.457	—	.566	−.566	—	—	—	—	.869
9. Growth in housing units, 1950–1960	.462	—	—	−.707	—	—	—	—	.885
10. Number of occupied housing units	.949	—	—	—	—	—	—	—	.991
11. Average value of building permits	.454	.476	—	—	—	—	—	—	.500
12. Number of occupied rental units	.765	—	.549	—	—	—	—	—	.948
13. Median rent	.543	—	—	—	—	—	—	—	.566
14. % housing units in structures with 3 or more units	.438	—	.621	—	—	—	—	—	.710
15. Total labor force	.948	—	—	—	—	—	—	—	.994
16. Women over 14 in labor force	.930	—	—	—	—	—	—	—	.968
17. % married mothers in labor force	.811	—	—	—	—	—	—	—	.718
18. Total assessed value of property in municipality	.862	—	—	—	—	—	—	—	.974
19. Median school years completed	—	.894	—	—	—	—	—	—	.874
20. Median family income	—	.852	—	—	—	—	—	—	.837
21. % families with incomes under $10,000	—	.868	—	—	—	—	—	—	.914
22. % white-collar	—	.928	—	—	—	—	—	—	.976
23. % professional	—	.956	—	—	—	—	—	—	.961
24. % clerical, sales	—	.591	—	—	—	—	−.610	—	.898
25. % craftsmen, operatives	—	−.792	—	—	—	—	—	—	.828
26. % laborers	—	−.848	—	—	—	—	—	—	.771
27. % service workers	—	−.809	—	—	—	—	—	—	.783
28. % housing of good quality	—	.556	—	—	—	—	−.589	—	.731
29. % homes owned	—	.400	−.568	—	—	—	—	—	.839
30. Average value of homes	—	.873	—	—	—	—	—	—	.874
31. % unemployed	—	−.711	—	—	—	—	—	—	.587
32. % women over 14 in labor force	—	−.454	.506	—	—	—	—	—	.660
33. Per capita value of property	—	.647	—	—	—	—	—	—	.748
34. Age of municipality (date incorporated)	—	—	−.566	—	—	—	—	—	.650
35. Median age of residents	—	—	.819	—	—	—	—	—	.916
36. % population under 5 years	—	—	−.827	—	—	—	—	—	.894
37. % population under 18 years	—	—	−.899	—	—	—	—	—	.936
38. % population over 65 years	—	—	.931	—	—	—	—	—	.917

Variables	Factors and Factor Loadings*								Communality: h^2
	Size	*Social Status*	*Family Structure*	*New Suburbs*	*Distance Density*	*Housing Vacancy*	*Race*	*Density Residual*	
39. Average family size	—	—	−.915	—	—	—	—	—	.930
40. % homes built pre-1940	—	—	.838	—	—	—	—	—	.863
41. % homes built post-1950	—	—	−.829	—	—	—	—	—	.821
42. % homes in 2-unit structure	—	—	.589	—	—	—	—	—	.698
43. Absolute growth, 1950–1960	—	—	—	−.872	—	—	—	—	.930
44. % growth 1950–1960†	—	—	—	−.874	—	—	—	—	.862
45. % growth of rental units, 1950–1960	—	—	—	−.711	—	—	—	—	.598
46. Distance from Loop	—	—	—	—	.751	—	—	—	.701
47. % housing vacant	—	—	—	—	—	.940	—	—	.923
48. % owned homes vacant	—	—	—	—	—	.686	—	—	.772
49. % rental units vacant	—	—	—	—	—	.735	—	—	.633
50. % non-white	—	—	—	—	—	—	.609	—	.485
Eigenvalue	10.804	10.794	9.449	4.071	2.053	2.189	2.037	1.233	
% *Variance*‡	23.48	23.40	20.54	8.85	4.46	4.75	4.42	2.68	92.58

Sources: Brian J. L. Berry and Robert J. Tennant, *Commercial Structure* (Chicago: Northeastern Illinois Planning Commission, 1965), Appendix A, "Socio-economic Classification of Municipalities in the Northeastern Illinois Metropolitan Area," Table A2, pp. 124–27. The data are from Northeastern Illinois Metropolitan Area Planning Commission, *Suburban Factbook*, rev. ed. (Chicago: Northeastern Illinois Planning Commision, 1961). The observations used in the study were the 147 municipalities with populations exceeding 2,500. All variables were transformed to base 10 logarithms.

*All loadings are from the "simple structure" solution resulting from rotation of principal axes factors to a normal varimax position. To facilitate interpretation of the table, loadings lying in the range $+.40 \geq a_{ij} \geq -.40$ have been omitted; this also led to deletion of Variable 51, Tax rate, which had a communality of .227 and all a_{ij} in the range selected for omission.

†Growth rates were coded 0.0 rather than 00 if the municipality was developed after 1950, resulting in a cluster of "outlying observations" which skewed variables such as No. 44. These observations gave rise to Factor 4, "New Suburbs."

‡These are percentages of the total *common* variance of the 51 variables used in the analysis (the common variance equals the sum of the communalities or the sum of the eigenvalues over all positive factors).

posed by Shevky and Bell and utilized, without testing for their validity, by McElrath and Barkey.

Factorial Ecology of Metropolitan Communities

In order "to provide a socio-economic framework within which the commercial structure of the Northeastern Illinois Metropolitan Area might be analyzed," Berry and Tennant undertook a social area factor analysis of the suburban portion of the metropolis.[61] Using some 50 variables and 147 municipalities with populations exceeding 2,500 in 1960 (but excluding the City of Chicago), a principal axes factor analysis of the 50×50 correlation matrix was performed, and some seven significant factors produced (Table 10–3).

The first factor, *size*, was not previously identified in social area factor analyses. It proved to be a function of the inclusion of many aggregate variables in the analysis: its theoretical significance is not great, except that population density, rental level, and value of building permits in 1960 all had medium loadings (their second or third highest factor loading) on this size dimension. The larger communities are those that are either close to the boundary of the City of Chicago or are industrial satellite towns (Waukegan, Elgin, Aurora, Joliet). These are the oldest communities, have had the longest opportunity to grow, were built to accommodate the highest densities, and have, as a result of their location at or near centers of employment, high rents and building values (consequences predictable from the theory of land values).

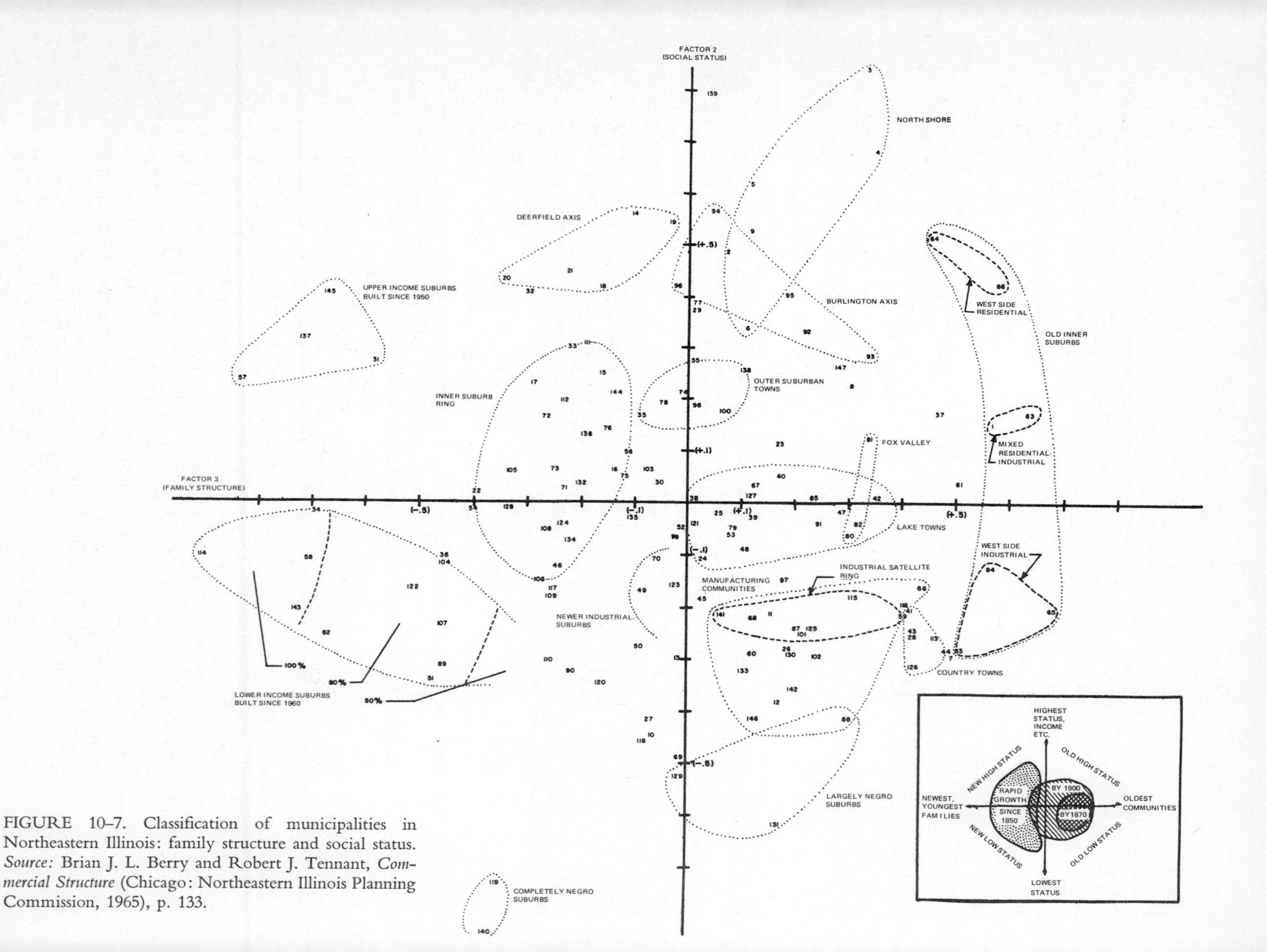

FIGURE 10–7. Classification of municipalities in Northeastern Illinois: family structure and social status. *Source:* Brian J. L. Berry and Robert J. Tennant, *Commercial Structure* (Chicago: Northeastern Illinois Planning Commission, 1965), p. 133.

The second and third factors extracted were the familiar Shevky dimensions of *social status* and *family structure* which, when combined in a two-dimensional graph (Fig. 10–7) go to make up *social space*. However, since the central city of Chicago was not included in the analysis, we cannot be sure that this diagram displays the complete range of social space—although enough satellite industrial cities, themselves microcosms of the wider metropolis, are incorporated in the study area.

The fourth factor, labeled *new suburbs*, identifies a growth dimension: the communities that scored less than −1 on this factor were new suburbs (built after 1950); those that scored negatively were small (or previously nonexistent) in 1950 and grew rapidly in the 1950's; those that scored high tended to be larger and to have grown less rapidly in the decade preceding 1960.

The fifth factor, *distance-density*, identifies the decline of population densities with distance from the central city (a relationship discussed in detail in Chapter 9). That the two variables which make up this factor did not load on the family structure dimension is probably a function of the star-like pattern of Chicago's growth that results in the location of communities with the same family structure at varying distances from the city center (radial rather than interstitial spacing of communities, for example) and from the inclusion of the industrial satellite cities, with older family structures, at the same distance from the Loop.

Housing vacancies (Factor VI) apparently formed their own distinctive pattern, unrelated to any of the other social, economic, or spatial variables included in the study. The authors regarded housing surpluses as a complex function of many forces[62] which combined to give its own special spatial distribution.

The final significant factor extracted was *race*, the third of the traditional indices of social area. Associated with the variable Percentage of Non-white Population were three others that help us to identify the influence of segregation in the housing and job markets: The greater the Negro proportion the more unsound was the housing, and the fewer were the workers employed in clerical and sales jobs.

Berry and Tennant's study, a carefully argued picture of the social geography of the suburban portion of the metropolis, is a foundation upon which the present analysis is built.

QUESTIONS TO BE ANSWERED

Several crucial questions need to be answered concerning the urban region under study—the metropolitan area of Chicago—in order to build the more general analysis desired:

1. What dimensions of differentiation of the urban population can be isolated if the range and mix of variables used is improved? If the study area is extended to include all of the functioning labor and housing market? If the analysis is performed using two sets of areal units: municipalities and "community areas,"[63] on the one hand, and Census tracts, on the other?
2. How do the dimensions of socio-economic space relate to those of physical space? How do the spatial patterns manifested by the various socio-economic factors compare with the spatial models of classical ecology?
3. What sort of social areas or communities characterize the metropolis? How are they located in the physical space of the metropolis?
4. How do the answers relate to the theory of residential choice outlined earlier?

It is to these questions we now turn.

METHODOLOGY

The social area factor analysis described here consists of not one but several separate factor analyses of data for community areas, municipalities and census tracts, the sequence and relations of which are set out in Fig. 10–8 together with their supporting graphic and cartographic interpretation. A systematic journey through the flow chart should reveal the ingredients that went into the analysis and the nature of the resulting product—a social geography of metropolitan Chicago.

In the first of the analyses, a set of variables describing the social and economic characteristics of residential groups in various subareas of the metropolis was selected from the many population characteristics available in the 1960 U.S.

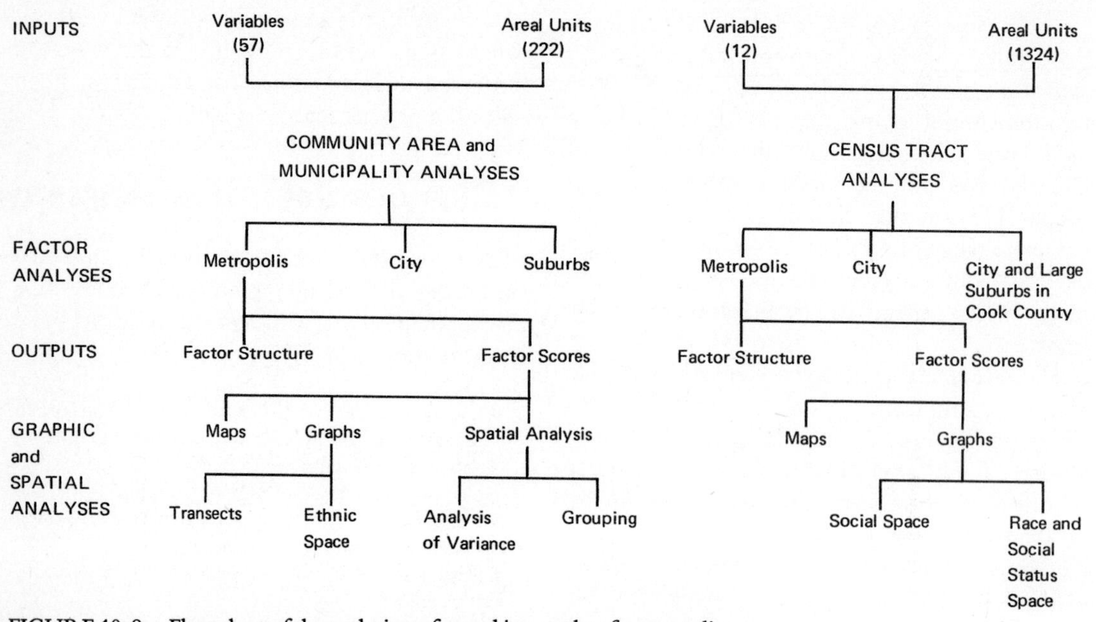

FIGURE 10–8. Flow chart of the analysis performed in a study of metropolitan Chicago. The factor structure output of the community area and municipality analysis was the basis for choice of the 12 variables used in the census tract analysis. *Source:* See caption for Fig. 10–3.

Census of Population. Such characteristics as age, racial or ethnic status, nativity, religious affiliation, income, occupation, and education apply to the population groups resident within an area; such attributes as age and size of the housing structures, the value of homes or their rental level pertain to the housing stock within an area; and such variables as the degree of overcrowding and the number of persons per household occupy the intersection of the two sets of characteristics, applying both to people and to housing. The names and definitions of the variables are set out in the Appendix to the chapter. They total 57 and include all of Shevky and Bell's variables with the exception of fertility.

The area studied is the Chicago Standard Metropolitan Statistical Area. The Northwestern Indiana SMSA is not included in the analysis, although is it part of the larger Chicago labor market (see Fig. 10–9). In the first set of factor analyses, the observations comprised the 75 community areas reported in the *Community Area Factbook*,[64] plus those municipalities with over 2,500 people reported in the *Suburban Factbook*.[65]

The 75 community areas blanket the City of Chicago, and the suburban portion of the metropolis is accounted for by the 147 municipalities. The communities included in the analyses comprise most of the incorporated places within Chicago's labor market or commuting field, though the degree of participation of such communities in the labor market of the central city declines with their distance from the central workplaces.

The steps in the analysis were as follows:

1. From an original matrix of 57 variables and 222 observations, a 57×57 matrix of the correlations between the variables (transformed to common logarithms for normalization) was calculated.
2. Factors were extracted from the matrix of correlation coefficients by the principal components method, to summarize the common patterns of variation among the 57 variables in a table of "factor loadings"—correlations between the original variables and the factors.
3. These factors were rotated to the normal varimax position in order to achieve "simple structure" in which

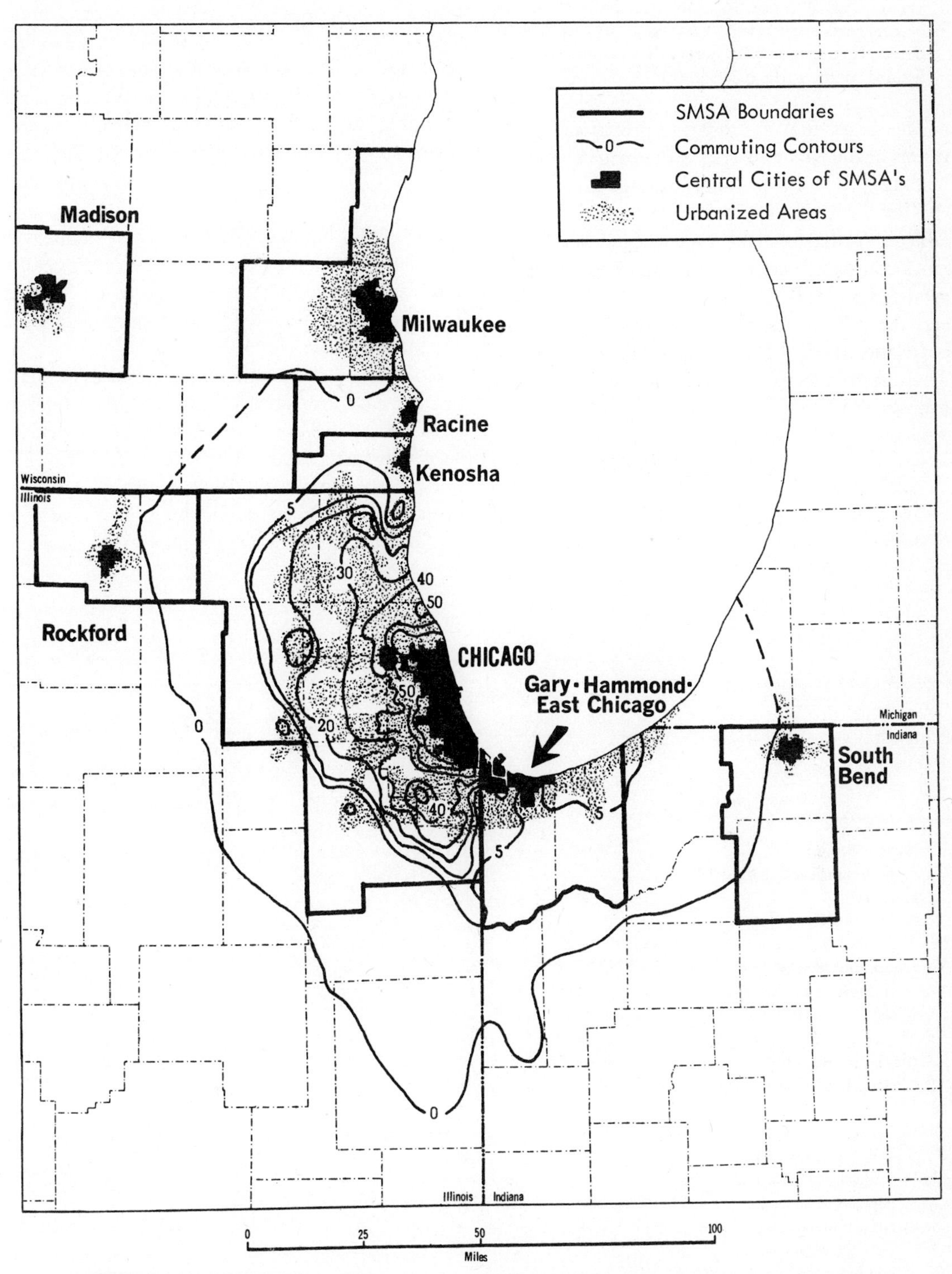

FIGURE 10–9. Chicago's commuting field and urbanized area: 1960. *Source:* Brian J. L. Berry, Peter G. Goheen, and Harold Goldstein, *Metropolitan Area Definition* (Washington, D.C.: U.S. Government Printing Office, Bureau of the Census Working Paper No. 28, 1968).

variables are allocated mutually exclusively to factors.
4. Factor scores were computed so as to allocate to each observation a value that gives it a position on scales defined by the particular factors.[66]

The basic tool in the interpretation of the results of the factor analysis is the matrix of factor loadings (Table 10–4). Only loadings greater than +.4 or less than −.4 have been included in the table (in order to make its structure clear). The rows consist of variables; the columns, of factors arranged in order of size of their eigenvalues; and the cell entries, the factor loadings, are the correlations of the variable with the factors. There are ten factors, the interpretation of which follows.

Factor I: Socio-economic Status

The first factor is undoubtedly an index of *Socio-economic Status*. Community areas or municipalities that score highly on this factor contain people with many years of schooling (Variable 36; loading, .845), much of it at college (Variable 37; loading, .868), in white-collar occupations (Variable 30; loading, .915), principally professional or managerial (Variable 30; loading, .930) but also clerical and sales (Variable 32; loading, .664), who earn, as a result, high incomes (Variable 27; loading, .787), many of them over $10,000 per annum (Variable 28; loading, .907), and who are able to live in high-rent (Variable 48; loading, .559) and sound housing (Variable 49; loading .453).

Conversely, the people who live in communities that have low scores on this first factor tend to have less education, are blue-collar workers, i.e., craftsmen and operatives (Variable 33; loading, −.874), or laborers (Variable 34; loading, −.595), or service workers (Variable 35; loading, −.501), who tend to earn low in-

TABLE 10–4

Factor Structure of 57 Variables in the Entire Chicago Metropolitan Area

*Number of Variable**	*Name of Variable*	*Socio-economic Status*	*Stage in the Life Cycle*	*Race and Resources*	*Immigrant and Catholic Status*	*Population Size and Density*	*Jewish and Russian Population*	*Housing Built in '40's; Workers Commute by Car*	*Irish and Swedish* Population*	*Mobility*	*Other Nonwhite Population; and Italians*
	Sums of Squares	10.166	8.068	7.445	6.210	4.252	2.154	1.693	1.532	1.363	1.194
31.	% professional and managerial employees	.930†	—	—	—	—	—	—	—	—	—
30.	% white-collar workers	.915	—	—	—	—	—	—	—	—	—
28.	% families with incomes over $10,000	.907	—	—	—	—	—	—	—	—	—
39.	Median home value	—	—	—	—	—	—	—	—	—	—
33.	% craftsmen and operatives	−.874	—	—	—	—	—	—	—	—	—
37.	% with 4 years of high school or more	.868	—	—	—	—	—	—	—	—	—
36.	Median school years completed	.845	—	—	—	—	—	—	—	—	—
27.	Median annual income	.787	—	.404	—	—	—	—	—	—	—
32.	% clerical and sales workers	.664	—	.417	—	—	—	—	—	—	—
48.	Median rent	.559	—	—	—	—	—	—	—	—	—
41.	% housing units in 2-unit structures	−.437	—	—	.405	—	—	—	—	—	—
19.	Canadian location quotient‡	.434	—	.414	—	—	—	—	—	—	—
43.	Population per household	—	.919	—	—	—	—	—	—	—	—
2.	% population under 18	—	.893	—	—	—	—	—	—	—	—
3.	% population over 65	—	−.891	—	—	—	—	—	—	—	—
4.	Median age of population	—	−.765	—	—	—	—	—	—	—	—
45.	% housing stock built before 1940	—	−.761	—	—	—	—	—	—	—	—
47.	% housing stock built 1950 and after	—	.743	—	—	—	—	—	—	—	—

Number of Variable*	Name of Variable	Socio-economic Status	Stage in the Life Cycle	Race and Resources	Immigrant and Catholic Status	Population Size and Density	Jewish and Russian Population	Housing, Built in '40's; Workers Commute by Car	Irish and Swedish* Population	Mobility	Other Nonwhite Population; and Italians
53.	% of women 14 and over in labor force	—	−.717	—	—	—	—	—	—	—	—
40.	% of housing units in 1-unit structures	—	.599	—	—	−.504	—	—	—	—	—
42.	% of housing units in 3- or more-unit structures	—	−.598	—	—	.481	—	—	—	—	—
44.	% owner-occupied housing	—	.585	—	—	—	—	—	—	—	—
57.	% workers commuting on foot	—	−.453	—	—	—	—	—	—	—	—
21.	Negro location quotient	—	—	−.750	−.501	—	—	—	—	—	—
7.	% nonwhite population	—	—	−.743	−.501	—	—	—	—	—	—
22.	Native white location quotient‡	—	—	.725	—	—	—	—	—	—	—
24.	% white Protestant population	—	—	.708	—	—	—	—	—	—	—
29.	% families with incomes under $3,000	−.437	—	−.667	—	—	—	—	—	—	—
34.	% laborers	−.595	—	−.645	—	—	—	—	—	—	—
51.	% unemployed	—	—	−.618	—	—	—	—	—	—	—
35.	% workers in service occupations	−.501	—	−.558	−.407	—	—	—	—	—	—
50.	% overcrowded housing units	—	—	−.535	—	—	—	—	—	—	—
12.	German location quotient‡	—	—	.526	—	—	—	—	—	—	—
49.	% sound housing units	.453	—	.509	—	—	—	—	—	—	—
18.	British location quotient‡	—	—	.486	—	—	—	—	—	—	—
55.	% workers commuting by bus	—	—	−.465	—	—	—	.400	—	—	—
9.	% population native-born of foreign or mixed parentage	—	—	—	.857	—	—	—	—	—	—
8.	% population native-born of native parentage	—	—	—	−.830	—	—	—	—	—	—
20.	Foreign stock location quotient‡	—	—	—	.828	—	—	—	—	—	—
25.	% white Catholic population	—	—	—	.760	—	—	—	—	—	—
10.	% foreign-born population	—	−.454	—	.655	—	—	—	—	—	—
11.	% Polish location quotient‡	—	—	—	.583	—	—	—	—	—	—
56.	% workers commuting by rail	—	—	—	−.390	—	—	—	—	—	—
16.	Czech location quotient	—	—	—	.362	—	—	—	—	—	—
52.	Total unemployment	—	−.454	—	—	.789	—	—	—	—	—
6.	% total unemployment	—	—	—	—	.787	—	—	—	—	—
1.	Population	—	—	—	—	.682	—	—	—	—	—
5.	Population density	—	—	−.418	—	.649	—	—	—	—	—
14.	Russian location quotient‡	—	—	—	—	—	−.837	—	—	—	—
26.	% Jewish population	—	—	—	—	—	−.793	—	—	—	—
46.	% housing stock built 1940–1949	—	—	—	—	−.458	—	−.600	—	—	—
54.	% workers commuting by car	—	—	.415	—	—	—	−.508	—	—	—
15.	Irish location quotient‡	—	—	—	—	—	—	—	−.787	—	—
17.	Swedish location quotient‡	—	—	—	—	—	—	—	−.430	—	—
38.	% families moved since 1955	—	—	—	−.448	—	—	—	—	.577	—
23.	Other nonwhite location quotients‡	—	—	—	—	—	—	—	—	—	.744
13.	Italian location quotient‡	—	—	—	.426	—	—	—	—	—	.494

Sources: Data for community areas are from Evelyn M. Kitagawa and Karl E. Taeuber, eds., *Local Community Factbook: Chicago Metropolitan Area, 1960* (Chicago: Chicago Community Inventory, University of Chicago, 1963). Data for municipalities are from Northeastern Illinois Metropolitan Area Planning Commission, *Suburban Factbook* (Chicago, 1964).

* The numbers are from the Appendix to Chapter 10, which lists the variables (and the substantive groups of variables) used in the analysis.

†The data for each variable are its correlations with the factors, i.e., its "loading."

‡The derivation of the location quotient is given in a footnote to the Appendix to this chapter.

comes, many of them below $3,000 (Variable 29; loading, −.437), and who live in low-rent housing.

There is a tendency for the immigrant Canadian population to cluster in the higher-status communities (Variable 19; loading, .434), and for duplex or two-decker housing to be found in lower-status communities (Variable 41; loading, −.437).

Almost all the variables traditionally regarded in sociology as indicators of class position or social status—education, occupation, and income—have either their highest (or their next to highest) loadings on this first factor. There also exists congruency between the personal indicators of social status (education, occupation, income) and the physical indicators of housing quality (value or median rent of home), as we suggested earlier in the discussion of residential choice.

At this point we will give only a brief verbal description of the spatial patterns of the various factors, reserving for a little later a more rigorous spatial analysis and test of theory.

The scores of the various communities of the metropolitan region on this scale of socio-economic status are mapped in Fig. 10–10, employing four roughly equal-sized classes. The highest status communities are found predominantly in the suburbs, along the North Shore, along the commuting railroads stretching out to the northwest, along parts of the commuting lines of the western sector (particularly along the Burlington railroad), and in a small southern subsector consisting of Homewood, Flossmoor, Olympia Fields, and Park Forest. Within the city, only the community areas on the northern margin, the Gold Coast fringe along the North Shore (somewhat obscured when community areas are the unit but rather clearer in the census tract analysis), Hyde Park, South Shore, and Beverly in South Side Chicago fall into the category of highest socio-economic status, and of these only Forest Glen (Community Area 12) falls in the highest octile.

The lowest status communities form a broad sweeping arc in the inner city, almost surrounding the Loop. These are the areas of blue collar residence close to the principal industrial areas of the metropolis.[67] Low status communities also cluster around the industrial areas of the Lake Calumet region within the city, and in Cook County to the south (Robbins, Posen, Dixmoor, East Chicago Heights, Sauk Village, South Chicago Heights, and Steger).

The middle status communities occupy the remainder of the populated metropolitan area: The higher middle status municipalities fill the gaps in the northern, northwestern, and western inner and outer suburban rings, and the lower middle status communities are along the Des Plaines River (with the exception of the lower-status communities of Highwood, where many of the military personnel from the Great Lakes Naval Base have their homes, Northlake, and Stone Park). The crescent of industrial satellites—Waukegan, Elgin, Aurora, Joliet, Chicago Heights—is also of lower middle status, on the average. The remainder of the southern suburbs tends to be of lower middle status.

The metropolitan area thus displays a complex pattern of socio-economic types of communities—a pattern, however, that is far from random. A complex exists of sectors, semi-sectors, sectors that are almost rings, and rings that display clear linkages between community type and environment. Thus: (1) the high status areas cluster at locations with amenities (the Lake Shore and the open spaces of the suburbs, away from the smoke and dirt of the factory areas); and (2) the low status areas lie close to the workplaces of their residents and in the areas of least or even negative amenity (the most pollution, the greatest mixture of land uses, the oldest and least desirable homes).

Factor II: Stage in the Life Cycle

An entirely different set of variables loads highly on the second factor. The high loadings exhibited by the variables family size and age structure lead one strongly to believe that this is a factor that identifies the Stage in the Life Cycle (also called Family Status) of a population group. Community areas or municipalities which score highly on this dimension are the areas of residence for families of fairly large size (Variable 43; loading, .919), with many children (Variable

FIGURE 10–10. Factor I: Socioeconomic status of population in metropolitan Chicago, 1960. *Source:* See caption for Fig. 10–3.

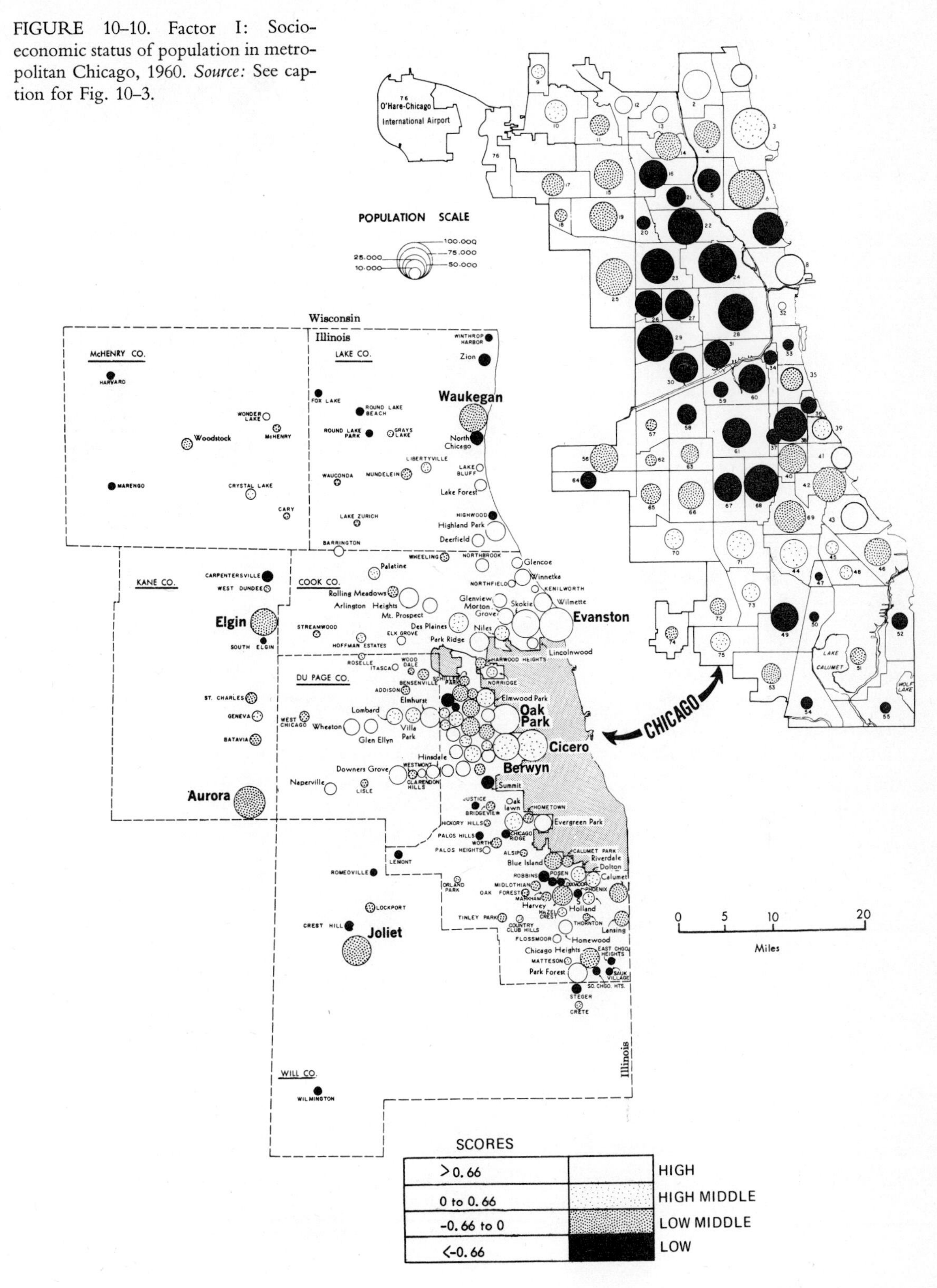

FIGURE 10–11. Factor II: Stage in the life cycle of population in metropolitan Chicago, 1960. *Source:* See caption for Fig. 10–3.

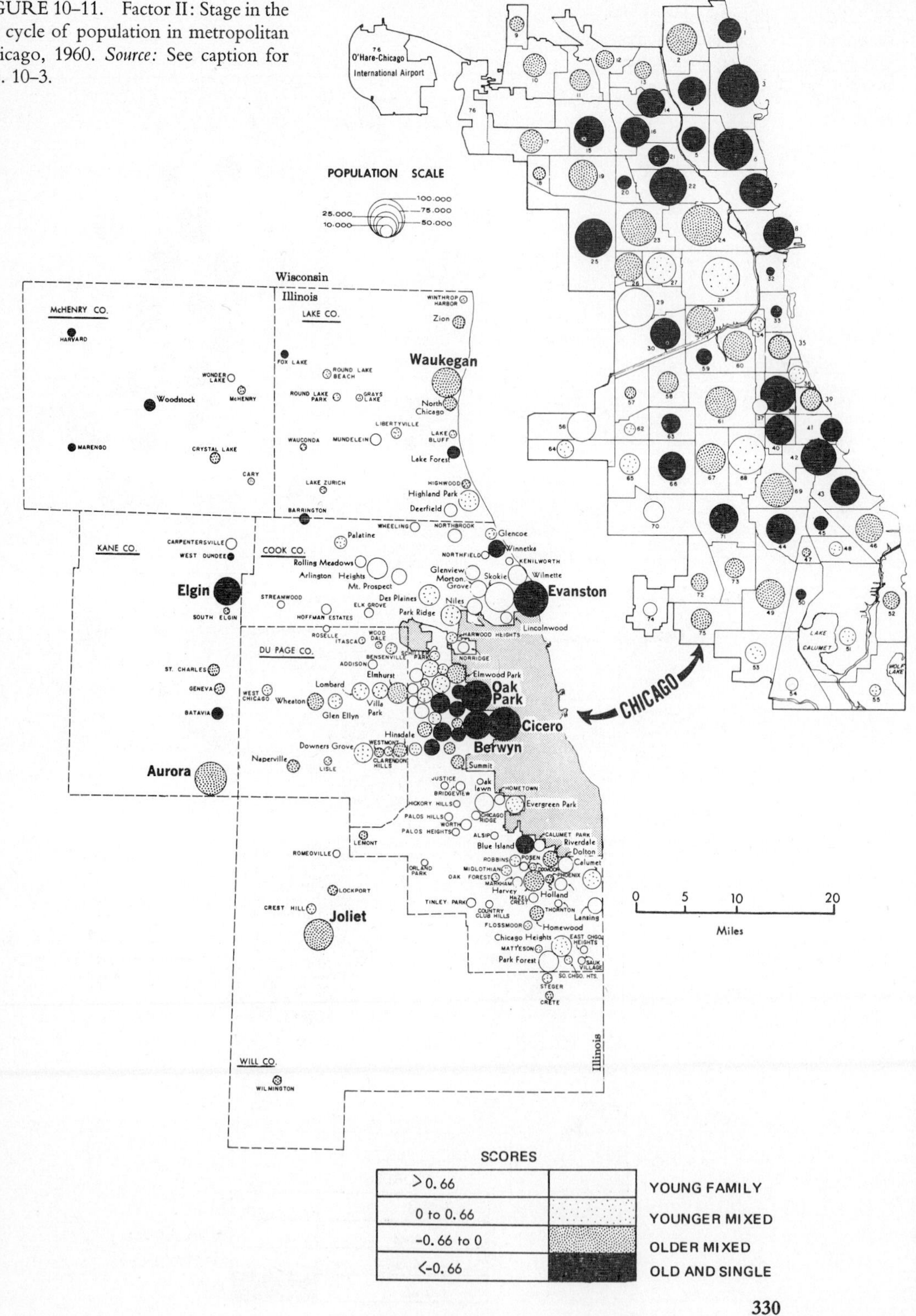

2; loading, .893), and few grandparents (Variable 3; loading, −.891). These families, in which the wives, fully occupied in child-rearing, tend not to work (Variable 53; loading, −.717), live in recently built (Variable 47; loading, .743), single-family homes (Variable 40; loading, .599), which they either own or are in process of buying (Variable 44; loading, .585). In communities which score low on this factor reside small families with few children (childless couples, couples who haven't yet started their families, couples whose children have left home, and single people), and with wives that work; families which tend to be older (Variable 4; loading, −.765), and which live in multi-unit structures (Variable 42; loading, −.598). These structures tend to be older (Variable 45; loading, −.761), made up of rental units, and close enough to their residents' workplaces so that a high proportion walk to work (Variable 57; loading, −.453).

The indicators used here to describe the characteristics of the age pyramid for the populations residing in the community areas and municipalities of the metropolitan region give only a crude picture of the age pyramid itself and act only as surrogates for the mix of family types,[68] but the fact that the variables selected, crude though they may be, do load highly on the same factor suggests that they do pick out the differences between community populations in terms of the stage in the life cycle at which they find themselves. The differences are a product of the migration of families in formation and dissolution, and of the aging of families in the process of maturation. That "subareas within the city [are] differentiated in their attractiveness to families of different types"[69] is attested to by the loading of most of the housing type variables on this factor, Stage in the Life Cycle.[70] Our expectations about the equivalency of individual social space and housing space (set out earlier) are thus borne out in terms of both the type and quality of housing.

The spatial pattern of Factor II is displayed in Fig. 10–11. The communities containing more than the average number of older, and of single people living in multi-unit structures are found predominantly in the central city and in the innermost suburbs (to the west of the central city, together with Evanston and Blue Island), with the one exception of the old industrial town of Elgin (also the location of a large state mental hospital, which tends to relate it more closely to this factor). Of this low-scoring group of community areas and municipalities, the lowest scoring (with scores below −1.15) are found along the North Shore, east of the Chicago River, in the very center of the city—the Loop, the Near South Side, Hyde Park, Washington Park, and the South Shore. These community areas are of very varying socio-economic status, ranging from the New North Side and Hyde Park at one extreme to the Near South Side and North Center at the other.

Not all the community areas within the city are low-scoring, however. Those on the south-western fringes have the young families characteristic of the suburbs, being the most recent parts of the city to be built up. In certain of the inner parts of the city, too, there are communities with young populations (North Lawndale, East Garfield Park, the New West Side, Armour Square, Fuller Park, Oakland, and Englewood). These communities are mainly Negro and comprise the West Side ghetto and the newer fringes of the South Side ghetto. They contrast strongly with high-scoring suburban communities in terms of their profiles on the original census variables, however (see Table 10–5). The population variables of the two sets of areas (city and suburbs) correspond fairly closely, class by class, but there are very marked differences in the housing variables. The non-white areas of the inner city, areas of recent in-migration of Negroes from the south (West Side) or from the existing ghetto (the fringe areas of South Side), contain young populations living in rented quarters in old, multiple-unit apartment buildings, whereas the young families of the white suburban areas live in and own new, single-family dwellings.

The contrast is a product of two influences. First, the purchase of a single-family home in

TABLE 10–5

Comparison of Inner City and Suburban Areas Scoring High on Factor II (Stage in the Life Cycle) in Terms of the Variables Loading High on that Factor

Community	*Octile**	*Population per House-hold*	*% Population under 18*	*% Population over 65*	*Median Age of Population*	*% Housing Stock Built before 1940*	*% Housing Stock Built 1950 and After*
29. North Lawndale (C)†	1	4.26	46.4	3.3	20.7	97.5	1.1
220. Park Forest (S)‡	1	4.00	48.0	2.0	21.0	0.0	71.0
37. Fuller Park (C)	2	4.31	44.7	4.4	22.5	97.5	1.7
90. Skokie (S)	2	3.60	39.0	5.0	30.0	11.0	78.0
27. East Garfield Park (C)	3	3.50	41.5	4.5	23.3	97.6	0.5
68. Englewood (C)	3	3.71	39.1	6.7	25.7	97.7	0.7
151. Lombard (S)	3	3.80	42.0	5.0	28.0	31.0	57.0
28. Near west side (C)	4	3.36	40.5	5.8	25.0	87.5	10.0
34. Armour Square (C)	4	3.64	40.1	8.3	26.2	86.2	3.9
36. Oakland (C)	4	3.27	46.3	4.7	21.9	87.3	4.5
173. Downer's Grove (S)	4	3.50	39.0	6.0	31.0	43.0	47.0

Community	*Octile**	*% of Women 14 and Over in Labor Force*	*% of Housing units in 1-Unit Structures*	*% of Housing units in 3- or More-Unit Structures*	*% Owner-Occu-pied Housing*	*% of Workers Commuting on Foot*	*% Non-white Population*
29. North Lawndale (C)†	1	42.4	7.4	74.1	7.4	6.0	91.4
220. Park Forest (S)‡	1	21.4	99.0	0.0	58.7	4.0	0.6
37. Fuller Park (C)	2	36.2	11.4	48.8	11.4	4.4	96.1
90. Skokie (S)	2	33.0	75.0	20.0	83.8	4.0	0.5
27. East Garfield Park (C)	3	39.3	6.8	77.1	6.8	10.1	62.0
68. Englewood (C)	3	41.1	19.2	48.6	19.2	5.5	69.2
151. Lombard (S)	3	30.7	94.0	3.0	88.9	5.0	0.1
28. Near west side (C)	4	33.0	13.0	75.8	13.0	16.4	54.4
34. Armour Square (C)	4	32.4	15.0	62.3	15.0	10.8	42.3
36. Oakland (C)	4	32.8	12.2	85.5	12.2	3.8	98.7
173. Downer's Grove (S)	4	31.9	93.0	4.0	86.6	7.0	0.3

Sources: Data for community areas are from Evelyn M. Kitagawa and Karl E. Taeuber, eds., *Local Community Factbook: Chicago Metropolitan Area, 1960* (Chicago: Chicago Community Inventory, University of Chicago, 1963). Data for municipalities are from Northeastern Illinois Metropolitan Planning Commission, *Suburban Factbook* (Chicago, 1964).
*The range of scores was divided into eight classes. It is assumed that the distribution of scores is approximately normal and that the classes are about equal in size—hence, octiles.
†C = City
‡S = Suburbs

the Chicago metropolitan area requires a minimum income level in order to meet mortgage requirements (which are higher for Negroes) and many of the family incomes in these inner-city, poverty-stricken communities fall below this figure.[71] Even when public bodies have intervened in the housing market in order to help families in this situation, they have built (with the one major exception of the Altgeld housing estate on the Far South Side of Chicago) apartment structures within the confines of the ghetto rather than single-family homes on the vacant land in the suburban ring.[72] Second, discrimination in the housing market operates to exclude would-be Negro home buyers from the predominantly white suburbs.

Surrounding the central city and the older inner municipalities is a ring of newer suburbs, whose residents vary somewhat in terms of their stage in the the life cycle, but which have generally positive scores. The newer suburbs with the youngest populations are found along the radial railway lines extending to the northwest, southwest, and south. Beyond this suburban ring are the satellite industrial towns and the rural service centers, whose older populations live in older, established settlements.

The spatial pattern of the factor Stage in the Life Cycle is thus generally concentric, except that the central older areas in fact stretch in a sectoral manner along Lake Michigan (one of the distortions imposed on the relative desirability of residential locations by the local geography) and that the younger Negro families are confined to the "new" ghetto areas.

This distribution of communities by the stage in the life cycle of their populations is reflected in the variation in housing types with distance from the center of the city. At the center of the city, land values are such as to necessitate capital-intensive use of land; if it is residential land, this necessarily means apartments. Further from the city center where land values are lower (because location rent has decreased), more land and less capital need be used; thus, two-family and town houses are found. At yet further distances where the land cost is yet lower, single-family homes predominate (see Chapter 9). The apartment districts prove attractive to older people, to younger single people, and to newly married couples who need less space and desire greater access to places of activity. The single-family homes in the suburban communities attract young families in the process of child-rearing, desirous of a spacious home with a yard around.[73] In this way, the concentric pattern of the factor Stage in the Life Cycle is related to the cost of access and hence to land values as they are affected by location in respect to the city center. The deviation of the Lake Shore from this concentric pattern can be explained by the higher land values and resultant capital-intensive development in response to the proximity to the Lake, an important amenity; the West Side ghetto is a deviation which has been shown to be a product of poverty and discrimination

Factor III: Race and Resources

The third factor to emerge from the analysis isolates the racial status of a neighborhood or community. We call this dimension Race and Resources because some of the variables which load on this factor identify racial or ethnic[74] status, and some are related to socio-economic status. Communities that score low on this factor contain residents (see Table 10–4) who are predominantly Negroes (Variable 21; loading, —.750; Variable 7; loading, —.743) who work as laborers (Variable 34; loading, —.645), in service occupations (Variable 35; loading, —.558), or have no job (Variable 51; loading, —.618). These occupations bring the residents of such communities low incomes (Variable 29; loading —.667), so that they cannot afford much housing (Variable 50; loading, —.535) or a car (Variable 55; loading, —.465).

Community areas or municipalities with high scores on this factor are at the opposite pole of the racial dimension; their populations tend to be white (Variable 22; loading, .725), native-born and Protestant (Variable 24; loading, .708), that small portion of the population which is of foreign stock as defined by the Census tending to be German (Variable 12; loading, .526), British (Variable 18; loading, .486), or Canadian (Variable 19; loading, .414). The residents of high-scoring communities tend not to work in the most manual or menial jobs (but rather more in clerical or sales occupations—Variable 32; loading, .417), and to be employed and to earn higher incomes (Variable 27; loading, .404), enabling them to live in sound and more spacious housing (Variable 49; loading, .509).

Digression on the necessary and sufficient conditions for particular factor structures to emerge in American cities: The third factor is thus not purely one of racial status, but rather one that identifies the association between racial status and the allocation of resources. It makes it clear that, given the same social status, the Negro will receive less education, a poorer job, less pay, and less for his money than a white person. This association between race and resources, though almost a truism in the American urban scene, has not been discussed in the literature of social area factor analysis. Thus, it may be profitable at this point to theorize about the kinds of factor structures that might be expected to emerge from a factor analysis of a set of socio-economic variables such as those we use in this analysis, and to ask ourselves under what urban conditions these various factor structures appear.

In Table 10–6 we consider the possible correspondences between sets of variables and factors. Three sets of variables are included in the analysis: a set of social and economic status indicators; a set of family status characteristics; and a set of minority group indicators. For the sake of simplicity, the only minority group referred to in this analysis is the Negro population of most American cities. The possible combinations range from a one-to-one correspondence of the variables and the factor, at one extreme (Combination 1), to undimensionality, all sets of variables loading on a single factor, at the other (Combination 5). A summary explanation of the types of combinations represented in Table 10–6 follows:

Type I. *Simple spatial segregation: there is an exclusive minority-group factor.* The minority group variable (or variables) loads on its own separate factor. No socio-economic or life cycle variables load highly on this factor. There are

TABLE 10-6

Combinations of Variable Sets and Factors

Sets of Variables

SES = Socio-economic Status
LC = Stage in the Life Cycle, or Family Status
MG = Minority Group (Negro)

*Factors: Q, Y, Z**

Combination 1†

Variables	*Correspondence*‡	*Factor*
SES		Q
LC		Y
MG		Z

Combination 2

Variables	*Correspondence*	*Factor*
SES		Q
LC		
MG		Z

Combination 3

Variables	*Correspondence*	*Factor*
SES		Q
LC		Y
MG		

Combination 4

Variables	*Correspondence*	*Factor*
SES		Q
LC		Y
MG		

Combination 5

Variables	*Correspondence*	*Factor*
SES		Q
LC		
MG		

Combination 6

Variables	*Correspondence*	*Factor*
SES		Q
LC		Y
MG		Z

Combination 7§

Variables	*Correspondence*	*Factor*
SES		Q
LC		Y Family Status
		Y′ Urbanization
MG		Z

*The symbols designate separate factors. Their order is of no significance. In actual studies, they will depend on the number of variables in each set, the study area, and the population.

†See text for an explanation of the various types of combinations.

‡Correspondence: Indicates highest loadings of variables on factors.

§See T. R. Anderson and L. L. Bean, "The Shevky-Bell Social Areas: Confirmation of Results and Reinterpretation," *Social Forces*, XL (1961), 119–24. The set of life cycle variables split into two subsets which load on separate factors, which Anderson and Bean call "family status" and "urbanization." There is a problem of interpretation of their factor loadings, stemming from the extent of the study area and of the range of study area population characteristics, since they dealt with only the central city of Toledo. There may, however, be a disassociation between the distribution of residential structures and the distribution of family types either because: (1) "subareas within the city are not differentiated in their attractiveness to families of different types" by the measures employed; or (2) the city is not differentiated by type of residential structure sufficiently for one type of structure to house one type of family unit (on a scale which can be identified by an analysis employing the areal units they used).

no secondary high loadings of such variables on this factor. Examples of factors identifying such simple spatial segregation are Factors VI (Jewish and Russian), VIII (Irish and Swedish), and X (Other non-whites and Italians) in the present study.

Type II. *The minority-group variable is part of a socio-economic status factor.* Minority-group status is a social status indicator. The minority group occupies the lower end of the socio-economic ladder,[75] but has a few members of high social status. The minority group variable (or variables) loads most highly on a socio-economic status factor. Examples of such situations are found in the factor structures of southern American cities.[76]

Type III. *The minority-group variable is part of the stage in the life cycle.* Minority group status is an indicator of family status. The minority group occupies one end of the family-status scale, having larger families and a younger population than the majority group. The minority-group variable loads most highly on a stage in the life-cycle factor. The factor structure of the central city of Miami displays this convergence of racial and family status,[77] but only because of the special nature of the study area, which excluded the younger and larger white families in the suburbs.

Type IV. *The minority-group variable is part of an allocation of resource factor.* The minority group is residentially segregated from the rest of the population, but occupies a position on the socio-economic scale midway between its positions in Type I and Type II situations. Members of the minority group are found in substantial numbers at every position, but in greater proportion at the bottom than the top (see, e.g., Table 10–7). The minority-group variable and those concerned with the distribution of resources (particularly those highlighting the lower parts of the distributions) load highly on the same factor, identifying a pattern of discrimination in the allocation of resources along minority-group (usually racial) lines. That is, at the same level of socio-economic status fewer resources are commanded by the minority group. However, discrimination is not as absolute as in the case of Type II factor structures. Our present Factor III (Race and Resources) is one example of a Type IV situation.

TABLE 10–7

Distribution of Incomes among White and Nonwhite Families in the Chicago Metropolitan Area

Income	*Percentage of Nonwhite Families*	*Ratio of Observed to Expected Percentage**
Under $1,000	34.6†	2.75
$1,000–$1,999	34.4	2.73
$2,000–$2,999	30.9	2.45
$3,000–$3,999	26.9	2.13
$4,000–$4,999	22.4	1.78
$5,000–$5,999	14.3	1.13
$6,000–$6,999	10.0	0.79
$7,000–$7,999	8.3	0.66
$8,000–$8,999	7.5	0.60
$9,000–$9,999	6.6	0.52
$10,000 and above	5.7	0.45

Source: U.S. Census of Population, 1960.
*The percentage of the nonwhite population is 14.8; the percentage of Negroes is 14.3. The percentage of the nonwhite population expected in each class, on the assumption that white and nonwhite incomes are distributed alike, is 12.6.
†The figures probably *underestimate* the concentration of the Negro population in the lower income categories for several reasons: (1) The "other nonwhites" included in the table probably have a more favorable distribution of incomes than the Negro; (2) the average Negro family is larger than the white; and (3) Negro families in the lower-income groups tend to be larger than white families of equivalent income, whereas in the upper-income groups Negro families tend to be smaller than white families of equivalent income.

In Combination 6, the socio-economic status variables split into those identified with "pure" status and those related to discrimination in the allocation of resources.

In certain cases, however, and this study is one of them, the sets of variables divide into two or possibly more components (Combinations 6 and 7 in Table 10–6, Type IV in the list above). We deliberately included, in the socio-economic set, variables which measure the proportion of an area's population employed in the lowest-status jobs, with incomes below the poverty line, and living in poor housing. Since the Negro population suffers a disproportionate share of the city's manual and menial jobs, low incomes, and slum housing, these variables loaded on the same factor as the minority group indicators. Thus, the dimension identified is not simply one of pure racial segregation, but also one of systematic inequality in the allocation of resources between the two principal racial groups,[78] the tragic meaning of which is being clarified in the unrest and violence in the black ghettos of urban America.

However, the inequality is far from absolute. There are large numbers of Negroes in white-collar jobs and in middle-class neighborhoods (Chatham, Hyde Park, South Kenwood, South Shore, Morgan Park), who have reached these positions since the wave of Negro in-migration from the South began during World War I. The point is perhaps made best by Table 10–7, in which the distribution of income by race is given. Negro families tend to be concentrated in the lower-income classes, but there are not insignificant numbers in the higher-income brackets. As a result, two separate factors result from a factor analysis of the socio-economic and minority group variable sets, in contrast to the collapse of these sets to one factor in the studies of the American South already referred to.

With these considerations in mind, we can proceed to specify the conditions that must necessarily exist in the urban system for a minor-

TABLE 10–8

Conditions for the Existence of a Minority Group Factor

Factor Condition	*Type of Variables Used*	*Necessary Conditions*
Separate minority group factor.	Proportion of the subarea population in the minority group. Measures of the relative concentration of minority groups.	1. That the characteristic(s) differentiating the minority group from the rest of the population be of perceived significance in the social system, that is, that the urban population be truly heterogeneous; 2. That the minority group be residentially segregated from the rest of the population,* on a scale observable by the measures used in the analysis
Disassociation between minority group membership and socio-economic status.	Measures used above for minority group; measures of education, occupation, income, and the distribution of resources.	1. That the minority groups be residentially segregated from the rest of the population,* on a scale observable in the analysis; and either: 2. That there exist little or no association between minority group status and socio-economic status; or 3. That if there be some association between social class and minority group status, that *a.* The minority group still span most of the social-status range, though it may be concentrated at the lower end of the range; and *b.* A fairly full range of housing accommodation quality be available for families within the residentially segregated area.
Disassociation between the minority group and the stage in the life cycle dimensions.	Measures used above for the minority group; measures of age distribution, family size, and fertility.	1. That the minority group be residentially segregated from the rest of the population on a scale observable in the analysis; and either: 2. That there exist little or no association between minority group status and family status; or 3. That if there be some association between family status and minority group status, that *a.* The minority group still span most of the family status range, though it may be concentrated at one end of the range; and *b.* A fairly full range of housing accommodation types be available for families within the residentially segregated area.

*As a result of discrimination in the housing market or through choice of residential neighborhood.

ity group factor to be extracted in a social area factor analysis. The conditions are laid out in Table 10–8 in a format analogous to that used to present Janet Abu-Lughod's findings (Table 10–2). For there to emerge a separate minority group factor (Combination 1, Table 10–6) not only must the minority group be spatially segregated (at the scale of the areas of observation used in the analysis) but there must exist little or no association between minority-group status and either socio-economic or family status. In heterogeneous societies, minority groups marked off from the rest of the population by highly visible characteristics are usually both spatially segregated and unequally treated by the majority group.[79] This was as true for the immigrants who arrived in America's cities from Europe as it was for Negroes who migrated from the south to northern cities. However, as the European immigrant groups moved up the social ladder they had a choice.

> [T]hey could move their enclaves to more comfortable environs or, as individuals, leave the enclaves and become members of the community at large. Negroes—forever marked by their color—could only hope for success within a rigidly delineated and severely restricted ghetto society. No physical wall has encircled the black belt. But an almost equally imperious wall of hostility and discrimination has isolated Negroes from the mainstream of Chicago life. Under such conditions, Negroes have tried, often against impossible odds, to make the best of their circumstances by creating a meaningful life of their own, but they have done so, not out of choice, but because white society has left them no alternative.[80]

Thus, in most American cities there is considerable association between socio-economic and racial status (less in northern and western cities, and more in southern cities). The effect on their respective factorial ecologies has already been discussed in some detail.[81]

The spatial pattern of Factor III: Chicago's ghetto. The spatial pattern of scores on Factor III (Fig. 10–12) is a familiar one. The lowest scoring tracts identify the limits of Chicago's ghetto.[82] The ghetto consists of three main parts: South Side, West Side and the western part of the Near north. In addition, there are enclaves to the south—eastern Morgan Park, a long-established, middle-class, Negro neighborhood, the Altgeld public housing estate in the Riverdale community area (part of the ghetto exported to the city's periphery), Robbins and East Chicago Heights (blue-collar Negro suburbs); to the west—Maywood, and part of LaGrange; and to the north—the Evanston ghetto. A discussion of the origin and spread of the Negro ghetto is not appropriate here,[83] but some comments on the spatial pattern of Negro neighborhoods may be in order.

The Negro population is predominantly concentrated in the central city (Table 10–9), more so than any other large population group within the metropolis. Within the city, the ghetto is not concentrated in a ring around the central business district but rather forms two main wedges which spread from the center for some six miles to the west and some ten miles to the south. The Negro residential district has evidently spread from the original "ports of entry," along the paths of least resistance: the middle-status sectors containing housing within reach of Negro incomes happen to be the sectors occupied by white residents with sufficient means to move in the face of Negro influx.[84] The well-established European immigrants in lower-class districts have traditionally resisted encroachment on their enclaves by Negroes, and the high-status districts have been beyond the range of Negro pockets. The West Side ghetto is currently spreading into middle-class Austin (but not into Cicero, a working-class, strongly Slavic community), and south of 67th Street the South Side area of Negro residence broadens out to occupy the middle class sector between the Rock Island and Illinois Central railroads.

The originally middle class neighborhoods near the center of the city which became areas of Negro residence towards the beginning of the century have long since decayed into slums, except where public authorities have intervened to build what they define as physically adequate housing. However, the incidence of decay diminishes with increasing distance from the center of the city. South of the Loop, social and family status rise,[85] and Negro neighborhoods comprised of single-family homes are reached

FIGURE 10–12. Factor III: Race and resources in metropolitan Chicago, 1960. *Source:* See caption for Fig. 10–3.

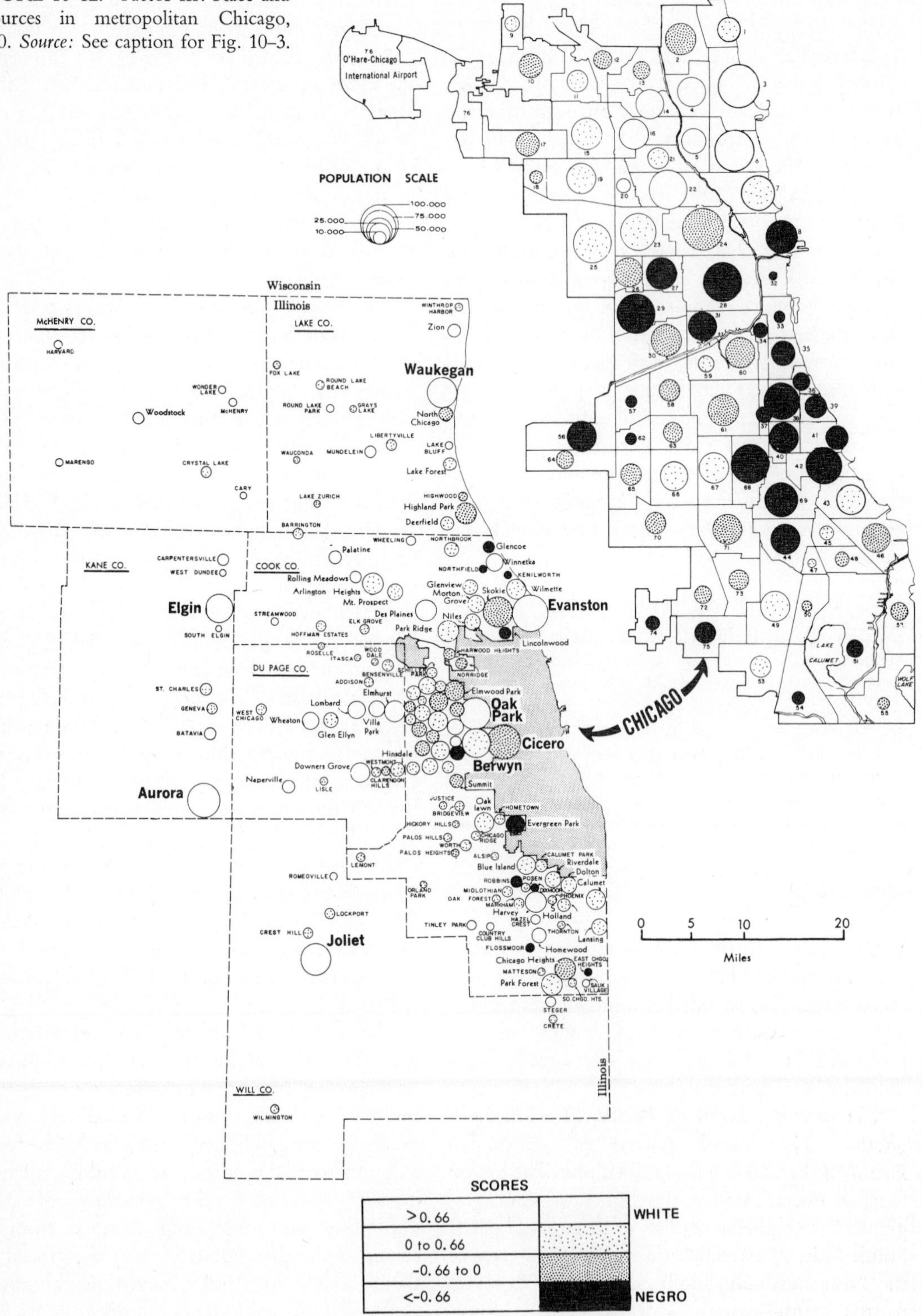

TABLE 10–9

Suburbanization of Various Population Groups in the Chicago Metropolitan Area: 1960

	Population (in Hundreds of Thousands)	*Percentage Living in City*	*Percentage Living in Suburbs*	*Rank Order in Terms of Suburbanization*
*Foreign Stock**				
Polish	340.0	76	24	11
German	293.1	55	45	6
Italian	211.9	64	36	8
Russian	129.2	75	25	9
Irish (from Eire)†	113.5	75	25	10
Czech	108.3	46	54	2
British (from U.K.)†	105.1	49	51	4
Swedish	98.0	53	47	5
Canadian	72.0	48	52	3
Total foreign stock	1,990.1	63	37	—
Native white	3,310.8	45	55	1
Negro	890.2	91	9	13
Other nonwhite	29.8	84	16	12
Total population	6,220.9	57	43	—

Source: Northeastern Illinois Metropolitan Planning Commission, *Suburban Factbook* (Chicago, 1964).
*Foreign Stock includes both foreign-born persons and native-born persons of foreign or mixed parentage, i.e., first- and second-generation immigrants. The nine most numerous groups were selected for analysis.
†The definition of Irish is "coming from Eire." In previous censuses there had been confusion over the definition of Irish. In the 1960 Census, immigrants from Northern Ireland were considered British, since Northern Ireland is part of the United Kingdom of Great Britain and Northern Ireland.

towards the margins of the city. *South Side Chicago is indeed a microcosm of the wider urban region, a veritable "Black Metropolis," though as Spear points out, not by choice.*

Factor IV: Immigrant and Catholic Status

The fourth factor to emerge from the factor analysis (and the first "non-Shevky-Bell" dimension) is that labeled Immigrant and Catholic Status in Table 10–4. On this dimension communities are differentiated in terms of the place of birth and the religious affiliation of their populations. Areas range from those with a large proportion of foreign stock and a large proportion of Catholics, at one extreme of the scale, to those with a population composed mainly of native Americans with native-born parents, adherents to some Protestant order, at the other.[86]

Communities or municipalities scoring high on this factor tend to contain populations with the highest concentrations of foreign stock (Variable 20; loading, .828), either foreign-born (Variable 10; loading, .655) or native-born of foreign or mixed parentage (Variable 9; loading, .857), who tend to be Polish (Variable 11; loading, .583), Czech (Variable 16; loading, .362), or Italian (Variable 13; loading, .426), and are members of the Catholic Church (Variable 25). Areas that score low on this dimension are the homes of predominantly native-born Americans (Variable 8; loading, —.830), who also tend to be non-Catholics. The very lowest-scoring communities are Negro (Variable 21; loading, —.501 and Variable 7; loading, —.501); these areas contain virtually no foreign-born residents, whereas the higher-status white suburbs do house some foreign-born Chicagoans.

This ethnic dimension is relatively free of association with the socio-economic status or family status sets of variables (except for a loading of .405 on the two-unit housing variable).[87] However, there appears to be some association between racial status and the Immigrant and Catholic factor, as was noted above. In fact, when the study area is reduced to the City of Chicago, through the exclusion of the suburbs (containing a much higher proportion of whites and native-born non-Catholics than the city) the two factors collapse into one, epitomizing the polarization of the central city.

The map of Immigrant and Catholic factor scores (Fig. 10–13) presents a clear-cut pattern. The highest scoring communities are found in the northwest sector, the southwest sector, and the Calumet regions of the City of Chicago, and in the inner western suburbs together with the innermost northwestern (Norridge, Niles, Lincolnwood) and southwestern (Summit, Evergreen Park) municipalities. The lowest scoring areas are the Negro ghettos and the Negro suburbs, plus a number of the North Shore, satellite crescent, and outer suburban communities. The remainder of the northern sector of the city, several middle class communities in

FIGURE 10–13. Factor IV: Immigrant and Catholic status in metropolitan Chicago, 1960. *Source:* See caption for Fig. 10–3.

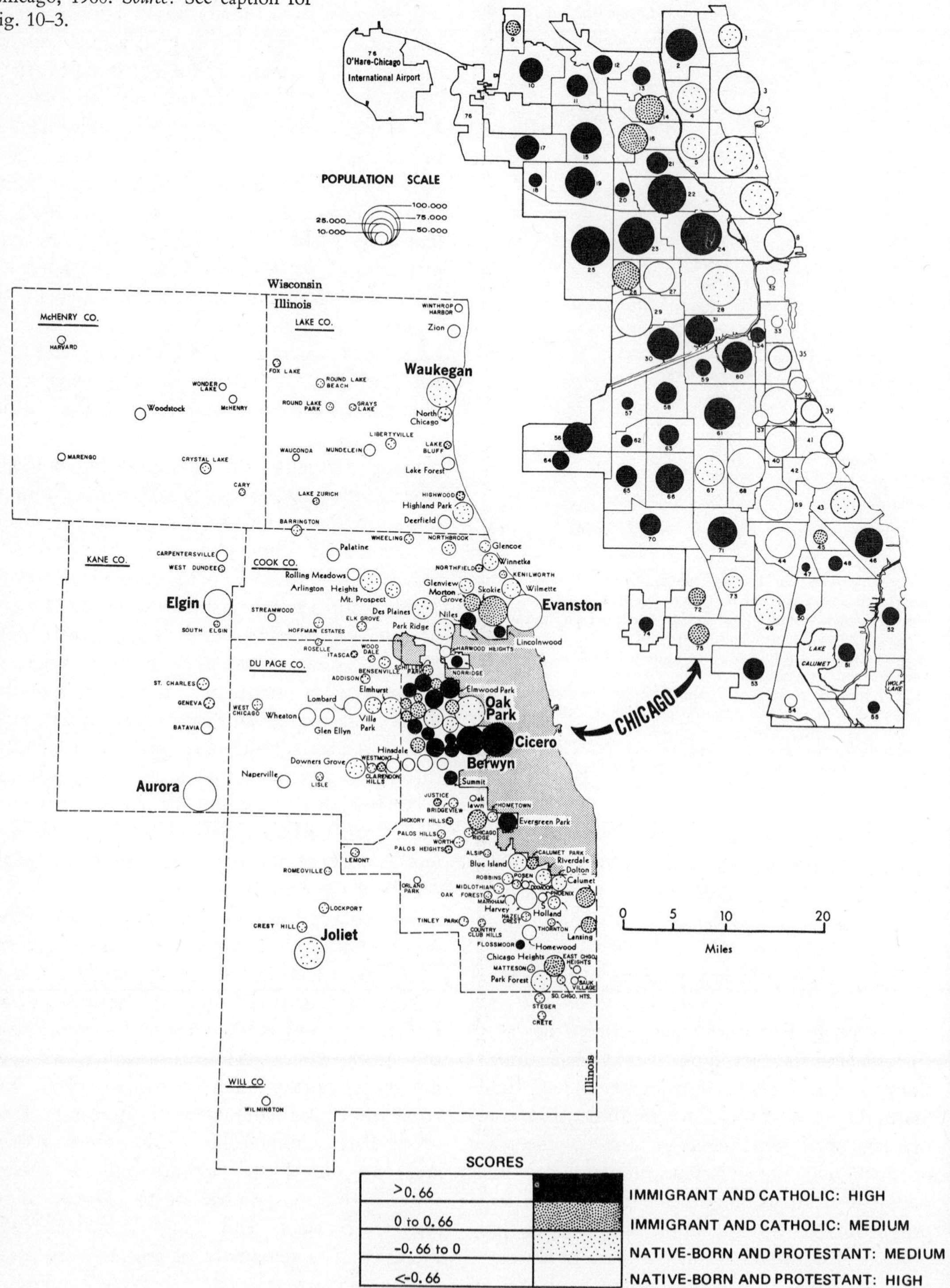

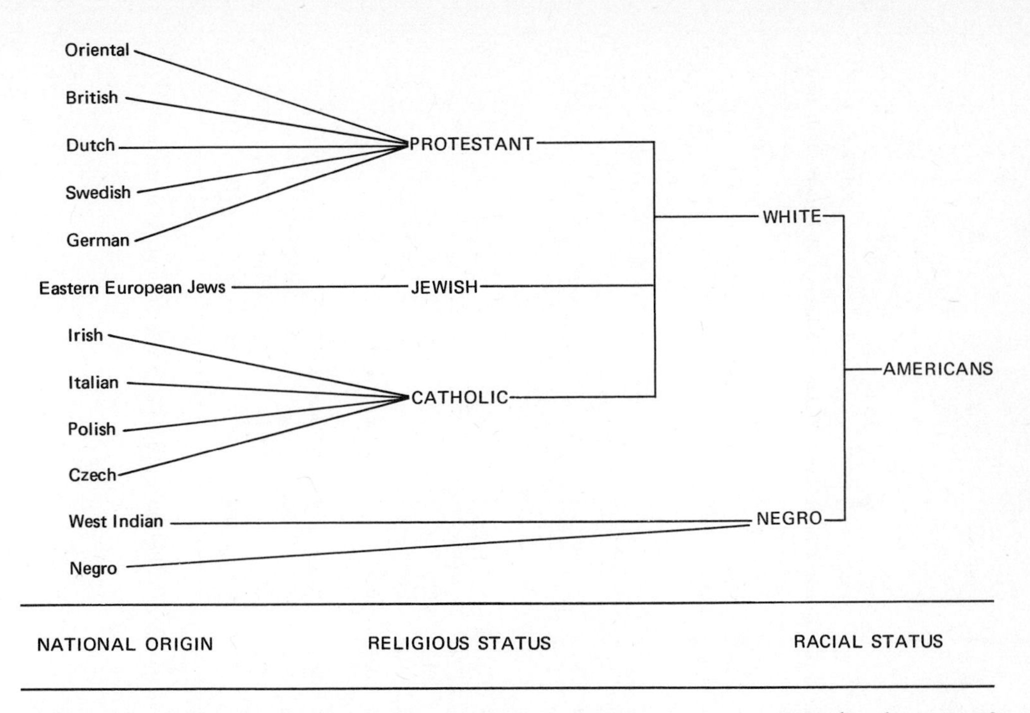

FIGURE 10–14. The polarization of ethnic groups in contemporary America. Note that the status of some groups is, as yet, unresolved. Puerto Ricans and Mexican-Americans at present make up part of the lower class, of which the Negroes form the largest group. But, with time, they may move into the working-class Catholic group. Only the principal connecting paths are shown in the diagram. Other paths may be important: Germany, for instance, has contributed members to each of the three white groups. *Source:* Based on Nathan Glazer and Daniel P. Moynihan, *Beyond the Melting Pot: The Negroes, Puerto Ricans, Jews, and Irish of New York City* (Cambridge, Mass.: The M.I.T. Press, 1963).

the far south of the city, and the majority of the suburbs score in the low middle range, indicating that some foreign-born inhabitants and some proportion of Catholics reside there, but not in great numbers.

A comparison of the maps of Socio-economic Status and Immigrant and Catholic Status (Figs. 10–10 and 10–13, respectively) reveals that: (1) within the city, areas that score high on Factor IV score low on Factor I; (2) within the Immigrant and Catholic sectors, status rises with distance from the center of the city; and (3) the highest status suburbs in the inner western sector tend to have the fewest Catholics and immigrants. Thus, in microcosm, is the process of assimilation of the foreign-born immigrant into the fabric of American life laid out on the map. We see that this process has proceeded far enough for there to be little general association between nativity and Catholicism, on the one hand, and social status, on the other, although in general the Catholic European immigrants and their descendants occupy the broad range of working-class and lower middle class America. Political power is theirs, but the pyramids of economic power remain in the hands of those who came before them or who climbed the ladder faster.

Some general discussion of the behavior of the racial and ethnic variables in the analysis is appropriate here. Nathan Glazer and Daniel Moynihan propose, in their work on the population groups of New York City, that the division of American society into groups defined by country of origin is in process of breaking down. The result is not to form one homogeneous American society but some four subsocieties (see Fig. 10–14), each an amalgam of race, national origin, religion, and class.

The deepest cleavage is along racial lines, into black and white, black being a color just a little darker than pinkish white and leading to

TABLE 10–10

Correlations among Location Quotients for Ethnic Groups, and Variables Showing Religious Affiliation

	Polish	*German*	*Italian*	*Russian*	*Irish*	*Czech*	*British*	*Swedish*	*Cana-dian*	*Foreign Stock*	*Negro*	*Other Non-white*	*Native White*	*Percent-age of Catholics*	*Percent-age of Pro-testants*	*Percent-age of Jews*
Polish	1.000															
German	.060	1.000														
Italian	.120	.095	1.000													
Russian	.107	.075	–.035	1.000												
Irish	–.027	.148	.046	–.002	1.000											
Czech	.171	.025	.053	–.042	–.011	1.000										
British	–.177	.261*	–.059	.084	.265	–.048	1.000									
Swedish	–.116	.301	–.020	.136	.208	–.061	.405	1.000								
Canadian	–.186	.192	–.084	.074	.123	–.075	.500	.326	1.000							
Foreign stock	.465	.347	.315	.319	.213	.246	.122	.197	.011	1.000						
Negro	–.230	–.398	–.181	–.127	–.165	–.153	–.414	–.314	–.336	–.537	1.000					
Other nonwhite	–.103	–.025	.070	–.004	–.049	–.048	–.031	–.022	.002	–.028	.028	1.000				
Native white	–.023	.243	.014	–.051	.017	.020	.371	.201	.364	–.024	–.796	–.030	1.000			
Percentage of Catholics	.382	.289	.319	–.075	.281	.256	.172	.142	.064	.671	–.561	–.066	.185	1.000		
Percentage of Protestants	–.006	.258	–.003	–.073	–.109	.046	.295	.187	.325	–.087	–.646	–.013	.812	–.018	1.000	
Percentage of Jews	.046	.084	–.081	.623	–.023	–.064	.137	.175	.145	.391	–.117	–.013	–.112	–.069	–.258	1.000

Source: Northeastern Illinois Metropolitan Planning Commission, *Suburban Factbook* (Chicago, 1964).
*Correlation coefficients significant at the .05 level are underlined. Many of the coefficients for the ethnic groups are rather low because data was not compiled for the smaller suburbs. Means were substituted for missing data, and the level of the correlation was somewhat reduced.

the subjective classification of a person as nonwhite, with all its implications in contemporary America. Within white society, the various ethnic minorities are polarizing into three groups. The *Protestant* group contains the original settlers of America as well as many groups which are neither white (the Chinese, the second and subsequent generations of whom are among the most educated of Americans), nor Protestant (agnostics, atheists, or the apathetic who meet some of the other criteria for membership of the group).[88] The *Jewish* group is perhaps more clearly distinguished: even nonreligious persons with Jewish parents feel themselves to be Jews, and the cohesiveness of the group has in the past been maintained by anti-Semitic discrimination and by the comparative rarity of marriage outside the group. Within the *Catholic* group, there is a strong identification with the religious faith, and the Church has a strong influence over group mores through the parochial school system and its teaching on matters such as birth control, which the other faiths leave to individual conscience.

Do people who pray together stay together? From a matrix of correlation coefficients amongst a set of variables measuring the degree of concentration of the various racial, ethnic, and religious groups (Table 10–10), the primary residential associations between the groups which Glazer and Moynihan suggest American society is tending towards and the component ethnic groups have been extracted (Fig. 10–15).[89] The figure does in fact bear out, in spatial terms in the Chicago metropolis, Glazer and Moynihan's suppositions (based on New York). Poles, Italians, Irish, and Czechs tend to be concentrated in areas which also show high Catholic percentages; Swedes, Britons, and Canadians, in neighborhoods with high percentages of Protestants;

FIGURE 10–15. Primary residential associations of population groups in the Chicago SMSA.

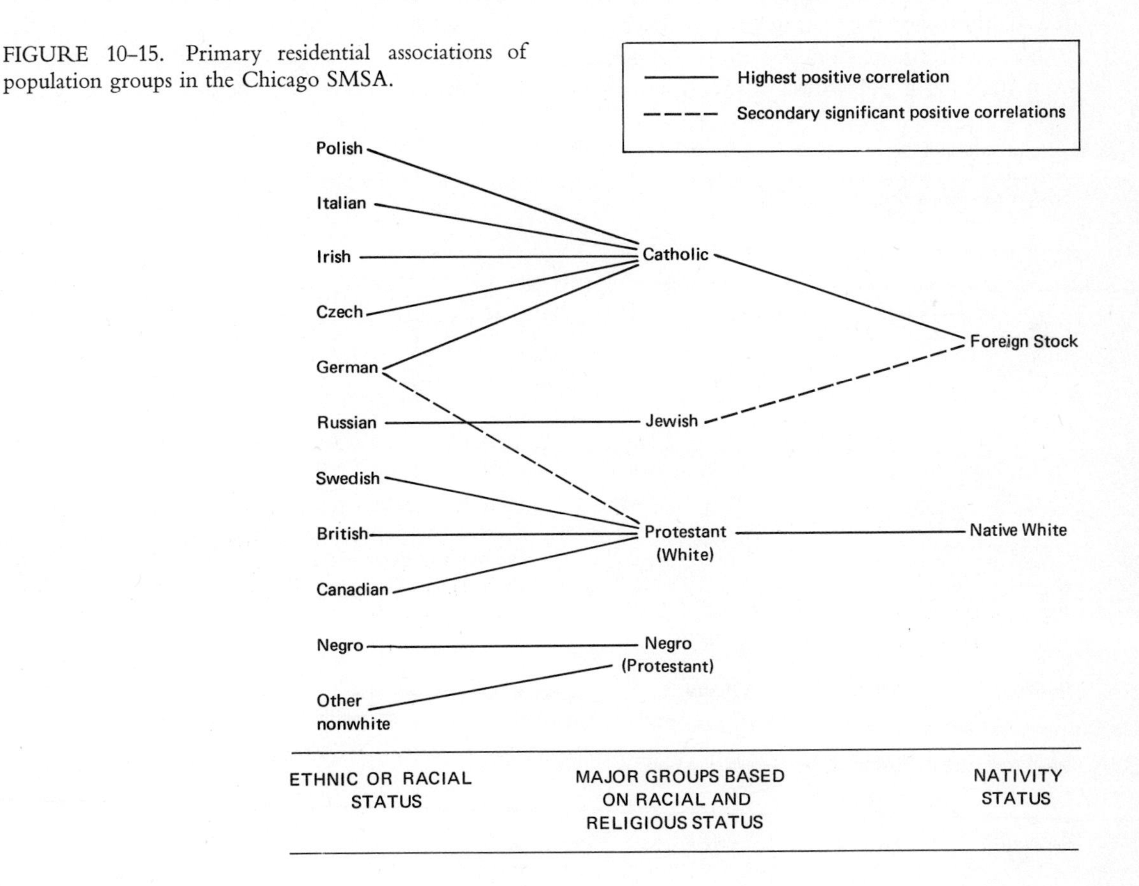

Russians, in neighborhoods with high percentage of Jews. National origin is a good guide to religious status except among the Germans, a group which has significant proportions of both Catholics and Protestants, reflecting the mixed religious character of Germany itself.

A second figure (10–16) shows that the pattern of group residential association is not quite as simple as Fig. 10–15 suggests. The Irish and German are members of the basic pair British-Canadian, rather than the Polish-Czech set. The Russian group forms a poorly associated member of the British-Canadian set. The Negro population stands completely on its own, having no positive correlation with any of the other groups, excepting other nonwhite groups—which, however, are more closely associated with the Italian group. The high degree of segregation of the Negro population is further emphasized by extraction of the negative correlation sets from the correlation matrix of Fig. 10–16, which shows that all the other population groups (except the "other nonwhite group") are most disassociated from the Negro population. This structuring of the associations of the population groups makes it easier to comprehend the emergence of two major "ethnic" factors (a Race and Resources factor loading negatively on the set of Negro variables and positively on the British and Native-white location quotients, and an Immigrant and Catholic factor loading positively on Polish, Czech, and Italian location quotients), and three minor ethnic factors (described in the ensuing paragraphs).

Factor V: Size

Our fifth factor, size, is the one that emerged as the most important in Berry and Tennant's analysis.[90] This dimension is of lesser importance in terms of its contribution to the total variance of the data matrix in this study, accounting for only 7.5 per cent (see Table 10–11), in contrast to 23.5 per cent in the previous study (Table 10–3), largely because fewer aggregates of variables were included in the present analysis, but also because size could be regarded as a significant attribute of politically defined suburban and

Positive Correlation Sets
(using basic pairs and highest positive correlation method)

Irish
Native white
British
Canadian
Swedish
Russian
German
Polish
Italian
Czech
Other nonwhite

Negro

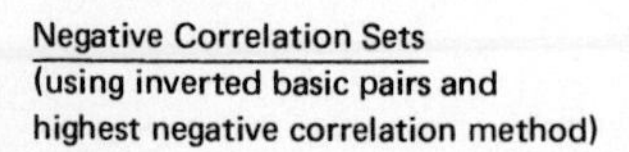

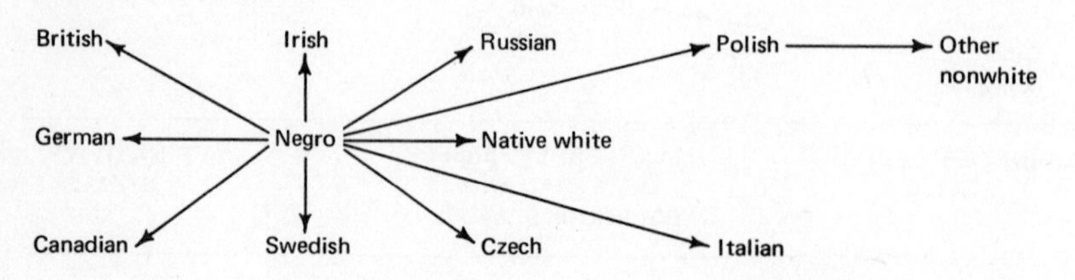

FIGURE 10–16. Associations among ethnic groups. *Source:* The positive correlation sets are outlined using the method described in Peter Haggett, *Locational Analysis in Human Geography* (New York: St. Martin's Press, Inc., 1966), p. 283.

TABLE 10-11

The Ten Factors and Their Respective Contributions to the Total Variance of Data in the Present Study of Chicago

	Factor	*Sums of Squares Accounted for (%)*
I	Socio-economic Status	17.8
II	Stage of the Life Cycle	14.2
III	Race and Resources	13.1
IV	Immigrant and Catholic Status	10.8
V	Population Size and Density	7.5
VI	Jewish and Russian Population	3.8
VII	Housing Built in 1940's, Workers Commute by Car	3.0
VIII	Irish and Swedish Population	2.6
IX	Mobility	2.4
X	Other Nonwhite Population, and Italians	2.1
		77.3

Source: Primary data.

satellite municipalities but could not be so regarded in respect to the set of areal units defined for statistical purposes in the central city (the community areas). Density is strongly associated with size as in the previous study, with respect to the suburbs, and with respect to the community areas of the city, as well, for technical reasons. But the range of sizes of the community areas is not great, since Burgess was attempting to define a set of communities in the behavioral sense: the concept of "community" set minimum and maximum limits on the size of the area.[91] Given a broad equality in the extent of the community areas, it follows that the denser community areas also have the largest populations. An accounting relationship is at work.

The populations shown in previous maps, in a sense, map this factor. Thus, no separate map of Factor V is presented here, and discussion of the distribution of the population within the urban region is postponed until later.

Factor VI: The Jewish Population

The third subpopulation factor (the others were Factors III and IV) identifies the relative spatial concentration of Chicago's Jewry. Communities which scored low on this dimension have disproportionate concentrations of Jews (Variable 26; loading, —.793), of whom a large proportion are of Russian origin (Variable 14; loading, —.837). High-scoring areas contain virtually no Jews.

The principal areas of Jewish residence within the city are found some eight or so miles north and south of the Loop, along or near the Lake Shore (Fig. 10–17). Rogers Park, West Ridge, Lincoln Square, North Park, and Albany Park, on the North Side, have scores of less than —1.15; Lakeview has a score of —.92; and West Town, of —.70. South Shore, Burnside, Calumet Heights, and South Deering, on the South Side, have scores of less than —1.15 (higher than the North Side communities); and Hyde Park had a score of —1.06. In the suburbs, the concentration in the northern part of the city continues into Lincolnwood, Skokie, Morton Grove, Glencoe, Highland Park, and Highwood. The low-scoring communities of Jewish concentration range widely in social status, from Burnside at the lower end of the scale to Glencoe and Highland Park at the other. This wide range explains in part why the Jewish minority group does not load on the Socio-economic Status factor. The other reason is that they are too small and concentrated a group to be equated with any one bracket of the social ladder.

Most of the rest of the metropolitan communities have few Jewish or Russian inhabitants. Many of the suburbs in the western sector score positively on this dimension, especially Cicero, Berwyn, and River Forest (suburbs which score high on Factor IV and contain notable concentrations of first-, second-, and third-generation Slavic immigrants, probably antipathetic to the presence of Jews in their communities).

In 1950 and earlier, a map of the Jewish population would have looked very different. The existing concentrations of the group would have been present, but there would have also been a concentration on the West Side, particularly in North Lawndale, the original ghetto, and the Near West Side, the area of second-generation settlement. A process of racial turnover took place between 1950 and 1960 in North Lawndale,

FIGURE 10–17. Factor VI: Jewish and Russian population in metropolitan Chicago, 1960. *Source:* See caption for Fig. 10–3.

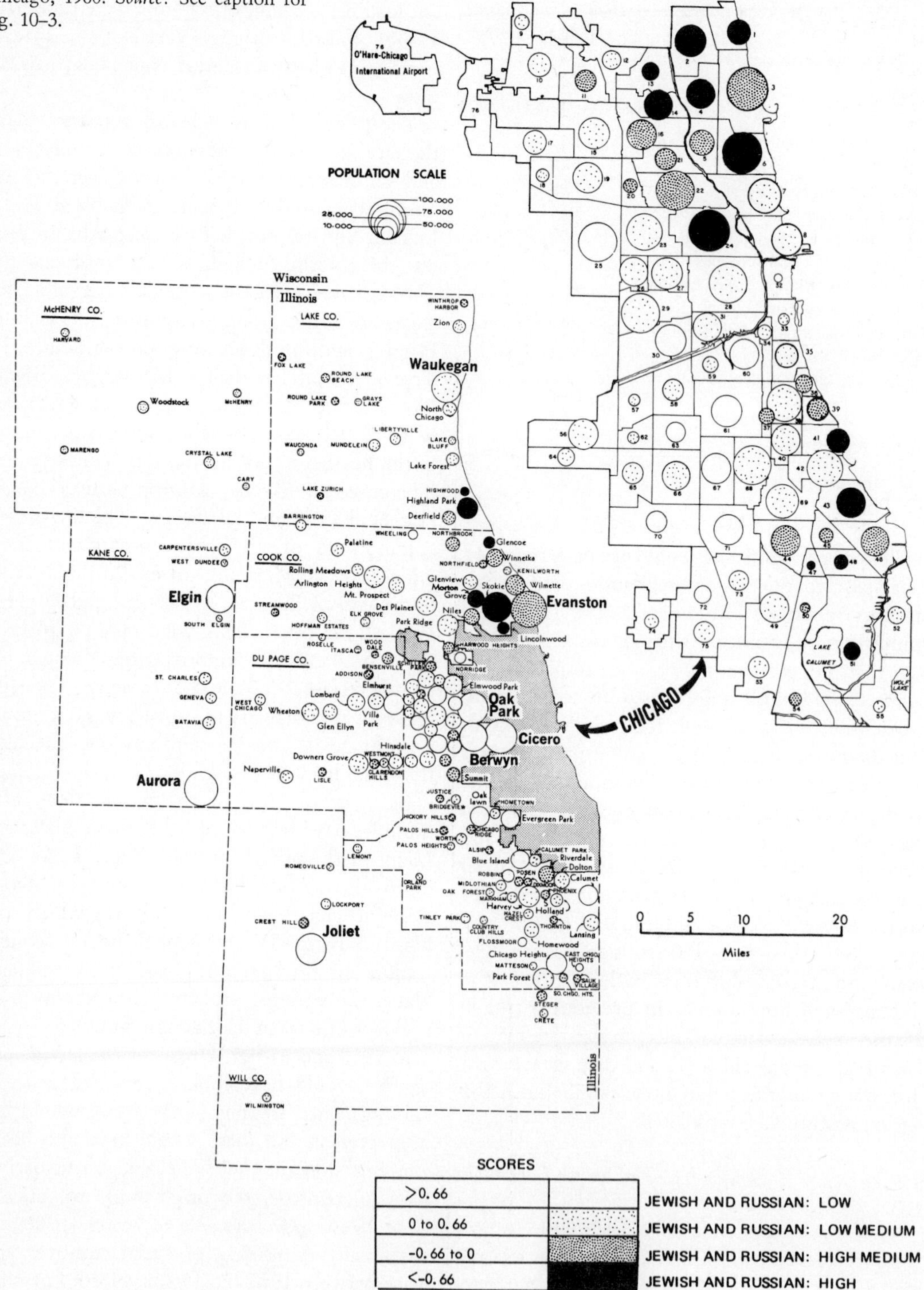

however, and the area's population is now almost completely Negro. The same process of racial transition is now taking place in South Shore.

Factor VII: Housing Built in the 1940's

From the seventh factor we learn that people in communities built in the 1940's commute by car (Variable 46; loading, —.600 and Variable 54; loading, —.508) and not by bus (Variable 55; loading, .400). The 1940's were an unusual decade in the housing market: there was little new construction during the war, and FHA and VA loans were instituted later. As a result, the pattern of growth was probably distorted (a point we shall come back to later on). The modes of commuting within the metropolis are influenced by spatial considerations not included in this study, and thus do not fit happily into our analysis.[92] Factor VII may represent a longitudinal factor which is obtruding in the cross-sectional analysis, but for the purposes of the present study it must be regarded as a special and hardly interpretable dimension of no theoretical significance.

Factor VIII: The Irish and Swedish Population

The eighth factor to be extracted is the fourth of the minority group dimensions. Communities with particularly low scores on this factor contain concentrations of first-, second-, and probably later-generation Irish immigrants (Variable 15; loading, —.787) who, at the metropolitan level, are associated with concentrations of persons of Swedish origin (Variable 17; loading, —.430). Figure 10–18 shows these communities (clustered in the southwest part of the city, in Austin and Oak Park; and along the Lake Shore, in Uptown, Lakeview, and Lincoln Square). Communities containing few Irish or Swedes are the satellite cities, including Chicago Heights, and the strongly Czech and Polish wedge from the Lower West Side out to Berwyn).[93]

However, neither the factor itself nor the geographic association between the Irish and Swedes is, to use Sweetser's term, "stable"[94] if the study area is altered. The factor emerges only at the metropolitan level. At the city level, the Irish and Swedish location quotients both load positively on the Socio-economic Status factor, and in the suburbs they both load on a factor distinguishing certain European ethnic groups from the rest of the population.

Factor IX: Mobility

Factor IX is the first factor that is composed of the principal loading of one variable only, i.e., mobility. There are no intermediate loadings greater than + or —.400 to aid us in identifying the correlates of mobility. But the map (Fig. 10–19) offers us better clues. The communities in which higher than average numbers of families have changed homes since 1955 are in two broad groups: the high-rise, apartment areas along the lake Shore which clustered at the upper end of the social status scale (high status) and at the lower end of the family status scale (small families, old or young), and a narrow ring of suburbs about twelve miles from the Loop, the zone of the fastest population growth (communities on the rapidly rising limb of an S curve) interrupted only by a few radii of older growth—the North Shore sector and part of the Oak Park sector.

This pattern results from the movement of two groups within the metropolitan area: young families in the process of formation or expansion, moving into their new suburban homes;[96] and single persons and couples (young and old) without children moving into and out of the Lake Shore apartment areas.[97] This pattern of movement is closely associated with Stage in the Life Cycle, a factor that was earlier proposed as responsible for differentiating the metropolitan space by type of family, given the existence of differentially attractive housing types in the various parts of the city. That the variable, mobility, does not load on the factor Stage in the Life Cycle, is due to the nonlinearity of the association between mobility and family status as well as to other factors which influence the pattern of movement.

The map also suggests that mobility may be linked to social status: within the city, people in

FIGURE 10–18. Factor VIII: Irish and Swedish population in metropolitan Chicago, 1960. *Source:* See caption for Fig. 10–3.

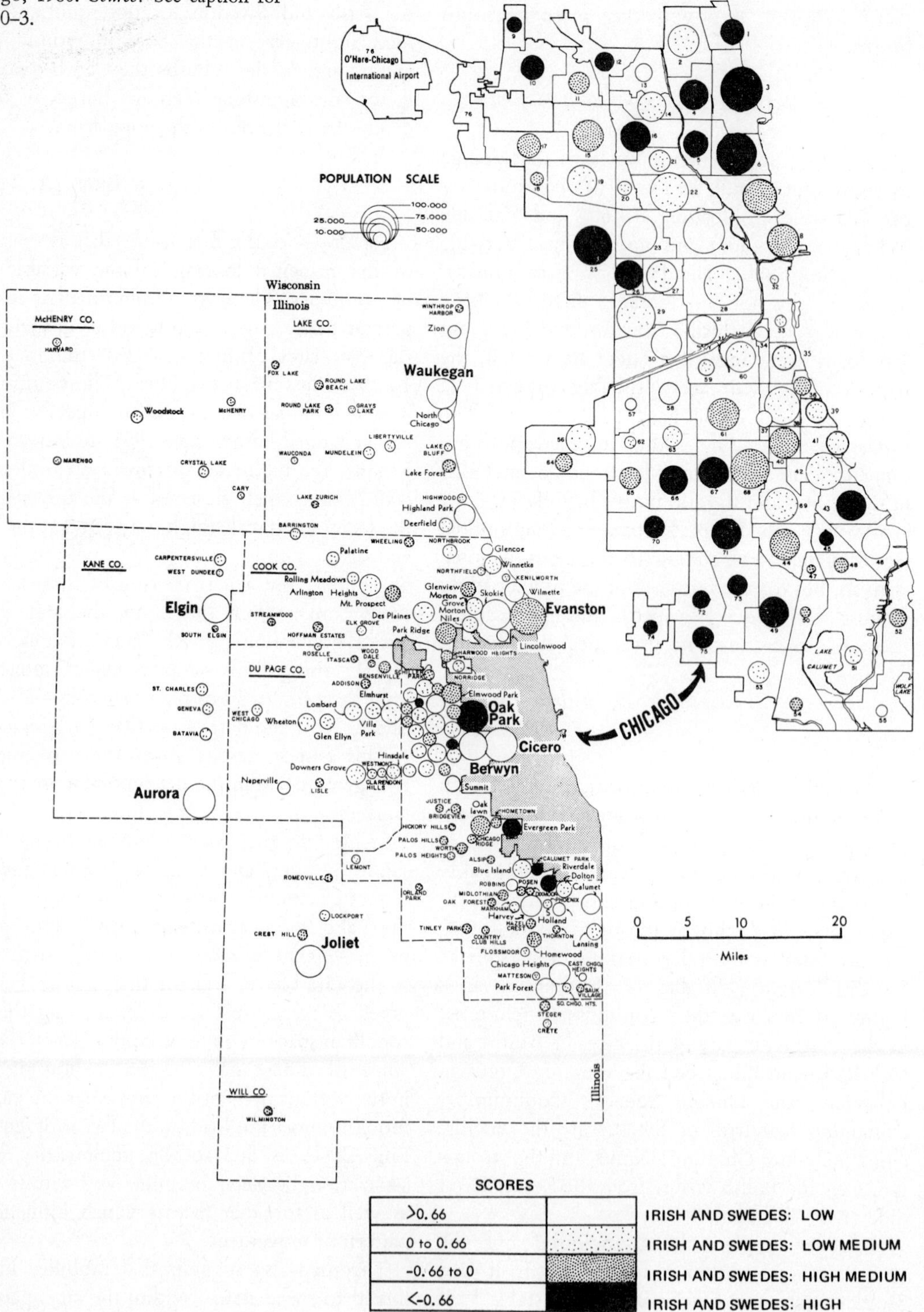

FIGURE 10–19. Factor IX: Mobility in metropolitan Chicago, 1960. *Source:* See caption for Fig. 10–3.

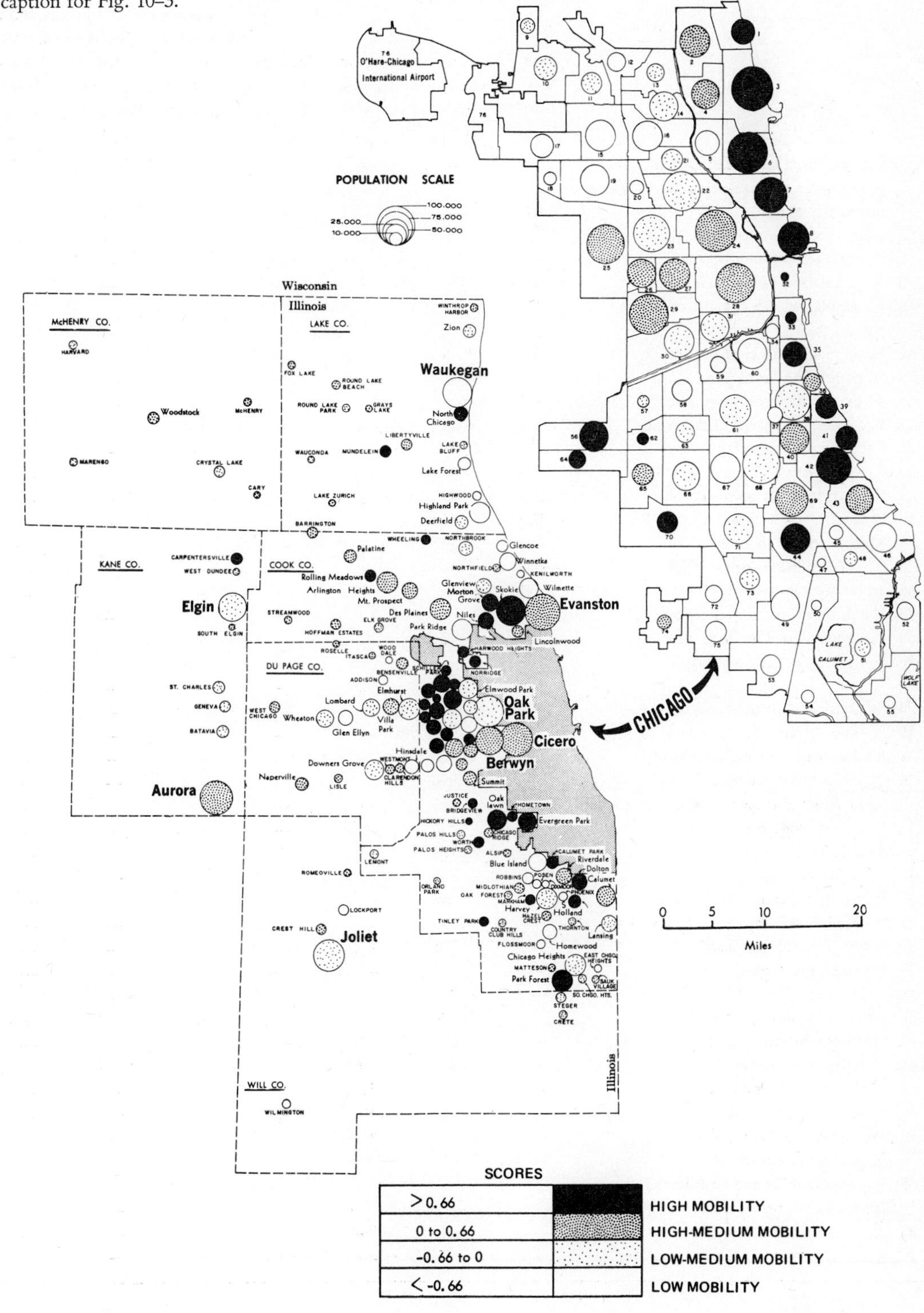

TABLE 10–12

Factor Structure: City of Chicago (57 Variables)

Variable	Race and Resources	Socio-economic Status	Stage in the Life Cycle	Population Size and Density	Other Nonwhite Population; Workers Commute by Foot	Jewish and Russian Population	Housing Built before 1940; Workers Commute by Rail
Sums of Squares	16.496	13.644	6.872	5.099	2.937	2.266	1.957
52. Foreign stock location quotient*	.949	—	—	—	—	—	—
7. % population native-born of foreign or mixed parentage	.942	—	—	—	—	—	—
53. Negro location quotient*	−.927	—	—	—	—	—	—
8. % population foreign-born	.917	—	—	—	—	—	—
40. % population (white) Catholic	.908	—	—	—	—	—	—
6. % population native-born of native parentage	−.808	—	—	—	—	—	—
41. % population (white) Protestant	.883	—	—	—	—	—	—
5. % population nonwhite	−.873	—	—	—	—	—	—
54. Native white location quotient*	.855	—	—	—	—	—	—
17. % workers in service occupations	−.772	—	—	—	—	—	—
43. Polish location quotient*	.768	—	—	—	—	—	—
33. % unemployed workers	−.709	−.543	—	—	—	—	—
44. German location quotient*	.696	.415	—	—	—	—	—
10. % families with incomes under $3,000	−.679	−.533	—	—	—	—	—
9. Median annual income	.651	.630	—	—	—	—	—
20. % families moved since 1955	−.648	—	—	—	—	—	—
45. Italian location quotient*	.647	—	—	—	—	—	—
48. Czech location quotient*	.644	—	—	—	—	—	—
32. % overcrowded housing units	−.636	−.626	—	—	—	—	—
26. % owner-occupied housing	.605	—	−.555	—	−.454	—	—
31. % sound housing units	.570	—	−.454	—	—	—	—
24. % housing units in 2-unit structures	.524	−.410	—	—	−.410	—	—
19. % with 4 years of high school or more	—	.966	—	—	—	—	—
18. Median school years completed	—	.954	—	—	—	—	—
12. % white-collar workers	—	.896	—	—	—	—	—
13. % managerial and professional employees	—	.853	—	—	—	—	—
14. % clerical and sales workers	—	.794	—	—	—	—	—
30. Median rent	—	.793	—	—	—	—	—
51. Canadian location quotient*	—	.765	—	—	—	—	—
38. % workers commuting by bus	—	−.735	—	—	—	—	—
11. % families with incomes over $10,000	—	.733	—	—	—	—	—
50. British location quotient*	—	.730	—	—	—	—	—
21. Median home value	—	.725	—	—	—	—	—
16. % laborers	—	−.707					
49. Swedish location quotient*	—	.736	—	—	—	—	−.431
15. % craftsmen and operatives	—	−.667	—	—	—	—	—
47. Irish location quotient*	—	.604	−.400	—	—	−.440	—
4. Median age of population	—	.549	.516	—	—	—	—
29. % housing stock built after 1950	—	.502	−.484	−.438	—	—	—
23. Population per household	—	—	−.984	—	—	—	—
2. % population under 18	—	—	−.848	—	—	—	—
35. % of women 14 and over in the labor force	—	—	.760	—	—	—	—
36. % workers commuting by car	—	—	−.746	—	—	—	—
22. % housing units in 1-unit structures	—	—	−.668	−.411	—	—	—

Variable Sums of Squares	Race and Resources	Socio-economic Status	Stage in the Life Cycle	Population Size and Density	Other Nonwhite Population; Workers Commute by Foot	Jewish and Russian Population	Housing Built before 1940; Workers Commute by Rail
28. % housing stock built 1940–1949	—	—	−.642	—	—	—	—
3. % population over 65	—	—	.634	—	—	—	—
25. % housing units in 3- or more-unit structures	—	—	—	.455	—	—	—
1. Population	—	—	—	.962	—	—	—
34. Total unemployment	—	—	—	.953	—	—	—
56. % of total population	—	—	—	.925	—	—	—
57. Population density	—	—	—	.823			
55. Other nonwhite location quotient*	—	—	—	—	.686	—	—
39. % workers commuting on foot	—	—	.510	—	.605	—	—
46. Russian location quotient*	—	.406	—	—	—	.787	—
42. % Jewish population	—	.440	—	—	—	.760	—
27. % housing stock built before 1940	—	—	.571	—	—	—	−.580
37. % workers commuting by rail	−.421	—	—	—	—	—	−.504

Source: Evelyn M. Kitagawa and Karl E. Taeuber, eds., *Local Community Factbook: Chicago Metropolitan Area, 1960* (Chicago: Chicago Community Inventory, University of Chicago, 1963).
*For calculation of the location quotient, see the footnote to the Appendix to this chapter.

the lower status areas are less mobile than people in the higher status Lake Shore areas. However, in the blue-collar ghetto (a very wide sector of the inner city) mobility tends to be greater than in the ethnic areas of the northwest and southwest. The contrast in the mobility rate may be related to the differences in the white and Negro housing markets: pressure for housing for Negroes is intense, prices for equivalent accommodations are higher, and Negro families move frequently,[98] probably in a ceaseless search for a decent home.

The mobility pattern, it is tentatively suggested here, is a complex amalgam of influences, the most important of which relate to the principal dimensions of the social area which have emerged in this study—socio-economic status, family status, and racial status.[99] A careful experimental design and program of research would, however, be needed to test these ideas.[100] What is certain is that the simple causal connection made by the classical ecologists between levels of social disorganization and levels of mobility is too narrow an explanation of the mobility pattern.

Factor X: Other Nonwhite and Italian Population

The tenth factor, the fifth minority group dimension, is, like Factor VIII (Irish and Swedish Population), a somewhat unstable dimension, probably for technical reasons. Only in the community areas of the city was it possible to separate the nonwhite group into Negroes and other nonwhites; in the data for the suburbs the nonwhite group is treated as a whole and regarded as a surrogate for the Negro population. Thus, the emergence of an Other Nonwhite and Italian factor at the metropolitan level is somewhat specious (see Table 10–4 for the loadings of these two variables on this tenth factor). However, the dimension *Other Nonwhite* does persist at the city level (see Table 10–12). The Italian location quotient goes to make up part of a collapsed Race and Resources–Immigrant and Catholic factor in the city analysis. There is some small positive association between the distribution of other nonwhites (mainly Orien-

TABLE 10–13

Factor Structure: Chicago Suburbs (56 Variables)

Variable	*Socio-economic Status*	*Stage in the Life Cycle*	*Immigrant and Catholic Status*	*Race and Resources*	*Population Size and Density*	*Poles vs. Anglo-Saxons*	*European Ethnic Groups*	*Housing Built in 1940's; Workers Commute by Car*	*Jewish and Russian Population*	*Overcrowded Housing; Workers Commute by Rail*
Sums of Squares	10.790	8.112	4.973	4.056	4.006	2.329	1.688	1.582	1.394	1.257
13. % professional and managerial employees	.944	—	—	—	—	—	—	—	—	—
12. % white-collar workers	.915	—	—	—	—	—	—	—	—	
19. % with 4 years of high school or more	.896	—	—	—	—	—	—	—	—	—
21. Median home value	.891	—	—	—	—	—	—	—	—	—
9. Median annual income	.883	—	—	—	—	—	—	—	—	—
18. Median school years completed	.881	—	—	—	—	—	—	—	—	—
11. % families with incomes over $10,000	.881	—	—	—	—	—	—	—	—	—
15. % craftsmen and operatives	−.850	—	—	—	—	—	—	—	—	—
16. % laborers	−.844	—	—	—	—	—	—	—	—	—
17. % workers in service occupations	−.798	—	—	—	—	—	—	—	—	—
33. % unemployed workers	−.602	—	—	—	—	—	—	—	—	—
14. % clerical and sales workers	.588	—	—	.446	—	—	—	—	—	—
31. % sound housing units	.533	—	—	—	—	—	—	—	—	—
30. Median rent	.451	—	—	—	—	—	—	—	—	—
3. % population over 65	—	.939	—	—	—	—	—	—	—	—
23. Population per household	—	−.885	—	—	—	—	—	—	—	—
27. % housing stock built before 1940	—	.875	—	—	—	—	—	—	—	—
2. % population under 18	—	−.836	—	—	—	—	—	—	—	—
29. % housing stock built after 1950	—	−.819	—	—	—	—	—	—	—	—
4. Median age of population	.410	.746	—	—	—	—	—	—	—	—
25. % housing units in 3- or more-unit structures	—	.680	—	—	.428	—	—	—	—	—
26. % owner-occupied housing	—	−.661	—	—	—	—	—	—	—	—
24. % housing units in 2-unit structures	—	.657	—	—	—	—	—	—	—	—
10. % families with incomes under $3,000	−.525	.619	—	—	—	—	—	—	—	—
22. % housing units in 1-unit structures	—	−.610	—	—	−.450	—	—	—	—	—

35. % women 14 or over in the labor force	—	.554	—	—	—	—	—	—	—	—
52. Foreign stock location quotient*	—	—	.853	—	—	—	—	—	—	—
6. % population native-born of native parentage	—	—	−.835	—	—	—	—	—	—	—
7. % population native-born of foreign or mixed parentage	—	—	.829	—	—	—	—	—	—	—
8. % population foreign-born	—	—	.798	—	—	—	—	—	—	—
40. % population Catholic	—	—	.652	—	—	—	—	—	—	—
42. % population Jewish	—	—	.442	—	—	—	—	—	.441	—
54. Native white location quotient*	—	—	—	−.847	—	—	—	—	—	—
53. Negro location quotient*	—	—	—	.791	—	—	—	—	—	—
5. % population nonwhite	—	—	—	.721	—	—	—	—	—	—
41. % population (white) Protestant	—	—	—	−.695	—	—	—	—	—	—
34. Total unemployment	—	—	—	—	.856	—	—	—	—	—
56. % of total population	—	—	—	—	.846	—	—	—	—	—
1. Population	—	—	—	—	.817	—	—	—	—	—
57. Population density	—	—	—	—	.647	—	—	—	—	—
50. British location quotient*	—	—	—	—	—	−.598	—	—	—	—
43. Polish location quotient*	—	—	—	—	—	.591	—	—	—	—
51. Canadian location quotient*	—	—	—	—	—	−.565	—	—	—	—
44. German location quotient*	—	—	—	—	—	—	.640	—	—	—
47. Irish location quotient*	—	—	—	—	—	—	.556	—	—	—
20. % families moved since 1955	—	—	—	—	—	—	−.428	—	—	—
38. % workers commuting by bus	—	—	—	—	—	—	.378	—	—	—
45. Italian location quotient*	—	—	—	—	—	—	.361	—	—	—
49. Swedish location quotient*	—	—	—	—	—	—	.357	—	—	—
28. % housing stock built 1940–1949	—	—	—	—	—	—	—	.633	—	—
36. % workers commuting by car	—	—	—	—	—	—	—	.495	—	—
39. % workers commuting by foot	—	—	—	—	—	—	—	−.490	—	—
46. Russian location quotient*	—	—	—	—	—	—	—	—	.624	—
48. Czech location quotient*	—	—	—	—	—	—	—	—	−.553	—
32. % overcrowded housing	—	—	—	—	—	—	—	—	—	.584
37. % workers commuting by rail	—	—	—	—	—	—	—	—	—	−.473

Source: Northeastern Illinois Metropolitan Planning Commission, *Suburban Factbook* (Chicago, 1964).
*For the calculation of the location quotient, see the footnote to the Appendix to this chapter.

tals) and Italians within the city, but not enough to warrant making any definitive statement of affinity. For these reasons a map is not reproduced here.

Variation of the Factor Structures with Differences in Study Area: The City and the Suburbs

In order to gain a better understanding of the influence of the study area chosen on the factorial ecology of a city, two further factor analyses were performed, using the same variables and same units of observation but with different study areas: (1) the City of Chicago; and (2) the rest of the metropolitan area, i.e., the suburbs.

A detailed discussion of the factor structures (Tables 10–12 and 10–13) is not attempted here. The interpretation of the factors and their labeling proceeded along lines similar to those already described, and the process can be repeated by the interested reader. It is the similarities and differences among the factor structures in the three study areas—metropolis, city, and suburbs—that we shall discuss.

Results and discussion. The major factors that emerged in the metropolitan, city, and suburban analyses are laid out in Table 10–14 in a form that aids comparison. Some five factors are common to all three analyses (Table 10–15). The only exception among the principal factors is Immigrant and Catholic Status. In the city, this factor combines with Race and Resources to form one bipolar dimension, the immigrants and Catholics being at one end of the scale, the Negroes at the other. At the metropolitan level there are two sets of Protestant, native-American communities (the largely native-white suburbs and the Negro ghetto), and these are at the opposite end of a Nativity and Religion dimension from communities which have concentrations of Catholics and Americans of foreign stock. Two factors are required to describe the great differences between such communities. In the central city, where the white communities tend to be Catholic and to contain concentrations of Americans of foreign stock, and where there are few native, white, Protestant areas of any magnitude, only one dimension is needed to describe the spatial variation of the racial, ethnic, native, and religious characteristics of the city's population (see the map of the City of Chicago in Fig. 10–13).

The common factors vary in their relative importance. Because of the collapse of two factors into one, and because the Negro group forms a much larger segment of the city's population, the Race and Resources factor accounts for more of the total variance in the city analysis than in the metropolitan or the suburban analyses. Socio-economic Status and Stage in the Life Cycle maintain the same position, relative to each other, in all three analyses. Family Status, in particular, explains a fairly constant proportion of the total variance, practically the same set of variables loading most highly on this dimension. The factor of Size and Density emerges in all three analyses for reasons already outlined, as does the Jewish and Russian factor. The longitudinal and other minor ethnic factors are more susceptible to variation as the area and population studied are changed, because the range of variation of each of the relevant sets of variable sets is so different in the suburbs. The age range in the two sets of communities is very different, for example. It may also be true that the residential association of ethnic groups within the city may break down as future generations move to the suburbs. A more detailed discussion and analysis of some of these ideas should, however, await further study.

An Analysis Based upon Census Tract Observations

The areas used as units of observation in the foregoing analyses are less than fully satisfactory. Certain community areas, such as those along the Lake Shore and those closest to the Loop, are very heterogeneous. Certain intermediate factor scores obtained for these communities may merely mean that they contain populations (living in different subareas) which are at opposite ends of the spectra. Another investigation, using the widely available data about the census tract, was therefore indicated, since the ideal solution—data about individual households, which could

TABLE 10–14

Community Area and Municipality Analysis: Summary

Metropolis		City		Suburbs	
Factor	*% Variance*	*Factor*	*% Variance*	*Factor*	*% Variance*
I Socio-economic status	17.8	Race and resources	28.9	Socio-economic status	18.9
II Stage in the life cycle	14.2	Socio-economic status	24.0	Stage in the life cycle	14.3
III Race and resources	13.1	Stage in the life cycle	12.0	Immigrant and Catholic status	8.7
IV Immigrant and Catholic status	10.8	Population size and density	9.0	Race and resources	7.1
V Population size and density	7.5	Other nonwhite population; workers commute on foot	5.1	Population size and density	7.0
VI Jewish and Russian population	3.8	Jewish and Russian population	4.0	Poles *vs.* Anglo-Saxons	4.1
VII Housing built in 1940's; workers commute by car	3.0	Housing built before 1940; workers commute by rail	3.4	European ethnic groups	3.0
VIII Irish and Swedish population	2.6			Housing built in 1940's; workers commute by car	2.8
IX Mobility	2.4			Jewish and Russian population	2.4
X Other nonwhites and Italians	2.1			Housing overcrowded; workers commute by rail	2.2
% 57 factors	77.3		86.4		70.5

Source: Tables 10–14 through 10–24 are from Philip Rees, "The Factorial Ecology of Metropolitan Chicago" (Master's thesis, University of Chicago, 1968).

TABLE 10–15

Community Area and Municipality Factor Analysis

	Consistent Sets of Factors in Order of Eigenvalues								
	I	*II*	*III*	*IV*	*V*	*VI*	. . .	*IX*	. . .
City	R + R*	SES†	LC‡	S + D§		J + R‖			
Metropolis	SES†	LC‡	R + R*	I + C♯	S + D§	J + R‖			
Suburbs	SES†	LC‡	I + C♯	R + R*	S + D§			J + R‖	

Source: See note to Table 10–14.
*Race and resources. †Socio-economic status. ‡Stage in the life cycle. §Size and density.
‖Jewish and Russian. ♯Immigrant and Catholic.

be aggregated as flexibly as desired—is available only rarely,[101] and not through current censuses.

Because of the labor involved in dealing with adequate samples of the population of the some 1,324 census tracts in the Chicago metropolitan area, the authors decided to use only some of the 57 variables employed in the analyses of community areas and municipalities. Schmid and Tagashira's findings were adopted,[102] and some 12 variables that loaded most highly on one of the three social area factors of the Community Area and Municipality analysis (Socio-economic Status, Stage in the Life Cycle, and Race and Resources) were selected for use in the census tract study. The set of 12 variables included two having to do with education; two having to do with occupation; three having to do with income; two, with age; one, with family size;

one, with race; one, with housing age; and one, with housing quality (see Table 10–16).

Results. The rotated factor matrix (three-factor solution) for the entire metropolitan area is set out in Table 10–17 for all the 1,324 census tracts employed and in Table 10–18 for only those 1,243 tracts with complete data vectors.[103] There is little difference in the solutions except that Variable 29, Percentage of Families with Incomes under $3,000, loads on the first factor in Table 10–17 and the third factor in Table 10–18, and that the second solution (in which tracts for which data are missing are eliminated) explains, not surprisingly, more of the total variance than the first solution (84, rather than 79 per cent).

The factors that emerge from the analysis have been labeled (as in the Community Area and Municipality Analysis) Socio-economic Status, Stage in the Life Cycle, and Race and Resources. The socio-economic variables (education, occupation, income, housing quality) load most highly on the first factor; age and family size, on the second factor; and race (Negro) on the third. However, associated with the third factor are a number of high secondary loadings of some of the socio-economic variables—unemployment, income, and housing quality (percentage substandard). Thus, the third factor identifies not merely the spatial segregation of the Negro population but also the discrimination in employment, income, and housing that is associated with such spatial segregation.

Reversing the argument, we can say that the way resources are distributed among the urban population is a function of two underlying influences: (1) a social status scale that is defined primarily by a person's educational achievement and occupation; and (2) a set of constraints that prevents members of a minority group (in this case, black Chicagoans) from achieving rewards concomitant with their social status.

In general, therefore, the results of our two analyses (based on Community Area and Municipality, on the one hand, and on Census Tracts, on the other) agree. On closer inspection, how-

TABLE 10–16

Factor Structure of Entire Chicago Metropolitan Area: 12 Variables, All 1,324 Census Tracts

Variable	*Socio-economic Status*	*Stage in the Life Cycle*	*Race and Resources*	*Communality*
Sums of Squares	4.472	2.676	2.311	
36. Median school years completed	.920*	−.011	−.048	.850
30. % white-collar workers	.846	−.220	−.203	.805
28. % families with incomes over $10,000	.771	−.096	−.484†	.837
27. Median annual income	.746	−.059	−.510	.820
47. % housing built after 1950	.697	.434	−.168	.702
29. % families with incomes under $3,000	−.646	−.167	.597	.802
49. % substandard housing‡	−.627	−.197	.488	.670
51. % unemployed workers	−.618	−.035	.566	.705
43. Population per household	.032	.928	−.045	.864
2. % population under 18	−.133	.867	−.064	.773
3. % population over 65	−.102	−.847	−.241	.786
7. % population Negro§	−.227	.172	.876	.848

Source: See note to Table 10–14.
*Principal or highest loadings of a variable on a factor.
†Secondary loadings of greater than ±.400 of a variable on a factor.
‡The complement of Variable 49, % Sound Housing Units was chosen, i.e., % Substandard = 100 minus % sound.
§% Population Negro was calculated in this analysis rather than % Population nonwhite, which was used in the Community Area and Municipality Analysis.

TABLE 10–17

Expected and Observed Factor Structure: Entire Chicago Metropolitan Area, 1,324 Census Tracts (1960)

Variable	*Socio-economic Status*		*Stage in the Life Cycle*		*Race and Resources*	
	E*	O†	E	O	E	O
36. Median school years completed	1‡	1			(2)	
30. % white-collar workers	1	1				
28. % families with incomes over $10,000	1	1				2
27. Median annual income	1	1			2	2
47. % housing built after 1950		1	1	2		
29. % families with incomes under $3,000	2§	1			1	2
(49.) % substandard housing	2	1	(3)#		1	2
51. % unemployed workers	(2)‖	1			1	2
43. Population per household			1	1		
2. % population under 18			1	1		
3. % population over 65			1	1		
(7.) % Negro population					1	1

Source: See note to Table 10–14.
*E = Expected factor structure, based on Community Area and Municipality Analysis.
†0 = Observed factor structure, based on census tracts.
‡1 = The highest loadings in the factor analyses are on this factor.
§2 = Second highest loadings, over ±.400.
‖(2) = Second highest loadings, between ±.300 and ±.399.
#(3) = Third highest loadings, between ±.300 and ±.399.

TABLE 10–18

Factor Structure: Entire Chicago Metropolitan Area, 1,324 Census Tracts (Incomplete Observations Omitted)

Variable	*Socio-economic Status*	*Stage in the Life Cycle*	*Race and Resources*	*Communality*
Sums of Squares	4.595	2.925	2.534	
36. Median school years completed	.951*	−.017	−.056	.907
30. % white-collar workers	.869	−.017	−.235	.868
28. % families with incomes over $10,000	.781	−.100	−.519	.889
27. Median annual income	.754	−.058	−.542	.866
47. % housing built after 1950	.691	.461	−.211	.736
49. % substandard housing	−.636	−.158	.508	.692
51. % unemployed workers	−.625	−.020	.603	.755
43. Population per household	.016	.946	−.064	.900
2. % population under 18	−.142	.933	.010	.891
3. % population over 65	−.085	−.880	−.197	.821
7. % Negro population	−.205	.202	.886	.869
29. % families with incomes under $3,000	−.640†	−.185	.646	.861

Source: See note to Table 10–14.
*Principal or highest loadings of a variable on a factor.
†Secondary loadings, greater than ±.400.

ever, some interesting differences emerge. Table 10–17 (containing the factor structure expected on the basis of previous analyses) reveals that the variables, Median school years, Percentage of white-collar workers, Percentage of families with incomes over $10,000, and Median income, load, as expected, most highly on the Socio-economic Status factor. Population per household, Percentage of the population under 18, and Percentage over 65 load most highly on the Stage in the Life Cycle factor; Percentage of Negroes and Percentage of families with incomes under $3,000 (see Table 10–18) load most highly on the Race and Resources dimension, all as expected. Two variables—Percentage of substandard housing and Percentage of unemployed—load most highly in the Census Tract analysis on the first rather than the third factor, as expected, but the secondary loadings are also very high on the third factor. The importance of the Race and Resources factor is thus very slightly exaggerated when community areas are the units used.

One variable only appears to behave substantially differently in the two parts of the study —that is, Percentage of housing built since 1950. Whereas in the previous analyses it was a member of a set of variables loading on the Family Status factor, with only its fourth highest loading on Race and Resources and its fifth highest loading on Socio-economic Status, in the present analysis it loads most highly on Socio-economic Status and second highest on the Family Status factor. Thus, the date at which housing was built proves to be not simply an index of housing type (the majority of housing built since 1950 in the metropolitan region being single-family, detached homes) but also of housing quality (the newer a home, the more it is worth). At the community area and municipality level, new housing in the inner city (on relatively small sites cleared of older buildings) was statistically swamped by the mass of older housing stock, whereas in the suburbs the new housing may cover whole municipalities. Housing projects in the inner city are not obscured when census tract statistics are used, however. Such new housing is not built for the young families who populate the new suburban subdivisions, but rather for the city's single person and small families of higher social status. What the two groups have in common is higher social status—hence the loading of the variable on Factor I as well as Factor II.

A comparison of the maps. Figures 10–20, 10–21, and 10–22 are maps of the various areas' scores on Factors I, II, and III, respectively.[104] The general patterns displayed in the maps closely follow those in the corresponding community area and municipality factor maps (Figs. 10–10, 10–11, and 10–12), which have already been described at some length.

The census tract maps, however, display some differences from the earlier maps. Since the mesh of the maps is finer, the North Lake Shore sector within the city is seen to be much narrower on the maps of both Factors I and II. Even so, the census tract is probably too gross to pick out the narrow strip of expensive, high-rise apartments along the North Lake Shore and the separate analogs on the South Lake Shore, Prairie Shores, Lake Meadows, East Hyde Park, and the fringe on the south shore of the lake, in which live older, wealthy residents, in smaller households than most of the city's population. The strip is only one block or one building wide in places, and the gradient of change from Gold Coast to slum is extremely rapid.

Also picked out by the finer census tract mesh is the fine pattern of racial differentiation in many community areas. On the Near West Side, for example, the Negro residential axes of Madison Street and Roosevelt Road are separated by white residential areas of Italian, Mexican, and Puerto Rican stock. Being based on the 1960 Census, the map of Race and Resources is somewhat dated at the time of writing. Figure. 10–23 is an attempt, based on a windshield survey, to update the picture of racial distribution to 1965. Since then, the Negro residential area has expanded further, into Austin from the West Side ghetto, and along the southern fingers of the main South Side ghetto into the middle class areas of southern Chicago.

Our use of the smaller census tracts also makes visible the internal differentiation within the larger suburbs and satellite towns, previously obscured. Each of the satellite towns (Waukegan, Elgin, Aurora, and Joliet) is seen to possess its

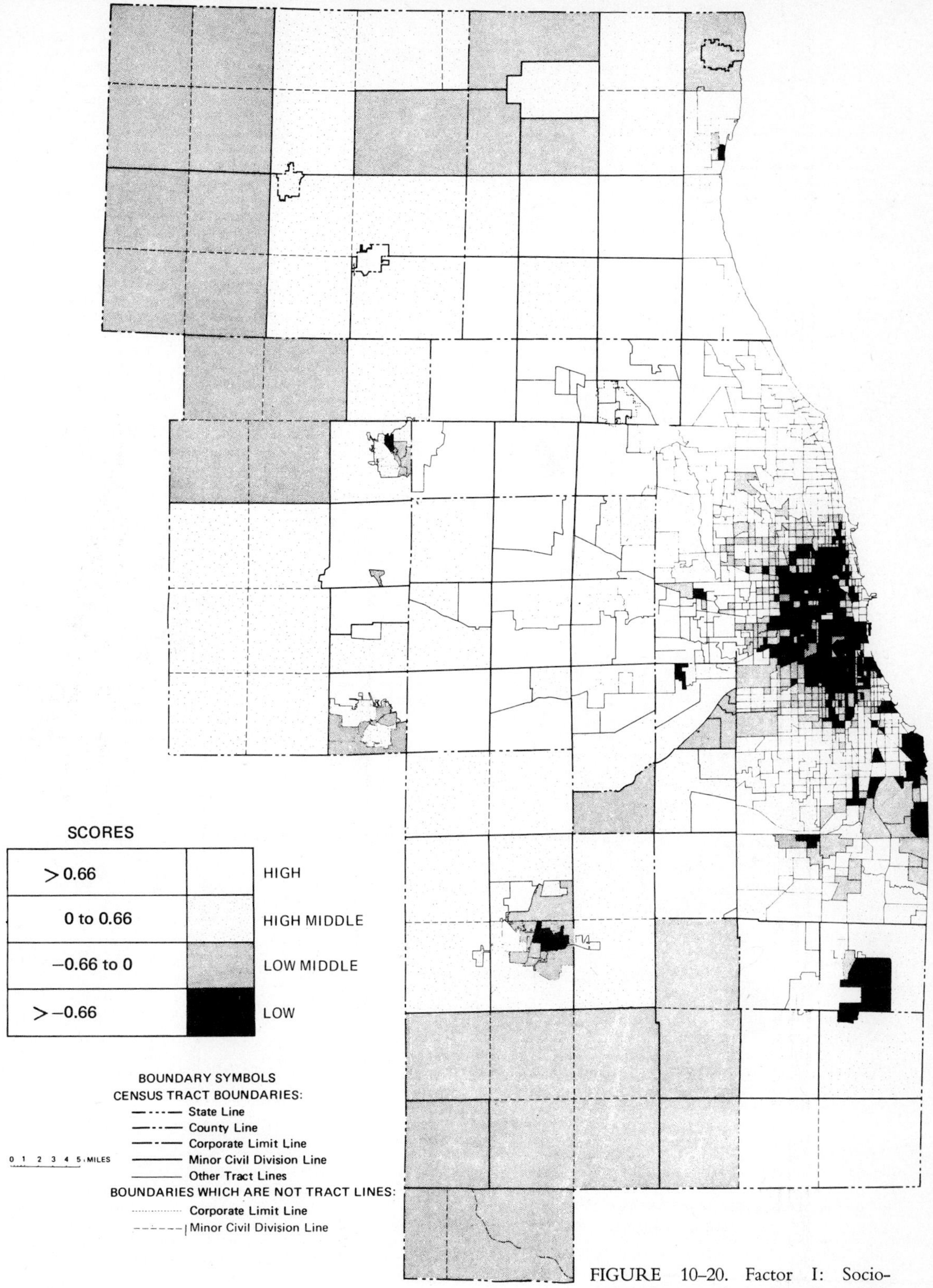

FIGURE 10–20. Factor I: Socioeconomic status in metropolitan Chicago, census tract analysis. *Source:* See caption for Fig. 10–3.

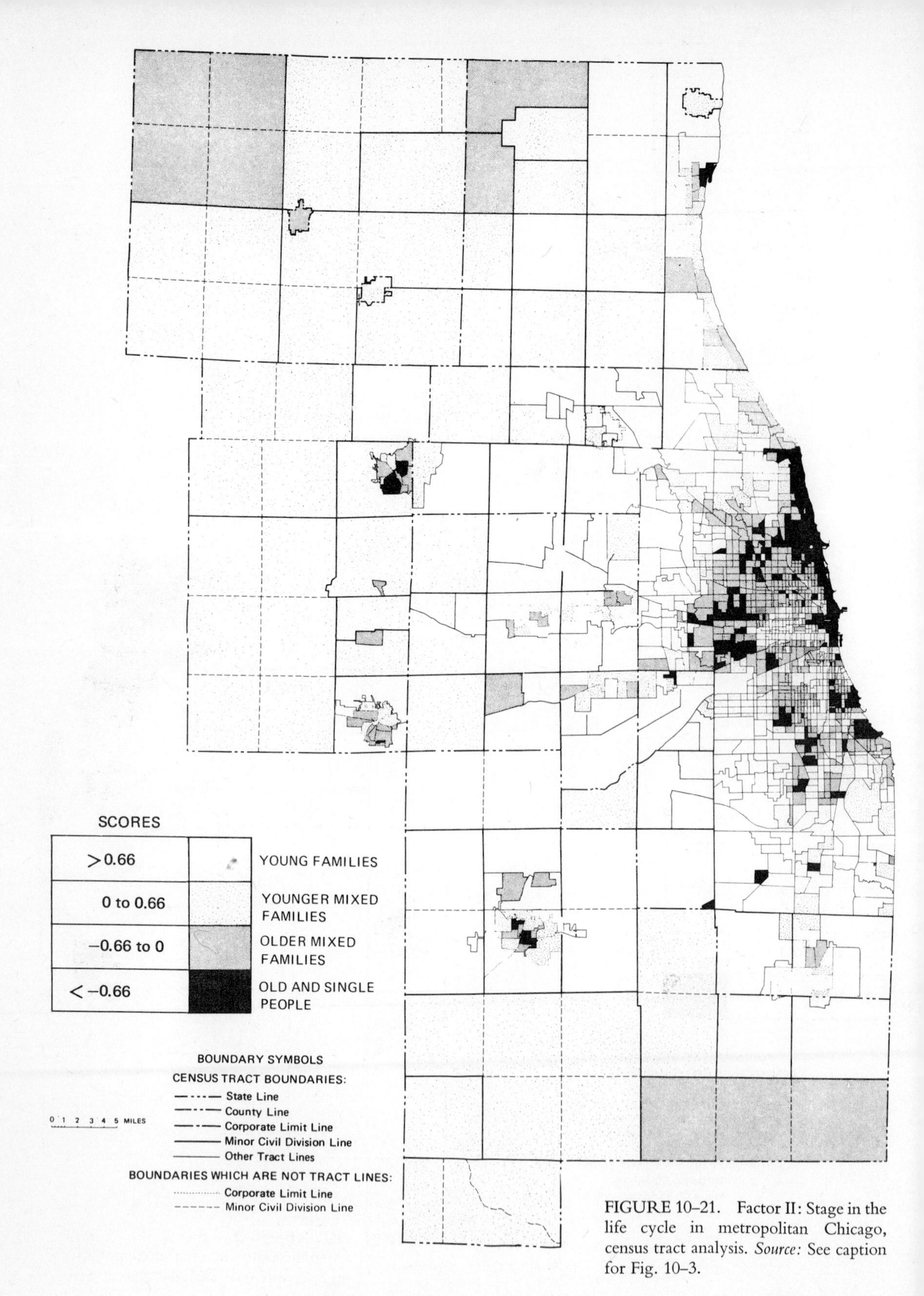

FIGURE 10–21. Factor II: Stage in the life cycle in metropolitan Chicago, census tract analysis. *Source:* See caption for Fig. 10–3.

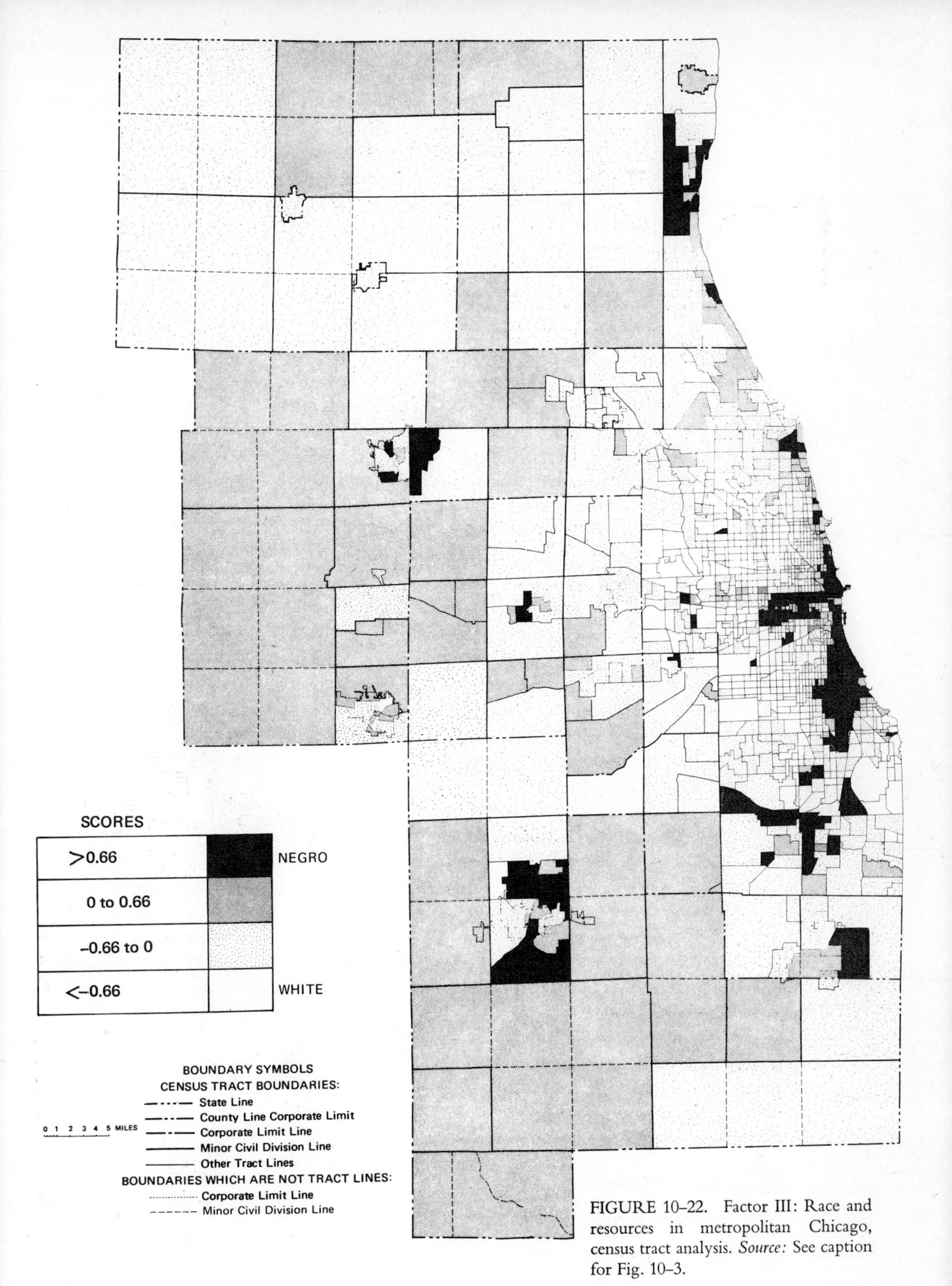

FIGURE 10–22. Factor III: Race and resources in metropolitan Chicago, census tract analysis. *Source:* See caption for Fig. 10–3.

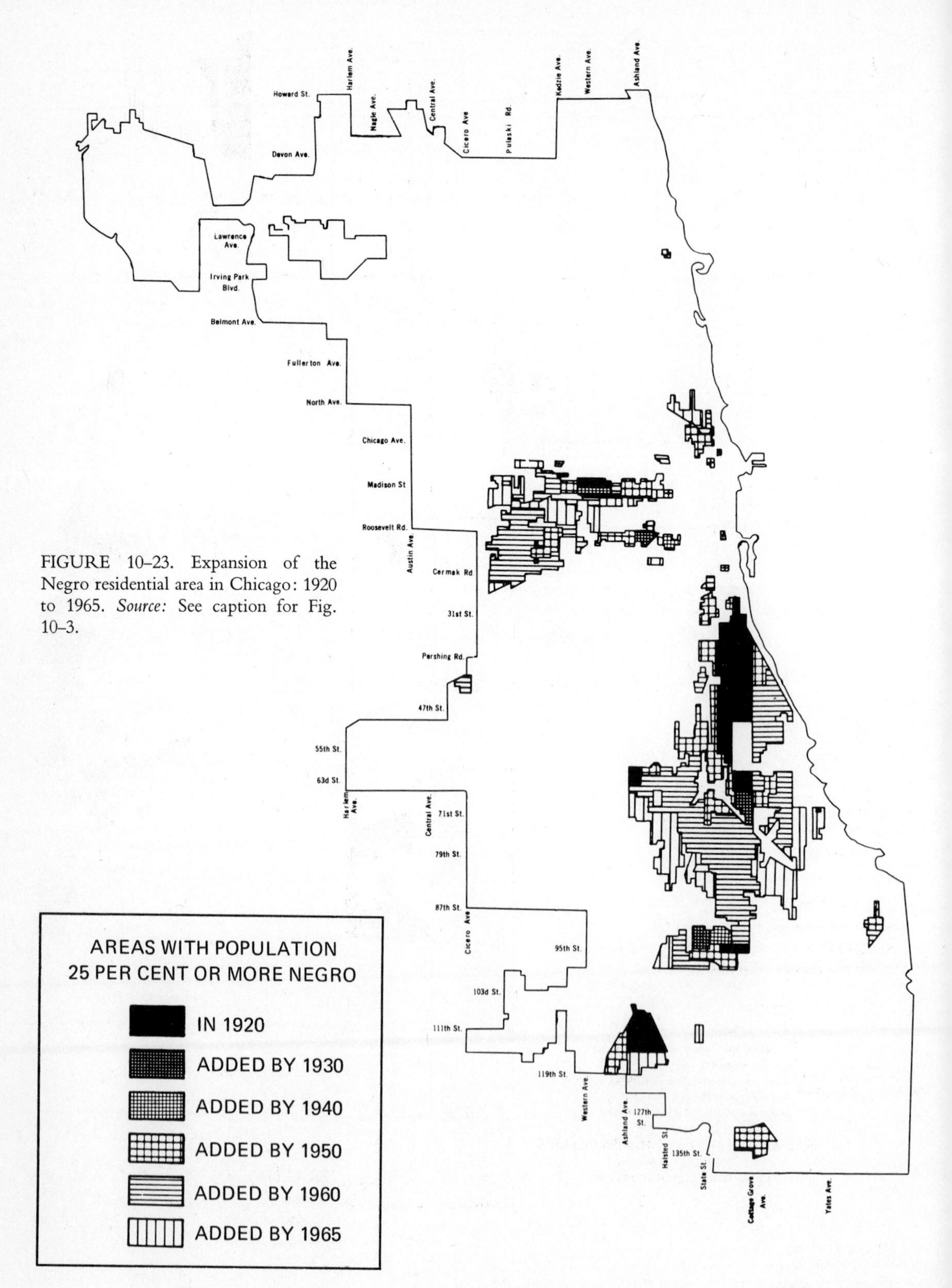

FIGURE 10–23. Expansion of the Negro residential area in Chicago: 1920 to 1965. *Source:* See caption for Fig. 10–3.

own social geography, a miniature of the wider metropolis.

The factorial ecology of the city as it emerges from an analysis of census tract data is summarized in Tables 10–19 and 10–20. A comparison of these with the expected factor structure (Table 10–21) reveals that the expectations are almost fully borne out, with the minor exception that the order of loadings of the variable, Percentage of families with incomes over $10,000, is reversed, indicating that even at the higher levels of social status there exist considerable barriers to Negro advancement. And finally Tables 10–22 and 10–23 set out the factorial ecology of the city and the large tracted suburbs of Cook County (those of over 10,000 population: Arlington Heights, Ber-

TABLE 10–19

Factor Structure in the City of Chicago: All 851 Census Tracts

Variable	*Race and Resources*	*Socio-economic Status*	*Stage in the Life Cycle*	*Communality*
Sums of Squares	3.858	2.849	2.791	
(7.) % Negro population	−.869*	.045	.282	.837
29. % families with incomes under $3,000	−.801	−.411†	.005	.810
27. Median annual income	.761	.462	−.201	.833
51. % unemployed workers	−.754	−.333	.087	.687
28. % families with incomes over $10,000	.698	.522	−.221	.808
(49.) % substandard housing	−.605	−.581	−.172	.733
36. Median school years completed	.176	.844	−.327	.851
47. % housing built after 1950	.249	.746	.230	.671
30. % white-collar workers	.366	.658	−.448	.767
43. Population per household	−.017	−.001	.950	.904
2. % population under 18	−.068	−.194	.878	.813
3. % population over 65	.479	−.062	−.743	.784

Source: See note to Table 10–14.
*Principal or highest loadings of a variable on a factor.
†Secondary loadings, greater than ±.400.

TABLE 10–20

Factor Structure in the City of Chicago: 790 Census Tracts (Incomplete Observations Eliminated)

Variable	*Race and Resources*	*Stage in the Life Cycle*	*Socio-economic Status*	*Communality*
Sums of Squares	3.979	3.099	3.022	
(7.) % Negro population	−.872*	.301	.064	.867
29. % families with incomes under $3,000	−.827	.033	−.431†	.870
27. Median annual income	.771	−.248	.481	.888
51. % unemployed workers	−.763	.179	−.342	.732
28. % families with incomes over $10,000	.711	−.271	.539	.869
(49.) % substandard housing	−.625	−.134	−.598	.766
43. Population per household	−.006	.956	.000	.913
2. % population under 18	−.169	.904	−.245	.906
3. % population over 65	.451	−.782	−.060	.819
36. Median school years completed	.160	−.381	.859	.908
47. % housing built after 1950	.266	.266	.766	.708
30. % white-collar workers	.365	−.514	.669	.845

Source: See note to Table 10–14.
*Principal or highest loadings of a variable on a factor.
†Secondary loadings, greater than ±.400.

TABLE 10–21

Expected and Observed Factor Structure: City of Chicago, Analysis of Census Tract Data

Variable	*Race and Resources*		*Socio-economic Status*		*Stage in the Life Cycle*	
	*E**	*O†*	*E*	*O*	*E*	*O*
(7.) % Negro population	1‡	1				
29. % families with incomes under $3,000	1	1	2§	2		
27. Median annual income	1	1	2	2		
51. % unemployed workers	1	1	2	(2)‖		
28. % families with incomes over $10,000	2	1	1	2		
(49.) % substandard housing	1	1	2	2	3#	
36. Median school years completed			1	1		(2)
47. % housing built after 1950			1	1	2	
30. % white-collar workers		(3)**	1	1		(2)
43. Population per household					1	1
2. % population under 18			(2)		1	1
3. % population over 65	2	2	(3)		1	1

Source: See note to Table 10–14.
*E = Expected factor structure, based on Community Area and Municipality Analysis.
†O = Observed factor structure, based on census tracts.
‡1 = Highest loadings in the factor analyses are on this factor.
§2 = Second highest loadings, over ±.400.
‖(2) = Second highest loadings, between ±.300 and +.399.
#3 = Third highest loadings, over ±.400.
**(3) = Third highest loadings which are between +.300 and ±.399.

TABLE 10–22

Factor Structure in the City of Chicago and Large Tracted Suburbs in Cook County: All 972 Census Tracts

Variable	*Socio-economic Status*	*Race and Resources*	*Stage in the Life Cycle*	*Communality*
Sums of Squares	3.447	3.414	2.700	
36. Median school years completed	.891*	.173	−.195	.861
30. % white-collar workers	.751	.338	−.330	.788
47. % housing built after 1950	.733	.246	.288	.681
(7.) % Negro population	−.040	−.876	.265	.840
29. % families with incomes under $3,000	−.513†	−.740	−.051	.814
51. % unemployed workers	−.445	−.714	.044	.710
27. Median annual income	.576	.689	−.140	.829
28. % families with incomes over $10,000	.615	.643	−.178	.823
(49.) % substandard housing	−.575	−.591	−.189	.715
43. Population per household	−.025	.025	.948	.899
2. % population under 18	−.198	−.012	.887	.826
3. % population over 65	−.099	.380	−.787	.774

Source: See note to Table 10–14.
*Principal or highest loadings of a variable on a factor.
†Secondary loadings, greater than ±.400.

TABLE 10–23

Factor Structure in the City of Chicago and Large Tracted Suburbs: 903 Census Tracts (Incomplete Observations Omitted)

	Socio-economic Status	*Race and Resources*	*Stage in the Life Cycle*	*Communality*
Sums of Squares	3.701	3.528	2.912	
36. Median school years completed	.920*	.160	−.218	.919
30. % white-collar workers	.777	.344	−.371	.859
47. % housing built after 1950	.745	.265	.298	.714
(7.) % Negro population	−.029	−.888	.287	.872
29. % families with incomes under $3,000	−.533†	−.769	−.043	.877
51. % unemployed workers	−.471	−.721	.113	.755
27. Median annual income	.601	.701	−.175	.883
28. % families with incomes over $10,000	.640	.657	−.208	.884
(49.) % substandard housing	−.597	−.603	−.157	.745
43. Population per household	−.034	.038	.952	.909
2. % population under 18	−.232	−.091	.916	.901
3. % population over 65	−.080	.343	−.835	.821

Source: See note to Table 10–14.
*Principal or highest loadings of a variable on a factor.
†Secondary loadings, greater than ±.400.

wyn, Calumet City, Chicago Heights, Cicero, Des Plaines, Elmhurst, Evanston, Harvey, Maywood, Oak Lawn, Oak Park, Park Forest, Park Ridge, Skokie, and Wilmette). In terms of the relative positions of the factors and the loading of variables on those factors, the factorial ecology of the city and the large suburbs falls midway between that of the city and the metropolis (Table 10–24).

TABLE 10–24

Relative Importance of Factors in the Census Tract Analyses

	Factors in Order of Their Eigenvalues		
	I	*II*	*III*
All tracts			
City	R&R*	SES†	LC‡
City and large suburbs	SES	R&R	LC
Metropolis	SES	LC	R&R
Omitting incomplete observations			
City	R&R	LC	SES
City and large suburbs	SES	R&R	LC
Metropolis	SES	LC	R&R

Source: See note to Table 10–14.
*Race and resources.
†Socio-economic status.
‡Stage in the life cycle.

LIGHT CAST ON THE RELATIONSHIPS BETWEEN SOCIAL AND PHYSICAL SPACE

The social area dimensions originally proposed by Shevky and Bell, together with the Immigrant and Catholic Status factor, make up the principal dimensions by which community populations within the Chicago metropolitan region vary (see Tables 10–25 and 10–26). Five factors, the minority group and ethnic dimensions, identify spatial segregation. The reasons for such segregation are various: discrimination in the housing market; income-related immobility; recency of arrival in the city; choice. A scaling dimension (Size) provides a measure of the importance of the individual units of observation with which to weight them. Two longitudinal factors describing some aspects of change in the metropolis are included among the dimensions, one of which, Mobility, is of such interest and complexity that it is treated separately in Chapter 11.

Some five of the dimensions were consistent, appearing in each of the study area analyses. A sixth, Immigrant and Catholic Status, was present at the metropolitan and suburban levels of analysis, but combined with the Race and Resources factor at the city level to form a single dimension which occupied the end of the scale opposite to Negroes.

TABLE 10–25

Summary of the Factors in the Metropolitan Chicago Factor Analysis

	*Factors**	*Sums of Squares (%)*
Community Area and Municipality Analysis		
I	Socio-economic status	17.8
II	Stage in the life cycle	14.2
III	Race and resources	13.1
IV	Immigrant and Catholic status	10.8
V	Population size and density	7.5
VI	Jewish and Russian population	3.8
VII	Housing built in 1940's; workers commute by car	3.0
VIII	Irish and Swedish population	2.6
IX	Mobility	2.4
X	Other nonwhite and Italian	2.1
		77.3
Census Tract Analysis		
I	Socio-economic status	37.3
II	Stage in the life cycle	22.3
III	Race and resources	19.3
		78.9

*Alternative names used in the text for some of these factors are: I, Social Status; II, Family Status; III, Racial Status; and IV, Nativity and Religion.

TABLE 10–26

Sets of Factors Appearing at the Metropolitan Level

Groups of Factors	*Sums of Squares (%)*
1. Modified social area dimensions (I, II, III)	45.1
2. Principal dimensions (I, II, III, IV)	55.9
3. Minority group or ethnic dimensions (III, IV, VI, VIII, X)	32.4
4. Scale dimension (V)	7.5
5. Longitudinal or time-related dimensions (VII, IX)	5.4
6. Consistent (in three study areas) dimensions (I, II, III, V, VI)	56.4
7. Special factors (only appear in metropolis) (VII, VIII, IX, X)	
8. Factors of some generality (I, II, III, IV, VI)	59.7
9. All factors with eigenvalues over 1.00 (I, II, III, IV, V, VI, VII, VIII, IX, X)	77.3

Of the ten factors (with eigenvalues greater than 1) some five factors were considered to be of some generality—the principal dimensions, and the Jewish population factor. These are factors which might be expected to emerge in factorial ecologies of many American cities, not just Chicago. The form in which the social area dimensions emerged (Combination VI of Table 10–6, and Type IV, described earlier in the chapter) is probably fairly typical of metropolitan areas in the United States outside the South, to judge from the frustration, unrest, and violence that such a form breeds. A dimension of Nativity and Religion would probably emerge in a smaller number of American cities, those in the industrial northeast which contain substantial numbers of European Catholic immigrants of the first, second, and third generations. In a smaller subset of northeastern cities, a common Jewish population factor would probably also emerge.[105]

Other dimensions, special factors, may be specific to the Chicago metropolis alone. The minor ethnic factor will probably differ considerably from city to city,[106] and some will be associated with part of the socio-economic set of variables, just as is the Negro in this and other studies.[107]

A visual inspection of the maps of factor scores also indicates that the spatial pattern of Socio-economic Status is sectoral, that of Family Status zonal, and that of Race clustered to sectoral, with the qualification that the simple geometric model of sectors, zones, and segregated areas is distorted by the metropolitan growth pattern and by the existence of secondary nuclei of workplaces in the urban region. We should now look more closely at the spatial patterning of the dimensions and ask whether the theoretical expectations are met by empirical observations.

The Transects

A series of axial and concentric transects were laid across the SMSA (Fig. 10–24). Scores on Factor I (Socio-economic Status), Factor II (Family Status), and on the variable, Percentage of Negroes (the essential ingredient of Factor III)

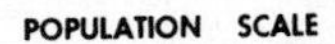

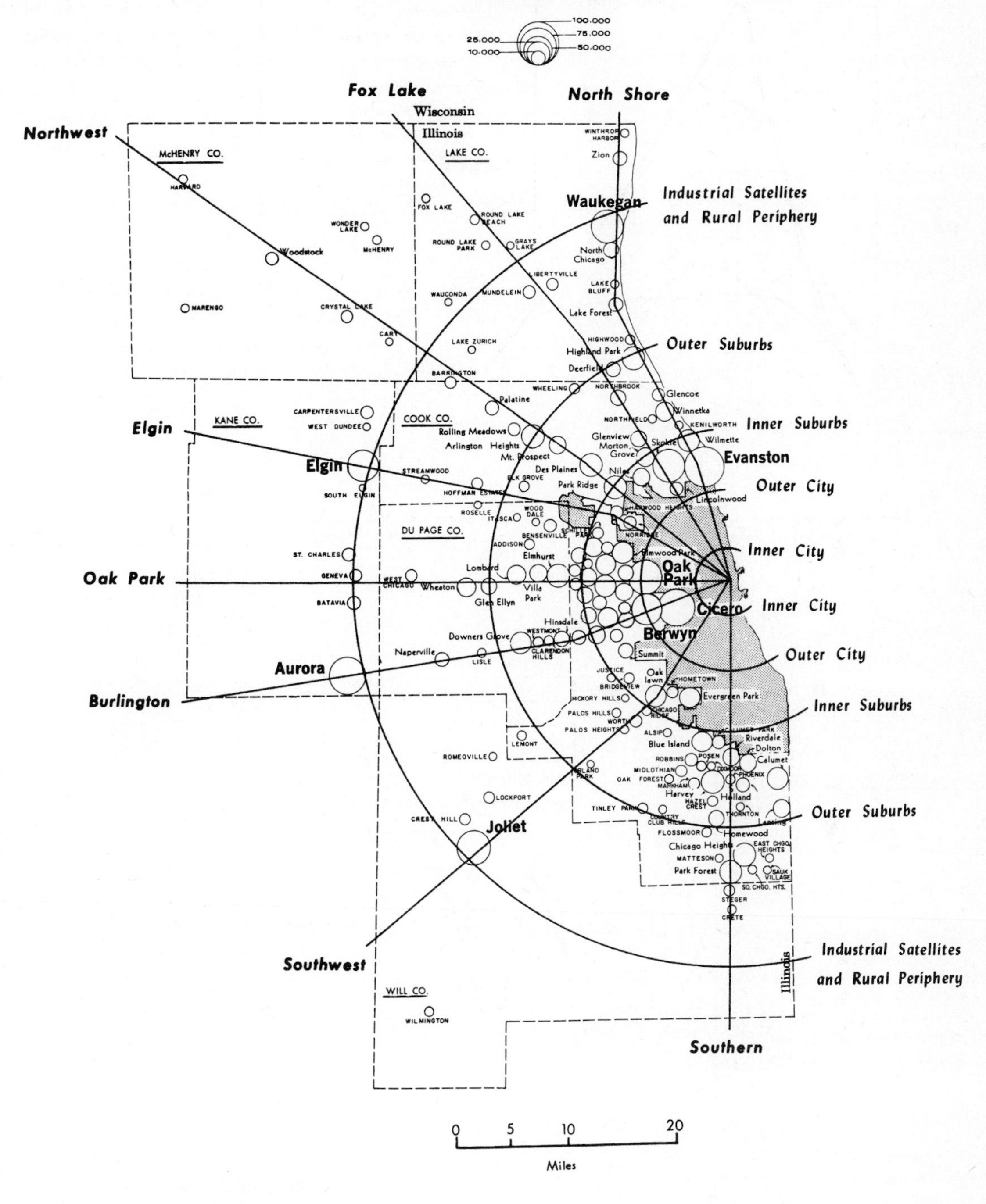

FIGURE 10–24. Transects across the metropolis.
Source: See caption for Fig. 10–3.

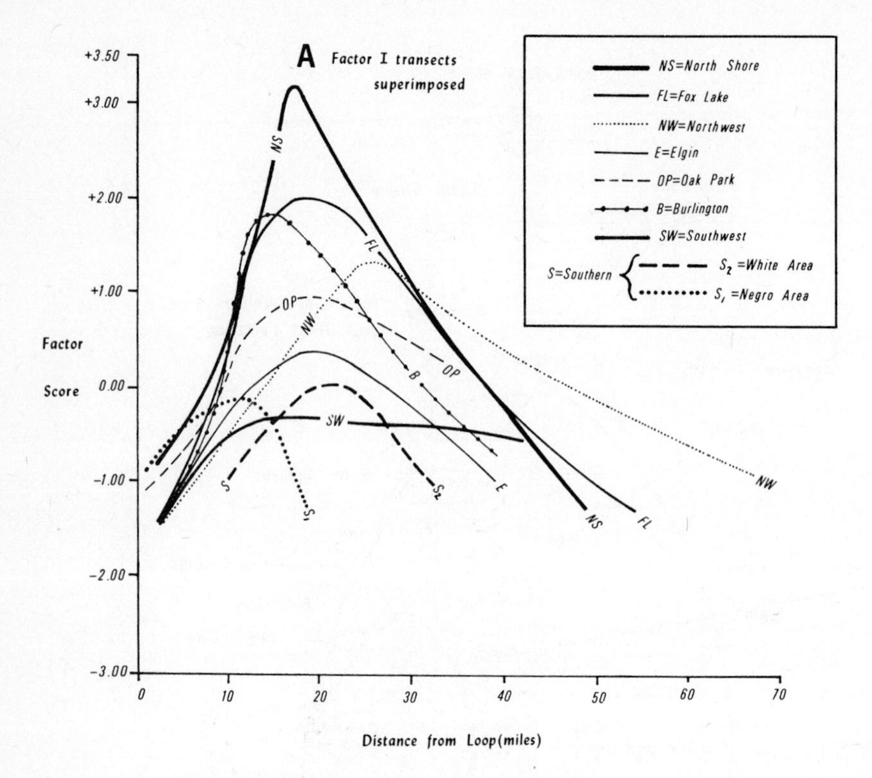

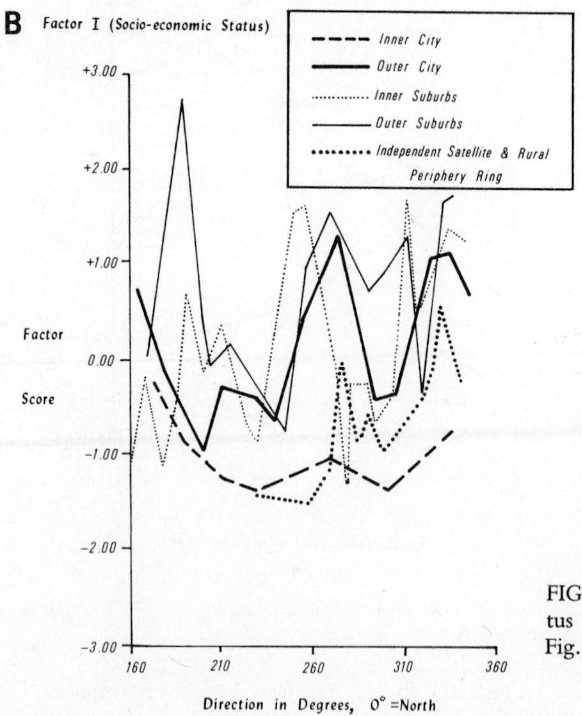

FIGURE 10–25. Socio-economic status transects. *Source:* See caption for Fig. 10–3.

were separately plotted for communities lying at or near to the transect lines in Figs. 10–25 to 10–27.

The Socio-economic Status transects show a fairly consistent pattern from sector to sector: a rising limb from the city center to the inner suburbs, and a falling limb from the inner suburbs to the rural periphery. The rises and falls are steeper in the higher status sectors (the North Shore, Fox Lake, Northwest, and Burlington transects). There are considerable differences between sectors in their over-all position (Fig. 10–25*a*) but, as the form of the individual transects indicates, there is also considerable zonal variation within each sector. Over-all, the zones do separate themselves out by Socio-economic Status score (Fig. 10–25*b*). The only exception to the sectoral differentation of the level of rise and fall of the Socio-economic Status factor is in the southern transect, where there appear to be two patterns. The Negro communities of the South Side have their own curve, separate from that of the white communities. It may be, however, that it is the concentration of blue-collar workers created by the Calumet industrial area that results in the low status of both the white (Roseland and West Pullman) and the Negro (Phoenix) residential areas, creating a sag in an otherwise consistent curve.

The Family Status curves, similarly, vary by zone and sector, though the sectoral variation seems less pronounced than that of Socio-economic Status or Median Income. Many of the curves, however, show not just one point of inflexion, as do the Factor I curves, but two points. The Northwest, Elgin, Oak Park, and Burlington transects all show the existence of a younger population with large families in the innermost parts of the city. The reasons for such a population in the West Side ghetto have already been outlined: its recent in-migration, poverty, and discrimination. In the white areas of the inner city, there is also poverty and recency of arrival, but not discrimination, and the "ecological distortion" (large families living in small, unsuitable homes), is thus of a lesser magnitude.

The third set of graphs re-emphasizes the fact of the spatial segregation of the nonwhite population. Five of the eight sectors contain virtually no Negroes. The North Shore sector contains some, even outside the small ghettos of the Near North and Evanston, but the Negro population is concentrated in the main in the inner portions of the western sector (Oak Park transect) and the southern sector.

An Analysis of the Variance of Socio-economic Status and Family Status

In order to make a more precise test of the spatial patterning of the two most important social dimensions, a series of analyses of variance were undertaken along the lines first suggested by Anderson and Egeland.[108] These authors selected (on a semi-random basis) 16 census tracts in each of four cities, positioned in one of four 30° sectors and in one of four zones relative to the city center. Their results are presented in Table 10–27.

Anderson and Egeland, in using a "Prestige Value Index,"[109] found that there was considerable interaction between cities and sectors because similarly positioned sectors were equated in the design, although it was not necessarily true that they were of similar status. The sector of highest prestige might be to the west in one city, to the north in another, to the east in a third. Therefore, the hypothesis that the dimension varied in a sectoral fashion was tested separately for each city (Table 10–27, Part *A*). In Akron, Dayton, and Syracuse, only the sectoral variation proved to be significant; in Indianapolis, both sectoral and zonal variation proved significant, though the sectoral variation was the greater.

Their Urbanization Index varied principally by zones, only city-to-city variation also achieving significance (Table 10–27, Part *B*).

A similar analysis was made of Chicago data, using not the Shevky-Bell indices of social rank and urbanization but rather the Factor I (socio-economic status) and Factor II (family status) scores which have already been interpreted as approximating the first two social area dimensions, and not a sample of the census tracts but rather all the community areas and municipalities used in our previous analyses. The results (Table 10–28)

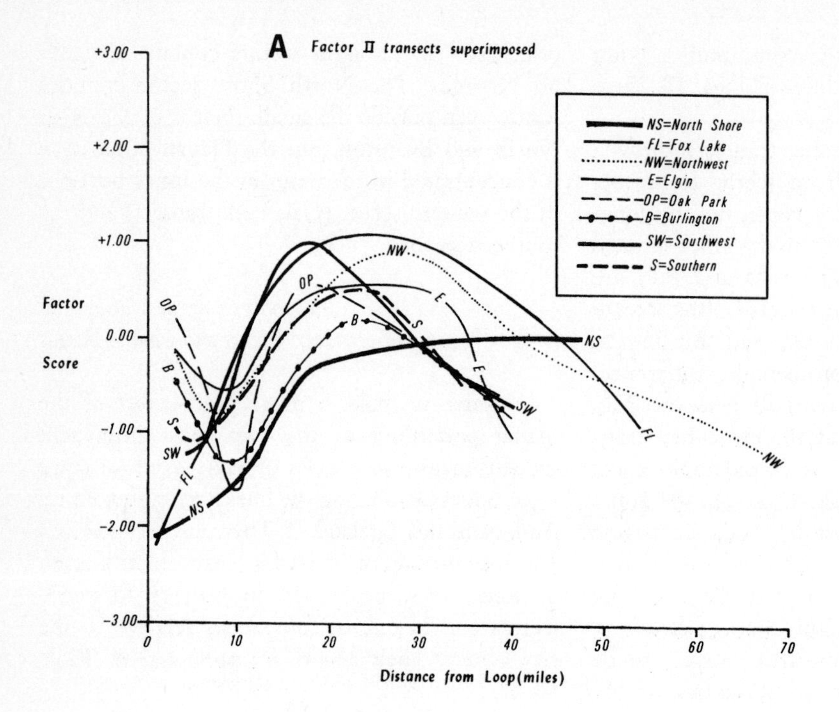

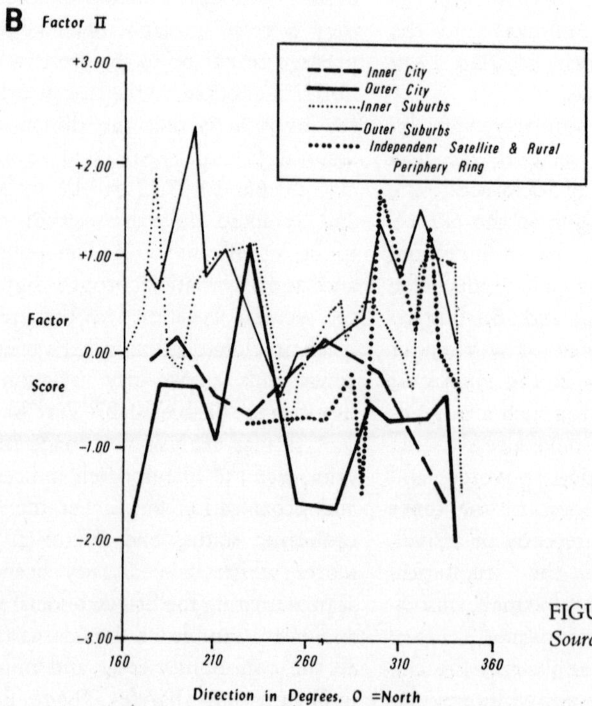

FIGURE 10–26. Family status transects.
Source: See caption for Fig. 10–3.

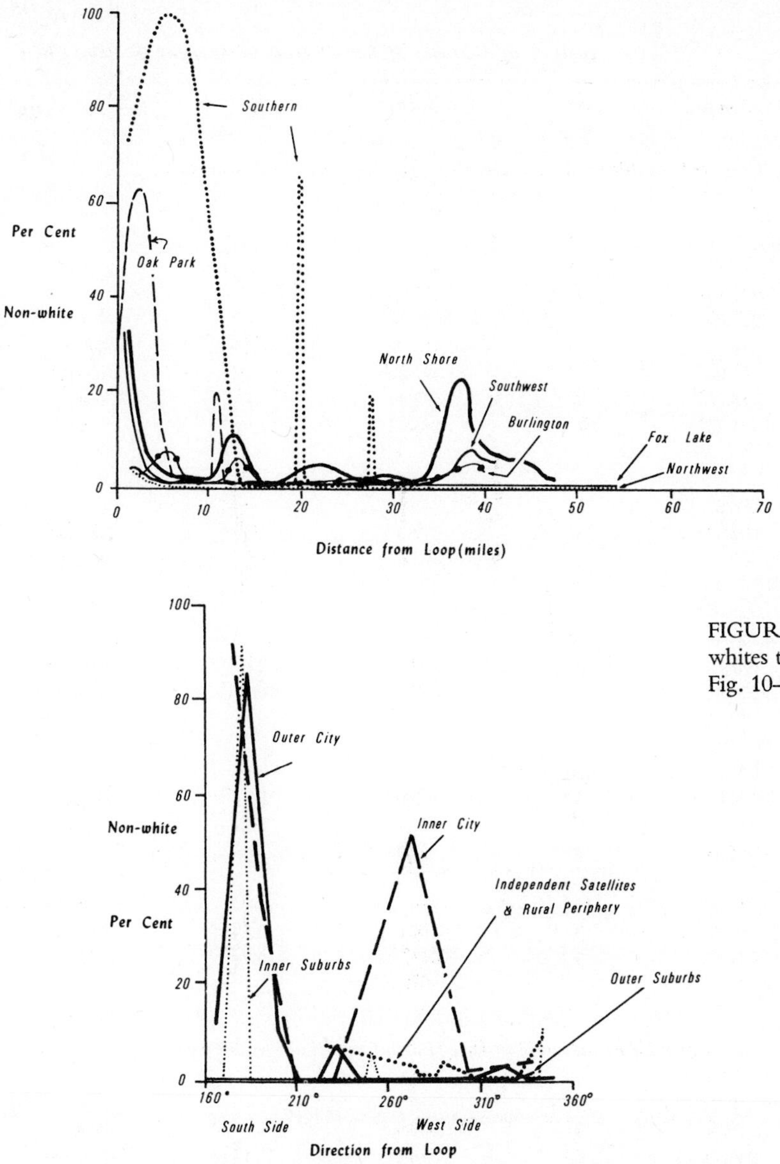

FIGURE 10–27. Percentage of non-whites transects. *Source:* See caption for Fig. 10–3.

confirm the interpretation suggested by the transect graphs: both socio-economic status and family status vary significantly by both sectors and zones.[110] Both Burgess and Hoyt were correct when they described the socio-economic population pattern of cities as respectively zonal and sectoral: they had both based their original work on Chicago where their hypotheses held simultaneously. If all the communities in the SMSA are included in the analysis (Part *A* of Table 10–28), then in fact zonal variation is slightly more significant than sectoral. However, if the two outermost zones are excluded from the analysis (they lie outside the most active metropolitan labor and housing markets), sectoral variation is of greater significance. Similarly, the importance of zonal variation in the total variation in the family status factor is enhanced if the analysis is restricted to the city and the suburban zones of the metropolis (Part *B* of Table 10–28). In any case, zonal variation of family status is more important than sectoral.

TABLE 10–27

An Analysis of Variance of Social Area Dimensions in Four Cities

Source	*Sum of Squares*	*df**	*Mean SS†*	*F‡*	*Decision on H_0§*
A. *Analysis of Variance for the Prestige Value Index (Equivalent to Factor I in Present Study)*					
The cities together					
Total	32,154.24	63	—	—	—
Between cities	1,810.77	3	603.59	—	—
Between sectors	1,835.76	3	611.92	—	—
Between distances	1,907.26	3	635.75	—	—
Cities × sectors	19,224.79	9	2,136.09	12.16	Reject
Cities × distances	1,775.02	9	197.22	1.12	Accept
Sectors × distances	858.92	9	95.44	.54	Accept
Residual	4,741.73	27	175.62		—
The cities separately					
Akron					
Total	7,698.8	15	—	—	—
Between distances	897.9	3	299.3	1.93	Accept
Between sectors	5,407.6	3	1,802.5	11.64	Reject
Remainder	1,393.4	9	154.8	—	—
Dayton					
Total	4,816.4	15	—	—	—
Between distances	607.8	3	202.6	2.88	Accept
Between sectors	3,576.4	3	1,192.1	16.97	Reject
Remainder	632.1	9	70.2	—	—
Indianapolis					
Total	5,011.3	15	—	—	—
Between distances	1,694.9	3	565.0	5.77	Reject
Between sectors	2,435.0	3	811.7	8.29	Reject
Remainder	881.4	9	97.9	—	—
Syracuse					
Total	12,817.0	15	—	—	—
Between distances	481.7	3	160.6	0.54	Accept
Between sectors	9,641.6	3	3,213.9	10.74	Reject
Remainder	2,693.8	9	299.3	—	—
B. *Analysis of Variance of the Urbanization Index (Equivalent to Factor II in Present Study)*					
Total	49,639.0	63	—	—	—
Between cities	4,816.3	3	1,605.4	5.68‖	Reject
Between sectors	948.4	3	316.1	1.12‖	Accept
Between distances	28,418.6	3	9,472.8	33.49‖	Reject
Cities × sectors	3,864.0	9	429.3	1.62	Accept
Cities × distances	1,692.2	9	188.0	.71	Accept
Sectors × distances	2,756.6	9	306.3	1.16	Accept
Residual	7,142.9	27	264.6	—	—
Pooled error	15,275.8	54	282.9	—	—

Source: Theodore R. Anderson and Janice A. Egeland, "The Spatial Aspects of Social Area Analysis," *American Sociological Review*, XXVI (June, 1961), 396–98, with the permission of the authors and editor.

*Degrees of freedom.

†Sum of squares accounted for by differences between means.

‡Variance-ratio, *F*.

§Decision relating to the null hypothesis (H_0) that the means are not significantly different.

‖Since the interactions were not significant, the main effects were tested from the pooled error estimate (residual plus the interactions).

TABLE 10–28

Chicago: An Analysis of Social Area Factors in Chicago

Source	*Sums of Squares*	*df**	*Mean SS**	*F**	*Probability of a Greater Difference at Random*	*Decision on H_0*†*
	A. Analysis of Variance of Factor I (Socio-Economic Status)					
Using all zones‡						
Within cells	132.223	191	0.692	—	—	—
Between sectors§	27.758	4	6.940	10.024	0.001	Reject
Between zones	36.156	5	7.231	10.446	0.001	Reject
Sector × zones	22.337	20	1.117	1.613	0.053	Accept
Using only zones 1 to 4						
Within cells	126.583	172	0.736	—	—	—
Between sectors	36.715	4	9.179	12.472	0.001	Reject
Between zones	23.990	3	7.997	10.886	0.001	Reject
Sector × zones	14.437	12	1.203	1.635	0.086	Accept
	B. Analysis of Variance of Factor II (Family Status)					
Using all zones						
Within cells	112.721	190	0.593	—	—	—
Between sectors	24.589	4	6.147	10.361	0.001	Reject
Between zones	58.041	5	11.603	19.557	0.001	Reject
Sectors × zones	21.847	20	1.092	1.841	0.019	Accept
Using only zones 1 to 4						
Within cells	100.704	170	0.592	—	—	—
Between sectors	28.228	4	7.057	11.913	0.001	Reject
Between zones	55.091	3	18.364	31.000	0.001	Reject
Sectors × zones	15.721	12	1.310	2.212	0.013	Accept

Source: Primary data.
*See definitions in footnotes to Table 10–27.
†Level applied for $H_0 = 0.01$.
‡Zones are: (1) Inner city; (2) Outer city; (3) Inner suburbs; (4) Outer suburbs; (5) Industrial satellites; and (6) Rural periphery.
§Sectors are: (1) North Shore; (2) Northwest; (3) West; (4) Southwest; and (5) South.

If we compare the between-sector and between-zone variances in a number of different sized cities for which we have analyses of variance, some interesting though very tentative findings emerge (Table 10–29). There appears to be a regular ordering, by size of city, of the relative contributions of zones and sectors to the variation in socio-economic status and family status. For the larger the city the greater the importance of zonal variation of socio-economic status as compared with sectoral variation, although sectoral variation remains the more important in all the cities. Similarly, the larger the city the greater the importance of sectoral variation of family status, as compared with zonal variation, though zonal variation remains, by far the more important in all the cities. The only exception in this size-governed continuum would seem to be Toronto, where sectoral variation of socio-economic status is almost completely dominant. The reason may be that some of the variables contained in the set of socio-economic variables, which in Chicago load on a Socio-economic Status factor, in Toronto make up a separate Household and Employment Characteristics factor with an extremely strong zonal pattern of spatial variation.[111]

The influence at work that leads to a mixed sectoral-zonal pattern of socio-economic status in Chicago is clear. Virtually all of the inner city,

TABLE 10–29

Relationship of* F *Ratios for Socio-economic Status and Family Status to Population of City

Urbanized Area	*1960 Population*	*Socio-economic Status: Factor I**	*Family Status: Factor II†*
Chicago-Northwest Indiana	5,959,000	1.148	2.602
Metropolitan Toronto	1,824,481‡	30.000	10.696
Indianapolis	639,000	1.437	29.902
Dayton	502,000	5.892	
Akron	458,000	6.031	
Syracuse	333,000	19.889	

Sources: Data for Chicago and Northwest Indiana from Table 10–28, Parts *A* and *B*, Zones 1 to 4; data for metropolitan Toronto from Table 10–27, Anderson and Egeland; data for Indianapolis, Dayton, Akron, and Syracuse from Robert A. Murdie, *The Factorial Ecology of Metropolitan Toronto, 1951–1961: An Essay on the Social Geography of the City* (Department of Geography Research Paper No. 116, University of Chicago, 1968), Table VII-4.
*Between sectors *F*; between zones *F*. †Between zones *F*; between sectors *F*. ‡1961.

with the exception of a narrow Lake Shore fringe north of the Loop and a discontinuous Lake Shore strip south of it, is of low status (See Figs. 10–10 nad 10–20). The formerly high-status districts, the Madison Street axis and Douglas-Oakland-North Kenwood, which made the former patterning of socio-economic status strongly sectoral, were invaded (in the ecological sense) by lower-status groups, converting the inner city into an almost zonal, lower-status area. The sectoral pattern persists most clearly in the city when racial and ethnic status are considered (Figs. 10–12 and 10–13), since the lower-status group that came to occupy the middle-to-higher status sector was black, and the original lower-status sector continued to be occupied by whites. This ecological process has probably, accepting the tentative evidence of such a small sample of cities as contained in Table 10–29, proceeded further in those cities that have a larger and longer established Negro minority. Since all the cities in the group are in the North, size serves as a suitable surrogate for the process. Thus, Murdie's statement that:

> Economic status and family status tend to be distributed in sectoral and concentric patterns respectively, while ethnic status tends to form "groupings" which can be superimposed on the cellular structure created by the sectoral and concentric patterns.[112]

needs modification. There is a subsidiary variation in socio-economic status by concentric zone, and in family status by sector, though this subsidiary variation is important only in larger cities. The transects presented earlier for Chicago (Fig. 10–25) showed a clear zonal variation of socio-economic status within each sector. We have suggested that this was partially a product of a group process of racial succession, but it may also be a product of individual behavior—in particular, a consequence of the variation of individual or family income with stages in the life cycle. The rising limbs of the transects reflect the fact that suburban residents are at or approaching the peak of their earning capacities and that the inhabitants of the inner city are either young, single, and yet to achieve their maximum income, or old and "over the hill" in terms of earning capacity, or large poor families which could not afford the move to a single-family home towards the urban periphery. The falling limbs of the socio-economic transects as distance from the city's center increases are probably a product of the decline in the proportion of urban-based residents closely involved in the metropolitan economy and the increase in the proportion of rural-based residents not so intimately tied to the functioning metropolis.

The sectoral variation of family status is, in most of the cities in Table 10–29, of much less importance than the zonal, with the exception of Chicago. There the elongation of the district of rented apartments suitable for occupation by individuals or older families, as well as the ecological succession referred to earlier, may be the influences at work.

The Spatial Patterns of the Remaining Factors

The variance of the remaining factors in our study (III to X) was not subjected to analysis, but it would be useful to summarize their patterns of spatial variation.

The Race and Resources factor and the Immigrant and Catholic factor both exhibit a pattern of areal segregation that is tending to develop into a sectoral pattern, at least within the city and the inner suburban zones, as the size of the groups grow. Some of the reasons for these patterns were discussed earlier.

The Size and Density dimension has a clearly concentric arrangement; denser and larger communities being near the city center, and less crowded and smaller communities being further away.

The minor ethnic dimensions (Jewish Population, Irish and Swedish Population, and Italians and Other Non-white Population) all display the tendency of their respective population groups to cluster in one or another part of the city—sometimes, as in the case of the Jews, in widely separated but spatially analogous communities.

Factor VII, Housing Built in the 1940's, identifies and dates a zone of growth in the inner suburbs, and Factor IX, Mobility, displays a complex pattern of sectors and zones.

LIGHT CAST ON COMMUNITIES IN THE METROPOLIS

Earlier we postulated that the like choices of like individuals or families, catered to by the like outputs of the housing market, would produce a set of communities homogeneous with respect to the characteristics of their inhabitants, the nature of the housing stock, and by implication with respect to the way people lived within the community. The problem is now to define a set of such communities and to arrange the communities in some meaningful typology.

Spatially Defined Communities

The approach of the classical ecologists leads us to define such homogeneous communities at the intersection of sectors and rings (Fig. 10–28). In the inner city, on the North Side, there is a higher-status (factor score: 0.123), older (factor score: −2.865) community. In the southwest sector the older population in the equivalent cell is of lower socio-economic status (factor score: −1.127). However, although the integrated spatial model does have some over-all validity for the metropolis, the variance within the cells is very large (as evidenced by the standard deviations recorded in Fig. 10–28). It may well be that the spatial divisions which we have selected do not group the observational units into the "best" (most internally homogeneous and externally heterogeneous) set of types of community.

Social Space and Social Areas

An alternative route would be to use the social space dimensions rather than those of physical space to group the observational units, in the manner of social area analysts Shevky and Bell. They divided their Social Rank Dimension into four categories, and the Urbanization Index similarly, forming some sixteen classes which they plotted on a census tract map.[113] An analogous procedure can be followed for the two most important dimensions of our own factorial ecology.

If Factor I (Socio-economic Status) scores are plotted along the vertical axis of a graph and Factor II (Family Status) scores are plotted along the horizontal axis, then the space so formed is called *social space*. All the census tracts used in our Metropolitan Factor Analysis are plotted in Fig. 10–29. Distinguished on the diagram are those tracts that lie in the city of Chicago and those that lie in the rest of the metropolis. By and large, the suburban tracts lie to the upper right of the city tracts; the remaining metropolitan tracts, lying within concentrations of city tracts, are generally those of the industrial satellites and rural periphery.

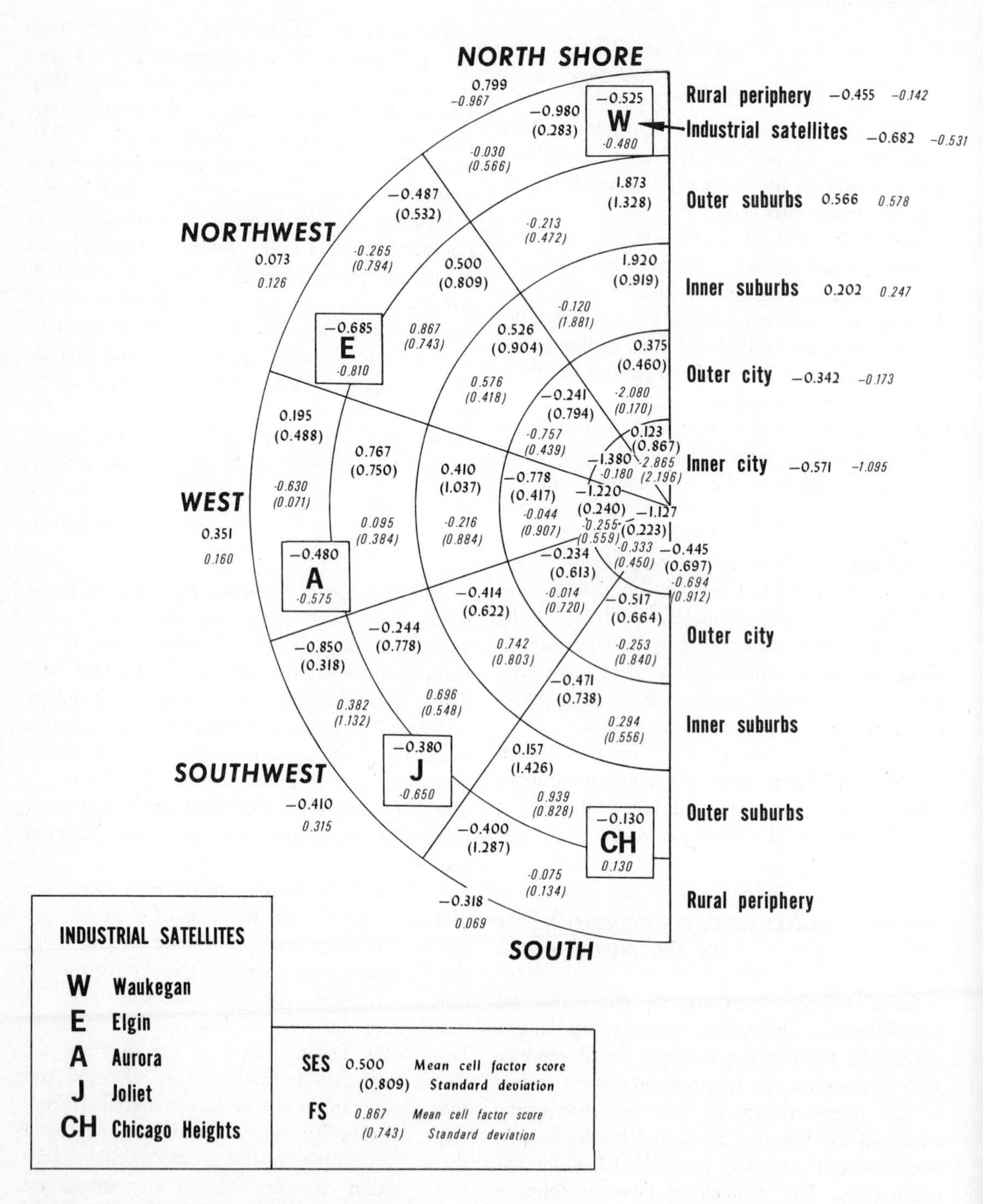

FIGURE 10–28. Spatially defined communities.
Source: See caption for Fig. 10–3.

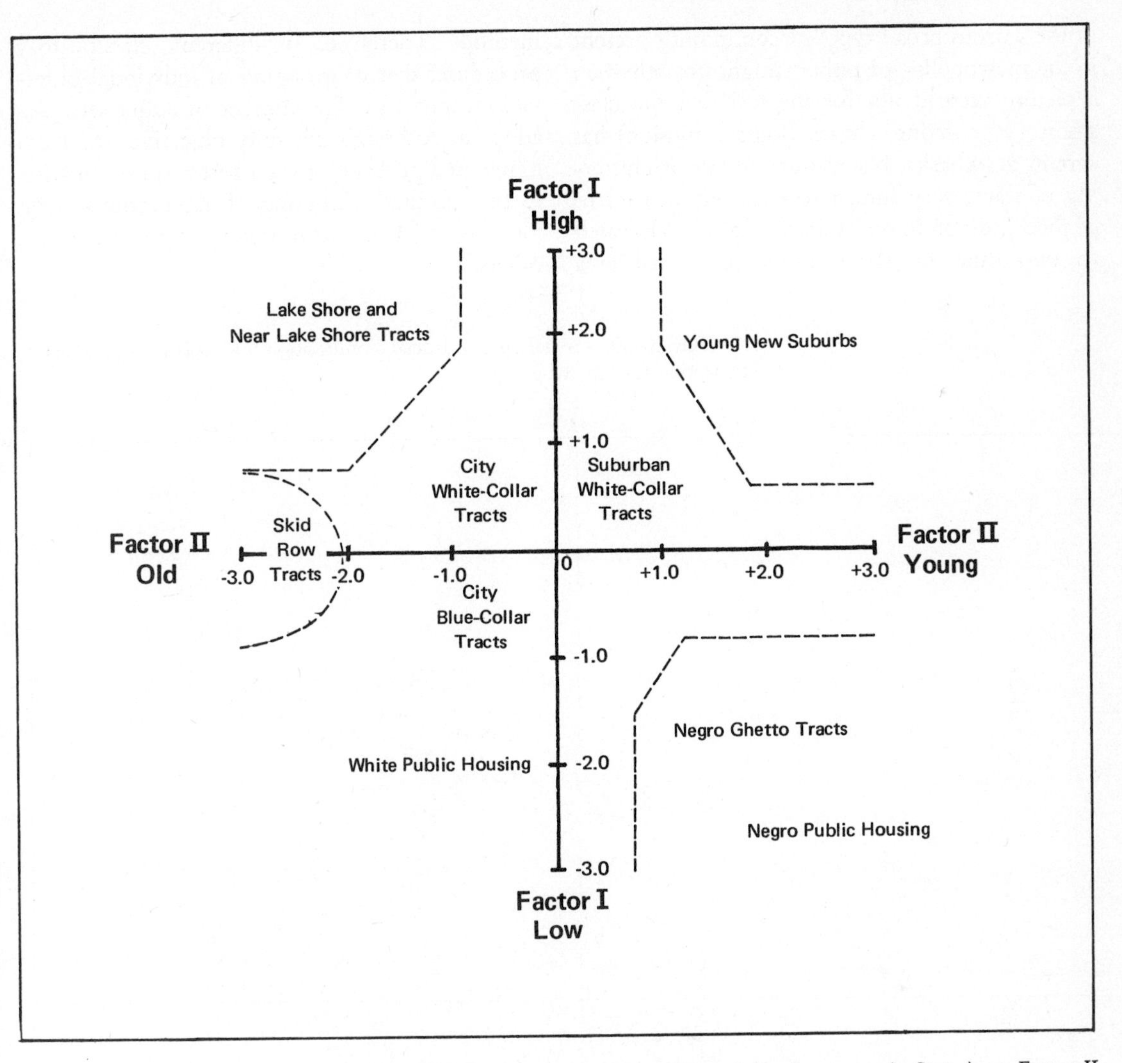

FIGURE 10–29. Social space: Factor I (Socio-economic Status) *vs.* Factor II (Stage in the Life Cycle). *Source:* See caption for Fig. 10–3.

Tracts with over 50 per cent of their population Negro are also distinguished in the social space of Fig. 10–30. They tend to be concentrated in the lower-right quadrant (poorer; younger and larger families), but the concentration is not so overwhelming that racial status becomes an index of socio-economic or family status. Negro tracts do spread over most of the metropolis's social space, and the emergence of a third factor, a product of the spatial segregation of the Negro population, is indicative of this spread. However, the concentration of Negro tracts in the lower-status ranges results in the second, "resources," component of the third factor.

Following the procedure of the social area analysts, we can divide social space up into a number of categories, which when plotted on a map, are called *social areas* (Fig. 10–31). Though the categories employed are very general (only the four quadrants of the graph of social space are used, for cartographic clarity, although a more detailed breakdown is perfectly possible) the map provides a consistent summary picture of the various broad types of community present in the metropolis—or rather, might provide such a picture were it not for the fact that the classificatory procedure chosen (logical division) has certain drawbacks. Natural groupings or clustering of tracts very similar to each other in terms of their position in social space might be allocated to two different classes using the social area method. Therefore, a different classificatory procedure, that of grouping of individual observations into a smaller number of larger sets, was adopted. Although not fully objective, the technique used probably gives a better approximation to the "natural" clustering of observational areas into homogeneous community types than most others.[114]

FIGURE 10–30. Social space: Racial composition of census tracts. *Source:* See caption for Fig. 10–3.

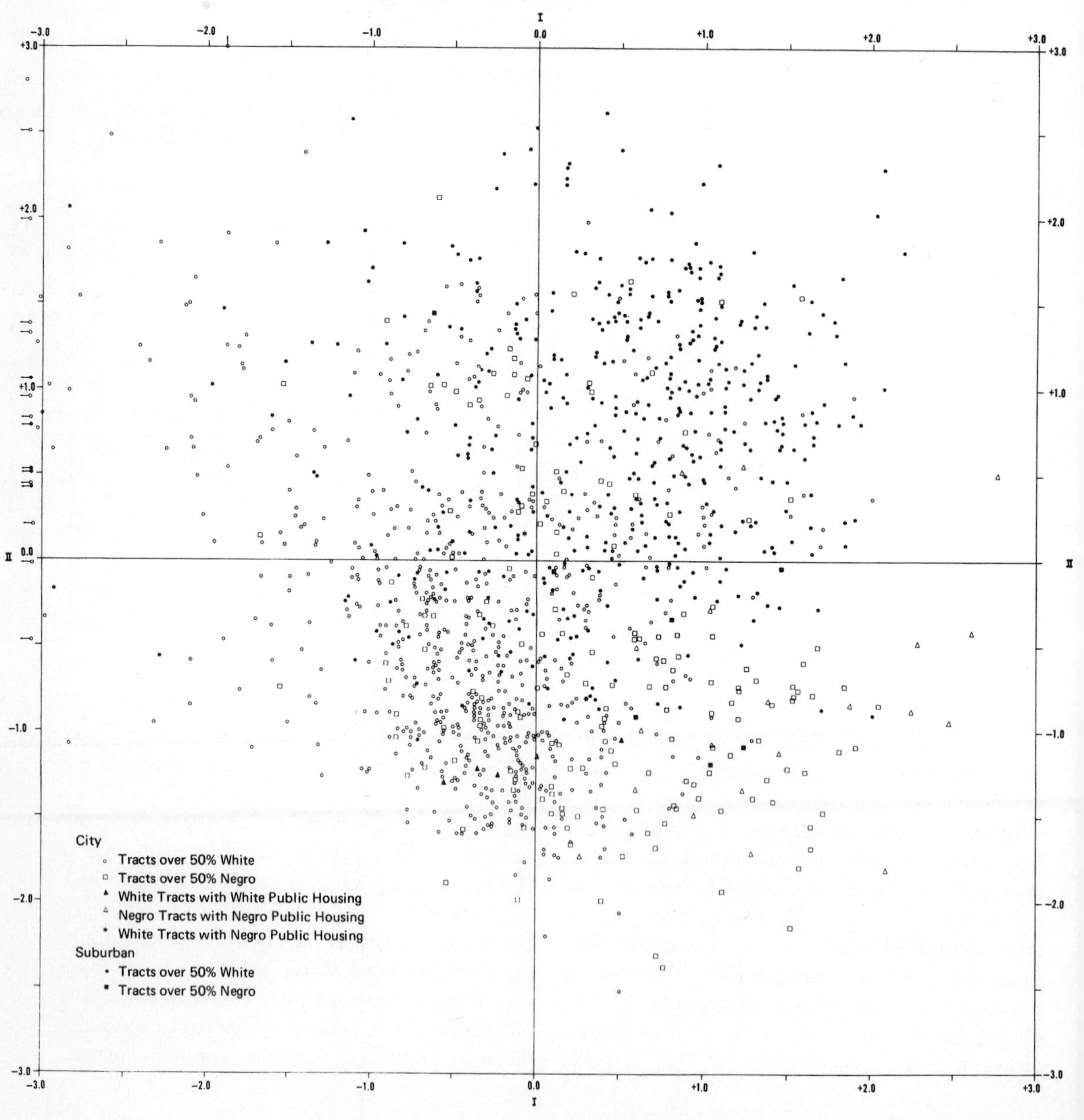

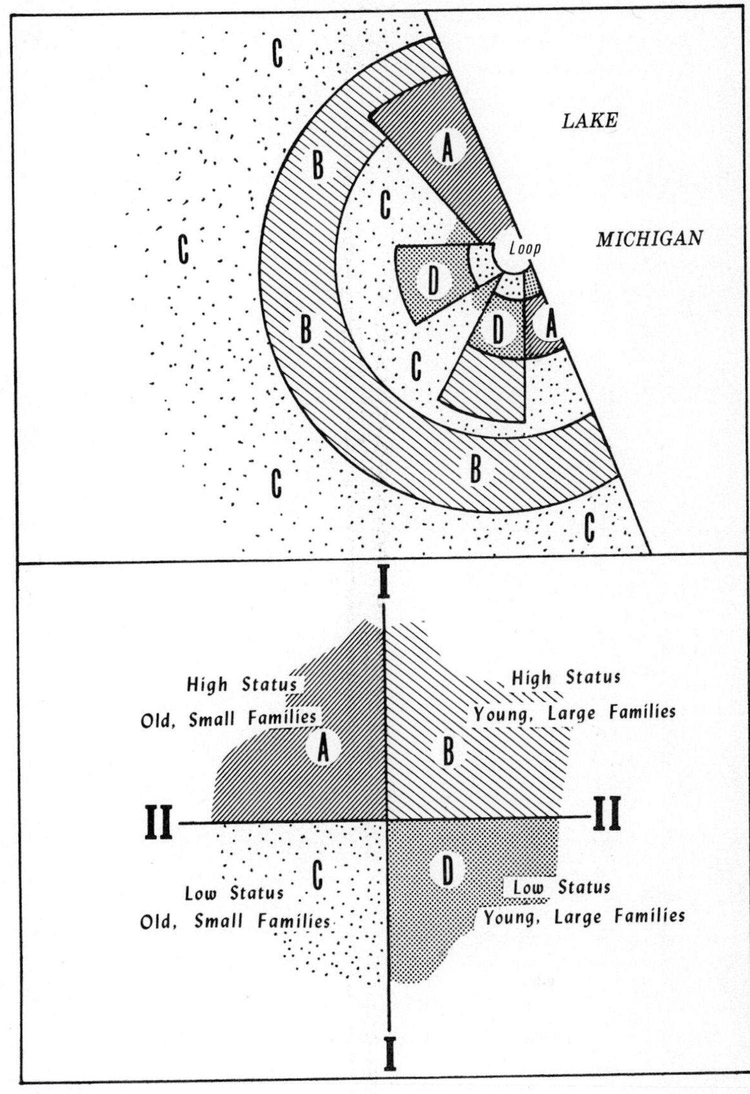

FIGURE 10–31. Social areas of the Chicago metropolis. *Source:* See caption for Fig. 10–3.

Community Types

It proved impossible to use census tracts in a fully computerized grouping analysis since there were too many of them for the existing programing capacity, and community areas and municipalities were used instead. The "grouping tree" is presented in Fig. 10–32. This shows that several small groups combine into one large group at an early stage in the grouping process. The large group then pulls into itself the remaining communities in successive steps one at a time. Decision as to which grouping stage to adopt is difficult since those stages which contain a small, feasible number of groups all consist of one large group and many single member groups or isolates.

A somewhat arbitrary procedure was therefore adopted to define a small number of reasonably sized groups. The grouping tree of Fig. 10–32 was retraced to step 140, at which the large majority group is merely a collection of medium-sized groups. The 18 groups with more than two

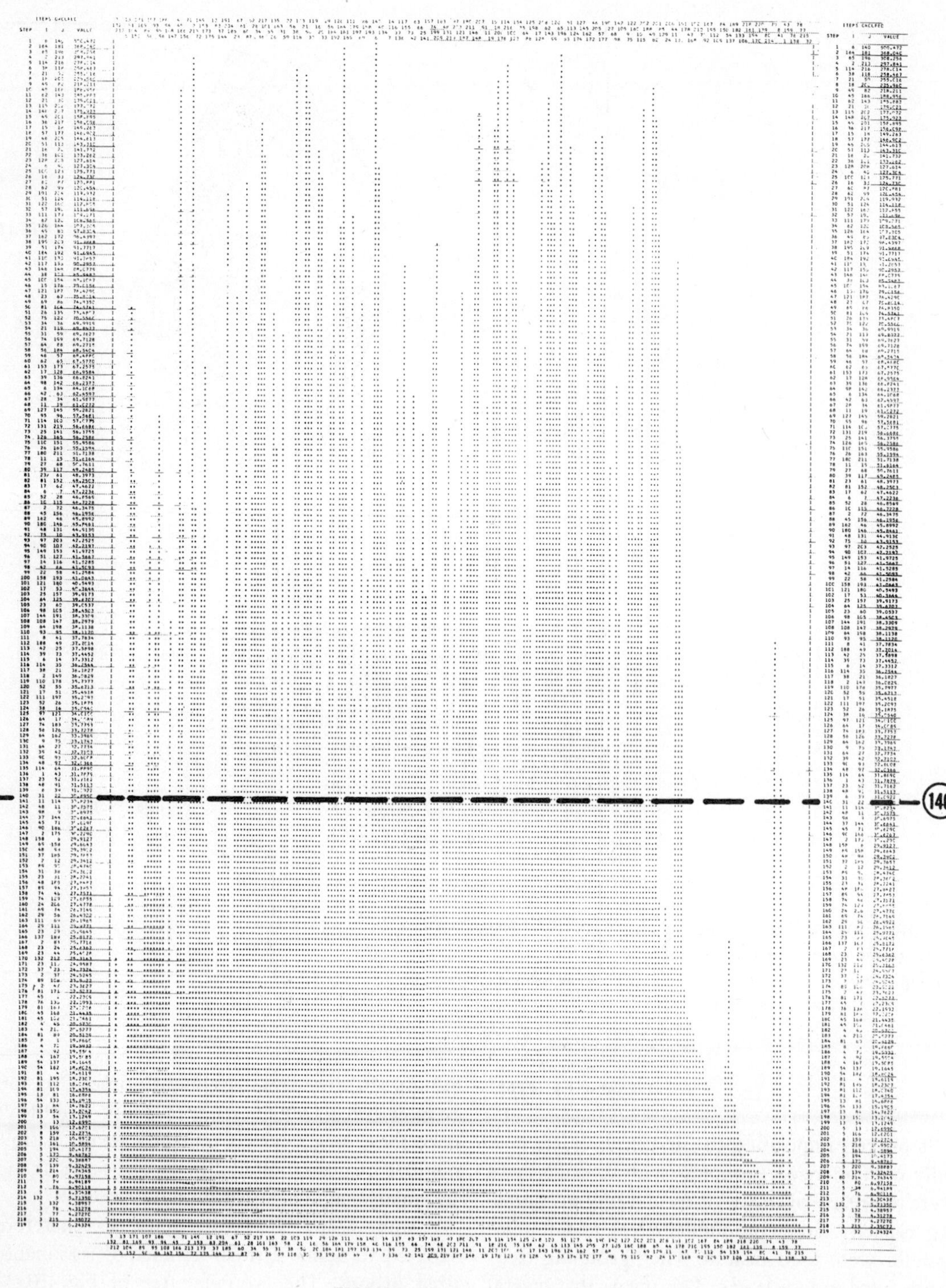

FIGURE 10–32. Grouping tree. *Source:* See caption for Fig. 10–3.

members defined at this grouping stage were chosen as the nuclei of larger groups; isolates were assigned to the nucleus the approximate centroid of which was closest. Exceptions were made in the case of two isolated clusters and two very isolated areas. The groups thus formed are displayed in social space in Fig. 10–33, and the group members are listed in Table 10–30. The resulting grouping solution, though by no means an optimum one, at least serves as some indication of what could be achieved in terms of community typology through the application of fairly objective classification methods.

The characteristics of the groups are fairly self-evident from their positions in social space. The first group, for example, is characterized by a fairly high-status population that is older and less familial than the rest of the population. The members of the group are found in high-status sectors about 7 or 8 miles from the Loop in all cases. Members of Group III (consisting of high-status, familial communities) are found further out from the city center in high-status sectors. A contrasting group, XVI, of low status and about average family status, occupies three distinct locations in the metropolitan region: the inner city; parts of the Lake Calumet area; and parts of the rural periphery of the SMSA. Similar description of the characteristics and the spatial distribution of the other groups is left to the reader. The analysis presented here contains no conclusive statement about metropolitan community types; further research is needed.

Racial and Ethnic Spaces

The socio-economic space of the Chicago metropolis in 1960 had not simply two or three dimensions, but ten, of which five were of some generality, at least with respect to cities in the industrial northeast of the United States.

The pressure of time did not permit the extension of the grouping analysis used above to three, four, five and ten dimensions, as originally planned, but an examination of some of the other two-dimensional spaces presented here (forty-five are possible) will serve to show how the metropolis is divided into communities on bases other than that of social space.

If the Race and Resources factor is plotted against Socio-economic Status (Fig. 10–34), a clear polarization of white and Negro tracts is evident. There are very many tracts to the left of the diagram (the white tracts), and a concentration of tracts towards the right (the predominantly Negro tracts). The generalized contours of the proportion of a tract's population that is Negro reveal that few tracts are integrated, and that those few tend to be of higher middle status rather than of lower status. But so few tracts, in fact, are integrated that it is difficult to argue that integration is more possible at higher socio-economic levels.

Public housing is located in two positions in both social and ethnic space: a few projects containing elderly white residents are clustered in the lower part of the bottom left quadrant of both Fig. 10–29 and Fig. 10–34; most of the public housing units, however, are located in the lower part of the bottom right quadrant of social space and ethnic space, and are occupied predominantly by Negro families. These clusterings are not unexpected in view of the maximum income limit set for project residents.

Further evidence of the polarization of racial and ethnic groups is provided by Fig. 10–35, a plot of Factor III against Factor IV (in community areas and municipalities), which may be called, in the broadest sense, *ethnic space*. There is the clear separation of white and black that was noted above, and also a separation between heavily Catholic and foreign-born communities, on the one hand, and Protestant and native-born, on the other. Those communities clustered in the right half of the graph are found on the northwest side, southwest side, and in the Calumet region in the city, and predominantly in the western sector of inner suburban Cook County in the rest of the metropolis. The remaining communities in the urban region are found in the upper left quadrant, with the exception of the North Shore suburbs, which contain rather higher percentages of Negroes than most of the white suburbs.

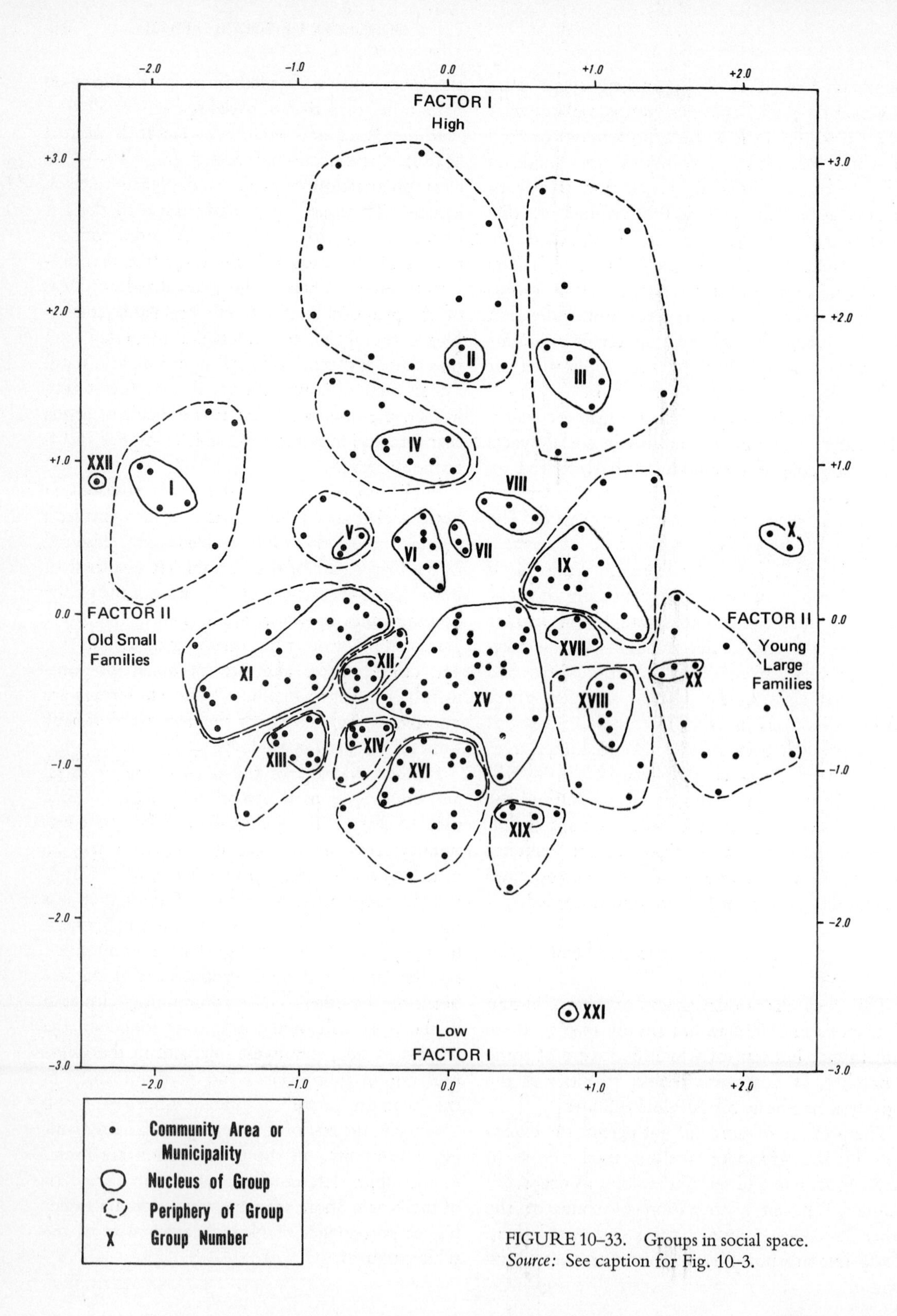

FIGURE 10–33. Groups in social space.
Source: See caption for Fig. 10–3.

TABLE 10–30
List of Group Members

Group Number		Group Members
I.	*Nucleus:*	Rogers Park, Near North Side, Hyde Park, South Shore
	Periphery:	Uptown, Evanston, Oak Park, Berwyn
II.	*Nucleus:*	Highland Park, Park Ridge, Glen Ellyn
	Periphery:	Kenilworth, Winnetka, Glencoe, Lake Bluff, River Forest, Riverside, LaGrange Park, Western Springs, Hinsdale, Clarendon Hills
III.	*Nucleus:*	Skokie, Glenview, Northbrook, Deerfield, Mount Prospect
	Periphery:	Wilmette, Lincolnwood, Northfield, Arlington Heights, Westchester, Palos Heights, Flossmoor, Park Forest
IV.	*Nucleus:*	West Ridge, Beverly, Elmhurst, Wheaton, Downers Grove, Homewood
	Periphery:	Forest Glen, North Park, Lake Forest, LaGrange, Naperville
V.	*Nucleus:*	Avalon Park, Geneva, Brookfield
	Periphery:	Auburn, Gresham, Barrington
VI.	*Nucleus:*	Edison Park, Norwood Park, Morgan Park, Crystal Lake, Elmwood Park, Riverdale, Crete
VII.	*Nucleus:*	Libertyville, Des Plaines, Broadview
VIII.	*Nucleus:*	Palatine, Itasca, Lombard, Evergreen Park
IX.	*Nucleus:*	Calumet Heights, Niles, Mundelein, Norridge, Roselle, Hillside, Berkeley, Villa Park, Oak Lawn, Orland Park, Dolton, South Holland, Hazel Crest
	Periphery:	Morton Grove, Elk Grove
X.	*Nucleus:*	Hoffman Estates, Country Club Hills
XI.	*Nucleus:*	Lakeview, Lincoln Park, Albany Park, Austin, Kenwood, Washington Park, Woodlawn, Gage Park, Chicago Lawn, Washington Heights, Woodstock, McHenry, Elgin, West Dundee, Forest Park, Maywood, St. Charles, Batavia, Blue Island
	Periphery:	Lincoln Square, Chatham, Cicero
XII.	*Nucleus:*	Jefferson Park, Portage Park, Montclare, Belmont-Cragin, Aurora, Joliet
	Periphery:	Greater Grand Crossing, Waukegan
XIII.	*Nucleus:*	Irving Park, Hermosa, Avondale, South Lawndale, Near South Side, Grand Boulevard, Pullman, Fox Lake, Marengo, Harvard
	Periphery:	North Center
XIV.	*Nucleus:*	Roseland, Highwood, North Chicago, Lemont, Wilmington
	Periphery:	Logan Square, Brighton Park
XV.	*Nucleus:*	Dunning, East Garfield Park, Douglas, South Chicago, South Deering, West Pullman, Archer Heights, West Elsdon, Clearing, West Lawn, Englewood, Winthrop Harbor, Wauconda, Grayslake, Lake Zurich, Cary, Harwood Heights, River Grove, Franklin Park, Schiller Park, Bensenville, Woodale, Melrose Park, Bellwood, West Chicago, Lyons, Westmont, Lisle, Stickney, Lockport, Midlothian, Oak Forest, Harvey, Calumet City, Chicago Heights
XVI.	*Nucleus:*	Humboldt Park, West Garfield Park, Near West Side, Armour Square, Oakland, East Side, Hegewisch, Bridgeport, New City, West Englewood, Zion, Round Lake Park, South Elgin, Summit, South Chicago Heights
	Periphery:	West Town, Lower West Side, Burnside, McKinley Park, Round Lake Beach, Phoenix, Steger
XVII.	*Nucleus:*	Mount Greenwood, Hickory Hills, Tinley Park, Lansing
XVIII.	*Nucleus:*	Garfield Ridge, North Lake, Bridge View, Justice, Alsip, Worth, Calumet Park
	Periphery:	North Lawndale, Palos Hills, Posen, Thornton
XIX.	*Nucleus:*	Stone Park, Crest Hill, Dixmoor
	Periphery:	Fuller Park, Robbins
XX.	*Nucleus:*	Wheeling, Hometown, Markham
	Periphery:	Ashburn, Rolling Meadows, Addison, Streamwood, Carpentersville, Romeoville, Sauk
XXI.	*Nucleus:*	East Chicago Heights
XXII.	*Nucleus:*	The Loop

Conclusions

A combination of social and ethnic spaces would enable us to make a more complete classification of communities within the metropolis on the basis of community of outlook as well as correspondence of social and physical characteristics. This is left to another publication,

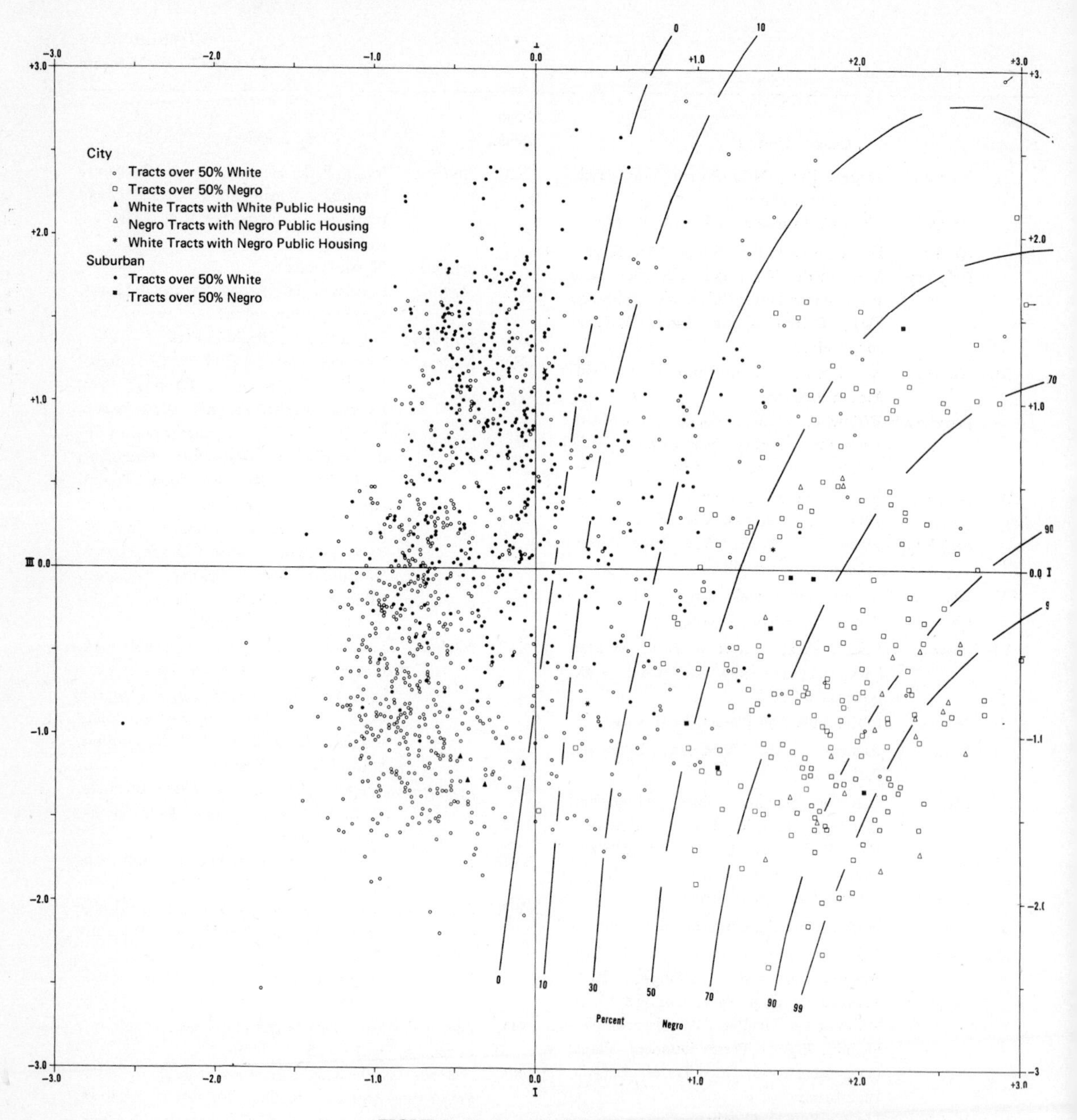

FIGURE 10–34. Social space: Factor III (Race and Resources) *vs.* Factor I (Socio-economic Status). *Source:* See caption for Fig. 10–3.

for we are content to recapitulate the principal findings reached so far.

At the outset we suggested that the classic hypotheses concerning the internal structure of the city (developed with special reference to Chicago) were not conflicting models in the present-day context but were complementary. It was postulated that:

1. Social rank and economic status indicators vary predominantly by sector of the city.
2. Family status and age structure indicators vary principally with distance from the city center.

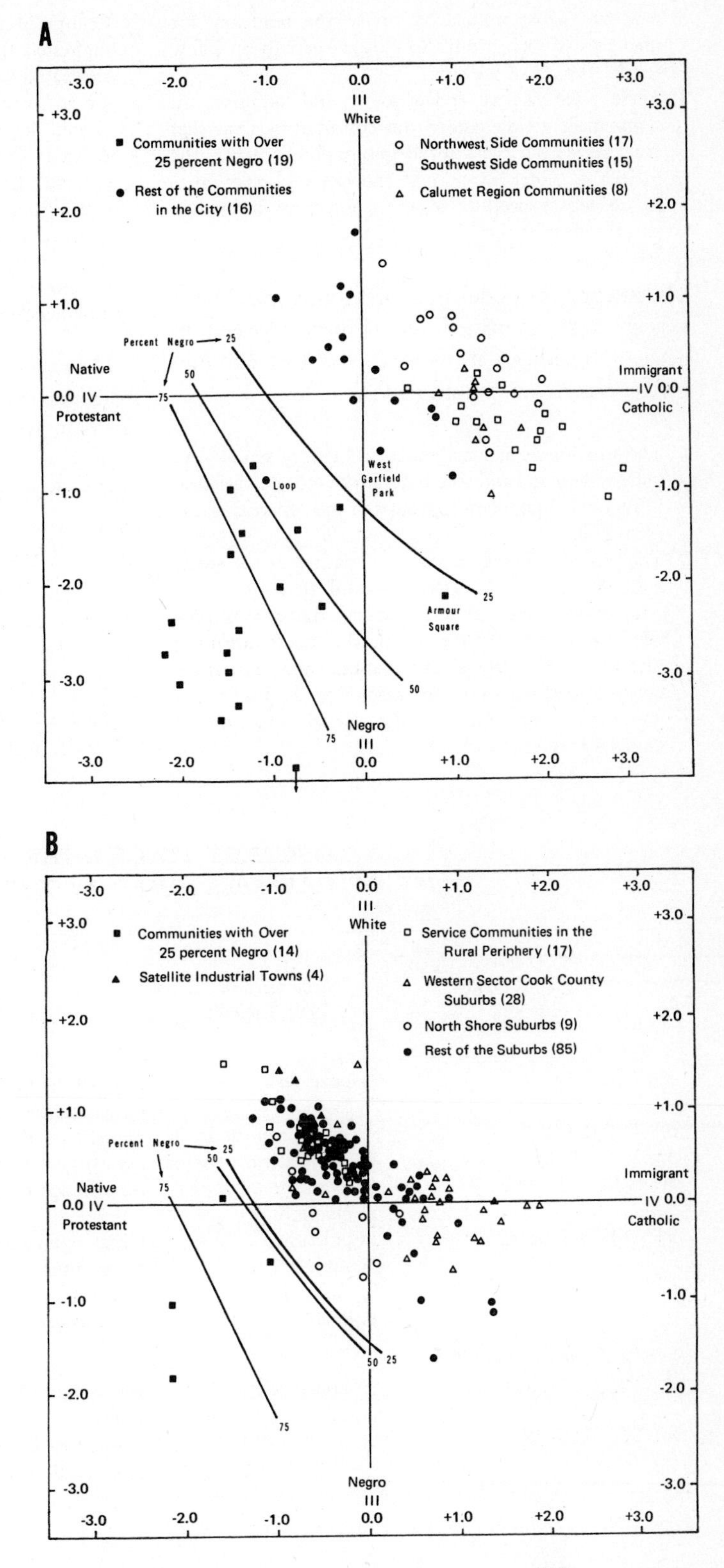

FIGURE 10–35. Ethnic space. *Source:* See caption for Fig. 10–3.

3. Minority group indicators reveal the tendency for members of such groups to cluster spatially in a few restricted parts of the city.
4. These patterns are independent and additive, in summation giving rise to the community areas that characterize the city's social geography. Further, the pattern of differentiation of the city's population is an aggregate product of the choices of individual households of type and place of residence.

The integrated model thus previously postulated was in part confirmed and in part revealed in need of qualification to serve for the Chicago metropolis. It was found that:

1. The dimensions of social status and family status were independent and additive contributors to the variation of residential population groups in the subareas of the metropolis.
2. The principal mode of spatial variation of the social status dimension was sectoral, and that of family status zonal, but zonal variation was almost as important as sectoral in the case of social status (confirming that many of Burgess' observations were not mere fancies), and sectoral variation was a minor but important contributor to the spatial variation of family status.
3. Comparison with similar studies of smaller cities suggested that this mix of spatial patterns might be associated with the size and stage of development of a city, since the smaller a city, the closer it approximated the integrated model postulated earlier.
4. A series of independent minority-group dimensions emerged from the analysis, but the most important, that distinguishing the Negro population, was undoubtedly associated with the set of socio-economic status indicators in a way that clearly revealed the pattern of discrimination along racial lines in the midwest metropolis.

The nature of the factorial ecology that emerged from the analysis lent strong support to, though not conclusive proof of, our view of the city as a product of the actions of home suppliers and home demanders. And the dimensions of differentiation that emerged have even wider significance. They showed that, *within the limits of the technology and resources at their command, people choose to minimize, through living apart from those unlike themselves, the possibilities of conflict because of class* (Factor I), *generational* (Factor II), *racial* (Factor III), *and religious or national* (Factors IV, VI, VIII, and X) *differences.*

APPENDIX TO CHAPTER 10: LIST OF VARIABLES USED IN THE ANALYSES

Number	*Abbreviation Used in Computer Analyses*	*Name Used in Text Tables*	*Definition*
Demographic characteristics			
1.	POP 1960	Population	Population in 1960 of community area, municipality, or census tract
2.	PUNDER 18	% population under 18	Percentage of the population under 18 years of age
3.	POVER 65	% population over 65	Percentage of the population over 65 years of age
4.	MEDIAN AGE	Median age of population	Median age of the population, in years
5.	POP DENSITY	Population density	Gross population density, in thousands of persons per square mile
6.	PTOTAL	% of total population	Population of the community area or municipality as a percentage of the total metropolitan area population
Racial and ethnic characteristics			
7.	PNONWHITE 60	% non-white population	Percentage of the population which was non-white, in 1960
8.	PNATIV, NATIV	% native-born of native parentage	Percentage of the population born in the U.S. of parents born in the U.S.

Number	Abbreviation Used in Computer Analyses	Name Used in Text Tables	Definition
9.	PNATIV, FOR*	% population native-born of foreign or mixed parentage	Percentage of the population born in the U.S., with at least one parent born in a foreign country
10.	PFOREIGNBORN*	% foreign-born population	Percentage of the population born in a foreign country
11.	POLISH LQ†	Polish location quotient	A measure of the concentration of Polish foreign stock* in the area
12.	GERMAN LQ†	German location quotient	A measure of the concentration of German foreign stock* in the area
13.	ITALIAN LQ†	Italian location quotient	A measure of the concentration of Italian foreign stock* in the area
14.	RUSSIAN LQ†	Russian location quotient	A measure of the concentration of Russian foreign stock* in the area
15.	IRISH LQ†	Irish location quotient	A measure of the concentration of Irish foreign stock* in the area
16.	CZECH LQ†	Czech location quotient	A measure of the concentration of Czech foreign stock* in the area
17.	SWEDISH LQ†	Swedish location quotient	A measure of the concentration of Swedish foreign stock* in the area
18.	BRITISH LQ†	British location quotient	A measure of the concentration of British foreign stock* in the area
19.	CANADIAN LQ†	Canadian location quotient	A measure of the concentration of Canadian foreign stock* in the area
20.	FOREIGN STOCK LQ*†	Foreign stock location quotient	A measure of the concentration of foreign stock* in the area
21.	NEGRO LQ†	Negro location quotient	A measure of the concentration of Negroes in the area
22.	NATIVE WHITE†	Native white location quotient	A measure of the concentration of native whites in the area
23.	OTHER NON-WHITE†	Other non-white location quotient	A measure of the concentration of other non-whites in the area
Religious characteristics			
24.	PPROTESTANT	% white Protestant population	Percentage of the population which is white Protestant
25.	PCATHOLIC	% white Catholic population	Percentage of the population which is white Catholic
26.	PJEWISH	% Jewish population	Percentage of the population which is white Jewish
Income characteristics			
27.	MEDIANINC	Median annual income	Median annual income of families in 1959
28.	POVER 10,000	% families with incomes over $10,000	Percentage of families with annual incomes of over $10,000
29.	PUNDER 3,000	% families with incomes under $3,000	Percentage of families with annual incomes of under $3,000
Occupational characteristics			
30.	PWHITECOLLAR	% white-collar workers	Percentage of the labor force in white-collar occupations
31.	PPROF/MANG	% professional and managerial employees	Percentage of the labor force in professional and managerial occupations

Number	Abbreviation Used in Computer Analyses	Name Used in Text Tables	Definition
32.	PCLERK/SALES	% clerical and sales workers	Percentage of the labor force in clerical and sales occupations
33.	PCRAFT/OPER	% craftsmen and operatives	Percentage of craftsmen and operatives in the labor force
34.	PLABORER	% laborers	Percentage of laborers in the the labor force
35.	PSERVICE	% workers in service occupations	Percentage of the labor force in service occupations
Educational characteristics			
36.	MEDSHOOLYRS	Median school years completed	Median years of schooling completed by the population aged 25 years and over
37.	4YRS+HS	% with 4 years of high school or more	Percentage of the population aged 25 years and over with 4 years of high school education or more
Mobility			
38.	PMOVED	% families moved since 1955	Percentage of families not living in same home as in 1955
Housing			
39.	HOME VALUE	Median home value	Median value of one-unit, owner-occupied homes
40.	PONE UNIT	% housing units in 1-unit structures	Percentage of housing units that are single family homes
41.	PTWO UNITS	% housing units in 2-unit stuctures	Percentage of housing units in two-unit structures
42.	PTHREE UNITS	% housing units in 3- or more-unit structures	Percentage of housing units in three- or more-unit structures
43.	POP PER HSLD	Population per household	Population per household (family size)
44.	POWNOCCUPIED	% owner-occupied housing	Percentage of housing units that are owner-occupied
45.	P BEFORE 1940	% housing built before 1940	Percentage of housing units built before 1940
46.	P BUILT 40–49	% housing built 1940–1949	Percentage of housing units built between 1940 and 1949
47.	P AFTER 1950	% housing built 1950 and after	Percentage of housing units built in 1950 and after
48.	MEDIAN RENT	Median rent	Median monthly contract rent of rented housing units, in dollars
49.	PSOUND	% sound housing units	Percentage of housing units that are sound and have all facilities
50.	POVERCROWDED	% overcrowded housing units	Percentage of housing units occupied by more than one person per room
Employment characteristics			
51.	PUNEMPLOYED	% unemployed workers	Percentage of the labor force unemployed
52.	TOT UNEMP	Total unemployment	Total numbers unemployed
53.	PWOMEN IN LF	% women 14 and over in labor force	Percentage of women aged 14 and over in the labor force
54.	PCAR	% workers commuting by car	Percentage of the labor force commuting to work by car
55.	PBUS	% workers commuting by bus	Percentage of the labor force commuting to work by bus

Number	Abbreviation Used in Computer Analyses	Name Used in Text Tables	Definition
56.	PRAIL	% workers commuting by rail	Percentage of the labor force commuting to work by rail
57.	PFOOT	% workers commuting on foot	Percentage of the labor force commuting to work on foot

Sources: Data for community areas are from Evelyn M. Kitagawa and Karl E. Taeuber, eds., *Local Community Factbook, Chicago Metropolitan Area, 1960* (Chicago: Chicago Community Inventory, University of Chicago, 1963); data for municipalities are from Northeastern Illinois Metropolitan Area Planning Commission, *Suburban Factbook* (Chicago, 1964); data for census tracts are from Department of Commerce, Bureau of the Census, *U.S. Census of Population and Housing: 1960, Final Report PHC(1)–26, Census Tracts, Chicago, Ill., Standard Metropolitan Statistical Area* (Washington, D.C.: Government Printing Office, 1961).
*The term "foreign stock" refers to the foreign-born and native-born of foreign or mixed parentage, taken together.
†The location quotient for each community area or municipality is constructed as follows:

$$LQ_{ij} = \frac{\dfrac{g_{ij}}{\sum_{j=1}^{m} g_{ij}}}{\dfrac{P_j}{\sum_{j=1}^{m} P_j}}$$

where: LQ_{ij} = the location quotient for population group i in area j
g_{ij} = the population of group i in area j
$\sum_{j=1}^{m} g_{ij}$ = the total population of group i in the metropolis
P_j = the total population in area j
$\sum_{j=1}^{m} P_j$ = the total population in the metropolis

FOOTNOTES TO CHAPTER 10

1. *American Journal of Sociology*, XLII, No. 2 (July, 1936), 1–15.

2. Harvey N. Zorbaugh, in "The Natural Areas of the City," *Publications of the American Sociological Society*, XX (1926), 188–97, provides a detailed definition of the term "natural area" as used by the Chicago school of urban ecologists.

3. Such tests involved mapping social data for a set of areal units for the city, and cumulating the particular indices by concentric rings around the central node of the city (the central business district). For some good examples of such research see Robert E. L. Faris and H. Warren Dunham, *Mental Disorders in Urban Areas* (Chicago: University of Chicago Press, 1939).

The tests were never really satisfactory, as Leo Schnore has pointed out in "On the Spatial Structure of Cities in the Two Americas," Chapter x in *A Study of Urbanization*, eds. Philip M. Hauser and Leo F. Schnore (New York: John Wiley & Sons, Inc., 1965). Schnore includes a very extensive bibliography of such papers.

4. For example: Harvey Zorbaugh, *Gold Coast and Slum* (1929); Nels Anderson, *The Hobo* (1923); E. Franklin Frazier, *The Negro Family in Chicago* (1932); and William F. Whyte, Jr., *Street Corner Society* (1943); all published in Chicago by the University of Chicago Press.

5. Ernest W. Burgess, "The Growth of the City: An Introduction to a Research Project," in *The City*, eds. Robert E. Park, Ernest W. Burgess, and Robert D. McKenzie (Chicago: University of Chicago Press, 1925).

6. Louis Wirth, "Urbanism as a Way of Life," *American Journal of Sociology*, XLIV, No. 2 (July, 1938), 1–24.

7. "Primary modes of interaction" involve face-to-face contacts between people in a whole span of roles; in "secondary modes of interactions" the contact is still face-to-face but in a specialized role only; in "tertiary modes" of contact (through letter or phone), even the face-to-face element is missing.

8. Oscar Lewis, in "Further Observations on the Folk-Urban Continuum and Urbanization with Special Reference to Mexico City," Part A of Chapter xiii in *A Study of Urbanization*, suggests that, as secondary and tertiary modes of interaction increase, the primary mode remains strong, along with the bonds of kinship.

9. Perhaps most progress has been made in the field of juvenile delinquency. Clifford Shaw and Henry McKay, *Juvenile Delinquency and Urban Areas* (Chicago: University of Chicago Press, 1942), show that juvenile delinquency is a deviant subculture with its own pattern of activity, rewards and sanctions, which is, like other cultural systems, passed on from generation to generation. For a first-hand account by a participant, see Claude Brown's *Manchild in the Promised Land* (New York: The Macmillan Company, 1965).

10. Homer Hoyt, *One Hundred Years of Land Values in Chicago* (Chicago: University of Chicago Press, 1933); and *idem, The Structure and Growth of Residential Neighborhoods in American Cities* (Washington, D.C.: U.S. Government Printing Office, 1939).

11. The variables were:
   1. Average rental for the block
   2. Percentage of residential structures that are 35 years old and over
   3. Percentage of dwelling units owner-occupied
   4. Percentage of residential structures in need of major repairs or unfit for occupancy

5. Percentage of the dwelling units that have no private bath
6. Percentage of persons that are of a race other than white
7. Percentage of dwelling units having no central heat
8. Percentage of dwelling units that are overcrowded

—*The Structure and Growth of Residential Neighborhoods*, p. 34.

12. *Ibid.*, pp. 118–19.

13. See Maurice R. Davie, "The Pattern of Urban Growth," in *Studies in the Science of Society*, ed. George P. Murdock (New Haven: Yale University Press, 1938), pp. 131–61, reprinted in *Studies in Human Ecology*, ed. G. A. Theodorson (New York: Harper & Row, Publishers, 1961).

14. Brian J. L. Berry, "Internal Structure of the City," *Law and Contemporary Problems*, XXX (Winter, 1965), p. 115.

15. Theodore R. Anderson and Janice A. Egeland, "Spatial Aspects of Social Area Analysis," *American Sociological Review*, XXVI, No. 2 (June, 1961), 392–98.

16. It is not surprising that Hoyt emphasized the sectoral pattern, dealing as he was with such housing attributes as these.

17. Map 12 in the Community Renewal Program's, *An Atlas of Chicago's People, Jobs and Homes* (Chicago, Renewal 1963) gives a picture of the distribution of industrial land use in Chicago in 1960.

18. This link was discussed in Chapter 9 of the present book. Concomitant with the decline in land values with increasing distance from the city center is a decline in the intensity of residential construction, leading to a gradient in home types from high-rise apartments near the center, through low-rise apartments, row houses, and duplexes, to single-family houses in the suburbs.

19. The figure is highly simplified in that only three axes of growth are shown, whereas, in fact, six major and three minor axes (along the commuting railroads) would be a better approximation.

20. This "multiple-nuclei" concept was suggested by Chauncy D. Harris and Edward L. Ullman, in "The Nature of Cities," *Annals of the American Academy of Political and Social Science*, CCXLII (November, 1945), 7–17.

21. See John R. P. Friedmann and John Miller, "The Urban Field," in Chapter 2 of the present volume.

22. The present section is couched largely in terms of the private housing market since the public sector occupies only a small and woefully inadequate portion of that market in most American cities. If our discussion were of a European city, then the public sector could not be excluded.

23. Personal preferences about the appearance of the home and the surrounding neighborhood have been investigated by George L. Peterson in "Subjective Measures of Housing Quality: An Investigation of Problems of Codification of Subjective Value for Urban Analysis" (Ph.D. dissertation, Northwestern University, June, 1965); *idem*, "A Model of Preference: Quantitative Analysis of the Perception of the Visual Appearance of Residential Neighborhoods," *Journal of Regional Science*, VII (Summer, 1967), 19–31; and *idem*, "Measuring Visual Preferences of Residential Neighborhoods," *Ekistics*, XXIII (March, 1967), 169–73.

24. Herbert Gans, *The Levittowners* (New York: Pantheon Books, Inc., 1967), Table 2, p. 35.

25. A product of the independent developer's decision about what to build.

26. See Zorbaugh, "The Natural Areas of the City."

27. The travel savings resulting when the low-income worker lives close to his job tend, in a market economy, to accrue to the landlord, who is able to charge the worker location rent. The total rent that the landlord is able to demand is not large, however, because the amenities in a location close to industrial workplaces are so few and the quality of the dwelling is so poor. Thus, the total rent per dwelling unit, made up of location rent and amenity rent (which may even be negative), is usually not high.

28. A much more elaborate theoretical discussion of the residential location decision process is contained in Lawrence A. Brown and Eric Moore, "The Intra-Urban Migration Process: An Actor-Oriented Model" (Unpublished paper, Department of Geography, University of Iowa, April, 1968), part of an ongoing research project on "Intra-Urban Migration in Its Spatial Context."

29. These are discussed in R. N. S. Harris, G. S. Tolley, and C. Harrell, "The Residence Site Choice" (Unpublished paper, Department of Economics, University of Chicago, 1967).

30. See Scott Greer, *The Emerging Metropolis* (New York: The Free Press, 1962), Chapter iv, "The Community of Limited Liability."

31. See Allan H. Spear, *Black Chicago: The Making of a Negro Ghetto, 1890–1920* (Chicago: University of Chicago Press, 1967); and St. Clair Drake and Horace Cayton, *Black Metropolis* (New York: Harcourt, Brace & World, Inc., 1945).

32. Eshref Shevky and Marianne Williams, *The Social Areas of Los Angeles: Analysis and Typology* (Berkeley and Los Angeles: University of California Press, 1949); Wendell Bell, "The Social Areas of the San Francisco Bay Region," *American Sociological Review*, XVIII (February, 1953), 29–47; Eshref Shevky and Wendell Bell, *Social Area Analysis: Theory, Illustrative Application, and Computational Procedures* (Stanford, Calif.: Stanford University Press, 1955).

33. The methods of construction are detailed in Shevky and Bell, *ibid*, pp. 54–58.

34. See Amos Hawley and Otis D. Duncan, "Social Area Analysis: A Critical Appraisal," *Land Economics*, XXXIII No. 4 (November, 1957), 337–45; and Otis D. Duncan's Review of *Social Area Analysis* by Eshref Shevky and Wendell Bell, *American Journal of Sociology*, LXI, No. 2 (July, 1955), 84–85.

35. Wendell Bell, "Economic, Family and Ethnic Status: An Empirical Test," *American Sociological Review*, XX, No. 1 (February, 1955), 45–52.

36. Maurice Van Arsdol, Santo F. Camilleri, and Calvin F. Schmid, "The Generality of Urban Social Area Indices," *American Sociological Review*, XXIII, No. 2 (June, 1958), 277–84.

37. Such research presupposes the availability of a large, high-speed computer and an operational program for the factor analysis, if large data matrices are to be factor analyzed. The absence of such resources has (presumably) meant the continuing use of the Shevky-Bell indices. A full bibliography of the research up to 1964 is contained in Scott Greer, "Bibliography: Social Area Analysis" (Department of Sociology, Northwestern University, May, 1964, Mimeographed). A recent typical example is D. T. Herbert, "Social Area Analysis: A British Study," *Urban Studies*, IV, No. 1 (February, 1967), 41–60.

38. Recent reviews of all types of social area analysis, including many recent studies in factorial ecology, are to be found in Robert A. Murdie, *The Factorial Ecology of Metropolitan Toronto, 1951–1961: An Essay on the Social Geography*

of the City (Chicago: University of Chicago, Department of Geography Research Paper No. 116, 1968); and Janet Abu-Lughod, "A Critical Test for the Theory of Social Area Analysis: The Factorial Ecology of Cairo, Egypt" (Paper, Department of Sociology, Northwestern University, February, 1968).

39. Berry, "Internal Structure of the City."

40. For an outline of factor analysis for the layman, see Rudolph Rummel, "Understanding Factor Analysis," *Journal of Conflict Resolution*, XI (December, 1967), 440–80; the more mathematically inclined should see Harry Harman, *Modern Factor Analysis* (Chicago: University of Chicago Press, 1960).

41. See Van Arsdol, Camilleri, and Schmid, "Urban Social Area Indices."

42. Calvin F. Schmid and Kiyoshi Tagashira, "Ecological and Demographic Indices: A Methodological Analysis," *Demography*, I (1964), 194–211.

43. The term "Skid Row" originated in the depressed waterfront of Seattle during the town's years as a lumber center, when flophouses, saloons and the like lined the lumber "skids" used to convey logs downhill to Puget Sound.

44. The urbanized area and commuting field of Chicago are shown in Fig. 10-9. The study area that was chosen was, in fact, the SMSA, which, although it does not coincide exactly with the one proposed, is a close approximation. The few outlying rural service settlements and industrial towns that were included in the analysis served as a useful contrast to the urbanized area communities without fundamentally distorting the factor structures.

45. Frank L. Sweetser, in "Ecological Factors in Metropolitan Zones and Sectors," in *Quantitative Ecological Analysis in the Social Sciences*, eds. Mattei Dogan and Stein Rokkan (Cambridge, Mass.: The M.I.T. Press, 1968), considered the influence of the boundaries of the study area on the factorial ecologies that emerged in his studies of Boston and Helsinki. He divided his study area into concentric rings and sectors and performed separate factor analyses for each ring and sector. But he failed to relate the similarities and differences of the factor structures in the various zones of the metropolis to the effect that such a zonation would have on the variation and range of values of his variables.

46. W. S. Robinson, "Ecological Correlation and the Behavior of Individuals," *American Sociological Review*, XV (June, 1950), 351–57; Herbert Menzel, "Comment on Robinson's 'Ecological Correlation and the Behavior of Individuals,' " *American Sociological Review*, XV (October, 1950), 674. Both articles are reprinted in *Studies in Human Ecology*, ed. G. Theodorson (New York: Harper & Row, Publishers, 1961). See also Otis D. Duncan, Ray P. Cuzzort, and Beverly Duncan, *Statistical Geography: Problems in Analyzing Areal Data* (New York: The Free Press, 1961).

47. See Leo A. Goodman, "Some Alternatives to Ecological Correlation," *American Journal of Sociology*, LXIV (May, 1959), 610–25.

48. Peter Goheen, *The North American Industrial City in the Late Nineteenth Century: The Case of Toronto* (Department of Geography, Research Paper; Chicago: University of Chicago, *in press*).

49. *Ibid.*

50. Murdie, *The Factorial Ecology of Toronto* (*in press*).

51. Brian J. L. Berry and Robert A. Murdie, *Socio-economic Correlates of Housing Condition* (Toronto: Metropolitan Planning Board, 1965).

52. A study of the factorial ecology of Chicago in 1930, 1940, and 1950, and for the decades, 1930 to 1940, 1940 to 1950, and 1950 to 1960 is in progress by Alan Hunter, "Communities and Community Areas in Chicago" (Ph. D. dissertation, University of Chicago, in preparation).

53. Poul O. Pedersen, *Modeller for Befolkningsstruktur og Befolkningsudvikling i Storbyomrader Specielt med Henblik pa Storkobenhavn* (Copenhagen: State Urban Planning Institute, 1967).

54. Frank L. Sweetser, "Factor Structure as Ecological Structure in Helsinki and Boston," *Acta Sociologica*, VIII, No. 3 (1965), 205–25; *idem*, "Ecological Factors in Metropolitan Zones and Sectors."

55. Abu-Lughod, "The Factorial Ecology of Cairo"; and Brian J. L. Berry and Philip Rees, "The Factorial Ecology of Calcutta," *American Journal of Sociology*, LXXIV, No. 5 (March, 1969), 445–91.

56. Abu-Lughod, "The Factorial Ecology of Cairo," p. 21.

57. Those studies, that is, that do not use a severely underbounded or overbounded study area.

58. Abu-Lughod, "The Factorial Ecology of Cairo," p. 30.

59. Dennis McElrath and John Barkey, "Social and Physical Space: Models of Metropolitan Differentiation" (Paper, Northwestern University, 1964).

60. Walter Kaufman, "Social Area Analysis: An Explication of Theory, Methodology and Techniques, with Statistical Tests of Revised Procedures, San Francisco and Chicago, 1950" (Ph.D. dissertation, Northwestern University, 1961).

61. Brian J. L. Berry and Robert J. Tennant, *Commercial Structure* (Chicago: Northeastern Illinois Planning Commission, 1965), Appendix A, "Socio-economic Classification of Municipalities in Northeastern Illinois Metropolitan Area."

62. They are areas of new construction not yet occupied; older areas in decline; areas which have characteristically high rates of population turnover and thus have a substantial pool of unoccupied housing units at any point in time."—Berry and Tennant, *Commercial Structure*, p. 120.

63. "Community Areas" are areal divisions of the City of Chicago originally established by Ernest Burgess in the 1920's, and for which sets of statistics have been compiled in *The Community Fact Book* (Chicago: Chicago Community Inventory, University of Chicago) for 1930, 1940, 1950, and 1960.

64. Evelyn M. Kitagawa and Karl E. Taeuber, *Local Community Factbook: Chicago Metropolitan Area, 1960* (Chicago: Chicago Community Inventory, University of Chicago, 1963).

65. Northeastern Illinois Metropolitan Area Planning Commission, *Suburban Factbook* (Chicago, 1964).

66. As many factors were produced as there are original variables, but most of these explain very little of the variance of the original data. Only factors with eigenvalues of greater than 1.0, that account, therefore, for more of the total variance than a single variable, were usually regarded as significant. The original data matrix was thereby collapsed from one comprising 57 variables $\times$ 222 observations to one of r factors $\times$ 222 observations, where r is the number of significant factors. The task of the social area analyst is to interpret the meaning of the various factors, both in terms of the variables that "load" highly (that is, correlate highly with) on particular factors, and that are relevant in terms of prior theory and concept. See Rummel, "Understanding Factor Analysis," and Harman, *Modern Factor Analysis*, for much fuller accounts

of the conceptual and mathematical foundations of factor analysis.

67. Fig. 13, p. 70, in Brian J. L. Berry, *Commercial Structure and Commercial Blight* (Department of Geography Research Paper No. 85, University of Chicago, 1963), shows the relationship between the inner-city industrial areas, blue-collar neighborhoods, and family income (bearing in mind which of the nonresidential areas are parks, universities, or airports).

68. Communities display double peaks in their age distribution, rather than the simple distribution we have assumed in our discussion here.

69. See Table 10-2. The quotation is from Abu-Lughod, "The Factorial Ecology of Cairo."

70. Variables 40 and 42, direct measures of housing type, load on Factor II, as do Variables 45 and 47 which relate to the age of the housing stock and are indirect measures of housing type in the case of Chicago. Variable 41, the percentage of housing in 2-unit structures, loads on Factor I, however, because it tends to be associated very largely with the blue-collar areas of the city.

The *Master Plan of Residential Land Use of Chicago* (Chicago: The Chicago Plan Commission, 1943) notes (pp. 36, 48) that the largest of all the residential Type-of-Structure areas (namely: tall apartment houses, walk-up apartments; mixed structures including apartments; mixed two-family and single-family structures; and single-family structures) is the one containing a mixture of single-family homes and two-flat structures. It covers 62 square miles and lies mainly to the west of the high-status, high-rise apartment areas near the lake. A comparison of the distribution of this type of structure area (in Fig. 32 of the Master Plan) with the distribution of lower-status communities (see Fig. 10-10) reveals that the distributions are associated.

71. This influence probably also operates in the white housing market. Large families with unskilled wage earners or mothers with illegitimate children are forced by circumstances to seek housing where the short-term cost is lowest, in the inner-city, high-density, apartment districts.

72. This contrasts with public housing policy in Britain, where "out-of-town" municipal housing "estates" have always complemented slum clearance and inner-city housing redevelopment.

73. Gans argues that the nature and cost of the home are the most important determinants of residential location. See *The Levittowners*, p. 35, Table 2.

74. There is some confusion over the term "ethnic." In the strict sense, following its derivation from the Greek "ethnos," a nation, it means "pertaining to a foreign national group or group marked out by the language it uses." The meaning has been extended to cover all groups sharply differentiated by national origin, language, or racial characteristics (as, e.g., Bell's "ethnic status"). Here, some attempt will be made to retain the original meaning of the word.

75. The situation may be reversed, however, in certain societies. In Montreal, for example, the English-speaking minority occupies the higher end of the socio-economic scale, and variables identifying this group load highly on a socio-economic status factor. See Geoffrey Cliffe-Phillips, John Mercer and Yue Man Yeung, "The Spatial Structure of Urban Areas: A Case Study of the Montreal Metropolitan Area" (Paper, Center for Urban Studies, University of Chicago, March, 1968).

76. Van Arsdol, Camilleri, and Schmid, in "Urban Social Area Indices," found a simple spatial segregation factor to be present in Atlanta, Birmingham, and Louisville in 1950. More recent studies of the latter two cities and of Shreveport, Louisiana, employing a wider range of variables (1960 data) found, however, that the variable Percentage Nonwhite loaded most highly and negatively on a general socio-economic status factor. See the following unpublished Papers, all written at the Center for Urban Studies, University of Chicago, in March, 1968: Yehoshua Cohen. "The Urban Ecology of Birmingham, Alabama"; Philip Peters, "The Urban Ecology of Louisville, Kentucky"; and Howard Spodek, "The Urban Ecology of Shreveport, Louisiana."

77. See Bruce Caswell, "The Urban Ecology of Miami, Florida" (Paper, Center for Urban Studies, University of Chicago, March, 1968).

78. The origins of this inequality and the physical confinement of the Negro population to the ghetto are traced in Spear's *Black Chicago: The Making of a Negro Ghetto*. An exhaustive analysis of Negro Chicago in the late 1930's is contained in Drake and Cayton's sociological classic, *Black Metropolis*. The story, in spatial terms, is extended to 1950 in Otis Duncan and Beverly Duncan, *The Negro Population of Chicago: A Study of Residential Succession* (Chicago: University of Chicago Press, 1957).

79. One contrary case may be the position of the Indonesian immigrant in the Netherlands. See Christopher Bagley, "Racial Barriers: (1) Holland Unites," *New Society*, XI, No. 284 (March, 1968), 339–40.

80. Spear, *Black Chicago*, p. 229.

81. Comparative research into the ecologies of a set of some thirty or so North-American cities is in progress at the Center for Urban Studies, University of Chicago.

82. The units used, community area and municipality, are not particularly suited to the delimitation of the Chicago ghetto. The Near North Side, the Near West Side, Kenwood, Hyde Park, and Morgan Park are communities containing both Negro and white neighborhoods. A more detailed spatial picture is provided by Fig. 10–22.

83. See Spear, *Black Chicago;* Stanley Lieberson, "Comparative Segregation and Assimilation of Ethnic Groups" (Ph.D. dissertation, University of Chicago, 1960); and Pierre de Visé, "Chicago at Mid-Century: Social Status and Ecology" (Working Paper, No. II.7, Chicago Regional Hospital Study, February, 1966), pp. 15–18.

84. Richard L. Morrill, "The Negro Ghetto: Problems and Alternatives," discusses ghetto expansion as a constrained process of block-by-block diffusion. He also points out that other groups, such as Orientals, Mexican-Americans, and Puerto Ricans are also forced by a variety of pressures to live in restricted areas. Morrills' paper is reprinted in Chapter 11.

In Chicago, the distribution of Spanish-speaking Americans parallels but does not coincide with that of the Negro population. Mexican-Americans are concentrated in the Near West Side (the strip dividing the Madison Avenue Negro residential axis from the Roosevelt Road axis), the lower West Side, and South Chicago near the steelworks. Puerto Ricans are concentrated in the same Near West Side area, in West Town, and away from the lake in the North Side community areas near the Loop.

85. As Frazier makes clear in *The Negro Family in Chicago*.

86. The most extensive study along ecological lines of the

assimilation of European immigrants into American urban life is Stanley Lieberson, *Ethnic Patterns in American Cities* (New York: The Free Press, 1963). See also David Ward, "The Emergence of Central Immigrant Ghettoes in American Cities, 1840–1920," *Annals of the Association of American Geographers*, LVIII, No. 2 (June, 1968), 343–59.

87. A number of smaller loadings of magnitude comparable with that of the Czech variable (not reported in Table 10–4) are of interest in positioning those population groups that tend to contain the highest proportions of immigrants and Catholics on the social and family status scales. Factor IV has a loading of .324 associated with Variable 33 (% Craftsmen and Operatives), indicating that high-scoring areas on the factor tend to contain skilled or semi-skilled blue-collar workers (working class), and a loading of .392 on Median Age (Variable 4), suggesting that immigrant areas contain a somewhat older population than average (as a result of the reduction of immigration from its peak in the first quarter of this century).

88. The WASP's (White Anglo-Saxon Protestants) are a subgroup within the larger Protestant division.

89. It is not suggested here that such a correlation matrix represents the best way to study the degree of spatial association or segregation between population groups. The correlation matrix is used because it forms part of the output of the University of Chicago MESA 85 factor analysis program. For a discussion of the range of methods available for measuring spatial segregation, see Donald J. Bogue, "Segregation: A Model for Multiple Criteria Measurement and Multiple Variable Explanation" (Paper, Department of Sociology, University of Chicago, October, 1967).

90. Berry and Tennant, *Commercial Structure*.

91. Hunter, in "Communities and Community Areas in Chicago," re-examines the criteria which Ernest Burgess originally used to delimit the community areas of Chicago, and attempts to assess how closely the set of areal units so defined corresponds to the behavioral communities now in existence.

92. In Chapter V, "Estimating Future Mode of Travel," of the Chicago Area Transportation Study's *Final Report, Volume II: Data Projections* (Chicago, 1960), the factors that affect people's choice of mode of travel to work are considered:

> [T]he appropriate location and probable use of each mode of transportation is determined by certain functional requirements. Among these requirements are land use, density of development and such consumer characteristics as automobile availability, ability to drive, plus the age, sex, and type of work of the traveller [p. 52].

93. The Czech location quotient has a positive loading of .236 on this factor.

94. Sweetser, "Ecological Factors in Metropolitan Zones and Sectors."

96. This is largely a white phenomenon. The corresponding movement of the black population is into the middle-status neighborhoods on the southern fringes of South Side Chicago.

97. The Lake Shore area was identified as the principal area within the city for the reception of immigrants from outside the metropolitan area by Ronald Freedman in his *Recent Migration to Chicago* (Chicago: University of Chicago Press, 1950). The area was still an important immigrant reception area in 1960 for whites while the West Side ghetto and eastern Woodlawn have become the ports of entry for Negro immigrants.

See Maps 32, 33, 34, and 35 in *An Atlas of Chicago's People, Jobs and Homes* (Chicago: Community Renewal Program, 1963) for a detailed breakdown, by census tract, of mobility patterns in the city. A picture of movement at the broad scale of city, rest of the metropolitan area, rest of the U.S., and rest of the world is provided by Pierre De Visé in "Chicago at Mid-Century: The Population Base" (Working Paper II.6, Chicago Regional Hospital Study, July, 1967), pp. 7–11.

98. Evidenced by the very high turnover of pupils in ghetto schools.

99. A very similar discussion of the reasons for the movement of people in the city is contained in James W. Simmons, "Changing Residence in the City: A Review of Intra-Urban Mobility" (Paper, Department of Geography, University of Toronto, 1968).

100. Peter Rossi's *Why Familes Move* (New York: The Free Press, 1955) would serve as an excellent starting point for such a research design.

101. See Goheen, *The Case of Toronto*.

102. See the general discussion on Variables, in their "Ecological and Demographic Indices."

103. Data was not gathered, coded, and punched for a few variables in a few tracts because the population failed to meet sample size requirements. The same criteria were adopted as were used in Kitagawa and Taeuber's *Local Community Factbook*. The values of variables were not calculated at all if the base (persons, families, or housing units) was less than 50 units. If the base was somewhere between 50 and 199, values were calculated only when the census data was complete, the items used were % Negroes, % Substandard housing, Population per household, % Population under 18, and % Population over 65; sample census items were not used.

104. *An Atlas of Chicago's People, Jobs and Homes* contains census tract maps of many of the individual variables employed in the present factor analysis. See: Map 25, Median years in school; Map 27, Median income; Map 37 (in part), Substandard housing; Map 31, Unemployment; Maps 15 and 16, Population under 18 and over 65, respectively; and Map 22, Percentage of Negroes.

105. The maps in Wilbur Zelinsky's "An Approach to the Religious Geography of the United States: Patterns of Church Membership in 1952," *Annals of the Association of American Geographers*, LI (June, 1961), 139–93, provide some estimate of cities in which these two dimensions would emerge.

106. For example, a Puerto Rican factor might emerge in New York, a Cuban in Miami, a Mexican in Los Angeles, and a Japanese in Seattle, assuming the conditions outlined in Table 10–8 were met.

107. The Puerto Rican factor in New York would probably be of this nature. See Glazer and Moynihan, *Beyond the Melting Pot*, pp. 86–136.

108. Theodore R. Anderson and Janice A. Egeland, "Spatial Aspects of Social Area Analysis," *American Sociological Review*, XXVI, No. 2 (June, 1961), 392–98.

109. Anderson and Egeland regard Shevky-Bell's social rank index as indicative of the prestige of a neighborhood rather than as a measure of its economic status, on the grounds that there exist some well-known discrepancies between the prestige of an occupation on the one hand and the income commanded by the practitioner, and income fluctuates with

stage in the life cycle. The dependence of income on factors other than social status (discrimination in particular) was noted in the present study of Chicago.

110. The findings of McElrath and Barkey, "Social Space and Physical Space," reported earlier, were confirmed only partially. Their Urbanization Index varied by both zone and sector, as does the Family Status factor of the present study, but their Social Rank Index varied only by zone, whereas the Socio-economic factor in the present study varies by both sector and zone.

111. The Between Zones F/Between Sectors F ratio for this factor is 58.5. See Murdie, *The Factorial Ecology of Metropolitan Toronto*, Table VII-4.

112. *Ibid.*, p. 168.

113. For another example see Herbert, "Social Area Analysis: A British Study."

114. Such a grouping procedure was first applied to a geographic problem by Brian J. L. Berry in "A Method for Deriving Multi-Factor Uniform Regions, *Przeglad Geograficzny*, XXXIII (1961), 263–82. A variant of his method, based on an algorithm devised and a program written by Peter M. Neely, is employed here. For a review of the various alternatives available and their relative merits, see Philip M. Lankford, "Regionalization: Theory and Alternative Algorithms" (Master's thesis, University of Chicago, 1968).

CHAPTER 11

behavioral bases of changing social space: individual mobility and waves of succession

INTRA-URBAN MOBILITY*

We now turn to intra-urban mobility—to decisions of individuals, to the processes that result from large numbers of such decisions, and to the results of the processes, as seen in patterns of stability or change in social space. Only in this way can we come to grips with the dynamics of urban social geography. Individual mobility is the mechanism by which change is generated. The driving energy involved is impressive. About 20 per cent of the population of the United States changes residence between one year and the next. Although many moves are made by a small number of highly mobile people, 40 to 50 per cent of the entire population moves within a five-year period. Given the magnitude of this movement, the distribution and characteristics of the population are remarkably stable; the in-migrants to an area, for the most part, resemble the out-migrants in numbers and attributes. Over a sufficient time, however, the migration process is an important instrument in altering the spatial patterns of social and demographic variables, and under certain conditions it leads to dramatic short-run changes in small areas, such as the almost instantaneous growth of a new subdivision, or the expansion of a racial ghetto.

An important but relatively neglected subset of these changes in residences are those which take place within a metropolitan area.[1] As Table 11–1 shows, the majority of moves are of this type. Measured in one-year intervals, the intra-county mobility rate is 12 to 13 per cent or about two-thirds of all moves.[2] Many of these relocations

*Reprinted from James W. Simmons, "Changing Residence in the City: A Review of Intra-Urban Mobility," *The Geographical Review*, LVIII (1968), with the permission of the author and editor. The study was aided by a grant from the Canadian Council on Urban and Regional Research.

TABLE 11–1

Migration in Urbanized Areas in the United States: 1955–1960 (in Percentages of Population)

Residence in 1955	*Central City*	*Fringe*	*Total*
Same house as in 1960	48.5	47.5	47.8
Different house in U.S.	47.5	50.0	48.0
Same county	33.6	28.7	31.4
Different county	13.9	21.1	16.6
Same state	5.7	10.1	7.3
Different state	8.3	11.0	9.3
Abroad	1.8	1.4	1.6
Moved, residence in 1955 not reported	2.5	1.1	1.9

Source: Bureau of the Census, *Census of Population, 1960: Subject Reports,* "Size of Place," Final Report PC (3)-1B, Table 1 (Washington, D.C.: U.S. Government Printing Office, 1963).

take place within the same block or the same neighborhood, but longer moves within the city determine most of the population growth or decline in different parts of the urban area and virtually all the changes in relative income levels and ethnic or racial concentrations [in these subareas].

. . .

Although the general process of migration has been widely studied and several excellent reviews are available,[3] the concepts and findings have limited application to movements within urban areas, since economic opportunity, the mainstay of migration theory at the international and interstate level, is largely irrelevant for movements within a commuting area, or for any patterns of gross migration. As a result the investigation of intra-urban mobility has been primarily the realm of the sociologist rather than the economist. The various facts of the topic, however, cover the whole range of the behavioral sciences, and may be synthesized under three headings. First, *who moves*? What information do we have about the sociological and psychological characteristics of movers? Is it possible to predict the mobility rates of various subcategories of the population? An extension of this question is *why do they move*? What social-psychological and economic factors actually trigger a move by a given household? Here the emphasis is on the study of the single decision-making unit. Finally, the almost completely neglected question, but of the greatest concern to students of urban spatial structure, is *where do they move*? What spatial regularities are these in the relocation process? How does the household go about finding a new place to live? What is the interaction between the supply of various kinds of housing and the demand by various consumer units?

Who Moves?

The great proportion of intra-urban residential movement reflects the high mobility of certain demographic groups within the population. The spatial distribution of demographic characteristics is a major factor in differentiating mobility rates throughout the city and, as will appear later on, the housing and access requirements of various life-cycle groups dominate the patterns of flow.

Data sources. Virtually all of the research on intra-urban relocation done prior to 1950 was concerned with the measurement of mobility rates. Urban sociological theory in the 1920's and 1930's stressed the role of mobility as a cause of urban social problems, but the absence of census data on rates of movement meant that each investigator had to develop his own measures. Caplow reviews the early studies in some detail, revealing the wide variations in mobility rates derived for different cities at different times and using different sources.[4]

The general impression gained from these works is that of a considerably higher degree of intra-urban mobility in the first quarter of the century. One study over time, that of Albig using city directories, found a steady decline in intra-urban mobility rates, from over 50 per cent per annum from 1903 to 1910 to 20 per cent from 1930 to 1932,[5] and Goldstein also identified a decline, although not so marked.[6] On the other hand an unpublished study by Rossi, based on longitudinal mobility records of households, indicates continuously increasing intra-urban mobility.[7] The measurement techniques are so diverse and imperfect that it seems unlikely the question will be resolved.

Once the Bureau of the Census began to gather systematic measures of mobility on a nationwide basis, the flood of consistent data allowed researchers to turn their attention to the study of process. *The Census of Population: 1940* asked about place of residence in 1935 although it did not aggregate moves for areas smaller than a county. *The Census of Population: 1950*, however, provided information on movers, both intra-county and inter-county, for urban places and census tracts during the year 1949 to 1950.[8] *The Census of Population: 1960* broadened the categories (see Table 11–1) and extended the time period to five years, 1955 to 1960.[9] For longitudinal comparisons, the *Current Population Survey* has produced annual estimates of national and regional mobility rates since 1948, although no data are provided for specific cities or parts of cities.[10] Their data indicate very little fluctuation in intra-urban mobility rates between 1948 and 1965.

Mobility rates for subpopulation. The census materials make it possible to obtain information on gross migration rates for different subsets of the population, defined either on the basis of destination (decennial census) or on socio-economic characteristics (*Current Population Reports*).[11] The major factor causing differential mobility rates is the life cycle stage (Fig. 11–1),[12] which obscures the effects of economic level or culture. Annual intra-county mobility rates for children under five are high, about 20 per cent. They decline for teenagers, maximize at over 30 per cent for people in the young twenties, and decline again to a rate of less than 10 per cent for people over 45 years of age.[13] The life cycle effects lead to many of the apparent variations in mobility rates for different areas, or different socio-economic groups, since the differentials due to occupation, income, and so forth, are minor, as Table 11–2 reveals. A slight tendency towards greater mobility for lower income groups complements the lower migration rates for this class. Farmers and the self-employed have lower mobility rates, and the same is true for home owners. Their investment creates a larger threshold to overcome before moving, and the very fact of ownership may indicate a psychological commitment to an area.

FIGURE 11–1. Annual intra-county mobility rate and migration rate for the United States by age and sex, for the population 1 year and over: March, 1965. *Source:* Primary data.

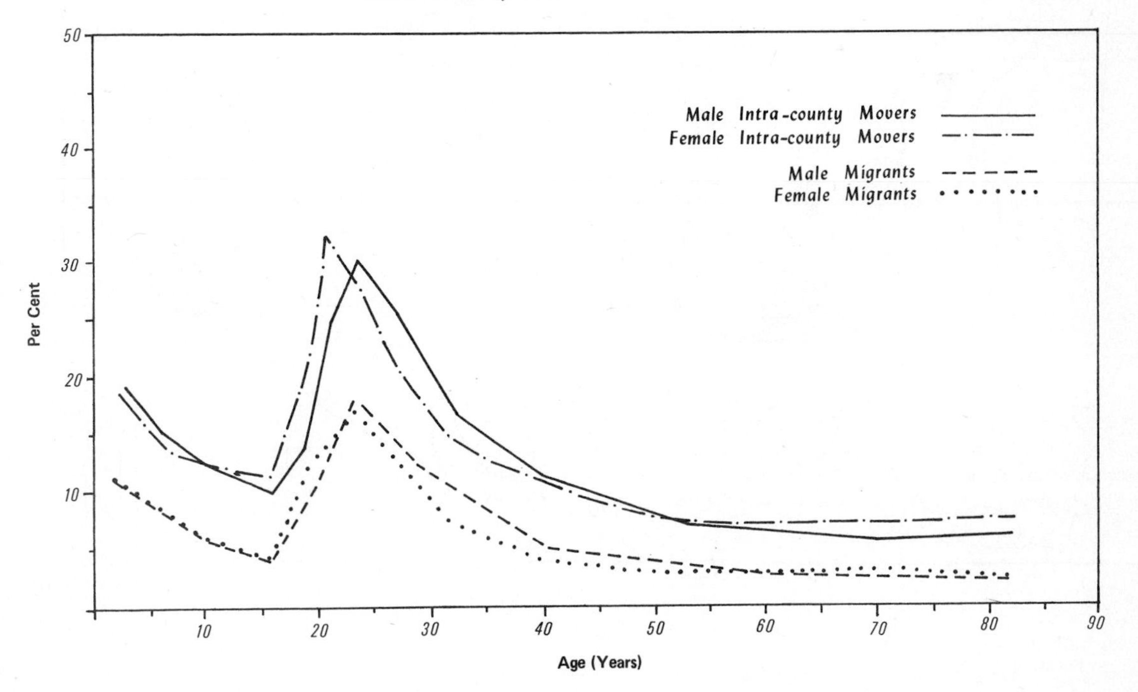

TABLE 11–2

Annual Intra-urban Mobility Rates for Subpopulations (Males)

	Age				
	18–24	*25–34*	*35–44*	*45–64*	*65+*
Education (years)					
0–8	—	24.1	14.2	8.5	6.6
9–11	—	26.2	10.7	7.8	5.2
12	—	18.9	11.1	7.0	5.4
13 or more	—	19.4	10.3	7.5	5.9
Occupation					
White-collar	27.2	19.9	9.4	6.3	3.0
Manual	30.4	22.9	12.0	8.2	5.9
Service	25.6	25.5	16.7	9.0	5.9
Farm	15.9	11.1	9.5	6.8	2.0
Employment					
Self-employed	15.9	14.1	8.1	4.8	2.5
Wage and salaried	28.8	22.0	11.5	8.1	4.7
Unemployed	22.3	26.4	17.2	11.7	—

Source: Bureau of the Census, *Current Population Reports: Population Characteristics*, Series P 20, *Mobility of the Population of the United States* (Washington, D.C.: U.S. Government Printing Office, 1966), No. 150, which has used a national sample of 30,000 homes.

The spatial distribution of mobility. Figure 11–2 shows mobility rates within the metropolitan area. Rates of total in-movement are generally highest in the city center, reflecting the demographic pattern, and in the most recently developed suburbs, where, of course, virtually everyone is a newcomer.[14] Where data are available the distribution of out-migration is of more interest, since this measure is not as sensitive to the addition of new housing. Rates of out-migration in the city center are about double those of the suburban area, and Moore was able to explain about 60 per cent of the variation by distance.[15] Mobility rates are also slightly higher in low-income sectors of the city.

The measurement of mobility used in Fig. 11–2 is in-movers from the central city as a percentage of population, and it features a sharp decline at the boundary of the city, indicating the magnitude of short-distance moves [but see also Chapter 8 of the present volume]. The dominant impression obtained from any examination of the spatial

FIGURE 11–2. Percentage of population moving into the Toronto area from central city: 1955–1960. *Source:* Prepared by J. W. Simmons from Canadian census data.

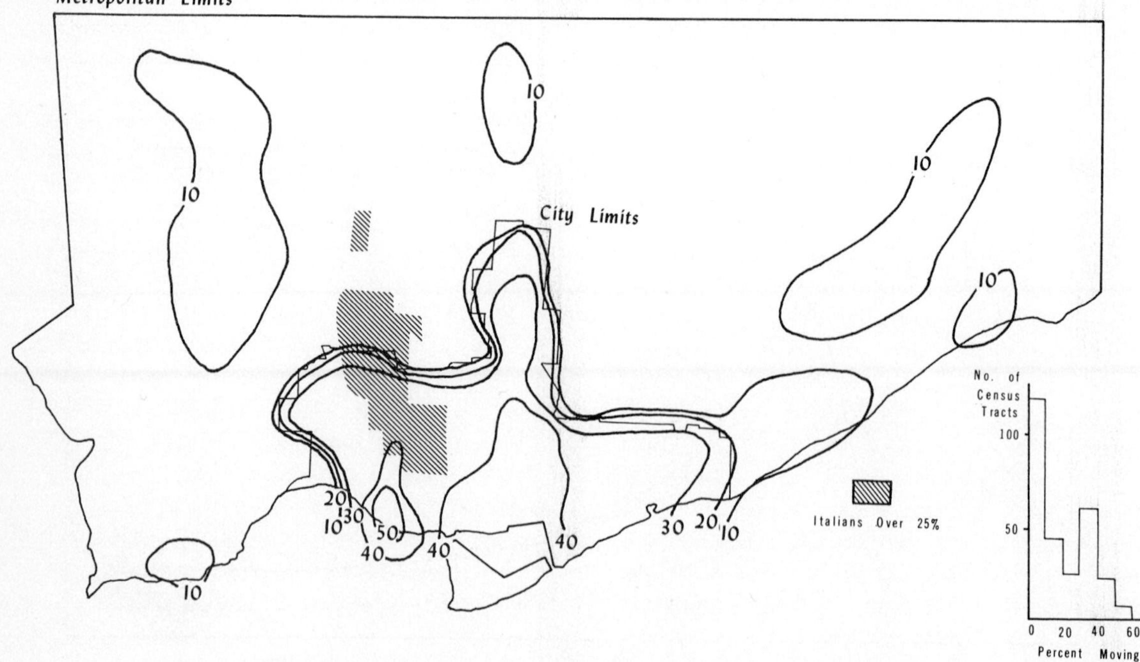

distribution of mobility rates is one of a high degree of movement into all parts of the metropolitan area.

The size and growth rate of the city. A measurement problem common to all migration studies is the effect of the size of observation units.[16] Cities with larger populations provide more migration opportunities; greater area allows people to move farther without crossing boundaries.

The other factor tending to increase mobility within a city is its growth rate. Rapid growth stimulates new housing investment, creates a ready market for older property, and accelerates processes of suburbanization, invasion, and succession. In Canadian cities where $(N = 17)$, for example, the percentage of intra-metropolitan movers, from 1956 to 1961, using as a base the population of 1956, can be expressed as a function of city population and growth:

$$\text{Per cent Movers} = -29 + 10 \log \text{Population} + 0.45 \text{ Growth Rate}$$

Population explains 52 per cent and growth explains 26 per cent of the variation of the intra-metropolitan migration rate. The former [population] is an irregularity due to the kind of measurements taken; the latter [growth] accelerates movements which take place for other reasons.

Why Do They Move?

The motivation for changing residence within the city varies with the characteristics of the mover. The preponderance of movers in the age group fifteen to twenty-five weights the over-all pattern towards their particular needs and dissatisfactions, but other subpopulations, such as the aged or the residents of a particular part of the city, may move for quite different reasons. The pressure of housing needs generated by life-cycle changes causes the majority of moves, producing high rates of out-movement in all parts of the city. A great deal of social change can take place without significantly altering the mobility rate, but a variety of social factors may modify the out-movement of certain kinds of subpopulations in certain areas.

The decision to move may be examined from several points of view. The social psychologist sees the household as acting under various kinds of stress; the economist views the move as maximizing satisfaction of a set of utilities; and the human ecologist treats it as an element in a large pattern of movements, as part of the processes of growth and succession. From any point of view, the process is complex, involving, on the one hand, the needs and values of the household as they change over time and, on the other hand, the changing characteristics of the environment, encompassing home, neighborhood, and alternative locations.

Types of social change. In order to overcome the demonstrable time and money costs of moving, some kind of attraction or dissatisfaction is required. The most obvious factors are those kinds of social change which alter the relationship between a household and its environment. The environment may be altered by such things as blight, invasion by different cultural groups, or increased land values; while the household may change in age, size, or income. More likely, both household and environment are changing simultaneously, and at varying rates. Following [the framework of the previous chapter] three major clusters of social variables may be examined for their contributions to the generation of mobility: life cycle, including demographic characteristics and life-style; economic status, combining measures of income, occupation, and education; and segregation, the variables identifying ethnic or racial origin and religion.[17]

LIFE CYCLE. All evidence indicates that the most powerful factor in inducing people to change their residence is change in the set of demographic characteristics called the "urbanization" or "life-cycle" factor. Rossi, after his intensive series of interviews and follow-up studies on residential relocation concluded, "The findings of this study indicate the major function of mobility to be the process by which families adjust their housing to the housing needs that are generated by the shifts in family composition that accompany life cycle changes."[18] The sharp variations in mobility rates shown in Fig. 11-1 reinforce Rossi's statement.[19] The life-cycle stages account for at least five of the eight or nine moves which might be expected in a lifetime, as the household forms, grows, ages, and disperses. The cluster of moves in a quick succession during the age bracket 15 to 25 is evident. Although some of the life-cycle adjustments occur through inter-county migrations, many people have much more complex life cycles, including several moves at certain stages, such as childhood, maturity, and marriage. Most movers are dependents, following the movement of the head of the household; so the family characteristics rather than those of the individual are the critical factor. Rossi classified about one-third of the moves which he studied as involuntary, coming in the aftermath of other major events, such as eviction, marriage, death, or sudden loss of income.[20] Of the voluntary moves, the most common pressure is the need for space for a growing family. Less frequently there is a later adjustment back to a smaller unit when the family is grown, although often this move is not made until the household is broken up by death or illness.

Often, in combination with the housing adjustment, the family may choose or be compelled to adjust its neighborhood environment. For instance, a young man may flee the suburbs for a mildly bohemian area, change it for a more respectable town house district at marriage, and seek a new low-density suburb for the children. Low density, new housing, and particularly the opportunity to own rather than rent attract the young family. Several studies of the adjustment of low-income families to different kinds of neighborhoods indicate that the loss of kinship and familiar neighborhood contacts create severe problems which can lead to return movements.[21] On the other hand, the variety of life-styles already experienced by middle-class householders may give them more flexibility. It is difficult, on the basis of research to date, to differentiate changes in life-style due to changes in physical environment from changes which reflect change or a desire to change the life-style.[22]

For the most part, any change in neighborhood demographic characteristics, most frequently a general aging of the population, coincides with the change taking place in the household. Even if a particular family were out of phase with the age structure of the neighborhood, it seems unlikely that this form of stress would be sufficiently severe to lead to a move. Possible generators of mobility are the demographic changes associated with the redevelopment cycle in the central city. Old houses are converted to rooming houses or high-rise apartments for young single people, increasing the neighborhood density. These areas, however, comprise only a small part of the city and generally undergo gradual adjustments in the wake of out-movements for other reasons.

Economic status. This dimension includes income, occupation, and certain housing variables. Since urban areas are strongly differentiated with respect to class, a person who changes his social status might be expected to change the location of his residence. However, Lipset and Bendix find that only 30 per cent of North Americans change from the social class in which they were raised (using *two* class categories), requiring residential relocation once in the lifetime of one-third of the population.[23] Even if three times as many social class categories were used, only one move per lifetime would be explained. Perhaps more effective are the income changes which may take place throughout a lifetime without altering relative social class. Each household reaps the advantage of the annual 2 to 3 per cent increase in the standard of living, and while working in the same job a man's disposable income may increase as he gains seniority and shifts expenditures away from appliances and children towards housing and other goods. The effect is to remove the cost constraint which may have restricted the adjustment of housing needs. During the same period, of course, the original housing, even if adequate in size and location, becomes less attractive relative to the over-all housing stock. In this way, housing "filters down" to low-income groups while people "filter up" to better housing.[24]

Table 11–3 demonstrates the general ineffectiveness of changing economic status in generating mobility. The majority of moves adjust housing within a neighborhood of similar characteristics. About 80 per cent of intra-city movement takes place within census tracts of the same class or adjacent classes.[25] A greater tendency for higher-

TABLE 11–3

Moves Among Social Areas (in Percentages)

Social Class	Destination I	II	III	IV	V	Total
I	63.8	12.0	11.3	8.2	4.8	100
II	8.2	51.0	20.6	13.3	6.8	100
III	6.1	18.8	50.4	16.7	8.1	100
IV	5.1	13.0	21.0	52.7	8.1	100
V	4.1	13.2	17.3	17.4	48.1	100

Source: Sidney Goldstein and Kurt B. Mayer, *Metropolitanization and Population Change in Rhode Island*, Publication No. 3, Planning Division, Rhode Island Development Council (Providence, 1961), p. 51.

income people to move outside the city limits accelerates the filtering-down of housing opportunities, with a net movement of lower income groups into higher income areas.

It is also possible for the economic status of the neighborhood to change as one social class displaces another, the rich buying out the poor, or the poor making life uncomfortable for the rich. In most instances, these movements are gradual and do not increase the rate of migration. Even urban renewal projects, which may relocate thousands from a given area during a period of two or three years, account for only a small portion of the total mobility in a city.[26]

Ethnic and racial change. The variations in the experience of different cultural groups in the city have generated a complex and often contradictory body of theory about their intra-urban movements.[27] The assimilation processes undergone by European ethnic minorities in the nineteenth and early twentieth centuries are less and less relevant to present-day groups, who have different problems and who live in a city with different patterns of interaction and opportunity. The Negro ghetto is larger and more permanent than those of any of the earlier groups, while at the same time many recent European immigrants avoid the ghetto stage entirely.

The traditional ethnic community had a core area where much of the assimilation took place, the successful immigrant moving out socially and spatially, either as an individual or with his countrymen. If the flow of immigration from the source slackened, the core area itself might relocate, particularly if spatial assimilation had been a group process. The net effect was a continual decline in the concentration of each ethnic group. The movements in space of ethnic groups, whether early or recent, have not had appreciable effects on mobility rates. The moves of members of the ethnic group reflect the normal reasons for moving, such as the need for better housing, so that the communities expand gradually.[27] The ethnic factors act only as a constraint on the number of possible alternatives, expanding the question of "where?" rather than "why?"

The expansion of Negro ghettoes in northern U.S. cities increases mobility more dramatically. Typically, the highly segregated and rapidly growing Negro area can only expand into nearby white neighborhoods.[29] If the whites panic, the turnover takes place very rapidly, affecting up to 75 per cent of the dwellings within two or three years. The mobility rate increases as the normal rate of white out-migration (about 50 per cent in five years) is accelerated by racial and economic fears; but, as in any neighborhood, the most mobile elements, the young and the renters leave first. The crucial stage in the changeover is not the acceleration of white out-migration, but the almost total cessation of white in-migration.[30] Negro in-migrants of the same socio-economic level as the whites fill the vacuum.[31] Even in a city the size of Chicago, with a large and rapidly growing negro population, the number of moves stimulated by racial shifts is a small proportion of the total moves. An examination of the census tract data for the South Side of the city (Fig. 11–3) reveals that about 10 per cent of the tracts were affected, and that those tracts had mobility rates less than 50 per cent higher than the normal rate and generated from 3 to 5 per cent of all movement in that part of the city.[32] [A more detailed treatment of the spread of the ghetto is presented later in this chapter.]

Individual adjustment. The final set of factors which induce a change of residence reflect the individual's problems in adjusting to his environment, beyond the effects of physical needs and the constraints of class and culture outlined above. Personal conflicts with neighbors may make an area untenable; some persons are chronically

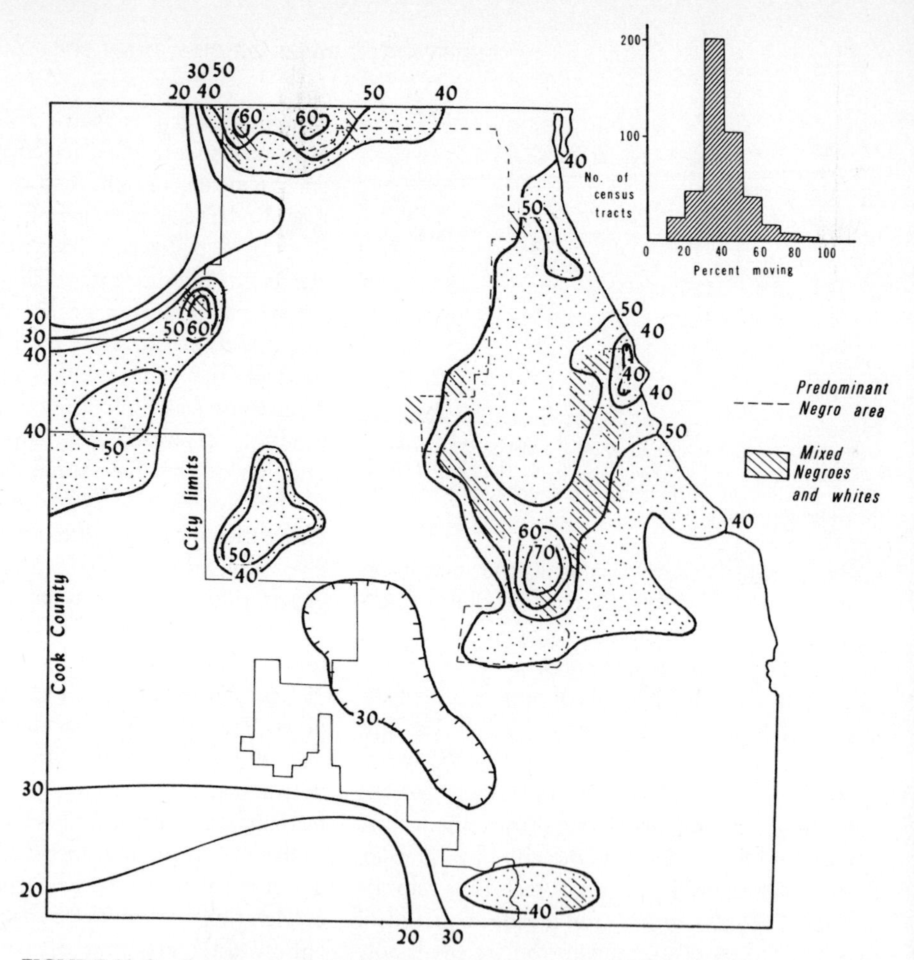

FIGURE 11–3. Percentage of population moving into South Chicago from the central city: 1955–1960. *Source:* Department of Commerce, Bureau of the Census, *Census of Population and Housing: 1960, Census Tracts*, Final Report PHC (1)–26, *Census Tracts: Chicago, Illinois* (Washington, D.C.: U.S. Government Printing Office, 1961).

unsatisfied with their environment; others appear to err in their evaluation of alternative neighborhoods or to be unable to adjust their life style to a particular environment.

Evidence for these personal aspects of mobility is provided by Rossi, who found it necessary to evaluate the household complaints about a dwelling, as well as life cycle and tenure information, in order to predict mobility.[33] The complaints generated by the differences between expectations and reality as perceived by the household were not predictable from any socio-economic measures. They involve the individual's perception of cost, the characteristics of the dwelling space, and the immediate social and economic environment. Only a small proportion of complaints concerned location, in the sense of access, and these had little effect on mobility. In order to explain expectations of movement, Lansing and Barth combined two social variables, age of household head and crowding, with three attitude variables, satisfaction with housing, neighborhood, and access, and obtained results confirming Rossi's work.[34]

Some light is shed on the source of complaints in Table 11–4, which shows the discrepancies in the perception of housing by residents of areas and an outside observer. Agreement is best, however, for the most significant complaints variable, the dwelling unit space. Rossi also associated

TABLE 11–4

Area Characteristics and Their Perception by Residents

	Area				
Ranking	*I*	*II*	*III*	*IV*	*Attribute*
Observed	4	1	3	2	Location
Perceived	3	2	1	2	
Observed	1	2	3	4	Physical facilities
Perceived	2	3	1	4	
Observed	2	3	1	4	Dwelling unit space
Perceived	1	3	2	4	

Source: Peter A. Rossi, *Why Families Move* (New York: The Free Press, 1955), pp. 26–30.

mobility with the perceived difference in social class between residents and their neighbors.[35]

The personal aspects of the decision to move are the most difficult component to evaluate, although current exploration of the perception of the environment may be of some assistance.[36] A theoretical structure is provided by Wolpert, who has designed a behavioral model of migration.[37] The tendency to migrate is stable for the various social and demographic groups reflecting their "thresholds of utility," the degree of differentation of *place utility* between the origin and possible locations sufficient to make them move. "Place utility" is the measure of attractiveness or unattractiveness of an area, relative to alternative locations, as perceived by the individual decision maker.[38] The utility of a site also varies with the demographic and social characteristics of the individual.

Thus place utility both initiates relocation and determines the location, but location is also determined by the *theory of search behavior*. The individual evaluates alternatives with which he is familiar: places nearby, the location of friends and relatives, areas visited in travel, described by mass media, or alternatives investigated in a systematic search. Generally, the alternatives are clustered around one or two locations. The decision process is complicated by the possibility of time lags after changes in the household-environment relationship, the tendency to minimize uncertainty, and the alternative of adjusting to the existing situation.

In a later paper, Wolpert enlarges the concept of threshold of utility into a strain-stress model in which an individual migrates as a form of adaptation to stress exerted by his environment.[39] This stress has two elements—the change in the individual over time (his earlier attributes operated on a series of change parameters), and stress exerted by the environment. . . .

To provide some concept of the relative weights of these factors, one must realize that within a moderately growing city more than 50 per cent of the intra-urban mobility results from the changing housing needs generated by shifts through the life cycle. Abu-Lughod and Foley estimate that about 30 per cent of intra-urban moves are involuntary, 10 per cent following the creation of new households, and 20 per cent resulting from demolition, destruction by fire, or eviction.[40] Perhaps another 10 per cent reflect social change other than the life cycle, such as social mobility and ethnic change of the family (assimilation) or the neighborhood (invasion). All studies reject the effect of job location as an important reason for moving.[41] The most important aspect of the housing adjustments are the size and facilities of the dwelling unit, followed by the social environment of the neighborhood. Physical site and access to the over-all urban structure are relatively unimportant.

Given the universally high rate of out-mobility generated by life cycle factors, changes in the number and characteristics of the population within a certain area generally reflect a change in the pattern of in-migration.

Where Do They Move?

Knowing why a family moves tells us very little about its final destination, as is apparent when maps of intra-urban migration are studied.[42] Flows and counterflows criss-cross the urban area, and the major regularities, the tendencies to move nearby and within the same sector, are determined by the procedure for seeking a new home rather than the reason for leaving the old. New factors are taken into consideration once the decision to move has been made. The selection of a new home depends not only on demand conditions, the priorities which the family assigns to different housing characteristics, but also on supply constraints, the cost and quantity of different types of housing in different parts of the city. Also significant is the search procedure by which the family examines and evaluates alternative locations.

The housing market. Both the demand and supply sides of the housing market are highly differentiated.[43] The supply, or housing stock, can be categorized into submarkets by such variables as tenure, number of rooms, age, or location; and the demand in each submarket is a function of the characteristics of the urban population such as income, age, family size, and place of employment. The demand submarkets have varying degrees of independence from other submarkets, for often a family will find it difficult to choose from two quite different alternatives, such as an aging duplex in a central location or a suburban bungalow. Housing surveys and the economics of the construction industry provide the supply schedules for each submarket and knowledge of past behavior patterns and surveys of consumer preference generate housing demand curves for various subpopulations.[44] Grigsby has constructed matrices which show shifts of households between demand submarkets,[45] and relations between demand and supply categories.[46] Given the number of variables differentiating both the housing and households, matrices relating demand and supply become very complex. However, the complicated combinations of housing alternatives are simplified by the fixed supply of housing stock in the short run and by the correlations between the various housing characteristics. For instance, the majority of the smaller dwelling units are for rent, and older housing is found near the city center. Certain cross-categories are nonexistent, such as the two-acre residential lot in the central business district.

The individual household chooses from the housing available in the various submarkets at one time,[47] but relatively little is known about the complex decision process. Data such as in Table 11–5 are available, but vary so much with the survey methods—the questionnaire and the timing—that they are almost useless. Any hierarchy of criteria will still be hypothetical.[48] Cost undoubtedly plays a major role. Each household has a housing budget which is a function of its "normal" income, defined as the long-run expected income of the family.[49] A crucial option is whether to own or to rent, a decision which is related to both income and life-cycle characteristics. The other important life-cycle consideration is the amount of space required. Social factors such as access to downtown, a familiar neighborhood, or an ethnic community, further complicate the decision. Different kinds of families will have different priorities and will structure their decision accordingly.

TABLE 11–5

Factors Considered in the Selection of New Homes

	Rossi	*Lansing and Mueller*	*Gans*
Dwelling			
Space	51%	32%	2
Design	50%	—	11
Cost	19%	14%	23
Other	16%	—	(value) 48
Neighborhood			
Social	6%	22%	3
Location	26%	31%	8
Other	9%	—	—

Sources: Peter H. Rossi, *Why Families Move* (New York: The Free Press, 1955), p. 154; John B. Lansing and Eva Mueller, *Residential Location and Urban Mobility* (Ann Arbor, Mich.: Institute for Social Research, 1964), p. 21; and Herbert J. Gans, *The Levittowners* (New York: Pantheon Books, 1967), p. 35.

Spatial aspects of the housing market. The division of the housing stock into location submarkets does not, in itself, severely reduce the supply of available dwelling units. Mobility rates indicate that some form of housing is available at virtually every location within the city and that there is a minimum of 30 per cent turnover in occupance every five years. Generally a wide range of cost alternatives exist throughout the city as well, if one is willing to trade off size for price. Only in a few cases—the $300,000 mansion, the 50¢ flop house, or the seventeenth century home—would cost or quantity alone define the location. The location constraint operates in conjunction with other variables, so that the requirement of living in a certain neighborhood becomes difficult only when housing of a certain size or standard is specified.

More often, location comes so far down on the hierarchy of criteria that the final location of a home is the result of decisions about other factors. Submarkets may be defined at all levels of the decision criteria. One can consider in turn the submarket of cheap housing, cheap apartments, cheap suburban apartments, and so forth. A submarket at any level is not necessarily confined to one location, since cheap housing, for instance, can be found in several areas of the city. Generally, as the submarket is defined more and more precisely, the spatial contiguity of housing characteristics restricts the number of possible locations until the final decision focuses on a single site. Each criterion in the housing decision process has spatial implications because of the distribution of that phenomenon.

Since changing housing needs are the dominant reason for moving, it is not surprising that housing characteristics are more important than location factors in selecting a dwelling. The spatial distribution of housing of various kinds will affect the direction of flows. Although an increasing variety of housing tenure and size exists throughout the city, as old houses are subdivided, new apartment buildings are erected in older residential areas, and new suburbs include multifamily units from the beginning, the range of choice is restricted in two ways: Housing in the central part of the city, particularly the single-family dwelling, is old in style and amenities, leading to its rejection by some families; and densities are much higher in the central areas as well, following the variations in land costs, although often the choice of density by a family is not explicit but follows such decisions as whether to seek a single-family house and how big a lot is required.

In the discussion of various factors affecting the location decision which follows, it should be remembered that the relative importance placed on access, space, and so on varies with the household and, thus, by neighborhoods. People who live downtown have already opted for access, while suburban dwellers have placed more importance on space and quiet.

Propinquity. Despite the apparent logic of the hierarchy of criteria, the best single factor to predict location of a new residence is the location of the former house. All evidence indicates the importance of distance from the mover's origin in differentiating housing alternatives. Most moves are short, within familiar territory, reflecting satisfaction with the neighborhood and the location with respect to the urban structure. For example, a number of studies show that about one quarter of all moves take place within the census tract, a very small area indeed (see Table 11–6).[50]

The great number of local moves, adjusting housing needs within the same social area, mask long moves which involve a change in the social environment of the mover. The short moves may produce a net spatial change in one direction (as suggested by the process of decentralization)[51] or may just be a random milling about. They do provide a high density of opportunities for in-migrants throughout the whole metropolitan area and indicate that the household should be

TABLE 11–6

Family Migration: Providence, R. I., 1950–1959

	Social Class of Origin					
Destination	*I*	*II*	*III*	*IV*	*V*	*Total*
Within tract	18.3%	20.0%	22.5%	28.1%	29.1%	24.2%
Within city	35.1	38.3	46.0	48.6	45.6	43.9
Outside city	46.8	40.7	31.5	24.6	25.2	31.9
Totals	100%	100%	100%	100%	100%	100%

Source: Sidney Goldstein and Kurt B. Mayer, *Residential Mobility, Migration and Commuting in Rhode Island*, Planning Division, Rhode Island Development Council (Providence, 1963), Table 18.

able to satisfy its housing requirements relatively easily.

Beyond the immediate neighborhood, the decline of moves with distance become more irregular as other factors, such as the location of housing alternatives, come into play. It is possible, however, to describe the probability of relocation of a migrant as a function of distance, and several formulations have been suggested, with varying theoretical bases and empirical demonstrations.[52] All the suggested distributions feature a sharp decline at first which then levels off.[53] Although few curves have been fitted to urban areas, the general relationship that seems to hold best (despite the distortions introduced by the patterns of social variation in the city) is the Pareto equation: in-migration/population $= a/\text{distance}^b$, where a is a constant and the exponent b summarizes the frictional effects of distance on migration. Calculated parameters to be found in the literature include: Asby (Sweden, 1950), $b = 1.6$; Cleveland (1933–1936), $b = 2.5$;[54] and, from Albig's study of small midwestern cities in 1930, $b = 1.8$.[55] This decline of destinations with distance beyond the immediate neighborhood suggests that short moves may reflect imperfections in the housing market as well as the network of social contacts, especially since the discussion to follow will stress the relative unimportance of location. As suggested by Wolpert's concept of the search procedure, or in another form by Stouffer's intervening opportunities, alternatives nearby are more likely to be evaluated than distant ones. Rossi found that almost 50 per cent of all locations were obtained through personal contact.[56]

Cultural constraints. The tendency to locate in the same neighborhood may reflect the requirements, voluntary or involuntary, of being near people of similar origin or interest, or of access to certain institutions. The most prized residential sites in the city often are not intrinsically different, but represent a set of linkages and access to wealthy people and the organizations which serve them. Minority cultural groups are also sensitive to linkages. Entire Jewish communities have been transplanted from the old urban core to the suburbs as they climb the economic ladder.[57] Negroes find tremendous internal and external forces opposing their movement out of the ghetto.

The effect of the cultural constraints is to emphasize movements within sectors as demonstrated in the table prepared by Caplow[58] and the maps in Green's reports.[59] Households are able to adjust their housing and access costs without crossing the sectoral boundaries as defined by nonresidential land uses or the location of other income and cultural groups. The tendency for high-income movers to relocate within the same sector formed a central part of Hoyt's theory of residential structure.[60] Hoyt suggests a number of reasons why this should be so: the importance of site characteristics such as shore lines and of fast transport lines, both of which are essentially sectoral phenomena; and the cumulative effect when high incomes attract prestige commercial establishments and community leaders, in turn attracting high-income residents.

People in higher socio-economic groups tend to move greater distances (Table 11–6). More of them move outside the census tract, outside the central city, and outside the metropolitan area. Their evaluation procedures are likely more thorough and involve a more complex set of constraints. The cost of moving for families of this type, estimated to be at least 10 per cent of house values,[61] requires a substantial change in dwelling or environment to make it worthwhile. At the lowest end of the income scale, however, the slightest financial crisis may prevent the payment of rent and require relocation, and any modification in the family structure creates pressures for adjustment.

Thus, people tend to maintain the same sort of income or ethnic environment as they move. Moves of the upwardly mobile or ethnic families who are rapidly assimilating are less easy to predict, but they form only a small part of total moves. The time lag may be of considerable importance. Movers select a neighborhood according to their perception of its characteristics in the near future, characteristics which may resemble the neighborhood they leave as it was five, ten, or twenty years ago. The degree of contiguity in space of income and cultural area will also have an effect. A city may have only one high-income area or it may have half a dozen, providing varying numbers of alternative locations.

Access relative to the rest of the city. The consensus of various studies of consumer preference is that the location of the house is generally less important than the characteristics of the dwelling itself. The location has three aspects, which for most people have the following order of importance: (1) the social environment, such as nearness of friends and institutional amenities; (2) the physical environment, including quiet, maintenance and design; and (3) access to the city as a whole or to the set of work places.[62] After trying unsuccessfully to explain differences in stated access preference by means of income, life cycle, and family activity measures, Lansing and Barth concluded that access was relatively unimportant to most people and that location decisions reflect other kinds of preference, such as privacy, cost, and type of dwelling.[63] Yet access becomes an important factor in the location decision if only because of the constraints it imposes on the supply side. The supply and demand for access have generated consistently declining housing costs along the continuum of submarkets moving outward from the city center to the suburbs, as Alonso and Wingo have shown theoretically, and Brigham, Muth, and Seyfried have demonstrated empirically.[64] This pattern reflects the differential access to the rest of the city. Housing costs also vary sectorally with changing access to higher social class amenities, and sometimes with certain site characteristics such as water frontage or elevation. Although Yeates has demonstrated a steady decline in the effect of access over time as the reduction of transport costs reduced the importance of centrality and man-made amenities outweigh natural advantages, the strong radial variation in housing cost remains.[65]

Most of the demand of residential areas in the city center is generated by a relatively small number of families. Considerable evidence indicates that the great majority prefer to live farther rather than closer to the central business district, finding the quiet, the spaciousness, and the general suburban image more attractive than downtown.[66] The people seeking a centrally located residence are a special group. Those having a wider choice, the white middle-to-high income group, are older and have family structure and employment characteristics different from their counterparts in the suburb. The most significant difference is the almost total absence of school-age children.[67] Although access is important to this group,[68] they are concerned with the availability of social amenities rather than employment.[69]

The high cost of access to downtown is not a response to overwhelming demand but a result of competition from other land uses and a slowly increasing demand on the residential side, with a fixed or decreasing supply of housing. Almost all the net addition to the city's housing supply occurs in the outer, suburban parts of the metropolitan area. The number of units added by increased density on residential land in the central area is compensated for by the removal of other residential units to accommodate the expansion of other land uses. At the same time, the demand for central locations increases as the metropolitan area grows.

The result of this imbalance is a continuing increase in housing costs in the city center as the city grows,[70] amplified by the perceptions of future urban development as seen by investors. The constant cost isopleth moves steadily outward, requiring outward movement for families with constant income and constant housing needs.

The movement outward from the city center because of personal preferences and cost is abetted by the large proportion of total housing opportunities found at the outskirts of growing cities. A city growing at 10 per cent per year, with an over-all annual mobility rate of 20 per cent, will generate one-third of all housing opportunities at the outskirts of the city. It can be shown, using some simple assumptions and calculus, that the great majority of the population will have many more housing opportunities away from the city center rather than towards it. The result is a persistent net movement outward as the city grows, as Table 11–7 indicates. About 10 per cent of the 1956 population of the central city moved across the city limits, but in the next five years many other moves within the city and the fringe had

TABLE 11–7

Gross Movement Patterns in the Toronto Metropolitan Area

	Destination		
	Fringe	*Central City*	*Total*
Fringe	343,500	17,900	361,400
Central City	63,000	197,800	260,800
Total	406,500	215,700	622,200
Population			
1961	1,152,100	672,400	1,824,500
1956	834,400	667,700	1,502,300

Source: James W. Simmons, "Changing Residence in the City: A Review of Intra-Urban Mobility," *The Geographical Review*, LVIII (1968).

the same decentralizing effect. The outward bias shows up in Caplow's table[71] and Green's maps,[72] and was an important assumption in Burgess' discussion of city structure.[73]

Certain groups will have a much higher likelihood of outward movement—households with young children, tenants wanting to own, and people with preferences for low density areas. Alonso and Kain have tried to generate these various location decisions from economic theory, given different preferences for space.[74] Caplow notes that there is also a counter current—young people forming new households at the city center and older households ready to trade space for access.[75] No evidence to date demonstrates a greater propensity to out-migration on the part of higher-income groups.[76] It may have been true in the past, however. Rodwin points out that the importance of life-cycle stages in suburbanization must be modified by the constraints of income, transportation, and cultural values, which kept many of the earlier immigrant groups from participating in the outward movement.[77]

Access does play an important role in ordering the development of new suburban areas.[78] Virtually every model of urban growth introduces the effect of access, generally to the central business district but often to employment, shipping areas, schools, or highways as well. Several studies have developed empirical relationships. Hansen used density, access to city center, access to other residential areas, and access to jobs, to predict 87 per cent of the variations in a measure of development (new dwellings/possible sites).[79] All variables were strongly correlated with the dependent variable and each other. Chapin and Weiss have evaluated the effect of different growth factors in a series of multiple regressions. Sixty per cent of the amount of urban development in a given area could be explained by eight factors: poor land, access to work areas, assessed value, distance to major street, distance to school, residential amenities, sewers, and zoning—listed in order of importance.[80] A study by Kaiser, developing the model further, indicates the order of contribution to development to be: socioeconomic rank, contiguous residential subdivision, public utilities, zoning protection, and access to employment.[81] The changes in order, together with the propinquity effect noted earlier, suggest that urban growth may be related primarily to access to residential areas which serve as sources of migrants, and that access to the city center is meaningful only to the extent that it acts as a surrogate for this measure.

The journey to work. The relationship between job and residence is a particular form of access which is defined for each employment location. All families are concerned to some extent with their location relative to the central business district, but only a few hundred may care about their relationship with any particular outlying industrial area. Although few people decide to move in order to be closer to their jobs, the place of employment may act as a constraint when it comes to selecting location. Several studies show a weak but consistent decline in the employment field with distance.[82] Lansing notes that only 36 per cent of movers had explicitly defined a maximum journey-to-work travel time in searching for a new home, although 92 per cent of those had kept within the limit.[83]

A number of factors offset the apparent attraction of reduced travel time to work. Most drivers enjoy the journey to work; many more don't mind it;[84] a majority would prefer to live farther out rather than closer to downtown, the main employment center.[85] Many members of the labor force do not make the location decision but follow the head of the household. Others, such as retail clerks or handymen can find employment nearby wherever they live. For the entire population, trip lengths tend to increase with each move, reflecting the residential decentralization process.[86] The only workers who consistently relocate closer to their jobs are those employed in the suburbs, so that continuing decentralization of employment may lead to the increased importance of job location in predicting residence location. Job changes and residence have approximately the same frequency of occurrence.[87]

Data which Goldstein and Mayer obtained from the 1960 census reveal the interactions between commuting and migration. Of those who worked in the central city, over 25 per cent moved outward away from their jobs, outnumbering (9,000 to 6,000) those who worked outside the central city and moved out, presumably reducing the journey to work. The probability of outward movement is much higher, however, for the latter.

Information on the differential effects of the journey-to-work constraint on different income groups is inconsistent. Lansing indicates very little difference; Lapin indicates a longer work trip for middle-income clerical, sales, and blue-collar workers; while Lowry and Duncan find higher-income people more widely dispersed from job locations.[88]

Typical of the kinds of data available on the journey-to-work link are those presented in Figs. 11–4, 11–5, and 11–6, showing the residential distribution of the employees of the Argonne National Laboratories in Chicago. There are clear differences in the distances traveled by sexes, races, and occupational groups, with the effects of segregation particularly apparent, but occupational groups also differ in the status level of community of residence.[89]

Future Research on Individual Mobility: Problems and Implications

The spatial differentiation of attributes of urban residents is largely the result of the cumulation of intra-urban moves made by the city's inhabitants. Unfortunately, the bias in the available data has focused urban research on the static distributions instead of on the processes which generated these patterns and the decisions which accumulated to the processes, yet so many of the significant urban phenomena—social segregation, the housing market, and urban growth, for instance—operate through the mechanism of intra-urban mobility, that it merits continuing systematic study.

Perhaps the most remarkable aspect of intra-urban mobility is the stability of the spatial structure of social characteristics despite high rates of mobility throughout the city. The tendency of movers to relocate nearby and the immobility of housing investments maintain the spatial equilibrium, but occasionally a dramatic social change within a neighborhood is a reminder of the complexity of the adjustments between form and process leading to social differentiation. The equilibrium between in-migration and out-migration involves a great variety of factors: physical characteristics of the city, economic conditions, and particularly the values and perceptions of the population—and these factors may contradict or reinforce each other in innumerable combinations.[90] [Two cases of dramatic change are explored later in this chapter.]

Data needs. Critical needs for better understanding of intra-urban location are regular, consistent measures of area-to-area flows. Current census data which give mobility rates for in-movers, identifying a limited number of origins, are useful but not sufficient. The development of models which will explain and predict patterns of flow and, hence, spatial change within the city will require the full flow matrix, identifying flows from every spatial subdivision of the city to every other subdivision. The problems of filing and storing such information become enormous, since n areas generate n^2 possible flows, and one metropolitan area might include twenty to thirty communities (10^3 flow dyads) or several hundred census tracts (10^5 flow dyads). Recent technological advances now make it possible.[91] The problem of gathering an adequate sample from interviews or city directories overwhelms the private researcher, particularly when it is desirable to obtain socio-economic information at the same time.[92] The most promising avenue is the compilation of change-of-address data gathered for other purposes but capable of modification to provide the neces-

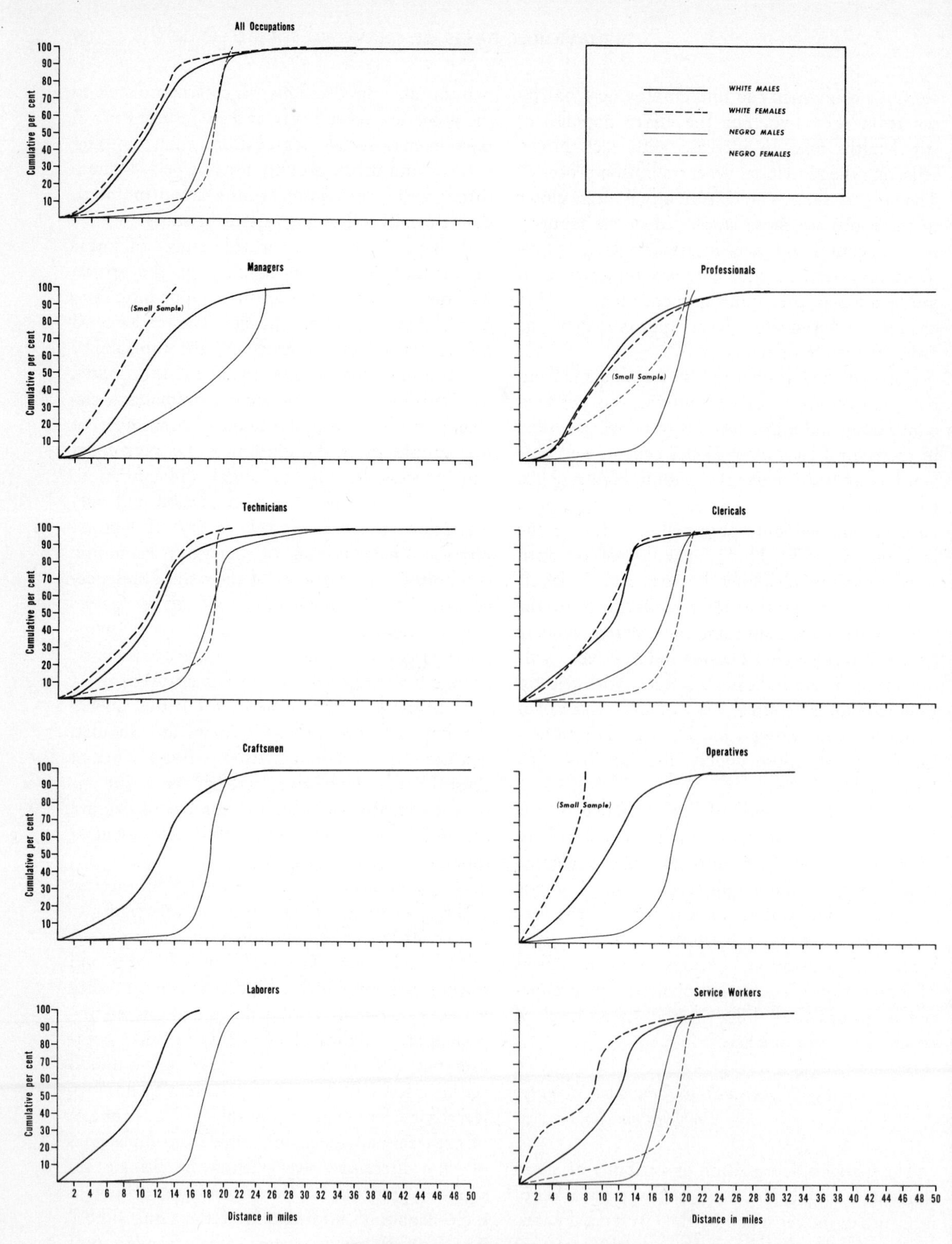

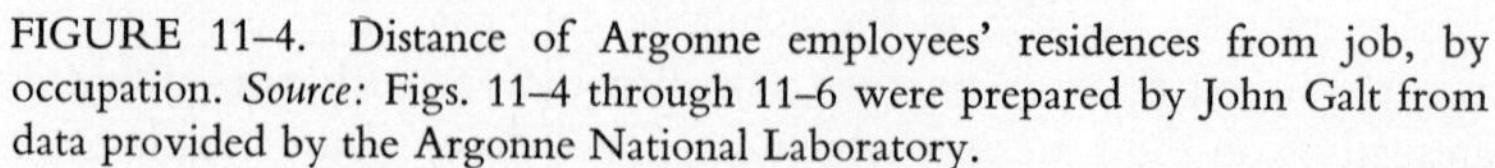

FIGURE 11–4. Distance of Argonne employees' residences from job, by occupation. *Source:* Figs. 11–4 through 11–6 were prepared by John Galt from data provided by the Argonne National Laboratory.

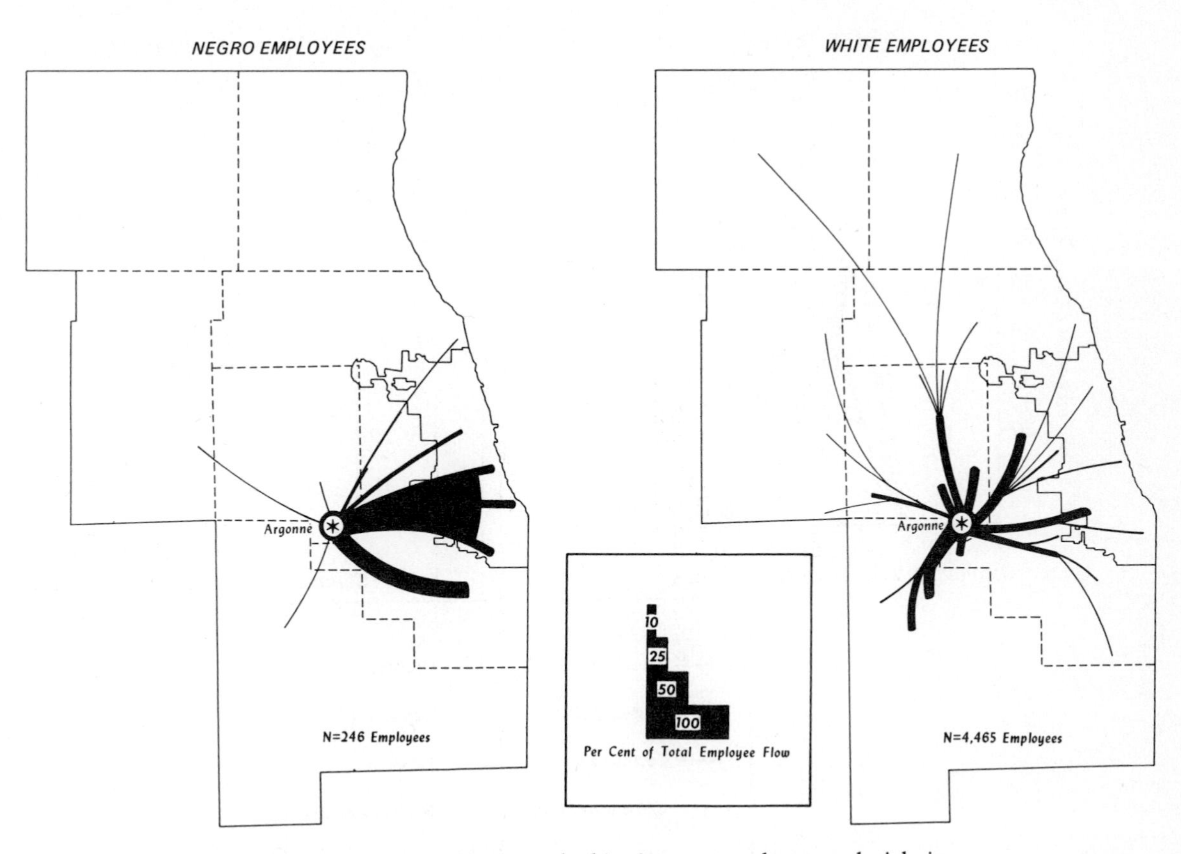

FIGURE 11–5. Flows of Negro and white Argonne employees to the job site.
Source: See caption for Fig. 11–4.

sary variables. Public utilities data, transportation studies, and various kinds of government files have been used.

The other necessary set of variables is housing measures, available on a small-area basis and classified by the critical aspects of the location decision—cost, tenure, number of rooms, and quality. These measures of opportunity, when combined with existing data on the social characteristics of the population, can be used to predict the volume of in-movers and out-movers.

The preference structure. Although the accumulation of the above data should lead to better models of intra-urban migration in the short run, the prospects over a longer period are much more uncertain. Although the housing needs of the population under thirty-five dominate the mobility pattern, a large hazy area of perception, preference, and institutional effects is also involved. The attitudes towards a given neighborhood can shift more rapidly than the physical characteristics of the area, and the actions of planning boards, real estate associations, and mortgage brokers are capricious.

It is increasingly apparent that virtually all the elements which enter into location decisions reflect the unstable perceptions and evaluations of needs and opportunities of individuals, which are shaped in turn by the values and habits of various subcultures. Households with similar social characteristics but different life styles use and prefer widely differing housing and neighborhood conditions. Even such a basic element as size of house is perceived differently, some households preferring very large units, and others, even those capable of affording other alternatives, living in a

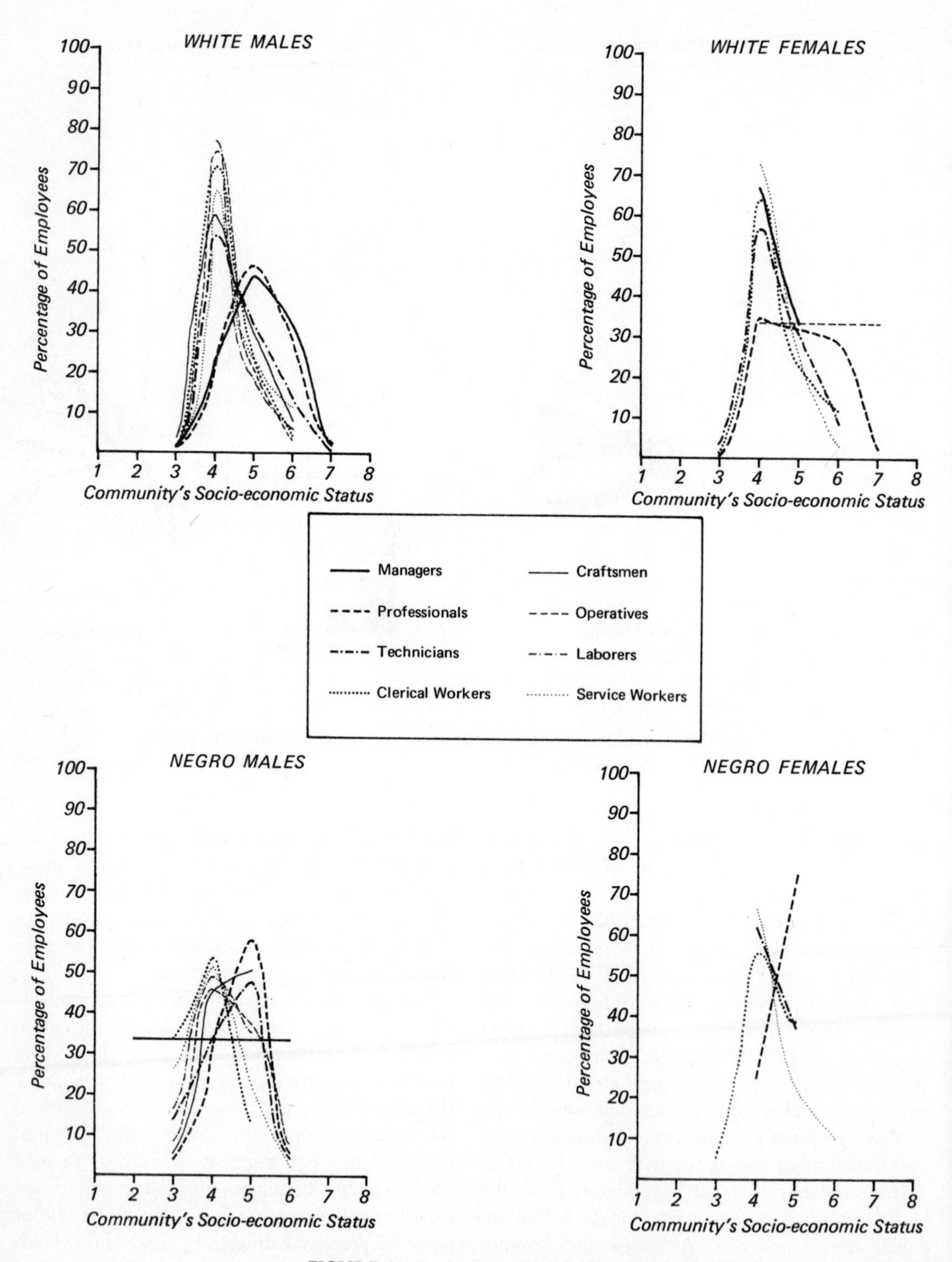

FIGURE 11–6. Socio-economic rank of community of residence of Argonne employees, by occupation. *Source:* See caption for Fig. 11–4.

small number of rooms.[93] Location preferences are more obviously tied to the background or aspirations of the household. The problem of planners in trying to design urban environments on the basis of such a tenuous structure of likes and dislikes is brought out forcefully in *Environment for Man*,[94] a collection of papers which demonstrates clearly the uncertainties and conflicting interpretations of human needs as seen by professional planners. In the absence of rigid functional requirements for urban residential areas, the alternatives seem to be either the esthetics of the professional planner or the preference of the man on the street as interpreted in the market place. The possible payoffs in understanding and modifying preferences are enormous. A shift in middle-class norms regarding the value of access to downtown could be more significant than all the urban renewal to date; changing attitudes towards land tenure could modify the suburban landscape; and a desire for a greater variety of social contacts would alter spatial distribution of the whole city.

Two Case Studies of Massive Social Change

*I. CHANGING POPULATION AND ITS IMPACT ON PUBLIC ELEMENTARY SCHOOLS IN OAK PARK, ILLINOIS**

As suggested in the foregoing review, the redistribution of population through migration and mobility has a vital impact on the age structure of a community. Mobility is the mechanism by which a family's housing is brought into adjustment to its housing needs. Housing needs are determined by the life cycle of the family. In time, a new family tends to increase in size and income, and to become more sensitive to the social and physical environment. It tends to move from smaller to larger dwellings, from mobile, family-less areas to neighborhoods where family living is the typical pattern.

Different kinds of housing areas vary in their ability to accommodate the changing needs of families. Some are suitable to a wide range of needs while others are not. Densely built, mobile areas in the central city offer "limited purpose" dwellings—small rental units, least adjustable to changes of family households. These areas are suitable only for the earliest and final stages of the family cycle.

The single-family home areas, located in the less dense, peripheral parts of the central city and suburbs, offer large dwelling units which can meet the space needs of a family through all life-cycle changes. It is easier to adjust to a surplus of space than to overcrowding.

Households of large families found in mobile areas tend to be broken families, or poor families, or families of residentially segregated minorities. As the general level of income rises, more growing families are able to move out of mobile areas into single-family home areas. Increasingly, then, mobile areas become refuges for broken families, the poor, and the segregated.

With the downgrading of the mobile areas, single-family neighborhoods sharing regional facilities like shopping centers, high schools, and public transportation with mobile areas are affected. Middle-class white families tend to leave these previously stable neighborhoods for homes in more homogeneous school-attendance areas. By and large, these families are replaced by lower-income families and individuals. Because the new group cannot always afford to pay for the middle-class housing, the neighborhood gradually becomes converted from an area of large, owner-occupied, middle-class housing units to one of small, renter-occupied, lower-class housing units. Often, too, this transition is accompanied either by conversion of existing structures to the new use, or by new apartment development.

In Chicago, there is a correlation between older population, dormitory communities with a higher family income, and slow population growth, on the one hand, and a high proportion of white-collar labor force, on the other. Many areas with a predominantly younger population

*This case study was completed by Pierre de Visé, Research Director of the Hospital Planning Council of Metropolitan Chicago.

TABLE 11-8

Age Distribution of Population of Oak Park: 1950 to 1966

	Age Group	1950	1956	1960	1966	Net Change 1950–1956	Net Change 1956–1960	Net Change 1960–1966
	0–4	4,770	4,584	4,788	4,411	−186	+204	−377
	5–9	4,033	4,498	4,524	5,012	+465	+26	+488
	10–14	3,242	4,221	4,517	4,992	+979	+296	+475
	15–19	3,265	3,293	3,816	4,509	+28	+523	+693
Subtotal:	0–19	15,310	16,596	17,645	18,924	+1,286	+1,049	+1,279
	20–39	16,541	14,084	12,962	14,042	−2,457	−1,122	+1,080
	40–64	24,230	22,929	21,356	19,634	−1,301	−1,573	−1,722
	65+	7,448	7,717	9,130	8,938	+269	+1,413	−192

Source: Tables 11–8 through 11–10 and 11–12 are from primary data compiled by Pierre de Visé, Research Director of the Hospital Planning Council of Metropolitan Chicago.

are industrial communities of lower income or rapidly growing communities of all income levels. The more balanced economies and more mature housing areas of the outlying satellites are characterized by a middle-aged population.

In 1950 to 1960, Oak Park was one of the communities in the oldest age-group category—one of twenty-five communities, all but two of which are located in an arc approximately eight miles from Chicago's Loop, starting at Rogers Park on the North Shore and terminating at South Shore on the southern littoral [refer back to the maps in Chapter 10]. Like many of the others, Oak Park reached maturity in the 1920's. Its life cycle unfolded a full generational course in the 1930's and 1940's, during which its population aged substantially. A new generational cycle began in the 1950's, however, during which the young (under 20) increased sizably, young adults (20 to 39) and middle-aged adults (40 to 64) decreased substantially, and older adults (65 and over) increased moderately. These trends were modified further in the 1960's by the large immigration of young adults and a net loss in older adults, marking a significant turning point in the village's life cycle history (see Table 11–8).

The net changes in age groups shown in the last three columns of Table 11–8 are not wholly attributable to differential rates of migration of these age "cohorts." Differences in the number and rates of births and deaths would particularly affect net difference in the very young and very old age groups. We applied cohort survival rates to estimate loss by deaths in each age group and have obtained net residuals attributable to net migration which closely parallel the net population changes reported in Table 11–8. The total number of births, deaths, and net migration in Oak Park for the three time periods surveyed in Table 11–8 is summarized in Table 11–9.

TABLE 11-9

Components of Populatian Change in Oak Park: 1950 to 1966

	1950–1955	1956–1960	1960–1966
Births	5,565	5,571	6,209
Deaths	3,711	3,680	4,609
Natural increase	1,854	1,891	1,600
Migration	−4,057	−2,124	−1,400

Source: See note to Table 11–8.

Areas with unusually high proportions of both young and older populations are not necessarily differentiated from areas with a more normal age composition by the average measure of median age. The median simply divides the age distribution into two equal groups. This cautionary word is certainly appropriate for Oak Park, whose populations' median age remained 40 through the 1950's even though the proportion of both young and old substantially increased. Oak Park's proportion of young and old populations resembles Chicago's white population much more than that of the suburbs (see Table 11–10).

TABLE 11–10

Distribution of White Popultaion: 1960 (by Percentage of Age Groups)

	Oak Park	*Other Suburbs*	*Chicago*	*Metropolitan Area*
Under 18	26.8	35.6	28.3	33.2
18 to 64	58.2	57.7	60.5	57.8
65 and over	14.9	6.7	11.2	9.0
Median age (in years)	39.9	29.5	35.7	32.0

Source: See note to Table 11–8.

An aging population is the normal manifestation of the life cycle of a residentially mature community like Oak Park. Changes toward younger population are more typically associated with residentially newer communities whose housing stock is rapidly growing. Purchasers of new housing are families with school-aged children who bring down the average age of a total population which includes a wider and older age range of residents.

Mature communities whose proportion of young people gets larger rather than smaller are communities undergoing a new life cycle. Such renewal is generally hastened by racial or ethnic transition from a higher to a lower social stratum. The transition may be from white to Negro, from old immigrant Catholic (Irish, Polish, Italian) to new immigrant Catholic (Ukranian, Spanish-American), or from old immigrant Protestant to old immigrant Catholic. Depending on the rapidity of turnover, the process of racial or ethnic transition is accompanied by various degrees of socio-economic downgrading of the population and the residential environment. If the housing stock and character of the community is not readily adaptable to the needs of the incoming population, fundamental adjustments like urban renewal, private construction, or functional conversion may result in widening the range of housing types and increasing the mobility rate of the community.

The changes in Oak Park were of this kind, and may be ascertained from school population records. Oak Park is one of only two communities outside the central city that experienced such changes in the decade from 1950 to 1960 (see Fig. 11–7).

The communities which experienced the greatest increase in the proportion of school-age population are the old and new Negro communities of the Near West and South Sides within the central city. On the immediate periphery and in the main paths of the expanding wedges of Negro population are found the communities with the next most rapidly increasing school-aged population. All but two of these communities (Near North Side and Hyde Park) remained stable racially, but they became younger because they received young white families fleeing racially transitional areas one to three miles closer to downtown Chicago. Oak Park and Maywood, the only suburban communities on this select list, are in the main path of westward Negro movement.

Similar evidence may be found in the median age statistics. The old Black Belt of 1940 has an aging population, succeeded by transitional areas in which the median age has been generally reduced by 10 or more years. These areas are immediately surrounded by white areas whose populations are aging. About two miles or so beyond the transitional borders, we see white communities with populations whose median ages are dropping 5 to 10 years. The communities received white in-migrants from the transitional areas in the 1950's, just as Oak Park is receiving such in-migrants in the 1960's. Thus, although the median age of Oak Park's population remained constant from 1950 to 1960, it can be expected to show marked reductions for the period since 1960.

Origins of Oak Park In-migrants and Destinations of Out-migrants

Although there is net out-migration of the total Oak Park population, age differentials in migration have resulted in the net in-migration of school-aged population. We have examined the record of public elementary school in-transfers and out-transfers for the school years 1965–1966 and 1966–1967 with a view to determining the residential origins and destinations of these transferring students.

Transfers from schools in the South Austin community, directly east of Oak Park, accounted for most of the students transferring in from other public schools. In the two years, 32 in-

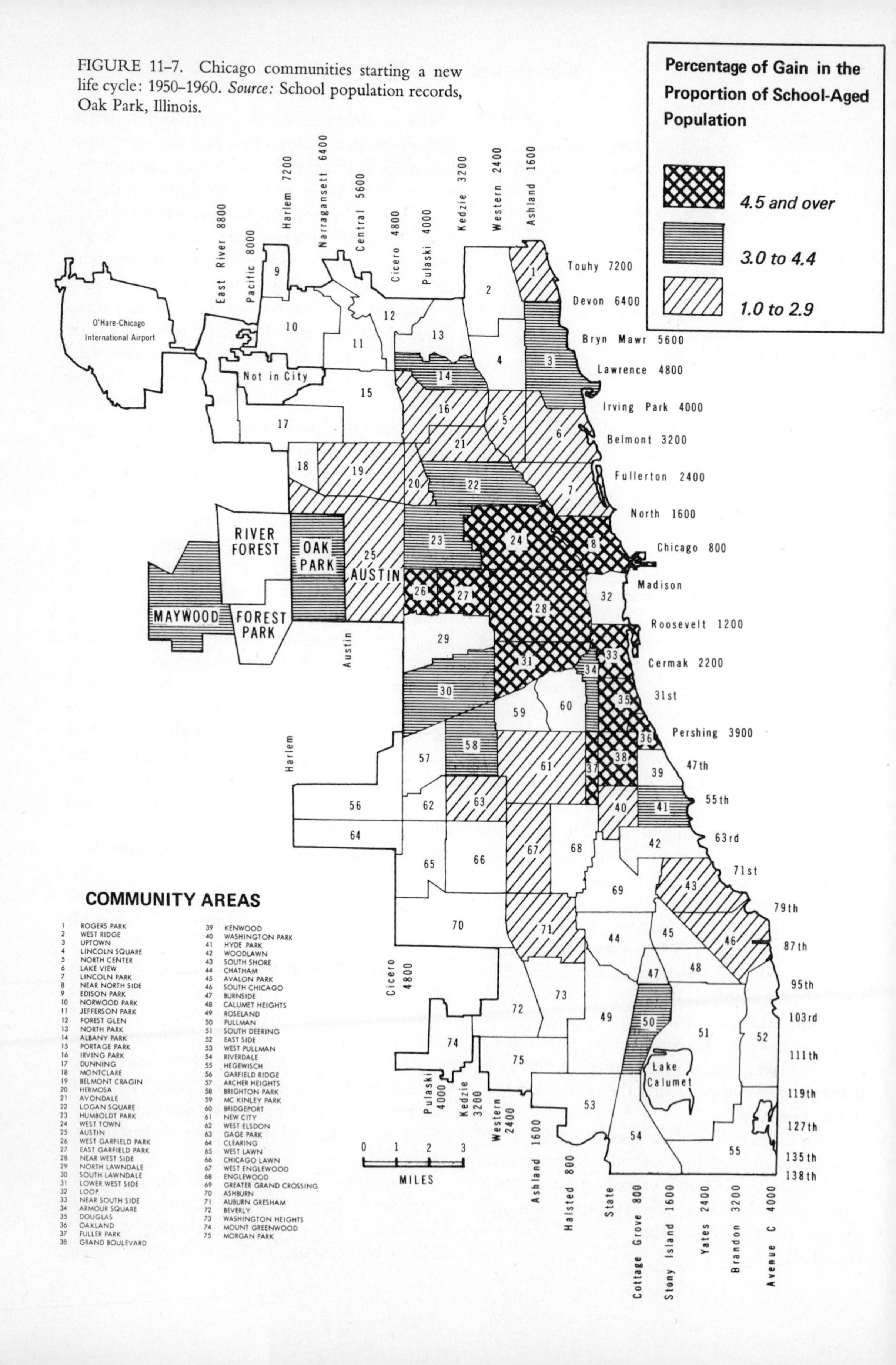

FIGURE 11-7. Chicago communities starting a new life cycle: 1950–1960. *Source:* School population records, Oak Park, Illinois.

transferring students came from Emmet, 10 from Lovett, 9 from Nash, 6 from May, and 3 from Sayre. (These are transfers after the first day of school, perhaps a third of all transfers. First-day transfer records were not available.) Total in-transfers for the two years were as follows:

In-transfers from:	*1966–1967*	*1965–1966*
Illinois	315	315
Out-of-State	101	76

According to a questionnaire survey, undertaken as part of the investigation, "ethnic and other changes in neighborhood" was the main reason the parents of students coming from within Illinois moved from the previous neighborhood, and "deteriorating school problems" was the second reason. "Good schools" were the main factor influencing the choice of Oak Park, and a "stable residential area" was the second factor.

Surveys of out-transferring students made in prototypic West Side Polish and Italian Catholic schools confirmed the pattern of westward movement caused by racial transition.[95] Both transfer groups studied, one just south and one just north of the West Side Negro belt, tended to move out of ethnic neighborhoods that were changing racially, into nearby western suburbs that were somewhat more ethnically heterogeneous.

An examination of new locations of students transferring *out* of Oak Park public elementary schools in the academic years 1965 to 1967 revealed a concentration of movements to suburbs immediately to the west of Oak Park, predominantly River Forest, Forest Park, Elmwood Park, Elmhurst, and Lombard. In contrast, it is interesting to note that 40 of the 72 parents who answered the survey question on future moves indicated a preference for a northwestern or northern suburb, and only one chose a western suburb. "Change in residential character" was the principal reason cited in answer to the related question: "What do you think might cause you to move from Oak Park, in order of importance?"

Thus, a clearly centrifugal pattern of relocation, from east to west, is discernible in the four groups of transferring school children. Flight from the expanding Negro western sector, implicit in the concentration of residential origins of those transferring, is made a more explicit explanation of mobility in answers to questionnaire items regarding reasons for leaving former address, for selecting Oak Park, and for possibly leaving Oak Park.

Migration, Religious Affiliation, and Parochial Attendance

In a 1967 Religious Survey of Oak Park, it was reported that, between 1947 and 1967, there was a downward shift of 13.8 per cent in old-line Protestants, 2.9 per cent in Lutherans and Reformed Christians; and a gain of 11.7 per cent in Roman Catholics, 1.2 per cent in Jews, and 2.2 per cent in Greek and Russian Orthodox[96] (see Table 11–11).

TABLE 11–11

Major Denominations of Residents of Oak Park and River Forest: 1946 to 1966

Denomination	*1946*	*1958*	*1961*	*1966*	*Nonresidents 1961–1966*
Old-line Protestant	39.9%	33.1%	30.8%	28.1%	21.4%
Lutheran and Reformed Christian	13.0	10.7	10.5	10.2	9.6
Other Protestant	8.2	10.8	10.7	9.8	9.7
Roman Catholic	35.5	43.0	45.2	47.0	55.3
Jewish	1.5	2.8	2.8	2.7	2.2
Greek and Russian Orthodox	—	—	—	2.2	1.8

Source: Merlin L. Clark, "1967 Religious Survey of Oak Park and River Forest, Illinois," prepared for the Oak Park-River Forest Council of Churches.

This religious shift toward Catholic in-migrants notwithstanding, parochial school enrollment in Oak Park has gone down substantially, while public school enrollment has gone up. As shown in Table 11–12, the proportion of elementary school children in parochial schools has declined from 43 to 35 per cent since 1960.

TABLE 11–12

Public and Parochial Elementary School Enrollment: Oak Park Residents, 1960 to 1968

School Year Ending	*Public*	*Parochial*	*Total*	*Percentage Parochial*
1968	5957	3160	9117	34.7
1967	5637	3212	8849	36.3
1966	5397	3283	8680	37.8
1965	4997	3510	8507	41.3
1964	4700	3525	8225	42.8
1963	4690	3520	8210	42.9
1962	4578	3450	8028	43.0
1961	4656	3441	8097	42.5
1960	4600	3452	8052	42.9

Source: See note to Table 11–8.

We hypothesize that incoming Catholics are more prone to send their children to public schools in Oak Park for the following reasons: (1) the incoming Catholics have a lower income than the old Catholic residents; and (2) The recent decision of the Catholic School Board to reduce class size has resulted in a curtailment of first- and second-grade admissions.

There is some evidence, from a variety of attitudinal surveys, that the desire to enroll children in a parochial school increases with socioeconomic status. The accessibility of desirable Catholic schools is also a factor in parochial school enrollment. Thus, in neighborhoods which have a shortage of desirable parochial school capacity, as in rapidly growing "ecumenical" suburban areas and racially mixed inner-city areas, the proportion of the parochial school population will fall considerably below the proportion of the Catholic population.

The hypothesis that upwardly mobile Catholics tend to send their children to high-grade public schools finds support in the parallel tendency of Catholics to move from national parishes into "WASP" (White Anglo-Saxon Protestant) communities. To the extent that Oak Park still has the reputation of having an excellent public school system and predominantly Protestant residents, it may attract a considerable number of Catholics who are upwardly mobile in these two aspirations. This hypothesis is given further credence by two answers to our questionnaire. Half the new pupils come from Catholic homes, and their parents' stated as their principal reason for choosing a public school, the "good quality of public schools."

Transfers from Oak Park Catholic Schools have made up between a third and a fourth of all in-transfer students to Oak Park public schools in the last three years. In our survey of other than first-day transfers in 1965–1967, Ascension sent 33 pupils, St. Giles sent 13, St. Catherine sent 11, and St. Edmund sent 4. When we add these numbers of Catholic school transfer students to Catholic students entering the public schools as transfers from other communities, over two-thirds of Oak Park public school in-transfer students are from Catholic families.

Not only in Oak Park, but in other suburban and Chicago communities as well, public schools have had to increase class sizes from 25 to 30 or more to accommodate Catholic transfer students. In the entire Chicago area, the proportion of elementary school pupils in Catholic schools fell from 30 to 24 per cent between 1957 and 1967, while the proportion of Catholic population remained constant at 42 per cent. Catholic school transfers increased precipitously in 1967 with the new archdiocesan policy of restricting first-grade class size to 45 that year, and to 40 in 1968. Of the 11,446 transfers in 1966–1967, 7,555 were from Catholic schools in Chicago and 3,891 from suburban schools. Three-fourths of these out-transfers were involuntary.[97]

An examination of recent changes in Oak Park parochial school enrolment by grade, reveals that first grade drop-outs account for the bulk of total declines in enrollment between 1966–1967 and 1967–1968 (55 out of 59), confirming the restrictive effect of the new Catholic policy of limiting first grade class size.

Future Migration and Racial Transition

The western band of Negro population, whose widening wedge constricts at the Belt Line railroad from a 3-mile width to a half-mile wide funnel between the Lake Street and Congress elevated lines, now reaches as far west as Laramie, one mile from Oak Park's eastern limits.[98] We believe that this band will continue to be extended, through the 1960's and 1970's, by the movement of Negroes being displaced by urban renewal programs in the eastern and central segments of the band. We predict that while Cicero and Berwyn will continue to resist integration, Oak Park will admit Negroes. We predict that Oak Park will become 10 per cent Negro by 1975, and 25 per cent Negro by 1980.

We base this prediction on the belief that pressures for Negro housing will follow essentially the same geographic pattern of expansion between 1950 and 1968. The approaching wave of Negro population is now one mile away and is advancing at the rate of two blocks per year.[99] Oak Park will be a prime target of Negro expansion, we believe, because of its accessibility (provided by two elevated lines and a major expressway), its proximity to new employment centers (in the Melrose Park and Franklin Park area), its large number of large pre-war apartments, the reputation and quality of its schools, and the relatively liberal attitudes of its churches and other community organizations. We predict that most of the Negro in-migrants will be families of a size, age composition, and socio-economic character generally similar to those of the present incoming white families from South Austin.

The basis of these predictions is the research on ghetto expansion that follows.

*II. THE NEGRO GHETTO: PROBLEMS AND ALTERNATIVES**

"Ghettos," as we must realistically term the segregated areas occupied by Negroes and other minority groups, are common features of American urban life. The vast majority of Negroes, Japanese, Puerto Ricans, and Mexican-Americans are forced by a variety of pressures to reside in restricted areas, in which they themselves are dominant. So general is this phenomenon that not one of the hundred largest urban areas can be said to be without ghettos.[100]

Inferiority in almost every conceivable material respect is the mark of the ghetto. But also, to the minority person, the ghetto implies a rejection, a stamp of inferiority, which stifles ambition and initiative. The very fact of residential segregation reinforces other forms of discrimination by preventing the normal contacts through which prejudice may be gradually overcome. Yet because the home and the neighborhood are so personal and intimate, housing will be the last and most difficult step in the struggle for equal rights.

The purpose here is to trace the origin of the ghetto and the forces that perpetuate it and to evaluate proposals for controlling it. The Negro community of Seattle, Washington, is used in illustration of a simple model of ghetto expansion as a diffusion process into the surrounding white area.

From the beginning of the nineteenth century, the newest immigrants were accustomed to spend some time in slum ghettos of New York, Philadelphia, or Boston.[101] But as their incomes grew and their English improved they moved out into the American mainstream, making way for the next group. During the nineteenth century the American Negro population, in this country from the beginning but accustomed to servitude, remained predominantly southern and rural. Relatively few moved to the north, and those who did move lived in small clusters about the cities. The Negro ghetto did not exist.[102] Even in southern cities the Negroes, largely in the service of whites, lived side by side with the white majority. Rather suddenly, with the social upheaval and employment opportunities of World War I, Negro discontent grew, and large-scale migration began from the rural south to the urban north, to Philadelphia, New York, Chicago, and St. Louis, and beyond.

*Reprinted from Richard M. Morrill, "The Negro Ghetto: Problems and Alternatives," *The Geographical Review*, LV, No. 2 (July, 1965), 339–61, with the permission of the author and editor.

The influx was far larger than the cities could absorb without prejudice. The vision of a flood of Negroes, uneducated and unskilled, was frightening both to the whites and to the old-time Negro residents. As the poorest and newest migrants, the Negroes were forced to double up in the slums that had already been created on the periphery of business and industrial districts. The pattern has never been broken. Just as one group was becoming settled, another would follow, placing ever greater pressure on the limited area of settlement, and forcing expansion into neighboring areas, being emptied from fear of inundation. Only in a few cities, such as Minneapolis—St. Paul, and Providence and other New England cities, has the migration been so small *and* so gradual that the Negro could be accepted into most sections as an individual.

America has experienced four gigantic streams of migration: the European immigration, which up to 1920 must have brought 30,000,000 or more; the westward movement, in which, from 1900 to the present, close to 10,000,000 persons have participated; the movement from the farms to the cities, which since 1900 has attracted some 30,000,000; and the migration of Negroes to the North and West, which has amounted since World War I to about 5,000,000, including some 3,000,000 between 1940 and 1960 (Table 11-13). The pace has not abated. Contributing also to the ghetto population have been 900,000 Puerto Ricans, who came between 1940 and 1960, largely to New York City; about 1,500,000 Mexicans, descendants of migrants to the farms and cities of the Southwest; and smaller numbers of Chinese, Japanese, and others.[103] Economic opportunity has been the prime motivation for all these migrant groups, but for the Negro there was the additional hope of less discrimination.

TABLE 11–13

Major Destinations of Net 3,000,000 Negroes Moving North, 1940–1960 **(*Estimates Only*)**

New York	635,000	Washington, D.C.	201,000
Chicago	445,000	San Francisco	130,000
Los Angeles	260,000	Cleveland	120,000
Detroit	260,000	St. Louis	118,000
Philadelphia	255,000	Baltimore	115,000

The rapidity and magnitude of the Negro stream not only have increased the intensity and size of ghettos in the North but no doubt have also accelerated the white "flight to the suburbs" and have strongly affected the economic, political, and social life of the central cities.[104] In the South, too, Negroes have participated in the new and rapid urbanization, which has been accompanied by increased ghettoization and more rigid segregation.

As a result of these migrations, the present urban minority population consists, in the North and West, of 7,500,000 Negroes and 4,000,000 others, together 12.5 per cent of the total regional urban population; in the South, of 6,500,000 Negroes, 20 per cent; in total, of 18,000,000, 14 per cent.[105] The proportion is increasing in the North, decreasing in the South. Minority populations in large American cities are presented in Table 11–14.

TABLE 11–14

Minority Populations of Major Urbanized Areas: United States, 1960

City	*Minority Population*	*Total Population*	*Minority (%)*
1. New York City	2,271,000	14,115,000	16
Negro	1,545,000		
Puerto Rican	671,000		
2. Los Angeles	1,233,000	6,489,000	19
Negro	465,000		
Mexican	629,000		
Asian	120,000		
3. Chicago	1,032,000	5,959,000	17
4. Philadelphia	655,000	3,635,000	18
5. Detroit	560,000	3,538,000	16
6. San Francisco	519,000	2,430,000	21
7. Washington, D.C.	468,000	1,808,000	26
8. Baltimore	346,000	1,419,000	24
9. Houston	314,000	1,140,000	28
10. San Antonio	303,000	642,000	47
11. St. Louis	287,000	1,668,000	17
12. Cleveland-Lorain	279,000	1,928,000	15
13. New Orleans	265,000	845,000	31
14. Dallas-Fort Worth	252,000	1,435,000	18
15. Atlanta	207,000	768,000	27
16. Birmingham	201,000	521,000	38
17. Memphis	200,000	545,000	37

Sources: Department of Commerce, Bureau of the Census, *Census of Population: 1960*, I. chap. C, "General Social and Economic Characteristics"; II, *Subiect Reports*, "Nonwhite Population by Race" (Washington, D.C.: U.S. Government Printing Office, 1961).

The Nature of the Ghetto

If we study the minority population in various cities, we can discern real differences in income, education, occupational structure, and quality of homes.[106] For example, median family income of Negroes ranges from $2,600 in Jackson, Mississippi, to $5,500 in Seattle; and as a proportion of median white family income, from 46 per cent to 80 per cent, respectively. The United States median family income for Negroes in urban areas is only $3,700, as compared with $6,400 for whites, but it is more than double the figure for Negroes still living in rural areas, $1,750. It is not hard, therefore, to understand the motivation for Negro migration to the northern cities, where striking progress has really been made.

But the stronger impression is of those general characteristics which are repeated over and over. The ghetto system is dual: not only are Negroes excluded from white areas, but whites are largely absent from Negro areas. Areas entirely or almost exclusively white or nonwhite are the rule, areas of mixture the exception. The ghettos, irrespective of regional differences, are always sharply inferior to white areas; home ownership is less and the houses are older, less valuable, more crowded, and more likely to be substandard.[107] More than 30 per cent of Negro urban housing is dilapidated or without indoor plumbing, as compared with less than 15 per cent for whites. The ghetto is almost always in a zone peripheral to the central business district, often containing formerly elegant houses intermingled with commercial and light industrial uses. As poor, unskilled labor, Negroes settled near the warehouses and the railroads, sometimes in shacktowns, and gradually took over the older central houses being abandoned by the most recently segregated groups—for example, the Italians and the Jews—as their rise in economic status enabled them to move farther out. More than one ghetto may appear on different sides of the business district, perhaps separated by ridges of wealthy, exclusive houses or apartments.

The Negro differs fundamentally from these earlier groups, and from the Mexicans and Puerto Ricans as well. As soon as economic and educational improvements permit, the lighter-skinned members of the other groups may escape the ghetto, but black skin constitutes a qualitative difference in the minds of whites, and even the wealthy Negro rarely finds it possible to leave the ghetto. Color takes precedence over the normal determinants of our associations.[108]

In the southern city, Negroes have always constituted a large proportion of the population and have traditionally occupied sections, or wedges, extending from the center of the city out into the open country. Indeed, around some cities, such as Charleston, South Carolina, the outer suburban zone is largely Negro. Figure 11–8 depicts the ghetto pattern in selected cities.

The impact of the ghetto on the life of its residents is partly well known, partly hidden. The white person driving through is struck by the poverty, the substandard housing, the mixture of uses, and the dirt; he is likely to feel that these conditions are due to the innate character of the Negro. The underlying fact is, of course, that Negroes on the average are much poorer, owing partly to far inferior educational opportunities in most areas, but more to systematic discrimination in employment, which is only now beginning to be broken. Besides pure poverty, the pressure of the influx into most northern cities itself induces deterioration: formerly elegant houses, abandoned by whites, have had to be divided and redivided to accommodate the newcomers, maintenance is almost impossible, much ownership is by absentee whites. Public services such as street maintenance and garbage collection and amenities such as parks and playgrounds are often neglected. Residential segregation means *de facto* school segregation. Unemployment is high, at least double the white average, and delinquency and crime are the almost inevitable result. A feeling of inferiority and hopelessness comes to pervade the ghetto. Most important is the enormous waste of human resources in the failure to utilize Negroes to reasonable capacity. The real cost of maintaining the ghetto system is fantastic. In direct costs the city spends much more in crime prevention, welfare payments, and so forth than it can collect.[109] The ghetto is the key to the Negro problem.

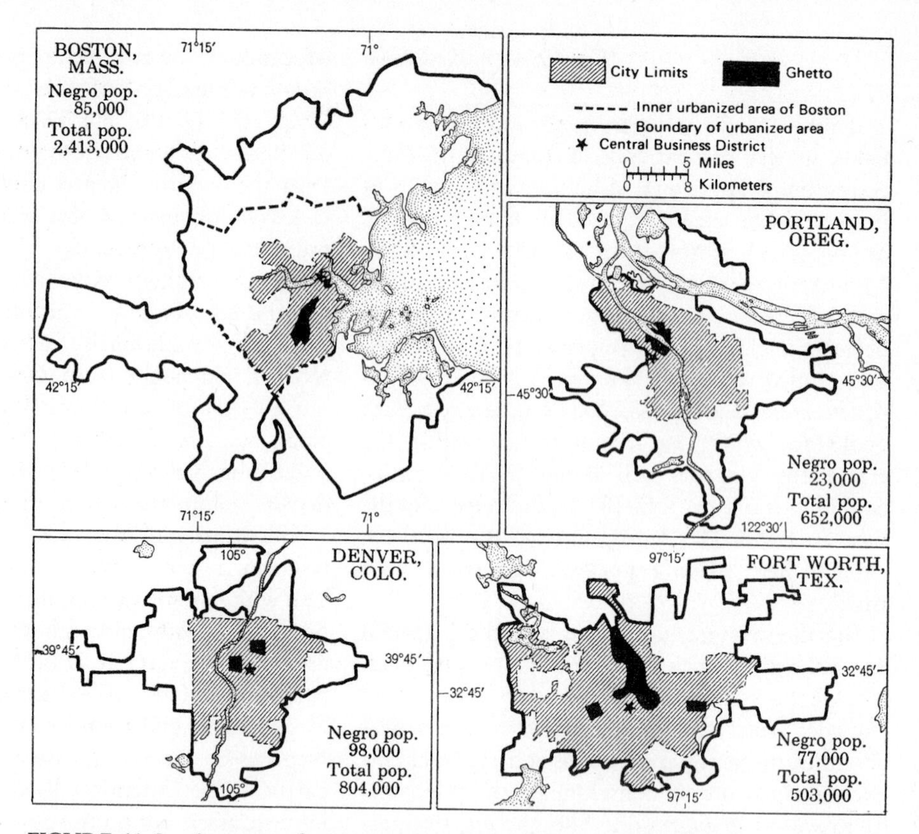

FIGURE 11–8. A group of representative ghettos. *Source:* Figs. 11–8 through 11–14*a* are from Richard L. Morrill, "The Negro Ghetto: Problems and Alternatives," *The Geographical Review*, LV (July, 1965), 339–61.

What are the forces that operate to maintain the ghetto system? Four kinds of barriers hinder change: prejudice of whites against Negroes; characteristics of the Negroes; discrimination by the real-estate industry and associated financial institutions; and legal and governmental barriers. Naked prejudice is disclaimed by a majority of Americans today. Today's prejudice is not an outright dislike; it is, rather, a subtle fear, consisting of many elements. The typical white American may now welcome the chance to meet a Negro, but he is afraid that if a Negro moves into his neighborhood it will break up and soon be Negro. Of course, on a national average there are not as many Negroes as that—only one or two families to a block—but the fear exists because that is the way the ghetto has grown. A greater fear is of loss in social status if Negroes move in. This reflects the culture-bred notion that Negroes are inherently of lower standing. Some persons are terrified at the unlikely prospect of intermarriage. Finally, people are basically afraid of, or uncertain about, people who are different, especially in any obvious physical way. These fears combine into powerful controls to maintain segregation: refusal to sell to Negroes, so as not to offend the neighbors; and the tendency to move out as soon as a Negro enters, in order not to lose status by association.

The Negro himself contributes, however unwillingly, to ghettoization. It is difficult to be a minority as a group, but more difficult still to be a minority alone. Consequently the desire to escape the ghetto and move freely in the larger society is tempered by a realization of the problems in store for the "pioneer" and hesitancy to cut neighborhood ties with his own kind. Few people have such courage. In most cities, even if there were no housing discrimination, the ghetto would still persist, simply because a large proportion of Negroes could not afford, or would be afraid, to leave. Most Negroes achieve status and acceptance only within the Negro community. Usually Negroes who leave the ghetto prefer Negro neighbors; the risk is that this number, however small, is enough to initiate the conversion to full-scale ghetto.[110]

The Negro today suffers from his past. The lack of initiative and the family instability resulting from generations of enforced or inculcated subservience and denial of normal family formation are still present and are a barrier to white acceptance. The far lower levels of Negro income and education, no matter how much they are due to direct neglect and discrimination by the white majority, are nevertheless a strong force to maintain the ghetto. Studies show that whites will accept Negroes of equivalent income, education, and occupation.[111]

The strongest force, however, in maintaining the ghetto may well be real-estate institutions: the real-estate broker and sources of financing. It has always been, and continues to be, the clear-cut, official, and absolute policy of the associations of real-estate brokers that "a realtor should never be instrumental in introducing into a neighborhood a character of property or occupancy, members of any race or nationality, or any individuals whose presence will clearly be detrimental to property values in that neighborhood."[112] Many studies have attempted to resolve this problem. In the long run, property values and rents exhibit little if any change in the transition from white to Negro occupancy.[113] Sale prices may fall temporarily under panic selling, a phenomenon called the "self-fulfilling prophecy": believing that values will fall, the owner panics and sells, and thus depresses market values.[114]

The real-estate industry opposes with all its resources not only all laws but any device, such as cooperative apartments or open-occupancy advertising, to further integration. Real-estate and home-building industries base this policy on the desirability of neighborhood homogeneity and compatibility. Perhaps underlying the collective action is the fear of the individual real-estate broker that if he introduces a Negro into a white area he will be penalized by withdrawal of business. There is, then, a real business risk to the individual broker in a policy of integration, if none to the industry as a whole. Segregation is maintained by refusal of real-estate brokers even to show, let alone sell, houses to Negroes in white areas. Countless devices are used: quoting excessive prices, saying the house is already sold, demanding unfair down payments, removing "For Sale" signs, not keeping appointments, and so on. Even if the Negro finds someone willing to sell him a house in a white area, financing may remain a barrier. Although his income may be sufficient, the bank or savings institution often refuses to provide financing from a fear of Negro income instability and retaliatory withdrawal of deposits by whites. If financing is offered, the terms may be prohibitive. Similar circumstances may also result when a white attempts to buy a house—for *his* residence—in a heavily minority area.

Through the years many legal procedures have been used to maintain segregation. Early in the century races were zoned to certain areas, but these laws were abolished by the courts in 1917. The restrictive covenant, in which the transfer or property contained a promise not to sell to minorities, became the vehicle and stood as legal until 1948, since when more subtle and extra-legal restrictions have been used.

Until 1949, the federal government was a strong supporter of residential segregation, since the Federal Housing Administration required racial homogeneity in housing it financed or insured. As late as 1963, when the President, by Executive Order, forbade discrimination in FHA-financed housing, the old philosophy still prevailed in most areas. Finally, many states, and not just those in the South, still encourage separation. Even in the few states with laws against discrimination in housing, the combined forces for maintaining segregation have proved by far the stronger.

The Process of Ghetto Expansion

The Negro community in the North has grown so rapidly in the last forty years, almost doubling in every decade, that even the subdivision of houses cannot accommodate the newcomers. How does the ghetto expand? Along its edge, the white area is also fairly old and perhaps deteriorating. Many whites would be considering a move to the suburbs even if the ghetto were not there, and fears of deterioration of schools and services, and the feeling that all the other whites will move out, reinforce their inclination to move. Individual owners, especially in blocks adjoining the ghetto, may become anxious to sell. The pressure of Negro buyers and fleeing white residents, who see the solid ghetto a block or two away, combine to scare off potential white purchasers; the owner's resistance gradually weakens; and the transfer is made.

The role of proximity is crucial. On adjacent blocks the only buyers will be Negroes, but five or six blocks away white buyers will still be the rule. In a typical ghetto fringe in Philadelphia the proportion of white buyers climbed from less than 4 per cent, adjacent to the ghetto itself, to 100 per cent five to seven blocks away.[115] Figure 11–9 illustrates the great concentration of initial entry of new street fronts in a band of two or three blocks around a ghetto. The "break" zone contains 5 per cent or fewer Negroes, but 60 per cent of the purchases are by Negroes. Typically, a white on the edge does not mind one or two Negroes on the block or across the street, but if a Negro moves next door the white is likely to move out. He is replaced by a Negro, and the evacuation-replacement process continues until the block has been solidly transferred from white to Negro residence. Expansion of the ghetto is thus a block-by-block total transition.

In this process the real-estate agent is also operative. If the demand for Negro housing can be met in the area adjacent to the ghetto, pressure

FIGURE 11–9. Distribution of purchases of homes by Negroes on the edge of the ghetto, showing initial entry onto streets: 1955. *Source:* Adapted from C. Rapkin and W. Grigsby, *The Demand for Housing in Racially Mixed Areas* (Berkeley: University of California Press, 1960), p. 76. See also caption for Fig. 11–8.

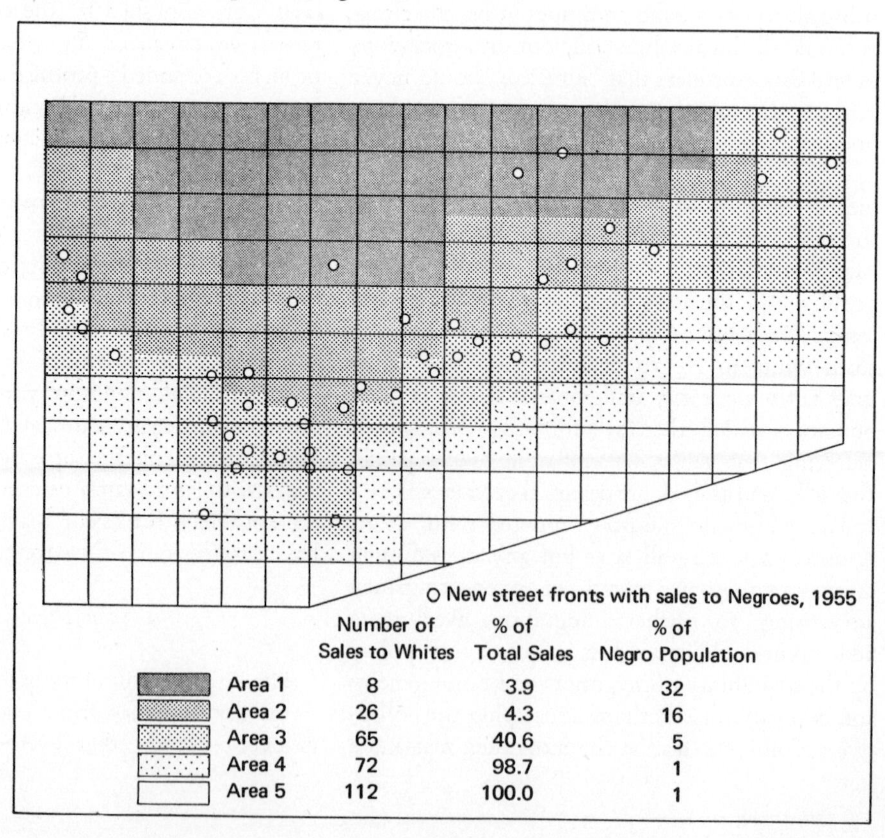

	Number of Sales to Whites	% of Total Sales	% of Negro Population
Area 1	8	3.9	32
Area 2	26	4.3	16
Area 3	65	40.6	5
Area 4	72	98.7	1
Area 5	112	100.0	1

to move elsewhere in the city will diminish. The real-estate industry thus strongly supports the gradual transition along the periphery. After the initial break, the real-estate broker encourages whites to sell. The transition is often orderly, but the unscrupulous dealer sometimes encourages panic selling at deflated prices, purchasing the properties himself and reselling them to Negroes for windfall profits. The probability of finding a white seller is high in the blocks adjacent to the ghetto but falls off rapidly at greater distances, as whites try to maintain familiar neighborhood patterns and conceive this to be possible if the Negro proportion can be kept small. The process of transition is destructive to both groups, separately and together. Whites are in a sense "forced" to sell, move, and see their neighborhoods disband, and Negroes are forced to remain isolated; and total transition reinforces prejudice and hinders healthy contact.

Spread of the Negro ghetto can be described as a *spatial diffusion* process, in which Negro migrants gradually penetrate the surrounding white area. From some origin, a block-by-block substitution or diffusion of a new condition—that is, Negro for white occupancy—takes place. The Negro is the active agent; he can move easily within the ghetto and can, though with difficulty, "pioneer" outside it. The white is passive, an agent of resistance or inertia. Resistance against escape of Negroes from the ghetto takes two forms: rebuff of attempts to buy; and diminishing willingness to sell with increasing distance from areas or blocks that already have Negroes. On the average the Negro will have to try more than once to consummate a sale, or, conversely, the owner will have to be approached by more than one buyer. Once the block is broken, however, resistance falls markedly, and transition begins. Although a complete model would take into account that a few whites continue to purchase in transition areas, the rate is insufficient, the net flow clear-cut, and the transition inevitable.

The proposed diffusion model is of the probabilistic simulation type.[116] It is probabilistic rather than deterministic for several reasons. We do not have sufficient definite information concerning the motivations for specific house-to-house moves of particular persons, but only general ideas concerning the likelihood of movement and how far. We are not dealing with a large aggregate of migrants, but with only a few individuals in a short period of time in a small area. If we had a thousand migrants, we could safely predict how many would move how far, but at the micro-level a probabilistic approach is required to evaluate individual decisions in the face of a complex of possible choices. Rather than determine that a specific migrant moves from one particular house to another, we find the probability of a typical migrant's move from a block to any and all other blocks, and we use random numbers to decide which destination, among the many possible, he chooses. We thus obtain a spatial pattern of moves, which spreads settlement into new blocks and intensifies it in old blocks.

The model is simulated rather than "real" because it does not purport to predict individual behavior of actual people, but to simulate or pretend moves for typical households. Simulation is a valuable technique in science and technology, in which a model is constructed to depict artificially certain *major* features of some real process.

The simulation of diffusion model is important in biology; in rural and general sociology, and in communications, and has been used in geography.[117] It is an ideal vehicle for the characteristics of ghetto expansion—a process of growth in time, concerning behavior of small groups in small areas in small units of time, in which a powerful element of uncertainty remains, even though the general parameters of the model tend to channel the results. This randomness is evident in the real situation, since we observe that the ghetto, like a rumor or an innovation, does not progress evenly and smoothly in all directions but exhibits an uneven edge and moves at different rates in different directions, here advancing from block to block, there jumping over an obstacle.

We do not expect the simulated patterns to match precisely the actual patterns. We do want the model to generate a pattern of expansion that corresponds in its characteristics to the real pattern, and we can satisfy ourselves of the correspondence by visual and statistical tests. The purpose and hope are to discover and illustrate the nature of the ghetto expansion process, in full knowledge that the detail of the ultimate step is omitted—how the actual individual decides between his specific alternatives. The omission is justified, because we know that the combined effect of many individual decisions can often be described by a random process. The real test here is whether the spread, over a period of time, has the right extent, intensity, solidity or lack of it, and so on.

The Model

A model of ghetto expansion must incorporate several elements: natural increase of the Negro population; Negro immigration into the ghetto; the nature of the resistance to Negro out-migration and its relation to distance; land values and housing characteristics; and the population size limits of destination blocks.

Beginning with the residential pattern at a particular time (in the Seattle example, 1940), migration and the spread of Negro settlement are simulated for ten two-year periods through 1960. The steps are as follows.

1. Taking into account natural increase for each period of the Negro population resident in the Seattle ghetto, at the observed rate of 5 per cent every two years.
2. Assigning immigrants who enter the study area from outside at the observed mean rate of 10 per cent every two years of the Negro population at the beginning of a period. These are assigned by random numbers, the probability that an area will be chosen being proportional to its present Negro population. Presumably, immigrants entering the area will find it easier to live, at least temporarily, and will find opportunities in houses or apartments or with friends, in approximate reflection of the number of Negro units available. After initial residence in the ghetto, the model allows these immigrants to participate in further migration.
3. Assigning internal migrants, at the rate of 20 per cent of the Negro households (including natural increase and immigration) of each block every two years, in the following manner:
   a. Each would-be migrant behaves according to a migration probability field (Fig. 11–10) superimposed over his block. This migration probability field can be shifted about so that each would-be migrant can in turn be regarded as located at the position indicated by X. The numbers in the blocks show where the migrant is to move, depending on which number is selected for him in the manner described below. Blocks adjoining position *X* each have three numbers (e.g., 48–50); more distant blocks have two numbers (e.g., 54–55); and the most distant have one number (e.g., 98). Since 100 numbers are used, the total number of these numbers used in any one block may be regarded as the probability, expressed as a percentage, that any one migrant will move there. Thus a movable probability field, or information field, such as this states the probabilities of a migrant for moving any distance in any direction from his original block. Probability fields are often derived, as this one was, from empirical observations of migration distances. That is, if we look at a large number of moves, their lengths follow a simple frequency distribution, in which the probability of moving declines as distance from the home block increases. Such probabilities reflect the obvious fact of decreasing likelihood of knowing about opportunities at greater and greater distances from home. Thus the probability is higher that a prospective migrant will move to adjacent blocks than to more distant ones. The probability field provides a mechanism for incorporating this empirical knowledge in a model.
   b. Randomly selected numbers, as many as there are migrants, are used to choose specific destinations, according to these probabilities, as will be illustrated below. The probability field as such makes it as likely for a Negro family to move into a white

1	2	3	4	5	6	7	8	9
10	11	12	13	14–15	16	17	18	19
20	21	22	23	24–25	26	27	28	29
30	31	32	33–34	35–37	38–39	40	41	42
43	44–45	46–47	48–50	X	51–53	54–55	56–57	58
59	60	61	62–63	64–66	67–68	69	70	71
72	73	74	75	76–77	78	79	80	81
82	83	84	85	86–87	88	89	90	91
92	93	94	95	96	97	98	99	00

FIGURE 11–10. A probability model of the Negro migration field. *Source:* See caption for Fig. 11–8.

area as to move within the ghetto. A method is needed to take into account the differential resistance of Negro areas, and of different kinds or qualities of white areas, to Negro migration. Modification of the probability field is accomplished by the following procedures.

(1) If a random number indicates a block that already contains Negroes, the move is made immediately (no resistance).

(2) If a random number indicates a block with no Negroes, the fact of contact is registered, but no move is made.

(3) If, however, additional numbers indicate the same block contacted in (2) in the same or the next two-year period, and from whatever location, then the move is made. This provides a means for the gradual penetration of new areas after some persistence by Negroes and resistance by whites. Under such a rule, the majority of Negro contacts into white areas will not be followed by other contacts soon enough, and no migration takes place. In the actual study area chosen, it was found that resistance to Negro entry was great to the west, requiring that a move be allowed there only after three contacts, if the simulated rate of expansion was to match the observed rate. This is an area of apartments and high-value houses. To the north and east, during this period, resistance varied. At times initial contacts ended in successful moves and transition was rapid; at other times a second contact was required. These facts were incorporated into the operation of this phase of the model.

4. There is a limit (based on zoning and lot size) to the number of families that may live on a block. Thus when the population, after natural increase and immigration, temporarily exceeds this limit, the surplus must be moved according to the procedures above. Obviously, in the internal-migration phase no moves are allowed to blocks that are already filled. The entire process is repeated for the next and subsequent time periods.

(a)

		2	2		
1	5	10	10	5	1
5	10	15	15	15	4

(b)

		1–2	3–4		
5	6–10	11–20 //	21–30	31–35	36
37–41	42–51 //	52–66 //	67–81 /	82–96 //	97–00

(c)

		f			
		2	2		
1	6	12	10e	5	1
5	12d	17a	16b	17c	4

FIGURE 11–11. An example of the use of the model. (*a*) Negro residents at start of period; (*b*) distribution of immigrants; (*c*) movement of migrants from three sample blocks. *Source:* See caption for Fig. 11–8.

Hypothetical Example of the Model

Immigration (1 and 2) in the above list. Let us assume at the start that the total Negro population—that is, the number of families—including natural increase, is 100, distributed spatially as in Fig. 11–11*a*. Here the numbers indicate the number of families in each block. Ten immigrant families (10 per cent) enter from outside. The probability of their moving to any of the blocks is proportional to the block's population and here, then, is the same in percentage as the population is in number. In order that we may use random numbers to obtain a location for each immigrant family, the probabilities are first accumulated as whole integers, from 1 to 100, as illustrated in Fig. 11–11*b*. That is, each original family is assigned a number. Thus the third block from the left in the second row has 2 of the 100 families, identified by the numbers 1 and 2, and therefore has a 2 per cent chance of being chosen as a destination by an immigrant family. The range of integral numbers 1–2 corresponds to these chances. The bottom left-hand block has a 5 per cent probability, as the five numbers 37–41 for the families now living there indicate. If, then, the random number 1 or 2, representing an immigrant family, comes up, that family will move to the third block in the second row.

For the 10 immigrant families we need 10 random numbers. Assume that from a table of random numbers we obtain, for example, the numbers 91, 62, 17, 08, 82, 51, 47, 77, 11, and 56. The first number, 91, falls in the range of probabilities for the next to the last block in the bottom row. We place an immigrant family in that block. The second number, 62, places an immigrant family in the third block from the left in the bottom row. This process is continued until all 10 random numbers are used. The final distribution of the immigrant families is shown by the small tally marks in various blocks in Fig. 11-11*b*. The population of blocks after this immigration is shown in Fig. 11–11*c*. Here the large numerals indicate the number of families now in the blocks. It should be made clear that the migrants could not have been assigned exactly proportional to population, because there are not enough whole migrants to go around. The first two blocks, for example, would each have required two-tenths of a migrant. In the probabilistic model, however, this difficulty does not exist.

Local migration (3) in the above list. Twenty per cent of the Negro families of each block, rounded off to the nearer whole number, are now taken as potential migrants. The rounding off yields a total of 19 families who will try to migrate from the blocks, as indicated by the italic numerals in Fig. 11–11*c*. In this figure, the large numbers indicate the resident Negroes. To illustrate, let us consider migration from the three blocks identified by **a**, **b**, and **c** in the bottom row. Random numbers are now needed to match against the migration probability field (Fig. 11–10). Let the random numbers now obtained from the table of random numbers be 49, 75, 14, 50, 36, 68, 26, 12, and 33. The first migrant from **a** is represented by the random number 49. This provides a location one block to the left of the migrant's origin, *X*, to **d**. The second migrant's random number, 75, provides a location two blocks down and one to the left, which is beyond the study area. We interpret this as moot, as though he were replaced by another migrant from outside the area. The third migrant's number, 14, provides a location three blocks up, location **f**. Since this block has no Negroes, this is only a contact, and no move is made at the time. This is indicated by a dashed line. Now let us proceed to migration from block **b**. The first migrant's number, 50, provides a location one block to the left, in block **a**, and the move is made. The second migrant's number, 36, provides a location one block up, in block **e**, and the move is made. The third migrant's number, 68, provides a location beyond the area. From block **c** the first migrant's number is 26, a location two blocks up and one to the right. This is an area with no Negroes, and only a contact path is shown. The second migrant's number, 12, provides a location three blocks up and two to the left. This location coincides with the contact made earlier by the third migrant from block **a**, and the move is made. The third migrant's number, 33, provides a location one block up and one to the left, or block **e** again, and the move is made. The net result of all this migration is the opening of one new block to settlement, the reinforcement of three blocks, and two lost contacts. The italic numbers in the figure show the number of migrants to the block, and the actual moves are shown by solid lines.

Northward Expansion of the Ghetto in Seattle

The ghetto in Seattle, with only 25,000 residents, is of course smaller than those in the large metropoli, and it may seem less of a threat to the surrounding area.[118] Nevertheless, the nature of expansion does not differ from one ghetto to another, though the size of the ghetto and the rate of expansion may vary.

The expansion of the Seattle ghetto is shown in Fig. 11–12*a*, in which the study area is also indicated. From 1940 to 1960, the Negro population in the study area more than quadrupled, from 347 families to 1,520. Except for a few blocks just north and east of the 1940 Negro area, expansion was into middle-class, single-family houses. To the west, where expansion was least, apartments offer increasing resistance and, to the northwest and along the lake to the east, houses reach rather expensive levels. Expansion was easiest along the major south-north and southwest-northeast arterial streets, and northward along

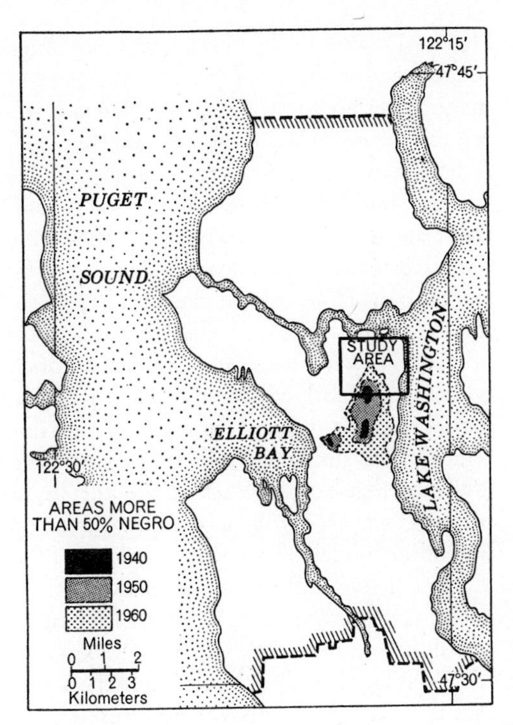

FIGURE 11–12*a*. The growth of the Seattle ghetto: 1940–1960. *Source:* Based on census data for the relevant years. See caption for Fig. 11–8.

FIGURE 11–12*b*. The growth of the northern part of Seattle's ghetto. *Source:* Figs. 11–12*b*, 11–13*a*, and 11–13*b* are based on Department of Commerce, Bureau of the Census, *Census of Housing: 1960*. Block statistics for Seattle. See caption for Fig. 11–8.

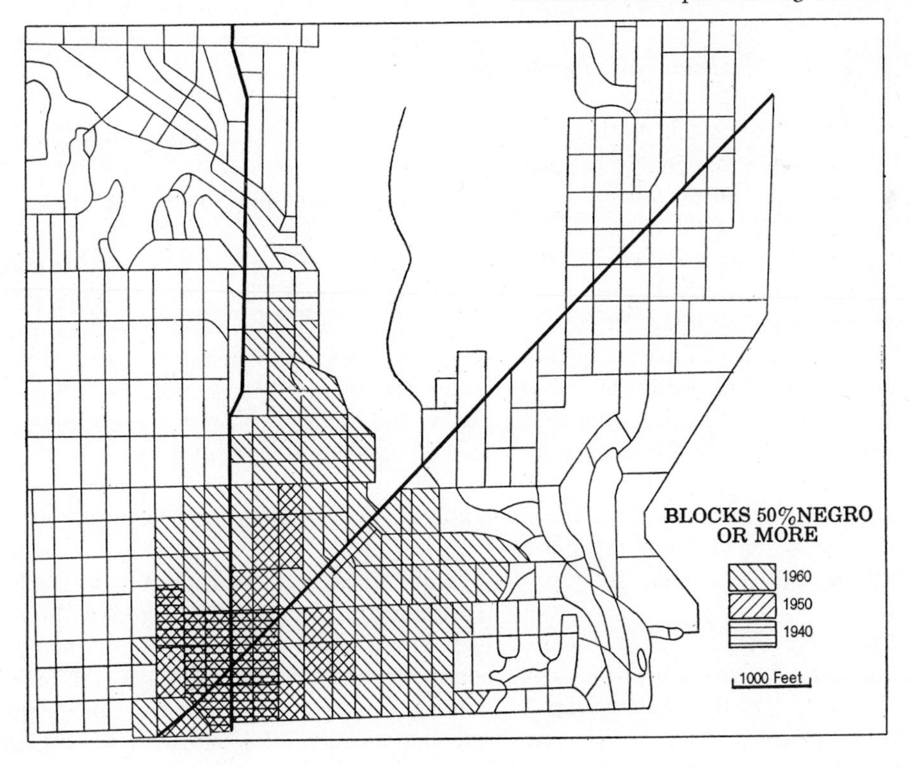

a topographic trough where houses and land were the least valuable. The solidity of the ghetto core, the relatively shallow zone of initial penetration, and the consequent extension of the ghetto proper are shown on Figs. 11–12*b* and 11–13*a* and *b*. As the ghetto became larger and thus more threatening, transition became more nearly solid.

The model was applied to the study area for ten two-year periods, beginning with the actual conditions of 1940 and simulating migration for twenty years. For each two-year period the natural increase of the Negro population was added to the resident population at the beginning of the period. Immigrants were assigned as in the model. Migrants were assigned according to the probability field (Fig. 11–10) and the rules of resistance. One example of the simulation of migration is shown on Fig. 11–14*a*, for 1948 to 1950. Typically, out of 147 potential migrants, 131 were successful and 16 made contacts, but only 8 of the movers pioneered successfully into new blocks. The results of the simulation are illustrated by Figs. 11–14*b* and *c*, which summarize the changes within two larger periods, 1940 to 1950 and 1950 to 1960.

Evaluation of the Results

A comparison of Figs. 11–13*a* and 11–14*b*, and of Figs. 11–13*b* and 11–14*c* showing actual and simulated expansion of the Seattle ghetto from 1940 to 1950 and 1950 to 1960, respectively, indicates a generally close correspondence in the patterns. The actual pattern extended more to the north and the simulated pattern more to the northwest. A field check revealed that neither the quality nor the value of homes was sufficiently taken into account in the model. Topography, too, was apparently crucial. By 1960 the Negroes were rapidly filling in the lower-lying, viewless land. The ridge and view properties remained more highly resistant. The model did not recognize the rapid movement northward along the topographic trough.

According to the most stringent test of absolute block-by-block conformity, the model was not too successful. Less than two-thirds of the simulated new blocks coincided with actual new blocks. However, the model was not intended to account for the exact pattern. Sufficient information does not exist. The proper test was whether the simulated pattern of spread had the right extent (area), intensity (number of Negro families in blocks), and solidity (allowing for white and Negro enclaves), and in these respects the performance was better. The number of blocks entered was close, 140 in the simulation, to 151 for the actual; the size distribution of Negro population was close; and similar numbers of whites remained within the ghetto (with the model tending toward too great exclusion of whites). This similarity, rather than conformance, indicated that both the actual and the simulated patterns *could have occurred* according to the operation of the model. This is the crucial test of theory.

A predictive simulation, as a pattern that could occur, using as the base the actual 1960 situation, was done for the periods 1960 to 1962 and 1962 to 1964 (Fig. 11–14*d*). A limited field check showed that this pattern is approximately correct, except, again, with too much movement to the northwest and not enough to the north. No prediction after 1964 has been attempted, because of risk of misinterpretation by the residents of the area.

Alternatives to the Ghetto

The model attempted merely to identify the process of ghetto expansion and thus helps only indirectly in the evaluation of measures to control the ghetto. We know that such a diffusion process is common in nature—the growth from an origin or origins of something new or different within a parent body. Reduction of this phenomenon would seem to require a great weakening of the distinction between groups, here Negroes and whites, either naturally through new conceptions of each other or artificially by legal means.

In ghetto expansion the process is reduced to replacement of passive white "deserters" by active Negro migrants. Is there an alternative that would permit the integration of minorities in the over-all housing market and prevent the further spread and consolidation of ghettos? Is it possible to

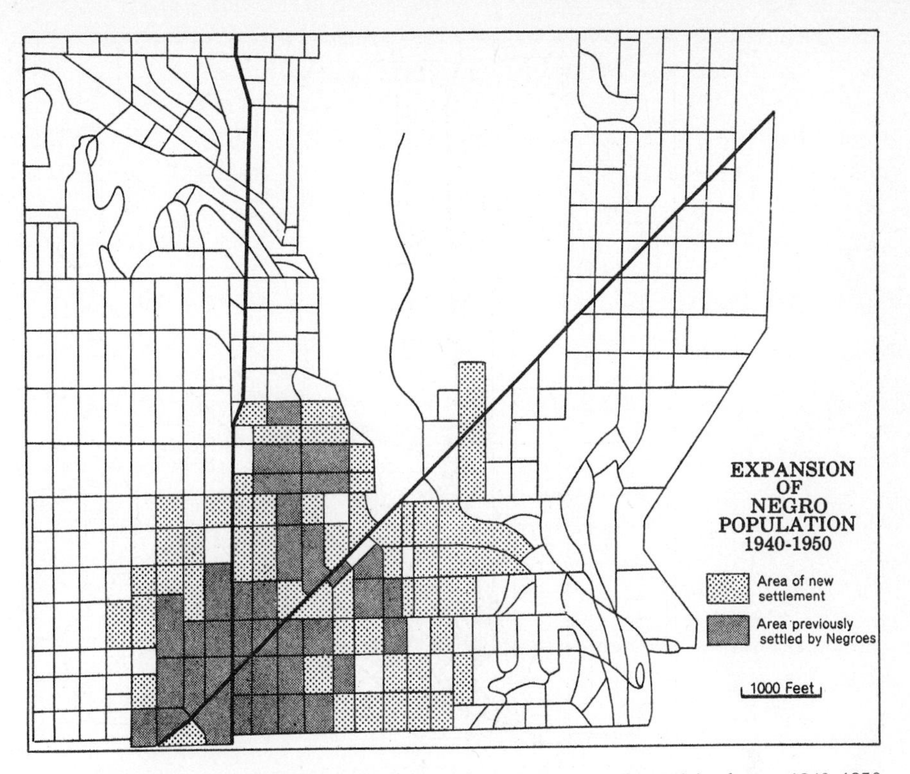

FIGURE 11–13*a*. The actual expansion of the northern part of Seattle's ghetto, 1940–1950. *Source:* See captions for Figs. 11–8 and 11–12*b*.

FIGURE 11–13*b*. The actual expansion of the northern part of Seattle's ghetto, 1950–1960. *Source:* See captions for Figs. 11–8 and 11–12*b*.

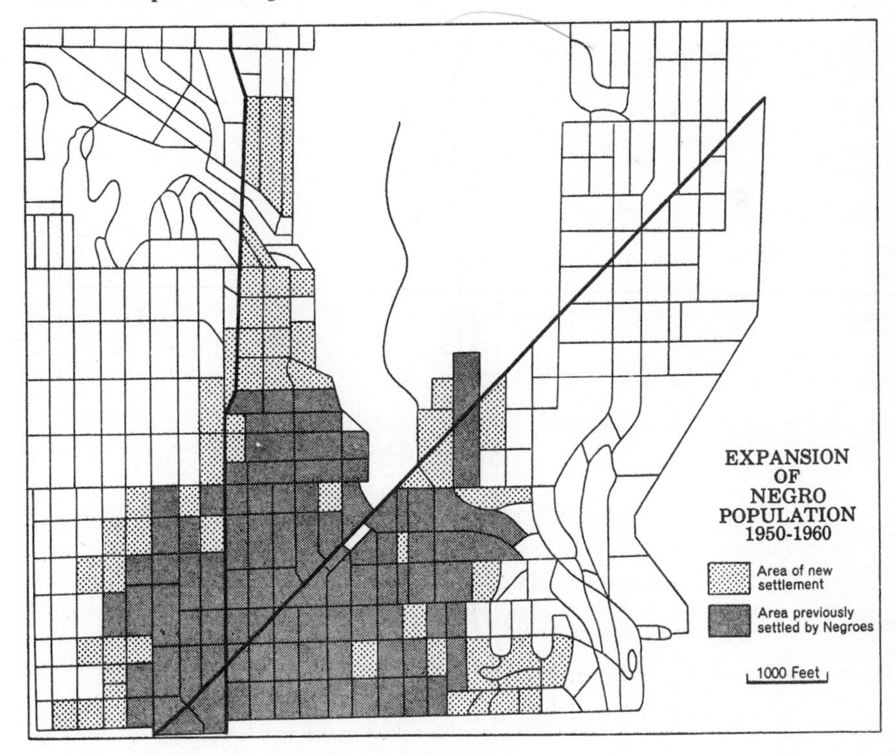

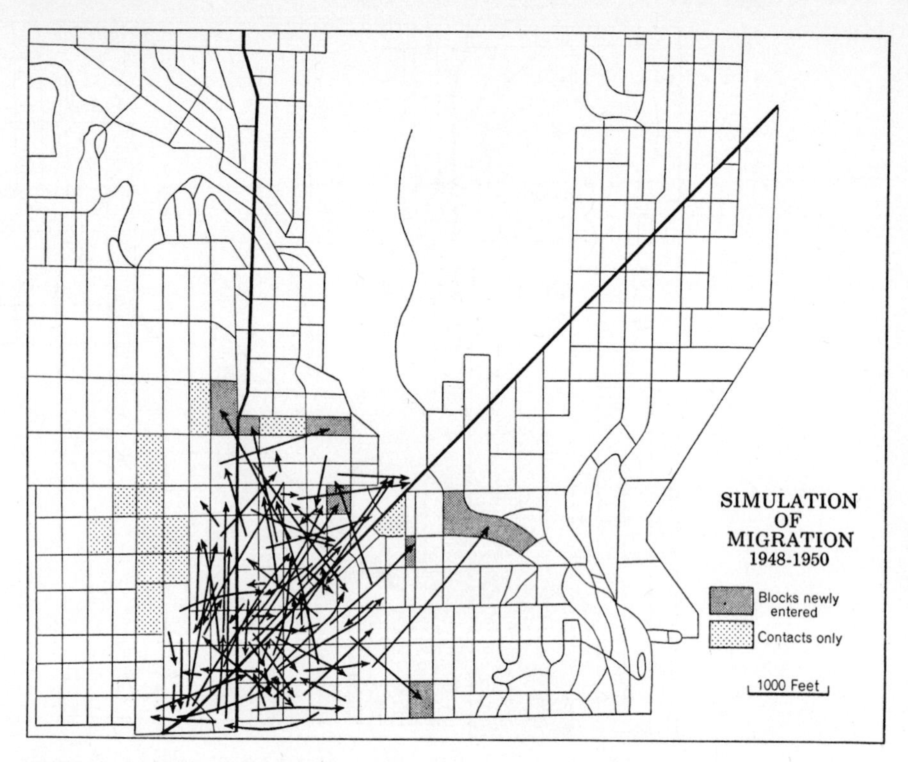

FIGURE 11–14*a*. A simulation of the growth of the northern part of Seattle's ghetto. Simulated migration: 1948–1950. *Source:* See caption for Fig. 11–8.

FIGURE 11–14*b*. A simulation of the growth of the northern part of Seattle's ghetto. Simulated expansion: 1940–1950. *Source:* See caption for Fig. 11–8.

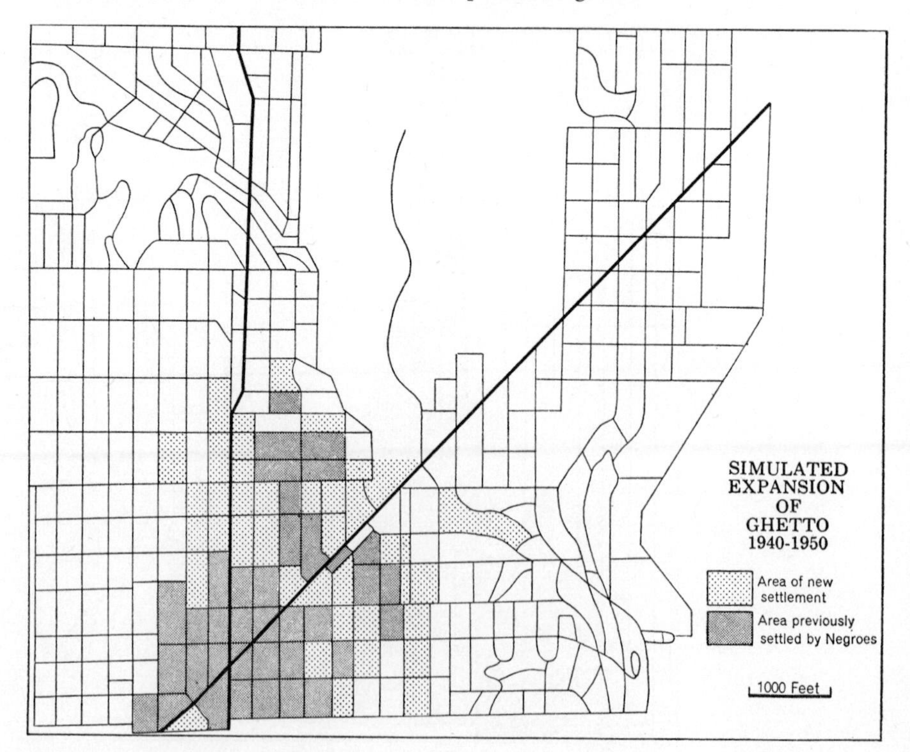

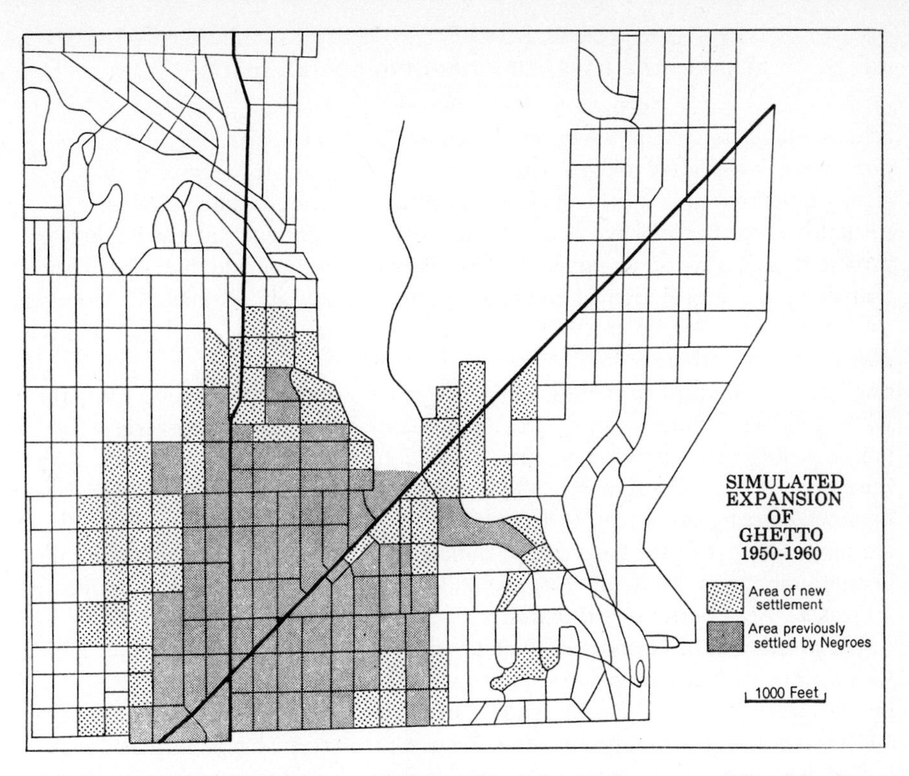

FIGURE 11–14*c*. A simulation of the growth of the northern part of Seattle's ghetto. Simulated expansion: 1950–1960. *Source:* See caption for Fig. 11–8.

FIGURE 11–14*d*. A simulation of the growth of the northern part of Seattle's ghetto. Simulated expansion: 1960–1964. *Source:* See caption for Fig. 11–8.

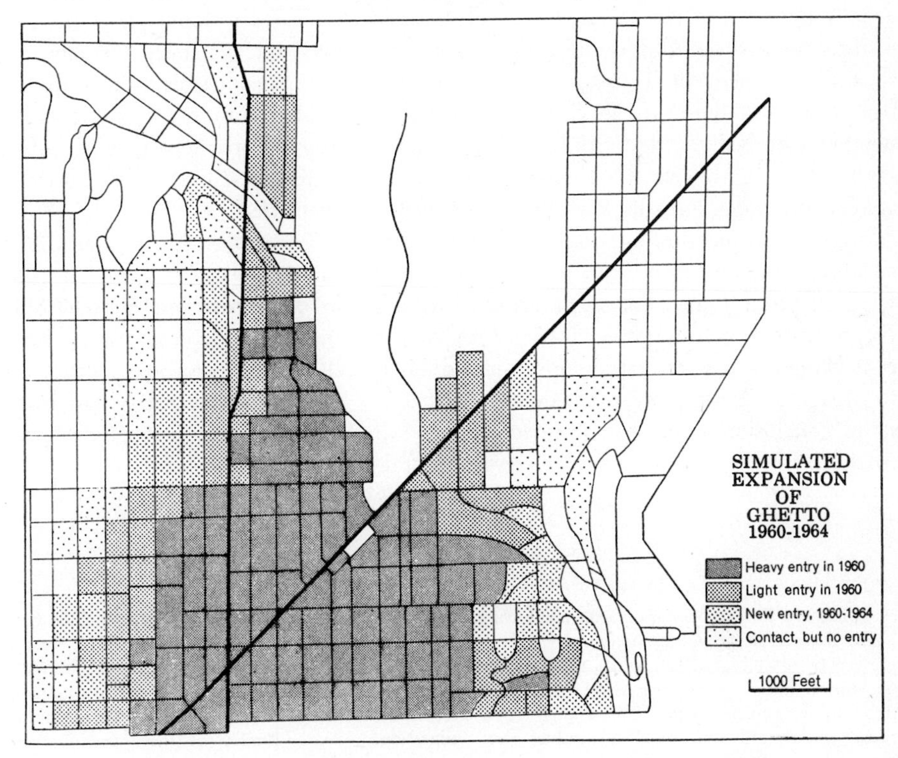

achieve stable interracial areas, in which white purchasers, even after Negro entry, are sufficiently numerous to maintain a balance acceptable to both? Three factors have been found crucial: proximity to a ghetto; proportions of white and nonwhite; and preparation of the neighborhood for acceptance of Negro entry.[119] Proximity to a ghetto almost forbids a stable interracial situation. Fear of inundation either panics or steels white residents. Only wealthy areas can maintain any interracial character in such a location, since few, if any, Negroes can afford to enter. Negroes entering areas remote from the ghetto are more easily accepted (after initial difficulties), because the great body of Negroes does not "threaten" neighborhood structures.

The proportion of Negroes in an area is critical for continued white purchasing. Whites are willing to accept 5 to 25 per cent (with a mean of 10 per cent) Negro occupancy for a long time before beginning abandonment—depending on such factors as the characteristics of the Negroes moving in, the proximity of the ghetto, and the open-mindedness of the resident white population. On the other hand, although the Negro is accustomed to minority status, he usually prefers a larger proportion of his own group nearby than the critical 10 per cent. Thus a fundamental dilemma arises, and there are in fact few interracial neighborhoods. For cities with low Negro ratios, say less than 10 per cent, the long-run possibilities are encouraging, especially with the rise of Negro education and income, increased enforcement of nondiscrimination laws, and the more liberal views of youth today. For urban areas with high Negro ratios, such as Philadelphia, with 20 per cent (40 per cent in the city proper), it is difficult to imagine an alternative to the ghetto. The same conclusion holds for southern cities. No spatial arrangement, given present levels of prejudice, will permit so large a proportion of Negroes to be spread throughout the city without serious white reaction.

Private interracial projects have begun integration and have been successful and stable, if few in number.[120] From these experiments it has been learned that white buyers in such developments are not unusually liberal but are a normal cross section. Also, the spatial arrangement that permits the largest stable proportion of nonwhites has been found to be a cluster pattern—small, compact colonies of a few houses—rather than dispersed isolates.[121] This makes possible easy contact within the minority group, but also good opportunity for interaction with the white group, while minimizing the frequency of direct neighbors, which few whites are as yet able to accept.

Integrated residential living will become more acceptable as Negroes achieve equality in education and employment, but housing integration will probably lag years or decades behind. At most we may expect an arrest of the extension of existing ghettos, their internal upgrading, and prevention of new ones. Experience certainly indicates a long wait for goodwill to achieve even internal improvement; hence a real reduction in ghettoization implies a governmental, not a voluntary, regulation of the urban land and housing market—that is, enforced open-housing ordinances. Everything short of that has already been tried.

The suggested model of diffusion-expansion still describes the dominant ghettoization pattern. In the future we may be able to recognize an alternative "colonization" model, in which small clusters of Negroes or other minorities break out of the ghetto and spread throughout the urban area under the fostering or protection of government.

FOOTNOTES TO CHAPTER 11

1. Henry S. Shryock, Jr., *Population Mobility within the United States* (Chicago: Community and Family Study Center, University of Chicago, 1964), p. 10, following the practice of the Bureau of the Census, restricts the use of the term "migration" for movements which cross county lines. This study, then, is primarily of mobility, rather than migration, although larger cities may include more than one county—if not as part of the city itself, at least as part of the Standard Metropolitan Statistical Area (SMSA). Many census aggregations refer to intra-county movements, but, for census tracts, data is compiled on an intra-metropolitan basis.

2. Bureau of the Census, *Current Population Reports:*

Population Characteristics, Mobility of the Population of the United States: March 1964 to March, 1965," Series P-20, No. 150 (Washington, D.C.: U.S. Government Printing Office, 1966).

3. See Walter Isard *et al., Methods of Regional Analysis* (New York: John Wiley & Sons, Inc., 1960), chap. iii; and Gunnar Olsson, *Distance and Human Interaction* (Philadelphia: Regional Science Research Institute, 1965). E. G. Moore, "Models of Migration and the Intra-Urban Case," *Australian and New Zealand Journal of Sociology*, II (April, 1966) 16–37, reviews the models available. Shryock, in *Population Mobility*, discusses data sources. Julian Wolpert, in "Behavioral Aspects of the Decision to Migrate," *Papers and Proceedings of the Regional Science Association*, XV (1965), 159–69; and Torsten Hägerstrand, "Migration and Area: Survey of a Sample of Swedish Migration Fields and Hypothetical Considerations on Their Genesis," *Lund Studies in Geography, Series B*, No. 13 (Lund, Sweden: Gleerup, 1957), 27–158, present important contributions to the theory.

4. Theodore Caplow, "Incidence and Direction of Residential Mobility in a Minneapolis Sample," *Social Forces*, XXVII (May, 1949), 413–17. Other good bibliographies are found in Sidney Goldstein, *Patterns of Mobility: 1910–1950* (Philadelphia: University of Pennsylvania Press, 1958), pp. 244–49; and Peter H. Rossi, *Why Families Move* (New York: The Free Press, 1955), Appendix A.

See also Janet Abu-Lughod and Mary Mix Foley, "Consumer Strategies," in *Housing Choices and Housing Constraints*, Nelson N. Foote *et al.*, (New York: McGraw-Hill Book Company, 1960), pp. 71–271. Studies deriving mobility rates include Andrew W. Lind, "A Study of the Mobility of Population in Seattle," *University of Washington Publications in the Social Sciences*, III (1925), 1–64; T. Earl Sullenger, "A Study in Intra-Urban Mobility," *Sociology and Social Research*, XVII (1932), 16–24; *idem*, "The Social Significance of Mobility: An Omaha Study," *American Journal of Sociology*, LX (1950), 559–64; William Albig, "The Mobility of Urban Population," *Social Forces*, XI (December, 1933), 351–67; *idem*, "A Method of Recording Trends of Urban Residential Mobility," *Sociology and Social Research*, XXI (1936–1937), 120–27; *idem*, "A Comparison of Methods for Recording Trends in Urban Residential Mobility," *Sociology and Social Research*, XXI, (1936–1937), 226–33; Sidney Goldstein and Kurt B. Mayer, *Residential Mobility, Migration and Commuting in Rhode Island*, Publication No. 7, Planning Division, Rhode Island Development Council (Providence, R.I.: 1963).

An incredible amount of data (eight 321 × 321 flow matrices) was assembled in the 1930's but remains largely unanalyzed: Howard Whipple Green, *Movements of Families within the Cleveland Metropolitan District*, Reports Nos. 3, 5, 7, 9, 11, 13, 15, 17 (Cleveland: Real Property Inventory of Metropolitan Cleveland, annually from 1934 to 1942). The data did stimulate, however, the seminal paper by Samuel A. Stouffer, "Intervening Opportunities: A Theory Relating Mobility and Distance," *American Sociological Review*, V (December, 1940), 845–67.

5. Albig, "A Method of Recording Trends." The decline is so marked as to overcome the various possible sources of error.

6. Goldstein, *Patterns of Mobility*, pp. 211 ff.

7. Quoted in Abu-Lughod and Foley, "Consumer Strategies," p. 161.

8. Bureau of the Census: *Census of Population: 1950, II, Characteristics of the Population* (Washington, D.C.: U.S. Government Printing Office, 1953); based on a 20 per cent sample of all households.

9. Bureau of the Census, *Census of Population: 1960, II, Characteristics of the Population* (Washington, D.C.: U.S. Government Printing Office, 1963), which used a 25 per cent sample. For census tracts, the origins differ slightly from the headings in Table 11-1: Central city of SMSA; Other part of SMSA; Outside SMSA. In addition, *The Census of Housing: 1960* (Washington, D.C.: U.S. Government Printing Office, 1961), identifies the date of movement into the present residence: 1958 to mid-1960; 1954 to 1957; 1940 to 1953; 1939 or earlier.

10. Bureau of the Census, *Current Population Reports: Population Characteristics*, Series P 20, *Mobility of the Population of the United States* (Washington, D.C.: U.S. Government Printing Office, Annually from 1948 to present), which has used a national sample of 30,000 homes.

11. Shryock, in *Population Mobility* chaps. x and xi, discusses mobility rates for sub-populations, using 1950 data.

12. John B. Lansing and Leslie Kish, in "Family Life Cycle as an Independent Variable," *American Sociological Review*, XXII (September, 1957), 512–19, point out that the stage of family formation is more accurate than age alone in predicting expenditure, housing characteristics and, undoubtedly, mobility. Most data, however, are tied to age, and the two variables are used interchangeably in this discussion.

13. The concentration of movement in a short period in the life span accounts for the phenomenon of repeated migration in which a single person or household moves several times during the period of study. See Sidney Goldstein, "The Extent of Repeated Migration," *Journal of the American Statistical Association*, LIV (December, 1964), 1122–32; and *idem*, "Repeated Migration as a factor in High Mobility Rates," *American Sociological Review*, XIX (September, 1954), 536–41; and Rossi, *Why Families Move*, p. 69.

14. Green, *Movements of Families within Cleveland*, Report No. 7, p. 55, has a graph which shows how mobility declines with ages of dwellings to about 25 years, and then increases.

15. Moore, in "Models of Migration," used data from Brisbane. Lind, in "Mobility of Population in Seattle," Fig. 1, shows the pattern of out-migration in Seattle, the highest rates, in the central area, being two or three times as great as the suburbs. Albig, in "The Mobility of Urban Population," finds the same pattern, but with the central area about 50 per cent higher. See also Elsie S. Longmoor and Earl F. Young, "Ecological Interrelationship of Juvenile Delinquency, Dependency, and Population Mobility: A Cartographic Analysis of Data from Long Beach, California," *American Journal of Sociology*, XLI (1936), 598–610; and Green's reports, *Movements within Cleveland*

16. The effect of size has been studied theoretically by G. Kulldorff, in "Migration Probabilities," *Lund Studies in Geography, Series B*, No. 14 (Lund, Sweden: Gleerup, 1955); and empirically by Bertil Wendil, "Regional Aspects of Internal Migration and Mobility in Sweden 1946–1950," *Lund Studies in Geography, Series B*, No. 13 (Lund, Sweden: Gleerup, 1957), 1–26.

17. See T. R. Anderson and J. E. Egeland, "Spatial Aspects of Social Area Analysis," *American Sociological Review*, XXVI (1961), 392–98; Brian J. L. Berry, "Cities as Systems within Systems of Cities," *Papers and Proceedings of the Regional Science Association*, XIII (1964), 147–63; and Robert A. Murdie, "Factorial Ecology of Metropolitan Toronto: 1951–1961," University of Chicago, Department of Geography Research Paper No. 116 (1969).

18. Rossi, *Why Families Move*, p. 9. Rossi was able to predict a large proportion of mobility on the basis of a Mobility Index based on age, household size, and type of tenure preference (p. 76).

19. Similar results were obtained by R. Wilkinson and D. M. Merry, in "Statistical Anlaysis of Attitudes to Moving," *Urban Studies*, II, No. 2 (May, 1965), 1–14; also Abu-Lughod and Foley, "Consumer Strategies," p. 155.

20. Rossi, *Why Families Move*, p. 135.

21. See, for instance, M. Young and P. Willmott, *Family and Kinship in East London* (London: Routledge & Kegan Paul Ltd., 1957); and Marc Fried, "Grieving for a Lost Home," in *The Urban Condition*, ed. Leonard J. Duhl (New York: Basic Books, Inc., 1964), pp. 141–71.

22. Rossi, *Why Families Move*, p. 135.

23. Seymour M. Lipset and Reinhold Bendix, *Social Mobility in Industrial Society* (Berkeley: University of California Press, 1959), Table 2–1. Goldstein, *Patterns of Mobility*, p. 185, found less than 50 per cent shifts among six categories over a ten-year period.

24. See the detailed discussion of the filtering process in William G. Grigsby, *Housing Markets and Public Policy* (Philadelphia: University of Pennsylvania Press, 1963), chap. iii.

25. Green, *Movements of Families within Cleveland*, Report No. 11, p. 63, obtained similar results in Cleveland.

26. For instance, in Chicago, from 1955 to 1960, about 80,000 persons were relocated for all city activities, including urban renewal, public housing, and expressways, out of a total of over 1,200,000 moves within the city. See Community Renewal Program, "Housing and Urban Renewal Progress Report" (Chicago, December 31, 1964), Fig. 7; and Department of Commerce, Bureau of the Census, *Census of Population and Housing: 1960, Final Report PHC (1)–26, Census Tracts: Chicago, Illinois* (Washington, D.C.: U.S. Government Printing Office, 1961).

27. The patterns of residential segregation are discussed in Davis McEntire, *Residence and Race* (Berkeley: University of California Press, 1960), pp. 9–101; and Stanley Lieberson, *Ethnic Patterns in American Cities* (New York: The Free Press, 1963). For particular cities, see Paul F. Cressey, "Population Succession in Chicago: 1898–1930," *American Journal of Sociology*, XLIV (January, 1938), 59–69; Richard G. Ford, "Population Succession in Chicago," *American Journal of Sociology*, XLVI (March, 1950), 156–60; Christen T. Jonassen, "Cultural Variables in the Ecology of an Ethnic Group," *American Sociological Review*, XIV (1949), 32–41; and John Kosa, "Hungarian Immigrants in North America: Their Residential Mobility and Ecology," *Canadian Journal of Economics and Political Science*, XII (1956), 358–370.

28. When the mobility rates for Metropolitan Toronto were plotted the large and recent Italian area (over 100,000 people; see Fig. 11–2) and its surroundings did not show greater mobility.

29. For discussion of the process in northern cities, see Otis D. Duncan and Beverly Duncan, *The Negro Population of Chicago* (Chicago: University of Chicago Press, 1957); Chester Rapkin and William G. Grigsby, *The Demand for Housing in Racially Mixed Areas* (Berkeley: University of California Press, 1960). Others have argued that the ghetto in Southern cities expands differently because access to the urban fringe allows Negroes to move directly into new housing.

30. The point is documented by Rapkin and Grigsby, in *Demand for Housing in Racially Mixed Areas*, pp. 52–72.

31. See Karl E. Taeuber and Alma F. Taeuber, *Negroes in Cities* (Chicago: Aldine Publishing Co., 1965), pp. 156, 180.

32. Census Bureau, *Census of Population and Housing: 1960, Census Tracts: Chicago, Illinois.*

33. Rossi, *Why Families Move*, p. 92.

34. John B. Lansing and Nancy Barth, *Residential Location and Urban Mobility: A Multivariate Analysis* (Ann Arbor, Mich.: Institute for Social Research, 1964), p. 18. Twenty-five per cent of the variation in expectation of movement was explained, in order of importance of the independent variables, as follows: age of household head; satisfaction with neighborhood; satisfaction with housing; crowding; and satisfaction with distance from the city center. The last variable was not significant.

35. *Why Families Move*, p. 34.

36. The general approach of individual perception of the environment is presented in two collections of papers: R. W. Kates and J. F. Wohlwill, eds., "Man's Response to the Physical Environment," *Journal of Social Issues*, XXII (1966); and David Lowenthal, ed., *Environment, Perception, and Behavior* (University of Chicago, Department of Geography, Research Paper No. 109, Chicago: 1967). Significant studies of urban phenomena include Kevin Lynch, *The Image of the City* (Cambridge, Mass: The M.I.T. Press, 1960); Robert L. Wilson, "The Liveability of the City," in *Urban Growth Dynamics*, eds. F. Stuart Chapin, Jr. and Shirley F. Weiss (New York: John Wiley & Sons, Inc., 1962), pp. 359–99; and George L. Peterson, "A Model of Preference: Quantitative Analysis of the Perception of the Visual Appearance of Residential Neighborhoods," *Journal of Regional Science*, XVII (1967), pp. 19–33. So far urban studies relate to the selection of neighborhood rather than motivations for moving.

37. Wolpert, "Behavioral Aspects of the Decision to Move."

38. Further evidence is provided by Peter Gould's "On Mental Maps," Discussion Paper No. 9, Michigan Inter-University Community of Mathematical Geographers, 1966. Gould obtained a consistent structure of location preferences for individuals.

39. Julian Wolpert, "Migration as an Adjustment to Environment Stress," *Journal of Social Issues*, XXII (1966), 92–102.

40. Abu-Lughod and Foley, "Consumer Strategies," p. 132. Peter H. Rossi, Why Families Move," in *The Language of Social Research*, eds. Paul F. Lazarsfeld and Morris Rosenberg (New York: The Free Press, 1955), p. 459, suggests slightly smaller values.

41. See Rossi, *Why Families Move*, p. 80; and Howard S. Lapin, *Structuring the Journey to Work* (Philadelphia: University of Pennsylvania Press, 1964), p. 163.

42. Maps of mobility desire lines are found in Lind, "Mobility of Population in Seattle," p. 28; Albig, *The Mobility of Urban Population*, pp. 352–53; and Green, *Movements of Families within Cleveland*, Report No. 9, p. 52. Caplow, "Residential Mobility in Minneapolis," p. 416, tabulated his data rings from the city center, in order to examine the degree of decentralization. No one has yet produced an urban counterpart to the remarkable work by C. Warren Thornthwaite, *Internal Migration in the United States* (Philadelphia: University of Pennyslvania Press, 1934) in which flow lines summarize the whole pattern of interstate migration; or the study by Daniel O. Price, "Distance and Direction as Vectors of Internal Migration: 1935–40," *Social Forces*, XXVII (January, 1948), 58–53.

43. One of the most stimulating discussions of the housing market is found in Grigsby, *Housing Markets and Public Policy*, chap. ii. Other studies which approach the housing market of a city from the point of view of supply and demand include Chester Rapkin and William G. Grigsby, *The Demand for Housing in Eastwick* (Philadelphia: Redevelopment Authority of the City of Philadelphia, 1960); *idem*, *Residential Renewal in the Urban Core* (Philadelphia: University of Pennsylvania Press, 1960); and Beverly Duncan and Philip M. Hauser, *Housing a Metropolis: Chicago* (New York: The Free Press, 1960).

44. The San Francisco Community Renewal Program has undertaken a project which will maintain and simulate the present and future supplies of housing stock and housing demand as a policy aid in renewal planning; see Ira M. Robinson, Harry B. Wolfe, and Robert L. Barringer, "A Simulation Model for Renewal Programming," *Journal of the American Institute of Planners*, XXXI (January, 1965), 126–34. Michelson analyzes the demand by one set of consumers, those likely to prefer downtown, high-rise apartments, in "Potential Candidates for the Designer's Paradise: A Social Analysis from a Nation-wide Survey," *Social Forces* (forthcoming).

45. Grigsby, *Housing Markets and Public Policy*, pp. 64–69.

46. *Ibid.*, pp. 51 and 54.

47. Grigsby, *ibid.*, p. 83, differentiates between the total stock of housing and the amount on the market at one time. Certain submarkets, such as owner-occupied, single-family dwellings, have a lower turnover rate than others, so that the supply of such housing available for rent or sale is disproportionately low at any one time.

48. The best information to date in this area is the national sample of interviews carried out by the University of Michigan, Survey Research Center, Institute for Social Research: John B. Lansing and Eva Mueller's, *Residential Location and Urban Mobility* (Ann Arbor, Mich.: Institute for Social Research, 1964); John B. Lansing and Nancy Barth's, *Residential Location and Urban Mobility: A Multivariate Analysis* (Ann Arbor, Mich.: Institute for Social Research, 1964); and John B. Lansing's, *Residential Location and Urban Mobility: The Second Wave of Interviews* (Ann Arbor, Mich.: Institute for Social Research, 1966). In an interesting gaming approach developed by Wilson, "The Liveability of the City," people are asked to spend a given amount of money on various housing features.

49. Margaret G. Reid, *Housing and Income* (Chicago: University of Chicago Press, 1962), finds that housing expenditures are tied more closely to average incomes than to actual incomes because of the short-term fluctuation in the latter. Housing expenditures form a higher proportion of income as income increases, and as tenure shifts from renting to owning (p. 378). See also the discussion by Louis Winnick, "Economic Constraints," in Foote *et al.*, *Housing Choices and Housing Constraints*, pp. 3–67.

50. Green, *Movements of Families within Cleveland*, obtained values of 31, 28, 30, 26, and 24 per cent moves within the same tract in Cleveland in 1933 to 1937; Caplow gives 25 per cent for Minneapolis, from 1940 to 1948; Albig's data, "The Mobility of Urban Population," indicates that 25 to 30 per cent of the moves in Danville, Rock Island, and Moline, Illinois, in 1929 to 1930, covered less than 1,200 feet. Lind, in "Mobility of Population in Seattle," p. 26, refers to the tendency to move about the same areas as resembling "milling" among cattle.

51. Richard Dewey, in "Peripheral Expansion in Milwaukee County," *American Journal of Sociology*, LIV (January, 1948), 120, states that most out-movement occurs by a succession of short moves, but provides no substantiating data.

52. By Kulldorff, "Migration Possibilities"; Hägerstrand, "Migration and Area," pp. 112–26; and Richard L. Morrill, "The Distribution of Migration Distance," *Papers and Proceedings of the Regional Science Association*, XI (1963), 75–84.

53. See the discussion of the migration field in Olsson, *Distance and Human Interaction;* and by Richard L. Morrill and Forrest R. Pitts, "Marriage, Migration and the Mean Information Field," *Annals of the Association of American Geographers*, LVII (December, 1967), 401–22.

54. Asby's and Cleveland's parameters are given by Duane F. Marble and John D. Nystuen in "An Approach to the Direct Measurement of Community Mean Information Fields," *Papers and Proceedings of the Regional Science Association*, XI (1963), 99–100.

55. This parameter was obtained from the data of Table 6 in Albig's "The Mobility of Urban Population."

56. Rossi, *Why Families Move*, p. 161.

57. The continuing effect of ethnic linkages is demonstrated for a number of cultural groups by Nathan Glazer and Daniel Patrick Moynihan in *Beyond the Melting Pot* (Cambridge, Mass.: The M.I.T. Press, 1963).

58. Caplow, "Residential Mobility in Minneapolis," p. 415. Dewey, "Peripheral Expansion in Milwaukee," p. 120, claims to have observed the same phenomena on the outskirts of Milwaukee.

59. Green, *Movements of Families within Cleveland*, Report No. 9, p. 52; Report No. 12, p. 54. Stouffer, "Intervening Opportunities," using the same data, found that directional variations and moves by ethnic groups disturbed his explanatory model, which was based on housing opportunities.

60. Homer Hoyt, *The Structure and Growth of Residential Neighborhoods in American Cities* (Washington, D.C.: U.S. Government Printing Office, 1939), pp. 114–18. Hoyt's conclusions are evaluated for Boston by Lloyd Rodwin, in *Housing and Economic Progress* (Cambridge, Mass.: Harvard University Press, 1961), chap. vi.

61. Grigsby, *Housing Markets and Public Policy*, p. 69.

62. Lansing and Mueller, *Residential Location and Urban Mobility*, p. 33; Lansing, *The Second Wave of Interviews*, pp. 48–56; and Abu-Lughod and Foley, "Consumer Strategies," p. 183.

63. Lansing and Barth, *Residential Location and Urban Mobility: A Multivariate Analysis*, p. 21.

64. Bernard Frieden discusses in detail the demand for access: *The Future of Old Neighborhoods* (Cambridge, Mass.: The M.I.T. Press, 1964), chap. iii and Appendix C; and the costs of access, chap. iv.

The references here are to William Alonso, *Location and Land Use* (Cambridge, Mass.: Harvard University Press, 1964); Lowden Wingo, Jr., *Transportation and Urban Land* (Washington, D. C.: Resources for the Future, 1961); E. F. Brigham, *A Model of Residential Land Values* (Santa Monica, Calif.: The Rand Corporation, 1964); Richard F. Muth, "Variation of Population Density and Its Components in South Chicago," *Papers and Proceedings of the Regional Science Association*, XV (1965), 183–89; Warren R. Seyfried, "The Centrality of Urban Land Values," *Land Economics*, XXXIX (1963), 275–84; and John D. Herbert and Benjamin H. Stevens, "A Model for the Distribution of Residential Activity in Urban Areas," *Journal of Regional Science*, XI (1960), 21–36.

65. Maurice H. Yeates, "Some Factors Affecting the Spatial Distribution of Chicago Land Values: 1910–1960," *Economic Geography*, XLI (January, 1965), 57–70.

66. Lansing and Mueller, *Residential Location and Urban Mobility*, p. 26; and Lansing, *The Second Wave of Interviews* p. 35; found three times as many people would prefer to live farther away from the city center than closer. Similar results were found by Theodore Caplow, "Home Ownership and Location Preference in a Minneapolis Sample," *American Sociological Review*, XIII (1948), 725–30.

67. Janet Abu-Lughod, "A Survey of Center-City Residents," in Foote, *et al.*, *Housing Choices and Housing Constraints*, Appendix; Michelson, "Potential Candidates for the Designer's Paradise."

68. Rapkin and Grigsby, *The Demand for Housing in Racially Mixed Areas*, found that 50 per cent of residents in sample areas near the city centers gave access as the major factor in moving to the area.

69. Lansing and Mueller, *Residential Location and Urban Mobility*, p. 28.

70. Wingo, *Transportation and Urban Land*, calls this "position rent."

71. Caplow, "Residential Mobility in Minneapolis," p. 416.

72. Green, *Movements within Cleveland*, Report No. 9, p. 53; Report No. 11, p. 54.

73. Ernest W. Burgess, "The Growth of the City," in *The City*, eds. R. E. Park, E. W. Burgess, and R. D. McKenzie (Chicago: University of Chicago Press, 1925).

74. Alonso, *Location and Land Use*, pp. 107–9; and John F. Kain, "Journey to Work and Residential Location," *Papers and Proceedings of the Regional Science Association*, IX (1962), 137–60.

75. Caplow, "Residential Mobility in Minneapolis," p. 416.

76. This hypothesis has been examined by Sidney Goldstein and Kurt B. Mayer, "The Impact of Migration on the Socio-economic Structure of Cities and Suburbs," *Sociology and Social Research*, L (1965); *idem*, "Population Decline and the Social Demographic Structure of an American City," *American Sociological Review*, XXIX (1964), 48–54; and Karl F. Taeuber and Alma Taeuber, "White Migration and Socio-economic Differences between City and Suburbs," *American Sociological Review*, XXIX (1964), 718–29.

77. Rodwin, *Housing and Economic Progress*, p. 103.

78. A summary and appraisal of the major urban growth models is contained in the review by the Traffic Research Corporation, *Review of Existing Land Use Forecasting Techniques* (Boston: Boston Regional Planning Project, 1963).

79. Willard B. Hansen, "An Approach to the Analysis of Metropolitan Residential Expansion," *Journal of Regional Science*, III (1961), 37–55. T. R. Lakshmanan, in "An Approach to the Analysis of Intra-urban Location Applied to the Baltimore Region," *Economic Geography*, XL (December, 1964), 348–70, obtained similar results.

80. F. Stuart Chapin, Jr., and Shirley F. Weiss, *Factors Influencing Land Development* (Chapel Hill: University of North Carolina, Center for Urban and Regional Studies, 1962).

81. Edward J. Kaiser, "Locational Decision Factors in a Producer Model of Residential Development," Paper presented to the Regional Science Association, Philadelphia, 1965.

82. Edward J. Taaffe, Barry J. Garner, and Maurice H. Yeates, *The Peripheral Journey to Work* (Evanston, Ill.: Northwestern University Press, 1963), p. 36 ff., explain 46 per cent of variations in commuter location as a function of population and distance. See also the discussion by Lapin, *Structuring the Journey to Work*, pp. 123–40; Ira Lowry, "Locational Parameters in the Pittsburgh Model," *Papers and Proceedings of the Regional Science Association*, XI (1963), 146–65; Beverly Duncan and Otis D. Duncan, "The Measurement of Intra-city Locational and Residential Patterns," *Journal of Regional Science*, II (1960) 37–54; John R. Wolforth, *Residential Location and the Place of Work* (Vancouver: University of British Columbia Geographical Series, No. 4, 1965); and J. R. Mayer, J. F. Kain, and M. Wake, *The Urban Transportation Problem* (Cambridge, Mass.: Harvard University Press, 1965), chap. vi, "Interrelationship of Housing and Urban Transportation." The latter also demonstrates the interaction of job location and type of housing structure in determining location.

83. Lansing, *The Second Wave of Interviews*, p. 74.

84. Thirteen per cent disliked the journey to work; 53 per cent enjoyed it; 34 per cent didn't care—*ibid*, p. 99. See also The Editors of Fortune, *The Exploding Metropolis* (New York: Doubleday & Company, Inc., 1958), pp. 79–80.

85. *Ibid*, p. 35; Abu-Lughod, "A Survey of Center-City Residents"; Theodore Caplow, "Home Ownership and Location Preferences in a Minneapolis Sample"; and Melville Branch, Jr., *Urban Planning and Public Opinion* (Princeton, N.J.: Bureau of Urban Research, 1942).

86. Goldstein and Mayer, "Residential Mobility in Rhode Island," p. 24; Lapin *Structuring the Journey to Work* p. 153; and Beverly Duncan, "Intra-urban Population Movement," in *Cities and Sociology*, eds. Paul K. Hatt and Albert J. Reiss (New York: The Free Press, 1957), rev. ed., p. 307.

87. See Gladys L. Palmer, *Labor Mobility in Six Cities* (New York: Social Science Research Council, 1954).

88. Lansing, *The Second Wave of Interviews*, p. 90; Lapin, *Structuring the Journey to Work*, p. 100; Lowry, "Locational Parameters in the Pittsburgh Model," p. 150; and Beverly Duncan, "Factors In Work-Residence Separation: Wage Salary Workers: Chicago, 1951," *American Sociological Review*, (1956), pp. 48–56.

89. John E. Galt, in "The Residential Distribution of the Employees of Argonne National Laboratory. Patterns and Implications" (Master's thesis, University of Chicago, 1968), shows that Negro employees travel half as much again between residence and work as white residents (an average of 9,170 miles annually vs. the white's 5,740 miles), because they are forced to reside in Chicago's Southwest Side ghetto.

90. In many ways, the development of spatial differentiation of social variables is analogous to the changes in the physical landscape. A useful discussion of the relationship between form and process in geomorphology is Richard J. Chorley's *Geomorphology and General Systems Theory*, U.S. Geological Survey Professional Paper 500-B (Washington, D.C.: U.S. Government Printing Office, 1962).

91. The Census Bureau has published data on intermetropolitan flows between SMSA's of over 250,000 population (101^2 flow cells): Department of Commerce, Bureau of the Census, *Census of Population: 1960, Subject Reports: Mobility for Metropolitan Areas, Final Report PC (2)-2c* (Washington, D.C.: U.S. Government Printing Office, 1963), Table 2. Berry has analyzed a 43000×4300 matrix of computer movements from census data: Brian J. L. Berry, *Functional Economic Areas and Consolidated Urban Regions of the United States*, Final report of the Social Science Research Council, Study of Principles of Metropolitan Area Classification (Chicago: University of Chicago Center for Urban Studies, 1967). Long before electronic data processing, Green produced, in *Movements within Cleveland*, annual matrices of flows among

321 census tracts (approximately 100,000 cells), using public utilities data.

92. Sidney Goldstein comments on directory data in "City Directories as Sources of Migration Data," *American Journal of Sociology*, XL (January, 1954), 167–76.

93. See Abu-Lughod and Foley, in Foote *et al.*, *Housing Choices and Housing Constraints,* chap. vii, "Consumer Preferences: The Dwelling."

94. William R. Ewald, Jr., ed., *Environment for Man* (Bloomington: Indiana University Press, 1967) is a report of a symposium sponsored by the American Institute of Planners.

95. Arthur Baker, "A Study of Polish and Italian Mobility in Chicago: 1954–1968" (Typescript, Department of Geography, DePaul University, June, 1968).

96. Merlin L. Clark, "1967 Religious Survey of Oak Park and River Forest, Illinois," Prepared for the Oak Park-River Forest Council of Churches.

97. Lois Wille, "Catholic Education in Ferment," *Chicago Daily News*, November 29, 1967, pp. 3 and 4.

98. Reported by Van Gordon Sauter, "Pressure on 6 Areas for Negro Move-In," *Chicago Daily News*, May 11, 1967, pp. 3 and 4.

99. Real Estate Research Corporation, "Preliminary Findings and Projections of Population and School Enrolments for Chicago, Illinois, 1970–1980." Prepared for Board of Education, City of Chicago, December 1967. [Editor's note: In the period March 1—May 31, 1969, 100 black families moved into Oak Park.]

100. Department of Commerce, Bureau of the Census, *Census Tract Reports, 1960, Ser. PHC (1)*, selected cities; *Census of Population: 1960*, II. *Subject Reports, 1960, Ser. PC (2): Nonwhite Population by Race; State of Birth* (Washington, D.C.: U. S. Government Printing Office, various dates).

101. Oscar Handlin, *The Newcomers*, New York Metropolitan Region Study, III (Cambridge, Mass: Harvard University Press, 1959).

102. Charles Abrams, *Forbidden Neighbors* (New York: Harper & Row, Publishers, 1955), p. 19.

103. *Ibid.*, pp. 29–43.

104. David McEntire, *Residence and Race: Final and Comprehensive Report to the Commission on Race and Housing* (Berkeley: University of California Press, 1960), pp. 88–104.

105. *Nonwhite Population by Race.*

106. *Census Tract Reports: 1960.*

107. McEntire, *Residence and Race*, pp. 148–56.

108. Abrams, *Forbidden Neighbors*, p. 73.

109. John C. Alston, *Cost of a Slum Area* (Wilberforce, Ohio: Wilberforce State College, 1948).

110. Chester Rapkin and William G. Grigsby, *The Demand for Housing in Racially Mixed Areas: Special Research Report to the Commission on Race and Housing* (Berkeley: University of Calefornia Press, 1960), pp. 27–30.

111. Nathan Glazer and David McEntire, eds., *Studies in Housing and Minority Groups: Special Research Report to the Commission on Race and Housing* (Berkeley: University of California Press, 1960), pp. 5–11.

112. McEntire, *Residence and Race*, p. 245.

113. Luigi Mario Laurenti, *Property Values and Race: Studies in 7 Cities: Special Research Report to the Commission on Race and Housing* (Berkeley: University of California Press, 1960); Homer Hoyt, *The Structure and Growth of Residential Neighborhoods in American Cities* (Washington, D.C.: U.S. Government Printing Office, 1939); Lloyd Rodwin, "The Theory of Residential Growth and Structure," *Appraisal Journal*, XVIII (September, 1950), 295–317.

114. Eleanor P. Wolf, "The Invasion-Succession Sequence as a Self-Fulfilling Prophecy," *Journal of Social Issues*, XIII (January, 1957), 7–20.

115. Rapkin and Grigsby, *The Demand for Housing*, pp. 56–80.

116. See Herbert A. Meyer, ed., *Symposium on Monte Carlo Methods*, University of Florida, March 16–17, 1954 (New York and London, 1956); Everett M. Rogers, *Diffusion of Innovations* (New York: The Free Press, 1962); and Warren C. Scoville, "Minority Migrations and the Diffusion of Technology," *Journal of Economic History*, XI (1951), 347–60.

117. See Torsten Hägerstrand, "On Monte Carlo Simulation of Diffusion," in *Quantitative Geography*, ed. William L. Garrison (Evanston, Ill.: Northwestern Studies in Geography, 1967); Forrest R. Pitts, "Problems in Computer Simulation of Diffusion," *Papers and Proceedings of the Regional Science Association*, XI (1963), 111–19.

118. See Calvin F. Schmid and Wayne W. McVey, Jr., *Growth and Distribution of Minority Races in Seattle, Washington* (Seattle: University of Washington, 1964); Walter B. Watson and E. A. T. Barth, *Summary of Recent Research Concerning Minority Housing in Seattle* (Institute for Social Research, Department of Sociology, University of Washington, 1962); John C. Fei, "Rent Differentiation Related to Segregated Housing Markets for Racial Groups with Special Reference to Seattle" (Master's thesis, University of Washington, 1949).

119. See Eunice Grier and George Grier, *Privately Developed Interracial Housing: An Analysis of Experience: Special Research Report to the Commission on Race and Housing* (Berkeley: University of California Press, 1960), pp. 29–30.

120. *Ibid.*, p. 8.

121. See Reuel S. Amdur, "An Exploratory Study of Nineteen Negro Families in the Seattle Area Who Were First Negro Residents in White Neighborhoods, of Their White Neighbors, and of the Integration Process, Together with a Proposed Program to Promote Integration in Seattle" (Master's thesis, University of Washington, 1962); Arnold M. Rose *et al.*, "Neighborhood Reactions to Isolated Negro Residents: An Alternative to Invasion and Succession," *American Sociological Review*, XVIII (1953), 497–507; and L. K. Northwood and E. A. T. Barth, *Neighborhoods in Transition: The New American Pioneers and Their Neighbors* (Seattle: University of Washington, School of Social Work, n.d.), pp. 27–28.

CHAPTER 12

internal structure: physical space

So far we have discussed social space and social mobility, making direct reference to physical space only in the sense of the geographic distributions assumed by different socio-economic types. Now we must come to grips with the most basic elements of physical space, *structures* and *land use*. Study of land use is what geographers and physical planners, in particular, have meant when they have talked of "the urban pattern." We first consider the spatial distributions of urban land uses, then changes in these distributions. Finally, various planning models are discussed, and the philosophy of model building is reviewed.

But today our concepts of physical space are confounded by an indeterminism that did not enter the consciousness of geographers and planners in the past. As we saw in earlier chapters, the meaning of the word "urban" is now by no means clear.

*THE URBAN PATTERN**

The Latin word *urbs* is related to *orbis*, the circle. Like the English "town" and the Slavic *gorod*, related to "yard" and "girdle," it denotes as the basic characteristic of the urban phenomenon the enclosure which separates it from the open country. This is the city as it has existed through recorded history: a static unit, confined and defined by its enclosing boundary, and with a definite pattern of its internal organization, in which each part has a stable and defined relation to the whole.

. . .

*Reprinted from Hans Blumenfeld, "The Urban Pattern," *Annals of the American Academy of Political and Social Science*, CCCLII (1964), 74–83, with the permission of the author and editor.

For 5,000 years, this was one of two forms of human settlement that predominated in all but the most scarcely populated areas of the globe: the city and the rural village. The vast majority lived in the latter, and most of the world's work was done there. The villages were largely self-sufficient, not only in agricultural products but also in such manufactured products and services as they required. The cities were the seat of the ruling elite—landowning, political, military, religious, commercial—and those who supplied them with goods and services; these constituted a small minority, hardly ever exceeding 20 per cent of the population. The "services" which, in exchange for food and raw materials, they supplied to the countryside were limited to military protection, dispensation of justice, and religious guidance. Urban trade was trading with other cities and with such other seats of the ruling elite as castles, manors, and monasteries, most of which, in the course of time, either disappeared or became the nuclei of cities.

This pattern changed radically only with what we rather narrowly call the Industrial Revolution, meaning the application of scientific methods to the processes of production and distribution. This resulted in two closely related and interacting processes: increasing division of labor and increasing productivity. Increasing productivity set more and more labor free for the production of manufactured goods and of services, and more and more productive activities were specialized out of the village economy and transformed into urban industries.

Increasing division and specialization of labor required increasing interaction and cooperation, both within and between establishments. This interaction required proximity. The presence of specialized workers attracted industrial and commercial establishments, and these in turn attracted other establishments and more workers. The process fed on itself. The great country-to-city migration began and is still continuing everywhere.

This great process of concentration was made possible by the development of powerful means of long-distance transportation and communication, primarily the steamship, the railroad, and the electric telegraph, which, for the first time in history, made it possible to assemble at one point the food and raw materials required to support the life and work of millions of people.

Although technology had revolutionized long-distance transportation well before the middle of the nineteenth century, goods, persons, and messages within these huge agglomerations still moved almost exclusively by foot or by hoof. This limited their size to a radius of about one hour's walking time, or three miles. Within this narrow perimeter, houses, factories, docks, and railroad yards crowded together.

Almost half a century passed before new technology revolutionized internal transportation and communication: the bicycle, electric traction applied to streetcars and rapid-transit trains, the telephone, followed by the internal-combustion engine applied to passenger cars, trucks, and buses, and by radio and television. The city could expand. While the original inbound wave of the country-to-city migration continues in full force, it is now met by a new outbound city-to-suburb wave. This wave of expansion, which started about a century ago, is still gathering momentum. The result of the interaction of these two waves is a completely new form of human settlement which can no longer be understood in the traditional terms of town-and-country or of city-and-suburb. The concentrated nineteenth-century city with its separate suburbs was a short-lived transitional phenomenon.

The emerging new form of settlement is the metropolis. . . . The essence and reason for existence of the metropolis is, as for its predecessor the city, mutual accessibility—primarily, though by no means exclusively, mutual accessibility of place of residence and place of work. The metropolis extends as far as widespread daily commuting extends, and no farther.

However, its influence extends over a wider area. . . . Here the influence is twofold. Because the metropolis is easily accessible as a supplier of goods and of business and consumer services and also as a market for their products, establishments and households prefer to settle in towns within these regions rather than in those remote from metropolitan centers. While isolated towns are losing population relatively and often absolutely, each metropolis is typically surrounded by a number of active and growing "satellite" towns, based generally on manufacturing plants which are often branch plants of or migrants from the metropolis.

But the pattern of the region is determined not only by those functions which are served by the metropolis but also by those even more rapidly growing and wider ranging ones which serve the recreational needs of the metropolitan population: summer cottages, lodges, motels, camps, picnic grounds, parks, and facilities for a growing variety of land and water sports, with a host of services to their users. The Stockholm regional planners define a vast "summer Stockholm" surrounding the "winter" metropolis, and a similar "summer metropolis" can be identified everywhere in America.

A strange reversal is taking place. For thousands of years, the countryside has been the main locus of production, while the city was largely a place of consumption. Now, all activities but the immediate cultivation of the soil—even the raising and feeding of the new "animal" that draws the plow—have been specialized and transformed into "urban" activities. The same process, abetted by the same transportation technology which at one pole transformed the city into the giant metropolitan concentration, has, at the opposite pole, dissolved the village into ever fewer and more widely dispersed farms. But, over wide areas, though not everywhere, the dwindling farm population is being replaced by a different group, those who "retire" to the countryside. The vast majority of these retire only for short periods, week ends or a few weeks of vacation, but a growing number are permanent residents. This is true not only of the insignificant numbers of gentlemen-farmers but of many people of modest means, living on pensions, insurance, or other transfer payments, often supplemented by various services to tourists. . . . Casual observation indicates [the] growing significance [of this phenomenon]. With increase in leisure time, it may ultimately influence the pattern of the metropolis itself.

For the present we are dealing only with the area of regular daily commuting, and only with its most frequent form, the "mononuclear" metropolis. There exist other metropolitan areas which are "polynuclear," resulting from a process for which Patrick Geddes coined the term "conurbation," and defined as the growing together of several important independent cities. This has occurred in areas of old and dense urban developments which had already expanded rapidly during the early phases of the Industrial Revolution. The English Midlands, the "Randstad Holland," and the Rhine-Ruhr concentration are the three major examples. In other areas of equally old and dense urban development which, however, started their transformation only at a later stage of the Industrial Revolution, one city increasingly assumes a dominant central role. Cases are Stuttgart for Württemberg, Zurich for northwestern Switzerland, and Milan for Lombardy. They become increasingly similar to the metropolitan areas in younger countries which started out from a single big city such as Chicago or Melbourne.

Many observers believe that the process of conurbation is now repeating itself on an enlarged scale in the United States, notably along the Atlantic seaboard from Boston to Washington. However, analysis of available data shows that daily commuting between the metropolitan centers located on this axis is quite insignificant and that intervening areas show densities which are, on the average, very low compared to those within the major metropolitan areas. The following discussion will therefore deal only with the single monocentric commuting areas as the "archetype" of the metropolis, recognizing, however, that its boundary with the region is fluid and tends to expand.

Characteristics of the Metropolis

The developing pattern of the transmutation of the traditional city into the metropolis can be understood best by identifying their essential differences.

1. The metropolis combines with the traditional city function of central leadership the traditional function of the countryside to provide the bulk of material production.

2. As a result, as a country reaches the "developed" level, the majority of its population is now, or soon will be, living in metropolitan areas or, at least, in metropolitan regions. The population of the individual metropolis is much larger than that of the city. The biggest metropolis, New York, contains ten times the population of the biggest preindustrial city, Imperial Rome.
3. This larger population is dispersed over a much larger territory. With a radius of thirty miles it comprises a hundred times more land than the area determined by the three-mile radius of even the biggest foot-and-hoof cities.
4. This vast territory contains not only "urban-developed" land but also extensive "open" areas, parks, golf courses, country clubs, institutional campuses, even farms and forests.
5. Places of work and places of residence are located in separate areas.
6. Residential areas are segregated according to class or income of their residents.

This last-named difference calls for some comment. At first sight, it seems paradoxical that democratic capitalism should have produced a pattern so contrary to democratic ideology. In preindustrial societies, a large part of the "lower" classes lived on the premises of their masters, as slaves or domestic servants. The alley dwellings of Washington and other southern cities still reflect this older pattern. Elsewhere, as in Chinese cities, ambulant craftsmen worked and often slept in the compounds of their wealthy clients. Almost everywhere in preindustrial cities hovels are found next to or behind palaces. This did not disturb the "upper" classes. Their status was secured by family, title, rank, speech, manner, and clothing. In contemporary American society, these no longer determine status. Only financial status remains and is documented by conspicuous consumption. The decisive status symbol is the residence in the "good neighborhood," legally protected by zoning and fiercely defended against any intrusion of nonconforming elements, structural or human.

7. Finally, and only fairly recently, there is another reversal of an historical trend. Previously, as manufacturing specialized out of the peasant village and proliferated, the old elite-service city had become the industrial city, with industrial workers forming the majority of its population. Now, the same process of increasing productivity and specialization leads to a proliferation of mass services, business services specializing out of production for the market and consumer services specializing out of households. Now, industrial workers are predominant and growing in number primarily in the satellite towns of the metropolitan regions. In the metropolis itself, manufacturing employment is decreasing relatively and sometimes absolutely. Generally, two-thirds or more of the labor force works in a great variety of tertiary, or service, industries.

Pattern of Land Uses

As a result of these transformations, four basic types of land use can be identified: central business, industrial, residential, and open areas.

The historical core of the metropolis, the original "city," tends to remain its center. With the main lines of the transportation system oriented to it, this center remains the point most accessible to all parts of the metropolis and therefore attracts all those functions which serve the entire area. Partly attracted by these, partly for historical reasons, all those functions which require mutual contact also concentrate here, typically in office buildings. These two basic central functions attract others which serve them, such as eating and drinking places and parking facilities.

The resulting competition for space, both within the center and on the transportation facilities leading to it, leads to a displacement from the center of all those uses which require relatively much space and can also function elsewhere. These are primarily those dealing with goods, manufacturing, and warehouses, but also retail stores, consumer services, and residences.

As the metropolitan population grows and spreads out, outlying sectors accommodate sufficient population and purchasing power to support "second order" services of their own, notably retail, but also most consumer and some business services. With continuing growth, the quality of the second order moves up, leaving a narrowing range of the "highest order" in the center. Similarly, second-order routine office functions also move out, leaving only the highest-order contact functions in the center. However, with the over-all growth of the metropolis, both types of highest-order functions are growing and are being augmented by others of still higher order which can only exist when the size of the total market has reached a higher threshold.

Thus, the center is undergoing a process of continuous selective adaptation to those functions for which it is uniquely suited. Surprisingly, this unending change in quality seems to produce stability of quantity. The number of persons entering the central areas of major American cities has remained constant over the last thirty years. During the last twelve years, the same constancy has been observed in Toronto, a younger and smaller metropolis. Congestion acts as the selective agent which maintains the balance. The center is always "choked" but never "chokes itself to death."

From the center outward, density of population and of all activities decreases. . . . Over time, this curve undergoes two typical modifications: it becomes flatter, and it becomes smoother. The increasing smoothness seems to indicate that the center, despite its relative decrease in quantity, increasingly dominates the entire area, superseding the influence of other, preexisting centers. The flattening results from a slow decrease of density in the inner and a rapid increase in the outer zones, each of which, however, finally stabilizes at a lower density than the previous one.

Within this basic pattern, modifications are brought about by topography and by transportation. Whenever individual transportation predominates, time distances tend to be proportional to straight-line distances, and the over-all form of the settlement tends to be circular. This was the case in the foot-and-hoof city. The development of suburban railroads brought a change, because the trips made by their passengers were performed by two means of radically different speeds: a train at thirty miles an hour and walking at three miles per hour. As the technology of steam railroads dictated few and widely spaced stations, a pattern of small circular dots developed, strung out over a considerable length of railroad line, with a small commercial center at each station.

With the electric streetcar, stops were far more frequent, and the speed was only about three times walking speed. So the dots merged into solid and shorter lines, with commercial concentrations at their intersections.

When the automobile brought about a sudden and unpredictable reversal of the secular trend from individual to collective transportation, the use of one means of transportation for the entire trip and at fairly uniform speed reproduced, on a vastly larger scale, the circular form of the foot-and-hoof city. The structured pattern of developed and open land, which had begun to emerge in the railroad and streetcar areas, was submerged in universal sprawl. "Developments" were scattered all over the metropolitan area, cutting up the open space into smaller and oddly shaped remnants.

The developments are of two major types: industrial and residential. The former, used for manufacturing, warehousing, and transportation, need relatively large areas of level land with good access to transportation by water, air, rail, and road. Residential areas are practically unrestricted in their choice of location and cover much more extensive areas. They are patterned by several factors: in particular, family composition, income, and race.

THE USE OF LAND IN THE CHICAGO AREA

The resulting pattern of urban land use may be seen in a case study of Chicago, taken from the final report of the Chicago Area Transportation Study (CATS)—the first of the large-scale metropolitan transportation studies that sought to explore systematic relationships between traffic and land use. In Chapter 13 we use more of this CATS report, to show the relationships between traffic, transportation systems, and land uses.

*The Chicago Area Transportation Study**

Of the 1,236.5 square miles in the area studied by the *Chicago Area Transportation Study* (CATS), 45 per cent is in urban use (see Fig. 12–1 and Table 12–1). The pattern revealed in

*Reprinted from the Chicago Area Transportation Study, *Final Report, I: Survey Findings* (Chicago: Western Engraving and Embossing Company, 1959), with the permission of the Agency.

TABLE 12–1

Areas and Percentages of Major Land Uses within the Chicago Study Area

Land Use Type	*Square Miles*	*Percentage*
Residential	180.6	32.1
Streets and alleys	146.1	25.9
Public open space	114.9	20.4
Transportation	50.7	9.0
Manufacturing	24.7	4.4
Public buildings	23.1	4.1
Commercial	21.1	3.8
Parking and miscellaneous	1.6	0.3
Total in urban use	562.8	100.0
Vacant or not in urban use	673.7	
Total study area	1,236.5	

the maps of the city has a definite structure: a semi-circular concentration, where nearly all the land is used, from which radiate five fingers of urban development, not counting the Indiana area.

Why has the Chicago area developed in this particular fashion? One reason is the raw fact of growth itself. From a small settlement at the mouth of the Chicago River, the urbanized area has grown out steadily in all directions, as shown in Fig. 12–1. Growth has been horizontal rather than vertical, because it evidently has been found cheaper, in this area, to absorb new lands into urban uses rather than to build up into the air. With faster and more versatile transporta-

FIGURE 12–1. Chicago area growth patterns. *Source:* Figs. 12–1 through 12–12 are from Chicago Area Transportation Study, *Final Report, I: Survey Findings* (Chicago: Western Engraving and Embossing Company, 1959).

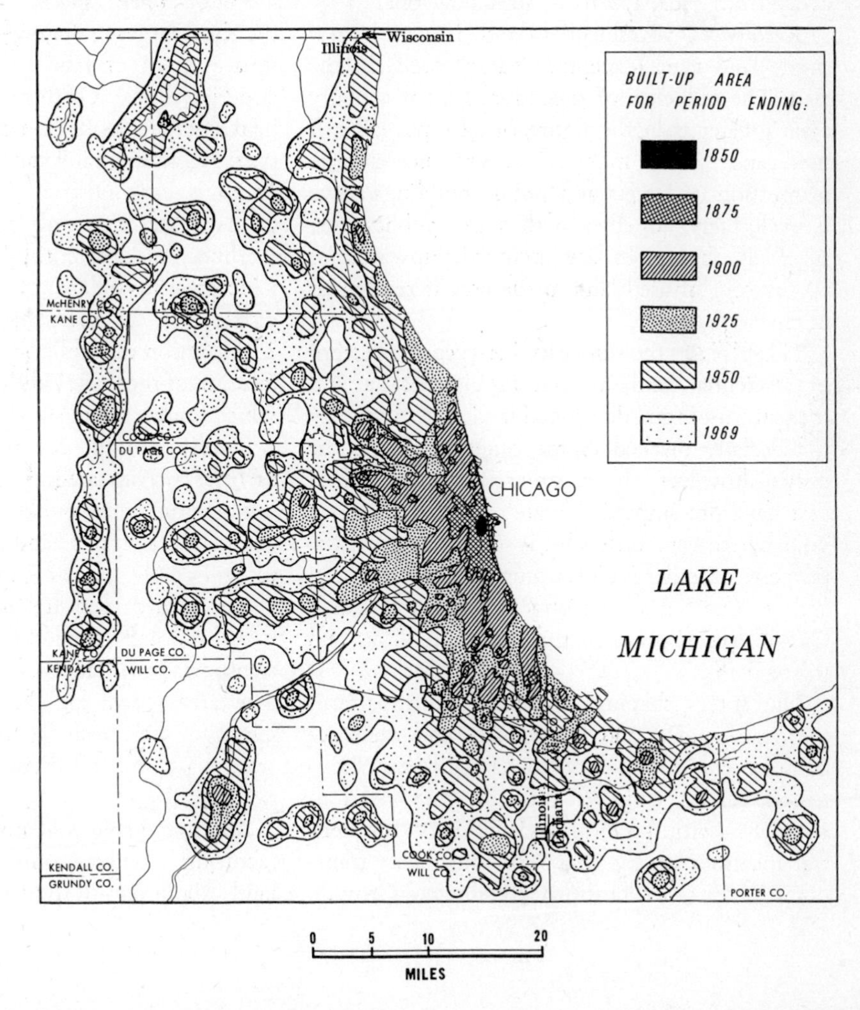

tion provided by the automobile, agricultural and vacant lands are being absorbed at an increasing rate and at lower densities.

The form of this horizontal expansion has been shaped by transportation even from earliest times. Horse cars and cable cars on State Street accelerated growth southward in the period from 1860 to 1875. The suburban railroad lines created fingers and islands of urban development. The latest wave of expansion, taking place in the age of the automobile, has filled out the railroad pattern and has extended the semi-circular area of complete development. The persistence of a particular form, even into a new era of transportation, can be explained by the process of growth. This is growth by accretion. Each new subdivision and each new commercial and industrial area is influenced by the great mass of the existing city, with no real prospect of breaking away from old patterns to start new ones.

Residences. Residential land is the largest single land type (excepting vacant land) in the area. The influence of residential land is actually even greater than the figure of 32.1 per cent of used land[1] would make it appear, since a large proportion of streets and public buildings serve it exclusively, together with some public open space. If these uses are included, upwards of 60 per cent of used land in the area is residential in character.

This explains the similarity between the pattern of residential land, as seen in Fig. 12–2*a*, and the pattern of total developed land. The similarity is especially marked in the outer areas. At the center, however, the commercial and industrial uses have pre-empted the land, so that there is a void where very little land is used for residential purposes. Similar voids occur in the industrial and commercial areas along the Sanitary Canal, Cicero Avenue, and in the forest preserves and major parks.

The forces shaping residential land patterns are easily understood. Residences and their accompanying land uses occupy large areas. Residences cannot compete—nor do they need to compete—with business and industry for central locations or for sites with particular transportation or other locational advantages. Growth, therefore, takes place on the outskirts where land is cheaper. Yet, residential activities cannot be dispersed completely; they must have good connections with the city where work opportunities and other necessary services concentrate. Hence they cling to the mass of the city as closely as possible and this is the reason why transportation, which provides the necessary connections, is so important in shaping urban development.

Streets. Streets use the second largest amount of land in the study area, 25.9 per cent of the total of used land (31.7 per cent, excluding public open space). The distribution of streets is almost exactly like the distribution of developed land (see Fig. 12–2*b*). In fact it must be, because, for land to be developed, it must have access and this is by way of streets. This is another way of saying that where there is development there must also be traffic.

Public open space. Public open space is the third largest category of land use, with 114.9 square miles of land devoted to this purpose (see Fig. 12–2*c*). Of this area, 69 square miles are held by the Cook County Forest Preserve District. An additional 9 square miles are held by the Chicago Park District. The remainder is taken up by cemeteries, golf courses, race tracks, and the like. The distribution of public open space in Chicago is irregular, not really well related to the distribution of population or residential land. The location of public open space depends on the location of those sites with certain natural qualities which make them suitable for recreational use.

Transportation, communications, and public utilities. The category of transportation, communications, and public utilities land takes up about half as much land as the public open space category. Of the 50.7 square miles in this use, about 16 are used for airports; the remainder is in railroad properties, miscellaneous other transportation facilities, and public utilities. The areas used for these purposes are highly selective: they occur at the airports and near the waterways and rail lines. Most of these areas are rail yards.

Manufacturing and public buildings. Manufacturing occupies only 4.4 per cent of the land. About one-third of all workers are employed

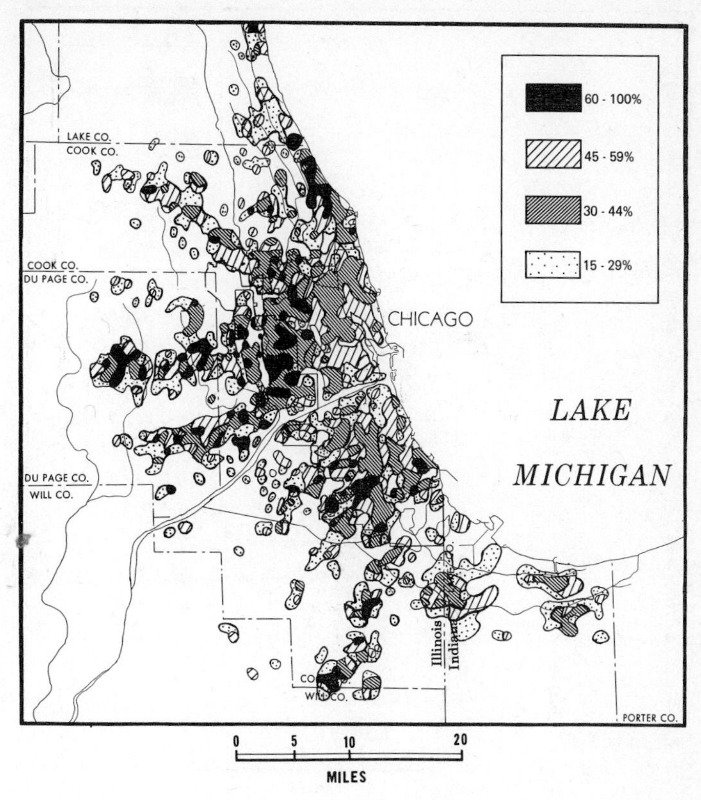

FIGURE 12–2*a*. Land use in the Chicago area (percentage per one-quarter square mile): residential land. *Source:* See caption for Fig. 12–1.

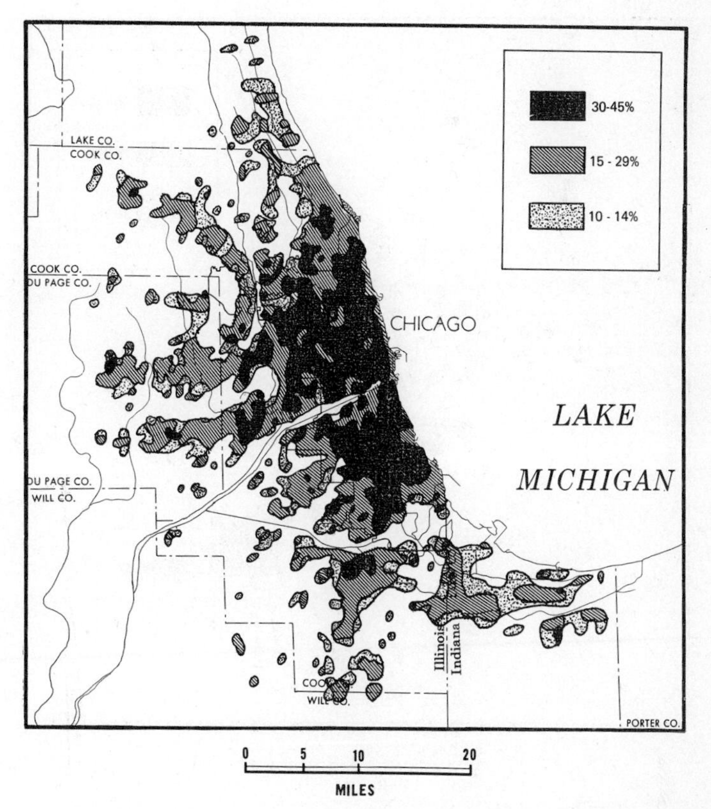

FIGURE 12–2*b*. Land use in the Chicago area (percentage per one-quarter square mile): streets and alleys. *Source:* See caption for Fig. 12–1.

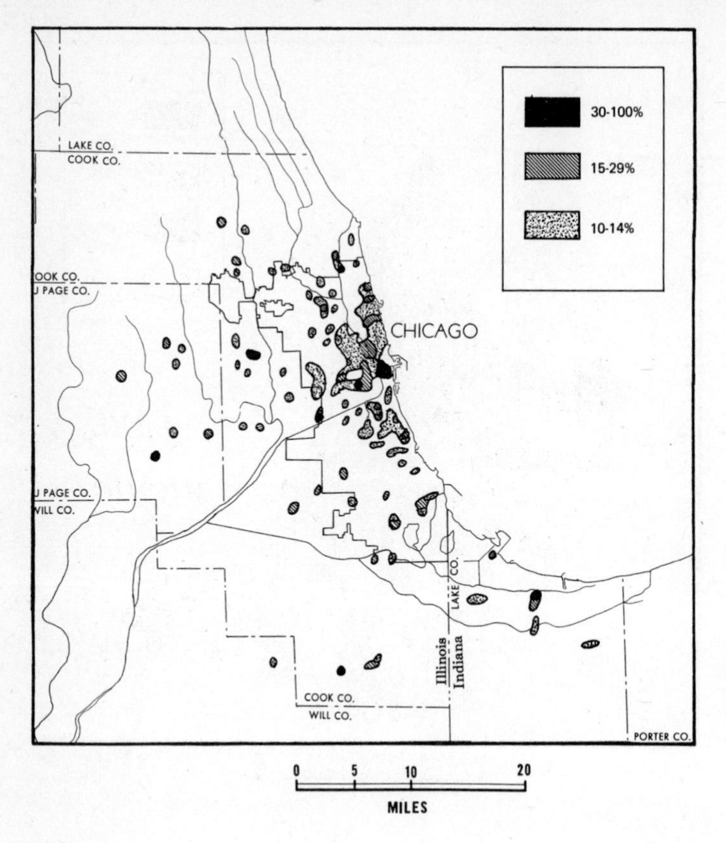

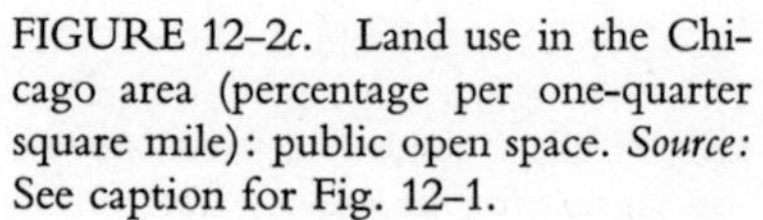
FIGURE 12–2*c*. Land use in the Chicago area (percentage per one-quarter square mile): public open space. *Source:* See caption for Fig. 12–1.

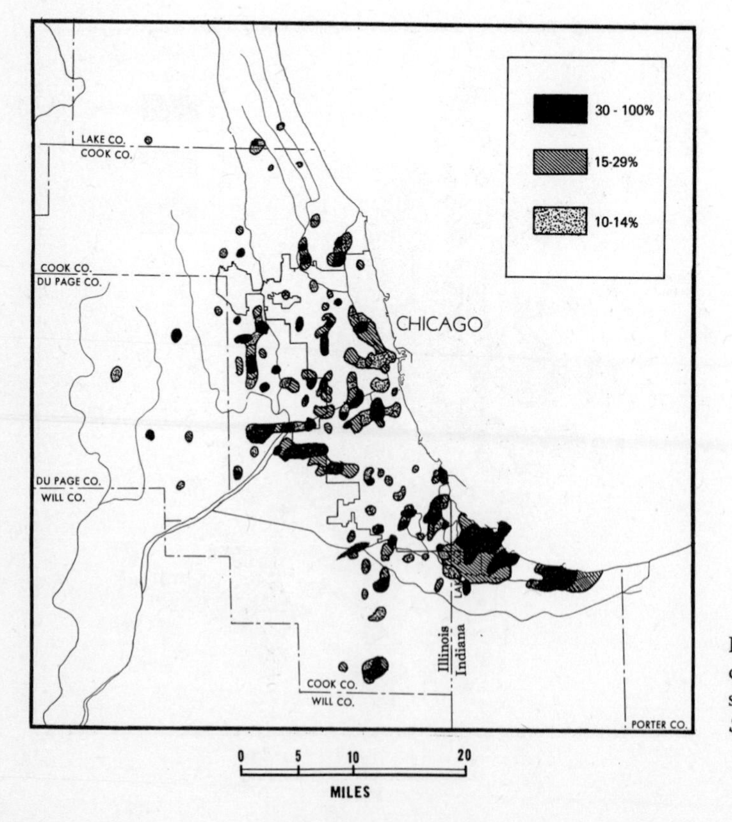

FIGURE 12–2*d*. Land use in the Chicago area (percentage per one-quarter square mile): manufacturing land. *Source:* See caption for Fig. 12–1.

in manufacturing, so that such land becomes something of a focal point for travel and its location is of great interest. Figure 12–2*d* shows the pattern to be closely related to that of land used for transportation.

While public buildings occupy nearly as much land as manufacturing, these lands are so evenly scattered around the area that no pattern is discernible.

Commerce. Commercial land encompasses a variety of activities, not just retail stores. Personal and business services, wholesaling, offices, automotive sales, and some contracting and building trades are included in the definition. Even with this broad definition, commercial land occupies only 3.8 per cent of used land (see Fig. 12–2*e*). The greatest concentration is in the Loop and its vicinity. With the exception of this concentration, commercial land is scattered lightly and evenly over the remainder of the developed area. The pattern of commercial land is explained by the functions of commercial activities, which are to bring buyers together with assortments of goods and services. Accessibility is thus the prime requirement and commercial land has always had an affinity for the central places which are closest to most people. The accessibility of the Loop area has been riveted down by the construction of mass transportation facilities which made this the time-center of the area, even if it is not the geographic center. The scattering of other commercial uses is simply a reflection of the fact that it is more economic to bring some goods and services closer to the consumers, at places which are central to smaller, less specialized, trading areas.

Figure 12–3 shows how the proportions of land in each of six major uses change as distance from the central business district (CBD) increases. Commercial land as a percentage of these six uses decreases from 28 per cent of the total at the CBD[2] to about 3 per cent of the total at 12 miles distance and remains at about this proportion further out. The amount of residential land increases to about 40 per cent of the total 8 miles from the CBD and remains more or less constant at about that

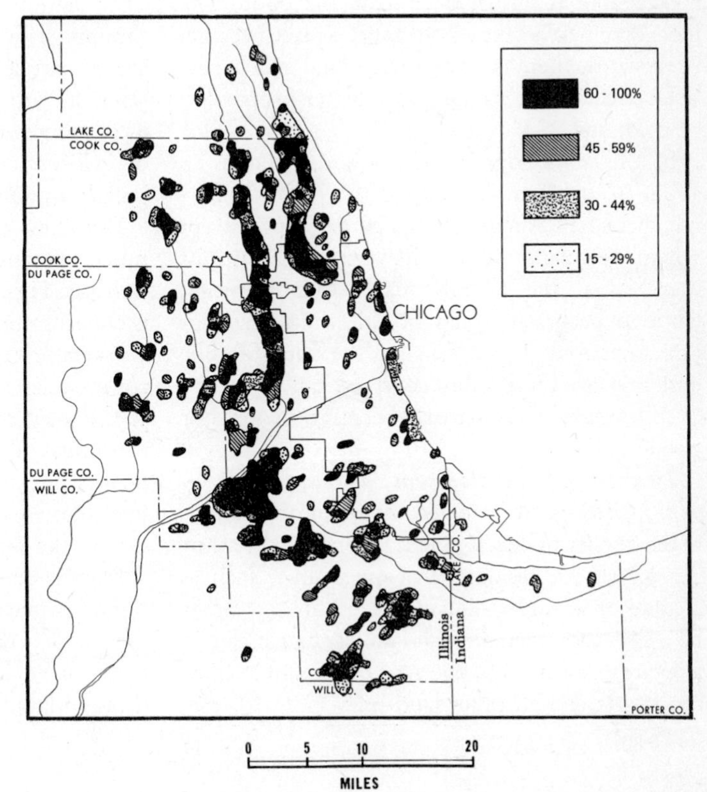

FIGURE 12–2*e*. Land use in the Chicago area (percentage per one-quarter square mile): commercial land. *Source:* See caption for Fig. 12–1.

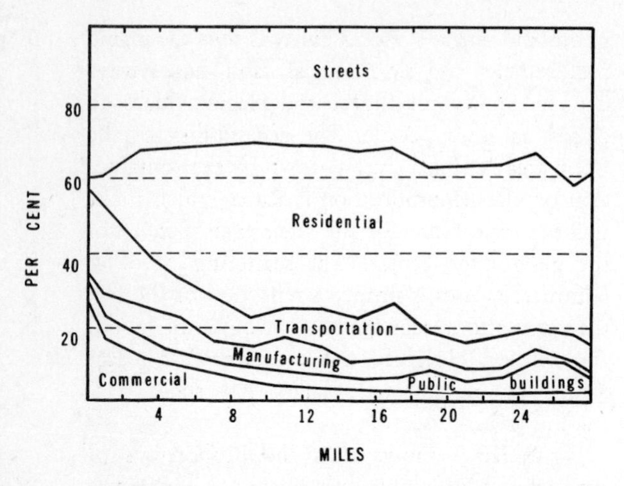

FIGURE 12–3. Six land uses *vs.* distance from the Loop. *Source:* See caption for Fig. 12–1.

level. Streets take up over 40 per cent of the land within 2 miles of the Loop, then decrease to about 32 per cent. Between 15 and 28 miles from the Loop, streets are a variable, but gradually increasing, proportion of the total. The variability occurs because transportation and public buildings are variable at this distance from the Loop. The increasing percentage of streets takes place because, in this area, there is more vacant land and hence, what streets there are take up a larger proportion of used land.

In this same figure, transportation takes up about 22 per cent of land at the urban center, but thereafter averages about 10 per cent, except where unusually large rail yards build up its share, as at the 17-mile mark. Manufacturing has two peaks, at 5 and 11 miles; elsewhere it remains about 4 per cent of the total. Public buildings are remarkably constant, but at 25 and 27 miles there seems to be a concentration of major public buildings.

Density of development as measured by population. One way of measuring variations in the density of development is to count the number of persons residing in a given area, such as an acre or a quarter-square mile: This can either be a *gross* area, including all land uses, or it can be a *net* area, restricted to one type of use and excluding streets and all other land uses.

The pattern of population density is related to age of development. When Chicago was in its most explosive period of growth, from 1860 to 1910, the principal means of travel was by mass transportation, along with some on foot and a minor amount by horse and carriage. These slow means of transportation required that houses be built close together, multi-family structures wherever possible. Slow transportation and high density dwelling mutually reinforced each other.

However, as the average speed of travel has increased over the years, more and more land has fallen within tolerable commuting distance and hence has become available for urban development. The automobile has been a dominant influence in bringing new land into the urban market. With these improvements in transportation, residential lots could be made larger and this has gradually reduced densities of urban settlement.

Population densities are often called "nighttime" densities, since they are true only for that part of the day when all the members of a family are at home. "Daytime" densities are different, since large numbers of persons are at work, shopping, or in school. Employment densities are a particular kind of daytime density, and refer only to the number of employees working in any given area. They do not include shoppers or visitors who may, in commercial areas, greatly outnumber employees.

Densities of commercial employment show much the same pattern as the densities of population (see Figs. 12–4 and 12–5). This employment is concentrated in the core area, with densities of workers exceeding 1,130 persons per acre of commercial land (700,000 per net square mile) at the very center. This shows the mutual reinforcement of mass transportation and high density. It was not an accident that elevated trains and steel-framed skyscrapers were developed side by side in the same period, 1884 to 1897.

Manufacturing employment densities show a similar pattern: the closer to the CBD, the higher the density of employment. Here again strong forces have influenced the density of development. Manufacturing employment had to be

FIGURE 12–4. The sectoral pattern of net population densities. Population density declines sharply from a peak equivalent to 78 families per net residential acre to between 4 and 5. *Source:* See caption for Fig. 12–1.

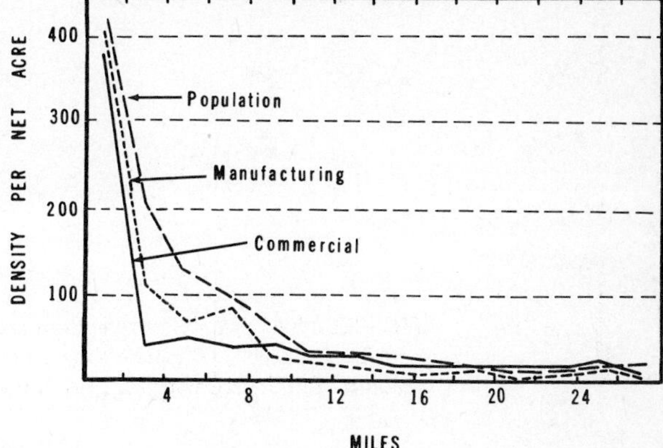

FIGURE 12–5. Population and employment densities *vs.* distance from the Loop. *Source:* See caption for Fig. 12–1.

dense in the nineteenth century, partly because factories had to be centrally located to obtain an adequate labor supply. Compact production arrangements were necessary because power was transmitted to machinery by means of belts and shafts. Further, with less mechanical power available, manufacturing required more employees per given unit of output.

Current technology modifies these effects. Power is transmitted to machinery by electricity. More power is available for each worker. The workers themselves travel by cars and require parking space. All these conspire to reduce the density of manufacturing employment.

. . .

Density as measured by floor area. A concentration of population or employment in any small area requires a similar concentration of buildings to shelter people and their activities. Density, therefore, can be measured in terms of square feet of floor area per acre of land, as well as by population density. Each measure has its own applications in analysis, forecasting, and planning.

Floor area measures are useful because they permit the study of establishments. This is a more direct and detailed index of the amount and kind of activity taking place on a parcel of land than is provided by land use measures. Floor area data are particularly valuable for planning and studying traffic generation in such areas as the CBD, where land is used so intensively and at such varying rates.

Although floor area was not inventoried for the entire CATS study area, the 295-square mile area which was surveyed in 1956 did contain 80 per cent of the population of the study area and an estimated 86 per cent of the total floor area. The breakdown of this floor area by types is shown in Table 12–2.

Put in human scale, the total floor areas in residences works out at about 940 square feet per dwelling place. (Measurements are exterior wall measurements and include all public halls

TABLE 12-2

Floor Areas Occupied, by Major Land Uses, within the 295-Square Mile Inventory Area

Type of Establishment	*Floor Area (in Millions of Square Feet)*	*Percentage of Total Floor Area*
Residential	1,301.0	58.4
Commercial	351.9	15.8
Manufacturing	309.5	13.9
Transportation	103.5	4.6
Public Buildings	162.5	7.3
Total	2,228.4	100.0

FIGURE 12–6. Model of total floor area. The 295-square mile area where buildings were measured contains 2,200,000,000 square feet of floor area. The vertical dimension of each block represents the amount of floor area within a grid of one-quarter square mile. *Source:* See caption for Fig. 12–1.

and stairs in apartment buildings.) This is very close to what might be expected, since new single-family houses average about 1,200 square feet and new two-bedroom apartments average about 720 square feet, both using inside measurements and not including public halls and stairs. Floor area for manufacturing workers runs a little over 300 square feet per worker.

The density of floor area in Chicago is dramatically portrayed in Figs. 12–6 and 12–7. These models, showing the total amount of floor area per quarter-square mile, illustrate perfectly how land is used more and more intensely as one approaches the center of the city, until in the actual CBD there is a boiling up of activity which towers over, and completely dominates, the entire metropolitan area.

In the four one-quarter square mile zones which comprise the Loop district, there are 92.3 million square feet of floor area. The single quarter-square mile bounded by State Street, Madison Street, the Chicago River, and Harrison Street, contains over 32,000,000 square feet of floor area. This is in contrast with the lowest blocks shown on the model, each of which represents 1,000,000 square feet of floor area per quarter-square mile.

FIGURE 12–7. Model of total floor area. The highest value shown on this model is 32,000,000 square feet. Grids of one-quarter square mile containing less than 1,000,000 square feet of floor area are not shown. *Source:* See caption for Fig. 12–1.

Since very few suburban areas approach this rate of land utilization, the model as a whole represents a good approximation of the whole study area, even though floor area measurements were not taken in most suburban and rural sections.

Readers familiar with the area will recognize the resemblance between the models and the actual skyline of Chicago. Both the Loop and the Near North Side stand out. The more intense use of land along the lake front can be seen in such special peaks as those caused by the dense apartment development at 51st Street and the Outer Drive, to the south. The remainder of the model shows a gradual lessening of densities, with the exception of a few isolated peaks. These peaks are caused, for the most part, by manufacturing concentrations.

To give these models and figures a scale which can be related to everyday experience, the ratio between floor area and land area can be used. Floor area ratios can best be described by example. If the total floor area in the Loop is divided by the Loop's net land area (excluding streets, public open spaces, and unusable land) a floor area ratio of 6.8 is attained. This means that if every net square foot of land in the Loop were covered with buildings, the buildings would average nearly seven stories in height. To attain such a ratio, many buildings must be twenty and thirty stories high. By contrast, the remainder of the City of Chicago seldom has a floor area ratio exceeding 1.5. For such a ratio, buildings must generally be two and three stories high. The suburban parts of the study area generally have a floor area ratio of less than .5.

Figure 12–8 does not show floor area but represents instead the number of "person trips" which terminate in each quarter-square mile on an average weekday. Compare this figure with the model of total floor area shown in Fig. 12–7. The similarity between the two is great, although, of course, not perfect. The concentration of floor area in the Loop is matched by an equal concentration of persons whose trips are destined to that spot. Elsewhere, there are much smaller amounts of floor area, fairly evenly distributed, and a similar even distribution of person trip destinations. The model of person trip destinations extends farther into the suburbs because the floor area survey was limited in extent. Even in the details there is comparability: for example, just west

FIGURE 12–8. Total "person trip" destinations. The destinations of 10,212,000 person trips, on the average weekday, are distributed throughout the study area as shown in this model. The highest blocks in the model represent 144,000 trip destinations per grid of one-quarter square mile; the lowest blocks, 5,000; and the shaded areas, less than 5,000 but more than 2,500. *Source:* See caption for Fig. 12–1.

FIGURE 12–9. Model of nonresidential floor area. The highest value shown is 29,700,000 square feet; grids of one-quarter square mile containing less than 1,000,000 square feet of floor area are not shown. Total floor area shown is 927,400,000 square feet. *Source:* See caption for Fig. 12–1.

of Lake Calumet is the former town of Pullman with its factories and shopping center, and this shows up clearly on both models.

This is a general demonstration of the truth in the basic assumption that travel is related to land use.

Figure 12–9 shows just the floor areas of nonresidential building uses. Nonresidential floor area is packed within a semi-circular area having a radius of about 6 miles, centering on the Loop.

The concentration of floor area in downtown Chicago is extremely high: 4.1 per cent of the total floor area measured is in the Loop, which has a land area of 1 square mile, or less than .1 per cent of the entire study area. Within the central area there are 16.2 per cent of the total floor area measured, 40 per cent of the commercial floor area, 20 per cent of the manufacturing floor area, and 36 per cent of the transportation floor area. This is in contrast with the fact that these areas, combined, contain only 1 per cent of the land area in the study area! This is the apex of density in land utilization.

Many of these lesser peaks of nonresidential floor area are active with the handling of goods and do not require so many people. This is one reason why the model of person trip destinations (Fig. 12–8) tends to be more even than the model of total floor area.

Figure 12–10 shows residential floor area. This is the complement of the model of nonresidential floor area; both of them, if added together, would produce the model of total floor area shown in Fig. 12–7. Naturally, where there is a great deal of nonresidential floor area, there is correspondingly less residential floor area.

There tends to be slightly more residential floor area just outside the central area. Also, greater amounts of residential floor area are found along the lake front, showing the advantage which has been taken of this desirable site, with its high degree of accessibility to the Loop via the Outer Drive. This pattern agrees closely with the population map.[3]

URBAN RETAIL STRUCTURE

The previous chapter fleshed out in some detail the socio-economic differentiation of the land used for residential purposes, by far the greatest amount

FIGURE 12–10. Model of residential floor area. Buildings measured contained a total of 1,300,000 square feet of residential floor area. The highest value shown is 8,400,000 square feet. Values of less than 1,000,000 square feet per grid of one-quarter square mile are not shown. *Source:* See caption for Fig. 12–1.

of urban land that is used, but for purposes which cannot compete with other urban activities. It is to these other activities that we must therefore now turn.

Commercial activities form a large part of the economic activity which occurs in urban areas, and they provide employment opportunities for a large number of urban dwellers. The most recent contributions to the theoretical examination of commercial structure are those of Brian J. L. Berry. Interest in the internal commercial structure of urban areas may be traced to his early interest in central-place theory.[4] As indicated in earlier chapters, Christaller's theory focussed upon locational and hierarchical systems of urban places. Berry applied similar ideas to the internal structure of urban areas.

When viewed in an abstract manner, cities can be thought of as "condensed" regions of population. In central-place theory, centers selling goods and services at retail locate in optimal positions with regard to a dispersed population. In urban areas, where population densities are much higher than in the case of a large region, the optimal locations of retail and service activities are much closer together. Nonetheless, a hierarchical structure of shopping centers develops. The number of classes within the hierarchy can be associated with the number of people in the urban area.

In rural settings we can envision a set of villages in a particular county, a smaller number of towns, and perhaps a county seat. The internal retail structure of the *villages* would most likely comprise one shopping area providing convenience-type goods. The *town* might contain two levels of shopping centers. The lower level would be "village-type" or "neighborhood" centers, since they provide convenience goods for the people living close by. The higher-order center, a prototypic central business district (CBD), the equivalent of a community shopping center in larger cities, provides banking services and more expensive and durable goods than the neighborhood convenience centers.

Finally, at the level of the *county* seat, three levels of commercial centers would be in evidence. Neighborhood centers again provide goods for people in the immediate vicinity. A second level in the hierarchy includes shops selling more durable goods. Finally, there is a well developed county-seat CBD selling a broad variety of dura-

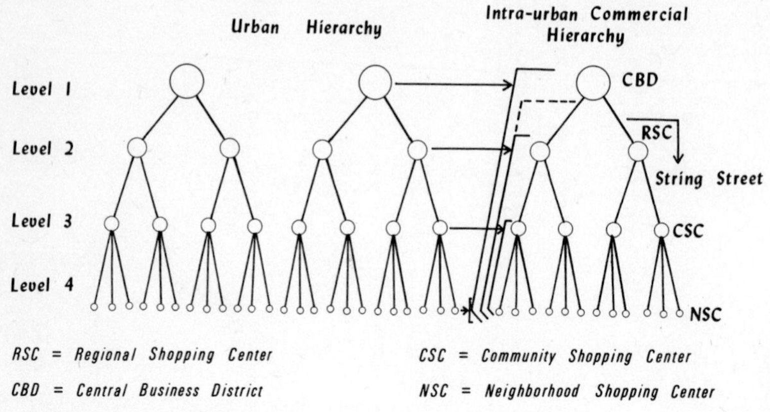

FIGURE 12–11. The urban commercial hierarchy. *Source:* See caption for Fig. 12–1.

ble goods and services that require relatively large populations to support them.

Figures 12–11 and 12–12 indicate the possible relationships between the urban hierarchy and the number and types of commercial centers within the urban area. In Chicago, however, Berry defined additional components of urban retail structure (Fig. 12–13). The distribution of both recent planned and older unplanned shopping centers is displayed in Fig. 12–14. Spreading between these are "ribbons" of highway-oriented businesses, along the mile and half-mile major arterial system.

There are several reasons for such an intraurban hierarchy of retail centers:

> (1)[F]rom the supply side, different commercial functions have different conditions of entry (thresholds), and thus demand minimum trade areas of different sizes for their support; and (2) on the demand side, consumers spend differing portions of their income on different goods and services, and purchase them with differing degrees of frequency. Low threshold, high frequency functions are found in lower level nucleations ("convenience goods centers"), whereas high threshold, low frequency functions are found in higher-level nucleations serving large trade areas ("shopping goods centers").[5]

We conclude that the hierarchical nature of intraurban retail structure may be attributed to the same process that generates systems of central places. The primary difference is the high density of households within cities.

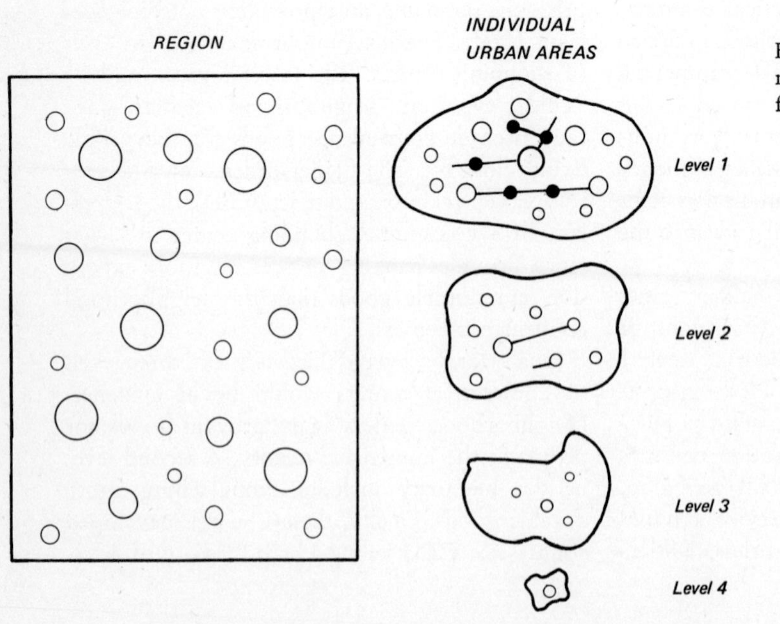

FIGURE 12–12. The regional commercial hierarchy. *Source:* See caption for Fig. 12–1.

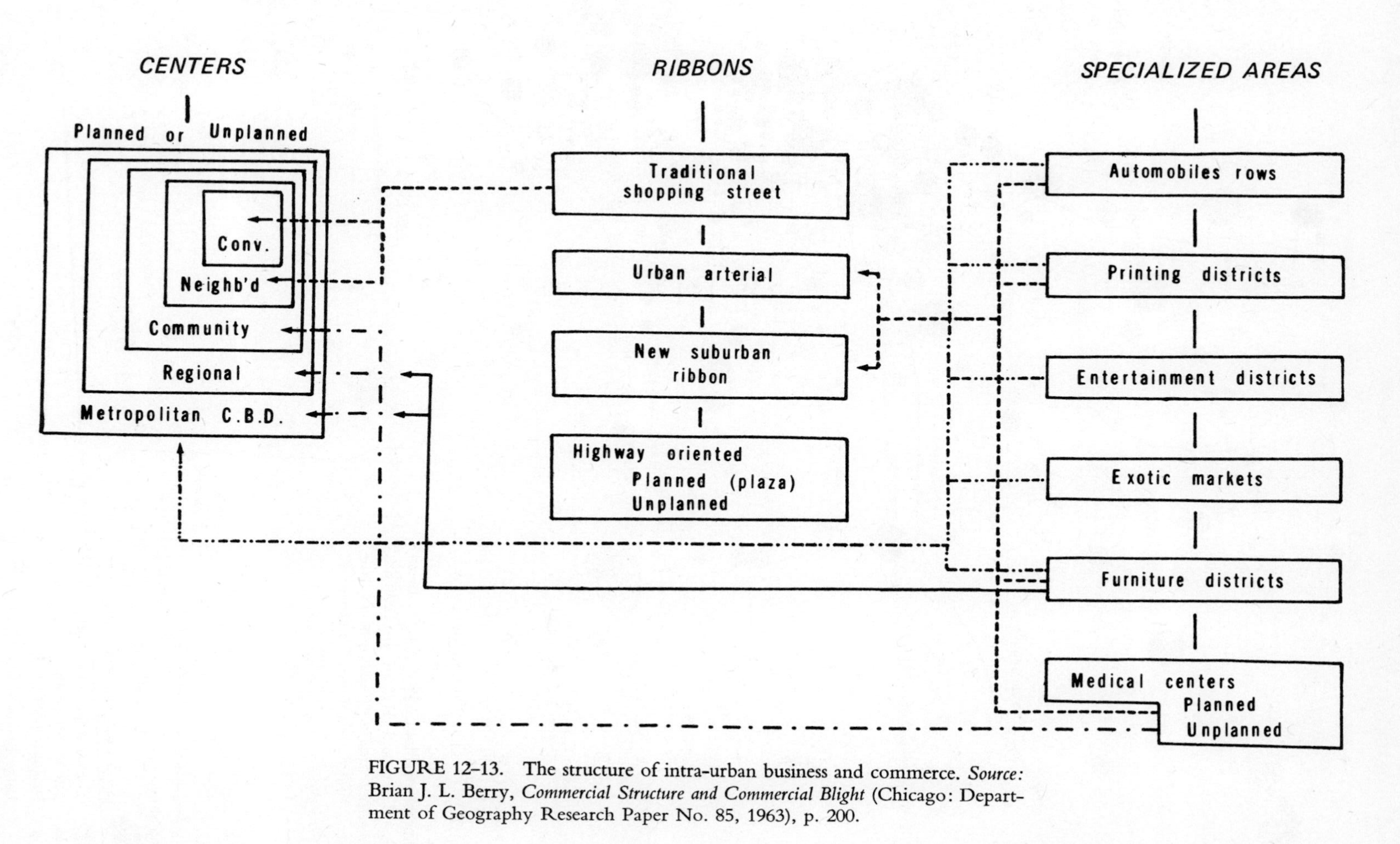

FIGURE 12–13. The structure of intra-urban business and commerce. *Source:* Brian J. L. Berry, *Commercial Structure and Commercial Blight* (Chicago: Department of Geography Research Paper No. 85, 1963), p. 200.

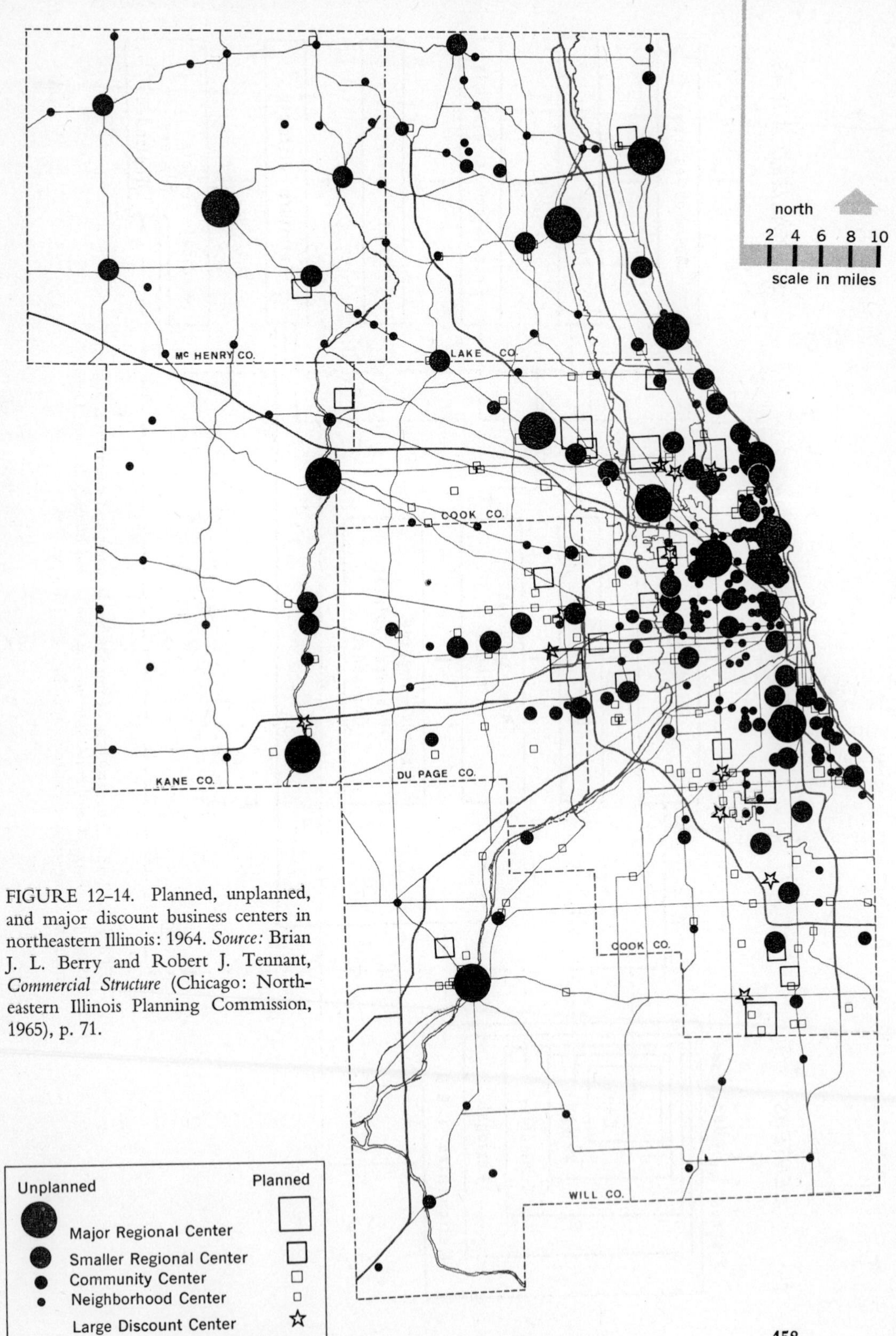

FIGURE 12–14. Planned, unplanned, and major discount business centers in northeastern Illinois: 1964. *Source:* Brian J. L. Berry and Robert J. Tennant, *Commercial Structure* (Chicago: Northeastern Illinois Planning Commission, 1965), p. 71.

LOCATION OF INDUSTRY WITHIN CITIES

The location of industry within cities often can only be understood after a careful examination of historical events. The complexity of these events and their impact on the spatial distribution of industry within cities make it difficult to establish a theoretical basis for intraurban industrial location. The following excerpt from the *Mid-Chicago Economic Development Study* of the Center for Urban Studies, University of Chicago, illustrates the impact of various factors on the location of industry in Chicago.

*Historical Evolution**

Chicago's spectacular rate of growth has obscured the fact that its original site had imposing topographical disadvantages for urban growth. While its harbor was as good as any on the south end of Lake Michigan and was strategically located for inland commerce, it was far from ideal. A sand bar kept large ships from using the Chicago River as a harbor until the Army Corps of Engineers cleared the channel in 1834. Thereafter, the narrow, crooked, shallow river required constant attention to keep abreast of the demands on it. Furthermore, land near the stem of the river was so low and poorly drained that it became a swamp-like morass of mud and water whenever it rained or the snow melted. Until the introduction of railroads in the late 1840's and early 1850's, the city was constantly plagued by muddy entrances and exits.

Chicago's early industrial growth was closely associated with the agricultural development of nearby areas, and with the need to satisfy the internal demands of the growing city. A western terminus for New York City commerce passing through the Erie Canal and the Great Lakes, Chicago was a meeting place for eastern finished goods and western agricultural commodities. Since fall crops were usually harvested just before the close of navigation on the Great Lakes, mud made it almost impossible for farmers to market their grain while it could still be shipped East. Mud likewise made it difficult to sell livestock at a time when both the advantages of summer feeding and Great Lakes markets were available. As a result, packing houses and grain elevators grew up to store agricultural commodities until they could be exported East after the spring thaw.

Breweries and bakeries soon sprang up, utilizing the abundance of grain to meet local demands. Similarly, printing, cabinetmaking, shoemaking, millinery and tailoring, carriage and wagon-making, and saddle and harnessmaking establishments were formed to satisfy local markets. But as employers, the building trades were more important than any of these. By 1856, Chicago had eighteen brick yards, nine marble and stone yards, fourteen planing mills, eight sash, door, and blind factories, and numerous lumber yards and shingle manufacturers.

Meanwhile, Chicago's aggressive civic and business leaders were attempting to exploit the city's locational advantages. In the early 1830's construction began on the Illinois and Michigan Canal, in hopes of connecting the Great Lakes to the Mississippi River and its tributaries. Although the construction of the canal was interrupted by the Panic of 1837, it was finally completed in 1848. Thereafter, the canal brought an increasing volume of bulk transport items into the city, while carrying away large amounts of lumber, farm machinery, and miscellaneous finished goods. The canal did much to attract the McCormick Reaper Works (which later became International Harvester) to Chicago.

By 1856, Chicago had become the leading lumber, livestock, and grain marketing center in the nation. Since the diameter of the city was less than 12 miles, every location in it was reasonably close to the city's primary transportation networks. Within the relatively compact city of 84,113 people, industry was widely scattered. The city's seventeen packing firms, for example, were scattered from what is now the 1600 block north to the 3500 block south of the city center, a distance of almost 12 miles.

The Chicago River, which divided the city into three parts, played a significant role in determin-

*Reprinted from *Mid-Chicago Economic Development Study, II: Technical Analysis and Findings,* The Center for Urban Studies, University of Chicago, 1966, with the permission of The Center for Urban Studies.

ing the spatial distribution of the industry in 1856. Open drawbridges over the main stem of the river retarded industrial development on the city's North Side, but both banks of the river were used for bulk storage. Almost every type of manufacturing flourished in the commercial center of the city. Farther south, at the edge of the built-up area, several heavy industries prospered. On the West Side, somewhat isolated from the main commercial district yet close to it, a growing number of industries clustered within a few blocks of the river.

One of the most interesting aspects of Chicago's 1856 industrial locational patterns was the slowness with which industrialists greeted the advantages of locating on railroad tracks. As early as 1835 the city's commercial leaders attempted to bring a railroad to Chicago, and by 1847, the Chicago and Galena Union Railroad Company was laying tracks. By 1856, Chicago, with thirty-two railroads entering the city over five major trunk lines, could justifiably claim to be the nation's leading railroad center. Yet it took the Panic of 1857 to make Chicago's industrial leaders see the locational advantages of the railroad. Faced with contracting local markets, many Chicago industries looked to regional markets to retain their prosperity. Increasingly they recognized the potentialities of the railroad for marketing their products on a regional basis.

The growth of the railroad industry created a natural market for iron and steel products. Engines, rails, cars, and even trestles required iron or steel. As a railroad center, Chicago was well situated to exploit this trade. Furthermore, the Illinois and Michigan Canal offered a means of transporting coal from southern Illinois to Chicago, while the opening of the Soo Locks in 1855 permitted freighters to bring iron ore to the city inexpensively. In 1857, Ward's Rolling Mill, a forerunner of the United States Steel Company, opened along the north branch of the Chicago River to re-roll iron rails. In 1865, America's first steel rails were rolled at that mill. Coming at a time of massive railroad expansion, Chicago's iron and steel industry grew rapidly. In 1868, the city's first blast furnace was put into operation; by 1879 Chicago produced more steel rails than any other city in the nation, and was among the nation's leaders in other types of iron and steel production.

Railroads also revolutionized Chicago's packing trade. The city's early livestock marketing was centered around taverns. The coming of the railroad splintered the trade among stockyards associated with various railroad lines. In June, 1864, the Chicago Pork Packers Association held a meeting to discuss the building of a union stockyard. On February 13, 1865, the Union Stock Yards & Transit Company was formed, and on Christmas Day, 1865, the Union Stock Yards were opened for business. Shortly thereafter, J. G. McCoy, an Illinois livestock shipper, conceived of a plan whereby Texas cattle drovers could meet Eastern cattle buyers on an equal footing. When Abilene, Kansas, was laid out in 1867, with marketing ties to Chicago, a critical step was taken that succeeded in keeping the meat packing trade in Chicago for nearly 90 years.

The Great Fire of 1871 caused extensive damage, but had little long-range effect on the city's industrial pattern. True, the extensive printing trade was almost completely burnt out, the numerous millinery and tailoring shops in the commercial district were destroyed, and such well-known firms as the McCormick Reaper Works and the Pullman Car Company were burned over. But nearly all these firms either rebuilt on the same sites or completed moves that had already been started before the fire struck. Instead of redirecting the locational trends and building patterns of the day, the fire intensified the trends that were already under way.

One important example of an emerging locational pattern that was accelerated by the Great Fire was the centrifugal growth of Chicago. As early as 1846, William Cullen Bryant observed that suburbs had begun to develop outside Chicago. By 1851, Chicago also had industrial suburbs. Horse-car railroads and commuter trains further encouraged the centrifugal movement of population long before the Great Fire. The fire did dislocate nearly half of the City's population, however, and many people settled down outside the burnt area rather than rebuild or move back into their old neighborhoods. Industrialists like Cyrus McCormick, who were planning to move their plants to more ample quarters, also hastened their moves.

The industrial land use patterns that characterize the City of Chicago in the twentieth century took form primarily between 1856 and 1886. The several diagonal streets assumed substantial commercial and light industrial significance. The Chicago River in the latter half of the nineteenth century became a strategic location for heavy industries, and railroads became an established factor in industrial location.

A profound technological revolution took place in America between 1860 and 1910. During that period an area as large as western Europe was put into cultivation; at the same time the percentage of the population employed on farms declined. Chicago agricultural implement firms played a key role in this revolution, and captured a large share of the agricultural implements market. Two firms, McCormick's and Deering's, made up the heart of Chicago's farm implement industry, which, in 1899, employed 10,245 people. In 1902, McCormick, Deering, and other establishments joined to form International Harvester.

Industrial consolidations. Amalgamations, mergers, and industrial consolidations became quite common throughout the United States after 1860. The excise tax on alcoholic beverages levied during the Civil War encouraged centralization of the distilling industry. Economies of scale in the agricultural implements industry were being exploited as early as 1870. Between 1870 and 1890, the number of tanning establishments in the nation declined by about three-quarters, although total production in the industry grew rapidly.

The years from 1888 to 1904 saw more significant consolidations than in any other period in Chicago history. The sash and door mills of the city amalgamated in the late 1880's. In 1889, another of a long line of consolidations occurred in the steel industry when the Illinois Steel Company was formed. A forerunner of the United States Steel Company, the firm brought together all of Chicago's major steel producers. Three years later, a large number of bakeries producing crackers, gingersnaps, and other package goods merged. In 1898 Union Carbide of Chicago and the American Steel and Wire Company were formed. Among major manufacturing industries in Chicago, only the furniture industry resisted amalgamation into giant corporations.

All of this activity accelerated the trend of a half-century toward large industrial organizations characterized by greater capital outlay and economies of scale. A shift from handicraft to modern manufacturing production methods, better geared to supplying regional and national markets, helped to produce a wave of consolidations and cleared the way for the exploitation of wider markets.

The centrifugal movement of industry. Between 1894 and 1915, the centrifugal movement of industry within the Chicago Metropolitan area began to pose a serious problem for the City of Chicago for the first time. Until then, annexations brought the new industries that had been built on the outskirts within the corporate limits. During that period, however, Chicago annexed only 12.88 square miles of additional land, even though its population increased by over 1,000,000 inhabitants and its suburban population grew by more than 300,000 people. To add to the problem, the number of industries moving to the outskirts of the city appears to have accelerated after 1903. Apparently land prices and taxes were fundamental causes, but the completion of the Elgin, Joliet, and Eastern Railroad (Chicago Outer Belt Line) in the late 1880's may have been a latent factor in drawing industry away from Chicago's central core.

World War I undoubtedly prolonged Chicago's period of rapid industrial development. Wartime restrictions on travel compelled many clothing and millinery buyers to patronize markets closer to home, and because of the city's central location in the nation, its garment industry benefited. The discovery of an inexpensive glue, combined with the timely blockade of competing German goods, catapulted Chicago's toy manufacturers into profitable production. Chemical research done by the universities of the region, along with private industrial research, enabled the city to capture a sizable share of the chemical market vacated by the severing of German imports. Thus, the war effort acted as a stimulant to Chicago's basic industries.

The twenty-five years between 1895 and 1920 were the Golden Age of Chicago's industrial development. The value of manufactured products more than doubled during the first two decades, only to double again by 1920. The number of people employed by manufacturing, as contrasted with handicraft industries, nearly doubled, while the total number of industrial establishments increased by more than 5,000. Indeed, 1919 was the peak year for Chicago industry in terms of the number of industrial establishments.

Planned industrial districts. At about the turn of the century, two planned industrial districts appeared in metropolitan Chicago. They were among the first in the nation.

The land for the original Clearing Industrial District, located just west of the 1890 city limits, was consolidated in the early 1890's by A. B. Stickney, president of the Chicago Great Western Railroad. His plans for a large railroad classification yard on the property were thwarted by the Panic of 1893. In 1898, plans for the land were revived when the Clearing Industrial District was formed. Because some of the competing railroads could not be induced to use the proposed yard facilities on a cooperative basis, and because technological advances in railroading produced more efficient use of railroad lands, the district officials decided to develop a portion of their property for manufacturing purposes. In 1907, they sold a large parcel of land to the Corn Products Refining Company. Beginning in 1909, some 530 additional acres were actively promoted for industrial purposes by the Clearing District.

The Central Manufacturing District was organized in 1890 by the Chicago Junction Railway and Union Stock Yards Company. It was twelve years, however, before the organization began to acquire land, and eighteen years before it actively developed its property—although the first district-financed building was built in 1905. Formed primarily to develop an area just north of the Union Stock Yards that had been somewhat bypassed by the City's growth, the District became so successful that a second tract was developed in 1916 on the south side of Pershing Road, west of the stock yards. Being located near the city's geographic center, where demand for land was high, both tracts were dominated by multistory buildings. Largely as a result of the increasing popularity of one and two-story factory structures, occasioned by the development of horizontal production-line methods, the Central Manufacturing District expanded its activities to peripheral locations to the south and southwest. By 1932, the district controlled six tracts containing a total of 851 acres.

Unlike the planned industrial towns of Pullman and Gary, the organized industrial districts did not provide housing and other complementary facilities. Able in some instances to use the city's sewer, power, and water services, the planned industrial district was particularly beneficial to small and medium-sized firms, giving them large-scale industrial security without sacrificing their individual identities. District promoters undertook the consolidation of small real-estate parcels into units large enough for plant sites, utilities placement, zoning, railroad linkage, and parking and loading. Such districts have generally been developed for light and medium manufacturing and warehousing, although industrial districts for heavy manufacturing are apparently becoming more popular.

By 1965, there were 23 planned industrial districts in Chicago, in control of 2,558 acres of land. Twenty-two of these districts, accounting for all but 48 acres, were located on the city's South Side. In contrast, there were 149 planned industrial districts in the metropolitan areas *outside* the City of Chicago, in control of 25,426 acres of industrial land.

Industry continues to undergo locational changes. During the 1920's and 1930's, most of Chicago's industries were still clustered within 5 or 6 miles of the Loop, where they could take advantage of the railroad and mass transportation networks converging there. Following the tendencies established more than a half-century before, they hugged the railroad tracks and the diagonally running streets, concentrated most heavily west of the Loop, and spread out along the two branches of the Chicago River. Heavy industry favored the South Side, while light industry, shipping goods in less-than-carload lots, favored sites to the north and west.

On the whole, industrial job opportunities within the City of Chicago declined slightly during the early Twenties. They recovered almost to 1919 rates toward the end of the decade, only to decline sharply during the Great Depression. Individual industries, of course, reacted in vastly different ways to the pressures of the period. Except in number of establishments, the confectionery industry grew rapidly throughout the 1920's, after a mild dip during the depression following World War I. The industry did not suffer as greatly as most other Chicago-based industries did during the Depression of the 1930's. The development and popularization of chain stores were a boon to the pre-packaged confectionery industry throughout the 1920's and 1930's. Later, supermarkets further increased the market for pre-packaged confectioneries.

The baking industry underwent a change during the first two decades of the century similar to that of the confectionery industry. Until about 1910, the trade operated almost entirely out of small, individually owned shops. Modern factory methods of baking, characterized by mass production and distribution, began to take hold before World War I. By 1934, seven Chicago baking firms employed more than 350 people each.

In contrast, Chicago's furniture and garment industries declined sharply after World War I. In 1885, Chicago was the nation's leading furniture manufacturing center. Located at a break in transportation between lumber-producing areas and expanding furniture markets, Chicago benefited by the sensitivity of the industry to transportation costs. Despite the construction of the American Furniture Mart in Chicago in 1924, which brought the leading furniture buyers of the world to Chicago, depletion of the forests near the Great Lakes began to cut deeply into Chicago's furniture industry during the 1920's and 1930's.

Prior to 1850, factory production of men's clothing was almost unknown. Even as late as 1879, most men's clothing was either made at home or custom-tailored. The revolution that produced the ready-made clothing trade began in this country about 1825; the invention of the sewing machine in 1846 gave it impetus, and the development of factory methods encouraged the growth of the "store bought" clothing trade. By 1899, 15 per cent of the men's clothing manufacturing establishments of the nation were located in Chicago. Between 1900 and 1905, the number of men's clothing manufacturing establishments in Chicago dropped from 905 to 504, yet the value of products and the number of wage earners continued to rise. The industry in Chicago reached its pinnacle, as measured by value of products, in 1920 to 1923. But between 1920 and 1925, a large portion of the industry was lost to Chicago, either by financial failure or by relocation. The development of the women's clothing industry in Chicago strongly paralleled that of the men's.

Between 1919 and 1939, Chicago's key industries were characterized by static or declining employment opportunities. Meat packing, primary metal processing, farm implements, and railroad-related manufacturing firms were faced with new competition, changing market conditions, and technological advances.

The tendency for many industries to seek new locations on the outskirts of the built-up area increased during the 1920's and 1930's. In 1920, Chicago was a city of kaleidoscopic neighborhoods where many languages were spoken, a broad range of creeds represented, and where many diverse groups lived. Heterogeneous and constantly changing, urban life defied the kind of order that scientific management was placing on the operation of industrial manufacturing concerns. Perhaps because the city was diverse and changing, it challenged established mores and beliefs and the philosophy of the "orderly" life. Some factory owners moved out of Chicago under the guise of improving the living and working conditions of their employees.

Many other considerations were involved in the steadily increasing trend toward the location of industry away from the central city between 1903 and 1929. Among them were: (1) the trend toward assembly line methods, which usually worked best on a single floor, rather than in loft buildings; (2) the development of economies of size, which could not be accommodated by the limited space available for expansion in the industrial core; (3) the need for special resources, such as a waterfront site, which could not be accommodated within the city; (4) the deteriorating condition of some structures within the industrial core, making it less expensive to build on virgin land than to tear down and rebuild on the same site; (5) the fact that some railroads were more ambitious in attracting and keeping industrial clientele along their rights-of-way than were others; and (6) considerations of insurance rates and similar cost factors frequently associated with a central location. The trend established in the first decade of the twentieth century toward industrial location in a northwesterly direction has prevailed into the 1960's.

Effect of public utilities. In the 1920's and early 1930's, Chicago's public utility services dramatically influenced industrial change in metropolitan Chicago. New machinery, new processes, and entirely new industries were the result of efforts begun as early as February 12, 1855, when the Illinois State Legislature passed a special act chartering the Chicago Gas Light and Coke Company. By the mid-1880's, eight gas, light, and coke companies were operating in Chicago. In 1887, seven of the eight firms were joined into what has since become the People's Gas Light and Coke Company (which was also the name of one of the firms involved in the merger). In October, 1931, the Natural Gas Pipeline Company of America, a subsidiary of People's Gas, completed its pipeline from the Panhandle natural gas fields of Texas and Oklahoma to Chicago. The replacement of manufactured gas by natural gas enabled People's Gas to provide a better product for less money. The gas used in Chicago today is entirely natural gas.

Electric lights and appliances were still a novelty in some neighborhoods when Samuel Insull began piecing together his utilities empire in 1892, thereby reducing electric rates in Chicago for all classes of users. By 1902, Chicago's electric rates were the lowest in the nation. Reduced rates and Insull's "hard sell" brought business to the Commonwealth Edison Company, which acquired its 200,000th customer in 1913. Insull did much to shape Chicago's industrial development in the 1920's. By 1935, however, Chicago's comparative advantage in electric rates was gone. The inability to produce hydroelectric power in the area prevented Commonwealth Edison from maintaining rates lower than those in places closer to hydroelectric generating stations. Since 1935, Chicago's industrial electric rates have improved in relation to other cities of 50,000 or more population. In addition, the Commonwealth Edison Company has recently embarked on programs that promise to increase Chicago's supply of electric power as fast as any potential demands might be made for such power without increasing the cost per kilowatt hour.

Comprehensive zoning. Just as improved public utilities affected industrial procedures and the types of industries that developed in the 1920's and 1930's, Chicago's first comprehensive zoning ordinance affected industrial location patterns. Passed on April 5, 1923, the ordinance tended to freeze land use patterns. Not until the 1940's, when motor transportation began to affect industrial patterns, did the city's industrial location pattern begin to change significantly.

The impact of the motor truck. Chicago is a major focal point of intercity motor truck transportation. More common carrier motor truck operators are located in Chicago than anywhere else in the nation.

Between 1925 and 1935, motor trucks became effective competitors of railroads in the movement of less-than-carload quantities. Unlike railroads, trucks had no fixed routes and could usually deliver merchandise from the door of the consignor to the door of the consignee without reloading and rehandling the shipment. Thus, lower costs and often quicker deliveries, with fewer damaged goods, became the hallmark of less-than-carload truck shipments. Even the Depression did not break the steady growth of motor truck vehicle registration. In 1935, the Motor Carrier Act brought the "for-hire" section of the trucking industry involved in interstate commerce under the jurisdiction of the Interstate

Commerce Commission. As common carriers, they were thereafter required to travel predetermined routes, charge constant and supervised rates, and meet federal standards. By 1949, Chicago-based companies owned 5.4 per cent of the motor trucks operated by Class I common carriers—2.1 per cent more than New York City; its closest rival.

After World War II, the advent of well-organized motor truck common carrier fleets, operating over an expanding system of first-class highways, altered industrial concepts about central city transportation advantages. Whereas transportation-sensitive industries had hitherto found it advantageous to locate near the center of railroad activity, motor trucks could now offer faster, cheaper, and more convenient service. Less-than-carload shipments no longer required costly and time-consuming rehandling. Furthermore, motor truck flexibility gave industrialists a greater choice of sites, thus enabling them to reduce their investments in "frozen" assets and to interchange land cost for labor and building costs.

Technological changes in the meat packing industry. The use of motor trucks for marketing livestock from farm to city and the development of elaborate, chain store distribution facilities, which depended on mass purchasing but not necessarily on purchasing at a central location, did away with much of the need for a large concentration of packers. By 1933, smaller packing centers were making serious inroads into Chicago's livestock packing complex.

The meat packing industry was one of the first to use assembly line methods of production. The industry, however, continued to utilize large numbers of unskilled and semiskilled workers into the 1950's. After World War II, a technological revolution swept the meat packing industry. Stunners, mechanical knives and hide skinners, power saws, and electronic slicing and weighing devices began to appear. By 1956, engineers had worked out the complete automation of sausage and bacon operations.

Labor productivity in the packing industry rose nearly 15 per cent from 1954 to 1958, while total man-hours declined 13 per cent. Nearly 18,000 production jobs were cut during that period.

In 1954, four Cudahy houses closed their Chicago packing operations. By 1960, all the major meat packers had shut down their Chicago operations. An estimated 30,000 employees were directly affected by the shutdown.

Decline in the city's agricultural implement industry. In 1959, the International Harvester Company announced that it was planning to stop production in its McCormick works, where 3,800 people were then employed. On October 1, 1961, the works were officially closed.

Slump in railroad and railroad-related employment. A substantial decrease in railroad employment occurred between 1939 and 1963, despite a substantial increase in the volume of freight traffic handled by railroads. In 1939, the railroads of the United States handled 338,900,000,000 ton miles of freight traffic. In 1963, they handled 621,700,000,000 ton miles of freight traffic, nearly double the annual pre-war volume. In spite of these increases, railroad employment in the United States dropped from a 1939 figure of 1,000,000 employees to under 700,000 employees in 1963. As the largest single railroad center in the nation, Chicago has experienced approximately the same percentage drop in railroad employment as the national average during this period.

The completion of the major belt railroad lines around Chicago just before the turn of the century led many primary metal processing and railroad equipment companies to locate along the belt lines outside the city limits. By 1934, more railroad equipment companies were located outside the city along the belt lines than in the central city. Hence, when the railroad industry experienced a serious decline after World War II, the loss in employment was felt by the entire metropolitan area. Chicago's South Side lost approximately 5,000 jobs as a result of the slump.

At the same time that competing forms of transportation and freight shipment were making inroads into Chicago's railroad industry, efforts were being made to integrate rail and motor freight movement. In 1926 the Chicago North Shore and Milwaukee Railroad experimented with the movement of loaded trucks on railroad flat cars. Over the next twenty years, several other attempts were made to establish "ferry-truck" or "ferry-train" service between Chicago and other midwestern cities. In 1953, the Rail-Trailer Corporation introduced a 75-foot flat car designed to carry two trailers and proposed to lease Trailer-on-Flat-Car (TOFC) equipment and perform terminal operations. Generally known as "Piggy-back," these operations brought about an ICC ruling on August 6, 1954. The ruling cleared the way for rail carriers to transport rubber-tired highway vehicles between rail terminals without ICC certification as an over-the-road carrier. A boom in TOFC operations, which is still under way, followed this ruling.

Containerized and integrated freight shipments, along with new dynamic railroad leadership, have recently had a wholesome effect on Chicago's railroad and railroad-related industries.

City planning. In 1964, only 12,659 acres, or less than 9 per cent of the city's area was zoned for heavy industry—a reduction of 18,470 acres, or 64 per cent, since 1923. Furthermore, nearly all the new public land uses for the city have been made in areas zoned for manufacturing, and residential areas have encroached on industrial zones.

In 1951, the Chicago Plan Commission outlined an industrial renewal program aimed at revitalizing 43.5 acres of blighted land bound by Polk Street on the north, Canal Street on the east, 15th Street on the south, and the Dan Ryan on the west. The "West Central Industrial Project" began to offer industrial sites for sale in 1956. By 1962, all the project sites had been sold by the Chicago Land Clearance Commission.

The response to the West Central Industrial Project did much to convince a skeptical public of the need for similar ventures. Central site locations still had economic advantages that were recognized by a sizable number of firms.

Expressways and urban sprawl. During World War II, Chicago's industrial and residential land use patterns were profoundly altered. Many new, large industrial plants were located on the periphery of the city, and high wartime wages, along with FHA and VA loans that favored new residential construction in the suburbs over inner-city construction and redevelopment, encouraged suburban development.

Pre-war pressures for superhighways into the central city were multiplied by a greatly enlarged suburban population. The decade prior to 1961 saw a host of expressway projects completed. Running directly through the city's major industrial complexes, the expressways were a mixed blessing. Hundreds of industries were dislocated, and many—like the garment industries uprooted by the Eisenhower and Dan Ryan Expressways—moved out of the metropolitan area altogether. The Dan Ryan Expressway bridge over the South Branch of the Chicago River reduced potential waterway traffic by its low clearance, which virtually prohibits much lake and ocean-going traffic from using the waterway to the west. On the other hand, expressways were an aid to motor vehicle common carriers and improved the competitive position of much of Chicago's industrial property.

Chicago's air traffic. In 1947, some 167,997 passengers were handled at Chicago's Midway Airport, making it the nation's second busiest airport, in terms of passengers, and the third busiest, in terms of passenger miles. In 1950, Midway became the second busiest terminal in terms of both passenger miles and passengers, and the following year it became the world's busiest airport in both departments.

At the very time when air traffic at Midway had achieved pre-eminence, construction was begun on Chicago-O'Hare International Airport, located 25 miles northwest of Chicago's Loop. On October 30, 1955, some commercial passenger flights were shifted to O'Hare, Midway having become too small for the city's needs and the runway demands of new jet aircraft. By July 10, 1962, all commercial passenger service to Midway was discontinued. In 1962, O'Hare became the world's busiest airport, a position it has since maintained. In 1965 O'Hare handled nearly 20,000,000 arriving, departing, and transferring passengers.

The loss of Midway Airport scheduled passenger service was a serious blow to industrial development on the South Side of the City.

Partial resumption of passenger activities and an increase in freight movements have taken place there since July, 1964.

Past and future. The gradual shift in reliance for job opportunities and city income on manufacturing industry rather than commercial enterprise took most of the nineteenth century.

As late as World War I, most Chicago industry was still more dependent on regional than national markets. The city's most prominent industries, however, had a national flavor as early as the 1850's. Meat packing, primary metal processing, farm implements, and railroad equipment gave character to the city's industrial growth. Fortunately for Chicago, its major industries were rising stars. In 1879, for example, 7,478 hands were engaged in Chicago's slaughtering and meat packing wholesale industries. By 1886, the number of wage earners in those industries had increased to 19,340 and, by 1919, had grown to include 46,474 wage earners and nearly 2,500 salaried employees.

By 1919, the rapid growth of manufacturing job opportunities in Chicago was arrested. It was not until the interjection of World War II defense demands that life was again put back into the city's industrial employment picture. After 1947, Chicago's industrial employment again leveled off and subsequently began to decline.

An important part of Chicago's unemployment problems stems from the character of its traditional key industries. Between 1919 and 1939, small and medium-sized industrial firms and service industries took up much of the employment slack left by declining or static employment opportunities in meat packing, primary metals processing, farm implements, and railroad-related occupations. World War II gave a second wind to some of the city's key industries, but once the war was over, new and displaced workers were left without jobs. Since World War II, technological advances, alterations in marketing patterns, and scientific discoveries have profoundly altered Chicago's make-up: the size, number, and kinds of industries have all undergone fundamental changes. Since 1950, 250 more establishments have moved out of the Mid-Chicago Economic Study Area than have moved into it, and those moving out have tended to be much larger than those moving in.

Chicago has long had the reputation of being a center of opportunity for workers short on skills. Along with other large industrial centers in the United States, it has represented the chance for the individual to move up the economic and social scale. The shortage of dynamically growing industries that will continue to produce jobs for unskilled and semiskilled workers has created a dilemma for the city officials of contemporary Chicago.[6]

Approaches to Generalization

While at first glance it may appear that order is lacking and locational classification of urban industry difficult, several authors have developed useful generalizations concerning intra-urban industrial location. For example, Allan R. Pred has defined what he feels are major classifications of industries and their locations within urban areas[7]:

1. *Ubiquitous industries concentrated near the central business district:*

> Ubiquitous industries, or those industries whose market areas are essentially co-extensive with the metropolis or a portion thereof, are usually highly concentrated near the perimeter of the central business district, especially if the basic raw materials are of a nonlocal inland origin. . . . [T]hese ubiquitous industries, perhaps more than any other group, still tend to have linked wholesaling functions; it is not surprising that they are nucleated in the traditional wholesaling district.[8] The concentration in these districts has been perpetuated as much by the friction of minimum distribution costs[9] as by the relative ease with which raw materials may be shunted about within the original railroad terminal area. Also, since food processing and wholesaling with stocks are classes of activity which require large amounts of space for the storage and handling of goods, abandoned warehouses and multi-story factory buildings near the central business district are apparently particularly attractive to large-scale food manufacturers wishing to enter the expanding local marketing.[10]

2. *Centrally located "communication economy" industries.* By "communication economy" industries, Pred means those industries in which face-

to-face contact among sellers and beween sellers and buyers is necessary. Pred offers, as examples of these kinds of industries, such personal services as provided by lawyers, advertising agencies, brokers, administrative offices, and industries such as the job-printing industry and New York's garment center.

3. *Local market industries with local raw material sources.* These industries comprise manufacturing plants which utilize locally produced raw materials for the production of goods to be sold within the urban area or its surrounding communities. Pred points out that this group includes industries that utilize raw materials which are byproducts or semi-finished products of other production firms within the city. These kinds of industries still seem to locate near the central business district, but peripheral locations are now being chosen.

4. *Nonlocal market industries of high-value products.* These firms manufacture items with a high cost per unit, for national or international markets. Because of their high cost, these products generally have a high value per unit weight and therefore location close to transportation and terminals is less important. This leads to a random intra-metropolitan distribution of firms.

5. *Noncentrally located "communication economy" industries.* According to Pred, this group:

> ... embraces those industries which imperatively cluster in noncentral locations in order to realize "communications." Such industries are generally highly scientific or technical. They are forced to nucleate in order to keep abreast of the latest innovations and forthcoming contracts; but unlike other industries oriented toward communication economies, they are virtually independent of the business and service activities associated with the central business district.[11,12]

Firms of this type are often involved in the aerospace industries, electronics, and "think tank" operations.

6. *Nonlocal market industries on the waterfront.* This classification is self-explanatory. Generally these firms are engaged in heavy industry, petroleum, refining, and other firms which are "oriented toward foreign, or nonlocal, waterborne raw materials, and thereby choose waterfront locations in an effort to avoid unnecessary transfer and trans-shipment costs."[13,14]

7. *Industries oriented toward national markets.* These are industries which have bulky finished products, and necessarily their locations are coincident with inter-urban transportation facilities.

THE CHANGING SPATIAL STRUCTURE OF INTRA-URBAN RETAIL ACTIVITIES[15]

Change in the locations, distributions, and intensity of all urban activities is continuous. Attempts to define processes related to this change are a necessity in sound geographic analysis. Elsewhere, in a study of commercial activities in Chicago, we have identified several aspects of urban change and their effect on the intra-urban spatial structure of commercial activities. Selections from that discussion follow.

Try as we may, growth and change cannot be discussed without reference to the simpler concept of equilibrium.[16] The equilibrium idea was introduced as relating to a state of balance between system (outlying commercial structure) and environment (demands for goods and services within the city), and between major components within both system and environment (the technological relations between numbers of types of establishments, numbers of establishments, and space demands and the number, sizes, trade areas, and locational patterns of business centers, ribbons, and specialized functional areas). Yet the point of balance is always shifting. There is a moving equilibrium. For each observed change, restoration of balance means that some compensating change in the opposite direction must take place. To maintain a state of equilibrium, then, the forces which are to be balanced must be of equal magnitude.

The models presented earlier described the equilibrium between system and environment at a point in time, the state of balance approximated between demands and supplies, *ca.* 1961. At this point in time a specific set of interrelationships within both system and environment also existed (technological characteristics of retailing, patterns of consumer travel behavior, and the like). If these internal aspects of system environment remain unchanged, then the models which have been presented can be used to account for compensatory changes in the system to offset changes in the environment.

Yet the internal arrangements of the system and environment, conditioned by technology, travel behavior, and the like, do not remain constant. Compensatory changes are thus initiated, not simply by the need to readjust to a given equilibrium position but to achieve new states of balance occasioned by technological and other shifts, in what was described earlier as "an incessant chase of a moving equilibrium."[17]

The situation can be likened to a child's seesaw. A balance is achieved if the weights on either end compensate each other. A shift in one of the weights must be counterbalanced by a shift in the other for balance to be maintained under any given location of the fulcrum and length of the plank. But the length of the plank is constantly being modified, as is the location of the fulcrum, demanding constant readjustments of the weights in the attempt to secure a balance. Short-run changes may be defined as those of the first kind: plank and fulcrum are constant, and a single state of balance exists that can be achieved by compensatory readjustments in weights. Long-run changes are those demanded by relocation of fulcrum and plank: they represent compensatory readjustments required to achieve the new state of balance.

Two periods in the development of Chicago's outlying business structure were identified. During the quarter-century from 1910 to 1935 the basic skeleton of ribbons and unplanned business centers emerged, and persisted thereafter in spite of the exigencies of excess capacity during the Depression years, and wartime shortages. At the end of the War, in 1945, an outlying business structure existed that represented a state of balance developed within the framework of the retailing technology and consumer shopping and travel behavior of the pre-Depression years. Moreover, the supply of retail facilities was adjusted to population and income patterns of a decade earlier. Short-run readjustments had been held in check during the period from 1935 to 1945 by the Depression, and then by war. Pent-up change of both long-run kinds existed. Population and income patterns had shifted and were shifting as peripheral development proceeded apace and drew off the city's middle-income groups to live automobile-oriented, suburban lives. Restrictive housing covenants were being lifted, permitting the spread of racial minorities, particularly the Negro, into the older, more modest, residential areas of the city.[18] In turn, the lower-income white families moved further out into the middle-income neighborhoods being vacated by the movement of higher-income groups to suburbia, in a familiar pattern of social change. Furthermore, long-run shifts were occuring in the technology of retailing and in consumer travel behavior. Reliance upon public transit was declining with more widespread use and ownership of the automobile. Automobile usage occasioned realignments of trade areas and interjected technological obsolescence into the older, unplanned centers, especially in the form of parking deficiencies. New forms of larger-scale business were emerging: the large supermarket, the super drug store, the laundromat, the drive-in. New concepts were being applied: the integrated planned shopping center[19] and the outlying medical center. Conditions were ripe for the postwar change that burst into the city.

Yet the change had to take place within the framework of existing retail developments. Additional demands in the peripheral areas of the city could be satisfied by new developments of centers and ribbons, adjusted to the newer modes of technology and retailing. But declining demands in the older, more central areas could not be compensated for by a counterbalancing reduction in capacity or by change in technology: the stores were there, with existing sizes and inadequate provision for parking. From this stems the first cause or manifestation of commercial blight: excessive capacity in the older parts of the city.

The assumption of a technological *status quo* is obviously questionable. Retailing is changing very rapidly—so rapidly, in fact, that many experts, such as R. L. Nelson of the Real Estate Research Corporation, argue that the entire commercial structure of American cities is obsolescent and needs drastic, dramatic redesign.[20]

An analysis by R. H. Holton, based on Census

of Business data for the period 1939 to 1958 in the United States, shows regional, size of center, and type of establishment trends.[21] Of interest are his arguments that:

1. The Census classification of commercial activities, based upon product sold, is imperfect because these activities are differentiated further by the services which the retailer adds to these goods and finances out of his gross margin.
2. The provision of these additional services depends upon the scale of establishment. If a retailer moves along his long-run cost function he changes the nature of his product, so that the larger-scale store is not just a larger store but a different one in the eyes of the customer. Hence, if the retailer is to expand his sales, he must do it not simply in terms of price reductions allowed by increasing scale, but, since the cost function is reversed J-shaped rather than U-shaped, also by adding extra, "non-price" inducements that foster product differentiation and attract more distant consumers. Such non-price inducements include advertising, breadth of selection, furnishings of the store, and servicing of customers' complaints.
3. But, as size of market increases, so does the number of atypical customers, to the point where new specialized functions can enter to satisfy these customers. Thus, for example, specialty shops appear to bite off a segment of a growing central business district (CBD) department-store market.

Examination of Census of Business data for 1939 to 1958 led Holton to conclude that the above arguments were verified in fact. He found:

1. Cost functions with the shape of a reversed-J.
2. Considerable increases in sales per establishment for forty classes of business in the period from 1939 to 1958, the mean increase being 111 per cent, and the median 80 per cent. The difference between mean and median is accounted for by very large increases in four categories: grocery stores (supermarkets); gasoline service stations; passenger car dealers; and department stores (whose sales increased by 200 per cent). It appears that retail trade is gravitating towards these uses: In 1939 they accounted for 50 per cent of in-store consumer goods retail sales; in 1954, 53 per cent; and in 1958, 57 per cent.
3. The fastest growing and wealthiest cities and regions of the United States have the largest sales per establishment, the largest growth in sales in convenience goods stores, but also more smaller specialty goods stores than poorer or less rapidly growing regions.[22]

Additional perspectives have been provided by J. E. Vance in a comprehensive overview of the forces affecting the commercial structure of American cities.[23] Vance listed the following influences:

1. Changing means of personal transportation, allowing more fluid circulation patterns to develop.
2. Changing purchasing power and tastes.
3. New types of housing, particularly the modern suburb, constituting very fertile ground for mass sales techniques centered in integrated shopping centers.
4. Imposition of land use planning through zoning, which appears to be reinforcing the trend towards integrated shopping facilities.
5. Changes in merchandizing, emphasizing increasing scale and mixing of lines, leading to fluid boundaries among establishment types and continual transformation of commercial districts.

These forces Vance saw as leading to increasing *commodity specialization* on the one hand (e.g., Steuben's glass shops) and increasing *locational specialization* on the other (i.e., fewer, larger supermarkets serving larger distributary areas than many smaller groceries, resulting in fewer, specialized supermarket locations rather than in more groceries diffused in larger numbers of locations). Furthermore, he argued that "as commodity specialization increases, so must locational specialization."[24] As Holton suggests, however, this statement can also be reversed, because the two are interdependent.[25]

Vance, who went on to apply his ideas in the San Francisco Bay Region, found that, in this example of an area of recent growth, highly developed, with integrated shopping facilities representing postwar technology, a locational equilibrium has been reached under the current conditions of residential distribution, transportation, and mass demand for goods. One of his conclusions is:

> [T]he CBD has become the mass seller to the inner part of the metropolis, the specialty seller to the entire city, and the office area for the region. In turn, the regional integrated center has become the mass seller to the individual suburb alone, with no other important function. And through this change it seems that there has been an adjustment to the urban dynamics of transportation and settlement which has restored locational equilibrium in commercial structure after two decades of instability and doubt.[26]

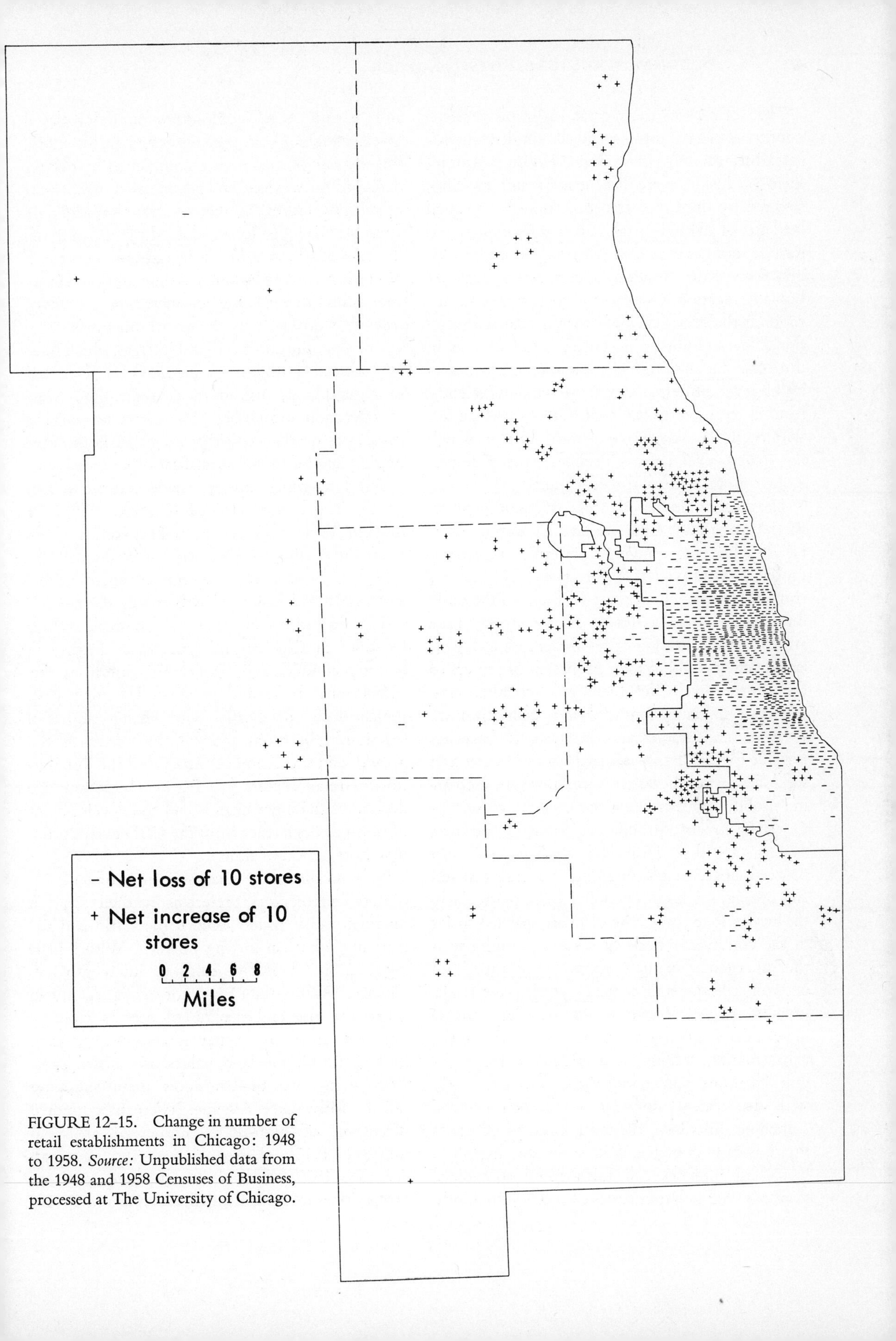

FIGURE 12–15. Change in number of retail establishments in Chicago: 1948 to 1958. *Source:* Unpublished data from the 1948 and 1958 Censuses of Business, processed at The University of Chicago.

The effects of transportation improvements upon commercial structure were singled out for special attention by Berry and Garrison.[27] Among their conclusions were that the increasing mobility fostered by improved transportation has enabled land uses of all kinds to take advantage of untapped scale economies previously held in check by transport costs, with a resulting specialization by function and location. One facet of locational specialization is the emergence of more specialized functional areas. Another is centralization of uses in the retail hierarchy, such that establishments in lower-level centers increase in scale sufficiently to need to move to the next higher-level center, with resulting progressive upward shifts in which the lowest-level centers decline, leaving fewer, larger, more widely spaced centers.

The theme of increasing scale of retailing repeats itself throughout these studies. Changing store types, changing buying patterns, increasing mobility, improved transportation facilities, and rising income levels all exert pressures in the same direction: to larger stores serving larger trade areas; to centralization of retail facilities in fewer, larger centers; and to the elimination of centers of the lowest level. Yet there are accompanying trends of specialization as well as centralization. As scale and trade areas increase, it becomes possible for smaller, specialized stores to enter and slice off a part of the larger stores' markets. Increasing mobility breaks down the need for clustering of establishment of different kinds in business centers, so that locational specialization can proceed apace (e.g., outlying medical districts and other specialized functional areas, particularly the automobile row). The ultimate reached so far in the combined effects of scale and mobility is the emergence of new forms of competition between ribbons and centers, which have traditionally played complementary roles. Large, independent discount houses are now entering the urban market, serving large trade areas from ribbon locations and competing very effectively with department stores in established centers.

Income shifts have the same kinds of effects as those attending increases in scale and mobility. Increasing incomes call forth more specialized stores, as well as larger stores of more basic kinds, and permit both commodity and locational specialization. As Holton suggested in his study, this increase of income is accompanied by greater demands for services, and is expressed on the part of existing stores, as they increase in scale, by attempts to engender product differentiation on the basis of services offered. In addition, new kinds of services emerge as tastes change and the ability and desire to consume an increasing range of services is provided by the greater incomes.

The opposite effect is found in areas which have experienced a decline in income. Localism has more emphasis, instead of centralization. Scale of operation diminishes; for stores of existing sizes, sales decline; and the degree of both commodity and locational specialization diminishes.

The long-run trends are made evident in Fig. 12–15. The central area of Chicago exhibits a marked decline in retail establishments. Concomitantly, the number of establishments in suburbia, located both within planned centers and unplanned centers, has been on the rise.

The evolutionary patterns of business center locations in Chicago are spelled out further in a study conducted by James W. Simmons (his conclusions are related in the following pages), which deals specifically with change in retail location.[28] Simmons showed the effects of the growth and succession of the city on the distribution of retail centers (see Fig. 12–16). Note the decline of the inner centers and the development of new centers farther from the CBD even during this short period of time.

Nelson called these successive rings of outlying centers "interceptors," referring to their position on main radial routes *between* the CBD and the growing suburban buying power.[29] With a little juggling, he finds five rings of interceptors in Chicago. While they may not occur exactly in rings, the rise and decline of centers rippling outwards from the center is an observed fact. In Fig. 12–17, the land values are shown since 1915 along one of Chicago's main shopping radials, Milwaukee Avenue. There is a gradual succession of high-rent commercial areas, as follows: 1915, Halsted Street and Chicago Avenue; 1925, Ashland Avenue and Division Street; 1935 to 1950, Kimball Avenue and Diver-

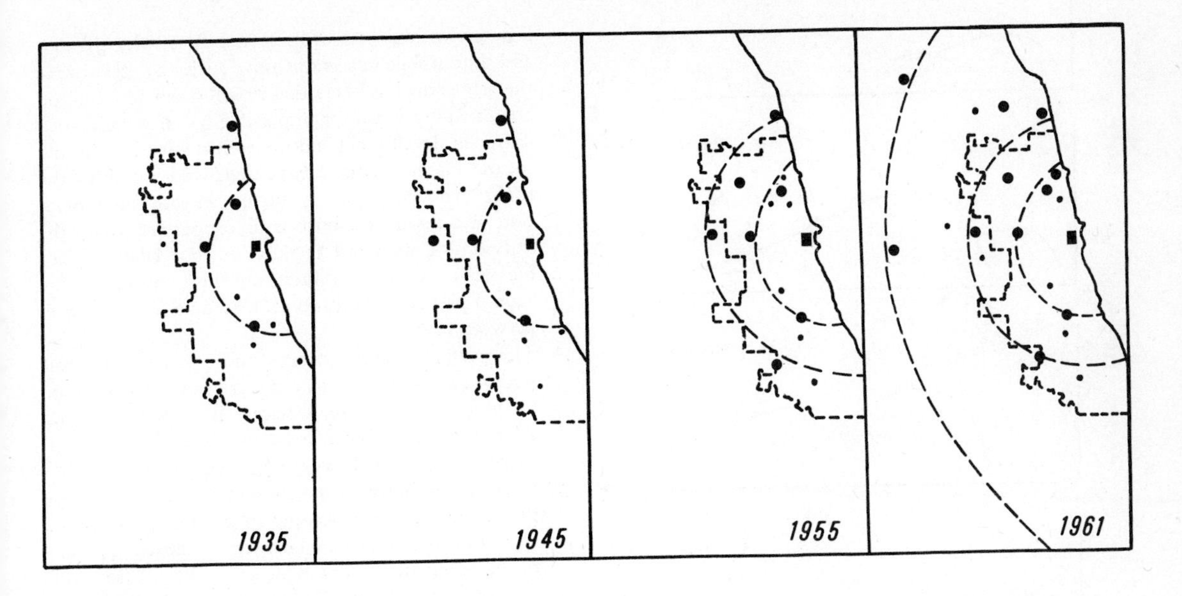

FIGURE 12–16. Major business centers outlying Chicago. *Source:* Figs. 12–16 through 12–18 are from James W. Simmons, *The Changing Pattern of Retail Location* (Chicago: Department of Geography Research Paper No. 92, 1964), pp. 141, 143, and 144.

sey Street; 1960, Irving Park Road and Cicero Avenue.

As each new center emerges, it siphons off shoppers before they can reach the next inward center. The inner centers then settle into a position of equilibrium, relying on their immediate trade area rather than on the outlying customers. As the zone of the wealthiest, high-consumption families gets farther and farther away from the CBD, it becomes easier for outlying centers to attract their trade, purely for convenience. This is a major reason for the relative decline of retail trade in the CBD.

At the same time, the decline of relative income in the equilibrium trade area due to the outward movement of high-income residents leads to a gradual decline in the outlying center. As Proudfoot noted, "Outlying centers rise and fall, become of major size or retrograde into the minor size class as the residential areas they serve improve or deteriorate."[30] The complete sequence of change as seen by Simmons may be illustrated by a series of hypothetical cross-sections of the trade area of a major outlying center (Fig. 12–18).

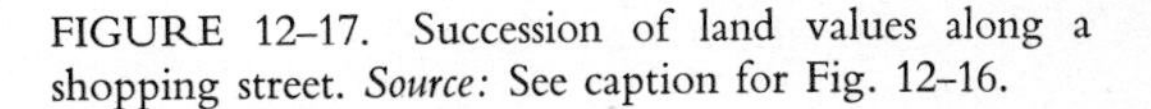

FIGURE 12–17. Succession of land values along a shopping street. *Source:* See caption for Fig. 12–16.

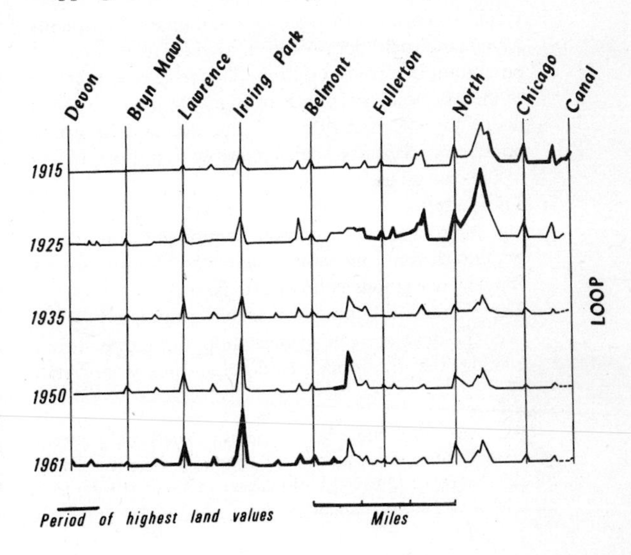

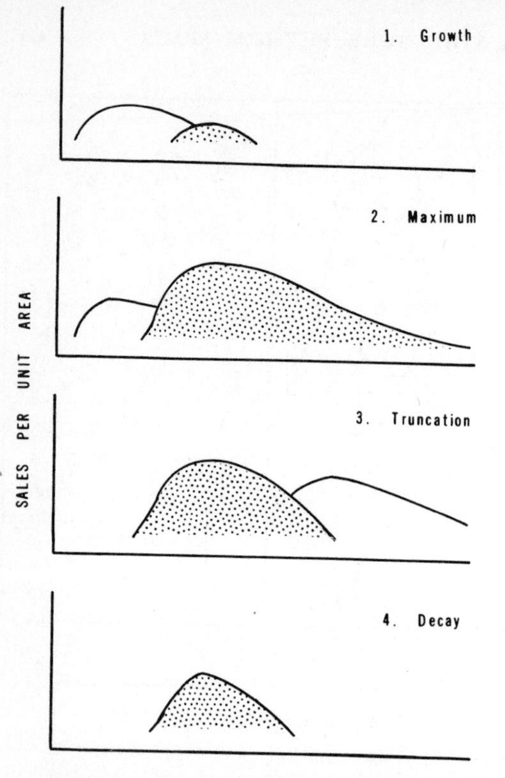

FIGURE 12–18. Life cycle of a business center. *Source:* See caption for Fig. 12–16.

*Conclusions about Changing Retail Locations**

The most compelling conclusions about changes in the retail pattern are as follows:

1. Rapid increases in the scale of retailing establishments have made them dependent on a wider trade area and on automobile transportation. The economic pressure to increase scale is more than balancing the customer's desire for specialization and the decrease in urban population densities which increase transport inputs to the customers.
2. The patterns of consumption have shifted towards higher-order goods in response to income and demographic changes, increasing the economic pressure on convenience goods conformations.
3. The planned shopping center has completely taken over the development of new shopping goods stores, making the traditional land-value theory of retail location within a center irrelevant. Needs for parking and automobile access are now such that the larger the center the less likely that it will occur in a builtup area, making it almost impossible for any unplanned center to develop beyond the community level in the future. Planned centers have destroyed a part of the traditional central place structure, in that the population of a town or suburb is no longer related to the position of its retail facilities in the central place hierarchy. Business centers are now avoiding the central parts of a built-up area, seeking the interstices between towns.[31]
4. The planned center defines more sharply its role within the hierarchy, since it carries only a minimum amount of low-order services. It is isolated from arterial uses, specialized areas, and office development, becoming specifically a *retailing* location.
5. Increased mobility by the consumer and the nature of the planned center is leading to greater specialization of retail conformations which serve a narrow segment of the population over a wide area. This specialization is occurring both by product, as in automobile, furniture, and medical districts, and by the socio-economic level of the consumer, as evidenced by the creation of fashion and discount centers. In the latter case the tendency is for whole centers to compete, rather than establishments within centers. In effect, all older retail concepts—specialization, competition, trade area, and so forth—are being applied to a different level, the center, rather than the establishment.
6. Small scattered stores in residential areas, neighborhood ribbons, and small walk-in centers are disappearing. Their decline is balanced by the expansion of urban arterial shopping and large independent markets and discount stores along major streets.
7. There is evidence that existing unplanned business centers are becoming more tightly defined, retreating at the peripheries but increasing in peak land value at the center. Functions are abandoning lower-order centers as they increase their threshold requirements.
8. There is a very close response by business centers, in terms of mix of business type, number of establishments, and extent of trade area, to the population and income characteristics of the district in which they are located. Changes in population and income are accelerating the decline of older retail patterns, especially the retreat of stores into business centers, leaving high vacancy rates in the older, continuous ribbon conformations.
9. Rings of centers mature and decline as the pattern of residential succession moves outward.

Much of the new retail pattern is a result of the increase in automobile ownership, producing the low-density suburbs themselves, leading to the success of the planned center with ample parking,

*Reprinted from James W. Simmons, *The Changing Pattern of Retail Location*, Department of Geography, Research Paper No. 92 (Chicago: University of Chicago, 1964), with the permission of the author and editor.

changing the spatial preference of the consumer and allowing the development of the overlapping hierarchies, enlarging the trade areas of stores to bring about economies of scale, and replacing the walk-in neighborhood ribbons by the suburban drive-in ribbons. In 1929, Rolph[32] could say that the size and concentration of stores could be traced to the public transportation structure, and Proudfoot,[33] stressed the importance of streetcar and "El" routes in determining the development business centers, but in 1963 it is the automobile which reigns, producing a significant difference in retail location requirements. A high degree of mobility has been attained by suburban dwellers of all income groups, which is more than overcoming the lower density in these areas (suburban densities range from 2,000 per square mile to 10,000, compared with urban densities of up to 80,000 per square mile) with the net result corresponding to the effect of increased density as predicted by Berry, "the higher the density of an area the greater scale of operation of any function, whether increased scale is expressed as: (1) increased size of establishment; (2) increased number of establishments; or (3) increased specialization of establishments within any particular functional type."[34]

The most important innovation has been the planned centers which both simplify and complicate the structure. The simplification comes from the rationalization of retail development as new projects are tailored to serve their trade area and located to do this most efficiently. As the residential areas are now designed by community units rather than single dwellings, shopping facilities are added by center instead of establishment.

CHANGES IN THE INTRA-URBAN LOCATION OF INDUSTRY

The decentralization of industry is also evident in major metropolitan centers, particularly those which experienced high growth rates in the nineteenth century. Moses and Williamson have analyzed industrial decentralization trends both empirically and theoretically.

*Bases of Decentralization**

The theoretical basis for the empirical research is as follows.

The city is divided into two areas: the core, where all economic activity initially takes place; and the satellite or residential zone surrounding it, where a known number of households are located. The satellite area is assumed to be a transport plane and all households are assumed to be identical in terms of tastes—they have identical utility functions—and income earned at the core.[35] An equilibrium distribution of households requires that each is maximizing utility subject to constraints on income and time, the entire satellite ring is settled, and no household can improve its level of satisfaction by changing location, meaning that all households are equally well off.

It is the price of land which must vary so that these conditions are met, since—as in the usual analysis of urban rent—incomes, transport costs, and the price of goods are fixed and known throughout the urban area. The result is a rent gradient—a function indicating the variation in the price of land as distance from the core varies. Since net income falls and the cost of goods rises as distance from the core increases, it can be shown that the rent gradient must decline with distance. Otherwise the equilibrium condition that utility is a locational constant would not be met.

Once the equilibrium distribution of households and the resulting rent gradient are established, a price gradient for labor—the wage-rate gradient—can be determined. It measures the wage a firm has to pay at various locations in the satellite area to switch a given number of workers from core employment to employment at those sites, other things given, including the rent gradient.[36] The form of the wage-rate gradient is not certain for all numbers of workers. It can, however, be shown to slope downward if a firm's employment were small relative to population in the

*Reprinted from Leon Moses and Harold W. Williamson, "Location of Economic Activities in Cities," *The American Economic Review*, LVII (1967), 211–22, with the permission of the authors and editor. Parts have been summarized by the present editors.

vicinity of a potential site. The remaining factor, price gradient, that for liquid capital, is invariant with respect to distance from the core. Capital is assumed to be perfectly mobile within an urban area so that the interest rate is a locational constant.

The above analysis leads to the conclusion that factor costs tended to be lower in the satellite area. If this is the case, it is evident that other conditions must account for the growth of the core-dominated city. The agglomerative economies associated with proximity to competitive and complementary firms and to service industries are usually advanced to explain concentration of economic activity in the core. The authors acknowledge their importance but wish to focus attention on the structure of transport costs in the nineteenth century, and the influence this structure had on the form of large cities. It is a thesis of this research that in the nineteenth century the cost of moving goods within cities was: (1) high relative to the cost of moving people within cities; and (2) high relative to the cost of moving goods between cities. Location in the satellite area involved moving away from the central goods-handling facilities of the city. In general, the increased costs of transporting inputs from and outputs to the core (for shipment to other areas) outweighed the savings from the lower factor prices associated with location in the satellite area.[37]

This in fact tended to be the situation during the period when the core-dominated cities grew. Firms received from and shipped to other regions a significant proportion of their inputs and outputs. The economies of scale in rail transport—the main mode for interregional goods movement—were such that the receiving and sending of such shipments were concentrated at one or, at most, a few large, centrally located freight terminals. Within cities, the movement of people was relatively efficient, being carried out by modes which were closely related to the railroad: trolleys and street railways. Intra-city movement of goods, however, took place by an inefficient mode, the horse and wagon. The cost of moving goods was, therefore, high relative to the cost of moving people. This relative cost relationship played a crucial role in the emergence of the core-dominated city. The lower transport costs associated with location in the core exceeded the reduction in cost possible from lower wages and rents at sites in the satellite area. A prerequisite for decentralization was the breaking of the transport tie to the core.

Only after technological changes occurred in transportation was the attraction of a noncore location strongly felt. The major change was the introduction of the truck, which reduced the cost of moving goods within cities. Its effect on the spatial structure of cities can, roughly, be divided into two phases. During the first, the motor truck was introduced and became the dominant form of intra-urban carriage, but inter-urban carriage was still done by railroads. In this period—the first two decades of this century—firms could leave the core but were still tied to it for shipments to and from other regions. This tie was weakened during the second phase, when improvements in the truck and in the interregional highway system meant this mode could be used for long-distance transport. The full impact of this change was probably not felt until the revival of a strong peacetime economy after World War II. The attractiveness of the satellite area in this period was increased by the automobile, which allowed firms to draw labor from a broad area.[38]

In summary, the theoretical analysis emphasized the effect of changes in transportation cost structure. It implied that decentralization should have begun, roughly, during the first two decades of this century when the motor truck was first introduced, though this period is not usually thought to be one of suburbanization. The first part of the empirical analysis examines this period. The second part provides a more extensive examination of the spatial rearrangement of firms during the post-World War II period—the period during which the impact of interregional transportation was felt.

Empirical evidence: the Chicago case. Empirical analysis of the movement of industrial firms in Chicago between 1908 and 1920 confirmed the theoretical analysis. While firms moved a short distance on average, the direction of movement was away from the core. The average distance from the core for firms which moved was 59 per cent greater in 1920 than it had been in 1908, having increased from .92 miles to 1.46 miles. In addition, the average origin (1908) distance for firms which moved was less than the distance for nonmoving firms. This agrees with the implication that the introduction of the motor truck had a greater impact on core area firms than those already located somewhat outside the core.

A second empirical analysis of the movement of industrial firms between 1950 and mid-1964 was conducted, utilizing a sample of 2,000 firms in Chicago. Preliminary investigation revealed that the distribution of origins fell off sharply as distance from the core of the city increased. One interpretation of this result is that inner portions of the city have become undesirable as locations, so that firms located there have a higher propensity to move. This conclusion is somewhat misleading in that it ignores the fact that zones near the core also are likely to have larger numbers of firms in them. The critical issue, therefore, is not whether number of origins declines with distance but whether the percentage of origins behaves in this manner.

To see whether number of firms or distance was more highly correlated with number of origins, regressions were run with origins in each zone as the dependent variable and these two factors as the independent variables.[39] The geographic divisions used were postal zones within the city of Chicago and suburbs outside it. When number of origins was regressed on each variable alone, number of firms provided a much higher explanatory power (coefficient of determination between .51 and .90) than did distance (coefficient of determination between .19 and .43). When the regression was run for both independent variables, number of firms had the higher explanatory power. The additional explanation provided by the distance variable was not significant in over half the cases. Thus, number of origins is highly correlated with number of firms in a zone. The coefficient for number of firms was from ten to twenty times as large as its standard error, i.e., the t ratio was between 10 and 20. Economic dispersal has not therefore occurred because firms that are closer to the core have a higher propensity to move. Instead, this propensity is fairly constant over the entire metropolitan area. Since this percentage of firms being "set loose" is relatively constant, the shifting pattern of industrial location must result from the spatial pattern of destinations—the percentage of firms which "set down" in each zone. Before turning to the analysis of this pattern of destinations, it is necessary to determine whether these firms are truly set loose from their origin site.

The preceding empirical work emphasized net change in distance from the core, i.e., distance from the core of a firm's destination minus its origin distance. Net change is a surrogate for the variation in land and labor costs and for the expense of maintaining linkages with the core which arose due to the move. A different measure of the connection between origin and destination is the distance actually moved by the firm. It reflects the costs associated with the linkage between these two sites. As distance moved increases, established ties with suppliers of raw materials and services, labor supply, and customers may be attenuated. Costs may then have to be incurred to establish new ties. If so, firms would not be set loose when they decided to move. Instead, there would be factors unrelated to the attributes of potential destination areas which influence whether location there is optimal. The distance which a potential destination is from the firm's origin appears to be a good proxy for these factors.

The distribution of firms falls off sharply when arranged by distance moved. The median distance moved for the four categories of firms[40] ranged from 4 to 6 miles. The relationship resembled that of a gravity model in which the number of interconnections between zones diminishes as the distance between them increases. A regression fitted to the data for all firms in the sample yielded a significant negative relationship between number of firms and distance moved, particularly when the latter was expressed logarithmically. The coefficient of determination was at least .50 in all cases and between .81 and .95 for the logarithmic form. Further insight into distance moved was obtained by examining various characteristics of the firms.

Size of the firm influenced distance moved.[41] Smaller firms tended to move shorter distances than larger ones. This would seem to support the conclusion that distance moved is generally short because it reflects the cost of moving. Larger firms can move longer distances, perhaps because they are more independent of suppliers or buyers at a particular location.[42] Size should therefore be taken into account when analyzing location patterns, since smaller firms may not be free to choose among all possible destination areas. Instead, they will be limited to those within a relatively short distance of their origin location.

Two conditions which did not seem to affect the pattern of distance moved were the origin distance of the firm and its industrial category. A regression with distance moved as a function of origin distance was run and the coefficient of determination was never as high as 6 per cent. The search for an industry effect had to be conducted in terms of the two-digit Standard Industrial Classification in order to have enough observations. At this level of aggregation it was found that the distribution of firms by distance moved for each industry was never significantly different (at the .05 level) from the distribution of all firms.

As part of the final analysis, a model was formulated to define the relationship between the number of destinations for Chicago firms and attributes of the destination areas. The basic model has the following form:

$$D = a + b_1L + b_2W + b_3T + b_4H + b_5V + b_6M + b_7C + u \qquad (1)$$

Where: D is the number of destinations per unit area; a is a constant; L is the distance of the zone from the origin area; W is the population density of the destination zone; T is the percentage of land in the destination zone used for transportation other than highway (a measure of accessibility to nonhighway transport); H is a nominal variable indicating whether or not a freeway or tollway is in the destination zone or one next to it; V is the percentage of vacant land in the zone which is zoned for manufacturing or commercial purposes; M is the percentage of land currently in manufacturing use in the destination zone; C is a nominal variable indicating whether or not this zone is within the city of Chicago (given a value of 1 if the zone is outside the city, 0 if not), and u is the error term.

This model was tested using 1950 to 1959 data. Results of this test can be seen in Table 12–3. The first two rows indicate the values when the equation was run for expansions at new locations and relocations, respectively, for the entire area (582 zones). As indicated by the coefficient of determination (r^2), this equation accounted for between one-fifth (.2152) and one-fourth (.2471) of the variation in the dependent variable. The only significant variables were distance, L, and percentage of manufacturing land, M. Before discussing them, it should be noted that all but one of the remaining coefficients have the expected sign. Other things equal, an increase in population or transportation land, the existence of a limited access highway near the zone or a change from the city to the suburbs will be associated with an increase in destinations. Only vacant land has an impact (negative) which is different from that expected. This may be because the inaccuracy of zoning definitions makes this variable a poor indicator of the availability of destination sites. The significant, positive coefficient for manufacturing land may indicate that this variable, instead, provides a measure of such availability. The significant, negative sign for the distance coefficient seems to indicate that it is a measure of the attraction of the core rather than a proxy for the rent gradient.

Though these explanations are logical, another more likely one for the signs of the latter two coefficients is suggested by the results of the distance moved analysis. Since most firms move short distances and most origins are near the core, distance and manufacturing land may merely be measuring the proximity of a zone to firms which are moving. Thus, increases in distance reduce the number of destinations since the zone is farther from firms which are moving. Similarly, as the percentage of manufacturing land rises, destinations rise, since more firms are located in that square. The ability of the equation to measure the influence of all the locational factors examined may be improved by introducing a variable for proximity. Two approaches suggest themselves. The first is to divide firms by size group and exam-

TABLE 12-3

Regression Results for Equation 1

Type of Analysis	r^2	Intercept: a	*Values of the Coefficients for the Variables*†						
			L	W	T	H	V	M	C
1. Expansion at new, total area	.2471	1.778	−.0956	.0177	.7671	.2260	−.6144	−6.8012	.1490
			(.0174)**	(.0116)	(.9306)	(.1607)	(.8615)	(1.2145)**	(.2458)
2. Relocation total area	.2152	1.501	−.0829	.0148	.3412	.2610	−.4791	4.5580	.1097
			(.0153)**	(.0102)	(.8187)	(.1413)	(.7579)	(1.0684)**	(.2612)
3. Expansion at new, north	.6600	.481	−.0354	.0362	−4.3679	.3317	−4.6234	42.9550	.2442
			(.0259)	(.0190)	(2.7080)	(.2662)	(4.3808)	(3.5370)**	(.4112)
4. Expansion at new, west	.4346	2.091	−.0349	−.0066	1.0869	.1451	−.4858	12.1229	−1.4064
			(.0292)	(.0241)	(1.1848)	(.2581)	(2.2110)	(2.3806)	(.5055)**
5. Expansion at new, south	.2801	1.303	−.0487	−.0064	3.1634	−.5261	−.0313	1.3638	−.0789
			(.0168)**	(.0103)	(.8577)**	(.1377)**	(.5625)	(.8369)	(.1994)
6. Relocation north	.5536	.121	−.0162	.0434	−1.7338	.1845	2.4800	24.9222	.1639
			(.0220)	(.0161)	(2.2997)	(.2261)	(3.7202)	(3.0032)**	(.3492)
7. Relocation west	.4662	1.482	−.0292	−.0052	.8782	.1422	−.5638	10.6777	−.9129
			(.0220)	(.0181)	(.8901)	(.1939)	(1.6613)	(1.7885)**	(.3797)**
8. Relocation south	.2521	.830	−.0358	.0028	2.2491	−.2696	.0988	.9438	−.0596
			(.0132)**	(.0081)	(.6727)**	(.1080)*	(.4412)	(.6564)	(.1564)

The number in parentheses below the value of the coefficient is the standard error. If the coefficient is significantly different from zero at the .05 level of significance, it is indicated by.
**Coefficient of Standard Error is significantly different from zero at the .01 level of significance.
†The variables are defined in the text.

ine the equation for each separately. A second is to introduce a measure of proximity of each zone to firms. This measure could be similar to the one suggested above for availibility of labor.

The importance of this and other improvements in the analysis can be seen from the results in the rest of Table 12–3. Equation (1) was fitted to data for each of three sectors into which the city was divided. This division was made because examination of the data indicated noticeable differences in these sectors, particularly with respect to manufacturing land. Though this variable had a significantly positive coefficient in all but one of the regressions, the sector with the highest percentage of such land, the south, had the lowest density of destinations. The reverse was true for the north.[43] The result of the division into sectors is a noticeable improvement in the explanatory power of the regression, particularly for the north and west sectors.[44] This improvement in the statistical results is not conceptually significant in itself. It indicates that there are critical variables that have not been included. It is hoped that with their identification it will be possible to obtain results for the entire study area that are as good as those that have been obtained for the somewhat arbitrary geographic subdivisions of it. One of these variables is suggested by the results of the sector analysis. As has been noted, zones in the southern sectors tend to have a higher percentage of manufacturing land than zones in the remainder of the study area. Manufacturing land always has a significant, positive effect on destinations yet the southern sectors attract the fewest number of firms. The explanation may be that zones in these sectors also tend to have a higher proportion of nonwhite population.

In summary, Moses and Williamson articulated a linear model of change in the location of industrial firms within metropolitan areas. Empirical analysis corroborated their hypotheses concerning transportation innovations and decentralization for the period 1908 to 1920. The authors concluded that new firms, rather than firms relocating from the central city, are principally responsible for the increase in the number of new firms locating in suburban areas during the 1950 to mid-1964 period. (Figures 12–19, 12–20, and 12–21 show the locations chosen by manufacturing

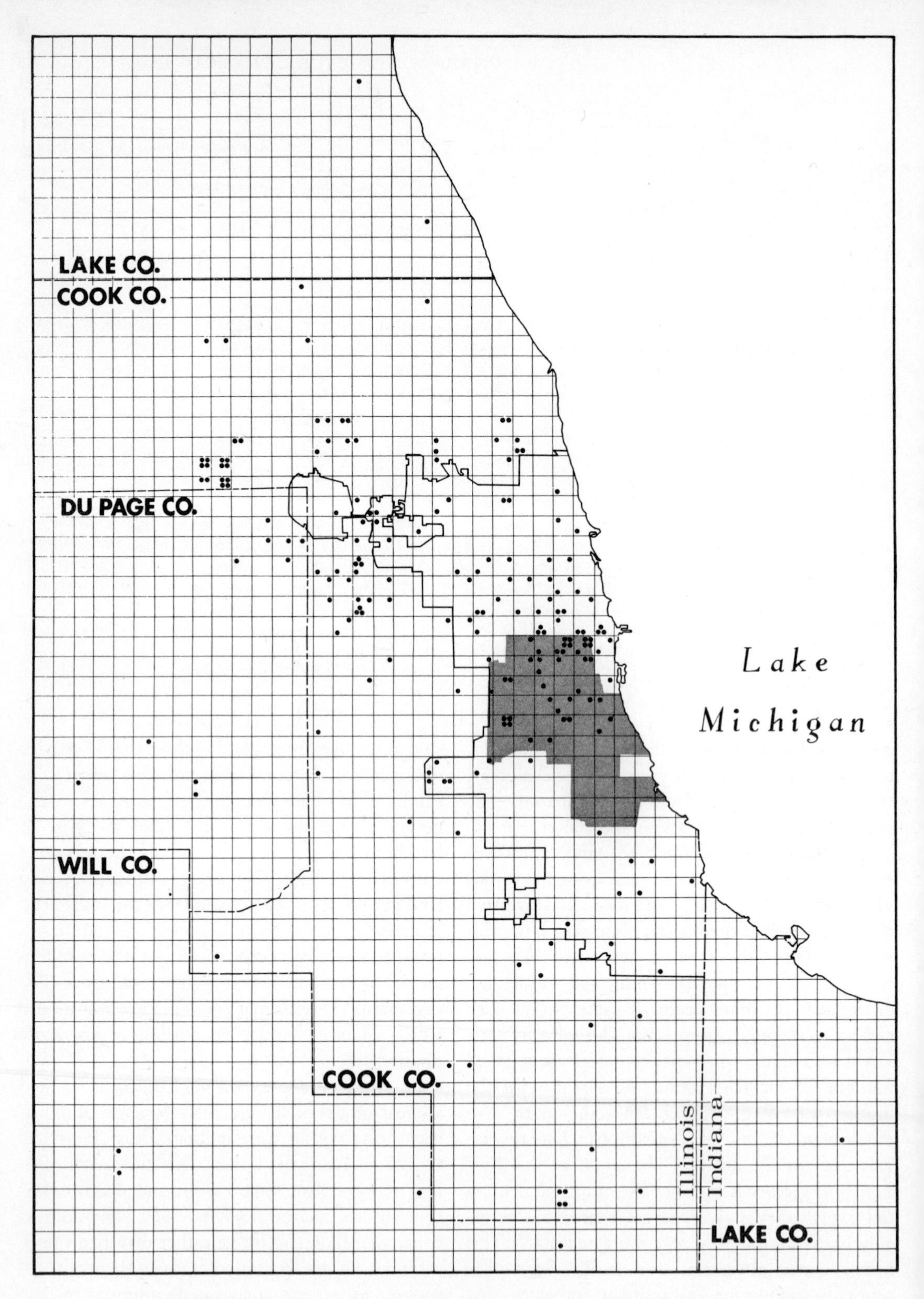

FIGURE 12–19. New industrial establishments locating within the Chicago area: 1950 to July 1, 1964. *Source:* Figs. 12–19 through 12–21 are based on original data provided by the City of Chicago.

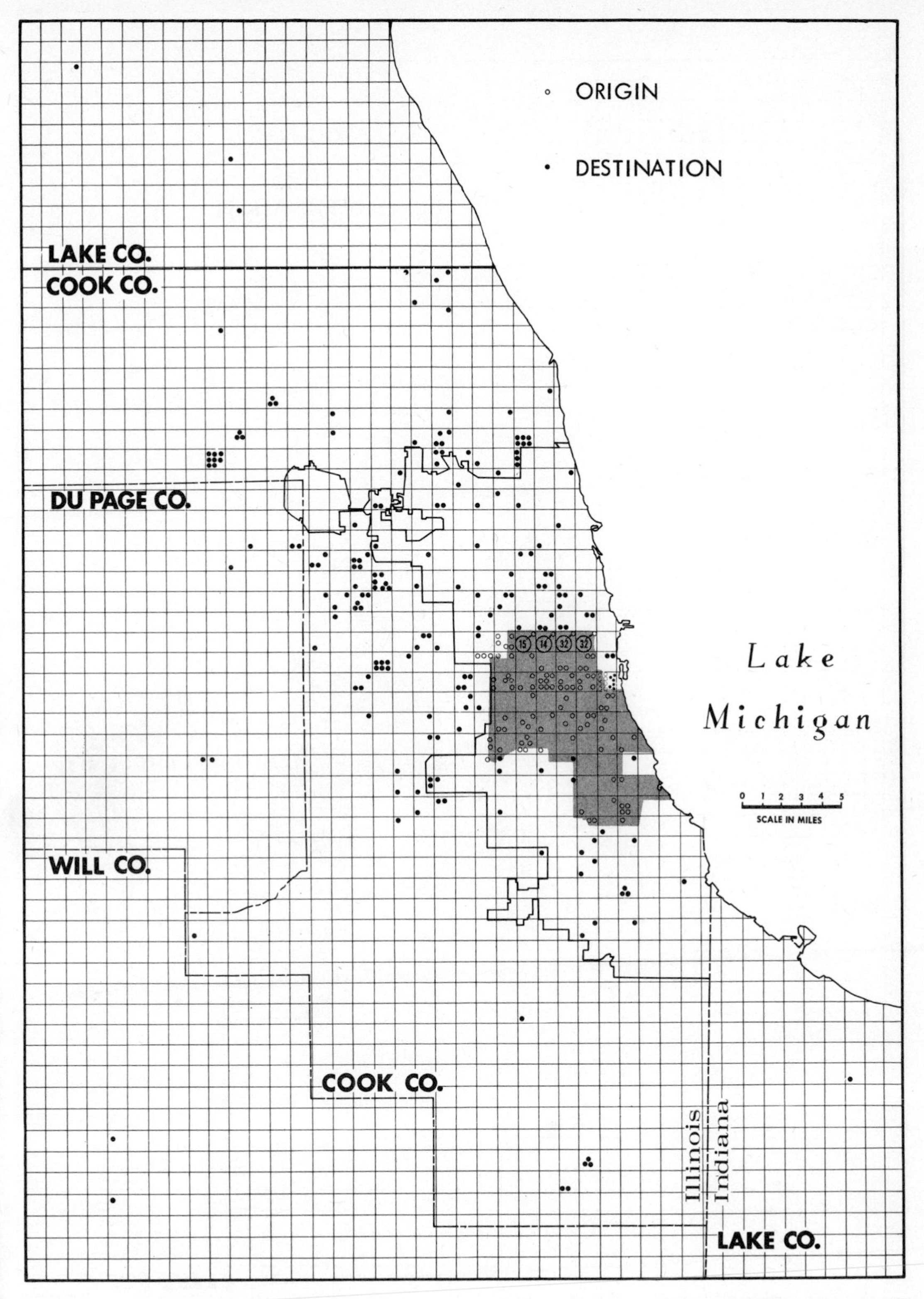

FIGURE 12–20. Expansion at new location by industrial establishments: 1950 to July 1, 1964. *Source:* See caption for Fig. 12–19.

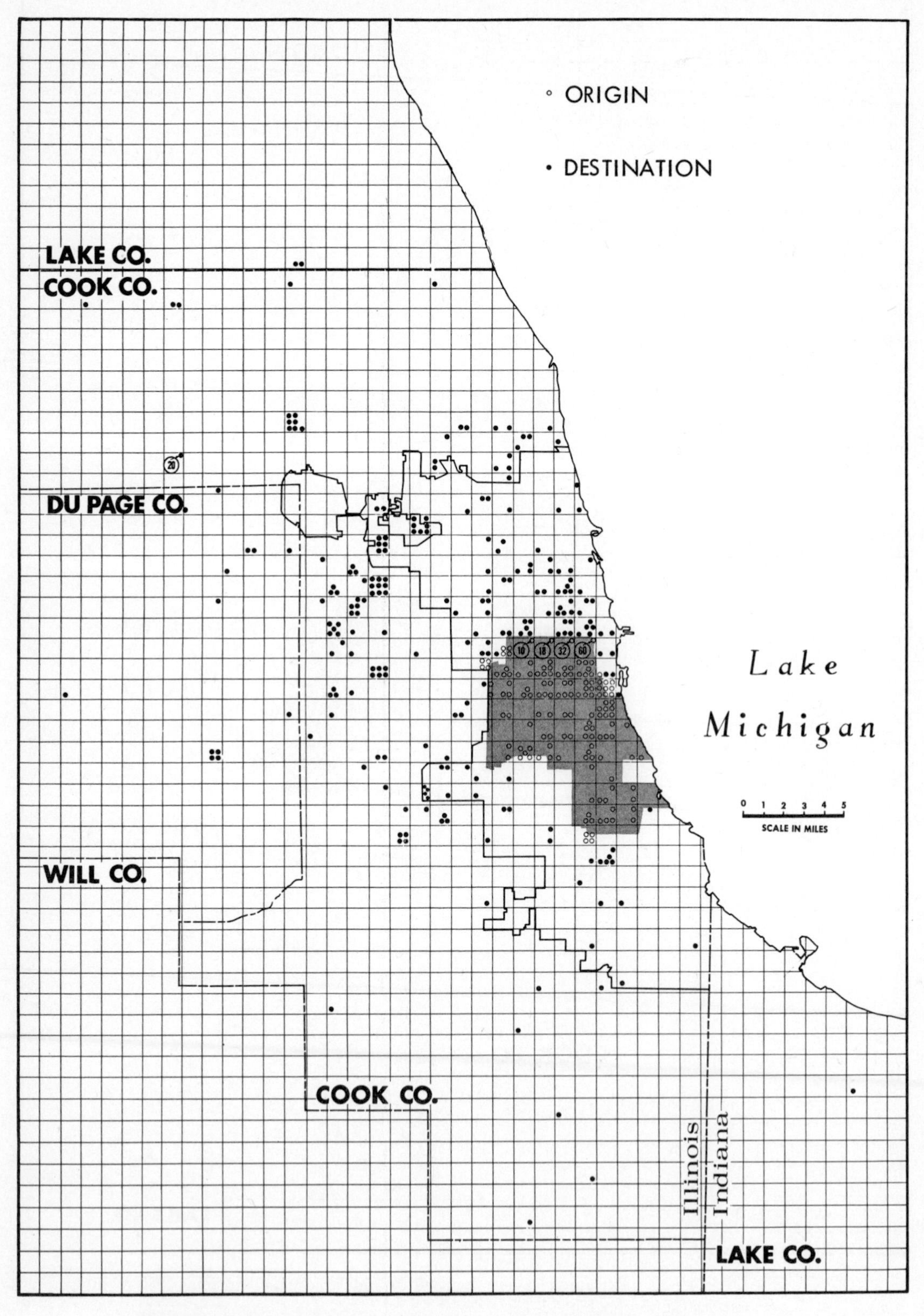

FIGURE 12–21. Relocation by industrial establishments: 1950 to July 1, 1964. *Source:* See caption for Fig. 12–19.

firms which were being newly established in the Chicago area, beginning branch operations outside the city boundaries, and relocating outside the city boundaries respectively.)

*PRIVATE REDEVELOPMENT AS A SOURCE OF URBAN CHANGE**

Private redevelopment is one means of effecting reutilization of urban land, through demolition of existing structures and new construction, or rehabilitation leading to better quality structures. The forces which lead to this kind of change and the economics of the process now need to be outlined, with special focus on processes and decisions affecting the individual property.

Through time, buildings have a tendency to *depreciate* in value, while *land tends to appreciate*.[45] With age and abuse, the value of any building, measured by net returns on investment or net capitalized income, declines steadily following an initial period of increase and equilibrium (Fig. 12–22). In contrast, urban land values tend to increase as the city grows and land use zones expand into areas of less intensive use. Although wide variations do occur in land values over time, and recent events suggest that in many areas of the city absolute declines have been recorded,[46] the theoretical argument for an increasing tendency still holds.[47] For any individual structure, whether the "rent" for land increases or remains relatively constant, as a proportion of total property value, it normally increases. As these two costs comprise the basic costs of redevelopment, the relative importance of each is critical to an understanding of the factors influencing such change.

In addition to the increasing divergence between land and building values for a particalar property, there is the important question of *rent differentials and gradients* and the relative rates of change in different properties and between areas. Earlier[48] the relationship between accessibility and transport costs, and the spatial patterns of new construction and "position" rent were discussed and evaluated. This discussion can now be related to the

*Reprinted from Larry S. Bourne, *Private Redevelopment of the Central City* (Chicago: University of Chicago, Department of Geography, Research Paper No. 112, 1967), with the permission of the author and editor.

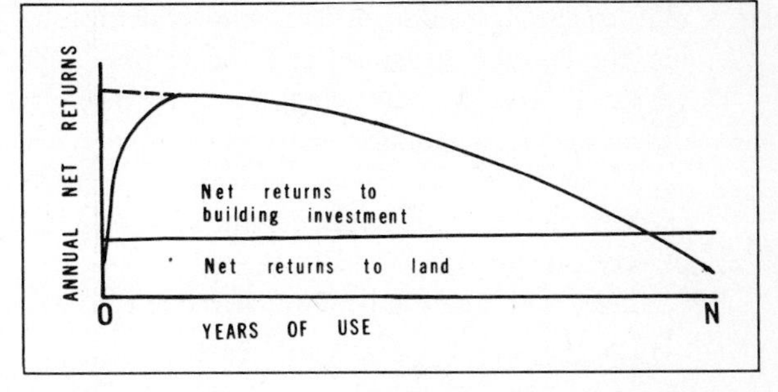

FIGURE 12–22. Expected net returns from investment in a new building. *Source:* Larry S. Bourne, *Private Redevelopment of the Central City* (Chicago: Department of Geography Research Paper No. 112, 1967), p. 27.

potential for redevelopment at any location through relative variations in rent through time. The effects of increasing land values on the feasibility of redevelopment depends on the relative increases in value of properties in competitive positions. An increase in the value of one parcel of land will, of course, decrease its attractiveness relative to all others.

Returning again to the individual property, the importance of the value of the land, compared to the building, in influencing the feasibility of redevelopment will tend to increase over time. However, this will only be a major consideration if all other properties undergo similar changes such that there is no shift in locational advantages. The effect of a rise in the cost of land on an investment in redevelopment will be to encourage the developer to substitute capital for land and thus to increase the intensity of use.

Economics of redevelopment and replacement. In economic theory, the replacement of structures can be defined by a set of cost-profit relationships. It can be assumed that property is held primarily for profit, and as Ratcliff comments, the individual owner is aware of "the possibility that some new use for his land may yield a greater return than the continued operation of the present use."[49]

The profitability of redevelopment is a function of the cost of redevelopment relative to the value of the property after redevelopment. The rationale for redevelopment depends on the individual owner's estimate of the anticipated income from a new structure, compared to the cost of that structure, the costs of removing or demolishing the existing structure, and the income that would be lost by removing that structure. In other words, demolition and replacement will occur, *ceteris paribus*, when anticipated income exceeds the cost of replacement and original investment lost.[50]

These conditions can be summarized as follows:

Let: V_1 = the market value of the existing property before redevelopment, consisting of S_1 the value of the site (land) and B_1 the value of the building

V_2 = the market value of the existing property after redevelopment representing the most profitable use of that site. This also may be broken down into S_2 the value of site, and B_2 the value of building

If the existing building represents the "highest and best" use then, of course:

$$V_2 = V_1 \tag{2}$$

Moreover: let C_2 = the cost of constructing this theoretically optimum building B_2

D_1 = the cost of demolishing the original building on the site B_1

Then:

$$S_1 = V_1 - B_1 \tag{3}$$

But if the building was fully depreciated, i.e., $B_1 = 0$, then:

$$S_1 = V_1 \tag{4}$$

If V_2 exceeds V_1 by more than the cost of demolition and new construction ($D_1 + C_2$), it will pay to demolish the building. In other words, redevelopment will be economically feasible for a *given property* when V_2 is greater than $V_1 + C_2 + D_1$. The most efficient course of action, in terms of the amount, type, and location of redevelopment, will be that which maximized the difference between the two, or that which maximizes profits. All other things being equal,[51] replacement will occur at the point of the cost-profit relationship which just compensates the owner for removal of the building. Generally, in a competitive market, V_2 will equal $S_1 + C_2$ if the developers profits are included in C_2.[52]

In many cases, however, the analysis is complicated by the differential reaction of individual owners to the possibility of greater profits from a given site. An owner may not redevelop his property even though it offers higher net returns in the long run, because of the prospect of higher development costs.[53] Others may hesitate to write off the current market value of their existing properties, and some may lack the financial means to do so. This is particularly true of small operators, because of the high costs of capital formation and the necessity of long-term financial commitments. Nevertheless, even though the operator may lose income, at least potential income, if he refuses to redevelop his property, his cost-profit situation allows him to continue on a profitable basis through the remaining economic life of the structure. These conditions slow urban change by adding to the difficulty of property conversion, and emphasize the conflict between fixed real estate resources and constantly shifting demands for space and locations.

Thus, within an economic context, replacement can be explained as a function of the balance between the market value of the present property and the market value less the cost of the new use for that property. The critical difference between the economics of land use succession in urban areas, compared to undeveloped rural or suburban areas, is the complex problem of increased costs resulting from the inherent value of the land and existing improvements[54] and the costs of demolition.

Empirical analysis of Toronto. An empirical analysis of the private redevelopment process in Toronto leads to the conclusion that the redevelopment process has produced a significant contribution to the structural inventory and spatial arrangement of land uses in the City of Toronto. Areas equivalent to 11 and 12 per cent of the land and building area of the city, respectively, underwent redevelopment during the period 1952 to 1962 inclusive. New construction and major structural modifications added some 46,000,000 square feet of floor space on over 8,300 properties, affecting over 1,400 acres of land. Among the more important features of this activity which substantiate the preceding generalizations are the following:

1. The *rate* of redevelopment (within unchanging city boundaries) has been 1 per cent a year in both land and floor area. Over time, the rate of change in the building stock has been increasing while that in land area has been declining.
2. Redevelopment is *concentrated* in those uses at opposite ends of the density scale, with apartments and offices the most intensive, and parking and commercial automobile among the least intensive. Over time, the differential in intensity between the two groups has been increasing.
3. Redevelopment is highly *specialized*. Apartment and office construction accounted for nearly 75 per cent of all floor area added to the building stock and the proportion increased sharply within the 1952 to 1962 period.
4. At the other end of the scale in terms of land area, commercial automobile and parking uses expanded most rapidly, accounting for nearly 25 per cent of the land area undergoing change.
5. Redevelopment reflects marked *shifts in land area requirements*. New industrial and warehousing construction in the city required more land than existing industries, while residential construction, 90 per cent of which is apartments, required considerably less land.
6. The increasing *scale* of land area required by new construction is also evident in that there were almost 50 per cent fewer properties in the redeveloped areas in 1962 than at the beginning of the study period.
7. Redevelopment is highly *selective* in the types of properties affected. About one-third of all new construction in the city took place on vacant land, and an equal proportion on properties occupied by single-family residential uses.
8. Yet, within the redeveloped areas, aggregating over 8,300 properties, all land uses expanded except low-density residential, with other low-density uses expanding largely at the expense of *vacant land*.
9. Each of the major types of redevelopment exhibits a *distinct spatial pattern* largely independent of all other patterns. When the change statistics for all types of redevelopment were factor analyzed, five basic patterns emerged, representing the major land use groups, and accounting for almost 62 per cent of the aggregate spatial variability in redevelopment.
10. Redevelopment is highly *localized*. The central core and northern sector of the city received about 35 per cent of all floor area added and 76 per cent of all office construction.
11. Specifically, the spatial pattern of apartment and office redevelopment is clearly *sectorial* rather than concentric. Apartments appear as *clusters* in the three higher income sectors of the city and offices are concentrated in the central area and in a northward extension following the subway through the highest income sector.
12. In the aggregate, the rate of redevelopment, measured as the proportion of total land area, drops sharply from a peak in the commercial core, reaches its lowest point in a concentric zone about 3 to 4 miles from downtown (the traditional "grey" area of stagnant conditions), and from this zone rises outward to the city boundary.

PUBLIC INVESTMENT AND URBAN CHANGE

Private redevelopment has focused on the central business district, placing less emphasis on areas located at some distance from the core. Obviously, there is less need for redevelopment in newer areas of the city that are normally found on the periphery. However, critical areas of need, the ghetto for example, are less likely to be chosen for private redevelopment because of the high financial risks. Since these risks are prohibitively large, public investment, usually in the form of urban renewal, has been the primary impetus for change in these areas. A second class of public improvements (investments in transportation, cultural facilities, and so forth) also has an impact on the spatial structure of urban areas, of course, but for purposes of this discussion we will focus on the renewal case. The substantial physical extent of public involvement in Chicago is indicated in Fig. 12–23.

*The Necessity for Urban Renewal**

The need for renewal is related primarily to the unsatisfactory state of the physical assets of the city. The condition and state of urban assets are the result of the functioning of the real estate

*Reprinted from Stanislaw Czamanski, "Effects of Public Investments on Urban Land Values," *Journal of the American Institute of Planners*, XXXII, No. 4 (July, 1966), 204–17, with the permission of the author and editor.

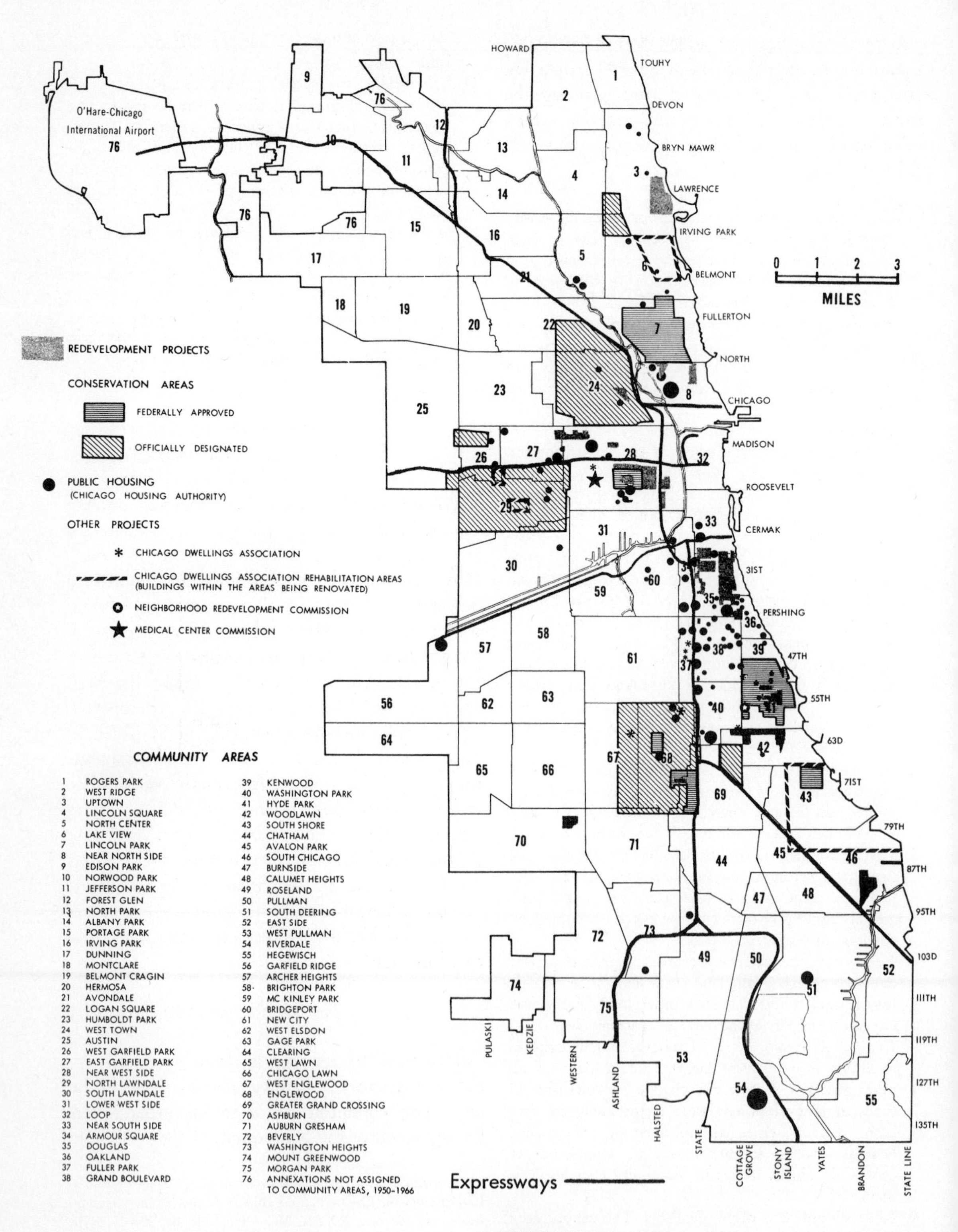

FIGURE 12–23. Chicago urban renewal and related activities: January, 1967. *Source:* Primary data.

market in the past. The public actions which constitute a renewal program must be evaluated and selected in relation to this market, upon which they exercise a profound influence. Usually, the areas coming under the direct effects of publicly financed actions are much smaller than those indirectly affected. In fact, one of the main objectives of an urban renewal program is to influence the functioning of the real estate market in such a way as to insure the fulfillment of certain general public welfare considerations.

One of the changes generated by public investment is an increase in land values. In the first stage of research into such changes in Baltimore, a structural model of land values in the city, for several land uses, was formulated. Three sets of independent variables were considered important in estimating land values: (1) accessibility; (2) physical factors; and (3) institutional factors.

Variable inputs to the structural models were:

X_1 = Estimated land value per square foot

accessibility factor:
- X_3 = Accessibility index

physical factors:
- X_4 = Lot size in square feet
- X_5 = Land use category
- X_6 = Degree of blight
- X_7 = Age of structures

institutional factors:
- X_8 = Existing zoning
- X_9 = Zoning change
- X_{10} = Potential change in use
- X_{11} = Ownership

Multiple regression analysis of these variables led to the following structural models for estimating land value:

All land uses: $X_1 = -47 + 3.06 \cdot X_3 + 4.92 \cdot X_7$ (5)

or $X_1 = -47 + 2.89 \cdot X_3 + 4.09 \cdot X_7 + 6.59 \cdot X_8$

Residential uses: $X_1 = 1 + 2.06 \cdot X_3 - 2.87 \cdot X_7 + 12.88 \cdot X_8$ (6)

Commercial uses: $X_1 = 63 + 4.73 \cdot X_3$ (7)

Industrial uses: $X_1 = 40 + 1.83 \cdot X_3$ (8)

Note the importance of accessibility in the above structural equations. Given the models, the next problem was to forecast land values for nine intensive land uses located in fourteen zones of the central city. The following sets of variables were utilized:

Variables to be estimated:
- W_i = Value in cents per square foot of land at location i in 1980, where $i = 1, 2 \ldots 337$
- T_i = Assessed value per square foot of land at location i in 1980
- A_i = Total index of accessibility at location i in 1980

Exogenous variables:
- $X_1 \cdot i$ = Value in cents per square foot of land at location i in 1964
- $X_2 \cdot i$ = Assessed value per square foot of land at location i in 1964
- $X_5 \cdot i$ = Land use of site i
- $X_7 \cdot i$ = Age of buildings on site i on an arbitrary scale
- P = Population of Baltimore Standard Metropolitan Statistical Area (SMSA) in 1980
- E = Total employment in Baltimore SMSA in 1980

Intermediate variables:
- E_u = Employment in urban oriented industries in Baltimore SMSA in 1980
- Y = Total personal income in Baltimore SMSA in 1980

Instrument variables:
- $I_{k \cdot j}$ = Index of urban functions k at any of the 14 centers j, operationally defined as 1/1,000,000 of the number of persons entering zone j in a year for purposes connected with urban function k
- d_{ij} = Distance in minutes by the best available means of transportation between grid point i and center j
- $X_8 \cdot i$ = Zoning on site i

The instrument variables can be manipulated to reflect alternative policy decisions made by city officials.

The first task consisted of estimating the values (for 1980) of the intermediate variables. Employment in urban oriented industries (E_u) had been also calculated in a previous study.[55] The regression equation of the form

$$E_{u(t)} = a + b \cdot P_{(t-1)} \qquad (9)$$

yielded an estimate of employment in the urban oriented industries for 1980 of: $E_u = 616{,}700$. An estimate of total personal income in the Baltimore SMSA was obtained by regressing past yearly income figures on total employment in the area. Best results were obtained by using least squares, straight-line regression, without time lags, of the form:

$$Y = -60.82 + 1.6222 \cdot E^{56} \qquad (10)$$

The necessary time series data were derived from a previous study.[57] This yielded an estimate of total personal income in 1980, Y_{1980} $8,100,000,000. Before any attempt could be made at determining the future values of the instrumental variables, an estimate had to be made of the total indexes of central functions combined over all centers. Obviously for each central urban function:

$$I_k = \sum_{j=1}^{14} I_{k \cdot j}{}^{58}$$

Eight functions were considered ($k = 1 \ldots 8$), namely: (1) offices (federal, state, and local governments, financial, commercial, real estate, professional services, and so forth); (2) cultural facilities; (3) amusements; (4) universities; (5) research and development; (6) specialized retail; (7) hotels and motels; and (8) transportation terminals.

Each of the indices of central function was regressed in turn against population P, using yearly time series data. In each case a scatter diagram was prepared. Three of the functions, namely, universities (4), research and development (5), and hotels and motels (7), were significantly correlated when a straight-line fit was attempted. The following parameters and related statistics were obtained:

$$\text{Universities: } I_4 = -16.88 + 1.4074 \cdot P; \; (R^2 = .90647) \qquad (11)$$

$$\text{Research and development: } I_5 = 22.95 + .2138 \cdot P; \; (R^2 = .86362) \qquad (12)$$

$$\text{Hotels and motels: } I_7 = 4.65 + .5769 \cdot P; \; (R^2 = .86638) \qquad (13)$$

As expected, the remaining 5 central functions were not significantly correlated with population, even though attempts were made at smoothing the data with a three-year moving average, using one- and two-year lagged relationships and various transformations.

On theoretical grounds one would expect trip intensity around transportation terminals to be positively correlated with the growth of employment in the urban oriented industries E_u typically concentrated near the center of the metropolitan area. A least squares, straight-line regression yielded the following result:

$$\text{Transportation terminals: } I_u = 11.77 + .5464 \cdot E_v; \; (R^2 = .70631) \qquad (14)$$

The remaining 4 variables may be assumed to vary directly with total personal income Y generated in the area. The following statistically significant results were obtained by applying in two cases a straight-line fit, and in two by using a logarithmic transformation.

$$\text{Cultural facilities: } I_2 = 66.33 + .2986 \cdot Y; \; (R^2 = .69668) \qquad (15)$$

$$\text{Specialized retail: } I_6 = 9.63 + .9716 \cdot Y; \; (R^2 = .79668) \qquad (16)$$

$$\text{Offices: } I_1 = -13.54 + .2424 \cdot \log Y; \; (R^2 = .64646) \qquad (17)$$

$$\text{Amusements: } \log I_3 = -62.36 + 1.4011 \cdot \log Y; \; (R^2 = .98000) \qquad (18)$$

By substituting estimated population for 1980 and the results of Eqs. (9) and (10) into Eqs. (11) to (18), the following indices for 1980 were obtained:

	Visitors per year (in thousands)
1. Offices	69.844
2 + 3. Cultural Facilities and Amusements	44.817
4. Universities	16.900
5. Research and Development	28.100
6. Specialized Retail	.900
7. Hotels and Motels	.200
8. Transportation Terminals	22.100
Total	182.861

The variables so far considered were all beyond the influence of planners or policy makers. Their future level depends largely, although indirectly, upon national and regional economic growth, local ability to attract new industries, and so forth. However, there exists in the system a set of variables which can be manipulated within broad limits by local decision makers.

First, the spatial distribution of urban functions between various centers depends largely upon urban renewal which may be directed either toward a fast and fairly complete rebuilding and rehabilitation of the core of the city or toward a number of other objectives. These objectives can often be attained by the use of less drastic tools than clearance and redevelopment. Such methods of controlling urban blight as code enforcement and conservation affect the spatial distribution of central urban functions differently from clearance and redevelopment. Direct public investments in certain key urban facilities also have effect.

Second, the time distances between various areas in the city could be considerably changed, according to various mass transit programs proposed. Of particular importance would be the proposed construction of a subway system.

Finally, zoning does affect land values and assessments, although to a somewhat lesser extent.

Six alternatives were considered, yielding in each case a different distribution of land values in the city. The differences in estimated mean land values and in assessed land values proved to be less spectacular although considerable. The mean estimated land value increased from 106.1¢ per square foot at present to 198.0¢ per square foot in the second alternative, which for a variety of reasons appears as the most likely one. This is, however, an increase of only 87 per cent over a period of fifteen years, during which considerable urban growth will take place. Table 12–4 illustrates the results.

TABLE 12–4

1980 Land Values Based on Alternative Policies

Alternative	*Description*	*Mean Estimated Land Value in Cents per Square Foot*	*Mean Assessed Land Value in Cents per Square Foot*
	Present values	106.1	61.6
1.	Construction of subway, present trends in renewal continue	199.4	121.1
2.	Strong renewal effort in Charles Center, State Office Bldg., and Johns Hopkins Hospital Areas	198.0	120.1
3.	Dispersion of central business district activities	176.2	106.5
4.	Development of peripheral nodes	196.3	119.1
5.	Investment concentrated in Municipal Center and Howard-Paca-Baltimore Area	206.5	125.5
6.	Development limited to Metrotowns	174.5	105.4

Using the first alternative, construction of a subway with present renewal trends continuing, a spatial distribution of estimated future land values was projected. This is illustrated in Fig. 12–24.[59]

Equally noteworthy is the increase in the assessment values. In the first alternative it would amount to some $400,000,000 for the whole city. Clearly, such an increase would be comparable to the financial burdens in renewal and subway construction.

The second and fifth alternatives envisage the development of a strong central business district (CBD) which would attract daytime population into the central part of the metropolitan area. They differ only in the location of the area of highest concentration of redevelopment efforts. In both alternatives revival of the core would be later followed, it is hoped, by an inflow of middle-income residents from the suburbs. An improvement in the social composition of the night population of the downtown area may help to stem the further progress of urban blight. The effects of these two alternative programs on urban land values are quite similar both in terms of their total impact and of their spatial distribution.

The fourth alternative, and the third even more so, have as their main objective the containment of blight. According to these alternatives some central urban functions will be introduced into

FIGURE 12–24. Projection of estimated land values per square foot for 1980: Baltimore, Maryland (assuming transportation). *Source:* Stanislaw Czamanski, "Effects of Public Investments on Urban Land Values," *Journal of the American Institute of Planners*, XXXII, No. 4 (July, 1966).

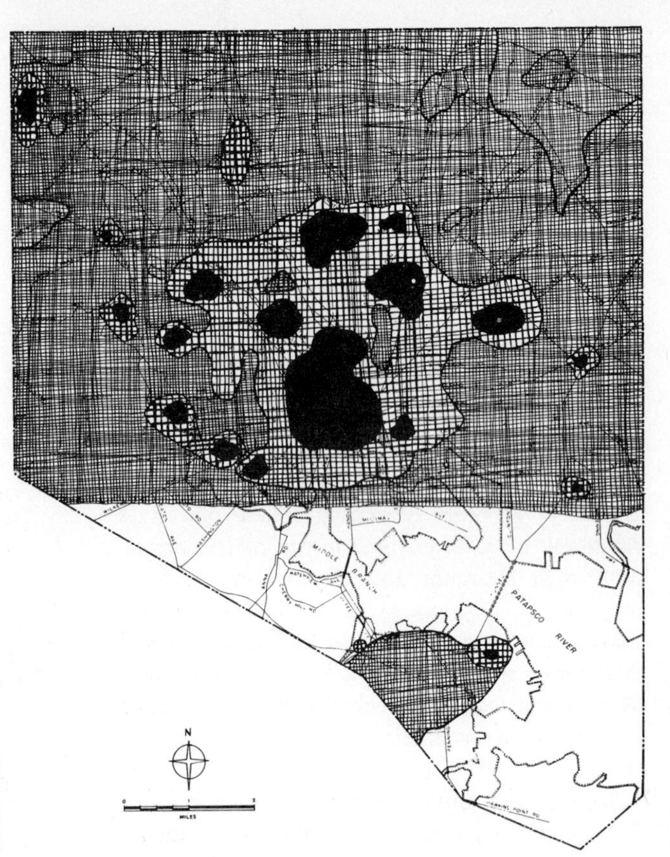

areas which immediately abut urban blight and which themselves are in danger of being engulfed by it.

The sixth alternative proposes to replace the CBD and the central part of the metropolitan area by developments outside of the city, along the Beltway. The new centers, called metrotowns, would be self-contained urban units of 100,000 to 200,000 inhabitants each, having besides residential also retailing, manufacturing (places of work), and recreational functions. In addition they would also fulfill certain central functions.

The impact of this alternative on urban land values would be most pronounced, particularly near the existing downtown area, where land values would hardly increase at all.

URBAN LAND USE MODELING

Czamanski, as we have just seen, has constructed a model capable of determing the impact of alternative public investment policy decisions on urban land values. There has been a variety of recent attempts by city planners and urban transportation analysts to develop macro-models of land use in urban areas, of which Czamanski's effort is a particular case. A classic overview of the strategies utilized and the types of urban models constructed has been provided by Ira S. Lowry.

*Model Design**

The model . . . may fall into any of three classes, depending on the interest of the client and the ambition of the model-builder. In ascending order of difficulty, these are: descriptive models; predictive models; and planning models.

DESCRIPTIVE MODELS. The builder of a de-

*Reprinted from Ira S. Lowry, "A Short Course in Model Design," *Journal of the American Institute of Planners*, XXX (May, 1965), 158–66, with the permission of the author and editor.

scriptive model has the limited objective of persuading the computer to replicate[60] the relevant features of an existing urban environment or of an already observed process of urban change. Roughly speaking, the measures of his accomplishment are: (1) the ratio of input data required by the model to output data generated by the model; (2) the accuracy and cost of the latter as compared to direct observation of the variables in question; and (3) the applicability of his model to other times and places than that for which it was originally constructed.

Good descriptive models are of scientific value because they reveal much about the structure of the urban environment, reducing the apparent complexity of the observed world to the coherent and rigorous language of mathematical relationships. They provide concrete evidence of the *ways* in which "everything in the city affects everything else," and few planners would fail to benefit from exposure to the inner workings of such models. They may also offer a shortcut to fieldwork, by generating reliable values for hard-to-measure variables from input data consisting of easy-to-measure variables.[61] But they do not directly satisfy the planner's demand for information about the future, or help him to choose among alternative programs. For these purposes, he must look to the more ambitious predictive and planning models.

PREDICTIVE MODELS. For prediction of the future, an understanding of the relationship between form and process becomes crucial. In a descriptive model it may suffice to note that X and Y are covariant (e.g., that the variable Y consistently has the value of $5X$, or equivalently, that $X = .2Y$); but when the aim is to predict the value of Y at some future time, the model must specify a causal sequence (e.g., that a one-unit change in the value of X will *cause* the value of Y to change by 5 units). If one is able to postulate the direction of causation, knowledge of the future value of the "cause" enables one to predict the future value of the "effect."[62]

Thus, the first task of the builder of a predictive model is to establish a logical framework within which the variables of interest to his client stand at the end rather than at the beginning of a causal sequence. (Variables in this terminal position are often described as "endogenous.") His second task is to make sure that those variables which stand at the beginning (prime cause, often called "exogenous") can be plausibly evaluated as far into the future as may be necessary. These requirements may enlarge his frame of reference far beyond that which would serve for a merely descriptive model.[63]

The second requirement is partly relaxed in the case of *conditional* predictions, which are in any case of greater interest to planners than the unconditional variety. The planner is ordinarily interested in the state of the world following some contemplated act on his part, or following some possible but uncertain event outside his control. The model may then be allowed to respond in the form, "if X occurs, then Y will follow," without explicitly asserting the likelihood of X's occurrence. But explicit predictions must still be made for other exogenous events, since these may reinforce or counteract the effects of the hypothetical change in X.

A special case of conditional prediction is called "impact analysis." Here, the interest is focused on the consequence that should be expected to follow a specified exogenous impact (change in X), if the environment were otherwise undisturbed.

PLANNING MODELS. Finally, there are planning models, a class whose technology is not far developed. A planning model necessarily incorporates the method of conditional prediction, but it goes further in that outcomes are evaluated in terms of the planner's goals. The essential steps are as follows: (1) specification of alternative programs or actions that might be chosen by the planner; (2) prediction of the consequences of choosing each alternative; (3) scoring these consequences according to a metric of goal-achievement; and (4) choosing the alternative which yields the highest score.

The best known species of planning model executes these steps by means of a "linear program," a computational routine allowing the efficient exploration of a very wide spectrum of alternatives—albeit under rather special restrictions as to permissible cause-effect relationships, and assuming complete information about alternatives and their consequences at the time of choice.

Perhaps more relevant to urban planners is the problem of making a sequence of choices, the effects of each choice conditioning the alternatives available for subsequent choices. Since, at each decision point, there are as many "branches" as alternatives available, the spectrum of possible final outcomes can easily become astronomical. If steps (3) and (4) above are programmed for the computer, it is feasible to trace a fairly large number of alternative decision sequences through to their final outcomes; and mathematicians have reported some success with "dynamic programs" for identifying optimal sequences more efficiently than by trial and error.[64]

Theories and models. [T]he model-builder's work begins with the identification of persistent relationships among relevant variables, of causal sequences, of a logical framework for the model. In so doing, he must develop or borrow from theories of urban form and process. Although "theory" and "model" are often used interchangeably to denote a logico-mathematical construct of interrelated variables, a distinction can be drawn. In formulating his constructs, the theorist's over-riding aims are logical coherence and generality; he is ordinarily content to specify only the conceptual significance of his variables and the general form of their functional interrelationships. The virtuosity of the theorist lies in rigorous logical derivation of interesting and empirically relevant propositions from the most parsimonious set of postulates.

The model builder, on the other hand, is concerned with the application of theories to a concrete case, with the aim of generating empirically relevant output from empirically based input. He is constrained, as the theorist is not, by considerations of cost, of data availability and accuracy, of timeliness, and of the client's convenience. Above all, he is required to be explicit where the theorist is vague. The exigencies of his trade are such that, even given his high appreciation of "theory," his model is likely to reflect its theoretical origins only in oblique and approximate ways. Mechanisms that "work," however mysteriously, get substituted for those whose virtue lies in theoretical elegance.

The theoretical perspective of the model builder is most clearly visible in the set of structural relations he chooses as the framework of his model. A neatly articulated model will consist of a series of propositions of the general form, $Y = f(U, V, X, Z \ldots)$.[65] These propositions embrace the variables in which he is interested and specify the ways in which these variables act on one another. For most models relating to policy issues, it is useful to classify the propositions in terms of their content, as technological, institutional, behavioral, or accounting.[66] While there may well be alternative sets of such propositions that convey the same meaning, the model builder is at least bound by rules of consistency (no contradictory propositions) and coherence (as many independent propositions as there are variables). Within these rules, his choice of structures is guided mostly by his sense of strategic advantage.

The pure theorist is often satisfied with the general forms indicated above, or with these forms plus a few constraints or restrictions. The model builder must be much more explicit, detailing the exact functional forms of his structural relations (e.g., $Y = \log U + a(V/X) - Z^b$); he must also fit his variables (Y, U, V, X, Z) and parameters (a, b) from empirical sources.

The strategy of model design. [S]trategic alternatives of design (a, b) are open to the model builder, choices which demand all his skill and ingenuity since they bear so heavily on the serviceability of his model to its predetermined purposes. Typically, these decisions must be made in an atmosphere of considerable uncertainty with respect to problems of implementation and eventual uses, and there are no clear canons of better and worse. Though the model builder can profit from the experience of others who have dealt with similar problems, he is to a large extent thrown back on his intuitive perceptions and his sense of style.

THE LEVEL OF AGGREGATION. Perhaps his most important choice concerns the level of aggregation at which he finds it profitable to search for regularities of form and process. While there is an accepted distinction between macro-analysis and micro-analysis, the differences between these modes of perception can be elusive. Neither is the exclusive property of a particular academic discipline, but in urban studies, macro-analysis is closely associated with urban geography, demography, social physics, and human ecology, while micro-analysis is typically the metier of economics and social psychology.

The geographers, demographers, ecologists, and social physicists prefer to deal with statistics of mass behavior and the properties of collectivities. The elements of a model based on this tradition are likely to be stock flow parameters, gravity or potential functions, matrices of transition probabilities.[67] Faced with the same *explanandum*, the economist is much more likely to think in terms of a market model, in which resources are allocated or events determined through competitive interaction of optimizing individuals whose behavior is predicated on a theory of rational choice. The social psychologist also works from a theory of individual choice, and has his own version of the market model—though it is less articulate because it embraces a much wider variety of transactions.[68]

The principal criticism of the macro-analytic approach is that its "theory" consists in large part of descriptive generalizations which lack explicit causal structure. Thus a macro-model of residential mobility may consist essentially of a set of mobility rates for population subgroups classified by age, sex, or family status, rates based on historical evidence of the statistical frequency of movement by the members of such groups. For purposes of prediction, one may assume that these rates will apply to future as well as past populations; but since the reasons people move are not explicit in such a model, the assumption of continuity in behavior cannot be easily modified to fit probable or postulated future changes in the environment of this behavior.

A second objection to macro-analytic approaches is that they do not lend themselves easily to financial accounting schemes. These are of particular relevance to planning models whose purpose is to distinguish among better and worse alternatives of policy or program. Strictly speaking, such distinctions can only be made if goal achievement is reducible to a single metric, and the most comprehensive metric available in our society, whether we like it or not, is money.[69] Thus, in choosing among alternative transportation plans, the objective may be to maximize net social return to transportation investments—for example, to maximize the difference between benefits to be derived from the investment and costs allocable to it. Even though a gravity model representation of the journey-to-work/residential location relationship may "work" in the sense of generating accurate predictions of population distribution and travel patterns, it will not yield financial data so easily as a market model of travel behavior and residential site selection, since the latter operates throughout in terms of price-defined alternatives faced by households.

The micro-analytic approach also has its problems. Chief among these is that a model based on the theory of rational choice can be implemented only if the chooser's system of relative values—technically, his "preference system"—can be specified in considerable detail. The search for an empirical technique to achieve this detailed specification has frustrated generations of economists, and approximations to date are both crude in detail and based on highly questionable operating assumptions. Lacking the ability to observe these preference systems directly, the modeler is restricted to a very meager menu of empirically relevant propositions concerning the complementarity and substitutability of economic goods, propositions deducible from general theoretical principles.

The second problem of the micro-analytic approach is the implementation of a comprehensive market model—one embracing the entire range of transactions which substantially affect the patterns of urban development and land use. Given complete information about the demand schedules of buyers and the supply schedules of sellers, the classical theory of a perfectly competitive market for a homogeneous commodity is simple enough, having a determinate solution for both the volume of transactions and the emergent price of the commodity. But the model builder is faced, empirically, with a congeries of interrelated markets, subtly differentiated commodities, imperfections in communication, and inequities of bargaining position, all of which rule out the easy mathematical resolutions of the classical case. The fact is that we are presently able to implement only quite crude and tenuous approximations of market models.[70]

THE TREATMENT OF TIME. Except for the simple descriptive case, a model usually purports to represent the outcome of a process with temporal dimensions. Beginning with the state of the (relevant) world at time t, it carries us forward to the state of that world at $t + n$; thus a land-use model may start with a 1960 land use inventory in order to predict the 1970 inventory. The way in which this time dimension is conceived is a matter of considerable strategic significance; the choice lies among varying degrees of temporal continuity, ranging from comparative statics at one extreme, through various types of recursive progression, to analytical dynamics at the other extreme.

At first glance, the choice seems to hinge merely on the question, how often need results be read out? But the issues go deeper, involving the model builder's perception of the self-equilibrating features of the world, represented by his model, the empirical evaluation of response lags among his variables, and his interest in impact analysis as distinguished from other types of conditional or unconditional prediction.

The method of comparative statics implies a conviction that the system is strongly self-equilibrating, that the endogenous variables respond quickly and fully to exogenous changes. The model's parameters, fit from cross-section data, represent "equilibrium" relationships between exogenous and endogenous variables; a prediction requires specification of the values of the exogenous variables as of the target date. The process by which the system moves from its initial to its terminal state is unspecified.[71]

Alternatively, comparative statics may be used for impact analysis, where no target date is specified. Assuming only one or a few exogenous changes, the model is solved to indicate the characteristics of the equilibrium state towards which the system would tend in the absence of further exogenous impacts.

Self-equilibration is not a necessary assumption for analytical dynamics, an approach which focuses attention on the processes of change rather than on the emergent state of the system at a specified future date. Technically, this type of model must be formulated as a set of differential equations, at least some of which include variables whose rates of change are specified with respect to time.

Implementation of such a model requires only specification of its structural parameters and the "initial conditions" of its variables. Thereafter, all processes are endogenous except time, and the time path of any variable can be continuously traced. The state of the system can be evaluated at any point in time. If the system *is* self-equilibrating, the values of its variables should converge on those indicated by analogous comparative statics; but without self-equilibrating properties, the system may fluctuate cyclically, explode, or degenerate.

Because comparative statics requires such strong equilibrium assumptions (seldom warranted for models of urban phenomena), and because analytical dynamics requires virtually complete closure (all variables except time are endogenous), most model builders compromise on recursive progressions. This method portrays the system's changes over time in lock-step fashion by means of lagged variables, for example:

$$Y_{t-1} = a + bX_t \tag{19}$$

$$X_t = c + dY_{t-1} \tag{20}$$

Starting with initial values for either X or Y, one carries the system forward by alternately solving Eqs. 19 and 20. Of course in this example, a bit of algebraic manipulation suffices to evaluate Y_{t+u} directly from a given Y_t; but the case is seldom so simple—and the model builder is likely to want to inject periodic exogenous changes into this recursive sequence.

THE CONCEPT OF CHANGE. Any model dealing with changes over time in an urban system must distinguish (at least implicitly) between variables conceived as "stocks" and variables conceived as "flows." A stock is an inventory of items sufficiently alike to be treated as having only the dimension of size or number—e.g., dwelling units, female labor force participants, acres of space used for retail trade. This inventory may change as items are added or deleted; such changes, expressed per unit of time, are called flows. A model builder may choose to focus either on the factors which determine the magnitude of each stock, or on the factors which determine the magnitude of each flow.[72]

Since a stock is by definition the integral over time of the corresponding flow, it must also have the same determinants as the flow. But if the model builder limits his attention to flows which occur over any short span of time, he can afford to take a number of shortcuts. Exogenous variables whose effects on stocks are visible only in the long run can be ignored or treated as fixed parameters. Whereas nonlinear expressions may be necessary to represent the long-run growth of a stock, marginal increments in the short run can often be represented by linear expressions. By accepting the initial magnitude of a stock as historically "given," one avoids the necessity of replicating the past and can devote himself to modeling the events of the present and near future.

Consider a model of retail location whose eventual application will be a five-year projection of the distribution of retail establishments within an urban area. The existing pattern (initial stock) of retail establishments in a large city reflects locational decisions made over the course of a century or more, during which time the transportation system, merchandising techniques, and patterns of consumption all have changed slowly but cumulatively. Most of the present stock of retail establishments will still be in operation at their present sites five years hence.

If the model builder is willing to organize his design around the *present* characteristics of the transportation network, of merchandising methods, of consumption patterns, his task may be greatly simplified. And the resulting model may be quite adequate for the prediction of short-run *changes* in retail location (say, as a consequence of population growth), even though it would not be able to recapitulate the city's history of retail development.

Clearly the model builder must weigh the advantages of such simplifications against the fact that his model will have a shorter useful life. Since its structure postulates stability in a changing environment, the model will soon lose its empirical relevance.[73] By way of compromise, many model builders make use of "drift parameters": structural "constants" which are programed for periodic revision to reflect changing environmental conditions, conditions which cannot conveniently be made explicit in the model.

SOLUTION METHODS. An integral part of the strategy of model design is a plan for operating the model—an algorithm or method of solution. This plan describes the concrete steps to be taken from the time that input data is fed to the computer until final results are read out. Four general methods are prominent: the choice among them is largely governed by the degree of logico-mathematical coherence of the model itself.

The neatest and most elegant method is the analytic solution. Ordinarily, this method is applicable only to models which exhibit very tight logical structures and whose internal functional relationships are uncomplicated by nonlinearities and discontinuities. In substance, the set of equations constituting the model is resolved by analysis into a direct relationship between the relevant output variables and the set of input variables. Intervening variables drop out of the "reduced form" equations. The paradigm system used above to illustrate recursion (Eqs. 19 and 20) can be solved analytically. For example[74]:

$$Y_{t+4} = (a + bc)(1 + bd) + (bd)^2 Y_t \qquad (21)$$

For models lacking complete logical closure, or whose structures are overburdened with inconvenient mathematical relationships, an alternative to the analytic solution is the iterative method. This method comprises a search for a set of output values which satisfy all the equations of the model; it proceeds initally by assuming approximate values for some of the variables and solving analytically for the remainder. These first-round solutions are then used as the basis for computing second approximations to replace the initially estimated values, and so on. Except for various degenerate cases, the solution values eventually "converge"—that is, further iterations fail to result in significant changes in the solution. Mechanically, the process is quite similar to recursive progression of a self-equilibrating system, but the iterative process need not imply either a sequence over time or a causal sequence. A drawback of this method is that it fails to signal the existence of alternative solution sets; a possibility that may have considerable importance for the interpretation of results.[75]

Ambitious models of urban processes may not meet the requirements for either the analytic or iterative methods of solution because of their scope: In the attempt to embrace a wide range of obviously relevant phenomena, one easily loses mathematical rigor and logical closure. For models of this class—loosely articulated "system analyses"—machine simulation may be the best resort. The model specifies an inventory of possible "events" and indicates the immediate consequences of each event for one or more variables representing a "stock" or population. A change in the magnitude of a stock has specified (endogenous) consequences in the form of inducing new events; but characteristically, the major source of new events is exogenous. Indeed, the more sophisticated simulations (Monte Carlo or stochastic models) generate exogenous events by random choice from a given frequency distribution of possibilities. The computer's principal task is to keep a running account of all stocks and to alter them in response to events. This method is less appropriate for explicit projections than for tests of the sensitivity of the model (and by implication, of the real world system represented by the model) to various possible constellations of exogenous events.

Finally, there is the method of "man-machine simulation," in which computer processing of input data is periodically interrupted, and the intermediate state of the system is read out for examination by a human participant. He may adjust intermediate results to correspond with his judgment as to their inherent plausibility, or he may use these intermediate results as a basis for a "policy" decision which is then fed back to the computer model as an exogenous change in values for specified variables or parameters. The human participant is ordinarily included for educational reasons—to give him practice in responding to planning problems—but on occasion, he is there simply because the model builder does not fully trust his model to behave "sensibly" under unusual circumstances[76] (see below, "Parameters").

Fitting a model. Once the model builder has selected a theoretical perspective, designed a logical framework large enough to encompass his objectives, and postulated the existence of enough emprical regularities to permit the resolution of his problem, his next task is to "fit" or "calibrate" the model. This task involves two types of transformation: the variables mentioned in the model must be given precise empirical definition, and numerical values must be provided for the model's parameters.

VARIABLES. The first transformation always involves compromise. A variable conceived in general terms (household income) must be related to an available statistic (median income of families and unrelated individuals as reported by the U.S. Census of 1960 on the basis of a 25 per cent sample), and the restrictions and qualifications surrounding the data must be carefully explored to be sure they do not seriously undermine the proposed role of the variable in the model (aggregation of medians is difficult; response errors may create serious biases in the data; sampling variability of figures reported for small areas may be uncomfortably large).

A variable included in the model because of its theoretical significance may not be directly observable in the real world, so that some more accessible proxy must be chosen. Thus, many land use models deal in "location rents" (defined as that portion of the annual payment to an owner of a parcel of land which is attributable to the geographical position of the parcel as distinct from its soil or slope characteristics, existing structural improvements, or services provided by the landlord), but empirical sources tell us only about "contract rents" (the total contractual payment of tenant to landlord). Can contract rents be statistically standardized to serve as a reliable proxy for location rents?

[There is] no formal canon of method for fitting variables although . . . some scattered principles [may] be observed.[77] More frequently than not, the problems encountered at this step force the model builder to back-track and revise parts of his logical structure to lessen its sensitivity to bad data or to make better use of what data is actually available. Since few published statistics are exactly what they seem to be from the table headings and column stubs, it is very easy for one inexperienced in the generation of a particular class of data to misinterpret either its meaning or its reliability.

PARAMETERS. The fitting of parameters—numerical constants of relationship—is necessary for two reasons: (1) theoretical principles and deductive reasoning therefrom are seldom sufficient to indicate more than the appropriate sign (positive or negative) and probable order of magnitude for such constants; and (2) since these constants are measures of relationship between numerical variables, the precise empirical definition of the variable affects the value of the parameter. For instance, the appropriate value of a labor-force participation rate depends among other things on whether the pool from which participants are drawn is defined to include persons 15 to 60 or persons 14 to 65.

Parameter fitting is a highly developed branch of statistical method.[78] The most common tool is regression analysis, the simplest case being the estimation of parameters for a linear function of two variables, $Y = a + bX$. From a set of coordinate observations of the values of X and Y, one can estimate values for a and b in such a way as to minimize the expected error of estimate of Y from known values of X.

If the model can be formulated as a set of simultaneous linear equations, an elaboration of this method can be used to locate "best fit" values for all parameters in the system.[78] Models fitted in this way are often described as "econometric," although the method is equally applicable to noneconomic variables. A significant drawback of econometric fitting is that the criterion of selection for the values assigned to each parameter is the best *over-all* fit of the model to a given array of data. The values generated for individual parameters are often surprising, yet it is difficult to look "inside" the fitting process for clues of explanation.

Alternatives to a comprehensive econometric fit can be described generally as "heuristic" methods. The model is partitioned into smaller systems of equations—some perhaps containing a single parameter—so that the parameters of each sub-system can be fit independently. This is in fact the typical approach, since few large models of urban form and process can be formulated as a single system of linear equations and still meet the objectives of the client.

Methods for obtaining estimates of the various parameters in these subsystems may vary considerably. A model ordinarily contains parameters whose function is nominal, and a model builder anxious to get on with his job may simply assign an arbitrary but plausible value to such a parameter. Where the context rules out direct methods for deriving simultaneous "best fits" even for the parameters of a limited sub-system, trial-and-error methods can be used to find a set of parametric values which seem to work. Or parametric values may be taken directly from empirical analogs, without regard for "best fit" in the context of the model.[80]

Finally, . . . model builders sometimes despair of finding a mathematically exact expression of relationship among certain of their model variables, so resort instead to "human" parameters. At the appropriate point in the operation of the model, intermediate or preliminary results are scanned by persons of respected judgment, who are asked to alter these outputs to conform to an intuitive standard of plausibility based on their experience in the field. The altered data are then fed back to the computer for further processing.

Testing a model. Fitting a model is analogous to the manufacture and assembly of a new piece of electrical machinery. A work team, guided by engineering drawings, fabricates each component and installs it in proper relation to other components, connecting input-output terminals. Along the way, considerable redesign, tinkering, and mutual adjustment of parts is inevitable; but eventually the prototype is completed. However carefully the individual components have been tested, and their interconnections inspected, a question remains about the final product: Will it really work?

Industrial experience indicates that the way to answer this question is to turn the machine on and apply it to the task at hand. This precept applies also to computer models of urban form and process, with the important reservation that it is extremely difficult to select a "fair" but revelatory task, or to establish clear and objective standards of performance.

The appropriate test for a model depends, of course, on its pre-determined function. It is unfair to ask a descriptive model to make a prediction, or a predictive model to find the optimal solution to a planning problem. But it is unfortunately the case that even an appropriate test may be infeasible.

The easiest model to test is the descriptive variety. Thus, for a model of urban form, the appropriate test would be its ability to replicate the details of an existing urban pattern on the basis of limited information concerning the area in question. Since most such models are built with a particular urban area in mind, and fitted with reference to this area's characteristics, one ordinarily has detailed observations (for example, concurrent and otherwise compatible inventories of land use, structures, human populations, business enterprises, transportation facilities, and so forth) against which the model's output may be checked. The limitations of the test should also be apparent. The model's structure and parameters may be so closely locked into the patterns evident in this particular area and time that its descriptive abilities may have no generality; applied to another city the model may fail miserably.

The appropriate test for a predictive model is to "run" a prediction and verify the details of its outcome. The more distant the horizon of forecast, the more stringent the test; it would be easy to predict the distribution of workplaces in Boston tomorrow if one were given today's inventory. But few clients have the patience to finance several years of model-building, then wait several more years to verify the model's first predictions. And even if one were willing to wait, there is the further problem that the model will almost certainly be designed for *conditional* predictions, and it would be remarkable indeed to discover in retrospect that all postulated conditions had been fulfilled.

The more accessible alternative is *ex post facto* prediction: Take the state of the world in 1950 as a starting point and apply the model by forecasting for 1960, then compare the forecast values to the observed values for 1960.[81] This procedure is likely to suffer from the same limitation of semi-circularity that plagues the testing of descriptive models. More likely than not, the predictive model was *fitted* to the recorded processes of change in 1950 to 1960. And if not, the reason is likely to be that comparable data are not available for the two dates. A predictive model is oriented to the problems of the future, and the model builder is anxious to feed his model the most recent additions to the menu of urban data—indeed, he may well initiate fieldwork on a new series to provide it with a balanced diet. Why limit his freedom by insisting that his model be able to subsist on the more limited menu available a decade ago?

The test of a planning model has two distinct phases. The first is a check on its ability to trace through the consequences of a given planning decision or set of decisions; this phase is a form of conditional prediction, and subject to all the hazards described above. The second phase is a check on the ability of the model to select an optimal result from a spectrum of alternative outcomes. It may fail to do so because: (1) shortcut methods may eliminate as suboptimal some outcomes which have more promise than they immediately show; (2) the evaluation of outcomes may be very sensitive to engineering estimates of cost or imputation of benefits, and these are intrinsically nebulous; or (3) the criteria of selection may be poorly stated, so that an outcome which would in fact be acceptable to the client is classified as unacceptable by the model.

"Sensitivity testing" is sometimes urged as a more accessible substitute for the performance tests discussed above; although it is easy to perform and applicable to a wide variety of models, sensitivity testing elicits indications of the "strength" of a model's design rather than of its descriptive or predictive or evaluative accuracy. The procedure is as follows: By varying the value of a single parameter (or even of an input variable) in successive runs of the model, one can measure the difference in outcome associated with a given parametric change. If the model's response to wide differences in parametric values is insignificant, this may be an indication that the parameter—and the associated network of functional relations—is superfluous. On the other hand, extreme sensitivity of outcomes to parametric changes indicates either that the parameter in question had better be fitted with great care, or that some further elaboration of this component of the model is in order—on the grounds that the analogous real world system must in fact have built-in compensations to forestall wild fluctuations in outcome.

*EXAMPLES OF URBAN MODELS**

Urban spatial organization is the outcome of a process which allocates activities to sites. In our society, the process is mainly one of transactions between owners of real estate and those who wish to rent or purchase space for their homes and businesses. These transactions are freely entered contracts, neither party having a legal obligation to accept the other's offer. These elements suffice to define a" market" in the economist's dictionary.

To be sure, there are exceptions to the general rule of the market. Governments exercise the power of eminent domain, although an independent judiciary controls the terms of forced contracts with at least formal obeisance to the standards of the market place. Transactions which are internal to an organization—between agencies of government, divisions of a corporation, or members of a family—are sheltered from the market. Nearly all urban governments impose negative constraints on land use and also levy real estate taxes, both of which may influence a potential buyer's interest in a particular site but do not constrain his freedom of contract.

*Reprinted from Ira S. Lowry, "Seven Models of Urban Development: A Structural Comparison," Paper prepared for the Highway Research Board, National Research Council, Conference on Urban Development Models, Dartmouth College, Hanover, New Hampshire, June, 1967, with the permission of the author. In this paper, Lowry examined urban land use models using the market for urban land, both buyers and sellers, as a frame of reference, and developed a land use model classification scheme useful to student and practitioner alike.

With exceptions as noted, the market process of transactions between willing buyers and willing sellers determines the spatial organization of urban activities in a very immediate sense. Since models of urban development must reflect the institutional arrangements of our society if they are to reproduce the results, a closer look at the market process will serve as point of departure for the analysis of alternative models. The salient features of the process can be vividly shown by a paradigm.

Consider a city whose territory is divided into many parcels of land, each of which may be called a "site." Most of these sites have structural improvements designed for some particular use. Each site has an owner who is free to sell or lease his property. His potential clients, whether households, business enterprises, quasi-public corporations, or governmental agencies, will be called "establishments."

A unit of time, the "transaction period," also should be defined. At the beginning of each transaction period, every establishment in the city reappraises the advantages of its present site as compared to other sites. Indeed, each establishment explicitly considers the merits of every site in the city and decides what dollar price it would be willing to pay for each. At the designated prices, then, the establishment would be indifferent among locations.

This set of "demand prices" can be displayed in matrix form, as in Fig. 12–25. The shaded cells in each row of the matrix indicate the initial location of each establishment; note that the establishment sets a price on that site as well as on all others.

Assume also that this matrix is published, available for inspection by the owner of each site. He scans the appropriate column of demand prices to identify the tenant who would be willing to pay the highest price for the use of that property during the coming transaction period. Naturally he deals with the highest "bidder," who may be the present tenant, the owner himself, or some third party. Some sites change hands and some establishments move to new locations, thus modifying the distribution of establishments in space. In Fig. 12–25, the location of each establishment at the end of the transaction period is

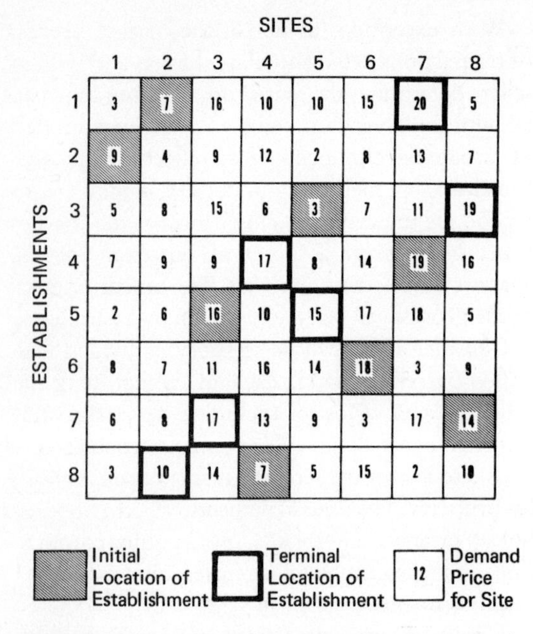

FIGURE 12–25. The urban land market: Demand prices for sites and locations of establishment. *Source:* Figs. 12–25 and 12–26 are from Ira S. Lowry, "Seven Models of Urban Development: A Structural Comparison." Paper prepared for the Highway Research Board, National Research Council, Conference on Urban Development Models, Dartmouth College, Hanover, New Hampshire.

indicated by a heavy border on the appropriate cell.

This paradigm, which could easily be elaborated to deal with unequal numbers of establishments and sites, illustrates in its essentials the economist's interpretation of the market for urban land. Competition among potential occupants determines the market price of land and each site goes to the highest bidder. Under the simplifying assumptions of the paradigm, there is an unequivocal *market-clearing solution* so long as no one establishment offers the highest prices for two or more sites. In the latter event, the solution depends on bilateral bargaining between the several site owners and this particular establishment, with the next highest demand price for each site providing a floor to each site owner's bargaining position.

Of course, the paradigm assumes a higher level of calculation and communication than exists in real markets. Few establishments ever make a thorough investigation of the full range of alternative possibilities, and none does so frequently. Except for occasional auctions, real-estate negotiations are conducted by offer and counter-offer; an establishment's "demand price" is always a closely guarded secret, and the floor to an owner's bargaining position is unstable unless he knows these prices. Real-estate leases do not conveniently expire simultaneously; thus only a portion of all establishments and of all sites are on the market at any one time.

It requires at least a small act of faith to assert, in view of these known market imperfections, that the actual allocation of urban sites to establishments is approximately that suggested by the market-clearing solution of the paradigm. But this theory offers a general and reasonably coherent account of the process by which urban land is allocated, and it has no serious intellectual competition—at least among analysts whose background is the discipline of economics.

The existence of a market-clearing solution does not depend on any particular assumption about the sources or pattern of demand prices except as noted above. Whatever method establishments use to decide on demand prices for individual sites, we need know only that they reach conclusions, i.e., that we have definite demand prices to enter into the matrix. But we are not interested in the market process *per se*; we are interested in the spatial distribution of activities within the city, a distribution that changes over time. This interest leads us to ask why different establishments will offer different prices for a given site, and why the same establishment will offer different prices for different sites. We want to know what regularities can be found in the matrix of demand prices, and how these regularities reflect in the market-clearing solution.

The abundant evidence of spatial patterns in our cities suggests a certain consistency over time and space in the evaluation of sites by establishments of a given type. Demand prices are not random numbers. In fact, we can with considerable confidence formalize the *evaluation function* by which they are determined:

$$P^{hi} = f(X_1^h, X_2^h, \ldots ; Y_1^i, Y_2^i, \ldots ; Z^{hi} h = 1, 2, \ldots, n) \tag{22}$$

where h is a particular establishment; i is a particular site; the price P that establishment h will offer for site i depends on a number of characteristics of the establishment $(X_1^h, X_2^h, \ldots)$, on a number of characteristics of the site $(Y_1^i, Y_2^i, \ldots)$, and on the location of the site with respect to the locations of other establishments $(Z^{hi},\ h = 1, 2, \ldots, n)$.

The formal statement is easy, but it is far from easy to identify and measure the relevant X's, Y's, and Z's. If we are dealing with households, for example, both reflection and observation suggest that income, number and ages of household members, and ethnic background are among the relevant X's. As for site characteristics, one would expect the size and shape and topography of the lot, the nature of its structural improvements, and the availability of utilities to be among the important Y's; we might also include microclimate and view, noise pollution, and even historical values attached to the site or the neighborhood. Prominent among the relevant Z's will be the most recurrent travel-destinations of household members—places of work, schools, shopping facilities, and the homes of friends.

These examples suggest both the number of possibly relevant variables and some of the difficulties of classification and measurement. There still remain the difficulties of determining a concrete form for the function which relates these variables to P^{hi}, and of specifying the numerical parameters of the function. These problems are not peculiar to the theory of demand for urban land. Economists have had scant success in giving empirical content to consumer preference functions in any context.

One group of variables in the evaluation function represents the characteristics of the site under consideration. Not all these characteristics are fixed. Raw land may be graded, utilities may be laid on, buildings may be erected, remodeled, or demolished. These actions are taken by site owners, sometimes to meet their own needs as occupants, often with a view to selling or leasing the site. Corresponding to the evaluation function by means of which establishments appraise sites, we can usefully postulate an *investment function* by means of which owners appraise the merits of site-improvements. At any point in time, the characteristics of a site are given; the owner must decide what improvements, if any, would be likely to raise his revenue by more than his outlay. Such an investment function might be written as:

$$E_j^i = g(C_j^i, P_j) \tag{23}$$

where i is a specific site; j is a specific bundle of site characteristics, some combination of the Y's which we encountered in the evaluation function; E_j^i is the expected gain from converting site i to condition j; C_j^i is the expected cost of imposing the jth bundle of site characteristics on site i, a cost which may well vary with the present condition of the site; and P_j is the current market price of sites in condition j.

The owner will choose an investment program which maximizes E_j^i; to do so, he must compare P_j and C_j^i for each alternative j.

As in the case of the evaluation function, it is easier to formulate the investment function in such general terms than it is to give it empirical content. Though the number of conceivable combinations of site characteristics which might be imposed on a particular site is infinite, only a cursory knowledge of the market will enable the owner to narrow the alternatives to a manageable set. For a given alternative, costs are readily approximated. The going price for that alternative is easily ascertained if it is currently offered on the market at sites in the geographical vicinity of i; the pioneer developer faces greater uncertainty.

The dynamics of the land market thus extend beyond the transaction period of the paradigm. Each period's market-clearing solution is examined by landowners for clues to profitable investments in site improvements. As improvements are installed on particular sites, establishments reevaluate these sites. The matrix of demand prices is thus altered, and a new market-clearing solution is in the making. The site owner's expectations of profit from the site improvements he has made may or may not be realized. Typically, too many developers respond to favorable market signals in one period, glutting the market with a particular type of improvement in the next period. Competition among landlords drives prices for this type of site improvement downward in the market-clearing solution.

The passage of time also brings changes in the number and types of establishments seeking locations. Existing establishments also change in their characteristics: households change in size, manufacturers acquire new production methods, retailers shift product lines. So long as some establishments are moving, the pattern of accessibility and contiguity changes for other establishments. These various changes in the argument of the evaluation function would cumulate over time to cause significant shifts in the demand-price matrix even though site characteristics were fixed.

There are also forces which stabilize the market. All other things equal, the existing location of an establishment is usually preferred to alternatives; for in adapting its activities to the characteristics of the site and vice versa, an establishment makes an investment which is seldom recoverable on the market. The search for alternative sites is tedious, transaction costs are high, and a move itself can be expensive. Consequently, few establishments are likely to move during any short period of time.

Classifying Models of Urban Development

From what has been said so far about the theory of the urban land market and the underlying evaluation and investment functions, it must be obvious that, while these provide a useful abstract framework for analysis, the theory could not readily be applied directly to a concrete case: the empirical problems would be overwhelming. Consequently, we resort to models of urban spatial organization. In this context, a model is the operational simplification of a theory which is necessary to fit our limited resources for empirical work. Not all models are explicitly derived from a more general theory; but if they work (and if the theory is correct), it should still be possible to interpret even an *ad hoc* model in terms of this theory.

One simplification which is characteristic of every model is aggregation. If one were to compile a matrix of the kind shown in Fig. 12–25, it would have thousands of rows and thousands of columns. Since these are models of urban spatial organization, the reasonable horizontal aggregation is to group contiguous sites into larger areas called "districts." The best way to group establishments is not so clear, but the usual practice distinguishes households, business enterprises, and government agencies, perhaps with subgroups among these broad categories of "activities." The sites and establishments of Fig. 12–25 have been thus grouped to create Fig. 12–26.

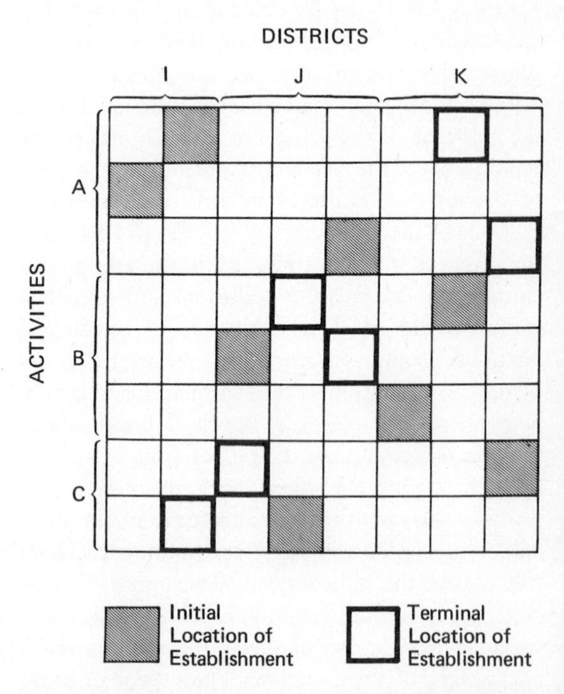

FIGURE 12–26. Changes in location and land use during a transaction period. *Source:* See caption for Fig. 12–25.

The illustration would have been better if a larger matrix had been used to begin with; but even the reduced 3×3 matrix of Fig. 12–26 will permit the principal points to be made if the reader will tolerate a rather casual treatment of discontinuities. Notice that the prices which were registered in the cells of Fig. 12–25 have not been carried over, but have retained the symbols which indicate both the old occupancy of each site and its new occupancy.

The rows and columns of the reduced matrix are significant. Since each column represents a district, the initial distribution of land uses (i.e., by type of user) in each district is indicated by the vertical pattern of shaded cells. Since each row represents an activity, the shaded cells of the row display the initial distribution of establishments belonging to this activity among the several districts. Vertically, the matrix displays *land use* patterns; horizontally, it displays *location* patterns.

The heavily banded cells also form vertical and horizontal distributions, representing land use and location patterns, respectively, at the end of the transction period. Moreover, initial and terminal distributions may be compared to derive additional patterns: vertically, these are patterns of *land use succession*; horizontally, they are patterns of *migration*.

The various patterns interlock, in the sense that each individual pattern implies others. Given an initial distribution of establishments among districts, a pattern of land use is implied. Given also a list of migratory movements, a new distribution of establishments among districts is implied, also a new pattern of land use and a certain pattern of land use succession. Whichever of these patterns we choose to manipulate, the others change by implication.

One clear difference among models of urban development, however, is just this choice. Some models focus on land use patterns, some on location patterns, a few on land use succession or on migration. The choice is important because it provides a focus for the ingenuity of the model builder. He strives for coherence in one pattern and neglects or subordinates the coherence of others. By this means, he radically reduces the number of relationships which enter into the determination of a solution to the model. Depending on the use to which the model will be put, such an incomplete solution may be adequate; but it is nonetheless incomplete.

. . .

Land use: the Chicago Area Transportation Study model. The method used by the Chicago Area Transportation Study (CATS) for forecasting 1980 land uses in that study area will serve as an example of a land use model. Of the models discussed, it is the earliest. It has a less formal structure than its successors, and *ad hoc* judgments are introduced at many points in the forecasting process. It is also unique among those to be discussed in that it was seriously used in conjunction with a transportation plan.[82]

The model is built around a strong system of land use accounting for small territorial subdivisions[83] of the study area. For each such district in turn, the future inventory of land uses is extrapolated from the initial inventory, according to rules (modified by judgment) specific to the kind of use. Six land uses are recognized: residential; commercial; manufacturing; transportation; public buildings; public open space; and streets. Vacant land is classified as residential, commercial, or industrial, according to its status under local zoning ordinances. Unusable land is also accounted for.

The initial land use pattern of each district is modified in six steps:

1. Specific parcels of land in some districts are designated for conversion to public open space and transportation uses (e.g., a new airport). The designations are based primarily on existing plans of public agencies for such development.
2. Commercially zoned vacant land in some districts is designated for shopping centers and heavy commercial uses. These designations are based on announced private plans and staff judgments.
3. Residentially zoned vacant land is designated for residential use. The amount so designated in each district depends on the location of the district and its residential holding capacity at existing or slightly modified net densities. The percentage of a district's holding capacity to be filled by 1980 is defined as a function of distance from the Central Business District (CBD), with sectoral and local modifications based on staff judgments.
4. For residentially oriented uses, per capita norms are applied to the estimated 1980 population of each district as determined in the third step. Thus, space for streets, local commercial facilities, public buildings, and recreation is set aside in each district.
5. Industrially zoned vacant land is designated for manufacturing use. The amount so designated in each district depends on the location of the district and its manufacturing holding capacity. Trends in net employment density in manufacturing establishments, both over time and by distance from the CBD, serve as the basis for 1980 forecasts of such employment density for each district; this projected density, in conjunction with the amount of industrial-

ly zoned space, determines the district's holding capacity. The percentage of this capacity to be filled by 1980 is defined as a function of distance from the CBD, with sectoral and local modifications based on staff judgments.

6. Since net activity density and acreage in each use have been explicitly predicted for each district, the implied population and employment totals for the district can be calculated. These are summarized for the study area as a whole and compared to independent projections of the area's population and employment. The land use forecast (acreage occupied) is then systematically modified so as to reconcile the implied activity total with the independent projections.

In terms of Fig. 12–26, this is clearly a column model. The inventory of land uses is projected for each district separately; the forecast is based on that district's initial inventory, its zoning map, and its location. The resulting tableau of land uses is modified by scaling the entries along each row so that they add to a control total. But the model avoids systematic comparisons of districts with respect to their merits as locations for establishments belonging to a given activity group; such comparisons are either highly generalized (distance from CBD) or else embedded in undocumented staff judgments (locations of shopping centers).

In its dynamic as well as its static aspects, land use accounting is much more rigorous than establishment accounting. Thus, there is a fairly explicit account of land use succession within each district, but no account whatever of the origins of new tenants of each district or of the destinations of those who leave.

In summary, the CATS model suppresses most horizontal relationships even at the level of aggregation implied by the reduced matrix of Fig. 12–26. Its implications for the full matrix of Fig. 12–25 are unguessable. We cannot say what structure of demand prices is consistent with the solution of the CATS model, nor can we infer much about the evaluation and investment functions which presumably motivate the establishments and land developers of Chicago.

. . .

Location: the EMPIRIC model. An interesting example of a model with a strong emphasis on locational patterns to the exclusion of other perspectives is the EMPIRIC, devised for the Boston Regional Planning Project by Traffic Research Corporation.[84] The model is designed to reallocate population and employment among the region's territorial subdivisions as the regional totals change over time and as local changes occur in the quality of public services and transportation networks. The territorial subdivisions are irregular in size and shape and many times larger than the twenty-three-acre cells of the University of North Carolina (UNC) model.

The model distinguishes two classes of population (blue-collar, white-collar) and three classes of employment (retail and wholesale, manufacturing, all other). The model is formulated as a set of simultaneous linear equations for each district, one equation for each population or employment variable. However, these equations do not directly estimate the number of households or employees to be assigned to each district at the target date. The dependent variable in each case is the change, during the forecasting interval, in the district's share of the regional total for that activity. After the model has been solved, these changes-in-shares are added into the shares held by each district at the beginning of the forecasting interval, and the revised shares determine the distribution of independently forecast totals for each activity group.

The determinants of each district's change-in-share of a given activity appear on the right-hand sides of the equations described above. They include concurrent change-in-share variables for each other activity and also variables which represent various site and accessibility characteristics of the district (existing activity distributions, quality of water service, quality of sewage disposal) constrain the solution of the equations so as to prevent "overdevelopment" of a district. Since the dependent variable of each equation is in any case a change-in-share of an unspecified regional total, the land use implications of this model's forecast of activity distributions do not in any significant way constrain the forecasts. In terms of the paradigm, EMPIRIC is *par excellence* a row model: the columns are left to fend for themselves.

Although EMPIRIC's equations solve for changes in the spatial distribution of the elements of each activity group, only net changes are explicit. The model does not comment on the pattern of inter-district flows necessary to produce these net changes. Needless to say, in view of the casual land use accounting, the model is also silent on the question of land use succession within each district.

There is a formal resemblance between the solution values of the EMPIRIC equations and the demand prices of the paradigm: a "score" is calculated for each activity in each district by means of a formula which greatly resembles the concept of an evaluation function. Conceivably, these scores might be interpreted as changes in demand prices which are subsequently added into the initial demand prices (base-year shares). But in any case, scores for different activities in the same district are never compared. Comparisons are horizontal rather than vertical, serving to allocate the establishments of a given activity among districts. The difficulty of finding a market interpretation for this method of allocation has already been indicated.

A hybrid: the Pittsburgh model. [Lowry's] contribution to the inventory of urban models was developed in the course of a study of the Pittsburgh Region, and is calibrated to data drawn from that study.[85] Although it could be described without great injustice as a location model, it has a stronger system of land use accounts than the preceding two examples, and the land use implications of each activity distribution serve as constraints on the distribution itself.

The model allocates three classes of retail employment and one of residential population among mile-square tracts of the urban region. The resulting pattern is claimed to be uniquely consistent with a given spatial distribution of basic employment. It is thus an equilibrium model with no time dimension.[86]

The model is formulated as a series of distributional algorithms, one for each activity. In the algorithm for residential distribution, each tract is assigned a score which reflects its accessibility to places of employment. A pool of households (whose number is consistent with total employment in the study area) is distributed among tracts in proportion to these scores. A maximum-density constraint, derived from the land use accounting system, limits the number of households which can be assigned to a specific tract, given the residential space available.

Retail employment is grouped into three activities, the number of employees in each being determined by productivity norms and the size of the regional market (number of households). The three groups correspond roughly with conventional hierarchical clusters—neighborhood, local, and metropolitan—which are functionally distinguished by the increasing territorial "range" of their markets.

For each retail activity, in turn, tracts are individually scored for their accessibility to consumer markets, i.e., to residential population and employment centers. The appropriate total of retail employment is then distributed among the tracts in proportion to these accessibility scores, with the proviso that the number of employees assigned to any one tract must be either zero or greater than a specified minimum.

The novel feature of the algorithm is an iterative process for achieving consistency between the spatial distributions of retail employment and residential population, each distribution entering (along with the distribution of basic employment) into the accessibility calculation for the others. The atemporal structure of the model naturally suppresses all questions of land use succession or internal migration of establishments.

Throughout the iterative sequence, the model carries a running account of land uses in each tract, beginning with fixed amounts assigned to exogenously located basic employment and fixed amounts of unusable land. Retail uses have next priority; each class of retail trade absorbs land at a fixed rate per employee so long as additional space is available; thereafter, retail densities automatically rise to accommodate the assigned number of employees.

For most tracts, however, the assigned complement of retail trade absorbs only a small fraction of the available land. The remainder is then classified as residential. In effect, households are the residual claimants of space in each tract. Residential density is a free variable which reflects rather than controls the household assignment up to the point at which the maximum-density constraint is violated.

The text of the report goes to some trouble to develop a market interpretation of the distributional algorithms without explicitly invoking land prices. In the case of retail trade, however, the effect of the algorithm is really to deny the relevance of land prices to retail location. Assuming that the accessibility scores indicate the relative volumes of business that can be done in each tract, the assignment of retail employment to tracts simply equalizes the volume of business per employee for all tracts; the assignment of retail land equalizes the volume of business per unit of space except in those few tracts where the assigned employment could not be accommodated at standard densities.

The case for a market interpretation of the method of residential distribution is somewhat better. Residential densities are not predetermined in the Pittsburgh model as they are in the CATS and UNC models. The accessibility score of a tract determines the number of households to be assigned there, and the average size of a residential parcel in the tract is jointly determined by this assignment and by the amount of residential space available after higher-priority uses have been accommodated. Residential density thus varies directly with the accessibility of a tract to places of employment; among tracts with equal accessibility scores, residential density varies inversely with the amount of space available.

These two results are generated by the model, not imposed upon it. The first result is clearly consistent with a market allocation of land given the assumption that accessible space commands a premium to which households adapt by living at higher densities. The second result is ambiguous; it would be clearly consistent with a market allocation only if accessibility fields did not overlap.

A striking feature of this model is its concentration on spatial relationships among different activities, to the exclusion of most other variables which seem pertinent to the market process described earlier. Households have no dimension except number; retail activities are only slightly more differentiated. Available space is described only by quantity and location; its historical development, as reflected in lot size or existing structures, is ignored. Virtually the entire machinery of the model is given over to the calculation of accessibility measures. The solution of the model is explicitly a *locational* equilibrium, constrained only by the availability of space.

Market demand: the Penn Jersey model. The builders of the models so far discussed were of course aware of the existence of a market for urban land, but their strategems are designed to avoid its explicit representation. We now turn to a model which undertakes this representation, although only for the market in residential land. It is a demand model because it limits the functions of landowners to choosing among prospective tenants; entrepreneurial behavior is suppressed.

The Penn Jersey model was originally formulated as a forecasting device for the Penn Jersey Transportation Study. Although the model was eventually abandoned by that Study in favor of other approaches, its development resumed at the Institute for Environmental Studies, University of Pennsylvania, under the guidance of its steward at Penn Jersey.[87]

In its first incarnation, the model was intended to link with other models dealing with nonresidential land and activities. The operations of the various models were to be sequenced so as to provide comprehensive forecasts of activity distributions and land uses within the region under study, distributions which were sensitive not only to changes in regional aggregates but also to changes in the transportation network. In the model's current development, its transportation features have been retained, but distributions of nonresidential activities are treated as independent parameters of residential distribution. The solution of the model is an atemporal equilibrium allocation of households to residential sites.

The data requirements of this model far exceed those of any of the models so far discussed. It calls for an inventory of households cross-classified by incomes, patterns of consumption preferences, and patterns of daily movement; and an inventory of all residential sites in the region, grouped into districts such that sites within a given district are homogeneous with respect to size of lot, type and quality of structure, and neighborhood amenities. For each district, accessibility to alternative destination-sets (the sets reflecting alternative patterns of daily movement) must be calculated.

These data are entered as arguments of an evaluation function similar in form to that presented earlier. Although the grouping of households and sites implies some repetition of entries, in principle the Penn Jersey model calculates the complete matrix of demand prices suggested by the paradigm (Fig. 12–25). The model then seeks the market-clearing solution which is interpreted as the "equilibrium" assignment of households to residential sites.

The solution is found by a linear program which assigns households to sites so as to maximize aggregate "rent-paying ability" of the region's population. This quantity was originally defined for an individual household as the household's budget allocation for jointly consumed housing and transportation *minus* the cost of obtaining these items in a given district if sites were free; in other words, it is the budget residual available for land rent. For a given pattern of daily travel, it is assumed that travel costs will vary with residential location. The cost of a dwelling unit which meets the household's standards would vary with the character of existing structures in a given area. Obviously this cost would be least when the appropriate housing is already in place, but, in principle, an existing structure could be remodeled or replaced. Thus the investment calculation attributed in my paradigm to landowners is here represented explicitly, but attributed to households evaluating sites.

In the current version of the model, this investment calculation has been suppressed. "Rent-paying ability" is replaced by "bid rent," a budget residual covering the entire residential package of site and structure (but not the cost of transportation), and households are not permitted to tamper with the given inventory of dwelling units. This modification was in part a response to certain mechanical difficulties in the linear program which threatened the integrity of the solution. Linear programing, an algorithm designed for continuous variables, does not readily cope with an assignment problem involving groups of households and groups of residential sites.[88]

An assignment of households to residential sites which maximizes bid rents is mathematically equivalent to the process by which the market-clearing solution was found in the paradigm; the reader can readily test this equivalence in the example offered by Fig. 12–25. Discussions of the Penn Jersey model have been much plagued by interpretations of this algorithm as an "optimizing" procedure. Depending on the reader's taste in welfare theory, the market-clearing solution may be endowed with social values, but surely these values do not derive from the algebra by which the solution is identified.

Designing a linear program appropriate to this assignment problem has proved difficult. Only recently have the architects of the model come to grips with an even more intractable problem, that of formulating and calibrating an evaluation function. This function is necessary to generate the matrix of demand prices; the linear program comes into play only *after* the matrix is available.

For the linear program, grouping households and sites is a means of reducing the assignment problem to dimensions manageable by present-day computer storage. For calibrating the evaluation function, grouping is essential to the statistical identification of preference structures, while selection of appropriate grouping criteria presupposes considerable *a priori* knowledge of these structures. It is not easy to break into this circle. The statistical identification of preference structures is the focus of current research on the Penn Jersey model.

With respect to that portion of the urban land market involving households and residential space, the Penn Jersey model closely approximates my land-market paradigm. (Indeed, that paradigm's construction was considerably aided by Herbert and Stevens' conceptualization of the assignment problem.) Within these limits, both row and column controls govern the allocation of a given pool of households to a given stock of sites. Because the solution is an atemporal equilibrium, it cannot comment on either the patterns of population movement or the incidence of land use succession en route to equilibrium.

FOOTNOTES TO CHAPTER 12

1. Public open space is considered as "used" land, but not as "developed" land. The distinction is necessary because public open space occurs in the Chicago region in very large parcels—an unusual and, in a sense, nonrecurring land use.

2. The two terms, Central Business District and Loop, will be used interchangeably. The Loop is considered to be the square-mile area centered on the intersection of State and Madison Streets; this district takes its name from the loop of elevated structures on Wabash Avenue, Lake, Wells, and Van Buren Streets.

3. The map referred to is in the Chicago Area Transportation Study, *Final Report, I: Survey Findings* (Chicago: Western Engraving and Embossing Company, 1959), pp. 12–27.

4. Brian J. L. Berry, *Commercial Structure and Commercial Blight* (Chicago: University of Chicago, Department of Geography, Research Paper No. 85, 1963).

5. *Ibid.*, p. 21

6. See *Mid-Chicago Economic Development Study, II: Technical Analysis and Findings*, The Center for Urban Studies, University of Chicago, 1966, pp. 4–13.

7. Allan R. Pred, "The Intrametropolitan Location of American Manufacturing," *Annals of the Association of American Geographers*, LIV (June, 1964), 165–80.

8. Industries not in this group are obviously also found in the mixed wholesaling and manufacturing district adjacent to the central business district. For a detailed geographical study of such a mixed district, see Marcel J. de Meirleir, *Manufactural Occupants in the West Central District of Chicago*, (Chicago: University of Chicago, Department of Geography, Research Paper No. 11, 1950).

9. For example, a relatively recent inquiry revealed that food processing firms in Philadelphia often select their sites with the intention of minimizing local distribution costs. See Institute for Urban Studies, University of Pennsylvania, *Industrial Land and Facilities for Philadelphia* (Philadelphia: City Planning Commission, 1956), p. 58.

10. Pred, "Intrametropolitan Location of American Manufacturing," pp. 174–75.

11. See James M. Hund, "Military and Industrial Electronics," in *The Industries of London since 1861*, ed. P. G. Hall (London, 1962), pp. 292–308.

12. Pred, "Intrametropolitan Location of American Manufacturing," p. 177.

13. For a discussion of "Port Industries," see M. Amphoux, "*Les Fonctions Portuaires*," *Revue de la Porte Oceane*, No. 54 (1949), 19–22; F. W. Morgan, *Ports and Harbours* (London: Hutchinson University Library, 2d ed., 1958), pp. 132–49. Also see W. A. Douglas Jackson, *Philadelphia's Water Front Industry* (Philadelphia: Department of Commerce, City of Philadelphia, 1955).

14. Pred, "Intrametopolitan Location of American Manufacturing," p. 178.

15. From Berry, *Commercial Structure and Commercial Blight*.

16. For an excellent discussion of the relations between growth and equilibrium, see Richard L. Meier, *A Communication Theory of Urban Growth* (Cambridge, Mass.: The M.I.T. Press, 1962).

17. Berry, *Commercial Structure and Commercial Blight*.

18. Although often more rapid were moves along "paths of least resistance" into adjacent higher-income communities, whose members were more likely to be able to make the jump to the suburbs.

19. In 1953, there were only 153 planned centers in the United States, yet by 1960 there were more than 4,000. These included 95 regional centers, each with 400,000 square feet or more floor area, 308 community centers, with 200,000 to 400,000 square feet, and over 3,200 neighborhood centers, with less than 200,000 square feet. Twenty of the regional centers had more than 1,000,000 square feet of ground floor area. See H. Hoyt, "The Status of Shopping Centers in the United States," *Urban Land*, No. 19. Similar data are available for Chicago from the Marketing Research Department of the *Chicago Tribune*.

20. R.L. Nelson, *The Selection of Retail Locations* (Chicago: F.W. Dodge Corporation, 1958).

21. R.H. Holton, "Scale, Specialization and Costs in Retailing" (Paper, School of Business, University of California, Berkeley, 1960).

22. For relevant supporting data, see R. D. Entenberg, *The Changing Competitive Position of Department Stores in the United States: by Merchandise Lines* (Pittsburgh: University of Pittsburgh Press, rev. ed, 1961).

23. J. E. Vance, Jr., "Emerging Patterns of Commercial Structure in American Cities," *Proceedings of the I. G. U. Symposium of Urban Geography*, Lund Studies in Geography, Series B, No. 24 (Lund, Sweden: Gleerup, 1962).

24. *Ibid.*, p. 493.

25. Holton, "Scale, Specialization and Costs in Retailing."

26. Vance, "Emerging Patterns of Commercial Structure in American Cities," p. 495.

27. Brian J. L. Berry and W. L. Garrison, "Cities and Freeways," *Landscape*, X (January, 1961), 20–23. See also W.L. Garrison *et al.*, *Studies of Highway Development and Geographic Change* (Seattle: University of Washington Press, 1959).

28. James W. Simmons, *The Changing Pattern of Retail Location*, Department of Geography, Research Paper No. 92, (Chicago: University of Chicago, 1964).

29. Nelson, *The Selection of Retail Locations*, p. 26.

30. Malcolm J. Proudfoot, "The Major Outlying Business Centers of Chicago" (Ph.D. Dissertation, University of Chicago, 1936), p. 231.

31. See Brian J. L. Berry, "The Impact of Expanding Metropolitan Communities upon the Central Place Hierarchy," *Annals of the Association of American Geographers*, L (June, 1960), 112–17.

32. Inez K. Rolph, "The Population Pattern in Relation to Retail Buying," *American Journal of Sociology*, XXXVIII (1932), 368–76.

33. Proudfoot, "The Major Outlying Business Centers of Chicago," Chap. iii.

34. Brian J. L. Berry and Harold M. Mayer, *A Comparative Study of Central Place Systems*, Report to the Office of Naval Research, 2121–18, Project NR389–196, 1961, Part 3, p. 9.

35. The assumptions are similar to those used by other authors who have analyzed urban land rents. For example, see William Alonso's study of land rent, *Location and Land Use: Toward a General Theory of Land Rent* (Cambridge, Mass.: Harvard University Press, 1964).

36. For a detailed development of the analysis concerning this gradient, see Leon N. Moses, "Towards a Theory of Intra-urban Wage Differentials and Their Influence on Travel

Patterns," *Papers of the Regional Science Association*, IX (1962), 53–64.

37. For a study of freight costs and their impact upon the New York metropolitan region, see Benjamin Chinitz, *Freight and the Metropolis* (Cambridge, Mass.: Harvard University Press, 1960).

38. The attractiveness of suburban locations was also enhanced by other technological changes during this period. For a discussion of such factors, see J. R. Mayer, J. F. Kain, and M. Wohl, *The Urban Transportation Problem* (Cambridge, Mass.: Harvard University Press, 1965). Improvements in data processing and communications, e.g., meant that firms could remain "near" other firms though they had moved many miles away.

39. Though the results were summarized without this distinction, there were actually four groups of firms examined. The division was by type of move, relocation or expansion, between 1950 and 1959 and 1960 to 1964. The latter division was made because the data for each period were gathered at different times by different groups, though from the same sources. In general, the results are similar for all four groups.

40. The four groups are, respectively, those relocating and expanding 1950–1959 and 1960–1964.

41. Size was measured by the cost of land and construction associated with relocation or expansion at a new site.

42. The regression of number of firms on distance moved provided a good fit for the small-sized categories but had a reduced and often insignificant coefficient of determination for large firms. In other words, the distribution of number of firms did not decrease sharply as distance moved increased for the latter group.

43. The number of destinations in both groups per square mile in the north, west, and south sectors, respectively, was 1.21, 1, and .54, while the percentage of land in manufacturing was 1.9, 3.1, and 4.4.

44. When the regression is calculated for each of the seven CATS sectors, the explanatory power is further improved, especially in the southern sectors. Except for one case, the coefficient of determination is over .40 and ranges as high as .74.

45. For example, see the arguments in Richard U. Ratcliff, *Urban Land Economics* (New York: McGraw-Hill Book Company, 1949).

46. The tendency for land values to decrease is by no means consistent or clearly understood. See, e.g., Wendt's study of central area land values in both San Francisco and Oakland, in which he contrasts the increasing values in the former area and the decline in the latter: Paul F. Wendt, *Dynamics of Central City Land Values, San Francisco and Oakland*, Real Estate Research Program, Research Report No. 18, (Berkeley: University of California, 1961).

47. The contention that land appreciates with time because of the inelasticity of supply is *not* valid for urban land as a whole. The land area available for most urban areas is essentially unlimited, given technological innovations. The tendency for land to appreciate can be attributed to generally increasing demands for land at given locations within the city. The amount of land for particular types of use, at any location, is essentially limited.

48. Larry S. Bourne, *Private Redevelopment of the Central City* (Chicago: University of Chicago, Department of Geography, Research Paper No. 112, 1967), pp. 17 ff.

49. Ratcliff, *Urban Land Economics*, p. 403.

50. A. H. Schaaf, *Economic Aspects of Urban Renewal: Theory, Policy and Area Analysis*, Institute of Business and Economic Research, Research Report No. 14 (Berkeley, Calif., 1960).

51. For example, we are ignoring completely the effects of variations in interest and mortgage rates, construction costs, and the like, which would commonly enter into an economic analysis.

52. Turvey argues that the division between land and building value, common in American assessment practices, is meaningless except in the case of long run equilibrium, as "no ordinary building is ever sold floating in the air"—Ralph Turvey, *The Economics of Real Property: An Analysis of Property Values and Patterns of Use* (London: George Allen and Unwin Ltd., 1957).

53. See Raleigh Barlowe, *Land Resource Economics: The Political Economy of Rural and Urban Land Resource Use* (Englewood Cliffs, N.J.: Prentice-Hall, Inc., 1958).

54. See Richard U. Ratcliff, *Real Estate Analysis* (New York: McGraw-Hill Book Company, 1961), p. 123.

55. Stanislaw Czamanski, *Economic Growth Forecast for Baltimore* (Baltimore: Urban Renewal and Housing Agency, 1964), pp. 39–40. The value of P (population) for 1980 is 2,423,000; of E (total employment) in 1980, 875,400.

56. Y was in millions of dollars.

57. Czamanski *et al.*, *Family Income and Current Consumption* (Baltimore: Urban Renewal and Housing Agency, 1965).

58. Actually, at this stage the number of relevant centers in 1980 was limited to 12. Pimlico race track and Fort McHenry were eliminated because they contributed very little to the final results.

59. It should be noted that areas of land values below 50¢, per square foot disappear altogether. The areas of highest land values are more extensive and numerous than in 1964. The CBD is still the largest area of highest land values, and now includes the state office complex. On the other hand, the northern part of the Charles Street corridor no longer belongs to the highest land values area. Another important development is the appearance of numerous islands of high land values near or around projected subway stations. The most remarkable development occurs at Johns Hopkins University campus. Some isolated areas to the west of the subway obviously benefit from its construction. On the other hand, some areas within the subway loop do not benefit, despite the general increase in land values.

60. Some model builders would freely substitute "simulate" for "replicate." All models are intended in some sense to simulate reality, but this usage is a source of some confusion in the literature since "simulation" has acquired another more technical meaning, descriptive of a class of algorithms. In this essay, the term is used only in the latter sense. See "Solution Methods," further on in the paper.

61. For example, traffic analysts use zonal interchange models to generate estimates of zone-to-zone traffic flows from inventories of the land uses in each zone. One prominent member of the profession is so convinced of the descriptive reliability of these models that he sees no further need for direct survey of traffic movements (Origin and Destination studies).

62. Philosophers of science view the concepts of "cause" and "effect" with jaundiced eyes. For lesser mortals these concepts are most helpful and not at all dangerous so long as they are applied within the framework of a system of interdependence. See Herbert A. Simon, *Models of Man* (New York: John Wiley & Sons, Inc., 1957), Chaps. i–iii.

63. No variable is intrinsically endogenous or exogenous.

These terms, like the statisticians "dependent" and "independent," merely define the position of a variable within a particular model. A further useful distinction can be made between exogenous variables subject to policy control and those which are not, and between endogenous variables of direct interest to the planner and those which are included only because they are necessary to complete the logical structure of the model. See Sidney Sonenblum and Lewis H. Stern, "The Use of Economic Projections in Planning," *Journal of the American Institute of Planners*, XXX (1964), 110–23.

64. The fundamentals and applications of linear programming are summarized in a very readable form by William J. Baumol, "Activity Analysis in One Lesson," *American Economic Review*, XLVIII (December, 1958), 837–73. A simple exposition of dynamic programming is not available but, for a brief account of the class of problems to which the technique is applicable, see Richard Bellman, *Dynamic Programming* (Princeton, N.J.: Princeton University Press, 1957).

65. The value of Y is a function of (depends on) the values of U, V, X, Z, and so on. For a gentle introduction to the notation and method of mathematical modeling, an excellent source is E. F. Beach's *Economic Models: An Exposition* (New York: John Wiley & Sons, Inc., 1957).

66. Some examples, in prose rather than symbols: technological—the maximum vehicular capacity of a roadway is a function of the number of lanes, the average distance between signals, and weather; institutional—disposable family income is a function of gross family earnings and the tax rate; behavioral—the level of housing density chosen by a family depends on disposable family income, the average age of family members, and the location of the workplace of the principle wage earner; accounting—total land in use is the sum of land in residential use, in retail use, in manufacturing use, and so forth.

67. The essays in George Kingsley Zipf, *Human Behavior and the Principle of Least Effort* (Reading, Mass: Addson-Wesley Publishing Company, Inc., 1949), Part 2, should give the reader a "feel" for the macro-analytic perspective in urban models. See also Gerald A. P. Carrothers, "An Historical Review of the Gravity and Potential Concepts of Human Interaction," *Journal of the American Institute of Planners*, XXII (January, 1956), 94–102; and Brian J. L. Berry, "Cities as Systems within Systems of Cities," Paper presented at the annual meeting of the Regional Science Association, Chicago, November, 1963.

68. For an excellent review of the theory of rational choice in a planning context, see John W. Dyckman, "Planning and Decision Theory," *Journal of the American Institute of Planners*, XXVII (June, 1961), 335–45. Any introductory text in economics will describe the micro-analytic underpinnings of demand and supply schedules and will also review a family of market models. The most ambitious micro-analytic model ever undertaken in the social sciences is described in Guy H. Orcutt *et al.*, *Micro Analysts of Socio-economic Systems: A Simulation Study* (New York: Harper & Row, Publishers, 1961). For models that embrace more than "economic" man, see Simon, *Models of Man*, or Paul F. Lazarsfeld, *Mathematical Thinking in the Social Sciences* (New York: The Free Press, 1954).

69. See Nathaniel Field, "Cost-Benefit Analysis in City Planning," *Journal of the American Institute of Planners*, XXVI (1960), 273–79.

70. It is Lowry's personal conviction—not shared by all members of the fraternity of model builders—that the macro-analytic approach to modeling urban form and processes shows the greater promise of providing reliable answers to concrete problems of prediction and planning. For a contrary view, see the forceful statement by Britton Harris, "Some Problems in the Theory of Intra-Urban Location," Paper prepared for a seminar sponsored by the Committee on Urban Economics of Resources for the Future, Washington, D.C., April, 1961, p. 16.

71. Descriptive models of urban form are nearly always static or "equilibrium" models and are sometimes used for quasi-predictions (comparative statics). For convenient examples, see Britton Harris, "A Model of Locational Equilibrium for Retail Trade," Paper prepared for the Seminar on Models of Land Use Development, Institute of Urban Studies, University of Pennsylvania, Philadelphia, October, 1964; and Ira S. Lowry, *A Model of Metropolis*, RM-4035-RC (Santa Monica, Calif.: The Rand Corporation, 1964).

72. Contrast the emphasis on stocks in the San Francisco Community Renewal Program model designed by A. D. Little, Inc., "A Simulation Model of the Residential Space Market in San Francisco," Paper prepared for the Seminar on Models of Land Use Development, Institute of Urban Studies, University of Pennsylvania, Philadelphia, October, 1964, with the emphasis on flows in Richard S. Bolan, Willard B. Hansen, Neil A. Irwin, and Carl H. Dieter, "Planning Applications of a Simulation Model," Paper prepared for the New England Section, Regional Science Association, Fall Meeting, Boston College, October, 1963, or with the several "Growth Allocation" models described in the *Journal of the American Institute of Planners*, XXXI (May, 1965).

73. See Russell VanNest Black, "Scientific Empirical Projections," *Journal of the American Institute of Planners*, XXVI (May, 1960), 144–45.

74. The reader is warned that Eq. 21 is not a general solution for Y_{t+n}, but merely the simplest expression for Y_{t+4}.

75. An example of the iterative technique is given earlier in this chapter.

76. A good bibliography on simulation methods is Martin Shubik's "Bibliography on Simulation, Gaming, Artificial Intelligence and Allied Topics," *Journal of the American Statistical Association*, LV (October, 1960), 736–51. M. A. Geisler, W. W. Haythorne, and W. A. Steger, *Simulation and Logistics Systems Laboratory* (Santa Monica, Calif.: RM-3281-PR, The Rand Corporation, 1962), offer a readable and quick review of the field with emphasis on man-machine simulation, or "gaming." Nathan D. Grundstein, in "Computer Simulation of a Community for Gaming," Paper prepared for the annual meeting of the American Association for the Advancement of Science, Denver, December, 1961, describes a "community game" for the training of planners and municipal administrators.

77. Special data problems encountered in modeling urban form and process are discussed by Britton Harris, "An Accounts Framework for Metropolitan Models," in *Elements of Regional Accounts*, ed. Werner Z. Hirsch (Baltimore: Johns Hopkins Press, 1964), pp. 107–27. See also Wilbur A. Steger, "Data and Information Management in a Large Scale Modeling Effort: The Pittsburgh Urban Renewal Simulation Model," Paper prepared for the Seminar on Models of Land Use Development, Institute of Urban Studies, University of Pennsylvania, Philadelphia, October, 1964.

78. Beach, in *Economic Models*, Part 2, provides an especially good introduction to statistical econometric methods.

79. The convenience of this method is so great that it is often applied to systems containing known nonlinearities, on

the grounds that a linear approximation is better than nothing. Simultaneous estimation of the parameters of nonlinear systems is possible, but more difficult; the outstanding example among land use models is Carl Dieter's program, POLIMETRIC, for fitting an exponential model with a great many parameters. (The model, but not the fitting method, is described in Bolan, *et al.*, "Planning Applications").

80. See John H. Niedercorn, *An Econometric Model of Metropolitan Employment and Population Growth*, RM-3758-RC (Santa Monica, Calif.: The Rand Corporation, 1963). His model is partitioned into three subsystems, each of which was fitted independently; the discussion on pp. 14–15 illustrates the variety of estimating methods ordinarily required to fit a model. See also Harris, "Some Problems," for a discussion of the "gradient search" method of estimating parameters.

81. Donald M. Hill, in "A Growth Allocation Model for the Boston Region: Its Development, Calibration, and Validation," Paper prepared for the Seminar on Models of Land Use Development, Institute of Urban Studies, University of Pennsylvania, Philadelphia, October, 1964, reports with unusual thoroughness on a test of this type for the EMPIRIC model developed for Boston by Traffic Research Corporation.

82. Sources are John R. Hamburg and Robert H. Sharky, *Land Use Forecast*, Document No. 32, 610 (Chicago: Chicago Area Transportation Study, 1961); and Chicago Area Transportation Study, *Final Report*, II (Chicago: Western Engraving and Embossing Company, 1960), 16–33.

83. These are "traffic zones" in the original. They will be called "districts" to avoid confusion with "land use zones" determined by municipal ordinances.

84. The account is based on Donald M. Hill, "A Growth Allocation Model for the Boston Region," *Journal of the American Institute of Planners*, XXXI (May, 1965), 111–20; and Donald M. Hill, Daniel Brand, and Willard B. Hansen, "Prototype Development of a Statistical Land Use Prediction Model for the Greater Boston Region," *Highway Research Board Record*, No. 114 (1965), pp. 51–70. There have been subsequent revisions of the model, not yet documented in quotable form. These pertain mostly to further disaggregation of both activities and territorial units; it is assumed they do not effect the structural features to be discussed here.

85. See the earlier discussion in this chapter. The method used for simultaneously estimating the parameters of all equations should yield regression coefficients that are true partial derivatives. However, the logic of these equations is puzzling. Since each district's population and employment variables are expressed as changes in shares, the fitted parameters fix relationships among these changes in *shares* without regard for the magnitude or even the sign of changes in the total regional volumes of the relevant activities. The fitted equations tell nothing about the relationships among changes in volumes for the activities within a district—eds.

86. A time-phased version of the model was developed by CONSAD Research Corporation. See John P. Crecine, *A Time Oriented Metropolitan Model for Spatial Location*, Community Renewal Program technical Bulletin No. 6 (Pittsburgh: Department of City Planning, 1964).

87. Lowry's direct sources are John Herbert and Benjamin J. Stevens, "A Model for the Distribution of Residential Activities in Urban Areas," *Journal of Regional Science*, II (February, 1960), 21–36; Britton Harris, *Linear Programming and the Projection of Land Uses*, Penn Jersey, Paper No. 20 (Harrisburg: Pennsylvania Department of Highways, n.d.); Britton Harris, Joseph Nathanson, and Louis Rosenberg, *Research on an Equilibrium Model of Metropolitan Housing and Locational Change*, and Britton Harris, *Basic Assumptions for a Simulation of the Urban Residential Housing and Land Market* (Philadelphia: University of Pennsylvania, Institute for Environmental Study, both dated 1966).

88. The issues are too complex for exposition here; but cf. Herbert and Stevens, "Model for the Distribution of Residential Activities," with Harris, *Basic Assumptions*, especially on the use of "subsidies" as a variable in the original model.

CHAPTER 13

movement

It is movement, the daily ebb and flow of people and traffic, that knits the social areas and functional zones of the metropolis into an integrated whole. Yet all contemporary discussions of movement in our cities are framed in terms of current and emerging difficulties and impedances.

"Every metropolitan area in the United States is confronted by a transportation problem that seems destined to become more aggravated in the years ahead," said Wilfred Owen, and his statement has been repeated many times by different authors.[1] What is the nature of the urban transportation problem? William Garrison has cited several critical problem areas:

1. *Much travel in urban areas is not as comfortable and convenient as we desire.* Vehicles are often noisy, too hot or too cold, and poorly ventilated; there may be delays and uncertainties, and many routes and facilities are unattractive.
2. *Many transit systems have fiscal difficulties.* In some the fare box will not bring in enough money to cover fixed and operating expenses and needs for new investment.
3. *Many facilities are grossly congested.* Five mornings a week and five evenings a week streets and transit facilities (and urban airports and sidewalks) are crowded; they do not operate efficiently and delays are frequent.
4. *Transportation restricts the quality of urban life.* Choices of living, shopping, playing, visiting and working places may be constrained because they are difficult of access. Limitations of the transportation system may restrict advances in housing, employment, education, and other urban activities.
5. *Enormous expenditures must be made in order to meet demands for urban transportation.* Urban highway investments are made at the rate of at least six billion dollars a year, and requirements for airports, mass transportation facilities and other transportation facilities also run into billions of dollars. The urban transportation problem requires meeting massive costs and the allocation of those costs.
6. *Urban transportation systems should be safer.* About one-half of our accidents and injuries in highway

transportation are in urban areas, and it is here that most pedestrian deaths occur. In some cities emissions from combustion pose problems.

7. *Urban physical distribution costs are high.* Congested streets delay truck movements.[2]

What is the context of movement patterns in metropolitan areas, within which these problems are set? Valuable background data are provided by studies in *urban transportation geography* such as were completed by the Chicago Area Transportation Study.

*THE NATURE OF MOVEMENT IN URBAN AREAS**

The CATS travel inventories were designed to represent travel undertaken in the Chicago region on the average weekday in 1956. Every trip made by a person or vehicle within the study area had to be represented. It was necessary, therefore, to consider the different kinds of trips being made and to find the most reliable and economical means of sampling each type. Obviously a complete enumeration of 10,500,000 daily trips was impossible.[3]

Trips made within a bounded region may be classified into three types on the basis of the location of their origins and destinations. A trip may have both origin and destination within the study area, or one end in and one end outside, or both ends outside.

Those trips having both origin and destination inside the study area were sampled in the "internal" travel surveys. These were broken down into two parts: the home interview survey which obtained data on trips made by persons (whether by automobile or public transportation), and the commercial vehicle survey which obtained data on trips made by trucks and taxis. Those trips with one or both ends outside the study area were sampled at the cordon line bounding the area. The cordon-line or external surveys were of two types: a roadside survey which sampled trucks, taxis, and private automobiles, and a survey of suburban railroad passengers.

The vast bulk of all trips made in the Chicago area have both ends inside the study area. Only 5.3 per cent of all trips made by persons, and 5.2 per cent of all trips made by vehicles, were recorded at the external surveys. Among the internal surveys, the home interview survey accounted for 94.7 per cent of all trips made by persons, and 78.4 per cent of all vehicle trips. Although the home interview survey was the most expensive to undertake, it provided data on the largest segment of average daily travel.

Home interviews were made at every thirtieth dwelling place throughout the study area, approximately 58,000 sample units. Using the dwelling place as the basic unit permitted the sample to be selected very carefully,[4] and the interview could be conducted without haste and hence more thoroughly. Another advantage of the home interview technique was that travel by all types of transportation could be recorded.

At each home, two kinds of information were obtained. The first covered the characteristics of the sample unit itself, including type of dwelling place, number of residents, sex and race of head of household, car ownership, number of drivers, and total number of trips made. This was, in effect, a sample census of population. The second type of information concerned the trips which were made by each member of the household. This included the address of each trip's origin and destination, trip purpose, land use at origin and destination, mode of travel (by automobile, bus, subway, elevated or suburban railroad), and time of departure and arrival.[5]

Commercial motor vehicles registered within the study area were sampled from lists obtained from the State of Illinois. Trucks were sampled at the rate of one in every fifteen (6.67 per cent). Taxis were sampled at the rate of one in thirty (3.33 per cent).[6] Interviews were conducted with the driver of each vehicle or with his dispatcher, and data similar to those obtained by the home interview survey were recorded.

*Reprinted from the Chicago Area Transportation Study, *Final Report, I: Survey Findings* (Chicago: Western Engraving and Embossing Company, 1959), with the permission of the Agency.

Trips, made by automobile, taxi, or truck, which had one or both ends outside the study area, were surveyed at a series of roadside interview stations set up on all the principal roads crossing the cordon line. When these stations were in operation, a sample of about 25 per cent of the [drivers of the] stream of vehicles in each direction was interviewed. Trip data about origin, destination, purpose, land use, and number of persons per car were recorded.

Finally, to insure completeness of coverage, a survey was taken of those persons commuting across the cordon line into the study area by suburban railroad. Inbound passengers were given postcards asking for information comparable with that obtained in the other travel surveys. The returns provided a sample in excess of 50 per cent of such travelers.

Number and Characteristics of Weekday Trips

Just over 10,500,000 "person trips" were made in the study area on the average weekday in 1956. Of these, 10,200,000 were made by residents and 300,000 by nonresidents.[7]

Vehicles made 6,100,000 trips within the cordon line. Of these, 5,900,000 trips were made by residents in their automobiles and by trucks and taxis registered in the area.

For most analytical purposes, the figures of 10,200,000 person trips and 5,900,000 vehicle trips will be used. This is partly because these trips are related to the resident population, and partly because these trips are directly related to the land area within the cordon line.[8]

Trip production rates. There were in 1956 over 1,667,000 occupied dwelling places in the study area. These units housed 5,170,000 persons, at an average rate of 3.1 persons per occupied dwelling place.

The population living in these dwelling places reported owning 1,342,000 automobiles. This is an average of .8 automobiles per occupied dwelling place; it can also be expressed as 260 automobiles per 1,000 population.[9] In addition to automobiles, 130,000 trucks and 5,600 taxis were registered and garaged in the study area. Trucks make up about 8.2 per cent of the total number of vehicles registered.[10] The total rate of vehicle ownership is 310 vehicles per 1,000 population (see Fig. 13-1).

If the total number of resident trips with destinations in the study area is divided by the number of persons, the figure of 2 trips per person per day is obtained. This is the equivalent of one tround trip per person on the average weekday. So, if 1,000,000 persons are added to the population of the study area, at least 2,000,000 additional trips will be made each weekday.

The average household's automobile in 1956 made about 3.7 trips per weekday, the equivalent of about two round trips per day. Trucks made 6.4 trips per day, on the average. This can be pictured as five deliveries and a return

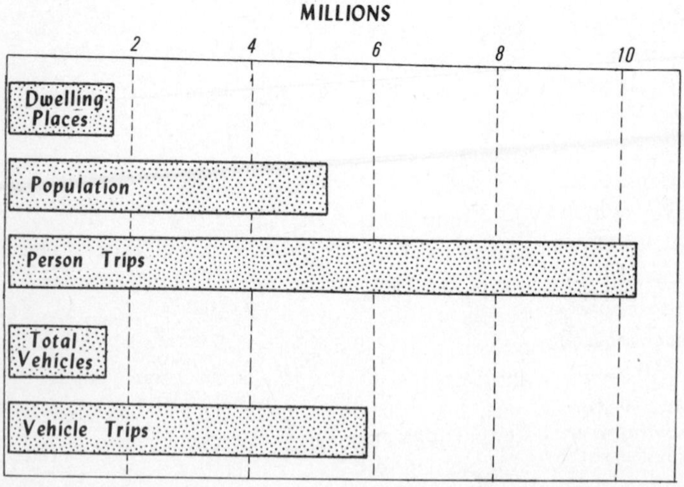

FIGURE 13-1. Total dwelling places, population, vehicles, and weekday trip production: Chicago area. *Source:* Figs. 13-1 through 13-8 and 13-10 through 13-15 are from the Chicago Area Transportation Study, *Final Report, I: Survey Findings* (Chicago: Western Engraving and Embossing Company, 1959).

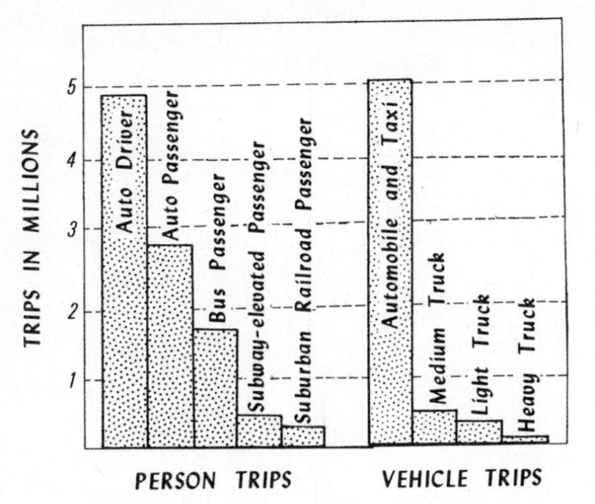

FIGURE 13–2. Person trips by mode of travel, vehicle trips by vehicle type: Chicago area. *Source:* See caption for Fig. 13–1.

to garage, or as three round trips, such as might be made by a coal truck. Taxis averaged 30.5 trips per day!

Mode of travel; vehicle type. Of all person trips, roughly three-quarters were made by automobile in 1956. One-quarter was made by all forms of mass transportation, including buses, subway and elevated trains, and suburban railroads.

Buses carried 16.5 per cent of all person trips—nearly 1,700,000 trips per day. Elevated and subway lines carried 480,000 trips (4.7 per cent of all person trips) and suburban railroads served 266,000 riders (2.6 per cent of all person trips) on the average weekday. As will be described later, these trips take on an added significance because of their length and their concentration in time and place.

Just over 63 per cent of all person trips made by automobile were made by automobile drivers. The average number of persons per car is therefore roughly 1.5. This does not include children under five.

Although comprising only 8.2 per cent of all vehicles, trucks made 13.9 per cent of all vehicle trips. The reason is that trucks make more trips daily per vehicle. Taxis, with 3 per cent of all vehicles, made 2.9 per cent of all vehicle trips. The remaining trips—83.2 per cent or about four-fifths of the total—are made by automobiles (see Fig. 13-2).

Purpose of travel and land use. The dominant trip purpose of persons is to home; 43.5 per cent of all person trips are made for this purpose.[11] Since an equal number of persons must leave home, almost 87 per cent of all person trips are anchored with one end at the home. This is a powerful influence in organizing travel patterns.

Work trips make up one-fifth of all person trips. Again, an equal number must come from work as go to work, and so it can be said that roughly 40 per cent of all person travel is work oriented.

Other trip purposes are individually much less important. Personal business trips and social-recreation trips each account for about one-tenth of all person trips. All other trip purposes combined, including shopping, school, ride, serve passenger and eat meal, make up about one-eighth of all person trips.

There is a strong and logical correspondence between trip purposes and the land use to which the trip is destined. While but 43.5 per cent of all person trips are returning to their homes, more than half of all person trips are destined to residential land. The reason for the difference is that a number of work and social-recreation trips are made to residential land. Work trips by domestics and servicemen and visits by families or friends are good examples. Residential land, like the home trip purpose, is of great importance in fixing the location of travel.

Trips made to service establishments and to wholesale and retail locations make up 24 per cent of all person travel. These types of activities fall in the broad category of commercial land use. Thus slightly more than half of those trips not bound to residential land are bound to commercial land.

All other land uses combined attract 21.1 per cent of all trips. Manufacturing (both durable and nondurable) gets 7.6 per cent of all person trips, and public buildings (schools, churches, post offices and the like) attract 7.7 per cent. The remaining land uses (such as public open space

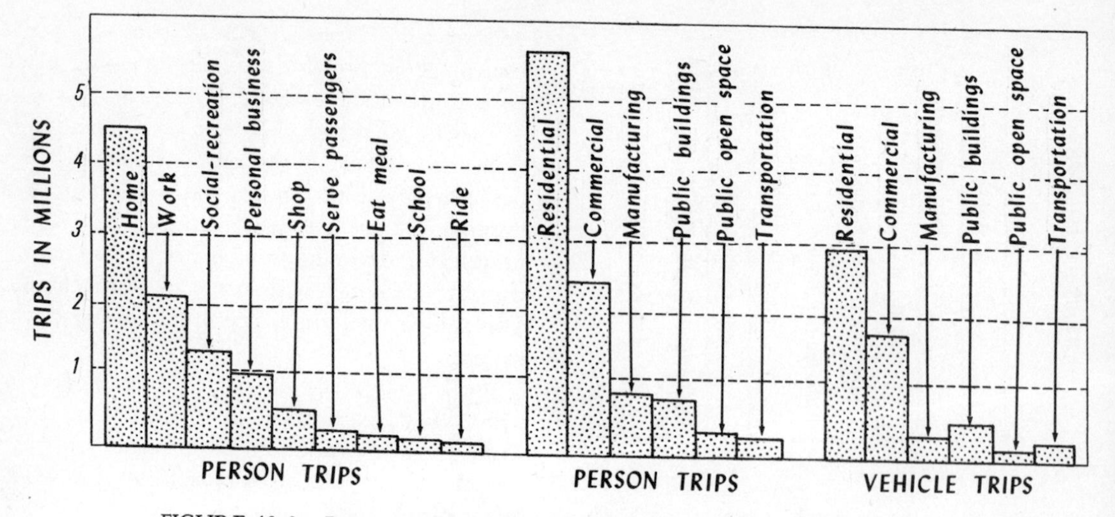

FIGURE 13-3. Person trips by purpose and land use, vehicle trips by land use: Chicago area. *Source:* See caption for Fig. 13-1.

and transportation) are minor generators of travel, as might be expected.

Vehicle trips[12] have a land use distribution similar to that of person trips. The similarity is natural because automobiles and taxis carry three-quarters of all person trips. As a result, slightly less than one-half of all vehicle trips go to residential land, whereas slightly more than one-half of all person trips go to residential land. On the other hand, more vehicle trips (28.8 per cent) go to commercial land than do person trips (24 per cent).

The difference between the land use distribution of person trips and vehicle trips is caused by three factors. First, 72 per cent of all truck trips are bound for nonresidential activities. Second, people use different modes of travel according to their trip purposes. For example, a smaller proportion of vehicle trips than of person trips is made to public buildings because more children go to school by bus than by car. And third, car loading varies for different trip purposes. Over-all land use distributions of person and vehicle trips are shown in Fig. 13-3.

. . .

Patterns of Travel in Time and Space

It is difficult for an individual, driving in a stream of traffic or traveling by bus or rapid transit, to see the orderliness in the travel patterns of which he is an infinitesimal part. But upon reflection, the principal patterns are obvious. He knows when and where traffic peaks are high or low, and when buses or trains will be most or least crowded. Clearly, he can only know this if travel patterns are repetitive in time and space.

Time. Throughout the year, the amount of travel taking place within the Chicago area is quite even. Figure 13-4 shows the daily vehicle counts of five permanent counter stations maintained by the Study, and also the average weekday and weekend travel for the mass transportation system operated by the Chicago Transit Authority. As shown in this figure, the variation about the annual average weekly travel seldom exceeds ± 12 per cent, despite the fact tht two out of the five permanent counter stations are subject to summer seasonal loads.

Although these particular street traffic and mass transportation data cannot be added together, it can be seen that when automobile traffic increases, mass transportation usage declines, and vice versa. Thus, there is a certain cancellation of peaks and valleys in travel, leading to an even greater steadiness in the amount of trip making within the Chicago area throughout the year.

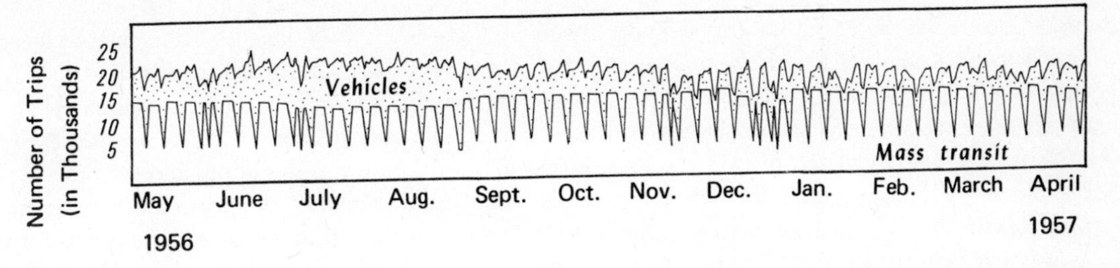

FIGURE 13–4. Variations in average daily travel on streets and in mass transportation: Chicago area, 1956 to 1957. *Source:* See caption for Fig. 13–1.

Within the yearly pattern there is a repetitive weekly pattern broken only by holidays. The variation of the days of the week about average weekday traffic is of the same order as the seasonal variations. Within the week, high and low traffic volumes differ by ± 5 per cent from average weekday travel. Mondays and Tuesdays are slightly under average; Friday is typically the busiest day. Weekend traffic is generally less than weekday traffic.[13]

In sum, seasonal variations in travel are slight. Variations in travel within the week are also slight. Both follow a regular pattern. All this is reasonable, since continuous activity is necessary if a large community like Chicago is to keep producing the goods and services which keep it alive. The concept of average weekday travel is therefore valid and can be used for planning purposes.

The fact is that the greatest variation in travel occurs within the day, and not within the week or year. The average 24-hour weekday has a regular cycle of travel, as shown in Fig. 13-5. The peaking of travel in the morning

FIGURE 13–5. Hourly distribution of different types of internal person trips: Chicago area. *Source:* See caption for Fig. 13–1.

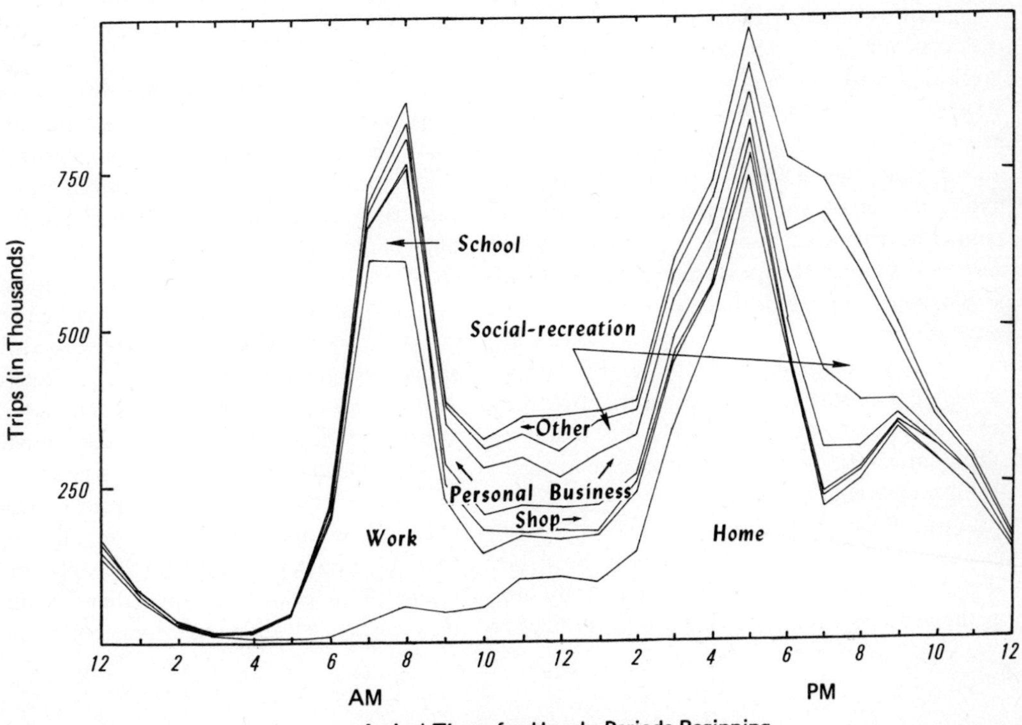

rush hour is twice, and in the evening rush hour two and one-half times, the average hourly travel. It is this peaking within the day which causes the most severe traffic problems.

Why travel is organized in this way is readily explained by the purposes for which travel is undertaken. At 4:00 in the morning, the urban area is very nearly at rest. From 7:00 to 10:00 A.M. there is a big surge of travel to work. This is matched by a slightly greater movement back home in the period 4:00 to 7:00 P.M. Other trip purposes have their own patterns. Personal business trips are fairly evenly spaced throughout the day, as are shopping trips. Social-recreation, as might be expected, peaks in the period between 6:00 and 10:00 P.M. While trips to work and home make up the greatest part of peak hour travel, other trip purposes, such as school, shopping, personal business, and social-recreation, combine to form 35 per cent of the morning peak and 25 per cent of the evening peak.

It can be seen that the reasons for the daily cycle of traffic are founded in the whole way of life of an urban society. Barring major catastrophes, or significant changes in social organization, it is unlikely that there will be any real shifts in this cycle. The times of the day when people eat, work and rest tend to be stable—basically, they are geared to the sun's rising and setting. Therefore, it is quite reasonable to use current data in forecasting time distribution of travel.

Space. Travel also has definite regularities in space. For example, during the average 24-hour period, the number of trips entering any given area equals, for all practical purposes, the number leaving that area. This principle is one which is supported by common sense. More people could not come into a small area than leave it, day after day, without accumulating an excess population very rapidly. In another example, if people leave a residential area they must also return to that same residential area during an *average* 24-hour period or else it would become deserted.

Empirical proof that arrivals equal departures during any 24-hour period is readily available. The number of persons entering the study area on the average weekday is 175,000. The number leaving is 177,000. This is a difference of less than 1 per cent. Of the forty-four districts making up the study area, only two had a difference between inbound and outbound travel of more than 1 per cent. One was the Loop, and the other district contained Midway Airport. Both districts are noted for their transient populations and for their intercity travel. Despite the difficulty of keeping precise records on travel in and out of such districts, the difference between inbound and outbound travel in each case was less than 2 per cent. In all these cases, the difference between input and output was always less than the sampling error.[14] Thus, as far as sample data can prove a rule, it has been demonstrated that inbound travel equals outbound travel from any area during the average weekday.

Related to the foregoing is the rule of directional symmetry of travel. Travel in one direction equals travel in the opposite direction for any 24-hour period. If 1,000 trips leave Evanston to go to Elmhurst, then an equal number will leave Elmhurst to go to Evanston within the same day.[15]

Table 13–1 summarizes trips both by purpose from and purpose to. It shows that 1,652,000 trips go to work from home and 1,581,000 trips return to home from work. This is a difference of about 4 per cent. About 405,000 trips go from home to shop while 432,000 go from shop to home. This is a difference of less than 7 per cent. Slightly more trips go to work than come home directly from work, while slightly more trips return to home from shopping than go to shop from home. Thus, a small percentage of trips do make a triangular trip from home to work and then to shopping. Only 5.2 per cent of all trips are unmatched triangular trips, computed on a purpose basis.[16] This shows that triangularity is quite limited and its importance should not be exaggerated.

Knowledge of the fact of directional symmetry, which almost amounts to a natural law, permits the transportation planner to deal with trips in one direction only, with full confidence that the number of trips in the opposite direction will so nearly be equal that equality may be claimed for all practical purposes. This fact

TABLE 13-1

Origins and Destinations of All Internal Person Trips: Chicago Area* (in Thousands of Trips)

	Trip Purpose at Destination								
Origin	*Home*	*Work*	*Shop*	*School*	*Social-Recreation*	*Eat Meal*	*Personal Business*	*Serve Passenger**	*Total*
Home	—	1,652	405	182	924	83	753	308	4,307
Work	1,581	290	28	3	27	57	42	1	2,029
Shop	432	5	55	1	23	4	24	—	544
School	159	7	1	1	5	4	2	—	179
Social-recreation	1,042	3	17	1	160	42	36	4	1,305
Eat meal	109	49	3	4	21	1	18	—	205
Personal business	689	26	38	1	99	20	145	2	1,020
Serve passenger*	307	1	—	—	6	—	2	26	342
Total	4,319	2,033	547	193	1,265	211	1,022	341	9,931

Source: Tables 13–1 through 13–6 are from the Chicago Area Transportation Study, *Final Report, I: Survey Findings* (Chicago: Western Engraving and Embossing Company, 1959).
*Includes trips involving "riding around." Types of trips are defined in ftn. 3, p. 554.

is well known to traffic engineers. Over a 24-hour period, directional travel on individual streets is equal and turning movements balance one another.

Trip length. Regularity of travel is evidenced in another important way: the number of trips made varies systematically with trip length. Short trips are made most frequently and progressively fewer are made as trip length increases. The frequency distribution of trips by length is extremely regular, as shown in Fig. 13-6.

It is worth speculating on the reasons why this occurs. First, there seems to be a natural conservation of travel costs, so that for any given objective, such as a trip to buy groceries, there is a strong tendency to buy at the nearest store. Then there is a tendency to relate the length of the journey to the reward obtained; for example, no one would drive 20 miles to buy cigarettes. Finally the trip maker has a whole spectrum of needs which range from daily needs, such as work, shopping, and school, to the less frequently felt needs for recreation, medical care, and vacations.

FIGURE 13–6. Distribution of internal person trips of different lengths and purposes: Chicago area. *Source:* See caption for Fig. 13–1.

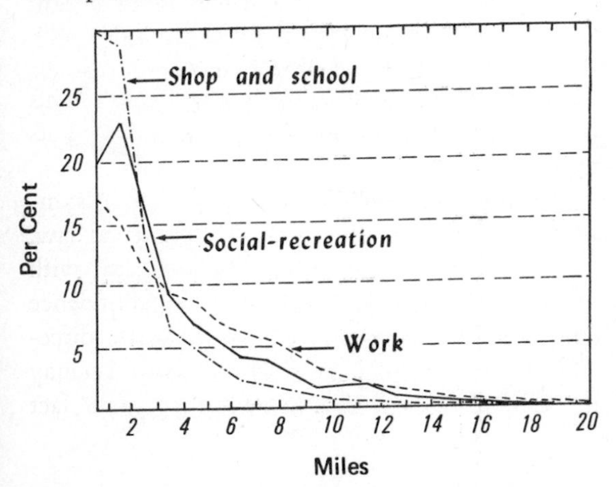

To meet people's requirements, stores, services, churches, factories, hospitals and colleges are located at different intervals throughout an urban area. Food stores are close together because people must buy food frequently. Department stores are farther apart because shopping trips for clothing and furniture are made less frequently. Moreover, each kind of urban activity has its own internal requirements which affect spacing, among which are the collection, handling, storage, and distribution of goods. Generally, the more specialized the activity, the farther it is located from the average traveler.

So the result is a balance between the requirements and travel costs of the trip maker, on one hand, and the requirements of activities on the other. This balance may operate to conserve total energy resources, or to maximize productivity. One evidence of this is the decline of trip frequency with increasing trip length.

Another way to see this is to examine trip length as related to trip purpose. As might be expected, purpose has a great deal to do with trip length. Shopping trips are usually short, averaging 2.8 miles in length. The longest trips are those made to work, with an average length of 5.3 miles. Trips to home average 4.4 miles in length; those made for social-recreational purposes are 4.3 miles in length.

The relationship between trip length and trip frequency is useful in estimating the ways in which trips will move between parts of the area in the future. For example, if Zone A is 2 miles from Zone B and 10 miles from Zone C, more trips will be expected to move from Zone A to B than from A to C. This, of course, is the simplest sort of example and does not include consideration of mode, time of travel, type of trip or land use connections, all of which influence the precise amounts of travel between zones.

The preceding data have shown that when dealing with large masses of trips, there do exist regularities in travel patterns. The behavior of a single person cannot be predicted successfully, but major transportation facilities are not planned for single persons or even small groups. They are planned to serve very large groups of travelers—perhaps of the order of 10,000 or more per day. The travel inventories show that travel habits of these large groups can be estimated reliably.

This orderliness in travel is useful for prediction. The reasons for regularity of travel are so tied in with all the living and working habits of an urban community that it is hard to imagine any sudden or substantial change. Plans based upon these relationships, therefore, are on a stable base.

The Location and Mode of Person Travel

The location of travel is dictated by land use; this is the simplest and most obvious of the relationships needed to understand and work with travel data. The number of trips coming to each small area within the Chicago region is determined by the kind, amount, and intensity of land use going on there. No more can come than will be served there by jobs or services; no more will go to live than there are houses to live in.

At this point it is necessary to distinguish between a trip as a single event and a trip as a journey having the property of length. When considering numbers of trips or the generation of trips, any trip is counted as one unit. But when considering the *amount* of travel which takes place in an area, trip length must be included in the measure. Amount of travel is therefore measured in vehicle miles of travel or in person miles of travel. It is a good representation of the impact upon, or use of, a transportation system, since each trip is appropriately weighted by its length.[17]

The miles of person or vehicle travel which take place within a defined area then become a function both of the number of trips which are destined there, and of the position of that area with respect to other land uses.

The amount of both through and local travel can be portrayed by the use of desire line maps. A desire line map shows the sum of all the straight lines connecting the origins and the destinations of all trips. The desire line is the shortest line between origin and destination, and expresses the way a person would like to go, if such a way were available. The desire line is, of course, unrealistic, but it is a simple, completely unbiased presentation and gives the viewer a strong impression of the location and magnitude of travel within an urban area.

Rapid transit. Although rapid transit represents less than one-twelfth of all person trips, and only one-sixth of the miles of person travel, the concentration of these trips makes rapid transit extremely important, especially to the Loop and the Central Area. Over 45 per cent of all trips to the Loop are made by rapid transit. Over 71 per cent are made by all means of mass transportation combined.

The other side of the coin is the dependence of mass transportation upon the Loop traveler as a source of income. About 54 per cent of all subway, elevated and suburban railroad passengers have an origin or destination in the Loop, and 81 per cent have an origin or destination in the Central Area. There is thus a strong mutual dependence between the commercial core of the region and rapid transit.

In no other part of the study area does rapid transit play so important a part. In District 11, which is the 12.4-square-mile area surrounding the Loop, only 14.2 per cent of all trips come by rapid transit, while 44.5 per cent come by both rapid transit and bus. The proportional use of both rapid transit and bus transportation declines rapidly with distance from the central business district (CBD), while that of the automobile rises steadily. The percentage of trips by rapid transit at the CBD is very high, but then declines rapidly to about 3 per cent of all trips, maintaining itself at this level until the cordon line is reached at a distance of nearly 30 miles. Bus trips have their biggest share of person trips within 10 miles of the Loop.

Rapid transit, by these tokens, is an extremely specialized type of transportation. These trips are long; subway-elevated trips average 7.2 desire line miles in length, and suburban railroad trips average 13.3 miles. By contrast, all internal person trips average about 4.3 desire line miles. As will be shown, rapid transit trips are mostly made in the peak hour. Over 70 per cent are between home and work. The starlike form of rapid transit radiates from the CBD and coincides exactly with the fingers of suburban development. Thus the connection with land use is clear. This is a unique pattern, showing specialization of both living and working areas organized around a fast means of transportation.

Buses. Bus trips crisscross and overlap each other within a relatively small area. The resulting pattern is compact, without the focus or strongly directional nature of rapid transit trips.

One reason for this pattern is that bus trips are short, averaging only 3.6 desire line miles in length. Half of all bus trips are less than 2.8 miles. Hence there is no real possibility of a unique focusing on the Loop. Another aspect of trip length is that while over twice as many trips are made by bus as by rapid transit, fewer person miles of travel are by bus.

Trips by bus passengers average slightly longer than automobile passengers (3.5 desire line miles) but less than automobile drivers (3.9 miles). Like them, bus trips have a smoothly declining frequency as trip length increases (see Fig. 13-7). Subway-elevated trips and railroad trips have special patterns; obviously very few people use these facilities for short trips.

Most bus trips take place within the city of Chicago, but there is some bus travel in the adjacent suburban communities.

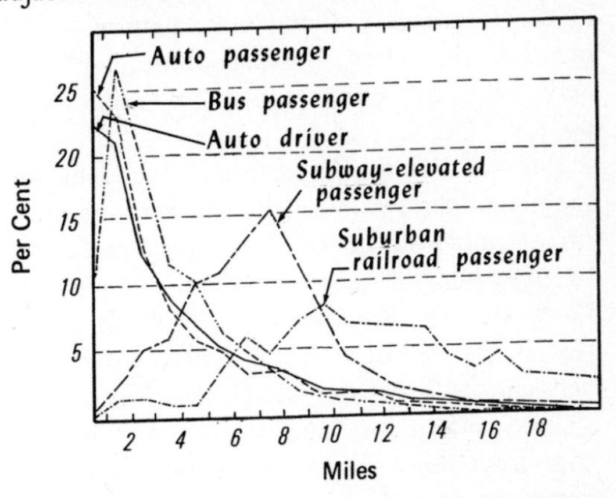

FIGURE 13–7. Length of different types of internal person trips: Chicago area. *Source:* See caption for Fig. 13–1.

The explanation for the limited extent of bus usage lies in the density of land use, and in car ownership. Bus service can be provided only where there are enough passengers to pay operating costs. (In some cases, profitable, heavily traveled lines can cover the losses of lightly traveled lines, but this principle cannot be extended too far.) There are enough passengers only in districts which have a certain density of development. This minimum density appears to be about 25,000 persons per net residential square mile. The areas where heavy bus usage shows up have these high densities. Where densities fall below this point, buses apparently cannot operate economically in local service.

Density and car ownership are closely related. Where residential densities are high, car ownership is low. Low car ownership is associated with greater use of mass transportation, particularly buses. It is worth noting that of those who used buses in the Chicago area in 1956, only 27 per cent could drive a car. By contrast, half of those using elevated-subway trains and two-thirds of those using suburban railroads could drive.

While bus trips are less specialized than rapid transit trips, they do not have the universal coverage of automobile travel. They are short trips which take place within areas of relatively high density. The use of buses on expressways in the future may change this pattern a little, but then the riders of express buses will probably have the characteristics of rapid transit users.

Internal automobile drivers. Resident automobile drivers produce 46 per cent of all the person miles of desire line travel made daily by residents; if passengers are included, this figure rises to 69 per cent of all person-miles of travel. As vehicles, automobiles produce 84 per cent of all the internal vehicle-miles of travel.

The pattern of internal automobile driver trip desire lines conforms exactly to the land development configuration of the urban area.

There is another way of demonstrating why travel patterns resemble land use patterns so closely. Most internal automobile driver trips—like bus or auto passenger trips—are quite short. Half are under 2.5 miles in length; one-fifth are under 1 mile in length. The shortest trips cannot depart from the urbanized area since both ends are bound to be at urban activities —a house, a store, or a factory. The longer trips are similarly constrained, but have the further property of being increasingly rare as they get longer. . . . It is as if the urban area were a magnet influencing not only the particles of trips but the paths by which they move.

Within 8 miles of the Loop there is a more even tone of density of auto driver trip desire lines. While there are ridges and valleys, they are not so apparent to the eye, especially when contrasted with the intense ridges of travel desire on the rapid transit and, to a lesser extent, the bus desire line displays. The location of the Loop stands out, but it does not have an intensity like that of the mass transportation modes.

The implication of these facts is that expressways and arterials built to serve the needs of automobile drivers in the Chicago area must be designed to provide service throughout the urbanized area. The focusing of all routes on a single point, such as the CBD, is not necessarily to be desired in view of the relatively wide dispersion of automobile desire lines.

Automobile passengers. The desire line pattern of automobile passenger trips is similar to that of automobile driver trips.

Automobile passenger desire lines have a lower over-all intensity than those of automobile drivers. There are only 56 per cent as many trips involved and, since automobile passenger trips have a shorter average length, only 51 per cent as many miles of travel.

Internal trucks. The pattern of truck trips is similar to that of all automobile driver travel but is more concentrated towards the center of the urban area. This concentration is caused to a great extent by the warehousing, commercial, industrial and truck terminal activities which are located within 6 miles of the Loop. The patterns of automobile trips and truck trips are sufficiently alike to suggest that no special treatment of trucks will be warranted in locating new highways.

While the spatial pattern of truck trips is not greatly different from that of passenger cars, trucks do travel at different times of the day. Auto trips are made to get people to places where they can do things, such as work. Hence, peaks occur before and after the work day (see Fig. 13–8). But the truck driver's trip is his work, and is conditioned by the hours of receiving, shipping and production workers. The truck is, in effect, an extension of the production line.

Truck trips are made mostly between 7:00 A.M. and 6:00 P.M. This corresponds to the 8-hour working day, with some overlapping caused by those trucks which operate on unusual schedules—milk trucks are a good example. There is a notable drop in truck traffic during the lunch hour, as might be expected. Taxis, which are shown in the same figure, begin their work later in the morning and spill over into the evening hours. This is to be expected because taxis normally operate on a two-shift day.

Truck trips have many of the same characteristics as person trips; they follow the same rules of travel behavior. Truck trip origins equal

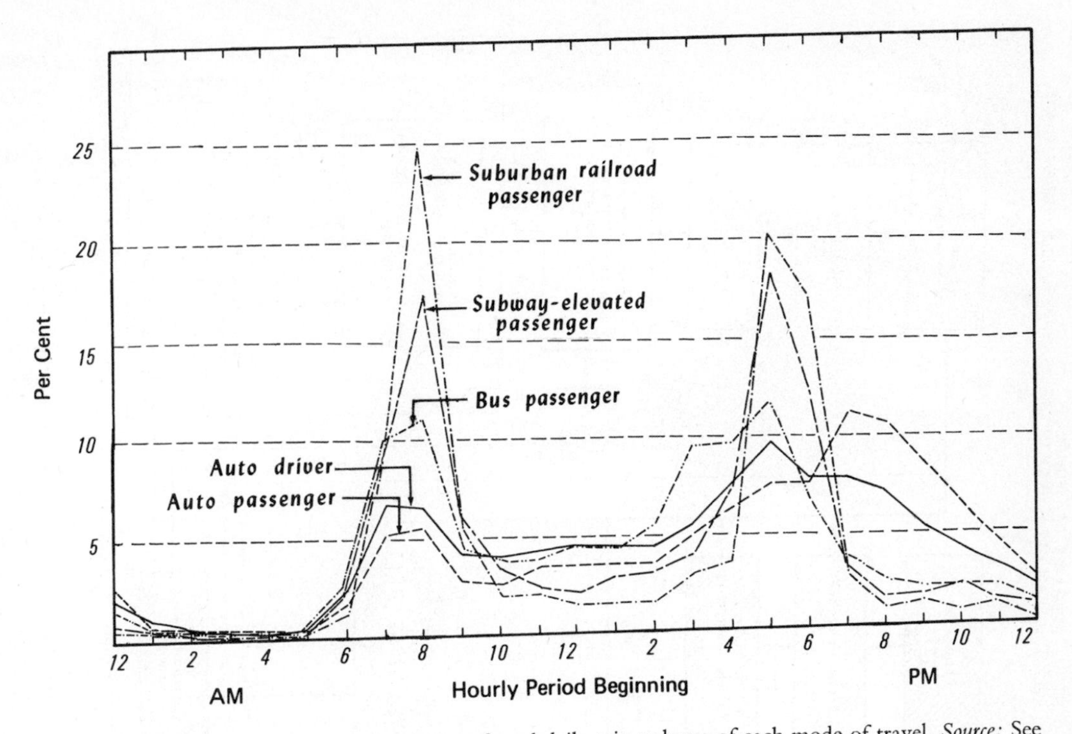

FIGURE 13–8. Hourly percentages of total daily trip volume of each mode of travel. *Source:* See caption for Fig. 13–1.

truck trip destinations for any area, within any 24-hour period. Symmetry of directional travel for trucks is a fact. But truck trips are substantially shorter than automobile trips. The average truck trip is 2.7, and the average taxi trip is 2.1, miles in length.

URBAN TRANSPORTATION PLANNING TECHNOLOGY

These basic data enable us to focus on current avenues of research and the urban transportation planning process. To place the various lines of research into an over-all context, a brief introduction concerning the structure of large-scale urban transportation studies seems appropriate. Figure 13-9 depicts the several phases of current urban transportation studies and the relationships between them.[18]

The first step in a transportation study such as was conducted in Chicago is a costly and time-consuming inventory of current conditions. Initially, the metropolitan area is divided into basic areal units. These units, normally designated "traffic zones," are the basic informational entities of the transportation study.

The distribution of urban population, usually aggregated to the traffic zone level, is defined for the study area. The intensity of economic activity within each of the traffic zones, defined either as the number of person employed in a particular activity or the number of square feet occupied by various activities, has to be determined for all zones, usually for a classification of from 10 to 100 different activities.[19] Number of vehicles owned within each of the zones is tabulated. An origin and destination survey, which includes interviewing a sample of the households within the urban area, is used to define present trip generation and current patterns of vehicular and person travel.[20] A land use survey classifies land uses within a traffic zone, into 10 to 100 different types of land use. The physical facilities of the existing circulation system within the urban area are inventoried.[21] Finally, the budget alloca-

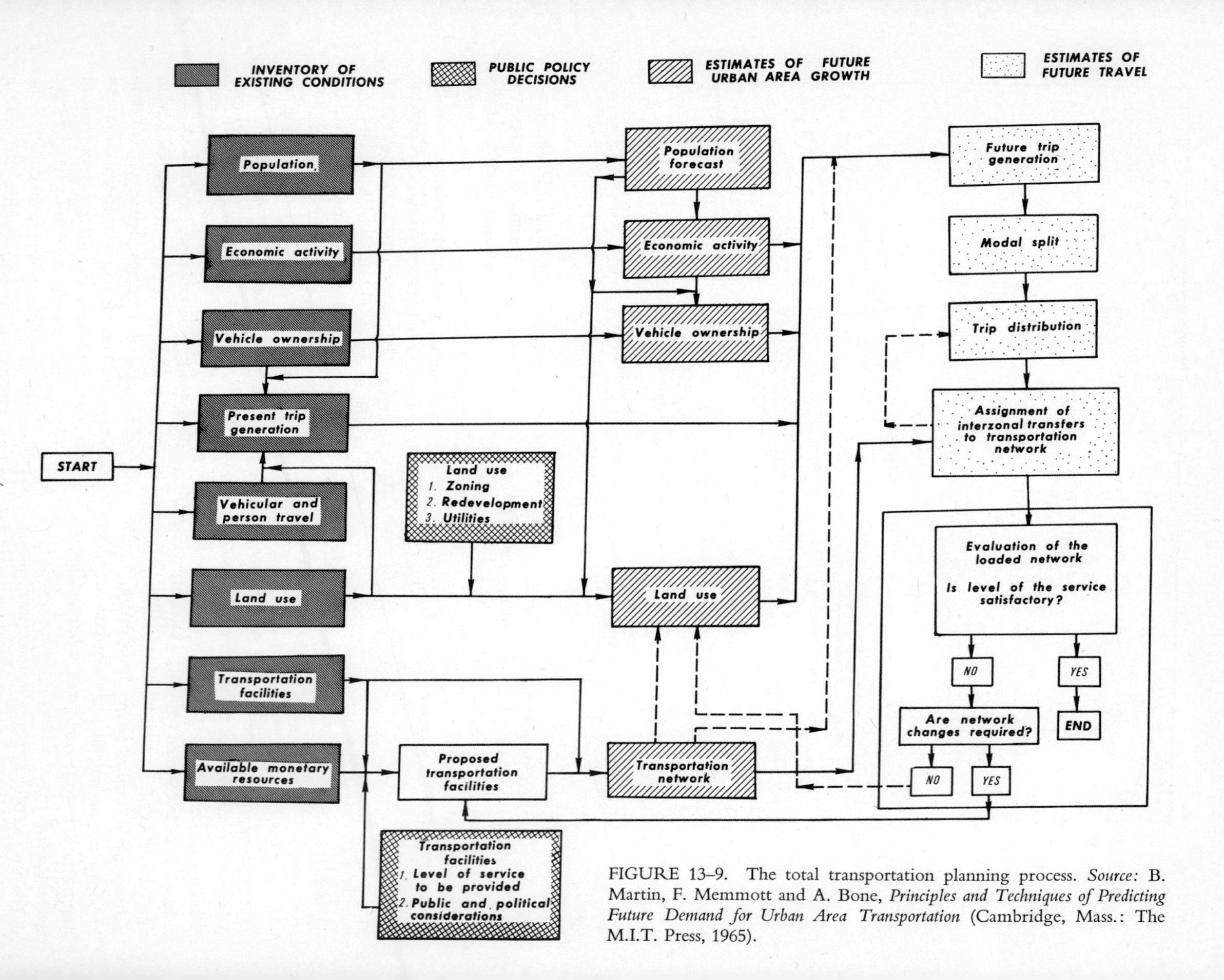

FIGURE 13–9. The total transportation planning process. *Source:* B. Martin, F. Memmott and A. Bone, *Principles and Techniques of Predicting Future Demand for Urban Area Transportation* (Cambridge, Mass.: The M.I.T. Press, 1965).

tion for transportation improvements is given or estimated.

Public policy decisions may be considered as constraints on the arrangement of land uses and on the developmental plans for changes in the transportation system. Current zoning laws and the location of utilities obviously constrain the kind of land use which can be located in different areas. Policy considerations concerning service levels for the transportation system as a whole and on its various links are obviously constrained by the budget. Public and political pressures for the construction of new routes or the addition of capacity on existing routes clearly must be a consideration in the transportation planning process.[22] Information on these elements is therefore added to the analytic package.

Given the information sets and the constraints, estimates of urban growth and development at future time periods must be developed. Population increases and decreases within traffic zones are generally estimated by an exogenous model. Forecasts of the intensity of economic activity and the kinds of land use within traffic zones are made (using models similar to those discussed in Chapter 12).[23] Estimates of vehicle ownership are also determined by an exogenous model.

The final stage of the urban transportation study is the forecasting of travel demands and travel patterns within the urban area. Models are developed to forecast the level of trip generation within each of the traffic zones, for households and nonresidential activities. Trip distribution models forecast the intensity of interaction between traffic zones. Assignment models determine the routes taken between zones and the level of utilization on each of the links of the network.[24] Modal split models determine the percentage of individuals who will use private automobiles or other kinds of transportation, primarily mass transit.[25]

Once these activities have been completed, urban planners and urban transportation planners can then evaluate the level of service required for the proposed transportation network at some future time period. If the level of service is satisfactory, i.e., above or equal to the level of service defined by policy makers, the proposed transportation facilities can be constructed. If not, and if budgetary constraints are such that new facilities cannot be constructed or the proposed construction of routes altered to increase the level of service, constraints on land use could be initiated to restrict traffic. In practice, the decision to alter the level of desired service is the solution, rather than the institution of additional constraits, however.

TRANSPORTATION DEMAND

The intensity of land use varies thoughout the metropolitan area. Because of this variation and the differences among the various land uses with regard to the number of trips which end and begin at them, information about the variation must be derived. The Chicago Area Transportation Study again provides relevant insights.

*Computing the Generation of Travel**

Trips are made for profitable purposes. While not all such profits are tangible, this does not mean that they are not real. A man leaves his home to go to work in a factory, and his earnings justify the cost of his journey; a woman drives to the library for a book and gets her reward from reading the book. At least 10 per cent of consumer income is spent for personal transportation; none of this would be spent if there were no rewards to be gained. Hence, the key to the explanation and understanding of travel lies in the rewarding activities which generate travel.

Land use is a convenient way to classify and study these trip-generating activities. The use of land is a tangible, stable, and predictable quantity which can be measured. . . .

Each person interviewed in the travel inventories was asked to identify the kind of establishment or land use at the origin and destination of each trip. In comparable travel surveys

*Reprinted from the Chicago Area Transportation Study, *Final Report, I: Survey Findings* (Chicago: Western Engraving and Embossing Company, 1959), Chap. v, ftn. 4, with the permission of the Agency.

in over 100 cities, this was the first case in which land use at each trip end was recorded. Responses permitted both person and vehicle trips to be classified by kind of activity or land use, using the same 10 major and 88 minor categories employed in the land use and floor area surveys. Table 13–2 shows all trips made by persons, broken down by six major activity types of their destinations.[26]

TABLE 13-2

Person Trip Destinations and Generation Rates by Type of Land Use

Type of Land Use	*Person Trip Destinations*	*Area (in Square Miles)*	*Person Trip Destinations (per Square Mile)*
Residential	5,606,527	180.6	31,000
Manufacturing	779,340	24.7	31,600
Transportation	280,270	50.7	5,500
Commercial	2,449,468	21.1	116,000
Public buildings	781,960	23.1	33,800
Public open space	314,833	114.9	2,700
Total	10,212,398	415.1	24,600

Source: See note to Table 13–1.

By dividing the numbers of person trips with destinations in a given land use category by the number of square miles of land in that category, rates of trip generation can be computed. This type of computation is used throughout to obtain the trip-generation rates which are necessary in estimating future trip making.

The rates shown in Table 13-2 are for the study area as a whole. Surprisingly, residential, manufacturing, and public building lands all generate trips at the same average rate—about 32,000 person trips per net square mile. Commercial land generates trips at nearly four times this rate. This identifies commercial land as being most likely to have a greater potential for traffic congestion, parking, and other transportation problems. Transportation land, which includes extensive railroad yards and airports, has a low rate of trip generation. Public open space, including the forest preserves and parks, is almost by definition a low generator of trips.

Gross rates, however, do not disclose the great variations in trip generation within the study area. There are extremely high rates of trip generation in the Loop—both of person trips and of vehicle trips. In the suburban areas, the number of trips destined to (i.e., generated by) each small area is quite low. In between these extremes there is a whole range of different rates. Clearly, the average trip-generation rates for the study area must be refined if there is to be an understanding upon which projection for small areas can be based.

In summary, the method for computing trip generation is to divide trips by land area. The variations in rates must be understood and hence need to be related to density as well as to type of land use. The objective for obtaining these more precise rates is to allow estimates of future trip making to be prepared for each of the 582 analysis zones comprising the study area.

Land use trip-generation rates. Trip-generation rates themselves—both person trips and vehicle trips—have been calculated for six major land use categories, and are related to those variables, such as density, which permit the rates to be used reliably in making forecasts of the trip generation of analysis zones. For convenience, the six major land uses are grouped into two types: residential and nonresidential land uses. This is useful in later stages of the estimation of future travel demand, because the movement of trips between residential and nonresidential land uses is dominant.

TRIP GENERATION OF RESIDENTIAL LAND. Table 13-3 shows the rates of residential trip generation which were computed from the 1956 inventories of travel and land use. The data are summarized to rings at different distances from the Central Business District (CBD) because such an organization shows most clearly the regular changes in the rates.

Residential trip generation rates exhibit an extremely regular decline as distance from the CBD increases. This drop is the result of two opposing factors, the first of which completely dominates the second. The first factor is the decline in number of dwelling places per net residential

TABLE 13-3

Person and Vehicle Trips Generated by Residential Land, by Ring*

Ring	*Average Distance from Loop (in Miles)*	*Person Trip Destinations (per Acre)*	*Vehicle Trip Destinations (per Acre)*
0	0.0	2,228.5	1,336.9
1	1.5	224.2	93.3
2	3.5	127.3	54.0
3	5.5	106.2	49.5
4	8.5	68.3	35.5
5	12.5	43.0	25.3
6	16.0	31.2	19.4
7	24.0	21.1	13.3
Study area average		48.5	26.1

Source: See note to Table 13-1.
*Each ring comprises a band of traffic zones arranged concentrically around the Loop at successively greater distances from the city center.

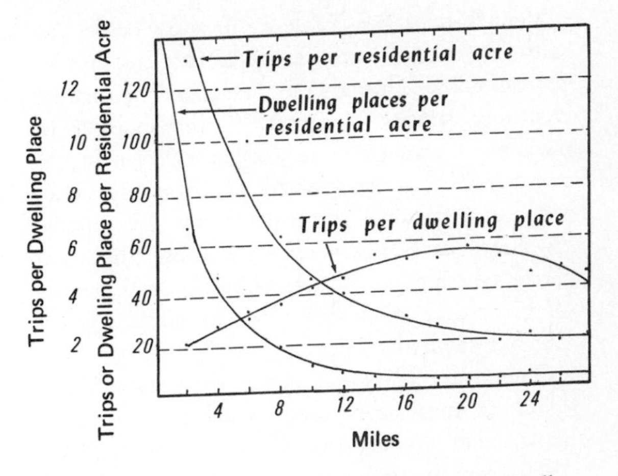

FIGURE 13-10. Destinations of person trips per dwelling place, frequency of trips, and density of dwelling places *vs.* distance from the Loop. Information was plotted at the midpoints of two-mile bands. Curves were hand fitted. *Source:* See caption for Fig. 13-1.

acre. Obviously, the fewer dwelling places per acre, the fewer trips will be made per acre.

Opposing the decline in numbers of dwellings is the increasing number of trips destined to the average dwelling place, with increasing distance from the center. The typical dwelling place, located 2 miles from the Loop, will generate about two person trips each weekday; the dwelling located 10 miles from the Loop will generate four person trips, while the typical dwelling 20 miles from the Loop will generate 5.5 person trips. These rates are shown in Fig. 13-10, which also indicates the interrelationship between the number of dwellings per acre and the number of trips per acre at various distances from the CBD.[27]

Why more trips are made to dwelling places which are located at greater distances from the CBD is not completely understood. One explanation may be that travel, like food and housing, is a type of consumption. Data indicate that the proportion of income spent for travel rises slightly as income rises,[28] and thus a higher-income family is likely to make more trips. It also may be cheaper, and is probably easier, to make trips in areas of lower density development than in high density areas, because of congestion on the streets and the difficulties of parking at both ends of each trip. Families are also larger in suburban areas (3.5 persons per occupied dwelling in the suburbs as against 3.1 in Chicago) and so create a greater potential of trip making per dwelling place. The net result, as seen in Fig. 13-11, is a higher rate of trip generation per dwelling place in areas of lower density.

FIGURE 13-11. Person and vehicle trip destinations per dwelling place *vs.* residential density: Chicago area. *Source:* See caption for Fig. 13-1.

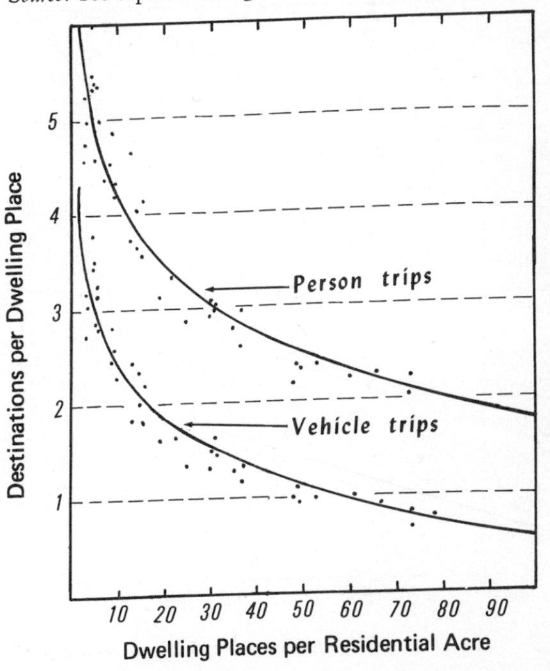

Vehicle trips (see Table 13-3) show a decline with increasing distance from the Loop, like person trips. This also is associated with two opposing factors: a decline in the number of dwelling places per acre and an increase in the number of vehicles owned per dwelling, with increasing distance from the Loop. Density of dwelling places per acre is the most important factor which gives the rate of vehicle trip generation its characteristic declining curve with greater distance from the Loop.

The steady increase in person trips per dwelling place as more cars are owned is completely reasonable: people do not buy automobiles to keep them in garages! Figure 13-12 shows the relationship between vehicle and person trip generation and the number of vehicles owned per dwelling place. It is impossible to escape the similarity between the curves of person and vehicle trips. This is reasonable, considering that 76 per cent of person trips are made by automobile, and automobiles account for 86 per cent of vehicle trips.

Since vehicle ownership is so significant for both person and vehicle trip making, it becomes necessary to know something about its geographic distribution. Within the city of Chicago, most small areas average less than 1 car per dwelling place—often as low as .4 cars per dwelling, which means that at least 60 per cent of the households in such areas do not own cars. Outside the city of Chicago, the average car ownership rate is generally over 1, sometimes rising as high as 1.6 automobiles per dwelling.

FIGURE 13–12. Person and vehicle trip destinations per dwelling place *vs.* automobile ownership: Chicago area. *Source:* See caption for Fig. 13–1.

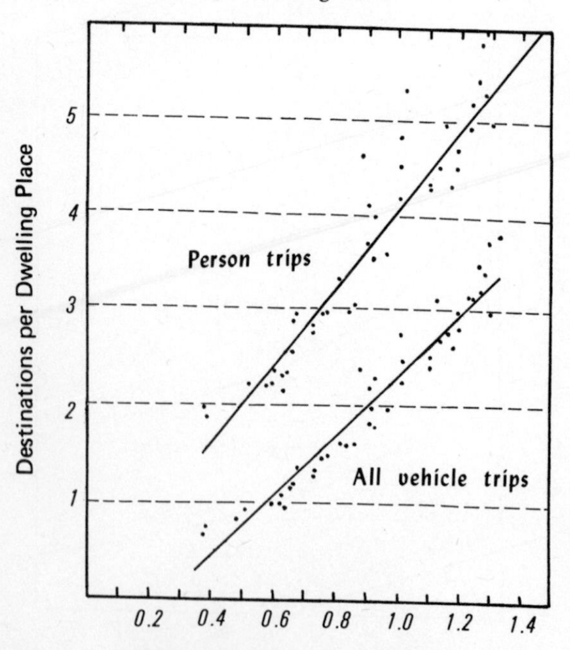

In the suburban areas, 8.8 per cent of all families do not own a car while 69.5 per cent own one car and 21.7 per cent own more than one car. In the city of Chicago, 40.5 per cent do not own a car while 52.2 per cent own one car and 7.3 per cent own more than one car. It is quite clear, therefore, that high residential density goes with low car ownership.[29]

Since families without cars still must make trips, it is apparent that such families will make more trips by mass transportation. (It is still possible for them to make some trips by automobile, either as passengers or as drivers of borrowed cars.) This connection between ownership and mode of travel will be developed more completely later on, but it can be seen that the figures of the very lowest automobile ownership coincide with the routes of subways and elevated trains—i.e., the lines of most frequent transit service.

In summary, trip generation rates of residential land show a steady drop with increasing distance from the Loop. The drop is consistent with the declining number of dwelling places per acre as distance from the Loop increases. Hence residential density is a powerful influence regulating the gross number of trips made to each acre of residential land. On the other hand, higher densities are associated with fewer trips made to each dwelling place, and with low car ownership. To the extent that density and car ownership can be anticipated in the Chicago region of 1980, there will be a firm basis for estimating trips to residential land.

TRIP GENERATION OF NONRESIDENTIAL LAND. About 45 per cent of all person trips and 54 per cent of all vehicle trips (trucks weighted) are destined to nonresidential land. The trips to each type of nonresidential land use were matched with corresponding land areas, and rates of trip generation for each type were then derived, as shown in Table 13-4.

The difference in trip generation rates between the nonresidential land uses lies in the nature of these activities. Commercial land requires not only workers, but customers. Customers stay in these establishments only for short periods, so the same space can accommodate many persons during the day. Public buildings in the central area also have many "customers"—lawyers, people paying traffic fines, and students in downtown schools. Elsewhere, public buildings land attracts fewer trips. Manufacturing land does not have many visitors; 91.6 per cent of internal person trips to this land are made by workers.[30] Transportation land generates few person trips per acre because it includes extensive railroad yards, railroad rights-of-way, and airports. Public open space, with its golf courses, cemeteries, parks, and forest preserves, naturally generates few trips per acre.

Like residential trip generation rates, these rates are at their highest at the CBD. From this peak they decline rapidly until a distance of about 3 miles from the Loop is reached. Here a curious reversal takes place: commercial land develops an increase in trips per acre, as distance from the Loop increases, to a secondary peak about 8 miles from the Loop. Thereafter, commercial trip generation rates decline steadily until the cordon line is reached. There are other, lesser reversals but they are not pronounced and do not affect the general trend of the remaining nonresidential land uses to have lower trip-generation rates with increasing distance from the CBD.

The variations in the rates of trip generation within the several nonresidential uses are the result of a number of factors. First and most important is the decreasing amount of floor space per acre of land with increasing distance from the Loop. Floor space is built to accommodate users; if there is less of it in any given area, there will be fewer trips made to that area, as a general rule (see Fig. 13-13). . . . Here, then, is an indication of the controlling influence of floor area on land area trip generation rates.

Floor area attracts trips in different amounts depending upon the type of use. As shown in Table 13-5, there are significant variations between the different types. Retail and service activities attract the most person trips per thousand square feet of floor area, while wholesale establishments attract the fewest. . . . The wholesale, manufacturing, and transportation establishments in the rings close to the Loop have a great deal of floor area but require fewer people.[31] Farther away from the Loop, retail and service uses attract more people.

TABLE 13-4

Person and Vehicle Trips Generated by Nonresidential Land by Type and by Ring

		Person Trips (per Acre)					*Vehicle Trips (per Acre)**				
Ring	*Average Distance from Loop (in Miles)*	*Manufacturing*	*Transportation*	*Commercial*	*Public Buildings*	*Public Open Space*	*Manufacturing*	*Transportation*	*Commercial*	*Public Buildings*	*Public Open Space*
0	0.0	3,544.7	273.1	2,132.2	2,013.8	98.5	1,081.1	103.4	728.1	461.0	62.3
1	1.5	243.2	36.9	188.7	255.5	28.8	162.5	54.6	194.0	116.5	26.2
2	3.5	80.0	15.9	122.1	123.5	26.5	64.2	30.6	116.7	50.9	22.7
3	5.5	86.9	10.8	143.3	100.7	27.8	66.0	14.7	132.1	46.4	17.5
4	8.5	50.9	12.8	212.4	77.7	13.5	43.8	12.4	165.4	33.8	11.6
5	12.5	26.8	5.8	178.7	58.1	6.1	23.4	7.1	150.2	29.3	4.4
6	16.0	15.7	2.6	132.5	46.6	2.5	14.7	2.9	111.7	24.2	1.8
7	24.0	18.2	6.4	131.9	14.4	1.5	15.7	6.4	115.3	7.2	1.0
Study area average		49.4	8.6	181.4	52.8	4.2	38.6	10.2	144.6	24.2	3.1

Source: See note to Table 13–1.
*Trucks are weighted.

FIGURE 13–13. Person trip destinations on nonresidential land. Over 4,600,000 person trips are destined for nonresidential land on the average weekday. The highest vertical value shown on the model represents 133,000 destinations, the lowest is 5,000. The shaded areas have values between 2,500 and 5,000 destinations per grid of one-quarter square mile. Approximately one-fifth of all nonresidential person trip destinations are within 2.5 miles of the intersection of State and Madison Streets. *Source:* See caption for Fig. 13–1.

TABLE 13-5

Floor Area Trip-Generation Rates, by Type of Activity

Type of Activity	*Internal Person Trips (per Thousand Square Feet of Floor Area*)*
Residential	3.2
Manufacturing	2.1
Transportation	1.9
Retail	7.0
Services	5.4
Wholesale	1.5
Public buildings	3.5
All types	3.3

Source: See note to Table 13–1.
*For the analysis zones for which the floor area data were available.

A number of other factors influence the generation of person and vehicle trips by nonresidential land. For example, the secondary peak in commercial trip generation in Ring 4 is caused by several factors. One is the composition of commercial land: in the Loop, retail and office uses are predominant; while in Rings 2 and 3, wholesale uses take on greater importance. Beyond Ring 3, retail and service uses become more important, and these generally attract a greater number of trips. Second, there is an increasing number of commercial trips per capita made by those persons who live at greater distances from the Loop. The location of major shopping centers may have an effect. Closer to the Loop there are fewer big centers, and some shopping needs are satisfied by walking; farther away, commercial land is less densely developed, with more parking space. This secondary peak in trip generation was also observed in Detroit.[32]

Once a nonresidential area has been completely developed, its density is likely to change only slowly. Moreover, the kinds of activities taking place there will tend to remain within the same generalized land use type. Therefore, existing rates of nonresidential trip generation per acre of developed land are going to be much the same in the future. Where substantial changes in density or use may occur, however, floor area data may be used to provide additional precision in estimating future trip making. Examples of such changes are redevelopment projects or the changes envisioned in the Central Area Plan of the Chicago Department of Planning.[33]

LAND USE LINKAGES. Land use has been shown to be related to trip making in reasonable and orderly fashion. In this sense, it is akin to the regularities of travel in time and in space. But it has a further usefulness: the explanation of trip linkages. Trip origins and destinations, predicted from land use estimates, provide part of the picture. Knowledge of which origins are likely to connect with which destinations is obviously critical in fashioning forecasts of travel.

Of all internal person trips, 76.1 per cent are between residential and nonresidential land. These are work trips, school trips, shopping trips, and miscellaneous other kinds of trips. They form the tide-like currents which sweep back and forth across the urban area each day, caused by the outer residential areas and the commercial and industrial core. Only one-sixth—16.7 per cent—of all person trips have both origin and destination on residential land. These are trips from house to house, such as social-recreation trips. The remainder, 7.2 per cent, have both origins and destinations on nonresidential land. These are trips from work to lunch, from work to retail stores, and so forth.

For vehicle trips, the linkage picture is somewhat different. While auto trips have much the same tendency to move back and forth from residential to nonresidential land, trucks tend to link the various types of nonresidential land together. Thus 61 per cent of all truck and taxi trips are from one nonresidential use to another. Eighteen per cent (milk trucks and the like), move between residential uses, and 20.8 per cent move between residential and nonresidential activities.

... Truck destinations are concentrated in the core of the Chicago region where commercial and industrial activities predominate. By contrast, all vehicle trip destinations and all person trip destinations show a much more extensive distribution throughout the urbanized area and illustrate how these trips are more evenly split between residential and nonresidential activities.

The way land uses are arrayed, whether in concentrated or dispersed fashion, has a great deal to do with the comings and goings of travel. Given an estimate of future land use, both intensity of trip generation and linkages between land uses can be estimated. This is another means of fastening down a reliable forecast.

Characteristics of the trip makers. Attention must be focused ultimately on people, who are the basic producers of travel. People create the stationary activities here called land uses. People also cause themselves to be moved about between these activities in automobiles and mass transportation vehicles, and create demands for the movement of goods in trucks. The characteristics of these trip makers are important. The volume of trips is related to human needs; while these may vary from family to family, there are similarities which are of considerable interest because they suggest the existence of ceilings on travel requirements. Studies of trip making by persons and by commercial vehicles are also useful because they allow total trip estimates for the region to be made from forecasts of population and vehicle registration. These estimates can be used to check the prediction of total travel arrived at by summing the land use trip estimates for all the small geographic areas within the study area.

TRIP MAKING OF FAMILIES. The number of trips generated by a family is not the same as the number of trips which are destined to a dwelling place on an average day. It is about twice the dwelling place trip-generation rate. This is because the trips made by the members of a family include those trips leaving the dwelling place as well as those arriving, and also include those trips made completely away from home. The total of trips generated by all the families in the study area equals the total number of person trips made by residents of the area, and so includes both their trips to residential and to nonresidential land.

The number of trips made by families is related to residential density. The lower the density of dwellings per net acre of residential land, the greater the trips per family. A family living in a house with a lot of 10,000 square feet is likely to make 9 person trips per day. A family living in an apartment house, with only 600 square feet of land as its share, is likely to make only 4 trips per day.

Congestion, which is obviously greater in denser areas, probably reduces travel as rust in a pipe reduces water flow. It takes effort to walk to a bus or to get a car out of an alley garage. Furthermore, the cost of travel is a real item in the family budget, and in high-density, low-income areas it probably operates to reduce trip making. Finally, high-density areas are more likely to have a variety of activities packed sufficiently close together so that vehicular trips are less necessary.

For similar reasons, the amount of trip making by families is related to car ownership. The higher the car ownership, the more trips—both person trips and auto trips—will be made on the average weekday. A one-car family is likely to make 7 person trips and 3.7 auto trips per day; a two-car family, 11 person trips and 7.3 auto trips per day; a family with no car, 3.1 person trips and less than .1 auto trips per day.[34]

As families make more trips, they make them for different purposes. Figure 13-14 shows that a typical family making 4 trips per day has half of its travel to and from work (one quarter to work, and one qurter from). The family which makes 10 trips per day makes only about one quarter of its trips to and from work. The additional travel is usually for a greater number of social-recreation, shopping, school, serve passenger, and "eat meal" trips.

FIGURE 13–14. Distribution of trips for different purposes and trip making per family. *Source:* See caption for Fig. 13–1.

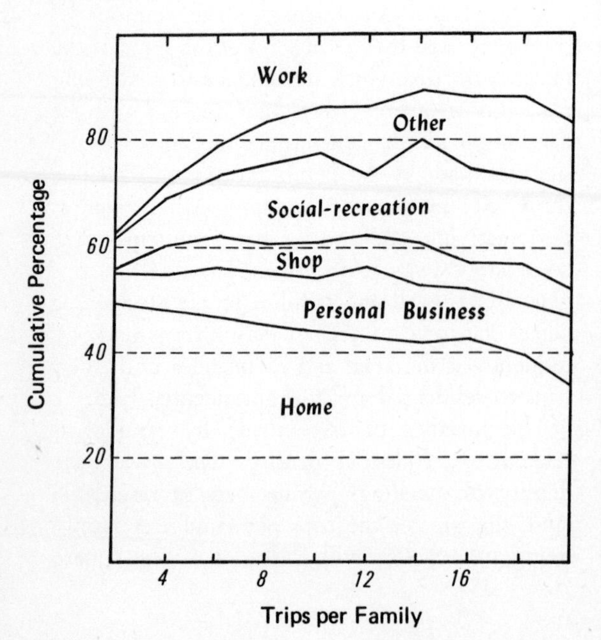

Those families who make more trips tend to make shorter trips on the average. The average trip length for a family making 10 trips per day is 4.1 miles, for a family making 6 trips per day it is 4.7 miles, and for a family making 2 trips it is 5.2 miles. This agrees with the trip-purpose distribution as shown in Fig. 13-14; those families making more trips have more shopping and social-recreation trips, which are shorter on the average.

This evidence reinforces the view that trip making by families is stable in relation to car ownership and density. Those families which reported making more trips also reported making the kinds of trips which go with higher income, more car ownership, and lower-density areas. All these things fit together closely. For significant shifts to be made in trip making, there would have to be disruptions in the proportions of income which are spent for travel—and for other purposes.

Trip making by commercial vehicles. Person trips can be estimated, using resident population forecasts and family trip generation rates. But similar estimates of trips made by commercial vehicles depend upon a separate estimate of future truck and taxi registrations. Against these registrations, trip-making rates can be applied. In 1956, trucks registered in the study area averaged 6.4 trips per weekday. Taxis averaged 30.5 trips.

Mode of travel. In 1956, people in the Chicago area made one quarter of their trips by mass transportation and three quarters by automobile. Why in this proportion? If the reason for reaching this collective decision is known, then it may be possible to estimate the proportions which will use mass transportation in 1980, a vitally important factor in preparing a transportation plan.

Many transportation studies have sought to determine choice of mode of travel by asking questions like: "*If* a certain type of transportation were provided, would you use it?" The reliability of answers to such questions is uncertain because of the difficulty of including within such questions all the factors which might influence a decision.

In Chicago a different basis for study was employed. There are in the study area thousands of different situations involving mass transportation, having varying types of service, of density, of car ownership, and of land use. The actual choices which people made as to the use of mass transportation or automobile could be related to these and other variables. From these collective decisions—presumably thoughtful ones, because they were made by people after years of experience—the factors affecting choice could be identified.

The inventories of travel provided data indicating that the geographic distribution of mass transportation trips is extremely orderly. Those zones with the lowest percentage of mass transportation trips are farthest from the Loop. Closer in, more mass transportation trips are made, and along the subway and elevated lines still higher percentages use this means of travel. The highest usage is at the Loop itself, where 71 per cent of all person trips arrived via mass transportation. Such regular patterns imply the existence of strong forces affecting mass transportation usage.

Density of land development appears to be a strong force. Where density is highest, the use of mass transportation is the highest; where densities are low, the use of mass transportation is low. Of course Chicago is not unique in this respect; it is well known that in older and more dense eastern cities the use of mass transportation is at a higher level, whereas low density places like Detroit and Los Angeles have much lower percentages of mass transportation use.

. . .

Automobile ownership is another factor. A family which does not own an automobile is most likely to use mass transportation if it is to make a trip (as defined) within the study area. A family which owns a car is less likely to use mass transportation, and still less likely if it owns two cars. Having made an investment in the automobile, it is natural that people want to use it. . . . Where there is great auto ownership, mass transportation is not used much. Along the lines of the subways and elevated trains, where more than 40 per cent of all trips are made by mass transportation, car ownership is generally below .4 cars per family—the lowest rate in the Chicago area.

Auto ownership and density are naturally closely related to one another, but not perfectly. So, knowing both factors provides an even greater understanding of mass transportation usage.[35] Of two areas having the same density but different automobile ownership rates, the one with the greater automobile ownership will have the fewer trips by mass transportation. Conversely, of two areas with the same automobile ownership, the one with a higher density will have more trips by mass transportation.

The use of buses is fairly well restricted to those areas which have high population densities. Intense bus usage is within 8 to 10 miles from the Loop. Within this area, population densities generally exceed 25,000 persons per net residential square mile, which is about 12 families per net acre.

Rapid transit usage is highly concentrated at the CBD. More than half the trips to the quarter-square mile bounded by Madison, State, and Harrison Streets and the Chicago River is made by rapid transit (some 75,500 trip destinations). Nowhere else in the study area are there more than 2,500 rapid transit trip destinations in any quarter-square mile. In fact, the vast bulk of all quarter-square miles—even those adjacent to the suburban rail lines—have less than 500 rapid transit trip destinations.

By these tokens, rapid transit is a specialized form of mass transportation. One of its components, the subway-elevated system, does serve areas of high residential density and low car ownership. Suburban railroads, however, connect the Loop with residential areas of medium to low densities and high car ownership. The extent of specialization is indicated by the increased average trip length, 7.2 desire line miles for sub-

TABLE 13-6

Characteristics of Residents Using Each Mode of Travel in the Chicago Study Area (in %)

Resident Characteristics	*Auto Driver*	*Auto Passenger*	*Bus Passenger*	*Subway-Elevated Passenger*	*Suburban Railroad*
Male	75	33	43	50	61
Auto drivers	100	36	27	48	66
Under 14 years of age	—	23	12	2	1
Over 65 years of age	3	5	8	6	4
Going to and from work	47	16	46	70	82
Going to and from school	1	5	13	4	2
Trips in four peak hours	30	25	39	56	72
Going to or from central area	13	13	39	80	83

Source: See note to Table 13–1.

way-elevated trips and 13.3 for suburban railroad trips, as against 3.6 for bus trips.

Other indices of specialization are shown in Table 13-6, which describes some of the more important characteristics of persons using the five modes of travel. Suburban railroads are quite specialized, not only by trip purpose, time and destination, but also because two-thirds of their riders are people who can drive. The fact that they do *not* drive points again to their long average journeys and concentrated destinations in the Loop.

Bus users appear to be more restricted in their capability to drive. Of all mass transportation users, they have the highest proportion of nondrivers, of women, and of the very old and very young. Subway and elevated passengers have characteristics more like those of suburban railroad passengers than those of bus passengers.

This evidence partially destroys the idea that people choose their mode of travel. Clearly, a very great number of transit users do not have any alternate choice. If careful examination of car availability were added, additional persons who can drive would also be found to be "captive" users. It appears that choice operates to the greatest extent for suburban rail users, and the obvious costs of driving and parking in the Loop would suggest that the rail mode is the better choice.

In contrast with mass transportation, Fig. 13-15 shows the destination of all internal person trips made by auto drivers. This model is remarkable for the evenness of distribution of automobile trip destinations, not only in the suburban areas, where there are very few mass transportation trips, but also within the inner area. Even the peaks are not extreme; the highest single quarter-square mile in the Loop is the target of 28,500 auto driver trips per day. Elsewhere, there are somewhat lesser but still substantial concentrations. The highest quarter-square mile in the Oak Park shopping center receives 15,400 such trips, that in Evanston receives 11,100, and the shopping center at 95th and Western receives 8,500.[36]

The evenness of auto driver trip destinations implies a dispersed travel pattern, and this is the case. Mass transportation is less dispersed and far more oriented toward the central area. Automobile trips can be dispersed because the automobile is an individual means of travel. Mass transportation must be more concentrated because it can serve efficiently only where there are sufficiently large groups of persons having common origins, common destinations, or common alignments of their journeys. So the extent of urban centralization versus dispersion will have its effect upon mode of travel.

In sum, the choice of mode of travel is one of the most critical choices which groups of people make regarding transportation. But it is not a free choice, and the data which have been obtained by survey indicate that decisions are made within tight limitations. The demand for

FIGURE 13–15. Model of automobile trip destinations. Automobile drivers made 4,945,000 trips (internal and external) with destinations in the Chicago study area. These destinations are quite evenly spread; the highest block represents 28,500 destinations, while the lowest stands for 2,000 destinations. Shaded areas have from 1,000 to 2,000 destinations per grid of one-quarter square mile. *Source:* See caption for Fig. 13–1.

mass transportation service is, above all, a function of the number of people living and working in an area. If there are many people, then mass transportation can operate effectively. If the level of population density falls below 25,000 persons per net residential square mile (and similar densities for nonresidential uses), it appears that mass transportation services and usage decline. Suburban railroads are exceptions to this rule; they depend upon a specialization of living place tied to a highly concentrated work place like the CBD. Automobile ownership is linked with density in affecting usage of mass transportation; the higher the automobile ownership, the lower the mass transportation usage. The two basic limits set by density and car ownership appear to be so reasonably related to mass transportation usage, economically and practically, that predictions can be based upon them.

NATURE AND VARIANTS OF TRIP GENERATION MODELS

The literature on trip generation may be placed under one of two broad categories: (1) household trip generation; and (2) nonresidential trip generation. The literature on household trips is extensive, and justly so, since approximately 80 per cent of all trips in urban areas begin or end at the home. Furthermore, a wealth of data has been collected through extensive home interviews conducted in urban transportation studies over the past two decades. The great majority of the empirical research dealing with travel behavior in urban areas has sprung from such data. Research into household travel demands usually attempts to derive specific socio-economic or locational factors which will be useful in the development of linear regression models which will estimate the level of transport demands by a particular household or groups of households. Generally, family size, income, vehicle ownership, occupation, distance to retail trade center, or surrogates of these variables have been used to produce estimates of trip production at residential sites.[37] Effective estimation or prediction of residential trip generation remains difficult at the present time, however, and many of the models developed up to now leave much to be desired in accuracy and reliability.

Examining the level of demand for transportation at nonresidential land uses is also important in the study of travel demand. Frank E. Horton has outlined the general nature of the models used for this type of investigation. While the discussion, which follows, deals primarily with commercial land uses, the general forms of the models are similar for all land uses and will give the reader insight into the makeup of the general models and several of the problems associated with them.

*Four Methods of Estimating Travel Demands**

Major urban transportation studies have used four different methods for estimating attraction levels. These models are as follows.

Land use method. In the land use method all trips ending at commercial land uses, regardless of purpose, are summed to derive magnitudes of consumer attraction. Several different models have been developed to estimate the number of commercial trips to particular areal units. In most instances these models are very similar in form to those used in the trip purpose models to be discussed later. A typical example of a land use based model can be found in the approach used by the Chicago Area Transportation Study (CATS).[38] CATS examined all trips to commercial land uses and found that, on the average, 70 per cent do not leave the zone in which the home place of the consumer is located. Therefore, CATS considered that 70 per cent of all commercial trips made by a zone's residents are local trips, and allocated them to the zone of origin. Consumer attraction (e.g., number of commercial trips) per square feet of commercial land use was then calculated for all major shopping centers as well as for the central business district or CBD (these centers are considered nonlocal commercial trip attractors). Using this rate, the remaining 30 per cent of each zone's commercial trips (those crossing the zone's boundary) were distributed to zones, according to the number of square feet of commercial activity located in each zone.

Trip-purpose models. In this set of models the number of trips made for particular purposes is to be estimated. Urban transportation studies are usually structured so as to include ten possible purposes for each trip reported on the home interview coding sheet. Trips made for each of the ten purposes are then aggregated to form from three to six purpose groups on the basis of similarities in land use at the destination or trip lengths. Models are then developed to estimate the number of trips ending in each zone for a particular purpose. The majority of the trip-purpose models allocate shopping trips to zones according to the intensity of commercial activity in each zone; where intensity is defined as number of commercial employees, acres of commercial land use, retail sales, or some other surrogate variable.

Regression models. Although regression techniques are extensively employed to derive estimating equations in the two models previously discussed, a number of urban transportation studies have also used regression models in order to make use of a much larger variety of independent variables which conceivably are useful in explaining zonal variation in consumer attraction. These models are frequently used for estimating the number of trips for a miscellaneous category of purposes or land uses in which shopping trips are often grouped. In many cases, aggregation of trips made for diverse purposes and the mix of independent variables confuse rather than clarify the process of consumer allocation.[39]

Analogy expansions. The analogy-expansion approach to estimating consumer attraction is similar to the trip-purpose method in that the attraction levels are defined as the number of trips for particular purposes. However, existing rates of attraction (measured in trips per square feet, trips per acre, or trips per employee) are calculated for *individual* zones, with no attempt to seek causative factors underlying the observed area-to-area differences in the particular rates. Zones are divided into those which are considered stable (no extensive changes in land use expected) and those in which it is anticipated that considerable commercial development will take place. In stable zones, the existing rate of shopping trips per acre is applied to the expected acres of commercial land use at some future time period. In zones which are expected to have considerable

*Reprinted from Frank E. Horton, "Location Factors as Determinants of Consumer Attraction to Retail Firms," *Annals of the Association of American Geographers*, LVIII (1968), 787–801, with the permission of the editor.

new development, an expansion factor (frequently derived from existing rates in zones with considerable commercial development) is applied to the expected acreage (or a similar variable denoting the intensity of commercial activity) at some future time period.[40]

TRIP DISTRIBUTION AND URBAN TRAVEL BEHAVIOR

Modeling the movement of individuals within the urban area has generally taken two forms, both of them similar in that they are both modified "gravity" formulations.

Gravity Models

The basic gravity model can be written as:

$$I_{ij} = G\frac{P_i P_j}{D_{ij}^b} \quad (1)$$

where: I_{ij} is the interaction between traffic zones i and j; G is a constant; P_i and P_j are populations of the respective areal units; D is the distance between i and j; and b is a constant.[41]

This basic model has been refined and adapted into the following form for transportation forecasting:[42]

$$T_{ij} = \frac{P_i A_j F_{ij} K_{ij}}{\sum_{j=1}^{n} A_j F_{ij} K_{ij}} \quad (2)$$

where: T_{ij} is number of trips from traffic zone i to traffic zone j; P_i is the trips produced by traffic zone i; A_j is the attraction at traffic zone j; F_{ij} is the friction between i and j; K_{ij} is a socio-economic factor. The attraction factor A_j is normally defined by some such surrogate as employment or land use within a particular traffic zone. The friction factor F_{ij} is given a value of either driving time or distance between traffic zones. The socio-economic factor is a variable which can be manipulated to force the model to conform to information derived in the origin-destination study.

This model is calibrated to define the travel in the current time period, as based on the sample data.[43] The attraction and friction factors are then estimated for the future time period, and the model is applied to examine the distribution of trips between zones at some future time period.

The second kind of model employed is called the "intervening opportunities model." Colin Clark and G. H. Peters have written an interesting discussion of this method of examining travel within cities, which follows.

*Opportunities Models**

So far as location theorists are concerned, attention has become increasingly focused on the idea of distance operating as a major constraint in shaping social conduct. An early effort in this field is associated with the name of W. J. Reilly.[44] In his study of the relative attractions of moderately sized American towns as shopping centers, Reilly came to the conclusion (often described as the Law of Reilly) that attractive power was measured by the town's population, divided by the square of the distance from the town to the area in question. This, of course, is an analog of Newton's Law of Gravity. More examination of the evidence on this problem was made during the 1930's, particularly by the distinguished German economist Lösch, who thought that distance raised to the power of 1.6 gave a better measure than the square of the distance.[45] Further examples of the use of gravity type formula are available in abundance, notably in the works of Zipf and Stewart.[46]

It was perhaps inevitable that sooner or later the method would be applied to the problem of describing inter-zonal movements of urban traffic. One of the early examples appears to be a study of Munich conducted in 1952 by Feuchtinger and Schlums, who used the products of populations of areas as a measure of "attraction" and divided by distance raised to the power of 1.69 as a measure of "resistance." Many attempts have been made to apply the method in American cities. Voorhees, and Carroll and Bevis were among the leaders in the field.[47] Various powers

*Reprinted from Colin Clark and G. H. Peters. "The Intervening Opportunities Method of Traffic Analysis," *Traffic Quarterly*, XIX (1965), 101–19, with the permission of the authors and editor.

of distance were discovered to hold for different cities and for different types of journeys, while efforts were also made to modify the basic nature of the resistance function in efforts to secure more adequate fits, notably in Toronto.[48] Similar work in Britain, by Tanner of the Road Research Laboratory, showed that a simple distance function of the type normally employed in gravity models definitely failed to fit the census data for the different London boroughs in 1951, showing movements between residences and work places, though a formula incorporating an inverse square (approximately) multiplied by a negative exponential of distance (i.e., a function of the form $\varepsilon^{-\lambda d}d^{-n}$) gave a better fit.[49]

Apart from all of the difficulties associated with obtaining a suitable resistance function, the question of how best to measure "attraction" has also raised problems. The population or work force of the sending area clearly must be included, along with population, job opportunities or retail employment in the "receiving" area, depending upon the nature of the travel flows which are being analyzed. The choice of a measure of attraction, however, also raises the question of what form of function is most appropriate. Normally the straight "product" is regarded as most useful but, as Mylroie has shown in her analysis of intercity movements, it may be preferable to use the product of the square roots in order to increase the degree of explanation attained.[50]

All of these features, the disaggregation of the data for purpose of journey, and the setting up of suitable "resistance" and "attraction" functions, raise immense computing problems. One can never be certain whether the use of one formulation might not produce "explanation" which is inferior to that which could be obtained by employing a somewhat different variant of the basic model. In the nature of the case, computation of alternatives is a long and costly process, often involving tiresome iterative procedures. Though the gravity model may have unexplored possibilities, it is not surprising that a thorough search for more suitable procedures is under way. Clearly this was the line taken by the organizers of the recently published Chicago Area Transportation Survey. Instead of relying upon a gravity model, it was decided to try out the idea of a member of the survey staff, Morton Schneider, and use what has come to be called the method of "intervening opportunities."[51]

The application of this method in Chicago, where it was first successfully tried out (Schneider subsequently tried it also in Pittsburgh[52] and is now at work in New York, while Tomazinis has attempted a similar approach for Philadelphia and in the subsequent Penn-Jersey study)[53] certainly required a computer, and even then constituted a heavy piece of calculation. But it does appear to be worth following up. In its first application it was possible only to analyze the traffic originating in one or two specified districts in Chicago, because of the sheer weight of calculation which had to be performed. All the destinations of traffic in Chicago on an average day—some ten million of them—had to be tabulated. The computer was then required (by a method known to traffic engineers) to estimate the average time required for a journey from the sample area under consideration to every one of these possible destinations and then to range the number of possible destinations in ascending order of time required for a journey to them. (Readers will note that the substitution of time, or sometimes cost, for distance is a common feature of traffic models, which has obvious advantages.)

The next step is the important one. Let us suppose that V_i represents the total trip origins from area i and that V_{ij} represents the number of these which terminate in area j. Any trip from i will have a certain probability of ending in area j, which can be represented as $P(S_j)$. In other words:

$$V_{ij} = V_i \cdot P(S_j) \tag{3}$$

Schneider discovered that the $P(S_j)$ factor is closely related to the total number of opportunities in area j and to the number of opportunities available in areas closer to area i than is area j. In other words, intervening opportunities have a controlling influence of decisive importance. In fact, the log of the number of journeys terminating in areas up to j was found to be inversely proportional to the number of intervening opportunities, while the log of the number of journeys beyond j is inversely proportional to the number of opportunities between i and j plus the number within j itself. The number of journeys terminating *within* j is, of course, given by the difference.[54]

It is perhaps of some interest to note that this idea, like the gravity model, also has an analog in physics and a predecessor in general location theory. The physical law concerns the principles governing the distribution of lengths of path of molecules in a gas, while the location theory example is normally referred to as "Stouffer's principle." This latter was derived after study of migration of families between census tracts in Cleveland, Ohio in the 1930's.[55] It was often thought that migration flows could be explained simply in terms of distance, but Stouffer held that distance is not the chief factor. Instead he found the number of people migrating a given distance to be proportional to opportunities at that distance and inversely proportional to the number of intervening opportunities. Stouffer went even further, arguing that the use of distance in any explanatory model is simply confusing the main relationship, which is between movement and opportunities, with the auxiliary relationship between distance and opportunities which is almost certain to be present. This point, as will be argued later, is of fundamental importance.

. . .

In Greater London, for an area of over 500 square miles and a population of over 10,000,000, a detailed cross-classification of residences and workplaces is given in the 1951 census (another census has been taken in 1961, though the results are not yet available; in any case, they are likely to be less finely classified since information was collected only on a sample basis).[56] As it stands, the data relate only to the numbers moving. There is no direct information relating to "accessibility" in terms of travel time or cost. However, since we are performing a test only at a highly aggregated level, we may take, as a measure of "opportunities," total employment available within succeeding radii of distance from the residential area under consideration, and then record the numbers of persons from this residential area working in each zone. Even so, a certain amount of arbitrary "splitting" was necessary, since the boundaries of some London boroughs sprawl untidily over the map, but in general this did not present severe problems.

The basic Schneider formulation was also altered somewhat in order to make for ease of treatment. A plot was made of the logarithm of the percentage of total journeys originating in an area, which terminated before or at a particular point on a cumulated opportunities scale.[57]

A final improvement in the method of analysis arose from a suggestion of Lieutenant Kain of the U.S. Air Force Academy and Rand Corporation. Journeys to work by women workers, he found, generally tended to follow a quite different law from those of men; women workers were much less willing to work at a distance from their homes. This undoubtedly was proved true by the Greater London data.

Figure 13–16 clearly shows how well the straight line, semi-logarithmic rule works in different types of English boroughs. In all, some seventeen diagrams were drawn for different types of boroughs, some central, some outlying, some rich, some poor. Two qualifications must, however, be made. In the first place, a careful examination of the diagrams shows that the number of people who find work in the immediate neighborhood of their homes tends to be greater than predicted by the general formula (i.e., there is a kink in the northwest corner). This may be due to two causes. First, the data refer to "all employment," and do not make a distinction between those who walk or cycle to work and those who travel by car and public transport. The two classes may possibly obey different "laws." Another possible cause, however, is that the data do not permit a very fine breakdown; a greater degree of disaggregation might have resulted in a better fit being obtained for shorter journeys. The second major qualification concerns the behavior of persons living in really outlying boroughs such as St. Albans and Watford, some 20 miles from Central London. As might have been expected, half or more of all people here find work in their own borough, and only a minority travel to work at a distance. The "kink" in these cases tends to be much more pro-

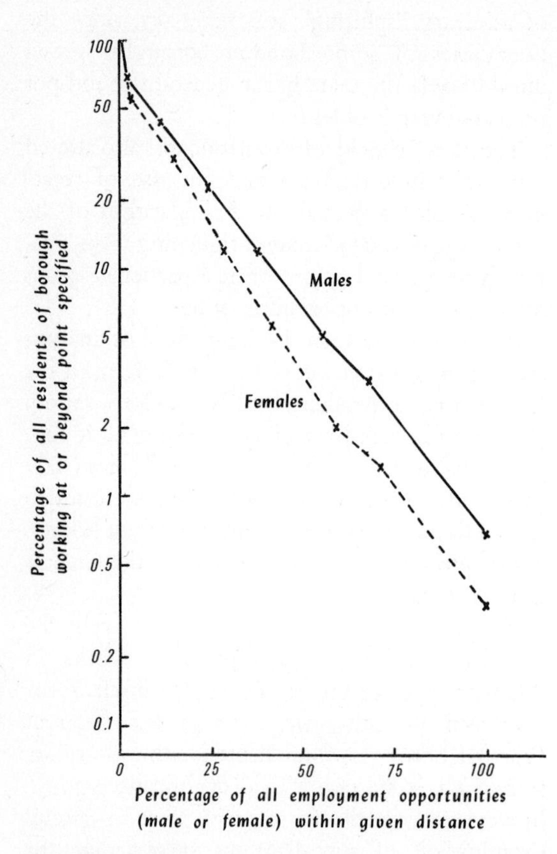

FIGURE 13–16*a*. Alternate employment opportunities in England: Kensington M.B. *Source:* Figs. 13–16*a* through 13–20 are from Colin Clark and G. H. Peters, "The Intervening Opportunities Method of Traffic Analysis," *Traffic Quarterly*, XIX (1965), 101–19.

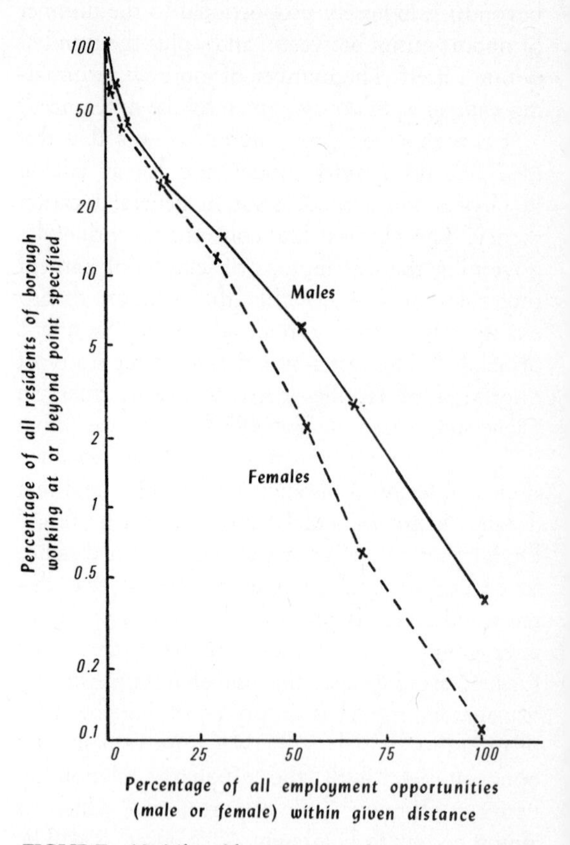

FIGURE 13–16*b*. Alternate employment opportunities in England: Deptford M.B. *Source:* See caption for Fig. 13–16*a*.

nounced; but even so the movements of the minority still follow the general "straight line" rule.

Given that distance appears to be an important variable in estimating interaction, people living on the peripheral areas of a city would have to travel farther for opportunities than those living in the central city. The distance factor will presumably act as an inhibitor, resulting in the slope of the opportunity line being steeper for residents of the outlying area. In short, the effect of distance might be expected to matter very considerably in determining travel patterns. The important point which emerges from the study, however, is that this is *not* the case. Distance does not have its expected effects (at any rate until it becomes large), and the slopes of the opportunity curves, in general, have a remarkable constancy. It is opportunities, as such, rather than distance, which provide the controlling influence.

Such a startling proposition clearly requires a strict test. For this purpose we may begin by looking at a case in which slight effects of distance are to be found. Residents of Kensington, since they are close to the center of London, have almost the maximum number of opportunities within a given distance. Residents of Deptford, which is situated nearer to the corner of the map, have

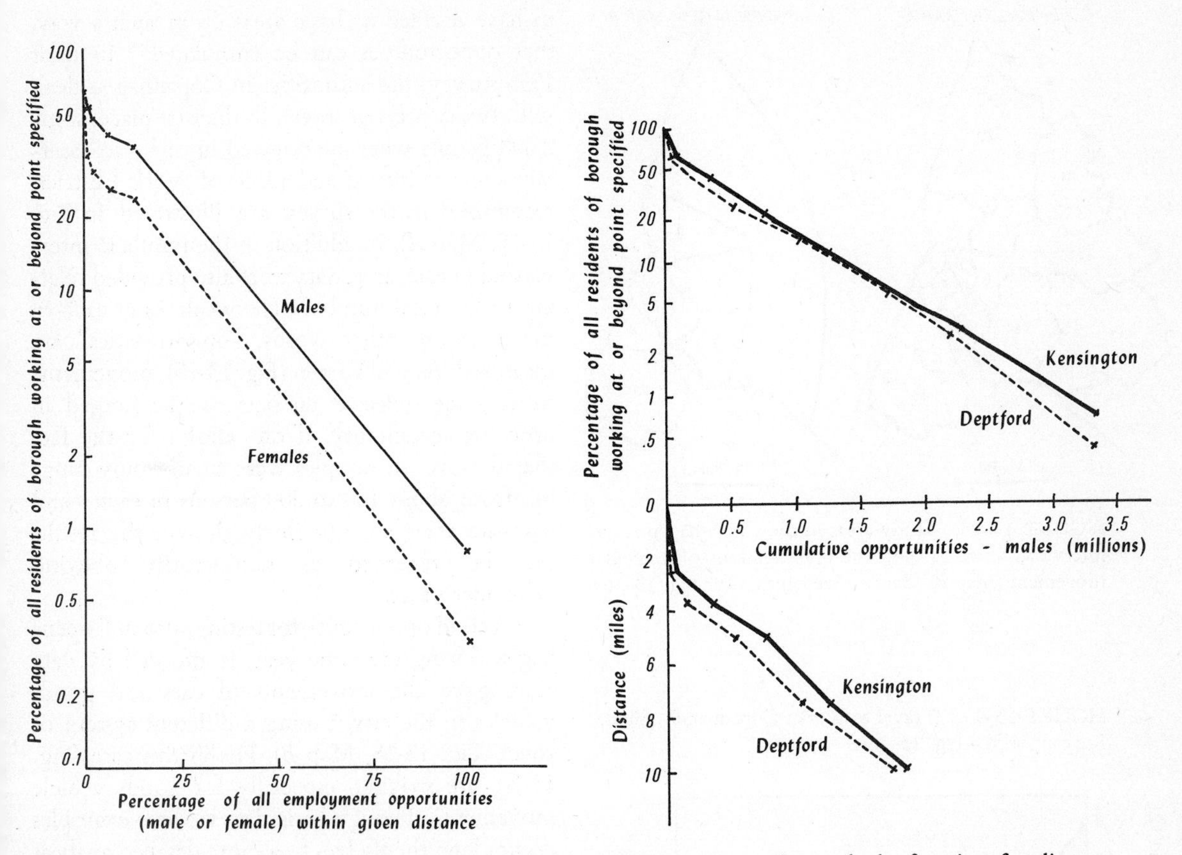

FIGURE 13–16*c*. Alternate employment opportunities in England: Epsom and Ewell M.B. *Source:* See caption for Fig. 13–16*a*.

FIGURE 13–17. The method of testing for distance and opportunity effects. *Source:* See caption for Fig. 13–16*a*.

to travel greater distances to reach any given number of opportunities (Fig. 13–17). As can be seen, the Deptford line has a slightly steeper slope. The lower half of the diagram shows that Deptford residents do need to travel farther to reach any given number of opportunities than do residents of Kensington. One would expect differences to become more marked as lines on the lower half of the diagram diverge. In fact, diagrams of this nature were constructed for each borough studied, and slight effects only were found in the other cases until one reached areas as far out as Feltham (some 12 miles from the center of London). Divergencies in the opportunities-distance relationship, in short, did *not* cause marked divergencies in the movement-opportunities relationship over a very wide area. Indeed, the evidence appears to be strong enough to support the proposition implicit in Schneider's principle that "distance does not matter."

It has already been stated that further information which is amenable to treatment by the Schneider method is difficult to obtain. Despite a strenuous search through the results of traffic surveys for a large number of cities, only one, Copenhagen, appears to possess a sufficiently elongated topography, and at the same time

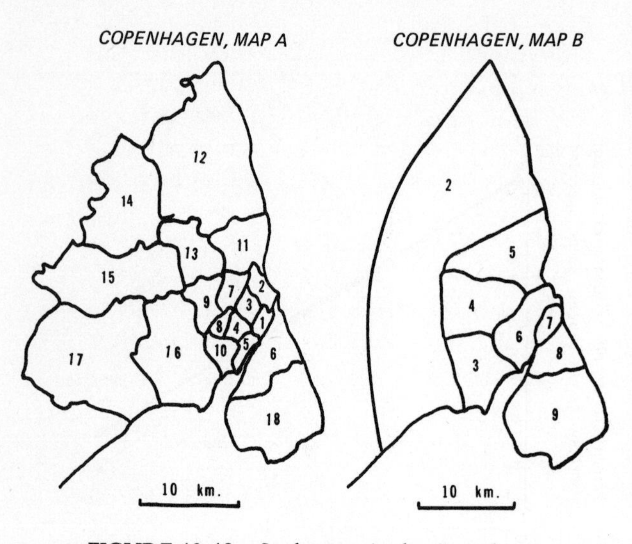

FIGURE 13–18. Study areas in the Copenhagen travel interviews (map *A*) and the investigations of vehicular movement (map *B*). *Source:* See caption for Fig. 13–16*a*.

FIGURE 13–19. Travel to work: Copenhagen. *Source:* See caption for Fig. 13–16*a*.

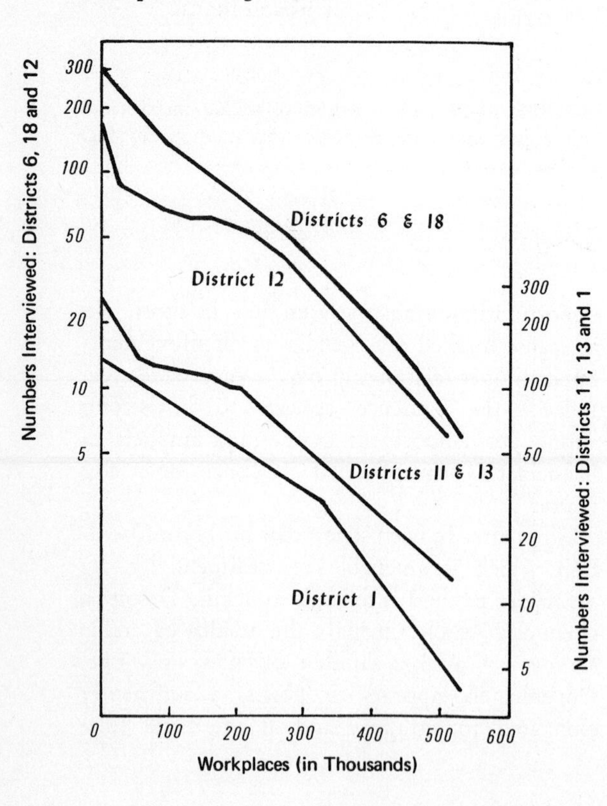

to have divided its basic areas up in such a way, that opportunities can be cumulated.[58] In their 1956 survey, the authorities in Copenhagen dealt with two aspects of travel. In the first place, some 2,000 people were interviewed in order to ascertain their residence and place of work (districts recognized in the survey are illustrated in Fig. 13-18, Map *A*). In addition to the numbers interviewed in each area, data were also provided relating to the total number of workplaces in each of the areas; in other words, "opportunities" are measured. As will be seen (Fig. 13-19), movements from a few selected districts can be ranged in order of accessibility. If one allows for the fact that the sizes of samples were small—only ranging from about 100 to 300 persons in each—and that the areas are not finely drawn, the results can be regarded as satisfactorily obeying Schneider's rule.

A second opportunity for testing, also in Copenhagen during the same year, is afforded by data relating to the movements of cars and goods vehicles in the city,[59] using a different system of zones (Fig. 13-18, Map *B*). Fits in this case (Fig. 13-20) are striking, especially for goods vehicle movements. Though basic data in these examples do not lend themselves to a more detailed analysis of the "distance *vs.* opportunity" effects, such as was carried out for London, it can, nevertheless, be said that the results reinforce our faith in the Schneider formulation.

It may be said in conclusion that the principle of "intervening opportunities" appears to be an important step forward in our knowledge relating to travel habits. At the very least it must further undermine our faith in the effects of distance, and it must surely force us to recast our thinking concerning the potential usefulness of gravity models.

HOUSEHOLD TRAVEL BEHAVIOR

The gravity and intervening opportunities models described above are two operational approaches to forecasting the zone-to-zone movement of urban inhabitants. Geographers have examined urban travel behavior in other ways

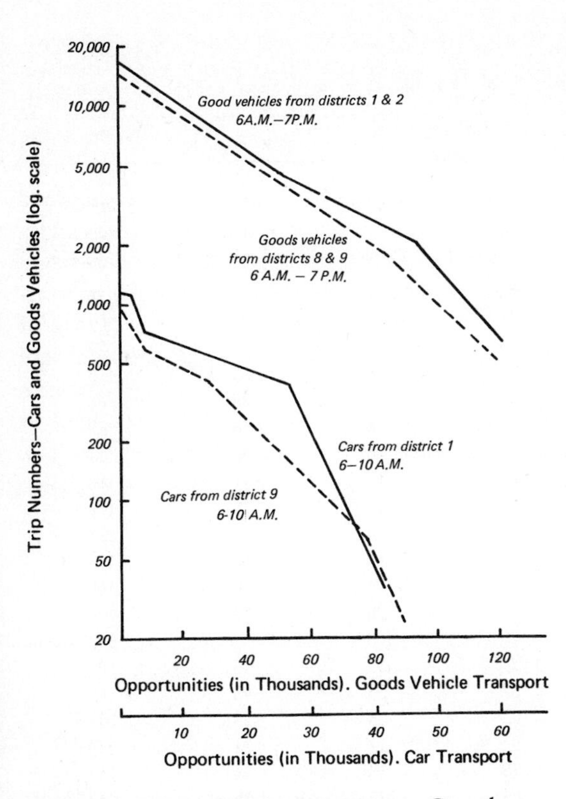

FIGURE 13–20. Vehicle movements: Copenhagen. *Source:* See caption for Fig. 13–16*a*.

as well. Duane F. Marble has discussed several problems associated with the detailed analysis of individual household travel behavior (as opposed to aggregate travel behavior) in a paper, parts of which follow.

*Individual Travel Behavior**

Many of the problems encountered in geographic research involve choice situations, and, because of the nature of the discipline, the alternatives in these choice situations are frequently spatial in nature. For instance, firms or industries may select from among a set of alternative locations and patterns of shipment and procurement; or a region may be thought of as attempting to choose an optimal production structure and set of trade patterns in light of its resource endowment and relative location within the over-all space economy. The examples cited are familiar ones to research workers in geography, and recently modest amounts of information have been developed, dealing with the theoretical structuring and empirical examination of these and similar spatial choice problems. Many of the important contributions in this area have been reviewed by William L. Garrison in a series of articles.[60] The planning implications of certain portions of this work have also been examined in a review article by Benjamin H. Stevens.[61]

Less familiar to many research workers are the structured patterns of spatial behavior exhibited by individuals or such small groups of individuals as household units. Although assumptions about the spatial behavior patterns of individuals are frequently incorporated into theories dealing with the spatial behavior of firms and industries (such as those found in central-place theory), these assumptions usually represent severe simplifications which have never been adequately tested to determine their degree of correspondence with real-world situations. For instance, note the explicitly stated assumptions about household travel behavior contained in the Herbert-Stevens model of residential location.[62] Another well-known example is contained in central-place theory, where consumers are assumed to desire only one good at a time and hence are concerned only with decisions pertaining to a limited number of single-purpose trips.

Recent empirical studies by Marble, Nystuen, and others have pointed out the complexities of individual travel behavior and stressed the need for further development of theoretical structures in this area.[63] Some notion of the deviations that occur between assumed and observed travel behavior can be obtained from an examination of Table 13-7. This table displays the combination of purposes to be expected within 100 trips, all of which include a stop at the specified business type. For instance, in the first category—auto

*Reprinted from Duane F. Marble, "A Theoretical Exploration of Individual Travel Behavior," in *Quantitative Geography*, Part I: *Economic and Cultural Topics*, eds. W. L. Garrison and D. F. Marble (Evanston, Ill.: Northwestern University Studies in Geography, 1966), pp. 33–54, with the permission of the author and editors.

TABLE 13-7

Structure of Customer Stops (per 100 Trips to a Specific Type of Business)

		Multiple-purpose Trips			
Type of Business	*Number of Single-purpose Trips*	*Number of Trips*	*Stops for Work Purposes*	*Stops for Social-recreation Purposes*	*Stops at Other Business Establishments*
Auto accessory	64	36	7	0	36
Theater	61	39	4	27	61
Grocery	60	40	3	14	27
Hotel	41	59	8	33	108
Ice cream	41	59	0	38	68
Dentist	38	62	8	8	62
Drug store	36	64	8	23	113
Supermarket	34	66	12	19	106
Doctor	33	67	10	6	112
Beauty shop	31	69	6	38	131
Tavern	29	71	50	21	179
Hardware and paint	28	72	4	8	188
Barber shop	28	72	28	11	128
Meat and vegetable	25	75	8	17	108
Auto repair	23	77	33	13	97
Gas station	18	82	33	45	65
Appliance store	17	83	25	25	283
Furniture store	17	83	17	11	245
Bakery	15	85	15	24	142
Restaurant	11	89	52	26	122
Real estate, lawyer and insurance	11	89	11	22	195
Utility company	11	89	21	4	269
Miscellaneous retail	11	89	24	46	208
Bank	8	92	48	20	190
Department store	7	93	11	20	151
Variety store	5	95	20	14	275
Clothing store	4	96	8	15	253
Laundry	0	100	38	8	238

Source: William L. Garrison *et al.*, *Studies of Highway Development and Geographic Change* (Seattle: University of Washington Press, 1959), p. 223.

accessories—64 single-purpose trips and 36 multi-purpose trips are noted. These latter trips contained 43 stops distributed between work purposes and stops at other business establishments. Furniture stores, further down the list, display an even higher dependence on linkages with other establishments, with 83 trips out of 100 involving other purposes. It seems only reasonable, then, to anticipate that behavior in a real-world situation will display a pattern of variation which is based on the goods involved as well as on differences between individuals or household units.

The present discussion offers no new, comprehensive theory of individual travel behavior; instead, it constitutes a preliminary exploration of some theoretical aspects of the situation. The problem posed here is not a simple one. Our personal experience, as well as many of the existing empirical studies, demonstrates that consumers are constantly engaged in a complex pattern of spatial operations involving, among other things, the choice of a residential site and the development of a set of intricate travel patterns in order to satisfy their day-to-day demands for goods and services. The present discussion deals with only one aspect of this problem, the day-to-day movement patterns exhibited by most individuals. This question, of course, is not unrelated to the problem of residential-site selection, since it is felt that a significant relationship exists between desired movement patterns and the amount individuals are willing to bid for specific locations as permanent residential sites. That is, a substitution relationship is postulated to exist between transport inputs to the household and residential land values.

A useful first step is to turn to the existing body of theory and examine items to be found there, even though they are few in number and unarticulated in structure. The first notion which is directly related to the problem of individual travel behavior is the concept of "space preference" set forth by Isard in his basic work on general location theory.[64] Isard admits that current concepts in general location theory are deficient in accounting for household-to-household and individual-to-individual variations in the level of transport inputs, but he does indicate that spatial relationships may not be the only factor of importance in determining individual spatial behavior patterns when he introduces the concept of individual space preference (which may be defined in terms of the individual's perception of distance and spatial relationships).

To illustrate this notion, consider two individuals placed in the same spatial situation and possessing identical levels of information. Despite the similarities in environmental structure, these individuals may well exhibit differing patterns of spatial behavior, and it is postulated that these differences in behavior patterns arise from the differences in the space preferences of the individuals involved. For instance, one of the individuals might have a high, positive space preference. His need for social interaction would be high, and he would tend to weight additional increments of distance rather lightly. It is not unreasonable to suppose that his choices of a residential site and a set of travel patterns would differ greatly from those made by the second individual whom we may suppose to have a much lower, but still positive, space preference, and who would weight distance increments much more heavily. These space preferences are determined by social, psychological, and cultural forces which are frequently exogenous to the general spatial system.

Huff has formulated a *sui generis* model of consumer space preference in an attempt to bring certain psychological concepts to bear on the topic.[65] A series of elements believed to affect consumer space preference were designated and, together with their postulated interconnections, formed into a "digraph" (directed graph). The vertices of the graph represented the behavioral determinants and the directed links connecting them to the postulated functional relationships. Connectivity analysis of the digraph, using a modified Shimbel-Katz index, indicated that age was by far the most dominant element in space preference, with personality, sex, education, mental synthesizing abilities, occupation, and income comprising the remaining influential factors (see Table 13-8). Cultural differences such as those discussed by Hall were not examined.[66]

TABLE 13-8

Relative Degree of Connectivity of Model Elements

Element	*Percentage of Total Connectivity*
Age	26.42
Personality	14.11
Sex	12.95
Education	10.01
Mental synthesizing abilities	10.01
Occupation	8.64
Income	4.83
Stimulus situation	1.55
Transport mode	1.21
Physiological drive	1.21
Geographical location	1.21
Ethnic affiliation	1.21
Reputation of source	1.05
Breadth of merchandise	1.05
Price of product	1.05
Others	Less than 1 per cent each

Source: David L. Huff, "Toward a General Theory of Consumer Travel Behavior" (D.B.A. dissertation, University of Washington, 1955).

Existing empirical evidence pertaining to household travel behavior appears to provide some small degree of substantiation to the notion that nonspatial factors play a significant role in determining individual movement patterns. Garrison's study of the travel habits of rural households showed that, in his study areas, the propensity to travel at any given time was distributed among households without any apparent relationship to the type of road service locally available, and that the frequency of shopping was independent of the distance from the shopping center, although the place visited was a function of distance.[67] Additional empirical investigations, by the present author, of the travel behavior of urban households generally supports these conclusions and, in addition, points out the importance of the socioeconomic structure of the household in determining such things as gross trip frequencies and total time spent away from the home.[68]

A second major concept encountered in existing theory is that potential returns in a spatial choice situation are a function of the decision maker's position with respect to other elements in the space economy and the ease with which he may undertake movements within this system.[69] Combining this with the concept of individual space preference would seem to lead to the following—Individual movement patterns are a function of: (1) the space preference of the individual in question; (2) his location within the over-all space economy; and (3) the relative ease with which he may move from place to place within the system. In the short run, it would seem reasonable to assume that, for a given individual, the first factor remains constant. The latter two items, however, may be expected to undergo variations at fairly frequent intervals, since any decision by the individual to undertake a movement automatically induces a variation in his relative location as well as in the set of movement paths available to him.

What about the conditions under which the individual makes his choices? If common terminology in the field of decision theory is followed, then an individual in a given spatial choice situation may be said to be acting in the realm of: (1) certainty, if each possible choice on his part is known by him to lead invariably to a specific outcome; (2) risk, if each decision leads to one of a set of possible specific outcomes, each of which occurs with a known probability; and (3) uncertainty, if any of the possible decisions have as their consequence a set of possible specific outcomes, but where the probabilities of these outcomes are completely unknown. An examination of current theory leads to the conclusion that individuals are normally assumed to act under conditions of certainty, and frequently with only a small number of alternatives open at any given time.

Available empirical information is extremely limited, but it does seem to indicate that these common assumptions regarding individual behavior in space are quite unrealistic. Not only are the observed behavior patterns much more complex (see Table 13-7 and related discussion), but apparently when individuals are placed in a spatial choice situation which is new to them, their decision-making operations are conducted at the level of uncertainty; as the individual indulges in various information-gathering activities, this state tends to approach the level of risk rather than certainty.[70] That is, the result of a growing familiarity with the environment in which a spatial choice situation is situated may be viewed as generating an *a priori* probability distribution over the set of potential outcomes.

The researcher who wishes to investigate various facets of this behavior system is confronted with the necessity of producing a model (since none now exists) of a rather complex decision situation.

The problems associated with examining individual travel behavior led Marble to suggest the use of a simple time-dependent probability model in a later paper.

*A Time-dependent Model**

Empirical investigations of person movements within a metropolitan region commonly define a trip as a movement between two locations. Associated with this point-to-point movement

*Reprinted from Duane F. Marble, "A Simple Markovian Model of Trip Structures in a Metropolitan Region," *Papers of the Regional Science Association*, Western Section (1964), with the permission of the author.

are a number of assorted characteristics—land use (a purpose) at the point of destination, land use (a purpose) at the point of origin, distance, travel time, mode, and so forth. Marble has pointed out that this view of the trip as an isolated and independent movement between two locations is at odds with the behavioral situation which generates the observed movement.[71] In almost all cases, the individual trip maker views his recurrent daily movements from place to place within the region as starting at a fixed location (normally his home base) and terminating—after a number of intermediate stops which may serve a variety of purposes—at the same location. This view of the person trip as a closed circuit has proven quite useful in several studies of travel behavior (see Garrison *et al.* and Nystuen[72]).

If this definition of a person trip is adopted, it proves useful to introduce at the present level of investigation a somewhat artificial dichotomy between notions of trip generation and trip structure. The former (see Oi and Shuldiner)[73] is normally held to deal with questions relating to number of trips made by the behavioral units, the factors which influence the level of travel activity, and so forth, while the latter considers the mix of purposes, modes, and so forth within a given trip or set of trips. In reality, the two are not independent, but we may consider them to be so as a first approximation.

One difficulty encountered in the study of questions relating to trip structure is the obvious heavy dependency of current decisions upon the previous spatial and temporal parameters of the trip. This dependency, together with the wide variety of factors operating to influence the decision maker in his choice, presents the potential analyst with a most complex situation. Marble has suggested that the decision process might be viewed as a stochastic game,[74] but this suggestion has only limited merit from an empirical point of view. What is needed is a simple model (or perhaps a set of models) which will permit the analyst to manipulate the major elements of this system without being forced into the additional problems rampant in a large-scale Monte Carlo representation.

The simplest time-dependent probability model available is the finite Markov chain. Its basic operation assumes that we have a finite collection of events or states, and our interest lies in the behavior of a process which moves from state to state in such a manner that if at any given time it is in state i, it will move to state j with probability P_{ij}. The distribution of these transition probabilities for movement from a specific state (say the kth) to all other states is given by the kth row of the transition matrix P. This matrix, together with an initial probability distribution, completely describes the entire process. The time dependence of this model is severely limited, but it is readily amenable to a wide variety of manipulations (see Kemeny and Snell and Harary and Lipstein[75]).

A SYSTEMS APPROACH TO URBAN TRANSPORTATION

Marble's research utilized the Markov chain model to examine empirically the trip purpose structure of urban households for both single and multi-purpose trips. The Markov model was successfully applied later by Horton and Shuldiner to movements between urban activities.[76]

Research in urban travel behavior by geographers has increased markedly in the past several years.[77] As geographers become more aware of the contributions they can make to this vital area of research, we can expect an even greater participation by urban geographers. One of the most recent trends in urban transportation is the trend toward the systems analytic approach to transportation problems. A simple and straightforward explanation of the systems approach to urban transportation has been given by Joseph L. Schofer.

*Systems Analysis in Transportation Planning**

Systems analysis is a term used to describe an approach to the study of large systems. A system may be characterized as a group of interdependent

*Reprinted from Joseph L. Schofer, "Systems Analysis in Transportation Planning" (Center for Urban Studies and Department of Systems Engineering, University of Illinois at Chicago), with the permission of the author.

elements which function together for a purpose. Systems analysis is not a tool for answering questions, but a viewpoint from which to ask questions. It evolved from the problems of operations research analysts during World War II. The operations researchers were concerned with developing the optimum, or most efficient solution, to a given set of problems. They began to realize, however, that in many cases the wrong problems were being solved. Often only a part of a system was optimized; this came to be known as "sub-optimization."

In order to ask the relevant questions, it was necessary to view the entire system under study in the proper perspective, rather than looking only at one or more of its elements. It became clear, however, that the reason that methods of sub-optimization had been accepted in the past was the extreme complexity of the most interesting systems under examination.

For example, the typical systems problem is the one of the chicken and the egg. Does transportation determine land use patterns? Or, is land use a function of transportation networks? The answer, of course, is that the relationship between transportation and land use operates in both directions. In the face of such complexities, new approaches were necessary. While they come under the name "systems analysis," many researchers will come to understand them as the only logical way to solve difficult problems.

In the most elementary sense, systems analysis consists of looking first at the whole, rather than at the parts. As an understanding of the functioning of the entire system is developed, the most logical ways to separate it into its components will be devised. The next step is the study of the interactions between the system elements. This will lead to the conclusion that the whole is greater than the sum of its parts, for the components themselves have limited meaning. It is only when they are seen in the context of the entire system, with its inputs, flows, interactions, boundaries, and outputs, that the parts will have their true significance.

Consider, for example, an effort to understand the operation of an automobile. It would certainly be difficult to examine a pile of spark plugs, pistons, gears, and wires, and to deduce from these the way in which the automobile functions, or the best way to evaluate its performance. Systems analysis would call for the examination of the vehicle in the context of its operating environment. The various parts could be studied in relation to the entire system. As the investigation progressed, parts could be removed and examined in order to determine their function and their relationship to other parts. Such an approach would eventually lead to an understanding of the automobile.

Transportation systems planning. The transportation system might be considered to include the fixed and movable facilities which make movement possible, the flows of resources and information which promote the operation, control, and planning of transport services, the functional groups concerned with planning the future states of the system, and the interfaces of the system with its social, political, and economic environment. An analysis of the transportation system must consider the impacts of system changes upon the various aspects of its environment. An analysis of this nature differs from the more traditional approaches to transportation planning, just as a partial equilibrium economic analysis differs from a general equilibrium study. The former would be concerned with the changes in the prices of transportation services which would result from a modification of the system. The latter would deal with the changes in the prices of *all* goods which would be affected by a change in the transportation system.

The ability to perform this kind of comprehensive analysis does not yet exist. Such an approach requires an understanding of the functional relationships between the transportation system and those elements of the environment which it influences. This understanding must be in sufficient detail to model the consequences of alternative plans. While some important system consequences can be modeled today, others cannot be measured or predicted, and still others remain unclear or unrecognized.

The difficulties associated with predicting and measuring the various consequences brought about by the transportation system, as well as the problems of combining incommensurate and immeasurable factors into a description of an alternative plan suitable for decision making, place severe demands upon the planning process and upon the methods for evaluating alternative transportation plans.

These complexities prevent the planner from attempting to optimize all of the various system consequences. Instead, he must describe the characteristics of these consequences with which the community residents would at least be satisfied. In other words, a rather detailed specification of system goals is required. These goals must reflect the nature of the acceptable system consequences in all of the relevant impact areas. The logical criterion for evaluating alternative transportation plans, given that they satisfy the comprehensive goal set, would be the minimization of total costs.

Figure 13–21 shows the goal-oriented transportation system planning process which is coming into general use. A comprehensive set of system goals is formulated. Then some alternative transportation plans aimed at achieving these goals are proposed. The proposed alternatives and information concerning existing and anticipated environmental conditions are inputs to a combined forecasting and testing process. The demand for movement is projected, and the operation of each alternative under the given demand conditions is simulated. At the same time, the various impacts of the proposed networks upon the environment are forecasted. All phases of the forecasting and testing process are interrelated, so that the projected travel demands, system operating characteristics, and system consequences are internally consistent. The results of the tests are multi-dimensional, for they might include operating costs, the expected number of accidents, impacts on urban form, and the various social, political, economic, and esthetic consequences of each alternative.

These test results are evaluated with respect to the set of system goals. Where necessary, plan revisions are accomplished. Finally, the goals may be revised and the process repeated in order to

FIGURE 13–21. The transportation system planning process. *Source:* Joseph L. Schofer, "Systems Analysis in Transportation Planning" (Center for Urban Studies and Department of Systems Engineering, University of Illinois at Chicago).

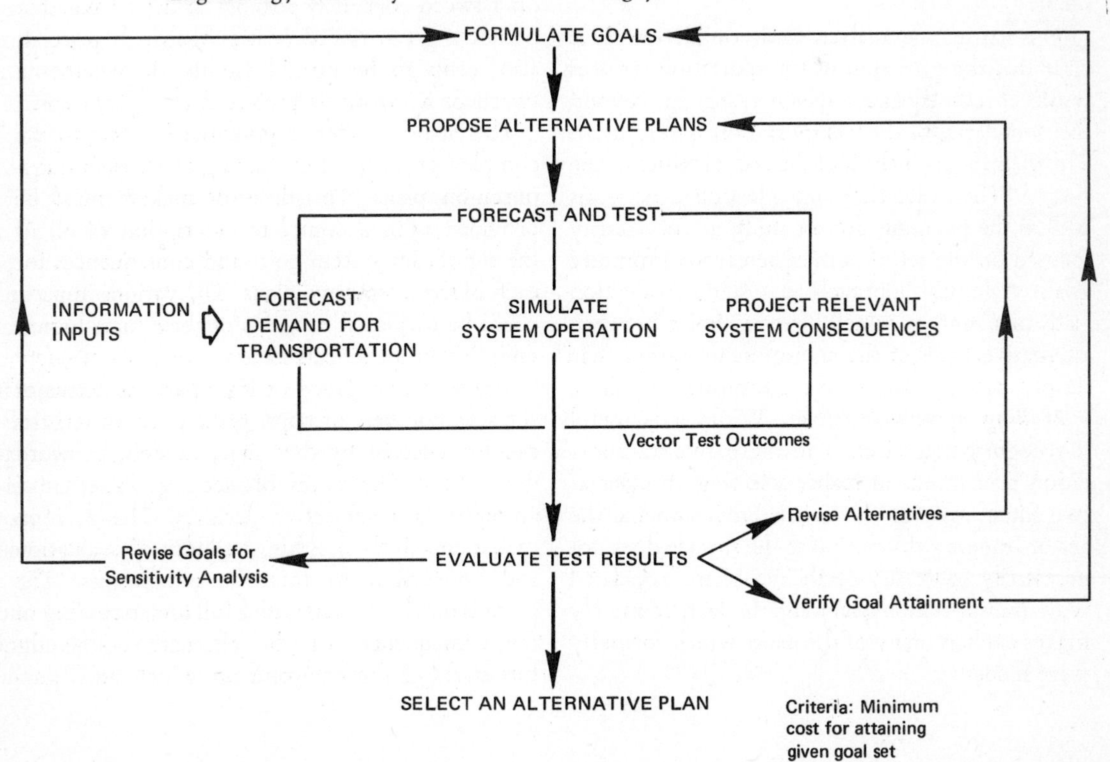

determine the cost-sensitivity of each system goal. The latter process is necessary in order to insure that the community recognizes the costs of setting goals at various levels. It may show that a slight revision in a particular goal would result in a considerable reduction in system costs.

System evaluation. The fixed performance-minimum cost evaluation criterion differs considerably from the traditional benefit-cost analysis. The strategy in benefit-cost studies is to select the system which provides the highest ratio of benefits to costs. Two alternative systems could differ considerably in their benefits and costs, and still have the same benefit-cost ratio. The criterion proposed here, in what is termed a cost-effectiveness approach, insures that each system performs at a minimum level consistent with the community goals. The performance or effectiveness of each alternative is fixed at an acceptable level.

An immediate conclusion is that the cost-effectiveness strategy amounts to an evaluation of system goals rather that simply a test of various alternative plans. The goals, of course, are specified levels of the anticipated system consequences. The plan selection process becomes the choice among possible future states of the urban environment.

This carries the analysis to a completion. It is clear that the provision of transportation services results in consequences which reach far beyond the boundaries of the transportation system itself. This calls for an analysis of the complexities of the system. The evaluation and selection process, as well as the planning process itself, are necessarily focused on the set of comprehensive community goals. A logical approach to systems evaluation leads to a strategy which forces a choice between alternative states of the environment, rather than simply between alternative transportation plans.

Making system decisions. While it is useful to recognize that selecting an alternative transportation plan means in reality selecting an alternative future state of the urban environment, the act of bringing this notion to the surface does not necessarily solve any of the problems associated with transportation planning. In fact, it merely makes explicit many of the issues which formerly were hidden.

There remains a number of most difficult questions to answer. For example, what is the conversion rate between human lives and the provision of open space? That is, is it worth sacrificing some safety features to build an expressway around, rather than through, a park? Equally difficult, what is the dollar value of a human life or an acre of park land? The values of lives and parks are incommensurate; they cannot be logically considered in common units. Likewise, is the provision of a sensually pleasing highway worth the additional cost? The latter question is even harder to answer, because it concerns an intangible—esthetic value. Highway safety can be measured in terms of lives saved or lost or accidents caused; parks can be measured in terms of acres or perhaps even the expected number of visits to them over a period of years. What is esthetically pleasing to one man, however, may not be so to another.

The solution to these measuring and scaling problems is not immediately obvious. It is clear, however, that decisions of this nature are being made every day. In fact, we might say that it is this type of decision which men make best. It is not possible to place a dollar value (not a price) on a tweed coat. It is possible to decide whether or not a given tweed coat is worth its price. It also seems to be possible to decide whether a tweed or a madras is preferred at a given cost.

This analogy offers a potential solution to the complex problem of evaluating alternative transportation plans. The decision makers must be provided with a complete description of all of the significant system costs and consequences for each of the alternative plans. The various impacts could be measured in terms of their most logical units: economic effects in terms of dollars; safety in terms of lives saved or lost; parks in terms of acres or numbers of trips. Esthetic characteristics can be reflected by drawings, models, or word descriptions. The process of selecting an alternative amounts to a subjective decision. The decision maker effectively uses his own units of evaluation and conversion to rate the alternatives. The point is that he does so with a full understanding of the consequences of the alternatives—the future states of the environment which he is purchasing—and in light of the community goals.

The systems viewpoint has not solved the problem. In fact, it has brought forth even more problems. The significance of such an approach is that it helps to eliminate blind decisions in which both the products purchased and the costs are not completely recognized. It is a complicated procedure because the systems involved are not simple. Properly used, the systems approach should provide for the logical and comprehensive planning of urban transportation facilities.

THE FUTURE OF URBAN TRANSPORTATION PLANNING

The recent application of systems analysis and other advances in urban information systems has led Garrison to speculate about the future of urban transportation planning, and specifically about the next generation of transportation planning models.

*Transportation Planning Models in 1975**

The short history of large-scale urban transportation planning studies may be said to cover two generations of models for planning. The first consists of models that distribute expected land uses and then allocate complementary transportation facilities; in second-generation models, transportation and land uses are allocated simultaneously in light of their effects upon each other. Second-generation models also stress choices among alternate development schemes and give more explicit recognition to development goals. While the utility and the momentum of these models will occasion their use for a number of years, and while each class of model will benefit from additional development, it is not too soon to consider suitable directions for the development of the next generation or generations of models. . . .

Information for models. Not much will be available in 1975 that is not already in view today, for a minimum of about ten years appears to be required to turn ideas into practice. This would seem to be an acceptable working rule both for recognition of social and scientific problems and for development of ways to meet these problems using planning, engineering, and scientific and policy tools. The gestation periods required for our community renewal and transportation programs provide examples of lags between problem recognition and action, and the lag between the development of linear programing and its widespread use provides a good example on the scientific side. This is a conservative claim, a claim that we will not go in directions that we cannot already foresee. This, however, does not solve the problem of which directions we might follow from among alternatives that we can see. The main thought of this discussion is that promising payoffs and subsequent model development are likely to result from the provision of better information for problem solving.

This hypothesis has a fairly simple argument underlying it, based upon an examination of alternatives. Present models embrace certain classes of decision processes. Decision makers strive toward certain goals using certain classes of information for their decision making. While we can speak quite articulately about goals and the measurements of goals and about formal decision-making schemes, it is difficult to believe that the next decade will see great strides in these areas. A fundamental fact about goals is that different people hold different goals at different times, and not much is likely to be done to simplify this situation. Decision makers are people, and they are not dynamic programing models, stochastic search procedures, or other kinds of mathematical optimization devices. Although further development of techniques will take place, by and large we will still have the same people juggling the same conflicting goals and attempting to reach them through the mix of decision mechanisms now in use.

With respect to information, however, it would appear that a considerable amount of development and new flexibility is in view. The urban data bank effort is evidence of certain preliminary stirrings in this direction and the rapid evolution

*Reprinted from William L. Garrison. "Urban Transportation Planning Models in 1975," *Journal of the American Institute of Planners*, XXXI, No. 2 (May, 1965), 156–58, with the permission of the author and the *Journal of the American Institute of Planners.*

of information display techniques is another bit of evidence that more and better information is on its way.... It is important now to restate the main point of this argument, which is simply that the degrees of freedom in model construction and implementation seem to lie mostly on the information side. While we may not know our goals much more clearly in the future and we may not have much more incisive decision-making devices, we can still improve our models by using much more and much better information.

There are those who claim that we already have more information than we know how to use, and it is granted that much information is available for the taking. The problem, however, is one of economy: the information is there, but it is expensive to obtain. Even some of our standard data sources lack desired features of economy. Consider, for instance, problems of scanning the Census of Business again, again, and again for bits of information on levels of employment and output. Each scan is expensive, and for small areas the quality of information is such that not much is returned from the effort. Although we have much information, it is expensive compared to what we can expect in the not too distant future.

It is not possible to say very much here about how new information systems are evolving, but several points can be mentioned. Development of computer hardware is central in the information revolution. Of equal importance is the development of various systems for using this hardware in efficient storage and retrieval procedures for urban data. Another significant matter is the development of various types of computer display systems: these are automated methods for displaying information inexpensively. Also important is the revolution in remote sensors. Active sensors, such as high frequency sound devices and radar, are already in use in urban transportation work and the potentiality for increased use of the visible light spectrum and of infrared reception is very great.[78] A related possibility is that of placing sensor equipment in orbital platforms such as those proposed in the Manned Orbital Laboratory Program. While this prospect may sound like something out of Buck Rogers, we should remember that we are looking ten years ahead and that we are already making use of some kinds of information from orbiting platforms such as NIMBUS and TIROS. In addition, work on pattern recognition is proceeding rapidly and there is every hope that efficient methods to reduce imagery will be available soon. Finally, it is important to mention our continuing experience with survey research. Information from this type of activity has become much more useful in the last decade or so, and there is every reason to believe that the efficacy of such survey research will continue to improve.

Planning for rapid adjustment and control. In order to look at implications of better information for the 1975 model it seems necessary to restate the situations which we must analyze in order to carry out effective transportation planning. High priority must be given to hour-to-hour fluctuations of travel, for much transportation capacity is installed to adjust to these variations, and the success or failure of transportation planning is judged here. A basic determinant of the pattern of these movements is the pattern of location of activities that generate traffic. Changes in this pattern must receive high priority.[79] Information is needed on the changing locations of residences, commercial organizations, industrial firms, government organizations, and other entities which may be thought of as generating transportation. From these two points of view, our requirements are for information relating to transportation movements that take place very frequently, say daily, and for information on movements that take place rather infrequently, say every dozen years or so when a family moves.

One has only to listen to the radio during the rush hour to realize that daily transportation movements are subjected to a whole series of random shocks. One day there is an accident on an expressway ramp, producing a distinctive pattern of results. Another day will see a fire near the elevated tracks, another day a thunderstorm, and another day a sports event. Such events, singly and in combination, occasion day-to-day fluctuations that result in lack of capacity on one day and excessive capacity the next, and in turn they yield all the grievances that drivers and transit riders recognize as the transportation problem. Everything is not viewed as random, of course. There is much regularity in day-to-day travel, but we visualize the day-to-day travel pattern as subject to a series of random shocks which have many origins and are difficult to predict.

The role of new information in models that might deal with these problems is already becoming clear. What is needed is sufficient knowledge of the state of the system to bring it under control. At a minimum, there should be some feedback between the state of the system and action by drivers and other users. If drivers could know the states of the traffic soon enough and correctly enough, they could take corrective action. If transportation planners could see random perturbations clearly enough, they might be able to see where additions of capacity could be made to ease some of the problems occasioned by these random perturbations.

In the 1975 model, one can visualize a vastly improved capability to deal with these rather short-run aspects of transportation control and transportation planning. The key to our approved ability to deal with these problems will be better knowledge of the state of the system.

It does not need to be argued that transportation investment may set off certain long-run effects through relocations of households, firms, and other entities that utilize the transportation system. Much current effort in construction of transportation models is directed to finding ways to forecast how such reaction takes place. Much of the necessity for long-range forecasting seems to result from our inability even to consider the development of self-adapting models. We are not now developing models that can keep close contact with what is happening and react very quickly to shifts in the states of affairs, in the manner of an automatic pilot which has an ability to accept information and keep an aircraft on course. In such a model, the goals actually realized will be better known. Perhaps our transportation planning models will depend less upon forecasts than upon abilities to sense states of development resulting from outside forces as well as from their own past actions. With sufficient information, this would surely be possible and may be one of the directions the 1975 model will take. The 1975 model should be less of a long-range forecasting device and more of a guiding device to keep development on course in light of a high level of information about what is happening. In comparison with current models, this model would use less history and more current information.

But even without a basic change in the structure of present models, 1975 models can be vastly improved by better knowledge about the relocation of activities that generate traffic. Present land use allocation models depend upon statistical parameters estimated from rather gross data for an insufficient number of past years. Any improvement in knowledge of the nature of the expansion of the city will provide much better estimates of parameters for models that we are now using, and this increased understanding would surely offer opportunities for vast improvements in our 1975 models.

. . .

. . . Of special significance will be our improved information on the hourly states of transportation movements. This information will provide better opportunities for development of models for command and control and for recognition of places where investment is warranted in view of—or in spite of—variations in patterns of use of capacity. It is also likely that better information will improve our ability to forecast the distribution of traffic-generating activities, either through better understanding of how organizations and households react to changes in transportation, or by couching our models in frameworks that reflect the flexibility made possible by better information.

A Final Word from the Authors

Exciting innovations in techniques and the increase in our understanding of the process of urban travel behavior will generate marked improvements in our capability to cope with current urban transportation problems. In time, these will lead to increasing control over the urban geography of the future. Since the next decades seem destined to become periods of consciously planned urban development, we challenge the reader to scan the pages of this book and ask himself where else within urban geography may latent bases be found for effective determination of desirable future states for our cities, bases waiting to be utilized and improved upon by the urban geographers and planners of the future.

FOOTNOTES TO CHAPTER 13

1. Wilfred Owen, *The Metropolitan Transportation Problem* (Garden City, N.Y.: Doubleday & Company, Inc., rev. ed., 1956), p. 2. See also, e.g., J. R. Meyer, J. F. Kain, and M. Wohl, *The Urban Transportation Problem* (Cambridge, Mass.: Harvard University Press, 1965).

2. William L. Garrison, "Solving Urban Transportation Problems," Address to the Annual Conference of Mayors, Dallas, June, 1966.

3. A "person trip" is defined as a one-way journey by a person traveling as a driver or passenger in an automobile, or as a passenger in a taxi, truck, or mass transportation vehicle taking the person outside the block of trip origin. A "vehicle trip" is defined as a one-way journey in an automobile, taxi, or truck taking the vehicle outside the block of trip origin. In this report, person trips are "linked trips," i.e., a person using two or more modes of transportation to proceed from origin to destination is considered as making only one trip, although most travel surveys consider each link as a separate trip. The mode of travel in a linked trip is defined as the mode having highest priority in the following list, taken in the following order: (1) suburban railroad; (2) subway-elevated; (3) bus; (4) auto-driver; (5) auto-passenger. When the driver of a car dropped or picked up a passenger en route to his main destination, the stop involving the passenger was eliminated. For further details, see *Coding Manual* (21,000) (Chicago: Chicago Area Transportation Study, 1956).

4. *Home Interview Sample Design* (Chicago: Chicago Area Transportation Study, 1958).

5. For further details, see *The Home Interview Manual* and *Coding Manual*.

6. *Truck-Taxi Sampling Procedure* (Chicago: Chicago Area Transportation Study, 1956).

7. The number of resident trips equals, for all practical purposes, the number of trips having destinations within the Study Area. The reason is that inbound nonresident trips are canceled by an equal number of outbound resident trips.

8. Person and vehicle trips overlap, since 76 per cent of all person trips are made in automobiles which are also included in the total of vehicle trips. Throughout the report these two separate, but overlapping, universes of person and vehicle travel will be employed as the basis for analysis and planning.

9. These figures do not include approximately 120,000 automobiles owned by business firms or governments.

10. This rate is lower than the rates of most large cities, but compares closely with those of Detroit and Cleveland.

11. This percentage is higher than found in most origin-destination surveys, because these trips are linked trips. All "change mode of travel" trips and many "serve passenger" trips have disappeared in the linking process.

12. Purpose is useful for studying travel of persons, but not for vehicles. Therefore, purpose and land use breakdowns are provided for person travel, but only land use breakdowns for vehicle travel.

13. It should be noted that on certain roads near the cordon line the heaviest volumes of trips do occur on weekend days, especially in the summer months, and these weekend volumes are influential in determining the future designs of such roads.

14. In dealing with sample data, there is always a range of error resulting from the fact that a sample, and not 100 per cent of the universe, was interviewed. Sampling error is a function of sample rate, number of events predicted, and size of the universe.

15. It might be argued that many trips are made from home to work and then to a shopping center before returning home, and that this kind of a triangular trip would destroy the directional symmetry of travel. It appears, however, that the quantity of this type of triangular trip is not sufficiently great. Moreover, if one person goes from Zone A to Zone B and then to Zone C before returning to Zone A, another person is likely to make the reverse triangular trip, going from A to C and then to B before returning to A. Thus, the two triangular trips cancel one another.

16. Precisely, the sum of the absolute differences between directional travel between pairs of trip purposes.

17. Alternate weighting systems could be used, such as weighting by time, to measure the duration of use of a transportation system.

18. For a detailed review of the transportation planning process, see R. Schofer and B. Levin, "The Urban Transportation Planning Process," *Socio-Economic Planning Science*, I (June, 1967), 185–97; R. M. Zettel and R. R. Carll, *Summary Review of Major Metropolitan Area Transportation Studies in the United States*, Special Report of Institute of Transportation and Traffic Engineering, University of California (Berkeley, 1962); and B. Martin, F. Memmott, and A. Bone, *Principles and Techniques of Predicting Future Demand for Urban Area Transportation* (Cambridge, Mass.: The M.I.T. Press, 1965).

19. For an example of the major and minor land use classifications used in urban transportation studies, see Paul Shuldiner *et al.*, *Non-Residential Trip Generation Analysis* (Evanston, Ill.: Northwestern University, Transportation Center Research Report, 1965), pp. 150–52.

20. For a complete discussion of the origin-destination survey, see Walter Y. Oi and Paul W. Shuldiner, *An Analysis of Urban Travel Demands* (Evanston, Ill.: Northwestern University Press, 1962), Chap. iii.

21. See Chicago Area Transportation Study, *Final Report, I: Survey Findings* (Chicago: Western Engraving and Embossing Company, 1959), chap. vi.

22. A solution for relieving this pressure is given by Gordon J. Fielding, "Locating Urban Freeways: A Method for Resolving Community Conflict," in *Geographic Studies of Urban Transportation and Network Analysis*, ed. Frank E. Horton, Northwestern University Studies in Geography, No. 16

(Evanston, Ill.: Northwestern University, 1968).

23. See, for example, Ira S. Lowry, *A Model of Metropolis*, RM-4035-RC (Santa Monica, Calif.: The Rand Corporation, 1964); and Donald M. Hill, "A Growth Allocation Model for the Boston Region" and George T. Lathrop and John R. Hamburg, "An Opportunity-Accessibility Model for Allocating Regional Growth," both in the *Journal of the American Institute of Planners*, XXXI (May, 1965).

24. For a discussion of assignment models, see W. Jewell, "Models for Traffic Assignment," *Transportation Research*, I (March, 1967), 31–46.

25. See Martin, Memmott, and Bone, *Predicting Future Demand*, pp. 115–26.

26. Greater detail about trip destinations in the commercial and manufacturing categories was dropped to permit comparison with the six land use types for which land area was measured. Streets and alleys, parking, and vacant land, for which land area measures were also obtained, do not generate trips as defined in this report.

27. There is a slight drop in trip making per dwelling place near the cordon line because of the influence of older and more self-contained communities such as Chicago Heights and Wheaton.

28. See *Forecasting Economic Activity: Consumer Expenditures* (Chicago: Chicago Area Transportation Study, 1958).

29. The coefficient of correlation r between net residential density and car ownership is $-.71$.

30. In the two inner rings, manufacturing trip generation is inflated because the loft buildings in which many manufacturing concerns are located often have commercial establishments on the first floor. Since the first-floor activity determines the land use of a parcel, this operates to reduce commercial densities and increase manufacturing densities. It should also be pointed out that the trips to commercial land in the Loop are low by the extent that workers in the Loop walk to stores during the day.

31. Note, however, that they require more truck trips.

32. See Detroit Metropolitan Area Traffic Study, *Report on the Detroit Metropolitan Area Traffic Study* (Detroit, 1955), Part I, p. 89.

33. See City of Chicago, Department of Planning, *Development Plan for the Central Area of Chicago* (Chicago, 1958).

34. These averages are computed directly from home interview data. Area averages rarely go below .4 or exceed 1.4.

35. The coefficient of correlation r between percentage trip origins by mass transportation and net residential density is $+.84$ and between mass transportation usage and car ownership $-.71$ (± 1.00 is perfect correlation). Knowing both density and car ownership increases the coefficient to .86 ($r^2 = .76$). These data provide a statistically significant basis for making estimates of mass transportation users.

36. These trips, of course, are not all shopping trips, and are affected by the other activities which happen to be grouped in a particular quarter-square mile.

37. For a detailed discussion of residential trip generation, see Oi and Shuldiner, *An Analysis of Urban Travel Demands*, chaps. iv and v.

38. Chicago Area Transportation Study, *Final Report, II: Data Projections* (Chicago: Western Engraving and Embossing Company, 1960), 43–44.

39. See, e.g., P. Shuldiner *et al.*, *Non-Residential Trip Generation Analysis*, p. 41.

40. For an example, see Wilbur Smith and Associates, *Nashville Metropolitan Area Transportation Study, I: Origin-Destination Survey and Major Route Plans* (New Haven, Conn.: Wilbur Smith and Associates, 1961), p. 67.

41. For a thorough discussion of gravity type models, see Gunnar Olsson, *Distance and Human Interaction: A Review and Bibliography*, Bibliography Series, No. 2, Regional Science Research Institute, (Philadelphia, 1965).

42. Southeastern Wisconsin Regional Planning Commission, *Land Use-Transportation Study: 1940*, II (Waukesha: Southeastern Wisconsin Regional Planning Commission, 1966), p. 63.

43. For a discussion of the calibration process, see *ibid.*, pp. 63–72.

44. W. J. Reilly, *Methods for the Study of Retail Relationships*, University of Texas Bulletin No. 2944 (November, 1929).

45. A. Lösch, *Economics of Location* (New Haven, Conn.: Yale University Press, 1954).

46. G. J. Zipf, *Human Behavior and the Principle of Least Effort* (Reading, Mass.: Addison-Wesley Publishing Company, Inc., 1949); and J. Q. Stewart, "Sociometry," *Geographical Review*, XXXVII (1947).

47. A. M. Voorhees, "A General Theory of Traffic Movement," *Proceedings of the Institute of Traffic Engineers*, 1955; H. W. Bevis, "A Model for Predicting Urban Travel Patterns," *Journal of the American Institute of Planners*, 1959; H. W. Bevis, "Various Issues of Chicago ATS," *Research News;* J. D. Carroll and H. W. Bevis, "Predicting Local Travel in Urban Regions," *Papers and Proceedings of Regional Science Association*, III (1957).

48. K. H. Dieter, "Distribution of Work Trips in Toronto," *Journal of the City Planning Division*, 1962. An exponential function, $\alpha e^{-\beta d}$, was found to provide the best fit with actual data of a 1954 traffic survey.

49. J. C. Tanner, "Some Analysis of Distances from House to Work Based on the 1951 Census Population," *Road Research Laboratory Notes* (Harmondsworth, Middlesex, *n.d.*), RN3366/JCT.

50. W. Mylroie, *Evaluation of Inter-City Travel Desire*, Highway Research Board, Bulletin No. 119 (Washington, D.C.: Highway Research Board, 1956).

51. See Chicago Area Transportation Study, *Final Report*, Vol. II, (Chicago: Western Engraving and Embossing Company, 1959), pp. 81–92.

52. For a description, see D. D. Witheford, "Zonal Interchange Reviewed," *Research Letter*, Pittsburgh Area Transportation Study, 2 (1960).

53. A. R. Tomazinis, *A New Method of Trip Distribution in an Urban Area*, Highway Research Board Bulletin, No. 347. (Washington, D.C.: Highway Research Board, 1962), pp. 77–99. This method differs in a number of respects from Schneider's formulation and for purposes of classification is often referred to as a "competing opportunities" model. Its main feature is the distribution of trips by successive bands, based on distance, rather than on the basis of travel time.

54. Mathematically the basic formula is given by $V_{ij} = V_i(e^{-LV} - e^{-L(V+V_j)})$, where V is the sum of all destinations line closer to i then j is to i, V_j is the number of opportunities in area j, and L is a factor varying with trip type.

55. S. A. Stouffer, "Intervening Opportunities: A Theory Relating Mobility and Distance," *American Sociological Review*, V (1940).

56. General Register Office, *Census, 1951: Report on Usual Residences and Work Places* (London: Her Majesty's Stationery Office).

57. Mathematically, we plotted log $(100 - \Sigma V_{ij}\, 100/V_i)$; where V_{ij} is the number of journeys from i to j, with j varying from zone or origin and moving cumulatively through the zones defined by concentric circles; and (V_i is the total journeys from zone i) against cumulated opportunities (total employment) in succeeding zones, expressed as a percentage of all opportunities in the total area covered by the calculation.

58. *Storkjöbenhavns Trafikanalyse*, 1956, and *Hjemminterview*, 1960 (Copenhagen: Department of City Planning).

59. *Storkjöbenhavns Trafikanalyse*, 1956, and *Nummerskrivning*, 1960 (Copenhagen: Department of City Planning).

60. William L. Garrison, "The Spatial Structure of the Economy," *Annals of the Association of American Geographers*, Part 1: XLIX (June, 1959), 232–349; Part 2: XLIX (December, 1959), 471–82; Part 3: L (September, 1960), 357–73.

61. Benjamin H. Stevens, "A Review of the Literature on Linear Methods and Models for Spatial Analysis," *Journal of the American Institute of Planners*, XXVI (May, 1960), 253–59.

62. John D. Herbert and Benjamin H. Stevens, "A Model for the Distribution of Residential Activity in Urban Areas," *Journal of Regional Science*, II (1960), 21–36.

63. William L. Garrison *et al.*, *Studies of Highway Development and Geographic Change* (Seattle: University of Washington Press, 1959).

64. Walter Isard, *Location and Space-Economy* (New York: The M.I.T. Press and John Wiley & Sons, Inc., 1956).

65. David L. Huff, "Toward a General Theory of Consumer Travel Behavior" (D.B.A. dissertation, University of Washington, 1959). Published in part as: "A Topographic Model of Consumer Space Preference," *Papers and Proceedings Regional Science Association,* VI (1960), 159–74.

66. Edward T. Hall, *The Silent Language* (Garden City, N.Y.: Doubleday & Company, Inc., 1959).

67. William L. Garrison, *The Benefits of Rural Roads to Rural Property* (Seattle: Washington State Council for Highway Research, 1956).

68. See Garrison *et al.*, *Studies of Highway Development;* and Duane F. Marble, "Transport Inputs at Urban Residential Sites: A Study in the Transportation Geography of Urban Areas" (Ph.D. dissertation, University of Washington, 1959), published in part in Isard, *Location and Space-Economy*, and as "Transport Inputs at Urban Residential Sites," *Papers and Proceedings, Regional Science Association,* V (1959), 253–66.

69. Isard, *Location and Space-Economy*.

70. See Alderson and Sessions, "Basic Research Report on Consumer Behavior" (April, 1957, mimeographed); and Brian J. L. Berry, "Pre-Equilibrium Consumer Connections and the Spatial Structure of Retail Business" (Paper, Department of Geography, University of Washington, 1958).

71. Marble, "Transport Inputs at Urban Residential Sites."

72. Garrison *et al.*, *Studies of Highway Development;* and John D. Nystuen, "A Theory and Simulation of Intra-Urban Travel," in Garrison *et al.*, *Studies of Highway Development*, pp. 54–83.

73. Oi and Shuldiner, *An Analysis of Urban Travel Demands.*

74. Marble, "Transport Inputs at Urban Residential Sites."

75. John G. Kemeny and J. Laurie Snell, *Finite Markov Chains* (Princeton, N.J.: D. Van Nostrand Co., Inc., 1960); and Frank Harary and Benjamin Lipstein, "The Dynamics of Brand Loyalty: A Markovian Approach," *Operations Research*, X (1962), 19–40.

76. Frank E. Horton and Paul W. Shuldiner, "The Analysis of Land Use Linkages," *Highway Research Record*, No. 165 (1967), 96–108; see also Frank E. Horton and William Wagner, "A Markovian Analysis of Urban Travel Behavior: Pattern Response by Socio-Economic-Occupational Groups," Working Paper Series, No. 3, The Institute of Urban and Regional Research, University of Iowa, 1968.

77. Besides the publications previously listed, the following are representative: Edward J. Taaffe, Barry J. Garner, and Maurice H. Yeats, *The Peripheral Journey to Work: A Geographic Consideration* (Evanston, Ill.: Northwestern University Press, 1963); Duane F. Marble, *Residential Location and Household Travel Behavior*, Highway Research Circular, No. 12 (1965); Edwin N. Thomas and Joseph L. Schofer, "Toward the Development of More Responsive Urban and Transportation System Models," *High Speed Ground Transportation Journal*, I (1967), 154–201; F. E. Horton, "The Utility of Trip Forecasting Models Based on Aggregated Land Use Data," *The Professional Geographer* (1967), 319–23; James O. Wheeler, "The Transportation Model and Changing Home-Work Location," *The Professional Geographer* (1967), 144–48; Karel J. Kansky, "Travel Patterns of Urban Residents," *Transportation Science*, I (1967), 261–85; Robert T. Aangeenbrug, "Automobile Commuting in Large Suburbs: A Comparative Analysis of Private Car Use in the Daily Journey to Work," Eugene D. Perle, "Urban Mobility Needs of the Handicapped: An Exploration," and Duane F. Marble and Sophia R. Bowlby, "Shopping Alternatives and Recurrant Travel Patterns," in F. E. Horton, ed., *Geographic Studies of Urban Transportation and Network Analysis.* Other references can be found in William R. Black and Frank E. Horton, *A Bibliography of Selected Research on Networks and Urban Transportation Relevant to Current Transportation Geography Research*, Research Report No. 28, Supplement to Horton, ed., *Geographic Studies.*

78. See, e.g., Duane F. Marble and Frank E. Horton, "Remote Sensing: A New Tool for Urban Data Acquisition," in John E. Rickert, ed., *Urban and Regional Information Systems: Federal Activities and Specialized Systems* (Akron, Ohio: Hirey Printing Co. and Kent State University, 1969), pp. 252–57; and Frank E. Horton and Duane F. Marble, "Regional Information Systems: Remote Sensing Inputs," *Technical Papers*, Proceedings of the 35th Annual Meeting of the American Society of Photogrammetry (1969), pp. 259–68.

79. See, e.g., Kenneth J. Dueker and Frank E. Horton, Working Paper Series No. 5, Institute of Urban and Regional Research, University of Iowa, 1969.

index